DATE DUE

NO 8 99			

DEMCO 38-296

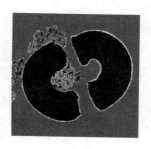

CHINA
A NATION IN TRANSITION

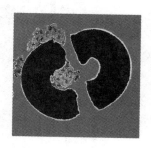

CHINA
A NATION IN TRANSITION

Expanded Reference Edition

Edited by

DEBRA E. SOLED

CONGRESSIONAL QUARTERLY INC.

WASHINGTON, D.C.

Copyright © 1995 Congressional Quarterly Inc.
1414 22nd Street, N.W., Washington, D.C. 20037

Printed in the United States of America
Cover design: Anne Masters Design, Washington, D.C.
Cover art: ''Welcome'' (no. two of twelve panels), by Wang Ming
Calligraphy: I-Chuan Chen
Typesetting: Cyndi L. Smith
Maps: Joyce Kachergis, Kachergis Book Design, Pittsboro, North Carolina

Photo credits: 8, 52, 54, 57, 64, 65, 67, 263, 295, National Archives; 11, An Keren/Xinhua News Agency; 13, 23, 27, 31, 35, 39, 41, 44, 50, 63, 86, 127, 266, Library of Congress; 72, 137, 241, 282, Xinhua News Agency; 80, UPI/Bettmann Newsphotos; 90, 307, Gerald Ford Library; 95, 99, 109, 170, 179, courtesy of the U.S.-China Business Council, Washington, D.C.; 115, 129, 135, 202, 206, 208, 239, 260, 288, 291, 299, Reuters/Bettmann; 141, 167, 180, 309, courtesy of the Embassy of the People's Republic of China; 146, Wang Jingde/New China Pictures, Beijing—Glofa Enterprises, New York; 154, courtesy of International Republican Institute; 201, Bush Presidential Materials Project; 253, Zeng Huang/Xinhua News Agency; 256, Wu Jun/Xinhua News Agency; 308, 309, Central Intelligence Agency.

Library of Congress Cataloging-in-Publication Data
China: a nation in transition / Debra E. Soled, editor.
    p.   cm.
  Includes bibliographical references and index.
  ISBN 0-87187-958-1 (pbk.).- -ISBN 1-56802-039-2
  1. China--History--20th century.   2. China--Politics and
government--1976-   3. China--Economic conditions--1976-   I. Soled,
Debra E.
DS774.C4414   1995   95-6048
951- -dc20   CIP

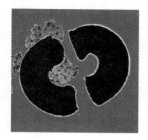

CONTENTS

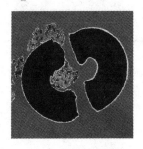

TABLES, MAPS, BOXES, AND CHARTS

A GUIDE TO SPELLING AND PRONUNCIATION

In 1978, the State Council of the People's Republic of China announced that it had decided to use the Chinese phonetic alphabet, called *pinyin,* to standardize the romanization of the names of people and places in China. The change went into effect on Jan. 1, 1979, and was subsequently adopted by most publications in the West.

Despite its obvious improvements over the previous system (Wade-Giles), the new system, too, poses problems for the reader unfamiliar with Chinese pronunciation. In addition, Chinese pronunciation, even by the Chinese themselves, is far from standardized, and can vary much more widely than is the case with English. Thus, those who use this pronunciation guide are cautioned that it represents, in many cases, only an approximation of the correct rendering of the actual sound.

The decision to change the system of romanization creates many problems for students of Chinese history, because so much has already been written about China using the old system of transliteration. Thus, a reader who might want to do further research on, say, the Taiwan Strait crisis of 1958, would search through recent literature in vain for any reference to an island named Quemoy, which is now rendered as "Jinmen" in the *pinyin* system.

This book mainly utilizes the *pinyin* system. However, references to some historical figures retain older spellings that may be more familiar to readers, such as Chiang Kai-shek and Sun Yat-sen, and references to Hong Kong and Taiwan employ the forms used locally there.

Pronunciation Guide

Most Chinese words consist of an "initial" and a "final." The initial is the consonant or pair of consonants at the beginning of a word. The final is the remainder of the word, beginning with the first vowel. Some words begin with vowels and have no initial—only a final.

To use this chart, look up the initial and final in their respective lists, and combine them. For example:

Shanghai:	initial "Sh" + final "ang"
	initial "h" + final "ai"
Deng Xiaoping:	initial "D" + final "eng"
	initial "X" + final "iao"
	initial "p" + final "ing"

Initials

b	**b**ay		p	**p**ay
c	ha**ts**		q	**ch**eer
ch	**ch**urch		r	leisu**r**e
d	**d**ay		s	**s**ay
f	**f**air		sh	**sh**irt
g	**g**ay		t	**t**ake
h	**h**ay		w	**w**ay
j	**j**eep		x	**s**he
k	**k**ay		y	**y**ea
l	**l**ay		z	rea**ds**
m	**m**ay		zh	ju**dge**
n	**n**ay			

Finals

a	**fa**ther		iong	**y** + w**o**man + **ng**
ai	**eye**		iu	**yeo**man
an	**on**		o	w**a**ll
ang	German G**ang**		ong	w**o**man + **ng**
ao	n**ow**		ou	**o**ld
e	h**er**		u	r**u**le
ei	**eigh**t		ü	f**ew**, French **tu**
en	n**un**		ua	q**ua**lity
eng	s**ung**		uai	w**i**fe
er	t**ar**		uan	q**uan**dary
i	s**ee**		üan	**u** + **ton**sil
ia	**A**s**ia**		uang	q**ua**lity + **ng**
iao	**yow**l		üe	sw**ea**t
ian	**yen**		ueng	sw**ung**
iang	**Yon**kers		ui	**way**
ie	**ye**s		un	w**on**
in	**in**		ün	French **une**
ing	s**ing**		uo	w**a**ll

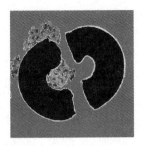

CONTRIBUTORS

Debra E. Soled, editor. Soled is a freelance editor with extensive background in Chinese studies. She has been an editor with M. E. Sharpe, Inc., *Current History* magazine, and Eurasia Press. She was coauthor and editorial director of *Christianity in China: A Scholar's Guide to Resources in the Libraries and Archives of the United States* and has edited and reviewed numerous reference and scholarly books on China.

Wendy Abraham. Chapters 1 and 2; she was assisted on chapter 2 by Xiaodong Wang. Abraham is on the faculty at New York University where she teaches courses on Middle Eastern and Asian studies.

Xiaodong Wang, who assisted in writing chapter 2, is a doctoral candidate in the History Department at the University of North Carolina at Chapel Hill.

Chi Wang. Chapters 3 and 4, with the assistance of Laura L. Wong. Wang is head of the Chinese and Korean Section at the Library of Congress and a professor of history at Georgetown University.

Laura L. Wong, who assisted in the preparation of chapters 3 and 4, previously was a staff member of the Asian Division's Chinese Section at the Library of Congress.

Marcia R. Ristaino. Chapter 5. Ristaino is East Asian acquisition specialist at the Library of Congress, where she has also served as senior research analyst, Chinese affairs, in the Federal Research Division.

Ray Bowen II. Chapter 6. Bowen is on the faculty of the Economics Department and is a fellow of the Center for International Studies at the University of Missouri—St. Louis.

Thomas W. Robinson. Chapter 7. Robinson is a specialist in Chinese, Russian, and Asian studies, and international relations. He has been associated in these areas with the American Enterprise Institute, the Rand Corporation, the Council on Foreign Relations, and the National War College. He also has taught at Georgetown University.

Sidney L. Greenblatt. Chapter 8. Greenblatt serves in the Office of International Services at Syracuse University. He also has taught at the State University of New York and was director of Asia-Pacific Consultants, an independent consulting group.

Gregory K. S. Man. Chapter 9. Man is a lieutenant colonel in the U.S. Army. He is a specialist on Chinese armed forces and in 1994 served as assistant army attaché in Beijing.

Robert Sutter. Chapter 10. Sutter is a senior specialist in international affairs at the Congressional Research Service of the Library of Congress in the area of U.S. policy toward Asia and the Pacific.

INTRODUCTION

As the twentieth century draws to a close, China is in the midst of a great transition. The country's enormous human potential at last is on its way to being harnessed to regain the glory of China during the best of its imperial age. Or is it? This sense of approaching destiny evokes a feeling of déjà vu. At the end of the nineteenth century, when the last of China's dynasties lay crumbling, many writers, historians, and politicians watched postimperial China with anticipation to see whether it would soon become what they had hoped—or feared.

Although observers disagree on whether the twenty-first century is likely to see a post-Communist China, it is certain that, whatever its political form, China at the millennium is far different from a century ago, a half century ago, or even a generation ago. The last hundred years have witnessed the country's tumultuous evolution from imperial, to republican, to Communist forms of government, and the last of these alone has itself changed radically in many ways. Moreover, the Communist leadership may be less able to impose its will on the society than it was in the past because China's social, political, and economic environments are becoming more variegated and dispersed. In addition to China's internal changes, the country is now ever-increasingly engaged with the outside world. Both China's fitful entry into the world community and the magnitude of effects the country's internal changes have on that community in economic, military, social, and environmental terms make crucial a more thorough understanding of China as it was, as it is, and as it may become.

Recent events have shown the effect that changes in China can have beyond its borders, in part because technology has made the world a smaller place. In the 1980s, radio and television transmitted from outside China began to provide information not available from the Chinese media; fax transmissions and electronic communication in 1989 enabled Chinese pro-democracy supporters to communicate not only with one another but with people outside China who were sympathetic to their cause. The example of the Chinese democracy movement inspired those living under Communist rule in Eastern Europe who yearned for greater political freedoms and thus may have set off a chain reaction that is still reverberating throughout the world. This kind of potential impact makes it imperative that people outside China other than specialists gain a better understanding of the forces and concerns that drive its behavior.

The next century will find China continuing its search for development and modernization, but not necessarily moving toward Western conceptions of either. As a proud civilization with a long history of following its own tune, China will likely arrive at different answers to modernization and development questions than many countries that have faced them before.

The question of whether China represents a unique civilization that must be treated as a special case or is one member of a diverse community of nations is an old one that will not be decided here. More importantly, by understanding the history that created contemporary China we may gain insight into where it is headed next. China's present-day decisions and behavior cannot be grasped in isolation from that history.

China: A Nation in Transition aims to provide an integrated approach to understanding China today, balancing an exploration of the historical tradition with an examination of recent developments. Written by specialists in China studies for the general reader, the chapters present objective analyses so that readers may begin to form their own perspectives; what is offered here is a framework to introduce the fundamental concepts, personages, events, and data for nonspecialist readers. Our purpose was to publish a text that will provide a broad audience with a comprehensive knowledge of China and will encourage readers to explore individual topics further through the works listed in the bibliography.

The book also serves as a ready reference for people seeking specific information on China. Textual discussions are supplemented by maps, tables, charts of the Chinese government and Chinese Communist Party structure, original documents, an extensive bibliography, a chronology of important events, and biographical profiles of important Chinese figures in the twentieth century.

The main text of the book is divided into two parts: a historical survey and a topical examination of issues in contemporary China's development. Part I consists of four chronologically oriented chapters on China, from its early history through the 1980s. Chapter 1 establishes the basic parameters of traditional China, its creation mythology, philosophies, culture, and concepts. China's imperial history is explored in sequence through concise discussion of the critical political, social, economic, and cultural developments of each period. A more expanded approach is used for the Ming (1368-1644) and Qing dynasties (1644-1911), which deserve special attention because they witnessed the decline of the imperial system and laid the groundwork for the modern period.

Chapter 2 analyzes the brief but all-important period of Republican China, when the country was not only reeling from the downfall of its centuries-old dynastic system but hastily dragged into international affairs before it was equipped to cope with them.

The first decades under a nonimperial form of government were filled with turmoil, yet also saw a cultural and social ferment influenced heavily, if not predominantly, by events outside China's borders. Chief among these influences was the spread from Europe of new political thinking, primarily in the form of communism emanating from the young Soviet Union.

The period that is the focus of chapter 3 was shaped mostly by Mao Zedong, who proclaimed the founding of the People's Republic of China in 1949 and was most responsible for its best and worst achievements during the state's first quarter century. China under Mao saw not only a recovery from decades of war and devastation but a progression of political movements aimed both at reversing the pernicious effects of China's decline and at consolidating Mao's personal grip on power. His reach extended after his death, when intensive jockeying took place to succeed him as top leader. Even after the leadership struggle was resolved, China still suffered the aftereffects of the most cataclysmic of Mao's campaigns, the Cultural Revolution (1966-1976). Recovery from that campaign required opening a re-evaluation of Mao himself, for the leaders recognized that China could not safely embrace its post-Mao future without bringing some closure to its Maoist past.

That post-Mao future began with the rise to power of Deng Xiaoping, as recounted in chapter 4. The time period covered in the chapter (1978-1989) is only about a decade, yet these few years contained irreversible changes that have put China on its track for the next century. Having secured the pinnacle of power, Deng carefully navigated the rocky shoals of economic development and political liberalization to allow the country to achieve greater prosperity. After decades of ideologically charged policies, Deng brought to economic decision making a pragmatic outlook that encouraged unleashing individual initiative in order to boost productivity and progress. But the genie of political relaxation had been released, and much of the decade was spent alternately trying to steer its course and trying to force it back into its bottle. Once popular demands for political change had begun to be expressed, Deng and his cohorts had difficulty channeling them for their own purposes.

The tension that resulted, in addition to pressures arising from the economic reforms and from popular reaction to government corruption, was manifested in mass demonstrations during the spring of 1989 in Tiananmen Square and elsewhere throughout China. The chapter gives an extensive description of developments leading up to the June 1989 Tiananmen incident, now a bellwether event in late twentieth-century Chinese history.

Part 2, which examines contemporary China from a topical perspective, begins with an analysis of what the author calls China's second revolution—political reforms and the quest for modernization. Chapter 5 describes China's current government system as well as the structure of the Communist Party, which not only infiltrates the central government but parallels it at every level. Through reforms, Deng has attempted to reduce duplication in the governance system and permit a younger generation to rise to prominence. However, the so-called third echelon leaders are competing not just with the entrenched old guard but with one another; factionalism, never absent from Chinese politics, has largely taken the shape of those supporting reform and those opposing it, either partially or entirely. No matter which side prevails, the Communist Party, rather than the state government, is likely to remain the arbiter of China's future course.

Chapter 6 probes the condition of China's economy after a decade of economic reform. Through extensive discussion and data, the chapter shows the progress made in terms of economic growth, modernization, and participation in the world economy and enumerates the obstacles to further growth. Many problems remain to be solved through further reforms, but these appear to be dependent on political decisions made at the top rather than solely on economic criteria. The economy continues to grow at impressive rates, however, as vividly shown in several of the tables that accompany the chapter, and appears to hold excellent prospects for continuing to do so.

China's engagement on the world stage is the subject of chapter 7, which systematically analyzes the determinants of China's foreign policy behavior. China's location and military strength have made the country a critical player in the great geostrategic questions of our times, while its size and influence give it a central place in the world. Yet in the post-cold war world, China looms less large in some respects and, like other countries, must recalculate its place in the world community—especially now that its ideological fraternity brother, the Soviet Union, has collapsed. What will the future bring? To answer this question, the author offers a fascinating exercise in alternative scenarios, sketching outcomes that would derive from various combinations of internal and external developments, and their foreign policy implications.

Chapter 8 describes the complicated mosaic of society and culture in contemporary China, where the traditional mores from a dynastic past have been overlaid with behaviors developed out of modern events. As is true of all countries, China's future direction is largely a function of its people and the events shaping their ordinary daily lives. This chapter examines various social issues, all of them affected in varying degrees by the reform process, such as the changing status of women, population trends, rural-urban migration, alienation in the wake of the loss of faith in communism, national minorities, social stratification, religion, and the use of political campaigns to effect social transformation. Although many aspects of China's unique culture remain, internal and external effects have produced a society that is beginning to resemble others to a greater extent than ever before.

The focus of chapter 9 is China's military and its attempts to transform itself from a guerrilla peasant militia to a modern, well-equipped fighting force able to project military might beyond the country's borders. The People's Liberation Army, according to the author, remains a poorly trained force with obsolete weaponry but has made strides in professionalizing its officer corps and acquiring more modern arms systems from Russia and the West. After a brief history of the PLA, the chapter describes the various branches of the military and the security issues China now faces. Like other groups in China, the military finds that its future prospects are tied to economic growth; reliant on its own efforts for funding, unlike in the past, the military has engaged in a variety of activities to boost its revenues. Arms sales provide a significant source of revenue but raise concerns over proliferation that complicate China's foreign relations. Although the PLA remains critical to maintaining the Communist Party's grip on power, to an increasing degree the PLA is trying to disengage itself from its long-standing internal political or ideological role and to concentrate on external security.

The last chapter explores China's relations with Hong Kong, Taiwan, and Tibet. The first of these has spent more than a century as a British crown colony, becoming a center of world finance and trade and experiencing a social and political climate shaped more by British common law than by Marx. But before the end of the decade Hong Kong will return to Chinese sovereignty, with as-yet uncertain effects on its ability to remain an economic powerhouse. The wrangling over the shape of the future relationship with the Chinese government has aroused widespread concern among the residents of Hong Kong, many of whom left the PRC over the past forty years for political reasons. Hong Kong will be a test case of China's recently enunciated doctrine of "one country, two systems," which China's leaders hope will allay fears over Hong Kong's future. The section on Hong Kong discusses the tensions that have plagued the transition to Chinese rule and the efforts by the territory's last British colonial governor to gain political rights for Hong Kong residents before his term ends.

The outcome in Hong Kong will greatly influence the prospects for a change in relations between China and Taiwan. A province of China until the island was ceded to Japan in 1895, Taiwan has developed a separate economic and political identity since the Nationalists set up a government there in 1949 after fleeing the Communist takeover of the mainland. Although they had been defeated by the Communists, the Nationalists have made a conspicuous success of their stewardship of the island, bringing prosperity and, later, political liberalization to the native inhabitants and the mainlanders who took refuge there. Both the mainland and the Taiwan governments have retained at least nominal allegiance to the goal of reunifying both territories. But the economic and political identities of the people living on either side of the Taiwan Strait have diverged significantly since

1949. For residents of Taiwan, particularly the younger generation, with no personal memory of the mainland, the idea of joining with (and being potentially overwhelmed by) the less prosperous, less politically open mainland remains a questionable proposition. China and Taiwan have recently opened economic relations, with the former learning from the latter's economic success but showing less interest in studying its successful transition to greater political democracy.

The chapter also includes a discussion of Tibet, which presents far different issues both for China and for the larger world community. Outside observers disagree on Tibet's historical status, but the Chinese government maintains that Tibet has always been within the boundaries of the Chinese state, even during dynastic times, and no government has recognized Tibet as a sovereign state. But, more than any other region incorporated into the Chinese empire, Tibet has retained a distinct, fiercely independent ethnic identity. China has had less success there than in any of its other outlying areas in sinifying the local population. In view of these conditions, and the disintegrative developments in post-Communist Eastern Europe, a separate examination of Tibet is valuable.

Under Chinese imperial rule, Tibet was largely permitted to go its own way because of its distance from Beijing; the Communist regime, however, has attempted to incorporate Tibet more fully and limit its expression of a separate social, cultural, and political identity. While relations with Hong Kong and Taiwan offer China economic benefits, China's interest in Tibet mostly concerns security. Chinese rule of Tibet has relied on coercion in the face of a local population with a strong ethnic identity in opposition to the Han culture. China's efforts to bring the territory under stricter control have inspired resistance and rebellion, which make the Beijing government struggle all the harder to retain its hold. Although an independent Tibet does not appear likely in the near future, advocates of Tibetan self-determination have raised international awareness of their cause, and Tibetan exiles have put a human face on what has historically been a remote community. The Tibetan situation has received relatively little notice, since the country has held less economic and strategic significance than Taiwan and Hong Kong. By focusing attention on Chinese abuses, Tibetans have rallied support for their cause, however, which they hope will be assisted by the trend toward democratization in other parts of the world. As yet, Beijing has given them little on which to build those hopes.

Looming over the course China will take in the next few years is the generational change taking place in its leadership. The death of Kim Il Sung in North Korea has focused new attention on possible repercussions following the death of China's paramount leader behind the scenes, Deng Xiaoping. Although officially out of power, Deng has maintained his commanding presence in Chinese politics, and the prospect of his passing has created uncertainty about the permanence of reforms. At this writing, Chinese leaders appear to be taking a hard line on matters of internal politics, such as release and treatment of Tiananmen dissidents, and putting on hold important decisions about the future of reform until the outcome of his passing is clear. At the beginning of 1995 it is not clear whether Jiang Zemin already has such a secure hold on power that the transition to a post-Deng era has in fact already happened; if this were true it would mean that Deng's demise represents the loss of a historical leader but will not occasion upheaval or crisis. An absence of chaos, the fear of which has motivated Chinese leaders over the centuries far more than has desire for progress, would be a welcome sign that China may have found a measure of the stability that eluded it at the previous turn of the century. This book is offered as a snapshot of China to hold up at the next one.

* * *

This book could not have been published without the help of several key individuals, including David Tarr, CQ books editorial director, who initiated the project and offered valuable encouragement, guidance, and support, along with others on the staff at Congressional Quarterly Books: Jerry Orvedahl, production editor; Talia Greenberg, editorial assistant; and Jamie Holland, photo research. Appreciation is also extended to Madelyn Ross, for editorial support and consulting on various aspects of the book, and to Maria Valdecanas, for research assistance and compilation of the chronology and profiles. Several advisers generously commented during the early stages of the project: David Buck, editor of the *Journal of Asian Studies* and professor of history, the University of Wisconsin-Milwaukee; Jan Prybyla, professor of economics, Pennsylvania State University; William Joseph, professor of political science, Wellesley College; June Teufel Dreyer, professor of politics, University of Miami at Coral Gables; and Steven Goldstein, professor of government, Smith College. Particular thanks are owed to Steven I. Levine, senior research associate, Boulder Run Research, for assistance above and beyond the call of duty from beginning to end. I am also grateful to the contributors, whose cooperation and interest in the book were indispensable to its realization.

Debra E. Soled, Editor
February 1995

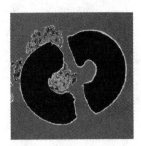

PART I

CHINA'S HERITAGE

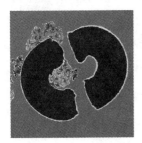

CHAPTER 1

IMPERIAL CHINA— ORIGINS TO 1911

The Chinese people, heirs to one of the oldest continuous civilizations on earth, have a history of close to four thousand years and a culture that has influenced neighboring East Asian nations for much of that time. Their cultural continuity and special social order allowed them to maintain a unique centralized Chinese state that held unlimited political authority through the rise and fall of many dynasties.

A panoramic view of Chinese history reveals not only the rise and fall of dynastic families dominating the throne, but continual cycles of political unity followed by periods of political and social chaos. Efforts to fend off periodic invaders from the north and even well beyond the Middle Kingdom, as China has called itself, have contributed to making the Chinese a self-sufficient people.

This chapter provides a brief overview of the personages and events that shaped dynastic China, followed by a more detailed look at China's last two dynasties, the Ming (1368-1644) and the Qing (1644-1911). It was during these last two dynasties that China's centuries-long isolation from the West ended, and its long road toward modernization and participation in world affairs began.

The Land

China is made up of twenty-one provinces, five autonomous regions (Xinjiang, Tibet, Inner Mongolia, Ningxia, and Guangxi), and three municipalities (Beijing, Shanghai, and Tianjin) and has two main river valleys: the Yellow River in the north (so named for its muddy color), and the Yangzi (Yangtze) River further south. Chinese civilization began in the North China plain and in the northwest, along the Wei and Fen river valley tributaries of the Yellow River. Throughout Chinese history, devastating flooding of the Yellow River, aptly dubbed ''China's Sorrow,'' has required the Chinese to construct canals for drainage, irrigation, and transportation in an effort to exert some control over its waters.

The fact that Chinese civilization began in the north is not surprising, due to the loess soil covering the northwest and the North China plain. Loess soil originates in the high pressure areas of the Central Asian plateaus, and has been carried by strong seasonal winds over the centuries toward the Pacific Ocean via the Gobi Desert and the northwestern steppes. As the wind gathers sand, it creates sandstorms over the northwestern mountains and the North China plain. The loose, sandy soil that accumulates as a result has at times reached depths of hundreds of feet.

Loess soil is rich, fertile, and easily dug into with simple tools, which made it easy for the people of this region to move from hunting and food gathering to agricultural cultivation of the soil, given enough water. The loose nature of the loess soil has been both a blessing and a curse to the Chinese, however, since it has also contributed to their longstanding problem of controlling the Yellow River, which carries a higher percentage of sediments than any other river. As a result, when its course breaks through the northwest mountains and levels off in the alluvial

Table 1.1   Dates of Chinese Dynasties

Dynasty	Date
Xia Dynasty	2205-1766 B.C.E.
Shang Dynasty	1766-1122 B.C.E.
Zhou Dynasty	1122-221 B.C.E.
Spring and Autumn Period	770-476 B.C.E.
Warring States Period	475-221 B.C.E.
Qin Dynasty	221-206 B.C.E.
Han Dynasty	206 B.C.E.-A.D. 220
Three Kingdoms	220-280
Western Jin	265-316
Eastern Jin	317-439
Southern and Northern Dynasties	386-589
Sui Dynasty	589-618
Tang Dynasty	618-906
Five Dynasties and Ten Kingdoms	907-960
Song Dynasty	960-1279
Yuan Dynasty	1279-1368
Ming Dynasty	1368-1644
Qing Dynasty	1644-1911

plain, its sediments settle and form sandbanks, raising the river bed and flooding adjacent lands.

Great skills in hydraulic engineering have been called upon to tame the Yellow River. The mythological sage-king Yu, founder of the legendary Xia dynasty (2205-1766 B.C.E.), was duly noted for being the first to control the great floods. Irrigation became an increasingly important concern as Chinese agriculture expanded into the Yangzi River basin and further south. Wheat was the traditional staple in the north, and terraced rice fields became a common feature of central and southern China, since rice requires flooded fields for long periods of time.

Geographically, China has long been isolated from much of the rest of the world. Its 4.2 million-square-mile territory is bordered on the north and west by underpopulated regions that came under Chinese political control relatively late in China's history. These include the mountainous region of Tibet in the southwest, the deserts of Xinjiang to the west, the barely arable region of Inner Mongolia to the north, and the fertile basin of Manchuria in the northeast. Central and southern China are bisected by vast mountain ranges, making those areas traditionally more difficult for political leaders to control. China's political center has thus been located primarily in the north.

Regardless of their differences, however, China's diverse regions were nevertheless long united in their basic beliefs and value system.

Chinese Creation Myths

According to Chinese mythology, the first man was known as Pangu. Tradition has it that Pangu lived for eighteen thousand years and created the space for man to live between Heaven and Earth. His remains were said to form the five sacred mountains of China.

Following Pangu were the three sovereigns—Fu Xi, Shen Nong, and Huang Di—who were lords of heaven, earth, and mankind. Together they taught the Chinese the various arts of civilization. Fu Xi taught the domestication of animals as well as hunting and fishing, and introduced the institution of marriage. He is also credited with the invention of musical instruments and the calendar. Shen Nong taught people to till the soil and use the plow, introduced markets for trade, and discovered the use of herbs as medicine. The legendary Yellow Emperor was the first to establish government institutions after defeating the barbarian Miao tribe. His wife, Lei Zu, originated sericulture, and is worshiped to this day as the goddess of silk. Huang Di's minister was said to have introduced the first written signs.

These three cultural heroes were followed by three great sage rulers, Yao, Shun, and Yu, who were all later held up by Confucius as model rulers of China's "Golden Age." Yao and Shun were said to be particularly virtuous and wise rulers who appointed only brilliant ministers and successors rather than their own sons. Yu, revered for having tamed a great flood, began the hereditary succession of rule, initiating China's long dynastic heritage. Yu is also credited with founding China's first dynasty, the Xia. As yet unsupported by archaeological evidence, the legendary Xia dynasty is, however, alluded to many times in later discoveries.

The Shang Dynasty (1766-1122 B.C.E.)

China's written history does not begin until approximately 1766 B.C.E. with the emergence of the Shang dynasty. Traces of unwritten history, however, go back much farther. A series of archaeological digs in the city of Zhoukoudian, thirty miles southwest of Beijing, between 1921 and 1937, unearthed "Beijing Man," estimated to be between 350,000 and 500,000 years old. He therefore lived during the Paleolithic era (ca. 1,000,000-12,000 B.C.E.). "Lantian Man," discovered in 1964 in Gansu Province, was determined to be 100,000 years older than Beijing Man. During this early time period the basic ideas of kinship, authority, religion, and art, still prevalent in China today, began to form.

The first identifiable Chinese appeared in north China during the Neolithic era (ca. 12,000-1750 B.C.E.), having evolved along the middle portion of the Yellow River, with possible links to Central Asia. The Yangshao culture, named after a village in western Henan Province south of the Yellow River, was first discovered in the 1920s. Also known as the "painted pottery culture," it is noted for its red and black painted pottery with geometric designs and ornamentation.

Because their primitive agricultural techniques quickly used up the soil, the Yangshao lived in small, temporary villages and moved frequently between sites. They displayed a knowledge of sericulture, and their graveside food vessels indicated a belief in the afterlife. This belief was a forerunner to the later practice of ancestor worship.

The Longshan culture, which followed the Yangshao in the latter part of the Neolithic period, is named for an archaeological site in Shandong Province. Longshan villages were larger, and inhabited for longer periods of time. Noted for their elegant pottery with primarily gray and black geometric patterns, indicating an indigenous cultural origin, the Longshan people domesticated dogs and pigs for food and maintained oxen and horses. The first village walls were built during this time.

Scapulimancy, the practice of heating bones and analyzing the resulting cracks to predict the future, was apparently practiced during the Longshan period. Family lineages, derived from large tribal clans, each set up their separate walled towns. It was some time during the period in which the Yangshao and Longshan cultures overlapped that Chinese civilization is considered to have its beginnings.

China's long dynastic history formally began with the Shang—the first dynasty for which there is literary as well as archaeological evidence. Although the earlier Xia dynasty is alluded to in written Shang records, no archaeological evidence for it has yet been found. The Shang is noted for its well-developed writing system, expertise in bronze casting, and the beginnings of a highly stratified society with a primitive form of ancestor worship.

In 1899 some farmers tilling their fields in the village of Xiaotun, outside the city of Anyang in northern Henan Province, found oddly shaped polished bones with cracks on the surface. Believing them to be dragon bones with inherent magical powers, the farmers sold them to local apothecaries, who in turn ground them into powder and offered them for sale as medicine. A Chinese scholar happened upon the bones and recognized the incisions as a form of early Chinese writing on what turned out to be oracle bones.

The writing on these oracle bones included both pictographs (pictorial representations of actual objects) and ideographs (more abstract representations of concepts). Tortoise shells and ox scapulae were both used for oracle bones, on which questions for the rulers were inscribed. The bones were then heated from underneath, and, depending on which way they cracked, an answer would be divined and then recorded alongside the original question.

Oracle bones served as the royal archives of the latter period of the Shang dynasty from the fourteenth century B.C.E. on, when the capital was located at Anyang. The royal house was referred to as Yin on the bones. Li Ji, the leading Chinese archaeologist at Academia Sinica (the archaeological section of China's Institute of History and Philology), systematically unearthed the oracle bones between 1928 and 1937. Professor Dong Zuopin, also of Academia Sinica, is credited with having deciphered approximately a thousand characters of their script. The basic principles of the Chinese writing system were discovered to have been already established by the Shang dynasty. The characters were originally pictographs and ideographs, depicting actual things or easily understood concepts. Later, as the written language developed, an element known as a radical, which indicates the general category of things, was combined with a phonetic element, which gives the probable pronunciation of the character. Altogether there are now 226 radicals and some 40,000 characters in the Chinese language.

The Shang dynasty, in addition to being noted for its well-developed writing system, marked the beginning of the bronze age. Shang bronze craftsmanship was unsurpassed in the world for the quality of its ritual vessels and weapons in particular. Horse-drawn chariots were also in use by this time.

The Shang kings had administrative as well as religious duties, and were considered intermediaries between the people and the unseen powers, holding undisputed sway over the Chinese world. The Son of Heaven, as the king was known, consulted diviners who interpreted oracle bones as advice from the royal ancestors and inscribed the results of their queries on the bones themselves.

According to Chinese historical records the Shang had twenty-eight rulers. The oracle bones reveal that Shang society was highly stratified, with the aristocracy leading superior lives. The ruling family used bronze vessels in court rituals to honor ancestors and placate spirits. Either a priest or the Son of Heaven himself would communicate with the ruler's ancestral spirits to gain their help and guidance. The ruler and his entourage of servants, diviners, scribes, the aristocracy, and members of the court all lived inside a walled town with a palace at the center. Farmers, who answered to the ruler or aristocratic lords, lived in surrounding villages and were expected to serve in the army. The king ruled through military strength rather than personal merit. Warfare was incessant, eventually contributing to the downfall of the dynasty. Human sacrifices of prisoners of war were common. Servants were sometimes buried alive to serve the aristocracy in the afterlife. The barbarism of the Shang is attested to by the many tombs containing decapitated skeletons.

It was long believed in China that two souls existed within each human being: an animal soul (*po*), which resided with the body after death, and a spiritual soul (*hun*), which left for the netherworld after death. Both required sacrifices to be placated. Spirits that never received sacrifices from descendants were believed to become "hungry ghosts" who would haunt the living, while those who received sacrifices helped their descendants. Thus began China's cult of the ancestor.

The origins of China's authoritarian pattern of government (political absolutism) can be seen clearly in the Shang dynasty. The ruling class had great power over others by virtue of its monopoly of bronze metallurgy. Those who possessed bronzes for ritual purposes had the sanction of *Shangdi,* or the Lord-on-High. The constant need for a unified defense against neighboring nomads led to the development of an absolute centralized state. The need for huge cooperative efforts to control the Yellow River was another source of the state's authority, with absolutist monarchs, supported by a bureaucratic class, ruling over a mostly peasant population.

The Zhou Dynasty (1122-221 B.C.E.)

The barbarism of the Shang dynasty was replaced by the emergence of humanism in the Zhou—a dynasty named after a former vassal state that overthrew the Shang. The leader of this rebellion has been identified in oracle bones as one who formerly served the Shang court. Human sacrifices used in burials during the Shang dynasty were replaced by clay figurines of people and animals that were entombed with the deceased along with furniture, cooking utensils, and anything else deemed necessary to serve the dead in the afterlife.

The Zhou was the longest dynasty in Chinese history, bringing with it the golden age of Chinese philosophy. The ethical world view of Confucianism emerged during the Zhou and has remained China's foremost philosophical system through the present.

While the Shang believed in *Shangdi,* the Zhou developed the concept of *Tian,* or Heaven. This new, more universal, concept of "Heaven" was soon followed by the concept of "morality." The introduction of these two ideas became the greatest legacy of the Zhou rulers, laying the basic foundation for the future Chinese system of government and society.

Concomitant to these two concepts was the notion of a "Heavenly Mandate," which posited that it was Heaven's will that a new dynasty should be created if the previous ruler proved unworthy. That this concept should have first appeared during the Zhou is not surprising, since it was also a way of legitimizing the overthrow of the long-ruling Shang. The idea of a Mandate of Heaven ensured that the ruler was to be considered the intermediary between Heaven and Earth. In fact, the Chinese character for "king" (*wang*) shows three horizontal lines representing heaven, man, and earth, and one vertical line connecting the three, symbolizing the role of the ruler. The idea of the Mandate of Heaven set a standard for government rule and thereby forever legitimized the people's right to overthrow a corrupt government.

Three early powers behind the Zhou dynasty are well known—King Wen, King Wu, and the Duke of Zhou. King Wen, a Shang dynasty court official renowned for his organizational skills, planned the original conquest of the Shang. King Wu, his son, was the first to lay claim to the newly conceived idea of the Heavenly Mandate, leading allied tribal leaders to defeat the Shang. However, he died in 1115 B.C.E., just seven years after proclaiming the Zhou dynasty. The Duke of Zhou, considered one of China's greatest statesmen, is credited with originating the idea of the Mandate of Heaven. He was also the leader of the armies that crushed a Shang rebellion to finally establish the Zhou rule.

Although the Zhou has been considered a feudal society, political control depended more on family ties, an extension of Shang tribal organization, than on feudal bonds. The various city-states within the Zhou domain became increasingly centralized, contributing to greater control over local government and a more routine form of agricultural taxation.

In 771 B.C.E., barbarians in alliance with rebel feudal lords overthrew the Zhou court and killed the king. They moved the capital east from Hao (near the present day city of Xi'an, known then as Chang'an) in modern Shaanxi Province to Luoyang, in modern Henan Province. This move precipitated the weakening of the Zhou court and the fragmentation of the empire. The ensuing period, sometimes referred to as the Eastern Zhou (770-221 B.C.E.), is further subdivided into the Spring and Autumn Period (770-476 B.C.E.), named after a famous historical chronicle written during that time, and the Warring States Period (475-221 B.C.E.).

The Zhou was also notable for moving China from the bronze age into the iron age, around 500 B.C.E., contributing to the refinement of weapons for war as well as the manufacture of farm tools. Coins were now produced and great public works begun, including flood control projects, irrigation systems, and canals.

Although the Eastern Zhou was notorious for its lack of political unity and its civil strife, it also marked China's golden age of philosophy, in response to the need for introspection and reform during a time of great political and social turmoil. Regional lords who competed to build strong armies and increase economic production needed more guidance from educated and skilled officials and teachers, recruited on the basis of merit. Many philosophers of the day also acted as advisers to the rulers on methods of government, war, and diplomacy. In their various ways, each of the philosophers of the Zhou dynasty dealt with questions of how best to live in a decidedly imperfect society.

Confucius

Confucius (551-479 B.C.E.), or Kong Fuzi, born in the state of Lu in present-day Shandong Province, was one such itinerant thinker. He believed that a person's ability and sense of morality, rather than birth, should be the basis for leadership. He advocated a society based more on universal human relationships than on feudal obligations. In particular he is known for having identified the "five major relationships" (father-son, emperor-subject, husband-wife, elder brother-younger brother, and friend-friend), which conceived of the individual and family as a microcosm of the society, the state, the country, and finally the universe itself. If each person acted according to his position in the family, harmony and peace would prevail. It is written in the *Analects,* sayings of Confucius collected by his disciples, that

Confucius (551-479 B.C.E.), Zhou dynasty philosopher and political reformer. Confucianism long served as China's official state doctrine and remains influential in China today.

"A man of benevolence, wishing to establish his own character also establishes the character of others, and wishing to be prominent also helps others to be prominent. In the end there will be self-perfection, family harmony, social order, and world peace. When the individual and society are in proper order, the Way is said to prevail."

A political reformer rather than a religious leader, Confucius embraced a highly stratified society as the key to the success of political systems and establishment of higher ethical standards. Confucius espoused the virtues of benevolence, righteousness, ritual (etiquette), filial piety, and harmony. His ideal man was a *junzi,* or gentleman, whose efforts at self-cultivation made him a "superior man." Confucius

believed that education, which alone could bring out the good in one who might otherwise be evil, should be available to all, regardless of economic background.

The final goal of all education was government service, and the body of works known as the Confucian Classics were later to become the basis of the civil service examination system, through which government officials were recruited until 1905. Although Confucius's ideas have influenced future generations of Chinese through the twentieth century, he himself never achieved an influential government position during his own lifetime, and died believing he was a failure.

Mencius (372-289 B.C.E.), or Mengzi, a disciple of Confucius who made major contributions to the development of Confucianism, believed that human nature is basically good. His idea that a ruler could not rule without the consent of the people led to the notion of "the right to rebel" against a ruler who did not take proper care of his subjects, effectively making him lose the Mandate of Heaven. He posited that people had an innate sense of right and wrong.

Another follower of Confucius, Xun Zi (300-237 B.C.E.), believed that human nature was innately evil and that people needed strict laws to guide them toward goodness. His belief that truly good government was based on authoritarian control rather than ethical or moral suasion led to the philosophy of Legalism, which promoted the interests of the state above all else and emphasized authoritarianism along with strict laws and punishments. The earliest Legalists were Han Feizi (d. 233 B.C.E.) and Li Si (d. 208 B.C.E.), who believed in the preservation of social order through the strict enforcement of laws. This philosophy was to play its greatest role during the following dynasty, the Qin. Legalists believed that strengthening the state was more important than looking after the welfare of the common people.

Laozi and Daoism

While Confucianism focused on the way of man and society, Daoism, the second most important school of Chinese thought, emphasized the way of nature. Laozi (literally "Old Master"), its purported founder, may never have existed, but the Daoist philosophy has exerted a great influence on the Chinese people and their arts. The concept of Dao is difficult to define. It has been compared to an uncarved block, and its essence is said to be eternal, absolute, and beyond space and time. According to this philosophy, harmony is achieved when the forces of yin (represented by the female, and the elements of passivity and darkness) and yang (represented by the male, activity, and lightness) interact and are well balanced.

Yin and yang are considered complementary, rather than opposite. In yin-yang theory all things rise and fall, integrate and disintegrate, but all are related. In the end, there is a unity between man and nature. For the Daoists a good life of simplicity, spontaneity, and tranquillity characterizes the natural state. The Dao, then, can be conceived of as the ultimate ordering principle of the universe.

Zhuangzi (ca. 369-286 B.C.E.), another famous Daoist philosopher, was less concerned than Laozi about seeing the Dao as a guide in life rather than as that which has a value intrinsic to itself. Whereas Laozi encouraged the ruler to return to a state of primitive simplicity, Zhuangzi did not concern himself at all with society or its reform, but rather believed it necessary to rise above it.

Mozi

The last major philosophical system to emerge during this period was known as Moism, based on the ideas of Mozi (470-391 B.C.E.), who believed in extreme utilitarianism and universal love. This latter notion ran counter to the basic Confucian virtue of filial piety, which held love and respect for one's own parents above almost everything else. His ideas about utilitarianism also ran counter to the Confucian emphasis on ritual and music, both of which Mozi considered wasteful. Mozi also regarded warfare as wasteful and espoused pacifism. He believed that people should obey their leaders and that leaders should follow the will of Heaven.

The Qin Dynasty (221-206 B.C.E.)

Warfare presaged the end of the Zhou dynasty, with various regional kings vying for control of the entire territory that was China. The regional state of Qin, with its harsh methods of government and citizen control, based on the ideas of Xunzi, proved the strongest and emerged victorious. The name "China" comes from this dynasty (pronounced "chin"), the first to unify the entire country.

Emperor Qin Shi Huang, its first ruler, was the first to centralize the Chinese government by dividing it into several administrative districts, each headed by one of the emperor's officials. Under the direction of Li Si, his able Legalist administrator, weights and measures were finally standardized, as was the Chinese writing system itself. Massive public works projects were undertaken, necessitating the conscription of slaves. Portions of the Great Wall, which had been built by various states in previous periods to keep out the northern Mongol barbarians, were connected for the first time, creating a wall five thousand kilometers long. What is known today as the Great Wall of China is actually four walls that were rebuilt or extended during the Western Han, Sui, Jin, and Ming dynasties.

More than four thousand miles of imperial highways were built. Approximately twelve hundred miles of waterways and canals were cut to facilitate water transport from the Yangzi River south to Guangzhou (Canton). The Qin Emperor began constructing his own tomb immediately after ascending the throne. The entrance to this huge tomb, first excavated in the 1970s in Xi'an, was found to contain thousands of terra-cotta warriors—each with a different costume, hairstyle, and facial expression. They still guard the main tomb of the emperor himself, which is as yet unexcavated.

In keeping with his totalitarian form of rule, the Qin Emperor decreed in 213 B.C.E. that all Confucian books and unofficial Qin historical chronicles were to be publicly burned. Confucian scholars were said to have been burned alive, and those who cited the Confucian Classics in order to criticize the government were executed. Neither praise for the past nor criticism of the present was tolerated.

Under such conditions, it is not surprising that as soon as the Qin Emperor died in 210 B.C.E., revolts immediately broke out across China. The Qin dynasty was overthrown by the first peasant rebellion in Chinese history, which erupted in response to the inhumane conditions of forced labor and heavy taxation needed to support its massive projects. In the year 206 B.C.E. the entire imperial library was destroyed during a period of civil unrest. The imperial system that had begun during the Qin, however, remained the basic pattern for Chinese government.

The Han Dynasty (206 B.C.E.-A.D. 220)

China enjoyed a long and peaceful rule during the next dynasty, the Han, whose capital was at Chang'an, or modern-day Xi'an. This dynasty was noted for westward territorial expansion and the use of the Silk Road for contact with Central Asia and Rome. Parts of what is now northern Vietnam and northern Korea were annexed by China toward the end of the second century B.C.E. During the Han the "tributary system" also emerged, wherein peace was maintained with non-Chinese states in the region by allowing them to remain autonomous in exchange for symbolic acceptance of Han rulership. Gifts were also exchanged and intermarriages arranged for this purpose.

Confucianism became the official state doctrine during the Han. The civil service examination, with the Confucian Classics as its foundation, was first instituted to recruit government servants. Books were particularly prized after having been publicly burned during the previous dynasty, and the Confucian Classics were reconstructed from memory by scholars. New types of poetry and historiography emerged, with Sima Qian's (145-?87 B.C.E.) *Records of the Historian,* a chronicle from the legendary Xia dynasty to that of the Han Emperor Wu Di (141-87 B.C.E.), becoming the style for all of the era's later historical writing. These histories had a particularly didactic tone, supporting the notion that the ruler of each dynasty could learn from the past. Although they provided facts and data based on the records of daily affairs from the court archivist, these writings exhibited little analysis within a conceptual framework, such as would exist today in works of a similar nature. Buddhism was also introduced from India during this period.

Inventions during the Han included paper and porcelain. Han rulers retained the basic administrative structure begun during the short-lived Qin dynasty, but created vassal states in some areas for political convenience rather than insisting on strict centralized control. Coupled with territorial expansion and overall peace, the Han was the first dynasty during which Chinese culture truly flourished. The Chinese have thus continued to use the word "Han" when referring to members of the country's ethnic majority.

From A.D. 9 to 24, Han dynastic rule was briefly interrupted by the reformer Wang Mang, who actually appointed himself emperor and began the "New" (Xin) dynasty. A relative of the empress dowager, Wang attempted to nationalize all land in the empire and prohibit private ownership of land or slaves. He reestablished state control over certain commodities, including salt, iron, liquor, timber, and fish in order to increase government revenues. Wang Mang also created granaries in various cities, which helped to stabilize prices and create a grain surplus in case of need during future famines.

The interests of the wealthy and powerful families throughout the country were threatened by such actions, however. Without the support of the central government Wang Mang's ideas for reform failed. Banditry resurfaced and famine ravaged the country, as years of official neglect of basic flood control and grain storage measures were felt.

In particular, a group known as the Red Eyebrows, who came from the imperial Liu family, raided villages and easily defeated Wang Mang's armies. Both peasants and gentry alike supported the Liu clan due to their connection to the Han ruling house. Eventually they captured the capital and killed Wang Mang, displaying his head in the marketplace. In the year A.D. 25, one of the rival Liu factions succeeded to the throne and began the Later Han dynasty, which lasted for another two hundred years.

By 220 the Han empire had collapsed under the weight of increasing corruption. With government centralization had come a greatly increased population and greater wealth, as well as rivalries and increasingly complex political institutions. A variety of domestic and external pressures contributed to

Numerous as-yet unexplored imperial burial mounds created for emperors of the Han dynasty (206 B.C.E.-A.D. 220) exist on the outskirts of the Han dynasty capital of Chang'an, now the modern city of Xi'an in Shaanxi Province.

its demise. Corrupt eunuchs gained power, a move that was protested immediately, though futilely, by scholar-officials. Great families gained even greater wealth at the expense of impoverished peasants, leading to widespread rebellion.

Popular religious cults spawned such groups as the Yellow Turbans, so named for the yellow kerchiefs worn around their heads. Yellow was a highly symbolic color for those who followed a magical offshoot of Daoism. According to naturalist concepts, yellow was the color of Earth, which was believed to follow the color red, representing fire, in the Five Agents theory. Fire was the agent, and red therefore the color, of the Han. The implication in wearing yellow was that there was to be both social and political change so that the poorer segments of society could be strengthened.

Although the Yellow Turbans did not succeed in overthrowing the government, other rebels followed their lead and helped weaken the already relatively powerless central government. Provincial military leaders were called in to help, but since the majority of them came from powerful local families, a type of "warlordism" emerged. These new warlords possessed not only military might but economic strength and social prestige as well. Eventually the emperor became a mere puppet in their hands, and was deposed in A.D. 220.

The Period of Disunion

The four centuries following the end of the Han dynasty were characterized by constant warfare among various states, gradual expansion to the southeast, and the development of Buddhism (first century A.D.) and Daoism. China was divided into the Three Kingdoms (Wei, Shu, and Wu), which reigned between A.D. 220 and 280. The Western Jin (265-316), with its capital at Luoyang, and the Eastern Jin (317-439), with its capital at Nanjing, were dynasties that briefly restored unity but were soon overrun by nomadic groups. With the removal of

China's capital to Nanjing, political fragmentation ensued and the sinification of non-Chinese increased in the north and among aboriginal tribesmen in the south. The Southern and Northern dynasties (386-589), were notable for dramatic sculptures of Buddhist figures carved in caves, as well as the invention of the wheelbarrow. Advances in medicine, cartography, and astronomy were also made during this period.

The Sui Dynasty (589-618)

China was unified politically for the second time in the Sui dynasty. Its centralized government, much more benevolent than that of the Qin, was still rather ruthless. The Grand Canal, the outstanding technological achievement of this dynasty, facilitated travel and trade by creating a waterway flowing directly from Beijing in the north to Hangzhou in the south.

The Sui leaders sought to reconstruct the Great Wall as well, but this only contributed to tyrannical demands being made on the people, who were already suffering under the burdens of great taxes and compulsory labor. Military campaigns against Korea in the early seventh century further weakened the dynasty, which finally collapsed as a result of popular revolts, disloyalty, and assassination.

The Tang Dynasty (618-906)

The apex of Chinese civilization and the heights of cultural achievement—even superior to those of the Han—were reached during the Tang dynasty. The Chinese government once again asserted political dominance over all of East Asia, now including Japan, thus expanding its territory and influence beyond that of the Han. Commerce flourished, and Buddhism, imported from India, now took root as a permanent part of traditional Chinese culture. An extensive system of roads was built. The entire era was seen as an aristocratic age in which a few powerful families had great influence over the state by virtue of their political and financial monopolies.

While at first military power was valued over moral or intellectual achievement, the civil service exam was soon perfected, allowing men of talent and Confucian training to enter public service. This new group of Confucian literati, or scholar-officials, did not pose the same destabilizing threat to the Tang rulers as the powerful aristocratic families during this era, because it held no private territory or base of power. In fact, the role of China's scholar-officials from the Tang dynasty through the end of the last dynasty in 1911 proved to be of paramount importance as a major link between the government and the people.

The Tang dynasty witnessed a golden age of Chinese literature and art. Poetry and painting flourished, with artists such as Li Bai, Du Fu, and Wang Wei all reaching unsurpassed heights of artistic achievement. The written word was made available to greater numbers of people through the invention of block printing.

Toward the middle of the eighth century, economic instability and military defeat in Central Asia marked the beginning of the end of Tang rule. Over the next five centuries the Chinese empire would decline steadily, allowing northern invaders to overthrow the dynasty after a long string of popular rebellions combined with military defeat and economic disasters.

With the downfall of the Tang, China was once again divided, this time into Five Dynasties in the north (907-960) and Ten Kingdoms in the south. Fraught with alien invasions and conquests, China was again forced to face its traditional enemies, the northern nomads, who had plagued it with raids throughout the dynastic era.

The Song Dynasty (960-1279)

The Song dynasty is divided into Northern Song (960-1127) and Southern Song (1127-1279), the latter period noting the year the Song court had to flee south to escape nomadic invaders. Song government was characterized by a centralized bureaucracy that employed civilian scholar-officials. Centrally appointed officials replaced regional military governors, enabling the emperor to have greater power than ever before.

Cities developed commercially as well as admin-

Detail from a Qing dynasty copy of the famous Song dynasty scroll "Spring Festival along the River." The scroll provides valuable insight into daily life and customs of the Song dynasty.

istratively, and the scholar-official class resided in the provincial centers alongside merchants, artisans, and shopkeepers. A new mercantile class of wealthy commoners arose, as printing, education, and trade spread between the coastal provinces and China's interior. For the first time neither the possession of land nor a government position was needed to gain wealth or prestige.

Paper production was further refined, gunpowder was discovered at this time, and the cruel practice of footbinding for young girls from wealthy families was initiated. Literature and philosophy flourished. With the invention of moveable type, literature became accessible to the masses for the first time, and various new literary genres emerged. Oral story-telling in the marketplace led to the development of the short story and the strange tales of Daoism. During the Tang dynasty the cultivated man was not only scholar but poet, painter, and statesman as well. Intellectuals during the Song dynasty con-

tinued this tradition but returned to the Confucian Classics for answers to philosophical and political questions. Buddhism was now seen as a foreign religion with little relevance to the problems faced by the Chinese.

Philosophically, neo-Confucianism took hold, reaching its height with the philosopher Zhuxi (1130-1200), who synthesized elements of Buddhism and Daoism with Confucianism. His ideas dominated official state ideology from the late Song through the nineteenth century. After being incorporated into the civil service examination system, Zhuxi's philosophy evolved into a rigid creed. The Confucian notion of the five relationships began to emphasize obligations of the subservient to the dominant. While stabilizing society, this interpretation inhibited development of premodern Chinese society, and greatly slowed down cultural and institutional change through the nineteenth century.

The Yuan Dynasty (1279-1368)

China's worst fears about invasion by its northern neighbors were realized in 1260, when the great Mongol leader Kublai Khan (1215-1294), grandson of Genghis Khan (1167?-1227), began his attack against the Southern Song. The Mongol Yuan dynasty, the first non-Chinese dynasty in the country's history, began barely a decade later.

The Mongols early on gave up the attempt to govern China through Chinese bureaucrats and traditional institutions, and soon monopolized all major government posts themselves. Ruling as unwelcome conquerors, the Mongols clearly discriminated against the Chinese throughout society, especially within the political sector. To avoid employing Chinese, non-Chinese from as far away as Central Asia, the Middle East, and even Europe were sought for positions for which no Mongol could be found. The Chinese were often sent to non-Chinese regions to work.

Ironically, Confucianism was reinstated for governmental practices. The Mongols even revived civil service exams based on the Confucian Classics after they had fallen out of use in the hope that these would help them somehow maintain order in Chinese society.

The Mongol rulers, about whom the Italian explorer Marco Polo would later write, ensured that China maintained contacts and cultural exchanges with the West. In keeping with this view, Christian missionaries from Europe were allowed free rein in China. Meanwhile, Chinese in the northwest and southwest were increasingly converted to Islam by Muslims from Central Asia.

A literary renaissance blossomed. The novel and the drama became highly developed, and the written vernacular was more widely used. The acrobatics much loved and performed by the Mongols influenced Chinese theater and later became an integral part of Beijing Opera. Travel literature, cartography, and geography, as well as science, all experienced an upsurge. Road and water linkages were reorganized and granaries were built throughout the empire to protect against possible famine. Beijing itself was rebuilt with new palace grounds, and the Grand Canal was completely renovated, with Beijing its last stop. All these improvements greatly facilitated commercial contacts between China and Europe. Scientific discoveries and architectural innovations were all exchanged, as were food and methods of cooking.

The Mongols maintained the most extensive land empire ever known, with China as only one of its provinces. But a combination of natural disasters, peasant uprisings, and rivalry among Mongol heirs all led to the demise of the Yuan dynasty and to the Mongol's retreat back into the northern desert by 1368. The rebels who returned the governance of China to Chinese hands did not wish for a social revolution, but rather the re-establishment of a truly Chinese dynasty under Confucianist influence. It is to this dynasty that we turn to begin a more detailed look at the emergence of modern China.

The Ming Dynasty (1368-1644)

Confucianism took its strongest hold in China after the Mongols were ousted from China, and along with it the civil service exams. In a swing of the pendulum back toward political control of its own destiny, China's xenophobic and isolationist sentiments quickly resurfaced.

The Ming dynasty represented the height of political and social conservatism. The stability of the dynasty lulled the Chinese into believing they had reached the apex of their civilization and that things foreign were neither welcomed nor needed. In the early part of the dynasty, the population remained steady at about 100 million. Politics, the economy, the arts, and society all remained unchanged for decades. As Ming conservatism made itself manifest in the civil service exams, independence of thought was no longer rewarded. This era of complacency, however, occurred just at the point in China's history when sixteenth- and seventeenth-century Portuguese, Dutch, Spanish, and English traders appeared, and when China faced a new form of imperialism closer to home, in the form of the Japanese. The Ming dynasty was to prove to be the last bastion of Chinese conservatism.

In the Ming dynasty, for the first time since the Han dynasty more than fifteen hundred years earlier, a peasant became the emperor of China. Zhu Yuanzhang, a peasant and one-time Buddhist monk from Anhui Province, turned to a rebel life upon seeing Chinese landlords and officials collaborate with the Mongols. His parents and older brother had died in a famine and his monastery had been destroyed in local fighting.

Illiterate until his early twenties, Zhu Yuanzhang worked with the Red Turbans and quickly became a local power in his own right, capturing Nanjing in 1356 and proclaiming it his capital. After a decade of consolidating power he took Beijing in the north and pushed the Mongols back into the steppes, establishing the Ming dynasty in 1368, with Nanjing as its capital.

Zhu Yuanzhang became known as Ming Taizu (r. 1368-1398), or the Hongwu Emperor. Although he never fully trusted intellectuals, he relied on capable advisers to administer his territory effectively, with the structure of government changed only slightly from that of previous dynasties. An able organizer and administrator, Ming Taizu quickly restored the viability of the government and the economy. Any changes he made had the effect of increasing the emperor's power and weakening potential opposition from civil servants.

As for his personality, Ming Taizu was known to be domineering to the point of being tyrannical. When he suspected his own prime minister, who was also a close friend, of plotting a rebellion, Ming Taizu not only got rid of the official but permanently eliminated the office of prime minister. He later elevated several grand secretaries from among those who had passed the highest level of the civil service exams, known as the *jinshi*.

The grand secretaries were sent for special advanced training to the Hanlin Academy, specially designed for scholars of the highest literary achievement. In an effort to control their power, however, they were given ranks lower than prefects at first, with no powers of decision or supervision over general affairs. Eventually, however, they formed a cabinet, and their ranks were raised in recognition of the great influence they had over the emperor.

Ming Taizu focused heavily on a defensive army with a complicated chain of command that effectively thwarted insubordination and rebellion. Military security was of paramount importance to him, and military status was made hereditary under his rule. Hundreds of garrisons were created throughout the country, mostly along the border areas as well as near Nanjing and Beijing. Each garrison was in charge of battalions of about a thousand men each, and each soldier was given a share of land to make him self-sufficient. This arrangement proved to be inadequate during long campaigns, however.

The Civil Service Exams

The most absolutist of any Chinese ruler up to that point, Ming Taizu attempted to redesign the civil service system in order to strengthen his own position and weaken the potential for opposition to the government. To ensure a representative segment of society sufficiently well educated to compete in the civil service exams, Ming Taizu established schools in each district, subprefecture, and prefecture of the country. Local exams were administered first, and those who passed were eligible to take the state examinations. Village schools cropped up everywhere, with the education of the entire rural population as the goal. Ming Taizu strongly identified with the common people and hoped to affect them more deeply than any previous Chinese government, but a lack of state funds prevented major change in popular education.

Ming Taizu also sought to create one ideology for the state. While he did not succeed in his own era, during the next emperor's reign the entire examination system became based on the neo-Confucian school of thought, using Zhuxi's commentaries on the Confucian Classics. A new edition of the Classics was commissioned and exam questions were based on this more recent interpretation, thus reducing and simplifying the learning to be tested on the exams.

Not only the content but also the form of the civil service exam was simplified. The "eight-legged essay," or *baguwen* style, was developed, which was supposed to make it easier for the candidate to order and express his thoughts and for the reader to grade the answer. Forced to conform to this essay form's elaborately parallel structure, candidates in the end paid more attention to the style than the content, which itself had already been simplified, inhibiting individual thought and creativity. Ming Taizu's final mode of restructuring the civil service system was to permit public beatings of officials who might previously have simply been demoted or fined. This graphically demonstrated the official's status as little more than a servant to the emperor.

To stifle opposition to his own rule, Ming Taizu ordered tens of thousands of wealthy families in the lower Yangzi Valley to relocate to poorer areas or to his capital at Nanjing, where they could be more closely watched. To promote conformity among the masses, he wrote six general precepts, known as the Six Maxims, to be followed by all. These taught respect for superiors, the need for moral guidance of youth, and contentment with one's lot in life. Rubbings of these maxims, which were engraved in stone, were given to every household in every village and were to be periodically read by the village elders to indoctrinate the entire population in the virtues of order.

Foreign Influence

After Ming Taizu's death his grandson took the throne, but he was soon challenged by his uncle, who commanded the northern armies at Beijing. His uncle won a bitter civil war and captured Nanjing. He soon moved the capital to Beijing, which became a capital city for the first time under Han Chinese rule.

The new emperor, known as the Yongle Emperor, built a new imperial city on the site of the old Mongol capital, keeping Nanjing as a second capital, which for the most part had only local jurisdiction.

The move to Beijing had far-reaching implications for the nation. In order to receive grain as a tax to support the government and army, the Grand Canal was restored, linking the Yangzi region to Beijing. Northern candidates for the civil service exam were now subject to larger quotas in order to maintain a regional balance within the bureaucracy, since more attention had traditionally been paid to intellectual pursuits in the south.

The south had indeed become more advanced, both economically and culturally. By moving the capital to Beijing, and creating a magnificent palace there, the Yongle Emperor ensured that northern invaders from the steppe regions would have to face a swifter and stronger northern military presence. He succeeded in holding off the Mongols for a time. Chinese territory once again expanded as Han Chinese moved into Yunnan in the southwest as well. Military campaigns in Inner Asia went as far north as the Amur River and as far south as Annam (as northern Vietnam was then called), making both Annam and Burma Chinese subjects.

The Yongle Emperor was even more successful with his maritime expeditions that sailed the China Seas and the Indian Ocean, reaching as far as the east coast of Africa between 1405 and 1433. Expeditions to Indochina and Malaya had begun during the Song dynasty, when the capital moved to the lower Yangzi area and served to strengthen the dynasty's prestige as well as to encourage trading between the countries. During the Ming dynasty this push southward continued as it had under the Song as well as the Yuan.

Most of these maritime expeditions were led by the famous Cheng He, a Muslim eunuch considered one of the greatest navigators and commanders in history. Seven missions, including as many as sixty-three ships and nearly thirty thousand men, stimulated large-scale reforestation around Nanjing in 1391, so that 50 million trees could be planted to prepare for the shipbuilding that would be required by future naval expeditions. The sailors, who were often gone for two or three years at a time, succeeded in increasing the prestige of the dynasty abroad.

Another reason for the expeditions was to encourage tributary relations to both increase the prestige of the Chinese empire and confirm the emperor's role as holding the Heavenly Mandate for all mankind. Foreign embassies from Annam, Japan, Korea, and Malaya all paid tribute. Several foreign rulers returned with the Ming ships as well, either as tributaries or as prisoners. The great importance placed on paying tribute to the emperor is best exemplified by the fate of approximately five thousand overseas Chinese who had failed to pay proper respects to the

Chinese when the mission reached Sumatra and were said to have been summarily massacred.

Decline of the Military and Maritime Expeditions

Maritime missions suddenly ceased after the Yongle Emperor's reign ended, leading some to believe that his primary motive had been to find the nephew whom he had previously forced off the throne and whose death had never been proved. Foreign relations soon became primarily defensive, and the expense of large-scale expeditions was no longer feasible when the Chinese had to defend themselves against the northern barbarians.

Another important factor that contributed to the cessation of maritime expeditions was court opposition by conservative officials, who believed that the very concept of expansion and commerce was anathema to the true Chinese spirit of government. Pressure from a powerful neo-Confucian bureaucracy eventually led to the revival of a strict, agrarian-centered society.

China's domestic situation was strained even before the Yongle Emperor died, with the power of the eunuchs becoming a serious source of competition for the kings. Since the Song dynasty, eunuchs had been restricted to functioning primarily as household servants. Although the first Ming emperor did not use them as administrators, during the Yongle Emperor's reign they participated in expeditions abroad and even acted as military supervisors elsewhere. Their supervisory roles in the administration of industry and finance made them a major political force.

The military system slowly depleted the state treasury surplus. Forces in the field withdrew from northeast Manchuria as well as south of the Great Wall after the Yongle period. In 1427 Annam was left independent. With the decline of the navy, China's coast saw a resurgence of piracy.

Important administrative issues were sorely neglected as a result of numerous factional disputes, especially after an incident in 1449 involving the young Chengtong Emperor (1436-1449). The emperor was advised by several eunuchs to chastise personally a Mongol leader of the Oirat tribes, a successor group of the Mongols, in response to their frequent raids against Chinese territory. The emperor was immediately imprisoned by the Mongols and, though finally released, he was so rattled by the affair that he created an entirely new, and expensive, military force in the form of the emperor's standing bodyguard garrisons. While the emperor had been imprisoned, however, a new emperoror had been enthroned. Upon the original emperor's release from the Mongols a succession crisis ensued, further poisoning the atmosphere in the already polarized and hostile court. The Chinese could clearly no longer control the tribal people of the steppes and began a defensive policy based largely on the new Great Wall they built to the south of the Ordos Desert.

Sixteenth-Century Ming China

The Chinese court in the sixteenth century was rife with factional disputes. The eunuchs gained power even over the grand secretaries, and the rulers themselves became increasingly derelict in their responsibilities toward the country. Local and provincial officials bribed eunuchs in order to retain their positions, and they in turn took large payments from the farming populace.

Foreigners made frequent border attacks. Mongols raided again in the north, and in 1550 succeeded in penetrating the Great Wall and gaining power near Beijing. The Japanese also menaced China, at first along the coast of Korea and then through raids on China's coastal communities, beginning in the thirteenth century and reoccurring again in the sixteenth, when they seized several offshore islands. In addition, Chinese outlaws conducted many raids in the sixteenth century, reflecting the failure of China's own government to control the situation.

After the Portuguese began to sail the Indian Ocean they reached Guangzhou in 1517 and then Ningbo, finally settling in Macao in 1557. Their advanced ships, navigating skills, and firearms earned them a degree of respect, although the Chinese quickly began to regard Europeans as barbarians like the Mongols, because they also pirated, looted, and killed.

Economy and Society During the Ming

By 1600 China's population had reached 150 million. This greatly increased population was able to sustain itself by taking advantage of new crops introduced by the European explorers in China's midst since the sixteenth century, including maize, sweet potatoes, Irish potatoes, and peanuts. Certain strains of rice, wheat, and sorghum were also grown more widely than before.

Commerce thrived, and a wealthy gentry class grew larger from the maritime trade. The towns of the lower Yangzi region, which had become centers of agricultural and commercial wealth, saw long periods of urban prosperity. Scholars began to gather with painters and poets for poetry contests and philosophical debates away from the court. Especially in the idyllic cities of Wuxi and Suzhou, they created magnificent surroundings for themselves, including gardens with waterfalls, artificial hills, and pavilions. Paintings of the Song and Yuan dynasties were collected by connoisseurs, who increased their value by adding their own seals and inscriptions.

Handicrafts began to develop and were bought by the court, the scholar-gentry, and the new business class. Colorful cloisonné enamel first appeared during the Ming on all sorts of objects, including dishes and vases. Decorative tapestry produced by weavers included reproductions of paintings and calligraphy on textiles. The Ming was also known for dark red carved lacquer with rich designs. But of all these, porcelain became the most famous of Ming crafts. Already manufactured during the Tang, Song porcelain was noted for its simplicity of forms and purity of colors. The fame attained by Ming porcelain in Europe is revealed in its Western name, "china," as if it represented the glory of the country itself. The style that made Ming porcelain famous was underglazed cobalt blue and white, although luminous white porcelain was also produced.

Economic development was evinced by the use of silver for money, which marked the beginning of a new fiscal era in which taxes were collected primarily in silver rather than in grain. Many surcharges, incidental taxes, and various new taxes had long beleaguered taxpayers and recordkeepers alike. The new Single Whip Tax, which introduced the concept of revenues payable in silver, noted on one bill all the various types of tax each person was obliged to pay. Its name was derived from the fact that the single statement received by each taxpayer replaced the one crack of the whip he had to suffer for the year.

As China's sixteenth-century economy grew, so did the availability of books and education. No longer were the literati the only ones to write poetry; merchants and artisans followed suit. The private life of the wealthy, full of scholarship, art, philanthropy, and the pleasures of food, began to take precedence over their official life.

The Confucian encouragement of self-cultivation reappeared, and emphasis began to be placed on the individual's capacity for knowing and containing good within himself. Wang Yangming (1472-1529) was the primary advocate of this philosophy, as originally defined by Zhuxi in the Song dynasty. Zhuxi's neo-Confucianism emphasized both the principle of reason and the principle of intuition. By understanding these principles and studying the Confucian Classics, people could overcome selfishness and partiality. One could identify with Heaven and the morality it represented and resist human desire through self-cultivation.

In contrast, the school of intuition emphasized the unity of the mind with the universe. This unity could not be achieved through study but through realization of an innate knowledge of what is good. It was this latter "School of the Mind" that Wang Yangming advocated, but with an additional concept: the unity of knowledge and action. His ideas gained prominence in private academies, further dividing the government from the scholars. In either case, there was a renewed emphasis on reviving Confucian ethics among the literati (scholar-elites) and re-establishing government integrity.

Because right action was the proof of true knowledge and knowledge was inseparable from action, one had to make a firm decision to follow the Way, including meditation and the practice of righteous works. Where Zhuxi emphasized orthodoxy and the importance of learning the Classics, Wang Yangming's thought implied a type of individualism in which every man had sagelike potential. Zhuxi's particular brand of philosophy produced learned men, while Wang Yangming's produced good men who had relied on methods of self-cultivation.

Wang was instrumental in establishing some of the academies that sprang up during the Ming, especially in the south, as centers for the serious pursuit of wisdom through the interaction between master and disciple. State schools, on the other hand, continued to emphasize preparation for the civil service exams. Wealth and status, likely within the grasp of graduates of state schools, were not the goal of Wang's academies, although they were often connected to political causes through the patronage of high officials. By emphasizing reform, academies posed a threat to the government and were put under closer state control.

The Arts

A clear division between the court and the scholar-elite could be seen in art and literature as well. The court produced great encyclopedic works of knowledge, rather than philosophical treatises. Court painters specialized in stylistically conservative details of flowers and birds. Technique was prized by court artists well above the expression of ideas or philosophical concepts, such as had been favored by Song artists.

Independent painters who flourished during the mid-Ming displayed great imagination. Foremost among them was Shen Chou (1427-1509), considered the founder of the Wu school of painting. The Wu school took its name from the ancient name for the city of Suzhou, home to many of these independent-minded painters. With the stress now placed on intuition via Wang Yangming's philosophy, painters of the Wu school used landscape imagery to express their philosophical ideas. This trend was also seen in longer poetic and philosophical inscriptions on Ming paintings, with their wildly imaginary scenes. The poet and painter Dong Qizhang (1555-1636) further classified painters into northern and southern schools, the latter representing the more independent-minded artists who displayed great spontaneity in their brushwork, were not controlled by the court, and expressed philosophical concepts with great skill.

Great advances were made in literature, as seen in the development of the prose novel. Previously literature had been written only by scholars for purposes of government records, biographies, philosophy, and history. Monks and priests had used religious literature since the advent of Buddhism. But as towns gained affluence and a new middle class of independent scholars and merchants emerged, demand arose for literature that would serve the purpose of entertainment.

The nature of the Chinese written word itself prevented works of literature and history from being accessible to the public, primarily because the written language differed vastly from the spoken language. Known as *wenyan* (literary speech), the written language was quite terse compared to spoken Chinese. It differed from the spoken language in its vocabulary, structure, and pronunciation. Even the scholar required years of learning to understand a *wenyan* text because thousands of characters had to be memorized and many expressions were used only in the written form.

Education gradually began to reach greater numbers of people as the spoken language, known as *baihua,* came to be used in written works. Woodblock printing and movable type, invented in China in the eleventh century, both improved greatly, making books more readily available.

Novels that appeared during the Ming dynasty became great cultural legacies, although the literati never acknowledged them as proper literature and never admitted to reading or writing them. Four novels from the Ming have become particularly famous. *The Romance of the Three Kingdoms* (Sanguo yanyi), a fictionalized history concerning power struggles of the chaotic late Han and immediate post-Han years, was the earliest historical novel. Chinese folk legend remains full of stories about the romanticized adventures of the great heroes and villains portrayed in this book. *Water Margin* (Shui hu zhuan), translated into English by Pearl S. Buck under the title *All Men Are Brothers,* is the Ming dynasty's second great novel. Set during the Song dynasty, it tells the story of the bandit leader Song Jiang and his 108 brothers in banditry who are Robin

Hood-like characters reacting to official corruption and oppression.

The novel known as *The Golden Lotus* (Jin ping mei), considered a pornographic satire and social commentary, revolves around the adventures of a pharmacist, his six wives, and his other paramours. In addition to its graphic eroticism, the novel provides great insight into the social life of a middle-class Chinese family.

The last great novel of the Ming dynasty, published around 1570, is *Journey to the West* (Xi youji), also known as *The Monkey King*. It concerns the legendary experiences of the historical Buddhist monk Xuan Zang, who spent sixteen years on a journey to India in search of religious texts in the first half of the seventh century. Accompanying Xuan Zang to India in the novel were a monkey and a pig, whose mischievous magical abilities aided the monk in achieving his goal. Sun Wukong, the monkey, has since become a well-known figure in Chinese literature and Beijing Opera.

These literary developments indicated a new level of popular culture and a wider reading public than ever before. In addition to the novel, the theater also gained popularity, with regional theaters portraying dramas of their own, especially in the south.

Christian Missionaries

Christian missionaries began to enter China in large numbers in the early sixteenth century. By mid-century the Portuguese had settled in Macao, then an uninhabited peninsula, where the first major order of Catholic missionaries, the Society of Jesus, was established. St. Francis Xavier, the first Jesuit missionary to attempt entry into China, was unsuccessful in persuading shipowners to take him to the mainland from the island he was on near Guangzhou; he died in 1552 after weeks of waiting.

Missionaries provided the Chinese with their first direct intellectual contact with Europe. For their part, the Jesuits attempted to gain a deep understanding of the Chinese language and culture and adopt Chinese ways of life as much as possible without denigrating the tenets of their own faith. In their ultimate goal of reaching the elite who had total power over the coun-

try at large, and in introducing their faith into a cultural system vastly different from their own, they found themselves siding with Confucian scholars against Buddhists and Daoists, and working within the existing Chinese value system, somewhat subordinating their own beliefs. Although the Chinese welcomed the Jesuits for their knowledge of science and contributions to astronomy and math, in the long run they considered the beliefs of Christianity disruptive to their society.

Matteo Ricci (1552-1610), the first Jesuit to set foot in China, arrived in Macao in 1582. Beginning in Guangdong Province in 1583, his mission to China lasted seventeen years. The Jesuits were eager to discuss Chinese philosophy, Christianity, mapmaking, astronomy, and scientific instruments. Ricci was successful in his contacts with the court and was invited to Beijing in 1600, where he ended up spending the next and last ten years of his life.

Thanks to Ricci's efforts, other Jesuits were given positions in the Bureau of Astronomy, which had been dominated by Muslims since the Yuan dynasty. The Jesuits compiled an imperial calendar, upon which religious and ordinary rituals were based. Ricci's success in proselytizing can be gauged by the fact that at the beginning of the Qing dynasty, 150,000 Chinese had become Catholics.

Reacting to Portuguese attacks on Chinese villagers later on, however, the Chinese increasingly came to distrust the Jesuits. When Franciscan and Dominican missionaries began testifying for Jesus at the marketplace and condemning Chinese ancestor worship as idolatry, the Chinese became visibly hostile. The Jesuit mission in Beijing became involved in factional politics and was routinely threatened with edicts of expulsion. The Jesuits also began to realize that young men were totally consumed with preparations for civil service exams, upon which their future life as literati depended, and that they were not as intellectually curious about Christianity as the Jesuits had hoped.

The Decline of the Ming

Like dynasties before it, the Ming collapsed under the weight of official corruption and court weakness, as well as famine and rebellion. Long wars with the Mongols and Japanese incursions into Korea in 1592 under Toyotomi Hideyoshi (1536-1598), not to mention harassment of Chinese coastal cities by the Japanese in the sixteenth century, greatly weakened Ming rule. Involvement of the Chinese army in uprisings in Annam and Burma necessitated great financial backing from the government treasury.

Factionalism and the power of the approximately one hundred thousand eunuchs were increasing, and various attempts to change long-held government administrative methods proved ineffective. Early in the seventeenth century government strength was put to the test with prolonged infighting between the eunuchs and scholars, just when the greatest strength was needed to deal with internal rebellion and invasion from the outside world.

Scholars who were part of the Donglin Academy at Wuxi, Jiangsu Province, strongly opposed the rule of the eunuchs, who had regained political influence under a previous ruler. However, they were severely persecuted by the eunuch Wei Zhongxian, who controlled the administration and secret police during the reign of the Tianqi Emperor (1621-1627). Wei not only closed the Donglin Academy but either imprisoned or executed several hundred scholars who opposed him. By appointing personal favorites to important posts, he ensured a corrupt system. After the Tianqi Emperor died, however, Wei was assassinated and his followers greatly weakened. Although scholars temporarily regained influence, the financial and political crisis only worsened, leading to the downfall of the Ming dynasty.

The greatest rebellion of the Ming dynasty was led by Li Zicheng (1605?-1645), an unemployed porter and former robber band chieftain possessing great leadership skills. Li traveled through several provinces with his men, looting and plundering as he went. While in Hubei he listened to various scholar-advisers and began a political organization with offices and ranks, appointed governors over some districts he controlled, and finally proclaimed himself emperor. He then attacked and conquered Beijing and appeared to have received the Heavenly Mandate after the last Ming emperor committed suicide. His bandit ways and widespread slaughtering did not

endear him to the scholar-elite, however, whose help he needed to run the country.

Wu Sankui, the northeastern army general in charge of the border pass at Shanhaiguan, tried to defeat Li Zicheng with the aid of Manchu leaders and in the process was accused of betraying China by joining the Manchus instead of holding them at bay at the frontier. His allegiance went to the Manchus instead of to Li Zicheng, probably because Li persecuted scholar-officials while the Manchus by then had accepted the Chinese system and used Chinese officials for major government posts. Wu obviously believed that Manchu rule would ensure order and protect the Chinese system of government.

Geographically the Manchus were in a prime location to conquer China, with the the southern portion of their territory extending into a Chinese agricultural region that had been settled since the Neolithic era. The Manchus conquered and incorporated into their territory the Tungus forest nomads in the west and the Mongol nomads in the steppes of the East. Under the rule of Nurhaci (1559-1626) they established a quasi-Chinese bureaucratic government even before encroaching on China proper.

Nurhaci, who had been the head of a small clan of Tungus forest nomads, rose to become a feudal lord in one of the frontier guards the Chinese had set up to maintain control and organize adjoining clans. When Chinese control weakened, Nurhaci defeated rival Tungus clan leaders and incorporated their clans into his own, growing force, simultaneously capturing Chinese towns, people, and officials whom he used as administrators. He thus transformed his own administration into a Chinese-style one, and moved his capital to Shenyang (Mukden).

By 1636 Nurhaci's successor took the dynastic title "Da Qing" and called his people the Manchu, most likely after the personal name of one of Nurhaci's ancestors, which was taken from the name of the Buddhist emanation Manjusri. Both Wu Sankui and the Manchus rose up against Li Zicheng, but rather than leaving after they entered Beijing, the Manchus stayed and did away with the last Ming contenders as well as any Chinese generals with new bases in the south who tried to revolt against the new Manchu dynasty.

The Qing Dynasty (1644-1911)

The Qing, China's last dynasty, was to be ruled by non-Chinese. The Manchus, although foreign, had served as officers to the Ming court and succeeded in using traditional Chinese cultural and administrative institutions during their long rule. Confucian court practices and temple rituals were continued. Rather than ruling in the fashion of conquerors, as the Mongols had done, the Manchus ruled almost as heirs to China's great civilization, continuing the use of the Confucian civil service exam for recruitment of government officials, and recognizing neo-Confucianism as the state ideology, stressing obedience of subject to ruler. The Manchu rulers also provided great support for extensive Chinese literary and historical projects.

All tribesmen became part of military groups identified by colored banners, in what was known as the banner system. Centrally appointed officials rather than hereditary chieftains administered Manchu, Mongol, and Chinese banners alike. The monarch and his appointed council ruled over tribal leaders. Nurhaci finally attacked Ming forces in Liaodong. Shenyang, occupied by his armies in 1621, became his capital in 1625. The Manchus extended their control to Korea, Inner Mongolia, and the Amur River valley, and named their state Qing.

Continuation of Ming Institutions

Several southern Ming princes opposed the Qing with military force, as did Wu Sankui and two Chinese generals who joined the Manchus early on while in Shenyang. Their revolts were quelled in 1681. The famous Ming loyalist Koxinga (Zheng Chenggong) maintained a final stronghold on the island of Formosa (Taiwan) until 1683, when Qing armies gained control of the island and began Chinese administration there for the first time.

While the Manchus adopted Ming government institutions and the Confucian civil service exam, a series of anti-Han measures were also enacted. Chinese were excluded from the highest government positions. Chinese officials were in the majority only outside Beijing, while only those with high military

rank were permitted in Beijing. Manchu banners were placed around Beijing, in major southern cities, and where the Grand Canal intersected the Yangzi River. Bannermen were allotted land and stipends and were administered as a hereditary group separate from the masses, similar to the Ming garrisons. In the Manchu system of dual government appointments, the Chinese did the bulk of the work, while the Manchus were in place to ensure Han loyalty to the Qing court.

The grand secretaries were promoted to the highest level of government and formally proclaimed a cabinet. In 1729 a grand council was also created to handle routine business, leaving the emperor to deal only with the most urgent matters of state. Three of the six grand secretaries in the cabinet were Manchu and three were Chinese. The six ministries each had Manchu and Chinese ministers.

To prevent Manchus from being absorbed into the greater Han culture, intermarriage was prohibited, as was trade or manual labor for Manchus, and Han Chinese migration into the Manchu homeland. Works deemed seditious were destroyed, and, in an attempt to eliminate from the record anything hostile to the Manchus, approximately twenty-three thousand works and parts of three hundred and fifty others were proscribed.

Manchu women were forbidden to practice the Chinese custom of footbinding. The Chinese were required to shave the sides of their heads and braid the remainder into a queue hanging down the back, as was the Manchu style, to show they acknowledged Manchu domination.

The Qing was particularly noted for three outstanding rulers: the Kangxi Emperor (r. 1662-1722), who unified the empire and whose reign was noted for its extensive peace and prosperity; the Yongzheng Emperor (r. 1723-1736), during whose reign Christianity was banned; and the Qianlong Emperor (r. 1736-1796), whose reign was most noted for territorial expansion through Tibet, Turkestan, Mongolia, and Manchuria, as well as the tributary nations of Korea, Burma, and Annam. Even Nepal was forced to recognize Qing superiority. All danger to China proper was therefore effectively eliminated from its border lands. The dynasty was also noted for domes-

Detail from the Imperial Palace, long the home of emperors in Beijing. The architecture of Beijing's Forbidden City follows traditional Chinese style, although it dates mainly from the Qing dynasty (1644-1911), when China was ruled by the Manchus.

tic prosperity. Together these three men made the dynasty strong for over a century.

Manchu Confucian Rule

The Kangxi Emperor commissioned a compilation of the Ming history and patronized works that established new standards of their kind, such as the *Kangxi Dictionary,* with more than forty-five thousand characters, and an encyclopedia of ten thousand chapters known as the "Synthesis of Books and Illustrations of Ancient and Modern Times."

The Qianlong Emperor, himself well educated in the Confucian Classics and whose calligraphy was nationally recognized, went even further to support learning. In addition to many reference works, he commissioned the largest compilation of Chinese traditional writings ever organized, called the "Complete Library of the Four Treasuries." This collection reviewed rare and valued books of the past, while those judged worth preserving were copied whole, including the best writings of the classics, history, philosophy, and literature. Upon completion, the library contained about 3,450 works in more than 36,000 volumes. Six additional copies of the library were made as well, and a bibliography of about 10,000 titles that had been considered for inclusion in the library was also compiled. This bibliography is the most complete index to the literature of its time.

China's greatest novel, *The Dream of the Red Chamber* (Hong lou meng) by Cao Xueqin, was written during this time. In it one can see the seeds of early protest against the Confucian family system in its tale of the life of a young hero and his female cousins living in a traditional family setting. The romance between the young hero and his frail cousin ends in tragedy because of the traditional notion of the importance of arranged marriages. Its style, portrayal of character, and well-developed narrative have made *The Dream of the Red Chamber* a classic of world literature. The last great novel of traditional China, *The Scholars,* also written at this time, satirized the scholars and officials of the world.

The Rites Controversy

Western soldiers, traders, and missionaries had begun to arrive in China even before the Qing, in the sixteenth century. By the beginning of the eighteenth century there were more than two hundred thousand converts to Christianity in China. Useful to the Qing government for their great knowledge of science, the Jesuits had been allowed to become directors of the Bureau of Astronomy, and they presented the throne with a great map of the empire in 1717.

The Jesuits differed from other Catholic orders not only in their degree of scholarship but also in their tolerance of various aspects of Chinese culture and traditional rituals, which were deemed unacceptable by other orders and eventually the pope. Disagreement between the Jesuits and other orders eventually became so marked that the Jesuits asked the Kangxi Emperor for his personal endorsement of their position on Chinese ancestor rites. However, in 1704 Pope Clement XI (r. 1700-1721) himself issued an edict against the Jesuit toleration of ancestor worship. The Kangxi Emperor, angered by Rome's interference, declared that only those missionaries who acknowledged his interpretation of the rites could remain in China. Many Jesuits stayed, but missionaries from most other orders left for Macao.

Kangxi's successor, the Yongzheng Emperor, banned Christianity altogether, considering it subversive. In 1723 all missionaries were banished to Macao except for those appointed to offices in the capital. Finally, in 1724 the Jesuits were told that their society was being dissolved by the pope. After the turn of the century, Christians were considered outlaws and attacked throughout China.

Rebellions and Secret Societies

Centuries of peace during the Ming dynasty had allowed China's ruling elite to become complacent and persuaded of their culture's superiority, an attitude that proved a liability when China was finally confronted by the West. Although eighteenth-century China reflected the epitome of prosperity, productivity and power abroad, by the nineteenth century China had begun to feel serious economic pressure domestically and would soon experience military threats from the foreigners in its midst. China's population exceeded 300 million, but the country had little industry or trade to absorb its abundant supply of labor. Increasingly scarce land led to great discontent and a resultant breakdown in law and order. Pirate ships, which had increased along the southern coast since 1800, attacked merchant ships and raided coastal settlements as they had during the Ming, proving that the coast guards were ineffective. With both the bureaucracy and the military weakened through corruption, secret societies emerged, combining anti-Manchu subversion and banditry. Social order became increasingly difficult to maintain.

Initially a response to the collection of taxes, a rebellion raged in the mountains of Hubei, Sichuan, and Shaanxi from 1795 to 1805, characterized by guerrilla-like raids on imperial forces and unsuccessful attempts to control villages. The largest rebellion

in close to a century, it took its name, the White Lotus Rebellion, from a sect of Buddhism that promised the advent of Buddha and salvation from present suffering.

Secret societies with their own religious doctrines now proliferated. Members were expected to defend and help each other, and took oaths in blood. In addition to the White Lotus Society in the north, the Triad Society took hold in the south, with the aim of overthrowing the Qing government and restoring the Ming.

Confrontations and Commerce with the West

Despite the attack on Christians, trade with the West continued. The Spanish joined the Portuguese in trading silver for Chinese silk in the newly conquered Philippine Islands. In the seventeenth century the Dutch and then the English became major traders in Asia, and eventually other Europeans built up trading relations with an officially designated group of Chinese merchants at Canton (now the city of Guangzhou), which became known as the Canton System.

Portuguese traders had initially monopolized foreign trade at the port in Guangzhou. Soon British, Spanish, and French traders followed suit and found they were expected to pay tribute to the Chinese emperor. The Chinese for the first time confronted Europeans who expected to be treated as political and cultural equals. China had treated only one European nation differently in its recent past—Russia—and then only for purposes of border security. The 1689 Treaty of Nerchinsk, China's first bilateral agreement with a European power, had ended a series of potentially threatening border incidents and served to create a mutually recognized border between Siberia and Manchuria along the Amur River. The 1727 Treaty of Kiakhta further delineated what remained of the eastern port of the Sino-Russian border.

After 1760 all foreign trade was confined to Guangzhou, and foreigners could only conduct trade with twelve officially licensed firms of Chinese merchants, known as "co-hongs" (a Western pronunciation of *gonghang*, or state-owned company). A supervisor appointed by Beijing made sure these merchants were responsible for the foreign ships and received fees.

By 1800 more than 20 million pounds of tea were exported to Britain through Guangzhou each year, while in the United States, the market for this novel new drink was growing. China also exported large amounts of silk and porcelain to the West. For its part, China appeared to neither want nor need anything from the West, thereby creating an unfavorable balance of trade for Westerners, especially the British. Foreigners therefore began to develop third-party trade. In particular, merchandise was exchanged in India and Southeast Asia for raw materials and semi-processed goods, for which there was a market in Guangzhou. Raw cotton and opium from India had become staples of Britain's China trade by the early nineteenth century. Although an official ban on opium existed, it was allowed in by corrupt bureaucrats and merchants.

The British East India Company, which had been given a monopoly of British trade in East Asia, discovered that the Chinese co-hong monopolists were not being held responsible for their debts to foreigners under China's commercial law. Soon irregular port charges surfaced as well. Coupled with their dissatisfaction with the Chinese treatment of prisoners and their inability to communicate with the Chinese government, the British pressured the Chinese to change their established ways.

The Macartney Embassy

In 1793 King George II of England sent the Earl of Macartney to Beijing to open an embassy, laden with more than six hundred presents for the emperor. The emperor at first interpreted the embassy as a tribute mission and acknowledged this sign of respect, not realizing that Britain's primary aim was to facilitate greater trade. Upon his arrival, Lord Macartney requested permission to trade at other ports in addition to Guangzhou, and to use the island depots near Guangzhou and Shanghai to store goods and refit ships. He also asked China to establish a fixed and printed tariff. Rather than kowtowing before the emperor, however, a practice that the Europeans considered demeaning, Lord Macartney knelt down on only one knee, as was British custom. The Chinese never responded to his three requests.

The Decline of the Canton System

Increasingly, private traders began to cut into what was previously the East India Company's monopoly in Guangzhou, creating confusion as to who actually represented the Western traders before the Chinese government. Seriously compounding this problem in Guangzhou was the expansion of the Chinese market for opium. Although long used for medicinal purposes in China, its use for enjoyment alone had been discovered only recently. Opium was initially combined with tobacco, which itself was introduced from the United States only in the seventeenth century. Later the upper classes began to smoke opium without tobacco, and soon both commoners and court officials alike took up the habit. Banned repeatedly by Chinese edicts, the price of opium fluctuated drastically and the profits from its sale were great.

In 1834 the British East India Company's monopoly of the China trade ended, and a superintendent of trade was appointed at Guangzhou to help the free traders. The superintendent's efforts to interact with local Chinese officials as equals were met with various forms of intimidation and attempts to cut off supplies to Westerners. After 1839 drastic prohibitory laws and measures against the opium trade were effected, following a decade of unsuccessful anti-opium campaigns. By then it was estimated that between two million and ten million people were addicted to opium in China, not to mention the havoc wreaked on society at large.

Exacerbating the situation in China was the fact that imports of opium in the 1820s and 1830s were paid for in silver, draining the country's silver supply. Commissioner Lin Zexu (1785-1850) was therefore sent to Guangzhou by the emperor with full authority to stop the opium traffic. Arriving in 1839, Lin first seized all illegal opium owned by Chinese dealers, then detained the entire foreign community in their factories, without servants. Lin managed to have approximately twenty thousand chests of illegal British opium confiscated and destroyed. The British retaliated, beginning the first Anglo-Chinese war.

The Opium War (1839-1842)
and the Unequal Treaties

The Chinese, who faced Western military power for the first time in the Opium War, were totally unprepared, and completely underestimated their enemies' capabilities. A British fleet terrorized China's coast, raiding and occupying cities at will in an effort to bring the Qing government to terms. The Chinese finally agreed to negotiate after Nanjing was threatened and major cities were blockaded, occupied, or bombed. The Manchu government was in no position to mobilize all available power, given the precarious domestic social order and the possibility that such large-scale military activity could threaten its own rule even more than could the British. The Chinese were disastrously defeated, and the image of their imperial power was destroyed.

The Treaty of Nanjing, signed in 1842 aboard a British warship by two Manchu imperial commissioners and the British plenipotentiary, was the first of a series of agreements signed with Western trading nations that became known as the ''Unequal Treaties'' and marked the beginning of China's ''hundred years of humiliation.'' Under the Treaty of Nanjing, the licensed co-hong monopoly system of trade was abolished, and Westerners were allowed to trade with anyone, upsetting the age-old practice of state supervision of trade. Five ports in addition to Guangzhou were opened to foreign trade and British residence. The island of Hong Kong was ceded to the British, and later a portion of the adjacent mainland was added as well. The tariff was fixed at 5 percent of the value of the goods and was not allowed to be changed without the agreement of both sides. Opium was eventually included in the tax schedule.

The treaty stipulated the practice of extraterritoriality, in which nationals of each party to the treaty were to be exempt from Chinese law, which they believed did not acknowledge the rights of the defendant and punished the guilty excessively. Christian missionaries were allowed to reside, lease or buy land, build houses, and practice in any of the provinces. Foreign ministers were allowed to reside in Beijing and communicate with the Chinese government as equals. Finally, huge indemnities were imposed on the Chinese.

The Treaty of Nanjing was followed by other unequal treaties as a result of further incursions and wars, resulting in increasing privileges to the foreigners in China's midst. It set the scope and character of China's unequal relationship with the West for the next century.

For all his efforts, Lin Zexu was exiled as punishment for his failed attempts to limit the opium trade through Guangzhou. Lin had been one of the few literati to foresee early on China's need for reform. After having Western books and newspapers translated for him by Chinese who had studied under missionaries, in order to learn more about the West, Lin concluded that modern guns and ships were essential if China was to protect itself and its heritage from Western barbarians. Lin's ideas were subsequently fostered by his friend and fellow scholar-official, Wei Yuan (1794-1856), in an attempt to show the Chinese how to use Western techniques to repel the Westerners. Neither, however, advocated any basic reform of China's established order itself.

Domestic Turmoil

Local villages were no longer safe from robbers and bandits. Soldiers and petty bureaucrats often had to be bribed for simple protection, although they, too, were guilty of stealing from the people. The economic situation in the country worsened with the high price of silver.

Both wealthy families and secret societies alike created self-defense forces, which also began to be used in disputes over the acquisition of land. Increased corruption and bureaucratic inefficiency weakened the leadership, all of which presaged a change in the dynastic cycle.

By the mid-nineteenth century China's domestic political problems were compounded by natural disasters, including droughts, famines, and floods. The Yellow River broke its dikes at least twenty times, affecting hundreds of thousands. The government had so neglected public works that the Grand Canal

Opium use became widespread in China during the early nineteenth century despite anti-opium campaigns and laws banning the opium trade. China's Opium War (1839-1842) was another unsuccessful attempt to stop opium from entering the country.

The Taiping Rebellion, 1850-1864

Hong Xiuquan (1814-1864), who initiated the Taiping Rebellion, was a village teacher of the Hakka minority from Guangxi Province who had taken and failed the civil service exam several times. After failing the exam on his third or fourth attempt, he experienced what today would be described as a nervous breakdown, claiming to have had visions in which he was taken to Heaven to meet the Heavenly Father, Mother, and Elder Brother, with the latter's wife and younger sisters. Hong claimed to have been made the Son of Heaven and charged with the mission of eliminating all those who misled people into worshiping false gods, and restoring the Kingdom of Heaven on Earth. After receiving a pamphlet from Christian missionaries in Guangzhou he reinterpreted his vision to mean that the Heavenly Father he had seen was God, and the Heavenly Elder Brother, Jesus. Although the missionaries refused to baptize him, realizing that he did not fully grasp the basic tenets of Christianity, Hong found a following among the Chinese, who did not question his differences with Christianity, such as the extended Heavenly family and the marital status of Jesus.

Hong's eclectic ideology was thus a mixture of Confucian utopianism and Protestant beliefs. He believed that the Confucian idea of filial piety was as important as love of others, and that man was originally good. Hong and his followers hoped to destroy the present government and set up their own in its place, recreating a legendary ancient state where peasants owned and tilled the land in common. Produce from the land was to be kept in storehouses established for each group of twenty-five families and distributed as needed.

Social changes espoused by Hong and his followers included segregation of the sexes and the elimination of slavery, concubinage, the drinking of wine, prostitution, opium and tobacco smoking, and gambling. Footbinding, judicial torture, and idol worship were also forbidden. Thousands of anti-establishment and anti-Manchu followers soon formed a military organization, with troops recruited from believers, armed peasant groups, and secret societies.

became impassable, leaving tens of thousands of boatmen unemployed. In the 1850s the Yellow River shifted course, flooding millions of acres of land and ruining thousands of communities. Since financial troubles and corruption had undermined the will to act, the Qing administration did little to initiate relief efforts.

Widespread unrest, especially in the south, also contributed to China's problems. South China had been the last area to yield to the Qing conquerors, and it was the first to be exposed to Western influence. Guangzhou had remained a hotbed of resentment toward foreigners since the Opium War. When Shanghai and other ports were opened commercial routes shifted, leaving widespread unemployment along the old routes. All these circumstances helped sow the seeds of the largest uprising in China's modern history.

Administratively, Hong's government was quint-essentially Chinese, with a ruler as autocratic as any in China's history using names of offices taken from the Classics and recruiting officials through examinations. Ideas of economic egalitarianism for the common people reflected classical ideals. Austerity was encouraged in a manner reminiscent of Mozi's ideas, and hatred of barbarians was a familiar theme.

Anti-Confucian elements soon surfaced in the Taiping Rebellion, such as the belief that the Four Books were a bad influence, and that the evil deeds of the devils went back to the teachings of Confucius. Ancestor worship and Confucian historical authority were rejected. This alone was enough to turn the literati against Hong's movement, whose tone was both militant and exclusive. All idols were to be smashed and all superstitions attacked head on. Little of the syncretic toleration for Buddhism, Daoism, and other cults remained. Relentless attacks on Confucianism and advocacy of radical social reform soon alienated China's scholar-gentry. These factors contributed directly to the rebellion's ultimate defeat.

The Taiping movement was influenced as much by Christianity as by popular novels, both in rhetoric and military strategy. Plain style in writing was promoted, rather than classical Chinese, which was understood only by the literati.

A military victory in Guizhou Province led Hong Xiuquan to proclaim his dynasty, called the Heavenly Kingdom of Great Peace (*Taiping Tianguo*), and name himself its Heavenly King. It is from the Chinese name for this state that the rebels became known to Westerners as Taipings. The next year they captured their first provincial capital in Hubei Province and then extended their influence south to Nanjing, altogether encompassing sixteen provinces.

The Taiping army never established stable base areas, however. Internal feuds, defection, and corruption gradually emerged among the Taiping leaders. Those considered disloyal were executed—sometimes numbering in the thousands. Hong also failed to win powerful allies. The Taipings considered the Europeans barbarians, and soon the Europeans had aligned with the Manchus. Wary of the uncertain Taiping regime, the British and the French preferred to deal with a weak Qing administration and support the Manchu imperial army. Most important of all, because of their strong religious doctrine and revolutionary aims the Taipings did not attempt to attract the educated class. For their part, the literati saw the Taipings, unlike the Manchus, as destroyers of their native civilization, hostile to the Confucian tradition.

In the end it was not the Qing army but the Chinese scholar-officials themselves who defeated the Taipings. It took fourteen years and more than 30 million deaths before the rebellion was completely crushed. Zeng Guofan (1811-1872), a holder of the *jinshi* degree from Hunan Province, saw the Taipings as a threat to the very soul of Chinese civilization. He was appointed imperial commissioner and governor-general of Taiping-controlled territories and organized a militia army paid for by local taxes. Other literati families contributed their forces as well, creating a new force under eminent scholar-generals who combined military training with Confucian indoctrination. Personally loyal to Zeng, the troops were carefully trained and highly motivated. In 1854 they were effective in preventing a Taiping force from returning to Hunan from Nanjing.

Li Hongzhang (1823-1901), a patron as well as a lifelong friend of Zeng Guofan, was another famous scholar-statesman turned successful military leader. He used his considerable diplomatic skills when dealing with foreigners, and by the 1860s the loyalist forces had improved their organization and were winning more victories. The government lightened taxes in some disputed areas, thus regaining the loyalty of their inhabitants. Meanwhile, corruption and a lack of discipline plagued the Taipings. In the summer of 1864 Hong Xiuquan committed suicide, paving the way for the final destruction of the Taiping rebels scarcely a month later.

Zeng Guofan's success made the emerging Han elite even more powerful, while simultaneously weakening Qing authority. Li Hongzhang was made a governor of the coastal provinces of his region. The combination of military and civil authority sparked the development of court rivalries.

By the time the Taiping Rebellion ended, not only were millions dead but towns and farmlands alike were completely in ruins. This, in turn, affected tax revenues. In the 1830s various other secret societies and floods further aggravated the already unstable social fabric. In some areas, officials were forced out by armed groups who attempted to administer various regions themselves, simultaneously raiding neighboring regions. Between 1853 and 1868 a group known as the Nian rebels dominated more than 100,000 square miles of rural China until blockades created by Zeng Guofan and continued by Li Hongzhang broke their hold on the peasants.

Various rebellions in the southwest (Yunnan) and northwest (Shaanxi, Gansu, and Chinese Turkestan) were initiated by Muslims whose hostility toward the Han after years of oppression by officials could no longer be contained. Russia now also sought more territory for trading purposes and tried to convince the Chinese that they had common interests in holding back the French and the British, thus justifying their expansion into Central Asia. The Treaties of Aigun (1858) and Beijing (1860) thus gave territory north of the Amur River and territory facing the Sea of Japan southward to the Korean border to Russia.

After 1860 foreign encroachments increased through a series of treaties imposed on China under a variety of pretexts, and gained a greater stronghold in the Chinese economy through an increasing list of concessions. Foreign settlements in treaty ports were treated as extraterritorial, their safety guaranteed by menacing warships and gunboats.

Foreigners also took over peripheral states that had given tribute to the Chinese emperor. France now colonized Cochin China (South Vietnam), and by 1864 had established a protectorate over Cambodia. Later, after its war against China in 1894-1895, France would take Annam as well. Britain gained control over Burma, and Russia had by now penetrated Chinese Turkestan (the present-day Xinjiang-Uighur Autonomous Region).

The Self-Strengthening Movement

Internal rebellions combined with the unequal treaties and external foreign threats caused the Chinese to reconsider ways to preserve their country, their heritage, and their dignity. And just as the need

to strengthen and change China gained urgency, one of the most powerful but conservative leaders in Chinese history came onto the scene. The Empress Dowager Ci Xi (1835-1908) entered the palace as a low-ranking concubine in 1861 and won the confidence and trust of the Xianfeng Emperor (r. 1851-1861). As the only one of his consorts to bear him a son, she acquired the title of empress dowager. For nearly half a century until her death in 1908, she held almost complete control over palace affairs, as regent for child emperors.

China's first major effort at self-reform, known as the Tongzhi Restoration, lasted from 1862 to 1874. It was named after the reign title of the new child emperor and begun by his mother, Ci Xi. An attempt to arrest the decline of the dynasty by restoring the traditional order, this was no true program of modernization. It served only to apply "practical knowledge" while reaffirming the traditional Chinese mentality.

Zeng Guofan was given increasing authority to deal with the remaining Taiping rebels, as were other regional leaders for various pacification campaigns throughout the country. Li Hongzhang and Zuo Zongtang (1812-1885), another eminent scholar-official, worked closely with government forces against the Taipings. These officials championed a cause they called the self-strengthening movement, which was first presented to the emperor by the scholar Feng Guifen in a series of essays written in 1860. The term "self-strengthening" referred to China's need to strengthen itself by including math, science, and foreign languages in its educational curriculum, as well as by building shipyards and arsenals. Zeng Guofan, taking the concept further, maintained that it included reform of government itself. Together, these leaders established modern institutions, developed basic industries and transportation and communication systems, and helped modernize the military.

A new organization, the Zongli Yamen, was formed in Beijing in 1861 to conduct foreign affairs and supervise diplomatic relations in the capital. A subcommittee of the Grand Council, the Zongli Yamen proposed experiments such as a college for Western learning, where foreign languages and Western science were taught. Special schools were opened in larger cities, and arsenals, factories, and shipyards based on Western models were established. Textile mills and schools with technical curricula developed as a result. European firearms were first used for training Chinese in 1862, and a navy yard was opened in 1867. Innovation became an aspect of both defense and foreign policy.

Western techniques were employed in the technical schools and machine shops established in the 1870s. Modern techniques were also used in the cargo and steam ships that began to operate under the China Merchants' Steam Navigation Company, established in 1872. These allowed the Chinese to dominate their own coastal trade and made it easier to transport rice from the south used as a tribute. These innovations also encouraged the development of coal mines that included short railways.

Both a modern Imperial Maritime Customs and its outgrowth, a modern postal service, emerged at this time. The former had been developed in the 1850s, when the Qing used foreigners to collect the revenues from foreign trade, and the latter served as a new source of government revenue.

Students were sent abroad for the first time by the government to learn Western methods. After the students went abroad, however, temptations proved great, and many abandoned their Chinese ways of dress and behavior. They were therefore recalled by the government within a decade, and considered to have failed in their mission.

For all their concern, the leaders of the self-strengthening movement failed to see the significance of the political institutions and social theories that had fostered Western advances and innovations. Moreover, change in China was a slow process because of its very size and the ratio of people to the available natural resources. Traditional Confucian attitudes, which glorified the past, further obstructed the adoption of basic features of modern life. Finally, rampant factionalism at court, consisting of the self-strengthening reformers on the one hand, and the eunuchs, increasingly used by the empress dowager, on the other, prevented China from reacting effectively to crises when needed. As a result, regional leaders were given some of the power normally held by the central administration.

The Foreign Presence, 1860-1894

The treaties of 1858 and 1860 allowed missionaries to travel and live where they wished in China, buying land and buildings as they pleased. Their numbers and the number of converts had increased tremendously, and their Western-oriented publications and schools were perceived by the Chinese as the antithesis of Chinese culture, and thus as a greater threat than its internal rebellions.

Unlike the controversial Jesuits who preceded them, the Jesuits of the nineteenth century were more inclined to condemn Chinese customs than to accommodate them. Their attitude contributed to greater suspicion and hostility toward foreigners in general.

Thanks to the unequal treaties, missionaries were also able to bypass the Chinese gentry, going directly to district magistrates with their concerns and thereby humiliating local officials. Ignorance, fear, and anger on the part of the Chinese mixed with foreign insensitivity and arrogance to create an explosive environment. Hostility in thought led to hostility in action in 1870, when it was rumored that a Catholic organization in Tianjin providing food for orphans had supplied the eyes and hearts of kidnapped children for use in magical rituals. A mob soon gathered in front of the French consul's residence, and killed him after he fired on them with Western weapons. Although foreign gunboats were called in to retaliate, Zeng Guofan's diplomatic intervention prevented further confrontation.

In 1870 the Chinese population numbered 400 million. There were also about 250 Catholic priests and 350 Protestant missionaries in China at this time. By the 1890s the number of priests had tripled and the number of Protestant missionaries had almost quadrupled. The foreign presence was also keenly felt through the addition of a half-million Chinese converts to Catholicism as well as 37,000 Protestants.

In the fourteen treaty ports that existed in the 1860s, curious young Chinese could observe and get a taste of Western urban life. While they understood

Ci Xi, the Empress Dowager of China (1835-1908), entered the palace as a concubine. She bore a son for the Xianfeng Emperor and eventually ruled China as regent for various child emperors from 1861 until her death in 1908.

Foreign Acquisition of Chinese Territory

Countries that had previously paid tribute to the Chinese emperor were one after another falling under the control of foreigners. Japan made the Ryuku Islands a prefecture of Okinawa while Russia and Great Britain gained more territories in the northwest, previously under Qing control. Japan attempted to gain Formosa in 1874, but the Chinese fleet was able to repel it.

Not long after this incident the British colonial government of India was able to mark the border between Burma and Yunnan Province, ending Burma's status as a tributary state. Through two prior invasions the British had already annexed portions of Burma. After the third Anglo-Burmese War (1885-1886), China was forced to recognize Burma as a British colony.

Vietnam soon followed a similar route, and after much fighting and resistance China was forced to acknowledge a French protectorate over Vietnam in 1885. Since the 1850s the French had controlled southern Vietnam and forced concessions by treaty in the north, despite resistance and rebellions. In the 1880s, when the Chinese were aiding the north Vietnamese rebels, the French attacked Chinese border towns, prompting China to declare a war that it eventually lost.

China's New Spirit

Foreigners were increasingly attacked within China as resentment at European aggression mounted. Not only did the literati object to the foreign presence, but ordinary Chinese were beginning to feel a common national bond and enmity toward foreigners. While some believed that Western technology could be combined with traditional Chinese values, others opposed any new technology, claiming that the age-old virtues of decorum and moral conduct espoused by Confucius were the best antidotes to what was conceived of as moral degeneration in the society at large.

Wang Tao (1828-1897?), an assistant to the eminent British sinologist James Legge and editor of a foreign mission press, contributed to China's aware-

that the foreign concessions gave opportunities to Chinese merchants, many Chinese resented the Western attitude of superiority and were angered by the Western monopoly on money and the good life. For their part, the Chinese resented providing the hard labor for Westerners while being barred from Western clubs. Many Chinese also looked down on the fact that wealthy Western businessmen did not evince an interest in intellectual pursuits like those of the Chinese intellectuals. The Chinese were therefore increasingly ill-disposed toward foreigners and began to draw the distinction between Western technological accomplishments and what they perceived as inferior Western culture.

ness of current affairs by founding newspapers and writing books based on what he learned in his extensive travels through Europe and Japan. Some of the things he espoused were truly revolutionary, such as an improvement in the status of women in Chinese society as well as the creation of a parliament, saying that the Classics themselves sanctioned reform. Each age was said to need its own institutions. His ideas attracted a wide reading audience, but the Chinese government was not ready to listen.

The Sino-Japanese War, 1894-1895

China and Japan soon battled over Korea, a Chinese tributary state of strategic value. For more than two decades, since Japan's newly modernized government had taken shape, the Japanese envisioned a different relationship with Korea to advance their own strategic interests: Either Japan should influence Korea and other East Asian nations so as to modernize and protect one another from Western imperialist nations, or Korea should simply be absorbed into the Japanese empire.

Strategically, Korea could have become a military base for Russia, which the Japanese sought to avoid at all costs. In the end, after a treaty in 1876 establishing relations in the modern era, Japan aided those Koreans who sought their help. When Japan became involved in factional disputes in Korean politics, however, the Chinese stepped in to contribute their help in domestic Korean affairs.

Both Chinese and Japanese troops were withdrawn in 1885 after intense rivalry arose, both countries agreeing not to redeploy troops without prior notification. In 1894, however, Korea specifically requested Chinese troops to quell a rebellion. Japan immediately sent its own troops, greatly exacerbating the situation. After the Japanese gained control of the palace in Seoul, China and Japan declared war on each other.

As happened in the Opium War, China soon discovered that it was no military match for Japan. Japan easily won the war, and the resulting Treaty of Shimonoseki (1895) forced China to cede Taiwan and the Penghu Islands to Japan. A huge indemnity of 200 million taels (a tael being equivalent to an ounce of silver) was paid to Japan. Japanese industries were allowed to be established in four treaty ports as well. Finally, China was forced to recognize Japanese hegemony over Korea.

Although China had a greater number of ships, it was hampered by its lack of military organization and leadership, as well as rampant misuse of funds. Rather than put funds toward the much-needed naval effort, the empress dowager was said to have preferred to furnish the Summer Palace outside Beijing and to finish a stately marble boat for her own pleasure. The Qing government's interest in reform was deeply in doubt.

Imperialist Inroads

Japan's military success signaled to the European nations that although China had enormous manpower, it was administratively and militarily incapable of defending itself, and that the regime itself might soon collapse. Eager to take a piece of the pie, the European powers quickly vied for portions of the country.

China, now forced to pay off the indemnity imposed by the Treaty of Shimonoseki, found that it had to borrow money from the Europeans, who considered the future revenues of the Chinese Imperial Maritime Customs strong security. Russia viewed any loans to China as a way of strengthening its own position there. It also proposed the construction of a railroad across Manchuria reaching as far as Vladivostok, which would serve to ally the two countries against further Japanese expansion. The Russians were permitted to station guards along the railway and held the rights of administration in the railway zone.

After two German priests were killed by bandits in a raid on a town in Shandong Province, a German naval squadron entered port and demanded compensation. As a result the Germans received a portion of Shandong for ninety-nine years and rights to railway building and mining in the province.

Many European nations now gained spheres of influence in China. Russia gained Manchuria, Germany took Shandong, Great Britain obtained the Yangzi River valley, and France, the territory around Vietnam. In 1898 Britain acquired a ninety-nine-year lease over the New Territories of Kowloon, increasing the size of its Hong Kong colony. At the time it was presumed that these spheres would soon become European colonies, as political events led China toward its own dissolution. In 1899 the United States proposed an ''open door'' policy in China to ensure that all foreign countries would have equal duties and rights in the treaty ports. All European nations, except Russia, agreed to this proposal.

National Resistance

China's national spirit proved resilient in the face of such dire circumstances. A movement of national resistance was begun by Kang Youwei (1858-1927), often considered the last great Confucian thinker. The movement of resistance thus began not among the mercantile class—whose interests were affected in the treaty ports—but from among the ranks of Confucian scholars. They were, after all, the primary guardians of China's heritage and felt an obligation to defend it at all costs.

Kang Youwei was learned not only in the Confucian Classics but in Buddhism, Western science, and philosophy. He conceived of human history in stages, progressing from chaos and great strife through greater unity and peace on a small level and finally to universal peace and harmony among all nations of the world. He believed that a common humanism united the various cultures of the world. For the Chinese, this humanism was, of course, to be found in Confucianism. In particular, the idea of ''public-spiritedness'' was to be found in one of the Confucian Classics, the Classic of Rituals (Li Ji).

Kang thus adapted Confucian thought to its new role in the modern world, believing firmly that without Confucianism, Chinese culture would surely perish. He went on to espouse the reform of the civil service exams, especially through the elimination of the eight-legged essay format, which stifled individual thought and creativity.

The Hundred Days' Reform

When Japan announced its conditions for peace in 1895, Kang organized more than twelve hundred graduates in Beijing to sign a confidential protest memorandum rejecting all the demands and requesting major governmental reforms to save the nation. Although the government had already accepted the terms dictated by the treaty, the Guangxu Emperor (1875-1908), nephew of the empress dowager, decided to listen to Kang's ideas on reform three years later, just as foreign powers were bidding to claim a part of China for themselves.

Kang's suggestions for wide-ranging institutional reforms within the Chinese government, which the Guangxu Emperor was willing to implement from June 11 to September 21, 1898 (hence, the term ''Hundred Days' Reform''), were rooted in the strong belief that China needed more than mere self-strengthening—it needed institutional and ideological change in order to survive.

Corruption within the government was attacked. The civil service and academic systems were to be made over, and agriculture, medicine, and mining were to be modernized, as was the defense establishment, postal services, and the entire legal system. Rather than neo-Confucian orthodoxy, practical studies were promoted. The court planned to send students abroad once again for firsthand observations of foreign methods and technical studies. Lastly, a de facto constitutional monarchy was to be created, based on the participation of the populace in government.

The empress dowager saw this attempt to reform the government institutions of the dynasty as too radical and a threat to her own power. With the backing of conservative officials at court, and the tacit support of the major regional military commander, Yuan Shikai (1859-1916), she had the Guangxu Emperor arrested in a palace coup d'état. Although Kang managed to escape, those close to him by either blood or ideology were arrested and executed. Kang Youwei himself managed to flee abroad.

The empress dowager took over the government as regent and quickly rescinded the new edicts. The Guangxu Emperor died his aunt's prisoner, never seeing the reforms come to fruition. The Hundred Days' Reform was the last attempt to move China into a modern nation-state without abandoning Confucianism as its guiding philosophy.

The Boxer Rebellion

The empress dowager and ultraconservatives at court supported the antiforeign and anti-Christian secret societies that now emerged as a sense of nationalism began to take shape in China. In northern China, the Society of Righteous Harmony (Yi he quan), whose earlier name included a term for "boxers" because of its members' habit of shadow boxing, took hold with a vengeance. In 1900, two years after their founding, the Boxers spread throughout northern China attacking missionaries, other foreigners, and even Chinese converts as far as Manchuria because they enjoyed certain special privileges. Relying on their strong convictions that many spirits from folk religions would serve as their protectors, the Boxers believed they were physically invincible, even in the face of Western military might. Many Boxers were recruited directly from the ranks of those who had lost everything in the devastating floods and droughts that had plagued Shandong Province, and had nothing left to lose.

These Boxers were soon joined by itinerant artisans as well as groups of female Boxers, said to possess magical powers. In June of that year they attacked the foreign concessions in Beijing and Tianjin with royal backing. Killing foreigners and Chinese converts alike, they targeted even those Chinese who merely owned foreign objects. They laid waste to the surroundings as well, destroying railroad tracks and telegraph lines. The reaction of local Chinese officials varied from protecting the foreigners in their midst and fighting the Boxers themselves, to actually encouraging Boxer activities. Attacks on foreigners and mission compounds continued in Shanxi, Hebei, and Henan provinces.

The foreign legation in Beijing, composed of Americans, British, Germans, Japanese, and Russians, quickly tried to barricade themselves in their quarters. Were it not for the lack of coordination with the Qing army troops and among the Boxers themselves, all foreigners might have been killed.

Boxer attempts to rid China of foreigners were met, however, with united Western might that quickly prevailed. As the Westerners began to occupy northern China, the empress dowager fled west, establishing a capital temporarily in Xi'an. The formal peace treaty, known as the Boxer Protocol, followed in 1901, overseen by Li Hongzhang just months before his death. Among other things, it suspended the examination system in the many cities where the Boxers had harmed foreigners, leading to abolition of the civil service exam system in 1905 at the instigation of the Chinese themselves.

The Chinese court was further ordered to execute many high officials and punish scores of others for their part in the rebellion. The Legation Quarter, the official offices and residences of foreign diplomats, had to be expanded, and war reparations were demanded. Foreign troops were to be stationed in China, and some Chinese fortifications were to be razed. No arms were allowed to be imported by China for two years. China was further required to pay an indemnity of 450 taels (about $330 million) to cover the loss of foreign life and property. (It would take China until the end of 1940 to pay off this sum, which, at 4 percent interest, then totaled close to $700 million.)

As a last-ditch effort to preserve dynastic rule and maintain the Mandate of Heaven, Ci Xi belatedly attempted to implement some of the reforms originally proposed by Kang Youwei. The very scope of the reform effort and its suddenness, however, in the end prevented its success.

Late Qing Reforms

The reforms proposed during this period all dealt with issues that would be crucial to China's political development in the twentieth century. Among the reforms attempted was the adoption of a constitution, which itself implied a representative assembly of the people. This would have single-handedly reduced the Qing emperor's political authority. The desire for such an arrangement was acknowledgment that the many new economic developments now emerging required greater regional autonomy than central control.

New government ministries were created between 1901 and 1906, including ministries of internal affairs, foreign affairs, and education, which took their place alongside the existing ministries of war, civil

The Boxer Rebellion of 1900, an attempt to rid China of foreigners, was met by united Western might that quickly prevailed. Here, American, British, and Japanese troops storm Beijing.

appointments, and rites. Advances were made in managing China's fiscal administration to bring more revenues under central control. The Qing government looked to Japan as a model in trying to harness new economic and political trends for its own purposes.

A boycott of trade with the United States in 1905 was one manifestation of the new-found patriotism among some Chinese. This patriotism was in part inspired by indignation among merchants and students that the United States was excluding Chinese laborers from immigration to its shores. Chinese patriotism was enhanced by observation of a fellow Asian nation, Japan, and its interactions with the West. Many Chinese came to respect Japan and its military

strength after its defeat of Russia in the Russo-Japanese War of 1904-1905, even though the war was fought primarily over a Chinese territory and China had no say in the matter. The mere fact that a smaller Asian state had defeated a large European one was inspirational.

Though fought mostly over a portion of Manchuria, the war had affected Korea as well. After Russia rejected a Japanese proposal to divide Manchuria into spheres of influence, Japan attacked Russian bases. Japan wanted to expand its influence in Manchuria while maintaining exclusive rights in Korea. Russia, however, sought to gain a foothold in Korea as well as expand its reach in Manchuria. Russia finally acknowledged Japan's upper hand in Korea (formally annexed by Japan five years later), in the 1905 Treaty of Portsmouth, and gave Japan a railway and leasehold in southern Manchuria. Russia also yielded the southern half of Sakhalin Island to Japan.

In 1906 an official Chinese mission went to Japan to consult with the creator of Japan's Meiji Restoration, Ito Hirobumi, about preparation of China's own constitutional government. The mission learned that it was not necessary to dissolve the emperor's powers to effect a change, but rather that all changes could come from the imperial powers in conjunction with a constitution that guaranteed the people a voice in the affairs of state. After this visit the empress dowager promised the Chinese a constitution, which was enough to bring the affairs of state into the realm of popular discussion.

Education, too, was greatly affected by late Qing reforms because, ever since the time of Confucius, it had been perceived as the key to good government leaders and a responsible citizenry. Toward the end of the Qing dynasty, school systems were set up at various administrative levels with the goal of preparing students to become officials. Major changes in China's educational system appeared, including the addition of Western subjects to the curriculum.

The civil service exam was resurrected in modified form, and graduates of China's new-style schools were allowed to sit for them as well. Students continued to prepare for the exams by studying traditional subjects, since most people were not yet convinced that the new educational fashions were beneficial for a career in government. But government reformers were already persuaded that the exam system had to be abolished if the new educational system was to have any chance for success.

At the same time that Western-style curriculum in the new schools allowed Chinese students to learn to think in a different way, translations of Western books were made available to the general public, introducing a new way of looking at the world beyond Chinese borders and new perspectives for looking at China itself. The most notable translator of foreign works was Yan Fu (1853-1921), who introduced T. H. Huxley, Herbert Spencer, and Adam Smith to Chinese readers. In his commentaries, Yan Fu noted the wealth and strength of the countries that had produced such great writers.

Japan was another major influence on Chinese attitudes. By 1907, eight to ten thousand young Chinese had gone to Japan to study. They found the cultural transition relatively easy because of Japan's geographic proximity and the familiarity of its language and customs. In addition, Japan had already opened up to Western scholarship. Most important, the Japanese supported the goals of the Chinese reformers, so the students found Japan a conducive atmosphere for training.

One great reformer, Liang Qichao (1873-1929), a student of Kang Youwei, had fled to Japan after the failure of the Hundred Days' Reform and from there propagated his ideas for social reform. He espoused Social Darwinism, which posited that the evolution of society came about through the struggling of nations and survival of the fittest. He said the Chinese people need to dedicate themselves fully to the nation's interests. Others in China simply called for ousting the Manchus, who were perceived as inferior to the Han Chinese. Interest in constitutional government mounted, with the young students leading the charge toward democracy.

Reforms during this last decade of the Qing dynasty also prompted military leaders to assume a greater role in politics. A renewed effort to build modern armies was made after Japan's victory, most notably, the creation of the Beiyang (Northern) Army. Totaling about 60,000 men, under the control of Yuan Shikai it became China's single strongest and most modernized military force. Yuan is also credited with the establishment of modern military academies in China; these academies provided the woefully lacking professional officer training and thus offered a new conduit for military advancement. Those who received further training in Japan returned to China imbued with a patriotism bred while observing their homeland from afar.

Revolutionary Stirrings

While Kang Youwei and Liang Qichao were promoting reform from overseas, other groups within China were ready for a violent overthrow of the government. Secret societies as well as organizations composed of the literati all agitated for change. Students banded together to form revolutionary groups, as did various army officers. Tens of thousands rioted against tax collectors, indicating that the time for a popular rebellion was at hand.

The vision of revolution in China was provided by Sun Yat-sen (1866-1925), or Sun Zhongshan, a medical doctor whose Western training and belief in Christianity, gained while studying in Hawaii, set him apart from other Chinese political leaders of his day. Deeply interested in reforming government, Sun eventually concluded that the Manchu government had to be overthrown for any reforms to be truly effective. Members of the secret society that he organized in 1894, known as the Revive China Society (Xing Zhong hui), joined him in an antigovernment uprising in Guangzhou the following year. The failure of this uprising led him to flee China so that he could work from overseas to collect money and establish a following for his organization and ideas.

Familiar with the government of the United States from his student days, Sun regarded it as the most advanced form of government in the world. He therefore sought to create in China a republic modeled after that of the United States. Although educated Chinese, steeped in the Confucian tradition, supported the efforts of Kang Youwei, younger Chinese who lived abroad and those who had studied in missionary or foreign schools eagerly listened to Sun's proposals for a complete overhaul of the Chinese government.

Japan's 1905 victory over Russia in the Russo-Japanese War spurred Chinese students to action. That year, while in Japan, Sun Yat-sen created the Alliance Society (Tongmeng hui), which combined various Chinese secret societies with a new group of Chinese—those studying in Japan. Within this group were men sent from regional military academies in China to learn Japanese military techniques. Well connected to the military leaders back in China, these students proved the key to Sun's ultimate success in overthrowing the Manchu government on October 10, 1911, and becoming the first president of the new Republic of China. The four-millennia-old dynastic system had finally come to an end.

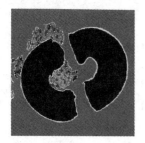

CHAPTER 2

REPUBLICAN CHINA (1911-1949)

The period from October 10, 1911, to October 1, 1949, is usually referred to as the era of Republican China. The search for a new political identity by the Chinese people began before the end of the Qing dynasty, with one group of reformers proposing a constitutional monarchy and another group of revolutionaries clamoring for a republic. For more than two thousand years, the Chinese had witnessed the replacement of one dynasty by another, while the basic political structure remained unchanged. The central feature of China's dynastic tradition was the country's image as equivalent to the family of the emperor, whoever he or she happened to be. Against such a background, the fact that Sun Yat-sen called his nascent government a Republic was indeed revolutionary in its implications, although he meant this as an ideal rather than a reality.

After only a brief tenure as premier of the fledgling republic, however, Sun Yat-sen was forced to give up his position, and China entered one of the most humiliating periods in its history. During this time, ordinary people had to submit to forces far beyond their control, from local small-time despots to gangs of roving bandits to warlords who acted like petty emperors. These problems were then compounded by the Japanese invasion, followed by a bitter civil war between the two biggest factions of the era, the Kuomintang (KMT, or Nationalist Party) and the Chinese Communist Party (CCP).

Sun Yat-sen and the Republic of China

The revolutionary period of modern Chinese history was ushered in by a mutiny among government troops in Wuchang, Hubei, on October 10, 1911. Foreseeing a bloody repression by the government, the soldiers, many of whom were members of Sun Yat-sen's Alliance Society (Tongmeng hui), launched an uprising and appointed their own military governor. Many other provinces soon followed the Hubei example. Returning from a trip to the United States and Europe, Sun Yat-sen became provisional president on January 1, 1912, in Nanjing, a city on the Yangzi River. Less than two months later, the last emperor of the Qing dynasty, the young Pu Yi, abdicated his throne in Beijing.

Sun Yat-sen, who came to be known as the "father of the country," was born to a farming family in a small village in Guangdong in 1866. Heavily influenced by stories about the Taiping rebel leader Hong Xiuquan, told to him by his uncle who had fought for the Taipings, he was also greatly impressed by Western ideas and values when his older brother, who had worked in Hawaii as an indentured laborer, paid for Sun's education at a local Christian school. Sun later studied medicine in Hong Kong and Guangzhou, but his desire to save the nation soon overwhelmed his interest in practicing medicine.

Sun advocated the Three Principles of the People (San min zhu yi)—nationalism, democracy, and the people's livelihood—which became the hallmark of his revolutionary doctrine and political platform. Nationalism was defined as a government run by the Chinese alone. The overthrow of the alien Manchu dynasty therefore became the first order of business for the revolutionaries, who rejected any foreign rule of China, no matter how sinified the foreigners. The second principle, democracy, based largely on Sun's

Sun Yat-sen (1866-1925), known as the "father of the country," led China into the post-dynastic era and in 1912 became the first provisional president of the Republic of China.

knowledge of Western democratic systems, posited the creation of a constitutional government and the obliteration of all class distinctions among the Chinese. The final principle, people's livelihood, hinged on a concern for the common good and material well-being of all China's citizens. Land rights were to be equalized, and the state would earn revenue from any future increases in the value of the land, which in turn would also be used for the common good. (Some have argued that Sun therefore advocated a form of socialism; in his conception, however, the interest of the people, not of the state, was paramount.)

The Three Principles of the People were to be implemented in three stages, so that political democracy could be realized more quickly. The first stage included a period of martial law, during which old political systems and customs would be destroyed.

The second period was one of phased constitutionalism, whereby the people would be trained to govern themselves. The final phase of enacting the Three Principles called for the implementation of a constitutional government.

Despite the sacrosanct position that the Three People's Principles hold in KMT ideology to this day, Sun Yat-sen's contribution to the Chinese revolution was mainly symbolic. The call for democracy reflected Sun's experience in the West, yet it took little account of the political and cultural realities of China. Even more problematic was Sun's emphasis on nationalism. This satisfied the anti-Manchu and anti-Western feelings prevalent among many Chinese at the time and was thus politically expedient. However, insofar as it aroused a patriotism and utopianism that blamed foreigners for everything wrong in China, it was self-exculpating and counterproductive in certain respects. And the idea of people's livelihood was just that, an idea that was never spelled out.

Sun soon found that his policies were no more successful than his ideas. In less than a year, he had to give up the provisional presidency in deference to Yuan Shikai, a former Qing general, who now possessed formidable military strength. Escaping persecution by Yuan, Sun fled back to his home province, but was betrayed by the local warlord, Chen Jiongming. Once again, Sun had to run away, this time to Japan.

Notwithstanding all these failures, Sun managed to go on to achieve extraordinary success with the founding of an influential military academy. Realizing that one reason for his futile effort to build a republic had been the lack of military power, in the early 1920s Sun set up the Huangpu (Whampoa) Military Academy near Guangzhou to train revolutionary cadets. Furthermore, he invited instructors from the Soviet Union and adopted the Red Army's structure in organizing a Chinese revolutionary army. Many twentieth-century Chinese politicians and administrators, to say nothing of generals, had their initial training at Whampoa. Sun appointed as president of Whampoa Chiang Kai-shek, who had received his military training at a Japanese army boot camp, where he developed an admiration for the efficiency of the Japanese military system.

In view of his attachment to democratic ideals, it is ironic that Sun eventually came to rely on the military for the realization of his goals. During this transformation, Sun seemed to orient his policy in a more practical direction and called for combining forces with the Russians, the labor movement, and the Communists. However, he did not live to see his dream fulfilled. On a trip to Beijing in the spring of 1925 to negotiate with his adversaries, Sun died of liver cancer at age fifty-nine. Just like Lenin, his fellow revolutionary in Russia who had died a year earlier, Sun left a muddled legacy to his revolutionary cause.

The Era of Warlordism and the First United Front, 1912-1927

From the downfall of China's last dynasty in 1912 to the establishment of the internationally recognized Kuomintang government in 1927, the country experienced a cultural renaissance as well as a search for new identity by political and military means. A short-lived attempt to re-establish another dynasty gave way to the fierce struggle among warlords. The KMT and the CCP emerged from the struggle as the two most powerful forces, and they in turn united with each other for a short time in order to eliminate the other contenders for power. At the same time, an examination of the country's past by the Chinese intelligentsia greatly influenced the struggle between the KMT and the CCP. Unable to attain a long-term modus vivendi with its Communist rivals, the KMT massacred tens of thousands of Communists. So ended the era of warlordism, as the first united front between the KMT and the CCP proved too fragile to withstand the intrinsic enmity between these two rivals.

Yuan Shikai and His "Emperor's Dream," 1912-1916

Yuan Shikai was the leader of the Beiyang Army, the most powerful military group in late Qing China. Considering himself the rightful heir to the Mandate of Heaven, Yuan was prepared to accept a superficial version of constitutionalism, provided that it did not undermine the military power that was the real basis of his authority. After accepting the presidency of the new republic from Sun, Yuan proclaimed Beijing the capital and agreed to uphold the constitution prepared by the revolutionaries. In reality, however, he filled his new cabinet posts with those whom he could control, and the few genuine revolutionaries in the government soon resigned. In reaction to plans to replace Kuomintang officials with military governors in the south, several officials tried to incite another revolution, but they were ill-prepared to deal with Yuan's superior military power. Yuan suspended the parliament in 1914, and the republic seemed stillborn.

China then found itself in a new predicament, having to fight against Western imperialist advances at perhaps the weakest stage in its nascent modern political development. At the beginning of World War I, China declared itself neutral. Japan, meanwhile, grasping the advantage that its alliance with Great Britain presented, sent troops to Qingdao, Shandong Province (then under German control), after declaring war on Germany.

In 1915 the Japanese government confronted Yuan Shikai with what came to be known as the Twenty-one Demands and instructed him to keep them secret. According to the demands, China was to recognize Japanese rights in Shandong as well as rights to property, commerce, industry, and residence in various portions of Mongolia. Most invasive of all, the demands stipulated that Japanese would have advisory roles in Chinese military and political affairs.

Word of the demands leaked to the Western press and Western diplomats. The Chinese tried to stall by insisting on reviewing each demand with the Japanese, line by line. The United States supported China in protesting the demands, but in the end Japan forced Yuan Shikai to accept them all with the exception of the potentially most insidious—a Japanese role in Chinese administrative affairs.

In addition to capitulating to Japan, Yuan also revealed an ideological anachronism that was characteristic of this turbulent period of transition and

The Era of Warlordism

With Yuan Shikai gone and numerous generals commanding independent armies, warlordism dominated the country between 1916 and 1927. Authority was forcefully taken by those who were often no better than bandits yet controlled vast expanses of land, in some cases equaling the size of an entire province. Those in control of Beijing and surrounding areas in the north commanded foreign diplomatic recognition.

It was a time of continual fighting and alliances and counteralliances among the various factions, whose main goal was to gain more territory and, hence, greater political power. But for most, the gains proved evanescent and did not truly increase control over the land. Life became even more intolerable for the average Chinese peasant. Taxes were imposed at will, as the warlords sought to obtain revenue by any means available.

While some warlords actually promoted programs for the public welfare, repairing roads, planting trees, and enacting measures against prostitution, gambling, and opium use, much of their motivation lay in an attempt to restore the old order rather than to pave the way for a truly new form of government. For the warlords, personal loyalty kept them in power—not, as the revolutionaries attempted to create, loyalty to the mere idea of democracy. Kinship, marriage, regional ties, and even school ties remained of paramount importance.

Yet the warlords also gave the era a colorful folklore. Sheng Shicai in Xinjiang took an interest in the livelihood of the Muslim population. He traveled to Moscow and was given Communist Party membership by Stalin. Han Fuqu in Shandong invited his illiterate peasant father to lecture his political and military subordinates, in order to help his followers "retain a sense of the commonfolk." Yan Xishan built a narrow-gauged railroad in Shanxi and was accused of attempting to hamper KMT efforts to unify China. His fellow provincials argued, however, that Yan acted to save money and prevent foreigners from exploiting Shanxi's rich coal mines. Chen Jiongming in Guangdong took an interest, with his Communist friends, in such issues as peasants' rent

Yuan Shikai (1859-1916), well-known military leader of the Beiyang Army, became the second president of the new Chinese republic. However, he suspended parliament in 1914 in the face of Japanese aggression and declared himself emperor in 1915. His death in 1916 ushered in the warlord era.

revolution. Conscious of his political isolation, he initiated a Zunkong (Venerate Confucius) movement, in an attempt to consolidate his rule. Meanwhile, he enforced strict censorship of publications and partisan activities. To cap off his extraordinary career, Yuan declared himself emperor at the end of 1915 and inaugurated the year of Hongxian (the Great Constitution) on January 1, 1916. His political enemies in the south deemed this an excellent excuse to begin another military campaign to topple him, and his allies and protégés in the north abandoned him to save themselves. The emperor's dream lasted less than a hundred days. Yuan had to cancel the monarchy in March 1916 and died shortly thereafter amid a storm of anger and derision.

and the spread of Marxism to China.

Warlordism also offered a political lesson for the democratic movement and republican ideals in China. On the one hand, warlords represented the continuation of feudal rule in China and thus impeded the country's development. On the other hand, warlordism demonstrated how easily China could fall into political confusion without a powerful central government. Thus, in many people's minds, warlordism became equated with democracy, since both were seen as posing the danger of insoluble and internecine conflict. Since many of China's political leaders today came of age during this era, the lesson has exerted great influence in China throughout the twentieth century.

The New Culture and
The May Fourth Movement

China also found itself in the midst of a profound cultural crisis during this period of political turmoil. By the turn of the century, superstition and rigidity had come to suffocate the thinking of both China's political rulers and the official literati. During the late Qing dynasty, for example, the Empress Dowager Ci Xi halted construction of the first Chinese railroad, reportedly because she regarded it as bad geomantic practice. And all aspirants for official government positions were required to write a *baguwen* (eight-legged essay), a form of writing that encouraged a slavish mentality rather than creative thinking. Responding to this type of stultifying orthodoxy, a group of intelligentsia launched the New Culture movement.

Cai Yuanpei, the first chancellor of Beijing University, had studied in Germany and was instrumental in sending thousands of Chinese students to Europe for study. His goals for Beijing University were not only to promote academic research but to make it the catalyst for the creation of a new Chinese social order. He strongly supported free expression and interchange of ideas. The faculty he hired all shared his sentiments, and Confucianism itself was called into question. Democracy, communism, and the promotion of rational thinking through scientific investigation were all advocated at Beijing University.

Cai appointed as dean of the School of Letters the scholar Chen Duxiu, whose reputation rapidly increased during his editorship of the influential magazine *New Youth* (Xin qingnian). Chen's article "Call to Youth," published in 1915, espoused the need for a new spirit and new culture to deal with the problems of Western imperialism that confronted China. *New Youth* became the focal point for the exchange of ideas among intellectuals, who viewed Confucianism as an outmoded philosophy that was useless for addressing the ills of modern Chinese society.

Hu Shi, a former student of John Dewey's at Columbia University, used *New Youth* as a forum for his own burgeoning ideas on language reform and the rejuvenation of literature. Hu's ideas reflected the pragmatism extolled by Dewey and emphasized constructive uses for doubt and criticism. In "A Preliminary Discussion of Literary Reform," he stressed the need for use of the Chinese vernacular, or everyday speech, rather than the classic literary style. Unlike Chen, Hu viewed the nascent literary revolution as an attempt to change literary form and style alone, divorced from politics and ideology.

An international event intervened, however, to radicalize the New Culture's literary debate and give birth to the famous May Fourth movement. The Treaty of Versailles, signed at the conclusion of World War I, transferred Germany's rights in Shandong to Japan. On May 4, 1919, more than three thousand students from various colleges in Beijing converged at Tiananmen, the vast Gate of Heavenly Peace in the heart of the city. The Chinese minister to Japan, a convenient target, was located and given a thrashing. The government arrested thousands of students, but intellectuals, politicians, and even some warlords expressed sympathy for the demonstrators. Workers and merchants began to join the intellectuals in a nationwide call for a solution to the problem of how to save China.

The twin slogans of "kexue yu minzhu" (science and democracy) captured the mood of the May Fourth generation. At the same time, a group of famous Chinese writers began to sharpen their criticism of the traditional society, especially Confucianism itself. The best-known of these writers was Lu Xun. By 1921, Lu Xun had published "Diary of a Madman'' and ''The True Story of Ah Q,'' both now mandatory reading for Chinese schoolchildren. In the first, the madman found that, from the era of Confucius to the 1911 Revolution, two words—*chi ren* (eating people)—actually leaped out from between the lines of Chinese history books. Chinese tradition was destroying the Chinese people. In the second, Lu Xun's most famous character, Ah Q, became a revolutionary with the lofty goal of expropriating his landlady's ivory-decorated bed. Unable even to sign his own name before being executed, Ah Q worried greatly about his ability to draw a circle in place of the signature he could not write. According to Lu Xun, China's backwardness was due first of all to the apathy and superstition that suffocated the intellectual life of its people. ''Ah Q has a lot of descendants who live among us today,'' Lu Xun declared ominously.

The concept of communism quickly entered the vocabulary of the New Culture movement. Li Dazhao (1888-1927), a talented professor of history, economics, political science, and law, and chief librarian at Beijing University, was instrumental in bringing this concept to the fore in this era. The son of a northern farmer who studied the Classics and attended college in Japan, Li Dazhao hired a young man from Hunan, Mao Zedong, as his library assistant. Li encouraged people to follow Marxism as a true science, insisting it was the epitome of egalitarianism in action. Li was successful in forming small Marxist study groups and training others in various organizational techniques for the purpose of pursuing political power.

Founding of the Chinese Communist Party, July 1921

Both Li Dazhao and Chen Duxiu had supported the students who marched during the May Fourth movement, and both had become followers of socialism. They were therefore eager to welcome Gregory Voitinsky, an agent from the Communist International (Comintern), upon his arrival in Beijing in 1920.

In 1919 Lenin had founded the Comintern in Moscow to coordinate and direct the policy and revolutionary efforts of Communist movements worldwide. Voitinsky, offering both money and organizational experience, found that his views were taken seriously in China. With his help, Chen Duxiu founded the Chinese Communist Party (CCP) in Shanghai, soon followed by the Socialist Youth Corps. Branches soon sprang up in other Chinese cities, with the one in Beijing headed by Li Dazhao and the one in Changsha headed by Mao Zedong. Meanwhile, in Paris, Zhou Enlai played a prominent role in organizing overseas Chinese students and workers into the young Chinese Communist Party.

The CCP was officially born at a meeting of twelve Chinese intellectuals in Shanghai in July 1921, and Chen Duxiu was elected secretary of the CCP's Central Committee. The party's immediate aim was to organize workers, the ''vanguard'' of the proletariat, who represented the revolutionary class, and increase their own membership with the ultimate goal of overthrowing the government.

From the very beginning, the CCP distinguished itself from the KMT and other political organizations in China by the tenacity of its view that it, alone, held the mandate of history and was the chosen instrument to effect revolutionary change in China. CCP members, who considered themselves the representatives of an exploited class and a repressed country, maintained a righteous attitude that whatever they did was justified by the miserable fate of China and its people. Accepting Marx's theory that society inevitably progressed from one stage to another, as well as Lenin's call for national self-determination, the CCP planned to implement socialism in China as its ultimate goal. Commenting on the birth of the party, Mao Zedong declared, ''The cannon roars of Russia's October Revolution sent us Marxism.''

KMT Alliance with the CCP: The First United Front

By 1923, members of the CCP were allowed membership in the KMT, in an attempt at both political and military cooperation by the two political groups in order to unify the country. Mao Zedong became a member of the KMT's Central Committee, in charge of training peasant agitators, while Zhou

Chiang Kai-shek became the leader of the Nationalist Party, or Kuomintang (KMT), upon Sun Yat-sen's death in 1925. He established a Nationalist government in Nanjing in 1928 and remained the KMT leader until his death on Taiwan in 1975.

Enlai and Nie Rongzhen taught at the Whampoa Military Academy. Although the KMT was badly split regarding the propriety of its alliance with the CCP, the reality of their common enemy, the Chinese warlords, forced this marriage of convenience on the two parties.

The Communists aimed eventually to take over the alliance, but their efforts were thwarted by Chiang Kai-shek, with the explicit approval of Moscow. Under Chiang's leadership, the Nationalist army evinced a greater sense of loyalty than ever before. Upon Sun Yat-sen's death in 1925, Chiang Kai-shek succeeded in becoming the leader of the KMT.

In order to eliminate the stronghold of the warlords in the north once and for all, Chiang Kai-shek planned a Northern Expedition, which he hoped would establish a Nationalist government in the process. All weapons and finances supporting the Whampoa Military Academy were controlled by Soviet advisers in Guangzhou, whom Chiang suspected would be loyal to his cause. Based on this, Chiang sought an early move northward in 1926, but not before he escaped an attempt on his life by Soviet advisers, who were quickly arrested.

Various power struggles erupted once again as the KMT army reached the Yangzi River area, culminating in the so-called April 12 massacre in 1927. In the end, the KMT managed to eliminate both its Soviet advisers and the Chinese Communist members in its ranks after destroying the Communist base in Shanghai and discovering a Communist takeover plot encouraged by Stalin. Finally, in 1928, a Nationalist government was established in Nanjing under the leadership of Chiang Kai-shek. The Communists, their ranks decimated by repeated Nationalist attacks, sought refuge from their former allies in the mountains of China's provincial border areas.

The Nanjing Decade, 1928-1937

The new Chinese government faced numerous challenges, with Japanese aggression against China posing the most immediate threat. Domestically, provincial militarists had to be eliminated to achieve the national unity needed to face the Japanese. The civil war with the Communists had to be dealt with as well. Amid all this turmoil, however, the Chinese economy eventually managed to stabilize and make strides in terms of both agricultural and industrial development.

Without pausing to consolidate his power base, Chiang quickly resumed his Northern Expedition. In 1928, after taking Beijing, the Nationalists were successful in gaining the cooperation of the warlord Zhang Xueliang. Li Zongren, the warlord of Guangxi, also pledged his support to Chiang. Feng Yuxiang, a warlord known as "the Christian general," together with Yan Xishan, became Chiang Kai-shek's "sworn brothers." Ultimately, Chiang and his "republican" government were able to convince an initially skeptical world that they were the only viable power in China, and foreign governments accorded recognition to the Nanjing regime. Countries like the Soviet Union and the United States voluntarily gave up many of their extraterritorial rights in China, and Chiang was able to capitalize on his diplomatic successes in consolidating his domestic rule.

The Manchurian Incident

In 1931, the Japanese created an incident that led to their occupation of Manchuria. Earlier, in 1894, the Japanese navy had defeated its Chinese counterpart and escalated Japan's intrusion into China, especially the northeastern area known as Manchuria. In 1905, the Japanese army defeated tsarist Russia in the Russo-Japanese War and further increased its presence in the area. Over the next two decades, the Japanese built railroads, mined coal, and produced steel in Korea and Manchuria, as part of a strategy to integrate mainland Asia into a Japanese-dominated system. Zhang Zuolin, the most powerful Chinese warlord in Manchuria, resisted the Japanese intrusion by superficially cooperating with the Japanese but secretly undermining Japanese hegemony in the area. Having defeated both the Manchu emperor and the Russian tsar, however, Japan was not going to allow a mere regional warlord to block its path toward Asian hegemony. In 1928 Zhang Zuolin was assassinated by Japanese army officers in Manchuria.

As the next step, the Japanese instigated a large-scale incident as the pretext for their direct takeover of Manchuria. On September 18, 1931, a bomb exploded on a railroad near the city of Mukden (Shenyang) in southern Manchuria. Accusing Chinese troops of deliberately destroying Japanese property and jeopardizing Japanese interests, Japan's Kwantung Army occupied Mukden, then all of Manchuria. In 1932 Tokyo engineered the establishment of a puppet state in Manchuria, known as Manzhouguo (Manchukuo). The dethroned last emperor of the Qing dynasty, Pu Yi, was drafted to serve as the puppet state's titular head and married to a Japanese woman. Japan's next goal was the five northern Chinese provinces. Under severe international pressure, however, the Japanese government decided to reach a truce with the Nanjing government. Beijing was temporarily saved from occupation.

Chiang Kai-shek, recognizing the urgent need to build up his armies, invited the services of German officers for this purpose. He also strengthened the role of the military in the Nationalist government, separating it from the civil government and greatly increasing the portion of national revenue devoted to national defense. Chiang ordered his troops to retreat when the Japanese attacked Shanghai, however, because he realized that his forces were not capable of prevailing over the technologically superior Japanese.

Another reason for this nonresistance policy was Chiang's continuing concern over the Communists. The Japanese and the Communists were both diseases, Chiang lectured his followers, but the former was that of the skin, while the latter was that of the heart. In order to drive out the foreign invaders, Chiang believed, China must first of all cure itself of the Reds. The Communists had been crushed in 1927, but not eliminated. Therefore, Chiang turned his back to the Japanese and instead launched five "bandit suppression" campaigns against the Communists.

Revival of Communist Bases

The Communist Central Committee went underground once again in Shanghai after being expelled from the KMT. The Comintern replaced Chen Duxiu, who was made the scapegoat for the CCP's failure and later expelled from the party, with Moscow-trained Qu Qiubai. At its next congress, held in Moscow in 1928, the CCP reaffirmed the need for armed struggle and declared the urban working class to be the true proletariat. The few uprisings subsequently launched by the CCP, however, failed abysmally.

The CCP's legendary Jinggangshan revolutionary base came into being during this period. After escaping from Nanjing in 1927, Mao Zedong organized the Autumn Harvest Uprising in Hunan, but his forces were badly defeated by Nationalist troops. Mao desperately needed to locate a site where his hungry and disappointed peasant soldiers could recuperate. Jinggangshan, a mountain located on the border between Jiangxi and Hunan provinces, seemed the ideal place. Mao persuaded two bandits who had occupied the area to let him stay, and, while there, he married an eighteen-year-old peasant girl.

Down the mountain, not far from Jinggangshan, a Communist-led military uprising on August 1 in the city of Nanchang flared briefly but was defeated. Zhu De, one of the chief organizers of the uprising, fled with his soldiers toward Guangdong and was nearly captured in a KMT ambush. Finally Zhu and Mao established contact and joined forces on Jinggangshan. They began to call their combined forces the Red Army of Peasants and Workers.

Zhu and Mao soon expanded their base areas. Although most of the warlords were ostensibly gone by this time, the reality of warlordism remained. Nominally appointed by the Nanjing government, local militarists continued to bicker with their neighbors over territory and influence. The Red Army was able to capitalize on this factionalism, establishing more bases in disputed areas. In the early 1930s, Mao and Zhu moved their headquarters from Jinggangshan into nearby Jiangxi Province.

Mao and Zhu called their bases "soviets," and in 1931 they established the Chinese Soviet Republic. They instituted radical agrarian reforms on the bases, in which land was confiscated from feudal landlords and other private landowners without compensation, and then redistributed among the poor peasants. Mao despised the rich local gentry, and blamed them for all the evils in China.

Even more radical were the political and ideological struggles launched during this time. Closely emulating political developments in the Soviet Union as well as influenced by the uncertainties of their harsh situation, the Communists instigated an anti-Trotskyite movement in several waves, intended to purge their ranks of those suspected of disloyalty. Soviet-trained Communists like Wang Ming and Bo Gu were particularly dogmatic and inflexible. They arrested, tortured, interrogated, and then executed many of their own comrades whose views differed from their own. Like the Nationalists in Nanjing, the Communists were certainly not trying to establish a democratic republic.

The Long March, 1934-1935

Distressed that his mortal foes had survived his earlier attempts to destroy them, Chiang Kai-shek once again marshaled his Nationalist forces to root out the Communists. The Red Army, however, had by this time mastered rural and mountain warfare and managed to defeat Chiang's first three "bandit suppression" campaigns, taking thousands of prisoners whom they indoctrinated with communism while expropriating their weapons.

Despite the Japanese invasion of Manchuria in 1931, the KMT launched two more Communist encirclement campaigns in the early 1930s. These were personally directed by Chiang Kai-shek, who swore to eliminate the Communists once and for all. Chiang employed new strategies and greater force than ever before. With the Red areas cut off from their supplies of grain and salt, the KMT soldiers relentlessly closed in on the Red Army by the spring of 1934. With the help of German military advisers as well as their own Whampoa-trained generals, the KMT and their modern military equipment finally overpowered the Communists.

On the Communist side, Mao was overruled by the Soviet-trained leaders who successfully advocated a foolhardy strategy of fighting the KMT troops head-on. As a result, the Red Army suffered heavy casualties. To make matters worse, intraparty purges led to the loss of many loyal and experienced Communist leaders. By the spring of 1934, the Red Army was forced to abandon its base in Jiangxi and begin the now famous retreat that would take the forces on an arduous and protracted journey of more than five thousand miles. Known as the Long March, this odyssey concluded in Shaanxi Province almost a year later, where the Communist troops were quartered in cave houses dug out of the loess soil.

Of the 100,000 who participated in the Long March, only about 20,000 endured to the end. Those who survived have been considered heroes throughout their lives, especially after the People's Republic of China was established in 1949. During their march, the Communists managed to gather popular support from many of the poor peasants whose villages they traversed. The Long March also secured Mao's position as leader of the Communist movement in China.

Chiang Kai-shek's New Life Movement

Chiang's purpose in seeking to eliminate the CCP was to establish his hegemony in China. He believed that he must not only defeat his enemies on the battleground but also win over "the hearts and minds" of the Chinese people from the CCP. Two additional factors encouraged Chiang to launch an ideological campaign in parallel with his military campaigns. The first was Chiang's hostility toward the New Culture and May Fourth movements. Although Chiang shared the students' concern about China's destiny and was as determined as they to "save China," he rejected the ideas of intellectuals like Lu Xun that there were fundamental problems within Chinese culture, particularly Confucianism. Instead, Chiang blamed foreigners for everything that was wrong in China, and proposed to revive China's "excellent traditions" in order to make the country strong again. Chiang's personal experiences also played a role in his point of view. While most of the May Fourth generation had studied science or liberal arts in Europe and the United States, Chiang went through military training in Japan. The only other foreign country in which he had set foot was the Soviet Union.

What made the Nationalists' ideological task even more imperative was the appeal of Marxism-Leninism, which the CCP had incorporated into its arsenal and seemed to wield with such dexterity to its benefit. Chiang Kai-shek had defeated the warlords relatively easily, in part because the struggle against them had been mainly military. By the early 1930s, however, the CCP and the Japanese had become Chiang's chief enemies, with the former representing a much more serious threat in his mind. Not surprisingly, Chiang was inclined to regard members of the CCP as traitors because they paid so much respect to a foreign doctrine—Marxism.

It was under these circumstances that Chiang began his New Life movement in 1934, just when he was on the verge of driving the Communists out of Jiangxi. In a series of lectures to his generals, delivered in the beautiful resort of Lushan along the Yangzi River, Chiang emphasized the importance of "order, harmony, discipline, and hierarchy." Chiang also warned of the danger of "liberalism," a trend that he accused the New Culture movement of fostering. The tone he adopted was not much different from the one assumed by the Communists half a century later, in the mid-1980s. In order to present himself as a model of proper behavior, Chiang would regularly pay his respects at the tomb of Sun Yat-sen, the "father of the nation," in Nanjing. When he happened to be in his hometown in Zhejiang, Chiang would also play the filial son, escorting visitors to his parents' tomb.

To a great extent, however, both Chiang's adoration of Chinese culture and his New Life movement were simple hypocrisy, if not a farce. In order to marry the Wellesley-educated Song (Soong) Meiling, a devout Methodist, Chiang promised to study the Bible and was baptized a Christian in 1930. Madame Chiang, using her connections with the YMCA, was to play a major part in the New Life movement too, educating the Chinese not to eat so noisily, for example. With the Japanese occupying Manchuria and thousands of Manchurian students demonstrating in the major cities, however, the New Life movement appeared trivial if not irrelevant to most Chinese, and it gradually sputtered out.

Economic Development During the Nanjing Period

In the early 1930s, the Japanese presence in China was still limited to Manchuria, while the Communists were confined to the rural hinterland. The Nanjing government controlled most of the core areas of China and enjoyed the allegiance of most of the erstwhile warlords as well as diplomatic recognition from foreign powers. This situation presented a golden opportunity for the Chinese economy to develop.

Financial reform preceded economic recovery and stabilization. T. V. Soong, Chiang's brother-in-law, was placed in charge of tariff reform and the establishment of the Central Bank of China. With the help of the United States, the Nanjing government won tariff autonomy in 1928 and received custom revenues that more than sufficed to underwrite the military budget. The government also worked hard to abolish internal transit taxes. It proved a formidable task since only four provinces could be considered fully under government control. Gradually, the fabi, a national currency, came to replace various other currencies.

The Nanjing government also tackled agricultural problems. In 1933, modern industrial manufacturing constituted less than 3 percent of China's gross national product, while the agrarian sector contributed more than 65 percent. One fundamental problem that had to be faced was the unfavorable ratio between population and food productivity. With the help of international specialists sent by the League of Nations, the Chinese conducted research in new seed varieties, pesticides, and fertilizers. To prevent floods, large numbers of peasants were mobilized to dredge the Yangzi, Yellow, and Huai Rivers. Tea, silk, and cotton production also increased dramatically.

The government's National Resource Commission played an important role in promoting modern industrial development. To create an industrial base that would sustain the nation's armed forces, the Commission issued a five-year industrialization plan that focused on establishing an industrial zone in China's interior provinces of Hunan, Hubei, and Sichuan. Heavy machinery, steel, and radio and electrical equipment were produced in the zone, as were coal, iron, zinc, tin, and copper. During the Nanjing decade, Chinese industry grew at an impressive rate of about 7 percent a year, comparing favorably with most other countries in the world. The transportation and communications infrastructure, urban services, and educational facilities also improved.

The Anti-Japanese War and The Second United Front, 1937-1945

China's national resistance efforts soon focused on the struggle against Japan's plans for military oc-cupation of China's coastal regions. The Japanese had moved into certain strategic areas in northern China under the pretext of combating communism, hoping to gain Nationalist acquiescence to Japanese control of these territories.

Although the Nationalists chose not to respond in a way that might have provoked open warfare, many Chinese students clamored for united opposition to the Japanese, rather than additional efforts to exterminate the Chinese Communists. The Communists openly courted the Nationalists with the intention of forming a second united front against the Japanese. Troops from Manchuria, whom Chiang had directed to crush the Red Army, quickly joined forces with the Communists instead, spurred by their desire to avenge the loss of their homeland to the Japanese. Zhang Xueliang, the former warlord of Manchuria, and Communist leader Zhou Enlai were key actors in forging cooperation between their forces.

The Xi'an Incident, December 12, 1936

When Chiang Kai-shek received word of the Manchurians' weakening resolve to fight against the Communists, he flew to Xi'an, Shaanxi Province, to discuss the situation with Zhang Xueliang. Shortly after his arrival, however, Chiang was arrested and held prisoner by Zhang Xueliang's forces. Angry at Chiang's policy of appeasing Japan, the Manchurians demanded that a second united front against the Japanese take precedence over fighting the Communists, and demanded that attacks on the Communists cease.

At this critical juncture, supporters of Chiang Kai-shek, including his wife and her brother T. V. Soong, flew to Xi'an, joined by Zhou Enlai and a delegation from the Communist Party. Zhou Enlai helped negotiate Chiang's release, in part following Stalin's orders. It took several weeks, but by Christmas 1936 Chiang Kai-shek had quietly agreed to the demands and returned to Nanjing amid an outpouring of public support. Under the terms of this uneasy truce, Communist-controlled territory and the Red Army itself were now to come under Nationalist leadership.

The Marco Polo Bridge Incident, July 7, 1937

Nationalist troops soon confronted the Japanese near the Marco Polo Bridge just outside Beijing. Although the Nationalists would have preferred a peaceful resolution of differences, they were forced into combat when it became clear that the Japanese intended to invade China city by city. When a Japanese soldier was found missing on the evening of July 7, 1937, the Japanese commander ordered his troops to attack the nearby Chinese soldiers, who returned fire, and an all-out war against Japan began.

The Japanese attacked first in the north, taking Beijing and Tianjin. They then moved south and attacked Shanghai. Finally, the capital of Nanjing fell to the Japanese. The looting, pillaging, killing, and general destruction by the Japanese in Nanjing was so horrendous that it became known as the "Rape of Nanjing." More than anything else, this event influenced foreign opinion in favor of the Republic of China.

By now more than a third of Chiang's crack, German-trained fighting units had been lost. Chiang adopted a policy of "exchanging space for time," offering limited resistance in the hope of retaining sufficient strength to await a favorable turn of events such as a change in the international situation. Meanwhile, the Communists could mobilize no more than two divisions of regular troops. Largely unable to attack the Japanese head-on, Mao directed his generals to adopt a strategy of guerrilla warfare. By the following year the Japanese had achieved dominance in the east and further inland along the Yellow River, as well as near Wuhan on the Yangzi River. Their new conquests also stretched as far south as Guangzhou.

Meanwhile, the Nationalists set up an interim wartime capital in Chongqing, deep in the southwestern province of Sichuan. There they re-established military bases, arsenals, and even reconstructed universities, although Chongqing lacked the sophistication and relative modernity of Nanjing or Shanghai. In the Nationalists' wartime refuge, modern, urban Chinese life was sharply juxtaposed against more traditional, rural Chinese ways. Adding to the inherent difficulties of this situation, rampant inflation

was quickly eroding national morale by the late 1930s. The euphoria of early wartime soon gave way to a mood of grim despair.

The international situation failed to develop as Chiang had expected. The French prevented rail traffic from entering southern China from Vietnam in June 1940, at Japan's request. To make matters worse, the Burma Road was temporarily closed by the British. And in April 1941 Japan signed a Treaty of Neutrality and Friendship with the Soviet Union, ending the possibility of further Soviet aid to the Nationalists, which had been substantial in the early years of the war.

By the time the international situation did begin to improve in 1941, Chiang's position was already gravely weakened by internal Chinese developments. Japan's forces were increasingly dispersed by its attacks against the United States at Pearl Harbor and the Philippines, as well as against the British and the Dutch in the Pacific. At the same time, the United States began to support the Nationalists with military aid. The Nationalists, however, squandered much of the U.S. and British aid they received and failed to adopt a more offensive posture against the Japanese, preferring to maintain a wait-and-see attitude. Morale among Nationalist troops fell to an all-time low as their own commanders' loyalty to the KMT came into question. War costs exceeded government revenues fivefold in 1941, contributing to the regime's mounting economic difficulties.

CCP Reform Movement in Yan'an

Unlike the Nationalists, the Communists were not dependent on access to urban industrial bases and their concomitant commercial benefits. Rather, Mao's troops were at home operating in remote rural areas. The Red Army easily won the allegiance .f large segments of the rural population by fighting directly against the Japanese in the northwest, and in doing so absorbed many peasants into its ranks. Moreover, the united front with the Nationalists made it possible, at least temporarily, for the Communists to relax their vigilance toward these perennial enemies and to concentrate on expanding their own political and military organizations.

China's war against Japanese aggression officially began with the Marco Polo Bridge incident of 1937 and did not end until the conclusion of World War II. Japanese atrocities in China throughout this period are well documented. This photo shows the ruins of a Chinese temple after Japanese bombing.

Peasant associations and village committees were organized in Communist-controlled territory to maintain order, and many peasants grew to trust the Communists. Membership in the Communist Party rose from 40,000 in 1937 to 1,200,000 in 1945; most of the new members came from the ranks of the peasantry. Large numbers of patriotic students also joined the party. Many training institutes, intended for political indoctrination more than for technical education, were established in Yan'an, the Communists' new base of operations in Shaanxi.

In 1942 Mao launched a major rectification cam-

paign *(zhengfeng)* aimed at unifying the philosophical outlook of the Communists and combining theory and practice in daily life. Theory referred to Marxism-Leninism, plus some of Mao's own writings, while practice referred to participation in the Chinese revolution. Mao also stressed that the party's leadership was paramount and that individualism should be subordinated to the needs of the people as a whole—the collective. Finally, literature and art were to be used to serve political ends. Mao's pronouncements on literature and art terminated what had earlier been a lively debate among various literary societies and well-known writers. In this respect, Mao and Chiang sang the same tune.

Study groups within the CCP were organized to read and discuss Mao's thoughts on these subjects. Within those study groups, individuals were encouraged to criticize one another and undergo self-examination. Public assemblies were held to apply peer pressure and extract confessions. All these measures were supposed to strengthen the unity of the Communists and their followers. Taken together, they represented the antithesis of democratic principles and politics.

Morale in the Communist army was kept high through such incentives as giving each soldier's family a plot of land, thus allowing their family to earn income while the soldiers were in the service. The conduct of those in the Red Army was to be exemplary, and a source of pride. Soldiers received many lectures on subjects reminiscent of the Confucian *Analects,* such as standards of conduct and political values, although the analogy was not made explicit. The Communists also held regular reading classes in an attempt to raise the literacy rate of those in the army.

In addition to strengthening the morale and literacy skills of its soldiers, the Red Army also taught them strategies of war. Mao's own essays on strategic warfare during the Yan'an days posited three distinct types of warfare to be used at different times. The first type was guerrilla warfare, whereby local forces attacked quickly and without warning, only to make an even hastier retreat to attack again elsewhere. The second type was mobile warfare, employed by the Red Army only when victory was assured. The last type of warfare, called "positional," was used to defend territory. Mao's famous aphorism, "Political power grows out of the barrel of a gun," expressed his belief in revolutionary warfare as an indispensable component of the revolutionary process.

Mao's commitment to the peasants was the most important component of his revolutionary strategy. Reforms in the political and economic spheres were relatively moderate at first, since he did not wish to alienate even the more prosperous of this important constituency. As more areas in North China were brought under Communist control, the Communists limited themselves to a third of the positions in the local governments they set up. The remainder consisted of equal numbers of left-wing supporters and independents.

All non-Communists in local political positions, however, were carefully selected to ensure their sympathy to the Communist cause. Cadres in the Communist Party had been active in forming local associations of people with mutual interests or backgrounds, such as women and peasants, thereby giving the party a direct line of communication for their own doctrines and ideas to the people. By extension, members of such associations relished the idea of being closely involved with those in political control. Such a system also promoted programs for the general good, such as literacy campaigns, which were successful on the local level.

Mao's major contributions to the transformation of Chinese politics included building an army controlled by the CCP and recruiting mass support for the cause of revolutionary change. Mao was able to adapt communism to China's environment by erecting a Leninist party on a peasant base. He divorced communism from the traditional Marxist emphasis on the urban, industrial proletariat and demonstrated that the peasantry could serve as the social foundation of revolutionary change.

In 1940 Mao wrote "On the New Democracy" to justify the united front with the Nationalists as a temporary phase, yet also to reaffirm the party's long-term mission: to liberate the Chinese peasant masses. The masses would be given a new life through the instrumentality of the party dictatorship. Absolute power in the hands of the CCP would enable it to transform the old order. This required the concentration of power within a centralized political party that enforced absolute discipline on all its members.

The United States and China During the War

The United States, hoping to combine forces with China against the common enemy, Japan, gave the Nationalist government more than $2 billion in aid between 1942 and 1946. President Franklin D. Roosevelt appointed General Joseph Stilwell, a brilliant

At the Communist base in Yan'an, Mao Zedong addresses a group of his followers.

yet intemperate infantry commander, as chief of staff to Chiang Kai-shek in early 1943. Stilwell and Chiang heartily detested each other from the outset. Chiang had to deal with an odd mixture of forces in his armies, including warlord armies whose loyalty was in doubt, the remnants of his German-trained elite forces, and masses of new recruits, many forcefully pressed into military service. General Stilwell wanted to use Chiang's forces for large-scale campaigns in both Burma and China. Chiang was concerned that any major military campaign would inflict staggering losses on the Chinese and in the end destroy both himself and the Republic of China. Most frightening to Chiang was Stilwell's intention to employ Communist forces in campaigns against the Japanese.

Casting about for a compromise, Chiang encouraged the United States to bomb Japan from Chinese-built bases. But in the summer of 1944, when the first attacks were launched, the Japanese swiftly counter-attacked, overrunning some of the Chinese air bases as well as defeating Chiang's ground forces. Stilwell was replaced after this disastrous turn of events, a move that was welcomed by Chiang. Americans were now split on support for Chiang's forces, however. Some argued that he and the Republic of China were ineffective and weak as well as hopelessly corrupt, while others contended that Chiang represented China's last hope and deserved to be supported against Communist insurgency at whatever cost. Policy makers in the United States continued to vacillate between these two extremes of attitude until the end of the war.

The Civil War, 1945-1949

Emperor Hirohito announced Japan's surrender on August 14, 1945. Although both the CCP and the KMT took credit for defeating the invaders, the Soviet Red Army and superior U.S. technology in fact played major roles in ending World War II in Asia. In mainland China, however, the renewed rivalry for national power between the CCP and the KMT started even before the defeated Japanese soldiers could return to their own country.

During the fall of 1945, the two competitors played a game of balance and negotiation. The KMT obviously controlled much larger territories and possessed superior military strength compared to the CCP. Apart from some relatively small and poor areas in Shaanxi, Hebei, Shandong, and Anhui, the rest of the country pledged at least nominal allegiance to Chiang Kai-shek. Even the Communists were compelled to recognize the dominant position enjoyed by the Nationalist government.

Support from the United States also gave Chiang an advantage in his attempt to subordinate his enemies. President Harry S. Truman, recognizing the strategic and economic importance of China to the postwar world order, tried his utmost to maintain peace in China. Unable to trust the CCP, Truman and his advisers entrusted their hopes for China and East Asia to Chiang Kai-shek. The United States equipped KMT forces with up-to-date weaponry, and American airplanes and battleships carried KMT forces to occupy strategic cities and railroad lines. At the same time, Truman sent to China America's most eminent soldier, General George C. Marshall, to mediate between the two warring parties.

Although feigning cooperation, both the KMT and the CCP preferred the battlefield to the negotiating table as the place to settle their differences. Mao Zedong went to the KMT capital of Chongqing for talks with Chiang in August 1945, and signed the "Double Ten Agreement" (so named for the date it was signed, October 10). Mao was even reported to have said "Long live President Chiang" at a banquet during his stay. But this superficial camaraderie failed to resolve two critical issues: Chiang refused Mao's demand for a free election, and Mao would not give up arms without a KMT guarantee to relinquish its one-party monopoly. Before the end of 1945, friction between Nationalist and the Communist troops broke out on the border of Hebei and Suiyuan Provinces (Suiyuan has since been incorporated into Inner Mongolia), a critical area because of

its proximity to Beijing, straddling China proper and Manchuria.

Once the window paper was pierced, as a Chinese saying goes, the two sides exerted every effort to eliminate each other. The Nationalists, who had the upper hand in 1946 and into 1947, launched a series of attacks against the Communists. Hu Zongnan, one of Chiang's elite commanders, attacked and occupied Yan'an in March 1947, a victory that brought Chiang considerable psychological satisfaction but little, if any, strategic advantage. Another of Chiang's generals, Fu Zuoyi, occupied Beijing. In places where he could not dispatch his own troops immediately, Chiang ordered the defeated Japanese solders to assume responsibility for maintaining order. Chiang hoped to effect the total national unification he had long dreamed of, and in the afterglow of the anti-Japanese war there seemed a better than even chance he might actually succeed.

The KMT leaders gradually realized, however, that they were badly overextended. After the famous Seventy-Fourth Corps had taken Shandong and Fu Zuoyi occupied Hebei, Nie Rongzhen, later one of Mao's ten marshals, occupied the Taihang Mountains and, in early 1948, "liberated" Shijiazhuang, the capital of Hebei. Luo Ronghuan took the Jiaodong Peninsula, the richer half of Shandong, and led his by-now veteran and high-spirited troops across the Bohai Bay to Manchuria. The Soviet Red Army's delay in evacuating Manchuria, which it had occupied in the last weeks of the war, also worked to the advantage of the Communists, who established control in the northern half of the region and filled out their stocks of weapons from Japanese arsenals that the Soviet troops turned over to them.

Chiang still controlled most of China in 1948, but Mao's strategy had begun to turn the tide of battle, which now began to flow rapidly to the CCP's advantage. In their liberated areas, the CCP started a large-scale movement to redistribute land, in order to gain the support of the peasants for the ongoing "liberation war." The ranks of the People's Liberation Army (PLA), as the CCP-led troops now came to be called, swelled with new peasant recruits as well as surrendering KMT troops. The new Communist soldiers were equipped with weapons captured from the

After the anti-Japanese war ended, the Nationalists and Communists fought a bitter civil war until 1949. Here, Zhou Enlai, Communist China's most famous diplomat, negotiates with the KMT in 1945.

Nationalists. While Chiang relied on airplanes to carry supplies for his troops, the PLA organized legions of peasant laborers who pushed wheelbarrows full of millet, shoes, quilts, pigs, and other foodstuffs and supplies.

The military balance now began to tilt toward the CCP side of the conflict. By November 1948, Lin Biao, Mao's youngest field commander, had completed his conquest of Manchuria, the most important industrial area of China. During the fall of 1948, Huang Wei, one of Chiang's ablest generals, was captured by the PLA. In the winter of 1948-1949, the combined forces of Lin Biao, Nie Rongzhen, and Luo Ronghuan took Tianjin, and Fu Zuoyi surrendered Beijing. Although the CCP had thus far captured only half of China, the KMT's major forces had been eliminated. Mao ordered his troops to cross the Yangzi River, and and the PLA occupied Chiang's capital city of Nanjing on April 23, 1949. By the end of the year, the PLA had captured all of China except Tibet and Taiwan. Chiang and the remnant Nationalist forces fled to Taiwan, and on October 1, 1949, in the name of the victorious CCP leadership, Mao Zedong proclaimed the establishment of the People's Republic of China.

From 1911 to 1949, engulfed in successive turmoil of various kinds, China never realized Sun Yat-sen's dream of a republic, partly because the country had never been united. When the CCP emerged victorious from the civil war, the question again arose as to whether China might be able to realize that dream under the new leadership of the Chinese Communist Party. The national flag adopted by the new country, which called itself the People's Republic of China, has five stars inlaid on a red background. While the big star symbolizes the CCP, the four smaller ones are said to represent the other political parties that were the CCP's partners in what purported to be a coalition government. Would that flag, so rich in symbolism, herald the long-awaited coming of democracy to China or would it usher in yet another era of political repression and social disruption?

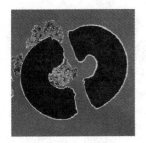

CHAPTER 3

MAOIST CHINA (1949-1978)

Early Years of the People's Republic of China, 1950-1957

The People's Republic of China (PRC) was formally declared in October 1949. As the leaders of the Chinese Communist Party (CCP) finally ascended to power, they brought with them considerable political and administrative experience, gained over decades of revolutionary struggle. Their legitimacy in the eyes of the Chinese people was strengthened by the significant progress made over the next few years in reconstructing the postwar economy, which had been burdened with hyperinflation, and in successfully reviving agricultural and industrial production. Legitimacy in the world's eyes, shaped by U.S. policy, would be absent for several decades to come, however. The CCP's association with the Soviet Union, the failure to link with non-Nationalist elements of the Chongqing government (which the United States had recognized), and the ensuing cold war effectively precluded U.S. recognition and support of the PRC for many years.

Great tasks lay before Mao Zedong (1893-1976) and the Communist leadership. To carry out their goal of transforming China's economy and society, Chinese leaders looked to the Soviet Union as a model, as well as a source of technology and aid. The Soviet experience offered structures for party and state organizations, models for urban-based and industrial development, and approaches toward collectivization of farming. At the same time, the CCP leadership consciously limited its scope of activities during the initial years of transition, implementing policies gradually. The CCP also sought to avoid the mistakes and excesses of the Soviet experience. Al-

though the Chinese Communist Party had long been dependent on Soviet support, it had sought to adapt Marxist-Leninist theories to Chinese realities from the very beginning. In particular, Mao's strategy based China's revolutionary struggle on the peasantry, rather than on the urban proletariat. And to help carry out his visions, Mao Zedong added a third theoretical source of ideas—Mao Zedong Thought.

Immediate Tasks of Nation-Building

The new government began by taking a united front approach, in which the proletariat was to join with the peasants, petty bourgeoisie, and national bourgeoisie to rule through a "people's democratic dictatorship." In addition to the Chinese Communist Party, non-CCP and non-Kuomintang (KMT) political parties sent delegates to the first Chinese People's Political Consultative Conference (CPPCC), an interim body that exercised the powers and functions of a national assembly until a system of people's congresses was established. The CPPCC approved a temporary constitution (the Common Program), elected Mao Zedong chairman of the People's Central Government Council and of the CPPCC National Committee, and determined administrative matters such as the national emblem and national flag.

Under the Common Program, which emphasized gradual change, the CCP utilized the existing base of officials and party cadres; capitalists were encouraged and helped to revive industrial production; various organizations, such as private and religious groups, provided needed services to the people. "Enemies of the people" were narrowly defined at this stage: imperialists, meaning Westerners and their enterprises; feudal forces, or landlords (less than 5 percent of the rural population); and bureaucratic capitalists, a small number of people who held large enterprises and were likely to have been connected to the KMT. Thus, in forming this united front, the Communist government sought to avoid alienating officials of the old regime, intellectuals, national bourgeoisie, rich peasants, and other potential opponents.

The CCP leaders consolidated power slowly, encountering pockets of resistance in places such as Tibet. China was temporarily divided into six military/administrative regions until formal government structures were established. In 1954, the Chinese People's Political Consultative Conference adopted a formal constitution, which outlined political and governing structures. The National People's Congress (NPC) was established as a permanent representative body. The NPC and its Standing Committee were elected by delegates, who were in turn elected by about 200,000 local assemblies. The NPC approved appointments to the State Council, and thus became the formal source of state authority; the CPPCC relinquished its legal power to become a deliberative and advisory body. However, the NPC's legislative authority was kept weak, and real power resided with the Chinese Communist Party.

Adopting the Soviet Political Structure

Looking to the Soviet model, the Chinese Communist Party formed a government structure in which power was vested in three organizations: the party, the government bureaucracy, and the People's Liberation Army (PLA). The CCP Central Committee, consisting of 100 to 300 members, is elected by the delegates of the party congress. Actual power in the central government, however, is held by the Political Bureau (Politburo), particularly its Standing Committee. Politburo members come from all three governing organizations. The key Standing Committee members in the first years of the People's Republic of China were Mao Zedong, party chairman; Liu Shaoqi (1898-1969), second-ranking leader and organizational development figure; Zhu De (1886-1976), commander-in-chief of the military; Zhou En-

lai (1898-1976), premier and diplomatic negotiator; and Chen Yun (1905-1995), economics and development expert.

In the party apparatus, the Secretariat oversaw all national and provincial-level party committees through a hierarchical structure. Directives were issued through the committees and carried out all the way through to provincial and local levels, which were mirrored in the central party structure. By positioning party cadres in influential positions in factories, farms, government offices, mass organizations, and educational institutions, the CCP was able to exert control over all aspects of political, economic, social, and cultural life. The State Council headed the government bureaucracy, which took care of running the country and, together with top officials in the government ministries, debated and made policy. Tensions developed from time to time between the party and government leaders, with the party dominating in most cases over time. The party-PLA linkage remained strong, shaped through years of revolutionary struggle. Top military leaders such as Zhu De, Lin Biao (1907-1971), Chen Yi (1901-1972), and Peng Dehuai (1898-1974), held important concurrent party positions. The Military Affairs Committee became the military's policy body and reported to the Politburo; it also directed the party committees that were a part of each military unit.

First Stage of Land Reform, 1950-1952

One key to the CCP's victory in the civil war had been its successful mobilization of the peasants, who comprise 80 percent of China's population. The CCP helped peasants solve practical problems and improve their standards of living, both of which the Nationalists had neglected. In the 1930s, half the land was held by rich farmers in some regions, while the bulk of the rural population were tenants or landless peasants. Rent paid in the form of 40 to 60 percent of annual crops and land taxes kept the peasants at subsistence levels.

The reallocation of land through CCP land reform measures had started in North and Northeast China, where the CCP built its base after 1937. The goal

The land reform movement was often characterized by violence and bloodshed, carried out by vengeful peasants and local party cadres. Some 2 million landlords are estimated to have been killed in the course of land reform in the early 1950s.

now was to transform China into a socialist society and economy. The CCP leaders saw agricultural reform as the first step to nation-building. They also recognized the need to remove the rural elite and destroy the local power structure. These goals were clearly stated in the Agrarian Reform Law of 1950:

The land ownership system of feudal exploitation by the landlord class shall be abolished, and the system of peasant land ownership shall be carried into effect in order to set free the rural productive forces, develop agricultural production, and pave the way for the industrialization of the new China.

To realize these goals, the rural population was divided into five classes: landlords, rich peasants, middle peasants, poor peasants, and agricultural laborers, with policies designed to benefit mainly the last two groups. A more equitable tax structure shift-

ed the burden to the rich, rents were reduced, and land was redistributed.

The land ownership system was not abolished without resistance or bloodshed. At local levels, people's tribunals led struggles against the landlords. Much of the violence was carried out by vengeful peasants and local party cadres, although authorized by the CCP. Some 2 million landlords are estimated to have been killed during these years. By 1952, land confiscated from the landlords and rich peasants was redistributed under the administration of the *xiang*, a group of several villages.

Improving the livelihood of a majority of the people in the countryside did much to bolster the credibility of the new government. For many, the expression "after liberation" (*jiefang yihou*) held genuine meaning, contrasting favorably with the destitution and widespread undernourishment of previous decades. Nevertheless, many scholars feel that the main achievement of agricultural reform was political, while the direct impact on productivity was more modest. Using both coercive and persuasive methods, the CCP built the base on which further social transformation through collectivization of agriculture could be implemented.

Reviving the Economy

A prerequisite to pursuing a modernization drive was to rebuild the rail and road infrastructure devastated during the war. During the first decade of the Communist regime, new rail lines were also built, particularly in the hinterland. Railways bridged regions in Outer and Inner Mongolia; Xinjiang and central China; and the major cities of Lanzhou, Chengdu, Chongqing, Guiyang, and Nanning in southwest China. Interior regions, rich in natural resources and raw materials, were now well connected to major industrial and coastal cities, such as Shanghai, Qingdao, and Tianjin.

The northeastern part of the country played a key role during this transition period as an industrial engine and a setting for experimentation. There, the Chinese inherited intact many industries that had been well developed by the Japanese when they occupied Manchuria (including the modern-day provinces of Heilongjiang, Jilin, and Liaoning) during the 1920s. The railway transport system in this region had also been highly developed by the Chinese Eastern Railway Company, a joint Chinese-Russian effort, in the 1890s. In 1949, the northeast was producing a third of China's industrial output, and by 1952 this proportion had soared to more than half.

At this early stage, some of the country's largest enterprises were being nationalized, especially foreign-held enterprises. China's traditional light industries, however, held mostly by private capitalists, were left alone. Under the Common Program, change was intentionally gradual, with an eye to allowing productivity to go forward without disruption. In line with the Soviet formula, the Chinese government investment program strongly favored industry over agriculture, and heavy industry over light industry. Yet the government also paid attention to the interdependent relationships between agricultural and industrial development. China's leaders saw the need to reform and strengthen the agricultural sector through land reform and collectivization before proceeding with substantial industrial reform. Agriculture could then support industrial efforts and serve as a tax base and as a source of foreign exchange; indeed during the early years of the PRC, 75 percent of China's exports were farm products and textiles (cotton and silk), while 90 percent of its imports consisted of machinery, equipment, and producer goods.

The relationship between agriculture and industry in China differed in two major ways from the Soviet model. First, care was taken, notably in the first Five-Year Plan (1953-1957), not to build the industrial sector at the peasants' expense. That is, the CCP's goals were not only to increase agricultural production but to continually raise the peasants' standard of living. The party leaders recognized that this was crucial to maintaining the stability necessary for steady production and strengthening mass support for the government. The CCP's power base was, after all, among the peasantry in north and northeast China. Furthermore, CCP leaders recognized the limitations of the Chinese agricultural sector compared with its Soviet counterpart—even at its most productive, China's farmers could never generate enough surplus to completely pay for industrialization. Therefore, the growth of the two sectors was somewhat more balanced.

In the countryside, land was now more equitably held and more of it was being put to productive use. Agricultural production and distribution were stable, which helped to raise nutritional levels. And by reviving the nation's industrial production, reconnecting the interior with the coast through infrastructure investments, and bringing inflation under control by 1952, the Communist leaders brought about a semblance of economic recovery and stability. This gained them broad support not only in their traditional rural base but in the urban sector as well.

Collectivization of Rural Society

The CCP's vision of transforming China's society and economy started with the countryside. Party leaders had already had considerable success in mobilizing the peasants in North China, and by 1952, approximately 40 percent of households in the liberated areas had been organized into mutual aid teams. In this first stage, peasants pooled tools and draft animals and labored together, particularly during the planting and harvesting seasons. During a further experimental stage, households and villages were organized into larger units of production and administration, called Agricultural Producers' Cooperatives. Land was pooled in these semi-socialist cooperatives, although individuals still held nominal deeds to the land.

The next several years saw cycles of intensive mobilization followed by relaxation of the collectivization process, as these efforts met with support or resistance. In addition, food was sometimes in short supply, grain transfers to urban areas were inefficient, and government procurement prices kept rising. When problems became obvious, many party leaders urged slowing down the process. But Mao firmly believed that stepping up mobilization was the only way to achieve social transformation of the Chinese peasantry. He urged intensive drives to collectivize agriculture, beginning in 1955. The entire Chinese countryside (with the exception of national minority areas) was to be organized under higher level, or fully collectivized, Agricultural Producers' Cooperatives in which land, as well as tools, was to be jointly owned by the cooperative. By 1957, China had nearly 800,000 cooperative farms with an average of 160 families (or 600 to 700 persons) in each.

It is difficult to credit the collectivization of farming with a rise in agricultural output. Farmers received wages based on calculations of the cooperative's projected output, regardless of contribution of land, draft animals, or other inputs. Some party leaders thought that farmers would be motivated to produce more if they had greater material incentives, but Mao's views prevailed. Moreover, although growth in rice and wheat output was stable, actual increase in yield was minimal. Increased output was more attributable to the increase in the amount of land being cultivated.

Although the Chinese looked to the Soviet Union for models, at the same time they sought to avoid the negative extremes of the Soviet experience. China's rich peasants were not eliminated as a class, as the kulaks had been in the young Soviet Union, although their property was confiscated with that of the landlords. The use of armed force, as occurred in the Soviet Union especially during the Stalinist period, was minimal in China. Landlords and rich peasants, however, were manipulated to serve as a focus of class struggle. Thus the Chinese government relied on mass participation and criticism by the poor peasants, rather than police force, to undermine the position and authority of the rich peasants. The goal was to break feudal relationships; the cooperative under party cadre leadership replaced families and clans as the basis of identification and loyalties.

Industrial Priorities Under the First Five-Year Plan

Although the first Five-Year Plan (1953-1957) was not formally approved and announced until 1955, much planning and implementation had already taken place by then. Key planners were Chen Yun, central planning expert on the Politburo; Li Fuchun (c. 1899-1975), State Planning Commission chairman; and Li Xiannian (1907-1992) and Bo Yibo (b. 1908), both finance and tax experts who also served terms as finance minister. The creation of the State Planning Commission and economic ministries in 1952 centralized planning power and authority; the Central Committee was highly involved in policy development. Regional and military authority were further reduced in 1954-1955 when temporary postwar administrative organizations were dismantled.

Overall, China made significant progress during the first Five-Year Plan (FYP), and economic measures point to success, especially in view of the country's devastation after decades of war. During this period, China's gross national product (GNP) increased 9 percent on average each year; industry grew at 13 to 14 percent annually; and agricultural output increased about 4 percent annually.

In the first Five-Year Plan period, CCP planners made an attempt to balance China's industrial base geographically. In contrast to the period before 1949, when factories in China had been concentrated in coastal cities, there was now a drive to build up new industrial centers in the northern, northwestern, and central parts of the country. Of the 156 planned projects in the first Five-Year Plan, nearly all were in heavy industry, such as iron and steel, electric power, and machinery. The Soviet Union transferred the latest technologies in the steel industry to plants to Baotou, Inner Mongolia; Wuhan, Hubei (Central China); and elsewhere. Other important large-scale plants included those producing automobiles in Changchun in the northeast and tractors in Luoyang, Henan. China also began to invest substantially in fuel exploration at this time, especially in the north and northwest provinces rich in coal, oil, natural gas, and other resources. The output of producer goods was impressive: production of machine tools doubled between 1952 and 1957; electric power generation increased tenfold.

Closely following the Soviet model, China's economic planners, under Chen Yun's leadership, emphasized large-scale, capital-intensive industries as the key to industrial modernization. In this respect, the Chinese closely followed the Soviet model. Some of the country's largest enterprises had been confiscated from foreign companies and Chinese industrialists, and were now state-owned and run. Many large industrial projects were undertaken with Soviet aid and technical assistance. China also adopted Soviet models of economic management and resource allocation. The focus was on producer goods—metallurgy, machinery, electric power, coal and petroleum, and chemicals—rather than consumer goods. Skipping over light industry and going directly to heavy industrialization was in line with Mao's own vision of rapidly catching up with the industrialized world.

During its first decade, the PRC depended on the Soviet Union almost completely to carry out its industrialization drive. The Chinese relied on the Soviet Union not only for the bulk of machinery and equipment they purchased but also for critical investment. During the heyday of Soviet presence in the 1950s, thousands of Soviet engineers, technicians, and managers were working throughout China at any given time, and many more Chinese technicians and workers went to Soviet factories for training. Be-

cause China's investment pattern during these years heavily favored heavy industry over light industry, the gap in their respective output values rose from a ratio of 3:1 in 1952 to 7:1 by 1957, reflecting the implementation of projects utilizing Soviet assistance.

The Search for a Chinese Socialist Model, 1958-1965

While China's first Five-Year Plan largely followed the Soviet model of development, the subsequent period was an attempt to forge China's own path to socialism. The second Five-Year Plan (1958-1963) had been designed to improve on the first FYP and included strategies that differed from the Soviet model but were thought to be better suited to China's circumstances and needs. The second FYP had hardly gotten under way, however, when Mao, under the banner of the Great Leap Forward, promoted policies to quicken development, especially the shaping of socialist man. Whereas political organizers and government administrators had been allowed relative latitude during the first FYP, after 1958 Mao took charge of formulating policies and determining the direction of China's development.

Mao's Great Leap Forward ultimately proved disastrous and caused great hardship, which prompted a period of retrenchment from 1959 to about 1962. Thus the essence of the second FYP, when it was revived, ultimately became an attempt to undo the damage and regression brought about by Mao's policies. It was then that the CCP leadership began to split into two main camps that can be characterized as "pragmatists" and "idealists."

The Second Five-Year Plan: A Vision of Balanced Development

In designing the second Five-Year Plan, Chinese planners wanted to avoid disruptions like those that had ensued from Mao's accelerated collectivization drive, including social problems resulting from the pace of radical changes and economic issues such as overplanting, and adoption of inappropriate tools and techniques. Ma Yinchu, then the president of Beijing

University, was among those recommending a more balanced course of development. Supported by the State Planning Commission, he urged that agriculture and light industry not be further neglected in China's development. Ma and many others argued for greater use of chemical fertilizers and more mechanization to increase agricultural yields; they also called for greater support for smaller industrial plants to address the growing problems of urban unemployment, especially in Shanghai and other coastal cities. The previous focus on upgrading large heavy industrial plants required a long time-frame, created new industrial centers, and did not alleviate unemployment in these traditional industrial cities.

The eighth party congress, which convened in 1956, signaled significant power shifts away from an emphasis on Mao and toward a more collective leadership, to guard against actions like Mao's 1955 collectivization drive, which had been implemented despite widespread opposition in the top leadership. The failure of the party congress to call for Mao Zedong Thought to become the party's guiding doctrine reflected this conscious move away from an emphasis on Mao's individual leadership. As a result, Mao retreated to a "second line" of leadership to focus primarily on policy considerations, professing to leave the "first line" of leadership, the day-to-day matters, to Liu Shaoqi and Deng Xiaoping.

Despite this professed retreat from a first line of leadership, Mao himself nevertheless remained highly involved. Mao's strategy included co-opting the military and the intellectuals. He also directed Chen Boda (1904-1989), his loyal theoretician, to start *Hongqi* (Red Flag), a journal devoted to propagating Mao's political theories. Mao was dissatisfied with the second Five-Year Plan (shaped mainly by the government ministries), feeling that it would move the country in a direction that would jeopardize the socialist transformation. Mao believed that Chinese society had become increasingly stratified under the programs of the first FYP, which had included implementation of a civil service grading system in the ministries, industry, and education.

To reassert revolutionary ideals, Mao resorted to his long-held belief in the value of mass mobilization and periodic political campaigns. The second Five-Year Plan was put on hold as a result, since Mao was determined to lead the country in a radically different direction. As first presented at the Qingdao Conference of July 1957, Mao advocated concurrent development of agriculture and industry, with increased mobilization and ideological fervor to achieve greater productivity. By advocating decentralization, he aimed to weaken the power of the central bureaucracy. He also convened party conferences, the Supreme State Conference, and the National People's Congress to further legitimize his agenda. Under such pressures from Mao, the National People's Congress and party congress gave their approval to the Great Leap Forward, attesting to Mao's power as an individual over the authority of China's political institutions.

The Great Leap Forward and Formation of People's Communes

Mao's visions, embodied in plans for a "Great Leap Forward," were adopted at the second session of the eighth party congress in May 1958 and became official policy at the August 1958 Beidaihe Conference. The new development strategy, which was referred to as "walking on two legs," aimed to build up a large-scale industrial base while utilizing small-scale technologies to maximize production in traditional industries and agriculture.

Key features of the Great Leap Forward were:

- fully mobilizing rural and urban labor through people's communes;
- consolidating socialist ownership;
- setting ambitious goals to replace a genuine planning process;
- experimenting with means to achieve these goals using, for example, so-called backyard furnaces to increase steel production;
- emphasizing rapid growth at the expense of quality and technical norms.

Another major aspect of the Great Leap Forward (GLF) was the organization of communal farming on a massive scale to enhance agricultural production. Even after the accelerated collectivization drive started in 1955, Mao felt that the transformation of the Chinese people into socialist men and women was inadequate. The peasants were therefore organized into even larger entities, called people's communes. The role of communes in furthering this transformation was clearly stated in the Central Committee Decision on People's Communes of August 29, 1958.

The people's communes are the logical result of the march of events. Large, comprehensive people's communes have made their appearance, and in several places they are already widespread. . . . The basis for the development of the people's communes is mainly the all-round, continuous leap forward in China's agricultural production and the ever-rising political consciousness of the 500 million peasants. . . . At the present stage our task is to build socialism. The primary purpose of establishing people's communes is to accelerate the speed of socialist construction and to prepare actively for the transition to communism. It seems that the attainment of communism in China is no longer a remote future event. We should actively use the form of the people's communes to explore the practical road of transition to communism.

The agricultural commune, consisting of about 5,000 households, was divided into brigades and smaller work units called teams. No major decisions were made at any of the three levels (commune, brigade, team) without party cadre involvement. There was no private property; income was calculated on projections of the commune's productivity as a whole. The commune handled all administrative matters and organized services, such as schools, banks, nurseries for infants, and homes for the elderly.

Within a short time, China's peasantry was reorganized into about 24,000 communes. The process of communization, shifting from a social unit of about 150 people to 5,000 households, greatly accelerated social change. Women were brought into the work force, as traditional household and childrearing tasks were now handled communally. The Red Flag Commune of Zhengzhou was held up as one of many "model communes." Consisting of more than 4,000 households, it was formed around the Zhengzhou Spinning and Weaving Factory.

The concept of social transformation through communalization was extended to factories in the cities and to the building of massive infrastructure projects, such as land reclamation and dams, that also involved a million students and large numbers of soldiers from the People's Liberation Army. Privately held factories were transformed into communes; after receiving some compensation, former capitalists found themselves salaried workers. All aspects of production and labor were determined by the commune; party cadres replaced skilled managers and technicians.

The "correctness" of the people's communes was affirmed by the sixth plenary session of the Eighth Central Committee, at which the newly announced targets revealed an ambitious but unrealistic vision. Great downward political pressure was exerted to meet the goal of "doubling output." Targets seemed to have been set arbitrarily with figures pulled from thin air, and output estimates were undoubtedly exaggerated in an attempt to approach these goals. As momentum grew, more conservative estimates, perhaps closer to reality, were voiced but then quashed for political expediency. Targets at various levels might be met, but at considerable cost, including severe demands on labor and food supplies and strain on the procurement and distribution systems.

China's plunge into disaster became apparent within a short time. Although 1958 was an unusually good year for agriculture, the sum of procurement and pricing policies, pressures to meet targets, and hoarding based on fear of unstable food supplies eventually caused great disruption and suffering in the countryside. Bad weather in subsequent years added to the difficulties, but was not the sole factor. People were at starvation levels in various provinces, and food shortages reached the cities. From a high of about 200 million tons in 1958, grain production in 1960 dipped to a low of 150 million tons (some estimates go as low as 143.5 million tons). It took until 1965 to climb back to the 1957-1958 production levels. Ironically, China's grain exports continued throughout this period, topping 4 million tons in 1959. Considering the domestic food shortages, this level of exports only increased the hardship experienced by the Chinese people. Government-controlled newspapers announced steel production

Rice harvesting on a people's commune in the 1960s. Communes relied mainly on traditional farming methods on a large scale. Despite serious problems, the commune system established in the late 1950s was not completely dismantled until the mid-1980s.

achievements on a virtually daily basis as the public was exhorted to produce more and more. Production reached only 8 million tons in 1958, rather than the ambitious 11-million-ton goal. And 3 million tons of this was steel that proved useless—produced in the backyard furnaces erected throughout the agricultural communes.

While some goals were undoubtedly achieved through massive mobilization, the failure of the backyard furnaces and ensuing widespread starvation were to become the lasting legacies of the Great Leap Forward. The famine took on serious proportions, especially in certain rural regions. Mortality rates had reached 25 per thousand in 1960 and were even higher in the countryside; 19 million people are believed to have died of starvation in that year alone. Political disaster appeared imminent if the government did not take immediate steps to address the grave situation.

Economic Adjustment and Recovery

Among the top leadership, Liu Shaoqi and Deng Xiaoping officially supported Mao's Great Leap Forward policies but many others did not. Just how aware China's top leaders initially were of the large-scale starvation and hardships in the countryside and the breakdown of the economy is difficult to ascertain. The famine was severely underreported at the time since sounding the alarm was equated with criticism of official policies, and such criticism was seen as a direct challenge to Mao's power. Considerable pressure was exerted at all levels to meet production targets at any cost. Under these conditions, falsification of figures had a snowball effect. Distant from the interior provinces, leaders in Beijing received reports in which figures fluctuated wildly and were no longer calculated with any consistent methods. Reports of the 1958 grain output, for example, ranged

The disastrous policies of the 1958 Great Leap Forward led to a period of economic retrenchment (1959-1962) and to increasing tensions among the Chinese leadership. Here, key Communist officials at the second session of the Second National People's Congress in April 1960 include (from left) Mao Zedong, Liu Shaoqi, Song Qingling (widow of Sun Yat-sen), and Dong Biwu.

from 375 million to 500 million tons. Nevertheless, when top leaders began to personally visit the provinces and report what they found, as did Peng Dehuai in Hunan and Chen Yun in Henan, the devastating reality slowly began to be known and, more significantly, discussed officially. By 1959, the Chinese Communist Party was ready to relax the policies of the Great Leap Forward.

Premier Zhou Enlai played a key role in initiating the recovery process, which was extended until 1965 under his influence. He drafted the "Urgent Directive on Rural Work" approved by the Central Committee in November 1960 to address the crises caused by the Great Leap. At the local level, it shifted decision making to the lower-level brigade and team units in the agricultural communes. At the central government level, Chen Yun, the most experienced economic planner, was brought back to power, having been ousted in the previous shakeups.

Although Mao allowed this relaxation of policies to take place, he did not admit to errors; indeed he argued that the problems were temporary or just due to natural calamities, such as bad weather. In the communiqué of the ninth plenary session of the Eighth Central Committee of the CCP (January 1961), Mao upheld the correctness of the Great Leap Forward:

The great achievements of our country during the past three years show that the party's general line for socialist construction, the Great Leap Forward, and the people's communes suit the realities of China. . . . Among the party and government functionaries, more than 90 percent work faithfully and conscientiously for the people; a few percent are bad elements, that is, landlord and bourgeois elements who have not yet been sufficiently remolded.

Lin Biao (1907-1971) rose quickly in the Chinese leadership during the late 1950s. He gained Mao's favor after the Great Leap Forward by strengthening political departments in the People's Liberation Army to ensure loyalty to Mao. Declared Mao's official successor in 1969, he was killed in a plane crash, reportedly fleeing after his plot to assassinate Mao was uncovered.

Mao Launches a Counteroffensive

Party and government leaders, especially the "organization-type" CCP leadership led by Liu Shaoqi, Deng Xiaoping, and Chen Yun, thought that advancing economic development after immediate recovery from the GLF years should take priority over perpetuating revolution. Mao, who viewed the post-GLF policies of "adjustment" as no more than a temporary expediency, decided to launch a counteroffensive.

Mao convened the tenth plenary session of the Central Committee at Beidaihe (a beach resort northeast of Beijing) in July 1962 with the objective of integrating his revolutionary views into the econom-

ic recovery plan. Through his Socialist Education movement, begun in 1962, Mao began to build up his base in China's institutions, making Maoist ideology a criterion for institutions at all levels. The first year of the movement was to concentrate on reforming the thinking of basic-level cadres, but it turned into a major purge. By the end of the three-year campaign, more than a million cadres had been dismissed. Liu Shaoqi was put in charge of education policies, weakening the education ministry and enabling Mao to penetrate educational institutions directly with his revolutionary agenda.

On a broader social level, Mao was critical of what he saw as the still influential feudal and capitalistic arts. He had long recognized the powerful role of literature in shaping people's thinking, and he now called on the CCP's top cultural and propaganda leaders to subject drama and literature to Marxist criticism. It was also at this time that Jiang Qing (1914-1991), Mao's wife, began to exert her influence in revolutionizing the arts. Her particular interest was in drama; she later guided the writing and production of the "eight model revolutionary plays."

The Rise of Lin Biao

Tensions continued to intensify, and Mao appeared increasingly determined to remove his opponents. Mao began to promote Lin Biao, grooming him as a possible successor. Lin's rise was quick. In May 1958, he was elevated to the Politburo's Standing Committee, the party's highest body. The following spring, as Sino-Soviet tensions were growing, Peng Dehuai, who had been a vocal critic of the Great Leap Forward policies and the commune system, visited the Soviet Union and Eastern Europe in his capacity as defense minister. Mao believed that Peng was garnering Khrushchev's support, since Khrushchev had also criticized the GLF approach as unorthodox. Peng's opposition to the GLF was therefore framed in terms of party unity and patriotism. Mao launched a campaign to criticize anti-partyism and anti-rightism, specifically targeting Peng. Mao then attacked Peng at the Central Committee's eighth plenum, held at Lushan in August. A month later,

Peng was dismissed, and Lin Biao was appointed defense minister.

After 1959, Lin Biao had gained Mao's favor by strengthening political departments in the PLA to ensure loyalty to Maoist thought and policies. The entire country was encouraged to look to the PLA and to "learn from Lei Feng," a model soldier who completely dedicated his life to "serving the people." The PLA published and distributed millions of copies of *Quotations from Chairman Mao,* also called the "little red book"; the beginnings of a Mao cult were emerging. By successfully incorporating Maoist thought into the military structure, Lin Biao, now China's top military leader, also enhanced his own power relative to other high-level leaders who might be considered potential successors to Mao.

The Cultural Revolution and Its Aftermath, 1966-1976

The Cultural Revolution, which eventually engulfed the entire nation, can be described as Mao's ultimate political campaign. In it, Mao mobilized the populace to carry forth his revolutionary vision. Millions of youth rallied to the cause, organizing into Red Guard units. Mao felt the need to destroy the Chinese Communist Party in order to build it up again according to his conception.

The Cultural Revolution was a complex phenomenon with many roots. The worsening of Sino-Soviet relations had pushed Mao to aim for fierce self-reliance and an independent road to communism and modernity. Ultimately, the Cultural Revolution was a power struggle between "pragmatists" and "radical Maoists" in the party, the government bureaucracy, the group promoting the Cultural Revolution, and the PLA. Mao, as an aging leader, was also trying to deal with the issue of succession, hoping to avoid a crisis like that faced by the Soviet Union in 1953, when Stalin died without naming a successor.

The Cultural Revolution would not be officially declared over until Mao's death in 1976, to be followed by a mass movement to "expose and criticize" Lin Biao and the "Gang of Four." At first, Chinese leaders were reluctant to interpret the Cultural Revolution in negative terms, but by the late 1970s, the official government line had acknowledged its destructive consequences and the Cultural Revolution was soberly described as the most severe reversal of the country's socialist cause to date.

The Course of the Cultural Revolution, 1966-1969

Chinese politics became increasingly personalized during the Cultural Revolution. Power was concentrated in three groups: the State Council, under Zhou Enlai, and the central ministries; the People's Liberation Army, under Lin Biao's leadership; and the Cultural Revolution Small Group, which included Mao's wife, Jiang Qing, and his trusted theoretician, Chen Boda. Over the course of the Cultural Revolution, Mao would constantly shift his support from one group to another. At the beginning, Jiang and Lin worked in close alliance, but conflicts of interest would cause one to turn on the other in the struggle for power and influence with Mao.

A flash point in the intellectual and ideological debates surrounding the beginning of the Cultural Revolution was a play entitled "Hai Rui Is Dismissed from Office" by Wu Han, which tells the story of the unjust dismissal of a Ming dynasty official. Controversy arose over the play's interpretation: Mao and many radical intellectuals interpreted this play as an allegorical critique of Mao's dismissal of Peng Dehuai in 1959. Peng Zhen (b. 1902, no relation to Peng Dehuai), a high party official and mayor of Beijing, had been assigned to lead the first five-person Cultural Revolution Small Group charged with making plans for a "cultural revolution." When called upon to criticize the play, he chose to emphasize its strictly historical context and defended playwright Wu, who also served as Beijing's deputy mayor. In response, Mao dismissed Peng Zhen in June 1966 and disbanded the Cultural Revolution Small Group. This was an example of Mao's efforts to utilize individuals who were sympathetic to his own views to bypass party process and to undermine party authority, including that of the Party Propaganda Department, then headed by Lu Dingyi (b. 1906).

Chen Boda was appointed to chair a new Cultural Revolution Group, which included Yao Wenyuan

Wall posters were plastered throughout China during the Cultural Revolution tracking political developments and strife. With the country's descent into chaos, Mao demobilized the Red Guards and sent many Chinese youth to labor in the countryside beginning in 1968.

(b. 1930), who had led the criticism of Wu Han's play; Jiang Qing; and Kang Sheng (1899-1975), a shadowy but influential figure in public security and secret police operations. These moves gave the radical Maoists far greater prominence in Beijing, adding to their existing media base in Shanghai. This grouping not only was dominated by Mao's supporters and radical intellectuals but reported directly to Mao through the Politburo—to which radicals would soon be appointed—rather than to the Party Secretariat.

As the speed and extent of the Red Guard activities intensified at Beijing University and other universities, and as confrontation moved to include the government ministries and agencies, party vice chairman Liu Shaoqi found himself in the awkward position of trying to prevent chaos in the midst of collapsing order while still trying to demonstrate

support of Mao's policies and fend off criticism of being "revisionist." He dispatched about 400 work teams to schools and various bureaucracies in an attempt to bring criticism back under party leadership, a commonly used tactic in earlier political campaigns. However, this ran counter to Mao's goal of realizing a complete shakeup of all institutions including top-level officials. At the same time, the Cultural Revolution Group had begun to identify high-ranking officials for criticism, while the military was increasing its presence and political role in the process of seizure of power in various institutions.

Eight massive rallies were held in Beijing in the fall of 1966, bringing together 13 million Red Guards from all over the country. The first three years of the Cultural Revolution were its most destructive: many intellectuals and party and government officials alike saw their lives destroyed and were driven to suicide or died from hardships or injury. Cleavages in society were brought into the open, as groups that supported the party establishment mobilized into their own mass organizations to counter the Red Guard movement and the central policies emanating from Maoist forces.

Mao called for a Central Committee plenum (the eleventh) in August 1966. Criticism focused on high-level party officials, including Liu Shaoqi and Deng Xiaoping; labels such as "Khrushchevite revisionists" were exploited to justify an all-out attack on them and their supporters. In this highly charged atmosphere, Zhou Enlai, the only top leader besides Mao to survive this movement without being purged, tried to minimize this overpersonalization of politics, as seen in his preference of the slogan "down with the line of Liu and Deng" over the more ominous "down with Liu and Deng." Later, Zhou Enlai also succeeded in protecting many bureaucrats in the government ministries from attacks by the Red Guards.

The Cultural Revolution Group, whose changing membership grew increasingly radical, took over the Party Secretariat, thus assuming Deng Xiaoping's substantial power base. Liu Shaoqi was demoted from the number two post of party vice chairman to number eight, and replaced by Lin Biao. Members of the Cultural Revolution Group were promoted to the Politburo, as were additional PLA marshals. Liu's fall was imminent: he was dismissed of all posts and expelled from the party in 1968. Sent down to the countryside, Liu died shortly thereafter in prison.

By 1967, the radicals had gained substantial power at the top levels. In their confidence, they began to call for the Cultural Revolution to be carried into the State Council and the People's Liberation Army. In fact, revolutionary rebels had already moved to seize the central ministries; after they took over the foreign ministry, nearly all of China's ambassadors were recalled. To protect themselves against the Red Guards' criticism, schools, factories, and labor unions reinforced their party apparatus by forming their own mass organizations. Though Mao initially gave his support to the Cultural Revolution Small Group and radical elements in the party, he later shifted his support to the PLA and State Council.

Although the Cultural Revolution Group and the People's Liberation Army worked closely in the first stage of the Cultural Revolution, conflicts over the PLA's role emerged as the movement progressed to the second stage, seizure of power. For a conservative force such as the military, whose objective was to maintain law and order, mass participation was not a working mode that could be easily adopted. The military became increasingly involved in civilian and political affairs: they occupied banking and mass media organizations and supervised transportation. Cleavages within the military came into the open. Local forces tended to defend the provincial and local party cadres and organizations, in part because of strong personal ties, while central directives were often weakly followed. Similarly, conservative and radical mass organizations clashed. The Wuhan incident of July 20, 1967, signaled a new level of danger. Radical mass organizations seized weapons to defend themselves from military suppression. Armed confrontation ensued with other organizations as well as with regional military forces, whose authority had recently been reduced by Lin Biao and the Cultural Revolution Group.

With the entire country in chaos and government structures under threat of collapse, Mao stepped in to slow things down in September 1967. He called for party apparatus to be restored—but under the more activist leadership of Yao Wenyuan. In the spring of

1968, Mao called for demobilization of the Red Guards; millions of former Red Guard youth were sent to the countryside (*xiafang*) as a result. Soon, following Zhou Enlai's skillful negotiations with the revolutionary committees that had installed themselves in the ministries, the central government's functions were restored. Mao then began to authorize limited criticism of excesses coming out of the Cultural Revolution.

A new party constitution was approved in April 1969 at the ninth party congress, with Mao Zedong Thought receiving a central place in the document. Lin Biao, as vice chairman of the Chinese Communist Party, was formally recognized in the constitution as Mao's successor. Other members of the Politburo's Standing Committee were Zhou Enlai, Chen Boda, and Kang Sheng; ranking sixth to eighth in the Politburo were Jiang Qing, Zhang Chunqiao (b. 1917), and Yao Wenyuan. Thus, both the Maoists and Lin with his military supporters could declare a victory. The Cultural Revolution had essentially wound down by 1969, although the power struggle continued.

The Fall of Lin Biao

After being declared Mao's successor in 1969, Lin Biao, bolstered by a strong military, acted quickly on his political ambitions and began building a power base in South China. Mao, who had become increasingly suspicious of Lin's intentions, had already shifted his support to Zhou in rebuilding the party, however. In August, Mao personally toured Central and South China to warn regional military leaders against getting involved in politics, thereby breaking any loyalties to Lin. It was clear that Lin was opposed to the perpetual revolution line advocated by the leftist radicals; he also questioned the wisdom of China's strong anti-Soviet policies, especially those that involved military confrontation and strategy.

In an attempt to thwart Lin's ambitions to succeed him, Mao initiated a mass movement to "expose and criticize" Lin in 1971. The "Gang of Four," as the radical Maoist leaders came to be called, next tried unsuccessfully to weaken Zhou Enlai's power base in the government and party. In the power shuffle, Deng Xiaoping, who had supported Liu Shaoqi, was removed from the Central Committee but not expelled from the party. The facts of what happened next are not clear, and it was not until much later that the party leadership presented its official statements on the matter. In Zhou Enlai's report to the tenth party congress given on August 24, 1973, Lin Biao was accused of three assassination attempts on Mao between 1970 and 1971. The official version of the affair was thus: "On September 13 [1971], after his conspiracy had collapsed, Lin Biao surreptitiously boarded a plane, fled as a defector to the Soviet revisionists in betrayal of the Party and country, and died in a crash at Undur Khan in the People's Republic of Mongolia." The pro-Soviet link, though dubious, presented Lin as counterrevolutionary, antiparty, and an enemy of the people. It also served to distance the PLA leadership from Lin, though many high-level military leaders were removed. Not surprisingly, Maoist radicals moved quickly to fill the vacuum.

Reconstruction: Pragmatists vs. Leftists

During Mao's remaining years, the issue of his succession intensified, with a jockeying for influence between pragmatic party leaders and the leftist radicals. Mao's health had deteriorated, and he was rarely seen in public. At the tenth party congress, a relative newcomer was elevated to the number three position: Wang Hongwen (c. 1937-1992), a young leftist worker from Shanghai who was to become the fourth member (along with Jiang Qing, Zhang Chunqiao, and Yao Wenyuan) of the Gang of Four. The Politburo was expanded, with only Zhou Enlai and Marshal Ye Jianying (1897-1986) left as moderate voices. Notably excluded was Chen Boda, who, having thrown his support to Lin Biao, fell with him.

Zhou's authority and leadership abilities were crucial in rebuilding the country's institutions and stabilizing the leadership in the early 1970s. With Lin Biao gone, Zhou pushed forward with modernizing programs based on sound management and central planning. He also took steps that would lead to reopening relations with the United States and therefore wider foreign relations.

On the ideological front, however, the leftists still prevailed. Isolated from power bases in the party, the government, and the military, they utilized the propaganda and media machinery to build their influence and champion their cause. They continued to disseminate official slogans such as "Learn from Dazhai" (a commune in Shanxi Province), which emphasized that the formation of agricultural communes was a correct policy. In late 1973, the leftists launched a "Criticize Confucius" campaign, using allegory as a means of attacking Zhou's programs and weakening his control of the State Council. At the same time, others began a campaign to criticize Lin Biao, probably to show support for Zhou. Thus a highly contradictory and confusing "Criticize Lin, Criticize Confucius" movement was carried out through major newspapers, wall posters, and other media. By the middle of 1974, the Politburo ended the campaign, which had no clear focus and had never gained momentum.

The central leadership seemed to place its priority on modernization and economic development. Many cadres and officials who had been victims of the Cultural Revolution were gradually being brought back despite the radicals' contrary agenda. The more moderate leaders concentrated on economic development. They succeeded, for example, in changing the basic agricultural accounting unit from the production brigade to the production team (the most basic unit in the three-tiered commune system) in an effort to spur productivity.

The moderates' efforts were dealt a severe blow when Zhou, diagnosed with cancer, became so ill that he had to leave office in June 1974. This left a vacuum that the leftists tried to exploit. Within a few months, however, Mao decided to bring back Deng Xiaoping, whose expertise was badly needed to deal with the rising labor unrest in various parts of the country—an appointment that clearly indicated Mao's faltering support for Jiang Qing and the leftists.

Among the rising leaders was Hua Guofeng, first party secretary of Hunan. Hua, named to the Politburo at the tenth party congress in 1973, was appointed vice premier and minister of public security in 1975. Not a strong leader, Hua would first side with the leftists and then move toward the pragmatists. At the fourth session of the National People's Congress in January 1975, Premier Zhou Enlai, who left his sickbed to attend, tried to bring the feuding factions together and move the country's economic development forward. Significantly, Mao did not attend; this has been interpreted as demonstrating his lack of support for the moderate policies being promoted. Despite Maoist exhortations to continue class struggle, party leaders and the state bureaucracy forged ahead with implementing economic development policies.

The Deaths of Zhou and Mao

Zhou Enlai's death on January 8, 1976, allowed the leftists once again to seize power and push out the military. Mao's choice to replace Zhou as premier was Hua Guofeng, rather than the pragmatic Deng or a high-ranking leftist. Hua was also appointed party first vice chairman at this time. Some have speculated that Mao chose Hua Guofeng to become premier in early 1976 as a compromise, to block the rise of Deng Xiaoping and to install Hua as an interim leader until the leftists could assume power after Mao's death.

Shortly afterward, in an unexpected turn, some 100,000 people came to lay wreaths in memory of their beloved leader Zhou Enlai during the traditional Qing Ming memorial festival in April 1976. Some also expressed support for Deng, who had been closely associated with Zhou. This show of support for Zhou, with its undertones of criticism of the leftists and even Mao, moved the central leadership to ruthlessly suppress the gathering. However, in dealing with the 1976 Tiananmen demonstrations, it was the local police, rather than the People's Liberation Army, who carried out the crackdown, suggesting that it was mainly the leftists, with Mao's consent, who were behind it.

Deng Xiaoping, who gave the eulogy at the memorial ceremony for Zhou, was subsequently attacked by the leftists and disappeared from public view, for the second time. At this critical juncture, Mao, who had suffered a stroke and could no longer speak, gave Hua three handwritten instructions.

First, Mao urged Hua to carry out work slowly. Second, he directed him to act according to past principles. Finally, Mao wrote, "With you in charge, I am at ease." Though the first two messages were made known to the Politburo immediately, Hua held onto the third as precious evidence of his legitimacy as Mao's successor. To Jiang Qing and her cohorts, Hua was no longer a potential ally but a significant competitor for power.

The leftist-controlled mass media initially portrayed the Tiananmen incident as "counterrevolutionary." Then, in a badly calculated move, they began to criticize Zhou Enlai; the Shanghai leftist newspaper *Wen Hui Bao* referred to Zhou as a "capitalist roader." This provoked public outrage and vocal support for Zhou, which translated into support for Deng Xiaoping, who, after being dismissed by the Central Committee in April, had retreated to his power base in the south.

Shortly thereafter, on September 9, 1976, Mao died. No constitutional process existed for the transfer of power, though Hua Guofeng claimed to have been given the mantle of leadership. When Hua became the new party chairman it appeared the succession crisis had been solved. But the battle remained to be fought between the leftists under Jiang Qing and the other, more moderate party and state leaders.

China entered gingerly into a new era without Mao Zedong. In addition to the deaths of three great leaders in one year—Zhou Enlai in January, military commander Zhu De in July, and Mao Zedong in September—China had experienced a devastating earthquake in the northern city of Tangshan just before Mao's death in September that registered 8.2 on the Richter scale. This disaster, which completely leveled the city, took the lives of more than half a million people. According to Chinese tradition, many interpreted such an event as the harbinger of great change.

Interregnum: Transition to the Post-Mao Era, 1976-1978

With the death of Mao Zedong in 1976, China stood at a major crossroads. How central was class struggle? Should China continue to follow a Maoist philosophy of self-reliance? China was being pulled in different directions, and a changing world called for adjustments in China's foreign policy. China had begun to normalize relations with the United States in 1972 and was now being drawn into complex global politics in Vietnam and Cambodia. Also crucial to China's future direction was the country's internal assessment of the politics of the Cultural Revolution led by Mao. Critics were hesitant in the first two years of the post-Mao era, since an official interpretation of the Cultural Revolution had not yet been made. Furthermore, with the long-term leadership succession still to be determined, Chinese were cautious about expressing any views that might be used against them in future campaigns.

The Fall of the Gang of Four

Mao's intimate involvement with the actions and policies of the Gang of Four is not in doubt, for without his personal endorsement, they could not have risen to power. Did they manipulate Mao, using his name to achieve their own ambitions; or was Mao utilizing them to fulfill his revolutionary visions in a China that seemed complacent? This debate will remain inconclusive.

What is clear is that, with Mao gone, Jiang Qing lost a buffer from her opponents and had new difficulty legitimizing her views. The leftists had only limited support beyond Mao. They still controlled the media and had garnered the support of local militia in important cities such as Shanghai, Beijing, Tianjin, and Guangzhou. They also had the support of Mao's nephew, Mao Yuanxin, a military leader in Shenyang. Members of the Gang of Four were supposedly planning a coup in which the militia forces would rise simultaneously, but their plans were exposed when other military leaders whom they tried to enlist informed Hua of these developments.

During this time, two groups were independently planning to launch a countercoup against the Gang of Four. One was led by senior party and military leaders, including Defense Minister Ye Jianying, who had pledged his support to Hua. The other was led by Deng Xiaoping, who was prepared to form a provisional Central Committee should the leftists succeed

in their plot. Deng met with numerous leaders at his headquarters in Guangzhou in southern China, including Ye Jianying and Zhao Ziyang, a rising star in Sichuan, and formed an alliance with regional military forces. In the end, the groups led by Ye and Deng allied themselves and prevailed, after gaining the support of Wang Dongxing (b. 1916), Mao's former bodyguard, who commanded the 20,000-member special 8341 military unit and whom the leftists thought was on their side.

At a series of highly contentious Politburo meetings held at the end of September 1976, each faction made proposals and counterproposals for top party and government positions. Believing that the Gang of Four would launch its coup on October 6, Deng, Ye, and Wang took quick action against them. Jiang Qing, Zhang Chunqiao, Yao Wenyuan, and Wang Hongwen were arrested early that morning. The four were permanently expelled from the party and removed from all posts. Four years would pass before their trial was held; they remained under arrest during that entire period.

The mass media vehemently denounced the Gang of Four and accused them of being counterrevolutionary conspirators. Now the four were branded as "ultrarightists" (despite their leftist views), meaning that they were against the people, the party, and the government. This was a tactical move on Hua's part to distance himself from potential criticism of his own previous activities and association with leftism. Thus Hua Guofeng, a previous unknown, became the leader of post-Mao China. Amazingly, this power struggle was resolved with practically no civil unrest.

Hua Guofeng as Leader

Hua Guofeng had been born of peasant background in 1921 and risen through provincial party ranks to the position of party first secretary of Hunan by 1970. Though lacking a power base and virtually unknown within the central party leadership until being elected to the Politburo in 1973, Hua was nevertheless named vice premier and minister of public security in 1975 and became premier in early 1976. Upon Mao's death, Hua also assumed the chairmanship of the Chinese Communist Party.

Hua Guofeng took over the helm of the party upon Mao's death in September 1976. Here, Hua presides over the third session of the Standing Committee of the Fourth National People's Congress, November 1976.

Hua faced three immediate challenges: legitimacy, the rehabilitation of Deng Xiaoping, and promotion of economic development. Believing that a smooth transition took priority over legal procedures, party leaders circumvented the constitutional process in proclaiming Hua their new head. They scripted the following compromise instead: in exchange for moving forward with the previously articulated Four Modernizations and bringing back Deng Xiaoping (who had the support of Defense Minister Ye Jianying and Vice Premier Li Xiannian), Deng and the others acknowledged Hua's leadership. Hua was now named to additional chairmanships of the Central Committee and the powerful Military Affairs Commission. Never before in China's history had one man held so many concurrent posts.

The power shuffle was promptly made official. At the third plenary session of the tenth congress of the Central Committee, held in July 1977, Deng was reinstated to the military, party, and government posts he had previously held, notably party vice

chairman and PLA chief of staff. At the eleventh party congress, convened in August, the coalition leaders of the countercoup—Hua Guofeng, Ye Jianying, Deng Xiaoping, Li Xiannian, and Wang Dongxing—were appointed to the Politburo Standing Committee. Although two-thirds of the Central Committee were re-elected overall, many members from mass organizations, brought in during the Cultural Revolution period, were not. The new, far more pragmatic congress would call for unity, discipline, and cooperation; modernization was a clearly articulated priority, as was development of government functions, particularly the legal system. A Discipline Inspection Commission was established to improve oversight over the greatly enlarged party membership and help rid the party ranks of Cultural Revolution leftists.

The Fifth National People's Congress convened in early 1978, in accordance with the requirement that this body approve the party's recommendations on government appointments. Key individuals who had been influential before the Cultural Revolution were brought back, including former Beijing Mayor Peng Zhen and economic experts Chen Yun and Bo Yibo. The Eleventh Central Committee elected four more Politburo members supportive of Deng: Hu Yaobang, who held high party positions; Zhou Enlai's widow, Deng Yingchao; General Wang Zhen (1909-1993); and Chen Yun.

Hua Guofeng's personal power was weak, even though he held the country's highest party, government, and military posts. Of the three key factions—those of Hua, Ye Jianying, and Deng Xiaoping—Deng's group was the strongest, with the moderate Ye leaning closer to Deng. Although Hua had been raised to prominence by Mao's personal influence, he did not have a power base of his own. Furthermore, his abilities fell short in leading China's Four Modernizations program. The Ten-Year Plan contained both unrealistic targets and poor planning. The resultant overinvestment in heavy industry and large-scale construction projects drained the government's finances. Behind the scenes, Deng was replacing Hua's supporters with his own group of moderate leaders, laying the groundwork for governmental reform, and strengthening relations with the outside world, particularly the United States. Though still heavily factionalized, a post-Cultural Revolution and post-Mao leadership group had begun to emerge.

Hua Out of Power

Hua could not maintain his hold on leadership in China for long. His ineptness, his retention of Cultural Revolution ideals, his interpretation of the 1976 Tiananmen incident as having been ''counterrevolutionary,'' and his support of Deng Xiaoping's ouster, were all marks against him. He blamed all of China's ills on the leftists, but held off criticizing the Cultural Revolution itself and tried to minimize his own involvement as head of public security.

Important policy decisions were made during the third plenary session of the Eleventh Central Committee (December 1978) that would make a clear break with the Maoist era. By condemning the two policies that were supposedly Mao's legacy—that of firmly upholding Chairman Mao's policy decisions and of unswervingly adhering to whatever instructions Mao had given (those who did so being called ''whateverists'')—the Central Committee had essentially invalidated Hua and his ''whateverist'' supporters. The Central Committee reassessed the 1976 pro-Zhou Enlai Tiananmen incident as entirely revolutionary and called Hua instrumental in suppressing it. This placed Hua in the position of having committed a grave error for characterizing it as counterrevolutionary.

Finally, in place of class struggle and Maoist idealism, the third plenum declared socialist modernization the nation's top priority. Deng was highly respected for his solid pragmatic administrative experience in association with the late Zhou Enlai, and he had the popular support that Hua lacked throughout the party apparatus, the military, and the general public. Industrial and agricultural policies advocated by Hua in his Ten-Year Plan were abandoned as unfeasible, poorly planned, and costly.

Thus, the plenum launched China on a new course, with economics in firm command and Deng as the leader holding real power. Within a few years, Deng and his supporters would remove those in Hua's faction from positions of influence. Thus in

June 1981 it came as no surprise when Hua Guofeng's resignation as premier of China was submitted and accepted at the sixth plenary session of the Eleventh Central Committee. To succeed himself as premier, Hua duly nominated Deng protégé Zhao Ziyang.

Party Politics Under Mao: The Philosophy of Perpetual Revolution

Throughout his tenure in power, Mao used political campaigns and other mass movements to achieve political ends and bring about social reform at the same time. These political campaigns grew out of Mao's conviction that to truly transform China, all levels of society must be inculcated with Marxist-Leninist thought and purged of old social patterns and ways of thinking. Thus, Mao skillfully used campaigns such as the Three Anti's and Five Anti's (1951-1952), the Hundred Flowers movement (1956-1957), and the Anti-Rightist campaign (1957-1958) to draw out and eliminate his political adversaries while gaining legitimacy for himself and his supporters. Ousting those identified as ''enemies of the people'' was more easily justified than the blatant use of power politics. Campaigns were also aimed at specific groups, notably intellectuals, in an effort to rid the country of alternative intellectual or political thought.

Whenever Mao felt the country straying from his vision, he did not hesitate to subvert policy formation processes and political structures to regain authority. An early example of this was Mao's insistence on a stepped-up collectivization drive in 1955, even though the government, the National People's Congress, and the majority of top party leaders had endorsed a slowdown. Disregarding the stand of the Politburo and official procedures, Mao went directly to party secretaries at provincial and subprovincial levels to mobilize support and have his directives issued and carried out.

Thus began an alternating pattern of intensification and loosening of pressures to enforce conformity to Maoist thought and a ''correct'' Marxist-Leninist line. Just what constituted such correctness was not always clear, for what was championed in one campaign would often be turned on its head in the next. Time and time again, those who voiced opinions and criticisms during one of the many campaigns would find themselves having to pay dearly when their views were interpreted adversely later.

Early Efforts at Transformation

Having finally achieved peace after decades of war, the Chinese people longed for stability by the early 1950s and were anxious to move forward in rebuilding their country. Between 1949 and 1957, party unity was stressed above all else, and a group leadership style provided for the stability under which China was able to achieve substantial economic progress.

The Chinese Communist Party, to its credit, maintained solidarity during its transition from fighting the anti-Japanese war of resistance and a civil war with the Kuomintang to ruling a new republic. Indeed, in contrast to the massive purges of the Soviet Communist Party during the Stalinist period, the CCP conducted only one major purge in the early years—that of Gao Gang and Rao Shushi in 1954. The official version alleges that the two were trying to form a separate regime but Western scholars believe that Gao was actually purged for trying to usurp central authority in Beijing.

Communist leaders recognized the immediate need to revive agricultural and industrial production, rebuild infrastructure, tend to health care and social needs, and reinvigorate the educational system. As a result, professionals, educators, and scientists, all in short supply, were allowed to function relatively undisturbed in their respective institutions, even though some were affiliated with foreign and religious organizations. Indeed, many intellectuals educated abroad were deciding to return to China to help with reconstruction. At the same time, many bureaucrats and officials from the previous government, needed for their expertise, stayed at their posts or moved into new positions in the Communist government. All were subjected to political education; they studied the thought of Marx, Engels, Lenin, Stalin, and Mao, as well as history and political economy from a Marxist-Leninist viewpoint. Such "re-education"

cannot be achieved simply, however, and numerous problems emerged in its implementation.

The party leadership launched its first major campaign in 1951—the Three Anti's (*San fan*) campaign against corruption, waste, and bureaucratism. Its target was urban cadres, especially those working in finance and economics. Shortly afterward, a Five Anti's (*Wu fan*) campaign was initiated, attacking capitalists and the national bourgeoisie as a class. Labeled counterrevolutionary, these individuals were accused of bribery, tax evasion, fraud, theft of government property, and leaking state economic secrets. Both campaigns also came to be directed at intellectuals, especially those involved in higher education, many of whom were accused of harboring Western bourgeois ideology and resisting the Soviet model of education. Furthermore, the nationalism that had been aroused by China's participation in the Korean War reinforced already strong anti-American sentiment.

A brief period of relaxation followed in 1953, as the extensive work of the first Five-Year Plan got under way. The goals of increasing productivity and building China's infrastructure received priority at this time, and the Chinese Communist Party allowed the ministries and central bureaucracy to take charge of program planning and implementation. A collective leadership style, which relied on those in the top leadership with development expertise, had left Mao—whose expertise lay in revolutionary and political movements and in formulating political theories based on the Chinese experience—in a position of less prominence. In the mid-1950s, Mao sought to utilize intellectuals and professionals in helping the country's collectivization and industrial drives, and especially in the drive to create a new socialist man in China. At the end of 1955, Premier Zhou Enlai voiced proposals to enhance the authority and respect given to intellectuals for their views and for their research, as well as to offer greater monetary and other incentives to improve their work. Hoping to arouse intellectuals' enthusiasm and more active participation, Chairman Mao made his famous speech in May 1956 to "Let a hundred flowers bloom, [and] let a hundred schools of thought contend."

The Hundred Flowers Movement

Mao's invitation for constructive criticism and intellectual debate had historical echoes in the rich intellectual traditions of the Zhou dynasty (1122-221 B.C.E.) as well as the intellectual dynamism of the May Fourth era in the 1920s. But in Mao's view, the Hundred Flowers movement's call for debate was to be restricted to the arts, literature, and the sciences; politics was supposedly insulated from criticism. Mao saw the utopian goal of selfless dedication to the greater good of the socialist state straying under the policies of the first Five-Year Plan and believed that a dose of "rectification" (*zhengfeng*) was needed to bring back a revolutionary perspective. In this campaign and in others to come, Mao looked back to his Yan'an rectification campaign of 1942-1944 as a model for personal socialist transformation.

China's intellectuals responded slowly; it took nearly a year after Mao's 1956 invitation for many to make their views public. Previous campaigns, particularly a 1955 movement against well-known writer Hu Feng (c. 1902-1985), had shown them the dangerous consequences of personal expression. Hu, a prominent literary figure in conflict with CCP cultural authorities since the 1930s, was cast as a dangerous counterrevolutionary. In the campaign initiated by Mao to discredit him, even peasants and workers were warned against "Hu Feng-ism." After only a brief reprieve from this campaign, Mao was now asking intellectuals to criticize party cadres and bureaucratic officials and to offer suggestions on how to change society.

As part of the Hundred Flowers movement, Mao encouraged criticism of the party's work, including "subjectivism," or copying unsuitable concepts and methods (for example, from the Soviet Union); "bureaucratism," or elitism and movement away from the masses; and "sectarianism," or an attitude of separation and superiority to nonparty members. Published writings began to appear, generating substantial discussion. Beginning with fictional depictions of arrogant and incompetent bureaucrats and identification of social problems and shortcomings of government policies, criticism moved to questioning the place of Maoist thought in science and aca-

demics. Some rallied to Hu Feng's cause—a direct criticism of Mao's policies. As the criticism came to be directed against the Chinese Communist Party regime itself, Mao quickly called off the Hundred Flowers movement after less than six months.

Some historians think that Mao may have genuinely believed that this effort at open criticism would generate an intellectual force to help promote China's social transformation. He hoped that China's intellectuals would contribute to formulating values to help forge China's path that were independent of those emanating from the Soviet experience. But in the end, the Hundred Flowers movement backfired, as the "blooming" allowed for the emergence of undesirable "weeds." Mao's methods were seen in hindsight as a cynical effort to manipulate intellectuals and identify Mao's opponents in the party and in the government.

At the same time, Mao's personal prestige was being diminished by the very successes of the first Five-Year Plan. The party—but not necessarily Mao himself—was credited with China's progress at this time. Mao, who in fact lacked such expertise, decided to strengthen his prestige by focusing on intellectual and artistic work—an area in which he had firm experience, especially from working closely with artists and literary figures in Yan'an on propaganda issues. But the Hundred Flowers movement had brought to the surface substantial dissatisfaction with the Communist regime, prompting Mao to return to a more negative stance and launch another campaign.

Anti-Rightist Campaign

To Mao, the very ideals of China's revolution were threatened by the critics who emerged during the Hundred Flowers movement. The Anti-Rightist campaign was launched to attack these critics, as well as anyone who held views—or was accused of holding views—that were antithetical to the socialist transformation of the Chinese people. Anyone who had associations with Western "bourgeois" culture and values, especially those educated abroad or at Western institutions in China, became a target. To be labeled a "rightist" meant political, professional, and personal disaster. This campaign was much more pervasive than previous campaigns, reaching into government bodies, factories, schools, universities, and all aspects of civil life. Condemnations by colleagues, forced mass criticisms, and self-criticism were widespread; some work units were even required to fulfill a 5 percent quota of people identified as rightists.

By the time the campaign wound down, 400,000 to 700,000 intellectuals had been stripped of their positions and separated from their families; many were sent to labor in factories and on farms. In this was a hint of things to come in the Cultural Revolution almost a decade later. The anti-intellectual slant of this campaign bolstered Mao's Great Leap Forward, in which the common man was held up as the ideal and in which "redness" (political correctness) was promoted over "expertise."

Mao's Ultimate Campaign: The Cultural Revolution

In announcing the Great Proletarian Cultural Revolution in 1966, Mao launched his plan to thoroughly shake up the system, as captured in the slogan "destroy the Four Olds"—old thought, old culture, old customs, and old habits—and to rebuild the country's political structures. By subjecting the party organization and government structures to attack from the outside, however, China's political system as a whole was weakened, both centrally and in the provinces.

The Cultural Revolution, undoubtedly modern China's most extensive political campaign, reached all levels of society: it disrupted the economy, political structures and functions, university and educational institutions, and foreign relations. During the most intense years, between 1966 and 1969, chaos reigned: political and governmental institutions were torn apart, with tragic consequences for numerous individuals.

The Cultural Revolution can be divided into three major stages. In stage one, which lasted from May 1966 to early 1967, a campaign to destroy the "olds" was intended to create a proletarian culture and undermine traditional Chinese elitist values, as well as the Western influences that had been incorpo-

rated into Chinese literature, arts, and scholarship since the 1920s. Soviet ideological influences were now also considered an "old." And traditional rural values, such as family and clan loyalties and the desire for private property were seen by Mao as obstacles to building a true proletarian culture. Mao was also dissatisfied with the party's efforts at fulfilling his directive to thoroughly link Mao Zedong Thought with work. He sought to remove from power those in the cultural establishment—university presidents, top figures in the Propaganda Department, leaders in the government ministries of culture, education, and higher education. To achieve this, Mao enlisted China's youth to form themselves into Red Guard units and "bombard the headquarters," meaning to attack party leaders and cadres and to reform those structures and their corresponding cultural and political values. Through such mass participation, Mao was able to weaken the authority structures of the political system and government administration, which he hoped to reshape for his own purposes.

In the second stage, lasting from 1967 through late 1968, revolutionary committees were formed that incorporated Mao Zedong Thought. During this time, the People's Liberation Army, under Lin Biao's leadership, was responsible for working with the committees to maintain law and order. This was not without conflict, however, especially when the momentum of criticism carried over to attack of PLA officers for not being sufficiently "leftist" in their thinking.

In the third and final stage, the process of rebuilding the Chinese Communist Party and its structures was supposed to be accomplished from the bottom up, starting with the revolutionary committees in universities, factories, communal farms, the party apparatus, and other institutions. This process was rushed, however, prodded in part by the fear of Soviet intervention, after the Soviet invasion of Czechoslovakia in August of that year. Having served their role, the Red Guards were disbanded and millions of students were sent down to the countryside to work. Rebuilding would take place without the mass participation originally envisioned.

Mass Mobilization in Daily Life

Mao believed that mass mobilization was essential to building socialism. Class struggle was regarded as central to the process of transformation and required unending political study sessions and self-criticisms. As a result, Mao Zedong Thought came to serve as the primary guiding principle in all aspects of daily life. People were encouraged to join organizations such as the All-China Students' Federation, the All-China Federation of Trade Unions, and the All-China Women's Federation. Membership in each of these numbered in the tens of millions. Rather than serving as a representative body for members' interests, these mass organizations were used more as vehicles for promoting party views and for carrying out political campaigns.

A person's work unit was the structure around which work and all aspects of daily life revolved. Party cadres serving as leaders determined work assignments (sometimes even to other provinces), housing and allocations of necessary items such as bicycles. They also gave permission for such personal matters as marriage and having children. Resident committees based on small neighborhood sectors in cities were another means of control.

Under the Communist regime, each person's business was everyone's business. Participation in political study sessions was required of everyone, as a member of a work unit, department, work team, or neighborhood association. Whenever a political campaign was under way, people had no choice but to take a stand on an issue, and they were frequently pressured to denounce family relations, neighbors, or colleagues as "class enemies."

Maoism in Education

One of the CCP's key goals was to eliminate illiteracy. Since education in traditional China was reserved for the elite, a substantial portion of the masses stood to benefit from the leadership's efforts to establish scores of primary and secondary schools throughout the countryside. For adults, there was a practical emphasis on vocational and agricultural training. The *minban* system of "people's schools,"

set up in the border regions during the civil war, was extended to the entire country. This system of basic education was designed to be run by local villagers, who would make the curriculum more relevant to their own needs and encourage more peasants to send their children to school. For technical training and higher education, the Soviet model, with its strengths in science and technology and close connections to industrial management, was adopted. At the same time, schools and educational institutions served as a powerful means of indoctrination. Beginning in the mid-1950s, political content became central. Particularly after the Hundred Flowers movement, Mao saw the necessity of gaining control over the universities to bring them into line with Marxist-Leninist precepts—and his own.

Universities and research institutions were to be run by committees led by party organizations. In the selection and promotion of university faculty and administrators, the correct political stance was now more important than qualifications, practical experience, formal credentials, or seniority. Likewise, class background became a key criterion for student admission. Whereas students from worker or peasant backgrounds made up about 20 percent of university admissions in 1951, they comprised 50 percent of admissions by 1960. In line with Mao's faith in the common man and goal of creating productive socialist laborers, programs were implemented to bridge intellectual and manual labor. Universities shifted emphasis accordingly from broad education to more practical and applied training, to produce technicians quickly and in large numbers. Professionals, academics, and scientists were sent to factories and fields to "learn from the masses"; unqualified, but politically correct technicians were put in positions of responsibility. Universities and research institutions were dealt a severe blow as the balance of ideology versus expertise shifted toward ideology.

Intellectuals, Arts, and the Media

Mao recognized the value of intellectuals and their potential for contributing to the revolution; at the same time he feared their capacity for holding up or even subverting his revolutionary vision. Hence a cycle of education, relaxation, repression, and re-education demonstrated that the process of mobiliz-ing intellectuals to support perpetual revolution was no simple matter. After the 1958 Anti-Rightist cam-paign, Mao issued a directive to train intellectuals for a new Communist state. He acknowledged that

[we] can't do without intellectuals. The proletariat must definitely have its own *xiucai* [graduates of the traditional imperial examinations who were often recruited for the bu-reaucracy]. These people must understand relatively more of Marxism-Leninism, and they must also have a certain cultural level, a certain amount of scientific knowledge and of literary training.

Zhou Yang (1908-1989), a leading Communist writer and theoretician in charge of party cultural and propaganda affairs, developed a framework for Chi-na's art and literature based on the Soviet concept of socialist realism. During the Great Leap Forward years, the Chinese Writers Union was urged to pro-duce works that were understandable and inspira-tional to the common person.

Mao used willing intellectuals and artists to prop-agate his views. Spearheaded by Mao's wife, Jiang Qing, theoretician Chen Boda, and Yao Wenyuan, all based in Shanghai, China's radical intellectuals con-demned many traditional forms of literature and dra-ma as perpetuating feudal ideas; instead, writers and artists were encouraged to create works imbued with "social realism."

A stage and movie actress during her youth in Shanghai, Jiang Qing joined the Communist Party in 1933. She met Mao in Yan'an, where she became involved in the arts and literature; they married in 1940. Beijing opera troupes and audiences had proved resistant to change despite Mao's 1942 speech "Talks at the Yan'an Forum on Arts and Lit-erature" and subsequent propaganda movements through the 1950s. Even at the Festival of Beijing Opera, held in the summer of 1964, top party propa-ganda leaders such as Peng Zhen and Lu Dingyi ar-gued that plays based on historical novels and myth-ological characters such as *Water Margin* (one of Mao's favorites) and *Journey to the West* still had a place in a new China.

Under Jiang Qing's initiative, however, China's rich tradition of Beijing opera and other dramatic forms was reduced to a handful of model revolution-ary dramas. These emphasized Maoist ethics and ex-tolled the virtues of model soldiers and workers in an idealized revolutionary society, heroes and heroines within themes of war, resistance, and standing up to oppressors. Ballet dancers wore military uniforms and carried rifles. During the Cultural Revolution years, audiences could see only Jiang Qing's model operas and ballets like *Taking Tiger Mountain by Strategy, The Red Lantern, The White-Haired Girl,* and *The Red Detachment of Women.*

All major forms of media—newspapers, publish-ing, television, radio—were controlled by the Chi-nese Communist Party. Policies were conveyed to the people in uniform fashion through the official party newspaper, *Renmin Ribao* (People's Daily), and regional newspapers. Publications were strictly controlled through methods such as licensing. The People's Liberation Army, which grew in political strength and importance throughout the early years of the PRC, became highly involved in publishing and had its own official newspaper, the *Jiefangjun Ribao* (Liberation Army Daily). During periods in which indoctrination of Maoist thought was intensi-fying, even nonpolitical publications, such as scien-tific journals, were obliged to include writings by Mao or quotations from the news announcements. Every shred of news and information was sifted through or approved by the government.

The Search for China's Revolutionary Path

To Mao, pursuing perpetual revolution and na-tion-building was inextricably linked through ideolo-gy: Mao Zedong Thought would help to mobilize the masses and connect them to the ruling elite, and this mobilization would lead to economic development. As envisioned in the programs of the Great Leap For-ward, economic, political, social, and cultural trans-formation would be carried out simultaneously. Mao was intent on institutionalizing his thought in hopes of ensuring that his revolutionary vision would pre-vail after his death.

Furthermore, the aim of self-reliance was formed in part as a response to China's deteriorating relations with the Soviet Union and Mao's view that, under Khrushchev, the Soviet Union was moving toward revisionism.

Mao never lost sight of his goal of moving China toward transformation to socialism and eventually communism. The more he felt that China was slipping from its revolutionary path, the more he increased political indoctrination. These were the seeds of the political campaigns he launched to manipulate supporters in the party and the military and those outside the formal structures, particularly in the Cultural Revolution. He believed that perpetual revolution, continuous class struggle, and guarding against "rightism" were essential in this process; but above and beyond all these, Mao sought also to maintain his own power.

Chinese Foreign Relations Under Mao

Two themes have had a major influence on the PRC's foreign relations: border security and relations with the Soviet Union. Having experienced a century of Western domination, which carved China into spheres of influence, and feeling further violated because of Japan's military offensive to make China part of its empire, the leaders of the People's Republic of China placed a high priority on sovereignty and maintaining secure borders. These goals have required constant vigilance.

The Korean War

China's first foreign involvement after the founding of the PRC was in Korea. The Korean War put China in direct opposition to the United States and triggered decades of mutual distrust between the two countries. From China's perspective, the United States became the aggressor when it intervened to push North Korean forces back from the north-south border, which the latter had crossed in June 1950. Concerned over how far the United Nations' forces would go—North Korea borders northeastern China at the Yalu River—China's leaders called on their nation that October to fight U.S. aggression and launch a campaign to "Resist America and Aid Ko-

rea." Support among the leadership was not unanimous but Mao's view prevailed, and with Peng Dehuai in command of the Chinese People's Volunteers, China soon entered the war.

For its efforts, China suffered substantial casualties and earned the enmity of the United States, which imposed an embargo on China and strengthened its alliance with Taiwan. At the same time, however, by challenging the most powerful state in the world, China raised its international stature. The war also aroused a nationalistic fervor that enhanced the CCP leadership's legitimacy and prompted China to define a more active global role.

Sino-Soviet Friendship and Split

From its inception in the 1920s, the Chinese Communist Party had been modeled on and nurtured by the Communist Party of the Soviet Union (CPSU). A treaty of friendship, alliance, and mutual assistance had been signed between the two countries in 1950. China based its first Five-Year Plan on the Soviet model for socialist construction, and turned to the Soviet Union for technology and aid.

Professed bonds of Soviet-Chinese friendship, however, barely masked a host of underlying hostilities. Ideological differences and territorial disputes would eventually lead to armed border clashes and severed relations. The Soviet Communists remained cool to Mao's efforts to redefine Marxism-Leninism and were displeased with the CCP's challenges to their leadership position in the socialist world. By the late 1950s, the friendship had begun to unravel.

Mao had always had reservations about Stalin's strategies for carrying out China's revolution. Nevertheless, after Stalin's death, Mao attacked the post-Stalin Soviet leadership as "revisionist," particularly after Khrushchev openly criticized Stalin and his "personality cult" at the twentieth congress of the CPSU in 1956. Mao also resented Khrushchev's overt criticism of the Hundred Flowers movement, China's communes, and the Great Leap Forward. Tensions increased to the point that in 1959 the Soviet Union canceled the 1957 New Technology and National Defense pact with China and recalled all Soviet technicians from Chinese projects. Signifi-

Sino-Soviet relations in the 1950s were marked by hostility over many issues. Although Mao distrusted Khrushchev and attacked the Soviet Union as revisionist, Khrushchev in 1959 attended the tenth anniversary celebrations of the founding of the People's Republic of China. With him (left-to-right) are Premier Zhou Enlai, President Liu Shaoqi, and CCP chairman Mao Zedong. The Sino-Soviet split became public shortly thereafter.

cantly, this also cut off China's access to technology and scientific data as well as to the assistance needed to develop the atomic bomb.

China and the Soviet Union continued to diverge ideologically. Branding Khrushchev's line "heretical," Mao advanced the position that only the Chinese Communists were true adherents to the doctrine they were now calling Marxism-Leninism-Mao Zedong Thought. Both the Great Leap Forward and the Cultural Revolution included strident anti-Soviet overtones. In a direct challenge to Soviet leadership in the socialist world, China's leaders offered the success of China's revolution as evidence of an alternative approach to revolutionary change. The CPSU espoused coexistence with the West; the CCP supported movements (and, in the U.S. view, fomented revolution) in colonial and anti-imperialist countries. The lack of Soviet support for China in the Taiwan Strait crisis (1958) and in China's border war with India (1962) heightened the differences between the two Communist giants.

Chinese and Soviet leaders also clashed on territorial issues. China still held strong and bitter memories of domination by imperial powers in the nineteenth century and invasion by Japan in the twentieth. Though the Soviet Union held a unique position as leader of the Communist world, tsarist Russia had nevertheless been one of the Western imperialist powers that had imposed "unequal treaties" on China. China resented Soviet support for Outer Mongolian independence from China in 1921, and Mao sought to recover territories he felt had been ceded to the Soviet Union through various unfair treaties. In 1963 Beijing published a list of lost territories, but Soviet leaders upheld the legality of treaties signed by tsarist Russia and Manchu China. By this point, China was loudly accusing Khrushchev of revisionism and criticizing him for capitulating to U.S. President John F. Kennedy in the 1962 Cuban missile crisis. Mao's "On Khrushchev's Phony Communism and Its Historical Lessons for the World," published in July 1965, infuriated the Soviet leaders and made it clear that the rift had become unbridgeable.

This war of words eventually escalated to armed confrontation. Both countries increased their troop presence along their 4,300-mile-long border. The Soviet military maintained a million troops, along with missiles and nuclear weapons; the Chinese posted a million troops and worked to develop second-strike capabilities aimed at Moscow and Leningrad. Soviet and Chinese troops clashed twice seriously in March 1969, causing international alarm. Numerous flare-ups continued along the border through the year, and by August, Soviet leaders had begun to hint at the possibility of launching pre-emptive strikes against China's nuclear installations. These events marked a shift in the perceived power balance, as it became increasingly clear that the Communist world was not a monolithic bloc.

Foreign Relations with the Third World

Despite being under the Soviet Communist Party's tutelage, the Chinese leadership under Mao had always maintained a degree of independence. On the ideological front, Mao stated that Communist parties could come to power only through violent revolution. Therefore, in encouraging self-reliance in liberation struggles, China was endorsing a challenge to both Soviet "revisionism" and U.S. "imperialist aggression." But in China's diplomatic forays, mainly under Zhou Enlai's leadership, China concurrently sought governmental relationships based on diplomacy, and developmental and strategic aid.

The 1955 Afro-Asian Conference, held in Bandung, Indonesia, defined the early phase of China's foreign relations. The "Bandung Spirit" endorsed self-determination for developing countries and encouraged them to avoid entanglement in superpower conflicts. China framed a policy of "peaceful coexistence" and, in a speech to the conference, Zhou En-

lai stressed that "[what] our nations in Asia and Africa need is peace and independence. We have no intention at all of pitting the nations of Asia and Africa against those of other regions." The "Five Principles of Peaceful Coexistence" endorsed by Zhou and Jawaharlal Nehru, premier of India—mutual respect of sovereignty, nonaggression, noninterference in one another's internal affairs, equality and mutual benefit, and peaceful coexistence—were to become the cardinal principles of China's future foreign policy.

The Chinese embarked on a "trade-and-aid" strategy toward countries in Asia, Africa, and the Middle East, rewarding those that proved friendly and helpful to China's strategic interests. Though limited in its own resources, China provided aid and technical support to infrastructure projects like the 1,860-kilometer Tanzania-Zambia railroad and the building of roads in Vietnam. Chinese aid to African states amounted to almost $3 million in the 1960s, a great deal of which went to develop communications and transport. Chinese medical teams were dispatched to serve African peoples in remote rural areas. In 1963, a substantial aid package was granted to the Burmese government, in part as a reward for not siding with India during the 1962 Sino-Indian conflicts.

By the early 1960s, China had begun to lend active and strategic support to independence and revolutionary movements in various third world countries, which also fulfilled China's own security interests. This more active role in African and Asian politics inevitably brought China into conflict with both the Soviet Union and the United States. Ideological differences between Chinese and Soviet leaders continued to grow as China carried its challenge to Soviet authority into the arena of third world countries. The Chinese helped trained guerrilla forces and provided arms and equipment to leftist uprisings in several African states, notably Tanzania and the Congo. To counter Soviet influence in Indonesia, the Chinese lent support not only to the Sukarno government (which was being wooed with generous Soviet aid) but also to the Indonesian Communist Party (PKI). The PKI, with Chinese encouragement, attempted a coup in 1965, which proved disastrous and resulted in arrests and deaths for most of the PKI ranks; Sukarno thereafter broke off relations with China.

China's foreign policy decisions toward countries in Africa and Southeast Asia, particularly Vietnam, were clearly shaped more by Soviet presence and influence there than by an understanding of or concern over the internal situation in those countries. Strong Soviet support of Hanoi, for example, prompted Beijing to look to Cambodia because of its potential as a buffer state. After the two countries established diplomatic relations in 1958 and signed a Treaty of Friendship and Mutual Nonaggression in 1960, China hoped to make Cambodia its client state. This became even more critical as the United States offered increasing military assistance to regimes in South Vietnam and Thailand.

The Chinese leaders employed other strategies as well to challenge Soviet leadership. They used the Afro-Asian People's Solidarity Committee as a forum in the 1960s to polarize its members into taking sides in the Sino-Soviet dispute. Although largely unsuccessful, these actions contributed to African distrust and resentment. The Chinese Communist Party also sought to build international influence through other Communist parties. It garnered the support of parties in North Vietnam, Japan, Indonesia, Albania, and Romania to boycott a Soviet-sponsored conference of Communist states in 1965, for example.

China's foreign policy strategies gradually shifted from an emphasis on revolutionary activities to a pursuit of governmental relations. In 1964, Beijing began to step up its foreign relations with countries that were members of what it called an "intermediate zone" consisting of independent and anti-colonial states in Asia, Africa, and Latin America, as well as with the industrialized countries of Europe and elsewhere. Tanzania under Julius Nyerere received a $2.8 million grant from China, plus a credit line of $42 million in 1964. China strengthened diplomacy with Pakistan in 1964 with a $60 million long-term, interest-free loan. In later years, China extended substantial political and military support to Pakistan, in part to bolster the latter's security against India, and in part to counter the strong Soviet support of India (the Indo-Soviet Treaty was signed in 1971). Pakistan would in turn be pivotal in facilitating the Sino-American dialogue that would lead to the 1972 normalization of relations. France was the first major European power to recognize the Chinese Communist government in this new atmosphere, establishing diplomatic relations in 1964.

Territorial security and ideological issues both came into play in China's relations with countries along its southern borders, particularly Vietnam, Laos, and Cambodia. Contrary to the Western perception of a "domino effect," the U.S. military presence in South Vietnam, the Philippines, Thailand, Taiwan, Japan, and South Korea caused China to feel encircled. U.S. support of the Lon Nol coup in Cambodia only strengthened China's resolve to support Cambodia's Prince Norodom Sihanouk and later Pol Pot. Aware of significant overseas Chinese communities throughout the region, Beijing also competed with Taipei (the new capital of the Kuomintang on Taiwan) for their favor. Unfortunately, this rivalry added fuel to the distrust indigenous peoples already felt toward Chinese residents, making it easier for regimes to treat Chinese residents harshly, as happened in Indonesia.

There was great concern among Chinese leaders that tensions in the region would ultimately spill over into an attack on China. After the U.S. Congress passed the Tonkin Gulf Resolution in August 1964, the United States launched massive air attacks against North Vietnam. Chinese leaders were faced with a dilemma: should they assist the North Vietnamese, as they had assisted the North Koreans in similar circumstances? Lin Biao's military and foreign policy view prevailed, and China advocated that countries must each fight their own "people's war." China's involvement in the Vietnam crisis in 1965 was thus limited to tactical assistance, and direct confrontation with the United States was avoided. Nevertheless, subsequent increases in the U.S. military troop presence and further U.S. involvement in Cambodia and Laos pushed China to support leftist Communist regimes in those countries.

China and Eastern Europe

Extending its own nationalist and independent stance, China challenged Soviet dominance in the socialist world as well. Publication of Mao's 1957 speech "On the Correct Handling of Contradictions Among the People," for example, presented an ideological challenge to Soviet policies in Hungary and Poland. In this speech, Mao argued that "nonantagonistic" conflicts of interest were natural under socialism and did not warrant authoritarian suppression. This speech substantially bolstered China's international prestige in the socialist world.

China maintained political relations with East European countries, but had particularly close relations with Albania and Romania, to whom China extended substantial aid. Most East European countries remained under firm Soviet influence, and their relations with China were shaped by Sino-Soviet friendship or rifts. Party-to-party relations were another means of influencing East European countries. China began to encourage nationalistic movements in the Soviet satellite countries, while suggesting that Soviet economic policies favored the needs of the Soviet Union over theirs. When the Soviet Union asserted its right of intervention as articulated in the "Brezhnev Doctrine" to justify the invasion of Czechoslovakia in 1968, China condemned the invasion.

China Flexes Its Muscles: Taiwan Strait and Indian Border

China's decision in 1958 to bomb the Taiwan Strait islands of Quemoy and Matsu, on which the Nationalist government on Taiwan maintained troops, must be understood in context of the Sino-Soviet relationship as well as China's fear of American military power in the region in the form of U.S. support for the Taiwan government. The act was a challenge to the United States and a test of the Soviet Union's commitment to China. Would the United States intervene to protect Taiwan? If it did, this could be construed as interference in China's civil war, raising the issue of sovereignty. At the same time, would the Soviet Union assist China if the United States carried out its nuclear threat?

China's unilateral actions angered Soviet leaders, who saw this as a breach of the 1950 alliance treaty, and brought the superpowers close to war. Still, Khrushchev publicly defended China. In a letter to U.S. President Dwight D. Eisenhower, he assured the United States that the Soviet Union would "do everything to defend, jointly with the People's Republic of China, the security of both countries." However, since this letter was not delivered until after the tensions had wound down, China interpreted Soviet support as less than genuine. The United States in fact did mobilize its forces to maintain a critical presence and pledged to defend Taiwan while issuing stern warnings to China. When it became evident that the United States was strongly committed to Taiwan, China eventually ceased its shelling of Quemoy. Superpower military involvement was avoided. Nonetheless, Beijing's brash actions and Moscow's mild support further widened the growing Sino-Soviet rift.

The late 1950s also saw territorial conflicts along the Chinese and Indian borders. This included sensitive areas in Tibet and the disputed Aksai Chin Plateau between Xinjiang and Tibet, through which China had built a highway for military use. In 1959, Tibetan unrest and independence movements came to a head; the PLA quelled the Tibetan rebellion and forced the Dalai Lama to flee to India. Indian leaders, like the British, had always favored an autonomous Tibet that would serve as a buffer zone, and they grew alarmed at China's strengthened military presence in Tibet. Territorial disputes continued, leading China to fight a brief but successful war with India in October-November 1962. The Chinese read the Soviet Union's neutral stance on the conflict as implicit support for New Delhi.

Relations with Other Countries

In spite of the United Nations-imposed trade embargo begun in 1951, the PRC developed relations with various countries during its early years. The Soviet Union was China's main trading partner, although China also had substantial trade with East European countries. The United Kingdom, Switzerland, and several smaller West European states recognized

Beijing beginning in 1950. Japan, Britain, and others maintained trade with China during these first two decades. Total Sino-Japanese trade amounted to over $2 billion between 1963 and 1967, strengthened by the signing of a five-year memorandum in 1963. During this period of relative isolation, however, China's official government relations with most non-Communist states were minimal, with the exception of the United Kingdom and France.

To strengthen China's influence abroad vis-à-vis the Soviet Union (and, to some extent, in competition with the Kuomintang government on Taiwan), China's leaders reached out to newly independent members of the United Nations and to the nonaligned countries—that is, those aligned neither with the United States and the West nor with the Soviet Union. China established diplomatic relations with fifteen newly independent countries between 1960 and 1965, and Zhou Enlai embarked on a high-visibility tour of eleven African and Asian states in 1963. For the most part, however, industrialized countries and those under U.S. influence deferred to the U.S. position on China. Hence it was not until 1972, when the United States began to normalize relations with China, that these countries would make similar moves.

Stand-off in Sino-American Relations

Mutual hostility pervaded the relationship between China and the United States from the time of the Korean War. The administration of U.S. President Harry S. Truman pursued a policy of containment, reinforced by the rise of McCarthyism. Under Secretary of State John Foster Dulles, the United States strengthened its Asian military bases, which stretched from Korea to Thailand, and firmed up defense alliances with Asian and Southeast Asian countries.

The signing of the 1954 defense pact with Taiwan solidified the cold war in Asia. To the Chinese, U.S. military support of colonialist and indigenous anti-Communist regimes that aimed to suppress people's nationalist movements confirmed their view of the United States as the number one imperialist enemy. China in turn supported leftist leaders and third

world regimes. China and the United States maintained no official government relations, although diplomats at an ambassadorial level occasionally interacted at international forums. The Chinese made initial moves in the mid-1950s to exchange ambassadors but discussions stalled.

To Washington, the Moscow-Beijing alliance established in 1950 represented a unified Communist world threat. In this context, the CCP-Kuomintang conflict was perceived to have global ramifications, encouraging the U.S. Congress to maintain strong support for Chiang Kai-shek and Nationalist China. Ultimately, however, it would be China's perception of the Soviet threat that would push China toward rapprochement with the United States. Though Washington and Beijing stood on opposite sides in the third world global-political wars during the Kennedy administration, Washington recognized that Sino-Soviet friendship had long since gone sour. In response to Soviet military suppression in Eastern Europe, China made overtures to the United States to guard against "provocative actions." Efforts to form nonaggression pacts were inconclusive, but the foundations for opening relations between China and the United States were beginning to be laid.

Reintegration into the World Community

Before the overtures between China and the United States to establish relations in the early 1970s, the United States had held fast to its policy of containment, formulated during the Truman and Eisenhower presidencies. On the domestic front, Senator Joseph McCarthy (R-Wis.) was spearheading the pursuit of supposedly Communist Americans in government, media, and other positions of influence. The strong China lobby in Congress that continued to support the Nationalist government on Taiwan also worked to prevent any American opening toward Beijing. Power dynamics in the Chinese-Soviet-U.S. triangle, however, began to shift in the next decade. The Sino-Soviet split erased the image of a united Communist bloc intent on world domination. During the 1960s, the United States sought rapprochement with the Soviet Union, rather than China, for two main reasons.

To the United States, the Soviet Union represented the greater military threat, and, in contrast to Beijing, Moscow maintained a stance of peaceful coexistence with the West.

China's slow change in policy toward the United States was motivated by its relations with the Soviet Union, which had continuously worsened through the 1960s. Chinese leaders watched the U.S.-Soviet rapprochement cautiously. Japan's economic power was also growing rapidly at this time, and China harbored concerns of a resurgence of its military might. Combining this concern with China's fear of a Soviet attack, including possible use of nuclear weapons, Chinese leaders decided to seek warmer relations with the United States. The time seemed right for leaders in both the United States and China to consider opening a dialogue.

The United States and China Reassess Their Relationship

Despite the disruption in government functions during the Cultural Revolution years, China's top leaders began to reassess its foreign policies and strategic interests at that time. Led by Zhou Enlai and supported by Mao, they believed that China would benefit by shifting from a dual adversary position (in conflict with both the United States and the Soviet Union) to one that was more equidistant. Accordingly, China softened its stance on self-reliance, as advocated by Mao, and instead began to seek greater participation in an interdependent world.

To support this reassessment of its strategic interests, China in the mid-1960s adjusted its world view to consist of three main categories: the two superpowers, developed countries, and less developed countries. The United States, previously viewed as the top imperialist enemy, was no longer perceived as a major military threat, particularly with expectations of its eventual exit from Southeast Asia. The Soviet military buildup and China's vulnerability formed the main basis for China's new foreign policies; China viewed the Soviet attack on Czechoslovakia in 1968 as a demonstration of Soviet willingness to use force against other socialist countries. If China chose to improve relations with the United

States, however, it would undoubtedly lead to broader Chinese diplomatic relations with other countries, which would help reduce the likelihood of Soviet aggression against China.

For his part, U.S. President Richard M. Nixon had to find ways to justify his diplomatic approaches to both the Soviet Union and China, especially considering his strong personal anti-Communist stance of the 1950s. In his televised debate with John F. Kennedy during the 1960 presidential campaign, Nixon had exclaimed "What do the Chinese Communists want? They don't want just Quemoy and Matsu; they don't want just Formosa [Taiwan]; they want the world." By 1967, he was evaluating China's world position more soberly: "Ten years from now the Communist Chinese . . . may have a significant nuclear capability . . . we are going to try to make the breakthrough in some normalization of our relations with Communist China." In moving the U.S. China policy forward, Nixon emphasized that global stability and peace would require China's participation. By June 1969, as the United States was beginning to withdraw from Indochina, he articulated the "Nixon Doctrine," which stressed each country's responsibility for its own defense.

In place of confrontation, Nixon was now advocating equilibrium. It was no longer a simple choice of either standing up to communism or being soft on communism. Nixon also presented his own new world view. Power in a bipolar world dominated by the United States and Soviet Union would gradually distribute itself among five power centers: the United States, the Soviet Union, China, Japan, and Western Europe. Concurrent with beginning the Strategic Arms Limitation Talks (SALT) with the Soviet Union to reduce the nuclear threat, Washington saw the benefit of bringing China out of its isolation.

The Nixon Initiative

Secret discussions between Chinese and U.S. government officials, especially national security adviser Henry Kissinger, paved the way for Zhou Enlai to issue an invitation for Nixon to visit China. In 1971 the United States lifted its trade embargo and gave its approval for the PRC to join the United Na-

By the early 1970s, the United States and China had begun to reassess their longstanding hostility. Following President Richard Nixon's historic visit to China in February 1972, many nations began to re-establish relations with China. Here, Nixon is greeted upon his arrival in China by Zhou Enlai.

tions, thus replacing the Nationalists, who had held the China seat in the UN since 1944. The U.S. table tennis team, then in Japan, received and accepted an invitation to visit China, where it was received by Zhou; thus was coined the phrase "ping-pong diplomacy." Romania had transmitted to Beijing Washington's wish to open a dialogue with China, and Kissinger made his secret trip to Beijing via Pakistan that July. After these initiatives, Beijing invited Nixon to visit China and he readily announced his formal acceptance in July 1971. Nixon arrived in Beijing on February 21, 1972, when he was greeted by Zhou and later received by Mao. Beginning with their historic handshake, the two world leaders reopened relations between their respective countries after more than twenty years of estrangement. The Shanghai Communiqué, signed on February 27, paved the way for the further development of relations.

The Shanghai Communiqué contains six major points. (For the complete text, see the appendix.) China's statement reiterates the PRC's claim to be the sole legal government of China. In its statement, the United States acknowledges that "Chinese on either side of the Taiwan Strait maintain that there is only one China, of which Taiwan is a part." While not challenging this view, the United States also did not take a position, except to support peaceful resolution of the Taiwan matter between the parties. For its part, the United States was eventually to withdraw its forces and military installations from Taiwan. The United States also endorsed the Five Principles of Peaceful Coexistence, first espoused by China in a 1954 Sino-Indian agreement concerning Tibet: respect for the sovereignty and territory of all states; nonaggression; noninterference in domestic affairs; equality and mutual benefits; and peaceful coexistence. Both countries agreed not to seek "hegemony" in the Asian-Pacific region and not to collude against third countries. Exchanges in science, technology, culture, journalism, and sports were to be facilitated, and both countries would aim toward further normalization of relations.

As cultural and other exchanges commenced, both countries quickly established liaison offices in each other's capitals as a prologue to embassies. The Chinese government gave two pandas to the National Zoo in Washington as a gift of friendship to the American people. China, eager for Western scientific knowledge and technology, as well as agricultural and industrial products, was an eager trading partner. Even as two-way trade grew, the United States maintained a significant trade surplus in those early years: a 10:1 U.S.-China trade ratio in 1973 increased to nearly 20:1 in 1974.

Tensions in Southeast Asia

Sino-Vietnamese tensions resurfaced after Vietnam's struggles with the West officially ended in the mid-1970s. Alliances and conflicts in the region became more complex, involving security issues and the larger Sino-Soviet conflict. The Vietnamese Communists in Hanoi had received Chinese support for years but after the Communist victory in 1975, a unified Vietnam perceived that China put its own self-interests first. This was demonstrated by China's February 1974 seizure of the Paracel (Xisha) Islands, a strategic chain in the South China Sea previously part of South Vietnamese territory.

Meanwhile, Cambodia's Khmer Rouge under Pol Pot defeated the U.S.-backed Lon Nol government in 1975 and the country's new regime shocked the world with its genocidal policies; it also took harsh actions against the ethnic Chinese and Vietnamese who had long resided in Cambodia. As early as 1977, Cambodian and Vietnamese forces clashed. China's support of the Khmer Rouge pushed Hanoi (isolated from the world because of U.S. policy) to seek support from the Soviet Union. In a cyclical manner, the increased Soviet presence in Vietnam increased China's fear of Soviet encirclement and pushed China into a deeper alliance with Cambodia.

Under Hua Guofeng's leadership, China entered into military agreements with the Khmer Rouge regime and promised significant economic aid over a period of years. The Chinese hoped that as a client state, Cambodia would serve as a buffer to counter the Soviet-backed Hanoi government. When Vietnam invaded Cambodia, it took a calculated risk: would the Chinese intervene knowing that Hanoi had the Soviet Union's support? The invasion then presented China with a dilemma: if China took military action, would the Soviet Union join in? Having developed a close relationship with the United States only recently, Chinese leaders believed that they were fulfilling a pledge to fight aggression and "hegemony," and that a strengthened U.S.-Chinese relationship would make Soviet intervention unlikely. During his visit to the United States in January 1979, Deng hinted at his willingness to exercise military power against Vietnam.

In December 1978, Vietnam launched a full-scale attack on Cambodia. By January, Vietnamese forces had taken the capital of Phnom Penh, and a Vietnamese-backed government headed by Heng Samrin was quickly installed. On February 17, shortly after Deng's return to China, the Chinese army attacked Vietnamese troops at twenty points along the border, to "teach them a lesson." The fighting lasted only sixteen days, and China was not able to achieve its declared objective of forcing the Vietnamese to withdraw from Cambodia. Casualties were high, the PLA lost large amounts of equipment, and the war was costly. Moreover, the need to modernize China's military became glaringly apparent. In the end, China's intervention had only pushed Hanoi closer to Moscow—just the outcome China had originally sought to avoid. As a result of the war, Beijing committed itself to supporting forces trying to rid Cambodia of the Vietnamese—including Pol Pot and the Khmer Rouge regime, which was almost universally shunned by the outside world for its extremism.

A New Interdependent World

The rest of the world watched the developing Beijing-Washington relationship carefully, and many took their cue from the U.S. initiative. Although Japan was surprised by what it called the "Nixon Shock" of 1972, Japanese leaders moved quickly to recognize Beijing, and Sino-Japanese diplomatic relations were established in September 1972. Japan still had to work through difficult issues, however, such as those presented by the 1951 U.S.-Japan Security Treaty, and how to continue Japan's cultural and economic relations with Taiwan.

Within a year, the Federal Republic of Germany, New Zealand, Australia, and Spain had joined in recognizing the Communist government in Beijing. Between 1971 and 1972, more than thirty states granted China formal recognition, and China became a member of the United Nations in 1971. Very few countries cut ties with Taiwan completely, even when they began to establish diplomatic relations with Beijing. Indeed, Taiwan's trade flourished, even though by 1977 the overwhelming majority of Taiwan's top trading partners did not maintain an embassy there. Instead, many countries set up unofficial organizations in Taipei to act as consular or trade offices, such as the Japan Inter-Exchange Association established in December 1972.

As Beijing re-established diplomatic relations with so many countries, its economic and trade relations grew quickly, and cultural, educational, and scientific exchanges flourished. U.S.-China relations progressed very little for the next several years, however, as each country focused on different priorities in domestic and foreign affairs. Issues related to Taiwan, particularly continued U.S. arms sales to Taipei and Beijing's lack of commitment to the principle of peaceful reunification, continued to be the major problem that would prevent full normalization of U.S.-China relations until 1979.

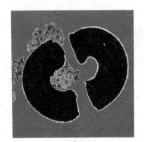

CHAPTER 4

DENG'S CHINA (1979-1989)

orn in Sichuan Province in 1904, Deng Xiao-ping studied in France and the Soviet Union during the 1920s. Deng joined the Chinese Communist Party in 1924, began his military career as a political commissar in 1929, and participated in the Long March. Closely associated with Mao Zedong, Deng was a member of the People's Revolutionary Military Council and the Central People's Government Council at the time of the founding of the People's Republic of China in 1949. Deng gained considerable administrative experience working with Liu Shaoqi and later Zhou Enlai, and proved a shrewd politician who carried himself in a direct, no-nonsense way.

After the exit of Hua Guofeng, Deng Xiaoping indisputably held top power in China, although he declined to occupy the top leadership positions. Instead, he formed a three-man leadership group composed of himself, Hu Yaobang (1915-1989), and Zhao Ziyang (b. 1919). This group was in charge of party, government, and military structures and activities, giving Deng the support needed to consolidate his power.

To solidify their legitimacy and move the country forward, China's leaders had to make a psychological break with the Maoist era. At the third plenary session of the Eleventh Central Committee, convened in December 1978, they abandoned Mao's approach to economic development, in particular, the communal agricultural system. In place of class struggle, isolation, and anti-intellectualism, they aimed for modernization in agriculture, industry, defense, and science and technology. Recognizing the need to acquire technology and knowledge from the West, China now began to pursue an "open door" policy, and Deng called for the country to define and pursue "socialism with Chinese characteristics."

Breaking with Maoist China

In making the transition to post-Mao China, it was necessary to reassess the legacy of Mao's leadership and the political, social, and economic ramifications. After the countercoup and arrest of the Gang of Four in 1976, China's leaders took several years to decide how to proceed with this politically sensitive reassessment. They viewed a trial of the leftists as essential for reinforcing the principle of the rule of law and demonstrating to the international community the change in China's political environment. But Mao's role in the Cultural Revolution and the rise of his wife, Jiang Qing (1914-1991), and her group would inevitably be questioned in the process, thereby putting Mao, though deceased, on trial as well. The difficulty was in deciding how to separate Mao and Hua from the charges against the leftists. Finally, the leaders decided to hold the trial of the Gang of Four first, and then later issue a separate assessment of Mao and his leadership.

The constitution was revised once again in 1978, to remove Maoist principles and policies that the leftists had written into the 1975 constitution. Important to China's new place in the post-Mao world were the Five Principles of Peaceful Coexistence, first articulated in the 1950s. The new constitution also spelled out the rights of ethnic minorities in China and declared the Cultural Revolution officially over.

Deng Xiaoping (b. 1904), who returned to power in 1978 after the Cultural Revolution ended, became indisputably China's most powerful leader after Hua Guofeng stepped down in 1981.

By 1979, the excesses and leftist idealism of the Cultural Revolution were being openly criticized by government officials and in the press. More important, the party officially acknowledged Mao's responsibility for leading the disastrous movement. Subsequently, the positive contributions of previously purged leaders, such as Peng Dehuai and Liu Shaoqi, were recognized. The party posthumously rehabilitated Liu in 1980 and reaffirmed him as a great leader, thus publicly negating the values of the Cultural Revolution.

Trial of the Gang of Four and Lin Biao

Even though Lin Biao had died in 1971, it was decided to hold a joint trial of the Gang of Four and Lin Biao. A special court consisting of thirty-five judges was created, and the trial of a total of ten defendants began in November 1980. The trial was held in secret; only a selected group of individuals could attend, and the foreign press was barred. All the defendants were accused of framing and persecuting party and state leaders, as well as party cadres and the masses. They were charged with attempting to overthrow the proletarian dictatorship, a serious violation of the Four Cardinal Principles, which were defined as keeping to the socialist road; upholding the dictatorship of the proletariat; upholding the leadership of the Communist Party; and upholding Marxism-Leninism and Mao Zedong Thought. The Special Court held them personally responsible for the persecution of 750,000 people over the course of the Cultural Revolution and for the deaths of another 35,000.

Jiang Qing's group was charged with plotting an armed uprising (on October 6, 1976), while Lin Biao was charged with plotting to assassinate Mao. The prosecutors tried to show that by framing Zhou Enlai and Deng Xiaoping, Jiang Qing sought to usurp party leadership and eventually take complete power. Throughout the trial, which lasted two months, Jiang Qing and others insisted that their actions were based on orders from Mao himself. Other defendants also claimed they were carrying out Mao's wishes. For her part, Jiang emphasized Hua's involvement as head of public security, particularly his central role in carrying out the suppression of the 1976 Tiananmen incident. The members of the Lin Biao group all pleaded guilty, saying they were acting on Lin's orders.

A consensus was finally reached at the end of January 1981. Jiang Qing and Zhang Chunqiao (b. 1917) were sentenced to death, though with a two-year suspension. Wang Hongwen (c. 1937-1992), Yao Wenyuan (b. 1930), and other defendants (including Chen Boda [1904-1989] and several high military officials) received lifetime prison terms. At the same time, the trial made a strong statement about Mao and the system that had allowed this group of radicals to assume such power from within. Prosecutor Jiang Wen openly blamed Mao for the Cultural Revolution and for failing to see through these two "counterrevolutionary cliques." His criticism was softened only by an acknowledgment of Mao's considerable revolutionary leadership. The conclusion: Mao had made mistakes, but his contributions outweighed these shortcomings.

Because China's legal code was weak, and its judiciary had little independence or authority, both the trial and its outcome were guided mainly by political considerations. A legal code had been enacted only in 1979, and China's leaders wanted badly to demonstrate to the world that the rule of law was becoming established in China. In this trial, however, guilt was largely assumed from the beginning. More important was the political significance of the trial's outcome: Mao's legacy was being reinterpreted, and Hua's political future was being undermined.

Assessment of Mao

A separate assessment of Mao's leadership and place in China's history was also necessary following the trial of the Gang of Four. Since Jiang Qing and the leftist intellectuals had held fast to their claims that they were acting on Mao's wishes and Maoist ideals, the verdict on them was by implication also a verdict on Mao. Furthermore, their contention that they were carrying forth true Maoist philosophy put the pragmatic leaders in a position where they could be perceived as challenging Mao Zedong Thought itself.

The Chinese Communist Party therefore began its assessment following the trial verdicts in 1981, using a policy of separating Mao's thought from his leadership qualities. It aimed to bring Mao down to a human level, and to reverse the personality cult that had been built around him. First the party began to include all of China's revolutionary experience under the rubric of Mao Zedong Thought and to acknowledge the contributions of many Communist leaders in addition to Mao. Next, they assessed Mao's leadership more objectively.

A 35,000-word document, "Resolution on Certain Questions in the History of Our Party Since the Founding of the People's Republic," was adopted at the sixth plenary session of the Eleventh Central Committee in June 1981. This document did not challenge Mao's position as the major revolutionary leader of the twentieth century, and indeed praised his brilliance and achievements up to the 1949 founding of the People's Republic. But the party resolution went on to contend that his revolutionary methods of perpetual class struggle and persecution of intellectuals were not suitable for socialist construction. Mao's many political campaigns were interpreted as having had a severe detrimental effect on China's development. In the end, the assessment of Mao was that his achievements had been "70 percent good, 30 percent bad." Furthermore, Hua Guofeng was criticized by name for perpetuating "erroneous theories, policies, and slogans of the Cultural Revolution." The resolution concluded that "obviously, under [Hua's] leadership it is impossible to correct 'leftist' errors within the party, and all the more impossible to restore the party's fine traditions."

Thus Mao's leadership in successfully carrying out China's revolution, his political thought, and his role in building the Chinese Communist Party were all upheld. The official recognition that Mao's revolutionary visions and methods could not, however, be applied to the current task of modernizing China enabled China's new group of leaders to seek a pragmatic path to socialist modernization. Hua's fate was also determined; whatever legitimacy he had was now erased. Hua and his supporters—called "whateverists" for blindly following Mao's decisions as previously stated—were excluded from the new order.

Deng Consolidates Power

Deng Xiaoping had begun to consolidate his power base in 1976 as he instituted reforms in China's political structures, which had been severely weakened during the Cultural Revolution. He would gradually but systematically get rid of Hua's supporters, and then Hua himself, while installing those who favored his pragmatic and reformist agenda. Deng saw an urgent need to strengthen government functions and procedures, many of which had broken down. The country had instead been operating on the basis of factional power, under which connections were all-important and individuals could exercise arbitrary authority. Mao had engineered the Cultural

Revolution by disregarding process and structure; his personalization of politics had allowed the leftists under Jiang Qing to rise to power. Deng hoped to prevent the repetition of such an event by strengthening government procedures and by keeping party, government, and military functions distinct. Beyond the need for consolidating his own power, Deng perceived that structural changes were essential for China's national development.

Changes at the Top Levels of Power

Significant personnel and policy changes made by the Eleventh Central Committee between 1978 and 1980 confirmed Deng's growing strength. While those aligned with Ye Jianying (1897-1986) lost some influence, Deng's real target was Hua Guofeng and his followers. Deng appointed his own supporters to top positions in both the party and the government; these would form the new collective leadership group. At this point Hua Guofeng was still chairman of the Chinese Communist Party, while Deng was party vice chairman. In early 1979, Hu Yaobang, a Deng protégé, was appointed secretary general of the Chinese Communist Party (a post that had been abolished during the Cultural Revolution) and simultaneously chief of the Propaganda Department. The latter position would ensure that Deng and his supporters could use the media to restrain the opposition.

To strengthen political structures and ensure continuity in China's leadership, Deng sought to bring in younger and more professional leaders, and make merit and professionalism the basis for promotion. The State Council was ordered to go through a process of reorganization and streamlining.

At the Fifth National People's Congress, convened in early 1978, Hua was reaffirmed as premier of the State Council, the top government position. Again, Deng deferred to Hua by taking the post of first vice premier. In 1979, the congress also appointed Chen Yun (1905-1995), Bo Yibo (b. 1908), and Yao Yilin (1917-1994), all economics experts, as vice premiers. Chen also headed the newly created State Finance and Economic Commission. A reshuffle of the Politburo came in February 1980 at the fifth

plenary session of the eleventh party congress. Mao's former bodyguard Wang Dongxing (b. 1916) and former mayor of Beijing Wu De (b. 1909), both members of Hua's group, were dismissed, while Zhao Ziyang, former party first secretary of Sichuan Province, and Hu Yaobang were appointed to the Politburo Standing Committee.

In line with his policy of separating party and government posts, Deng resigned from his government position of vice premier at the third plenary session of the Fifth National People's Congress in 1980. He retained the party vice chairmanship and remained on the Politburo. Six other vice premiers, five in their seventies, also resigned; among them were Chen Yun and Li Xiannian (1907-1992), who nevertheless retained their other posts. Hua's impending fall was evident when he was forced to resign as premier. Party involvement at all levels of the government bureaucracy was reduced. Top members of the State Council began to meet regularly to deal with daily administrative affairs. The party Secretariat was revived to focus on the day-to-day running of the party.

A New Generation of Leaders

One of Deng's particular strengths was that he kept a long-term view of China's development, specifically the need to recruit and groom a new generation of leaders. After all, the Long March generation was composed of people by then in their seventies and eighties. Deng also pushed for an end to the practice of life-long tenure in party positions and government positions; appointees were now limited to two terms. Through retirements and ongoing purges within the party, government, and military, Deng removed aging and ineffective leaders to make way for those who were younger and better educated, and who would more effectively carry out his economic reforms.

A sweeping three-year administrative purge of the party began in 1983 to re-educate, reorganize, and reregister the party's 40 million members. Many who had gained access to party and official positions during the Cultural Revolution period were workers, peasants, and soldiers who lacked the expertise in government and economic functions needed for modernization. Now, with a national focus on economic development, in which more authority was granted to enterprises and peasant families, many party cadres resented their diminishing privileges and status. Thus the administrative purge served a dual purpose: weeding out incompetent individuals and removing from the party apparatus those who did not support Deng's reform policies or still held Maoist values.

The government bureaucracy had become bloated, with functions duplicated across its various ministries, commissions, and agencies. Through merging some of these and strengthening others, the State Council could take on an increased role in management of the economy. For example, the State Agricultural Commission and State Capital Construction Commission were eliminated, their functions absorbed into the State Economic Commission. Various commissions and ministries that handled trade and international affairs were pulled together in a new Ministry of Foreign Economic Relations and Trade (MOFERT). The State Planning Commission was further strengthened. Accompanying the reorganization was a significant reduction in the number of positions, including ministers and vice ministers. In early 1982, several elderly deputy ministers were asked to resign.

With security of China's borders of paramount concern, changes were also needed to ensure a strong and effective military, especially after the years of privilege and entrenched power that had been the norm under the leadership of Lin Biao. Lin had eliminated ranks in the People's Liberation Army (PLA), which eroded discipline and effectiveness. As in many of China's other institutions, in the military expertise and professionalism had been accorded less weight than had personal connections during the Cultural Revolution period. As he had done in the party and the state government, over the next several years Deng removed men in the military who were incompetent, aging, and resistant to change. In December 1984, forty top PLA officers were asked to retire in an extensive sweep of the military. Because the PLA had become self-sufficient during the Cultural Revolution—operating its own schools, fac-

tories, newspapers, ports, and airports—the central government moved to bring more of these functions under civilian control. Understanding that whoever controlled the military controlled the country, Deng sought to build a strong military, but one that was under the party's direction.

The People's Liberation Army remained an institutional problem, however. Its Military Affairs Committee (MAC) had traditionally been the policy formation group, and the chairman of the MAC was thus head of the military. Care was given to keep the regional military leaders under strong central control. In 1982 the Central Military Commission (CMC) was established to lead the armed forces; it would be responsible to the National People's Congress, rather than to the party, thus promoting greater civilian control over the military. The MAC remained, however, and during the interim, Deng was chairman of both it and the CMC.

Solidifying the Reform Agenda

The Fifth National People's Congress took important steps in 1979 to solidify Deng's reform agenda. Agricultural development was declared the priority, and the nation's energies were to be directed toward socialist construction and the Four Modernizations. Local people's congresses were granted more authority in place of top-down appointments.

A code of law and administrative procedure was enacted in 1979 to protect individuals' rights against arbitrary official actions. A new criminal code was developed, in which "counterrevolutionary offenses" were more narrowly defined to refer only to those activities with an actual aim of overthrowing the government. China's judiciary, however, was kept weak and was still dominated by the party. A push for legal reform came from the open door policy, because laws and regulations were needed to facilitate economic activity and to encourage international business and trade.

Other changes were formalized in the revised constitution, which was deliberated by the Chinese People's Political Consultative Conference and ratified by the National People's Congress in December 1982. Significant points in the new constitution included: restoration of the post of president as chief of state, establishment of the CMC, restructuring of the state bureaucracy, and reduction of the power of the communes. Although the commune would continue to serve as an economic unit, the role of rural governance was returned to elected township officials.

By 1979, Deng Xiaoping had anchored his power base by bringing his supporters into the top levels of leadership. He used the process of restructuring party and government institutions to gradually move his opponents out, especially Hua Guofeng's faction. Having already been forced to resign from the premiership in 1980, Hua lost the position of party chairman in 1981. The position of party chairman was formally eliminated in the revised constitution of 1982; the general secretary would thereafter head the party.

When his subsequent position of vice chairman was eliminated under the 1982 constitution, Hua Guofeng essentially lost all power. Hu Yaobang now led the party, and Zhao Ziyang led the State Council. They and others proceeded to carry out Deng's structural and economic reform policies. Though the policy of separation of personnel in party and government was not strictly adhered to, the reforms greatly strengthened the independent functions in each. China was now in a strong position to proceed with economic reforms that would promote modernization.

Pursuing Modernization through "Socialism with Chinese Characteristics"

The break with the Maoist era had been made at the historic third plenary session of the Eleventh Central Committee in 1978: the priority was now explicitly declared to be economic development. To achieve this, as well as the Four Modernizations—in agriculture, industry, defense, and science and technology—the reformist leaders aimed to attract greatly needed capital investment and technologies through an open door policy. In setting these priorities, Deng was in many ways resuming the pragmatic work begun under Zhou Enlai's leadership in the early 1960s to remedy the ill effects of the Great Leap

Forward, and again in the mid-1970s to repair the country after the Cultural Revolution. The overriding goal of China's leaders was to modernize the country and raise the standard of living, which had actually declined since the 1950s. Broadening political freedoms, however, was not part of the agenda.

To maintain the party's legitimacy, China's reformist leaders had to reconcile the use of capitalist methods in a socialist country. The Four Cardinal Principles could not be violated, but they could be reinterpreted. Above all, what would be the direction of China's socialist road? To give the open door policy theoretical legitimacy, China's leaders declared that it would enhance China's capacity for self-reliant action and thereby further the socialist modernization process. The question was how to liberalize economic structures within a framework of centralized planning.

It soon became clear that much had changed in the global economy during China's Cultural Revolution decade of isolation. The point of comparison was not so much the Western capitalist countries but the widening economic gaps between China and the newly industrialized countries (NICs) in Asia. New approaches and a new set of incentives had to be adopted quickly for China to catch up. Leaders looked at the successful export-led growth strategies of the NICs, including Taiwan and South Korea, and realized that participation in the world's market economy would be essential to China's future. Egalitarianism was no longer held up as a national value. In a 1986 speech, Deng explained that "there can be no communism with pauperism, or socialism with pauperism. So to get rich is not a sin."

Experimental Economic Reforms

In the process of developing and defining "socialism with Chinese characteristics," experimentation was encouraged in the areas of agriculture, industry, education, taxation, and finances. The entire country's economic reform policies, formally implemented in 1984, were modeled after experiments in agricultural and industrial reforms first carried out in Sichuan Province and in several cities in other provinces. Agricultural production was once again fam-

Many agricultural reforms were first tried on an experimental basis in Sichuan Province in the latter half of the 1970s. Sichuan's provincial party secretary at the time, Zhao Ziyang, went on to become one of China's top leaders in the 1980s. Here, peasants in Sichuan sort and dry a new peanut crop in 1977.

ily-based. Whereas all enterprises had formerly been state-owned, collective and later individual ownership would gradually be allowed. Experimentation in taxation and labor management was carried out in state-owned enterprises with an aim to move them toward being self-sufficient, while stabilizing taxes on profits as a source of government revenues. Gradually, it became apparent that decentralization was needed to promote the desired "bottom-up" innovation, and more authority was accordingly granted to provinces, enterprises, and factory managers.

Zhao Ziyang, who was appointed party first secretary in Sichuan in 1975, had introduced new methods of production and organization within a framework of public ownership and a planned economy during his tenure in Sichuan. Material incentives were allowed, while merit and pay according to work replaced the egalitarianism of the commune ideal. Agricultural production was organized under a responsibility system based on the family or small group as a unit; entrepreneurial activity was encouraged. Factory managers were given more decision-making powers and allowed to experiment with management methods to achieve greater efficiency and productivity. Expertise in factories and in government work was given priority over cadre authority. Many state-owned enterprises were consolidated, especially at the provincial and local levels, where there was a great deal of duplication. Sichuan's increased productivity in the second half of the 1970s as a result of these changes was astounding.

Sichuan's successes boosted Deng's reform policies, which were gaining support at the top levels of leadership. A decentralized approach was proving effective in tapping the productive potential of the people and in enabling local authorities to respond better to local conditions. In 1979, the government allowed four cities to develop special economic zones, or SEZs: Shenzhen, Zhuhai, Shantou, and Xiamen—all in southern China. The Chinese hoped to attract foreign firms to invest in and establish operations in the SEZs through beneficial tax rates, lower import duties, and other incentives. The SEZs proved successful at attracting foreign investment and technology, replacing the more costly and less effective strategy of borrowing funds and importing technology. Enterprises in the SEZs were also allowed to experiment further with industrial reform.

These agricultural and industrial production methods were incorporated into a national model for achieving the goals of the sixth Five-Year Plan (1981-1986). Underlying this new master plan was the principle that China's economy would remain centrally planned and managed, but would make room for certain entrepreneurial activities and methods such as allowing prices to be determined by market forces. Goals were adjusted downward from the Ten-Year Plan to more realistic levels: overall growth targets were set at 4 to 5 percent a year; import and export growth was set at 9 percent and 8 percent, respectively. The government pledged to increase spending in education, science, culture, and public health; a $2.5 billion to $3 billion annual deficit was anticipated in the national budget.

Transformation of the Countryside

At the same time, China's peasants were ready to take initiatives that would transform the countryside. Previously, at the third plenum of the Eleventh Central Committee in late 1978, the basic agricultural unit of accounting had been returned from the brigade to the team. Now the family or small group was the basic unit of production. In what is often called the "household responsibility system," the family unit was to contract with the state to produce a certain amount on a land plot assigned to it. The family could retain any excess production, which could be consumed or sold in the many markets that were staging a comeback in rural life.

Rural collective markets, private plots, and sideline occupations—all were now officially recognized as important "supplements" to a socialist economy. The Central Committee approved twenty-five agricultural policies in 1979, including household sideline production; increased government loans and construction investment; increased government purchase prices; and promotion of chemical fertilizer use. The principles of "to each according to his work" and equal pay for equal work for men and women were reinforced. Accordingly, families and individuals eagerly began to grow cash crops and go into businesses providing transport, repairs, and other basic services. The standard of living rose for many, as family income was supplemented by such private activities.

Beginning in 1980, the government began to dismantle the agricultural commune system, a job that was finished by 1985. Fifty-six thousand communes were replaced by 92,000 townships; governance was returned to elected local officials. Even as early as 1979, the call to "learn from Dazhai," which had been widely held up as a model commune, ceased to be heard. Dazhai was further discredited as it became known that the model commune had in fact received substantial state subsidies and falsified its production figures. Communal ideals were no longer held up as guiding values; rather, individual efforts reaped individual rewards. However, the dismantling of the communes left a gap. Previously, these large organizations had undertaken infrastructure projects and provided certain human services within each commune. With structural reorganization slow in coming and government resources limited, important work such as irrigation projects, education, and health care were neglected or temporarily disrupted until provincial and local governments could once again build up their ability to function in such areas.

Industrial Reforms

China's state-owned enterprises were generally overstaffed and inefficient and often consumed high levels of scarce energy. Industrial reforms were needed to improve worker productivity, streamline enterprises through reorganization, and raise production standards. To boost efficiency and productivity, labor management reforms gave more authority to enterprise managers to hire, evaluate, and fire employees. The "iron rice bowl" (guaranteed life-long employment, regardless of productivity) was beginning to be challenged. Workers now contracted with the enterprise for specific jobs at specific wages and could be dismissed for laziness or incompetence. Duplicative enterprises were closed or merged with others, and some switched to manufacturing other products. In the countryside, the policy of consolidating small industries, especially those that made producer goods, was later found to have a negative effect on the self-sufficient nature of the rural economy.

After four years of experimentation with tax collection methods in hundreds of state-owned enterprises, the government adopted a new tax structure in 1983. Under this system, instead of turning over all their profits to the state, enterprises were assigned tax rates according to industrial categories, and a percentage of profits, typically 55 percent, was remitted to the state as taxes. The remaining small share of profits could be used by the enterprise in areas such as reinvestment or upgrading of equipment. With poor accountability and auditing procedures, however, many enterprises found ways to manipulate their accounting to reflect small profits as a way of minimizing their taxes.

Beginning in 1980, China's productivity began to rise steadily. The year 1983, for example, saw a 10.5 percent increase in industrial productivity and a 9.5 percent increase in agricultural productivity over 1982. Furthermore, heavy industry no longer dominated: by 1982, agriculture, light industry, and heavy industry were nearly equal in terms of contribution to overall output value. Grain output reached a high of 407 million tons in 1984, and then remained steady at an average of 395 million tons for the following four years. The value of agricultural and farm crops production nearly doubled between 1980 and 1986. As a result, food processing and other industries that utilized agricultural sources as inputs, such as sugar and cotton, could also grow. Exports of grain and produce—$1.4 billion in 1986—brought in foreign exchange. Concurrently, the savings from reduced grain imports (purchases of wheat from the United States fell from a high of $1.4 billion in 1981 to $30 million in 1986) allowed foreign exchange to be channeled toward high technology and other development-oriented imports. China's exports nearly doubled to $18 billion from 1978 to 1980, and continued to grow, reaching more than $30 billion by 1986. In terms of value, the export of manufactured goods increased, while primary exports steadily declined as a percentage of total exports. In the area of capital investments, special emphasis was placed on the energy and transportation sectors, improvement of which would spur economic development.

State revenues increased about 30 percent in the first few years of reform, even though the government encountered serious problems with tax collection. In making the transition to reform policies, however, government spending increased more dramatically than taxes, resulting in a deficit of about $11 billion in 1979 and about $8.5 billion in 1980. The government's overinvestment in construction and other large-scale projects begun under Hua Guofeng's Ten-Year Plan contributed heavily to the deficits. Under the new system in which enterprises reported profits and losses, the state-owned sector was incurring huge losses. It was officially reported that in 1978 about one in four was operating in the red (this estimate is probably low, since 40 percent were reported as incurring losses as late as 1991), thus continuing the need for substantial government subsidies. The situation was so grave that in 1981 the finance ministry issued $3.3 billion in ten-year bonds to raise revenues; the government also cut back on several major construction projects.

When economic reforms were first launched, the state-owned sector still employed about 75 percent of China's industrial workers. Many of the enterprises were overstaffed, and large numbers of employees were known to be idle. The government was anxious either to make the state-owned enterprises more efficient or to allow them to be privatized (i.e., become collectives), especially since the subsidies were a big drain on the government budget. Nevertheless, it moved slowly because of the massive un-employment already plaguing the cities. Layoffs from canceled construction projects and the fact that numerous youths were returning to the cities after having been sent to the countryside during the Cultural Revolution exacerbated the labor problems. China's leaders recognized the need to keep potential social unrest under control. Efficiency and adjustments came gradually, so that by 1984 the proportion of state-owned enterprises had fallen to 70 percent, and by 1989 to 56 percent. The difference has been made up by steady growth in collectively owned enterprises. Only a small portion, less than 5 percent, were privately owned enterprises, and these tended to be smaller in scale. The widely held view that China was becoming capitalist as a result of these reforms must therefore be qualified.

Structural Changes Formalized

In the government's drive to modernize and increase production, consumerism and the aim for material wealth were no longer considered incompatible with socialism, and by the mid-1980s, materialism had replaced egalitarianism as a guiding value in China. Success in carrying out reforms was uneven, but a comprehensive economic reform program was approved at the third plenary session of the Twelfth Central Committee in 1984. Measures included moving prices (both for producer activity and consumer activity) closer to a reflection of actual costs; reducing the authority of government officials while raising that of managers in enterprises; and developing structures and procedures to attract foreign aid and technology. A simplified distribution system also facilitated the flow of commodities between regions and between cities and the countryside. To keep up with the rising cost of living, in 1985 the government announced changes in the wage scale system for state workers, including educators, scientists, and doctors and health workers. The seventh Five-Year Plan (1986-1990), approved in April 1986 by the National People's Congress (NPC), called for transferring more power to local governments, but maintained the two-tier price system. In his speech to the NPC, Premier Zhao Ziyang acknowledged China's problems

in implementing economic reforms and indicated that the government would in 1987 restrict capital investments, consumption, and availability of credit.

Economic Aspects of the Open Door Policy

China initiated an unprecedented level of contact with the international economic community as a result of the open door policy announced in 1978. Trade volume was growing by leaps and bounds, although at first China was importing a great deal more than it was exporting. Furthermore, many of the exports were from the primary sector, especially petroleum. According to government statistics, with the exception of 1981 and 1982, China carried a trade deficit. The trade deficit rose to a high of $15 billion in 1985. With the export economy still underdeveloped, high-priced imports such as satellite stations, airplanes, and scientific instruments contributed significantly to the trade imbalance. During these transitional years, construction projects abroad and tourism served as important sources of foreign exchange. By 1984, tourism alone was bringing in over $1 billion a year.

The broadest experiments in industrial cooperation with foreign firms were carried out in the SEZs. Through joint ventures, the Chinese could learn the business organization methods and management techniques of their foreign partners. In addition to acquiring modern production technologies, the joint venture enterprises provided a setting for experimentation with labor management and new types of personnel relations.

Foreign Loans and Investment

Chinese businesses sought to attract funds and technology at various levels, beginning with government agencies, financial institutions, and commercial banks. Foreign loans became an important source of state revenues. From about 3 billion yuan in 1985, they leapt to 7.8 billion in 1986, doubling again to nearly 15 billion yuan (or about $4 billion) by 1989. Japan, for example, extended $1.5 billion in credits to China between 1979 and 1983; it emerged

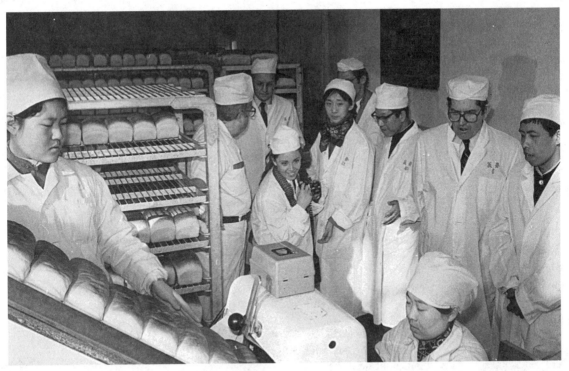

While much of China's foreign investment has come from Hong Kong, Western firms, enticed by the prospect of a billion consumers, have also been active since the early 1980s. Above is the 1983 inauguration of a Sino-American joint venture producing baked goods at Beijing's Yili Bakery and Confectionery.

as China's top source of loans, while Hong Kong was the top investor. Through joining the World Bank and International Monetary Fund in 1980, China also gained access to World Bank funds for large-scale and infrastructure projects, such as petroleum, energy, agriculture, education and research, and railway and port development.

The central government took further measures to liberalize the economy and give more authority to provincial levels of government in interacting with the outside world. In 1984, fourteen additional coastal cities (plus Hainan Island) were designated as "open cities" and allowed to carry out economic policies similar to those in the SEZs. The fourteen open coastal cities represented 60 percent of the nation's total industrial capacity, and it was hoped that favorable policies, plus well-established industrial bases, would help them attract foreign investment.

Shanghai and Tianjin were given the right to approve Sino-foreign contracts worth up to $30 million without the need for central permission, and other important cities, such as Guangzhou, were granted authority to approve projects involving smaller amounts.

From the beginning, most of the foreign investment came from Hong Kong firms and was concentrated in Guangdong and Fujian Provinces. Industrial projects were typically small-scale and labor-intensive and contributed little modern technology to the Chinese enterprises involved. Furthermore, the short-term nature of the projects meant that their impact on China's development plans was minimal.

Gradually, China allowed new incentives to be offered to attract more large-scale industries that utilized high technology and more advanced manufacturing processes from investors in a wider range of countries. The long-term commitment represented by such projects indicated growing confidence that the reforms being put in place would not change suddenly. Nevertheless, numerous structural problems obstructed the modernization process and China's ability to steadily attract foreign investment. Physical infrastructure, such as port facilities, transport, and communications, needed improvement. China needed to conform to international standards in banking, accounting, and other areas of economic management. Perhaps the most important difficulty was the perception by the international community of China's "legal gap."

Although China had made significant efforts since enactment of the 1979 Chinese-Foreign Equity Joint Venture Law to draw up more detailed laws and regulations, these were soon found to be lacking. Firms were reluctant to make large commitments in a country whose legal code was vague and often ambiguous. One positive step was the enactment of a progressive tax law in 1982, which levied a 20 percent minimum tax on annual profits, rising to 40 percent on profits over $590,000. Previously, tax rates were determined in each commercial agreement, a cumbersome and inequitable process. And in 1983, new regulations formally allowed joint venture products to be sold in China's domestic market, which greatly facilitated foreign firms' long-term marketing strategies. Moreover, a joint venture's board of directors gained the power to make many major business decisions that had previously been the purview of various government departments.

Still, inconsistency and weaknesses in structure and laws repeatedly became apparent, limiting investor confidence. In 1981, for example, Japanese and German firms in particular suffered substantial losses—not all of them compensated—when their Chinese partners canceled projects unilaterally. China's foreign trade partners also frequently complained about the fact that regulations were not clearly published, and varied by locale and industry. The China International Economic and Trade Arbitration Commission was established, but many foreign firms felt that a clear legal mechanism for solving disputes was still lacking.

Nevertheless, sizable foreign investment poured into the SEZs, particularly Shenzhen, located close to Hong Kong. Total direct foreign investment tripled from 1983 to 1985, when it reached $6.3 billion. (By 1992, that amount would reach over $11 billion, still maintaining a consistent pattern: approximately 70 percent of investment coming from Hong Kong, 10 percent from Japan, 4.5 percent from the United States, and the remaining 15.5 percent from other countries.) Most of this was in the form of joint ventures. Inexpensive and skilled labor in China was a plus, and the image of a billion potential and eager customers was a strong draw. Many foreign firms saw joint ventures as a means of gaining a foothold in the China market. Although the original intention was for SEZ products to be exported, approximately 70 percent of the goods produced in SEZs were actually being sold in China. This was because many consumer goods were unavailable in China, where citizens now had improved purchasing power. In recent years, new project agreements have placed a greater emphasis on exporting.

China's External Economic Activities

In addition to absorbing foreign investment and increasing two-way trade, China's reformist leaders embarked on their own "economic diplomacy." In late 1983, General Secretary Hu Yaobang, in his first visit to a non-Communist country, went to Japan to boost trade and economic relations. Premier Zhao Ziyang made his historic visit to the United States and Canada in January 1984. Hu then visited Australia, a major supplier of wheat and iron ore, in April 1985; in June, Zhao, accompanied by China's top economic planners and Deputy Foreign Minister Wu Xueqian (b. 1921), toured Western Europe. They successfully negotiated an economic cooperation agreement with Great Britain for 1986-1990, as well as an agreement on the peaceful use of nuclear energy to facilitate high-technology sales to China. An economic cooperation agreement with West Germany was extended to 1995.

By 1983, China had accumulated foreign exchange reserves of $14 billion, much of it from a booming tourism industry. Moreover, Chinese construction teams that formerly worked abroad as part of foreign policy programs now became an important means of earning hard currency. Chinese construction labor in the Middle East, for example, was earning China about $500 million annually. China was now in a position to look outward for investment opportunities. In addition to investments in the international financial market, China began to enter into overseas joint ventures in the mid-1980s. The goals of these ventures included securing stable supplies of raw materials and learning new management techniques, particularly for high-technology projects. Many of the partners were overseas Chinese from Hong Kong and elsewhere. Gradually, China has channeled investments into other developing countries, particularly in Southeast Asia, where projects include mining of iron ore and development of natural resources such as timber.

High-Technology Transfer and Military Cooperation

China was anxious to purchase high technology, including satellite tracking systems, computers, and earth stations for gathering geological data. This type of high-technology trade raises complex issues, however, since many technologies can be put to either civilian or military use. The developed countries therefore have competing domestic interests with regard to supplying high technology to developing countries like China: their firms are anxious not to lose out to international competitors, but their governments have security concerns. Thus selling these so-called dual-use items requires special governmental regulation, and sometimes intergovernmental oversight. The seventeen-member Coordinating Committee for Multilateral Export Controls (COCOM), created after World War II, regulated the transfer of high technology to Communist countries until 1994. To avoid overdependence on any one country, China sought and received high-technology cooperation from various developed nations.

France was among the first countries to sell nuclear reactors to China, in 1983. China's refusal to sign the Nuclear Nonproliferation Treaty, which the superpowers and many other countries had signed, and

China's unwillingness to open its facilities to inspections by the International Atomic Energy Agency were problematic for the United States, however. Moreover, the Chinese gave no firm assurance that they would not transfer potential dual-use technologies to third countries. China was believed, for example, to have been helping Pakistan and Algeria develop nuclear capabilities. China and the United States finally signed a nuclear cooperation agreement in July 1985. The U.S. Congress approved it, but not without attempts to detail specific restrictions, such as safeguards against weapons use. Vice President George Bush's visit to China that October cleared the way for government-to-government military sales to China under the Foreign Military Sales (FMS) program.

On the one hand, China was eager to step up its purchases of advanced weapons systems and communications systems from the United States, France, and other countries to modernize its military. At the same time, prompted by limited government allocations to the People's Liberation Army budget (which remained flat at an average of 16 million yuan annually between 1970 and 1981), the PLA began to shift research and development expenditures outside these budgets and accelerated the money-making activities of its defense industries. The Middle East became China's principal market for arms sales, especially with the start of the Iran-Iraq War in 1982. (It is estimated that between 1982 and 1989, China sold nearly $7.5 billion in arms to those two countries alone.) The United States in 1987 pressured China to stop sales to Iran of *Silkworm* missiles, which posed a threat to Persian Gulf shipping.

The Chinese have maintained their right to sell weapons. The foreign exchange earned through weapons sales was essential for furthering research and development in China's defense industries and for purchasing high-technology systems to fulfill the goal of modernizing the military. The value of arms deliveries from China between 1983 and 1990 totaled $13 billion; the high demand by Middle Eastern and other third world countries for the types of arms China can readily supply meant that armaments would continue to be an important export.

Impact of Economic Reforms on Society

Deng Xiaoping continued to prepare China for a smooth transition to the era when he and other revolutionary leaders will have passed from the scene and to ensure that China's institutions were strong enough to carry China's modernization drive into the twenty-first century. The reformers were persistent in pursuing their goal of modernizing China while trying to balance the interests of the central government with those of the provinces. The rapid change brought on by reforms created economic confusion, as well as some social and political instability.

As the Chinese people experienced more flexibility and options in their lives, their expectations also began to rise. And as in other developing countries, China's focus on rapid economic development created severe pollution and damaged natural resources, with few environmental interest groups active in the country to argue for more balanced policies. Thus China's leaders had to find ways to accommodate and yet control many complex forces, trying not to jeopardize China's progress, yet not to undermine their own political power at the same time.

Loosening Political Controls on People's Lives

Though the Chinese Communist Party held tightly to its monopoly of power, overall there was less intrusion in the personal lives of the Chinese people. Upon review of millions of cases of victims in the 1957 Anti-Rightist campaign and the Cultural Revolution, many of the rightist labels on individuals and their families were reversed, which strengthened support for the new leadership under Deng. To support the modernization drive, the value of intellectuals, education, and expertise (whether at universities, government offices, or factories) was recognized and upheld. Government controls over education, the press, and other spheres of life were loosened. Intellectuals and university students, buoyed by this atmosphere of openness, led a call for greater freedoms. In 1978 and 1979 this grew into a lively public discussion that became known as the Beijing Spring.

The possibilities of economic reforms and the open door policy seemed to capture the imagination of the Chinese people, and the Chinese economy grew in all sectors. With encouragement from the central government, provincial and local authorities undertook many new initiatives. But uncontrolled growth soon overheated the economy, leading to price instability and spiraling inflation. The decentralization process also weakened party control as well as the integrity of central financial and bureaucratic structures. Corruption and economic crimes were rampant. To try to remedy the negative aspects of openness and reforms, Deng launched an "Anti-Spiritual Pollution" campaign in 1983. However, social problems stemming from the rapid economic change continued; the people's growing dissatisfaction was expressed through increased social unrest. Deng's scapegoating of Hu Yaobang revealed the government's inability to deal with its myriad problems. In the meantime, a conservative force among the top CCP leadership was growing, though it remained committed to economic reform.

Democracy Wall and Beijing Spring

Intellectuals ventured to express and debate China's changes once it was clear that the Cultural Revolution had really ended, and they placed trust and confidence in a new leadership that seemed forward-looking. In Beijing, a spontaneous Democracy Wall sprung up in 1978, upon which individuals pasted wall posters and essays reflecting criticisms and views of current issues. Other cities created their own democracy walls and individuals copied and exchanged writings; newspapers and publishing were more open. At the beginning, Deng tacitly sanctioned such intellectual expression for two reasons. Much of the criticism was directed at discredited leftist policies of the Cultural Revolution and Gang of Four; thus the people's criticism helped reduce the legitimacy of Hua Guofeng and his moderate left faction. In addition, U.S.-China relations were advancing steadily, and the ongoing liberalization boosted China's human rights image abroad as Deng was preparing for his historic visit to the United States in late 1978.

This period of openness known as Beijing Spring was short-lived, however. When the party leadership itself began to be criticized, Deng moved quickly to put a stop to free expression. From early 1979 on, unofficial publications were restricted, contacts with foreign journalists were discouraged, and outspoken intellectuals and populist leaders were arrested. Furthermore, demonstrations and unrest were occurring throughout the country, fueled in part by former Red Guards, originally from the cities, who had been sent to the countryside. Many on family visits for the Spring Festival, or lunar new year, now openly refused to return to a peasant existence. The October 1979 trial of Wei Jingsheng, an electrician at the Beijing Zoo and a leader of the pro-democracy movement, was highly publicized as a warning to others. (For more on Wei Jingsheng, see Chapter 5.)

In November 1979 the Beijing municipal authorities closed down Democracy Wall, saying that it was causing chaos and that people were using it to attack both the socialist system and the leadership of the Chinese Communist Party. Authorities limited the right to write wall posters. The clampdown begun in early 1979 was formalized by an amendment to the constitution in September 1980, which included restrictions on freedom of speech. Though expression was curtailed, the government did not broaden its repression of intellectuals to the degree done in previous mass campaigns. In any case, educational and cultural exchanges with other countries under the open door policies mitigated the amount of control that the CCP could exert over people's thoughts.

Educational Reforms

Compared to the Maoist era, the period under Deng's leadership saw a renewed appreciation of education and expertise. Deng considered a highly skilled work force and an improvement in China's scientific and technological capabilities key to the modernization process. During the Cultural Revolution, colleges and universities emphasized technical training, to quickly produce a large number of people with a moderate level of expertise. By the 1980s, leaders realized the limitations of this approach for both long-term scientific research and applied technological innovations. Deng himself, for example, acknowledged the limits of ''barefoot doctors'' trained this way in public health work and high-level medical research. Party and government control over higher education and research institutions, particularly the Chinese Academy of Sciences, was loosened accordingly.

University entrance examinations were restored in 1977; admissions were once again based more on ability than political background; and a new system of scholarships and loans was introduced in 1986. University faculty were given more authority, curricula were revised, four-year university programs were put back in place, and graduate programs developed. The number of university students grew significantly after the Cultural Revolution; by 1989 enrollment had topped 2 million, double the amount in 1979.

After 1978, many students and workers in mid-career were sent abroad for advanced studies, particularly in the natural sciences and technical fields. However, many institutions in China did not fully utilize the knowledge and skills of these individuals after they returned. Many scientists had to work in outdated facilities, for instance, while returning students with business degrees often could not put their knowledge of monetary policies or management concepts to use because of weak infrastructure or institutional resistance. Indeed, many workers and staff accustomed to guaranteed jobs regardless of their performance felt threatened by students who had studied abroad and been exposed to broader ideas and new ways of problem solving. All this contributed to a questioning of governmental authority in various aspects of social and political life.

The Chinese government increased investments in universities and specialized schools, but improvements in basic education have lagged behind. Great strides were achieved during the Maoist era to universalize at least primary education. Yet even as recently as 1989, over 20 percent of the rural population were illiterate or semiliterate. Attracting qualified teachers to rural settings with meager school facilities and supplies and a lower standard of living than they are accustomed to is an ongoing problem. Many children in the countryside are pulled out of school at an early age to work.

The government has made it a goal to develop a better educated and better trained work force. Nine-year education (i.e., completing junior middle school) was made compulsory in 1986, but has been difficult to implement, especially in the countryside. Nationally, the number of students enrolled in junior middle schools is over five times the number in senior middle schools. About 70 percent of primary school graduates go on to junior middle school, but only a third of China's youth progress beyond the ninth year of schooling. Finally, even with a better-trained work force, greater industrial efficiency cannot develop unless workplace values and attitudes change as well.

Population Policy

Maintaining the country's population level has been taken seriously by its leaders. In the early 1980s, the Chinese government began to focus on population issues. The State Family Planning Commission was established, and the one-child policy put in place. Growth rates have been maintained, but effective enforcement has been difficult, especially in rural areas.

The revised Marriage Law of 1980 (updating the 1950 Law) promoted the modern concepts of free choice of marriage partners, monogamy, equal rights for both sexes, and the right to divorce, representing a break from the values of feudal China. At the same time, family planning was written into the law, and the marriageable age was raised to twenty-two for men and twenty for women. Beginning in 1980, the government encouraged later childbearing and implemented a one-child family policy. With two-thirds of the population under thirty years old—the "baby boomers" of the Cultural Revolution era—a push had to be made in the 1980s and 1990s to limit population growth in order to try to keep China's population at 1.2 billion in the year 2000. A State Family Planning Commission was accordingly established in 1981.

The Chinese government began to resort to coercive methods in order to carry out the one-child policy, including limited educational opportunities for the second child, income reduction, and fines for having more than one child. The commission started extensive educational programs on contraception and family planning. The message on billboards and other materials was that, girl or boy, one child is the ideal. Extreme coercive methods included involuntary abortions or sterilizations. Controlling population growth is especially difficult in the countryside, because of lower education levels, stronger traditional values that favor sons, and the economic practicality of large families in a family-centered farming economy. As bureaucratic authority weakened, however, some people openly defied the one-child restriction and raised larger families. Furthermore, under the responsibility system, land was assigned to families based on the number of working males, which worked as a disincentive to small families. The authorities also found that penalties and fines do not always serve as effective deterrents.

A one-child family policy had broad social ramifications. Parents and grandparents typically doted on the child, nurturing a generation of spoiled "little emperors." Under the Chinese tradition in which a woman takes care of her husband's parents in old age, the elderly with only a daughter (or no children) would have no one to care for them. Female infanticide grew to such alarming levels that it was declared a criminal offense in 1983. Changing employment patterns and the shifting of enterprises away from providing comprehensive welfare/retirement benefits contributed to family uncertainties. Even with the one-child policy, China's population continued its rapid growth. It reached 1.1 billion at the end of 1991, forcing authorities to revise targets for the year 2000. Despite criticism from other countries (notably the United States) for the harsh population control methods sometimes employed, China's leaders recognized that disaster would loom if long-term plans were not carried out to ensure the survival of 22 percent of the world's population on 7 percent of the globe's arable land.

In Maoist China, residence and movement were strictly controlled. Permission had to be obtained to move to a new locale, and a residence card issued by the Public Security Bureau was required for housing, employment, and schooling, and to obtain annual ration coupons. Migration to urban centers became more difficult to control in an open economy, however, in which employment mobility was greater and goods more readily available. As a result, large numbers of those without residence cards, known as the "floating population," swelled the population of China's cities. Growing unemployment and increased illegal activities contributed to urban problems and unrest.

Economic reform policies had a major impact on employment patterns in China. The shift toward manufacturing and exports encouraged a migration to urban and industrial centers. For the returning youth as well as laborers from the countryside, there were more urban employment opportunities in a more open economy, beyond those controlled by work units. The "floating population" has been estimated to comprise as much as 10 percent of the population in China's large cities. Unemployment emerged as state-owned and other enterprises were unable to absorb the surplus labor.

Rapid Economic Growth and Repercussions

During periods of relative economic freedom, the Chinese economy has periodically overheated, contributing to rising inflation, price instability, overinvestment, disruptions in supplies, and other problems. The government has generally responded by reimposing price controls, increasing wages of state workers, reducing government investments, and attempting to better control credit availability and money supply. Since the beginning of the open door policy, the central government has carried out three such periods of retrenchment to stabilize the economy: 1980-1981, 1986, and 1988.

During the first slowdown, in 1980, China had to reduce imports and government expenditures, in part because of the considerable expenses incurred during the 1979 war with Vietnam. Government investments, in particular, were scaled back, and in the years 1981 to 1984 the government deficits dropped to between 3 billion and 5 billion yuan, close to budgeted amounts. When restrictions were subsequently relaxed, however, the economy grew by leaps and bounds: between 1982 and 1985 annual growth in gross national product (GNP) was about 14 percent.

Inflation became a major problem, reaching more than 10 percent in 1985, while prices of nonstaples reportedly rose 50 percent.

Retrenchment policies in 1986 slowed growth to 8 to 10 percent, but had only a limited impact on inflation; retail prices continued to outpace real wages, particularly in the cities. At times the government moved to maintain price controls on some food and consumer goods to combat inflation. At others, it removed controls in an effort to allow the artificially low fixed prices to move closer to actual market prices. Price reforms announced in 1987 caused consumer panic buying, pushing inflation even higher. Inflation soared above 20 percent in 1988, and as high as 50 percent in some cities. Subsidies to consumers were insufficient; and at times when these were reduced or lifted, urban residents experienced hardships. Several retrenchment policies were approved in 1988, signaling a major power gain by the conservatives in the central leadership.

Overall, Deng and Zhao stressed development of the coastal provinces over the interior. This uneven development was something that Mao had specifically aimed to avoid by shifting industrial development to inland regions. Most peasants in regions well-endowed with natural resources saw their standard of living improve under the reforms, from both rising government procurement prices for agricultural products and engagement in sideline businesses. While many entrepreneurial families achieved success, becoming "ten thousand yuan" families, their numbers were small relative to the entire population. Growth in per capita income was steady and comparable, doubling between 1985 and 1992 from 400 to 800 yuan for rural residents and from 800 to more than 1,600 yuan for urban residents. Still standards of living lagged in the countryside, especially the resource-poor hinterlands of central and southwest China. Capital needed for development of the interior has been scarce: government investment was limited and foreign investment absent. A large portion of development project funds from agencies such as the World Bank, however, was targeted for these regions.

The government fought a losing battle to balance its budget; producer and consumer subsidies represented a considerable drain on state finances. Making state enterprises more effective and profitable proved difficult. Although the proportion of collective enterprises to state-owned enterprises was rising, many of the latter were still unprofitable. Statistics vary, but it is believed that government subsidies increased from about $10 billion in 1988 to $14 billion in 1989—or nearly 18 percent of all government expenditures. Into the 1990s, 30 to 40 percent of China's state enterprises were still reported as unprofitable, with another third suffering hidden losses. Even so, the Chinese government was extremely cautious about closing down inefficient plants, as laid-off workers would have limited alternatives. Rather than gamble with serious labor unrest, the government was left with little choice but to continue subsidies while experimenting with policies to improve those firms' profitability.

Instability during the rapid growth years of 1984 to 1989 led to increasing consumer price subsidies that absorbed 12 to 15 percent of tax and revenues (other sources estimate 1985's consumer subsidies as high as $16 billion, representing over 20 percent of state revenues). The government's financial difficulties continued despite various measures, and the annual deficit increased to about 9.2 billion yuan in 1989 and 14 billion in 1990. (Western analysts place deficits at much higher rates, increasing steadily from about 17 billion yuan in 1986 to nearly 35 billion yuan in 1988.) The government came to depend on loans and bond issues to cover the deficits. Efforts were also made to recentralize tax collection, since the provincial governments were not handling this effectively or properly.

The economy further heated up because of the availability of credit and relaxed money supply through special banks, a problem made worse by official corruption. The manipulation of prices was seen as partly to blame for bottlenecks in the flow of materials and supplies, and officials misused loan funds, engaging, for example, in real estate speculation. As early as 1981, Zhao Ziyang identified weak administration as a problem. In his report to the Fifth National People's Congress he stated:

[owing] to the inadequacies in our laws and regulations

covering the administrative and economic fields as well as in our management system, many weak links still exist. . . . At present, such criminal activities as graft, embezzlement, speculation, profiteering, smuggling and tax evasion are rife in some areas . . . What is particularly serious is that some economic units and some government functionaries connive at, shield, or even directly participate in these activities.

Many directors of enterprises used personal connections to obtain goods and supplies at fixed prices and to resell them at the much higher market prices, protected by corrupt party and government officials. Though the leaders continuously pledged to crack down on this and other forms of corruption, their efforts failed to achieve conspicuous results.

In 1988, several retrenchment policies were approved in an attempt to stabilize prices and supply, including the reimposition of price controls on basic raw materials, such as oil, electricity, and timber, and on shipping and rail transport services. Allowing provincial authorities to seek foreign investment and giving various banks greater lending authority led to high investment and rapid growth. To better regulate credit and the money supply, the government implemented structural changes in the People's Bank of China (the central bank) and other financial institutions; the bank thereupon devalued the yuan repeatedly, which benefited exports while making imports more expensive.

Weakening Central Control: The Struggle Against Spiritual Pollution and Economic Corruption

As the 1980s began, rampant corruption and increasing economic crime added to social instability that threatened the legitimacy of the Communist regime. Public support for China's principles and institutions had eroded. China began to suffer from a vacuum of social values: The egalitarian values of Maoist China had deteriorated after the Cultural Revolution, and a new set of guiding values had yet to be formed. For the time being, the aim of achieving material wealth was paramount. A tradition of respect for the law had not yet evolved, and embezzlement, tax evasion, foreign currency speculation, smuggling, and bribery were on the rise. *Guanxi,* or personal relations, often took the form of bribery and corruption. In this economic free-for-all, utilizing the "back door" of personal relations was often the most effective way of cutting through bureaucratic red tape; this widespread practice continued to make a mockery of procedures in many Chinese institutions.

The 1983 Anti-Spiritual Pollution Campaign

To combat the negative activities that came with economic reform and capitalist methods, the Chinese Communist Party launched an "Anti-Spiritual Pollution" campaign in 1983 to reverse the Western influences blamed for China's problems. The Chinese were urged to struggle against "bourgeois liberalization," while such Western-influenced phenomena as rock music were discouraged and even labeled pornographic. Deng defined "spiritual pollution" in an address to the Twelfth Central Committee as:

the spreading of various decadent and declining ideologies of the bourgeoisie and other exploiting classes and the spreading of sentiments of distrust regarding the cause of socialism and communism and the leadership of the Communist Party.

The effort to separate technological from spiritual values was reminiscent of imperial China's failed attempt to absorb Western technology without its corresponding values. The campaign coincided with the central party's three-year political purge to re-educate, reorganize, and reregister the party's 40 million members. This purge targeted the leftists who had swelled the party ranks during the Cultural Revolution and were proving resistant to Dengist reform policies. Thus Deng's definition of spiritual pollution, which included anything that could be construed as challenging the authority of the CCP, suggested the potential for another mass political campaign. Assurances were given that the campaign would not inhibit trade or cultural exchanges with foreign countries, however, and in any case, the campaign never gathered much momentum. Unlike previous campaigns of the 1950s and 1960s, Chinese society was no longer isolated from the world, and

people now had more control over their lives, making it difficult to force them to participate in such activities. By the end of 1983, Hu and Zhao had moved to end the Anti-Spiritual Pollution campaign.

Reassertion of Central Control

During the mid-1980s, China's top leadership began to polarize into reformist and conservative factions. The top levels of the Chinese Communist Party had sustained their collective leadership style through the first years of reform under Deng Xiaoping, Hu Yaobang, and Zhao Ziyang. Forced retirements and purges continued, and by 1985, the country had the beginnings of what was referred to as the "third echelon" of leaders—the first being the revolutionary-period leaders, and the second being leaders who had risen to power since 1949. Deng was now using administrative purges at all levels to remove party cadres, military leaders, and government officials from the second echelon, including those who were ineffective in implementing reform policies or felt to be active or passive obstructionists.

Deng did not seem satisfied with his hand-picked successors, however, despite their commitment to the reform agenda. Major personnel changes were made in late 1986, partly in response to the social unrest that was being manifested in various forms throughout the country. Hu Yaobang was forced to resign as general secretary in January 1987, and Zhao Ziyang was pressured by Deng to accept the position. At the thirteenth party congress, held in the fall of 1987, Deng resigned from the Central Committee, thereby relinquishing his Politburo membership and his seat on its powerful Standing Committee. Chen Yun and Li Xiannian were removed from the Central Committee's Standing Committee, and Peng Zhen from the Politburo.

Zhao Ziyang, formally elected general secretary at the party congress, set the tone by continuing to advocate Deng's economic reform policies. He was also made first vice chairman of the Central Military Commission, while Yang Shangkun (b. 1907) remained permanent vice chairman. Zhao resigned from the premiership, which he had held since 1980, and Li Peng (b. 1928) was named acting premier until his confirmation by the National People's Congress in the spring of 1988. Although Deng had essentially retired from formal leadership—he held only the important post of CMC chairman—he continued to exercise considerable power from behind the scenes. Leading the reform drive, Zhao emphasized that prices should be set more by free market forces such as supply and demand than by state control. He also sought to attract more foreign investment, promoted China's exports, and advocated creation of a civil service examination system so as to reduce party control over government administration.

The new seventeen-member Politburo included Zhao and Hu; vice premiers Li Peng, Qiao Shi (b. 1924), and Yao Yilin; Yang Shangkun, Hu Qili (b. 1929), head of the Party Secretariat, and Foreign Minister Wu Xueqian. Among the new members were Li Ruihuan (b. 1934) and Jiang Zemin (mayors of Tianjin and Shanghai, respectively). The five-member Standing Committee consisted of Zhao Ziyang, in charge overall; Li Peng, State Council; Qiao Shi, party affairs; Hu Qili, Secretariat and propaganda matters; and Yao Yilin, economic issues.

When he became premier, Li Peng's influence rose. Advocating a conservative approach to economic reforms and political liberalization, Li and other like-minded CCP leaders began to push for more centralized power. It was clear that the rising social unrest was related to the changes brought about by the process of rapid reforms, particularly inflationary pressures. More important, they believed the party's reduced role in the economy would inevitably lead to a loss of party influence in other spheres of national life. Thus a conservative group within the party and government advocated slowing the reforms and postponing further liberalization.

A shift in power from the reformists to the conservatives began to be evident with the latter's success in getting retrenchment policies approved in the National People's Congress in the fall of 1988. In March 1989, Premier Li Peng's report to the Seventh National People's Congress expressed the government's need to reassert central control over the economy and the political arena. Although there had been some talk of political reforms to promote democracy

as part of the seventh Five-Year Plan (1986-1990), no specifics had been given. Li Peng's group clearly indicated that China would not follow the Soviet path of glasnost and perestroika. Greater political participation would not accompany greater economic freedoms.

From Isolation to Active Foreign Relations

The pragmatic Chinese leaders of the 1980s recognized that increased political, cultural, and economic relations with other countries would be essential to China's modernization drive. Learning from the experience of the early years of the People's Republic, they sought to avoid overdependence on any one country. Having broken off relations with the Soviet Union, China's leaders were careful not to replace it with reliance on the United States and instead pursued an independent foreign policy. China's foreign policy from the late 1970s on can be characterized as an attempt to balance two strategies: pursuit of economic relationships with many countries to strengthen national development, while addressing China's security concerns. For the latter, China sought to build stronger friendships through trade. The opening of relations with the United States prompted a more open attitude toward Japan and West European countries; economic and political diplomacy converged. By the time Beijing and Moscow re-established relations in 1989, world power had become more equally balanced.

Full Normalization of Relations with the United States, 1978-1979

Although the pace of U.S.-Chinese relations had slowed since 1972, with U.S.-Taiwan relations still the major obstacle, progress toward full normalization accelerated at the end of 1978. The Chinese firmly expressed three conditions: the end of U.S. diplomatic relations with Taiwan; abrogation of the U.S.-Taiwan defense treaty of 1954; and withdrawal of U.S. military forces from Taiwan. Washington responded with its own basis for normalization: continued American commercial and economic ties with

Taiwan; insistence that China commit to resolving relations with Taiwan peacefully; and continued U.S. arms sales to Taiwan after U.S.-China normalization.

By 1978, President Jimmy Carter was prepared to end diplomatic relations with Taipei and recognize Beijing. Through Leonard Woodcock, then head of the U.S. liaison office in China, the United States presented a three-point proposal to the Chinese leadership in December 1978. The issue of arms sales remained unresolved; in spite of the evident disagreement, Deng was willing to set that issue aside in order to achieve normalization. Thus on December 15, President Carter announced that the United States and the People's Republic of China would establish full diplomatic relations on January 1, 1979; that official relations with Taiwan would concurrently end; and that the United States was giving the required one year's notice to Taiwan of its intention to terminate the 1954 Mutual Defense Treaty. Embassies in Beijing and Washington would be established on March 1, 1979, and the United States pledged to withdraw its remaining military forces from Taiwan within four months, while continuing unofficial cultural and commercial ties.

Deng was invited to the United States, and his January 1979 visit was successful in many ways. Three agreements were signed: on science and technology, cultural exchanges, and the establishment of consulates (San Francisco, Houston; Guangzhou, Shanghai). Americans were charmed by the image of Deng wearing a ten-gallon hat, and Deng was later selected as a *Time* magazine "Man of the Year."

The immediate reaction in Taiwan was heated. President Chiang Ching-kuo (Chiang Kai-shek's son) and government officials were offended that the United States had not consulted them before ending formal diplomatic relations. Protests were mounted at the U.S. embassy in Taiwan and elsewhere, but to no avail. The tide had decisively turned. In 1979, Congress passed the Taiwan Relations Act in which the United States declared its intention to maintain relations with Taiwan. To handle consular, cultural, and trade-related affairs, the United States set up its nongovernmental American Institute in Taiwan (AIT) in Taipei, while Taiwan set up the Coordinating Council for North American Affairs (CCNAA)

Americans were charmed by Deng on his historic January 1979 visit to the United States, which followed shortly after the United States and China normalized relations.

in Washington. A crucial point in the act was inclusion of the U.S. commitment to continue to sell arms "to enable Taiwan to maintain a sufficient self-defense capability."

With the diplomatic aspect of relations between China and the United States at last established, other aspects, particularly economic, could be attended to. After the issue of frozen assets from 1949 in both China and the United States was finally resolved in 1979, the two countries could proceed to work out details in their trade relations. A trade agreement was signed in 1980, and China was granted most favored nation (MFN) trading status; this allowed Chinese goods to have imposed on them U.S. import duties that were normal for most trade partners, a status that must be renewed annually by the U.S. Congress. Other agreements signed that year provided for direct airline service and port access in each country; called for limited growth in China's textile exports; and designated certain cities for the opening of additional consulates.

Under the Reagan administration, the issue of arms sales to Taiwan intensified as the United States continued sales rather than gradually reducing them. The Chinese leaders in Beijing were angered since these actions were a blatant reversal of the policy expressed in the 1972 Shanghai Communiqué. Beijing refused to commit to a statement of peaceful reunification with Taiwan, emphasizing the principle of sovereignty. During Premier Zhao Ziyang's January 1984 visit to the United States, the Chinese position was made clear. "We are seeking a peaceful settlement of the Taiwan question in good faith. But we cannot make a commitment to any foreign country that only peaceful means will be used . . . because this is China's internal affair and within China's sovereign rights." Nonetheless, China had begun to articulate the idea that there could be two political systems operating within one China, similar to the pledge made to Hong Kong that two economic systems would be allowed within one country after Hong Kong's reversion to China in 1997.

Sino-Soviet Normalization

After the intense border clashes in 1969, the Chinese and Soviet leaders maintained a more stable but still distant relationship. In 1970 and again in 1972, Moscow proposed entering into a nonaggression pact but Beijing, which was nearing an opening with Washington, appeared to be in no hurry, despite intensification of the Soviet arms buildup and positioning of missiles. Efforts at border negotiations stalled; even Romania tried to help mediate in 1974. In 1979, the National People's Congress decided to give the required one year's notice of intent to allow the thirty-year Sino-Soviet Treaty of Friendship, Alliance, and Mutual Assistance signed in 1950 to expire.

On the Chinese side, three obstacles remained to normalization of relations: the positioning of Soviet troops at their common border, the 1979 Soviet invasion of Afghanistan, and Soviet support of Vietnam's presence and policies in Cambodia. Throughout the

1970s, Beijing viewed Soviet actions as expansionist and saw the Soviet navy's presence in Vietnam's Cam Ranh Bay as a security threat. But similar to their phased approach to normalization with the United States, the Chinese leaders felt such political obstacles should not stand in the way of building economic and trade relations. In July 1985, the Soviet Union and China signed a $14 billion trade pact as well as an agreement for economic and technical cooperation that pledged Soviet assistance to the Chinese in building industrial plants and modernizing important sectors such as energy, coal, chemicals, and transport. By 1986 Soviet General Secretary Mikhail Gorbachev had begun to address withdrawal of troops from Afghanistan as well as from the Mongolian border with China. In response, Deng indicated China's willingness to consider normalization, in the event that Vietnamese troops were withdrawn from Cambodia.

Throughout 1987 the Soviet Union pushed for a summit meeting with China, while maintaining that it had only limited influence on Vietnam. Hanoi's 1988 announcement of plans to withdraw a large number of troops from Cambodia by the beginning of 1989 cleared the way for a summit meeting. Accordingly, in December 1988, announcements were made in both the Soviet Union and in China of a summit between Gorbachev and Deng, to be held in Beijing in mid-1989. Diplomatic relations were reestablished in May 1989. After the subsequent dissolution of the Soviet Union in December 1991, China signed bilateral economic and trade cooperation agreements with nearly all the former Soviet republics.

Sino-Soviet-American Power Balance

By the late 1980s, both China and the United States had perceived a greatly reduced Soviet threat in Asia. Both the Sino-Japanese Treaty of Peace and Friendship, signed in August 1978, and the Sino-American communiqué, signed in December 1978, emphasized opposition to efforts by any other country or group of countries trying to seek hegemony in the Asia-Pacific region—a message clearly aimed at the Soviet Union. Regional security concerns were relaxed as the United States and Soviet Union removed intermediate-range missiles from Europe and Asia.

China's warming relationship with the United States, and improving relations between the Soviet Union and the United States, put the three countries on a more equal footing. In the new power balance, China was to play an increasing role in maintaining stability in the region as the United States decreased its military presence. It was therefore in the U.S. interest to strengthen China's military as a counterweight to the Soviet army. Under the Foreign Military Sales (FMS) program, the U.S. government signed agreements beginning in the mid-1980s to sell more than $600 million in weapons to help modernize the People's Liberation Army.

For its part, the Soviet Union stressed a three-way balance of power to achieve Sino-Soviet normalization, in an attempt to reassure the United States that it was not working for a return to the 1950s cold war-era Communist alliance. Furthermore, the Soviet Union under Gorbachev's leadership signaled a retreat from expansionist policies through its apparent approval of political changes in Eastern Europe and its movements to withdraw Soviet troops from Eastern Europe and Afghanistan.

The three-way power balance also allowed China to pursue an independent foreign policy. China would become dependent on neither the United States nor the Soviet Union to counter the other, and its relations with other countries would be more independent. China pledged to uphold the Five Principles of Peaceful Coexistence. The twelfth party congress, convened in September 1992, articulated the core of China's foreign policy:

The Chinese Government pursues an independent foreign policy, firmly opposes hegemonism, and resolutely stands by all peoples who are subjected to oppression and aggression. China will never attach itself to any big power or group of powers, nor yield to any outside pressure. We support the non-aligned movement.

Unlike in the past, Beijing now tried to develop foreign relations with other countries on criteria other than challenging Soviet influence. South Asia is a case in point. China's support for Pakistan beginning in the mid-1960s was bolstered by the combination of Indo-Pakistani antagonism and strong Indo-Soviet ties. China began to make independent moves to improve relations with India in the 1970s. Exchange of ambassadors, broken off after the 1962 border war between the two countries, was resumed (India had recognized the Beijing government in 1950). Chinese support for Pakistan, nevertheless, remained strong; in 1988, 70 percent of Chinese aid to developing countries went to Pakistan.

Nearly all East European countries suspended party ties with China when China and the Soviet Union were hotly engaged in ideological disputes, but these ties were revived as part of China's opening to the world. China also continued to support third world countries, with whom China identified. Increased trade and economic relations became a more important vehicle than foreign aid for strengthening foreign relations. The 1980s can be characterized as a decade in which China actively pursued economic diplomacy with all states and ideology was no longer of central importance.

Economic Diplomacy and Trade Relations

In carrying out the policies of opening to the outside world, China adhered to expanding economic and technical exchanges and cooperation with both the industrialized and the developing countries. The more independent path was demonstrated by Zhao Ziyang's four-week tour of Africa at the end of 1982, followed soon thereafter by Hu Yaobang's visit to confer with the leaders of Communist parties in Romania and Yugoslavia, as well as Foreign Minister Qian Qichen's visit to other East European states.

Building trade and economic relations has been a central focus. China has sought cooperative agreements in science and technology as well as trade and loan agreements with the developed countries. Japan, China's principal trading partner, signed a five-year trade agreement in 1979 and extended $1.5 billion in low-interest loans to China. When Japan's prime minister, Yasuhiro Nakasone, visited China in 1984, a loan package totaling $2.1 billion over seven years was signed. In 1985, General Secretary Hu Yaobang, Premier Zhao Ziyang, and President Li Xiannian visited an unprecedented number of developed countries with the intention of strengthening trade relations.

Indeed, trade relations flourished through the 1980s, although Japan remained China's largest trading partner. Japan's exports in 1985 were valued at $12.5 billion, about 30 percent of all China's imports. Although Hong Kong's trade volume with China grew more quickly in the late 1980s, Japan remained an important supplier of electronics and machinery. A third of China's trade with European countries was with West Germany, whose two-way trade with China doubled between 1984 and 1989 to $5 billion. Its strongest exports to China were industrial machinery and scientific instruments.

In the early years of the open door policy, China sustained a trade deficit with the United States, even during the 1980-1981 retrenchment period in which government spending was curbed. Two-way trade increased rapidly, and according to U.S. Department of Commerce statistics, was in balance from 1983 to 1985. China's exports took off dramatically beginning in 1986, however. By 1989, Chinese imports from the United States had grown to $5.8 billion from $3.1 billion three years earlier, while its exports to the United States that year were more than double the level of imports, at $12 billion. In the early period, the top U.S. export to China was cereals, especially wheat, which averaged $1.4 billion in the years 1980 to 1982; cereals exports dropped considerably in subsequent years. By 1990, the top U.S. exports were transport equipment (especially airplanes), fertilizers, cereals, cotton, and specialized machinery.

Clothing and apparel, a low capital and labor-intensive industry, had become a major export for China. China's textile exports to the United States grew so rapidly in the mid-1980s that the United States moved to negotiate a bilateral textile trade agreement, under which China was to limit annual growth of apparel and textile exports to 3 percent beginning in 1988 for the following four years. Some Chinese enterprises circumvented these quotas, however, by shipping items as exports to Hong Kong, where they were relabeled and shipped onward to the United States. When values of such illegal transshipments are included, they show China's trade surplus with

the United States growing even more rapidly, doubling from about $3 billion in 1987 and 1988 to more than $6 billion in 1989 (and by 1993 it would multiply further, to $23 billion). China's ballooning trade surplus and continuing transshipments of textiles and clothing became flash points in U.S.-China trade relations.

China's two-way world trade volume grew at an astonishing rate during the 1980s. From 1982 to 1989 the total value nearly tripled, from $42 billion to $111 billion, most of it with Hong Kong, Japan, and the United States, according to China's customs statistics. As labor costs in other parts of East Asia climbed, many labor-intensive industries from these regions, such as apparel, shoes, and toys, shifted production to China in the form of joint ventures; the main sources of such investment were Hong Kong, Taiwan, and Singapore. China's economic reforms and export-led growth policies contributed to the country's high growth, even as growth in the East Asian NICs slowed down. China also benefited from the move by countries in East Asia, Australasia, and Southeast Asia to build up intraregional trade, partly in response to anticipated sluggish import demand from North America and Western Europe.

The Tiananmen Square Incident and Its Aftermath

Many of the forces and events leading up to the mass demonstrations in Tiananmen Square in the spring of 1989 reflected the rapid social change that had accompanied China's modernization drive and reintegration into the world community since the beginning of its open door economic policy in 1978. General expectations were rising, and people now had more means to shape their own lives. The rural social order was radically changed with the dismantling of the commune structure, which had been in place for about two decades. The return to the family as the unit of production concurrently reduced the instruments of government control over people's lives. Urban residents were hard-hit by inflation, which had risen to more than 20 percent in 1988. With the widespread reductions in the work force that came with restructuring, unemployment and underemployment contributed to unrest. Reforms had brought substantial change, and also economic confusion.

The granting of greater authority to local officials and enterprises had reduced the central government's ability to control both the economy and society. The administrative purge begun in 1983 further reduced the authority of party cadres and government officials. Some, for example, sought to maintain their power through other means in the new economic order—which included illegal activities. Under the two-tier price system for many commodities, including producer goods, many took advantage of opportunities to obtain goods at a controlled price and sell them at the higher market price. Furthermore, the rampant corruption, influence peddling, and ostentatious life-styles of officials and their family members added to the dissatisfaction and growing cynicism among the people. A large alienated group was the youth of the Red Guard generation, especially those seeking to return to the cities. As the previously strict control of population movements through residency permits and controls by one's work unit began to break down, more daring individuals gradually began to disregard such restrictions and return to the cities. This led urban populations to swell with returning students (many now in their twenties and thirties), unemployed workers, and peasants seeking work.

Social Unrest

Social unrest took several forms in the late 1980s. Worker unrest erupted, and although many of the incidents were localized they were increasing in number. It was student unrest, however, led by a new generation of university students, that would be articulated more clearly and spread more widely in influence. Before the Tiananmen Square demonstrations of 1989, some of the issues students rallied around could not be considered political, in terms of a consciousness of political rights. The xenophobic actions taken against African and other foreign students from the third world in 1986 and 1988, for example, stemmed from jealousy and a feeling of unfairness that their dormitories and living conditions were better than those of the Chinese students. Some

university students demanded greater student participation and representation in decision making; some demanded better food. Even the student protests in 1985 against Hu Yaobang for his close association with Japanese Prime Minister Nakasone had a xenophobic ring. In expressing fear of Japan's economic aggression (even though the central authorities encouraged Japanese economic investment in China), the protesters recalled images and emotions from Japan's military transgressions against the Chinese people in the 1930s and 1940s. In addition, the Japanese education ministry's plan to revise Japan's history textbooks and remove the notion of "aggression" in describing Japan's wartime activity and the term "massacre" to describe its brutal invasion and occupation of Nanjing during the 1930s evoked a highly emotional response in China. Carried away by romanticism, Chinese students likened themselves to the May Fourth-era student patriots who passionately protested China's forfeit of political rights to Japan in 1919.

Another focus of unrest was among Tibetans, who felt threatened by increasing numbers of Han Chinese settlers moving to Tibet with government encouragement. Protests grew in the late 1980s, culminating in the government's bloody repression in March 1988, in which numerous monks, nuns, and civilians were killed. Martial law was imposed on the Tibetan capital of Lhasa the following year and would not be lifted until May 1990. Beijing minimized the riots but their suppression left a bitter residue of emotion among an already disaffected minority population.

China's leaders considered the growing social unrest in various parts of China so serious that it was a factor in the decision to oust Hu Yaobang from the party leadership in 1987. As tensions rose in China, the government increasingly frowned on contacts with foreigners, and several foreign journalists were expelled from China beginning in 1987. Student demonstrations had become frequent and widespread. In Shanghai, for example, where popular support for the students was strong, some 50,000 marchers gathered in People's Square in December 1986 and became bold enough to issue four demands to their mayor: the right to debate and to put up posters, press coverage of the demonstrations, assurances of safety, and the legality of the protests. Large rallies took place in other cities, including Beijing and Nanjing. In some, participants tactfully insisted that their sentiments were nationalistic. They were fed up with corruption, but by expressing support for Deng and the Four Modernizations, they stressed their support for the socialist system. Hu Yaobang is believed to have been closely linked with the intellectuals and students who were calling for political change. Regardless of whether he could have better controlled the rising unrest or changed the circumstances, Hu ended up being forced to take the blame for not dealing with the student demonstrations effectively and was removed from his position as general secretary of the party in 1987.

Increasing Political Consciousness

Ironically, even though students had once denounced Hu Yaobang in the 1985 demonstrations against Japan, he was held up as a hero after he was removed from office for not having taken harsh measures against them. His death in April 1989 provided a focal point for social dissatisfaction: pro-democracy rallies that also expressed open criticism of the party leadership gathered in force, reminiscent of the April 1976 rallies commemorating Zhou Enlai. The support by many workers for these 1989 demonstrations was significant, as was the fact that intellectuals took an active role in supporting the students' calls for political rights and press freedoms; journalists were especially active.

The depth of political consciousness and breadth of mass support for the demonstrators grew and converged in the spring of 1989. Concurrently, hard-liners in the central government were gathering strength, shaping the eventual government response to the unrest. Hu's forced resignation in 1987 had been an early indication of the leadership's intolerance of student demonstrations. In April 1989 students at Beijing University, Qinghua University, and other schools launched a boycott of classes; at the same time the government banned Shanghai's *World Economic Herald*, which was publishing criticisms of the government. Rallies in Beijing were held al-

most daily, attended by over 100,000. Some other cities held their own rallies. Shanghai protests gained in intensity following an incident involving a train accident in which student protesters were killed; the train was subsequently set on fire, supposedly by outraged workers. Other cities experienced looting and vandalism as a form of protest.

Students came from throughout China to Beijing, onlookers began to join in, and journalists began to speak out. As the movement took on greater proportions, students increasingly began to address the concerns of workers and the general public, such as inflation and corruption among officials. Students formed a leadership group including Wang Dan, Chai Ling, and Wuer Kaixi and began a hunger strike. The hunger strike attracted sympathy and more direct involvement from Beijing's citizens, who brought water, medical, and other supplies to those at Tiananmen Square. In early May the student leaders demanded that government leaders open a dialogue with them—a demand dismissed by the government under hard-line premier Li Peng. Li and President Yang Shangkun declared martial law in parts of Beijing on May 20. Demonstrators were now calling for the resignation of Li, Yang, and Deng. Journalists, including the international press, paid little heed to restrictions. The demonstrations gained considerable momentum when art students installed a sculpture, the Goddess of Democracy, at Tiananmen Square on May 29 and 30.

The dynamics of the Tiananmen movement cannot be separated from developments in the Soviet Union, particularly Mikhail Gorbachev's visit to China in mid-May to sign the Sino-Soviet joint communiqué re-establishing formal relations between the two countries. China and the Soviet Union were actually heading in opposite directions at this time: the Soviet Union was moving toward openness and democratic political reforms, while China was not only retreating from economic reforms but tightening political controls. The students looked to Gorbachev's leadership with hope and admiration, and they knew that the international press focused on Beijing during the Gorbachev visit would lend visibility to their own cause. This powerful leverage in part made them bolder in their interaction with the Chinese government. The government, for its part, felt it could not afford to lose face by giving in to the demonstrators, especially with the entire world watching. In the end, the Chinese leaders took their chances on international opprobrium and dealt with the demonstrators harshly.

Hard-liners Gain Power: The Massacre at Tiananmen Square

While mass rallies were gaining momentum in Beijing and elsewhere, a power struggle was apparently being waged among the top leadership, with the military adding to the complex situation. General Secretary Zhao Ziyang appeared more conciliatory toward the demonstrators, while Premier Li Peng advocated a firmer approach. Although Deng had promoted increased liberalization, thereby boosting Zhao's position, he now seemed ultimately to agree with Li and the hard-liners on political matters. By the end of May, Zhao had been removed from office and placed under house arrest.

Various divisions of the People's Liberation Army were called in to put down the demonstrations. At first they were sent in unarmed, and the demonstrators tried to win them over to their cause. Seeing that this approach was ineffective in dispersing the crowds, party leaders then ordered the solders to be sent in heavily armed. Demonstrators seized buses and other vehicles to block the streets. Many vehicles were set on fire. With nearly all the international media in Beijing to cover Gorbachev's visit, much of the drama was televised all over the world. Speculation even of a pending civil war began to spread as various generals suggested their willingness or unwillingness to follow the central government's orders. But in the still dark morning hours of June 4, tanks rolled into Beijing and opened fire on unarmed demonstrators, prompting angered crowds to attack soldiers. Videotapes and firsthand accounts of the events were quickly transmitted internationally, though the media were temporarily blacked out in China. The government is believed to have called in divisions from other regions because it feared local military forces might be unwilling to fire on citizens, and disinformation was supposedly given to the out-

The 1989 Tiananmen pro-democracy demonstrations were the culmination of social unrest in China in the 1980s. Here, students erect a statue of the Goddess of Democracy in Tiananmen Square, just days before the massacre.

side troops to reduce the possibility that they might rebel against orders.

The days after the harsh quelling of the mass movement were chaotic. Attempts were made to restrict the movements of foreign journalists, though they were nearly impossible to enforce. Live transmissions through the Cable News Network (CNN) and the Columbia Broadcasting System (CBS) were stopped for several days. Exactly what happened or how many died and were injured will probably never be known. The Western press initially estimated as many as 5,000 deaths, with 10,000 injured. For several days, officials denied that the massacre had even taken place, although news of the attack reached other cities quickly. Eventually, the government acknowledged up to 300 deaths but claimed that most of the dead were soldiers. Chinese leaders minimized casualties among the demonstrators, while praising the soldiers and emphasizing the primary importance of restoring public order. Amnesty International later estimated that at least 1,000 had died in Beijing and 300 in Chengdu.

Protests were launched in numerous cities, in Hong Kong and Taiwan, and even in other countries. Unlike during previous mass movements, this time good telecommunications, particularly facsimile machines, played a crucial role in helping coordinate the student movement and providing information beyond the official government media, which the people had come to distrust. Several Chinese foreign ministry officials abroad, unable to uphold official statements on the events, held press conferences voicing support for the demonstrators; some resigned and applied for political asylum. In the subsequent weeks massive arrests of student leaders and demonstrators followed. The pro-democracy demonstrators were branded as counterrevolutionary; their activities were deemed antigovernment.

Aftermath

The Tiananmen incident was a turning point in determining the post-Deng leadership. Deng had already resigned from almost all party and government posts, and rarely appeared in public. His health had deteriorated greatly. Many question Deng's role in the Tiananmen events: were he and a small group of retired octogenarian leaders responsible for the decision to brutally put down the demonstration, thereby jeopardizing his reform and modernization program and risking international backlash? Or had the hardline leaders really called the shots, manipulating Deng, after gaining the edge over the moderate leaders in the Politburo? In any event, Deng appeared on national television on June 9 to defend the government's action and to emphasize law and order.

Later it became known that Deng had disregarded constitutional process and manipulated those in China's ruling institutions to preserve his power. It was up to the Standing Committee of the National People's Congress to decide on martial law, although partial martial law could be invoked by the State Council. The martial law Li Peng declared on May 20 was only for portions of Beijing, and there is some question as to whether or not the State Council actually voted on the matter. Moreover, although the NPC has the right to override the decree, it was prevented from convening until June 29. There appeared to be inside maneuvering of the Central Committee and NPC Standing Committee to support Deng's decision and quiet opposing views.

Placed under house arrest, Zhao Ziyang was no longer seen in public; other reformers thought sympathetic to Zhao and the demonstrators were purged. The fourth plenary session of the Thirteenth Central Committee was called promptly on June 23. China's leaders described the events as a "counterrevolutionary rebellion," the aim of which was to "overthrow the leadership of the Chinese Communist Party and to subvert the socialist People's Republic of China." Zhao Ziyang, they concluded, had made the mistake of supporting the turmoil and splitting the party. He was dismissed as general secretary, Politburo Standing Committee member, and first vice chairman of the Central Military Commission. Jiang Zemin (b. 1926), mayor and party secretary of Shanghai and Politburo member, replaced Zhao as general secretary. The Central Committee articulated China's pledge to continue its open door economic policies. Other "partial adjustments" were made: removal of Hu Qili from all posts, including the Politburo Standing Committee, and the removal of others on the Central Committee Secretariat who were Zhao supporters. Jiang Zemin, Song Ping (b. 1917), and Li Ruihuan were elected to the Standing Committee.

In November, at the fifth plenary session, Deng resigned his last official position as chairman of the Central Military Commission. Jiang assumed that position; Yang Shangkun was named first vice chairman and Liu Huaqing (b. 1917), vice chairman of the CMC. Vice Premier Qiao Shi, who was also a Politburo Standing Committee member and chairman of the Discipline Inspection Commission (which continued to play a central role in the aftermath of the Tiananmen crackdown), began to take on increasing prominence in China's leadership circles.

Leaders throughout the world condemned the actions of the Chinese government in dealing with the students and demonstrators, though in many ways these acts were more symbolic than substantial. As a response to the brutal crackdown and subsequent arrests, the United States and most developed countries imposed sanctions on China as a criticism of its leaders' violation of human rights. Government loans were denied; the U.S. government stopped its sales of military technology. The World Bank suspended consideration of China's loan requests of $780 million, and the United Nations passed a resolution condemning the Chinese government's actions. Sanctions were not uniform, however; many Asian states maintained open relations with Beijing.

Tensions between China and the United States were further strained by the Bush administration's decision to grant a special allowance for Chinese students to remain in the United States, and by U.S. protection of Fang Lizhi, a dissident astrophysicist, in Beijing. After first being expelled from the party and then unjustifiably accused of playing a major role in encouraging the student protests, Fang and his wife, Li Shuxian, had taken refuge at the U.S. embassy, and the United States resolved not to hand them over to Chinese authorities. But the hollowness of U.S. moral condemnation was revealed when the Bush administration sent two high-ranking officials secretly to Beijing in late 1989 for talks with Deng despite an official U.S. suspension of high-level contacts with China.

The Chinese government did not seem intimidated by world criticism, and its leaders strove to appear confident that "business as usual" would continue. China's leaders cautiously watched the political transformation in Eastern Europe, however, where Communist parties were falling from power. Particularly alarming was the revolt in Romania, China's long-time ally, in which President Ceaucescu and his wife were publicly executed. Official delegations between China and these countries decreased significantly after 1989. Fearing that movements in Eastern Europe might trigger mass political activism in China, the CCP strengthened its resolve to hold tightly to the reins of power. Believing that the decade of reform policies had allowed the economy to spin out of control, the conservative leaders wanted to regain political control over the economy and, therefore, over people's lives.

Stability and control were repeated as themes in official statements. The party's resolve to exert its power is reflected in Li Peng's televised speech to announce the lifting of martial law in Beijing on January 11, 1990.

This fact [i.e., lifting martial law] shows once again to the whole country and the whole world that the Chinese Communist Party, the Chinese government, and the Chinese people are capable of running their own affairs well and maintaining a long-term stable political, economic and social development. No matter what may happen in the world, we shall unswervingly follow the socialist road.

The CCP's gamble proved worthwhile: it strengthened its grip on power, and the negative repercussions of the Tiananmen massacre remained limited and brief. Japan took the initiative to restore China's place in the international community, advocating a resumption of loan disbursements to China at a July 1990 Group of Seven meeting. The World Bank and the Asian Development Bank quickly followed suit. Although the secret visit of U.S. officials to China was controversial, it nevertheless opened the way for Chinese concessions, such as the decision to allow Fang Lizhi and his wife to leave China.

The Persian Gulf War provided China with an opportunity to begin to regain world respect. As one of the five permanent members of the UN Security Council, China denounced Iraqi aggression and the invasion of Kuwait (even though China abstained from voting on resolutions against Iraq). World opinion of China shifted as the events of Tiananmen Square gradually faded from prominence. Economic relations resumed, and although China's trade volume dipped in 1990, it rebounded the following year. Japan, for example, signed a loan agreement pledging $7.7 billion to be paid out during 1990-1995. By 1990, tourism had climbed back to its 1988 level (earning the country $2.2 billion in foreign exchange) and China successfully hosted the eleventh Asian Games, demonstrating a continuing favorable international image. Indeed, business was carried on very much as usual.

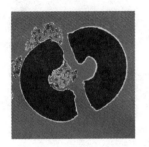

PART II

CONTEMPORARY CHINA

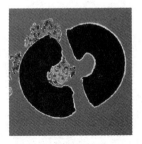

CHAPTER 5

POLITICS AND CHINA'S "SECOND REVOLUTION": THE QUEST FOR MODERNIZATION

In 1978, at the third plenary session of the Communist Party's Eleventh Central Committee, China officially embarked on a program of reform that was to lead into its "second revolution." The "first revolution" had been directed at defeating the Japanese, expelling foreign powers, pulling the country together, and providing the populace with a sense of national identity. Its success prompted its principal revolutionary leader and spokesman, Mao Zedong, to proclaim that, with this victory, the Chinese people had "stood up."

China's second revolution, the contents and principles of which have been developed and guided by twice-purged and rehabilitated leader Deng Xiaoping, has as its goal the creation, through comprehensive reforms, of what its leaders call "socialism with Chinese characteristics." Essentially, this concept emphasizes economic development; recognizes market mechanisms as vital to stimulating economic growth; grants central leaders and their macroeconomic policies a good measure of control over the reform process; allows China's economy to continue to become intertwined with those of developed countries; and maintains Marxism-Leninism-Mao Zedong Thought as the political frame of reference for these systemic changes. With all these measures in place, China forecasts the successful realization of the "Four Modernizations"—agriculture, industry, science and technology, and national defense—by the year 2000, transforming China into a relatively advanced industrialized country.

In the early 1980s, China's leaders coined another phrase to describe their reform efforts. They explained that China's reform program had "one center and two basic points." The "center" referred to economic reform and the opening of the country to the outside world, while the "two points" involved adherence to socialism and the Communist political system. Operating under strong influence from China's first revolution, with its predominant nationalistic impulses, its leaders remain determined to define their own course of development, in Chinese terms, no matter how much of their reform program is borrowed from Western developed countries. A prime example of this is the characterization of their present developmental level as the "initial stage" of socialism. By employing this ideological device, reform leaders attempt to rationalize the use of the capitalist market mechanisms required for China's economic growth, but at the same time maintain a strong connection with a socialist framework.

Whatever the device employed for maintaining a connection with its socialist past, China's reform efforts have been highly experimental and have provoked serious disagreements within both the leadership and populace. Some reform leaders have characterized their approach as "crossing the river by feeling for the stones." In general, the reforms have produced significant change and development, but also dislocation and hardship for many. In either case, the result has been a high degree of tension in society, punctuated by periods of retrenchment and conservative resistance. In short, the reforms have created a kind of dialectical relationship involving bold policy initiatives followed by periods of retrenchment. Nevertheless, the overall record of reform since 1978 shows a forward movement toward economic development.

The question arises as to how much stress the Chinese system can withstand and still maintain cohesion, identity, and viability. In China's sometimes desperate efforts to cure the "sick man of Asia" image that has plagued the country for much of the twentieth century, and to become a respectable member of the international community, China's leaders often appear to be working at cross purposes. On the one hand, they have encouraged outreach and the adoption of market-driven reforms; on the other, they have recentralized economic control and applied a heavy hand against dissenters and demonstrators seeking a greater popular voice in deciding China's future, the latter at a time when much of the world was moving toward more open communication and expression. Some of this behavior reflects disagreements among China's top leaders, but some can also be attributed to China's authoritarian past; the transitional nature of its present situation; China's commitment to defining an independent course of development within the context of Marxism-Leninism; and the size of the problem and challenges involved. China has not only the world's largest population but one that was long isolated from meaningful contact with the developed world.

Thus the outcome of China's second revolution may prove as daunting and uncertain as that of the revolution completed in 1949. To gain a better sense of the problem, it is first necessary to understand the nature and makeup of the key component of China's political system, the Chinese Communist Party. What are its ideological goals? How have these goals changed under Deng's leadership? What effect has the collapse of communism in the Soviet Union and Eastern Europe had on party confidence and direction? These questions are crucial because despite reforms, the Chinese Communist Party (CCP) continues to be the authoritative voice in all of China's affairs.

The Chinese Communist Party and Its Ideology

The Chinese Communist Party sets the course for the country to follow. It defines the general policy framework and then determines the content of the major issues involved. This accomplished, the party elects the leadership to oversee the implementation of its authoritative political program. In addition, the CCP develops and enforces measures to ensure the stability required to carry out the general program.

The Key CCP Bodies and Organizing Principle

According to the current party constitution, adopted in September 1982, the national party congress is the preeminent body of the CCP. The political report delivered at the congress by the CCP general secretary reviews the record and accomplishments since the previous congress and defines the political program to be followed for the next five years, until the next congress. The party congress concludes with the election of a new Central Committee, which, at its first plenary session, selects both a new Political Bureau (or Politburo) and the ultimate political body, the Politburo Standing Committee.

The party's key military body, elected by the Central Committee, is the Party Military Commission, which exercises its authority over military affairs through the General Political Department of the People's Liberation Army (PLA). The PLA includes the ground forces, navy, and air force (see Chapter 9 on the military).

The day-to-day party affairs of the Political Bureau and its Standing Committee are managed by the party Secretariat and its various departments. Members of the Secretariat are nominated by the Standing Committee and approved by the Central Committee. The Central Discipline Inspection Commission monitors the implementation of party policy and handles infractions of policy and rules by party organizations and members.

Chinese Communist Party Organizations

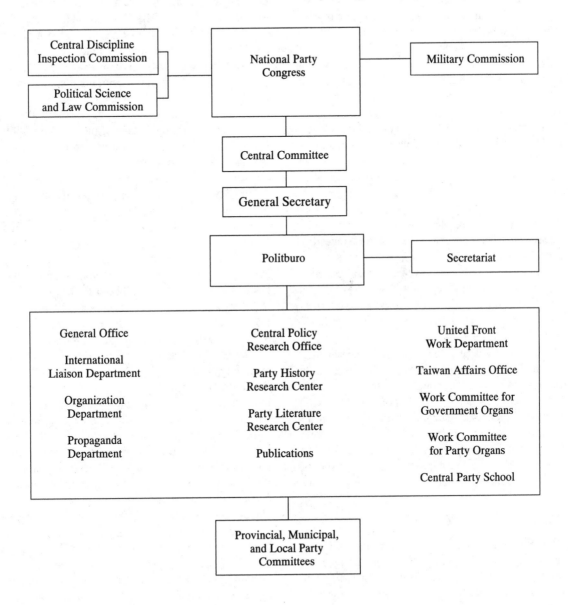

Source: Central Intelligence Agency.

Note: The Fourteenth National Party Congress convened October 12-18, 1992. The first plenum of the fourteenth congress convened October 19-20, 1992; the second plenum, March 5-7, 1993; and the third plenum, November 11-14, 1993. This chart represents the organization of the Chinese Communist Party as of February 1, 1994.

The party structure reaches down to lower levels in the form of party committees and congresses in China's twenty-two provinces, five autonomous regions, and three special provincial-level municipalities. It exists at county subdivisions and reaches down to the basic branch level, with the latter units being formed in factories, schools, offices, and neighborhoods. All of China's more than 50 million party members must belong to branch organs, in which they are informed about party goals and programs and learn to accept party discipline.

The political system at levels below the center operates according to the principle of democratic centralism. The democratic feature invites expressions of opinion on key policy issues from party members at all levels of the party structure. The purpose is to reinforce the concepts of investigation and broad consultation on the feasibility of party policy throughout the system. The results of these investigations are to be passed to higher levels to assist in policy formulation. The centralist feature requires subordinate levels to obey decisions from senior levels, and when a discussion or debate is resolved at the party center, all subordinate levels must then fall in line with these decisions.

The above describes the formal political system in China. There is also an informal system at both the central and local levels, composed of a web of influential networks that funnel political directives through a process of bargaining among relevant institutions, leading groups (see discussion below), work units, influential persons, and others. The outcome of this process determines the overall success of policy implementation.

The Fourteenth CCP Congress

The CCP's most recent party congress, the fourteenth, convened in Beijing on October 12-18, 1992, attended by 1,989 elected delegates. The party's reelected general secretary, Jiang Zemin, delivered a lengthy political report endorsing the reform program started by Deng Xiaoping in 1978 and authorizing new reform initiatives directed at setting aside central planning almost entirely in favor of market economics. Jiang also emphasized the need to continue integrating China's economy into the international economy. The elected leaders of both the new Political Bureau and its Secretariat are believed to favor Deng's reform agenda. The same can be said of most of the full members and alternate members of the Fourteenth CCP Central Committee. In short, this congress represented a significant victory for reformers over those who, in the past, have advocated gradual economic reform and a continuing commitment to plan, structure, and containment of economic change from the party center.

In another striking initiative, the congress abolished the Central Advisory Commission, a body established in 1982 to accommodate Long March veterans after their retirement from key positions while making room for younger leaders at the party's senior levels. But instead of lowering their voices, this Central Advisory Commission had become a forum for the elders' dissent from the reform program and a platform from which they could meddle effectively in policy affairs. Abolishing this formal party body has not meant that influential old leaders no longer influence key decisions, however: many have powerful and extensive personal networks that assure them of a continuing role in the political process.

The fourteenth party congress also succeeded in amending the 1982 party constitution to fully enshrine the reform agenda so that Deng's successors have at their disposal an authoritative basis from which to pursue reforms. The congress elected 189 full members and 130 alternate members to the Central Committee and a twenty-member Political Bureau (with two alternates) with a seven-member Standing Committee. The Standing Committee is headed by General Secretary Jiang Zemin and includes Premier Li Peng; Central Party School Head Qiao Shi; party propaganda chief Li Ruihuan; and new members Executive Vice Premier Zhu Rongji; vice chairman of the party Military Commission Liu Huaqing; and Hu Jintao, former party secretary of the Tibet Autonomous Region and a key figure in CCP organizational work. The newly elected party Secretariat contains five members. Qiao Shi was elected secretary general of the party congress.

Members of the Political Bureau and Standing Committee are younger than members of the previous body (average age about sixty-three years) and more than half are from technocratic backgrounds. China's prosperous municipalities and coastal regions, including Beijing, Shanghai, and Tianjin municipalities, and Shandong and Guangdong Provinces, each gained visibility through election of a member to the Political Bureau. The military was well represented on the Standing Committee by Liu Huaqing, a firm supporter of military modernization and professionalism. All seven of China's military region commanders and six of the political commissars were elected full members of the new Central Committee. Party General Secretary Jiang Zemin retained his position as chairman of the party's powerful Military Commission, again underlining the commitment to having the party firmly control the military. Provincial officials represented the largest single category of members on the new Central Committee, occupying 42 percent of the total. The average age of Central Committee members was fifty-six years.

Party Ideology under Mao

Marxism-Leninism provided China's early revolutionary leaders with a total ideology at a time when China had none. Confucianism had been discarded as having nothing to offer China in its search to climb out of poverty, humiliation, and repeated defeats. Marxism-Leninism had the distinct appeal of working within certain clearly defined laws and principles that, if correctly understood and applied, purportedly might be used to fathom the historical circumstances of China's predicament, and even to indicate a path for its salvation. The dialectics used to define situations where opposing forces were at work promised a progressive, forward-moving outcome—a comforting prospect to China's leaders facing chaos and defeat. This seemingly scientific approach to China's problems had the additional benefit of placing China in a universal framework that had already been applied to Western countries, and thus included an element of "modernization by association."

When China's first generation of revolutionary leaders came to power in 1949, Marxism-Leninism, for all its recommended universal science, began to

take on its own character in China. In addition to borrowing heavily from Stalinist economics, with the latter's emphasis on central planning and heavy industry, Mao Zedong (who eventually admitted to having no understanding of economics) emphasized the role of mass movements in achieving political, social, economic, and even human goals. He idealized the peasantry and whipped them into utopian campaigns such as the Great Leap Forward (1958-1960) at the cost of millions of lives. He targeted the Communist Party for transformation during the Great Proletarian Cultural Revolution (1966-1976), using rampaging Red Guards to destroy what he saw as party opposition to his policies.

Mao hoped to accomplish through human will what he could not accomplish through rational, well-thought-out social and economic planning. He mistrusted established institutions and people with expertise and training, finding them disparaging of his utopian goals and campaign style. Nevertheless, Mao's leadership of the successful Communist revolution made his role difficult, if not impossible, for his successors to ignore. To blacken Mao's image would call into question the party's own role and legitimacy. Therefore, while major revisions continue to be made to his multivolume "thoughts" in the form of new and authoritative published writings by Deng Xiaoping and others, the party's official ideology continues to be characterized as Marxism-Leninism-Mao Zedong Thought.

Ideological Differences Between Mao and Deng

When Deng Xiaoping came to power, he identified the "Four Cardinal Principles" guiding China's development as socialism; the dictatorship of the proletariat; supporting the party leadership; and Marxism-Leninism-Mao Zedong Thought. Nevertheless, declaring that reform is the necessary trend of history, Deng set goals for the modernization program that he hoped would be well established by the year 2000 and would engage the talents and energy of the entire population. Class consciousness and acceptable class background were to be replaced by initiative and expertise. Deng advocated a flexible approach to applying Marxist principles, even recognizing that Marxism, as the product of an earlier age, did not provide the means for addressing all contemporary problems. Rather, he called for a pragmatic approach aimed at producing desired and tangible results, captured in the famous phrase attributed to Deng: "It doesn't matter whether the cat is black or white, so long as it catches mice." Deng recognized the urgent need for an effective and efficient party and government system, staffed by trained cadres who could produce demonstrable results in support of his ambitious economic development program.

Stability was another requirement in Deng's program, to be guaranteed by the support of the military and security forces. Unlike Mao, who engendered chaos as a means to achieve his purposes, as expressed through his dictum "class struggle as the key link," Deng stressed order, leadership consensus, discipline, and adherence to party leadership. While participation, leadership, and policy formation in economic programs allowed for flexibility and innovation, politics remained under party control, with only relatively minor changes permitted.

One of the most significant political changes under Deng's leadership involved the institutionalization of the concept of collective leadership, an abrupt departure from Mao's cultivation of the cult of personality. Although collective leadership has become a reality, at least by institution and proclamation, Deng has not been able to work out a regular succession process, which the hierarchical Chinese Communist system by its very nature requires. While Deng holds no official position, his charisma, historic Long March association, and seminal role in post-1978 politics make him the pillar of the system, and thus its key point of vulnerability when he passes from the scene.

A major difference between Mao and Deng involves their approaches to the role of ideology. Mao saw its purpose as instilling selfless dedication, patriotism, and self-abnegation, as represented by the model soldier and martyr Lei Feng. Lei, who joined the PLA in 1960, died suddenly in public service. Using his purported diaries, the CCP held him up as an example of Maoist virtues for China's youth: pure motives, self-sacrifice, and willingness to follow whatever is decreed by the party and the army. Lei Feng campaigns have been resurrected in times of social turmoil, to instill discipline and restore social order. Mao relied on such campaigns for intense indoctrination of the populace. He regarded the media and its potential as the "tongue and throat" of the party, which could transform human nature for the better, as well as instill unthinking devotion to Mao and the party.

Maoist egalitarianism meant that all received the same rewards regardless of the quality of performance. Known as "eating from the same pot," this approach discouraged individual initiative, but guaranteed livelihood and care to all. Deng, on the other hand, advocates self-interest, individual initiative, material incentives, and "emancipating the mind" to new approaches, modern concepts and technologies—all relevant to the goals of modernization. While ideology under Deng is less personalized and doctrinaire, Deng, like Mao, views any challenge to the leadership of the CCP as a "forbidden zone."

The styles employed by Mao and Deng share other broad similarities. Mao is famous for mobilizing the masses to achieve his ends. Deng has also used this approach in a controlled way to speed up a reform drive or to counter resistance from the center. His celebrated tour of southern China in early 1992, during which he called for accelerating the reform agenda in a region sure to support this initiative, is one striking example of this tactic. Some of the reform leaders have even called for "going to the masses"—for calming rather than rousing purposes—in order to try to explain disastrous events such as what took place in and around Tiananmen Square in Beijing on June 4, 1989.

A key difference between Mao and Deng regarding mobilization of the masses, however, is the basic intent of each. Mao envisioned using collective action to achieve collectivist goals, often aimed at realizing some utopian program. Deng's motivation has been to stimulate individual action in pursuit of practical individual or family goals, above all that of private enrichment. In the end, of course, Deng's intent is to achieve his broad social program.

léi fēng zhēng dà zhe yǎn jing
雷 锋 睁 大着 眼睛
tīng zhe.
听 着。
    péng dà shū yòu shuō: "hái zi,
    彭 大 叔 又 说:"孩 子,
láo lao de jì zhù, zán men de
牢 牢 地 记 住, 咱们 的
jiù mìng ēn rén shì máo zhǔ xí, shì
救 命 恩 人 是 毛主席, 是
gòng chǎn dǎng, shì jiě fàng jūn.
共 产 党, 是 解 放 军。
nǐ yào tīng máo zhǔ xí de huà."
你 要 听 毛主席 的 话。"
    léi fēng diǎn dian tóu shuō: "wǒ
    雷锋 点 点 头 说:"我
yí dìng tīng máo zhǔ xí de huà!"
一 定 听 毛主席 的 话!"
tā bǎ péng dà shū de huà yí
他 把 彭 大 叔 的 话 一
jù yí jù quán jì zài xīn lǐ.
句 一 句 全 记 在 心 里。
    zài tǔ dì gǎi gé yùn dòng zhōng, léi fēng hé xiǎo huǒ bàn chàng zhe kuài
    在 土地 改 革 运 动 中, 雷 锋 和 小 伙 伴 唱 着 快
bǎn, dào chù xuān chuán dì zhǔ de zuì è:
板, 到 处 宣 传 地 主 的 罪 恶:

Mao used ideological mobilization campaigns to try to instill selfless dedication in China's citizens. This drawing shows the model revolutionary Lei Feng as a young boy being taught the virtues of Maoism. Lei Feng campaigns have been used periodically in China to restore social order and discipline in times of turmoil. Deng, in contrast, mobilized citizens in pursuit of practical goals rather than utopian programs.

In sum, official ideology now calls for support of the economic reform, but Deng is willing to tighten the ideological parameters whenever stability or reform goals are threatened by forceful expressions of individual rights, pluralistic politics, or bourgeois democracy. In that sense, Deng is the inheritor and supporter of Maoist political coercion and control.

The Impact of the Collapse of the Soviet Union

China's leaders remain convinced that their brand of socialism is embedded with "Chinese characteristics" and has thus become an evolution or perfection of socialism to a degree that will allow it to survive and overcome the fatal flaws that brought down the

Soviet system. Nevertheless, the Soviet experience has given China's Communist leaders pause. Their response in general has been to emphasize the essential need to deepen and accelerate economic reforms while maintaining careful control over political liberalization. They view the Soviet Union and the countries of Eastern Europe as examples of what can go wrong when economic policies fail and when political reforms are extended before a strong economic foundation is in place. The fate of these countries has even been described in internal party discussion as the result of the effects of what the Chinese call "peaceful evolution." Peaceful evolution is associated with the programs and ideals of Western spokespeople who call for multiparty democracy, recognition of individual rights and liberties, and an end to single-party Communist rule—all of which China's leaders see as provoking social breakdown and chaos.

Rather than allowing or promoting peaceful evolution toward political liberalization, China's party leaders advocate borrowing market reforms and applying them under strict party supervision with the purpose of moving society toward a fuller realization of socialism. Couching their arguments in Marxist terms and framework, they claim that only after this economic development has been attained can significant changes in the superstructure occur. In other words, they argue that a certain level of economic development must be reached before significant political and cultural change can take place without provoking unmanageable dislocations and chaos. Moreover, this complex developmental process must be guided and supervised by the Communist Party, which they see as the most knowledgeable protector of the people, the revolution, and the country.

Given China's experience under imperialism in the nineteenth and early twentieth centuries, its Communist leaders view Western recommendations for political liberalization with suspicion. Some see them as nefarious plans that will lead to the overthrow of their political system and socialism. Another factor affecting their convictions is the prevailing fear of any social instability reminiscent of costly Maoist campaigns such as the Cultural Revolution. China's leaders, and even the Chinese people, have a continuing fear of *luan,* or chaos, in society, which makes political and social liberalization in tandem with systemic economic reform a particularly worrisome undertaking. The limit of China's version of political liberalization involves official dialogue with institutions, interest groups, and newly privatized bodies engaged in promoting modernization goals.

In any case, the collapse of the Soviet Union is viewed as a negative example and has hardened many of China's key leaders, including Deng Xiaoping, against any immediate serious efforts at political reform. Rather, they have in effect linked the progress and extent of political reform to the success of their economic reform policies. They have, moreover, staked the legitimacy of the CCP leadership and continued rule of the Communist party on the successful outcome of their "second revolution."

Party-State Relations

The Chinese Communist Party has no credible competitor in the Chinese political system—no church, independent labor unions, or powerful private organizations. It does rely on certain mass organizations, the so-called democratic parties loyal to the CCP since 1949, and on professional organizations, to reach out to, penetrate, and mobilize the masses and integrate them into party-led programs and official political life. These organizations are led by party cadres who, in all their activities, provide the desired party image of presenting a united front with the CCP in matters of policy and participation. Mass organizations' affairs are supposed to be represented by the Chinese People's Political Consultative Conference (CPPCC), but are in fact carefully managed by the CCP Central Committee United Front Work Department. The CPPCC is a large umbrella organization that has committees at the national and local levels. Its diversity is apparent in its membership composition: the CCP, the Communist Youth League, the "democratic parties," All-China Federation of Trade Unions, All-China Women's Federation, All-China Federation of Industry and Commerce; representatives of minorities, of Hong Kong, Macao, and Taiwan, of overseas Chinese, and of out-

As China entered the 1990s, top leaders included (left to right) Premier Li Peng, President Yang Shangkun, and CCP General Secretary Jiang Zemin, shown here at the National People's Congress in April 1990.

standing intellectuals in science, the arts, journalism, and education.

CPPCC national meetings are usually held at about the same time as sessions of the National People's Congress (described in the next section) and help to provide a sounding board on national policies and promote consensus or a united front with party leadership and programs. The eighth CPPCC National Committee met in March 1993, electing a chairman, 15 vice chairmen, and a 288-member Standing Committee. The members of the eighth CPPCC National Committee total 2,093. The CPPCC plays an important symbolic role in multiparty cooperation and unity that the CCP is anxious to display and emphasize both at home and abroad.

Beyond this largely symbolic realm, party-originated policies are implemented through the state bureaucracy, which the party controls through its authority to appoint state leaders and supervise the implementation of policy. The development and supervision of policy are assisted by the existence of "leading groups" at the top levels of the party struc-

ture. These bodies are focused around certain policy clusters such as national security; political-legal affairs, including internal security, legislative, and judicial responsibilities; foreign affairs; government and economic matters; and other policy concerns.

Most of the Political Bureau's work is accomplished through these leading groups, which have at their disposal advisers and policy research bodies that gather information, research and debate policy options, resolve issues, and package the consensual end result for ratification by a meeting (usually once a month) of the Political Bureau. In addition, these functional groups provide an essential link between and among the far-flung bureaucracies. Members of the Political Bureau Standing Committee are active leaders of these groups. They often use their authority over a policy cluster as a power base for building their own strength and influence within the most senior levels of the party structure.

Policy research offices exist at all levels of the party structure, serving as a policy bridge to equivalent government organizations. These provide better statistical information and analytical reporting for the development and direction of policy at the top and, supported by lower level research bodies, make their findings available to senior levels. State ministries and commissions also have a network of research centers, which promote better state projections and policy planning. Government bureaucracies can better be held accountable, their performance examined for efficiency, and party policies more accurately evaluated for their suitability and realistic implementation. As economic programs unfold, accelerate, and proliferate, good information channels and resources have become a key asset for policymakers, especially in the highly complex arena of economic modernization.

The State Structure

As the party's commitment to systemic economic reform has deepened, the complexities of developing and carrying out policies has required that an interdependent relationship develop between the party and state structures. Economic and development issues have come to dominate the policy agendas and require frequent if not constant consultations, feedback, and even trade-offs between party-supervised state bureaucracies and their various subordinate levels.

The National Level

The largest and most senior level of the state bureaucracy, where most of the reform issues are at least debated and a sense of the country's mood concerning the reform program becomes apparent, is the National People's Congress (NPC). The 1982 State Constitution of the People's Republic of China defined the National People's Congress as "the highest organ of state power." Elected for a term of five years, the NPC, which meets only once a year, has a permanent Standing Committee that carries out NPC work when it is not in session. It also presides over NPC sessions, determines the agenda, and routes legislation and nominations for offices. Beginning in 1987, the Standing Committee acquired the right to enact and amend certain laws when the NPC is not in session. The Standing Committee, among other duties, supervises the work of the executive, the Central Military Commission, and the judicial organs. The Central Military Commission, established in December 1982, directs the armed forces of the country. The leaders who serve on this body are identical to those serving on its party counterpart, the Military Commission. Jiang Zemin is chairman of both, and the same persons serve as vice chairmen (2) and as other members (4). The Standing Committee also oversees the election of delegates to the NPC by the people's congresses at the provincial level, as well as by the PLA. Leaders of the Standing Committee are also influential members of the CCP.

The principal functions of the NPC are to amend the state constitution and enact laws; to examine and approve the national economic plan and state budget; and to decide on questions of war and peace. It also elects the president and vice president of the republic; the premier, based on the nomination of the president; the vice premiers, state councilors, and government ministers; the chairman of the Central Military Commission; the president of the Supreme Court; and the procurator-general of the Supreme People's Procuratorate. In 1993, the NPC passed amendments to the 1982 State Constitution that were identified as "a milestone in Chinese history" in that they included in this basic document the commitment both to "building socialism with Chinese characteristics" and to employing a market economy. These new concepts were accompanied by an equally firm commitment to uphold the Four Cardinal Principles as China "perseveres in reform and opening up to the outside world."

In March 1993, Jiang Zemin, already general secretary of the CCP Central Committee and chairman of the Central Military Commission, was elected president of the PRC at the first session of the Eighth National People's Congress. Political Bureau Standing Committee member Qiao Shi was named chairman of the 134-member NPC Standing Committee, which has within it a smaller group of 19 vice chairmen and a secretary general. Li Peng was re-elected to a five-year term as premier of the State Council.

The State Council, headed by the premier, is the highest organ of state administration. Its members

Government of the People's Republic of China

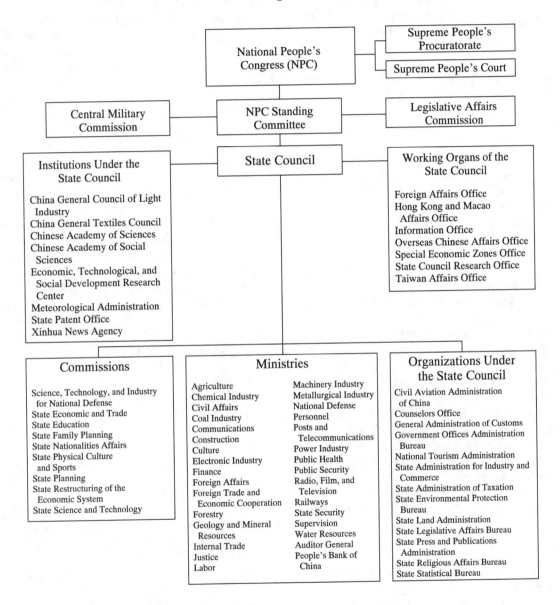

National People's Congress (NPC)

Supreme People's Procuratorate

Supreme People's Court

Central Military Commission

NPC Standing Committee

Legislative Affairs Commission

State Council

Institutions Under the State Council

China General Council of Light Industry
China General Textiles Council
Chinese Academy of Sciences
Chinese Academy of Social Sciences
Economic, Technological, and Social Development Research Center
Meteorological Administration
State Patent Office
Xinhua News Agency

Working Organs of the State Council

Foreign Affairs Office
Hong Kong and Macao Affairs Office
Information Office
Overseas Chinese Affairs Office
Special Economic Zones Office
State Council Research Office
Taiwan Affairs Office

Commissions

Science, Technology, and Industry for National Defense
State Economic and Trade
State Education
State Family Planning
State Nationalities Affairs
State Physical Culture and Sports
State Planning
State Restructuring of the Economic System
State Science and Technology

Ministries

Agriculture
Chemical Industry
Civil Affairs
Coal Industry
Communications
Construction
Culture
Electronic Industry
Finance
Foreign Affairs
Foreign Trade and Economic Cooperation
Forestry
Geology and Mineral Resources
Internal Trade
Justice
Labor

Machinery Industry
Metallurgical Industry
National Defense
Personnel
Posts and Telecommunications
Power Industry
Public Health
Public Security
Radio, Film, and Television
Railways
State Security
Supervision
Water Resources
Auditor General
People's Bank of China

Organizations Under the State Council

Civil Aviation Administration of China
Counselors Office
General Administration of Customs
Government Offices Administration Bureau
National Tourism Administration
State Administration for Industry and Commerce
State Administration of Taxation
State Environmental Protection Bureau
State Land Administration
State Legislative Affairs Bureau
State Press and Publications Administration
State Religious Affairs Bureau
State Statistical Bureau

Source: Central Intelligence Agency.

Note: The Eighth National People's Congress convened March 1993. This chart represents the organization of the Chinese government as of February 1994.

are appointed or removed by the NPC Standing Committee, upon recommendation of the premier. In March 1993, the newly approved Standing Committee, or cabinet, included the premier, four vice premiers, eight state councilors, and a secretary. Subordinate to this presiding body were the ministers in charge of ministries (29), ministers in charge of commissions (10), and heads of agencies with special functions (30). The State Council generally meets once a month, with twice-weekly meetings held by its Standing Committee.

The Standing Committee of the State Council is equivalent in rank to the CCP's Secretariat and Military Commission. Of course its members are already concurrently influential party members. The State Council, as the chief administrative organ of government, serves as the functional center of state power and a clearinghouse for government initiatives at all levels. Its principal responsibility is to develop the economic plan and state budget for deliberation and approval by the NPC. Other responsibilities involve drafting legislative bills and issuing and monitoring the implementation of administrative measures. In all these activities, the State Council is aided by various support offices and by leading groups, charged with researching a specific problem and providing a solution or working program to be submitted for State Council approval.

Another key body, established in late 1986, is the Ministry of Supervision, charged with overseeing the proper functioning of government organizations and officials, and handling the growing problem of corruption accompanying implementation of the reform agenda. A growing body of legal material is being developed to support the work of this ministry.

Local Administration

China's reform-minded leaders understand that for reform programs to be successful, there must be organizational means to involve and inspire those at the front line of government and production. Programs require broad mass support and a means of mobilizing that support for the purposes of both party and state organs.

Below the central level, China's administrative divisions include 30 provinces, municipalities, and autonomous regions, 115 prefectures, 1,894 counties, 476 cities, and 650 districts under the jurisdiction of cities. State institutions match those at the central level with people's congresses and standing committees at and above the county level. The administrative arm of these people's congresses are local people's governments, whose officials—governors, deputy governors, mayors and deputy mayors, heads and deputy heads of counties, districts and towns—are elected by people's congresses. The main purpose of the people's congress system is to make local government more responsive both to its constituents and to party and state programs. The former responsibility is achieved through the standing committees' power to supervise, inspect, appoint, and remove local administrative and judicial personnel. The latter is achieved by the standing committees' role as a conduit through which to convey party and state modernization programs and goals.

The county is a key operational level in the government system. The reform package of 1979 provided for the direct elections of deputies to people's congresses at the county level through secret ballots containing several candidates to choose from. During the more politically relaxed period of late 1986, central party officials announced experiments to allow broader participation even in key municipal elections. However, the conservative reaction provoked by subsequent student demonstrations, demanding broader democratic freedoms, effectively stalled these new initiatives, which might otherwise have allowed for substantive popular participation in governments above the county level. In the fall of 1993, official dissatisfaction was expressed over the open county-level elections of representatives to people's congresses, with some arguing that there had been a loss of control over these elections. Outspoken representatives elected at the county level were subsequently being elected to the more influential provincial-level people's congresses, where these representatives were making their sometimes-dissident voices clearly heard. The central leaders have expressed clear reservations about condoning or expanding open elections because power so transferred might be very difficult to reclaim in the future.

At the grass-roots level of government, in addition to urban neighborhood committees, the 1982 state constitution proclaimed the establishment of residents' and villagers' committees. These bodies were to meet certain public security, arbitration, and health services needs, as well as to better convey information to and from government organs. They carry the potential to keep the population better informed, but obviously can also serve as an additional means to monitor and control basic social behavior and attitudes. One theory is that these village-level committees, which have begun to receive added official attention, may become an indirect means to demand the attention and services of the otherwise ambitious and independent county-level bodies.

The Cadre System

The occasional inability of party and government cadres to successfully grasp and implement the often-complex reform programs and goals has required a careful and critical look at the government personnel system. The staffing of China's governing bodies promises to undergo a period of radical reform. One purpose of the reform is to replace the existing cadre (*ganbu*) system with something equivalent to the civil service systems that exist in many countries, with regularized and institutionalized procedures for selecting and grading officials. According to "Provisional Regulations on Civil Servants" promulgated by the State Council in September 1993, a new civil service system based on these regulations is to be established throughout China in "about three years."

The new system is to be designed to cure certain basic ills prevalent in the old cadre system. The selection of government functionaries is to be based on competitive examinations and exclude consideration of family or personal relationships, a fairly common practice in past years. If implemented, changing to a system rooted in rules and norms and away from one that depends on personal relationships will represent a systemic change in the way China conducts its official business. At the national level, relationships between veteran cadres based on family ties or long-standing relationships have driven the political process, causing decision making to be less rational, sometimes quixotic, and certainly difficult to predict. The same conditions exist at all levels of the party and government structure. Evidence of this practice is only more apparent at the center, where it receives the most attention and press coverage.

Selection on the basis of competence is posited on bringing into government younger, better educated, and talented personnel capable of handling and responding to challenging management issues and problems. This reform is to be strengthened by a feature identified as "cross-regional exchanges of civil servants." While the precise meaning of this new stipulation is not yet clear, it may well be aimed at reducing the likelihood of government officials building personal networks and power bases in their areas of operation. There is also a hint that the measure is directed at limiting the corruption that can come from the mutually beneficial, long-term relationships that spring from official support for new economic activities in a region.

The corruption issue, which has become a serious problem facing the reform leadership, may have inspired another major feature of civil service reform: a wage scale for civil servants that reportedly will bring their salaries to a level comparable with that of individuals working in commercial enterprises. The regulations will also include stipulations concerning the rights and responsibilities of civil servants, as well as a rational system of performance evaluation, which will provide rewards and penalties based on quality of work.

A frequently stated but difficult goal for the State Council to fulfill has been to rejuvenate, streamline, and downsize the entire government structure. Rather than getting smaller, as new reform programs are introduced, the government has tended to add research staff, technical advisers, and managerial personnel. Efforts to counteract this trend involve attempting to effect a massive retirement of veteran cadres. To eliminate aging and incompetent cadres, guidelines set age limits for key offices at all levels of the bureaucracy, thus bringing an end to lifetime tenure. This policy has met with significant resistance from those who see the new guidelines and requirements as a serious threat to their status and live-lihood. Creating an efficient, streamlined, and professional bureaucracy is likely to remain a vexing problem in the years ahead.

March 1992 Government Work Report

Just as the general secretary of the CCP gives the major address to the party congress spelling out the party's political program and goals for the next five years, the premier, at meetings of the National People's Congress, submits a report on the work of the government. In March 1992, Li Peng noted in his report that China began the first year of its eighth Five-Year Plan in 1991 and that same year completed a three-year period of economic readjustment aimed at controlling inflation and restoring economic health and stability.

In this comprehensive report, Li's assessments and recommendations regarding economic matters were notably conservative. After emphasizing that "only socialism can save China," Li forecast that modernization would be a lengthy process involving implementation of programs "stage by stage." Obviously required to reflect the impetus for accelerating economic reform and development provided by Deng Xiaoping's early 1992 tour of the southern provinces, Li advocated a faster pace of reform. But he described the focus of reform as mainly to increase efficiency, and singled out the less volatile area of agricultural reform for special attention. He projected a conservative estimate of 6 percent growth in the gross national product for 1992, a figure that later needed revision to 8 percent.

Party political reports and government work reports are usually the result of a great many debates, with the documents going through several drafts before the final version is submitted. This helps to explain why parts of the text often seem contradictory. In Li's report, while he called for speeding up reform, there is a pervasive emphasis on much milder remedies such as adjusting the economic structure, improving results, and planning for eventual growth rates. Li noted cautiously that the country had just come out of a period of rectification and that there

were still "some unstable factors in economic work."

Stating his points in good Marxist-Leninist terms, Li argued that the economic reform program is aimed primarily at changing the economic structure in order to liberate the productive forces. This goal is to be achieved by promoting the development of a "planned commodity economy." His use of the term "planned commodity economy" is revealing, underscoring his continued allegiance to a conservative economic strategy. In just a matter of months, however, the fourteenth CCP congress would enshrine the concept of the "socialist market economy," giving a much larger role to market forces in liberating the productive forces.

Li Peng's conservatism has often been associated with his mentor in the field of economics, Chen Yun. Chen, a powerful member of the first, or Long March, generation of PRC leaders, was famous for his theory of the "bird cage economy." According to Chen's theory, China's economy must function according to a centrally planned framework. Market forces must be restrained and contained within that framework, serving as a contributing but subordinate feature of the overall planned economic structure. But even Chen seemed to have moved beyond this approach by mid-1992, stressing the development of market-oriented aspects of the economic system and endorsing many of Deng's reform initiatives accelerating the pace of reform. Nevertheless, the late Chen's protégé, Li, remains on the conservative end of an economic spectrum that embraces, at opposite ends, state planning and market forces. In this respect, the term "conservative" refers to those who continue to follow certain aspects of Maoist orthodoxy (also sometimes called "leftists"), while "liberals" are those who support Deng's heretofore "rightist" economic reforms.

Another factor of importance in viewing Li's reform stance is that, as implementers of the party's economic policies, the premier and government organizations must face daily challenges and resistance from those who may be adversely affected by reform initiatives, or who generally resist change. Li and other government officials know that they will be held accountable for the progress of the reform agen-

Although his popular image suffered after the 1989 crackdown on Tiananmen demonstrators, Li Peng was re-elected to a second five-year term as premier of the State Council in 1993. Here, Li delivers his conservative 1992 government work report, warning against "bourgeois liberalization" and stressing the need for social and political stability.

da, a situation that inherently breeds a degree of conservatism. A rapid pace and radical reform measures elevate pressures in the system and even occasionally provoke bureaucratic sabotage and the undermining of disruptive programs. These are all challenges that reform managers must meet, handle, and often defuse. The difficulty and political sensitivity of the task frequently evoke a cautious response.

Li took a clear orthodox position on political matters in his 1992 government work report. He warned against the trend of bourgeois liberalization, saying that if allowed to develop unchecked, the consequences "will be dreadful to contemplate." To combat this pernicious threat, Li stressed the necessity of using the people's democratic dictatorship as a weapon to defend the socialist system. Like most of China's leadership after the events of June 4, 1989, Li repeatedly stressed that social and political stability are the prerequisites for success in reform and economic development.

Li's speech allowed for some superficial recognition of the goal of perfecting a democratic and scientific decision-making process and accepting more supervision from the people's congresses and their standing committees, as well as for building a socialist legal system. It gave more emphasis to developing a "socialist spiritual civilization," or the indoctrination of the populace in patriotism, collectivism, and values of the revolutionary generation. These include self-reliance and discipline, hard struggle, and serving the people. Socialist spiritual civilization is meant to balance the concomitant adverse effects of developing a vital "socialist material civilization" that have accompanied China's successful economic reforms. The latter pose the danger of promoting what in previous decades were referred to as "poisonous weeds," namely greed, apathy, corruption, and self-centeredness.

March 1993 Government Work Report

Premier Li Peng presented the report on government work to the first session of the Eighth National People's Congress on March 15, 1993, and the contents of that report contrast markedly with that provided one year before and discussed above. Overall, there is a celebratory tone to the 1993 report as Li describes the accomplishments of the five years that have passed since convocation of the Seventh NPC. In addition, Li and those who contributed to drafting this report needed to reflect the authoritative political program laid out at the fourteenth CCP congress in the fall of 1992, which emphasized a faster pace of reform toward the establishment of a socialist market economy.

The government report reads like a primer for those wishing to establish a market economy. It spells out a broad array of reforms to take place over the following five years, tackling such diverse areas as the enormous problems plaguing state enterprises, deepening price reform, developing the transportation and communications infrastructures, separating government administration from enterprise management, adjusting wage structures, reforming and expanding the banking system, revising the tax system, and learning to work with macroeconomic controls and other levers aimed at reining in inflation and an overheating economic system. In short, the work report is basically an economic document, with an unusual amount of detail for a report of this nature. Its consistency and thorough exposition of its subjects also suggested a broad consensus among party and state leaders that an economic reform program making use of extensive market features was the agreed-upon course for China's future.

In contrast to the 1992 report, Li does not even mention Mao Zedong Thought or the people's democratic dictatorship except as they are included in the Four Cardinal Principles, a term used only once in the lengthy document. Marxism alone is noted, and then with the recommendation that it be further developed and used as a training tool to develop theoretical workers. In this economics-focused document, the threat of bourgeois liberalization is replaced by a concern with economic crimes of corruption, bribery, and embezzlement. In place of the 1992 concentration on extensively publicizing heroic models typifying exemplary deeds, the new emphasis includes finding ways to build pride and self-confidence, education in national history and culture, and improving professional competence and performance. Rewards are to be based on one's work rather than one's need. All these values are, of course, very useful to a government bent on promoting economic modernization and development.

Just as evidence of orthodox Marxism-Leninism or even Mao Zedong Thought is largely absent from this 1993 government work report, the other extreme, political reform, also remains largely untouched. As in the 1992 report, mention is made of accepting supervision from the people's congresses and their standing committees. Vague statements call for "democratic consultations" with the people's consultative organs, democratic parties, and mass organizations. This brief section in the report concludes with a call to "unclog the channels" through which the government learns the views of the masses and urges enlivening democracy at the grass-roots level.

Economic Reforms

The general trend of China's reform program, initiated at the third plenum of the Eleventh CCP Central Committee in 1978, has been periods of initiative that move China forward, followed by periods of retrenchment and rectification. The periods of retrenchment have seemed to become milder with each occurrence, perhaps for several reasons: the reform program has produced some impressive results, and there is support for maintaining its momentum; those favoring more orthodox central planning methods are dying off or becoming less wedded to their positions; and the fate of the Soviet Union and Eastern Europe has served as a negative example of what occurs when societies fail to provide enough momentum for reform initiatives.

Early Stages of Reform

The first series of reforms, introduced between 1979 and 1984, involved revising China's foreign economic relations and instituting systemic change in the vast countryside. China needed to earn foreign exchange and import foreign technology in order to build a successful modernization program. Chinese students went abroad to learn modern skills and the country was opened up to tourism and foreign business. Along with technological information and know-how, however, China's newly opened door also let in the "flies and germs" of foreign political thinking and social ways, a development that angered conservative reformers and gave them arguments to use against further rapid reforms.

In the countryside, the reform program focused on decollectivization of agriculture, essentially replacing the people's commune system with a contract responsibility system under which households contracted with the state to supply a set amount of produce, beyond which they could sell any surplus on the local market. The incentive for more and better production under this new system is obvious. Peasant incomes increased, productivity improved, and the reform program gained substantial support for further expansion.

"Free markets," where produce could be sold at negotiated prices, appeared throughout China after the October 1984 Central Committee decision to create a mixed economy in which market forces could play a significant role alongside state planning.

In 1983, a period of backlash against some of the reform measures shifted into high gear, focusing on perceived threats to the party's Marxist-Leninist ideological foundation. There was concern over the emergence of rich peasants and growing disparities in rural incomes. Some regions appeared to be prospering more than others, and differences between rural and urban incomes and lifestyles were becoming increasingly obvious. Nevertheless, by 1984, the reform program experienced another burst of activity, with the new focus being placed on the urban industrial and commercial economy. It led to the enormously successful program for developing collectively and privately owned rural and township enterprises.

In October 1984, the "Decision of the Central Committee of the Chinese Communist Party on Reform of the Economic Structure" was issued. Its aim was to create a mixed economy in which market forces played a significant role while state planning

became more of a regulatory function rather than the singular directing agent in the economy. The most advanced of these new ideas were already being introduced in the four small coastal areas that had been designated "special economic zones," or SEZs, in 1980. In these new zones, foreign technology and investment, buttressed by special preferential taxes, tariffs, and other benefits, promoted export-oriented economic development. Market regulation became the primary feature of the SEZ economies (see Chapter 6 for further discussion).

These were radical concepts in the context of the times and carried with them many challenges to the existing social, economic, and political structures. For this reason, they provoked substantial resistance from different sectors of the population and from orthodox political leaders. Reforms bypassed the concept of state ownership of the means of production by leasing industrial and commercial enterprises to individuals and collectives. They included a "factory director responsibility system" that transferred much of the authority for economic decision making into the hands of new urban factory managers. The purpose was to create more efficient use of local resources, promote local initiative, and encourage the development and use of knowledgeable, responsible, and effective front-line producers. But at the same time, this shift in authority and responsibility for decision making threatened the role and status of party and government functionaries who had performed these roles in the past. Additional tensions resulted from the fact that this urban reform program was being implemented at a time when the party was also redefining its role vis-à-vis the government. Thus, the redistribution of decision-making authority became a source of conflict and tension, further exacerbated by the introduction of additional reform concepts.

To produce the desired "socialist planned commodity economy," the reform leadership began to introduce the concepts of a rational price system, securities markets, and stock exchanges—ideas that seemed to threaten the very heart of the socialist system. These reforms raised the specters of exploitation, speculation, and gross inequalities in wealth. The introduction of labor markets and contract systems promised rewards to those skilled and motivated but threatened the "iron rice bowl" of guaranteed lifetime job tenure for all. The formulation of the bankruptcy law seemed only to promise further hardship and unemployment for the work force. Some analysts even questioned how many Western-style reforms China could absorb and still be considered a socialist country. In short, so many changes severely challenged the familiar, ideologically unified thinking of the Maoist era, under which the state and its functionaries made all key decisions and provided (at least in theory) a fairly equitable means for China's masses to sustain life.

Even with conservative resistance, the enlarged economic reform program received the endorsement of the party's Central Committee at the thirteenth CCP congress in October 1987, but with a sense of restraint and a recommendation for gradual progress. The new party general secretary, Zhao Ziyang, explained that China was in the "primary state of socialism," which began in the 1950s and would last at least a century, after which socialist modernization was to have been accomplished. The tools to be used to accomplish this distant goal involved price and wage reform, joint ventures between Chinese and foreign investors, creation of more special economic zones, decentralization of decision-making authority in critical economic areas, and a host of other market-oriented reforms. The pace of the process began to be affected by the repercussions of freeing some prices and the resulting escalating rate of inflation caused mainly by panic buying. These dislocations, combined with the social and political upheaval that occurred during the first half of 1989, produced another period of economic retrenchment after the Tiananmen incident.

Decentralization of Decision Making

The household responsibility system and factory responsibility system are both examples of comprehensive reform initiatives begun in the 1980s to transfer economic decision-making authority to lower levels. These reforms reached into administrative areas as well and involved the apportionment of revenues and expenditures. The central government worked out with the provinces a five-year agreement that set the amount of revenues local authorities must remit to the central government annually. Amounts over those agreed upon could be kept for local use. In addition, provinces and lower level units could keep profits and earnings from factories and enterprises under their authority. Thus, the reforms permitted local units to acquire funds outside the usual channels, to become less focused on taking orders from higher levels, and to develop their own policies and programs for enhancing local wealth and development. The inefficient system of administrative distribution backed by a bloated bureaucracy was being supplanted by a bargained agreement responsive to local priorities. This fiscal and administrative reform encouraged local initiatives, built favorable support for the center's reform agenda, and encouraged local governments to expand their local economies.

The negative side effects of this policy have been the opportunities it provided for local corruption and exercise of poor economic judgment by unskilled local authorities. With the new relaxation of rules and diffusion of authority, local officials could decide for themselves such matters as which local construction projects to back, what licenses or fees to support or initiate, and how revenues might be spent. These new powers offered money-making opportunities that some local officials used to enrich themselves. Others, perhaps out of ignorance, invested local resources in wasteful construction projects, made poor investments, or engaged in local protectionism in ways that thwarted market development. Official corruption has become a major rallying point for those who do not benefit from the reforms and for those disgusted by the ostentatious behavior and wealth of local officials. More important, the widespread evidence of corruption has become a powerful weapon in the hands of orthodox conservatives at the center, who oppose or want to modify the reform programs.

With the center's policy agenda dominated by complex economic issues and with the decentralization of resources to lower-level units, the locus of economic decision making has become concentrated in the government bureaucracy. This has occurred largely because of the bargaining that has taken place between the center and the provinces over the distribution and disposal of resources, as discussed above. Ministry officials bargained with provincial leaders, and when a deadlock occurred the matter had to be resolved through the State Planning Commission, the State Economic Commission, or even handed up to the State Council or its Standing Committee, the pinnacle of economic authority, before a consensus could be reached to resolve the problem.

Until 1988, the State Planning Commission represented the central macroeconomic policies that might be applied to the economy while the State Economic Commission spoke for the interests of independent enterprises and market forces. In mid-1988, the State Planning Commission merged with the Economic Commission and in the following year, the State Planning Commission established an Economic Research Center to recommend ways to deal with inflation, price reform, and macroeconomic policy. At the same time, the State Commission for Restructuring the Economic System, established under Zhao Ziyang's tutelage in 1982, regained substantial influence in reforming the economic structure in urban and rural areas. This commission was staffed with more than two hundred economists and political scientists. Drawing from the best talent in these bodies, Executive Vice Premier Zhu Rongji, also the director of the State Council Economic and Trade Office, created his own body of advisers and assumed key responsibilities for managing the economic reform agenda. Under Zhu's leadership, the market side of the economy has gained importance along with a commitment to achieve a harmonious and interdependent relationship between the center and enterprises run by provincial and lower-level units.

The ongoing bargaining between central and local units and fragmentation of economic decision-making authority posed real challenges to China's bureaucratic system. Some have seen it as producing a fragmented system, pluralistic because of its composition of various competing interest groups and bargaining units. Without clear rules, procedures, or a developed legal system, the system sometimes functions chaotically, with unpredictable and changeable outcomes. The norms and procedures of government bargaining still lack a legal system with which to

standardize and validate bargaining behavior. Others see the system as one in which the center still plays a presiding role, refereeing and brokering deals between the central bureaucracy and provincial authorities. This view suggests that the arrangement was on balance more beneficial to the center, especially in that it created local support for the economic reform agenda and engaged the energies and participation of local authorities, thereby engendering a certain cohesion and achieving a major reform policy objective, regardless of the system's sometimes messy appearance. Whatever the accuracy of these two interpretations, the reform program created serious imbalances that required intervention to arrest.

Center-Provincial Relations

The shifting of economic decision making and budgetary authority often resulted in local levels' going their own way and disregarding central directives from Beijing. Emerging regional and local economic protectionism has threatened the smooth functioning of an integrated economy. In addition, the revenue-sharing arrangements often became distorted in the hands of local authorities in ways that decreased contributions to the center, seriously threatening the level of resources available to it.

To remedy the situation, the center in June 1993 began what it called an economic adjustment program under the direction of Executive Vice Premier Zhu Rongji, aimed at recentralizing control over the overheating economy. Zhu emphasized that the new program would not follow the traditional state planning methods used previously, but instead would emphasize macroeconomic control exercised through reforms in banking, taxation, investment, and the structuring of enterprises. The proclaimed purpose of the new program was to help bring about a stable balance by applying macroeconomic policies and fiscal and regulatory controls to the increasingly complex, varied, and chaotic market forces. Another goal was to break the cyclical boom-and-bust economic pattern, alternating between periods of rapid growth and overheating—leading to setbacks, austerity, retrenchment, and, ultimately, economic stagnation.

Banks, particularly those in high-growth areas such as Guangdong Province, have engaged in speculative loans for real estate development and in shifting money between financial institutions in order to evade loan ceilings. These transactions have often left banks critically short of cash. In some provinces, this has led banks, which are supposed to make state payments to farmers who must sell part of their produce to the state, instead to issue IOUs to the farmers. Beijing has repeatedly issued directives banning this practice, and in some provinces farmers have rioted in protest.

The reform adjustment program included monetary policies intended to control the supply of money and credit, determine the cost of obtainable funds, and guide the flow of funds through regulation of interest rates—in other words, to intervene in the economy in ways similar to those of key banks (that is, monetary policy-making banks) in developed economies. Another main goal was to ensure that lending and investment activities are based on market requirements and not on directives from local government administrators. To support these monetary reforms, in mid-1993, Zhu took over control of the central bank, known as the People's Bank of China, strengthening it, making it relatively independent, and placing it in charge of China's monetary policy.

The fiscal freedom enjoyed by the provinces through the revenue-sharing system often allowed provincial authorities to operate independently, even to withhold substantial tax revenues from the center. The agreements worked out by the center and local levels varied from region to region and, since they were negotiated to cover a period of five years, did not take into account changes in local economic conditions. The combination of administrative power and taxation and regulatory powers in the hands of provincial officials became a major challenge to the center's economic health and political power.

According to the new economic reforms, the center will try to rationalize the system through budgetary programs that ensure a regular system of revenue transfer to the center and make certain that government departments and localities observe spending limits imposed by the center. For example, if a bridge or other construction project is contemplated by the

local authorities, it must already appear in the local budget and cannot be arbitrarily funded out of revenues otherwise destined for the center. In 1993, the State Council passed a draft version of the state budget law that is to provide an authoritative basis for these policies.

New tax policies were to delineate clearly separate tax systems for the central and local authorities in order to reverse the decline in income for the central government that began in the late 1980s. It was also meant to help cut the escalating budget deficit and to help equalize tax rates among provinces, companies, and individuals. These tax reforms began to take effect on January 1, 1994.

Local money-raising schemes have been especially hard on the rural population. They have involved random demands for funds, illegal penalties, and excessive levying of taxes and fees, often for use in attaining targeted growth plans. These levies have provoked serious riots in certain rural areas. To alleviate the problem, the center issued a circular in 1993 abolishing forced contributions in the form of cash payments; confiscation of grain, livestock, and household goods; and forced labor services.

Agricultural income has not kept pace with urban enterprise income, which explains the mass exodus of rural workers into areas promising greater economic opportunity. It has been estimated that China has a surplus rural labor population of about 200 million, and that by the year 2000, 250 million rural workers will seek their livelihood in the cities. The "floating population" in the cities has put severe demands on China's already strained transportation system and has created serious burdens for municipal social services. The government's proposed remedy has been to step up efforts to build more small towns and encourage the development of township-level enterprises in order to help absorb the flow of rural workers out of the countryside.

To enforce the new package of reform policies on hesitant or recalcitrant provincial officials, Party General Secretary Jiang Zemin and Executive Vice Premier Zhu Rongji toured the provinces in July 1993 to enforce the dictum that "the regions must remain in absolute unison with the center." Some ten teams were sent to twenty provinces to restrain pro-

Throughout the course of reform in the 1980s and 1990s, central authorities have periodically tried to rein in capital construction budgets at the lower levels. According to 1993 State Council regulations, construction projects contemplated by local authorities cannot be arbitrarily funded out of revenues otherwise destined for the central government.

vincial cadres who had usurped too many powers in the name of practicing reform. These teams, including members from the CCP Organizational Department, Central Discipline Inspection Commission, and Ministry of Supervision, also investigated widespread evidence of official corruption and attempted to reverse market reforms that contradicted the new reform polices emphasizing strengthening macroeconomic control of the economy.

Enterprise Reforms

The most comprehensive and challenging reform policies have been those dealing with enterprises. Their focus has been on finding ways to invigorate state-owned large and medium-size enterprises, the backbone of the former socialist planned economy and among the economy's least productive and effi-

cient units. The goal was to make them competitive and responsible for their own profits and losses, so that their regular deficits would not continue to drain the state budget. Plans have involved the sale of small state enterprises; turning others into shareholding companies; recruiting managers and workers on the basis of expertise; and ending the concepts of an egalitarian wage system and the state as the main employer. These reforms were seriously hampered by lack of an effective labor market and failure to resolve the question of ownership of assets and property. Moreover, these kinds of transforming policy initiatives required additional social safety net programs such as health services, housing programs, and social security benefits for the massive numbers of workers and managers displaced and angered by these policies. Recent reform proposals have emphasized the development of tertiary, or service, industries to absorb workers displaced by reforms in the massive state sector.

China's central leaders often finalize their reform initiatives only after trying them out in pilot projects in several provinces or municipalities. By restricting the exposure of the new reforms to a few select areas, the results can be easily observed under somewhat controlled conditions, and any deleterious effects that might occur can be limited in their impact. Recent reform efforts developed on this basis have emphasized removing the government from all enterprise activity, including state-owned, collectively owned, foreign-invested, and township enterprises. The intention was to have enterprises respond to market forces rather than administrative directives issued by government officials. In some cases, governmental departments in overstaffed organizations were to be separated from all government connections and turned into commercial companies. Former government cadres working in these departments no longer functioned as administrative personnel entitled to state benefits. These reorganized departments included commercial bureaus, textile bureaus, foreign trade bureaus, and other governmental departments. Besides providing some degree of expertise to developing local enterprises, this reform has the additional possible benefit of reducing the state bureaucracy. Another objective of this reform was to remove government officials from exercising authority over the allocation of resources, low-interest loans, and renting low-priced land—areas where in the past official abuse of powers and corruption had been rampant. Under the new arrangement, these decisions were to be guided primarily by market forces.

At the national level, the State Commission for Restructuring the Economic System announced plans in 1993 to alter government functions so that government ministries would no longer interfere in the daily operations of enterprises. The new policy encourages enterprises to take part in market competition and depend on their own resources for development. Enterprises can make their own decisions in managing production and labor and in choosing where to invest earnings. The new role of government ministries involves developing broad policy for the entire industry of which enterprises are a part, and offering coordination services and guidance directed at development, industrywide. It also includes conducting inspections and exercising supervision over the industry.

Some ministries reportedly were being converted into semi-governmental councils. The former ministries of light and textile industries now act as a bridge between the industries and the government. They provide specialized industry services to enterprises, such as analysis and forecasting of domestic and overseas markets, investment guides, and other consultancy information and services. Also at this national level, restructuring is to have the additional benefit of cutting superfluous staff. The shape and content of these reforms was clarified at the third plenum of the Fourteenth CCP Central Committee, held in November 1993 and devoted to defining the structure of China's socialist market economy.

In the meantime, the development of the nonstate sector of the economy has achieved impressive results. Production of manufactured goods by rural and township enterprises is estimated to account for more than 40 percent of the gross domestic product, a condition similar to what exists today in France and Italy. This part of the reform program has enjoyed remarkable success. The more difficult program involves restructuring the governmental system to support and encourage a market economy. Staff cuts and shifting of missions and responsibilities directly challenge the power and influence of bureaucrats and their enclaves. Lack of past success in cutting the size of the bureaucracy provides clear evidence of the challenges ahead.

In the ongoing effort to build macroeconomic control over the economy while decentralizing enterprise management and making the latter responsive to market forces, it is unclear what role the party is to play in this transformation. Some discussion has described party organizations as serving as the "political core" of the state-owned enterprises with responsibility for explaining the new reform measures and seeing that they are executed, especially the directive that the enterprise manager assume full responsibility for the successes and failures of the enterprise. There is considerable room for conflict in this arrangement between party leaders in the state-owned enterprises and the enterprise manager in the shaping and execution of policy. This may help explain why official discussion and guidance on this topic remain general and vague.

In any case, one trend is clear: party-directed ideology plays a much diminished role in the economic reform program, especially since the fourteenth party congress endorsed the socialist market economy concept. Even such conservative party leaders as Li Peng and retired but still powerful octogenarian Chen Yun have expressed their support for the economic reform agenda. There is less emphasis on economic campaigns such as the Torch Program and the Spark Plan, reform programs that relied on Maoist mass mobilization techniques to promote scientific and technological development, introduce science and technology into the countryside, and modernize agriculture. The 1993 government work report omitted all mention of these programs, which had always been discussed and praised in similar past reports. To a large extent, this development reflects an awareness of the increasing lack of relevance of ideology to meeting the new challenges. The increased exposure of the population and its leaders to modern solutions and techniques has diminished the role and function of ideology. China's economy, attracting foreign capital and technology, has become closely linked to the world economy, placing it in a new, pragmatic, and nonideological setting. The fading of ideology also reflects the political changes taking place in China during the reform period.

Political Reforms and Challenges

The economic reforms required for directing China toward a market economy have caused serious tensions within the political system. Dismantling the old centrally planned economy, with its entrenched government system of administration, continues to present a major challenge for the reform leadership. The official Chinese press has referred to the task as "relocating the deity following demolition of the temple," the deity being China's political system (democratic centralism and the Four Cardinal Principles) and the temple being the old economic and administrative system. How can the leadership create a new system attuned to the requirements of the systemic reforms being introduced without disrupting political stability? How can the diverse and proliferating aspirations and demands of local and regional interests be satisfied—and contained? What means can be found to construct a policy consensus with which to consolidate the reform program while also maintaining the momentum required to move the reform program forward? These are key questions that the reform leadership must deal with and which reach into the political aspects of reform, an area that has experienced only partial change and will likely be the most difficult aspect of reform to construct and implement.

Early Initiatives of the 1980s

Reforms that can be considered political received the most attention and development during the 1980s. Their success evoked the energies and inspired the demonstrations that led up to the tragic events of Tiananmen Square in June 1989, after which political reforms took a back seat to a renewed drive for economic reform. An early step in the direction of political reform was Deng Xiaoping's emphasis on collective leadership, which became institutionalized with the re-establishment of the party Secretariat in 1980. This body contained younger leaders with credentials and experience in all the major substantive areas of governing, thus bringing to party leadership greater expertise and more reliable information. In a sense, the Secretariat became an early example of the many professional "think tank"-style organizations that would proliferate in both party and government structures in the 1980s. By managing daily party affairs, the Secretariat brought a greater sense of professionalism to the leadership by integrating many substantive areas in formulating policy. Its new organizational standing also helped the party exert pressure on the cumbersome bureaucracy to achieve desired results.

Another key political reform came with the 1982 party constitution, which abolished the post of party chairman, a position closely associated with the cult of personality fostered so assiduously by Mao Zedong. Under Chairman Mao, this paramount official position left Chinese society subject to the whims of an aging and increasingly irrational personality. Rather than concentrating power in the hands of one person, who in Mao's case was dedicated to effecting change by destabilizing, revolutionary means, Deng's goal was to broaden the base of policy making. Rather than having a CCP chairman, the party was to be led by a general secretary who would serve on the authoritative Political Bureau Standing Committee along with the heads of the military—the chairman of the party Military Commission and the government premier. By institutionalizing collective policy making that included the heads of the party, government, and military structures, some of the excesses of China's past, provoked by narrow, ill-informed, and despotic leadership, might be avoided.

Mao's status had already been reassessed in June 1981, when the CCP produced the lengthy "Resolution on Certain Questions in the History of Our Party Since the Founding of the People's Republic of China." This document, which represents a milestone in the passing of the Maoist era, condemned the ten-year Great Proletarian Cultural Revolution as a disaster for China and criticized Mao's role in it. In an overall assessment, Mao was judged mistaken in his policies 30 percent of the time, but his presiding role over the Chinese revolution was viewed as "correct" 70 percent of the time. After this, the "respectable" Mao became associated only with the early successes of the revolutionary period and with national unification.

The waning of Mao's political power was made apparent by the fact that his designated successor, Hua Guofeng, lost his presiding CCP position to Hu Yaobang at the same 1981 party sixth plenum. Hua was branded a "whateverist," or one who "supported whatever policy decisions Chairman Mao made and followed whatever instructions Chairman Mao gave." Hua had already been replaced as government premier in September 1980 by Zhao Ziyang, another Deng protégé, like Hu. Ironically, as China approached the centennial celebrations of Mao's 1893 birth, however, the country saw a revival of Mao's personality cult in the form of a "Mao Zedong craze." This curious phenomenon separated Mao from the ideology of Maoism, recreating Mao

as a comforting icon, whose likeness could be found hanging in taxi cab windows and appearing on commercial goods such as watches, yo-yos, and clocks.

Another institutional innovation initiated by Deng was the establishment of the Central Advisory Commission (CAC) at the twelfth party congress in 1982. This new central body, headed by Deng himself, provided him with the means to remove first-generation veterans from positions of real power. Many of these elders were opposed to Deng's reform program, disturbed by its contents and pace of implementation, or generally resistant to change.

Creating the CAC, which had counterpart bodies at all levels of the political system, was a step in the direction of sidelining the powerful opposition, but did not remove its influence entirely. With each failure or setback in the reform agenda, members of the CACs, together with representatives from the propaganda and media establishments whose influence had not yet been curtailed, brought pressures to bear against policymakers, often adorned in Maoist flourishes. Conservative members attempted to use the official campaign against "spiritual pollution" in 1983 and 1984, for example, to rectify what they considered decadent behavior and corrosive liberal thought brought on by the reforms and "open door" policies. These individuals had, and continue to have at their disposal, the rich legacy of Maoist thoughts and writings.

Reform at the Local Level

A notable degree of political reform has taken place at the subnational level, in the institutions of local government. Direct elections of deputies to local people's congresses, created at the county level in 1980, have strengthened local government. These elected people's congresses, working with local governments, have become a new forum for debate of reform issues affecting local interests and as such comprise a new area of "public opinion" that party and government authorities find necessary to at least consider in the shaping of policy. At the pivotal county level, key economic reform programs are implemented and monitored, and the success or failure of these initiatives is decided. The flexibility allowed by more open debate and elections provides a stimulus to local initiative, a sense of commitment to reform policies, but also a growing awareness of local political strength and autonomy.

This broadened participation in China's governmental and political process, although limited to local institutions, does serve as a precedent and area for experimentation in pluralistic and representational politics. It also provides the central authorities with an expanded forum for assessing both the potential and shortcomings of reform policies. These cautious first steps toward greater public participation in the political process seemed to represent a tentative opening up of China's political system. Extending to other vocational groups, such as workers' congresses, the leeway to examine, debate, and criticize policies applied in factories and to express their judgment of the performance of factory managers gives these groups a meaningful voice. These vocational and local governmental groups do not have real political power, but their new public voice does exert additional pressure on the governing system to be responsive in the interests of successfully carrying out the economic reform programs.

These steps toward realizing the goals of "socialist democracy" helped fuel a movement by the mid-1980s for increased freedoms and democratic practices. Literary output became prolific, and new serial publications appeared. An article in the official *Renmin Ribao* (People's Daily) even admitted that "we cannot look to the books of Marx or Lenin to solve all our problems today." Some of the most daring even began to question the presiding role of the CCP in the political system.

Massive student demonstrations throughout the country in late 1986 brought the situation to a head, with many students burning copies of official newspapers. When General Secretary Hu Yaobang refused to denounce the demonstrators or their intellectual mentors or to retreat from the political reform agenda, the strain on the center's leadership consensus became too great. At an extraordinary expanded Political Bureau session held in January 1987, Hu was removed from the post of CCP general secretary, no doubt upon orders from Deng, and replaced by Zhao Ziyang. The reportedly unanimous decision

gave the desired appearance that leadership changes in the political system no longer come about as a result of an arbitrary purge, but with the approval of a legitimate and authoritative institution. Partly to calm the enflamed atmosphere, now-General Secretary Zhao, heavily involved in the economic reform program, explained in the official press that the implementation of political reforms in China must be understood as a "protracted process."

The student demonstrations and Hu's removal gave Political Bureau conservatives like Chen Yun and Peng Zhen an opportunity to register their opinion that the reform program threatened to negate the socialist system in favor of capitalism. Their charges became part of an intense media campaign against "bourgeois liberalization" that sought to discredit Western political concepts and emphasize the importance of adhering to the Four Cardinal Principles. The more liberal Zhao, and even Deng, sought to limit the effects of this campaign in order to protect the progress of the economic reform program, especially at the county level. They wanted to avoid the serious disruptions that accompanied the earlier campaign against spiritual pollution in 1983 and 1984. In addition, a new consensus appeared within the central leadership: political reform should remain on the agenda, although Hu had permitted more of it than the system could bear and still maintain the stability required for continued economic reform. With Hu's departure, political reform could still be implemented, but at a slower and more considered pace than before. To do otherwise risked social chaos.

Zhao Ziyang was confirmed as CCP general secretary at the thirteenth party congress, where he also laid out the theoretical underpinnings for socialist economic development in the "initial state of socialism" concept. The newly elected Standing Committee began to show a balance between liberal and conservative forces as displayed by the following members: on the left side of the political spectrum, Zhao and Hu Qili, former mayor of Tianjin; on the right, Yao Yilin, minister of the State Planning Commission, and Li Peng, soon to be the confirmed premier. The elusive Qiao Shi is considered a centrist. Leading conservative Chen Yun was retired from the Political Bureau, replacing Deng Xiaoping as chair-

Large student demonstrations in 1986 and 1989 led to the fall from grace of two of China's top leaders: first, CCP General Secretary Hu Yaobang and then Zhao Ziyang, who had replaced him as general secretary. Both were considered protégés of Deng Xiaoping. Shown here on the rostrum of the 1987 National Party Congress in Beijing, left-to-right, are Chen Yun, Deng Xiaoping, Zhao Ziyang, Li Xiannian, and Hu Yaobang.

man of the Central Advisory Commission; Deng maintained his hold over the military by serving as chairman of the party's Military Commission.

The Tiananmen Square Incident of 1989

This was the new leadership lineup that would face the greatest challenge to the CCP since its rise to power—the democracy movement demonstrations of 1989. The 1989 events grew out of the still relatively liberal atmosphere accompanying political relaxation in the mid-1980s. The campaign against bourgeois liberalization in the early 1980s had been limited to a party disciplinary campaign, while literary creation and criticism continued to flourish. Students had demonstrated for demands such as a higher priority for education, press freedoms, and an improved legal system. Even the CCP's theoretical journal *Red Flag* was renamed *Seek Truth* (after Deng's slogan "Seek truth from facts").

The event that sparked the massive pro-democra-cy demonstrations in the spring of 1989 was Hu Yaobang's death in April of a heart attack. Hu, a former Communist Youth League leader, had become the symbol of political reform and democratization. At the official ceremony to mourn Hu's death, several thousand students gathered in Tiananmen Square to honor Hu, demand his political rehabilitation, and call for further democratic reforms. The student demonstrations continued for days, with growing numbers, provoking the official *Renmin Ribao* on April 26 to describe the Tiananmen demonstrations as "a grave political struggle confronting the entire party and Chinese citizens of all nationalities."

Rather than diminishing, the demonstrations continued to escalate, even in direct defiance of a government ban. Now numbering more than a hundred thousand, students congregated in the heart of Beijing, raising new demands for dialogue, enforcement of the PRC constitution and laws, and a crackdown on party corruption and nepotism. In commemoration of the famous May Fourth movement of 1919, a watershed event in the history of modern China and one initiated by students and intellectuals (see Chapter 2 for more discussion of the May Fourth movement), another enormous demonstration took place and was soon replicated in other cities around the country. On the eve of Soviet President Mikhail Gorbachev's visit (May 15-18), the first made by a Soviet leader to China since 1959, students occupying Tiananmen Square pledged to continue their demonstrations until their pro-democracy demands were satisfied and began a hunger strike to increase the pressure.

China's leaders were distracted by the Soviet leader's historic visit and its accompanying world media attention, as well as apparently deadlocked as to how to respond effectively to their growing civilian crisis. They finally renewed their efforts to contain and end the disturbances after Gorbachev's departure. Li Peng met with students in a televised meeting on May 18, followed the next day by Zhao Ziyang's personal visit to hunger-striking demonstrators in the square. The State Council backed up these initiatives, which failed to disperse the still-determined students, by declaring martial law in affected sections of Beijing, an action opposed by the demonstrators, who now called for Premier Li Peng's immediate resignation.

The situation began to deteriorate rapidly, with workers and intellectuals joining the ranks of students. Army personnel either refused to take action against the demonstrators or were blocked from doing so by barricades erected by the crowds to prevent access to Tiananmen Square. An event that caught world media attention was the statue of the Goddess of Democracy erected in the square on May 30 (another historic date in the history of China's revolutionary student movement).

Having allowed the situation to fester for almost two months, Deng Xiaoping finally chose to use decisive force against the demonstrators. One can now only speculate about the more positive outcome that might have occurred if the center had carried on an open dialogue with the students in the early stages of the demonstrations. But given China's political culture, developed over decades if not centuries, its leaders were not ready to respond generously and

with open minds to anything that appeared to challenge their authority, especially in full view of world media. Thus, on June 3-4, PLA troops forced their way through the barricades leading to Tiananmen Square, firing on the crowds and causing thousands of deaths and injuries. The tragedy was repeated on a smaller scale in other Chinese cities.

Once such drastic and costly action had been taken, it was necessary to depict the challenge posed by the students in the most serious terms, and to identify a key party leader for blame. On June 9, Military Commission Chairman Deng Xiaoping praised the performance of the army in quelling what he called a "counterrevolutionary rebellion" aimed at the "overthrow of the CCP." CCP General Secretary Zhao was notably absent from the televised gathering to hear Deng's pronouncement. Later that month, he was removed from all party positions and eventually charged with "splitting the party" by his handling of the Tiananmen crisis. At a party plenum he was replaced as CCP general secretary by Jiang Zemin, Shanghai's CCP leader and former mayor.

In what appeared to be an attempt to bestow on Jiang the backing and power needed to equip him for his place in the official seat of power, Deng in late June announced his theory of "cores of leadership," the first core being that headed by Mao Zedong, the second led by Deng himself, and the third by the newly installed leader, Jiang Zemin. In addition, a party plenum in November accepted Deng's request to resign as chairman of the party's powerful Military Commission and be replaced in this key post by core leader Jiang.

Post-Tiananmen Political Reform

The former head of China's official news agency in Hong Kong, Xu Jiatun, who left China after the Tiananmen catastrophe, described the Tiananmen incident as a tragedy for both the CCP and the Chinese government because of the high price paid in terms of politics and morality. One such price was the halt to meaningful political reform that occurred in the wake of Tiananmen. With the political reform wing of the leadership weakened, once again the conservative political arguments asserting that political freedoms only lead to social chaos gained credence. These arguments received added strength with the social and economic breakdown in Eastern Europe under increased political freedoms and later the August 1991 coup attempt in the Soviet Union. China's leaders responded to these events with enhanced conviction that the way to preserve their power and dominance was through increased and comprehensive economic reform. Only after a thorough overhaul of the economic structure, which would provide a good standard of living for most Chinese and give them a vested interest in the country's future, could the lid be lifted on serious political reform.

The immediate aftermath of Tiananmen brought renewed emphasis on political values and enhanced supervision of CCP party organizations by the CCP's watchdog Discipline Inspection Commission at various levels. Beijing exercised its powers by transferring party secretaries and deputy secretaries of several provincial party committees and rotating governors in order to neutralize the regionalism generated by reform programs and the discontent following the Tiananmen crackdown. But at the heart of the problem was the fear that democratic centralism, the basis of the political system, was being undermined by Western democratic methods of government. Senior leaders pointed to an antagonistic relationship between the Four Cardinal Principles and bourgeois democracy, emphasizing that CCP members must "keep to our own road." Party leader Jiang Zemin, in his 1991 speech on the CCP's seventieth anniversary, rejected all suggestions that a "pluralistic" political system be adopted in China. Another dimension was added by Qiao Shi, in charge of the legislative and security establishments, who claimed that as the economy developed, democratization would become a necessary policy, but it would have to follow China's own designs.

The economic retrenchment after Tiananmen and heavy emphasis on political values disturbed Deng Xiaoping, who, during his spring 1992 tour of the prosperous southern provinces, exclaimed that "ideology cannot supply rice." Thus began a campaign launched by Deng against anti-reform conservatives, whom he claimed were placing too much emphasis on the ideological dimensions of China's developmental strategies. With support from the so-called pro-reform pragmatist faction, Deng called for accelerated economic development and pronounced "low-speed development" as "equal to stagnation or even retrogression." Deng also made the revealing statement that there was not much to fear from the capitalist influences that seemed to infuse the economic reforms as long as "the political power is in our hands." His message was that economic construction took precedence over everything and that there would be no dangerous shifting or sharing of political power until that goal had been achieved.

The October 1992 fourteenth party congress was a clear victory for Deng's chosen course. The new Standing Committee of the Political Bureau contained only one clear conservative member, Premier Li Peng. The dismantling of the Central Advisory Commission, the conservative forum for Chen Yun and others, and the retirement from the Political Bureau Standing Committee of central planner Yao Yilin and personnel chief Song Ping were indicative of a clear victory for pragmatic economic reformers over the central planners and ideological conservatives. Elevation of five provincial or municipal party secretaries to membership on the Political Bureau from the strategic provinces of Guangdong and Shandong and the municipalities of Tianjin, Beijing, and Shanghai served the dual purpose of bringing their influence to bear against a reform-resistant central government and party bureaucrats while at the same time co-opting them into the central party establishment. With so much of the economic reform program's success dependent on the cooperation and effective performance of China's major regions, it became essential for the center to recruit such key regional leaders in policy-making circles.

In the spring of 1993, Li Peng's influence, already tainted by his association with the Tiananmen crackdown, was further diminished by severe health problems, thus helping to bring to the fore economic reformer Zhu Rongji. Zhu has become China's economic czar, whose future prospects depend on his successful handling of the seemingly contradictory policies of establishing macroeconomic control over China's overheated economy while pushing ahead with rapid economic reforms.

Other notable political developments during the spring of 1993 included Jiang Zemin's appointment as president of the People's Republic of China by the Eighth National People's Congress. With this office, Jiang acquired presiding authority over the party, state, and military, reminiscent of Mao Zedong's inclusive powers. As the "core leader" of the PRC's third generation of leaders, Jiang has now acquired, with Deng's blessing, all necessary powers to serve as his successor. Qiao Shi became chairman of the National People's Congress, making him China's chief legislator, a key role if and when this body takes on substantive political duties. With Qiao's background in legal and public security affairs, his appointment indicated a cautious approach to the sensitive area of political reform. Nevertheless, the stature he brings to this position reflected some movement in the direction of giving the "rubber stamp" parliament added powers and jurisdiction. Another member of the CCP's Political Bureau Standing Committee, Li Ruihuan, became chairman of the Chinese People's Political Consultative Conference. Li's appointment suggested the leadership's desire to give a stronger voice to this "flower vase" (that is, decorative and essentially powerless) body, and to increase communication and "political consultation" with non-Communist elements.

Human Rights

China has come under increasing international pressure regarding its human rights record, particularly since the Tiananmen crisis, which was followed by numerous arrests of participants and political dissidents. To respond to this criticism, and to explain and exonerate the government's official actions, the Information Office of the State Council prepared a "white paper" on "Human Rights in China," made available in November 1991. In this document, the authors state that the primary human right is the right to subsistence and economic development. The document also maintains that human rights are subject to different interpretations depending on the prevailing ideology of each individual country. Given China's twentieth-century historical context, defined by foreign incursions, war, and poverty, the determination

of China's leaders to define human rights on their own terms and to emphasize rights to economic well-being are perhaps not surprising.

The subject of human rights in China is viewed as a collective rather than individual issue, so that the individual acquires meaning only as he relates to the collective and, by extension, to the state. Deng Xiaoping, dismissing Western concepts of democracy, human rights, and freedom as tools of power politics and "hegemonism," has claimed that "state rights are much more important than human rights." This concept of human rights grows out of China's commitment to Marxism-Leninism as well as China's own imperial tradition, which did not promote an autonomous, private, or civil society. Operating within this context, China's leaders are determined not to accept a human rights construct that is rooted in foreign, Western democratic traditions and, as such, overlooks the particularities of China's own historical and developmental experience.

China's conservative leaders—including, on this issue, Deng Xiaoping—see a close connection between human rights issues and what they see as Western promotion of "bourgeois liberalization." Western democracies are charged with advocating a uniform standard of human rights for all countries. With respect to China, the imposition of a Western-defined human rights concept is viewed as part of a larger plan to undermine China's socialist system in favor of "peaceful evolution," or the gradual adoption of Western democratic governmental forms. As noted above, some have expressed their suspicions in the most stark terms, charging that Western agents are operating in China with the sole purpose of subverting the socialist system and its political leadership.

Because the issue of human rights is bound up with issues of national sovereignty and independence, China's response to Western pressures on human rights issues has been largely perfunctory. Chinese delegations have been sent abroad reportedly to explore and discuss the contents of human rights issues. Key political dissidents have been released from prison or had their sentences shortened, but with the timing of these events carefully attuned to achieve China's key foreign policy goals. Western reporters noted, for example, the release from prison several months early of China's most important democracy and human rights activist, Wei Jingsheng, who had been imprisoned for fifteen years for his leading role in the 1979 Democracy Wall demonstrations. (For a description of the Democracy Wall demonstrations, see Chapter 4.) The release came shortly before the International Olympic Committee was to make its decision on the location of the Olympic Games for the year 2000 for which China was a key contestant. After the Olympic Committee announced its decision (which did not go in China's favor), more arrests of political dissidents were carried out in key Chinese cities. A new State Security Law adopted in February 1993 became the basis for the arrest of several journalists charged with leaking state secrets to sources outside China.

The existence of the "global village" has made it harder for China's leaders to hide what in most Western countries are considered human rights abuses. The determination to open the economy to the outside world and to join international organizations has made domestic events more visible and accessible to outside media and visitors. Improved telecommunications have brought to China's population a more accurate and usually more friendly perception of the outside world, making it difficult for the propaganda ministry to portray foreign influence as wholly negative and polluting. The more positive popular perceptions of the outside world thus mitigate the conservative political influences to some extent. This new perception, however, must be balanced against evidence that there is general support for strict policies inside China. Most Chinese reportedly believed that the Tiananmen crackdown was necessary. Thus, the overall thrust of human rights policy in China most likely will continue to be responsive to internal concerns, not external pressures.

China's Prospects

The Legacy of Deng Xiaoping

Deng Xiaoping, in his cautious attempt to provide political leadership for China's "second revolution," has developed what might be seen as a unique political model. At its center is an emphasis on a collective and consensual leadership style. Deng has called on various officials holding major portfolios to play decisive leadership roles. He has expected them to maintain a balanced and cooperative leadership style, regarded as essential to ensuring the stability in the system required to pursue the all-important economic reform agenda. When Hu Yaobang failed to contain the divisive student demonstrations, he failed the test of a leader able to maintain the harmony and discipline necessary for keeping the political system in balance. Zhao Ziyang's error was labeled as "splittism," or showing personal concern for the interests of the students instead of considering as first priority the interests of the state and the survival of the challenged CCP. Zhao also revealed in his meeting with Gorbachev that Deng, even though officially retired, reviewed all major policy decisions. Although this was assumed by almost everyone, it is never officially admitted, given the recognized official decision-making structure already in place.

Deng's model thus seems to require leadership that can recognize tensions and problems in the system, debate them collectively at the highest level, arrive at and uphold a consensus solution, and then implement decisions with a firm hand. There must also be a careful balance between ideological initiative and reform policies, which has proved to be one of the most difficult aspects of Deng's leadership requirements. Deng himself has never hesitated to use campaigns for party discipline or to attack bourgeois liberalization, but only up to a certain point. And knowing just when to turn to a new direction or course correction in order not to stifle economic reform has been another subtlety that has sometimes eluded leader candidates. Leaders must also show innovation when dealing with otherwise intractable problems, as Deng did when he traveled to the prosperous southern provinces in 1992 to launch a campaign to mobilize support for accelerated reform, despite conservative resistance in Beijing. The Dengist model also requires that leaders demonstrate absolute loyalty to the CCP and its survival, and to furthering the progress of the economic reform agenda.

Deng has identified Jiang Zemin as the "core" of China's third generation of leadership and bestowed

The Fifth Modernization

China's best-known prisoner in the West until his release on September 14, 1993, Wei Jingsheng first attained prominence during the Democracy Wall movement of 1978-1979, when he published an essay that proposed adding to Zhou Enlai's touted Four Modernizations one more—democracy. An electrician by training and a former Red Guard, Wei wrote articulate appeals for democracy in the journal *Tansuo* (Exploration), which he edited. He used the journal as a platform for attacking the policies of senior leaders, including Deng, whom he called China's "new autocrat."

The Democracy Wall movement, the first outburst of dissent since the end of the Cultural Revolution, was so called because its primary manifestation was the "big character" posters pasted up on a wall in central Beijing—mostly handwritten posters airing citizens' grievances and political opinions. The notices were permitted for a brief period, but after the liberalized political atmosphere encouraged by Deng had achieved its intended effect of exposing his political enemies, the crackdown was swift. Wei was one of many jailed for inciting counterrevolutionary propaganda. Accused of divulging military secrets to foreign journalists, Wei was sentenced to fifteen years in prison (of which he had served more than fourteen when he was released).

The long jail term gave Wei an opportunity to develop his ideas on democracy and social, political, and economic development. From prison, he wrote letters to government and Communist Party leaders, explaining his concepts and suggesting ways to implement them. Many of these letters were published in the Hong Kong press after his release. They reveal Wei's relentless advocacy of a more enlightened political system to promote modernization and his view that economic development should not precede political democracy. The letters also show that, far from calling for the overthrow of the government or the party, Wei believes that democracy can develop only slowly in China through cooperation between the Chinese government and people—overthrowing the government, he cautions, could lead to autocracy and thus would not aid in democracy's development. Since his release Wei has been uncowed by renewed government pressure. One of the few Chinese dissidents to resist such intimidation, he has continued to publish political essays both in China and abroad.

In April 1994 Wei was detained by police reportedly for speaking out on human rights and for meeting with the U.S. assistant secretary of state for human rights, John Shattuck. As of December 1994, official charges had still not been filed and Wei was still being held incommunicado by the State Security Ministry.

---

on Jiang all major powers as CCP general secretary, PRC president, and chairman of both the party and the state Military Commissions. This action gave Jiang access to the resources and influence of China's three major bureaucracies. Jiang has made use of this opportunity, building his base and strength particularly in the military, where he has had the least exposure and where his influence will be sorely needed in the leadership transition after Deng's demise. Jiang has made key speeches to the troops, visited military regions, and no doubt played a key role in the post-Tiananmen reshuffle of military and police personnel.

Jiang Zemin's ideological cast has sometimes been conservative and even hard-line. He won Deng's praise for his firm handling of events during the spring of 1989 in Shanghai. When Deng called for an accelerated pace of reform beginning in 1992, Jiang again responded quickly with support. Jiang is Deng's choice to balance the top CCP leadership by holding the middle ground between conservative and still-influential Li Peng and the more liberal and fast-rising economic reformer Zhu Rongji. Jiang's military connections would be needed to provide the muscle to maintain this balance. Jiang may also be bland enough to be trusted not to initiate his own extensive reform programs after Deng's passing; such a program might threaten the direction chosen by Deng for China's modernization. The term *bland* is meant to convey the perception that Jiang, being from the provinces, was not tainted by the 1989 events in Beijing; he has not been identified clearly with any central leadership faction—liberal or conservative—and, having been educated in the Soviet Union, he comes from a technocrat background.

Deng also leaves behind a rich legacy of speeches and writing. The first volume of a three-volume collection, entitled *The Selected Works of Deng Xiaoping,* was published after Deng's consolidation of his power at the twelfth CCP congress in 1982 and became required reading for party members. Volume III, published in November 1993, clarified Deng's decisive role in the Tiananmen crackdown. Together these volumes, along with one entitled *Building Socialism with Chinese Characteristics,* provide guidance on economic policy, ideological questions, and foreign policy matters and, in effect, codify Deng's reform policies. They comprise an authoritative body of material that Deng's successor can employ to continue the reform program, and even quote to bolster his own legitimacy. At the same time, however, like any extensive and comprehensive collection of writings, Deng's works might also succumb to the imagination and pens of those who might want to write a different reform agenda. Certainly, Deng took similar leeway with some of Mao Zedong's writings in order to cast legitimacy on his own thoughts and programs.

Although Deng Xiaoping has designated Jiang Zemin his successor to lead and guide China into the next century, the success of designated successors at maintaining that status has been truly dismal. Mao's anointed successor, Hua Guofeng, proved to be only a bridge figure between Mao and the rehabilitated and charismatic Deng. Some observers have described Jiang as a similar kind of figure, only linking Deng to a future leader. Deng's first and second choices to succeed him, Hu Yaobang and Zhao Ziyang, failed the leadership test.

Because the Chinese political system lacks an institutionalized process for leadership succession, it must instead rely on the judgment and choice of the presiding and paramount leader. In Deng's case, although he did not even hold any official positions, he still served as the architect of leadership and policy consensus and the broker of deals both at the center and in the regions. Deng has led by virtue of his identity with the Long March generation, his immense political skill at mobilizing public support for his programs and disciplining the central leadership to follow his direction, and his personal charisma and style. But as Deng's health weakened in 1994, reportedly with only brief periods of lucidity, evidence of active factionalism in pursuit of strengthened personal power bases readily surfaced. The conferred mantle of leadership, based only on Deng's selection of the candidate, may not be enough in the period of transition after Deng's death or in a crisis situation during which Deng is incapacitated or gone from the scene. Deng's failure to put in place a succession arrangement based in law is further evidence of his inability to propose political and legal reforms at the same level of substance and creativity as his economic initiatives. Without putting a secure succession system at the center of China's political system, Deng may have planted the seeds for disruption or even the dismantling of his cherished reform structure.

Competing Forces in China's Future

The quest to realize the goals of China's "second revolution" has put China's political system under heavy stress. The commitment to work within the confines of a Marxist-Leninist political system limits the options to the quality and leadership of one political party and, as this arrangement plays out, one charismatic political leader. His predominance ensures that the legal system cannot readily regulate political institutions. Severe limits are placed on the expression of dissent, leaving the system without any effective escape valve at a time of rapid change and dislocation. The growing lack of ideological coherence with the introduction of so many market-oriented reforms evokes confusion and alienation for many. Thus, the question remains: can the system withstand the pressures produced by this ambitious reform agenda and still remain intact?

The system must cope with a variety of emerging interest groups bent on protecting their newly won gains. Many of these are provincial and regional economic powerhouses, some reportedly with military supporters. There are many other potential threats, however, from diverse sources including student and intellectual groups that have tasted the power of the streets and want more freedom of speech and clean, responsible government; dissidents who have gone abroad and voiced their criticisms in the press of China's political and human rights abuses; an overheated economy that still suffers from inefficient state enterprises and irrational allocations of resources; poorer regions of the country that are aware of the economic winnings of other parts of the country and want their share; competition and lack of job security that threaten a once modest but more secure lifestyle; minority groups who are responding to ethnic and religious tensions on China's borders and have found an audience with the Western press; a new and alienated generation that no longer responds to party ideology; and perhaps even the military, which desires a larger share of the budget for its own modernization programs.

What are the forces for stability and continuity that might contain and balance the sources of strain listed above? Most of the population is better off under Deng's reforms than ever before—some much better off. The standards of living for many have doubled within ten years. Opportunities seem to be emerging for real economic and social mobility. Chinese are freer to travel and move about the country and can make more choices about their future and lifestyle. The population (and leadership) has more access to accurate information about developments inside and outside China and thus is becoming more skillful, sophisticated, and more involved in the world community. Technological advancements and better medical care are reaching more of the population. Opportunities seem to be present at least at the village and county levels for expressing opinions and dissent, even if these channels are truncated at these levels and do not reach upward to real policy-making circles.

Added to the information revolution, the comprehensive economic reforms have tended to reduce the power of the state over the economy and by extension over the lives of the Chinese populace. Decentralization and its concomitant economic choices in the marketplace have led to other personal choices.

Religious, clan, and lineage organizations have re-emerged, particularly in rural areas. These events, of course, do not automatically lead to democracy or democratic institutions, but there does seem to be more flexibility and variety in Chinese life than previously experienced. Such developments have permitted the emergence of pockets of autonomous or civil society, free from preponderant state control.

Most Chinese want the reform program to work in order to make China's voice powerful in the world again. Whether this will happen is still far from certain, but the force of nationalistic sentiments is an important factor in its favor. The amorphous factor of nationalism has already been noted as a pervasive and motivating factor in China's policy behavior. China's many defeats and humiliations during the early twentieth century, along with its long and glorious history as a country that set the traditions and customs for others to follow, combine to strongly motivate China to seek renewed status in the world community. For China to accomplish this primary goal, the country must not break apart and fail in the course of the reform program. The pervasive fear of social chaos is one other aspect of this sentiment.

The next essential step is political reform, which Deng Xiaoping has left essentially undone. Deng's reputation will be lauded for innovations and progress in the realm of economic reform, and if the economy continues to prosper, it may provide a basis for political reform. The Chinese political tradition, as well as that of other Asian states with a grounding in Confucianism, seems to require a strong leader and centralized system to initiate and direct change while preventing social divisions. Speeches and volumes focused on political reform produced by such a leader might provide the impetus to political reform. Already, some laws and regulations exist on paper but have not been implemented. Zhao Ziyang and intellectuals of the 1980s became associated with a strain of reform that expressed admiration for the "new authoritarianism" they saw in Singapore, South Korea, and Taiwan. Under such a system, a benevolent dictatorship, headed by a charismatic leader and supported by technocrats and other experts, might lead China to enlightened state power.

After being suppressed following the 1989 democracy movement, local elections began to make a comeback in the early 1990s, holding out hope for further political reforms in China. Here, an elderly villager in Fujian Province casts her first vote in 1994.

Another scenario envisions future reforms directed at mending the bifurcated Chinese political system, divided as it is between the powerless representational people's congress system and the authoritative Chinese Communist Party system. With real powers based in a legal framework and awarded to the people's congresses, some of the pressures and tensions present in the political system might be relieved. The National People's Congress, for example, might function as a substantial legislature and balance the power of the CCP. But whether Jiang Zemin, as Deng Xiaoping's successor, is capable of bringing about such an elemental shift in political power is at least questionable.

Following the dictates of Marxism-Leninism, China's leaders have found it necessary to practice economic reform before taking on political change. The phrase sometimes used to describe this approach is "repairing the canal before releasing the water." Added to this ideological foundation is the factor of nationalism. In their tentative efforts at political reform, the commitment of China's leaders has been to maintain what they consider the authenticity of Chinese political institutions by having them defined and determined solely through accumulated Chinese experiences. As China's chief legislator Qiao Shi emphasized when questioned about future political reform, China "will not copy anything developed by a foreign country." With this as a premise, the future of political reform in China remains largely undefined. What might be expected is a more open, representational system permitting some basic freedoms. However, even a somewhat circumscribed party state in China is not likely to willingly forfeit any of its essential power in the key political arena.

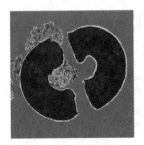

CHAPTER 6

THE DRAGON STIRS: CHINA'S ECONOMY UNDER REFORM

As it approaches the millennium, China ranks among the world's fastest growing economies, a prospect made all the more significant given its gigantic size. China's economy is undoubtedly among the world's largest in absolute terms. Using standards of measurement of the gross domestic product (GDP) based on purchasing power parity, the International Monetary Fund ranks China's economy a close third after only the United States and Russia, and ahead of Japan. Although China qualifies as an economic superpower, by many specific indicators it appears to be a developing—even preindustrial—economy. Strong growth is likely to continue in the near term, but there will be numerous challenges along the way.

China's economic system defies categorization into the standard economic types and cannot be understood strictly within the conventional framework of neoclassical economic theory. Its long history, culture, and the stark contrast between its gigantic population and natural resources and its scarce capital set the backdrop for China's institutions and performance and its prospects for growth and change.

Beginning in 1978, China's leaders promoted economic structural reforms to decrease material planning and increase use of market mechanisms, even employing practices associated with capitalism. At the same time, the leadership steadfastly maintained an official ideology of Marxism-Leninism tempered with elements of Maoism. The elements of central planning and central and local government control of the economy have largely evolved away from the Stalinist model, but these elements have by no means disappeared.

Geography and Resources

Population and Labor Resources

For China as for other countries, geography, resources, and population fundamentally shape the country's development. China is the world's most populous country; its absolute land area and other resources are also relatively large. Yet because of the size of the population, material resources are very scarce when measured in per capita terms. China's huge population and high average population density thus unavoidably are the key factors influencing economic conditions, policy choices, and future prospects.

In the richer agricultural plains and lowlands, rural population density exceeds that in most U.S. cities many times over. In large Chinese cities, crowds thicker than any ever encountered in North America or Europe fill everyday shopping streets and normal rush hour traffic. Some locations in the hinterlands may have relatively sparse population, especially in remote western mountains and deserts. Yet even in most of these areas, a walk in any direction will quickly encounter human habitation.

Indeed, China's absolute population is five times larger than that of the United States. Given their approximately similar land area, China's average population density, at over 119 persons per square kilometer, is more than four times the density of 27

Table 6.1   United States-China
Geodemographic Comparisons, 1990

	United States	PRC
Area (sq. km.)	9,400,000	9,600,000
Total population	249,924,000 [1]	1,143,330,000
Population density (persons/sq.km.)	27	119
Arable land (sq. km.)	1,900,000 [2]	957,200

Sources: U.S. Department of Commerce, Bureau of the Census, *Statistical Abstract of the United States* (Washington, D.C.: U.S. Government Printing Office, 1989, 1992). *Zhongguo tongji nianjian* (China Statistical Almanac), 1988, 1991.

[1] 1990 total.

[2] 1982 figure; includes cropland, idle cropland, and pasture.

persons per square kilometer found in the United States (see Table 6.1). China's population as of the end of 1993 was estimated at about 1,171,577,000, over 20 percent of the world's total population. The population is approximately 51.5 percent male and 48.5 percent female.

During the 1980s the population was weighted toward the young: in 1990, 38 percent of the population was less than 20 years of age, 50 percent of the population was less than 25 years of age, 59 percent less than 30 years, 66 percent less than 35 years, 74 percent less than 40 years, and 80 percent of the population was less than 45 years of age. This means that in the short term, people of an age to be in the work force will be relatively abundant, and a small proportion of the population will be dependent on them. If population growth is slow—within or near official targets—the population as a whole will age substantially and eventually the proportion of those dependent on the work force will rise, an effect seen already in Japan and Western industrialized countries.

Improvements in public health have contributed to the population's changing age composition. China's aggregate health statistics are very good on average. Most are comparable with middle- or high-income countries in the rest of the world.

Formal education is widespread at the earliest stages, but tapers off through secondary school. By 1985, 76 percent of females and 79 percent of males remained in school through the fourth grade. The

bias toward males becomes stronger at higher grades. In 1989, the ratio of females to males still in school at the end of primary school was 85:100, and by the end of secondary school the ratio drops further to 71:100. Both ratios are significantly higher than in 1965. As a proportion of the entire youth population, very few Chinese proceed to institutions of higher education, although in absolute terms they are still numerous.

The majority of China's population resides in the countryside and in rural areas attached to city administrative jurisdictions. In recent years, a substantial population shift toward urban areas has occurred, although perhaps not to the extent indicated by World Bank figures, which show urban population rising from 18 percent of the total population in 1965 to 56 percent in 1990. The discrepancy between official Chinese statistics and those reported by the World Bank may be explained in part by the significant amount of unauthorized, temporary rural-urban migration—called the "floating" or "transient" population (*liudong renkou*)—and in part by the fact that population residing within city jurisdictions is not necessarily urbanized, though it may have been included in World Bank totals as such. According to Chinese employment statistics, 60 percent of the entire labor force is employed in agricultural and other extractive activities—the primary sector of the economy. Since rural labor generally resides in rural areas, most likely with the family, the rural population is likely to be higher than the 44 percent suggested by the World Bank. Indeed, the rural household population figure of 903,220,000 persons in 1990 accounts for 80 percent of the total population according to Chinese figures.

The population in cities of one million or more remained at 9 percent of the total population from 1965 to 1990, but dropped as a percentage of urban population from 49 percent in 1965 to 27 percent in 1990. This suggests that China's increasing level of urbanization comes from the growth of smaller, peripheral cities and towns.

The "floating" population is a large category that might include people moving between urban areas, between rural areas, and between rural and urban areas. According to one estimate, more than 100 million rural residents in recent years have migrated to coastal or inland cities in search of work. They range from individuals and small groups making personal or professional business trips to transient rural laborers in search of temporary work, to those migrating illegally in search of permanent work. Perhaps the largest class is the transient labor in search of or proceeding to temporary work, because residency rules and the household registry system prohibit permanent relocation, but not temporary arrangements.

Several waves of Chinese migrations since the mid-nineteenth century (mainly to Southeast Asia, Indonesia, and North and South America) have distributed the Chinese diaspora throughout the world. While the general reasons for migration have varied, the Chinese expatriate communities, once established, range from economically viable to extremely successful. Generally referred to as "overseas Chinese," they were estimated to number between 25 and 50 million in 1993, including communities in the United States, Canada, Indonesia, Thailand, Malaysia, Singapore, Philippines, Vietnam, Burma (Myanmar), and elsewhere. Although this overseas Chinese population is only about 3 to 4 percent of the size of the PRC's population, the wealth of overseas Chinese is estimated at about two-thirds the size of PRC national income, while their family, professional, and especially financial ties remain very important to China (see Chapter 10).

Geography and Resource Distribution

China has a land area of about 9.6 million square kilometers (4.2 million square miles), about 2 percent larger than that of the United States (see Table 6.1). Also like the United States, most of China lies between 20 degrees and 50 degrees latitude. China's land is very high and mountainous, with more than half the area lying at elevations above 1,000 meters (about 3,300 feet) above sea level.

Compared to the rich croplands of the midwestern and coastal areas that cover more than 20 percent of the United States, less than 10 percent of China's surface is arable—amounting to less than 7 percent of the world's arable land area. China's cultivable area is low by comparison with the United States (see Table 6.1), even more so on a per capita basis. Chi-

na's arable land per capita is even less than the densely populated countries of the Netherlands, India, Japan, Indonesia, Egypt, Bangladesh, and South Korea. Much of the coastal and lowland cropland in China is used for paddy rice; the inland farm fields are in narrow river valleys and terraced up mountainsides. In the northwestern loess plateau lands of Shanxi and Shaanxi Provinces, all elevations are terraced.

China's population is most heavily distributed in the North China plain (about 270 million), the eastern Yangzi River basin and delta (about 230 million), and the South China plain and coastal areas (about 140 million), in the central Sichuan Basin (about 106 million), and in the Northeast China plain (about 100 million). China's population, arable land, and industrial development are generally skewed toward the eastern coast.

Freshwater resources are relatively concentrated in the Amur River (Heilongjiang) system in the northeast, along the two major east-west corridors of the Yellow River (Huanghe) and the Yangzi River (Yangzi Jiang or Chang Jiang) to the eastern coast, and the northwest-southeast corridor of the Pearl River (Zhujiang) to the southern coast. Small hydroelectric and irrigation dams are numerous. Large dams built on the Yellow River during and since the 1950s have been disappointing because of rapid siltation. The Yellow River contains so much silt from its path through the loess plateau that for some distance it flows in a channel created by the silt built up as high as 30 meters above the surrounding floodplain. Periodically this "hanging" section of the river jumps over and out of its raised banks and floods the vast areas below. A controversial project to build dams on the middle Yangzi River, in the planning stages for over twenty years, finally commenced in the early 1980s. The lower dam at Yichang has already been built, and construction on the remainder is under way. For the purpose of hydroelectric generation and downstream flood control, the project will eventually submerge the Three Gorges stretch of the river in eastern Sichuan as well as much farm and residential land in the province. Opponents of the project question whether the combination of known and unanticipated ecological, economic, and social consequences will be worth the returns from the dams, which will produce the world's largest reservoir to date.

China's climate is generally temperate, though it ranges from monsoonal in the tropical southeast to cool in the mountainous forests of the far northeast. Temperature ranges are widest in the arid Gobi and Taklimakan Deserts covering vast areas between Mongolia in the north, the arid Tibetan plateau and the Himalayan range in the southwest, and the Kunlun and Tian ranges in the west. Timber reserves are sparse, as there is proportionately little natural woodland area. Some mineral reserves—including many strategic metals—are abundant, but ferrous ores are not.

China's energy reserves are fairly large, equivalent to approximately 500 billion tons of standard coal, or 400 years' supply at 1990 rates of consumption. Eighty percent of the reserves are coal, much of it deposited in northern and northwestern China. The northeast has known oil reserves close to transportation routes, while reserves in central China appear to be small and those in the Taklimakan desert of Xinjiang Province are somewhat remote. The expectation that oil might be extractable from the South China Sea and from new wells in the seabed off the Pearl River delta may have increased China's concern regarding the disputed Spratly, or Nansha, Islands.

Income and Living Standards

How well does China feed, clothe, and otherwise provide for its population? During the early years of the PRC, the record was relatively good, although domestic political disruptions periodically interrupted progress until the substantial institutional changes initiated in 1978 began to take effect. Over the long run, average annual growth of production since shortly after 1949 has been a respectable 8 percent, and average annual growth of real per capita GDP was 7 percent during the 1980s. These rates are relatively high and remarkable by international standards, but they conceal wide fluctuations as well as urban-rural and interregional disparities.

The rate of economic activity recovered relatively rapidly during the 1950s from the ravages of the war with Japan and the civil war, as the nation concentrated on reconstruction. By the mid-1950s, China had made substantial progress in growth of output and national income per capita.

Policy problems in the late 1950s disrupted this good start, however. On the supply side, the drastic and accelerated collectivization of agriculture in the people's commune movement, bad weather conditions, and the Great Leap Forward campaign to boost domestic production through encouragement of local small-scale industry at any cost led to regional famines and a 5 percent decrease in national population during 1960, one of the largest recorded famines and population drops in a short period in history.

Policy adjustments helped improve growth from 1962 to 1966, but the Cultural Revolution policies of 1966 through 1976 disrupted economic activity, inhibiting supply recovery and growth. Despite these policy blunders, real growth of gross agricultural and industrial production did reach a substantial average annual rate of 8 percent over the 1952-1976 period, increasing in every year except for 1961-1962 and 1967-1968.

Gross output is only part of the picture of economic growth, however. On the demand side, the population and therefore the number of consumers grew rapidly over the same period. During the late 1950s a policy debate over population management was resolved in favor of a simplistic, perhaps naive reapplication to China of Stalin's policy for the Soviet Union. That country clearly suffered a severe labor shortage, especially in Siberia. The Stalinist policy emphasized the labor potential of the population, subsidizing and otherwise encouraging childbearing to that end. When actively pursued in China, this policy resulted in population growth from the 1950s through the early 1970s sufficient to keep the rate of per capita real income growth low.

During the first three decades of the PRC, the rate of investment in heavy industry as a proportion of national income often exceeded 30 percent. By some estimates, the country's low income growth, combined with high industrial investment, resulted in stagnation or even some decline in consumption and general living standards from the 1950s to the 1970s.

The Chinese economy predictably suffered from

production disincentives and other economic dys-function, a tendency toward frugality and asceticism in Chinese culture notwithstanding. Compared to the United States or other developed industrial countries, conditions for the average family in urban areas were spartan at best, while average material conditions in rural areas could best be described as undiscernible from previous centuries.

Urban housing had been neglected in both the Sta-linist planning phases and Maoist campaigns. From the late 1950s through the 1970s, the housing short-age reached crisis proportions despite repeated cam-paigns to rusticate portions of the urban population. The Stalinist plans de-emphasized investment in the production of many consumer durable and nondura-ble goods. By the 1970s, the average urban nuclear family felt fortunate to have one room of only a few square meters at most as housing. The building would probably be masonry or reinforced concrete and was unlikely to be decorated beyond the basic plaster or painted concrete. Kitchens and lavatory facilities were shared by several families in court-yards or hallways. Electricity depended on over-extended power grids, and brownouts were frequent. Cold running water depended on electrical supply. Heating and cooking was generally by coal or coal briquettes. Where available, natural gas was general-ly supplied by large (about five-gallon) refillable steel bottles. Where piped, it was subject to variation in supply, as was electricity. A bicycle had the status a family car would have held in the United States during the 1950s, mechanical wristwatches and cam-eras were major status symbols, and possession of appliances on the order of radios and sewing ma-chines was the highest conceivable goal of house-hold consumption.

Rural housing depended on each locality's tradi-tional construction methods. Masonry was favored in many regions, but other traditional materials, includ-ing the yaodong dwellings neatly carved into the loess banks of north-central China, remained wide-spread. Harvested stubble—the stalks of grain crops—was a major source of cooking and heating energy, though coal or wood might be used near pro-duction sites. In relatively warm regions, methane gas generated in closed wet compost (sewage) tanks

served as household energy supply. The ingenuity of traditional construction made the most of any com-bustion. Heat from the cookstove is channeled through the kang—a masonry platform used for seat-ing and sleeping, and as a heat reservoir. Where available, electrical supply was generally by small generator, which depended on the availability of oth-er energy supplies and generator parts. Since the pro-portion of marketed output was small as a percentage of rural production throughout China, rural cash in-comes tended to be very low except for rural house-holds near major cities. Even fabric for clothing might be woven in the household or by a neighbor. The ownership of a radio was beyond the expectation of the average household. But rural dwellers did and still do enjoy one advantage over urban households: relative lack of constraint on building space.

Food supply and consumption was mostly grains and grain-equivalent food sources such as tubers. Vegetables, much less meats and fishes, were rele-gated to a role as condiments to the main grain prepa-ration, except for the abundant preparation of cere-monial nongrain dishes during holidays and other banquet occasions.

After a transition period during the mid-1970s, the emerging economic reform program in late 1978 and early 1979 revealed a new, materially pragmatic economic philosophy. During the 1980s specific pol-icies advanced the fundamental reform goal of eco-nomic rationality within the context of China's na-tional condition and needs. China achieved consistently higher rates of growth in national in-come per capita after 1980 through aggressive pur-suit of economic growth, on the one hand, and imple-mentation of population control policies, on the other.

In the 1980s, rapid transformations occurred in the incomes and consumption patterns of many ur-ban and rural residents. In urban areas, the state em-barked on a decade-long program to "catch up" with the backlogged demand for housing and workspace by erecting high-rise apartment and office complexes within the traditional cities and, in suburban areas, increasing the per capita living space. Many rural dwellers embarked on collective or private construc-tion of housing with their new savings. Attention early in the reform period to the need for increased investment in light industry, combined with rapidly growing disposable incomes, led to rising expectations for consumer good availability, quality, and type. During the 1980s and 1990s, urban households increasingly pursued the acquisition of televisions—first black-and-white, then color—washing machines, refrigerators, electronic audio-video equipment, higher grades of furniture, interior decoration, and even air-conditioners. Motorcycles and automobiles would seem to be next in line, but regulations and spatial and other constraints restrained the average urban household's personal acquisition of these large consumer durables.

Rural households followed similar trends. In some rural areas convenient to markets and employment opportunities, the rate of growth of incomes and consumption has been much faster than even in urban areas. However, on average and in remoter rural areas, the growth of rural incomes lags behind that of urban areas.

The diet of urban and rural dwellers substantially improved. The consumption of nongrain vegetable and meat products increased in both quality and quantity compared to pre-1980 standards. By the late 1980s most rationing schemes for grain (staples) and nonstaples were phased out.

Comparisons of growth in income and living standards in China both before and after 1978 depend on the base period, currency of valuation, and other indicators. The World Bank reports Chinese gross national product (GNP) per capita, for example, as measured in nominal U.S. dollars, rising by an average annual rate of about 2 percent, from $230 in 1978 to $370 in 1990, implying a decline in real income as measured in 1978 dollars. The absolute dollar value of GNP per capita would place China among the lowest income countries in the world, near to Haiti and Ethiopia.

That analysis, however, suffers from the devaluation trend of the yuan (or renminbi) relative to the U.S. dollar over the period of comparison. When measured in yuan terms, the results appear quite different, and more in keeping with China's higher rankings in other living standard indicators such as longevity and health.

China's economic growth ambitions have been stated explicitly. In 1982, the twelfth congress of the CCP set the goal of quadrupling 1980 GNP by the year 2000. Over twenty years this would require an average annual real GNP growth rate of a little more than 7 percent. At about 15 percent average annual growth, national income and GNP in nominal renminbi more than quadrupled from 1980 to 1990, and per capita nominal GNP grew at 13 percent. However, these do not take price inflation into account. Adjusting for changes in prices, real GNP grew at 9 percent during the decade, and real per capita GNP grew at about 7 percent. In other words, measured in Chinese currency at comparable prices, real income per person grew on target for the first decade of the proposed twenty-year reform program.

Reforms in the Rural Economy

Evaluation of post-1978 reform policies varies widely among analysts both inside and outside China. Major issues include interpretation of the intent and effects of the institutional changes beginning in the late 1970s and continuing into the 1990s.

The "economic structural reform" program has not yet liberalized all markets. In rural China, agricultural activity has been decentralized and is managed largely at the household level. Private and collective rural enterprises have undergone tremendous, albeit uneven, growth since 1978. Yet, more than fifteen years after the inception of the post-Mao program of economic structural reforms, banking and finance remained largely state-owned and operated, as does most large-scale industrial capital. Production for export is encouraged—and rewarded—by administrative design, as is direct foreign investment. Further reforms and readjustment of profit remittances, taxes, wages, and prices have all been discussed or attempted.

Pre-1978 Agricultural Production

China is the world's single largest grain producer: in 1990 agricultural output contributed about a third of GDP, using about two-thirds of China's labor force.

Table 6.2   China's Gross Domestic Product by
Sector, 1990

	Value (hundred million yuan [1])	Percentage of total GDP
Primary sector	5,024	28
Secondary sector	7,829	44
Industry	(6,981)	(40)
Construction	(848)	(5)
Tertiary sector	4,818	27
Communications and Transport	(956)	(5)
Commerce	(944)	(5)
Total	17,686	100
GDP per capita	(1,558)	—

Source: 1991 Zhongguo tongji nianjian (China Statistical Almanac), Table 2-12.

[1] 1991 current value.

At about 366 million tons of grain per year in 1989, China produces about 30 percent more grain than does the United States (284 million tons). If the grain-equivalent of root crops is also included, China's total production of 506 million tons is about 70 percent higher than that of the United States, at 302 million tons.

China's dominance extends to specific crops and to nongrain production and processing: China leads the world in rice, tobacco, hogs, and brewing, to name a few. It probably holds the largest stocks of grain, although given its large population, the per capita stocks and surplus are not large.

Fertilizer consumption (262 tons per hectare) is high by comparison with the low-income countries, but close to that of the United States (250 tons per hectare) and lower than that of countries with the largest farm subsidy programs. Yields per hectare in China's grain production are 4 tons per hectare, low only when compared with 4.5 tons in the United States and even higher yields in Japan and some members of the European Union (EU)—which all have agricultural production subsidies. China's high yields and huge crops are to some extent the result of "green revolution" seed types, technical improvements in scale, machinery, and irrigation during the

1960s and 1970s, and the availability of subsidized inputs such as fertilizer; mostly, however, they are due to multiple cropping and intense labor input by the huge rural population, which is confined largely to the pursuit of agricultural production.

By the sheer volume and the amount of labor involved, rural grain, oilseed, fibers, and other crops form the backbone of China's traditional economy and—arguably—its current economy. Beyond providing food and materials for subsistence of the rural population, the agricultural sector has been exploited as a major source of "surplus"—taxable production—to be used for the urban economy and development. Traditional landlord-tenant relations served to extract a surplus for the purpose of supporting the urban population. Beginning in the 1950s, China's state grain procurement system and rural commune structure functioned to tap agricultural output at low costs and, in conjunction with state monopolized commerce, compulsory grain ration coupons for urban residents, and administered prices, maintained grain supply at low relative prices. In turn, the state collects revenues from state industry with high relative output prices in the form of state enterprise profit remittances. The revenues are reallocated by the state, especially for industrial investment.

Agricultural production was organized under "production teams" and "production brigades"—township or village organizations under the township-level "communes"—from the beginnings of the commune movement in the late 1950s until the post-1978 liberalization. Production decisions were managed by team and brigade leaders. Rural residents assigned to the teams and brigades earned workpoints according to age, gender, and, to some extent, contribution of time and effort. The real income value of a workpoint was calculated as a share of net team or brigade earnings when the actual product was harvested and delivered to the state according to a contract to fulfill a quota at state-set prices. The system did not engender effective incentives for increasing productivity, since everyone gained regardless of individual effort or contribution. The commune system clearly violated the economic maxim that agricultural production management generally is most efficient at the household level.

Table 6.3   China's National Income by Sector, 1990

	Value (hundred million yuan [1])	Percentage of total NI [2]
Agriculture	5,000	35
Industry	6,610	46
Construction	822	6
Transportation	705	5
Commerce	1,405	10
Total	14,542	102
Income per capita	1,271	—

Source: 1991 Zhongguo tongji nianjian (China Statistical Almanac), Table 2-13.

[1] 1991 current value.

[2] Percentage exceeds 100 due to rounding.

Rural "sidelines"—processing and other cottage industries in rural households, and small-scale factories—have a long tradition dating from China's dynastic period. Sideline production grew significantly during the republican era, including fiber and textile production. The independent pursuit of such activities was increasingly discouraged beginning with the collectivization movement of the 1950s and continuing through subsequent political campaigns in the 1960s.

"Rural small-scale enterprises" were emphasized again during the late 1960s and early 1970s, but only as a means to encourage rural communes (once again called townships) and brigades (now again called villages) to establish small industrial collectives. The small industries were intended to assist agricultural production by manufacturing fertilizer for crops and cement for the concrete required for rural infrastructure. Some employment was generated and some economic efficiency gained, notably in decreased transportation costs due to production of chemically unstable fertilizer and heavy cement closer to their place of use. Nevertheless, China's small-scale enterprise policy during the 1960s and 1970s was ultimately influenced by the Stalinist goal of extracting agricultural surplus to support industrial growth.

Post-1978 Agricultural Reforms

Communes and production brigades persisted as the officially sanctioned rural organizational form for almost twenty years. Some production improvements were achieved under the commune system through economies of scale. In the best instances, these appear to have been dependent on other favorable, complementary circumstances (for example, high-quality land and other favorable production conditions, proximity to transportation and large markets). In the more controversial case of the model commune at Dazhai, great achievements were reportedly attained through "self-reliance" but according to later allegations, the results were actually due to donations of exceptionally large amounts of labor and capital investment from the state or the military. By the late 1970s, general stagnation of rural production and incomes throughout China had been acknowledged as a critical problem.

To address the problem, the state turned to decollectivization—delegating production decision making downward to the household level—and increased use and manipulation of markets. During 1979-1983, the "household production responsibility" system (*baochan daohu*), or "household contracting system," was tried first as an experiment and then promoted and approved as the officially sanctioned method of organizing rural agricultural production. The commune system was dismantled. Direct state investment in rural agricultural infrastructure decreased. Instead, arable land was assigned to households, who then took responsibility for production decisions. Households did not receive full-fledged property ownership, however. Rather, they received the right to farm the land and dispose of surplus as they pleased in return for meeting production quotas and tax obligations. This managerial arrangement had been briefly tried in certain areas during the early 1960s, but it was otherwise unprecedented since the agricultural collectivization and communization movements of the mid- and late 1950s. In any case, the post-1978 household responsibility system greatly improved production incentives.

The state manipulated agricultural procurement quotas and prices to raise the returns on farm produc-

Table 6.4   China's Employment by Sector, 1990

	Number of employees (10,000s)	Percentage of total employment
Agriculture, timber, fisheries	34,177	60
Industry	9,697	17
Commerce (wholesale and retail)	2,937	5
Construction	2,461	4
Transportation and communications	1,469	3
Education and culture	1,458	3
State and party organizations	1,079	2
Housing management and public works	637	1
Public health	536	1
Banking and insurance	218	0.4
Science and technology	173	0.3
Mining	100	0.2
Other	1,798	3
Total	56,740	100

Source: 1991 Zhongguo tongji nianjian (China Statistical Almanac), Table 4-4.

tion. Rural producers still had mandatory quotas to deliver to the state at low state-set prices, but they could ask much higher prices for above-quota output. Various schemes were used for determining the "negotiated" prices for above-quota production, but the critical feature was that these prices were set higher in order to elicit increases in the quantity supplied.

Output gains from the initial reorganization of agricultural production were great, averaging about 8 percent over the six years from 1979 to 1984. Agricultural productivity and incomes also grew. While changes in weather contributed somewhat to the variation, the policy and institutional changes of the reform period dramatically affected Chinese agricul-

tural production, achieved some efficiency gains, and thereby rapidly raised output.

This growth did not persist, however. Over the period 1985-1989, the average growth rate of all agricultural output fell to about 3 percent, and for crops alone was close to zero. Several explanations have been advanced for this sudden change in the rate of growth of agricultural output. The gains from the managerial changes due to reforms appear to have raised production to a new plateau by 1984, when it began to stagnate. Indeed, some attribute more than half the increased output during 1979-1984 to improved production incentives under the household production responsibility system.

Some observers believe the state deliberately manipulated agricultural management and economic planning policies first to expand and then to restrict growth. In conjunction with the decollectivization and proliferation of the household production responsibility system, for example, quota and pricing policy changes initially caused acceleration in the growth of output. As grain and other surpluses increased and state deficits rose due to the subsidized retail sales of foodstuffs to urban consumers, the state moved to reduce its involvement further by curtailing the use of mandatory planned quotas. This allowed households to invest in higher return nonagricultural production. Under these conditions, the lowering of procurement prices by the state then caused stagnation of grain output.

Price policy changes raised the return to agricultural production from 1979 to 1984, then subsequently lowered it after 1984. State investment dropped and was not replaced by household investment. Households may have been reluctant to invest in farm/agricultural capital because of uncertainties over the duration of property rights and higher returns to nonagricultural investments in the growing private and collective "rural township enterprises." The household production responsibility system weakened incentives to engage in collective investments in the form of water conservancy and irrigation projects. The number of new projects and maintenance of deteriorating projects declined commensurately. While the household production responsibility system strengthened production incen-

Table 6.5   China's Employment According to Organization Type, 1990

	Number of employees (10,000s)	As percentage of all labor	Percentage in industry	Percentage in agriculture
State enterprise [1]	10,346	18	8	1
Township collective enterprise [1]	3,549	6	3	0.1
Individual enterprise [2]	671	1	n.a.	n.a.
Other ownership type	164	0.3	n.a.	n.a.
Rural village laborers	42,010	74	6	59
Total employment	56,740	100	17	60.1

Source: 1991 Zhongguo tongji nianjian (China Statistical Almanac), Table 4-4. Discrepancies in totals are due to rounding. Industry percentage and agriculture percentage do not sum to equal percentage of all labor because service sector activity is not included.

Notes: n.a. = not available.

[1] includes permanent workers and staff.

[2] *Getihu* means self-employed, single-family enterprise under special legal rules.

tives, the division of collective land into fragmented family plots decreased the scale of production. In some locations, for the purpose of meeting egalitarian objectives, the land was divided into very small parcels so that one family's holdings might consist of several scattered, minute plots. Although the household production responsibility system has been considered a fairly thorough decollectivization, in fact village-level leadership remains fairly strong and influential in the assignment of production contracts and conduct of collective activities such as crop planning, infrastructure construction, and plowing. Yet another aspect of administrative control is found in the persistent and resurgent role of local government in agricultural production.

Another analytical perspective emphasizes the direction of the effects of managerial changes resulting from the post-1978 reforms. In this view, the gains to be had were exhausted by about 1984. Continued growth requires further institutional changes in ownership rights, contract law, and development of a legal system with effective mechanisms of dispute resolution and enforcement.

Initially, the duration of farming rights was short—contracted for one to three years—or unspecified. Households lacked incentives to conserve so the increasing incidence of low rates of investment, soil depletion, and other types of damage became a concern to policy makers. Eventually, the lease period was extended for up to fifteen years in some areas

to address this problem. The marketing system remained firmly under state control, while the institutional arrangements for holding grain stocks remained in an uncertain transition. The state continued its control of stockpiles but producers as well held substantial stores. Urban ration coupons and subsidies for grain were not phased out until much later, in the early 1990s.

As reforms during 1979 and the early 1980s delegated aspects of production decision making downward to households, the state also endeavored to increase agricultural output through direct manipulation of prices and a policy of encouraging certain free market activities. Agricultural procurement prices administered by the state monopoly were adjusted, generally upward. Also, restrictions were eased on the private marketing of certain amounts and types of agricultural and cottage industry products (handicrafts). Eventually the state completely relinquished monopoly control over most agricultural product marketing, with the exception of a few "strategic" commodities such as major food and oil grains, and some fiber crops. Rural producers contracted with the state to supply certain amounts of these products at "negotiated" prices, but aside from meeting these quota sale obligations and taxes, they were free to make all other production and sales decisions.

While state agricultural procurement prices were adjusted upward to encourage output, food subsidies to urban consumers were increased to soften, at least temporarily, the impact of higher food prices on the urban household budget. During the early 1980s, the net share of food subsidies increased rapidly as a portion of the state's fiscal expenditure. The compulsory procurement system was abolished in 1985, but a drop in grain production was followed by a quick return to mandatory grain delivery contracts. Further "experiments" with the management of agricultural production and marketing were conducted across large parts of China beginning in 1988 and continuing into the early 1990s, including higher procurement and retailing prices, decreased supply of subsidized grain to urban areas, increasing the role of market allocation of agricultural inputs by removing subsidies, and various other means of shifting responsibility for financing of grain consumption from the state to the consumers.

Problems may arise from the increasing labor reallocations in combination with low contract prices for grain and other staple crops. In "suburban" rural communities, nonagricultural employment brings much higher cash incomes than even "upscale" agricultural pursuits such as production of vegetables and other nonstaple foodstuffs, while the grain production contracts are a binding constraint. Local urban authorities view the resultant allocation of higher quality labor (young, male) away from agriculture as a problem when the output of nonstaple foodstuffs (and therefore urban consumer choice) suffers. The reform period has seen a persistent interregional disequilibrium of grain demands and supplies. Grain surpluses can be reallocated at subsidized prices to "suburban" rural populations to encourage production of nonstaple foodstuff cash crops. Since the increased "suburban" nonstaple production then attracts itinerant rural-rural labor migration, the "problem" of depletion of agricultural labor is thus pushed back into more remote areas.

As state deficits grew during the early 1990s, the state began to issue nonnegotiable promissory notes and has had difficulty paying them off, leading to some rural unrest. By early 1993 outstanding IOUs for contract grain amounted to 2.75 billion yuan. By the late 1980s the reforms, combined with a long period of relatively favorable weather, had so stimulated agricultural production that in some years the authorities faced excess grain supplies and inadequate transport and storage facilities. Because of a 1992 decision to phase out the grain ration coupon system for urban residents, the future development of agricultural product marketing and the extent of the state's role remained uncertain. Without complementary reforms in land ownership and transfer, the role of the market in the allocation of agricultural products is likely to continue to be limited by the authority of state agencies.

Surplus Rural Labor

As much as 80 percent of China's population resides in rural areas outside the large cities. Any attempt to address the need for more efficient and increased economic activity would have to address rural areas, where underemployment, low incomes, and shortages of capital, material resources, and opportunities are generally more acute. In other economies comparable to China's, the difference between urban and rural incomes attracts far more migrants from rural areas to industrial urban areas than there are new urban employment opportunities.

Since dynastic times, China's traditional approach to this problem has been to maintain strict urban residency rules and records (*hukou zhidu*, or the household registration system), in combination with other mechanisms, to prevent surplus rural labor from permanently moving to large cities. The system has broken down at times, especially when government has been weakened by other stresses, but has functioned more often than not throughout history. Researchers have documented its relative efficacy during the period of economic development since the 1950s, taking into consideration China's exceptional demographic experience.

Under the system, virtually all voluntary labor migration—rural-urban and even rural-rural—is temporary. Household registrations cannot be legally changed, except by a woman marrying into a different jurisdiction or by certain professionals, largely university entrants and graduates. The rural unit (family, village, township, county) becomes the welfare provider for the reserve of surplus labor under this system. This maintains downward pressure on the relative productivity of rural labor and therefore tends to keep the earnings of rural labor low compared with urban labor. Full employment will not come from increases in the number of farm jobs; quite the contrary, opportunities for agricultural income growth will come only with reduction of the labor input to agriculture given China's already extremely high ratio of rural population to arable land.

Because estimates of underemployment range as high as 30 percent, the "overhang" of surplus labor in the Chinese economy, especially rural labor, presents a serious challenge to any policy that seeks to liberalize population movements. The short-run costs of relaxing residency and other rules, combined with the rural-urban wage differential, could cause a rural surplus labor force of as much as 100 million to press into cities that at present only barely manage to accommodate 300 million residents. Some of the post-1978 economic reform measures as initially proposed might be expected to produce such a result. In fact, while the urban economy has incorporated large amounts of rural-origin labor during periods of high labor demand since 1978, that same labor has been returned to the countryside through traditional control mechanisms during periods when urban demand for labor has subsided.

The residence registration system is not the only reason for the relative lack of rural-urban migration. Rural nonagricultural employment has also played a prominent role. The promotion of rural industrial and service activities has provided employment opportunities in rural and township jurisdictions, as well as increases in rural incomes, tax revenues to the state, and foreign exchange earnings.

The Growth of Township and Village Enterprises

Rural enterprises have their most recent origins in the "rural small-scale enterprise" policy of the 1960s and early 1970s. During the 1980s, "rural township enterprises" (*xiangzhen qiye,* also translated as "township and village enterprises," or TVEs)

grew rapidly, although not always smoothly. The growth of TVEs since the 1980s illustrates both a degree of liberalization of official rules and the flexibility of entrepreneurship in China and at the same time the rigidity and persistence of more traditional planned or state institutions.

The rapid development of nonagricultural, nonstate enterprises rapidly boosted output and employment outside the traditional urban industrial and service economy. During the post-1978 reform period, the number of TVEs nationwide first fell from 1978 through 1983, and then suddenly increased more than tenfold between 1984 and 1986, grew more slowly until 1988, then remained approximately constant through 1990. In terms of employment, TVEs grew steadily from 1978 to 1983, grew rapidly from 1984 to 1988, and then declined slowly until 1990. By 1990, the total labor force employed by TVEs numbered over 90 million. The total output value and tax remittances of TVEs grew continuously from 1978 to 1990, however. The value of fixed capital net of financial liabilities also grew in every year from 1978 to 1990. Profits grew every year except for dips in 1981, 1986, 1989, and 1990.

The growing role of TVEs in the economy results from both increased market forces and new policies within the framework of the planned economy. Some market components have been grafted onto a persistent, albeit reformed, command economy. TVEs have variously been established as collectives or private enterprises, but are subject to regulation by local and central government agencies. Some have even been converted into local government enterprises and vice versa. While TVEs grew rapidly, they also at times fell into rapid decline because of policy changes in such areas as access to capital, access to input and output markets, or because of increased competition following liberalization of commercial policy regarding larger urban enterprises. Substantial evidence suggests that TVEs may be treated as a flexible residual sector, to be released or restricted according to the state's short-run needs much as other rural industries have been in the past. Clearly, with some exceptions in terms of technology and quality control, TVEs offer significant efficiency gains to the Chinese and international

China's state-owned enterprises have been a focus of industrial reforms in the 1980s and 1990s. At the same time, the rapid rise of township and village enterprises, or TVEs, has helped to absorb excess labor resulting from agricultural and industrial reforms.

economies. In the political arena, however, the future of TVEs is less certain. When TVEs come into direct competition with larger enterprises for finance, inputs, and output markets, the TVEs are eventually likely to be the losers. As rural and grass-roots institutions, TVEs are at somewhat of a political disadvantage. Given their scale of production and likely technological level, TVEs may produce lower quality products.

Government at all levels expects to keep TVEs under close administrative watch and extract "surplus revenues" (that is, taxes) from them. Should they achieve substantial economic independence and momentum free of the state sector, the TVEs would be difficult to control because of their dispersion.

Reforms in the Urban Economy

Reform of Urban Industry, Commerce, and Services

The reform of urban industrial, commercial, and service enterprises lagged behind that of agricultural production. More than a decade into the economic structural reforms, most large industrial enterprises were still state-owned and managed, and the bulk of state enterprises still relied on economic planning for their budget and substantial proportions of their input requirements and output wholesaling. Economic plans have focused on future urban, industrial, and other reforms, but implementation sometimes lags behind or becomes sidetracked by difficulties. Fundamental challenges to the reform process lie at the core of the urban industrial economy.

From late 1978 through the early 1980s, on an increasingly widespread scale, state enterprises experimented with a variety of reforms, including profit retention, "economic responsibility systems," cost accounting, the use of bank loans to replace unilateral capital grants, depreciation fund retention, wage and salary bonuses, various incentive schemes, contracting and subcontracting schemes, replacement of profit remittances by taxation, and other administrative rearrangements.

Reform experiments during the late 1970s and early 1980s explored the potential for improving allocative efficiency by increasingly incorporating elements of market allocation into the industrial and commercial system, and by opening the nation to freer movement of goods and services domestically and internationally. In October 1984, the Economic Structural Reform Program Resolution of the State Council proposed pushing industrial, commercial, and service reforms further, together with banking, finance, and other major sectors. However, major obstacles were in the way.

Pricing, for example, presents a serious, perhaps central, economic challenge. Correct "scarcity" prices—prices reflecting the true social cost of a good or service, and generally the outcome of competitive markets—are necessary to improve allocative efficiency as enterprises experiment with various incentive and financial schemes. If the enterprises respond to state-set administrative prices, serious economic inefficiency could result as enterprises pursue "profits" under liberalized administration. This applies not only to the price of outputs but also to that of variable inputs like labor and materials as well as capital and real estate. But during the three decades predating reform in the People's Republic of China, correct "scarcity" prices were generally obscured, and the necessary economic and legal institutions of private property ownership and capital markets had been essentially eliminated.

The architects of China's economic structural reform program confront a central problem: where should the economy begin to establish "scarcity" prices? Lacking mature institutions of competitive

market pricing, simply declaring price reform would, at best, allow only muddled progress. A solution to the pricing dilemma can be found only partially in international market prices. The sheer size of China's economy will itself affect international market prices—the rest of the world would be adjusting together with China. As this became increasingly apparent, during the mid-1980s China's policy makers drew back from grand schemes and adopted a gradual, incremental approach to economic and pricing reform.

Before the reforms, prices had been determined administratively according to a long-standing system classifying goods into "materials" and "commodities," which were further classified according to the planning level responsible for the goods. Through the late 1970s and 1980s, a dual-track system of pricing was implemented. A specific quantity or proportion of production of a given good would be sold to planned recipients according to the state-set administered price. The remainder was sold at "flexible" prices. This applied to materials and commodities throughout the various categories, except those that were liberalized completely and removed from the planning process. Beginning in 1978, the proportion of production sold under the plan at administered prices fell, and in some cases even the absolute physical quantities under planned allocation declined. Producers of final products adjusted production and began to realize higher returns from sales in markets with rapid growth of demand; with improved production flexibility, they reduced their reliance on the supply of inputs at planned quantities and prices. The amount of "unplanned" output varied widely by product type, and the process was by no means complete by 1993. Nevertheless, the improved incentives to produce products in demand, together with other planning and policy changes, contributed to substantial growth of production.

During the mid-1980s, Chinese policy makers named the resulting system a "socialist commodity economy with unique Chinese characteristics." However, as serious incompatibilities between components in the evolving system became manifest, the long-run disadvantages of this passive and piecemeal process of reform became clearer.

Incompatibilities emerged, for example, between the fiscal system—essentially a component of the persistent Stalinist-type planned economy—and reform objectives. Despite the political campaigns and other tribulations of the three decades since the founding of the PRC, by 1979 the core of industrial and commercial activity continued to follow the Stalinist model. Under this model, the fiscal system relied mostly upon each state-owned industrial and commercial enterprise remitting the majority of its accounting profits to the state. Sales taxes contributed only a small share. Income tax did not apply to the vast majority of the population during the 1960s and 1970s, and despite its (re)institution during the 1980s it still lacked an effective regular collection mechanism. The social security function was borne by the enterprise (for the urban employee) or the family (for the urban dependent and all rural residents), and there was no social security tax before the 1990s, nor any other unemployment tax. Reforms that relaxed strict accounting and financial discipline and stopped requiring the remittance of all revenues to the state threatened the state's key source of fiscal revenue. At the same time that enterprise profit retention and other reforms reduced state revenue, the agricultural price adjustments were causing state expenditures on subsidies to balloon.

In principle, this fiscal pinch was to be resolved during the mid-1980s by eliminating the profit remittance system and converting fiscal revenue collection to state collection of taxes on enterprise profits. But this is not what happened, because of simultaneous reforms that decentralized enterprise budgetary responsibility downward to lower levels of government and eased the way for state enterprises to form relationships with subsidiary and private or semi-private subcontracting enterprises. To encourage the growth of economic activity, local governments often gave newly formed collective and private enterprises tax holidays. Subsidiaries and subcontractors often qualified for tax holidays too. The coincidence of these processes allowed some state enterprises to make their subsidiaries into profit centers, while running "losses" on their own accounts. As large state enterprises, they expected the government to subsidize their operations. Not to do

so or to close them down might lead to social disorder. The state continued to subsidize them, as it already had for some time in many cases. When state ministries and corporations had difficulty budgeting the subsidies, state enterprises operated on credit from banks and from one another under the continuing system of soft finance. State enterprises running persistent deficits may still have been net contributors to the economy, individually or as a group, if their subsidiaries and other affiliates ran profits and paid enough fees and (eventually) taxes to offset the subsidies taken by the "parent" state enterprise. Nevertheless, high economic costs are still incurred as state enterprises exploit economic monopolies and legal and political advantages to extract monopoly rents, and by allocative distortions caused by the subsidies. These inefficiencies compound the legacy of "self-sufficiency"—redundant and inefficient investment across industries and regions and other inefficiencies inherent in the old planned economy.

State rules and regulations, labor mobility constraints, and allocative or (increasingly) market competition for material inputs continue to limit urban state industrial enterprise expansion. At the same time, the relative difficulty of obtaining official permits and investment fund allocations from the state constrain urban and rural private and collective enterprises. Affiliation and subcontracting relationships between urban state enterprises and "subsidiary" urban and rural private and collective enterprises increasingly emerged as the most practical solution given the institutional constraints of the system. From this relationship, nonstate urban or rural enterprises obtain relatively low cost capital and technology as well as employment opportunities, while the state enterprise expands its production at lower cost and becomes more competitive by not having to provide such relatively high urban wages and "social welfare benefits" as housing, health care, and pensions for the incremental labor. State enterprises can also use the nonstate affiliate to obtain perhaps some tax relief or tax holidays, for market access, and to collect substantial monopoly rents by (re)sale of subsidized materials/products. This "internal colonization" uses the stature and privileges of urban state enterprises to extract economic

The reform of China's large state enterprises, like this phosphate fertilizer plant in southwest China, is an urgent task for the 1990s.

rents from rural township and village enterprises. Economic gains in output, employment, and allocative efficiency from these arrangements notwithstanding, this system does not contribute to competitive market efficiency. Further, it finesses the implications of an additional, critical feature of the traditional state enterprise—as an all-encompassing social unit.

Choosing a feasible path for state enterprise reform is complicated by the role of the enterprise as more than just an employer. The urban enterprise also serves as an all-encompassing social unit that provides the individual's and the family's legal status, housing and retirement benefits, and the channel to health care, education, and other social services. Most reforms have been implemented through the enterprises, even reforms of the enterprise's function. For example, since the early 1990s, a social security tax on wages and salaries is assessed at the enterprise level. International historical experience suggests that, if relatively stable economic growth continues, social welfare functions of the urban state enterprise may in the long run be "inflated" out of significance as the population pursues alternative, market-oriented solutions to these needs. Indeed, the process began early in the reform process in the markets for some retail consumer goods, and the "stock market" experimentation of the early 1990s suggests that future progress in capital markets and other factors markets may arrive in China sooner than the experience of other countries would indicate.

Private Markets: Consumer Demand and the Economy's Response

Household consumption increased rapidly as the result of the combination of rising incomes, the establishment and growth of markets for nondurable and some durable consumer goods, and the rapid growth of agricultural and light industrial output. Beginning in 1978, improving living standards became a central theme of the economic structural reform program. It signified that the Chinese leadership recognized the necessity of departing—in principle—from the Stalinist theme of selfless sacrifice by the population to achieve the goal of strengthening the socialist economy as measured by growth of heavy industry. In the PRC, the Soviet Union, and even in capitalist countries, it has proved feasible to mobilize a population to accept such moral arguments and endure personal economic sacrifice in the face of perceived external threat but, with the possible exception of wartime, the appeal has worked only for short periods. As consumption suffers over the long term the mechanism eventually breaks down. The erosion of economic incentives reduces enthusiasm for undercompensated work, and thereby defeats the goal of boosting production.

Early in the reform program, a two-pronged plan-and-market approach was taken to the problem of raising the standard of living. In the state sector, investment in heavy industry was reallocated to light industries. New management policies encouraged the formation of collective and private enterprises. The collectives and private businesses tended to be in light industrial manufactures and services, thus helping to increase the availability of goods and services. The formation of retail markets for agricultural and manufactured consumer goods was encouraged. State and collective enterprises were allowed to allocate a large proportion of their capacities to the production of "off-plan" output. While they would have the burden of marketing this output at whatever the market price turned out to be, they would also obtain the incremental benefits in profits. Eventually inputs were also allocated in this manner, a certain proportion at planned prices and the rest at market prices.

Variety and availability of products grew rapidly as producers became more sensitive to evolving consumer demands, expressed through a liberalizing commercial system. The expression of consumer demand in the marketplace, met by planned and market increases in supplies, was especially noticeable in foods, clothing, household appliances, and household electronics.

The expression of household demand was constrained, however, by the limitations of reform in property ownership and personal finance. In general, households divide disposable real income between expenditure for current consumption and saving for wealth formation. Current consumption expenditures are for food, clothing, housing services, and recreation. Wealth formation by saving or property purchases sets current income aside for future consumption. The savings might be used for purchases of consumer durables, education, retirement, or other needs. Current consumption and wealth accumulation can overlap in areas such as housing.

A household's ability to accumulate wealth through saving depends on the existence of banks, stock and bond markets, and a real estate market. But under the Stalinist-type planned economy, all real estate is public property, and the banking system serves the material plan. The state also provides most social welfare services to urban households through the enterprise of employment, and to rural households through the village/brigade or county/commune—to the extent provided. Education and health care are provided by rationing.

In the planned economy, the state broadly usurped the role of private household investment in property by providing standard housing to urban dwellers at low nominal rent charges and by prohibiting the formation of a market for real estate and housing. In banking and finance, the state has offered savings accounts at moderate nominal rates of interest. Nonnegotiable government savings bonds, with mandatory purchase targets, were sold through enterprises to urban residents. During periods when the rate of inflation remained below the nominal return on savings accounts or bonds, households would willingly place savings in them. When inflation exceeded the nominal rate of interest paid, however, households would prefer to purchase durables or even nondurable goods rather than hold onto cash in a savings account. This, in turn, exacerbates inflation.

Throughout the 1980s, housing remained under strict state control, while banks, as under the planned system, lacked access to competitive capital markets.

Banks therefore could not offer competitive assets to households, nor could households turn to investment in real estate as their real disposable income rose. Sales of "residency rights," increases in the nominal rents charged to residents, and the exchange of fees between residents engaging in locational swaps began late in the 1980s, but did not constitute a real estate market. During the early 1990s, the state authorized plans to increase rent charges. Over a period of years, rent would be raised from a fraction of a yuan per square meter per month to over a yuan and then to over two yuan. Although this would help the state withdraw some cash from circulation, rationalizing the use of housing services remains another matter. Even at the planned charge of over two yuan per square meter per month, rent would barely cover the thirty-five-year depreciation of the reinforced concrete high-rises. Neither maintenance nor scarcity rents would be reflected in the highest planned charges. Rural households, which have access to building sites, were able to use savings to purchase building materials and thereby make direct investment in housing stock.

Limited quantities of stocks and bond issues reached an experimental stage at specific, highly publicized locations. By the early 1990s, stocks and bonds remained largely experimental, and their widespread use by financial institutions and eventually households remained to be realized.

The relative lack of asset markets or other outlets for wealth formation by urban households led to disproportionately high spending on luxury goods such as fancy clothing, banquet entertainment, and consumer electronics. This rapid growth of consumption of apparently luxury goods seems deeply inconsistent with the reported income levels over the same period, even after adjustments are made for exchange rate distortions. To a certain extent, this reflects the outpouring of frustrated savings in the relatively advanced, developed consumer goods markets, because of the relatively poor absorption capabilities of the unreformed financial system and housing sector. The "luxury paradox" may be viewed from another perspective, however: consumers who buy luxuries are comfortable with the fulfillment of their other, more basic needs. As early as 1986, the rapidly in-creasing varieties and types of basic and luxury consumer products were mostly sold at market prices. In this regard, the first decade and a half of the economic structural reform program was largely successful.

The "Underground Economy"

Under the Stalinist-type planned economy, the extent of markets in the allocation of resources is deliberately limited. The focus of planning is to allocate investment capital, material inputs, most outputs, and, in China, labor. The plans attempted to be comprehensive but could not meet all real-world contingencies. Under the planned economy, various forms of quasi-legal and illegal extra-plan commerce—the "underground economy"—tied up loose ends, met unanticipated needs, and exploited disequilibrium administrative prices.

During the post-1978 reform period, the underground economy is difficult to document, but two major trends can be discerned. On the one hand, planned economic expansion and liberalization of commerce removed much economic activity from the underground economy and placed it in the open economy. On the other hand, the growth of the economy opened new commercial possibilities including some not officially sanctioned. Unsanctioned activities might range from those that simply crossed into gray areas not well defined by rules, to those that are objectionable on moral or social grounds.

Among the gray areas, an increasing challenge to planned allocation will be mounted in the form of price competition by the nonplanned sectors. For example, in railway transportation, the pressure or temptation to use railcars to move goods consigned by the highest payer may lead to "delays" in the shipping of planned products at lower, administratively set shipping charges. The planning authority may view this as a corruption of the system, although in terms of economic efficiency this may also be a social gain, assuming that the products in question are otherwise routine and legal. Indeed, insofar as an original stated goal of the economic structural program is the eventual replacement of the planned economy by the market economy, such a phenomenon is a goal of the reforms. Another gray area problem is foreign currency trading, discussed in detail below.

Graft and corruption of officials are often criticized by both domestic and outside observers, although they might not always agree on the definitions of "graft" and "corruption." Like the underground economy in general, documentation of corruption during the post-1978 economic reform period is hard to find, especially across periods. But studies under way have shown evidence of growth of clear diseconomies and illegal economic activities that are morally or socially objectionable. In particular, accounts indicate increases in prostitution and the trafficking, retailing, and consumption of narcotic drugs.

Challenges to Future Growth

Bottlenecks in Transportation

Traditional nonmechanized means of transportation are still used widely. The porter, wheelbarrow, bicycle, and animal-drawn cart are very important, although mostly for relatively short distances.

Modern, mechanized transportation—including rail, highway, water shipping, air, and pipeline—measured in ton-kilometers and passenger-kilometers, grew more rapidly than output during the mid-1950s. Its growth slowed during the early 1960s, and recovered (along with output) to grow at about the same rate as output during the 1970s and 1980s.

Railroads

Modern transportation within China has generally been by rail. However, from 1979 to 1988, the rail share of non-ocean freight shipping dropped from 73 percent to 59 percent, and the rail share of passenger transport fell from 63 percent to 53 percent. Nevertheless, the absolute levels rose rapidly from 1979 through 1990, achieving average annual rates of growth of 10 percent and 9 percent for freight ton-kilometer and passenger-kilometer traffic, respectively.

Beginning in early 1978, China began to emphasize the upgrading of existing railway lines. Al-though new routes continued to open, the rate of new route opening during the 1980s was only about 350 kilometers per year compared with the average rate of 1,000 kilometers per year from 1952 to 1979. From 1978 to 1989 railroads struggled to keep up with the demands of rapid overall economic growth.

About half of China's fleet of locomotives run by steam, with the remainder diesel or electric. Substantial numbers of locomotive engines were imported through the 1970s and 1980s, including 420 U.S. diesels during the 1980s. Almost 1,000 new diesel or electric locomotives were produced in China each year during the early 1990s, with production accelerating over time. Overall, from 1980 to 1990, average annual growth of China's total locomotive fleet was about 3 percent, with the freight car fleet increasing at about 3 percent, and the passenger railcar fleet at about 5 percent.

Trains are very crowded, undoubtedly because of the slow relative growth of capacity and low nominal freight charges and passenger ticket prices compared with the demand for freight space and seats. Freight and passenger rates rarely increased before the 1980s, and increases since then have not raised charges to equilibrium market price levels. The shortage of freight space leads to long delays and increasing corruption in the freight railway system. Passenger tickets are rationed by various nonprice measures, and there is an active, albeit illegal, "scalper" market. Passenger car crowding is exacerbated by the fact that much private business transportation relies on the passenger trains. Individuals buy passage on a passenger train, bringing large amounts of baggage, which is actually not personal effects but consumer goods for retail (re)sale.

This use of passenger cars for trade is even conducted to and across the borders into Russia for sale in Russia and the other former republics of the Soviet Union and Eastern bloc. It is much more costly in terms of space and energy consumption to have a human courier with every one or two bale-sized bundles of clothing, for example, than it is to ship the bundles in a freight car—the human courier requires many times more air and space in the car than the freight alone would require. Overcrowding of passenger cars is an inevitable side effect. The large sums of cash carried by the private traders also occasionally attract thieves and robbers. Nevertheless, China relies heavily on rail transportation. During the 1980s, in railway freight ton-kilometers moved, China was a close third behind the still-extant Soviet Union and the United States. In passenger-kilometers traveled, China was a close third behind the Soviet Union and Japan.

International rail lines through the north and northeast connect to Mongolia and Siberia, and eventually to Moscow; a newly completed line through Xinjiang proceeds to the border with Kazakhstan; rail lines south through Guangdong and Yunnan connect to Vietnam, but otherwise the land borders are not crossed by rail connections.

Highways and Motor Vehicles

Extensive building of highways, as measured in route length, took place at an average annual rate of about 11 percent from 1952 to 1965, slowing to an annual rate of about 4 percent from 1965 to 1978 during the Cultural Revolution period. After 1978 the annual rate declined to 1 percent, in part because of the upgrading of existing important routes, so that unsurfaced dirt roads decreased from 39 percent to 17 percent as a proportion of roads from 1979 to 1988. While still rare, a few limited access expressways have been constructed around several large cities and over short stretches in metropolitan areas. Some of these highways, mostly in areas like the coastal special economic zones, are financed by foreign investors as an adjunct to or as part of joint ventures or other investment.

The overland motor highways to the borders cross into Mongolia from Heilongjiang Province; Kazakhstan, Kyrgyzstan, Tajikistan, and Pakistan from Xinjiang; Nepal from Tibet; and Burma (Myanmar) and Laos from Yunnan Province. The building of these and many of the long inland routes constituted substantial engineering accomplishments.

China's motor vehicle production, which numbered about 400,000 per year in the mid-1980s, serves the domestic market for large trucks, agricultural tractors, and some passenger vehicles. By

international standards, however, it is relatively inefficient.

Annual imports of vehicles have fluctuated rapidly since rapid growth began in 1983, but after 1986 the volume averaged about 90,000 per year. Tariffs and other charges double to quadruple the price of an imported vehicle compared with its probable free market price. The establishment of Chinese-foreign joint ventures in this area has not overcome vehicle production problems; by some accounts the Chinese partners have experienced difficulties providing parts at competitive prices, or sometimes at all, so expensive imported parts kits continue to be used. Foreign investors remain optimistic about the market as incomes grow for a substantial number of households. They are hopeful that their efforts in China will pay off in the future if they obtain or increase their share of the domestic market, or perhaps as an international production strategy.

The stock of all nonmilitary motor vehicles, including private and public nonmilitary large and small trucks, buses, vans, cars, and transport tractors, grew from about 178 million in 1980 to about 551 million in 1990, at an average annual rate of 12 percent. One indication of the growth of the motor vehicle stock in China is the rapid increase in traffic and traffic congestion. Beginning in the mid-1980s, China established zoning rules restricting traffic types (for example, no truck or agricultural tractor traffic was allowed in parts of Beijing during busy daytime hours) and intersection improvements to respond to the congestion problem. A serious constraint on further growth of urban vehicle use will be the high real opportunity cost of roadway and parking space in densely populated areas.

Water Transport

Small-scale traditional and mechanized shallow-draft water transportation is widespread and very important along China's 109,200 kilometers of river, canal, lake, and marsh systems. The major routes accommodating larger vessels are the Amur River in the northeast, the Yangzi River flowing eastward, the Pearl River in the south, the 700-year-old north-south Grand Canal between Hangzhou and Beijing, and seaways along the eastern coast of China. The average annual growth rate of passenger utilization was about 6 percent from 1980 to 1986 but by 1990 fell back to only 0.3 percent after a steep decline beginning in 1988. Freight tonnage utilization grew at an average of 10 percent annually between 1980 and 1988 but fell to about 7 percent by 1990.

The huge Three Gorges project to build dams on the middle Yangzi River, which had long been in the planning stages, got under way in earnest in the 1980s. Intended mainly to increase hydroelectric generation capacity and improve flood control downstream, it would also allow shipping to pass through reservoirs where the difficult rapids of the Three Gorges stretch in eastern Sichuan once lay. Domestic and international controversy has followed the project, but the transportation aspects have not been as contentious as issues of silting, environmental impact, and community dislocation.

International water transportation links include the major seaports of Dalian, Qinhuangdao, Tianjin, Yantai, Qingdao, Shijiu, and Lianyungang on the Bohai and Yellow Seas; seaports up the Yangzi River and Shanghai, Ningbo, and Wenzhou on the East China Sea; Fuzhou and Xiamen on the Taiwan Strait; and Shantou, Guangzhou, Zhanjiang, Haikou, and Dongfang (Basuo) on the South China Sea. China has also built several oil pipelines since the 1960s that carry large quantities of crude and refined oil and relieve pressure on rail and road links.

Air Transport

During the late 1980s air traffic grew more rapidly than any other form of transportation in China. The distance of domestic routes served grew from a low base of 160,323 kilometers in 1985 to 329,493 kilometers in 1990, at an average annual rate of about 16 percent. Beijing, Shanghai, and Guangzhou each have official international airports and handle most of the country's international traffic. However, the number of exclusively civilian airports at which jets larger than a Boeing 737 may land increased from only 10 in 1985 to 47 by 1990. The size of the passenger aircraft civilian fleet remained almost constant from 1980 to 1990, growing from 404 to 421,

although capacity was likely gained through altering the fleet makeup toward larger, more modern craft. These figures may underestimate the number of large airports and the size of the aircraft fleet used for nonmilitary purposes, since some airports are used jointly by civil and military aviation authorities, and during the mid-1980s the military began to compete with the civil aviation administration for commercial traffic.

Rationalizing Energy Consumption

In absolute terms, China's energy consumption is much below that of the United States and other high-income countries. Energy consumption per capita in China is comparable to middle-income countries—in 1987 it was only 8 percent of the U.S. level, for example. The physical units of energy consumed per dollar of GNP have been calculated to be very high by comparison with any other country. Possible explanations for China's apparently high relative energy consumption advanced by the World Bank include the relatively high share of energy-intensive heavy industry in China's economic activity, poor access to new energy-saving technologies and processes developed in other countries, and lack of incentives to conserve. Furthermore, as noted above, the steady devaluation of the yuan relative to the U.S. dollar alone would downwardly bias the dollar-denominated value of Chinese income by as much as a factor of two or three. Over time, this would continue to distort dramatically upward the ratio of energy consumed per dollar of GNP.

Although the technology level is undoubtedly important and improved price incentives would certainly help, the suggestion of negligent and flagrant material waste of energy appears counterintuitive in light of the generally frugal nature of the Chinese. Re-examination of the statistics reveals an alternative explanation for the apparently high relative consumption. Compared with other countries—especially developed industrial economies, but even many developing economies—the degree of monetization of economic exchange as a proportion of all economic activity is low in China. Thus the ratio of energy use per dollar of GNP may appear to be high because, compared with use in other countries, in China energy is used to produce a higher proportion of real goods and services not captured in GNP measurement.

Banking, Finance, and Money Management

Banking and Monetary System

Both before the initiation of the structural reform program in 1978, and since that time to the extent that the planned state sector has persisted, China's banking system simultaneously acts as the accountant for planned economic activities and government expenditures as well as the dispenser of planned credit.

Under the planned economy, the banking and monetary system serves the material production plan. On the supply side, capital for investment in building and productive equipment is granted rather than lent, and "working capital" is provided at low or zero interest. Most transactions must be made through the banking system, and little cash is used except for enterprise payroll and rural agricultural procurements. In principle, all monetary transactions, including the use of cash, are made as accounting actions according to the material plan. On the demand side, production of consumption goods follows the plan. Any difference between income and consumption would be absorbed by either compulsory savings or, if there is any flexibility in consumer goods prices, by inflation. The People's Bank of China and its branches accepted household savings and time deposits, paying relatively low nominal interest rates. Nonnegotiable government bond issues were sold through state enterprises, generally in compulsory and egalitarian fashion.

Under the plan, the banking system performs some of the accounting activities of a treasury, as well as central bank, commercial, development, and savings bank. In principle, all these activities are closely dictated by the plan.

Such a banking system supports planned economic and development goals by channeling investment to target sectors. However, it also has some serious shortcomings. Notably, the lack of a capital market means that the cost of capital is not explicit; once past basic development goals, the optimal direction is no longer apparent. Also, the lack of a capital market and related asset markets implies the lack of a financial channel for the accumulation of household wealth. This may lead banks and enterprises to be neither willing nor able to use prices, interest rates, and other financial information for the purpose of making socially rational economic decisions. In fact, authorities resorted to repeated decrees in which they admonished enterprises to reduce overextension of infrastructure construction projects and unanticipated budget deficits.

Against this background, the reform program policies intended to promote economic efficacy face a monumental task. While the theoretical gains in efficiency are clear, the means to bear the costs are not apparent. In the financial sector, monetary authorities and banks would require risk and return assessment techniques and autonomy to pursue an independent, profit-seeking policy in a fractional reserve system. Households would (and increasingly do) require reliable financial instruments in which to hold their savings, and channel these back into business investment. To meet these needs, capital markets would have to be developed with workable and enforceable definitions of ownership and transfer. Firms would require hard budget accounting and real financial penalties, including bankruptcy rules. This, in turn, would raise difficult questions about the nature of urban residency, housing, unemployment compensation, labor mobility, social security, and so forth, which are still provided through the urban enterprise. Any new non-enterprise-based systems would require funding, which in turn implies the implementation of a fiscal system to replace the remittances of profits from state-owned enterprises. In the absence of further institutional development, bankruptcy rules cannot be implemented without incurring unbearable transition costs.

The requirement that reform policy address these issues was raised, in principle, at least as early as October 1984, in the Economic Structural Reform Program Resolution of the State Council, and much progress has been made in the discussion and design of solutions since then. Bankruptcy, copyright and intellectual property, real estate and residential rights, and financial issues have all been addressed by the State Council and local authorities. But the actual development and implementation of these new regulations and institutions is not yet complete, and their extent and efficacy remain to be seen. During 1992 and 1993, the Central Committee of the CCP announced its intention to proceed further with economic structural reforms. It plans to "corporatize" the few large enterprises that will remain state-owned and to create some "joint-stock enterprises." Many smaller state enterprises might be completely privatized by unspecified means. Market pricing, already applicable to 90 percent of prices for final goods, may be extended to labor, some property, and finance, including interest rates. These changes aim to gain control of economic fluctuations through macroeconomic policy instruments and at the same time further decrease administrative commands. The Bank of China may reduce its other activities and focus on allocation of credit according to business feasibility.

Foreign Currency Exchange

Throughout the 1980s, the Bank of China gradually adjusted the fixed exchange rates between the Chinese renminbi (RMB) and foreign currencies, generally devaluing the RMB against major convertible currencies (see Table 6.6). The RMB was devalued from 3.7 yuan to the dollar in 1986 to 4.7 in December 1989; within a year, it was further devalued to 5.2 yuan to the dollar, and by the end of 1993 it had reached 5.8 yuan.

Since about 1980, the approximately annual RMB devaluations against the U.S. dollar were significant, averaging about 12 percent per year from 1981 to 1992, but not traumatic. This gradual and regular approach has brought the RMB closer and closer to market value without incurring the costs of major price and inflation shock to the domestic economy, with the possible exceptions of the 41 percent devaluation in 1984 and the 27 percent devaluation in 1989.

Certainly, inflation has occurred as a result of both international exchange rate effects and domestic

Table 6.6   Yuan-Dollar Exchange Rates

Year	Chinese yuan per U.S. dollar	Change in value (percent of previous year's rate)
1970	2.4618	—
1971	2.4618	0.00
1972	2.2401	-9.01
1973	2.0202	-9.82
1974	1.8397	-8.94
1975	1.9663	6.88
1976	1.8803	-4.37
1977	1.7300	-7.99
1978	1.5771	-8.84
1979	1.4962	-5.13
1980	1.5303	2.28
1981	1.7455	14.06
1982	1.9227	10.15
1983	1.9809	3.03
1984	2.7957	41.13
1985	3.2015	14.52
1986	3.7221	16.26
1987	3.7221	0.00
1988	3.7221	0.00
1989	4.7221	26.87
1990	5.2221	10.59
1991	5.4342	4.06
1992	5.7518	5.85
1993	5.8000	0.84
1994[1]	8.5301	47.07

Source: International Monetary Fund, 1994. The reported exchange rates are the official rates at the end of the period.

[1] As of September 1994.

policy and cycles, but it alone has not caused any unmanageable crises. Even the 1989 Tiananmen crisis, although in part attributable to domestic fiscal problems and resulting inflation, cannot be placed at the doorstep of currency devaluation.

However, the downward bias in the dollar-denominated annual GNP and GNP growth figures is important from the viewpoint of evaluating economic growth. The use of the dollar figures by the World Bank results in deceptively paltry growth rates.

Throughout the 1980s, the state gradually devalued the RMB and at the same time maintained multiple exchange rates, under which foreigners purchased RMB at a higher dollar rate than that applied to convertible currency income from international trade by Chinese enterprises. The "official rate," applying to the supply of foreign currency by foreign private individuals and business and by Chinese private individuals, kept the RMB at its highest value relative to foreign currency. An "internal rate" applying to Chinese firms sanctioned to handle foreign currency set the RMB at a lower value relative to foreign currency. The two rates moved down together, but at a differential throughout the 1980s. At times, the official rate valued the RMB as much as 200 percent higher than the internal rate. Officially approved "currency swap centers" opened as early as 1985 in the Shenzhen Special Economic Zone (SEZ) and later elsewhere. "Black market" trading tapped an increased supply of foreign currency by private foreigners and Chinese by paying at the internal rate. By maintaining the two rates, the state banking system extracted "consumer surplus" from foreigners selling foreign exchange at the higher official rate, but may also have garnered a higher total quantity of foreign exchange by tolerating "black market" trading at the internal rate.

This black market for foreign exchange existed throughout the 1980s. Reflecting the official dual exchange rate, the black market RMB generally traded for less than the official rate, albeit at a diminishing differential over time. During the mid-1980s, over a hundred "gray market" currency "swap centers" relieved some of the pressure on the RMB by allowing officially sanctioned currency trading at flexible, usually lower-than-official, rates. The rates varied from center to center, sometimes widely. Between 1988 and 1991 the savings banks branches of the Bank of China began to allow citizens to exchange currency and to open convenient passbook savings accounts denominated in foreign currency, without any of the previous documentation, exchange rules, or withdrawal restrictions. This rationalization of currency handling helped to remove from circulation some of the "high-powered" money—foreign exchange already in use by the general public since the early 1980s—and presented an increasing challenge to monetary policy management.

In June 1993 controls on swap center RMB rates were ended. In November 1993 the Bank of China announced a plan to eliminate the dual exchange rate

system, and on January 1, 1994, China officially announced that foreign exchange rates for the RMB would be unified with a view toward complete convertibility sometime in the future. How the swap center rates will be reconciled and how they will be unified with the official rate remain to be seen. If past policy is a guide, the RMB will continue its gradual devaluation.

Nascent Stock Markets and Other New Capital Sources

"Stock exchanges" and "bond exchanges" that allow trading in domestically issued stocks and bonds became a new feature of the reforming economy during the early 1990s. The Shanghai securities exchange opened in December 1990 and the Shenzhen securities exchange opened in July 1991. Experiments with various "shareholding systems" date back at least to 1987, and in some cities "securities exchanges" allow bond trading by the government only. Fewer than a hundred companies actually sold stocks at the new Shanghai and Shenzhen exchanges. Thousands of other companies have sold or issued shares to employees, but these shares generally are not yet negotiable. Of the stocks for sale at the Shanghai and Shenzhen exchanges, "A" shares are for sale only to domestic individuals and institutions, while "B" shares are for sale only to foreigners and must be purchased with U.S. or Hong Kong dollars. The amount of capital attracted through the "B" shares remains small compared with the amount of foreign financial investment channeled into China through direct foreign investment, which is discussed below.

China's new securities markets have experienced some growing pains. Excess demand for financial instruments is enormous: in 1992 thousands of people waiting in line to apply to buy new issues in the Shenzhen exchange rioted when they failed to obtain forms. Opportunities for financial fraud exist in the new market; a recent pyramid scheme bond scandal cost investors $175 million and involved at least 120 senior officials. Even small mistakes, such as the misquotation of prices by brokers, may lead to multibillion-yuan losses. The legal system struggles to

Stock exchanges that allow trading in domestically issued stocks and bonds, like this one in Shenzhen, became a new feature of the reforming economy during the early 1990s. At the same time, China's banks are undergoing reform and becoming increasingly specialized.

keep up with developments in finance and assets markets. The markets shared in the boom as U.S. and other Western investors flocked to offshore markets during the early 1990s. Nevertheless, the establishment of stock and bond markets, even on an "experimental" scale, is necessary for the future development of capital markets and increased rationalization of resource allocation. For that reason, the new securities exchanges hold promise for the success of the economic structural reforms.

Foreign Trade and Investment: China in the World Economy
Historical Background and Policy Trends

Upon the establishment of the PRC in 1949, Stalinist-type central planning was adopted: foreign trade was by design isolated from the domestic sector and its main purpose was to serve domestic economic goals. Domestic commerce employed nonconvertible currency; foreign investment was all but absent,

with the major exceptions of Soviet technology and equipment transfers through late 1950s, and China's substantial export of development technology and/or military assistance to selected third world nations and groups in Asia and Africa between 1960 and 1980. Self-imposed trade constraints reinforced a U.S.-led cold war trade boycott of China dating back to the early 1950s.

Trade under this planned economy essentially followed an "import substitution" development strategy. An exception was the large-scale grain imports beginning in the 1960s, necessitated by the post-Great Leap Forward policy disaster. The next major exception was the decision to import large turn-key industrial plants in the mid-1970s, followed by the post-1978 Dengist "open door" policy reform programs.

China's trade grew rapidly in the late 1970s after the reopening of diplomatic relations with Western nations and eventually the United States, and abandonment of the longstanding U.S.-led trade boycott.

Beginning in 1978, China undertook a momentous policy change away from import substitution and toward export promotion. Exports have grown rapidly as a result. Textiles have consistently been a large foreign exchange earner for China.

New industrial capacity, developed under the planned growth strategy of the 1960s and 1970s, fueled rapid growth of both traditional light industrial exports and nontraditional heavy industrial exports such as machine tool equipment and chemical products. For a short period during the late 1970s, the Four Modernizations program promoted capital imports of turn-key plants, following the legacy of Stalinist emphasis on resource extraction and heavy industry. Subsequently, the decision to pursue retrenchment and scale back investment in heavy industry discouraged imports of capital in the form of turn-key plants.

The pivotal strategy change of the post-1978 reform program increased emphasis on exploitation of comparative advantage and mutual gains from trade. This led to massive increases in light industrial production and exports, especially textiles and service exports (tourism, contract labor crews, air transporta-

tion). Priority was accorded to imports of necessary material inputs, encouragement of technology acquisition and direct foreign investment.

The rapid turnabout of policy and performance constituted a momentous change in development strategy, away from import substitution and toward export promotion. Export constraints became external—in addition to the constraint of effective demand, much of China's exports came under the various tariff and nontariff restrictions applied to developing economies in general by developed industrial economies. China's exports were rapidly incorporated into existing multilateral protectionist conventions employed by developed economies such as the Multifiber Arrangement (MFA) associated with the General Agreement on Tariffs and Trade (GATT). Although initially China did not officially join GATT, it became subject to its rules and practices, such as MFA nontariff barriers that cap the

Table 6.7   China's Balance of Payments (in current U.S. dollars, millions)

Year	Exports[1]	Imports[1]	Current account[2]	Capital account	Balance of payments
1982	(23,637)	(-18,900)	5,674	631	6,305
1983	(23,186)	(-20,711)	4,240	-98	4,142
1984	(26,716)	(-26,748)	2,030	-1,892	138
1985	(28,163)	(-40,755)	11,417	8,977	-2,440
1986	(29,583)	(-37,172)	-7,034	4,986	-2,048
1987	(39,120)	(-38,880)	300	4,483	4,783
1988	(45,877)	(-49,972)	-3,802	6,176	2,374
1989	(47,770)	(-52,750)	-4,317	3,838	-479
1990	(57,322)	(-46,706)	11,997	50	12,047
1991	(65,824)	(-54,297)	13,272	1,265	14,537
1992	(78,757)	(-73,799)	6,401	-8,461	-2,060

Source: 1993 International Financial Statistics Yearbook (Washington, D.C.: International Monetary Fund, 1993).

[1] Merchandise, f.o.b., plus services.

[2] The current account includes merchandise exports minus imports, net flow of services, net flow of income, and private and unofficial unrequited transfers. The current account, therefore, does not necessarily exactly equal exports minus imports.

growth of textile exports and bilateral or unilateral tariff rules. These forms of trade protection have been shown to restrict real incomes in general and those of developing economies in particular. Nevertheless, China's post-1978 move from relative autarky to restricted trade certainly increased real income for China and its trading partners.

During the post-1978 decade, the average annual rate of growth of China's trade, at about 13 percent, was more than 50 percent higher than the already high 9 percent average annual growth in national income. The rapid growth of national income is associated with—if not caused by—China's opening to increased trade. In total volume of exports, China rose from below the top thirty nations to become one of the top twenty. China's simultaneous massive increase in imports—although sometimes running China's current account into deficit (see Table 6.7)—was accomplished without incurring excessive dependence on foreign borrowing. By 1990, China's foreign exchange reserves amounted to more than 50 percent of the size of external debt (not counting short-term credits), and the ratio of external debt to exports amounted to less than one to one, far below the ratios in excess of three to one found in the floundering economies of some countries in Latin America or Eastern Europe. As one of the largest or the

largest country in many categories, China is in a particularly advantageous position to gain from trade growth. Despite many remaining problems, international trade liberalization undoubtedly is among the most successful components, if not the most successful and critical component, of the post-1978 reforms.

The opening to increased trade in the 1980s, which occurred largely through existing trade bureaucracies, led to increased imports of both reduplicative capital equipment and technology and consumer goods. The central government's convertible currency reserves were depleted in cycles, depending upon the current degree of administrative liberalization or tightening. Domestic commercial bottlenecks further exacerbated waste as the imported capital equipment and technology frequently remained idle in the domestic shipping network for excessive periods, sometimes years. Some companies allowed to trade under the liberalization measures proved unable to fulfill contracts. Granting greater autonomy to local and lower-level trading units, while leaving other rules unreformed, led to problems of coordination and compatibility. The already poor port infrastructure was further limited by unreformed labor laws (such as caps on the growth of wages paid to state workers). As a result, when delays forced ships to moor offshore for days, contract clauses were trig-

Table 6.8   Major Product Categories in China's Imports, 1990 (percentage share of total imports, c.i.f.)

Product category	Percentage of total imports
Food and animals	6
Nonfuel raw materials	8
Petroleum products	2
Chemical products	13
Basic manufactures [1]	17
Machinery and transport equipment [2]	32
Miscellaneous manufactures	4
Other	18
All categories	100

Source: The Europa World Yearbook 1993 (London: Europa Publications, 1993).

[1] Includes iron, steel, textile yarn, fabrics, and other similar raw materials.
[2] Includes specialized manufacturing machinery, telecommunications equipment, electrical equipment, motor vehicles and parts, and other transportation equipment.

Table 6.9   Major Product Categories in China's Exports, 1990 (Percentage share of total exports, f.o.b.)

Product category	Percentage of total exports
Food and animals	11
Nonfuel raw materials	6
Petroleum products	8
Chemical products	6
Basic manufactures [1]	20
Machinery and transport equipment [2]	9
Miscellaneous manufactures [3]	20
Other	20
All categories	100

Source: The Europa World Yearbook 1993 (London: Europa Publications, 1993).

[1] Includes textile yarn, fabrics, nonmetallurgical mineral products, and other similar products.
[2] Includes telecommunications and audio equipment and electrical machinery and equipment.
[3] Includes clothing, accessories, footwear, and other similar products.

gered requiring the state trade bureaucracy to pay large fines for delays. A consolidation and restructuring plan in 1988 aimed to address some of these problems by reducing the number of organizations authorized to conduct international trade.

Composition of Trade

One decade into the economic structural reform program, the product makeup of China's trade generally reflects China's factor endowment and comparative advantage in the production of labor-intensive goods. Capital equipment and some industrial inputs dominate China's imports (see Table 6.8). Light industrial products and semiprocessed intermediate goods comprise the majority of China's exports (see Table 6.9). Some observers, pointing to the rapid growth in exports of electrical machinery and telecommunications equipment during the late 1980s, have raised questions as to whether these categories are in any way subsidized. But subsidies may not be the only reason for this rapid growth. Nontariff barriers on goods with a low unit price often stimulate exporters to move "up-market" into higher value-added products.

Direct Foreign Investment

An integral component of China's opening to the international economy has been the policy of attracting direct foreign investment. New laws and regulations implemented between 1978 and 1990 aimed at creating the necessary climate and channeling foreign investment into high-priority sectors. By 1990, almost thirty thousand contracts (in principle worth over US$40 billion) had been signed, with over $20 billion in investment already utilized (see Table 6.10). The level of foreign investment rose even more dramatically in the 1990s: China utilized more than $11 billion in foreign investment during 1992, and during 1993 $111 billion more was pledged, with $26 billion actually utilized.

Production at joint ventures (Sino-foreign business arrangements utilizing direct foreign investment) is responsible for a disproportionately high and growing share of the country's export earnings. The special economic zones (SEZs) have been major recipients of direct foreign investment, but joint ventures operate at many other locations as well. There is generally a coastal and southern bias—most foreign investment is concentrated in Guangdong Prov-

Table 6.10   Direct Foreign Investment (DFI) in China, 1979-1993

Year	Contracted DFI (U.S. $, billions)	Average contracted DFI per project [1] (U.S. $, millions)	Total utilized foreign investment [1] (U.S. $, billions)	Total utilized DFI (U.S. $, billions)	Utilized DFI as percent of foreign investment
1979-1982	$ 7.0	$ 7.6	$ 12.5	$ 1.8	14 %
1983	1.9	4.1	2.0	0.9	45
1984	2.9	1.6	2.7	1.4	52
1985	6.3	2.1	4.7	2.0	44
1986	3.3	2.2	7.3	2.2	30
1987	4.3	1.9	8.5	2.7	32
1988	6.2	1.0	10.2	3.7	36
1989	6.3	1.1	10.1	3.8	38
1990	7.0	1.0	10.3	3.8	37
1991	12.4	1.0	11.6	4.7	41
1992	58.7	1.2	19.2	11.3	59
1993	111.4	1.3	36.8	26.0	71

Source: Zhongguo tongji zhaiyao 1994 (Statistical Abstract of China) (Beijing: Statistical Publishing House, 1994), 110.

[1] DFI plus borrowing from abroad.

ince and, to a lesser extent, other coastal areas such as Fujian, Zhejiang, and Jiangsu Provinces and the city of Shanghai.

Many of the investments have been successful, but others have experienced difficulties. The degree of success has depended largely on the partners' compatibility of expectations. Foreign businesses entering joint ventures with international experience are more likely to arrive at a feasible and mutually satisfactory project. Large-scale projects are less likely to produce rapid results. Infrastructure and institutional arrangements generally differ from those in the foreign partner's home country. In the mid-1980s, for example, the U.S. partners of the Beijing Jeep joint venture felt compelled to extract confidential agreements from the highest levels of government allowing Beijing Jeep to convert RMB earnings into dollars at the internal rate. McDonnell Douglas, IBM, Volkswagen, Occidental Petroleum, General Motors, and many other large corporations have made large direct investments; however, they pale by comparison with the quantity and composition of investments by Japanese, Taiwanese, and other Asian and European corporations.

One area of significant foreign investment activity has been oil and gas exploration. Many foreign firms have signed offshore oil exploration and development contracts that include drilling rights, with a duration of up to thirty-five years. Japan, the largest purchaser of Chinese crude oil, has been a major investor; others include American oil companies like ARCO.

Investment from Japan and elsewhere has also been channeled into heavy industrial development projects such as the Baoshan Steel Mill near Shanghai, which has the capacity to produce 10 percent of China's steel production. The Daya Bay Nuclear Power Plant in Guangdong was built in a joint venture project with a Hong Kong firm. Other nuclear energy projects have attracted interest from Canada, France, Russia, and the United States.

A substantial proportion of the direct foreign investment coming from overseas Chinese has been from firms in Taiwan and Hong Kong that are responding to rising labor costs in their own countries and the relative ease of management in China, despite political obstacles. Former factory workers from Hong Kong have fanned out in Guangdong Province to manage new factories; successful Taiwan businesses propose major industrial investments in Fujian Province; and investors from South Korea manage factories in Tianjin and other northern and

Table 6.11   Sources of Direct Foreign
Investment in China, 1992
(percent of total)

	Contracted	Utilized
Hong Kong	69.0%	68.2%
Taiwan	9.5	9.5
United States	5.4	4.6
Japan	3.7	6.4
Macao	2.6	1.8
Singapore	1.7	1.1
Thailand	1.2	0.8
Other	6.9	7.6
Total	100.0	100.0

Source: Calculated from *Guoji shangbao* (International Commerce), no. 4 (1993), cited in *China Newsletter,* no. 105 (July-August 1993), 19-21. Adapted from N. T. Wang, ''The Role of Foreign Direct Investment in Reform and Development in China,'' Columbia University, East Asian Institute Report, December 1993, 11.

Table 6.12   U.S. Merchandise Trade with China,
1978-1993 (U.S. dollars, billions)

	U.S. imports from China	U.S. exports to China	Net trade balance	Gross trade
1978	$ 0.3	$0.8	$ 0.5	$ 1.1
1979	0.6	1.7	1.1	2.3
1980	1.1	3.8	2.7	4.9
1981	1.9	3.6	1.7	5.4
1982	2.3	2.9	0.6	5.2
1983	2.2	2.1	-0.1	4.3
1984	3.1	3.0	-0.1	6.1
1985	3.9	3.9	0.0	7.8
1986	4.8	3.1	-1.7	7.9
1987	6.3	3.5	-2.8	9.8
1988	8.5	5.0	-3.5	13.5
1989	12.0	5.8	-6.2	17.8
1990	15.2	4.8	-10.4	20.0
1991	19.0	6.3	-12.7	25.3
1992	25.7	7.5	-18.2	33.2
1993	31.5	8.8	-22.7	40.3

Source: U.S. Department of Commerce.

northeastern cities. Some multinationals, bringing marketing expertise, have joined forces with Asian investors to set up some of the most successful manufacturing plants throughout coastal China.

Some of the ''foreign'' direct investment may actually be money belonging to state enterprises in China that has been quietly channeled out of China through offshore subsidiaries and then back into joint ventures in China in order to obtain tax holidays and other concessions granted only to ''foreign'' investors. It is not clear what proportion of investment originates from such sources.

The Special Economic Zones

Special economic zones are an integral part of China's open door policy, which is in turn a key component of the reform program. When first inaugurated at four coastal locations in 1979—Shenzhen, Shantou, and Zhuhai in Guangdong Province, and Xiamen in Fujian—the SEZs were modeled on export-processing zones like those set up in Taiwan more than a decade earlier. Since then, Hainan and other areas have achieved similar status.

The basic goal was straightforward: SEZs would provide a special environment for combining domestic labor and some domestic materials with foreign capital, advanced foreign technology, and foreign-

supplied materials to produce exports in order to earn foreign exchange. China would gain from the increased investment of modern foreign capital and the opportunity to learn about foreign technology, from the increased economic activity and income generated by the zones, and especially from the opportunity to increase exports and thereby generate higher foreign exchange earnings. The foreign investors would gain higher returns than they could elsewhere from the low relative costs of labor and land rental, tax exemptions and tax holidays, lower import duties, and even the ability to set up 100 percent foreign-owned firms. Although they could not buy land, they could obtain leases for forty years or more.

The SEZs have experienced spectacular growth, despite being subject to many of the same and some additional policy and macroeconomic cycles that affect the rest of China. Despite attracting the lion's share of direct foreign investment and generating sizable foreign currency earnings, however, SEZs have not become the magnets for advanced foreign production technology and the powerhouses of export manufacturing that had been originally envisioned. Rather, much of the SEZ growth has occurred in con-

Table 6.13   China's Major Sources of Imports
(ranked by share of 1991 imports)

Origin of imports	Percentage
Hong Kong	27%
Japan	16
United States	13
Taiwan	6
Germany	5
CIS	3
Canada	3
France	3
Australia	2
Italy	2
Indonesia	2
Singapore	2
United Kingdom	2
Malaysia	1
Switzerland	1
Netherlands	1
Thailand	1
Belgium	1
Brazil	1
All others	8
Total	100

Source: The Europa World Yearbook 1993 (London: Europa Publications, 1993).

Table 6.14   China's Major Export Markets
(ranked by share of 1991 exports)

Destination of exports	Percentage
Hong Kong	45%
Japan	14
United States	9
Germany	3
South Korea	3
Singapore	3
CIS	3
Netherlands	2
Italy	1
Thailand	1
France	1
United Kingdom	1
Pakistan	1
Taiwan	1
Australia	1
Canada	1
Malaysia	1
Macao	1
North Korea	1
Indonesia	1
Belgium	1
United Arab Emirates	1
All others	4
Total	100

Source: The Europa World Yearbook 1993 (London: Europa Publications, 1993).

struction, real estate speculation, currency trading, and the importation of final goods and services in circumvention of more generally applicable import policy. The SEZs have had a positive effect in showcasing the stimulative effect of outward-looking policy, but other aspects, such as illicit commerce, are of dubious economic benefit.

Other Foreign Borrowing

China rejoined the International Monetary Fund (IMF) and the World Bank (the International Bank for Reconstruction and Development) in 1980. Membership in the IMF provides short-term borrowing privileges to meet balance of payments difficulties, and the bank offers long-term development loans at subsidized rates of interest. Moreover, a country in relatively good standing with the IMF projects a positive image of credibility and economic soundness to the private investors of the world.

Since 1980, China's borrowing from international private banks, particularly in the form of trade credits, has grown rapidly. By 1990, China had generally avoided taking on excessive international debt obligations. At about $53 billion in 1990, the country's total external debt was less than 80 percent of the value of annual export earnings and less than 15 percent of the value of GNP. China's borrowing and debt service have been conservative relative to China's foreign exchange reserves, current account net earnings, foreign government credits, and direct foreign investment. The funds have been used fairly responsibly for infrastructure and productive capital investment.

Competing in the Developing Asian-Pacific Economy

China has much in common historically, culturally, and even developmentally with Asia's newly in-

Table 6.15   China's Foreign Trade Volume,
1982-1993 (in U.S. dollars, billions)

	Imports	Exports	Trade balance	Total trade
1982	19.3	22.3	+3.0	41.6
1983	21.4	22.2	+0.8	43.6
1984	27.4	26.1	-1.3	53.5
1985	42.3	27.4	-14.9	69.7
1986	42.9	30.9	-12.0	73.8
1987	43.2	39.4	-3.8	82.6
1988	55.3	47.5	-7.8	102.8
1989	59.1	52.5	-6.6	111.6
1990	53.4	62.0	+8.6	115.4
1991	63.8	71.9	+8.1	135.7
1992	80.6	85.0	+4.4	165.6
1993	104.0	91.8	-12.2	195.8

Sources: Chinese Customs Statistics; State Statistical Bureau (SSB).

Note: Trading partners consistently report higher Chinese export figures because they include values of exports shipped through Hong Kong, and they slightly lower Chinese import figures because Chinese customs includes the cost of insurance and freight.

Table 6.16   The Value of Two-Way Trade between China and Selected Countries and as a Proportion of Total Trade, 1987-1992 (in U.S. dollars, billions)

Year	Total trade	Hong Kong	Japan	United States	Germany (FRG)	Soviet Union
1987	$ 82.7	$22.2 (26.8%)	$16.5 (20%)	$ 7.9 (9.6%)	$4.4 (5.3%)	$2.5 (3%)
1988	102.8	30.2 (29.4%)	18.9 (18.4%)	10 (9.7%)	4.9 (4.8%)	3.3 (3.2%)
1989	111.7	34.5 (30.9%)	18.9 (16.9%)	12.3 (11%)	5.0 (4.5%)	4.0 (3.6%)
1990	115.4	40.9 (35.4%)	16.6 (14.4%)	11.8 (10.2%)	5.0 (4.3%)	4.4 (3.8%)
1991	135.6	49.6 (36.6%)	20.3 (15%)	14.2 (10.5%)	5.4 (4.0%)	3.9 (2.9%)
1992	165.6	58.1 (35.1%)	25.4 (15.3%)	17.5 (10.6%)	6.5 (3.9%)	5.9[1] (3.6%)

Sources: Chinese Customs Statistics, State Statistical Bureau (SSB).
[1] Represents trade with Russian Republic only.

dustrialized countries (NICs). Although there are major differences, China increasingly challenges the NICs in at least two regards: the relative abundance of relatively good quality, low-cost labor, combined with a persistent export-promotion development policy.

As the economies and incomes of the NICs have grown, so has the cost of labor in them. The NICs have adapted, as have others before them, by moving out of labor-intensive, low value-added production into increasingly higher value-added production. By comparison, China's labor force swamps that of all the NICs together and indeed that of any other country in the world. Even under the most optimistic growth scenario, most of China's labor is likely to remain relatively inexpensive for the foreseeable future. China, then, is in a position not only to take over a substantial share of labor-intensive production, but even fundamentally to alter the price structure as it enters world markets.

Indeed, shortly after the reforms began in late 1978, this process of international reallocation began with exports of products made by state enterprises. Chinese textiles and textile product exports to the United States rose in quantity from a negligible amount to become the major U.S. source of supply in

less than four years. China was prevented from taking an even larger share of the market only by the quotas imposed by the United States. Anecdotal evidence suggests that by the late 1980s Chinese clothing producers had developed routing and relabeling through third countries to increase sales despite the specific country-of-origin MFA caps.

Ties between China and the NICs and other Asian countries, including Australia and New Zealand, are strengthening under China's open door policy. Hong Kong was China's largest trade partner in terms of both imports and exports during 1991, followed by Japan and then the United States. Taiwan was the fourth-largest source of China's imports. Indonesia, Singapore, Malaysia, and Thailand all supply China with substantial imports. In 1991, South Korea and Singapore were the fourth- and fifth-largest destinations of China's exports; Taiwan, Malaysia, North Korea, and Indonesia were also major recipients. Indeed, not only is China's economic role becoming increasingly prominent compared with the NICs, but it is a key player in the world economy's fastest growing region. U.S. trade with Asia during the early 1990s far outstripped U.S. trade across the Atlantic. While the United States, Europe, and even Japan fell into recessions between 1991 and 1993, the real national incomes and trade activity of Asian states—excluding Japan, but including Australia—grew at healthy average annual rates of 5 to 12 percent.

The Future of Economic Reform

Numerous challenges and obstacles lie in the path of economic reform. Economists in China and elsewhere have pointed out the potential efficiency gains from making the allocation of resources more rational. Yet some of these policy recommendations have negative side effects or costs. While economists generally acknowledge such costs, they are often at a loss to develop alternative policies to meet these costs.

In the post-reform Chinese economy, economic cycles continue to exert relatively widespread and increasing effects. The rapid growth of the economy has not been accompanied by development of commensurate fiscal or monetary policy tools. Periods of boom leading to overextension of investment plans, price inflation, fiscal budget deficits, and international balance of payments difficulties occurred in 1983-1984, 1987-1988, and again in 1992-1993. Typically, the boom is followed by retrenchment—broadstroke policy actions intended to cool the economy, such as price and wage freezes, cutbacks of working capital budgets and investment grants, and reimposition or tightening of import restrictions.

The consequences of the economic retrenchment periods are recessionary. But unlike business cycle recessions in major capitalist economies, which can be persistent and difficult to break out of, China's economy in the post-1978 reform period has required only relaxation of the restraints to recover and resume growth.

The more serious challenge to China appears to be keeping the growth rate from becoming excessively high and leading to the boom-related problems of inflation and deficits. Inflation, in turn, may at some level actually lead to declining real income and a recession—unlike the policy-induced retrenchment—that is completely out of control.

Other problems that remain to be resolved by economic reforms include:

- the market-related macroeconomic business cycle and the yet-to-be-fulfilled need for enhanced fiscal (effective tax system, government spending plan, and working and significant bond market) and monetary (hard budget constraint fractional reserve banking system, working bond market) tools to meet the new challenges of a market system;
- the relative decline of the effectiveness of the state's revenue-collecting apparatus, the state monopoly of commerce together with administrative prices enforcing an agricultural-industrial price differential;
- the potentially huge transaction cost of establishing and operating a new comprehensive tax system to replace the method of the planned economy in which revenue collection took place through the conveniently focused industrial profit remittance system;
- creation of the revenue sources and administrative institutions necessary for making explicit transfer payments and handling the transaction costs of administering the systems that would be required to handle social security, health-care needs, and the dislocation costs that would accompany increased labor mobility and reduced administrative security of employment;
- enormous savings deposits—approximately $200 billion in savings at the end of 1992, or roughly 50 percent of the size of that year's GNP—held in accounts bearing low nominal interest and sometimes negative real interest rates, which constitute a serious "overhang" in potential purchasing power and, if released in goods and services markets, a threat to macroeconomic stability.
- the economy has not yet generated the degree of industrial employment growth necessary to absorb the huge rural labor surplus and avoid the release of that labor on the space-constrained urban economy as residency rules are relaxed;

- there are no institutions or revenue sources sufficient to generate the transfer payments necessary to sustain the segment of the population that might earn a market wage less than subsistence should a further relaxation of traditional institutions of income redistribution occur;
- for various possible reform policies, for political leaders, and from a policy-making perspective, while the net economic gains of new measures might outweigh costs over time, the fact that the costs may occur before the gains may present an insurmountable barrier to policy implementation;
- the prospect of relaxation of state control over the real estate market threatens possibly severe political, economic, and social costs (highlighted in public housing in developed countries and urban ''barrios'' in other developing economies) attendant to removal of the linkage between employment and provision of residence and housing.

From 1978 to the early 1990s, Chinese leaders generally kept these and other problems at bay, while making spectacular progress in economic growth and some aspects of institutional change. Although there are bound to be inefficiencies and dislocations in the meantime, institutional development will have a chance to proceed as long as substantial and stable economic growth continues. Perhaps ironically, the evolution of these competitive market institutions depends in part on the ability of the state administrative system to remain in authority to promote and enforce favorable conditions. While the political implications of China's measured, incremental style of economic reform may not be acceptable to all observers, it has produced dramatic real growth on an unprecedented scale. China's record to date compares favorably with the results of paths pursued in other major economies striving to reform.

CHAPTER 7

CHINESE FOREIGN POLICY
POST-TIANANMEN

The Tiananmen incident of June 1989 was a major event in twentieth-century Chinese history, as well as one of the causes of the downfall of communism in many countries thereafter. As such, it influenced Chinese foreign policies significantly, since those policies derived from the country's greatly altered domestic situation and from the consequent international changes and attitudes toward Beijing. When coupled with the other sea changes in international relations in the several years afterward—the end of the cold war, the breakup of the Soviet Union, and the consequences of the Persian Gulf War—Chinese foreign relations began a new era after Tiananmen.

China's startling economic success of the early 1990s greatly augmented its raw power—which naturally influenced Beijing's regional and global status and policies. Indeed, China's recovery from the isolation inflicted on it immediately after the Tiananmen incident was so rapid as to indicate, by the mid-1990s, that a historic change had occurred in how other nations viewed that country and how, in turn, Beijing's rulers approached the outside world. The very fact of the massive Beijing demonstrations in 1989 indicated that the Communist rulers had lost their right to sole rule in China. Moreover, the way China's rulers handled the citizenry—through massive, brutal, and indiscriminate use of force—opened the prospect that they themselves would eventually fall from power, to be replaced (whether at one stroke or gradually) by a form of government and an ideology more representative of the wishes of the

Chinese people. That, by itself, would augur the greatest change in Chinese foreign policy since the Communists came to power in 1949, maybe even since the fall of the Qing dynasty in 1911. And, despite China's ascension to superpower candidate status, until these changes became definitive in China, the international community would hold the Beijing regime at arm's length and regard its intentions with suspicion. That would be all the more true as China began to project its newly created power abroad.

Chinese foreign policy post-Tiananmen is not only the product of the important events between 1989 and 1991 but also of the prior forty years of Beijing's relations with the outside world, to say nothing of causative factors farther back in history. Before considering the country's policies toward the various relevant states and issues during the 1990s and forecasting likely alternative Chinese policy futures for the early twenty-first century, it is necessary to look briefly at earlier causative factors in Chinese foreign policy.

Causative Elements in Pre-1989 Chinese Foreign Policy

Tiananmen marked the beginning of the third period of modern Chinese foreign policy. The first was coterminous with Mao Zedong's rule, 1949-1976, and the second was coterminous with the economic reform movement of 1977-1988, led by Deng Xiaoping. Each showed the influence of a few domestic and international determinants that changed in relative weight, but not in number or character, between periods. The same held true after the Tiananmen incident. Thus, establishing a historical and causative base is useful for understanding Chinese foreign policy after 1989.

In looking at China since 1949, three domestic and three international determinants can be seen as having combined to shape the formulation of Chinese foreign policy. In the domestic realm, these were: the primacy of politics, the weight of the past, and the importance of ideology. The three international factors were: the foreign policies of the states that mattered to China, the structure of the international system, and China's calculation of its relative power and interests.

Domestic Determinants of Foreign Policy under Mao

Revolutionary Politics. Under Mao, Beijing's foreign policy was determined mostly by domestic factors. The first of these was revolutionary politics. With a well-thought-out Leninist ideology, a quarter-century of battle-hardened experience, internal political unity, a pliant Chinese population, and solid administrative experience, the Chinese Communist Party (CCP) could set forth an activist foreign policy. Its goals were national unity, socialist revolution, export of Communist ideology, anti-Americanism and pro-Sovietism, and restoration of Chinese primacy in Asia. These goals stemmed principally from Mao's own domestic actions and his personality. The well-known swings in foreign policy during these years also stemmed directly from similar swings in domestic politics (see Chapter 3). China's excessively close relations with the Soviet Union during the early to mid-1950s followed from the need to emulate and implant Soviet political and economic institutions and processes in China; the 1958 Taiwan Strait crisis grew out of the Great Leap Forward; the overreaction to Soviet "perfidy" in the early to mid-1960s was a natural concomitant of the 1960-1962 "three lean years" of post-Great Leap Forward disasters; and the isolationist foreign policy of 1966-1976 was part and parcel of the Cultural Revolution. Mao's personality—his campaign style, insistence on revolution above all, megalomania, and paranoia—informed much of Chinese foreign policy during this period and prevented a more rational, national interest-centered policy from emerging. (Only when Zhou Enlai could exert direct influence over foreign policy did national interests dominate, and then only for short periods.)

Weight of the Party's Past. Second was the weight of the party's past, particularly the 1921-1949 era in which basic policies were determined through trial and error in seeking the "correct" revolutionary path to power. First, the Maoist domestic strategy for revolutionary success was applied to the international environment, as set forth in Lin Biao's 1965 pronouncement on people's war. Second was the early experience of a three-sided balance of power, in which the Chinese Communist Party, usually the weakest element, allied and re-allied itself with the second strongest member of the group to avoid destruction. Mao successfully pursued such a strategy in 1949, with his first foreign policy act, which was to ally China with the Soviet Union against the United States, guaranteeing Beijing's security for more than a decade.

Mao was less successful when he forgot the lesson of triangular international relations (by equating the Soviet Union with the United States in the 1960s as China's twin enemies), after which China had no choice in the 1970s but to seek security with the United States. Thus China became a firm believer in security as a function of power, alliance, and manipulation in a tight balance of power.

The distant past was also important. That China was economically backward, had suffered from imperialist overlordship, and had had a history in Asia of cultural supremacy and political centrality, all influenced the post-1949 goals of development, anti-imperialism, and national assertion. Some Chinese policy orientations originate even farther back. Maoist military strategy owed much to the ancient Chinese military strategist Sun Zi and the romantic heroism of such novels as *Romance of the Three Kingdoms* and *The Water Margin*.

Ideology. The third domestic determinant was ideology. Marxism-Leninism-Maoism clearly influenced general policy directions, and sometimes pushed matters to extremes. This can be seen in adulation of the Soviet Union in the early 1950s, total rejection of Moscow after the 1960 break, rabid anti-Americanism in the 1950s and 1960s (see Chapter 4), and wide-scale acceptance of moving close to the United States when dictated by anti-Soviet necessity in the 1970s and 1980s. Ideological blinders caused Mao to misjudge badly other states' foreign policies and domestic developments, particularly those of the United States.

Foreign Determinants of Chinese Foreign Policy under Mao

An understanding of what the party and Mao were attempting at home clarifies many aspects of China's foreign policy, and explains what otherwise seemed to be bizarre, irrational behavior. The three domestic determinants outlined above explain most of the direction, timing, and specifics of Mao's foreign policy. Other causative elements remained outside this framework, however, for China still existed within an international system of states. It had to obey the ''laws'' of that system and was influenced by its structure and by the foreign policies of the other states that were important for Beijing.

The International System. The most influential element of the international framework during Mao's tenure was the cold war between the United States and the Soviet Union. Mao had to lean toward Moscow during the height of American cold war power in the 1950s, found some room for maneuver when Washington and Moscow were ''contending'' during the 1960s, and had to lean back toward Washington in the 1970s when Moscow threatened invasion (see Chapter 4).

Soviet-American systemic domination determined much of Beijing's foreign relations with other nations, international institutions, global issues, and revolutionary movements, once it was apparent where China stood at a given time in relation to the superpowers. China's otherwise inexplicable policy over the decades toward, for instance, such entities as the Thai Communist Party, the North Atlantic Treaty Organization (NATO), Ethiopia, the Shah of Iran, and the revolutionaries in Angola could thus be rationalized. Indeed, Chinese foreign policy in many areas could be derived this way, even without detailed local knowledge.

Asian Regional Dynamics. China also had to conform to the structure and processes of the Asian regional and international systems. Nuclear weapons were a key to national security and international prestige; therefore China had to acquire them. It did so at great national cost by 1964, with marked effect on its subsequent relations with the superpowers and its Asian neighbors. The shape of the international system was greatly altered after World War II: power flowed out of Europe and Japan into the hands of the superpowers, and the postcolonial third world developed into independent states. China thus found it had to devote most of its attention to the United States and the Soviet Union, could largely ignore Europe and Japan, and discovered a major opportunity to appeal to the third world as a prospective ally. In Asia, China found that, beginning in the 1970s, military power counted relatively less and economic power more, as the export-oriented newly developing ''Four Tigers'' (Hong Kong, Taiwan, South Korea, and Singapore), together with the United States and Japan, came to dominate the region. If China had to play economic catch-up just to stay in the game, under Mao it chose not to. Moreover, in each Asian subregion, a balance of power was in place that included Washington and Moscow as security guarantors through alliances with the major regional powers, which were not overly friendly to Beijing. Asia was thus led by those at its periphery, while China, literally its center, was all but excluded. China did become a member of the Asian regional system, which was an important advance, but it had to conform to the system's structure and rules, which were made by others.

China's Changing Power and Interests. The final international determinant was the relationship between China's changing power and interests. Domestic power increased substantially merely as a result of reunification in 1949 under a strong government, as well as the accretions of economic and military power in the quarter-century thereafter. The normal and inevitable consequence of power augmentation is a corresponding increase in the range of national interests. Beijing's international behavior under Mao was a textbook illustration of this central verity of international politics. Obeying this "Iron Law of International Relations," Beijing used its new power to involve itself in situations and disputes ever farther from its geographic boundaries, becoming militarily involved in the territories of all its neighbors (for the first time in its history), participating actively in the diplomacy of other global regions and the strategic triangle and contending with Moscow for control of the international Communist movement, trading with distant countries, and establishing diplomatic ties with most nations.

As China thus expanded its foreign policy horizons, other international actors reacted correspondingly, accommodating Beijing's activism and interventionism but also erecting barriers to keep perceived Chinese expansionism in check. This was done mostly by the United States—in Korea, the Taiwan Strait, and Vietnam—but also by the Soviet Union, Japan, India, and many of the nations in Southeast Asia. Thus, with sufficient time and countervailing power available, a balance of power in Asia and beyond was created that kept Maoist power expansion within acceptable limits.

Unlike during the Maoist period, Chinese foreign policy under Deng Xiaoping did not coincide neatly with his period in power, since the combination of startling domestic developments (the Tiananmen incident) and international changes (the end of the cold war, the general collapse of Communism, and international reaction to Tiananmen) occurred in 1989 and signaled a major shift in Chinese foreign policy. But the six determinants of Chinese foreign policy remained, while changing in their content and relative weight. These major modifications and important new trends considerably altered China's foreign relations after Mao.

Foreign Policy under Deng: Economics Becomes Primary

Domestic Determinants of Deng's Foreign Policy

The most important domestic change was replacement of Maoist radicalism by Dengist pragmatic moderation and a corresponding shift from the primacy of politics to that of economics. Beijing's foreign policy thus became driven by whatever appeared good for China's economic development. The domestic reforms of decollectivization, partial return to the profit incentive and price as resource allocators, mixed state, collective, and private ownership, and pragmatic access to markets, technology, and goods were all reflected internationally in terms of the "open door" to investment, technology transfer, trade, and training. Beijing's foreign policy was summed up by the twin goals of peace and security, since they maximized the probability of high growth and since their opposites, war and threat, would destroy China's best and perhaps only chance to modernize. Deng also deradicalized politics by retiring his revolutionary colleagues, ousting the Maoist radicals, bringing in new and more qualified leaders, installing a new generation of modernizing, counter-revolutionary successors, and building up a mass support base among the peasantry and increasing sectors of urban society (see Chapters 4 and 5).

The weight of the past continued to be important, but stress on the revolutionary tradition was dampened while traditional Chinese culture, hitherto suppressed, was restored. Anti-Westernism was de-emphasized and the customs, habits, and practices dominant before 1949 made a strong comeback under the rubric of modernization. China thus began to look like it had in the late 1920s: variegated, lively, and differentiated, a mixture of the traditional, transitional, and the modern. The ideological heritage was revised as well. The pragmatic and "scientific" aspects of Marxism were stressed ("seek truth from facts" and "practice is the sole criterion of truth"), and Marxism was downgraded to only one determinant of modern thought ("Marxism cannot resolve all our problems"). Maoism was criticized and no longer widely studied. But Leninism (that is, contemporary Machiavellianism) was retained as the party's philosophy of organization (although even this suffered in practice, as membership criteria were relaxed, decision making shifted to government ministries, party popularity declined greatly, and the pragmatic aspects of Leninism supplanted the dogmatic). These allowed Deng to justify the host of economic, administrative, legal, and foreign policy changes basic to his reform program.

International Determinants of Deng's Foreign Policy

The domestic changes described above propelled China onto an entirely new international course and continued to explain most of the direction and variation in Beijing's foreign policy. But changing international determinants also helped to configure the new direction. Within the strategic triangle, Beijing's decision to downgrade the Soviet threat after 1978 reflected its re-evaluation of Russian military intentions as more benign. This led to major policy changes, such as allowing China to reduce its dependence on the United States. Beijing gradually distanced itself from Washington politically, even as the economic relationship deepened. China's relations with the United States henceforth were complex and contradictory, as political tensions coexisted with increasing economic interdependence. Sino-Soviet détente also re-emerged and the road to eventual rapprochement was laid down. Here too, relations became increasingly complex. Beijing denounced the Russian military bear and spoke of the "three obstacles" (Afghanistan, Vietnam, and the Sino-Soviet border problem) that Moscow would have to overcome before genuine friendship could be attained. On the other hand, China and the Soviet Union improved economic ties and steadily moved toward settling the border question. In both the American and Soviet cases, marginal changes constituted the core of Chinese foreign policy and pointed the way to the future.

On the basis of such "relative equidistance," China constructed a "new" policy of independence and supplied the foundation for the third major variation in Deng's foreign policy: renewed interest in the third world. The inequities between the superpower-dominated strategic triangle and the third world convinced Deng that the downtrodden "masses" would determine the international system's future and would eventually accept Beijing as their natural leader. Thus, China generalized its concept of people's war to include among the globe's "masses" all people of the third world, and any Chinese action that would strengthen third world nations against the first and second worlds. As a result, China began a program of military transfer and sale of conventional equipment, nuclear technology, and missiles to the Middle East, sided whenever possible with the third world "Group of 77" in the United Nations against Washington and Moscow, and began to market Chinese economic goods in earnest to many developing countries. The general idea was to convince all within the strategic triangle that China had the support of the third world and was thus a force to be reckoned with.

The international economic system also changed and hence influenced Chinese policy. The enormous explosion of trade and investment, economic interdependence, the post-1974 oil crises, the dollar recycling phenomenon, and the massive increase in global debt all changed the rules of the system. China had to order its economy and its foreign policy according to these new rules, laid down by the Group of Seven advanced industrial democracies and by the General Agreement on Tariffs and Trade (GATT). And since Beijing was a member of neither group and since the engines of production, invention, finance, and technology were concentrated in the market economies of Europe, North America, and Northeast Asia, Deng would have to redirect his country's economic policies to sell to these countries, appeal to them for investment capital, and open whole regions of China (mostly the coast and the southeast) to massive foreign economic (and other) influences. To modernize, China therefore became interdependent.

In global military affairs, further revolutions occurred, as weapons emerged of extraordinary accuracy, power, and speed. Military high technology changed the nature of warfare, such that only those possessing it could hope to wage, win, or deter wars. That presented China with a dilemma. Deng wisely deferred military modernization, reasoning that fielding an up-to-date military before the necessary scientific, technological, and industrial conditions existed would bankrupt the country (see Chapter 9). But pursuing military self-reliance and not using hard currency earnings to buy weapons and military technology abroad might make military modernization take decades, during which time the Soviet Union and the United States might continue to threaten China and also move ahead themselves to the next generation of military technology. Beijing then could neither leapfrog nor approach superpower levels and could well be consigned to permanent inferiority.

The final international determinant, the power-interest nexus, also varied, driven by China's desire to augment its power. Power is the composite of four elements: diplomacy, the economy, culture, and military prowess. China enhanced its capabilities in all four. In diplomacy, Deng kept China out of war, managed the post-Mao transition, revamped the economy, and kept the United States as China's residual security guarantor without knuckling under to Washington, and extracted considerable technology from Washington at little cost. He also opened a line to Moscow, reintroduced China to the third world, and learned the ropes of the latter-day cold war international system. These diplomatic achievements enhanced Chinese power.

In the economic realm, a breakthrough was made. Growth accelerated on the basis of domestic reforms and the open door international economic policy, accompanied by improved technology and large increases in industrial production and the availability of consumer goods (see Chapter 6). Internationally, China became a major trading nation, an importer of technology and exporter of machinery, a force in international economic institutions, and a center of regional commerce. China's economic interests correspondingly enlarged: it wanted freer trade (for itself); more careful integration of other states' economic policies (to protect itself from capitalist business cycles); and a liberalized flow of technology and its scientific, technical, and student carriers (so long as the noxious "spiritual pollution" was left at dockside). China used trade as a device to approach states, far and near, with which it had little prior contact, and

continued a small but showcase foreign aid program.

Chinese culture, suppressed by Mao, was now allowed to re-emerge, refurbished. The result, in terms of tourism, the media, and the performing arts, meant that the world could enjoy China *qua* China without a Marxist-Leninist-Maoist overlay. China aided this transformation by emphasizing the traditional, even in the midst of modernist transformation. With a more balanced mix of tradition and modernity, Beijing was more likely to remain at peace with its neighbors. Cultural renaissance thus greatly enhanced Chinese national power.

As for military power, at first glance China seemed to have made little progress. The military budget stagnated, the military was embarrassed because of its Cultural Revolution-Lin Biao errors, its leadership was elderly and tradition-encrusted, its ranks were poorly trained and equipped, and its production base had shrunk. Beijing could not have fended off a concerted Soviet attack and was even vulnerable to being bested in border conflicts with India and Vietnam (to say nothing of the United States, had it chosen to make life difficult). But China's military budget was the world's third largest, its missile force constantly grew and was modernizing and dispersed, and its troops were younger, better trained, and somewhat better equipped than before. Accordingly, dividends began to accrue. China became a central constituent in Asian subregional balances of military power, Beijing's nuclear missile capability was taken into account in Washington and Moscow, the Chinese navy emerged onto the open seas for the first time since the Ming dynasty, spare production capacity was used to assist distant states, and nuclear cooperation was initiated with some nations, particularly Pakistan. For a country with allegedly manifold military problems, China was in reasonable military shape and was rapidly setting the stage for major expansion (see Chapter 9).

Hiatus in the 1980s

With this huge augmentation in gross national power, China ought to have pursued its interests more vigorously, but during the late 1980s a hiatus appeared in which Chinese foreign policy became nonthreatening and inclined toward the status quo. The first reason for this was the success of Dengist pragmatism, which seemed to work so well that few wished to interfere. Since all agreed that rapid economic development must continue, the opening to the West would be maintained, and the absolute priority accorded to modernization would not be modified through military adventurism or a new hard line. Foreign policy would continue to emphasize cooperation, participation, and even an acceptable degree of interdependence. The fact that many Asian nations increased their power even faster than did China also contributed to the foreign policy hiatus. As the interests of other regional powers expanded, it became more difficult for China to insert itself into new arenas, situations, and disputes. The best example was Japan, which had no projective military power but had become an economic superpower. Everywhere China found that Japan led in production and trade of high-quality, high-technology goods. The same was true of Asia's Four Tigers and even India. China could only continue to upgrade its technology, serve as an export platform for relatively low-technology, low-wage goods, earn more hard currency, and integrate more of its productive capacity with Hong Kong and Taiwan. That again meant interdependence and also learning how to navigate the new world of tariffs, marketing agreements, joint ventures, and comparative exchange and interest rates. Once the country had grown enough, in the 1990s, China would help call the tune. But not in the late 1980s.

The same was true outside Asia. Some regional issues—for instance, in the Middle East—were still too complicated for China to understand fully, and Chinese power was still insufficient to allow Beijing to play a major role with the superpowers. Lacking requisite policy instruments (ships, aircraft, banks, broadcast facilities, and tourists), China used the only instrument of policy that it had in quantity and that was desired by many states: military equipment and technology, especially nuclear know-how and missiles. This was, of course, playing with fire, and Deng knew the superpowers might rule China out of bounds or precipitate a crisis over Beijing's dealings,

in these regards, with Algeria, Pakistan, Iran, Iraq, Saudi Arabia, and Syria. But he got away with such a policy during most of the 1980s, although not after 1989.

The final reason for the hiatus was the domestic consequence of the Deng reforms. Beginning in 1987, gaining force in 1988, and bursting forth in 1989, the economic and then the political situation careened out of control. In retrospect, the Tiananmen incident had many causes: high inflation, political corruption, widespread urban dissatisfaction, student demands for political liberalization, decades-long resentment against party misrule and massive mistakes, reform-caused dislocations, and disunity within the top leadership (see Chapters 4 and 5). When brought together they precipitated huge popular demonstrations in many cities over several months, follow-on martial law, and finally the tragic and unnecessary repression in June 1989. The foreign policy consequences were immediate, although the regime tried to act as if nothing much had changed and continued to cooperate in regional and global security and economic matters. (An ironic symbol was continuation of negotiations with the Soviet Union, which were brought to fruition just before the incident, with Soviet President Mikhail Gorbachev's visit to Beijing in the midst of the demonstrations.) Thus the second major period of Chinese foreign policy, which should have concluded in the mid-1990s with Deng's death, ended abruptly in mid-1989.

Chinese Foreign Policy 1989-1991: Transition to the Post-Deng Era

Beijing's definitive, if temporary, arrival onto the world scene as a global power in the 1980s was interrupted by several events of worldwide impact between 1989 and 1991, including the Tiananmen incident itself; the downfall of communism in Eastern Europe and the Soviet Union; and the Persian Gulf War as an indication of the new global security equation. Each severely affected China domestically as well as internationally. It was only in 1992 that China begin to recover its confidence and use its rapidly growing power to claim its place as a principal in international affairs.

The Tiananmen Incident

Tiananmen symbolized the beginning of the end of Communist rule in China, contributed to the end of Marxism-Leninism globally, and affected China's foreign relations in two ways. Domestically, it temporarily halted reformism and elevated the power of the elderly conservative ideologues, their neo-Maoist philosophy, and the power of the army in the political arena. Leadership composition therefore changed: the Zhao Ziyang-led economic reformers were thrown out and their opposites, symbolized by Yang Shangkun, stepped back in. In foreign policy, their inclination was to close the door to the outside world, as fear of external political and cultural influences overcame the new leadership's desire to import technology and capital. Economic recentralization did stop inflation, but it also reduced growth rates, postponed many foreign purchases, and induced a beggar-thy-neighbor foreign economic policy. A crisis followed in China's relations with many countries, particularly the United States.

The causal relationship between domestic determinants and foreign policy was also demonstrated when China attempted to break out of this relative isolation, beginning in mid-1990. Leadership changes (the return of the reformers, now led by Zhu Rongji), ideological modifications (''market socialism''), and renewal of economic reforms (initiated by Deng's visit to Shenzhen in the Hong Kong hinterland, in early 1992) all indicated restoration of the pre-Tiananmen policy line: diplomatic engagement, support of international organizations, issue-based cooperation, and renewed emphasis on investment and trade. But many nations were not about to let Beijing off the hook so quickly or lightly. Various countries, led by the United States, had applied sanctions to China to show their revulsion and disgust at the Tiananmen violence. These sanctions isolated Beijing further and began to be lifted only gradually. Deng attempted to placate the United States without losing too much face (for example, by allowing dissident Fang Lizhi to exit the country in mid-1990), sought substitute non-American sources of capital and technology, and tried to form an anti-American international coalition. He succeeded moderately well in the first two efforts, but the last, which had little chance of success, was torpedoed by the gulf war and the disappearance of the strategic triangle that followed the 1991 collapse of communism in the Soviet Union and that country's subsequent breakup. Beijing thereupon retreated to a cautious, step-by-step policy of all-around accommodation, careful reopening of investment and trade, and positioning China as a reasonable and responsible country. On the other hand, it retained enough confidence in the permanent influence of its new power to make known that, henceforth, Beijing would not be taken for granted—it would defend its own (expanding) interests and would negotiate from a position of strength. Its gradual re-emergence from isolation demonstrated the partial success of that policy, as did its resistance to the United States over economic relations, security issues, and human rights.

This restorationist foreign policy swing would have been more nearly complete and would have borne fruit earlier if not for the influence of post-1989 international events. When combined with the aftereffects of Tiananmen, they delayed into the mid-1990s China's full acceptance and participation in global affairs commensurate with its new power. The first, communism's downfall, graphically clarified the true relationship between modernization and revolution, the twentieth century's two major trends, and in 1989-1991 revealed its full meaning for China. Economic and political revolution were now clearly linked, with economic development now a necessary condition for political revolution. No longer was political revolution the prerequisite for economic development. Whenever economic and political modernization moved out of step with each other, breakdown and violence would occur and revolutionary resynchronization was needed. This is what happened in China in 1989, and further disorders would be inevitable until the two components of modernization were reconnected to develop in parallel.

These trends directly influenced post-1989 Chinese foreign policy. The party realized that its time in power as an unreconstructed Marxist-Leninist entity was limited; that economic growth meant marketization; and that the party's only hope was to manage those changes and to change with them. Foreign policy had to vary accordingly. For instance, the influence of individual personalities would have to decline since the party would try to represent the entire range of groups and forces in the new Chinese society; ideology and the weight of the past would also vary, as a mixture of nationalism and traditionalism gradually replaced Marxism and revolutionary heroism; a cacophony of groups, interests, and orientations would make Chinese foreign policy more difficult to formulate, Beijing would take longer to react to international events, and its previously sharply defined policies would blur. The Deng ruling group also realized that, to harmonize political and economic modernization, ensure high economic growth, and continue political stability, China would have to retain good relations with the market democracies for a considerable period. That meant keeping the door open to investment, trade, and technology transfer, as well as tolerating foreign cultural and political influences. But the door must not be opened too wide, for fear of losing control. Thus a centrist foreign policy was adopted of avoiding conflict with the overwhelmingly powerful market democracies and playing for time until China was much stronger.

Impact of the Persian Gulf War

The gulf war marked the division between the cold war era and its successor. First, the strategic triangle was replaced by a loose, informal arrangement among five power centers—North America, Greater Europe, Russia, China, and Japan—with its own characteristics, including ad hoc rather than formal alliance ties. Second, marketization, democratization, and interdependence dominated world affairs. China had no choice but to bend in those directions. Third, at the same time, practically all nations, large and small, felt the need to pay primary attention to solving domestic problems, and their domestic affairs consequently dominated foreign policy concerns. China was, in this regard, no different from the others. Fourth, technological change in all fields became the central driving force. Technologically advanced nations, and those that were progressing most rapidly, would dominate, and China, for the sake of

its own international survival and influence, had to be one of them. And last, "global" issues such as the environment, for example, began to appear on the international stage.

These trends and forces carried particular implications for China. Beijing would have to cooperate in loosely cobbled international arrangements to solve such important problems as the North Korean nuclear issue, the "peace process" in Cambodia, and nonviolent solutions to territorial questions, including Taiwan (further detailed below). China was not considered qualified to lead Asia into a post-cold war regional security system (as neither Japan nor Russia could take on the job, the task would continue to fall to the United States, which placed an additional constraint on Beijing's freedom of maneuver). If ad hoc, laissez-faire activities formed the core of Asian security relations, China would have to cooperate with the other major powers and not opt for a policy of splendid isolation. Asian (and global) international relations would tend to be focused on economic, not security, issues while the geographic focus of Asian economic activity would change from Northeast and East Asia to Southeast and South Asia and even Asiatic Russia. Nations would derive their power and prestige from high rates of growth, expanding gross national product (GNP), per capita income, and technological prowess rather than such traditional measures of power as military size, population, territory, and level of production. China's "natural" advantages, while still great, would count for relatively less until the country could rank high in the former set of attributes as well as the latter.

The gulf war and the overwhelming U.S.-led victory epitomized these implications for China. The speed and overwhelmingly technological character of the allied victory shocked the Chinese military: despite much progress, it had a great, perhaps increasing, distance to go before it would be able to compete with the militaries of the market democracies (see Chapter 9 on the military). The integral power of democratization, marketization, and interdependence was brilliantly displayed to China, leading directly to Deng's decision to renew rapid economic reform. Beijing was also impressed that the United States did not exploit its victory for anti-Chinese purposes (something that would have been easy, given the massive amounts of military equipment China had earlier supplied to Iraq). Rather, the Allies were grateful for Chinese neutrality. China could thus breathe easier, renew its emphasis on development, trade, technology transfer, diplomatic participation, and power projection. That is what it did, once the direct impact of Tiananmen on international attitudes was past. A new phase of Chinese foreign policy was therefore about to open.

Given the limits and opportunities described above, China embarked on a "new" foreign policy beginning in 1992. The same domestic and international influences that had played a role in policy under Mao and Deng remained a factor, but their contents were now vastly different. As a result, foreign policy after 1992 differed considerably from that of even a decade earlier. A general outline of that policy can be derived from analysis of China's relations with the states that were most important for Beijing—the United States and the former Soviet Union—and the leading nations of the subregions of Asia—Northeast, East, Southeast, and South Asia. Relations with regions farther afield, such as the Middle East and Europe, while of increasing importance, were still most efficiently subsumed under these three categories.

U.S.-China Relations at the Beginning of the Post-Deng Era

Even before Tiananmen, China's relations with the United States had entered into a gentle decline, the product of Beijing's 1989 decision to gradually distance itself from Washington and to begin an equally cautious rapprochement with the Soviet Union. The June 1989 events both accelerated the separation and tilted it downward drastically. But it was hardly Tiananmen and China's intrastrategic triangular policy that caused such a sea change; it was as much the product of long-term Chinese policies that increasingly irritated the United States and finally impelled the White House to call Deng to account. China's "offending" activities covered the waterfront of Sino-American relations, from national security issues to economics and human rights.

National security issues included:

- China's surreptitious sale in 1982 of a large nuclear reactor to Algeria for production of nuclear weapons, outside the rules of the International Atomic Energy Agency (IAEA);
- China's transfer to Pakistan of nuclear weapons technology, missile technology, launchers, and missiles, outside the rubric of the Missile Technology Control Regime (MTCR);
- China's sale to Iran, Iraq, and Saudi Arabia of various missiles, destabilizing the military equation in the globe's most volatile region;
- China's unwillingness, until pressed hard, to join the Nuclear Nonproliferation Treaty (NPT), to agree to MTCR rules, or to place export of nuclear materials and technology under IAEA inspection;
- China's practice of deliberately setting its security policy just outside international rules.

Economics issues included:

- China's deliberate impeding of imports through market-restricting measures and import substitution policies, while emphasizing exports and amassing a large hard-currency surplus;
- the multitude of restrictions placed on foreign companies in China;
- China's practice of deliberately and massively mislabeling textile products to circumvent import restrictions;
- China's purloining of intellectual property as a national policy;
- China's export of prison labor-made goods and denial of this when queried;

Moral/ideological issues included:

- China's continuing arrests, incarcerations, denials of procedural safeguards, arbitrary interference in personal affairs, restrictions on travel and emigration, and widespread denial of basic civil rights;
- China's practice of cracking down on anyone suspected of participating in the Tiananmen incident or of harboring opinions unfavorable to the regime;
- China's continued severe repression in Tibet and Xinjiang.

Tiananmen brought these issues to a head, and the United States imposed a broad variety of sanctions on the Deng regime in an attempt to coerce Beijing into making satisfactory policy changes in all these areas. This Deng was not about to do, at least not without resistance, for submission to the United States would destroy China's entire foreign policy program, to say nothing of threatening the party's domestic policy and its central role in Chinese society. A standoff thus emerged.

Historical Sino-American Relations

Resolution of these problems and amelioration of bilateral relations in general required placing both in the context of some 200 years of Sino-American relations. First was the economic interest, emerging earlier in the American case (the chimera of the China market) but existing in the Chinese instance by the late 1800s with the country's early efforts at economic development. Second were security interests, which the United States discovered in 1898 with the notion that a united and strong China could be useful as an element in the Asian balance of power, and which China found somewhat later, in the idea that the United States could, if properly treated, become an important counterweight against foreign (for example, Japanese) military threats. Finally was the moral, or ideological, component, which existed for America from the onset of the missionary movement in the early nineteenth century, and in the Chinese case much farther back with the idea of the cultural supremacy of Chinese civilization and hence of keeping America morally (ideologically) at arm's length.

While there was thus a rough parallelism in interests on both sides, content varied considerably. That, as well as unrealistic expectations in both capitals, was a principal cause of the roller-coasterlike course of relations, especially after 1949 (see Chapters 3 and 4). Moreover, neither side successfully defined a steady long-term policy toward the other, although there was always talk about deep, lasting friendship between the two peoples. Instead, during the 1950s and 1960s, ideological differences and the cold war led to confrontation. Overdependence during the

1970s on the common Soviet military threat and the personal relations among the top Chinese and American decision makers led to a false sense of togetherness. And the downgrading in the 1980s by both Washington and Beijing of the other's strategic utility, together with American misreading of the political consequences of the post-Mao economic reforms and China's assumption that a generous America would continually transfer technology and capital without requiring full compensation, meant that disappointment was imminent on both sides.

Mapped onto this evolution were several secular trends. On the American side, China policy varied between the extremes of excessive idealism and blunt realism. Sometimes, such as during the 1978-1987 period, there was rough balance, as anti-Soviet reality remained important and idealism (the idea of evolutionary democracy in China) returned to a central place. But as human rights-based idealism progressively dominated U.S. policy and as the Soviet threat receded, American policy evolved toward stressing global multipolarity and interdependence. China's role in this scenario was clearly small, at least until Beijing became strong enough to join the ranks of leading trading states, which did not occur in the 1980s. On the Chinese side, Beijing was slow to cast off its neo-Maoist isolationism and was therefore constantly forced to trail behind the West in accepting international norms. It did well in the economic and security realms but poorly in human rights. China also put off U.S. policy makers with its constant anti-imperialist rhetoric, stress on sovereignty and self-determination, and a foreign economic policy that pushed domestic growth at foreign expense. China and the United States were thus increasingly out of phase.

The weakening basis of the relationship in the late 1980s was, however, temporarily masked. In the United States, the government fostered the false impression that ties with China were improving, and the populace willingly accepted the notion that Deng Xiaoping was a political as well as economic reformer. In China, the party, eager to restore its sense of autonomy within the strategic triangle by moving away from Washington, failed to keep the balance in its relations with the United States through compromise on economic issues and greater efforts to adhere to international standards of behavior regarding arms sales, trade, and human rights.

Had Tiananmen not occurred, Sino-American relations might have achieved a "soft landing," balancing the decline in importance of the strategic component with the rise in weight of the economic element. Whatever might have been, however, certain historical lessons were apparent. First, each country would have to seek a rough balance between security, economic, and moral/ideological interests in bilateral relations, without overly depending on any one of these components. Second, Beijing and Washington had to move into phase with each other internationally and to better understand each other's domestic situations. Third, they needed to eschew the factor of personality, clearly define their objective national interests, and communicate those ideas directly to the other side. Fourth, both sides needed to understand that the changing power balance between the two countries would always affect their foreign policies and hence their bilateral relations. Sophisticated power calculations would have to be performed constantly on both sides and implications drawn directly for changing national interests.

Downward Spiral after Tiananmen

Nevertheless, the Tiananmen incident did take place, leading to a downward spiral in relations for the next several years. Not only did Washington focus on the various Chinese "sins" cataloged above, but Beijing usually tried to avoid addressing them on their merits. Moreover, the several international developments previously noted cast the relationship adrift from its relatively comfortable moorings of the previous decade.

With no new principles to guide U.S.-China relations through uncharted post-cold war waters, with the anti-Soviet security component at least temporarily removed as a factor in bilateral ties, and with China having suffered an obvious if temporary decline in international prestige after Tiananmen, the United States concluded that it could base its policy on a combination of economic and human rights interests. Indeed, the White House, influenced by congressio-

nal demands to use the economic relationship as a lever to force human rights changes in China, made the annual renewal of China's most favored nation trade status (tariff treatment equal to other American trading partners, or MFN) a test of how far China could be pushed in U.S.-desired moral directions.

For a time, coincident with the Bush administration's tenure and extending into the early Clinton administration, the United States was largely able to have its way with China. Bush pursued a so-called good cop (himself)-bad cop (Congress) approach to Deng. He argued that it was better for Beijing to move as far as it could toward satisfaction of Bush's own list of demands lest a much more stringent set be approved by the Congress, MFN be lost, and the relationship be shattered. The reason China compromised, of course, was the diminution of its power after 1989. So, reasoning that when China recovered its strength, it could more successfully resist being pushed around by the United States, Deng focused on economic development as the quickest and most effective means to augment Chinese power, and through trade, to get U.S. attention.

First, however, the downward spiral had to be halted. This was not so easy, as each side took actions that greatly displeased the other and that gave ammunition to those leaders in each capital disinclined to an overly close relationship with the other. In China's case, the post-1991 economic recovery and then the 1992-1994 boom in investment and exports gave the United States pause, as China suddenly emerged as a principal trading state and as the International Monetary Fund re-evaluated dramatically upward (by adopting the so-called purchasing power parity measure) China's GNP to some $1.5 trillion (see Chapter 6). But by the same token, the U.S.-China trade imbalance grew to gigantic proportions (close to $20 billion by the end of 1993) and showed no sign of tapering off. No matter that an increasing portion of that imbalance was caused by different definitions of exports and by the immense movement of low-wage industry from Taiwan and Hong Kong to the mainland. The fact was that China's stance of protecting its industries and promoting its exports remained an important source of the problem. China also continued to resist American human rights de-

President George Bush, a long-time supporter of improved Sino-American ties, went to China in February 1989. He was forced to preside over a downward spiral in U.S.-China relations over the next several years, however, after China's suppression of the Tiananmen democracy movement in June 1989.

mands, making only last-minute token gestures, and continued to transfer missile components to Pakistan and other materials of mass destruction to the Middle East. On the American side, confusion in China policy continued, as illustrated by swings between the extremes of neglecting and overvaluing China, failing to strike a balance between subtle pressure and confrontation, and placing the Taiwan Relations Act above the three communiqués (1972, 1978, and 1982) that formed the basis of their ties.

The most important near-term question was whether the downward spiral had indeed been halted and replaced by early 1993 with a series of ebbs and flows in the relationship. If so, new foundations would have to be planned and constructed, including balancing (on both sides) between emphasis on peaceful political evolution and economic development, and finding a new security tie to replace anti-Sovietism. The U.S. side would need a replacement for its sanctions-based policy, which was already

wearing out as an efficient means of influencing China's domestic and foreign policies, while the Chinese side needed to understand the dysfunctional effects on the United States (to say nothing of its Asian neighbors) of its unwarranted and deliberate exercise of its newly created power.

Favorable conditions did exist. Neither side threatened the other militarily. The three communiques remained in effect. Domestic interests now predominated in both countries. Under Bush but much more clearly under Clinton, the United States was increasingly selective about involving itself in international security operations and inclined to coordinate rather than dominate global affairs. Like China, the United States was concentrating on solving its economic problems. Finally, in 1991 China renewed its interest in economic reforms, continued to seek international stability and peace as the best conditions for domestic development and stability, remained at least somewhat flexible diplomatically, and sought

By 1993 both China and the United States were taking steps to resolve some of their outstanding tensions. President Clinton met with Chinese president Jiang Zemin in November 1993 at the Asia-Pacific Economic Cooperation conference in Seattle, the highest level contact between the two countries since 1989.

to join rather than fight the market-oriented international economic system.

A New Rationale in the 1990s

The hard issues of the relationship—human rights, arms sales, nuclear weapons proliferation, the future of Hong Kong and Taiwan, and the panoply of economic differences—remained to be addressed frontally. In the security realm, a new rationale slowly began to emerge: to construct a new U.S.-Chinese-Japanese strategic triangle (China's preferred solution) or to quadrilateralize it by including Russia (favored by some in the United States), but in any case to cooperate in building a new Asian security regime or subregional security arrangements; and to work together in defusing the highly dangerous North Korean problem despite different approaches and interests.

In the area of perceptions, both nations continued to try to understand each other's domestic situations better, through enhanced analysis, continued schol-

arly exchange, and a major effort to come to terms with the complicated nature of each other's political processes. Washington would have to understand that it could not remold China in its own image and that most other nations would not join the United States in such an endeavor. Rather, the United States would have to replace its polarized post-Tiananmen policy regarding China and strive for a more balanced mix of realism and idealism without, however, eliminating the democratic component. China would have to demonstrate movement toward democracy by concrete acts and also learn to accept international (not just American) criticism of its internal order. Finally, China would have to learn to take advantage of global trends: interdependence, environmentalism, global détente, much greater importance of information and technology, the universal drive to democratize, and the demilitarization of ideology.

The prospect for further crises remained. President Clinton's early stance of making renewal of MFN conditional only on a long list of human rights demands seemed at first to guarantee a confrontation and possible loss of this central economic tie just when China was beginning to open its domestic market. Fortunately, Clinton thought better of such a one-sided strategy in mid-1994 and went beyond, once and for all, the annual renewal battle by "delinking" it from human rights policy. On the Chinese side, the question was how to avoid thumbing its nose at the West in several realms, including further weapons sales to unsavory Middle Eastern governments and to Pakistan. China also needed to modify its harsh stance on British proposals for furthering democracy in Hong Kong (see Chapter 10), to slow down its own arms buildup especially through purchase/transfer of Russian military systems and technology, to stop its continuous end-running of U.S. restrictions on certain imports, to resist the temptation to raise additional import barriers, and to ease off on further forcible suppression of political dissent in China. It was not clear that Beijing possessed the willpower to make all, or even most, of these changes. A third danger to U.S.-China relations stemmed from an event over which neither nation had full control, such as a crisis on the Korean peninsula, strong movement in Taiwanese politics toward declaring independence, and outbreak of Indo-Pakistani conflict over Kashmir. If any of these events occurred, the U.S.-China bilateral relationship would be severely tested.

Compared to security and human rights issues, economic relations appeared relatively simple to manage. First, every economic problem was potentially solvable on its merits. Indeed, difficulties in contemporary Sino-American economic relations were no different in kind, and to some extent magnitude, from those typically encountered between nations at similar stages of their respective economic development. Second, the way to overcome them was to address their merits by intensive negotiations. The problems, of course, were real: figuring out what the actual U.S. trade deficit with China was, taking account of the influence of the Hong Kong and Taiwan factors; investigating the changing four-sided relationship between China, Hong Kong, Taiwan, and the United States (detailed in Chapter 10); deciding whether, and to what extent, China's unfair trade practices were deliberate, cyclical, or progressively

resolving themselves with time; addressing specifics of American complaints about accessing the China market (tariffs, import and foreign exchange restrictions, inadequate intellectual property protection, restrictions on the activities of American service companies); and problems relating to importing Chinese goods into the United States (massive export subsidies, violation of American textile quotas, and the convict labor question). By 1994 measures were being adopted by both sides to deal with all these economic issues, although changing Chinese regulations constantly imposed new challenges. Behind these developments, the rapidly increasing size and activism of the Chinese economy, as well as the more obvious complementarity of the two economies, made it likely that politics—the use of economic relations for political purposes on either side —would gradually intrude less. The future of Sino-American relations would then tend to revert to determination by domestic political and national security issues over the medium to long term (as discussed in the last section below).

Post-Tiananmen Relations with the Soviet Union and Russia

China's relations with the Russian empire, the Soviet Union, and the Russian Republic and the Central Asian successor states go back even farther than do its contacts and ties with the United States. Formal ties between the Chinese and Russian empires were established in the 1689 Treaty of Nerchinsk, although trade had taken place intermittently via the Silk Road since the time of the Roman empire and direct contacts had begun in the mid-1640s. The next two centuries saw a series of treaties defining the Sino-Russian border ever more closely, as the Russian empire expanded and the Chinese contracted and declined.

By the late nineteenth century, Russia was the most aggressive of the European imperial powers attempting to subvert China through trade and investment and playing European power politics in East Asia. By the early twentieth century, however, the Russian empire was also near collapse and had suffered defeats in wars with Japan (1904-1905) and

Germany (1914-1918). Russian influence in Asia between these dates was nearly absent, reviving only when the Bolsheviks came to power in 1917 and began to carry their revolutionary message to China. Soviet power was maximized in the early to mid-1920s through organizational and ideological assistance to the nascent Chinese Communist Party and material assistance to the Kuomintang. After the Communist-Nationalist split of 1927, however, Russian influence again declined precipitously (see Chapter 2).

Moscow also found that the domestic problems that followed collectivization, industrialization, and the purges of the 1930s and the impending threat from Nazi Germany took priority over participating in Asian security relations and in the internal Chinese struggle for power. Soviet power did not recover until the end of World War II, when the Soviet Red Army, in accordance with the Yalta Agreements of 1945, invaded Manchuria, overcame the Japanese Army in a short but intense struggle, and occupied Northeast China until May 1946. Electing to withdraw rather than emplace a local Communist government in power (in contrast to what it had done in North Korea and Eastern Europe), Moscow nonetheless influenced the Chinese civil war of 1946-1949 through supply of equipment and training to the Communists. And in 1950, Stalin signed a thirty-year treaty of alliance with Mao, designed to cement ties between the two Communist giants and thus confront the United States and its allies with an impregnable fortress.

The well-known story of Sino-Soviet relations from 1949 to 1989 is divided into four phases. The first, 1950-1959, saw cooperation and close ties peak in the early part of the decade, level off thereafter, and then decline rapidly in the last years. The symbolic way stations were Mao's early 1950 trip to Moscow culminating in the alliance treaty and enabling China to fight the Korean War with Russian assistance and security guarantee; the Khrushchev trip to Beijing of 1954 to straighten out the problems created by Stalin's attempt to turn the 1950 treaty into an instrument of control over China; the Chinese criticism in 1956 of the Kremlin's handling of Stalin's legacy, which began the public phase of ideo-

logical rivalry and struggle for control of the international Communist movement; the Soviet tearing up of the so-called atom bomb agreement in 1959 and its withdrawal of advisers in 1960, dealing a severe blow to China's nuclear ambitions and industrialization strategy; the competition within the Communist movement, 1960-1966; disagreement over how to react to the American intervention in Vietnam, 1965-1968; the border dispute, lasting from the mid-1960s down to 1989; Soviet military buildup along the border from 1967, confronting China with insuperable military power and casting Beijing into Washington's waiting arms during the 1970s and early 1980s; the Soviet invasion of Afghanistan of 1979, engendering further Sino-American cooperation; and finally the decision on both sides to seek rapprochement, leading to the Gorbachev visit to Beijing shortly before Tiananmen, in May 1989.

Throughout these three centuries, China evolved a series of interests and policies toward what has been termed Central Eurasia (Russia and the five Central Asian successor states of the former Soviet Union), depending on its relative power vis-à-vis Moscow. When China was weak or weakening, its policy was either to protect itself from Russian encroachment or to use Russia to counterbalance the imperialist Western powers. Hence, Beijing had little choice but to move back and forth between Russia and the West, leaving little room for a policy toward Russia based on more general principles and necessitating instead a diplomacy of tactics and movement. This also explains its attitude to Moscow during most of the 1970s and the early 1980s. When China felt stronger, it pursued a policy of cooperation or competition with Moscow, depending on how the Beijing rulers evaluated their power relative to Moscow and their general international standing. This was the case in most of the 1950s, 1963-1965, and from the mid-1980s to Tiananmen. The first years of the Cultural Revolution, 1966-1969, were a special period during which China isolated itself. Its policy toward the Soviet Union consisted of ideological and military opposition, no trade, and diplomatic contact only out of necessity. A foolish and self-defeating policy, it took no account of power realities and brought on border incidents in 1969, massive Soviet military buildup and threat, and rapprochement with the United States largely on American terms.

Rapprochement

China's post-Tiananmen relations with Russia and the Central Asian successor states provide a textbook example of the application of altered Chinese foreign policy specifics based on reaction to the four major post-1989 developments noted earlier. Accordingly, Beijing pursued four goals toward the former Soviet Union. Politically, it attempted to prevent Moscow, Tashkent, and the other capitals from establishing overly close ties with the United States, Europe, and Japan. Nothing would be more disastrous for China than an institutionalized league of global market democracies, making Beijing fully dependent on states of a fundamentally different character for technology, capital, and markets. Such a group could eventually convert itself into a security community directed against Beijing. Indeed, Deng watched nervously as first Gorbachev and then Russia's elected president, Boris Yeltsin, began to attend the annual meetings of the Group of Seven countries. His response was to establish diplomatic relations with all the successor states and develop reasonable political relations on the basis of resolution of existing disputes and development of economic ties. The longer term political goal was to so tie the relevant successor states to China as to make unlikely their full integration with the market democracies. That was difficult, since in the systemless post-cold war global and Asian political arrangement, universal marketization and eventual democratization appeared probable. China thus had to strike a careful midpoint between its own preference for balances of power, on the one hand, and learning how to use such new levers of international influence as interdependence, technology, and participation in international institutions, on the other.

In security matters, China's Central Eurasian policy was equally cautious: existing security issues, such as border disputes, should either be settled or put aside. China also desired agreement on security arrangements assuring mutual noninterference, pledges not to direct security assets against one another, and joint opposition to potentially threatening military arrangements elsewhere. Finally, Beijing perceived an opportunity to obtain high-technology Russian military systems and technology at much reduced prices, which could greatly assist in shortening the period of danger from American post-gulf war military domination and perhaps even help China draw close to the American level. The trick was to use Russian military assistance and sales to stay out of harm's way as China's economy grew rapidly, prepare for China's own Asian military preponderance, and avoid frightening Central Eurasia into a global anti-Chinese alliance.

Economically, China adopted a three-pronged policy toward the successor states. First, it sought to maintain and then enhance trade relations with Russia and establish and then expand trade with Central Asia. This could only mean exchange of Chinese consumer goods for Russian producer goods and primary products and, absent meaningful exchange rates, more barter and border trade. Second, China wished to set up more permanent economic relations through trade treaties and most favored nation tariff treatment. And third, Beijing took advantage of the increasingly desperate Russian economic situation by purchasing Russian technology on very favorable terms and by offering hard currency in exchange for know-how, assembly lines, plans, and technicians.

Finally, China initiated a new ideological approach. This was not easy, given the post-Communist orientation of the successor states and their ideologically confused mixture of nationalism, religion, modernism, and anticommunism. Beijing could only minimize the differences between these and its own still-Communist, incipiently authoritarian, and increasingly chauvinistic orientation. That meant a complex policy toward Soviet successor nations, which ranged from Catholic to Orthodox to Islamic religions, from fully democratic to confusedly authoritarian to potentially militaristic polities, and from a simple social class structure characteristic of developing societies to highly differentiated modern societies. Such a policy would also have to be sophisticated, patient, innovative, and understanding; qualities that Deng and his associates did not always possess in the requisite abundance.

Soviet president Mikhail Gorbachev's May 1989 summit in China was a significant step toward building a new and positive relationship between China and the Soviet Union, although it was overshadowed by the massive demonstrations taking place in Beijing at the time.

For obvious reasons, Beijing had to center its attention on relations with Russia/the Soviet Union. The most interesting and commanding fact is the continuity of Chinese policy toward Moscow throughout the turbulent early post-cold war period, a continuity mostly reciprocated by Moscow during both the Gorbachev and Yeltsin periods. Gorbachev had, in his well-known Vladivostok and Krasnoyarsk speeches (respectively in 1986 and 1988), fundamentally altered Soviet policy toward China, from opposition on every front to accommodation, compromise, and renewed friendship. The Chinese leadership, having for nearly three decades resisted Soviet encroachments, threats, and war preparations, now gradually warmed to Gorbachev's advances. By 1989, the process of Russian bending to Chinese demands for proof of their good intentions (the so-called three obstacles—withdrawal of Russian forces from Afghanistan, Mongolia, and Vietnam) and negotiations on the Sino-Soviet border question had both proceeded far enough to schedule the break-through May summit meeting, with its accompanying and equally startling joint communiqué.

The accident of the timing of Gorbachev's China visit, in the midst of the massive Beijing demonstrations that led two weeks later to the Tiananmen repression, should not detract from the results. Essentially, Beijing and Moscow agreed to put aside their ideological and security disputes and start anew. But the agreement did more than clear the deck; it was a significant step toward building a new and positive relationship. The communiqué read much like a nineteenth-century agreement of alignment, if not outright alliance. The two sides pledged not to use or threaten force against each other and agreed to solve the border question peaceably. They also agreed to resist "actions and attempts by any state to foist their will on others and to seek hegemony in any form anywhere." This could only be directed against the United States.

The Chinese premier, Li Peng, went to Moscow in April 1990. During this visit the foreign ministers of both countries signed an agreement to further reduce forces along their common border, while Li and his Soviet counterpart, Nikolai Ryzhkov, initialed a broad economic, technological, and scientific agreement that formed the basis of much of the practical improvement in relations thereafter. The next year, Jiang Zemin, the CCP general secretary, went to Moscow and signed another wide-ranging joint communiqué. Again, although international conditions had drastically changed, this further warming of bilateral ties was startling. Now the Soviet Union and China reduced their border forces further, stepped up military contacts, reiterated their opposition to "hegemonism," and agreed to take similar approaches to most issues. This was followed, in early 1992, by settlement of the most important (eastern, riverine) portions of the border question and later that year by a further joint declaration signed during Yeltsin's visit to Beijing. This was not a party-to-party announcement (since by then the Communist Party of the Soviet Union had been outlawed following its failed August 1991 coup attempt) but a more authoritative state-to-state declaration. It repeated the pledges made previously and went on to announce that "neither party [government] should join any military or political alliance against the other party, [or] sign any treaty or agreement with a third country [read the United States] prejudicing the sovereignty and security interests of the other party," and concluded that each would constantly consult the other at all levels on all international issues, that they would continue border force reductions, and that they would "maintain military contact."

Based on these foundations, a material aspect to the new security tie quickly developed, wherein much Soviet military equipment, military technology, and even whole assembly lines for late model Russian tanks, fighters, computers, and other relevant equipment were sold to China. Similar ties were re-established in many other fields, such that full normalization was achieved, trade blossomed, science and technological delegations visited frequently, tourism arose for the first time, and students and cultural troupes were exchanged in increasing numbers. Thus Russian and Chinese influence over each other's lands experienced a renaissance (the first

such wave of influence had occurred during the early 1950s).

Commonality of Interests

Why did China and Russia find it necessary to go to such lengths, why did China not feel unduly threatened by domestic Russian changes, and why did other nations (particularly the United States) not react in a justifiably negative manner? First, both China and Russia worried about a post-cold war, post-gulf war world possibly dominated by the United States. A commonality of interests emerged, as China increasingly regarded the United States as its security opponent while a rapidly weakening Russia needed to buttress its international position. Second, although international isolation drove Beijing to Moscow, China could hardly be enthralled by a Soviet Union that had given away its East European empire, allowed marketization and democratization to supplant central planning and Leninism, and lost control of its own internal order. Thus the two formed an arrangement of convenience between a Eurasian continental have-not and a temporary international pariah, reminiscent of the German-Soviet Rapallo Treaty of 1922. Third, exchange made economic sense: Moscow had on Russian soil much leftover but first-class military equipment beginning to rust and becoming obsolete. Overconcentration on military production had also left Russia with insufficient consumer goods, a decaying infrastructure, and an unworkable economy, whereas Beijing lacked modern military systems. Finally, the larger purpose of Chinese foreign policy—to make the world safe for Chinese economic development and expansion of Beijing's influence—was satisfied by these arrangements and helped clear the way for the more challenging competition with the United States and Japan in Asia and beyond. Better to have Moscow on one's side, even if it was temporarily down and out.

Two developments further buttressed Sino-Russian rapprochement. On the one hand, deterioration of the Russian domestic scene accelerated after the August 1991 coup attempt. If post-Communist Russia had been successfully marketizing and democratizing, Deng Xiaoping and his group might legiti-

During Premier Li Peng's visit to Moscow in April 1990, Li and his counterpart, Nikolai Ryzhkov, initialed a broad economic, technical, and scientific agreement that formed the basis of much of the practical improvement in relations between their two countries thereafter.

mately have feared such a nation. But as that was not the case, and as China continued to grow rapidly economically and remained stable politically, such a concern did not materialize and probably would not for some years. On the other hand, the market democracies did not become overly apprehensive about the new Sino-Russian ties. Washington largely ignored the situation, being too busy encouraging East European decommunization, keeping Russia afloat, and dealing with increasingly critical domestic concerns. The last thing Washington wanted was to worry about Eurasian border problems and a replay of strategic triangular politics. Japan and the other leading Asian nations took an economics-and-trade-first attitude toward China, had other regional concerns, and concluded that a rapidly weakening Russia renewing ties with a rapidly marketizing China did not present a threat. Cause for concern would have been created if China, under no threat from its Eurasian

continental hinterland, had become ultra-powerful and threatened its Asian neighbors, and if Russia had recovered its strength sufficiently to add its resources to China's. But this did not happen, at least not yet. Moreover, the opinion was also widespread—in North America, Europe, and Asia—that post-Tiananmen China would eventually go the way of post-Gorbachev Russia. Besides, these governments reasoned, if Russia possessed an excessively large military arsenal, it would be better to sell it to China and other Asian nations than to continue to deploy it west of the Urals or allow unstable Middle Eastern potentates to bid for it.

Beijing did face potential dangers and opportunities in the five Central Asian successor states of the former Soviet Union: Kazakhstan, Uzbekistan, Turkmenistan, Tajikistan, and Kyrgyzstan, though not immediately. After initial hesitation caused by general unfamiliarity with these regions and by post-August coup confusion in the now-disintegrating Soviet Union, China, like all other nations, offered diplomatic recognition to Alma Alta (later called Almaty; the capital has since moved to Akmola), Tashkent, Ashgabat, Dushanbe, and Bishkek. But it would take time for China to open embassies, train staffs, and gain experience in and with these new states. Like other states, China did not know what to do about Central Asian ethnic strife and problems between local inhabitants and Russians, and decided not to get involved for the time being. Beijing's rational interest was served by looking favorably on a region both divided against itself and opposed to Russia, since potential trouble would then avoid China's borders. Finally, the last thing Beijing wished for was for the five states to adopt—together or separately—an Islamic fundamentalist ideology and form of government, since China had its own restive domestic minority populations in its western provinces and Islamic fundamentalism was gaining popularity in many areas. As a result, Deng and his associates chose to watch, but not participate in, Central Asian volatility. In 1992 China initiated trade, diplomatic, and cultural ties with the five successor states and these ties developed gradually thereafter. This would be the better road to take until the Central Asian picture became clearer, until China's own political situation was stabilized, and until Beijing's post-Tiananmen international image improved. The action in the short term was likely not to be in Central Asia but elsewhere—in Northeast Asia, Russia, Europe, and North America, internationally, and, more importantly, in domestic politics and economics.

As in the case of the United States, the longer term future of Chinese relations with Central Eurasia would be a function of the same set of domestic and international trends and forces noted above. The difference was that the domestic situation in Russia and the Central Asian states was much more volatile, and hence less predictable, than in the United States.

China's Relations with Important Asian Regional States

China's post-Tiananmen Asian policy revolved around its relations with the important states in each subregion—Northeast, East, Southeast, and South Asia—as well as certain continuing policy issues.

Sino-Japanese Relations

Japan has always presented China with its most important regional foreign policy problem. Beginning with the Meiji Restoration (1868), Tokyo was accurately perceived as China's only regional rival of consequence. Japan early on became a model for many Chinese modernizers as the first results of late nineteenth-century Japanese modernization became apparent. Later, as China proved unable to follow a similar path and the Qing empire declined, fell, and was replaced by the disunity of warlordism, Japan became a threat. It defeated China in war in 1895, participated in imperialist interference in the immediate pre-World War I period, and took advantage of that conflict and the absence of the European powers to impose the infamous Twenty-One Demands on a prostrate China (see Chapters 1 and 2). Prevented by allied intervention from dominating China at the war's end, and hemmed in by the American-led Washington Naval Treaty, Japan then reverted to a kind of modernist model for many of China's early revolutionaries, Nationalist and Communist alike. But Tokyo's own domestic political situation was not sufficiently stable, and by the late 1920s to early 1930s Japan became rabidly imperialist toward China, invading Manchuria in 1931. In 1937 Japan embarked on full-scale war, invading China proper and occupying most populated areas of the country until the end of World War II. The brutality of that occupation, as well as the huge and costly, if largely unsuccessful, Chinese resistance, largely formed Chinese attitudes toward Japan. Only with Tokyo's final defeat in 1945, occupation by the United States, and forcible conversion to a market democracy during the late 1940s did China relax, if only a bit, its fear of Japanese militarism. And because until 1972 Japan was constrained by the cold war and American insistence that it not enter into diplomatic ties with China, Beijing had little firsthand knowledge of the enormous benefits that reforms had brought to Japan. Only after that point, and only with the equally huge economic and trade strides that Japan took toward becoming an economic superpower, did most Chinese once again view Japan with something other than fear.

Therefore, not surprisingly, China's policy toward Japan did not change much as a consequence of Tiananmen or the other major events that propelled the world into a new era at the end of the twentieth century. Fortunately, Beijing and Tokyo did not have to begin from scratch at that point, for China's anti-Soviet needs of the late 1970s had at least produced a peace treaty with Japan in 1978. This, along with recognition earlier in the decade, provided a base on which to build. Sino-Japanese relations could remain mostly within the economic realm because of China's need for investment, trade, and technology and Japan's plentiful possession of all these, combined with the absence, thanks to Japan's security treaty with the United States, of any Japanese military threat to China. Each area of bilateral relations—political, security, and economic—presented potential problems. But both governments deliberately downplayed difficulties and sought common ground. Relations were therefore excellent on the surface if potentially troubled just beneath.

During the cold war, the question of what to do about the Soviet Union dominated Beijing's policy toward Japan. Indeed, since Tokyo was closely allied to Washington, Japanese autonomy was not likely nor did China desire it. The situation began to change in the 1980s, as Japan and the United States agreed on a division of labor in the security realm, with Japan increasing its martial (''self-defense'') capabilities and taking the principal role in sea control for 1,000 miles from Tokyo Bay. Progress in Sino-Japanese relations was stalled by a series of eruptions, however. Problems included controversy over the treatment of Japan's occupation of China in Japanese high school textbooks, scandal over Japan's handling of the memory of the Nanjing massacre and other World War II atrocities against China, an emerging Chinese trade deficit with Japan, Prime Minister Yasuhiro Nakasone's more outward-oriented foreign policy, large yearly increases in Tokyo's defense budget, and Japan's ascendance to the top reaches of global economic leadership (symbolized by its membership in the Group of Seven) and the concomitant

threat to Beijing of economic isolation. Added to these bilateral concerns were changes in the structure of international relations foreshadowing the end of the cold war: declining American and Soviet prestige because of growing domestic problems, decline in the Russian military threat to China, and the economic rise of both Japan and the European Community, presaging global multipolarity.

The combination of bilateral problems and these international events could have driven Tokyo and Beijing apart. But the major changes in 1989 and beyond, in China, Russia, and globally, reversed that drift. For separate reasons, both capitals decided to maintain and, if possible, improve their bilateral relations. China needed to break out of post-Tiananmen isolation, forestall any U.S.-led global alliance, set the stage for its own emergence as a superpower, and above all continue rapid economic modernization. Japan needed gradually to supplement the security treaty with a multilateral Asian-centered instrument that would include China, sustain and perfect the global free-trade regime and broaden its Asian component, and continue fostering a market-centered Asian economy based on high growth rates everywhere. Together, these would provide for Japanese national security and promote a bigger Japanese economy. As administration of these policies dovetailed, short-term tensions declined. Trade, loans, and investment supplied a convenient cushion for absorbing Japanese worries about a powerful China and Chinese concerns over a remilitarizing Japan. Two-way trade, in line with the general explosion of China's economy, increased greatly after 1991, to $39 billion in 1993. More than $30 billion in loans were extended to China in the thirteen years after 1978, and contracted Japanese investment in China ballooned from less than $1 billion on an average yearly basis until 1991 to $4 billion in 1993.

However, this overall improvement of Sino-Japanese relations masked continuing problems. China worried that Japan would freeze it out of what it perceived to be a ''new world order'' centered upon the triangular relations between the developed market democracies of North America, Europe, and East Asia. It therefore tried to substitute a China-Japan-United States triangle in which Beijing would balance between Tokyo and Washington and thus maximize its security and influence. But no such triangle came into being and instead, Washington came first with Tokyo, as it did with Beijing. Beijing would have to deal with Sino-Japanese issues, bilateral and multilateral, on their merits, including: Tokyo's tendency to put China a distant second to the United States in overall foreign policy terms; obtaining a seat for Tokyo on the United Nations Security Council; roles of the Asia-Pacific Economic Cooperation (APEC) forum and the Association of Southeast Asian Nations (ASEAN); Asian security; and transfer of U.S. *Patriot* missiles to Japan as part of the Reagan administration's Strategic Defense Initiative. Most of these were matters in which Beijing was only a marginal player. Tokyo worried not just about how to face a strong China for the first time in the 2,000 years of Sino-Japanese contacts but also about the opposite prospect—post-Deng instability in China. Japan was unsure how to integrate China into international institutions not of China's making—renewal of the NPT and the MTCR, how to promote responsible Chinese participation in solutions to such regional problems as North Korean nuclear weapons development and UN registry of arms sales, and how to overcome the disjunction between the relative proportions of trade with each other (for China, trade with Japan was about 15 percent of the total while for Japan, trade with China was only about 6 percent). Lastly, Tokyo was increasingly concerned about China's military projection potential.

As for China, it worried about whether the security treaty with the United States would continue to block Japanese remilitarization, how to maintain Japanese aid, trade, and investments despite the resultant inequitable economic consequences, and how to expand its influence and power without overly disturbing Tokyo. None of these matters was likely to shake the foundations of Beijing-Tokyo relations in the coming years or to alter significantly the status quo enforced by both sides in the meantime. What was more likely was quiet evolution, with the siren of economic advancement competing with the dangerous fog of evolving competition as both countries emerged onto the world stage as full-fledged superpowers.

China's Relations with Korea

Korea presented an opportunity as well as an issue for China in the 1990s. The opportunity was provided by South Korea's desire to establish formal diplomatic relations with China, to further its economic well-being through trade with Beijing, and to reinforce its position vis-à-vis North Korea concerning both defense and the North-South reunification process. With the exception of reunification, these goals coincided with China's own. When Seoul traded formal recognition of Taiwan for official relations with China in 1992, Beijing perceived an opportunity to isolate Taiwan further and to take advantage of South Korea as a nearby, large, and untapped source of capital, technology, and markets. And China—like all other states—was increasingly troubled by Pyongyang's isolation and belligerence. The major issue was North Korea's nuclear weapons production program, but Beijing also found disconcerting the North's *juche* (self-reliance) ideology, Kim Il Sung's monarchist pretensions, Pyongyang's highly threatening military position and policy toward the South, and its faltering economy. The problems confronting China were: how to achieve a diplomatic and economic breakthrough with Seoul, how to prevent a collapse of the Kim family regime while encouraging it to change both its basic structure and its fundamental policies, and how to decrease the probability of conflict on the peninsula and stop the North's nuclear weapons development program while still offering residual security guarantees to Pyongyang.

The Northeast Asian international situation also, for the first time, gave China room to maneuver. The improvement of Sino-Soviet (Russian) relations meant that China no longer had to compete with Moscow for Pyongyang's favor. Further, because of the decline in Russian-North Korean relations, which predated the end of the cold war and the disintegration of the Soviet Union, Pyongyang depended increasingly on Beijing and thus gave the latter room to maneuver in its approach to Seoul. Another factor was Moscow's own success in opening diplomatic relations with South Korea; this also moved Beijing more rapidly in the same direction. Finally, the deterioration in Sino-American relations did not drive

Beijing and Pyongyang too close together. Rather, Washington and Beijing realized that the North Korean problem had to be dealt with, and that only the United States and China could provide the incentives, positive and negative, to maintain peace on the peninsula.

Moving from opposition to accommodation with Seoul was relatively easy. Seoul and Beijing, using Hong Kong as a neutral meeting ground, had already established informal contact in the late 1970s, through trade, tourism, sports, and diplomatic contacts. Once the nadir of China's post-Tiananmen isolation was past and the various internal and international motivations (described above) began to take hold in Beijing, China approached South Korea directly. Trade, only $40,000 in 1978, had surged to $5.8 billion by 1991. Trade offices were established in the two capitals in late 1990, South Korea assisted China's (and Taiwan's and Hong Kong's) entrance into APEC, and in late 1991 South Korea extended most favored nation treatment to China, soon followed by an investment treaty. Secret talks were held concerning diplomatic ties, and formal relations were announced in August 1992. A flurry of high-level state visits then took place, most occasioned by the North Korean problem. The South Korean president, Roh Tae Woo, went to Beijing in September 1992; Chinese Foreign Minister Qian Qichen went to Seoul in May 1993; consulates were opened in Shanghai and Pusan in July; the new South Korean foreign minister, Han Sung Joo, went to Beijing in October 1993 to sign agreements on military attachés, aviation, fisheries, and the environment, and to open more consulates; the newly elected South Korean president, Kim Young Sam, and Jiang Zemin met at the Seattle APEC summit in November; and in March 1994 Kim Young Sam, accompanied by several cabinet ministers, visited Beijing to exchange views on North Korea and to sign trade, industrial cooperation, cultural exchange, and aviation agreements. Meanwhile, trade exceeded the $10 billion mark in 1993, making South Korea China's seventh-largest trading partner, and South Korean investment in China exceeded $600 million, mostly in the nearby Chinese provinces of Shandong and Liaoning and the centrally administered city of Tianjin.

Taiwan was a short-term loser in this process. In response to Seoul's switch of Chinese diplomatic partners, Taipei severed all diplomatic, trade, and transport ties with South Korea, even though trade, tourism, and diplomatic contacts were important to both sides. Before the cutoff, trade totaled $3 billion per year, while afterward it declined by about $700 million annually. After surprisingly prolonged negotiations, the two sides in July 1993 agreed to establish informal ties similar to those in place between Taiwan and most other political entities, with diplomatic embassies replaced by unofficial but quasi-diplomatic missions. Thereupon, airline and shipping links were restored, tourism recovered, and cultural exchanges were renewed. After the loss of South Korean diplomatic ties, Taiwan was totally isolated in Asia in the formal sense, since by then Indonesia, too, had restored formal ties with Beijing. But little had changed in real terms, except that Chinese and South Korean diplomats could see each other openly and Taiwan and South Korean diplomats had to take care as to which formal names they used for each other.

For China, maintaining reasonably close ties with Pyongyang and assuring the security, political, and economic future of North Korea were more challenging tasks. Beijing fell out with Kim Il Sung not only because of the international changes mentioned above but also because of the vastly different domestic directions the two nations began to take in the 1980s. China marketized, North Korea remained frozen in socialist planning; China internationalized its economy, North Korea stressed economic autarky; China rejected most elements of Marxism-Leninism-Maoism, North Korea proceeded even further into the Stalinist dead end; China stressed pragmatism, North Korea underlined *juche;* China "came alive" socially, North Korea remained in the deep slumber of stultified and artificial social distinctions. On the other hand, Beijing was worried that the multiplying problems in the North might cascade into regime collapse, as had happened in Eastern Europe. The parallels were arresting: a stagnant polity revolving around artificial adulation of one man (or one family, in the Kims' case); a meaningless ideology; an economy slowing to the point of stopping altogether; a foreign policy that sparked increasing regional and global opposition; and a society so totalitarian that individual and state faced only zero-sum choices as to their respective futures. Deng Xiaoping and his colleagues cajoled and counseled Kim to follow their lead, but to no avail. They threatened, then began to withdraw economic ties by insisting on payment in hard currency. Chinese leaders made plain that their country would in no manner cooperate with, or countenance, Northern aggression against the South. And when, in the early 1990s, Pyongyang even engendered firefights along the China border, resulting in loss of life on both sides, Beijing made firm what had previously been vague: it recast the security tie as a residual guarantorship to be operationalized only if the North were about to be overcome in a South Korean-American invasion.

The consequent decline in Sino-North Korean relations could be seen in the international economic arena. Chinese aid to Pyongyang, once generous, diminished to nothing. Two-way trade, large for Pyongyang if not for Beijing, shrank to only several hundred million dollars, most of it on a barter basis. Military assistance, once a mainstay of the relationship, declined to near zero, as China refused Kim's request for advanced equipment and as Chinese training teams were gradually withdrawn. Only in the case of oil and grain exports did China maintain North Korea's supplies—about a million tons of oil and 800,000 tons of grain a year. Even here, however, China demanded a mixture of hard currency and hard goods in exchange. North Korea made a pass at opening free trade zones and encouraging foreign investment at strong Chinese suggestion and after Deng showed Kim what could come from such places as China's Shenzhen Special Economic Zone. But this effort was stillborn, as Pyongyang surrounded such initiatives with self-defeating restrictions and as foreign businesses assessed the Northern economic situation as uninviting.

The nuclear issue and the attendant Northern military threat to the South, the impending succession to Kim Il Sung, and eventual Korean reunification posed additional problems. Beijing was no more enthusiastic than any other nation about Pyongyang's nuclear weapons program. It wished neither to see

such weapons in the hands of such an unstable regime nor to deal with the consequences of subsequent proliferation in Northeast Asia or of North Korean nuclear exports to pariah regimes elsewhere. Deng, like South Korean, Japanese, and American leaders, feared the North would kindle another Korean War by suddenly attacking the South with its large and aggressively positioned army, possibly in connection with the succession struggle or as part of Kim's promise to reunify the country by 1995. China realized that a conflict might eventually involve its own forces, thereby causing another several decades of separation from the United States, to say nothing of the high amount of casualties and destruction involved.

The immediate question was how to stop Kim Il Sung from acquiring nuclear weapons. That posed a critical problem, since Kim would not listen to advice from any quarter and was no longer dependent—as he had been previously—on Russian nuclear assistance. Instead he was proceeding strictly on the basis of domestic efforts and what technology and equipment could be purloined internationally. China could only gradually distance itself from Kim, offer to carry messages to the Great Leader from the United States and the rest of the international community, and try to maximize its own influence in Pyongyang by appearing to hold back the U.S.-led effort to open North Korea's nuclear facilities at Yongbyon to inspection by the IAEA. But that was increasingly a losing game, as inspection deadlines came and went between 1992 and 1994, and as the United States, at last perceiving the reality of the North Korean threat, began a concerted effort to bring Kim to heel. At some point, China could be forced to choose between vetoing a UN Security Council sanctions resolution, thus precipitating a further major crisis with the United States and, concomitantly, with the rest of the international community, or going along with the UN, putting Kim in a corner out of which he could emerge only by starting a war or being overthrown himself. If Beijing had a "strategy," it was one of delay in the hope that Kim would die soon, his son, Kim Jong Il, would be ousted in a palace coup, and that the next government (probably a military administration) would come to its senses and give up the nuclear option. The problem was that history usually does not proceed in such a rational manner. Even though Kim died in June 1994, his son's fate initially remained unclear. Succession could still touch off a civil war in the North, with the probability that peninsular conflict would escalate. Or the North Korean economy might collapse, introducing the prospect of an Eastern Europe-like society-versus-state confrontation that could be resolved only by replacing the Kim dynasty, and North Korean communism, with a strong anti-Communist regime and instantaneous Korean reunification under Southern leadership.

Beijing thus had no more a concerted winning policy toward North Korea than did any other state. Like other interested parties, it could only hope and play for time.

China's Relations with Taiwan

Taiwan was China's other major problem in Asia. As in the North Korean situation, Beijing was not in control of events, which stemmed largely from trends internal to the island. Moreover, Deng and his associates had few options of their own. Having long wedded their approach to reunification to the "one country, two systems" model, they found that it was the United States, in the end, that stood in the way of reincorporating Taiwan into the Chinese body politic on Beijing's terms. The Taiwan issue regained prominence in the 1990s because of, first, the victory of democratization in Taiwan, with the attendant rise of Taiwanese nationalism, decline in the Kuomintang, and the inevitable trend toward independence; second, the Chinese option of using force to achieve reunification, which for the first time since the 1950s emerged as more than a theoretical possibility; and third, the emergence of the so-called Greater China economic region comprising southeastern coastal portions of China, Hong Kong, and Taiwan, and sometimes expanded to include other areas with strong overseas Chinese influence. (For an extended discussion of Taiwan and Hong Kong, see Chapter 10.)

Beijing has always considered its policy and actions toward Taiwan a domestic matter, a temporar-

ily unsettled remnant of the Chinese civil war. In 1950, Beijing prepared to mount a full-scale invasion until prevented by American actions related to the Korean War. Later, China made two attempts without much success (in 1954 and 1958) to take back at least portions of the territory under Kuomintang control. Because the United States had extended security guarantorship to Taiwan in the 1954 security treaty with the island, Beijing could do nothing concrete to extend its sovereignty except reiterate its claim to this province. The question thus stood at the heart of Sino-American differences for more than two decades after 1949.

After the Beijing-Washington rapprochement of the early 1970s, however, some room for maneuver was gained as a result of three developments: 1) the United States agreed not to contest Beijing's assertion that "Taiwan is a part of China" in the 1972 Shanghai (and subsequent) Communiqué(s); 2) the United States in 1978 switched its diplomatic recognition from Taipei to Beijing and allowed the security treaty with Taiwan to expire, substituting the somewhat weaker Taiwan Relations Act in 1979, which merely asserted the American interest in a peaceful settlement of the dispute; and 3) the United States and China agreed in 1982 to long-term limits on the kind, quantity, quality, and duration of American arms to be supplied to Taiwan. But so long as China was not prepared to risk possible defeat at the hands of U.S.-assisted Taiwan forces in a frontal attack against Taiwan, it could not make good on these favorable developments.

The situation began to change in the 1980s. First, Taiwan became increasingly isolated internationally, as most countries moved their embassies to Beijing. While substitute quasi-diplomatic trade and cultural missions were maintained in Taipei, Taiwan came to depend even more on the United States for its security and international representation. Second, China began to increase its power, prestige, and military capabilities, the product of its marketization and economic internationalization policies. Although China's military modernization was initially delayed (by budget cuts and the triple setbacks, after 1989, of the display of U.S. high-technology military operations in the gulf war, the decline in the PLA's military prestige after Tiananmen, and the disappearance of communism almost everywhere), the general augmentation of Chinese military forces into the 1990s began to tilt the military balance in the Taiwan Strait increasingly toward China. Third, Taiwan made a calculated change in its China strategy by allowing trade with, investment in, and travel to the mainland. Soon, many Taiwan industries moved important portions of their facilities to nearby Chinese provinces, trade (indirectly, through Hong Kong) across the strait grew exponentially, and millions of Taiwan residents visited China. Taipei benefited from this change by making China partly dependent on the continued flow of Taiwan capital, resources, and people, but the policy also carried the reciprocal danger of bringing economic dependence on a China that was many times larger and would continue to grow into an economic superpower. Fourth, the domestic political situation on Taiwan also changed, again by deliberate decision of its Kuomintang-run government. By opening the country to democracy in the 1980s, and then extending it through a carefully structured set of ever-widening elections and constitutional changes in the 1990s, the island became a working democracy. The implication, however, was that the island's native Taiwanese majority (about 80 percent of the population) would find voice independent of the Kuomintang, bring to power their own representatives, and pursue a policy of independence from the mainland. They began to do just that in various early 1990s elections, through the now-legalized Democratic Progressive Party (DPP). Although it did not win a majority in any of the elections (the Kuomintang convinced many that a vote for the DPP would invite a Chinese military attack along with independence), the DPP nonetheless crept up in percentage terms and looked like it might come to power eventually.

Finally, Taiwan decided to take two political initiatives. On the one hand, Taipei moved to negotiate with Beijing, indirectly and cautiously. First it established the Straits Exchange Foundation (SEF), to work on such questions as social and cultural exchanges, trade, transport, and communications, as well as to explore the basic issue of reunification in the longer term. Concomitantly, Taiwan initiated internal political changes that included issuing Guidelines for Reunification in early 1991 to legally end the state of hostility with the mainland, and enacting laws in 1992 governing details of contacts with China. On the other hand, Taipei set out to expand, to the extent possible, its international political status, within the constraints of its continuing policy of declaring itself the government of all China. Taiwan sought membership not only in the relevant international economic institutions, including the World Bank and GATT, but also international political institutions, especially the United Nations, and to convince other states to recognize Taipei as an independent political entity. It did so on the express basis that the island was a major trading state and that, as a democracy, it deserved recognition by other states of like political system. Taipei understood that the losses in recognition that it suffered in the early 1990s (particularly from South Korea and Saudi Arabia) would have to be made up. It did so also buttressed by the decision of the United States in late 1992 to sell 150 high-performance F-15 jet fighters to Taipei (thus violating, in spirit if not in letter, the 1982 Sino-American communiqué on American sales to Taiwan), France's simultaneous move to sell 60 *Mirage* 2000 jet fighters to Taipei, and Taiwan's collateral purchase of much naval, air defense, and associated high-technology weapons systems. These transfers went far to redress the military imbalance, if only for a few additional years until Chinese military modernization and quantitative advantage would take hold once again. International political isolation would force it either to depend on the United States exclusively or face a massively powerful Beijing alone, or both.

Under the rubric of Taipei's "pragmatic" or "flexible" diplomacy, these changes did impart some welcome dynamism to cross-straits relations, relax tensions to some extent, and buy at least some autonomy and time for Taipei. China reacted by issuing statements, declarations, and White Papers on the Taiwan question. These began in 1979 with the call to establish direct mail, trade, and air links with Taipei as well as exchanges of persons, cultural groups, and sports teams, and continued in 1981 with the well-known Ye Jianying nine-point proposal for reunification on apparently generous terms of autonomy for the island. Beijing continuously asserted its sovereignty over Taiwan and reiterated its right to use force if it so chose, upheld the principle of "one China, two systems," and offered to negotiate terms of reunification on a party-to-party (but not government-to-government) basis.

In December 1991, China established an Association for Relations Across the Taiwan Strait (ARATS) to work with Taiwan's SEF, and in September 1993 issued a White Paper summarizing its Taiwan policy over the previous decades. This made clear that Taiwan must accept Beijing's suzerainty or face the use of force, and registered China's opposition to Taiwan's arms purchases and its attempt to participate in international political organizations. After several preparatory meetings (the first time since 1949 the two sides had sat down together), the heads of SEF and ARATS, Koo Chen-fu and Wang Daohan, met in Singapore in April 1993. The two signed agreements on relatively minor but symbolically important matters (notarization and mail) and agreed on mechanisms to facilitate further meetings. Despite this seemingly promising beginning, problems remained: the White Paper represented a step backward in mainland policy and was poorly received on Taiwan; a series of hijackings of Chinese airliners to Taiwan caused both sides to delay further talks; Taiwan's attempt to enter the United Nations met with full opposition from Beijing; second thoughts arose in Taipei as to the wisdom of moving too close to the mainland economically; and several untoward incidents threw a temporary chill over cross-straits relations. Taiwan attempted to impart new dynamism in its foreign policy by a new version of pragmatism in which its president, Lee Teng-hui, made "vacation" trips to the Philippines, Indonesia, and Thailand in early 1994 and by issuing its own White Paper in June on relations with Beijing.

Despite persistence of this standoff in 1994, some things were clear. First, Beijing's rapidly increasing power, including military, would eventually place the mainland in a position to overwhelm the island. Second, despite Taiwan's enviable economic record and its global economic status far out of proportion to its geographic and population size, it would eventually be dwarfed by China. The latter could, if it so chose, use that economic difference to squeeze the island further. While in the early 1990s China needed Taiwanese investment and trade more than did the latter (which entered into economic relations more for prophylactic political reasons than from a straight economic calculus), the island could only become increasingly dependent on the mainland economically unless it consciously sought to redirect its trade and investment. Third, Taipei's drive to re-enter the United Nations, undertaken mostly for domestic political reasons, was not likely to succeed, although Taipei was likely to gain entry to international economic institutions. Fourth, Taiwan would continue to be dependent on the United States for its security. No program of armaments alone, however well financed, could purchase military security. And it was not at all clear that, in its moment of need, Taiwan could count on the kind and level of direct American military support needed to defeat a determined mainland military thrust. Finally, the political trend toward independence and empowerment of the DPP in Taiwan meant that a cross-straits crisis would surely come. With Beijing's Taiwan policy tied to its Hong Kong policy, and the latter trumpeted as a good first instance of the "one country, two systems" policy, Taiwan appeared to be "safe" until at least mid-1997. Moreover, a working democracy on Taiwan could well turn the heads of other such states, in Asia and elsewhere, and lead to strong representations in Beijing to eschew use of force. But toward the close of the 1990s or in the first years of the new millennium, Taiwan could face negotiating reunification largely on the latter's terms. In that sense, Beijing's policy of strengthening itself, isolating Taiwan, and waiting looked like a winning strategy.

China and Hong Kong

Compared to Taiwan, Hong Kong should not have been a major issue for China. In 1984, Britain and China agreed, in a Joint Declaration, that all of the colony would revert to Chinese sovereignty in mid-1997, that a special administrative region would be set up there with a high degree of political and administrative autonomy, and that Hong Kong's capitalist and sociolegal systems would basically not change for fifty years beyond that point (see also Chapter 10). It also provided for a local constitution and political and administrative institutions to be put in place through a China-drafted Basic Law, which provided for at least some degree of popular representation in the Legislative Council (LegCo). Moreover, through its increasingly active shadow government—the local branch of the Xinhua (New China) News Agency and the many front groups and media organs set up and controlled by it and Beijing's State Council office of Hong Kong (and Macao) affairs—China exercised increasingly broad and direct powers in the colony. Finally, through party directives, Deng Xiaoping's own pronouncements, and negotiations with London and the Hong Kong governor, China made clear that while Hong Kong would continue to play its historic role as political and economic gateway between China and the outside world, Beijing and not Hong Kong or London would be the final arbiter of activities there and would not allow the Basic Law or any of Hong Kong's institutions to deviate significantly from Chinese structures or policies. All that was required, therefore, was to hold things together until 1997—soothing local concerns, maintaining economic confidence, fending off foreign pressures—and waiting.

That all changed after the Tiananmen incident in 1989. For the first time in Hong Kong's British-ruled history, the populace came alive politically. Massive protests against the Beijing slaughter took place immediately after June 4. The Hong Kong head of the Xinhua News Agency, Xu Jiatun, who acted as China's unofficial representative in Hong Kong, defected to the United States. Even the principal Communist Party newspaper in the colony, *Wen Wei Pao*, joined in universal condemnation of the Beijing government. The United Democrats, the colony's first real political party, were able to capitalize on these overtly expressed anti-China sentiments. Two years later, they won a stunning victory in the LegCo elections, returning all eighteen of their candidates while shutting out those backed by the Xinhua News Agency. Britain, aided by a change in Conservative Party leadership, appointed a new governor of Hong Kong, Christopher Patten, in 1992, and charged him with

introducing as much democracy as the situation would allow.

Immediately, in October 1992, carrying out London's mandate, Patten proposed political changes—all within the Basic Law—to extend the franchise, elect more of the sixty-member LegCo by contested election (either directly or through functional constituencies), and increase the power of LegCo and Executive Council (ExeCo) members.

Beijing's reaction was immediate and negative. It denounced the governor's proposals as violations of the Joint Declaration and the Basic Law, terming them "completely unacceptable." It threatened to overturn all British-created legal and political institutions upon Chinese recovery of the colony in 1997. It mobilized the Xinhua-directed united front organizations in opposition. It appointed its own group of Hong Kong "advisers" and began setting up a Preliminary Working Committee and subgroups in Hong Kong that had the makings of a more nearly formal shadow government. It did conduct an extensive round of talks with Britain during 1993, but torpedoed them in December 1993 when Patten finally tabled his reform program. It attempted, with some success, to divide various groups within Hong Kong and to enlist, through promises, blandishments, and clearly corruptive approaches, the all-important business community. It threw up roadblocks to slow down projects, such as construction of a new Hong Kong airport and container terminal, and stated that all contracts, leases, and franchises that straddled 1997 would be nullified unless approved by China. It threatened to stymie the 1995 LegCo elections. Through republishing Deng Xiaoping's 1982 remark that China might take over the colony before 1997 and by training a PLA force to be stationed in downtown Hong Kong, China directly threatened to abrogate the entire transition process. For all intents and purposes, China declared Patten persona non grata in March 1994 when he introduced the second reading of his political reform bill and continued to snipe at the governor. Finally, it held up progress on amending the colony's legal system to conform to the Basic Law, sniffed at statements by Hong Kong's financial secretary, Hamish Macleod, that Britain would probably transfer to the post-1997 Chinese administration a surplus of about $35 billion, and tightened its censorship noose around Hong Kong by arresting its journalists in China on trumped-up charges.

These numerous initiatives bespoke Beijing's new self-confidence, indeed arrogance, stemming from its growth in economic power, especially after 1991. The fact that Hong Kong was also becoming so interdependent on China, particularly nearby Guangdong Province and the Shenzhen Special Economic Zone, made Beijing feel that it could increasingly dictate terms. Indeed, after going into a tailspin after Tiananmen, Hong Kong's bellwether Hang Seng stock market index recovered to historic highs, passing the 10,000 mark in 1993. Hong Kong's economic growth continued near the 5 percent level, employment was full, and the panic emigration in 1989-1991 slowed considerably. More importantly, Hong Kong businesses moved much of their manufacturing operations to the mainland, where land and labor were much cheaper, such that fully a third of the colony's GNP came from such operations and some 5 million Chinese citizens were on the payrolls of Hong Kong corporations. Hong Kong investments in China (again, mostly in Guangdong and mostly in infrastructure projects) rose to $40 billion, and China stood in first place in terms of Hong Kong's exports and second in terms of China's exports. For its part, China invested heavily in Hong Kong and could, by 1997, own about a fifth of all property there. Economics and politics seemed, therefore, to be moving in opposite directions.

The working assumption in Hong Kong appeared to be that, whatever political crisis might arise, China would have its way in the end and that it was in Beijing's interest to maintain Hong Kong as a viable economic entity. Short-term indicators appeared to support this notion. The aphorism was spread that Hong Kong's interest in democracy existed only so long as the stock market continued to rise. In the medium to longer term, however, the success of Beijing's policy of progressive political subversion of the colony and separation of economics from politics would depend on other factors, not all of which were in CCP hands. The democratic impetus in Hong Kong, having finally gained voice in 1989, could not be easily overcome. The British government still had

three years left to administer the colony. It retained the power not merely to fine tune the transition but alternately to face down the Chinese government. Events in China could change outcomes drastically: Deng's passing could precipitate a prolonged Chinese power struggle in which Hong Kong might be left alone, or China's economic development could get entirely out of hand, again seeming to favor a laissez-faire approach to Hong Kong affairs. China's "one country, two systems" policy toward Taiwan was hostage to the success of that same policy toward Hong Kong. Jeopardize the latter and Taiwan could escape; better, therefore, not to rock the Hong Kong boat unduly. And the United States and Sino-American relations were increasingly important factors. If Washington, as was likely, continued to emphasize human rights, economic development, and political change in China, it would also continue to have an important interest in a Hong Kong that was successful politically as well as economically. (Indeed, the 1992 Hong Kong Relations Act passed by the U.S. Congress contained provisions linking trade with political progress in the colony and the subsequent Special Administrative Region.)

Probability still pointed to a reasonably successful, if rocky, transition for Hong Kong to Chinese rule. It also indicated the continued value to China, after 1997, of a relatively autonomous Hong Kong. But it was doubtful whether Beijing would countenance a Hong Kong that was seriously out of step, especially politically, with the rest of China. In that respect, the hope for this world city, artificial though it might be, was to be found in the pace and direction of political liberalism in China.

China and Southeast Asia

If Chinese policy toward Northeast and East Asia seemed fraught with dangers and disappointments, Southeast Asia after 1989 was an area of relative success for Beijing. China normalized its relations with its erstwhile foe, Vietnam, cooperated with the major powers and the regional states in the Cambodian peace process, re-established working ties with Indonesia and Singapore, and made its economic influence felt. Problems did exist: China's policy toward the Spratly Islands ownership question and the associated issue of oil exploration rights was not only unhelpful but distinctly threatening; Beijing's ties with the repressive military government in Burma (Myanmar) offered the only international support for that unpopular regime; and China's military buildup, arms sales policy, and increasingly assertive foreign policy caused much concern among the regional states. Many believed that China intended to convert the region into its own sphere of influence. As with Hong Kong and Taiwan, time would tell which avenue China would take: neighborly cooperation stressing economic ties or expansionism through threat or use of military force.

From the early 1960s through the 1980s, China's principal goals in Southeast Asia were to rid the region first of superpower dominance and then of the threat of regional hegemonism. The first was partially accomplished when the United States withdrew from Vietnam in the mid-1970s. China, as well as the Soviet Union, assisted Vietnam in its war of independence, which, however, saw replacement of U.S. influence in Vietnam with that of the Soviet Union. Moscow signed an anti-Chinese treaty of guarantee with Hanoi and stationed strong forces on Vietnamese soil. Together with Hanoi's conquest of the South in 1975, this led to the emergence of Vietnam as Southeast Asia's most powerful military state. Vietnam not only continued its domination of Laos but took over Cambodia by force, ousting the Khmer Rouge in late 1978 and completing its domination of Indochina. China's second goal, to rid Southeast Asia of regional hegemonism, was realized gradually, beginning with the Chinese invasion of Vietnam in early 1979. It ended a decade later with the Chinese ouster of Vietnamese forces from some of the Spratly Islands in 1988 and Vietnamese withdrawal from Cambodia in late 1989. Soviet withdrawal from the region followed from internal Russian weakness, the consequent end of the cold war and downfall of communism in the Soviet Union, and the Sino-Soviet rapprochement of 1989. That, along with U.S. support through the United Nations, laid the groundwork for the 1991 Paris Agreement formalizing a ceasefire among the various warring factions in Cambodia (including the Khmer Rouge) and for the U.S.-sponsored "peace process" in that country. China was not only a principal backer of those changes but even contributed a PLA unit to help keep the peace before the 1993 elections. In this way the civil war in Cambodia formally ended, though not the Khmer Rouge threat, and a new government of national unity was constituted under Prince Norodom Sihanouk.

The question then emerged as to whether China would use its new position of strength in Southeast Asia to begin converting the region into an exclusive Chinese sphere of influence or whether it would be content with becoming the good neighbor to the north. A benign policy had its attractions, at least for a while. Beijing's general orientation, immediately after 1989, was to get back in the good graces of the world community as well as to prepare for what many in China saw as a coming contest with the United States. That meant downplaying and possibly settling rivalries and disputes around its periphery, upgrading diplomatic ties, and taking care not to allow the country's burgeoning power to frighten the region into putting up a united front against China or inviting the United States to return. Moreover, the post-cold war era changed most countries' focus from security concerns to questions of economic development. That was obviously so in China itself, but it was also the case in Southeast Asia. If China wished to exert its influence in that region, it would have to do so through use of such relatively new (for it) economic tools as trade, investment, and aid. Besides, Southeast Asia possessed much of use for China's own development: raw materials, trained labor, markets, and capital (especially from the large overseas Chinese communities in most Southeast Asian countries). Finally, if Southeast Asia were to be seen as an example of exemplary Chinese behavior, the Chinese cause elsewhere would be easier to advance. A benign policy appeared reasonable and rational for Beijing, and it mostly pursued such a policy after 1989. But this did not explain many of China's activities in the region, which instead seemed more assertive, expansionist, even neoimperialist. There was, foremost, the complex Spratly Islands question. Both the mainland and Taiwan were co-claimants with Vietnam, the Philippines, Malaysia, and Brunei over all or part of these scattered reefs and atolls. China's claim was on paper only until 1970, when the PLA navy began survey and meteorological operations in the Paracel Islands. These activities were extended in early 1974, when the navy—perceiving South Vietnamese weakness and American disinterest—seized those Paracel Islands that were under Southern control. Thereafter, much construction work, mostly of a military nature, was conducted there. During the following years, China waged a "battle of documents" with Hanoi over legal ownership and completed the ouster of Vietnamese forces by 1979. The next year, Chinese air and sea forces began to show themselves in the Spratly Islands, first conducting familiarization and scientific cruises and flights (thus asserting Chinese sovereignty) and, after a mid-1980s hiatus explained by the delicacy of ongoing rapprochement negotiations with the Soviet Union, began a major push southward in 1987. Patrols were constantly sent out, and in 1988 channel, port, storage, and road facilities were constructed on Fiery Cross Shoal and less permanent facilities on other reefs. These provoked repeated confrontations with Vietnamese forces that had occupied other parts of the Spratlys. Finally a major naval battle took place in March 1988, which China won. Thereafter, Vietnam continued to claim the islands, garrisoned some of them, girded for further combat, and protested against Chinese occupation of those in its possession. Further semi-military operations took place in the mid-1990s, as China sent naval ships to blockade Vietnamese drilling sites in waters claimed by Hanoi and as both countries moved drilling rigs into place.

Having thus established a controlling military presence, Beijing's strategy changed. China wanted to re-establish at least working relations with the outside world after the Tiananmen incident in 1989, and to appear reasonable as to the use of diplomacy versus force concerning ownership of the islands. Thus, in August 1990, Premier Li Peng proposed discussions on joint development of the Spratlys, and suggested that all parties put aside, at least for economic purposes, their various claims of sovereignty. As this occurred at the nadir of post-1989 Chinese foreign relations, the Chinese diplomatic purpose seemed to be to ride out the shock of Tiananmen, the collapse of communism, and charges of Chinese expansionism,

as well as to soothe the suspicions of ASEAN members concerning Beijing's intentions during the delicate negotiations over Cambodia. By 1992, however, these concerns had largely been overcome, and military and legislative consolidation of control resumed. Thus, in February 1992, the National People's Congress passed a territorial waters law that included the Spratlys and the Paracels (as well as the Diaoyu Tai in the East China Sea, disputed by Japan, which calls them the Senkaku Islands), established transit regulations around them, and threatened to oust military operatives of foreign governments. Finally, in May 1992, China negotiated a deal with an American oil drilling company, Crestone Corporation, for exploration rights in an area also claimed by Vietnam. Significantly, China stated that it would use all necessary military force to protect Crestone's operations, thus presumably undercutting, if not entirely neutralizing, American concerns about Chinese expansionism and rights of maritime transit through the South China Sea.

Oil exploration questions uncovered a second Chinese motive for expanding into the South China Sea area. Onshore oil production was not expanding at a rate equivalent to the country's GNP growth, and China faced a prospective shift from being a modest oil exporter to a major importer. Since the mineral potential of these islands was enormous (despite disappointing near-term discoveries), China's economic interest was clearly to make good on its claim to as much of the region as possible. Beijing's expansionist naval interest thus became economic as well as territorial. That did not sit well, of course, with the other Spratly claimants. It drove Vietnam into the waiting hands of ASEAN, an attraction already manifest following the Cambodian settlement and Hanoi's desperate economic situation. Equally important, the other claimants openly suspected China of territorial ambitions. After 1992 all ASEAN members began to acquire new military hardware to counteract the perceived rise of a Chinese military threat and to consult together (and with the United States) as to how to cope with it. Soon a mini-arms race was taking place in Southeast Asia, fueled in part by the new Chinese maritime presence. Those concerns could only grow during the rest of the decade, as

Beijing continued to acquire and field modern military systems. In Southeast Asia, the most-watched trend was Chinese acquisition of Russian Su-27 jet fighters and its progress in learning how to conduct air refueling of such craft. Once that was accomplished, China would definitively be able to dominate the Spratlys against all comers, save a determined U.S. naval opposition.

Beijing's relations with ASEAN members and Indochina would have deteriorated had the Spratlys and the related military question been the only issue. Fortunately for Beijing, China's participation in the Cambodian settlement helped abate general suspicion of China's intentions. As long as Vietnam was allied with a militarily strong Soviet Union and Vietnamese troops controlled Cambodia, all of Southeast Asia was threatened by Moscow-Hanoi domination. But as long as China and the Soviet Union opposed each other, and the United States and China cooperated against Moscow, the way was open to a coalition of these two external powers with the indigenous nations of the area. That also opened the region, for the first time, to general Chinese influence. Beijing was quick to take advantage of the situation. The most important task was to secure Thailand from invasion by the Vietnamese divisions on its frontiers after 1978—which meant opening arms supply to Bangkok, using Thai territory to shore up the Khmer Rouge remnants along the Thai-Cambodian border, and stationing a strong Chinese force along the Sino-Vietnamese border. These put China in a position to replace the United States as Thailand's security guarantor. Fortunately for both countries, China had already bent to Thai demands that it cut its ties with the Thai Communists (who then atrophied, severed from their principal support base). China went further, however, in expanding trade with Thailand in the 1980s, especially by purchasing Thai rice. China also moved to improve relations with other ASEAN members, principally Singapore and Indonesia, both of which opposed Hanoi's ambitions and feared the Soviet naval and air presence on Vietnamese soil.

Thus, with only a few elements still missing, the stage was set for settlement of the Cambodian problem through withdrawal of Vietnamese forces and empowerment of a new government in Phnom Penh, which was accomplished with relative ease. First the Soviet Union withdrew from cold war competition, exhausted from forty years of competing with the West. The downfall of communism in the Soviet empire, including Moscow itself, finalized the Russian decision to exit Southeast Asia and end its support of Vietnamese imperialism. Second, since Vietnam could not sustain its occupation and feed and clothe its own people at the same time, it sought a way to withdraw gracefully. Finally, the United States sponsored the UN "peace process," which resulted in the October 1991 Paris Agreements on a Comprehensive Political Settlement of the Cambodian Conflict. Since China was now the only major external Asian military power in the region, the only question remaining was how it would use that power.

Beijing began a process of rapprochement with Hanoi, progressively lowering its border military threat and opening up the border to extensive trade so that Vietnam could resume its historic role as Southeast Asian tributary to China. In Cambodia, China diminished its military supply tie with the Khmer Rouge, supported the post-settlement Sihanouk-led coalition government, even hosted a meeting of the Cambodian Supreme National Council in Beijing, and initiated trade and transportation ties. As for Malaysia, China allowed, as in Thailand, the 1989 demise of the Malaysian Communist Party by ceasing its support, though by that late date the local Communists had long since become only a nuisance to Kuala Lumpur. Given Beijing's need for good economic ties and whatever additional capital the Malaysian overseas Chinese could support, relations could only improve from there.

A similar conclusion obtained regarding Indonesia. The Suharto regime had long been wary of Chinese intentions stemming from Chinese and Communist Party of Indonesia support of a 1965 antimilitary coup attempt. It therefore did not restore "suspended" diplomatic ties with Beijing for nearly three decades. It finally did so in 1990, on the basis of domestic political and economic confidence gained in the interim as well as the realization that a powerful China had to be dealt with. Its suspicions of Chinese policy goals nonetheless remained. In 1990 Singapore followed Jakarta's lead and established diplomatic ties with Beijing—a switch for its leader, Lee Kuan Yew, who despite his and most Singaporeans' Chinese ancestry and Confucian orientation, had also been deeply suspicious of the Chinese potential for ethnic Chinese-based subversion.

Indeed, the 1990s saw economics largely replace security as the leitmotif of China-Southeast Asian relations. Economic development, investment, trade, and comparative rates of growth became primary, and diplomacy therefore became economic diplomacy. The question for China was whether its gathering economic strength would allow it to exercise a principal role in the region or whether regional economic development would proceed largely on the basis of indigenous resources and economic contacts among all the major external economies. As of the mid-1990s, the latter appeared more likely. ASEAN was well on its way to becoming a full-fledged economic community, whose trade with China, while increasing rapidly, was still behind that with Japan and the United States. Intraregional institution-building and the emergence of "natural economic regions" across national boundaries became new and important factors. External investment, especially from Japan and, increasingly, Taiwan, more than made up for the transfer of capital from the region by overseas Chinese businesses to China. In a word, interdependence was a fact of life in Southeast Asia.

Japan, not China, had grown into the most important outside player in Southeast Asia. Despite Tokyo's World War II involvement in the region, most Southeast Asian nations prefer dealing with Japan to seeing China grow in military as well as economic power. While Beijing had some advantages in competing economically with Tokyo in the region—principally low labor costs and proximity—it would be some time before Chinese products achieved the quality and technical appeal of Japan's (to say nothing of those from North America and Europe). China had to petition the Asia-Pacific nations, including those of Southeast Asia, to join the Asia-Pacific Economic Community and the Pacific Basin Economic Community (PBEC), and was beholden to them, and thus to their assessment of China's good behavior and the performance of its reformist economic program, for entrance into GATT.

In the end, China's uphill struggle to be accepted in Southeast Asia would still depend on how it comported itself in the security area. Beijing's intransigent attitude concerning the Spratly sovereignty question did not help, nor did China's negative attitude toward building security institutions in the area, as well as in the Asia-Pacific region as a whole.

Finally, there was the question of Burma. Under self-imposed isolation for over three decades, Burma since the late 1980s had been ruled by a vicious military junta that killed many citizens in cold blood in a 1988 uprising. A self-appointed set of leaders who refused to accept the results of the 1991 elections, the Rangoon "State Law and Order Restoration Council" (SLORC) depended entirely on Chinese military support for its continuation in office. Beijing transferred more than $1.5 billion of military equipment to the junta, which used it to suppress the popular will. China, Burma's primary trading partner, engaged in wholesale felling of Burmese timber with appalling environmental results, cooperated in opium growing and export operations in the "Golden Triangle," encouraged SLORC to hunt down and kill ethnic minority opponents of the central regime, and ceased its support of White and Red Flag Communist insurgents. The Burmese situation was ripe for tragedy, as the democrats under Nobel Peace Prize-winner Aung San Suu Kyi prepared for another try at ousting the military and as the latter attempted to cling to power. Not only was China SLORC's only friend, it also used its position to extract military base-like privileges from Rangoon. China in 1994 was assisting Burma in port construction and improvement on the Bay of Bengal and the Andaman Sea. Some thought these were at least Chinese listening posts to look in on Indian naval activities and perhaps were proto-military bases. If so, further charges of Chinese expansionist intents would be raised, this time by South and Southeast Asians together.

China and South Asia

Since the late 1950s South Asia has been an area of direct Chinese influence and involvement. China's role was also relatively constant for several decades from 1959, opposing and often threatening India and supporting New Delhi's regional nemesis, Pakistan. Beijing's approach to South Asia was also strongly configured by the cold war: it had to choose between regional clients of the United States and those of the Soviet Union, and when it changed its position within the strategic triangle, its policies toward regional clients of the superpowers varied accordingly. The major question for Beijing, however, was what to do with India, a nation too large, powerful (at least potentially), and culturally distant for China to embrace, despite early protestations of common third world interests. The territorial question, above all, prevented Indo-Chinese relations, from the late 1950s to the mid-1990s, from becoming anything more than formally correct. Similarly, it was the Indo-Pakistani standoff over Kashmir, from 1948, that prevented any united South Asian approach to China and that gave Beijing the opportunity to become a regional player through support of Islamabad.

China's South Asian policy was therefore circumscribed and channeled from the beginning. Two events set New Delhi firmly against Beijing: the border conflict in 1959 following Indian discovery of a China-constructed road in the Aksai Chin connecting Xinjiang and Tibet on the Indian side of the McMahon Line, and the Chinese invasion of the North East Frontier Agency (NEFA) in 1962. China's good relations with Pakistan emerged as a result, as China as well as the United States, for different reasons—anti-Soviet in the American case, anti-Indian in the Chinese instance—became Islamabad's security guarantors, despite more friendly Sino-Indian relations during the Bandung Conference (Five Principles of Peaceful Coexistence) period of the early 1950s. The situation was frozen when the Soviet Union signed an anti-Chinese defense agreement (euphemistically termed a "friendship treaty") with India in 1971. Only beginning in the late 1970s, as part of Deng Xiaoping's opening strategy, did China attempt to improve ties with India. Given these problems and the successful Indian effort in the meantime to build up its defenses against China (including possession of nuclear weapons from 1974), this strategy achieved only modest success.

Deng's motives were a desire to draw New Delhi away from Moscow, to make its peace with the hegemon of South Asia, and to gain Indian agreement on the Chinese version of the Sino-Indian border. That fit well with Beijing's "antihegemony" (that is, anti-Soviet) policy after the Soviet-Vietnamese Treaty of 1978 and the Sino-American recognition agreement of the same year. It also coincided with the desires of the then Indian government (under Morarji Desai) to improve ties with both the United States and China. These efforts, which saw some Indian attempts at compromise on the territorial issue, foundered with the Chinese invasion of Vietnam in early 1979, the successful Soviet blocking action, and finally Desai's resignation in mid-1979.

India was placed in a difficult position, however, by the Soviet invasion of Afghanistan in late 1979, as Moscow presented a major security threat to Islamabad and provided further opportunity for China to support Pakistan. That it did, with much military equipment (although no formal treaty of guarantee) and with Sino-American cooperation to arm and train the Afghani mujahedin in Pakistan. As for India, it had no choice but to distance itself, at least somewhat, from Moscow over Afghanistan. Beijing thereby saw further opportunity to entice India into the grand anti-Soviet coalition being constructed, separately but in parallel, with Washington, and to forestall Moscow's attempt to weld its Asian clients—principally Vietnam and India—into its own anti-Chinese alliance system. China thus softened its verbal support of Pakistan on the Kashmir issue, sent many high-level officials to New Delhi, touted the peaceful coexistence line, and obtained Indian agreement to reopen border talks. But this offensive foundered, as had the first, on the rocks of a determined Russian counteroffensive (which vastly stepped up Moscow's economic and military assistance to New Delhi) and also on Indian Prime Minister Indira Gandhi's determination not to move so far away from the Soviet Union as to jeopardize India's fundamental requirement of a Soviet security guarantee against China.

The situation began to change in the early 1980s, as Beijing gradually promulgated its "independent foreign policy." This meant in essence lessening emphasis on the Soviet threat, initiating a rapprochement with Moscow, distancing itself within the strategic triangle from the United States, and re-emphasizing Beijing's third world credentials. This new policy was assisted by ongoing Russian military difficulties in Afghanistan, initial signs that Vietnam would consider withdrawing from Cambodia, and (most importantly) Russian signals—beginning in early 1982 with Soviet President Leonid Brezhnev's Tashkent speech—that Moscow would like to improve relations with Beijing. This constrained India to open, at least slightly, to China, lest it eventually find itself without Soviet (to say nothing of American) protection against a vastly stronger and more active China. Verbal support came from both sides, especially the Indian after Rajiv Gandhi's accession to office following his mother's assassination in late 1984, and many high-level visits to both capitals again took place. The Soviet Union, pursuing a similar goal vis-à-vis China, could only reduce—although hardly eliminate—its opposition. Indeed, Moscow had to work hard to convince New Delhi that their bilateral ties would not suffer as Moscow and Beijing moved closer, a task made more difficult by the Indo-Chinese border crisis of 1986-1987 at Sumdorong Chu valley. This sent the Indians scurrying to Moscow for reassurance, which was not forthcoming. The Soviet Union, of course, tried to have it both ways: improvement of ties with China and maintenance of very good relations with India. There followed a near-blizzard of high-level visits among the three countries, as Soviet President Gorbachev visited New Delhi twice (in 1986 and 1988), the three foreign ministers moved rapidly back and forth, and Gandhi visited China in late 1988. These contacts continued through 1990.

But once again, major improvement in relations eluded the two Asian powers. This time, it was obviously not the Russians who stood in the way, for they had proceeded to full rapprochement with China by May 1989. Rather, it was a combination of Chinese domestic events, a change in Chinese policy on the territorial issue, China's attempts to establish closer ties with India's regional dependencies, Sri Lanka and Nepal, and its further military assistance to Pakistan. Domestically, Beijing was in grave difficulty as

a result of the Tiananmen events of 1989. It could only gird for the worst, in terms of U.S.-led international criticism, and hope for the eventual dawning of a new forgive-and-forget era. The change in Beijing's stance on the territorial question was surprising and distinctly unhelpful. Beginning in 1960, both sides had proceeded on the basis of Zhou Enlai's offer to trade Indian claims in the NEFA for Chinese claims in the Aksai Chin. In 1986, China withdrew this offer and substituted the demand that India had to make concessions in the NEFA while China was prepared to give way, at least marginally, in the Aksai Chin. That essentially halted the border talks. By attempting to improve relations with Sri Lanka and Nepal, even on the seemingly innocuous basis of the ''Principles of Peaceful Coexistence,'' Beijing called into question, in New Delhi, the purity of its intentions to better ties with India. In the 1970s, Beijing chose strongly to support Sri Lanka's government in its struggle with the Tamil insurgents, in the face of Indian opposition to Sri Lanka's effort to escape Indian dominance (and the latter's consequent arming of the insurgents on Indian territory). India called China on its support for Colombo, and Beijing had to step back, both in 1986 and especially after the Sri Lankan capitulation to India in mid-1987.

A similar outcome occurred regarding Nepal. That mountain kingdom had always been under India's (and Britain's, before it) watchful eyes but had also always wished at least to diversify its relations, if not achieve full foreign policy independence from India. In 1988, Katmandu made one of its periodic tries by agreeing to purchase Chinese military equipment, sold by China's supposedly autonomous (but actually PLA-run) North China Industrial Corporation. This enraged New Delhi, since if the process were allowed to go forward, China could gradually wean Nepal away from dependency on India—although Nepal was obligated by the 1950 Indo-Nepali Treaty to purchase arms only from New Delhi. When Nepal refused to rescind the Chinese purchase upon Indian demand and also declined to eschew further such purchases, India came down hard. It refused, in turn, to extend trade and transit treaties with Katmandu and then, in early 1989, blockaded the country. At first, Beijing supported Katmandu by trucking in essential supplies and by aid grants. It even sent Premier Li Peng to Nepal in late 1990 to continue Chinese talk of peaceful coexistence. But in the end, China could not but pull back. First, India proved too strong for China within New Delhi's own sphere of interest. Second, China's post-Tiananmen image did not allow Beijing to take a threatening attitude toward an important neighbor, at least until memories grew dim, especially over a relatively important matter to India. And third, the Nepalese internal situation changed much to Chinese detriment when, in early 1990, the government was overthrown after the anti-monarchist democratic movement in Katmandu. Nepal thereupon willingly capitulated to India, and Chinese influence declined.

Pakistan, however, was another matter. There, Islamabad and Beijing maintained the confluence of interests established a quarter century earlier. China needed Pakistan all the more after the Sri Lankan and Nepalese setbacks, and arming Islamabad was the only way Beijing could draw growing Indian power away from itself. Pakistan also remained China's principal means of access to the Middle East, geographically and ideologically. For its part, Pakistan had only China for its security support, once the United States began to pull back after the Soviet Union ended its occupation of Afghanistan. China therefore saw to it that Pakistan received a steady flow of Chinese military equipment. In the late 1980s, this meant production in Pakistan of the F-7 jet fighter and the most advanced Chinese tank. But then China transferred Chinese missiles, missile technology, and nuclear weapons technology and materials to Islamabad. By the late 1980s, it was increasingly apparent that India was providing itself with a number of nuclear warheads (by the mid-1990s, said to number more than sixty). Pakistan had already begun to acquire its own nuclear capability, but it needed external support. This China proved willing, if foolishly, to provide. The problem was that Beijing had, in 1984, signed the NPT, and had been more or less coerced by the United States and others into adhering to the MTCR. China would therefore have to skirt the edge of these agreements, or be found in violation of them, if it wished to support the Pakistani nuclear weapons program. If China

were found out, of course, it would not only drive India further away but enrage the United States and other signatories of these major international agreements. Beijing took the chance anyway, because Pakistan remained China's only means to remain an internal player of South Asian politics. The transfers— of nuclear technology, possibly nuclear production-related equipment, equipment needed to set up in Pakistan a Chinese-supplied M-11 missile capacity, and probably the missiles themselves—were discovered by the United States, using a combination of intelligence methods.

The consequences were a halt to Indo-Chinese rapprochement, major exacerbation of Sino-American tensions during the early 1990s, and an end to U.S. military assistance to Islamabad. Beijing hardly needed either of the first two results, given the many other areas of emerging disagreement with Washington and the still tentative nature of its otherwise improving ties with New Delhi. By the mid-1990s the ongoing crisis had still not been resolved, although China continued to deny American allegations and apparently did either slow down or periodically stop missile transfers. This proved to be but one example among several in the arms transfer arena in which China deliberately went to the edge of international legality: in this case, Beijing claimed the missiles in question had a range of just less than 300 kilometers, the threshold for the MTCR being 300 kilometers. Such maneuvering irritated the United States. But as nuclear weapons and missiles were the only tool China had to continue its role as a principal outside player in South Asia, Beijing chose not to back down completely. The cost was high: not just another thorn in the American side but a factor in the Indian decision to accelerate its own missile program. By the mid-1990s, therefore, New Delhi had not only fielded the short-range *Prithvi* but had moved far to perfect and eventually deploy the intermediate-range *Agni* missile. Thus China's lack of foresight produced an emerging nuclear arms race with India and put another obstacle in the path of eventual Sino-American settlement.

Perhaps by way of partial compensation, and in light of its post-Tiananmen isolation, China agreed to continue efforts to "normalize" relations with India.

This led to establishment of working relations at various political levels, trade and other cooperative economic ventures, and various other kinds of contacts, but it did not mean convergence of perspectives and interests, or full settlement of disputes. India also found it useful to proceed in that direction, noting China's rapid increase in power and potential for superpower status, and its own domestic difficulties in many spheres. These difficulties included budgetary (defense budgets began to decline), ethnic (the Kashmir problem began to heat up again, on top of rising disunity among castes and regions in general), political (the Congress Party fully lost control, especially after the assassination of Rajiv Gandhi in 1991), and economic issues (only in the early 1990s did India finally initiate its own opening to international investment and begin to liberalize its economy). The result was resumption of talks on the territorial issue. Thus, the Rajiv Gandhi visit to Beijing in 1988, coupled with the Congress Party's resolution, late in that year, not to insist on return from China of all territory claimed by India and seized by China, resulted in establishment of the Joint Working Group. This body met six times as of 1994, agreed on a number of confidence-building measures in the disputed areas, and established the basis for exchange of premiers: Li Peng went to New Delhi in late 1991 and Indian Prime Minister P.V. Narasimha Rao visited Beijing in September 1993. The two sides signed an important agreement that same month designed to reduce the probability of accidental conflicts along the border. It also set forth the goal of drawing a detailed map of the line of actual control and established the principles of minimum and agreed-on force levels and of staged force reductions.

This détente extended to other areas. Various high-level political, economic, and military exchanges took place, nongovernmental contacts expanded, and scholarly and cultural exchanges proceeded. Trade, historically very small, began to grow, although it remained below the $1 billion a year level and—given lack of complementarity between the two economies and large transport difficulties—looked unlikely to rise precipitously. Agreements on communications, science and technology, and the environment were signed. More con-

sulates were opened. Nonetheless, China's unwillingness to jettison its anti-Indian entente cordiale with Pakistan (despite Beijing's increasing reluctance to support Islamabad's position on Kashmir) remained a key limitation. India also differed with China on human rights questions, a reflection of differences between the two societies as well as the political character of the two regimes. China disagreed with India's support of a comprehensive nuclear test ban treaty. And then there was the question of Tibet (Beijing suspected New Delhi both of stirring up trouble in Lhasa and of favoring Tibetan independence) and India's granting of long-term asylum to the Dalai Lama. Above all, both states realized that they were fated always to be competitive, if not actually opponents. The only question was the extent to which changing relative power in both nations allowed China to continue to play a big role in South Asia or India increasingly to exclude Chinese influence and have the region for itself.

General Themes in China's Future Foreign Policy

Chinese foreign policy post-Tiananmen has been the policy of transition, of ad hoc reactions to trends and forces not clearly understood in Beijing—or, for that matter, in most other quarters. The complexity and inchoate nature of the emerging situation, inside China and out, make any sure statement about the future nearly impossible.

Nevertheless, two generalizations might be offered concerning the future of Chinese foreign policy. One is that, providing China avoids the many domestic and international pitfalls noted above, it should emerge as a global superpower in the early twenty-first century. The question then will be whether, in the interim, Beijing will have learned to use its new power not merely to achieve its foreign policy goals but to conduct its foreign relations in a peaceful, reasonably rational, and responsible manner. In other words, will China become a full member of the world community, accepting global standards of behavior, or will it still try to argue that it should be exempt from the rules of the new international system? In that case, China will become a threat not only to Asia but to many other states and thus will need balancing and deterring. That itself will go far to configure Asian and international relations, unfortunately missing the opportunity to construct a higher order system and precipitating matters back to a balance of power. If the former situation obtains, China could become a regional and global leader, sharing that mantle with the other superpowers of the twenty-first century. Then the future of Chinese foreign policy, in terms of its goals and the amount of trouble avoided, will be bright. In the mid-1990s, however, there is no easy way to determine which path China will choose. But if history is a guide, relatively greater weight ought to be given to the unpalatable alternative. Countries, given sudden large accretions of power, almost always pose threats to their neighbors and have to be reined in by a coalition of outside forces.

Second, the domestic and international variables that inform Chinese foreign policy have changed greatly in their relative weight since the end of the cold war. Internally, economics has all but replaced politics as the most important factor. The role of personality has been greatly attenuated. The generally positive weight of the pre-1949 party past has been largely replaced by the negative influence of the Great Leap Forward, the Cultural Revolution, and the Tiananmen incident. The party itself is transforming itself into a neo-Marxist, quasi-socialist, proto-democratic institution, gradually rejecting the Leninist-Maoist extreme. It would not be surprising if it were to fall of its own weight before that transition is complete. The weight of the more distant past is now more important and is rapidly combining with modernist culture—the product of rapid economic development—to overcome party culture. The role of the military will continue to decline within the party as new claimants to power arise. Ideology will continue to move toward cultural nationalism. The international system and its rules of behavior will also continue to be a wild card influencing China, internally and internationally. The various revolutions (military, economic, political) noted previously will foil Beijing's attempt to conduct a domestically driven foreign policy. The rise (or restoration) to global prominence of Europe, Japan, and Russia and the continued presence everywhere of the United States will short-circuit any chance of easy regional Chinese overlordship and will place severe limits on unpalatable Chinese behavior elsewhere. Finally, the newly emergent factors of power will discourage any Chinese attempt to conduct its future foreign policy on the basis of simple, quantitative power calculations.

Toward the New Millennium: China as a World Power?

Predicting the future is nearly impossible. There are too many variables, the "weights" and sequence of which are unknown, unmeasurable, or changing rapidly with time. Determining all alternative futures for Chinese foreign policy during the remainder of the 1990s and into the twenty-first century would require consideration of the domestic determinants discussed above (politics, economics, and society; weight of the past; and ideology); various external determinants (policies of the other relevant states; nature and trends in the international system; and changes in China's power and interest structures relative to other important states); China-related issues including Korean reunification, Taiwan, the Sprat-lys, and the like); and various time frames (short term, up to two years; medium term, up to five years; or long term, more than five years). The number of ways these variables can be combined quickly mounts to several hundred. Nevertheless, there are ways to choose among them, as some alternatives are clearly more relevant and probable than others. Moreover, for analytical purposes, short- and long-term prognoses may be forgone as too quickly dated and too murky, respectively, in favor of concentrating on the medium term, when useful distinctions between constants and variables can still be made. The relatively small number of scenarios that result can be extrapolated to sketch out some of those that are missing. If one further limits the categories in each set of determinants to three and combines them in a reasonable manner, the number of alternative Chinese foreign policy futures can also be reduced greatly. That is the method used here, which begins with three realistic scenarios of China's mid-term future (that is, until the year 2000), each with distinct foreign policy implications.

Scenarios of China's Future and Their Foreign Policy Implications

1. Continuation of Economic Reforms Amid Slow Political Evolution

In this scenario, economic factors would continue to dominate politics. The succession would see a younger, somewhat less ideological but highly nationalistic generation of leaders come to power. Maoist-style Marxism would continue to erode in favor of a combination of pragmatism and Confucian values, as in Singapore. Leninist central party rule would be stretched increasingly thin by the rise of new centers of regional and local power, declining interest in party membership among youth, and new or resurgent groups and classes (entrepreneurs, an urban middle class, better-off farmers, intellectuals) outside the party. To retain ultimate control, the party would have to become an institution increasingly representative of corporate, class, and geographic groups. Leadership would become factionalized along fault lines reflecting the new, dynamic divisions of society and economy, with finely balanced, shared power and no dominant, charismatic individual at the top. The economy would continue its march toward marketization, growth rates would remain reasonably high (about 5 percent a year), the opening to the outside would be maintained, international investment and trade would increase (although at a pace considerably reduced from the early 1990s), and the degree of economic interdependence would rise. While corruption, large population movements, uneven interprovincial development, and inflation all would continue to plague such a regime, it would not succumb to their collective influence. This scenario represents a continuation of the situation and trends in the mid-1990s. Although many problems would

occur, none would pose an insuperable challenge to such a regime.

2. Conservative Restoration and Halting or Reversal of Economic Reforms

Unlike the first scenario, in this alternative the succession would bring to power a combination of party ideologues, authoritarians stressing top-down order and obedience, and military leaders as kingmakers. Economic reforms would cease, an attempt would be made to reimpose the discipline of central planning, private enterprise would come under suspicion as subversive, the open door would be at least partly closed in an attempt to control external influences, and China would no longer look with favor or indifference on economic interdependence. Growth rates would therefore plunge as foreign investors and traders pulled out and as the efficiencies of the marketizing economy were sacrificed to the "iron rice bowl" and central directives. Social freedoms, such as they were during the Deng era, would be greatly constrained, and the party-army would rule by force and ideological conformity to neo-Maoist Leninism with a strong admixture of nationalism. The many emerging economic inequities and the increasing looseness of society of the Deng period would be dealt with by attempting to restore the status quo before 1978, although that would be impossible and would merely exacerbate tensions. Lacking either social or economic constraints, China would see corruption become the norm. Society and economy would increasingly be set against polity, resulting in a series of crises and explosions. Such a regime could maintain itself in power for a considerable period, but only at the cost of eventual economic collapse, pulverization of society, popular uprisings out of desperation, and bloody overthrow in the end.

3. Political Decay, Loss of Economic Control, and Societal Unrest

If the succession did not produce a new leadership of definite character and program, an extended political crisis could ensue. That would progressively weaken party rule and lead to a combination of petty personalism at all levels, corruption, and periodic but unsuccessful attempts at reform followed by repression. China would spiral downward, with power spread over a wide geographic area but a narrow range of authority. The society would break loose from political control, with a creative upsurge but near chaos in terms of the norms of social order. Marxist ideology would be replaced by a free-for-all competition of many ideas, although Confucian values would predominate. The economy would regionalize, with some provinces looking mostly outside China for gains in wealth, others depending on their own resources, and still others ranging between interdependence and autarky. Major economic crises would therefore follow as the country began to pull apart. The central government would lose control and govern in name only, with the consent of powerful provincial (possibly military) figures. This alternative could occur under Communist rule, increasingly nominal though it might be, or in a post-Communist period.

Each of these domestic scenarios would be associated with a differing foreign policy. The reformist authoritarian regime described in the first scenario would continue a policy favoring interdependence, the open door, and participation in existing international institutions and construction of new ones. As it gained in self-confidence and international respectability, it would increasingly assert itself in its relations with Asian neighbors and issues. It would project its power, including military power, at ever-farther distances from China's border, and involve itself in issues and areas where it had not previously played a role. It would therefore attempt to change the status quo in its favor, but because it would work within institutions and with other nations, its presence and policies would not necessarily be regarded as threatening. Because issues could not be addressed, much less solved, without China, Beijing would not look kindly on attempts by the United States or Japan to limit or circumscribe its range and degree of influence. China would possess a veto over all important international changes in Asia and improve its capabilities and interests in global concerns and issues outside the region. This is a formula for the acceptable growth of China into Asia's leader, along with Japan, of reduction of U.S. influence in Asia to that of a (still powerful) outsider that is no longer the region's leader, and emergence of Beijing as a world power. Depending on how far toward po-

litical pluralism this China were able to proceed, its policies would be akin to those of Japan during the later Meiji period: proud, aggressive, and demanding its place in the Asian and the global sun.

The conservative repressive regime described second would lean toward a neo-isolationist, mercantilist foreign policy, emphasizing the virtue of self-sufficient military security instead of rejecting such a zero-sum approach in favor of the mutual benefits of security cooperation. Such a regime would center its policies on the balance of power game, leaning to one side and then the other in a three-state system composed (in Chinese eyes) of the United States, China, and Japan. Likewise, in the economic sphere, the open door would swing nearly shut as the military-authoritarian junta attempted to rid Chinese society of undesirable foreign cultural influences and would stand aloof from trends toward interdependence and construction of new multilateral economic institutions. Just enough international economic contact would be allowed to enable China to extract maximum benefit at minimal cost. Given the extreme emphasis on neo-Maoism and nationalism, Beijing would view the outside world as generally hostile and would, consequently, be quite willing to use its military power to support its international goals, taking a narrow view of national sovereignty as the basis for use of its power abroad. Perceiving the world as threatening, China would act in like manner: China would threaten punishment for alleged misdeeds, carry out such retributive acts with regularity, and thus come to be regarded itself as an all-around threat. Beijing would thus become the "bad boy" of Asia, engendering over time (and reluctantly) a coalition of states throughout the region seeking to contain China until its internal order, and hence it foreign policy, changed for the better. This China might be similar in its foreign policy to that of the Soviet Union during the two decades after Stalin's death: xenophobic and always preparing for some showdown; a giant pariah state, but too important to ignore.

The decaying regime described last would perhaps be the easiest for foreign states to deal with, for a China with that sort of internal order would be dependent on the benevolence of other nations. It would thus willingly go along with multilateral diplomatic and economic initiatives. On the other hand, its international weakness would cause its foreign policy to swing rapidly and unpredictably between extremes. Increasingly, its diplomatic policies would be made in foreign capitals, especially Tokyo and Washington, while its economic orientation would follow those of the London and New York financial markets. In this largely open society, foreign influence would penetrate the borders with little hindrance, thus further disorganizing the internal order. China could easily experience an economic crash, causing food shortages and large population movements (including huge numbers of refugees fleeing across national borders) and requiring massive international assistance. An environmental crisis brought on not only by decades of neglect but triggered by several poor harvests could precipitate such an overall downturn. This China's foreign policy would be akin to that of the China of the late nineteenth and early twentieth centuries: the playground (if they so chose) of the relevant great powers. The difference would be that a massively more powerful China, even if internally weak, would be much more difficult to push around or, if it collapsed, the burden on the international community would be extremely heavy.

International Scenarios

If the number of useful alternative internal Chinese futures is large, the same is obviously true of China's external environment, except that the variants are even more numerous. The same problems of limiting them to a small number also obtain, and what follows can illustrate only some of the relevant possibilities. Moreover, in order to link the three internally driven alternative Chinese foreign policy futures to those flowing from international developments, the number of combinations must be further reduced, and therefore seemingly arbitrary choices will have to be made. The criterion for exercising those choices is their real world relevance to important China-related issues. But because there is only one actual future, the scenarios examined must still be regarded as mostly for illustrative purposes.

1. Continuation of 1990s Trends

This configuration of the international system is a more or less straight line projection of the international situation of the mid-1990s. The states most relevant to China are the United States, Japan, Russia, and possibly India. The most relevant regional actors are Korea, Taiwan, ASEAN augmented by Vietnam, and Pakistan. No major conflict would occur, although there would be plenty of subregional, ethnic, and internal civil conflicts. No new regional security systems—either collective defense or collective security—would emerge, and the major powers would address issues in an ad hoc, laissez-faire manner. The international economy would grow at a moderate rate, with a unifying Europe, a growing North America, and a dynamic Asia setting the pace. The United States and Japan, both mostly concerned with internal restructuring but increasingly at odds over economic matters, would continue residual cooperation under the security treaty and would persist in efforts to address, and slowly settle, economic disputes. U.S.-Japanese relations would still constitute the basis, however fragile, for overall Asian security and continued Asian economic growth. Russia would slowly recover its unity and, therefore, its strength and self-confidence, but not sufficiently to allow Moscow to be a major participant in Asian affairs. The center of dynamic Asian growth would continue to shift southward to Southeast Asia, where a marketizing Vietnam would enter ASEAN on the latter's terms. India, growing at around 5 percent a year and continuing its reformist opening to trade and foreign investment, would become even more the economic giant of South Asia and dominate subregional security.

2. International Systemic Disintegration

The worst-case alternative to continuation of the mid-1990s situation would be international systemic disintegration. In this case, subregional and other conflicts would not be successfully addressed by the major powers or by international organizations. Consequently, the incidence of violence, internal and international, would rise exponentially. Most nations would refrain from quelling various types and levels of disturbance, pleading the need to solve internal problems. The international economic system would become unstable as security concerns mounted and the movement toward greater interdependence and institutionalization would cease. Since all nations would be forced to look only to their own security, existing alliances would sunder or not be established, alignments would become less meaningful, the arms race would escalate everywhere, and beggar-thy-neighbor economic policies would replace cooperative, low-tariff regimes under GATT. The cornerstone of Asian security, the U.S.-Japan Security Treaty, would fall as Washington and Tokyo split on a range of economic and security issues. Japan would rearm and pursue an independent foreign policy. Russia would come under fascist rule and possibly link up with China. ASEAN would not be able to coalesce because of ethnic differences and nationalism and would therefore fall prey to great power subversive ethnic or economic activities. India would make its own way as best it could, but ethnic and communal conflicts would prevent it from projecting its power beyond its borders. This near-Hobbesian world would not even be capable of forming a balance of power system for short-term security, although it could eventually evolve into one. Nuclear proliferation would be the rule, not the exception. International environmental protection efforts would fail for lack of national wills to cooperate.

3. International Systemic Integration

The best-case alternative to continuation of the mid-1990s situation would be international systemic integration. In that case, the major powers, in concert or acting through the United Nations, would cope with internal and cross-border violence. Gradually, the incidence of conflict would decrease. The resultant breathing room would promote construction of regional collective security organizations (or sometimes, collective defense institutions, depending on the degree to which one or more of the major powers chose to project military power). The United Nations would be reformed under major power leadership, with a more representative Security Council (a single European Union seat and a new seat for Japan, augmented security powers, and limitation on the veto). International arms control regimes would be agreed to, including a strong international institution limiting the spread of nuclear and other weapons of mass

destruction. The U.S.-Japan Security Treaty would be revised into a genuine alliance, economic as well as security-oriented. Asia would thus be stabilized, with a successfully democratizing and marketizing Russia welcomed to the region as an important player. The relevant Asian powers would join in working out plans for an Asian collective security organization. ASEAN (now with Vietnam as a full member) would establish common economic institutions and move toward becoming a regional security community as well. The degree of economic interdependence, and its institutional base, would gradually rise. The United States would seek to restore its place as global leader, but now as facilitator of movements toward regional collective security, economic interdependence, and environmental protection.

Integrating Domestic and International Determinants of Chinese Foreign Policy

The combination of three internally generated Chinese foreign policy alternatives and three international systemic futures generates nine possibilities. None are inherently unrealistic, all have foreign policy aspects that must be considered, and therefore each is addressed in turn.

1. Permutations of a Reformist-Authoritarian Regime

Combined with a Straight-Line Projection of the Mid-1990s International System. The foreign policy proclivities of this combination would beget a Chinese foreign relations regime most nearly in congruence with Beijing's foreign policy goals laid out previously for such a regime. China's best chance at becoming Asia's principal power and a world power in every sense is through this combination of internal and external determinants. Such a combination would also maximize opportunity for peaceful settlement of several key regional issues, largely although not exclusively on Beijing's terms: the twin Korean questions (North Korean nuclear weapons and Northern succession/reunification); Taiwan (eventual agreement on terms of reunification); Hong Kong (peaceful retrocession); and the Spratly Islands question (negotiations, led by China, for joint oil exploration but no near-term ownership settlement). The Burma and Kashmir problems would remain in abeyance.

Combined with International Systemic Disintegration.   This combination would be a mixed blessing for Beijing. On the one hand, it would be more or less free to expand or consolidate its military influence beyond China's geographic borders, since Japan and the United States would be mostly preoccupied with each other, militarily and economically, and Russia could find its only safety in concert with China. That could mean outbreak of a new Korean war, since the United States would have less capacity to defend the South. Such a recipe could, however, be disastrous for China, in that the United States might still choose to fight, and a repetition of the previous Korean conflict could bring the United States and China to blows. It could also mean a nuclearized North Korea and, hence, eventual possession of such weapons by Japan and even Taiwan. That could also mean early return of Hong Kong on stringent Chinese terms. It could, most importantly, mean that Taiwan might try for independence (given the highly unsettled nature of international relations) and hope for U.S. military support in the then inevitable Chinese mainland attempt to overcome the island by force. It would probably mean that China would be able to make fast its assertions of sovereignty over the Spratlys, since ASEAN would be unable to resist, especially with no assurance of U.S. or Japanese support (the latter would come, if at all, too late, since Japanese rearmament would take years). And no international coalition against such an aggressive China could be built. China might even bring Burma more fully into a status of dependency, including construction of full-fledged Chinese naval bases on Burmese soil. On the other hand, and aside from the obvious Chinese involvement in one or several conflicts at a still-inconvenient time, such a combination would not accord with other Chinese interests, chiefly economic. A disorganized international economic system would constrain Beijing to amend its reformist economic program in favor of greater degrees of economic autarky. Interdependence, a mainstay of the reformist economic platform, would disintegrate,

with serious consequences for China. Some provinces might still be able to benefit, but China's economy as a whole could not but be hurt, and Beijing's ability to orchestrate general economic progress and therefore the party's ability to remain in power would be undermined considerably. In sum, this combination would be superficially attractive and tempting to China, but eventually damaging to it, internally as well as internationally.

Combined with International Systemic Integration.   This combination would be more to the benefit of China, Asia, and the world. Of benefit to China would be the probable absence of conflict, especially as concerns Korea, the peaceful return of Hong Kong, and general acknowledgment in the region of China's status as one of the three or four major powers. With security, stability, and propitious conditions for all-around economic development, China could continue to grow with reasonable rapidity or to mitigate, through continued high rates of foreign investment and trade volumes, domestic economic downturns or high growth-induced political or economic crises. China would have an excellent chance of cooperating with the other major powers in constructing a stable intra-Asian security system, regional and global international economic institutions, and a revamped United Nations on which it could help put its stamp. On the other hand, Chinese security expansion would be bounded. A cooperative China would probably have to chance Taiwanese independence (and, seeing its opportunity, a DPP-led Taipei might seize it). It would have to withdraw its extravagant claims to the Spratlys, join a new international regime to modernize Burma, and put aside any further thought of making Southeast Asia its exclusive sphere of influence. In other words, a China on such good behavior would have to curtail its ambitions and sublimate its power drive, diverting its energies into internationally acceptable channels.

2. Permutations of a Conservative Repressive Regime

Combined with a Straight-Line Projection of the Mid-1990s International System.   This combination would find the world slowly but steadily becoming more unfriendly and constrictive. Beijing might be able to move its political boundaries steadily outward, since China could still grow in power and since the other powers would be so busy with other concerns as not to be able to coalesce against an obviously unpalatable Chinese regime. But any Chinese move to use force, in any of the several conflict-laden instances noted previously, would be proof positive of China's "real" goal of regional domination and be the signal for construction of a grand coalition to contain Beijing. Moreover, a Chinese regime of that character would find it much more difficult to rule at home and to augment the nation's economic power. An increasing percentage of GNP would go into military hardware procurement and training, and correspondingly less would go to economic and social betterment of the populace. The Beijing regime would thus feel threatened both internally and internationally, and adopt a "circle-the-wagons" foreign policy reminiscent of the disastrous period just after Tiananmen. That in turn would only lead to a vicious circle of charges and recriminations and growing Chinese isolation. Indeed, a China of this sort could well help bring about early solution of U.S.-Japanese differences, Moscow's decision to opt for joining a league of anti-Chinese market democracies, Indian movement in the same direction, and coalescence (under benevolent and approving American and Japanese eyes) of ASEAN-Vietnam as a full economic community and nascent anti-Chinese security community. Beijing could, to be sure, coexist for some time with such an Asia, but it could hardly prosper, and it would probably lose what chance it might have had to extend its influence efficiently, at least until the nature of the regime changed for the better.

Combined with a Disintegrated International System. In this scenario, little or nothing would stand in the way of China. Using the greatly augmented power available to it and not fatally (at least not yet) injured by its own regressive economic system and the weakened international economy, China would expand militarily. The greatest danger would be to Taiwan, which could find itself shorn of its American guarantee, not able to claim Japanese protection,

and unable to depend on a renewed Russian threat to China. This Chinese regime might also be more willing to bankroll and support North Korea, given the renewed ideological affinity the two would have for each other and the opportunities provided by the general international disorganization. It would not be impossible to imagine a jointly planned, but separately executed, attack against South Korea and Taiwan. Such a regime would also hesitate little before incorporating Hong Kong by force in advance of 1997 or ousting by force the Vietnamese and the ASEAN claimants from those of the Spratly Islands they garrisoned—all in the name of taking advantage of the international situation before it changed to China's disadvantage. Southeast Asia might have to become subservient to a militarily expansionist China, which would close off the South China Sea to whomever it wished and bring Burma fully under Chinese control. China would thus become imperialist, in a situation reminiscent of Asia in the first half of the twentieth century, when Japan, temporarily seeing no obstacles in its path, found reasons to expand. Expansion would eventually spell the end of this regime, for the threatened states—at least the major powers—would probably recover sufficiently to restore the status quo ante or at least establish a line beyond which China would not be permitted to cross. That would spell war or cold war and, combined with internal political and economic decay, would eventually lead to the regime's downfall, as happened to the Communist Party of the Soviet Union.

Combined with International Systemic Integration. This combination would make life much harder for China much sooner. The resources would be available more or less immediately to stave off a potentially imperialist China through a collective security organization led by the United States and Japan. If China did not join at the outset in those efforts and thus prick its own balloon, it could find itself the object of an Asian regional defense organization, to which Russia, Vietnam, ASEAN, and even India might belong. Taiwan would thus be secured militarily and would probably be able to declare independence and join the league of market democracies.

Hong Kong's post-1997 society and economy would be able to survive, if not immediately prosper, since the former colony's traditional entrepôt and window-on-the world functions would be of value to the Beijing rulers. North Korea might continue to exist, shielded by Beijing, but would not be able to invade the South. Its Kim dynasty rulers could only wait out their last days before succumbing to a combination of popular overthrow and Southern takeover and reconstruction. China would find it tough going in international political and economic organizations, particularly the United Nations and the World Trade Organization (the successor to GATT). In both arenas Beijing would constantly face a coalition of the whole in opposition to its interests. A similar lineup would exist in Asian and trans-Pacific regional institutions. In sum, incipient Chinese imperialism would be forestalled.

3. Permutations of a Decaying Regime

Combined with a Straight-Line Extrapolation of the Mid-1990s International System. This combination would not be instantly disastrous for such a regime, although unpleasant surprises could confront both Beijing and its neighbors. The degree of international influence on such a China, and thus over its foreign policy, would surely increase. But the pace would be modulated by the manifold problems, domestic and international, outside China's borders and by the relatively gentle slope (in all probability) of China's downward slide. The relatively relaxed international atmosphere would, in fact, be beneficial to this regime's foreign policy, since it would not be able to take advantage of external opportunities or, indeed, to involve itself in international situations to any major extent. Its interest would be served by keeping out of harm's way and hoping that international crises or the possibly predatory policies of foreign powers would not require a Chinese response that would further destabilize internal affairs. The problem, however, would be that Beijing would not, generally, be a party to settlement of international problems of innate concern to itself. Thus, the Korean questions might be overcome, and a new security equation appear in Northeast Asia, without major Chinese input. China might have to pull back from

the Spratlys. Most importantly, Taiwan could perceive its opportunity and opt for independence, safe in the assumption of continued American security backing and the small likelihood of Chinese military intervention. (That, of course, might be a recipe for tragedy, as even a decaying Beijing regime might have enough power, unity, and purpose to turn around by surprise and send its still large and relatively modern forces across the Taiwan Strait.) Another difficulty for China would be that the other major powers would, perhaps unwisely, discount China's power. Arms control agreements and regional economic or security institution-building might therefore occur with little or no Chinese input or participation. That would isolate Beijing within the region or require its unwilling assent. In sum, this combination would make China somewhat less difficult to live with but also be fraught with the twin dangers of sudden crises on the one hand, and of emergence of otherwise avoidable longer term difficulties, on the other hand.

Combined with International Systemic Disintegration. This combination could increase the danger dramatically. The operative question would be: which would decline more rapidly, China or its international environment. Decay, after all, does not equal collapse, although one could eventually lead to the other. Decay could also signal transformation of the internal Chinese political scene through replacement, whether gradual or instant, of party rule by some more liberal form of polity, even if that were one or another version of authoritarianism and not necessarily democracy. If the rate of downward drift (before systemic transformation took place) in China were slower than that of the external world, Beijing might be tempted to project its power abroad faster and farther than in the other two internal alternatives. This would be the equivalent of the Soviet Union engaging in ''defensive imperialism,'' as it did on several occasions (East Germany, Poland, Hungary, Czechoslovakia, and Afghanistan) on the way to systemic downfall. China could thus strongly involve itself in Korea, possibly leading to collision with the United States if the latter were also in a position to take part in a North-South conflict. Beijing could also take military action against a Taipei at the verge of independence, and could thus also find itself in confrontation with Washington. In like manner, it could project its still-modernizing military power further into the Spratlys or take advantage of Southeast Asian security disorganization to make Burma into a full dependency. But if China's rate of downward drift were more rapid than that of its international environment, quite different outcomes to crises, and therefore a much more quiescent, cooperative Chinese foreign policy, would result. The problem would be that comparative rates of decline would be difficult to evaluate. Miscalculations on all sides would be easy to make. Hence, the danger of disaster would be high.

Combined with International Systemic Integration. This could lead to Chinese isolation or possibly to desperate Chinese efforts to avoid such a fate. China's internal situation might deteriorate so greatly that the outer world would decide to leave China to itself until it recovered sufficiently to warrant reestablishing contact with a successor regime, as was the case during China's warlord period early in the century. If Taiwan saw China's internal decay as providing its chance at independence, there would be a danger that Beijing would quickly, but blindly, attempt to forcibly prevent the island from slipping away. In either case, Chinese foreign policy would be made mostly in the capitals of the other major powers. Structural changes in the international security and economic systems would be initiated and carried out by others and China would be proffered the results on a take-it-or-leave-it basis. Since crises would be avoided in this alternative (with the significant possible exception of Taiwan), China could at least address its internal problems without fear of untoward external involvement. That would prolong the domestic transition and provide at least some support for further marketization and movement toward democracy. Moreover, although construction of higher-order international institutions would proceed largely without strong Chinese participation, China would be pulled further into mutually beneficial economic interdependence and provided with an institutional framework for its elemental security needs. The country could thus benefit from this combination, or at least mitigate or stretch out the problems produced by this type of regime.

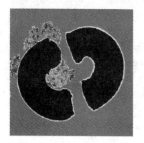

CHAPTER **8**

SOCIETY AND CULTURE
IN CONTEMPORARY CHINA

The "liberation" of China in 1949 marked the beginning of a program to revolutionize all of Chinese society and restructure the beliefs and values of its vast populace. This chapter focuses on government policies, their impact on society, and the public response to them as China has experienced social and cultural transformation. The analysis is broken down into discussions of the population, intergenerational relations, women, class and status, ethnicity, religion, and the social problems facing contemporary Chinese society.

Some analysts believe Chinese society and culture are unique, while others emphasize the similarities between China and other countries. Chinese society is different from others in three main respects: its incomparably large population size, its long, continuous cultural history, and its method of mobilizing people for social change through the use of campaigns. Yet in its struggle to modernize and in its experience with Communist-inspired revolution in the twentieth century, China is also like many other societies. Before these features of Chinese society are discussed, an explanation of China's campaign method of social mobilization is useful.

Campaigns as a Tool of Social Policy

Policy making in China can be viewed in at least two ways. The first, as in most other countries, is that policy is formulated by legislative or executive organs of government and is implemented through administrative subunits as laws, regulations, or guidelines. A second approach, which overlaps with the first, uses propaganda to mobilize the masses to achieve an objective established by leaders of the Chinese Communist Party. Through branch party units in every organization and at all levels of the system, vertically integrated for tight planning and coordination, citizens are taught the ideological goals of the campaign, singled out either for their activism or their deviance, and rewarded or punished for their performance.

This system owes its origins mostly to the organizational model bestowed on China and other societies in Eastern Europe and Asia by ideologues and organizational experts from the Soviet Union. But it also has roots in China's indigenous organizational style, developed over thousands of years of centralized bureaucratic imperial rule. Imperial rule, however, never reached as deeply into the lives of the people as did the party/state in China after 1949. The campaign system blends Chinese philosophy, collectivist social behavior, and social psychological precepts involving "face," shame, and social control into a unique method for mobilizing masses of people for social change. This form of social organization and change served as a model for other societies, like North Korea, to follow.

Thousands of campaigns (sometimes called "movements") have taken place in China since 1949. Some serve short-term, mundane policy purposes, such as collection of the harvest. Most have consequences for individuals and organizations, like deepening the presence of party organizations in the countryside in the case of the campaigns to collectivize agriculture. Some have consequences for whole groups, for instance, the elimination of landlords as a social class by the end of the land reform movement in 1953.

Campaigns can be seen in terms of both their planned outcomes—such as the elimination of sparrows in urban China in the early 1950s—and their unanticipated outcomes—such as the replacement of sparrows by insect pests, the removal of "capitalist roaders" from party and state ranks during the Cultural Revolution, and near civil war in the closing years of that movement. Many campaigns (such as the Anti-Rightist campaign of 1957 or the Anti-Lin Biao, Anti-Confucius campaign of 1972-1974) were aimed specifically at identifying and punishing ideological and political deviants. Some campaigns have been so pervasive that they stand for whole blocks of modern China's chronology and history. The Great Leap Forward from 1958 to 1960 and the Cultural Revolution from 1966 to 1976 are examples.

The campaigns of the late 1950s and mid-1960s cannot be understood without reference to the crisis of succession to Chairman Mao Zedong and factionalism among top-ranking officials of the party and the state. Some analysts believe that the Hundred Flowers movement of 1956-1957 was Mao's failed attempt to use the intelligentsia to criticize and reform party and state bureaucrats. But intellectuals took their mission too much to heart, and their scathing critique of single-party rule led to the government's punitive reaction known as the Anti-Rightist campaign.

The Cultural Revolution, spurred by the personality cult surrounding Mao, sought to undo the urban bureaucracy that supported both party and state systems. Led by the Gang of Four (Mao's wife, Jiang Qing; Shanghai leaders Yao Wenyuan and Zhang Chunqiao; and security guard Wang Hongwen), young Red Guard units were formed to find and punish class enemies. Schools and factories closed. Young rebels clogged transportation systems, bringing transport of critical goods to a halt. Red Guards turned first on prominent individuals as targets. Gradually, the Gang of Four became unable to distinguish between genuine rebels and those who merely

assumed this posture as an excuse to engage in violence. The Red Guards had armed themselves with heavy weapons including artillery, and eventually they turned on one another in an explosion of intergroup violence that threatened the country with full-scale civil war. The Gang of Four was arrested in 1976, after Mao's death. Despite their pernicious influence, it is remarkable how much the movement depended on Mao's charisma and how shallow a social infrastructure the Gang of Four had actually created.

The campaign method continued to be utilized after the Cultural Revolution. Movements were launched to control bottom-up pressures in 1978 and 1986—including the 1979 anti-democracy campaign and the 1983 campaign against "bourgeois liberalization"—and in 1989, when the "re-education" campaign was initiated after the Tiananmen incident. But these movements have not attracted the commitment and energy that people were willing to give to the party/state system before the Cultural Revolution. Social control of deviance, which always contained an element of coercion, has now given way to much more potent demonstrations of naked power, and reform has, in many ways, undermined the vertical integration of the 1950s and 1960s on which this system of mobilization depended. Greater social and geographic mobility among the masses, local innovation and initiative, and growing familiarity with standards of living outside China have led to new horizontal linkages and organizational initiatives that are not so easily displaced by central control. These issues are discussed further below in terms of policies aimed at social change.

Population Trends

As of December 1, 1993, China's population totaled 1,171,577,000, the largest national population on earth. The majority of Chinese belong to the Han ethnic group. Less than 2 percent are Zhuang, and other minorities each comprise less than 1 percent of the total. China's official language is Mandarin Chinese (*putong hua*), which is based on northern dialects. The characters used to write Chinese (*hanzi*) are fairly uniform, but the spoken language includes many mutually unintelligible local dialects other than Mandarin, such as those that are spoken in Shanghai (Shanghainese) and Guangzhou (Cantonese).

Less than 10 percent of the land in China is arable, and in recent years the desert has been steadily encroaching on what remains of cultivable land. Massive mountain chains, the Tian Shan, Altai Shan, and Himalayas, intersect with hot deserts of Inner Mongolia and the cold desert plateau of Tibet to dominate China's interior.

The distribution of China's population reflects these physical conditions. More than 75 percent of the population resides in twelve provinces and three special municipalities on China's east coast. The country's transportation, industrial, educational, and other service infrastructures, as well as the majority Han population and best-educated labor force, have historically been and continue to be concentrated in China's coastal cities and provinces. Most of the nation's fifty-five minority groups reside in the far less densely populated regions of China's northwest and southwest. Though potentially rich in natural resources, these areas of the country have the least developed infrastructure. (For more on population density and distribution, see Chapter 6.)

China's vast population is still growing, but the pattern of growth has shifted over time. Before the Communist victory in 1949, population growth was characterized by high birth rates, high death rates, and a low rate of natural increase. Between 1840 and 1949 China's population expanded, on average, only .26 percent a year, rising from 410 to 540 million. Since 1949, however, China has undergone a major demographic transition marked by sharply reduced mortality rates and moderate rates of birth and natural increase. This relatively stable pattern has been broken only once since the Communist takeover in 1949—mortality rates skyrocketed in 1960, after the Great Leap Forward's radical effort to revolutionize the countryside led to the falsification of grain production statistics and caused a devastating famine in China.

The 1990 census data reaffirmed the overall stability of rates of birth and natural increase, as well as the ratio between births and deaths. Crude death rates

were recorded as 8 per thousand and birth rates at 21 to 22 per thousand between 1982 and 1990 (1982 was the date of the most recent census preceding the census of 1990). In 1990 the mortality of infants under five years of age was low, approximately 29 per thousand males and 40 per thousand females. Maternal mortality was 44 per 100,000 live births in 1980. Natural increase was pegged at 1.5 to 1.6 percent, and the fertility rate held at 2.5 percent for the whole country. Despite the stability in this pattern, the figures were cause for concern. To assure the nation's ability to support its population, particularly in the face of the baby boom of the 1960s, China sought to reduce population growth to 1.2 billion by the turn of the century. At the 1990 rate of growth, however, population totals are more likely to be somewhere between a low estimate of 1.3 billion and a high estimate of 1.8 billion by the year 2000.

More recent data suggest that fertility in China is falling. In 1990 crude birth rates were calculated at 21.1; in 1991, 19.7; and in 1992, 18.2 per thousand. Earlier estimates were based on an average of six children each for Chinese women over an entire lifetime, but more recent estimates, based on 1991, 1992, and 1993 reports, bring total fertility rates to 1.9 births per woman. Other figures support this important trend. The average age at the time of first marriage is climbing (now 22.2) and the proportion of women marrying at early ages is declining. In 1950 more than 40 percent of Chinese women were married by the time they were eighteen years old versus 3 percent overall in 1988 (less than 4 percent in rural China alone). The rate of contraceptive use (reported as 83 percent in 1993) and sterilization rose rapidly between 1988 and 1991. These changes may account for the differences between high and low projections for the year 2000. Since baby boomers of the 1960s are now in their reproductive years, China's population by the year 2000 will still exceed the target figure of 1.2 billion.

By the second decade of the twenty-first century, the number of children in the lowest age group (under five years of age) will begin to decline. Assuming more equitable access to economic opportunity, birth rates, described as "moderate" in 1990, are likely to register new lows in the twenty-first centu-

China's population, approaching 1.2 billion, is the largest national population on earth. The population is expected to age substantially as China enters the twenty-first century.

ry. In that event, population growth would level off around 2025.

Although age composition is currently weighted toward those under age 45, China is also gradually aging. Since 1949, Chinese men and women are living longer. Longevity has increased about a year and a half each year since 1949. Demographers calculated life expectancies at 71 for women and 69 for men in 1990. Thus, along with changes in fertility and birth rates, the age structure of China's population is undergoing a long-term, dramatic change. If these shifting patterns continue, by the second decade of the twenty-first century the proportion of young people in China's total population will shrink, a sign of the second major demographic transition since 1949. The population will likely be characterized by low birth rates, low rates of mortality, and low rates of natural increase. (For a discussion of the effect of this demographic transition on labor resources, see Chapter 6.)

The One-Child Policy

The potential for a second demographic transition now rests, in part, on the success of one of China's most controversial policies: the one-child policy. From 1949 until 1979, birth control depended on a combination of policies aimed at improvement of maternal and child care, the distribution of contraceptives, and propaganda for later marriage. Although early campaigns from 1953 to 1958 and from 1962 to 1966 had some impact on birth rates, there were obstacles to success. In the early and mid-1950s, the traditional preference for sons was backed by family and clan organizations that threw their weight against party-sponsored birth control. Despite the pressure of women's associations to embody birth control in state policy, there was resistance within party ranks. Intellectuals who advocated state planning for population control were attacked during the Anti-Rightist campaign of 1957 and again during the course of the Cultural Revolution from 1966 to 1976.

It was not until 1971 that population growth targets were included in the nation's five-year plans. A new campaign pressed for late marriage, longer spacing between births, and fewer children (*wan, xi, shao*); the campaign was implemented using all available means of social control, with particular emphasis on the supervisory role of women's associations at every level of governance. State advocacy of family planning became part of the new constitutions of 1978 and 1982, while the 1980 Marriage Law committed every couple to practice birth control. An explosion of population growth in the 1960s and 1970s made it clear that these strategies, however effective, were too little, too late. Hanging over policymakers' heads was the possibility that China's population would grow by 13 million to 15 million each year. Those numbers would have a devastating impact on the country's hopes for modernization and development. The proposed solution, implemented in 1979, was the one-child policy.

The one-child policy in its initial stages required 95 percent of married couples in cities and 90 percent of rural couples to sign one-child certificates pledging to have only one child. Material and nonmaterial incentives and disincentives were tied to the policy. Those who took the pledge would receive income, housing, health care, employment, pension, and educational benefits for themselves and their child. Those who failed to do so would suffer penalties. By 1985 nearly 30 million such certificates had been signed. There were exceptions to these rules; China's minorities, for example, were exempted. The 1990 data, however, show that minorities grew at a rate nearly three and a half times the rate among the Han, and, as a consequence, the exemptions are being reversed.

The one-child policy depends, at least in part, on the availability of incentives and the meaningfulness of penalties. In rural villages with depressed incomes, negligible educational benefits, and poor health care, there are few incentives, and the penalties are virtually meaningless. In some areas of the country, the implementation of economic reform in the late 1970s removed the foundations for the incentives that might otherwise have supported the one-child policy.

There are also multiple ways to circumvent the policy. One worrisome counterstrategy is to hide the birth of females in order to assure that "only" children are recorded as males. Some families have secretly sent daughters to distant locations where they are out of reach of party and state monitors. Their births are not recorded. Forced to recognize resistance within a year of first implementing the policy, officials in rural areas retreated from their one-child goal to allow families to have two children.

Even with these caveats, the one-child policy is a serious effort and a major factor in low population growth rates. The agents of the one-child policy go far beyond propaganda: the policy is linked to techniques of campaign mobilization at every level of organizational structure in which citizens of China are involved. Women are empowered through women's associations to monitor other women's menstruation cycles, pregnancies, and birth control usage, and to administer rewards, and disincentives. Intense social pressure is used to persuade women to abort unscheduled pregnancies. Intense persuasion often turns into coercion when cadres get carried away with their missions. Both forced abortions and forced sterilizations have resulted from excessive zeal. In general, however, the program is contributing to the downward trend in birth rates, and it is likely to be applied with greater vigor to regions and peoples who have been either partially or wholly exempted.

This approach does have notable inequities. Women bear the burden of compliance as the agents and the targets of the policy, even though it is the patriarchs, and often the mothers-in-law with whom they are allied, who force wives and daughters to have children they do not want. The one-child policy militates against an age-old pattern in which sons are valued over daughters. The birth of additional children also maximizes family labor power and minimizes chances of family dissolution. The one-child policy has drawn the ire of critics because it is assumed to be responsible for lopsided sex ratios in China by encouraging female infanticide, an unanticipated consequence of its implementation. Sex ratios

China's one-child policy is linked to techniques of campaign mobilization at all levels of society. While several groups have found ways to circumvent the policy, it has contributed to a downward trend in birth rates.

in the 1990 census are imbalanced (106.6 males per 100 females), and the practice of female infanticide has a long history in China, but most demographers argue that the 1990 data represent underreported births rather than female infanticide.

Technology has armed patriarchs and traditionalists with new weapons, the impact of which is still being weighed. China is now producing ultrasound B machines, for example, at the rate of approximately 10,000 per year. These supply an illegal market for prenatal sex identification. Amniocentesis and chorionic villi sampling were also in use as of 1993, but the extent of their application for sex identification is not yet known. If the single-child policy succeeds in reversing traditional preferences and fighting off technologies aimed at its defeat, it will be a major achievement.

Controlling Migration and Rural/Urban Balance

China's urban infrastructure is concentrated on the east coast. The remainder of the country remains predominantly rural, and much of rural China is isolated and poor. The uneven distribution of human power and resources led Mao Zedong to define the resolution of the contradiction between coast and interior as one of the principal goals of the Chinese Communist Party and state system. Many strategies have been employed to stem the flow of population from the interior to the coast and from the countryside to the city. There have also been efforts to shift human and material resources into the interior and to encourage the formation of small- and medium-size cities in every part of China. In one such attempt to redress the imbalance between city and countryside, Shanghai's party and state apparatus relocated more than 45 percent of the city's industrial base, including skilled labor, between 1949 and the beginning of the Cultural Revolution in 1966. The interior cities of Xi'an and Lanzhou were among the principal beneficiaries. These efforts have employed varying degrees of coercion and persuasion. On close examination, all reveal the tension between the central government's desire for control and the needs, interests, and commitments of the citizenry at the local level.

By the mid-1950s, control of migration from the countryside rested on a system of residence passes, rationing, and surveillance. Work units and neighborhood committees were required to register and monitor residents. These organizations also became the sources of ration certificates for the purchase of food, clothing, and raw materials as well as for the use of transportation facilities. Work units and neighborhood committees frequently altered the certificates to prevent fraud. Rural migrants found it difficult to survive without access to goods and services. If they were lucky, relatives, friends, and schoolmates who received urban benefits might help them out.

Whenever population pressures, periodic famines, or floods sent waves of people into the cities and overwhelmed the system of control, city residents, public security forces, and the police were mobilized to force unwanted migrants back to the countryside. These measures, successful in the short run, have failed to stem the general tide of rural-urban migration. Between 1982 and 1990, approximately 90 million people became urbanites. Although part of the increase in east coast urban population is attributable to the absorption of contiguous suburban areas within city boundaries (a reflection of the economic transformations experienced by suburban regions formerly classified as "rural"), demographers credit much of the increase to migration rather than the reclassification of administrative boundaries.

The city of Guangzhou demonstrates how easily the system of control can be overwhelmed when faced with mass and sudden migration. On the eve of the Chinese New Year celebrations in February 1989, rural migrants exploded into one of China's most prosperous cities under the new economic reforms. The city's population of 3.5 million increased by 2 million in less than a month. At the peak of this spontaneous infusion of population, more than 100,000 migrants poured into the area each day. Guangzhou and other cities of the increasingly prosperous South and East China regions were ordered to close their gates to new arrivals. Trains to the city were suspended; illegal migrants were rounded up, herded onto available trains, and returned to their homes. The example of Guangzhou indicates how fragile the balance is between rural and urban society in the face of rapid economic and political change.

This chaotic pattern of population migration co-exists with a more stable, long-term trend toward the growth of small and medium cities. But while small cities and towns in the interior have been growing, coastal cities are particularly advantaged by their links to the international marketplace. Since the implementation of the "open door" policy in 1978, the coastal cities have bargained successfully for a greater role in the economic modernization of China.

"To the Countryside"

Political campaigns, although principally designed to serve ideological and organizational purposes, have also served as a means of controlling the movement of China's people. Campaigns of the early and mid-1950s mobilized students, teachers, and administrative and party cadres to go "to the countryside" and develop the hinterland. Unlike stints of short-term, voluntary labor, these mobilizations celebrated deliberate and permanent downward mobility as a sign of willingness to share the lives of the peasantry. Such efforts helped to meet the general goal of balanced development and installed Han populations in minority regions. Many intellectuals found the experience exhilarating. For them it was a spiritual and material journey from a stigmatized bourgeois identity to a socialist persona. Most important, it legitimated the active participation of young intellectuals in China's national project.

The efficacy of political campaigns as a means of controlling certain segments of the population was demonstrated anew with the Anti-Rightist campaign of 1957. This ideological movement segregated China's intelligentsia by class. Those from bourgeois or landlord families were sent into the countryside as "rightists" and "counterrevolutionaries" and subjected to harsh physical labor for indefinite periods of time. Their education, careers, and family lives were shattered by this forced migration. The Anti-Rightist campaign, followed by the Cultural Revolution (1966-1976), made temporary exiles of nearly 20 million people.

By 1978, exiles sent down during the Cultural Revolution began to return to coastal cities, swelling the ranks of "youth awaiting employment" (*daiye qingnian*). Their return placed an enormous burden on the national budget. The central government's effort to cope with the strain stimulated the inauguration of a private sector in the urban economy. In this case, political and economic forces converged to enhance the role of the cities in the south and along the east coast. Now at the forefront of modernization and change, these cities suffer the consequences of overcrowding, pollution, and corruption.

Age and the Politics of Intergenerational Relations

China has a young population. In this respect it is not unlike many other nations undergoing rapid economic development, and, like other nations, its population is gradually aging. This change affects society in many ways. In terms of mortality, the number of industrial accidents may decline as the average age of factory workers increases. At the same time, death from diseases, particularly cancer and respiratory ailments, will probably claim more lives. Indeed, statistics already reflect an increase in deadly cancer and respiratory ailments in urban China, while diseases of the digestive track still play a key role in rural mortality.

Veneration of the aged, filial piety, and the centrality of family have always ensured that the aged would be cared for by their heirs. A corollary of shifts in age structure and attitudes toward the aged places a new burden on the state to maintain the elderly.

Ideological Piety, Age, and the Cultural Revolution

Changing age structures have political and social implications. The Chinese Communist Party utilized veneration for the aged to achieve its goals. At the same time, it attempted to instill a new veneration, not unlike filial piety, for the workers and peasantry and for the legendary accomplishments of the Chinese Communist movement. Throughout the 1950s and 1960s, peasants and workers of advanced age were hailed as role models for the young. Many of them were honored as heroes and exemplars of Communist virtue.

Frequently these older people were called upon to tell their stories in schools and places of work. They attended role model conferences and were publicly acclaimed. Their histories were recorded and compiled by young people, who acquired revolutionary merit through this act. The self-esteem of those fortunate enough to have been accorded such adulation was undoubtedly enhanced, while there is ample evidence that those peasants and workers not selected as role models also derived pleasure and confidence from propaganda that paid them homage.

The highest social and economic privileges were reserved for those who served the Chinese Communist movement. These men and women were ranking party, army, and administrative cadres who joined the party and served the state at strategic junctures in its history. Classified by "revolutionary age," starting with the founding of the Chinese Communist Party in 1921, party and state cadres were placed in a rank order that established salary levels, pensions, access to chauffeured limousines, and opportunities for schooling, including access to travel and education abroad for themselves and their dependents. This system was most effective in creating and sustaining gerontocratic rule, and its disassembly since reform in the late 1970s has been a painful process.

Intergenerational Relations and the Manufacture of Deviance

Age could be a distinct liability for people whose family histories were infected with an ideological virus. Labels or "hats" (literally, duncecaps) were imposed on families with links to the Kuomintang or to Western countries before and after 1949. As mass campaigns followed one after another in the 1950s and 1960s, the catalog of ideological sins expanded, as did the numbers of the accused. After the Hundred Flowers campaign and the subsequent Anti-Rightist campaign, young intellectuals were labeled as one of the "five bad elements," the general term for stigmatized groups in Chinese society. The Cultural Revolution witnessed the invention of such new generic labels as "snakes and monsters" for the ideologically deviant.

The sons and daughters of those who had been "capped" inherited this negative status just as the sons and daughters of revolutionary heroes inherited privileges. While rectification campaigns provided opportunities to "uncap" those who had been erroneously labeled, it was difficult to reverse a verdict. Once the verdict was entered into personnel records of schools and enterprises, it became an easy matter to flag the records of those whose family backgrounds would make them targets for the labeling process. The recurrent identification of the sons and daughters of "capped" parents as deviants led party activists to conclude that ideological deviance was heritable and inescapable.

The sociological import of the process of labeling is demonstrated by a phenomenon that occurred first in 1957 and again during the Cultural Revolution. It was known as the thesis of being "naturally red and naturally black" (ziran hong, ziran hei). A frustrated popular response to the repeated confessions of elderly intellectuals, this thesis held that class was innate and intellectuals were incapable of reform. Both Mao Zedong and Zhou Enlai publicly denounced this idea as incompatible with basic party principles on educability. Nevertheless, it persisted and was a powerful demonstration of the system's ability to manufacture deviance.

Those who were accused of being class enemies or ideologically stigmatized had very limited options. They could seek to escape China, risking imprisonment and possibly death. Or they could accept their fate as permanent outsiders and endure constant persecution. Some found niches within the system where they could win acceptance in spite of the ideological labels in their records. Some found respite and recognition in the countryside, where their skills were valued above their political credentials. The young, however, were actively encouraged by the party to denounce their elders and prove their commitment to the party and Chairman Mao as ideological activists. This course also held dangers, but it was very tempting for many young people who saw it as giving them a chance to obtain the power and status they were denied as birthright.

During the Cultural Revolution, people from families with power fared no better than those from stigmatized families. Factionalism and the determination of Chinese Communist Party leaders to purify class ranks led to attacks even on members of the political elite. The Gang of Four sought out "capitalist roaders" in the party and state apparatus and pitted the young against their elders in the name of loyalty to Mao. The Cultural Revolution stretched the fissures in Chinese society between and within groups. This movement stimulated class conflict and exacerbated intraclass, cross-generational antipathies as well. It made uneasy and unlikely partners out of Red Guard rebels of diverse backgrounds, who resorted to factional warfare to resolve their differences. Finally, the People's Liberation Army used its superior weaponry to bring the Cultural Revolution to a close.

Gerontocracy and the Aftermath of the Cultural Revolution

At the end of the Cultural Revolution in 1976, there was an attempt to reform the grip of the older generation on the party. In 1949 approximately 26 percent of party members were under twenty-five years of age; by the early 1980s only 5 percent were this young. Leading a reformist coalition, Deng Xiaoping pensioned off large numbers of aging cadres. A "third echelon" of more than 160,000 "reserve" party cadres under age forty-five provided a recruitment pool at every level of administration. By 1987, the party counted 13 million new members, two-thirds of whom were under thirty-five years old.

This singular attack on gerontocracy had its limits. Senior party cadres frequently promoted their children into the ranks of the "third echelon." On the eve of the demonstrations at Tiananmen in the spring of 1989, young activists mocked this abuse of the reform effort as an initiative of the "party of the princes" (*taizi dang*). The return of the old guard to power at the time of the violence at Tiananmen stifled follow-up measures, although there is evidence that the "reserves" have ascended into mid- and higher-rank positions since 1989.

After the arrest of the Gang of Four, intellectuals and professionals who had been sent to the countryside for re-education and hard labor returned to their universities, laboratories, and enterprises. Some came back to higher salaries, enhanced status, and, in many cases, restored family properties. Students whose training had been interrupted by the Cultural Revolution were permitted to take university entrance exams and complete missing course work. For a few years in the early and mid-1980s even the marital prospects of intellectuals improved. Their progress was checked, however, by budgetary restraints on the growth of educational institutions, and more importantly, by the failure to launch and sustain a political reform agenda.

The Tiananmen demonstrations of 1989 were the culmination of protests against corruption, nepotism, and authoritarian rule. The Tiananmen incident in June dealt a severe blow to the ideals of both older and younger intellectuals and professionals. The Tiananmen demonstrators, most of them students, represented older moderate reformers and radical reformers, as well as the young revolutionaries who advocated total systemic transformation.

In the wake of Tiananmen, the status of intellectuals underwent even greater changes. Chinese students abroad contemplated long-term exile. At home, they faced repression and ideological re-education. Older intellectuals, with few options available, occupied what was left of the ramparts of academic institutions. Marital prospects for intellectuals declined again. Many who were cleared of wrongdoing escaped academe, the site of repeated anti-intellectual campaigns, to assume posts in the burgeoning new economic sector created by the open door policy. A new rift was thus introduced between the generations in the early 1990s.

Intergenerational Relations in the Countryside

The context for intergenerational relations in rural China starts with the collectivization of agriculture. From the mid-1950s until the 1970s, peasant producers were mobilized into ever-larger collective farming enterprises. Private ownership gave way to collective ownership. Membership in early collectives, called "mutual aid teams" and "lower-level agricultural cooperatives," was voluntary, but voluntarism gave way to coercion thereafter. Remuneration for farm work and the division of labor was by plan. Although peasants had access to private plots, state policies and ideological campaigns limited private production and open market sales. The state was the principal purchaser of farm products. In the late 1950s, an attempt was made to organize the peasantry into people's communes—multifunctional, self-sustaining collective communities. China's entire farming population was eventually divided into 24,000 such communes.

The social ramifications of these policies were considerable. Most important was that the collectivization of agriculture brought the party/state system directly into the lives of China's peasantry. The resistance of family and clan to central control certainly remained, but was muted. Everything from road repair to birth control and health care reached rural populations through the communes; so did ideological mobilization. But overzealousness led to some of the most unhappy failures of the commune system, such as the campaign to produce backyard steel, efforts to universalize deep planting, attempts to replace separate family dining patterns with communal mess halls, and the attempt to break women out of the confines of the family and into communal labor. These failures were partially responsible for the massive famine of the early 1960s that followed the Great Leap Forward.

Starting in the early 1970s, in an effort to improve farm productivity, the countryside witnessed both the dissolution of the commune and the devolution of economic decision making from collective systems to heads of households through the so-called household responsibility system. By and large, these reforms seemed to serve the interests of elder patriarchs. Their authority over matters concerning women and the young in their families was substantially enhanced. Some men decided to remove their children from rural schools and utilize their labor, since produce could now be sold in the free market. The maintenance of grain reserves, roads, schools, medical facilities, and irrigation dikes suffered. Old marriage customs, banqueting, fortune-telling, and lavish birthday and wedding celebrations began to return as the Maoist normative order disappeared. In suburban areas close to major metropolitan centers, families abandoned agricultural work to enter the service sector or perform contract labor. Where egalitarian lifestyles once predominated, income differentials began to appear.

In remote rural areas, the redistribution of authority may have had little if any impact. People in abject poverty were already locked into traditional patterns of authority weighted in favor of aging heads of households. In areas along major rail and roadways, closer to urban centers, new income-generating possibilities were sufficiently diverse to give the young and the old, women and men something to negotiate about. The younger generation brought significant additions of labor power and productivity to the family and thus could claim a voice in the division of labor and profit and in decisions about marriage, residence, and career. Later marriage meant that women had more labor power to allocate to their natal families.

Equally important, no matter what their attitude toward the events at Tiananmen in 1989, rural families share a deep hunger for the material trappings of modernity. Eager to catch up with the rest of the world and unwilling to wait patiently for China to modernize, even remote towns and villages work to acquire the consumer goods and styles that seem the epitome of modern taste. Taste is now being defined by the urban young. Cynical about ideology and alienated from politics, they look unabashedly to Taiwan, Singapore, and the West for models of dress, deportment, product quality, entertainment, and lifestyle.

Chinese Communism and the Emancipation of Women

The pursuit of gender equality in China predates the history of the Communist Party. The Taiping Rebellion of the late nineteenth century served as an early model of the struggle to free women from such feudal practices as concubinage, foot-binding, prohibitions against widow remarriage, and the "three obeisances": to fathers, husbands, and sons. The Taiping Rebellion armed women and placed men and women warriors under female commanders as a step toward achieving the Taiping millennium. Taiping leaders later abandoned these goals but subsequent revolutionary movements drew upon them for inspiration. Early revolutionary movements to overthrow the Qing dynasty included women who became heroines and martyrs to their cause. Women joined men in mobilizing support for a revitalized China.

The Republic of China, under the leadership of Sun Yat-sen, came into existence in 1911. Women were already entering the burgeoning urban industrial labor force and joining Nationalist (Kuomintang) associations for the emancipation of women. They were also prime candidates for recruitment into the Chinese Communist Party after its formation in 1921. Laboring under grossly exploitative conditions, women could be found in both leadership and rank-and-file positions in the urban labor movement. The young Mao Zedong played a key role in mobilizing women students against the warlord governor of Hunan. Both his early writings and his statements in support of women, including their education abroad, revealed a sensitivity to women's issues. Mao made the emancipation of women a priority in his plan to build a socialist society.

In 1927 Chiang Kai-shek, Sun Yat-sen's successor as leader of the Kuomintang, engineered a massacre of left-wing workers in Shanghai, which not only decimated the CCP membership but frightened off potential members. The result was a decline in the number of enrollees in the Communist Party, particularly women, who formed the majority of those workers. Under the leadership of Mao Zedong and Zhu De, the Communist Party core retreated to the mountains of Jiangxi Province, where many peasant women were recruited. As members of the Jiangxi Soviet (1930-1934), these women were assigned to leadership roles and encouraged to improve the status of women by rewriting regulations dealing with distribution of land and marriage and divorce.

The retreat from Jiangxi and the Long March (1934-1935) took a heavy toll on both men and women. Women suffered the largest losses, but the years in Yan'an provided sufficient respite to re-establish the party's commitment to them and resuscitate the cause of women's emancipation. Women played critical roles in the anti-Japanese war (1937-1945) and land reform efforts both before and after 1949.

By 1949, the CCP had accumulated more than twenty-five years of experience in the cause of women's emancipation. Despite the ideological commitment to equality, ambiguities in party policy and practice were already apparent before 1949. Both the ambiguities and the commitment continued to inform interpretations of the party's approach to gender relations.

During the early history of peasant mobilization, there were already complaints that women's concerns and the female leaders who expressed them were being deliberately ignored because of the party leadership's desire to woo male heads of households to the Communist cause. In Yan'an, as the party pursued wartime united front policies designed to draw support from every sector of society against the Japanese, women's demands for an end to feudal marriage practices were muted. Although this position was reversed after the Communist victory, episodes like these gave credence to the charge that the party, principally composed of men who were themselves socialized in a patriarchal society, was acting as a superpatriarch. Women were denied agency as the party determined the time and extent of women's emancipation, and nationalism took precedence over feminism.

Marriage, Divorce, and Family

With the Marriage Law of 1950, however, the party's commitment to women was announced clearly and unambiguously. Drawing on the marriage reg-

ulations of the Jiangxi Soviet, the law gave men and women equal right to enter into a free-choice, monogamous marriage. The new code banned arranged marriages and conferred investigatory powers on marriage registration organs to prevent parental or third-party interference. Minimum legal ages for marriage (eighteen for women and twenty for men) were established by law. Bigamy, concubinage, and child marriage were banned; prohibitions against widow remarriage were outlawed. Local government was made responsible for the registration of marriages and divorces in cases of mutual agreement. Contested divorces were subject to mediation and an appeals process. Special protection was accorded to marriages involving People's Liberation Army soldiers.

In cases of divorce involving children, the best interests of the children constituted the basis for the division of property and responsibility. Both parties to a divorce were made responsible for mutual economic support in the face of financial crisis. Where wives had custody of the children, former husbands bore responsibility for support; where husbands held custody, this duty was not reciprocal. The Marriage Law declared that each party to a marriage had equal right to hold a job, equal access to society, equal status at home, and equal right to possess property and dispose of property. Both parties shared the responsibility for constructing a socialist society.

Apart from the special protection of soldiers' marriages, the law was advanced and progressive. When it was replaced by the Marriage Law of 1980, its basic provisions were reiterated. The duty of family planning was added to the list of responsibilities assumed by the parties to a marriage. As in many societies, however, the problem was not in the provisions of the law but in their implementation.

The Marriage Law was drafted while a civil war was being waged, which in itself indicates the importance attached to it and the role of women in its drafting and promulgation. The law was made available to cadres implementing land reform so that the redistribution of confiscated land and tools would give substance to legal guarantees of property rights for women. There were, however, impressive obstacles to its implementation.

When the campaign method was applied to the Marriage Law's implementation, both the overzealousness of its proponents and the passions of the resistors, in and outside the party, led to the victimization of women. Many women who sought to take advantage of the provisions of the law, particularly widows seeking remarriage, were killed or driven to commit suicide. Some women committed suicide because their husbands, often party members, connived with local cadres to dissolve unwanted marriages. Both the agents and the targets of the law were steeped in family and clan dominion over marriage and marital customs at a time when the party's organizational infrastructure in rural China was still weak and transitional. Ten thousand women were reported to have been murdered or to have committed suicide in South China in 1951. By 1955, the numbers had jumped to seventy thousand or eighty thousand, and even these are likely to have been underestimates.

Some analysts have pointed out that during the civil war, the peasantry found common cause with the Chinese Communists no matter what the shape of their policy. This generalization may be based on peasant response to land reform, the civil war, and the anti-Japanese war, but it clearly did not apply to the implementation of the Marriage Law. Furthermore, the Marriage Law continued to meet intense resistance into the mid-1950s.

When the Marriage Law was promulgated, the Chinese Communists were just emerging from their guerrilla base areas in the hinterland to assume control of the cities. They were not anticipating the complete collapse of the Kuomintang's forces. Many cadres, including young intellectuals who joined Mao Zedong and Zhu De in Yan'an, expected to spend a considerable portion of their lives in rural China. They married peasant women and then found their mates ill-adapted to the urban posts to which they were reassigned after 1949. Some sought divorce; others maintained the fiction of marriage and sought better-educated, urban companions. The pages of *Zhongguo Funu* (Women of China) in the mid-1950s carried letters from across the country responding to cases of high-ranking party and administrative cadres who had abandoned their spouses. This too may have informed male cadres' willingness to

use the provisions and procedures of the Marriage Law for their own ends. By 1953, the emphasis had shifted away from campaigns to implement the law toward the use of more gradual education and propaganda on its behalf.

There was, however, another subtle shift toward accommodation with more conservative social forces. Radical land reform targeted landlord and rich peasant families. Land reform cadres mobilized peasants to attack their exploiters in "speak bitterness" rallies. The children and spouses of targeted individuals were often pressured to denounce parents and spouses publicly. Executions followed, and the redistribution of land and possessions closed the process. Although excessive force was condemned, it was not far-fetched to conclude that the party intended to do away with the family altogether. In the course of urban campaigns to remove capitalist families from control of productive assets, similar techniques called "tiger beating" were employed. These tactics also aroused fears that the party was assuming an antifamily stance. To mollify such fears, party leaders leaned toward compromise.

There were other considerations as well. The nationalization of industry and the collectivization of agriculture were difficult undertakings by any accounting. More violence and resistance accompanied the collectivization of agriculture between 1953 and 1955 than is generally acknowledged. There was a strong temptation then to effect some compromises with the family and clan system in order to maximize cohesion. Furthermore, the shift from guerrilla war strategy and tactics before 1949 to responsibility for state and society as a whole led party leaders toward the management of change within a larger framework of order and stability.

Finally, the Sino-Soviet alliance in the 1950s yielded massive new projects to build industries in the cities. Either because they sought to avoid collectivization drives in the countryside or because they were attracted to new job openings in the city, rural laborers, mostly male, headed for urban centers. Their fear that they might be competing with women for places in the labor force helped to produce a new emphasis on family, family stability, and women's responsibilities as housewives. Women were urged to abandon the workplace and return to the family. An emerging literature defined the new socialist family as the nucleus of post-liberation society and the protection of its interests as a primary responsibility of the party and state. In news articles and guidebooks, "semi-arranged marriages" were legitimized, and the responsibilities of women for home care and child-rearing received special emphasis. On the eve of the Hundred Flowers movement of 1957, a little-known movement to "prettify" women urged women to break out of their blue worksuits, the unisex uniform of the day, to wear skirts, colorful blouses, scarves, and stylish shoes. The subsequent Anti-Rightist campaign reversed this initiative, however, and, after a brief respite in the early 1960s, Red Guards used their authority in the early stages of the Cultural Revolution to punish women who had long hair or wore makeup, bell-bottom slacks, colorful blouses, or Hong Kong shoes.

The domestication of women was also offset in the mid- and late 1950s by expanded opportunities for education, including higher education, and the recruitment of women into the growing ranks of the All-China Women's Federation and the Communist Youth League. The latter served as a training ground for political activists and an organizational support system and recruitment base for the Chinese Communist Party. Their combined impact on attitudes and values of urban youth was particularly significant. Furthermore, these organizations, the organizational infrastructure that underlay rural cooperativization, and the communes by the late 1950s, gave the party/state system additional leverage over the rural families and clans that resisted women's emancipation.

Comradeship and Companionate Marriage

The cultivation of comradeship throughout the party/state system played an important role in gender relations. The concept of "comradeship" has its most proximate origins in Marxist-Leninist ideology, but it also resonated with traditional family values in the relationships between "elder brothers" and "younger sisters" before marriage. Comradeship offered a degree of cross-gender intimacy not common

among outsiders to the family and, at the same time, cast men in the role of the protectors of their "younger sisters." These attitudes and values helped to pave the way for cooperative work relationships in every type of urban setting. Equipped with the values of comradeship, the Youth League could legitimize its role in organizing parties and dances for young people and serving as a channel for matchmaking. Companionate marriage, outside the control of parents but with their tacit consent, received an added boost from urban party and Youth League organization and values.

Comradeship was a limited instrument for the achievement of sexual equality. The concept was itself flawed by its emphasis on women's need for protection. If women "held up half the world," in the parlance of the times, they did so without complete agency. Since women were considered an exploited collectivity, deviance among women could be explained only in terms of manipulation by landlords, counterrevolutionaries, and bad elements. For that reason, women needed the protection of the party/state system.

In the countryside, the notion of comradeship came up against entrenched patterns of sexual segregation. Radical experiments in the late 1950s, designed to release women from household labor to participate in the management of the people's communes, failed. The attack on families of the intelligentsia that accompanied the Anti-Rightist campaign once again raised the specter of an antifamily drive, and such attacks were repeated during the Cultural Revolution. Spouses denounced each other in an effort to keep at least one spouse safe from criticism, punishment, hard labor, possible imprisonment, and torture. Some intellectuals were permanently removed from the marriage market because of the ideological labels they carried. Thus, comradeship and all it entailed was undermined by political and ideological factionalism.

The zigzag course of what is often described as the "two-line struggle" between bureaucratization and routinization, on the one hand, and revolutionary class struggle, on the other, also influenced marriage practices. In the mid-1950s, when young engineers held pride of place as both "red and expert" (that is, both ideologically committed and technologically skilled), they also occupied a place of prominence in the marriage market. In the course of the Great Leap Forward, peasant activists displaced engineers. The cycle of preferences continued into and beyond the Cultural Revolution. In the 1980s, following the implementation of the open door policy and economic reform, a new group reached preeminence in the marriage market: young, promising entrepreneurs.

The Impact of Reforms on Marriage

By the 1980s, the marriage market was also undergoing other types of radical change. With the introduction of the household responsibility system, peasant families who had the resources and skills were released from their dependence on the land they had farmed for generations. While some men took advantage of the opportunity to contract out their labor, leaving women in charge of farming, some young women took the opportunity to leave their villages for brighter economic prospects in the city. The distances they traveled were considerable.

In the mid-1970s, a veritable flood of young women from northern Jiangsu entered Beijing to seek work as housemaids in the homes of intellectuals. The very notion that women would assume roles that would have been ideologically unacceptable in times past was an indication of how radical a change this was. The Beijing Women's Federation took responsibility for placing women into the right households and for overseeing contracts and work conditions. Their rationale for doing so was that rural women needed intermediate safe havens from which they might gradually make their way into the modern commercial and industrial sector. Housemaids could take courses via television in their spare time and become accustomed to modern city life without suffering its worst features. Their presence led, however, to protests from intellectual women over the age of thirty-five, who argued that the young women from Jiangsu were attracting older men and ruining older and more independent women's prospects for marriage or remarriage. The

Women's Federation, which was already acting as a dating and counseling agency for middle-aged unmarried and divorced women, had to balance such complaints against the needs of young women migrants from the countryside.

There were indications that the pace of change also quickened in the 1980s. Divorce rates, though never very high, had been climbing since the end of the Cultural Revolution. These rates were affected, in part, by an epidemic of "rash" marriages that followed the Cultural Revolution. These marriages probably reflected young people's hunger for pair relationships over the ideological ties that had bound the violently contentious Red Guard factions. It also reflected a rebellion against delayed marriage.

Other changes were also taking place. In 1985 some thirty-eight thousand divorces were registered in Beijing. While these numbers are small, their significance was more than numerical. An analysis of the cases demonstrates that most involved charges of physical abuse taken to court by rural women against their husbands. This situation marks a radical change in traditional and even modern values. Until that time, rural women were the least likely to bring divorce cases to court, and abuse, tolerated for so long by men and women, was the charge least likely to make it into the courts. These cases, then, marked a significant shift in women's self-assessment and consciousness.

Reports in the 1990s suggest a new phenomenon. The number of women who have never been married and are not seeking marriage seems to be increasing. Men are reported to be suffering from bouts of "bronchitis." They can neither spit out their bitterness (*tu ku*) nor swallow it (*chi ku*), to use the terms of the exploited classes at the time of the Communist takeover. If they wish to find a marriage partner, all they can do is try to clear their throats, sputtering, "Ahem! ahem!" in a fruitless effort to avoid having to deal with independent women who have minds of their own. This type of anecdote suggests that, in the multiple transformations that have governed marriage and marital choice, a second wave of feminist consciousness may now be at hand. This consciousness does not rest on comradeship or on any of the ideologies of the past.

Attitudes toward Sexuality

Evidence for the emergence of a second wave of feminism can found in survey research being undertaken principally by women researchers in China. In 1990, the Shanghai Center for the Study of Sexuality and Society published a summary of a survey undertaken by five hundred researchers in fifteen provinces and cities and twenty-four districts, involving twenty-three thousand respondents. The provinces and cities from which they drew their sample included every major region of the country; minority and Han regions, urban and rural settings, small and large cities were all participants. This work concentrated on three groups: unmarried middle school students, unmarried university students, and married couples.

The study showed that young people are maturing earlier and acquiring greater sexual knowledge at younger ages than in earlier decades, although the degree of understanding varies by region. Children from urbanized coastal regions have greater access to sex education and better knowledge of sexuality than do those from China's interior. University students are more sexually active than has generally been assumed. Their attitudes are a source of concern to the researchers because they are guided neither by customary inhibitions nor by Marxist-Leninist-Maoist ideals. A substantial proportion of these students felt that mutual consent was sufficient basis for intimate relations; few regarded moral responsibility or the danger of sexually transmitted diseases as a serious constraint.

Among married couples, the most startling finding was that more than a third of respondents (in a sample in which women were disproportionately represented) believed they would have been happier if they had married someone else, although more than 90 percent regarded their marriages as "physically satisfying" or "adequate." The apparent contradiction is resolved when the definition of satisfaction is taken into account: that is, a so-so husband, a place to live, clothes to wear, and food to eat. Expectations defined by the past mingle with dreams about the present in this fascinating account of married life.

To sum up the findings, significant percentages of men and women, both urban and rural, have shifted their attitudes from opposition to generally greater tolerance of premarital sex, divorce, and open sexuality. This study warrants particular attention because it gives a rare, intimate glimpse into microsocial aspects of the transition to a postrevolutionary society. The willingness of respondents to offer candid opinions on such topics is also testimony to both the ingenuity of the researchers and the open-mindedness of their subjects.

Some aspects of sexual behavior are linked to political campaigns. The large-scale movements of young people from city to countryside in the aftermath of deviance-control campaigns was particularly difficult for women, who were subject to sexual harassment and exploitation by corrupt and arrogant local cadres and criminals. Statistics are not readily available, but novels, short stories, and autobiographies attest to the incidence of violence against women.

The surveys tell us relatively little about sexual harassment and exploitation in the workplace, particularly in joint venture assembly industries established in China's special economic zones (SEZs) and other areas as part of the open door policy. These enterprises, whose employees are principally young women, are relatively free of interference from central government authority. The managers of SEZ enterprises honor regulations designed to protect women employees largely in the breach. Reports suggest that sexual harassment and exploitation are commonplace. In addition, the SEZs have achieved some notoriety as sites for prostitution and sexually transmitted diseases. While the government and popular attitudes have tended to attribute these phenomena, including the spread of AIDS, to Western influence and presence, surveys like the one discussed here recognize that the lack of sex education at home also plays an important role.

Women and the Workplace: Reform and Its Limitations

Outside the SEZs, in urban state and collective enterprises, the situation of women is ambiguous at best. The ambiguity stems from the state's tendency to regard women as wives and mothers in need of special protection (discussed above) instead of co-equal citizens whose contributions to the society and economy are at least as important as their reproductive capacities.

The protection of women's reproductive role is embodied in legislation introduced in the 1950s and the late 1970s and in regulations enacted in 1986 and 1988. Under the terms of labor insurance regulations, women must retire at fifty; men, at sixty. Efforts to equalize the terms of retirement have failed. Health care and labor regulations passed in 1986 and 1988, respectively, impose limits on the work women can perform. They cannot work at high altitudes or in areas with low temperatures, and they cannot be required to work in cold water if they are menstruating. They cannot be ordered to work overtime or during the night shift if they are pregnant or nursing. They may not perform work that is classified as high grade (in an eight-grade system) during menstruation, pregnancy, and recovery. This provision restricts women's access to higher wages.

Furthermore, enterprises must provide rest facilities, health-care facilities, child care, and nursing rooms if they employ more than a hundred women. Apart from being denied certain kinds of employment, women's productivity is thus defined by their reproductivity, and the cost of providing appropriate benefits leads employers either to deny eligible women job opportunities or to pay women partial salaries to stay out of the work force for periods ranging up to two years. This situation contradicts the 1982 constitution's guarantees of equal rights for women and equal pay for equal work.

Privatization of industry and the migration of men into the cities in search of work once again pits men against women in the intense competition for a place in the work force. Protectionism, however commendable in other terms, reduces women to a prevailing stereotype shared, unfortunately, by both men and women. The stereotype defines women as the weaker sex, whose capacities are innately limited. In a nationwide survey in 1991, 30 percent of women agreed that women were less capable than men. Thus, despite the strides women have made in education, industry, and the professions, there are still traps awaiting them, even in the sectors of the economy most favorable to women's interests.

The attitudinal and behavioral challenges to women's worth in the workplace has led to yet another indicator that many women are responding to bias as part of a second-wave feminist movement to redefine women's place in Chinese society. Debates about protectionist legislation, improvements in enforcement of equal treatment under the law, consciousness raising, and self-empowerment are the tactics of choice. They have supplanted the "storming techniques," so common in ideological campaigns, that sought to mobilize women as co-equals in the establishment of a Communist social order. Those techniques carved out temporary roles for women on the front line of the revolutionary cause, but their position was purchased at the price of long-term economic and social stability, gender equality, and gender justice.

In rural China, reform brought about a transformation in women's working lives. Women were already working in sideline production, in the raising of pigs for sale on the open market, and the cultivation of private plots; but with the institution of the responsibility system in agriculture, many women moved out of agriculture and into full-time posts in town and township industrial enterprises. While both men and women were involved in this transition, the number of women who made the transition to rural industry is impressive. In 1987 women made up 35 percent of the total labor force in rural industry. In the coastal provinces where open door policies produced a booming export trade, women played even more prominent roles. Nearly 48 percent of the workers in rural industry in Fujian and 43 percent in Jiangsu in 1987 were women. Free of economic dependence on their husbands and earning fixed incomes, these women occupy the frontiers of a new social order.

Women constitute a large part of the mobile labor force migrating from rural locales into towns and cities and filling posts in the processing sector. Many have become innovators, opening their own businesses and creating the basis for a nascent service sector. They are also at the bottom of the wage scale, working longer hours than their counterparts in most other societies, in unstable jobs. Nevertheless, the

Despite improvements in the status of women in China, the practice of patriarchy continues in rules of residence and patterns of inheritance.

new roles they play are preferable to those offered in agriculture. More importantly, the rewards for creative and innovative involvement in the emerging commodity economy pay dividends at home. Male peasants, recognizing the value of women's participation in the system, are sharing household work, supporting the education of their daughters, and deliberating on matters of joint concern. Self-empowerment and self-worth are also outcomes of the greater participation of women in the modern sector.

Despite these signals of improvement in the status of women, there are still gross imbalances in employment. In 1986, the distribution of women employed in a sample of villages, provinces, regions, and cities found that women made up more than 36 percent of transfer labor in the east, about 21 percent in central China, and 14 percent in the west. Women are predominantly in lower-level, lower-paid jobs or jobs with low levels of prestige, and they are paid

less than men despite the rhetoric of equal pay for equal work. The practice of patriarchy continues in rules of residence and patterns of inheritance. And the protectionism that applies to women in the industrial sector extends to rural women as well, including the pressures to return home. While modernization and the dissemination of more varied occupational opportunities holds promise for women, there is no certainty that modernity brings equality in its wake.

Social Stratification in China

The establishment of the People's Republic of China in 1949 signaled the triumph of Marxism-Leninism in China and of the thesis of class struggle. The definition and characterization of class background and affiliation were critical in the determination of life chances, particularly at the time of radical land reform, and in the course of countless ideological campaigns since 1949. Indeed, the campaign process is inseparable from the creation of social stratification in China. Campaigns were instruments for labeling individuals with class designations, imputing motives and behavioral predispositions to them, and punishing them for manifesting the backgrounds and predispositions with which they were labeled.

Rural and Urban Stratification

In the countryside, the traditional four-class model of landlords, rich peasants, middle peasants, and poor peasants served as the skeleton on which Mao Zedong overlaid Marxist and Leninist ideological and political predispositions as well as his own interpretation of peasant psychology. He deepened the analysis of rural social structure by distinguishing between upper- and lower-middle peasants. Wedded to feudalism and resistant to the transfer of power in the countryside, landlords and rich peasants were considered little better than counterrevolutionaries and traitors. Upper-middle peasants wavered in their sympathies, while lower-middle and poor peasants were considered the motive force, once effectively organized, for revolutionary social change.

In the North China guerrilla base areas that nurtured the legendary Eighth Route Army, there was little to distinguish between the material possessions of landlords and those of ordinary peasants. But Mao's vision resonated with the poor, who understood, in their own terms, that it was not material possessions but access to power—the power of money through control of loans, the power of the gun through police and hired thugs—that distinguished exploiting from exploited classes. As for the connection to the feudal social order, exploiters and the exploited shared commitments to family and clan, customs and traditions, rules and rituals, and ideals that were not so far removed from the neo-Confucianism of the premodern era as ideological rhetoric made it appear.

By the end of land reform in 1953, landlords had been virtually wiped out as a class, while the ranks of rich peasants were sharply reduced. Land redistribution did much to improve living conditions for the poor and middle peasant allies of the Chinese Communist Party. Collectivization of agriculture served to maintain minimal distances between strata in rural China. There were exceptions, however, including former guerrilla base areas that were left behind in the revolution's sweep into the cities and other mountain and desert enclaves too far from the center of control to have felt the tides of change.

Urban social structure in 1949 was more complicated than the situation in rural areas. There were capitalists, petit bourgeois intellectuals and shopkeepers, workers, enterprise managers, labor gang bosses, soldiers, police, lawyers and judges, loansharks, pimps, prostitutes, and racketeers. Former Kuomintang officials helped to maintain order and secure the transition from military to civilian rule at every level of the urban system.

In a series of campaigns in the early and mid-1950s, which proceeded while China was engaged in the Korean War, urban society was leveled. The property of capitalists was expropriated, and former Kuomintang police, military, and civilian officials were purged of their posts or exposed to front-line fire in Korea. Labor gangs were dismantled as Soviet-style mass organizations took form. The doctrine of the dictatorship of the proletariat, embodied in the provisions for the handling of counterrevolutionaries and traitors in the criminal code, gave muscle to urban social control. The underworld was decimated by imprisonments and executions. Prostitutes underwent thought reform. Soviet-style central planning and the ration, subsidy, and eight-grade wage system put a common floor underneath the bottom strata of China's urban social structure.

The leveling of both rural and urban society allowed Mao Zedong to believe that a basic consensus had been achieved by the late 1950s that would allow the dictatorship of the proletariat to continue to be applied to counterrevolutionaries and traitors, but not to the resolution of differences among the remainder of the country's socialist citizenry. If this was a genuine assessment of the situation, it was rudely disturbed by the Hundred Flowers movement of 1956-1957, in which intellectuals, encouraged and even prodded by Mao Zedong, launched a critique of the Chinese Communist Party. Some analysts regard the criticism as an early, unsuccessful attempt by Mao Zedong to launch a cultural revolution against an increasingly bureaucratized, urban party/state system. Exacerbated by the struggle for succession, class warfare was revitalized in the Anti-Rightist campaign of the summer of 1957. It was in use again in the Great Leap Forward campaign from 1958 to 1959. A campaign designed to check the emergence of a new rich peasantry resuscitated the idea of class conflict in the countryside in the early 1960s. That idea reached its most extreme expression during the Cultural Revolution.

The ensuing years of reform reveal a society that can no longer be described using either traditional or Marxist-Leninist and Maoist terms of reference. There is a new rich peasantry in the countryside, but their wealth rests on a combination of specialized agricultural production and diversified investment in township industry, trade, and services. They can no longer be defined solely in terms of their stake in the land. Successful entrepreneurs in the cities are making mountains of money, but they are doing so through interregional joint ventures and subcontracting projects that combine private initiative and collective institutions. They are mastering managerial skills by building horizontal links between different sectors of the economy. Itinerant skilled and unskilled workers, migrating into towns and cities, are defining a new working class. Part of that class are workers in collective and private enterprises. In addition, a large group of "floating workers" or casual laborers—who work on no established contract, at the fringe of legality—has formed among rural migrants to the cities. They take their place in an urban labor force of approximately 150 million.

Income Inequality

Evidence of income inequality is not hard to come by. More than 70 million peasants in western and interior provinces of China were said to be living in dire poverty in 1990, and disparity is evident even between households in the same locale as an expression of differential resources and skills. In some regions where the distance between top and bottom incomes was once approximately 3:1, the ratio has increased to 5:1. Reform, however, has produced rapidly rising incomes and rising living standards overall, and as part of the constant cycle of change, increases in rural purchasing power have exceeded urban rates of increase, first in 1986 and again in 1989.

It may not, however, be actual income differential that has the greatest impact on the expectations and concerns of China's populace. Many of China's urban citizens suffer from "red eye disease" (*hongyan bing*). This term refers to the envy felt by urbanites who see peasants enjoying more living space than they do, as well as luxury goods, tourism, comfortable travel, and cash to spare. Expectations are changing so significantly that the central government must attempt to cope with conflicting demands for control of inflation, subsidization of housing and transportation, gender equality, and price control as new groups with uncertain prospects take form.

What is most interesting about changes in social stratification is that new alliances are being formed and new organizational linkages are taking place that challenge the vertical, hierarchical order of the past. These changes define new, more innovative roles for trade unions, youth organizations, and women's federations as they take on service roles to meet the needs of more diverse constituencies. The motives and political inclinations of these diverse constituen-cies cannot simply be imputed as they were at the time the People's Republic was founded in 1949.

Minorities and Religion in China

According to the 1990 census, China's fifty-five minorities account for only 8 percent of the country's total population (see Table 8.1). That proportion, however, amounts to more than 91 million people, the majority of whom are from regions that span the length of China's border with Russia, the new Central Asian states, and Mongolia. The minority population presents something of a paradox in the study of Chinese society. While the groups classified as minorities are quite diverse in terms of population size, language, customs, beliefs, and lifestyle, they share the distinct characteristic of being quintessentially "other"—exotic, even erotic, non-Han peoples. At the same time, the term *minority* sometimes refers to groups of people now indistinguishable from the Han, such as the Manchus and the Zhuang. Both have intermarried with Han Chinese over a considerable period of time. Neither have distinctive customs or language that mark them off from the Han. Thus, the general category of "minority" refers both to groups that have integrated almost entirely into Han life and to those with quite distinct cultures, languages, and customs.

In terms of the historical relationship between the Chinese Communist Party and the minorities, the differences between groups are substantial. Before 1949, Han organizers were aided by committed Marxist comrades from Mongol, Korean, and Hui (Muslim) backgrounds. The help of these minority groups in assuring the party's survival during the Long March is partly recognized in the autonomy they have been granted since. The establishment of a relationship with the peoples of Xinjiang and Tibet took longer and was complicated by the hostility of Tibetans to repeated occupation by Han colonizers of every stripe during the past century.

The elaborate process by which minority status is conferred allows room for negotiation between interested groups and central government authorities. The stakes can be quite high since classification as a minority brings subsidies, special educational opportu-

Table 8.1 China's Ethnic Composition, 1990

	Number (millions)	Percent of total population
Han	1,042.50	91.96
Zhuang	15.50	1.37
Manchu	9.82	0.87
Hui	8.60	0.76
Miao	7.40	0.65
Uighur	7.21	0.64
Yi	6.57	0.58
Tujia	5.70	0.50
Mongolian	4.80	0.42
Tibetan	4.60	0.41
Bouyei	2.54	0.22
Dong	2.51	0.22
Yao	2.13	0.19
Korean	1.92	0.17
Bai	1.59	0.14
Hani	1.25	0.11
Kazakh	1.11	0.10
Li	1.11	0.10
Dai	1.03	0.09
Others	5.70	0.50
Total	1,133.59	100.00

Source: 1990 census.

The Hui, or Muslims, like this elderly man from Xi'an, are among China's major non-Han population groups. Minority status has conferred on China's ethnic groups special educational opportunities, subsidies, and, for a time, exemption from the one-child policy.

nities (including access to higher education through the National Minority Institutes), support for publications and dissemination of information in minority languages, and, for a time between 1979 and 1990, waiver of the one-child policy. Most important, classification as a minority provides administrative autonomy. In the centralized party/state system, autonomy is never assured, but it has been taken seriously in the interests of China's interethnic united front and the security of China's frontiers, where significant minority populations reside.

From 1949 to the late 1950s, the party made serious efforts to recruit minorities under Mao Zedong's dictum that autonomous minority leadership was essential to the success of the party's mission in minority territories. Han cadres lived and worked among minority people, created minority councils, relied on minority advice and opinion, and succeeded in establishing a system where genuine autonomy was briefly enjoyed. Out of this effort came a group of reliable minority allies, particularly among the Mongols. At

rare moments in history, cross-border ties among minority peoples were treated as benefits rather than liabilities.

During the mid-1950s, when China made a bid for third world leadership under the policy of "peaceful coexistence," the minorities and their religious leaders served as models of China's willingness to accommodate autonomy and cultural difference. As the architect of the Five Principles of Peaceful Coexistence, Premier Zhou Enlai was particularly sensitive to the importance of the role of minorities and their leadership. He was unable, however, to stave off the much more chauvinistic approach to Beijing's relations with minorities that occurred when the Cultural

Revolution took its toll on minorities and religious institutions.

The benefits conferred on China's minorities must therefore be weighed against the burdens they bear. Most occupy territorial domains along China's 5,000-mile border with Russia and the new Central Asian states, on the Tibetan Plateau separating China from India, Pakistan, and Afghanistan, or in the Himalayan border lands of China's extreme southwest bordering on Vietnam, Burma (Myanmar), and Nepal. All these regions have historically had contested boundaries, and all have been sites of military conflict since 1949. In the course of China's various regional conflicts, minority peoples who share identities across porous boundaries have either been pitted against one another or have found themselves in the unenviable position of being the targets of hostile forces on both sides of their borders. The Korean War, the Sino-Indian border campaign of 1961, the Sino-Soviet conflict of the late 1960s, and the Sino-Vietnamese conflict of the 1970s and 1980s have been cases in point.

Minorities and Party Policies

Poverty is the continuing burden of the minorities in border regions. Although they occupy areas rich in natural resources, including oil and mineral reserves, China's minorities are rarely the principal beneficiaries of development. The process of modernization has been hampered by the long distances to ports and markets and the high cost of transportation in areas of limited accessibility.

But there have been other barriers, too, including the slow spread of medical services to minority regions, the incompatibility of the nomadic and semi-nomadic lifestyles of many of the minorities with the urban orientation of the Han, prejudice and discrimination, sheer arrogance, and abuse of administrative authority and power. During the Great Leap Forward, Muslim Hui were forced to eat pork in communal dining halls. This and many other examples of ignorance and arrogance illustrate how collaboration in the early and mid-1950s had given way to "Great Han chauvinism" by the late 1950s.

The barriers to collaboration were many between Han and non-Han minorities. Few Han cadres spoke non-Han languages. Living conditions in some nomadic regions were extremely trying. High altitude sickness afflicted Han cadres and the PLA soldiers who occupied Tibet in 1950 or moved into Tibet to suppress rebellion in 1959, and the dependents of Han cadres and soldiers who moved into minority regions. In Tibet, collaborators with the Han risked mutilation and death at the hands of fellow Tibetans.

However difficult conditions were, the response of the Han in the course of the Great Leap Forward was harsh. Cadres promised to eliminate vestiges of feudalism within three years by forcing changes in everything from dress to beliefs and customary practices, a process that struck minority regions particularly hard. The effort failed. In its aftermath, the party was sufficiently sensitive to call off the Anti-Rightist campaign in Tibet and refrain from implementation of radical reforms, although these compromises were undone by the Cultural Revolution.

Religion and Secularism

During the Cultural Revolution, impatient with the segregated minority elites produced by earlier compromises, Han chauvinist Red Guards launched attacks on traditional minority leaders and the remnants of separate minority beliefs, customs, and practices, and the institutions that supported them. Mosques, temples, and churches were destroyed, and monks and nuns defrocked, beaten, and tortured. Libraries were torched and artifacts and statuary defaced in an orgy of violence against the remnants of "feudalism."

A trend toward secularism among the young was already under way before the Cultural Revolution, and it has continued since 1976. Secularism among China's approximately 14 million Muslims has been a continuing phenomenon, for example, despite the rise of Islamic fundamentalism elsewhere and occasional signs of its influence on Chinese believers. The constitution's protection of the freedom to believe or not to believe in religion was used as the basis for campaigns designed to eliminate "superstition." Deep, historically driven antipathy to popular religions as sources of rebellion or foreign domination have frequently justified suppression of religious practices and institutions throughout China.

Yet, despite these secularist trends, the tenacity of religious believers has been demonstrated at every interlude between campaigns. The rebuilding of temples and monasteries has proceeded apace in the era of reform. To the genuine commitment of religious believers has been added the monetary incentive of religious tourism. Older women among the devotees of the Buddhist goddess Guanyin mix with wealthy tourists from Taiwan at the Guanyin Temple on Putuo Island. Pilgrims, mostly women, climb the five sacred mountains, attend religious fairs, and visit sites all over China, singing the praises of Guanyin. Overseas Chinese investors have refurbished Buddhist, Daoist, and Confucian shrines, while reformist leaders, Deng Xiaoping in particular, have committed the resources of the state to rebuilding the Tibetan monasteries and training lamas, monks, and nuns.

Since the end of the Cultural Revolution, party policy has cautiously returned to a revival of autonomous rule and at least a rhetorical commitment to equal treatment and developmental priority for minorities. School reform is also under way. Nine years of schooling is now mandated in minority regions to counter the effects of illiteracy and the household responsibility system, which encourages parents to withdraw students from school to maximize productivity. But the burden of providing institutional and financial support for such reforms falls heavily on resource-poor local governments. New efforts being made to diversify labor pools might best be described as China's effort at affirmative action.

By the late 1980s, China was sending delegations of reformers to the United States to study not only job-training programs, affirmative action, and human resource management but also the role of Native American peoples in the federal system, their challenges to the U.S. Constitution, and the elements of autonomous governance in this setting. While these efforts were interrupted by Tiananmen, and while China is deeply defensive on matters ranging from Tibet to human rights for dissidents of all backgrounds, the efforts provide starting points for further steps toward a balance between autonomy and economic and social integration. The difficult question is whether this or any conceivable regime can break the patterns of the past to embark on a new joint venture between Han and non-Han minorities. Some analysts reviewing popular literature and art depicting minorities note that minority women are usually portrayed as exotic and sexually enticing, often graphically presented in nude or seminude form, and described as free of the constraints that affect their Han sisters. The persistence of these stereotypes makes obvious the persisting "otherness" of minorities in the eyes of the Han. Perhaps, as the issue of sexuality and politics enters public discourse, the "otherness" of minorities may be dispelled.

Reform and the open door policy have revived interest in the roots of Han society and beliefs, and thus in Confucianism and the neo-Confucian legacy. Courses on these subjects became popular in major urban centers, particularly in Beijing. An offshoot of this interest among conservative reformers was an inquiry into the role of Confucianism in the modernization of the Japanese, Taiwanese, and Singaporean economies. Chinese leaders set out on a search abroad for the formulas—captured in the expression "the new authoritarianism"—that would ensure economic reform and preserve authoritarian rule.

Equally important is the re-emergence of secret sects, fortune tellers, and mediums. The Yi Guan Dao (the Way of Basic Unity society), depicted as the most dangerous and traitorous of China's secret societies, has been hounded by police and public security for years, and its leaders executed or dispersed. Similar repressive measures have been used to control the rise of mediums. Cynical about ideology and alienated from traditional religions, young people, including disgruntled Red Guards, began to turn to popular cults at the end of the Cultural Revolution. They were among the first to breathe new life into the Yi Guan Dao and other secret societies that have returned to prominence despite continuing repression.

Revival of Western Religions

The Christian churches have also witnessed a revival, but fear of Western proselytism and foreign manipulation has dampened their prospects since the Tiananmen incident. Catholicism, Protestantism, Russian Orthodoxy, and Judaism were given a new lease on life with the implementation of the open door policy. In 1978, a conference held in Kunming broached the possibility of revival by recommending the study of comparative religions. Interest was renewed through the Institute of World Religions of the Chinese Academy of Social Sciences. Colleges and universities in the United States with historic ties to religious institutions, including Yale University and St. John's University, re-established relations with their sister universities in China. Religious tourism received an extra boost as former Western missionaries returned to China to visit the communities they had once served.

As in the case of Islam and China's indigenous religions, churches were rebuilt and seminary training restarted. By the late 1980s, fifty-seven bishops served 112 Catholic dioceses. Some 1,100 priests worked in over 1,000 churches and 2,300 chapels. An average of 47,000 baptisms were reportedly performed each year. The total number of Catholics in China was estimated by Chinese authorities at 3 million in 1989. As of 1987 there were reportedly 4,044 Protestant churches and 16,900 meeting places, 4,500 professional church workers, more than 26,000 lay workers, and nearly 15,000 volunteers, centered principally in Henan, Zhejiang, and Fujian. They served an estimated 5 million people. By contrast, the Russian Orthodox faithful and descendants of the Jewish community in Kaifeng, Henan, formed minuscule though interesting communities. The number of Christians, which includes the merely curious as well as the committed, should be considered carefully, since the former were quick to retreat in the face of yet another round of repression beginning in 1989. By the time of these reports, the open door policy had revealed that, despite persecution, true believers had gathered in secret underground religious circles for years preceding reform. Their organizational ingenuity was testimony to the tenacity of their commitment as well as to the continuing tension between Western religion and the party/state system well after the open door policy was promulgated.

Because of its continuing commitment to the Holy See and renewed contact with (as well as material and financial support from) Catholics outside China, the Chinese Catholic community in January 1990 was charged with violation of the "Three Self" policy (self-propagation, self-administration, and self-support), which in the 1950s separated the Chinese church from the Vatican. For their part, Protestants were accused of contravening the constitutional freedom "not to believe" because of their illegal distribution of "superstitious" literature, their proselytism, and their underground organizations. As in the early 1950s, Protestant churches were also labeled instruments of noxious Western influence, including bourgeois propaganda on human rights and democracy. The Tiananmen incident put a chill on religious reconstruction and revival, reigniting tensions between churches and the party/state.

Social Problems after Tiananmen: Crisis of Identity

The single most serious issue confronting the current regime is the erosion of popular commitment to the goal of building a Communist society. Alienation from the party/state system and from the ideology that legitimated it began well before the Tiananmen incident. The upheaval that marked the Cultural Revolution and the re-education, rustication, and democracy movements that came after it have produced deep fissures in China's social fabric.

Every stratum in Chinese society—from the intelligentsia to party and state cadres, to the employees of state enterprises, and the rural peasantry—felt the shock waves of the Cultural Revolution. They struck both men and women, the Han majority and non-Han minorities, the well-to-do and the poor, the young and the elderly.

In the years after the Cultural Revolution, enrollment in both the party and its Youth League fell precipitously. Young people from varied backgrounds were demonstrating their lack of interest in careers in the party and in the government. Studies conducted in recent years demonstrate that middle school and college students, whether from the coast or the interior, prefer movie stars and singers as role models to the Communist heroes and heroines promoted by propaganda organs. Other surveys rank classes in ideology at the lowest end of student preference. Students have opposed attempts to reintroduce ideological training. All the evidence available suggests that it was the violence at Tiananmen that marked the withdrawal of urban youth from mobilization politics, and that ideological re-indoctrination after the Tiananmen incident has failed to reverse young people's sense of betrayal or their alienation from politics.

Alienation from the party/state system was most obvious in acts of overt resistance to authority in the months immediately after the Tiananmen incident. University students dropped bottles out of the windows of their residence halls in a symbolic attack on Deng Xiaoping (*xiaoping*, a homonym with Deng's given name, means ''little bottle''). Anonymous posters appeared on college campuses denouncing the leadership of the Chinese Communist Party and the PLA. In Beijing a rumor spread that Romania's recently executed dictator, Nicolae Ceaucescu, was not dead but had escaped to China. He could be reached by dialing the number (06) 04-1989 (June 4, 1989).

Wang Juntao, former editor of the prize-winning Shanghai paper the *World Economic Herald,* sued the Chinese Communist Party for depriving him of his freedom to publish. The family of a student killed by troops at Tiananmen mounted its own protest against the party/state system. Most recently, Beijing University students posted a notice in 1994 that the time had come to remove the ideological labels visited upon the organizers and demonstrators at Tiananmen.

The interrelationship between alienation and resistance is also manifest in the remarkable efforts of bureaucrats, workers, peasants, and public security and military personnel to provide safe haven and secure escape routes for leading Tiananmen dissidents. Less dramatic demonstrations of alienation and resistance come from post-Tiananmen ideological campaigns. Little of the commitment and none of the fervor of earlier ideological movements have been reflected in these attempts to mobilize the masses in anticorruption campaigns.

Since the Tiananmen pro-democracy movement of 1989, China has experienced a major economic boom but also mass alienation from the nation's party/state system and its founding Communist ideology.

There is some evidence that alienation, resistance, and social innovation are interrelated. Students who flooded back to the cities between 1976 and 1978, after having been ''permanently'' assigned to the countryside, were engaged in massive resistance. During the period of reform, as ''youth awaiting employment,'' they, along with other déclassé elements, constituted an alienated group of sufficient size and potential threat to lead the government toward privatization of the economy, which would create more employment opportunities.

The weight given to signs of alienation and acts of resistance depends on the larger context in which those signs and acts take on meaning. Is the current emphasis on making money, publicly espoused by citizens in every walk of life, a sign of alienation from the ideologies of scarcity that have dominated the People's Republic of China since its founding? Or is it simply an expression of an age-old, culturally rooted pragmatic drive temporarily sidetracked by China's Maoists and hard-line conservatives? Several authors point out that capitalism took root far more effectively in China than in Russia, once the party/state apparatus no longer blocked entrepreneurs.

Tiananmen dissidents who announced they were turning away from politics for good to embrace money-making were clearly expressing their alienation from the system, and placing self-interest above the interests of the collective. The motives and intentions of peasants, workers, and intellectuals migrating to Guangzhou, the center of open door economic development, are more ambiguous. Rapid economic growth in the south in general, and Guangzhou in particular, acts as a magnet to pull in hundreds of thousands of migrants from other parts of the country. But there are also push factors at work, including the slow pace of reform and persistent support for moribund state enterprises in the more conservative north. Migrants may also be expressing their alienation from failed policies. While that alienation does not necessarily constitute a source of dissidence, much less political rebellion, it is an added impetus for change and a signal of the public's dissatisfaction with the current situation.

There are also signs that many of the cultural attributes that distinguished China may be weakening.

Surveys of Chinese youth by Chinese researchers show that young people are becoming very competitive and much less mindful of the collective than their predecessors. Sexuality, repressed and treated as an illegitimate topic of public discourse earlier, is now on young people's agendas, and sex appeal looms much larger than earlier mores permitted. Among the young, China's work ethic may also be diminishing. The young expect to live better lives without working "too hard," and, at least according to the surveys, contemporary youth do not trust anyone over thirty. Filial piety and respect for the elderly may be losing ground. There is, then, strong evidence of a shift in identity that the policies pursued since 1949 have helped to produce. But the product is not the ideal of revolutionary men and women committed to the realization of a Communist society dreamed of by the party's founders. The identities that are emerging are multiple and ambiguous. They are as much a product of the misdirection and unanticipated consequences of policy initiatives as they are of the revolutionary ideals that led to the founding of the state in 1949.

Chinese society is deeply influenced by values that are not indigenous, but imported. These ideas strike a resonant chord because indigenous experience has given many people a new confidence in the possibility of change, and because the trauma so many have suffered militates against closure and dogma. China is now joining world culture and sharing in all the ambiguities with which the rest of that world must cope.

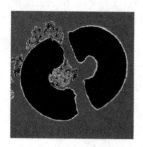

CHAPTER **9**

MODERNIZING THE
CHINESE MILITARY

The People's Liberation Army (PLA) of today is not yet an up-to-date force able to deploy rapidly to conduct regional operations in support of China's interests. Yet it is much more than merely a well-trained internal security force.

The PLA that invaded Vietnam in 1979 to teach the Vietnamese a lesson was an obsolete military giant. Although the force has been reorganized and streamlined since then, the PLA remains a poorly trained military armed with obsolete weaponry. However, the Chinese military has benefited from the fall of the Soviet Union. China's most significant military threat, the Soviet military, has been decimated, although it is attempting to remain cohesive in the face of tremendous political and social upheaval. Former Soviet defense industries and institutions, struggling to survive in the post-cold war era, welcome Chinese buyers of their technology and weapons. Smaller regional neighbors who are currently surpassing China's military technology base and deploying more sophisticated weaponry are concerned with facing a modernizing PLA developing indigenous military production capabilities and acquiring state-of-the-art weapons systems from Russia and the West.

Although these systems and technologies will help modernize the PLA, serious roadblocks remain to be overcome in many areas, including personnel, training, doctrine, defense industries, technology, arms sales and proliferation, and basic military capabilities, before China can become more than a regional military force.

The History of the PLA

The Chinese military (ground, air, naval, and strategic forces), collectively known as the PLA, was born in the mountainous region of Jinggangshan in Jiangxi Province on August 1, 1927. This "Chinese Workers' and Peasants' Red Army," commanded by Zhu De and Mao Zedong, began by fighting a guerrilla war against the Kuomintang (KMT, or Nationalist Party) forces led by Chiang Kai-shek. Forged during the Long March in the 1930s to escape the KMT's Communist suppression campaigns, the PLA went on to help defeat the Japanese in 1945 and then to drive the KMT to Taiwan in 1949. The formation of the People's Republic of China (PRC) in October of that year made China's new leaders realize the need to transform their primitive peasant army into a modern military force. Using massive Soviet aid, the Chinese began modernizing their military during the 1950s with new equipment, weapons, and technical advisers, particularly after incurring tremendous personnel and equipment losses during the Korean War (1950-1953).

These actions were seen in the West as part of a monolithic Communist drive for global domination. Western fears of a radical China allied with Moscow seemed to be realized when the PLA adopted Soviet military organizational structures, strategies, and tactics in the form of the 1954 establishment of a National Defense Council, the Ministry of National Defense, and thirteen military regions. In addition, China's defense industry, officers corps, military

The People's Liberation Army flourished during a period of military professionalism in the 1950s. Here a tank unit of the PLA parades in Tiananmen Square on National Day, October 1, 1952. As China entered a period of isolationism in the 1960s, the military began to emphasize ideology over modernization.

ranks, and uniforms were established or reformed based on the Soviet model.

The PLA flourished during a period of military professionalism from 1953 to 1958 under the leadership of Peng Dehuai. However, the military's new emphasis on a Soviet-style modernization created tensions between the Chinese Communist Party (CCP) and the military. The CCP wished to de-emphasize military professionalism in favor of Mao's belief in revolutionary purity, economic development, and the supremacy of men over weapons. This economic, ideological, and personality struggle led to the 1959 CCP plenum at Lushan. At this plenum, Lin Biao, who supported the party's position, replaced Peng Dehuai as minister of defense. Soon after Lin's political ascension, the Soviet Union withdrew from China in 1960 for political, economic, territorial, and ideological reasons. Among China's concerns were Moscow's moves toward peaceful co-

existence with the West, reluctance to provide China with ballistic missile technology, and lack of support for China's desire to recover Taiwan. (See also Chapters 4 and 7.)

Chinese military development began a new stage after the Soviet withdrawal, which disrupted China's defense industry and weapons development, and led the country to stress self-reliance. Sino-Soviet relations deteriorated almost to the point of war in 1969. Coinciding with the chaos of the Cultural Revolution, armed clashes occurred at Zhenbao Island on China's northeast border with the Soviet Union, formed by the Amur and Ussuri Rivers.

In the 1970s, Beijing viewed Moscow as a continuing long-term threat and thus moderated its radical stance and improved relations with the United States and the West. Chinese leaders felt threatened by Soviet political, military, and economic activities in Afghanistan, India, Mongolia, Vietnam, and along the Sino-Soviet border, which were perceived as Soviet attempts to encircle China.

This threat, coupled with China's military weakness and Mao's waning health and power, forced China's mid-decade decision to modernize the PLA. In 1975, Premier Zhou Enlai proclaimed as national policy the Four Modernizations—a program designed to ensure agricultural self-sufficiency, turn China into an industrialized country by 2000, expand its indigenous scientific and technological sectors, and achieve military parity with advanced powers by the middle of the next century.

Mao's death in 1976 led to a dramatic national shift toward pragmatism, modernization, and opening up to the outside world. Relations with the West improved, and military contacts developed with the United States and Western Europe to offset the Soviet threat. China supplied weapons to the Khmer Rouge and other Cambodian groups to counter Vietnamese operations in Southeast Asia. In addition, Chinese leaders developed close relations with and sold weapons to Burma and Thailand. China used weapons sales in the Middle East and supported Afghan rebels to make diplomatic inroads and partially finance its military modernization efforts. A massive reorganization of the PLA in the 1980s allowed the consolidation of military regions from thirteen to seven, formation of twenty-four group armies from thirty-six field armies, demobilization of one million troops, significant acquisition of military technology, and many other improvements.

Since the collapse of communism in the Soviet Union and Eastern Europe, the Soviet threat has been replaced with a severely diminished Russian military threat. The Russian military, struggling to remain united in the face of fourteen new states vying for the spoils of the former Soviet Union, is involved in internal political battles as well as having difficulty finding food and housing for its soldiers and their families. At the same time, the United States and the rest of the West are reducing their military forces and spending. So China can once again look northward for military technology and hardware acquisitions as it attempts to modernize its defense forces and reach levels equivalent to those of advanced countries within the next half century.

Threats and Goals in the 1990s

The threat of a global superpower conflict has receded in the 1990s while the dangers of regional rivalries, ancient antagonisms, territorial disputes, religious conflicts, and regional political realignments have become more prevalent and explosive. Within China, instability caused by economic turmoil, minority unrest, or a succession struggle after the death of Deng Xiaoping remains a concern and threat to the viability of the CCP.

For the remainder of this century, Chinese leaders do not project a confluence of external political, economic, or military forces that could threaten China's security. The United States is perceived to be China's primary long-term strategic threat. As the sole remaining global superpower, the United States has political, economic, cultural, and military influence that poses significant dilemmas for Beijing. In order to become a global actor, China requires American trade, financial investments, technological assistance, production expertise, and military forces in Asia to maintain regional stability. At the same time, Beijing fears Washington's cultural influence and global military power.

Within the region, Chinese leaders consider the following situations possible long-term threats:

- Japan's economic and technological strength, which provides a ready foundation for Japanese remilitarization and a potential for the development of nuclear military power;
- Taiwan's independence, which China perceives as a direct threat to its national sovereignty;
- Russian military forces in Asia, which, though weakened by political turmoil and the struggle to survive, have been enhanced with the deployment of additional weapon systems from Europe such as the Su-27/*Flanker,* nuclear-capable *Backfire* bombers; T-80 tanks; and improved artillery;
- conflict in Korea, which would disrupt regional stability and Beijing's economic reform programs, or a reunified, democratic Korea, which could economically and ideologically threaten China;
- Islamic fundamentalism, which could provoke more intense unrest in Xinjiang;

• conflicting territorial claims with India and Vietnam, which could cause armed conflict in the South China Sea or in the Himalayas.

In Asia, China's leaders continue to see the United States as the short-term guarantor of regional security and the arbiter of regional disputes. If the United States falters in this regional role, Beijing hopes to be positioned to assume the role of Asia's military and political leader by the early decades of the twenty-first century. Beijing expects that gradual economic reforms and the acquisitions of Hong Kong in 1997 and Macao in 1999 will provide significant boosts to its national economic power. Militarily, China continues modernization efforts to strengthen its military options to defend its sovereign rights and interests within the region and assert its territorial claims. The military will also be employed to preserve the leadership of the CCP and maintain Chinese values and institutions.

Doctrine and Strategy

In order to meet threats and attain its strategic goals, Beijing has been attempting to transform the PLA from what began as Mao's infantry army of revolutionary peasants into a relatively professional military, beyond the force improvements and technological upgrading that took place during Mao's tenure as national leader. This force is currently equipped with post-Korean War weapons such as the Type 59 (Soviet T-54) tank, *Romeo* submarine, and F-7 (MiG-21) fighter. The PLA is supported by a developing defense industry and technological base and is gradually moving away from active political participation.

Although the PLA remains firmly committed to deterring nuclear attack or a massive invasion, the changes in Beijing's threat perception since the end of the 1980s have redefined the country's military strategy to focus on a limited, flexible, and rapid response to a regional conflict or foe. Under the precepts established by this more outward-looking military doctrine, called "Local War," success on the battlefield will require the employment of sophisticated weapons and specially tailored, highly mobile

forces to make rapid gains by achieving an early tactical advantage. Actual combat operations will be intense and focused on specific tactical objectives. The emphasis will be on decisive military operations to achieve specific political objectives because it is presumed that the adversary will view the cost of continued conflict as unacceptably high. This doctrine emphasizes rapid reaction, limited conflict, flexible response, preemptive action, and limited power projection to China's strategic borders. At present, China defines its strategic boundary as its territorial interests in the Spratly Islands and on its border with India. However, the construct is open-ended and could easily be applied to "defending" other interests. The doctrine of Local War will likely remain the guiding philosophy for modernization priorities of the PLA, especially for its naval and air forces.

However, the PLA's evolving Local War doctrine will only supplement, not replace, China's current official military doctrine—People's War Under Modern Conditions—which is based on Mao Zedong Military Thought. Mao's military thought incorporated his studies of the peasant rebellions of eighteenth- and nineteenth-century China; the experiences of the PLA in the civil war with the KMT (1927-49) and during the anti-Japanese resistance war (1937-1945); and the concepts of numerous military strategists such as Napoleon, Clausewitz, and especially Sun Zi (*The Art of War*, circa 350 B.C.E.). In Mao's view, the PLA was victorious against the larger, better-armed KMT and Japanese forces because it relied on popular support and used tactics that continually adapted to the overall situation.

People's War is a doctrine for defending China against various types of war, ranging from a surprise long-range nuclear strike combined with a massive ground invasion to a conventional ground attack with limited objectives. The doctrine is premised on participation of the whole populace and mobilization of all the country's resources for as long as it takes to defeat any invader. The doctrine of People's War is meant to assure both the Chinese people and any potential invader that in war there will be neither surrender nor collaboration, and that even if China's military forces were defeated, widespread and unremitting resistance would continue until the invader

生命不息，冲锋不止
CHARGE THE ENEMY TO THE LAST BREATH

The Maoist doctrine of People's War is premised on participation of the whole population and mobilization of the country's resources. It is meant to deter potential enemies by making it clear that any invasion of China would be an expensive proposition with no chance of success. This 1970 poster shows a People's Liberation Army fighter defending Chairman Mao and the motherland, in reference to the Sino-Soviet border skirmishes of early 1969.

withdrew. Ideally, China's main forces, using modern conventional tactics, would carry out a strategic withdrawal supported by guerrilla operations until the invading forces were overextended and dispersed. When this occurred, China would then concentrate its forces to annihilate the enemy. In part, the People's War doctrine is meant to deter potential enemies by making it clear that any invasion of China would be a very expensive proposition with no chance of a satisfactory resolution.

Although People's War remains the primary doctrine for the defense of the Chinese nation-state, the leadership in Beijing is constantly striving to find a proper balance between the concept of People's War and the development of professional forces capable of fighting a modern conventional local war. China realizes that the preservation of its territorial integrity and the Mandate of Heaven (political power) depend on its ability to prevent encroachment of its territory and to maintain political control. The CCP has demonstrated its willingness to use military force to pursue its core interests and objectives throughout its history (see Table 9.1). Despite its avowed defensive orientation, Beijing rationalizes its offensive actions, such as the month-long 1979 assault into Vietnam, as actions to ''counterattack in self-defense.''

China's security strategy reflects the country's national interests and presents a broad plan for achieving the national objectives that support those

Table 9.1 Internal and External Crises, 1927-1989

Internal		External	
Crisis	Year	Crisis	Year
Chinese Civil War	1927-1949	Korean War	1950-1953
War with Japan	1937-1945	Sino-Indian conflict	1962
Taiwan Strait crisis	1958	Sino-Soviet border	1969
Cultural Revolution	1965-1975	Paracel Island skirmish	1974
Gang of Four purge	1976	Sino-Vietnam border	1979
Tiananmen incident	1989	Sino-Indian border	1989

interests. The key national interests that the strategy seeks to assure and protect include:

- to defend the territory of China;
- to support China's foreign policy objectives;
- to deter attack by any country and, should deterrence fail, to bring any war to a conclusion favorable to China;
- to maintain internal security.

Closely related to these national interests is the PLA's military strategy. As stated by Liu Huaqing, vice chairman of the Central Military Commission (CMC), in an August 1993 article in *Jiefangjun Ribao* (Liberation Army Daily), the mission of the PLA is "to keep our territories, territorial waters, territorial airspace, and oceanic interests free of infringement; to safeguard the unity of the country; and to defend the security of the country." Military strategy concerns not only the use of military power in war but also the use and political utility of military power to maintain peace and reach national goals.

Resources of the PLA

In order to develop the modern military forces necessary to defend China's territorial and strategic interests, Beijing continues a military modernization program that is attempting to downsize the PLA and provide its forces with younger, better-educated troops; more opportunities for realistic training; and state-of-the-art weaponry.

Defense Funding

An essential element in China's military modernization efforts will be economic growth, which in turn will provide funds for the PLA. Beijing has identified the next ten years as a unique period of relative peace and stability in which the economy can grow and the military can continue to modernize. In an attempt to match the world's modern military forces, China has increased defense expenditures by as much as 20 percent a year since 1989; this trend continued with the official 1993 defense budget of 42 billion yuan (US$8.1 billion), a 22 percent increase over the 1992 state outlay of 37 billion yuan (US$7.1 billion). Moreover, Beijing's official defense budget does not reflect true overall defense spending for the PLA. Aside from the defense budget, the state budget itself contains money for military research and development, special funds for major military purchases, and other supposedly nonmilitary spending for the PLA. In addition, commercial PLA activities, arms sales, and nuclear technology sales all contribute to China's military revenues. Estimates of total revenues and expenditures are extremely imprecise, ranging from $11.5 billion to $20 billion for 1992. These defense outlays will increase as China's national economic growth in the 1990s is projected to be in the range of 7 to 9 percent.

However, the PLA will continue to be constrained by fiscal shortages. As Major General Wan Qikan, president of the Academy of Military Economics in Wuhan, stated in an interview published in the June

29, 1990, issue of *Renmin Ribao* (People's Daily), "As the rate of increase in military spending has been lower than that of price increases in recent years, to maintain the stability of the army, we had to increase the proportion of living costs in national defense spending and relevantly cut the proportion of purchases and maintenance of weapons. The decrease in spending and increase in prices means a drop in purchasing power by a wide margin." As an example, military funding as a percentage of the state budget fell from 17.7 percent in 1977 to 8.4 percent in 1992. In addition, inflation has eaten away at the purchasing power of the Chinese defense budget. The 22 billion yuan spent in 1988 had much less purchasing power than the 17 billion yuan of 1977, even using a conservative Chinese annual inflation rate of 10 percent. Beijing is attempting to counteract these shortfalls with increased state funding. These funds will be dedicated to raising the standard of living for its troops; acquiring limited numbers of high-technology weapons and systems; and reorganizing the force. Funds for unit construction, training, and subsistence will continue to come from PLA and individual unit enterprises and other sources.

Personnel

The PLA's primary expenditure since 1989 has been on improving the living standards of its soldiers, to try to overcome the increased perception among China's populace that service in the PLA reduces one's ability to attain a better standard of living. During its first fifty years of existence, the PLA was one of the few institutions to provide Chinese youth with the means to improve their standing in society. The PLA offered opportunities to join the CCP, to move into the cities, and to gain the prestige of serving in the "people's" army. However, even before the 1989 Tiananmen incident, the prestige and opportunities for advancement obtained by joining the military were evaporating. Thus conscript quotas have not been met, and problems have emerged in retaining younger officers and specialists.

The new recruits worry PLA leaders because of their unsatisfactory physical and educational condition. Educated urban recruits are needed to operate the increasingly technological systems being developed for the PLA. However, city youth bring increased disciplinary and motivational problems. Because of economic reforms, urban youth have better prospects for getting ahead in the civilian economy than they would by joining the PLA. City youth who do join are likely to have less stamina and be unfamiliar with military life. Meanwhile, China's hardy rural youth, who comprise the majority of the PLA's recruits, do not have an adequate educational background. Most rural recruits must initially be sent for basic education before they can attend basic military training. To entice qualified youth into joining the PLA, Beijing has initiated a series of programs including building new barracks and facilities for units; a GI Bill-type program of benefits for Chinese soldiers; and continued civil-military programs meant to restore the popular prestige of the PLA. Whether these and other efforts will succeed in recruiting and retaining the educated, yet ideologically malleable, personnel the PLA requires for modernization remains unclear.

Defense Industries

China's defense industries are central to PLA modernization. Like defense industries elsewhere, those in China are undergoing a massive conversion from military to civilian production priorities. Because the PLA is unable to fund a large-scale rearmament of its forces with modern weaponry, and because most Chinese conventional military products are uncompetitive in weapons markets, defense factories are turning to the production of civilian consumer goods in order to survive. How much income is realized from this production is difficult to determine (pharmaceutical production alone is thought to earn about $1 billion a year), and even Chinese authorities are concerned that the rapid growth in these activities might spiral out of control.

The majority of China's defense factories manufacture motorcycles, refrigerators, and other consumer goods, including satellite television dishes, cellular telephones, and contact lenses, but key factories and R & D centers continue to modernize and build a foundation from which state-of-the-art weapons can be produced to rearm the PLA. (One of the military's more unusual ventures is a popular Shanghai disco co-owned with a Hong Kong investor.) The 1991 Persian Gulf War reinforced the PLA's assessment that its combat capabilities and weaponry are inadequate for local war operations on a modern battlefield. The PLA has given increased priority to the introduction of technology and the purchase of patent and production rights from abroad. Additional resources are being funneled into China's indigenous weapons programs from civilian production and government reserve funds.

For a short time after June 1989, the restrictions the West placed on military and financial transactions with China hampered PLA weapons development and defense production. But the fall of the Soviet Union continues to provide China's defense facilities with significant opportunities for the acquisition and purchase of advanced Russian defensive military technology, hardware, and production expertise. China's leaders are well aware of the importance of self-reliance in weapons modernization. Their future defense needs must be met basically from within the Chinese homeland, with assistance from selective purchases of foreign military technology and weaponry. The PLA, for the immediate future, will have to use many outdated weapons and await the fruits of China's economic growth to fund the deployment of indigenous or foreign advanced weaponry to its combat units.

To attain a self-sustaining weapons modernization program and an upgraded military force, without a significant infusion of funds, China's defense R & D is being closely coordinated with that of the civilian sector to the benefit of both. Technology imported for the civilian sector will be used for defense purposes whenever possible and vice versa.

The Commission for Science, Technology, and Industry for National Defense (COSTIND) manages China's military R & D and production efforts. The COSTIND's primary responsibility is to direct the design, building, and testing of military hardware. COSTIND governs the following ministries and organizations responsible for producing industrial equipment for civilian use and for China's military production:

- China National Nuclear Corporation, responsible for all nuclear research and weapons production. This ministry has received the most consistent financial and technological support from the central government.
- Aviation Industries of China (AVIC), responsible for aeronautic systems, except ballistic missiles. AVIC supervises a significant industry that produces, maintains, and replaces over 5,000 military aircraft and at least 500 aircraft belonging to the civilian fleet.
- The Ministry of Electronics Industry, responsible for electronics, telecommunications, and navigational equipment production.
- The North China Industrial Group (NORINCO), responsible for all munitions and conventional military hardware production. The hardware includes infantry weapons, tanks, armored personnel carriers, ammunition, mortars, rocket launchers, antiaircraft guns, and some tactical missiles.
- The China State Shipbuilding Corporation (CSSC), responsible for shipbuilding and naval construction.
- China National Space Industry Corporation, responsible for ballistic missile production and satellite launching. There is an overlap between the China National Nuclear Corporation and China National Space Industry Corporation in the production of ballistic missiles.

China's entire military production system is undergoing a massive reorganization, which is projected to help resolve coordination problems among many different agencies. Moreover, attempts are being made to eliminate waste and inefficiency. Many ministries and their enterprises are being spun off into independent commercial enterprises while others are being consolidated or eliminated. The national economic reforms and requirements for the PLA to fund many programs with internal resources have led to geometric growth in the number of enterprises under the direct control of Chinese military units. Although many of these PLA companies are making money using the unit's troops, vehicles, resources, and connections, others are losing money because of mismanagement. These enterprises are prime breeding grounds for corruption, nepotism, and greed.

Technology Transfers

Since 1980, Chinese policy statements have stressed the need for improving existing facilities, importing technology rather than finished goods, and renovating defense factories through selective purchase or acquisition of key technologies and systems rather than through the purchase of entire plants. An essential COSTIND task continues to be to import technology to renovate and upgrade essential defense factories and weapons systems whose products and capabilities remain far below prevailing international standards.

Beijing faces two major impediments to effective technology transfer. First, there have been problems with assimilating technology within specific factories because of a lack of training or attempts to introduce technology into inappropriate situations. These problems can be resolved over time with better education, training, and experience. Each year tens of thousands of Chinese students and technicians go abroad to study foreign science and technology, and their return to China is beginning to provide significant benefits for Chinese technological development.

The second major impediment is the Chinese economic system itself. Most of China's defense industrial and technological system remains constrained by rigid centralized planning and control, overemphasis on production, lack of incentives for innovation, excessive compartmentalization, and an irrational price system. These can be resolved only by systemic change. Change has begun, and its success depends on the political skills of Chinese leaders attempting to carry it out. The more fully the economic reforms are put into practice, the more likely it is that technology transfer will succeed in China.

China's military planners have given priority in technology imports to electronics and telecommunications as well as missile, air defense, and mobility systems. Naval and aviation technology and systems to support the PLA's ability to conduct local war operations are of the utmost importance to Beijing.

Even with reforms and higher priorities in the technology arena, Beijing will not achieve self-sufficiency in military technology in the near future. China will continue to acquire equipment from abroad on which R & D costs have already been paid and technical problems resolved. China's policy of selective importation of technology and weapons remains the PLA's key to being able to leapfrog from its deployment of 1950s, 1960s, and early 1970s weapons to the development of weapons incorporating post-Persian Gulf War technologies.

For the near term, the PLA's principal source of military technology and hardware will be Russia. In 1989, Moscow's withdrawal from Afghanistan, its termination of military and economic subsidies to Vietnam, and its reduction of forces in Mongolia and along the Sino-Soviet border led to a series of bilateral meetings to promote economic and military cooperation. Beijing and Moscow have a mutual interest in modernizing their economies, resolving historic territorial disputes, and improving trade and military sales. Since most of China's weapons are based on Soviet designs, it will be more cost effective and less complicated for the PLA to integrate arms and technology from Russia into its defense industry and military units. Both sides have held trade fairs, exchanged high-level military visits, and signed several agreements to promote trade, joint ventures, technology transfers, and limited weapons sales. Even before June 1989, the Chinese had already begun negotiations for the purchase of Soviet military equipment. This represented a shift away from China's plans in the 1980s to use Western technology for its military modernization.

Arms Sales

Before 1980, China provided weapons at low ''friendship'' prices to third world countries with compatible ideological views and strategic goals. After 1980, the PLA altered its arms sales strategy from one based on ideology and politics to one based on profits in order to make China's defense industry more economically viable, to purchase foreign military technology, and to modernize its obsolete weaponry.

Chinese weapon sales increased rapidly during the 1980s. While continuing to sell weapons at relatively low prices to certain friendly states, China began to make profit-motivated sales to Middle Eastern countries. In particular, China became a significant arms supplier to both combatants in the Iran-Iraq War. Between 1982 and 1989, China became the world's fifth-largest arms exporter behind the United States, the Soviet Union, Great Britain, and France by selling inexpensive, relatively simple weapons. Sixty percent of Chinese arms sales in the 1980s went to Middle Eastern countries and annual arms exports reached a high of $2.6 billion in 1988. Numerous trading corporations were established within China during the 1980s to handle arms exports and facilitate the import of foreign military technology. In 1984, these corporations began displaying their products at international exhibits designed to encourage sales of Chinese weapons and to facilitate technological imports.

The Tiananmen incident, the disintegration of the Soviet Union, and the Persian Gulf War intervened, however, eliminating Chinese arms sales advantages and drastically reducing sales to a total of up to $200 million in 1992. Reacting to the Tiananmen incident, most Western countries suspended contracts that helped modernize Chinese weaponry. After the fall of the Soviet Union, a flood of more advanced Soviet and East European weapons entered the arms market at costs competitive with Chinese systems. During the Persian Gulf War, Chinese weapons employed by Iraq did not fare well against weaponry of the U.S.-led coalition. In addition, current customers of Chinese arms have complained about the maintainability, workmanship, and effectiveness of their purchases.

Although Chinese weapons have lost much of their competitive advantage, Chinese arms deliveries or contracts in the 1990s have included:

- F-7/*Fishbed* (MiG-21) fighters and Type-85 tanks to Pakistan.
- 6 frigates for Thailand, the first four of which are *Jianghu IV* class-equipped with Chinese weapons and systems and the last two, multipurpose ships with a mixture of Western weapons and systems.

- Over $1 billion in Chinese military equipment to Burma (F-6/*Farmer* fighter aircraft, *Shanghai* naval patrol boats, antiaircraft guns, ground-based radar systems, small arms and ammunition).

The PLA will not regain its competitive arms sales advantages in the near term. China's conventional arms sales are expected to remain stagnant until its defense industries can produce weapons attractive to world buyers.

Weapons Proliferation

China's conventional weapons may have lost their sales advantages and prestige, but Beijing's missile, chemical, and nuclear technology and selected systems remain attractive to third world buyers barred from Western supplies. This is of increasing concern to the United States and others, especially the proliferation of such weapons and systems to volatile regions like the Middle East and South Asia.

China's foreign ministry would like to curtail sensitive arms sales in order to improve Beijing's international image. This conflicts with the PLA's interest in promoting aggressive arms sales as a means to generate currency. For several years, the Chinese argued that since China was not a founding member of the Missile Technology Control Regime (MTCR) it was therefore not obligated to follow MTCR restrictions. In 1992, however, China's foreign minister, Qian Qichen, sent a letter to U.S. Secretary of State James Baker stating Beijing's intention to follow the MTCR guidelines. These guidelines, implemented in 1987, prohibit sales of missiles capable of delivering a payload of 500 kg to a distance of at least 300 km. Since China's M-9 missile has a 600-km range and the M-11 has a stated 300-km range and can carry a nuclear warhead, the transfer of these two systems or technology could violate MTCR restrictions.

This disagreement has expanded beyond the diplomatic and military leadership in Beijing to affect China's international relations, especially with the United States. In 1991, Chinese M-11 launchers were reportedly sighted in Pakistan, and M-11 missile technology deliveries were reported in 1992. The United States responded in August 1993 by imposing sanctions targeted against Chinese missile and space companies and organizations involved in M-11 technology sales to Pakistan. Because of the sale of M-9 and M-11 missiles and the possible transfer of chemical weapons precursors (base materials), proliferation will remain a major stumbling block to improved U.S.-China relations. China signed agreements in the early 1990s to build nuclear reactors in Pakistan and Iran, although Western countries have denied nuclear cooperation to those countries, which are suspected of developing nuclear weapons.

Politics and Leadership

The PLA is commanded by the CCP's Military Commission. The party Military Commission has traditionally been one of the principal centers of national power in Communist China. It is from the Military Commission that the CCP controls the gun (PLA), which in turn serves as a significant force for stability in China. The current Military Commission chairman is Jiang Zemin, who concurrently serves as general secretary of the CCP and president of China. Although he holds the three most important posts in China, Jiang is regarded as a compromise leader who will not retain significant power after the death of China's ruler from behind the scenes, Deng Xiaoping.

Whether the succession to Deng is peaceful or violent, the PLA, led by the Military Commission, will not decide who will lead China. It will, however, have a voice in the decision and ensure that the CCP leadership's choice is installed. Two PLA leaders who will have significant influence over the PLA's political support are the Military Commission vice chairmen, General Liu Huaqing and General Zhang Zhen. General Liu, former director of the Navy and COSTIND, is thought to be the equipment and R & D chief for the PLA. General Zhang, a former president of the PLA National Defense University, is thought to be the personnel, strategic doctrine, and training chief for the PLA. Both in their late seventies, the two men were appointed to provide stability for the PLA in case of a succession struggle. In relatively good health, both have the experience and re-

lationships required to guide the PLA through political turmoil. Moreover, neither is in the "running" to replace Deng.

Lower-ranking PLA leaders, while aware of the political machinations in Beijing, are more interested in the PLA's modernization. Like other national armed forces, the PLA has many constituent interest groups, from operators and technocrats to strategists and political commissars. Each has its own goals and powers, yet recognizes the danger of factionalism and the need for the PLA to remain unified in the face of any crisis. Throughout its history, the PLA has served as a stabilizing force for China and the CCP. It was the PLA that initially won over the Chinese people in 1949, restored order after the chaos of the Cultural Revolution, and carried out the party leadership's directives during the spring 1989 disturbances.

Although reports that elements of group armies were fighting with one another during the Tiananmen incident later proved unfounded, the Military Commission instituted a drive immediately afterward to increase PLA ideological indoctrination. This program, along with a revitalized campaign to strengthen civil-military relations, was intended to ensure the PLA's reliability and loyalty to the CCP. As much as 50 percent of all PLA training time was taken up with political ideology training after the spring of 1989. A post-Tiananmen editorial in the *Liberation Army Daily* on the three revised PLA regulations (Internal Management, Discipline, and Formation Drill) signed by Military Commission Chairman Jiang Zemin in June 1990 states that "the new regulations stress the party's absolute leadership over the army and the principle of strengthening the army politically."

The Old Guard, veterans of the Long March in the 1930s, continued the struggle to maintain the unity of the PLA and thereby preserve the single force within China capable of maintaining national stability. A June 1990 article in Hong Kong's *South China Morning Post* (SCMP) quoted Yang Shangkun, then executive vice chairman of the Military Commission and president of China, as saying, "unity is the lifeline of the army. Now we must put this into practice." A later SCMP article stated that this call for military unity came directly from Deng Xiaoping during an informal meeting with the Military Commission in late May. Deng is quoted as having said, "the unity of the army is the lifeline of the republic. If the army is unified, it signals that the entire country is stable."

While hoping to instill political correctness, support for the CCP, and unity in the PLA, the CCP is also concerned with other national problems that have an impact on the PLA's capabilities, most prominently, corruption. The traditional problem of corruption is festering within the military and throughout Chinese society. Thanks to increased contacts with outside manufacturers and agents and its role as the guarantor of party supremacy, the PLA has become even more fertile ground for corruption, influence peddling, and nepotism. Corruption is rampant, programs to overcome corruption are not easily implemented, and resources are taken away from the military to line the pockets of those with *guanxi* (personal relations). The CCP has initiated a national campaign to stamp out corruption. The PLA and other national organizations have held meetings and established investigations. So far those targeted include only mid-level leaders, while senior leaders and their offspring have been largely spared. This current campaign cannot succeed unless corruption is eliminated at the highest levels of the CCP, the PLA, and the Chinese economy, however. High-level corruption will allow economic, social, and political corruption to continue at all levels of Chinese society.

Regionalism is a second potential problem for the PLA. Some observers fear that as the economic reforms take hold in the provinces, China will dissolve into regional economic entities. However, China is unlikely to follow in the footsteps of the Soviet Union and dissolve into several disparate nation-states. Although Tibet and Xinjiang Province have significant minority populations, the majority of China remains Han Chinese. Having carefully observed the turmoil and the economic situation in Russia and the other former Soviet republics, China does not want to go down the path of regionalism.

Military Forces

The total armed forces of the PRC are defined as the integration of the PLA, the reserves/militia, and the People's Armed Police (PAP). The PLA is more than an army. All Chinese military service organizations—the Army, Navy, Air Force, and Second Artillery Corps—are integral members of the PLA. Three general departments—General Logistics (GLD), General Political (GPD), and General Staff (GSD)—provide overall operational leadership to the PLA. The COSTIND, a general departmental-level organization, supervises weapons research and development and coordinates the military with the civilian sectors of the economy.

In peacetime the PAP is under the administrative and operational leadership of the Ministry of Public Security. In times of war or crisis, the PLA regains operational control over the PAP. China's reserves and militia come under the operational leadership of the PLA at the military district level but remain under the administrative control of provincial and local leaders at the People's Armed Forces District level.

Armed Forces

The armed forces of the PRC are organized into seven military regions (MR), each capable of using its own service branches to carry out combined arms operations across an entire spectrum of military missions within its area of responsibility. In specific cases, such as in the Sino-Vietnamese conflict in the late 1970s and early 1980s, two or more MRs can be combined into a front command to conduct operational campaigns.

China's armed forces in each region are organized into four categories of units that are assigned specific missions. The PLA group armies or combined arms armies are the highest-level tactical organization for battle operations. Military districts serve as the PLA's link to provincial and autonomous region governments. Garrison district commands were the key to China's People's War concept, defending territory and conducting warfare within a specific locale. However, these units are being eliminated or consolidated into reserve forces as the external threat to China recedes. Independent units are assigned to a military region to conduct specialized missions such as the Air Force's Fifteenth Airborne Army in Jinan MR, the Marine Brigade in Guangzhou MR, and the independent PLA units assigned in Tibet and Xinjiang for internal security and special terrain operations.

China has determined that its force posture, fielded equipment, and infrastructure are not optimally tailored for the localized conflicts it judges likely to occur at its strategic boundaries. In an effort to correct these deficiencies, it is expected to expand several relatively new programs. China is experimenting with smaller, more mobile rapid reaction units equipped with more sophisticated weapons such as helicopters. Key group armies such as the Thirty-Eighth (Beijing MR) and Thirty-Ninth (Shenyang MR) have been designated rapid deployment units along with selected divisions in each MR. Elements of the Air Force's Airborne Army and the Navy's Marine forces have also assumed rapid reaction missions.

Without the funding required to rearm the entire PLA with modern weapons and equipment, the CMC is concentrating its limited resources on enhancing the weapons, training, and leadership of its best units—the rapid reaction forces, Second Artillery, Navy, and Air Force. While awaiting additional funds and resources, the remainder of the PLA will support the economic programs of the military, train its military service personnel, and reorganize its units.

One combat multiplier that has been reformed and is meeting significant success in the PLA is military training. In the past, PLA training operations were characterized as set piece exercises with little freedom of maneuver for the individual trainee, commander, or unit. To solve training problems, the leadership unveiled a new training regulation in July 1990. This training regulation, which outlines specific individual, unit, and combined arms training, is the most comprehensive and specific to date. The regulation is designed to promote military-wide standardization, which has been lacking in the past. Furthermore, the regulation establishes strict standards for evaluating unit progress in training and prescribes

detailed methods for higher headquarters to test subordinate units. The early 1990s witnessed a dramatic increase in Chinese reporting on the growing frequency, size, and complexity of PLA training. However, foreign military experts have not been allowed to examine or report on PLA training exercises to determine the true extent and realism involved in PLA training. PLA ground, air, and naval units have conducted training exercises in the same location at the same time. It is unclear, however, whether these units conducted realistic joint operations with viable command and control links.

Nuclear Forces

China is the world's fourth-largest nuclear power, possessing a small but credible nuclear deterrent force. The nuclear forces are operated by the 100,000-member Strategic Missile Force or Second Artillery, which is controlled directly by the Military Commission through the General Staff Department. China's nuclear forces, in combination with the PLA's conventional forces, serve to deter both nuclear and conventional attack. Chinese leaders have pledged never to be the first to use nuclear weapons, but they have accompanied this pledge with a promise of a certain nuclear counterattack if attacked. China maintains its nuclear retaliatory capability by dispersing and concealing its nuclear forces in difficult terrain, improving the mobility of its systems, and hardening its missile silos.

Beijing's current missile force consists of more than 100 mobile CSS-2 intermediate-range ballistic missiles (IRBM), which use storable liquid propellants to launch a one- to three-megaton warhead to almost 3,000 km. It also has a few transportable CSS-3 limited-range intercontinental ballistic missiles (ICBM), which are CSS-2s with a second stage that can propel a one- to three-megaton warhead to 7,000 km. The PLA has as many as twelve silo-based CSS-4 ICBMs, which can strike targets throughout the United States, Russia, and Europe with a four- to five-megaton warhead or three to four multiple independently targetable re-entry vehicles (MIRVs). The Second Artillery has on hand an aging stockpile of less than 100 nuclear bombs that can be delivered on

Table 9.2   China's Strategic Nuclear Forces

Category	Number
Active duty personnel	100,000
ICBMs	
CSS-4	7-12
CSS-3	10
IRBMs	
CSS-2	44
MRBMs	
CSS-5	2
SRBMs	
M-9/M-11	Unknown
SLBMs	
JL-1	14

Source: The Military Balance: 1992-1993 (London: Brassey's for the International Institute for Strategic Studies).

equally aging B-6/*Badger* or A-5/*Fantan* bombers that would probably not survive in hostile airspace. China possesses one *Xia*-class nuclear-powered ballistic missile submarine (SSBN) with twelve tubes for the JL-1 submarine-launched ballistic missile (SLBM). The solid propellant JL-1 has a range of about 2,000 km. Although the JL-1 was successfully test-launched from the *Xia* SSBN in 1988, it is unclear whether the SSBN is currently equipped with the JL-1 or is awaiting a follow-on missile.

As discussed above, China has developed the M-9 and M-11 short-range ballistic missiles (SRBM) for the international arms market and for deployment in a tactical nuclear mode to PLA field artillery units. For the future, China is developing solid propellant MRBM and ICBM missiles to provide more mobile and reliable systems with faster launch times using less manpower and equipment. These new systems are expected to replace the obsolete CSS-2, CSS-3, and the older CSS-4 missiles.

Ground Forces

China's ground force army, the largest in the world, is composed primarily of light and motorized infantry and includes a newly established aviation corps. Other ground combat and combat support units conduct infantry, artillery, armor, engineer, antiaircraft, antichemical, and command, control, and communications (C3) missions. The ground force is organized into 24 group armies. The PLA has 72 infantry, 12 tank, 2 mechanized, and 7 artillery divisions available for group army or independent operations.

China's ground forces can conduct an effective defense against any conventional attack within Chinese territory. However, the PLA has a very limited ability to project military force beyond its territorial boundaries. Chinese deficiencies in logistics, combat transport, air defense, armor, communications, air support, doctrine, and training severely limit the army's power-projection capabilities. In 1993, rapid reaction units such as the Thirty-Eighth and Thirty-Ninth Group Armies, the Fifteenth Airborne Army, and specified regional divisions conducted mobilization and mobility training exercises to develop their capability to react rapidly to a crisis.

During the 1989 Tiananmen incident, the PLA marshaled and deployed an estimated 200,000 troops to Beijing. This movement of troops may appear impressive, yet it does not translate into enhanced PLA ground force projection capabilities by the year 2000, as the operations in the capital revealed many deficiencies. The 1989 operation was conducted using Civil Aviation Administration of China (CAAC) passenger aircraft flying to and from secured airfields. Units from outside the Beijing MR moved with minimal combat equipment, and the mission was an internal security operation against unarmed civilians. With little riot control training or equipment, PLA ground units and their leaders tragically employed overwhelming armed force against the demonstrators. The PLA will remain the ultimate guarantor of stability and continued rule by the CCP, but the mission of internal security has been given to the People's Armed Police (PAP).

The focus of the PLA ground forces remains modernizing both its main and regional forces to conduct warfare on the modern battlefield. The premier unit for the ground forces is the combined arms or group army. Each PLA main-force group army typically includes approximately 46,000 troops in up to four divisions. Each division includes infantry, armor, artillery, air defense, antichemical defense, signal,

Table 9.3 China's Ground Forces

Category	Number
Active duty personnel	2,300,000
Reserve personnel	1,200,000
Infantry divisions	
Main force	72
Reserve, independent, garrison, border	35
Tank divisions	12
Mechanized divisions	2
Artillery divisions	7
Airborne divisions	3
Tanks	9,500
Armored personnel carriers	3,000
Artillery (guns/howitzers)	1,000
Multiple rocket launchers (MRLs/SSMs)	5,300
Surface-to-air missiles	1,500
Attack helicopters	8
Cargo/utility helicopters	43

Source: The Military Balance: 1992-1993 (London: Brassey's for the International Institute for Strategic Studies).

engineer, and air support units. In general, a group army consists primarily of motorized infantry divisions supported by an armor brigade, artillery division or brigade, and a variety of combat support and combat service support units. Although the group armies are supposed to reflect a move to integrated joint operations, the lack of equipment and training inhibits this capability.

Regional forces consist of full-time PLA troops organized as independent divisions for border and garrison missions. Garrison divisions are mostly static, artillery-heavy units deployed along the coastline and borders in areas of likely attack. The PLA garrison divisions are gradually being demobilized or converted into reserve units or coastal defense units. Because China faces a reduced external threat, the PLA has little requirement for these units designed to stand and fight in designated locales, although the garrison units assigned to major urban localities are an exception. Outside Beijing these city garrisons serve to reinforce the PAP in an internal security crisis and assist PLA main force units. In Beijing, the city garrison serves to protect the CCP leadership, reinforce the PAP, and assist the PLA if required.

The PLA's main force and regional ground units deploy many obsolete but serviceable weapons. In China's armored units, the Type 59 (Soviet T-54) continues to be the primary tank. Of late 1950s vintage, the Type 59 has been followed by evolutionary enhancements resulting in the Type 69, 79, 80, 85, and 90 tanks. With cannon, optics, and range-finder upgrades modeled on Western technologies, these tanks have been produced principally for foreign sales. Only a limited number (200 to 300) have been deployed to PLA armor units. Prototype tanks to replace the Type 59s have been under development for more than fifteen years with the help of various countries. Problems facing the Chinese include lack of funding to produce enough tanks to replace thousands of Type 59s and the lack of success in reverse engineering the Soviet T-72 or being able to integrate foreign systems into an indigenous prototype that can be produced as a viable tank for the next century.

Chinese towed artillery and multiple-rocket launchers have strength in numbers and have achieved significant systems and ammunition enhancements. However, self-propelled (SP) systems continue to face difficulties. The Type 83 152mm SP was assembled for the 1984 National Day Parade, then taken back to the factory to solve integration problems. Only now is this system being deployed to key artillery units. The PLA's towed artillery has capabilities similar to those of the best in the world. For example, the WAC 21, a state-of-the-art 155mm system developed for export, might be deployed to replace the PLA's 152mm systems. Chinese artillery has also been helped by the acquisition of counter-battery radars from the West.

Air defense artillery (ADA) gun systems, from heavy machine guns to 100mm antiaircraft guns, remain the backbone of PLA ADA units. Three surface-to-air (SAM) systems have been deployed in limited numbers to tactical units, the HN-5 infrared (IR) guided, shoulder-launched variant of the 1960s SA-7 *Grail*, the HQ-61 radar-guided SAM, which is a reverse engineering of the 1970s *Sparrow*, and the S-300 or SA-10 that the PLA bought from Russia. Several battalions of S-300 SAMs have been delivered and are being deployed to replace the CSA-2 or SA-2 SAM belt around Beijing.

The PLA's aviation corps is a mix of Soviet (MI-4, 6, 8, and 17) and Western (*Gazelle, Blackhawk, Dauphin,* and *Frelon*) systems. Testing and experimentation continues on lift and antiarmor capabilities and tactics. The most significant problem for PLA army aviation is keeping helicopters and other technically complex machines and weapons operational. The Chinese apply maintenance only when the system is nonoperational. Preventive maintenance, a fairly new concept to the PLA, is not performed regularly. The PLA has had several catastrophic *Dauphin* and *Blackhawk* mishaps as a result.

The PLA ground forces have some R & D ventures in progress to address PLA weapons and equipment deficiencies. These consist primarily of developing antitank and antiaircraft missiles, armor-piercing ammunition, helicopters, trucks, jeeps, automobiles, tank fire-control systems, engines, and turrets for the ground forces. For example, China imported about 500 helicopters from the Soviet Union during the early 1960s, but by 1980, these needed to be replaced. In urgent need of new helicopters for both civilian and military sectors, China has acquired various Western helicopters. In the early 1990s, China imported approximately 300 helicopters from the United States, Russia, France, Australia, and Germany, including eight *Gazelle* helicopters equipped with HOT antitank missiles.

For the remainder of the 1990s, the PLA will have very limited power-projection capabilities. Away from China's rail lines and airfields the PLA would revert to an infantry force. While extremely tough individually, these forces lack adequate logistical, transport, air defense, communications, armor, and air support to fight a modern battle. Development of rapid reaction units in each group army, enhanced training, and the eventual fielding of modern weaponry will result in limited Chinese ground force projection capabilities in the next decade.

Navy

The PLA navy (PLAN) ranks as the third-largest in the world. Headquartered in Beijing, it consists of three fleet commands: the North Sea Fleet, based at Qingdao, Shandong Province; the East Sea Fleet, based at Shanghai; and the South Sea Fleet, based at Zhanjiang, Guangdong Province. The majority of China's three fleets are made up of patrol and coastal combatants. These vessels are effective for coastal defense but ineffective on the open seas.

In the 1970s, when approximately 20 percent of the defense budget was allocated to naval forces, the navy grew dramatically. Modernization continued in the 1980s at a somewhat reduced rate. In light of China's economic conditions and international strategic environment during the late 1980s, the PLAN's strategy shifted, placing greater emphasis on the development of more capable coastal forces and the ability to operate in regional seas. In the 1990s, the Chinese navy intends to add forward depth to its national strategic defense mission. This strategy calls for the navy to protect the forward edge of China's territorial claim in the South China Sea and be prepared, if necessary, for a "localized naval war" against states in the region.

The PLAN has only fifty-six principal combatants. *Luda* destroyers and *Jianghu* frigates, while good, older designed hulls, have significant problems with on-board weapons, equipment, and powerplants. The Chinese navy is trying to upgrade these platforms with both indigenous and foreign systems and powerplants. Key deficiencies and areas of development are in air defense, surface-to-surface missiles, electronic warfare, C3, and in integrating these systems into a viable fighting ship. The PLAN's success in deploying the *Luhu* destroyer as a follow-on to the *Luda,* and the *Jiangwei* frigate as a follow-on to the *Jianghu,* will be essential to China's future capability to protect its territorial waters and claims.

Like its combatants, the PLAN submarine force is one of the largest, yet most obsolete, in the world. China has one operational *Xia*-class SSBN and one converted *Golf*-class test bed submarine equipped to launch the JL-1. Four *Han*-class SSNs are operational but do not operate far from their ports. The

Table 9.4   China's Naval Forces

Category	Number
Active duty personnel	243,000
Reserve personnel	49,000
Destroyers	16
Frigates	36
Submarines	100
Amphibious ships	52
Mine warfare ships	40
Patrol boats	411
Torpedo boats	173
Missile boats	216

Source: The Military Balance: 1992-1993 (London: Brassey's for the International Institute for Strategic Studies).

principal tactical submarine is the *Romeo*-class diesel. This 1950s-vintage, Soviet-designed submarine was totally scrapped from the Soviet Navy. Some Chinese *Romeos* are being retired, and all its *Whiskey*-class submarines have gone to the scrapyard. Both the *Hans* and *Romeos* are fitted with dated sensors and weapons. As a partial replacement for the *Romeos,* the PLAN has been negotiating with Russia to purchase a small number of *Kilo*-class diesel submarines. Such an acquisition would greatly advance submarine technology in China and provide an advanced sonar and weapons platform for the fleets.

The PLAN's amphibious fleet is a result of the 1970s building program. Little was built or added in the 1980s. The Navy has the organic sealift for one infantry division with tanks for a thirty-day deployment. This could provide enough force for a South China Sea Spratly Islands operation, but nothing larger. In addition, hundreds of civilian merchant and fishing vessels could be employed to transport troops in a nontactical operation.

PLAN aviation can cover Chinese ports and installations, but the lack of aerial refueling capability prohibits coverage of fleet operations beyond the limited range of land-based naval fighter aircraft. In addition, most aircraft are limited to daytime operations. The PLAN aviation force is gradually being modernized with the deployment of C-601 air-to-sur-

face missiles on the B-6/*Badger* bomber and the fielding of a new fighter-bomber, the FB-7.

The PLAN's R & D ventures consist primarily of developing antiship missiles, air defense systems, antisubmarine warfare systems, and electronic countermeasure systems. China is improving propulsion systems, gun-loading systems, air surveillance, and fire control radar systems with outside help. The PLAN has received gas turbine engines, air surveillance systems, antisubmarine torpedoes, and mine countermeasure technology from the West and Russia.

To re-equip their obsolete submarines, the Chinese have sought bids from numerous Western countries and Russia for sonars, radars, communications, data processing, propulsion plant, periscopes, batteries, and weapons-handling equipment. For example, the *Han*-class nuclear attack submarine is believed to be fitted with French sonars.

Even with these enhancements, the PLA Navy remains a coastal defense force. However, the PLAN has slowly developed a regional defensive capability so it can now conduct viable operations against Vietnamese-held islands and atolls in the South China Sea. For the remainder of the 1990s, any Chinese naval operation beyond its territorial waters would be constrained by the lack of ship-mounted air defense systems, poor antisubmarine warfare, and inadequate replenishment.

Air Force

The PLA Air Force (PLAAF), established in 1949, has the world's largest collection of 1950s-technology Soviet aircraft. The second-largest air force in the world behind Russia, the PLAAF has as its primary mission the defense of China's airspace. Most PLAAF aircraft are assigned to this air defense role. A few aircraft are assigned to interdiction and close air support, and a limited number dedicated to military airlift and reconnaissance capabilities. Although its large number of aircraft is impressive, the PLAAF's lack of modern capabilities for sustained night operations, all-weather operations, and aerial refueling makes it obsolescent. The PLAAF is estimated to have 500,000 personnel.

Table 9.5   China's Air Force

Category	Number
Active duty personnel	470,000
Reserve personnel	220,000
Interceptors	2,475
Bombers	335
Ground attack	419
Reconnaissance	79
Electronic warfare	3
Antisubmarine warfare	22
Transport	196
Helicopters	132
Combat support	328
Operational support	980
R & D/Storage	920

Source: The Military Balance: 1992-1993 (London: Brassey's for the International Institute for Strategic Studies).

In peacetime, the Air Force Directorate, under the supervision of the PLA General Staff Department, controls the PLAAF through air army headquarters located with, or in communication with, each of the seven military region headquarters. In war, control reverts to regional commanders. The military region air force (MRAF), the PLAAF service component command of the MR, provides administrative and operational leadership for the air force commands, armies, divisions, and regiments within the MR jurisdiction. These regiments are organized under four mission areas: air defense, ground attack, bombing, and independent air operations.

The military reorganization and streamlining of the forces in the mid-1980s resulted in major personnel reduction and transfer of support and technical functions to the newly created civil service. In the 1980s, the PLAAF made serious efforts to raise the education level and improve the training of its pilots. Training emphasized raising technical and tactical skills in individual pilots and participation in combined-arms operations. Flight safety has also been emphasized.

The PLA Air Force's capabilities continue to be seriously hindered by obsolete airframes and power-plants. China's 2,700 F-6 (J-6) fighters are based on the Soviet MiG 19/*Farmer,* which began production in the late 1950s. This aircraft is the backbone of the Air Force. A possible replacement aircraft under development, called the *Xin Jian* (new fighter), will have mid- to late-1970s design technology comparable to the F-16.

The first PLAAF F-7s were Soviet MiG 21F/*Fishbed* fighters delivered to China before 1960. A proven fighter, only 300 have been deployed. Improved versions such as the F-7/*Airguard* have been upgraded with foreign radar, heads-up display, computer, radios, and IFF (identification friend or foe) systems. Several versions of the F-7 fighters are being refitted by Western firms such as General Electric Corporation/Marconi and Grumman. However, these aircraft will not be produced in sufficient numbers to replace the F-6 *Farmers.*

Development began on the F-8 (J-8) interceptor in the late 1960s. The F-8-I *Finback,* a modernized version of the F-7, has been developed into the F-8-II with Western technology. Under the U.S. Peace Pearl program, the F-8-II was to have been a steppingstone to a next-generation fighter. This project has been terminated, however, because of financial, technical, and political difficulties.

The Q-5 (A-5) began in 1958 as a design to transform the MiG-19 into a supersonic, single-seat, twin-engine, close air support aircraft. A prototype flew in 1965, and several were deployed to the flying units. Some were sold to North Korea and Pakistan in the 1970s and 1980s. Under a 1986 contract, the Q-5 was upgraded with Italian avionics and an improved Chinese engine. A Q-5K prototype agreement exists between the Chinese National Aerotechnology Import and Export Corporation (CATIC) and Thomson-CSF. The all-French avionics includes Thomson-CSF heads-up display and laser range-finder, inertial navigation system, radar altimeter, Crouzet wind speed unit, and Omera video camera. The aircraft is being produced mainly for foreign sales but some Air Force and Navy Q-5s can be refitted in the future.

The most significant acquisition by the PLAAF has been the purchase and delivery of twenty-six Su-27/*Flanker* long-range fighters. Chinese pilots and support personnel have trained in Russia and are completing advanced training in central China.

These state-of-the-art, fourth-generation aircraft will provide a leap in aircraft technology from the second generation F-7.

China's bomber force is dependent on the 1960s-vintage B-6 *Badger*. Because of its slow speed and poor electronic countermeasure capability, it is unlikely to survive in a modern aerial arena. C601 missiles will help the B-6's standoff capabilities, but lack of aerial refueling limits any fighter protection for China's bomber force.

Of China's 420 transports, 300 are Y-5 *Colt* biplanes. Some *Tridents* are available for VIP and special cargo flights, and there are limited numbers of Y-7 and Y-8 aircraft based on the Soviet An-12 and An-24 transports. A major acquisition for the PLAAF has been the purchase of ten Il-76 transports. The Y-8 is being developed in several variants for refueling, airborne electronic warning, and surveillance missions. The post-1989 cutoff of Western contracts and military assistance has hindered these programs. As in 1989, CAAC, China's civil aviation administration, stands ready to support PLA operations with all its aircraft and crews.

The Air Force has serious technological deficiencies. Some progress has been made in aircraft design with the incorporation of Western avionics, initial development of flight refueling capabilities, increased all-weather capabilities, and the production of a high-altitude surface-to-air and air-to-ship missile. To address these deficiencies, the PLAAF R & D ventures are concentrating on upgrading aircraft with new fire control and navigation systems. In the late 1980s, Chinese fighter avionics were being upgraded in a collaboration between CATIC and Western avionics firms.

The Chinese aircraft industry is turning increasingly to Russian technology sources in order to update its avionics program. The expanding defense industrial relationship between the PLA and Russia's aircraft industry leads to daily reports and rumors of contracts for MiG-31 coproduction, fighter engine sales, additional Su-27 sales, and thousands of Russian scientists and production engineers assisting in Chinese aeronautics developments.

Paramilitary Operations

Reserves

Under the guidance of the 1985 Central Document No. 22, China began to make reference to the National Defense Reserve Force. In theory, these reserve units are integrated into the orders of battle of group armies and other active force units as augmenting or roundout units. Roughly 80 percent of the forty reserve divisions identified thus far are infantry. Most reserve divisions have been formed in the three military regions adjacent to the Sino-Russian border.

Active-force PLA officers and local government and party leaders are the commanders and cadres of reserve units. Soldiers and lower echelon officers are drawn from a two-category reserve personnel pool. Category 1 personnel are expected to be physically fit, politically reliable eighteen- to twenty-eight-year-old men and women trained in basic and specialized military skills. Category 2 personnel are between the ages of twenty-nine and forty and have little recent military training. In wartime, category 2 personnel would serve to round out personnel for reserve units or would be organized to conduct civil defense in their local areas.

In peacetime, category 1 personnel conduct basic and specialized military training with PLA assistance and perform coastal/border defense in some areas. Both category 1 and 2 personnel assist public security forces and provide disaster relief. These peacetime tasks are administered by military district, local party, and government offices.

The reserve force has increased China's military capability only modestly. Nonetheless, it is better organized, better trained, and more capable than the militia. The doctrinal and organizational framework being established for the reserve force will increase the PLA's wartime capability. The keys to translating the force's potential into a fully realized capability are continued development of reserve training, organization, and mobilization. Barring a drastic change in China's national priorities, the process of reserve force development will be slow.

Since 1989, the PLA has established a viable foundation combining its militia and reserve forces.

A sizable reserve force composed of such specialized elements as antiaircraft, artillery, communications, engineers, antichemical warfare, reconnaissance, naval, and air detachments is being assembled. Military training for these units has been conducted in training bases in nearly 2,000 counties and cities throughout China. The tactical and operational capabilities of the reserves are being enhanced.

Militia and People's Armed Police Force

The PLA militia is controlled by the PLA at the military district (provincial) level and by People's Armed Forces Departments, which evolved to civilian control at the county and city levels as part of the reduction in force. A smaller force than in Mao's era, the militia consists of approximately 4 million armed and 6 million general or ordinary militia. In peacetime the militia's principal tasks are economic production, periodic military training, and maintaining the internal security of China's localities. In time of war, the militia would supply reserves for mobilization, provide logistical support to the PLA, and conduct guerrilla operations behind enemy lines. Many of these wartime missions are being assumed by the PLA's reserve forces, and a considerable downsizing of China's enormous militia force is expected.

The People's Armed Police (PAP) was formed in 1983, when the PLA transferred its internal security and border defense units to the Ministry of Public Security. In its first major test, in May and June 1989, the PAP failed to control the demonstrators in Beijing and was replaced by main force units. A year of intensive riot-control training and acquisition of specialized equipment enabled the PAP to perform its internal security missions adequately during the 1990 Asian Games and the anniversaries of the Tiananmen incident, in the face of no opposition. In wartime, the armed police, as part of China's armed forces, perform border defense and support functions for the PLA.

Accomplishments and the Future

China's military modernization program has succeeded in increasing China's status as a regional military power. Reforms in organization, doctrine, education and training, and personnel practices have brought the PLA closer to its objective of molding a modern combat force capable of waging combined arms warfare. Although PLA capabilities still lag behind advanced-country levels, the lack of immediate potent adversaries on China's borders means that defense modernization will be a long-term program, lasting well into the next century. Actual improvements to date have been slow and incremental. Staffing has been reduced, the reorganization has established a solid foundation to build on, and some excellent R & D and think tanks have been established.

The bulk of China's military modernization will involve the indigenous upgrading of its research, production, and manufacturing capabilities, while continuing to acquire technologies and weapons from the West and Russia. Defense science and industry have become more closely integrated with their civilian counterparts and begun producing more civilian goods while modernizing PLA weaponry with foreign technology. China is expected to continue to avoid large-scale imports and to concentrate on importing limited quantities of items that it cannot produce itself. From there, it will pursue reverse engineering to develop products for domestic use or foreign markets. While selectively pursuing imports, the Chinese are dealing with multiple sources of foreign technology, effectively playing them against one another.

Although new military weapons are emerging from Chinese development facilities with great fanfare, these weapons are not rolling off production lines and being fielded to China's soldiers, sailors, and airmen. As in other sectors, much emphasis is being placed on symbolism. The Navy's *Xia*s and *Han*s are symbolic vessels that rarely depart from their ports. If China should acquire an aircraft or helicopter carrier, it, too, would be just a symbol.

To fund its military modernization efforts, the PLA will continue to pursue arms exports. These sales, especially weapons of mass destruction, challenge the United States and the West, which place an increasingly high priority on the reduction of arms

Although People's Liberation Army capabilities still lag behind those of advanced countries, the lack of immediate potent adversaries on China's borders means that China's defense modernization will be a long-term program. Here, primary school students attend military training in Hangzhou, Zhejiang Province, 1993.

proliferation. Even though proliferation will remain a serious subject of contention between China and the United States, both states are committed to building an enduring relationship.

While the PLA modernizes and its capabilities to defend the homeland improve, there should be little anxiety about the PLA's ability to conduct effective military power projection operations beyond the Spratly Islands. Internal economic troubles, political succession uncertainties, minority unrest, and social fluidity provide a fertile breeding ground for future crises, any of which would undoubtedly retard and possibly derail the PLA's effort to modernize and professionalize. Therefore, with the exception of senior military leaders such as Liu Huaqing and Zhang Zhen, the PLA is trying to disengage itself from politics and concentrate its attention on military tasks and ensuring the stability of the nation.

For the future, China must depend on the military professionalism and leadership of the Army, Navy, Air Force, Second Artillery, and defense industries to bring the PLA into the modern world. The PLA's leaders hope that economic reforms will eventually produce technologically advanced military production facilities. While China's military leaders do not want to become involved in divisive political or ideological turmoil, they will continue to serve as the ultimate guarantors of party rule.

Note: The views expressed in this chapter are those of the author, Lieutenant Colonel Gregory K. S. Man (U.S. Army), and not necessarily those of the Department of Defense.

CHAPTER **10**

CHINA'S RELATIONS WITH HONG KONG, TAIWAN, AND TIBET

Tumultuous developments in twentieth-century China have reflected strong nationalistic and anti-imperialistic currents of thought that have focused the attention of the Chinese leadership and popular opinion on the importance of Chinese reassertion of control over territories that were historically part of the Chinese empire. Hong Kong and Taiwan were among the territories "lost" to British, Japanese, and other foreign expansion in the nineteenth century. The Manchu dynasty in its waning years showed the depth of this sense of empire and control by dispatching troops to reassert its claim to Tibet in the face of British encroachments in the early 1900s. Later, Chiang Kai-shek's Nationalists were uniform in asserting their claim to Taiwan, Hong Kong, Tibet, Mongolia, and other "lost territories."

Mao Zedong's Communists were no less adamant in their defense of territorial claims, although they—unlike the Nationalists—bowed to realities of power and Soviet wishes in accepting Mongolia as an independent country. The wide swings of Sino-Soviet relations during the Maoist period—from close alliance to military confrontation—had an effect on China's territorial claims, with Mao for a time in the 1960s appearing to reassert Chinese claims to vast reaches of territory taken from imperial China by tsarist Russia in the nineteenth century.

Territorial Issues in Post-Mao China

As Chinese revolutionary ardor declined coincident with the rise of more technocratic and pragmatic nation-builders to leadership positions in post-Mao China, the ideological vacuum was filled to some degree by the new leaders' appeals to nationalistic and territorial claims. In particular, China's success in reaching agreement with Great Britain in 1984 to restore Hong Kong to Chinese rule in 1997 was clearly viewed by Chinese leaders as a major accomplishment in China's century-long quest for restoration of appropriate rights and dignity in the modern state system. Strong nationalistic sentiment has also motivated Chinese efforts to maintain a hold on territories like Tibet, which have been subject to repeated episodes of internal ethnic dissent that have received sympathy and support from around the world. Nationalistic feelings also help to explain Beijing's stance that Taiwan, which has been separate from mainland control since 1949, should be reunited with China under terms giving Beijing sovereign control.

The collapse of the Soviet Union and its empire of "captive nations" in Europe and Asia, the decline of the international Communist movement, and the complete undermining of the cold war international structure of foreign affairs have had a major impact on China's international security environment. This, in turn, has had serious consequences for China's nationalistic and territorial claims. On the one hand, the changes discredited the Communist rulers of China, who seemed to underline their political weakness and illegitimacy by having to resort to massive armed force in order to curb pro-democracy demonstrators in Beijing's Tiananmen Square and other

Chinese cities in June 1989. Perhaps of more importance, the breakup of the Soviet empire gave a strong boost to numerous nationalist and ethnic groups previously held in check by Moscow to assert their claims to autonomy and independence. Their example was followed by others in areas important to China's leaders. In particular, dissidents Tibet continued to agitate for greater autonomy and independence. Meanwhile, activists in Hong Kong pushed for greater local autonomy under the general framework of the 1984 Joint Agreement on the Question of Hong Kong, also known as the Sino-British Joint Declaration. And in Taiwan, politicians calling for Taiwan self-determination and independence gained more prominence and a significant share of political power.

The collapse of the cold war international order also reinforced an emerging trend in Asian and world politics. Not only were governments being held increasingly accountable to the demands of those governed but the measurement of success was increasingly economic. That is, the legitimacy of governments rested increasingly on their ability to encourage economic development and a better material life for their people. Authorities in Hong Kong and Taiwan, two of Asia's emerging economic "tigers," had long followed this route in charting economic success. Post-Mao Chinese leaders began to recognize this political logic in the late 1970s, pursuing internal market-oriented economic reforms and outreach to the developed world unprecedented in modern Chinese history.

The result of these trends has been a convergence of Chinese entrepreneurs in Hong Kong, Taiwan, and coastal China that created the most economically vibrant part of the world by the early 1990s. The concept of "greater China" came into vogue based on rapidly growing investment from Hong Kong and Taiwan to mainland China, and increasingly from mainland China to Hong Kong as well, and on the burgeoning trade between and among Hong Kong, Taiwan, and mainland China. It was premised on a sometimes vague notion of the coming together of economic, political, and cultural interaction among formerly separate elements of the Chinese diaspora.

A careful analysis of the interactions among these parties indeed showed closer economic and cultural convergence. By the late 1980s, Hong Kong and coastal China had become each other's largest outside investor and major trading partner. Taiwan investment and annual trade with mainland China by the 1990s each had reached around $10 billion and growing fast. Travel among the three grew enormously, especially as Taiwan eased restrictions on travel to the mainland. People in all three entities had a better understanding of one another's societies and unique cultural features. Nevertheless, there were clear limits as to what effect economic convergence and greater human interchange would have on political and other relations. Thus, as people in Hong Kong reassessed the politics in Beijing after the 1989 Tiananmen incident, they were more inclined to abandon political apathy in favor of an activist approach pushing for greater Hong Kong autonomy under the Sino-British agreement of 1984. In Taiwan, greater contacts with the mainland did little to bridge the tremendous gap in living standards and outlook, while Taiwan's greater economic development and political freedom encouraged supporters of Taiwan's formal independence from mainland China.

Whatever importance the concept of "greater China" had for integrating formerly separate elements of the Chinese diaspora, it was of little relevance for Tibet, where Chinese rule was based on physical control and historical precedent. Beijing saw a strategic need to keep control of this area, which despite its remoteness is essential to the defense and control of western China.

Chinese leaders used material incentives to encourage Tibetans to conform to central government-approved behavior and to work with existing authorities. But the rise in material well-being under Chinese rule was of less importance to many Tibetans than the fact that Chinese authorities—after several decades of often brutal and capricious repression—were determined to control and integrate Tibet into China in ways Tibetan partisans saw as destroying Tibetans' freedom and national identity. The repeated evidence of continued resistance to Chinese rule showed the limitations of China's strategy toward the region.

Hong Kong

Hong Kong has a population of almost 6 million, 98 percent of whom are ethnic Chinese. The colony was acquired by Britain from China in three stages: Hong Kong Island (32 sq. mi.) by the Treaty of Nanjing in 1842; Kowloon Peninsula and Stonecutters' Island (3.75 sq. mi.) by the First Convention of Peking in 1860; and the New Territories (365 sq. mi., consisting of a mainland area adjoining Kowloon and 235 adjacent islands) by a ninety-nine-year lease under the Second Convention of Peking in 1898. Consequently, most of the land area of Hong Kong was scheduled to revert to China in 1997, while Hong Kong Island and Kowloon Peninsula theoretically were to remain British in perpetuity. Beijing regarded all of Hong Kong as part of its territory, held illegally under British administration—a view it announced formally to the United Nations in 1972.

Hong Kong's Rise to Prominence

Hong Kong began its rise to prominence as a preeminent commercial center in East Asia after Shanghai was taken by Communist forces in 1949 and began to decline as an international economic market. The large number of people from the People's Republic of China (PRC) who sought refuge in Hong Kong and the subsequent cut-off of much entrepôt trade between China and the West as a result of the embargo during the Korean War led to the development of textile and other light manufacturing industries in Hong Kong.

At first Hong Kong purchased only limited amounts of food, building materials, and fuel from the PRC for local consumption, but its growing industries created new needs, causing Hong Kong to become a major importer of PRC products including such vital supplies as water, foodstuffs, and fuel. In the early 1980s, imports from China amounted to almost $6 billion, one-fourth of Hong Kong's total import bill. Hong Kong exports to China were much lower in value, which gave the PRC a favorable balance of trade that, along with remittances by Hong Kong Chinese to relatives in the PRC, accounted for around 30 to 40 percent of China's overall foreign exchange earnings. According to a well-known adage in the region, "Hong Kong is a unique machine capable of turning PRC pigs and chickens into U.S. dollars."

After Great Britain withdrew most military forces east of the Suez Canal during the 1960s, Hong Kong's security rested even more on Chinese restraint and goodwill than on the very limited power of British forces in the colony. There was considerable uncertainty over the future of Hong Kong in the latter 1960s, when violence associated with the most radical phase of "Red Guard Diplomacy" during China's Cultural Revolution threatened to spill over and jeopardize stability in the colony. As Maoist influence faded, however, increasingly cordial, practical, and extensive ties developed between the colony and the PRC. Transportation markedly improved and visits increased, encouraged by official representatives of both sides. The British governor of Hong Kong made his first trip to the PRC in March 1979, and Chinese leader Deng Xiaoping told him that "investors in Hong Kong should put their hearts at ease" over Chinese intentions toward the colony.

Subsequently, British officials and Hong Kong business leaders repeatedly sought assurances from Chinese officials regarding the future of the territory after the scheduled lapse of the lease on the New Territories in 1997. PRC officials freely echoed Deng's instruction and pledged that Hong Kong's social and economic system would not be adversely affected; they implied that China was not anxious to push the British out and govern the territory directly.

China's cautious approach to the neighboring Portuguese territory of Macao seemed to underline Beijing's reluctance to interfere strongly in Hong Kong. After the 1975 military coup in Portugal and Lisbon's withdrawal from overseas holdings, Macao was the only Portuguese territory to retain its governor in office—this was because China refused to discuss the future of Macao with Portugal, and independence for the territory did not appear to be a viable option. When Portugal and China established diplomatic relations in 1979, the PRC made clear that it regarded Macao as Chinese territory under Portuguese administration. In Western legal terms, Macao remained a territory and Portugal was sovereign. In both interpretations, Macao had no international personality itself and its relations were subject to the de jure approval of the president of Portugal and the de facto tolerance of China, which continued to exert extensive influence in the territory through a network of pro-PRC Chinese leaders there.

Sino-British Accord of 1984

By 1982, the impending end of the lease governing the New Territories (in 1997) began to have a direct impact on individual property leases, mortgages (often made for fifteen years), and other financial and real estate arrangements in Hong Kong during 1982. This prompted British authorities to raise the issue again in discussions with Chinese leaders at the time of British Prime Minister Margaret Thatcher's September 1982 visit to China. The visit produced agreement between China and Britain to "enter into talks through diplomatic channels with the common aim of maintaining the stability and prosperity of Hong Kong." But the visit was also marked by pointed differences over the current legal status of the territory. In addition, Deng Xiaoping reportedly told Prime Minister Thatcher in September 1982 that a Sino-British agreement on Hong Kong had to be reached within two years. Beijing subsequently announced that if the agreement were not reached within that time, China would announce its plans for the territory unilaterally. This represented an implicit threat presumably designed to keep the British from dragging their feet in the negotiations.

After many months of secret diplomatic communication, the two sides issued a joint statement on July 1, 1983, announcing the start of formal talks on Hong Kong's future. The talks continued into 1984 and were supplemented in June 1984 by discussions of a working group of Chinese and British diplomats trying to come up with a draft agreement by Bei-

Chinese Pledges Regarding Hong Kong's Future

- After China regains full sovereignty and administrative control of Hong Kong in 1997, the territory will become a special administrative region of China under Article 31 of the Chinese constitution.
- Hong Kong will enjoy a high degree of autonomy, with local people administering the city. Beijing has raised the possibility of local elections to select senior local authorities.
- Hong Kong's present capitalist socioeconomic system will remain unchanged for at least fifty years after 1997.
- Hong Kong's legal structure will remain basically unchanged except that the highest court of appeals will be located in Hong Kong instead of London.
- Local and expatriate civil servants, including police officers and administrators, can retain their jobs.
- Hong Kong's status as a free port and international financial center will remain unchanged.
- The Hong Kong dollar will remain a separate and freely convertible currency.
- Residents will enjoy the right of free speech, assembly, press, and the freedom to travel.
- Beijing will be responsible for Hong Kong's foreign affairs, but will maintain its separate status in international organizations and in international agreements. It will be allowed to issue its own travel documents.
- The Hong Kong government will be responsible for public security, to be maintained by the local police force.
- The economic interests of Britain and other countries will be respected.

jing's September 1984 deadline. In the meantime, the Chinese gradually released details of their plans for Hong Kong informally, mainly through reports from Hong Kong residents who met with senior Chinese leaders over this period.

Press reports and the limited Chinese and British disclosures about progress in the talks showed that London was forced repeatedly to give way to Chinese demands during the course of the negotiations. First, some observers in London and Hong Kong had initially hoped that China would accept a renewal of the lease on the New Territories or allow the status quo to continue after 1997, but China's determination to recover complete sovereignty over all of Hong Kong soon dashed these hopes. Second, by late 1983, it had become clear that the British had been compelled to accept in principle China's sovereignty and administrative control of Hong Kong after 1997, and had agreed to negotiate on the basis of China's general plan for the territory. Third, during a visit to Beijing in April 1984, British Foreign Secretary Geoffrey Howe agreed to a timetable in accord with China's deadline, calling for a draft agreement by September 1984, a debate in the British Parliament in the autumn, and ratification by year's end. Howe then went to Hong Kong, where he reported that it would be "unrealistic" to expect the British to retain an administrative role in Hong Kong after 1997.

In mid-1984, it was disclosed that London was under pressure to accept a Chinese proposal to establish a joint liaison group to oversee developments in Hong Kong before 1997, thereby giving China a vehicle to influence developments in the colony prior to formal takeover. Foreign Secretary Howe again traveled to Beijing and Hong Kong in late July in an effort to bridge differences. He reported that the Chinese were more accommodating than in the past. In particular, while Britain accepted China's proposal for a joint liaison group, both sides explicitly stated that the group was not to be an "organ of power," but would serve only as a consultative body between the Chinese and the British over Hong Kong issues. Moreover, Howe indicated that the British had obtained China's agreement that the proposed Sino-British accord would contain detailed provisions governing future administration in Hong Kong and would be considered an international agreement legally binding on both China and Great Britain.

The agreement reached on September 26, 1984, known as the Sino-British Joint Declaration, was in

Hong Kong's small land area is home to a population of almost 6 million, 98 percent of whom are ethnic Chinese. The Sino-British Joint Declaration of 1984 paves the way for China's resumption of sovereignty over the territory in July 1997.

accord with British expectations and paved the legal path for British withdrawal. It also ended any remaining doubt over whether or not Hong Kong would become Chinese territory—it would. Faced with strong Chinese insistence on regaining sovereignty over the territory, Britain had felt compelled to give ground repeatedly in the course of the negotiations; this approach, along with some Chinese compromises, led to the 1984 agreement that seemed to many to hold promise for a smooth transition to Chinese rule under the proposed ''one country, two systems'' framework.

Great Britain attempted to negotiate the best deal it could get from China regarding the future of Hong

Kong. The agreement contained various specific Chinese commitments to preserve Hong Kong's British-style laws and institutions and to allow Hong Kong to continue to prosper as an autonomous economic entity with its own freely convertible currency and its distinctive standing in international economic affairs. Nevertheless, British officials acknowledged that London had few contingency plans in the event China did not fully uphold the accord in the years ahead. Foreign Secretary Howe reportedly said that the agreement relied on trust between Britain and China, rather than on tangible guarantees of its implementation.

Hong Kong-China Economic Interdependence

The next several years saw continuous Sino-British interchange under the framework established by the 1984 agreement. Tens of thousands of higher paid, capable Hong Kong residents left each year for opportunities elsewhere—a ''brain drain'' of serious proportions. Nonetheless, incremental progress was made toward incorporating the various Chinese reassurances and promises into the PRC Basic Law, passed in 1990, that is to govern administration of Hong Kong after 1997. A minority in Hong Kong objected to the way Britain and China continued to deal with Hong Kong's fate without input from the people of the colony. But perhaps of even more importance for the future of Hong Kong was the ongoing rapid development of a very close and interdependent economic relationship between Hong Kong and the newly opened regions of coastal China, especially neighboring Guangdong Province.

Thus, by the late 1980s, ten years of PRC economic openness and reform had begun to change the nature of the mainland's relations with Hong Kong. As in the past, Hong Kong remained one of China's top trading partners as well as one of China's major economic conduits to the rest of the world. But the level and scope of Chinese foreign trade was growing rapidly, far surpassing the considerable growth rate of the Chinese economy as a whole. In short, this meant that trade with Hong Kong was even more important than it had been in the past. Similarly, Hong Kong continued to account for 30 to 40 percent of

China's foreign exchange earnings, but the level and scope of those earnings were also growing faster than the economy as a whole.

China's post-Mao "open door" to economic investment provided entree for Hong Kong entrepreneurs and other foreign investors working through Hong Kong-based companies. Sixty to seventy percent of external investment in mainland China consistently came from Hong Kong. Capitalists in the colony were particularly attracted to economic opportunities in nearby Guangdong Province. Because of space constraints and a limited and increasingly expensive labor force, Hong Kong entrepreneurs began to move processing, manufacturing, and other activities to nearby parts of Guangdong Province. By 1988, Hong Kong manufacturers directly employed two million workers in Guangdong. By the 1990s, the number of manufacturing employees working for Hong Kong enterprises in mainland China was reportedly more than twice the number of such workers in Hong Kong.

Guangdong's geographic proximity, large labor supply, substantially lower wage rates, and overall lower costs of production bolstered Hong Kong's international competitiveness. Hong Kong's special access to Guangdong and, through Guangdong, to China as a whole increased its attractiveness to foreign businesses anxious to benefit from Hong Kong's export advantages and gain greater access to China's domestic market.

For its part, Guangdong benefited greatly from its Hong Kong connections. A key success story in China's modernization program, Guangdong achieved spectacular double-digit growth rates in the 1980s, comparable to those achieved by Japan in the early 1950s, Taiwan in the late 1950s, and South Korea in the early 1960s. Moreover, in achieving this growth rate, Guangdong had to overcome challenges not faced by these countries. As part of Communist China, Guangdong labored under greater economic and political constraints than did these dynamic Asian economies. In addition, the province was confronted with an international trading environment decidedly less favorable to the kind of export-driven growth that had contributed to Asian economic success stories in earlier years. Its proximity to Hong Kong,

however, gave Guangdong a special asset. Guangdong benefited from Hong Kong's high general management skills, well-developed financial and services sectors, and the excellent information network that enabled Hong Kong to respond rapidly to changing conditions in overseas markets.

As time went on, the interconnectedness between the mainland and Hong Kong economies grew into a two-way street. In particular, mainland China's level of investment in Hong Kong came to far surpass that of other countries. Beijing's stake in the health and vibrancy of the territory's economic status and prospects grew accordingly.

Sino-British Tensions over Hong Kong in the 1990s

The developing pattern of economic interdependence and political accommodation (especially by the British side) might have continued steadily toward 1997 had it not been for the political crisis in mainland China posed by the 1989 Tiananmen incident. Moreover, the end of the cold war led Britain and others to recalculate the importance of their relationship with Beijing in the post-cold war world. While these events in fact did little to upset the broad trend of growing Hong Kong-China economic interconnectedness, they laid the groundwork for a serious Sino-British confrontation in the 1990s over the future course of governance in Hong Kong.

China's June 1989 Tiananmen Square incident led to a nationwide crackdown on dissent, and became a major turning point in Sino-British relations over Hong Kong. Up to that point, the British and Chinese had settled into a pattern of generally cooperative interaction over Hong Kong, following the difficult bilateral negotiations that preceded the joint Sino-British Joint Declaration of 1984 governing Hong Kong's reversion to Chinese sovereignty in 1997. Subsequently, British officials reportedly considered political reforms that would grant the people of Hong Kong greater autonomy in the period leading to 1997. But London moved cautiously, in part out of concern over Chinese government objections to granting the Hong Kong government a political status distinct from that of the PRC after 1997.

The Tiananmen Square crackdown led to demonstrations in Hong Kong involving more than one million residents protesting the PRC government's action. People in the territory became influential supporters of dissidents in the PRC and helped to smuggle out political critics and information that proved damaging to the Beijing regime's standing at home and abroad. This changed British and Chinese calculations over Hong Kong in several ways.

For the British, the so-called politically apathetic Chinese people in Hong Kong were now showing a keen interest in politics. Many pressed for more support from London to establish better safeguards against possibly capricious and repressive PRC government action toward Hong Kong after 1997. Hong Kong's increasingly important middle class of professionals and business people began to prominently suggest that representative government in Hong Kong be strengthened and expanded.

For China, the demonstrations and subsequent action of people in Hong Kong raised a major security concern. They heightened PRC sensitivities over any action by the British or others that could be seen as fostering political or other conditions in Hong Kong at odds with Beijing's definition of stability.

British Actions to Reassure Hong Kong

To reassure the residents of Hong Kong and avoid unduly antagonizing Beijing, British authorities took several steps, including passing a Bill of Rights for Hong Kong citizens; granting an additional fifty thousand Hong Kong residents with close ties to Great Britain the option to emigrate there; and encouraging countries like the United States, France, and others to grant more generous immigration options to Hong Kong employees of their institutions and businesses in Hong Kong. Elections for the eighteen contested seats of the Hong Kong Legislative Council (or LegCo) were held on schedule in 1991 and were won by vocal critics of China. Beijing opposed many of these measures, but acquiesced after they were completed.

There were two key elements of the British plan for reassuring Hong Kong after the Tiananmen incident. The first involved construction of a large, complicated, and expensive airport project that would demonstrate confidence in the territory's future. The second involved obtaining Chinese agreement to allow those Hong Kong legislators elected before 1997 to serve out their terms after China took over in July 1997, a concept referred to as the "through train."

Almost from the outset, the airport plan and the "through train" met with serious Chinese objections. Chinese leaders were able to call international financial support for the airport into question by asserting that they had not been adequately consulted on the project and that its financing might have to be reviewed after 1997. Attempting to move the airport project forward, Britain began negotiations with China. These talks bogged down, however, amid Chinese charges that Britain was planning to spend Hong Kong's treasury surplus before 1997 on airport contracts that would benefit British firms. Meanwhile, Chinese commentators made clear that Martin Lee and other LegCo members who were open critics of the PRC would be excluded from the "through train" in 1997.

In an effort to cut through the difficulties over the airport and the "through train" and to get these programs back on track, British Prime Minister John Major in September 1991 became the first Western head of government to travel to Beijing after the Tiananmen incident. Many observers noted that Chinese treatment of Major was humiliating—Major was required, for example, to review the troops at the site of the massacre at Tiananmen Square. Although Major managed to sign a memorandum of understanding with Beijing over the airport, Chinese officials continued to voice reservations that made it difficult to move ahead with the project.

Under the circumstances, Britain decided to shift the style if not the substance of its policy toward Hong Kong. The more cautious policy of the recent past, solicitous of PRC concerns and fearful of antagonizing China, was put aside in favor of a more direct approach under the leadership of Hong Kong Governor Christopher Patten. The new governor's fall 1992 proposal to broaden representation in LegCo was a notable case in point. The Chinese had privately asked for consultations before the governor

In July 1992 the British sent a new governor to Hong Kong, Christopher Patten, shown here reviewing an honor guard upon his arrival in the colony. Patten's bold steps to promote democracy in Hong Kong have brought him into frequent conflict with Beijing.

went public with the new plan. The governor proceeded to announce the plan first, however, calling on the Chinese to consult. (Privately, some British observers noted that if Britain had followed past practice, there would have been consultations according to PRC wishes, which probably would have blocked or diluted Patten's reforms.) Subsequently, Patten proceeded with his planned reform despite strenuous PRC objections, saying that he remained willing to discuss the issue with China. The Chinese objected to the Hong Kong government's representation in talks proposed by the British side. Compromise was reached in mid-April 1993 allowing new Sino-British talks on Hong Kong. Some British observers in Hong Kong believed that new talks with

Beijing would do little to solve the problem, however, as the Chinese would try to block the reforms that Patten was determined to carry forward.

China's Reaction

Chinese observers close to the Hong Kong situation stated that Beijing was well aware and suspicious of the new direction in British policy after the Tiananmen incident. The Chinese government reportedly was willing to acquiesce in British actions over the Bill of Rights, passports, and other steps, but the airport was a different matter, given its size and the amount of money involved (over $15 billion). Governor Patten's actions regarding political reforms despite Chinese objections greatly increased Chinese anger and attracted a barrage of Chinese rhetoric and other pressure focused on the governor.

In general, Beijing was put in the position of reacting to British actions. Up to 1989, relations with Britain over Hong Kong had been satisfactory from China's point of view, but subsequent British actions, described above, deepened Chinese suspicions. Knowledgeable Chinese officials thought the British intent was to create a quasi-independent political entity in Hong Kong by 1997 that Beijing would be required to recognize, with the more representative LegCo under Patten's program as a central element in the plan. Beijing argued that Patten's changes would complicate Chinese reassertion of sovereignty in 1997; make more difficult Beijing's delicate task of trying to run the territory effectively after 1997; and in the meantime divide political opinion and reduce business confidence in the territory. They charged that London was promoting these reforms out of vengeance and anger stemming from its being compelled to withdraw from Hong Kong. Some Chinese officials saw the British actions as part of a broader Western conspiracy against China, which included U.S. and French efforts to shore up Taiwan's separation from the mainland through new arms sales and other means.

Competing Policy Priorities

British government objectives in the situation appeared fairly straightforward to observers in Hong Kong. Governor Patten and officials in Hong Kong and London wanted to assure Hong Kong residents of more representative institutions before 1997. British officials had given this goal lower priority in the past, reflecting in part their own desire to run colonial affairs, the apparent apathy of people in Hong Kong regarding politics, and concern over Beijing's possibly critical reaction. Meanwhile, British officials hoped that their shift in approach after 1989 might set a pattern for Britain's remaining years in Hong Kong, wherein Chinese government officials would be less inclined to meddle in administrative and other affairs of the territory until 1997.

Given Beijing's strident reaction to Patten's plan, British officials recognized that their policy ran the risk of igniting a protracted confrontation with Beijing that could seriously upset Sino-British relations and possibly affect business and popular confidence in Hong Kong. They apparently judged, however, that Hong Kong residents and businesses would weather this storm and that longer-term interests in stability required that the newly politically energized people of Hong Kong be given a greater voice in their own political affairs.

Britain appeared to be in a better position to push this political objective than it had been during the previous decade, which saw London repeatedly give way to PRC demands on political, economic, and other issues regarding Hong Kong. For one thing, the people of Hong Kong were seen as better prepared to deal with PRC warnings and threats. In the 1980s, such Chinese rhetoric would have sent business and public confidence down sharply, but Hong Kong residents were now said to be accustomed to Beijing's posturing and to have prepared necessary contingency plans. For another, a considerable number of people in Hong Kong were organized and mobilized to push for greater political rights. Any British retreat would surely be excoriated by them and by press and interest groups in Hong Kong, London, and elsewhere that favored greater democratization in Hong Kong. Meanwhile, Britain's economic stake in Hong Kong—which might be jeopardized by confrontation with Beijing over political matters—was relatively small. China, Japan, and the United States had much larger economic interests in the territory. Many of the so-called British firms in Hong Kong were actually more representative of the interests of Hong Kong resident shareholders than of British citizens. Although Britain had a growing stake in the emerging China market, Chinese threats to link its handling of British business on the mainland with London's policy toward Hong Kong worked against China's broader interest in winning Western support for its membership in the General Agreement on Tariffs and Trade (GATT) and other organizations. Finally, Governor Patten's assertive stance in favor of political rights was well received in Britain and the West. He and the British government were widely depicted in Western media as principled advocates of democracy working against forces of reaction and repression in Beijing.

Hong Kong public figures were split sharply over Patten's plan and China's reaction. On one side were elected legislators like Martin Lee, who strongly supported Governor Patten and warned of popular reaction in Hong Kong if the British were to back down. On the other were more conservative politicians, like LegCo member Allen Lee, who seemed to consider it unwise to jeopardize Hong Kong's future relationship with the PRC for the sake of possibly short-lived broader representation for Hong Kong citizens in their government. They strongly favored a return to the previous British policy of accommodation regarding PRC demands.

Beijing's policy goals focused on broad political principles as well as practical matters of stability and control in Hong Kong. Beijing saw Patten's plan and his method of operation as high-handed, insulting, and contrary to earlier understandings reached between Chinese and British officials over Hong Kong. In this view, the governor's actions seemed implicitly designed to challenge PRC sovereignty and control over Hong Kong after 1997 and, as such, they elicited strong Chinese feelings regarding the evil intent of British and Western imperialism in China.

As a practical matter, Beijing had very large economic, political, and other interests in Hong Kong and reportedly was concerned about its ability to manage the complicated situation there after 1997. Dangers included possible Hong Kong support for people and groups seen as subversive by the PRC; the difficulty of managing the complicated political, economic, and social welfare institutions of a highly sophisticated entity like Hong Kong; and the worry that instability or political polarization in Hong Kong would negatively affect the billions of dollars of investment of PRC companies in Hong Kong and the more than $30 billion of Hong Kong investment in China's economy.

Possible Outcomes

Tensions remained high in 1994, as LegCo narrowly passed Patten's reforms and China stepped up efforts to establish a separate administration. Beijing pledged to derail Hong Kong's "through train" and political reforms when it took control in 1997, but it also tried to reassure the colony by easing the way for progress on construction of the new airport and related facilities.

The conflicting objectives and relative power of the Chinese and British suggested that the crisis could continue for some time. Critical variables included the level of support for Patten in LegCo; business and public confidence in Hong Kong; foreign reaction, especially from the United States and Japan; and possible new initiatives from London or Beijing.

One scenario would see LegCo continue to support the governor. The Chinese, presented with a fait accompli, would be forced to acquiesce as they did in the face of the Hong Kong-passed Bill of Rights and expanded immigration provisions in 1990. In reaction, Beijing would be expected to step up its recent efforts to establish its own bodies of Hong Kong citizens to serve as "advisers" on Hong Kong affairs. This would presumably deepen PRC involvement in Hong Kong matters, but could be looked upon with some equanimity in Hong Kong. In particular, such advisory panels would expose Beijing even more closely to the complexities of running Hong Kong's efficient administration structure and educate Chinese leaders more fully on the need to avoid disrupting China's vast stake in Hong Kong.

A second scenario would involve talks leading to a compromise on Patten's political reform. This could involve compromises by both the British and Chinese governments. Resumed talks leading to compromise were favored by many U.S. businesses and others in Hong Kong who believed that the political impasse negatively affected Hong Kong's stability and their interests in the territory.

A third scenario would see Beijing take more substantive action. Chinese officials made clear that they were prepared to set up a separate administration for Hong Kong (the "second kitchen") if Patten's planned reforms went through or if the impasse continued. Other options included concrete action to pressure Hong Kong until it accommodates PRC interests. Some could be heavy-handed (cutting off water or food supplies); others could be more subtle (refusing to accept the return of illegal Chinese immigrants to Hong Kong or refusing to endorse the airport plan). All present heavy risks for the extensive PRC economic interests in Hong Kong.

Beijing's preferred outcome would involve LegCo's refusal to pass Patten's reforms. This would presumably show that Chinese pressure was sufficient to cause the Hong Kong representatives to back away from programs opposed by the PRC. Beijing would hope for such an outcome to discredit Patten and result either in his removal or retirement, or a change in his approach back to the more accommodating posture of previous British governors.

Taiwan

According to Chinese sources, migration from China to Taiwan began as early as 500 C.E. Taiwan seems to have been known, albeit vaguely, to China's Song dynasty historians as early as the tenth century. Dutch traders first claimed the island in 1624 as a base for Dutch commerce with Japan and the China coast. Dutch colonists administered the island and its predominantly aboriginal population until 1661. The first major influx of migrants from the Chinese mainland came during the Dutch period, sparked by political and economic chaos on the China coast during the twilight of the Ming dynasty and at the time of the Manchu invasion.

In 1664, a Chinese fleet led by the Ming loyalist Zheng Chenggong (known in the West as Koxinga) retreated from the mainland and occupied Taiwan. Zheng expelled the Dutch and established Taiwan as a base in his attempt to restore the Ming dynasty. He died shortly thereafter and, in 1683, his successors submitted to Manchu control.

Manchu China ruled Taiwan as a frontier district until it was declared a separate Chinese province in 1886. During the eighteenth and nineteenth centuries, migration from China's coastal provinces of Fujian and Guangdong steadily increased, and Chinese supplanted aborigines as the dominant population group. In 1895, a weakened imperial China ceded Taiwan to Japan after the first Sino-Japanese war.

Taiwan

Background to the Economic "Miracle"

During its fifty years of authoritarian colonial domination (1895-1945), Japan expended considerable effort in developing Taiwan's economy, laying the foundation for Taiwan's later industrial development. Also under Japanese rule, a government-supported school system spread literacy, giving Taiwan an educated labor force. In 1945 Taiwan reverted to Chinese rule. Toward the end of the civil war on the mainland, as the Communists under Mao Zedong began to consolidate their victories, some two million Chinese refugees fled to Taiwan, predominantly military officials, bureaucrats, and business people. After the Communist victory, Nationalist President Chiang Kai-shek established a new "provisional" capital in Taipei in December 1949. Just before retreating to Taiwan, Chiang Kai-shek secured a revision of the constitution granting him broad powers under a system of martial law, including the ability to

Foreign trade has been a major factor in Taiwan's rapid economic growth since the 1950s. The composition of Taiwan's exports has changed from predominantly agricultural commodities to 90 percent industrial goods. Here, Taiwanese workers check television receivers coming off the assembly line.

restrict freedom of assembly, free expression, and political activities. President Chiang remained in office on Taiwan until his death in 1975, although by 1972 power had effectively been transferred to his eldest son, Chiang Ching-kuo. The younger Chiang became premier in 1972 and president in 1978, serving until he died on January 13, 1988. The organization of Taiwan's ruling party, the Nationalist Party or Kuomintang (KMT), closely parallels that of the government at all levels, with key government and party posts often held by a single individual. Like its counterpart on the mainland, the Chinese Communist Party (CCP), the KMT is modeled on Lenin's Bolshevik Party and is responsible for determining policy.

Since the 1950s, Taiwan's economy has changed from being primarily agricultural to mostly industrialized. Taiwan's per capita income is estimated at more than $10,000 per year. The economy distributes wealth in a balanced way that gives all major sectors in society an important stake in continued economic progress.

Foreign trade has been a major factor in Taiwan's rapid growth over the past forty years. The value of trade roughly tripled in each five-year period since 1955 and increased nearly fourfold between 1975 and 1980. Foreign investment, mostly from the United States, Japan, Western Europe, and overseas Chinese in many countries, helped introduce modern technology to the island in the 1960s. Taiwan's exports have changed from predominantly agricultural commodities to 90 percent industrial goods. Raw materials and capital goods account for more than 90 percent of all imports. Taiwan also imports more than 75 percent of its energy needs. The United States and Japan account for more than half of Taiwan's foreign trade, and the United States is Taiwan's largest trading partner. Other important trading partners are Hong Kong, Kuwait, Saudi Arabia, Germany, Australia, Indonesia, and, most recently, mainland China. The lack of formal diplomatic relations with all but a few of its trading partners has not hindered Taiwan's rapidly increasing commerce. The maintenance of a large military establishment, which absorbs about 6 percent of the gross national product (GNP) and accounts for about 30 percent of the central budget, places a substantial but manageable burden on Taiwan's expanding economy. For much of the 1970s and 1980s, GNP rose at an annual average of 9 percent in real terms.

The growth of Taiwan's trade in recent years has led to large trade surpluses, particularly with the United States. Taiwan's resulting large foreign-exchange holdings and inflationary pressures have persuaded authorities to relax controls on the outflow of capital. The political decision in the late 1980s to allow greater interchange with mainland China has prompted rapid growth in trade and investment from Taiwan to the mainland. Exports from Taiwan to the mainland accounted for nearly 90 percent of their almost $7 billion in bilateral trade in 1992. In that same year, $1 billion in direct foreign investment in China, representing 9.5 percent of China's total foreign investment, came from Taiwan.

Social Stability:
Key to Taiwan's Development

Social stability was often credited with creating the necessary conditions for Taiwan's rapid economic development and with helping to avoid political disorder. While many observers admired Taiwan's social stability, others were less sanguine, pointing to the role of the government's strong internal security apparatus in limiting social unrest. The tightly controlled political system, combined with generally good economic conditions, conservative values, and traditionally strong family ties, helped to guarantee the relative docility of the labor force, a major factor in the island's economic advancement.

The island's family-centered social structure was generally suitable for the kinds of small-scale enterprises that have been the backbone of the island's economic success up to the present. But the tightly knit family structure in Taiwan may prove incompatible with the broader-scale economic enterprises Taiwan is said to need to remain competitive in the international economic environment. If so, the result could be a decline in prosperity, which in turn could cause social and political tensions that may undermine the island's stability.

Taiwan's government officials have attempted to use policy to provide opportunity for economic and social advancement. There is a direct relationship between the government's economic policies and the rise of new middle-class groups. Through the promotion and expansion of the public and private sectors, state development strategies pushed small landowners into the ranks of the urban industrial worker class or the middle class, which emerged as the mainstay of this newly industrialized capitalist society. By 1980 only 18 percent of the island's employed population engaged in farming activities, the vast majority of them on a part-time basis. At the same time, the emerging working and middle classes have an increasingly visible social and political impact. The key lesson of these changes for the people of Taiwan is that the majority of the middle classes, old and new, have come from lower-class groups and have benefited from the upward social mobility of the postwar period. However, the rise of the middle classes leads to growing expectations. If class structures were to solidify as a result of less rapid economic growth or other changes, frustration and anxiety could result for both the middle classes and those below them.

Modernization on Taiwan

Economic modernization lies behind many of the important social and political changes on Taiwan in recent years. This rapid economic transformation reflects complex relationships among economic growth, income distribution, and productivity. Another crucial factor in the solution of economic problems over the past thirty years has been the effectiveness of the government's role; government policies have fostered innovation, nurtured flexibility in the economy, and provided encouragement and incentives.

These administrative efforts can be classified into three categories. First, the government pursued policies to restructure economic incentives, particularly through the redistribution of property rights. Second, government policies shifted resources from low to high value-added products by inducing more competition, channeling the flow of economic activity in new ways, and facilitating the role of markets. Finally, the government inaugurated policies to achieve equilibrium within the economic system by offsetting certain kinds of scarcities. The government remains strongly committed to using its power to facilitate economic growth. The state continually intervenes in the market through new legislation and policies aimed at providing stable growth and ensuring that the gap in income distribution between rich and poor sectors of society does not widen as growth takes place. The state also strives to minimize unemployment and maintain stable price levels.

Taiwan's physical resources are limited. The island's economy is heavily dependent on foreign trade for the raw and finished materials with which to produce goods and services for domestic use and foreign sale and for its supply of energy. Some economic experts caution that Taiwan may not be able to maintain the rapid export growth rates of the recent past and that, therefore, because of its high dependency on foreign trade, overall economic growth rates may begin to decline. Export income constituted around 55 percent of GNP in 1994, making the trend of international protectionism particularly worrisome and adding weight to the arguments of those who see a relatively gloomy future for Taiwan.

Perhaps of even greater importance is the decline in labor discipline, social stability, and political orderliness that has accompanied political democratization on Taiwan in recent years. Some foreign investors are becoming less attracted to Taiwan because of rapidly rising labor costs and the difficulty in getting decisions from government leaders who must now work with more representative legislative and administrative bodies. Meanwhile, Taiwan's growing democratization and freedom have made

greater trade and investment with China possible, but have also raised the possibility that Beijing might use such links to gain political or other concessions from Taipei.

Over the long run, Taiwan seeks to maintain high growth rates and high productivity, keep unemployment and inflation low, and protect its balanced income distribution. Many factors make Taiwan's prospects for achieving these goals favorable. Taiwan's business firms and households have great resiliency, are frugal, strive to be efficient and highly productive, and—perhaps most important—remain ready to respond and adapt to new market forces. It is this flexibility that should enable the economy to continue to outperform most other economies in the coming decades. Given social and political stability and peaceful conditions along the Taiwan Strait, Taiwan should be able to upgrade productivity in its manufacturing and service sectors; continue to have high savings and make the necessary investment in new capital to improve economic performance and product quality; and maintain markets in foreign countries by which to earn the foreign exchange needed to purchase necessary raw materials and products from abroad.

Political Liberalization

Under Chiang Kai-shek's leadership, the government ruled in a sometimes harsh, authoritarian fashion. It pursued policies of a strong national defense against the Communist mainland and of export-oriented economic growth. It tolerated little open political dissent. In the 1970s, the United States and most developed countries recognized the PRC and broke official ties with Taipei. Under international pressure, Taiwan withdrew from the United Nations and lost its right to the "China seat" in most international bodies.

These international setbacks challenged a major source of the Nationalist regime's political legitimacy. It became harder to argue that people on Taiwan should accept and pay for an elaborate central government administration that included a majority of representatives who were elected on mainland China before the Communist victory there and Nationalist retreat to Taiwan in 1949. Nationalist leaders, especially Chiang Kai-shek's son, Chiang Ching-kuo, emphasized other elements in support of the Nationalists' rule, noting in particular the leadership's successful supervision of Taiwan's dramatic economic progress. Chiang and his associates also were at pains to bring more ethnic Taiwanese to power—the 85 percent of the island's population whose roots in Taiwan predate the influx of two million "mainlanders" in the 1940s and 1950s. The vast majority of the Nationalist Party's rank and file were Taiwanese, and important local dignitaries, including Taiwan's current president, Lee Teng-hui, were raised to high positions.

A combination of international and domestic pressures accelerated the pace of political reform in the mid- and late 1980s. Authoritarian rule was overthrown in the Philippines and South Korea. Encouraged by the events, Taiwan opposition leaders announced in September 1986 that they had formed a formal opposition party, the Democratic Progressive Party (DPP). Although the Nationalist authorities considered this step illegal under terms of martial law, they took no repressive action and allowed oppositionists to campaign in a December 1986 election under their new banner. At the polls, the DPP candidates received about 22 percent of the vote, an increase over the 17 percent received by opposition politicians who ran without party affiliation in the last such election in 1983.

President Chiang Ching-kuo ended martial law in July 1987. The opposition shifted its focus to calls for an overhaul of Taiwan's National Assembly, Legislative Yuan, and Control Yuan—important legislative bodies still dominated by mainlanders elected more than forty years earlier. The opposition also called for the direct popular election of the president and the right of Taiwan people to determine their international status. Upon taking office in 1988, President Lee Teng-hui reaffirmed a commitment to reform that would legalize opposition parties and restructure parliamentary bodies. In December 1989 elections, the Nationalist Party won 65 percent of the vote and the DPP more than 30 percent.

By early 1991, several major changes were taking place on Taiwan:

- May 1991. President Lee delivered on his promise to end the state of civil war with the PRC and the associated "temporary provisions" that had given Nationalist leaders "emergency" powers to deal with dissent and other issues.
- December 1991. All National Assembly members and members of other legislative bodies elected in the mainland retired. An election was held on December 21 to fill 325 seats in a new National Assembly. The Nationalists won 71 percent and the DPP about 24 percent of the vote.
- 1992. The new National Assembly began what turned into a long process of revising the constitution. Based on public debate in Taiwan, revisions were expected to focus on issues relating to how the president is elected; how the central government relates to provincial and local governments; and whether the central executive should have a presidential system, a parliamentary system, or some other system. At present, the central government has important aspects of both presidential and parliamentary systems, which lead to ambiguity about the respective powers of the president and the prime minister in particular. The actual outcome of initial revisions did not deal with these problems but did enhance the power of the National Assembly relative to other government bodies.
- December 1992. For the first time, elections took place for the Legislative Yuan. The Nationalist Party did poorly, winning only 53 percent of the vote while the DPP won 31 percent. By combining with Nationalist Party members who ran without party endorsement, the Nationalists controlled 103 seats in the new legislature, the DPP 50 seats.
- 1994. The mayors of Taipei and Kaohsiung and the governor of Taiwan Province were directly elected for the first time by popular vote on December 3.
- 1996. An election to determine the president is to be carried out under whatever terms are set forth in the constitutional revision.

Taiwan's Role in World Affairs

Backed by a vibrant economy and an increasingly internationalized political and social atmosphere,

Taiwan has made remarkable progress toward democratization in the 1990s. Here, Taiwan's ruling Nationalist Party opens a congress to debate democratic reforms at the National Assembly Hall. In the country's first elections to the Legislative Yuan, held in December 1992, the Nationalist Party won just 53 percent of the vote.

Taiwan has emerged in the 1990s as an increasingly important actor in world affairs. As in the past, the main obstacle to Taiwan's playing a greater role relates to Beijing's strong opposition to Taiwan's gaining official status as a separate entity in international affairs. Recent trends in Taiwan, in Taiwan-mainland relations, and in international developments, however, suggest that Taiwan will make greater progress in establishing itself as an important force in world economic, social, and political affairs in the years to come.

Beijing is not without influence in this situation, particularly as its vast and rapidly growing economy exerts extraordinary influence on decision makers throughout Asia and the world, including Taiwan. The wider range of political forces in Taipei includes those who advocate extreme positions on self-determination and independence that could jeopardize

Taiwan-mainland stability and promote conflict across the Taiwan Strait. Nonetheless, the economic and political changes on the mainland seem to reinforce a moderate stance toward Taiwan based on growing economic interdependence. In Taiwan, voters and politicians have had several opportunities in recent years to stake out extreme political positions, but have invariably chosen a moderate course designed to avoid unnecessary tension while sustaining and strengthening Taipei's de facto independent status.

Historically, Taiwan's importance in world affairs has been as an area acted upon by others, rather than as a significant force in its own right. This was true when it was a frontier province in Manchu China; a colony directly administered by Japan; a recovered territory administered, sometimes harshly, by Nationalist forces from the mainland; and an ''unsinkable aircraft carrier'' and anti-Communist out-post in the U.S.-backed containment system directed at Communist China in Asia in the 1950s and 1960s.

Taiwan's continued strong dependence on the United States was underlined at the time of the shift in U.S. policy in Asia beginning in the late 1960s. At this time, a convergence of strategic needs drove Beijing and Washington closer together, leading to the Sino-American rapprochement seen during President Richard Nixon's 1972 visit to China. In the interests of solidifying U.S. relations with Beijing in the so-called great power triangle of U.S.-PRC-USSR relations, U.S. leaders increasingly accommodated Beijing's demands regarding U.S. policy toward Taiwan. Throughout the 1970s, the United States gradually cut back its military presence in Taiwan and in 1979 it ended official relations, including the U.S.-Taiwan defense treaty, in order to establish formal relations with Beijing as the sole legal government of China.

The U.S. shift was accompanied by a massive decline in Taiwan's international standing, as scores of countries switched diplomatic relations to Beijing and Taiwan was excluded or withdrew from the UN and other international organizations. The official presence in both countries was replaced by the unofficial American Institute in Taipei, representing the United States, and the Coordinating Council for North American Affairs (CCNAA), representing Taiwan in Washington. In September 1994, the Clinton administration reaffirmed the policy of not treating Taiwan as a sovereign country, yet supported Taiwan's effort to join GATT and agreed to allow the CCNAA's name to be changed to the Taipei Economic and Cultural Representative Office in the United States.

Beijing endeavored to capitalize on its enhanced stature and Taipei's growing international political (but not economic) isolation. It followed a carrot-and-stick policy of concurrent gestures and pressures designed to bring Taipei into formal negotiations on reunification. The PRC's success in negotiating the 1984 Sino-British Joint Declaration on Hong Kong prompted Deng Xiaoping and other senior PRC leaders to hold up the "one country, two systems" approach used in that accord as a model for Taiwan's reunification. Deng and others promised that not only would the political, economic, and social system in Taiwan be guaranteed, as in the case of Hong Kong, but that Taiwan would also be able to maintain its separate defense forces.

The PRC "stick" took various forms. Taipei leaders were warned—sometimes with allusions to possible PRC use of force—against undue delay. Americans and others with unofficial contacts with Taiwan were repeatedly pressed to cut back ties in sensitive areas, especially the sale of weapons. They were also warned against efforts to boost Taiwan's international standing through membership in international governmental organizations. Beijing came out strongly against any effort by Taiwan to declare independence.

Taipei responded by seeking greater legitimacy through elections and other democratic practices noted above; at the same time, it took a variety of pragmatic steps in an effort to increase Taiwan's stature in world affairs without fundamentally challenging the "one China" principle so critical to a minority of Nationalist Party leaders and, more importantly, to Beijing. This resulted in several substantial adjustments in Taiwan's international and internal policies:

- Taiwan began to break new ground in the field of "substantive diplomacy." This involved establishing increasingly close, albeit ostensibly unofficial, relations with countries that had switched official recognition to Beijing. Taiwan's relations with Japan after 1972, and the United States after 1979, provided models for these extensive unofficial ties.
- Taiwan began to show flexibility over its claim to be the sole legitimate government of China and by the late 1980s had moved to establish official ties with some governments that continued to officially recognize the PRC. Taipei was also markedly more flexible in seeking membership in official international organizations that recognized the PRC as the legitimate government of China.
- While continuing to promote close interchange with the United States, Taiwan used its growing economic stature to broaden relations with a wide range of other developed and developing countries.

• Internal reforms were strongly emphasized in Taiwan to build political legitimacy at home as well as to enhance Taiwan's image abroad as a more politically attractive partner to many democratic developed states, notably the United States. The reforms also opened the way to greatly increased Taiwan contacts with the mainland—a trend that helped to ease tensions and buy time for Taiwan to come up with a viable approach for dealing with the mainland over the longer term. At the same time, they served to build Taiwan's economic power and influence, supporting a trend wherein Taiwan was no longer largely an entity acted upon by others but was increasingly using its economic and other influence in world affairs to promote its own interests and concerns.

Prospects for Taiwan

Some basic factors appear on balance to argue for optimism when assessing Taiwan's prospects. These include Taiwan's generally effective and attractive political, economic, and social situation. While Taiwan's administration has been buffeted by competing interests and has demonstrated the rough and tumble political process of a new democracy, the net result of recent policies has been to strengthen the legitimacy and resolve of the authorities in charge. They have proved capable of charting effective economic, social, and political reforms and other policies that add to Taiwan's strength and influence in world affairs.

A review of Taiwan's economic position in the thriving East Asian region shows Taiwan entrepreneurs serving as important catalysts for East Asian growth and Taiwan in general providing a model for development attractive to many developing countries. Taiwan businesspeople seem to be uniquely efficient and effective in promoting growth and making deals in East Asia. They and their government are not passive, but are seen as aggressive and constructive actors promoting trade and investment in areas where others might fear to go.

In the realm of international arms sales, Taipei has adroitly exploited a combination of factors to greatly improve its military capabilities while undermining the PRC-backed international arms embargo against it. The post-cold war environment has led to a massive arms glut and a "buyers' market" favorable to those like Taipei that have the cash to buy what they want from hard-pressed world arms merchants. Taipei's democratic progress has also contrasted with Beijing's continued authoritarianism to improve Taipei's political image among decision makers in the United States and Western Europe, who hold the key to access to the modern military equipment and defense technology desired by Taiwan.

Taipei leaders have been adept in adjusting their policies on sensitive global issues in order to substantiate their argument that Taiwan is a responsible actor in world affairs deserving of respect commensurate with its size and influence. Thus, Taipei's efforts to conform to world trading practices on difficult issues like intellectual property rights, market access, and re-evaluating Taiwan's currency policies are designed not only to avoid retaliation from major trading partners, notably the United States. Rather, Taiwan leaders consciously accommodate these trends in order to build their case for Taiwan's entry into GATT and other world economic bodies. Similarly, Taipei leaders are well aware that striking a cooperative posture on other transnational issues including crime, drugs, terrorism, refugee support, and environmental issues builds goodwill among world leaders, and thereby indirectly boosts Taiwan's standing among these politicians.

Although the sophisticated, often technocratic Republic of China leadership in Taiwan has been instrumental in steering Taipei's course in world affairs, the roots of Taiwan's success go deeper than that. In particular, rising educational and economic standards on the island have accompanied the trend toward democracy in recent years. Taiwan government decision makers are now required to reflect the increasingly sophisticated middle-class values of the people on the island. These popular attitudes are also more international because of the relatively free flow of information and frequent travel of many in Taiwan. The result has been more sophisticated Taiwan popular attitudes toward world politics, especially toward relations with the mainland.

The challenge of legitimation Taiwan faces in the international system can be met by a broad and expanding web of international contacts. On the one hand, the challenge often prompts Taiwan citizens to press their government to increase Taiwan's official stature in world affairs. For some in Taiwan, this requires Taiwan to move toward de jure independence. Faced with continued strong PRC opposition, however, people in Taiwan until now have pragmatically sought their sense of international identity through international contacts in business, culture, and education as well as politics. Under these circumstances, Taiwan citizens may be more likely to assert their identity and sense of legitimacy through other avenues short of a total break with mainland China.

These trends and variables could change, however, disrupting or upsetting the generally sanguine view of Taiwan's future noted above. Dangers include:

- A breakdown of effective political decision making to a point where domestic and foreign investors no longer seek opportunities in Taiwan.
- A further and protracted decline in the economic dynamism of the United States and other important markets for Taiwan exports.
- A heavy-handed PRC effort to use leverage provided by Taiwan's investment in the mainland or other factors to force Taiwan to the negotiating table regarding political reunification.
- A headlong push by the DPP and other independence advocates of an official Taiwan stance endorsing independence—a stance that would likely elicit a forceful PRC response.

Tibet: A Case Study in Minority and Security Issues

The case of Tibet poses lessons for China far different from those of Hong Kong and Taiwan, which are viewed by post-Mao leaders as arenas of important economic opportunity. Economic levers are used to reinforce trends of convergence between the mainland and Hong Kong and Taiwan, which have an immediate payoff in substantial improvement and advances in Chinese mainland growth. In fact, Chinese policies toward Hong Kong and Taiwan are as much

or more influenced by the economic benefits such relations have for mainland China as they are by nationalistic or security concerns.

The Tibetan situation, in contrast, generally follows the pattern of Chinese relations with its minority peoples located in remote areas that are important for Chinese security but far from main lines of logistical support and communications. Chinese policy is dominated here by nationalistic concerns and a perceived need to control remote border regions that might otherwise fall under the influence of foreign or domestic forces inimical to central government rule. Chinese leaders today are very conversant with the many examples from China's long history of rulers who were weak or ineffective in managing minority affairs and controlling these regions, and whose regimes suffered or were overthrown as a result.

In these parts of the country, the central government uses economic, political, and military means to maintain power. Optimally, Beijing hopes to win over sufficient followers among the local people to ensure control without large outside Chinese government presence. Vigilance is constant to sustain central control, with sufficient local support to ensure the need for minimal central government personnel and resources.

In areas like Tibet, however, where many local people oppose PRC rule, the Communists have resorted to more direct coercion, involving public security and military forces when they feel it is necessary. In addition, economic, social, and other programs are designed to benefit and co-opt ambitious Tibetans willing to accommodate themselves to Chinese rule and work within the existing system. These economic and other programs are seen largely as a net drain on government resources, without significant importance as an incentive for greater growth in the rest of China.

Twentieth-century Chinese governments have paid even more attention to minority questions than did their predecessors. With the rise of nationalism, concepts of the nation-state, national unity, and the citizen replaced traditional ideas of ruler and subject and raised new questions about the role of minority peoples in a modernized Chinese society. China's new leaders were determined to eliminate past social injustices, and the Nationalists and the Communists promised equality for all citizens of the new nation. It was, moreover, ideologically important for these contenders for power to demonstrate the viability of their new political systems by raising the social status and standard of living of all citizens, Han and non-Han alike. Both Sun Yat-sen and Mao Zedong, in his early writings, acknowledged the discrimination suffered by minorities and advocated "self-determination" as the means of redressing the situation. (Both quickly retreated, however, from the implication that minorities had the right to declare themselves independent.)

Attention also focused on perceived foreign threats to the strategic areas in which many minorities lived. Manchu, Nationalist, and Communist leaders all viewed British machinations in Tibet and Russian moves in Mongolia with considerable anxiety. Indeed, the Chinese launched military strikes into Xinjiang, Tibet, and other border regions to keep these areas fully within the Chinese sphere of influence. The people of these regions suffered from the campaigns in terms of both the destruction of life and property and the loss of their accustomed autonomy.

Tibet's Struggles in the Twentieth Century

The Tibet Autonomous Region (TAR) covers the area between the Himalayan and Kunlun mountains. When the PRC refers to Tibet, it means the TAR. When the Dalai Lama speaks of Tibet, he refers to the broader area in which ethnic Tibetans reside, including the TAR as well as the high plateaus of Qinghai, Gansu, western Sichuan, and northernmost Yunnan provinces.

During the twentieth century, Tibet was isolated politically, economically, and geographically from China proper until the 1950s, maintaining de facto autonomy under the claimed sovereignty first of the Qing dynasty and then of the KMT government. Chinese of many political persuasions (including KMT authorities) traditionally have regarded Tibet as an integral part of China. No third country has ever formally recognized Tibet as a sovereign nation, independent of China. When the Communists came to power with the establishment of the PRC in 1949,

Nationalist Chinese representatives in Tibet were expelled. In October 1950, the People's Liberation Army (PLA) began a drive to gain control of the area around Tibet's capital city of Lhasa and most of central Tibet, which was completed in 1951. That May, the Chinese government signed the seventeen-point "Agreement on the Peaceful Liberation of Tibet" with Ngapo Ngawang Jigme, then governor of Chamdo and later chairman of the People's Congress of the TAR. (The agreement was later accepted by the Dalai Lama, but has been repudiated in recent years as having been signed under "coercion" without proper authority.)

Tibetans rebelled against the PLA in 1959. Upon suppression of the rebellion, the Dalai Lama and tens of thousands of his followers fled to India in March 1959, and the PLA began to establish more direct control over Tibet. Tens of thousands of Tibetan rebels were killed in the fighting, and perhaps as many as a hundred thousand were imprisoned. The period from 1959 to 1976 was the worst in the history of the Tibet-central government relationship. Anti-Han Chinese sentiment among Tibetans was increased by the brutal suppression of the Tibetan rebellion and extensive persecution of religious followers. The situation was exacerbated by the serious famine in much of China in 1960-1961. Southwest China was particularly hard hit. In Sichuan alone, the population fell by 5.9 million, or 8.4 percent, from 1957 to 1962. The population group probably most affected was the Tibetan minority in the mountainous northwestern part of the province.

Given the fragile nature of Tibet's agriculture (only 2,300 square kilometers, or 0.18 percent, of Tibet's area is cultivated), the fighting and emigration related to the Dalai Lama's escape in 1959, and the Sino-Indian border war of 1962, a 275,000-person decrease in the population of the TAR between 1953 and 1964 seems quite credible. Comparable decreases for other provinces with significant Tibetan minority populations are also likely.

From 1966 to 1976, during the Cultural Revolution, the central government made a strong but unsuccessful effort to eradicate Tibetan nationalism as a political force. During this period, virtually all temples and religious buildings were destroyed throughout China. The Tibetan refugee community estimates that more than 6,200 Tibetan monasteries were razed. That figure almost certainly includes monasteries located outside the TAR in Sichuan, Qinghai, Gansu, and Yunnan. Sources in the TAR estimate that about 2,700 monasteries were open in the TAR before 1959.

Beginning with the installation of Hu Yaobang as general secretary of the Chinese Communist Party in 1980, Tibetan relations with Beijing began a slow recovery from the nadir of 1959-1976. In May 1980, Hu and newly appointed Vice Premier Wan Li visited Tibet on an inspection tour. After the visit, Hu proposed reforms aimed at easing tensions between Tibetans and Han Chinese and bringing more Tibetans into the government and party. After 1980, control was relaxed over religious observances. Major religious activities (for example, the Lhasa Grand Prayer ceremony), which had not been observed for twenty years, were allowed to resume. The Tibetan economy benefited from reform measures, including the dismantling of the commune system, investment in tourism and related infrastructure, and efforts to develop trade relations with other provinces and internationally.

These trends continued until the latter 1980s, when a series of violent demonstrations and conflicts alarmed PRC authorities and exacerbated Chinese-Tibetan relations. Communist authorities did not refrain from live-fire volleys to disperse threatening crowds, torture, and large-scale imprisonment in order to suppress the dissent. Foreign observers found it increasingly difficult to travel to Tibet. Reports that filtered out through the Tibetan exile community painted a bleak picture of repression and widespread human rights violations.

Post-Tiananmen Tensions

The June 1989 Chinese repression of pro-democracy demonstrators in Beijing and other Chinese cities seemed to substantiate the charges of the Dalai Lama and his followers about the ruthlessness of the PRC regime in Tibet. In recent years their charges, usually supported by extensive documentation, have revolved around several issues, including:

- deliberate Chinese government efforts to limit the size of Tibet to the TAR, when the actual historical area of Tibet is much larger;
- abusive Chinese treatment of thousands of Tibetans said to be held as political prisoners, and disproportionate use of capital punishment against Tibetans;
- deliberate Chinese government efforts to encourage greater Han migration into the TAR and to promote the assimilation of Tibetans into the mainstream of Chinese society (the Dalai Lama made this issue of cultural survival the central point of his presentation to world leaders in 1993);
- strong restrictions on Tibetans' religious practices, especially significant gatherings of believers, and use of informers, torture, and other methods in an attempt to intimidate Tibetan monks and other religious leaders to acquiesce in Chinese rule;
- a reported large (more than 200,000) presence of Chinese troops in the TAR.

At present, the realities of coercive power clearly limit the immediate prospects of advocates of greater Tibetan self-rule or independence. Nevertheless, the Dalai Lama and the Tibetan exile community have made considerable progress in changing international opinion, especially in the developed world, on this issue. Beijing leaders have been forced by public opinion and leaders in the West to be more accountable about the human rights situation in the TAR. As noted above, no government has formally challenged Beijing's sovereignty over Tibet, although the U.S. Congress and other world bodies have gone on record in support of Tibetan independence.

Some Tibet self-determination/independence advocates are hopeful that recent world trends will continue to support their cause. Specifically, if the regime in Beijing were to weaken and collapse as have other Communist regimes in recent years, conditions might be ripe for the emergence of a democratic Chinese government that presumably would hold out greater hope for Tibetan independence partisans.

Note: The views in this article are the author's and not necessarily those of the Congressional Research Service.

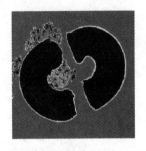

REFERENCE MATERIALS

BIOGRAPHIES

CHRONOLOGY

DOCUMENTS

BIBLIOGRAPHY

The Leaderships of the People's Republic of China and Taiwan

People's Republic of China

President: Jiang Zemin
Vice President: Rong Yiren
Chairman of the State Council (Premier): Li Peng
Vice Premiers: Zhu Rongji, Zou Jiahua, Qian Qichen, Li Lanqing
Minister of Agriculture: Liu Jiang
Minister of Chemical Industry: Gu Xiulian
Minister of Civil Affairs: Doje Cering
Minister of Coal Industry: Wang Senhao
Minister of Communications: Huang Zhendong
Minister of Construction: Hou Jie
Minister of Culture: Liu Zhongde
Minister of Electronics Industry: Hu Qili
Minister of Finance: Liu Zhongli
Minister of Foreign Affairs: Qian Qichen
Minister of Foreign Trade and Economic Cooperation: Wu Yi
Minister of Forestry: Xu Youfang
Minister of Geology and Mineral Resources: Zhu Xun
Minister of Internal Trade: Zhang Haoruo
Minister of Justice: Xiao Yang
Minister of Labor: Li Boyang
Minister of Machine-Building Industry: He Guangyuan
Minister of Metallurgical Industry: Liu Qi
Minister of National Defense: Chi Haotian
Minister of the People's Bank of China: Li Guixian
Minister of Personnel: Song Defu
Minister of Post and Telecommunications: Wu Jichuan
Minister of Power Industry: Shi Dazhen
Minister of Public Health: Chen Minzhang
Minister of Public Security: Tao Siju
Minister of Radio, Film, and Television: Ai Zhisheng
Minister of Railways: Han Zhubin
Minister of the State Auditing Administration: Lu Peijian
Minister of the State Commission for Economic Restructuring: Li Tieying
Minister of the State Commission for Science, Technology, and Industry for National Defense: Ding Henggao
Minister of the State Economic and Trade Commission: Wang Zhongyu
Minister of the State Education Commission: Zhu Kaixuan
Minister of the State Family Planning Commission: Peng Peiyun
Minister of the State Nationalities Affairs Commission: Ismail Amat
Minister of the State Planning Commission: Chen Jinhua
Minister of the State Physical Culture and Sports Commission: Wu Shaozu
Minister of the State Science and Technology Commission: Song Jian
Minister of State Security: Jia Chunwang
Minister of Supervision: Cao Qingze
Minister of Water Resources: Niu Maosheng

Taiwan

President: Lee Teng-hui
Vice President: Lee Yuan-zu
Premier: Lien Chan
Vice Premier: Hsu Li-teh
Minister of Economic Affairs: Chiang Ping-kun
Minister of Finance: Lin Cheng-kuo
Minister of Foreign Affairs: Frederick Chien
Minister of Justice: Ma Ying-jeou
Minister of National Defense: Chiang Chung-ling
Governor, Central Bank: Liang Kuo-shu

Note: Compiled in February 1995.

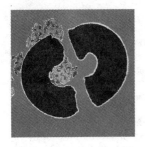

BIOGRAPHIES

Biographies of five prominent Chinese leaders—Deng Xiaoping, Jiang Zemin, Lee Teng-hui, Li Peng, and Mao Zedong—are given below. Following these are thirty-six shorter biographical sketches of other notable individuals.

Deng Xiaoping (1904-   )

Although in failing health and holding only the official titles of chairman of the Song Qingling Foundation (Song was Sun Yat-sen's widow) and chairman of the Chinese Bridge Association, Deng by the mid-1990s was still thought to be among China's most influential leaders. He is credited with bringing about China's post-1978 economic reforms and with leading the country onto the path of modernization.

Deng was born in 1904 in Sichuan Province. At the age of sixteen, he traveled to France on a work-study program. While attending the University of Lyon, he became involved in the overseas Chinese student movement and joined the Chinese Communist Party (CCP) in 1924. In 1926, Deng went to Moscow to continue his studies. He returned to China later that year and taught at the Xi'an Military Academy. He helped establish the Seventh Red Army and became its political commissar in 1929. Deng also established the Guangxi Soviet and later merged his army with Mao's forces. During an internal power struggle in 1933, Deng was stripped of his posts.

After the Long March, Deng again rose to the rank of political commissar within the army. In 1945 he was elected to the CCP Central Committee. He spent the war years taking part in campaigns in southwest China. When the CCP emerged victorious in 1949, Deng stayed in the southwest to help with postwar reconstruction.

In 1952, Deng became one of five vice premiers in Beijing and began to rise within the party and government hierarchies. He was named to the Politburo in 1955 and became secretary general of the Central Committee in 1956. During the years of the Great Leap Forward (1958-1960), Deng cautioned against taking extreme measures. Instead, he stressed the need for decentralizing the bureaucracy and became known for his pragmatism. When Mao temporarily stepped aside in 1961, Deng—together with Liu Shaoqi—took on the responsibility of repairing the damage caused by the Great Leap Forward.

When the Cultural Revolution began, Deng became one of its primary targets. Not only was Deng considered an enemy of the Gang of Four, but he was also later attacked as part of the entrenched party bureaucracy. He was stripped of his posts in 1966 and sent to the countryside to perform hard labor.

In 1973, as China began a limited opening to the outside world, Deng was reinstated as vice premier, in part because he had ties to Zhou Enlai. After Zhou's death in 1976, Deng was again dismissed, although he was reinstated to all his posts in 1977, after the fall of the Gang of Four.

After his second comeback, Deng's main nemesis was CCP Chairman Hua Guofeng, who basically supported continuing Maoist policies. Deng consolidated his support during the third plenum of the Eleventh National People's Congress (NPC) in 1978, but did not officially take power until 1981.

Since wresting power from Hua, Deng has stressed the Four Cardinal Principles and sought to build "socialism with Chinese characteristics." He has consistently pushed for pragmatic policies and advocated economic reform. In contrast to his support for changes in the economic arena, Deng's support of political reform has been far less secure. In 1983, he launched a campaign against "spiritual pollution" (negative cultural influences from the West) and in June 1989 ordered the crackdown against students and workers in Tiananmen Square.

Although he retired from all official posts in 1989, Deng continues to have much say in major central decisions. His well-publicized 1992 trip to southern China, including the Shenzhen Special Economic Zone, is credited with rekindling the spark of economic reform after the Tiananmen incident, and his endorsement of a return to the policies of rapid growth was considered critical at the 1993 party plenum.

Jiang Zemin (1926-   )

Appointed chairman of the National People's Congress and general secretary of the Communist Party after the Tiananmen incident of June 1989, Jiang Zemin became nominally the most powerful man in China in the early 1990s. Jiang spent most of his career in Shanghai until his meteoric rise beginning in the late 1980s.

Jiang was born in August 1926 in Yangzhou, Jiangsu Province, to an affluent intellectual family. He received his primary education at an American missionary school and joined the CCP in 1946, a year before graduating from the electrical engineering department of Shanghai's Jiaotong University.

When the People's Republic was founded in 1949, Jiang was working at a factory in Shanghai. He worked in various Shanghai factories for the next three years and in 1955 underwent training at an automobile plant in Moscow. When he returned to China, he was put in charge of the Changchun No. 1 Motor Vehicle Plant. In the 1960s he held positions as deputy director of the Shanghai Electrical Appliance Institute and director of the Wuhan Thermal Engineering Machinery Institute. In 1971, Jiang was named deputy director and later director of the foreign affairs bureau of the First Ministry of Machine Building, a post he held until 1979.

By 1980, Jiang was serving as vice minister of the Administrative Commission for Import and Export Affairs and two years later became secretary general of the commission. Beginning in 1981, Jiang concurrently served as vice minister and then secretary general of the State Foreign Investment Commission.

Jiang was made a full member of the Central Committee in 1982. During the next year, he was confirmed as vice minister of electronics industries and, later, deputy head of the State Council Leading Group for Electronics Industries. Jiang returned to Shanghai in 1985 as mayor and deputy party secretary of Shanghai municipality. He became party secretary of Shanghai in 1987 and was elected to the Politburo later that year. In Shanghai, Jiang experimented with various economic reforms while maintaining strict political control. He allowed development of a stock exchange, for example, but chose to close down the controversial *World Economic Herald* when its views became too politically liberal during the tumultuous spring of 1989.

When Zhao Ziyang was removed as general secretary of the CCP in 1989, Deng Xiaoping brought Jiang from Shanghai to take over the position. In October 1992, Jiang was added to the Politburo Standing Committee and became chairman of the Central Military Commission. In March 1993, when he was named president of the People's Republic of China (PRC), he became nominally the most powerful man in China, holding the country's highest government, party, and military titles.

Many attribute Jiang's rise to power to the elder leadership's need to find a figurehead to balance conservative and moderate forces. After four years at the height of power, however, Jiang had yet to gain the firm support of many of the various factions within the leadership and establish his own strong power base.

Lee Teng-hui (1923-   )

Lee Teng-hui succeeded Chiang Ching-kuo as president of Taiwan in 1988, becoming the first native Taiwanese to hold this office.

Lee was born in 1923 north of the city of Taipei. Raised in a rural area during the Japanese occupation, Lee is said to have been unsettled by the backward conditions of the countryside. During his college years, Lee took a strong interest in agriculture and was awarded a scholarship to study at the Imperial University in Kyoto, Japan. After graduating, he returned to Taipei. He taught at Taiwan University until 1952 and then studied agronomy at Iowa State University.

In 1957, Lee began his public service career in Taiwan as a specialist for the Joint Commission on Rural Reconstruction, where he worked to improve conditions within rural communities. He went again to the United States, this time to receive a doctorate in agronomy from Cornell University. When Lee returned to Taiwan, he was put in charge of the Joint Commission on Rural Reconstruction and is said to have spurred growth in the agricultural economy.

Lee attracted the attention of President Chiang Ching-kuo with his policies to stimulate the rural economy, and Chiang offered Lee a post within the administration. By 1978, Lee had become mayor of Taipei and, in 1981, governor of Taiwan Province. As governor he worked to introduce regional planning and to streamline the administrative bureaucracy.

On May 20, 1984, Lee was named vice president under Chiang Ching-kuo, making him the highest-ranking native Taiwanese in the government at the time. When Chiang died in January 1988, Lee succeeded him as president of the Republic of China. He has since worked to continue economic growth on Taiwan and to facilitate steps toward democracy. In addition, Lee has taken concrete steps to improve relations with the mainland by institutionalizing cross-straits discussions on social and cultural relations and trade. He has also allowed increased visitation between residents of the island and China. Though Lee has continued to support eventual reunification, many within his government, citing the disparities between China and Taiwan, have increased their calls for Taiwan's independence.

Li Peng (1928-   )

Nominally the second most powerful leader in China in the early 1990s, Li Peng rose through party ranks because of his personal and factional ties. He has a strong tech-

nical background and received training in the Soviet Union.

Li was born in October 1928 in Chengdu, Sichuan Province. His father, Li Shuoxun, was an early Communist Party leader who took part in the Nanchang Uprising of 1927 and worked closely with Zhou Enlai and Deng Xiaoping. When Li Peng was three, his father was executed by Kuomintang (KMT) forces and his family taken in by Zhou Enlai.

When Li was thirteen, Zhou sent him to the Communist base in Yan'an. He joined the party in 1945. The next year he was named party secretary of the Harbin Oil Company. In 1948 he was sent with other offspring of CCP leaders to the Soviet Union, where he studied for six years at the Moscow Power Institute.

From 1955 to 1960, Li worked in the Jilin Fengman Hydroelectric Power Plant, among the largest electric power stations in China at the time. He was soon promoted from engineer to chief engineer and deputy direc-

tor of the firm. In 1961, Li was named chief engineer of the Northeast Power Bureau and director of the dispatcher's office. After four years, Li became head of the Beijing Electric Power Administration.

Li remained at the Beijing Electric Power Administration during the years of the Cultural Revolution. He became vice minister of electric power in 1979 and was promoted to minister in 1981. In 1982 the ministry merged with the Ministry of Water Resources, and Li became vice minister and party secretary of the newly established Ministry of Water Resources and Electric Power.

Li gained a seat on the Central Committee in 1982 and was named a vice premier of the State Council in 1983. Two years later, he was named to the Politburo and put in charge of the State Education Commission. In 1987 he was elected premier of the State Council and a member of the Politburo Standing Committee. From 1988 to 1990 Li chaired the State Commission on Economic Restructuring.

Li is considered a conservative among China's current leadership and is frequently associated with Chen Yun and others who want to slow the pace of reform. He is also associated with the declaration of martial law during the Tiananmen incident of June 1989. Because of weak health, Li disappeared from public view for a few months in early 1992, although he reappeared that summer and continues to serve as premier.

Mao Zedong (1893-1976)

Often cited as the major figure of twentieth-century Chinese history, Mao was responsible for founding and leading the People's Republic of China during its first three decades. Since his

death, Mao's role has been re-evaluated because of the negative effects of the Great Leap Forward and the Cultural Revolution. While still seen as the greatest figure in modern Chinese history, many now also acknowledge Mao's serious past mistakes.

Mao was born in Shaoshan, Hunan Province, on December 26, 1893. One of four children, Mao was raised in a relatively prosperous family and educated in the Chinese classics. His relationship with his father was often strained and, at the age of sixteen, Mao left home to continue his studies.

Mao went to Changsha to participate in the 1911 Revolution as a student volunteer. In 1912 he returned to school but dropped out after six months, believing he could learn more on his own. He began reading Western and Japanese writers and developed a sense of nationalism. Like others at the time, he began looking for ways to explain China's weakness.

In 1918, Mao moved to Beijing to join the May Fourth movement. While working as a clerk in the Beijing University library, Mao met Li Dazhao and Chen Duxiu, who were soon to found the Chinese Communist Party. Mao moved back to Hunan in 1921 and established a branch of the Socialist Youth Corps in Changsha. He fled to Guangzhou in 1923 when local authorities began to suppress the Communist movement. While there, Mao became director of the Peasant Movement Training Institute, an organization that taught students how to work among the peasantry. Mao's experiences at the institute influenced much of his later emphasis on peasants as China's primary revolutionary force.

After the split between the KMT and the Communists in 1927, Mao went underground and joined the forces of General Zhu De in the Jinggang mountains of southern China. Meanwhile, other leaders worked to build the Communist movement in urban areas. The CCP established its headquarters in Shanghai, but in 1932 was forced to retreat. Urban Communist leaders, including Zhou Enlai, encountered Mao and Zhu at what came to be known as the Jiangxi Soviet.

Internal battles for control at the Jiangxi Soviet temporarily unseated Mao from his position of power in 1933. After Chiang Kai-shek's army forced the Communists to retreat from Jiangxi and undertake the Long March, Mao regained control and established a new base in Yan'an, Shaanxi Province.

Chiang's passive approach to Japanese attacks on China provided a rallying point around which the Communists could build support among the Chinese people. When Chiang's forces did confront the Japanese, they were forced to retreat to the city of Chongqing in southwest China. Mao used this retreat as an opportunity to build up his own base of support, taking over local governments and consolidating Communist power throughout most of northern China. Mao set forth fundamental strategies and left actual administration in the hands of subordinates.

During this time, Mao formulated some of the basic principles that would govern Chinese communism under his leadership. In 1938, he wrote "On Protracted War," in which he asserted that China's forces should not spend all their energy defeating the invading Japanese forces, but should save some strength for the ultimate goal of beating the Nationalists. Another such work was "On the New Democracy," written in 1940. In this essay, Mao claimed that because of the conflict with Japan, China would have to postpone its dream of socialism. The country first had to go through a "national-democratic"

stage, taking allies wherever they could be found. Only after the Japanese threat passed could it move toward socialism.

Through these and other works, Mao was able to explain to the peasants and average party members why he took certain steps. In doing so he built party morale and legitimized the cause of revolution. When the war with Japan ended in 1945, Mao's armies were ready to take on the Nationalist forces.

The Nationalists, for their part, were in a weak position. Their battles with the Japanese had left them demoralized and near disintegration. On October 1, 1949, the Communists emerged victorious and the People's Republic of China was founded, with Mao as head of state.

During the first ten years of the PRC, Mao continued to rely on the organizational techniques he developed before 1949. Subordinates were again given responsibility for administrative tasks, and China looked to the Soviet Union for political, military, and economic support.

Despite many achievements, Mao in 1958 decided to abandon the Soviet model and take the country along a different road of development. Plunging the country into the Great Leap Forward, Mao claimed that China could industrialize by its own efforts and swiftly catch up with the West. The Great Leap policies proved disastrous, however, and neglect of China's agricultural base led to massive starvation.

By 1961, Mao had recognized that the country was in serious trouble and stepped down as head of state. Liu Shaoqi took over the reins of power and, working with Deng Xiaoping, set out to undo the damage and reestablish more conventional economic planning methods.

Mao staged a comeback in 1965, however, claiming that Liu and Deng had betrayed the ideals of socialism. In an effort to mobilize society to move once again toward socialist goals, Mao enlisted the support of Chinese youth, who were to help remove the "four olds" from society and build up a revolutionary force. The result became the chaos of the Red Guards and the Cultural Revolution. Liu and Deng were purged, while Mao's wife, Jiang Qing, and her radical supporters amassed great control, and the army, led by Lin Biao, took over the government.

The fury of the Cultural Revolution began to die down in the early 1970s. Seeing that the Red Guards were becoming too unwieldy, Mao sent the youth to the countryside to learn from the peasants. Moderate leaders like Deng Xiaoping were allowed to return to their posts, and the country slowly opened up to the outside world. In 1971, China replaced Taiwan in the United Nations. Mao later welcomed Henry Kissinger and Richard Nixon to China as guests and took steps to normalize relations with the United States.

By the middle of the decade, however, Mao's health was deteriorating. The radicals under Jiang Qing began increasing their power and campaigned for the relatively unknown Hua Guofeng to succeed Mao. (Because Zhou Enlai was also in frail health, he was not considered for the post.) The result was a contentious transition coalition combining the radicals under Jiang Qing with the newly rehabilitated and reform-minded members of the party under Deng. Mao died in September 1976, less than eight months after the passing of Premier Zhou Enlai and General Zhu De. Immediately after Mao's death the Gang of Four was arrested by the more pragmatic elements within China's leadership. They feared that Mao's widow would use her husband's death to consolidate her own power. Hua Guofeng took power but was soon challenged by Deng Xiaoping and his supporters, who succeeded in removing Hua from the party leadership in 1981.

In an attempt to make sense of the horrors of the Cultural Revolution, many posthumous debates were held regarding Mao's role in China's recent history. In its 1981 Resolution on Party History, the party proclaimed that Mao had been a great man but had not been infallible. Borrowing from the calculations made of Stalin's record in the Soviet Union, the resolution concluded that 70 percent of what Mao had done was right, and that only 30 percent of his actions were a mistake. The centennial anniversary of Mao's birth was celebrated in 1993, amid a surge of Maoist nostalgia in China.

Bo Yibo (1908-   )

An economic planner, Bo Yibo was born in 1908 outside Shanghai. After studying at Beijing University, Bo joined the CCP in 1926. After 1949, Bo served in several economic and finance positions including minister of finance, chairman of the State Construction Committee, vice premier, and chairman of the Scientific Planning Commission. He was purged during the Cultural Revolution but rehabilitated in 1978. He was again named vice premier and was later elected to the CCP Central Committee. Considered a relative conservative among China's leaders, Bo has made numerous cautionary statements regarding economic reform and the pace of economic development since the late 1980s.

Chen Boda (1904-1989)

As Mao Zedong's personal and political secretary, Chen Boda was responsible for writing many of Mao's speeches. He also produced his own extensive writings on the applicability of Marxism to China. Born in 1904 in Fujian Province, Chen studied in Moscow and served the Communists during the Yan'an years. After 1949, he became a prominent figure in the CCP propaganda department and became editor of *Hongqi (Red Flag),* the Central Committee's ideological publication. When the Cultural Revolution began, Chen was made head of the Cultural Revolution Group and named to the Politburo Standing Committee. In 1970, Chen was imprisoned for allegedly conspiring with Lin Biao to overthrow Mao. He was put on trial at the same time as the Gang of Four and imprisoned for his activities. Chen died in September 1989.

Chen Yun (1905-1995)

Chen Yun focused most of his career within the Chinese leadership on economic planning and China's industrial structure. A one-time protégé of Liu Shaoqi, Chen differed with Deng Xiaoping on the pace and scope of economic development beginning in the early 1980s.

Born in 1905 in Jingbu County, Jiangsu Province, Chen received little formal education, but in 1921 moved to Shanghai and trained as a typesetter. He began his career as a labor organizer under Liu Shaoqi. Together with Liu, Chen was one of the leading initiators of the anti-imperialist May Thirtieth movement of 1925. Chen joined the Chinese Communist Party in 1925 and by 1927 had joined the Jiangxi Soviet. There he worked in the Organization Department and was elected to the party Central Committee in 1931. In 1934, he was named to the Politburo and joined the Long March. During the war with Japan, Chen served in various economic positions and on the Revolutionary Military Council under Mao.

In 1935, Chen traveled to Moscow and attended the seventh congress of the Communist International (Comintern), returning in 1937. He stayed in Xinjiang for a year, working with Soviet economic officials and technicians. He joined the Communist base of Yan'an in Shaanxi Province in 1938 and was named head of the Organization Department and later head of the Central Committee's Rural Work Department.

During the next five years, Chen's work in economic development helped strengthen the Communist position in northern China. After the Communist victory over the Nationalists in 1949, Chen was named vice premier and minister of heavy industry. In 1952 he was identified as a member of the State Planning Commission and, with Zhou Enlai, conducted negotiations with the Soviet Union regarding the Manchurian railway and the Port Arthur naval base. Chen was named to the Standing Committee and Politburo in 1956.

Chen disappeared from high-level positions during the Cultural Revolution but reappeared in 1975. He became a vice chairman of the party in 1978, when he was also appointed to the party's Central Discipline Inspection Commission. Chen was appointed a vice premier and chairman of the State Finance and Economic Commission in 1979.

By 1986, three volumes of Chen Yun's works had been published. He was relieved of his posts on the Standing Committee and Politburo in 1987 but was named chairman of the Central Advisory Commission. In his later years, Chen became an advocate of a more moderate pace of economic reform and a balanced sectoral development strategy and often disagreed with Deng Xiaoping over the pace and scope of economic reform.

Chiang Ching-kuo (1909-1988)

The eldest son of Nationalist leader Chiang Kai-shek, Chiang Ching-kuo succeeded his father as president of Taiwan in 1978. During his tenure as president, the younger Chiang sought to strengthen Taiwan's economy, assimilate the native population, and lessen the authoritarian control of the government.

Born in 1909 in Zhejiang Province, Chiang received his elementary education in Zhejiang and Beijing. During a short period of cordial relations between the Kuomintang and the Communists, Chiang went to study at Sun Yat-sen University in Moscow, graduating in 1927. Because his father had engineered a massacre of Communists in Shanghai in 1927, however, the younger Chiang was virtually held hostage in the Soviet Union until 1937, when the CCP and the KMT again agreed to work together in opposition to the Japanese invaders. Although Chiang met his wife during his years in the Soviet Union, his experiences and observations of life there reportedly led to his virulent anti-Communist stance in later life.

Upon his return to China, Chiang worked in several mid-level positions in the rural areas, earning a reputation for ruthless efficiency and honesty. He served in both the Sino-Japanese War (1937-1945) and Chinese civil war (1945-1949). With the defeat of the Nationalists in 1949, Chiang fled to Taiwan with his family. He was named his father's personal aide and served as head of the political department of the Ministry of National Defense, overseeing the political commissars and the secret police. Later, Chiang was named to the Standing Committee of the Kuomintang and appointed head of the Chinese Youth Anti-Communist National Salvation Corps.

Chiang continued to rise within Taiwan's government. In 1958 he was named to the cabinet as minister without portfolio. He continued to control the security apparatus and took over the management of veterans' affairs. In 1965, he was named minister of national defense and proclaimed "heir apparent" to the presidency. In 1972, as the elder Chiang's health began to deteriorate, Chiang Ching-kuo was named premier and began to assume responsibility for daily government operations. He was elected chairman of the KMT in April 1975 after his father's death and president of the Republic of China in March 1978.

As chairman and, later, president, Chiang concentrated on the economy and attempted to assimilate the native Taiwanese with the "mainlanders" by appointing Taiwanese to key government positions. Though he was committed to the ideal of a "united" China, Chiang focused mainly on improving the standard of living on the island. He also took steps toward political liberalization. He allowed formation of an opposition group, the Democratic Progressive Party (DPP), and lifted martial law in 1987.

Chiang died on January 13, 1988, and was succeeded as president by his chosen heir, Lee Teng-hui.

Chiang Kai-shek (1887-1975)

After being defeated by the Communists in 1949, Generalissimo Chiang Kai-shek and his Kuomintang forces retreated to the island of Taiwan. In doing so, they established the Republic of China, which they claimed as the true government of both the island and the mainland. Until his death in 1975, Chiang sought to reunite the island with the rest of China and saw Taiwan as only a way-station before his return to power on the mainland.

Chiang was born in 1887 in Fenghua County, Zhejiang. The death of Chiang's father in 1894 left the family in difficult financial straits. In 1905, Chiang studied Chinese philosophy in the nearby city of Ningbo. Like many young Chinese of the time, he concluded that China's lack of military strength had led to its exploitation by Western powers. He therefore enrolled in the Baoding Rapid Course School, China's first modern military academy, in 1907. Upon graduation, Chiang was awarded a scholarship for study in Japan. In 1908, he joined the Tongmeng hui (Alliance Society), Sun Yat-sen's secret revolutionary society.

Chiang returned to China after the outbreak of the 1911 Revolution and worked over the next decade in the revolutionary forces. From 1918 to 1920 he was based in Shanghai, where he worked with Sun Yat-sen. In 1924, Chiang was named commandant of Sun Yat-sen's newly established Whampoa Military Academy outside Guangzhou. Both the Communists and the Nationalists gathered at Whampoa, allied under the leadership of Sun Yat-sen.

When Sun died in 1925, the unity between the two groups deteriorated and a power struggle broke out. Chiang emerged as Sun's successor and struck out against the CCP, further undermining the alliance. He was named commander-in-chief of the National Revolutionary Army and tried to consolidate his power during the Northern Expedition. Chiang's attempts failed, and he was challenged by the left wing of the Kuomintang, based in Wuhan. He attacked the Wuhan government after it tried to strip him of power. The Communists retaliated and forced Chiang to retire in September 1927. By the end of

1928, however, Chiang had returned to capture Beijing and establish a Nationalist government in Nanjing. China was nominally unified.

Chiang's armies were not equipped to fight the Japanese, however, and growing discontent over his policies strengthened the Communist movement. With the start of World War II in the Pacific, Chiang received aid from U.S. forces. Despite such assistance, Chiang was not able to gain the upper hand. Civil war broke out in 1946, and in 1949 Chiang was forced to retreat to the island of Taiwan.

Chiang gradually took control of the island and built up a government staffed by those who had fled the mainland with him in 1949. During his stay on Taiwan, he continued to claim that he was the legitimate ruler of all of China and that Taiwan was the only true seat of China's government. With U.S. support, Chiang rebuilt the war-torn economy on Taiwan. He took steps to industrialize the island, although the government remained authoritarian in nature. Throughout his tenure, Chiang did not abandon the goal of eventual Chinese reunification. He nurtured relations with the United States and distanced himself from the Communist leadership on the mainland. Chiang died in 1975, leaving control of the country to his son, Chiang Ching-kuo.

Hua Guofeng (1920-   )

Chosen to succeed Mao Zedong, Hua served as party chairman from 1976 to 1981. During his tenure, Hua saw the fall of the Gang of Four and the rise of the more moderate group led by Deng Xiaoping.

Born in 1920 in Jiaocheng County, Shanxi Province, reportedly to a relatively wealthy peasant family, Hua left to join a guerrilla unit in 1937. He probably joined the Communist Youth League at that time. Though born with the surname of Su, Hua changed his name while fighting with the Anti-Japanese National Salvation Vanguard during the 1940s. (His adopted name uses three of the nine characters in the Anti-Japanese Vanguard's name.) Hua joined the CCP in 1940 and, at the end of World War II, became head of his county's party committee and political commissar.

After the founding of the People's Republic, Hua was transferred to Hunan Province to oversee land reform efforts, and later was put in charge of forming rural cooperatives in Xiangtan. He was named head of the provincial culture and education office in Changsha in 1956 and the next year took charge of the CCP United Front Department in Hunan.

Hua was promoted again during the Great Leap Forward, becoming vice governor of the province. Hua's strong support of Mao's policies won him Mao's favor and led to other promotions in 1959. By 1960, he was the senior leader in Hunan. Hua retained these positions but

also returned to Xiangtan from 1961 to 1966, this time as local party chief, to rebuild the economic infrastructure there. As the American presence in Vietnam escalated in the late 1960s, Hua and the leaders of other southern provinces were tasked with preparing for possible war. Hua took steps to train his militia and supply food to what would be the front. He emerged as chief provincial spokesman on foreign affairs.

When the Cultural Revolution began in 1966, Hua rose to fill positions left by purged party leaders. In 1968 he was appointed vice chairman of the Hunan Revolutionary Committee. Elected to the CCP Central Committee in 1969, he became first secretary of Hunan Province in 1970 after a provincial power struggle. After Lin Biao's failed coup in 1971, Hua was summoned to Beijing to serve directly under Zhou Enlai as chief of staff on the State Council.

Hua was named to the Politburo in 1973 and placed in charge of culture, education, science, and technology. By 1975, he had become the sixth-ranking vice premier and minister of public security. He succeeded Zhou Enlai as premier on Zhou's death in 1976, as neither pragmatist Deng Xiaoping nor leftist Zhang Chunqiao could garner enough support to take the position.

When Mao died later that year, Hua continued his meteoric rise, taking over as chairman of the CCP. As Mao's chosen successor, Hua was obliged to continue Mao's agenda. He and his supporters became known as the "whateverists" because of their position that "whatever Mao said was right."

Hua's group was challenged, however, by a more reform-minded group led by Deng Xiaoping. Having first-hand experience of the suffering and hardship caused by the Cultural Revolution, Deng's group was intent on reforming the party, coming to terms with the destruction wrought by the Cultural Revolution, and strengthening the country economically. A political power struggle ensued, and Deng formally replaced Hua in 1981. Hua has remained in relative political obscurity since that time.

Hu Jintao (1942-   )

A native of Anhui Province, Hu graduated from Qinghua University. During the Cultural Revolution, he worked at the Ministry of Water Resources and Electrical Power and later within the Gansu Provincial Construction Commission. In 1980, he entered the Central Party Young Cadre Training Program and was later appointed secretary to the Communist Youth League Secretariat. In 1982 he became an alternate member of the Central Committee and in 1985 was elevated to full membership, making him the youngest member at the time. Hu served as secretary of the Tibet Autonomous Region Party Committee beginning in 1988. He has been a member of the Politburo Standing Committee and Secretariat since 1992 and has also served as president of the Central Party School and vice chairman of the party's Organization Department.

Hu Qili (1929-   )

Hu Qili, born in 1929 in Yulin County, Shaanxi Province, joined the party in 1948. After graduating from Beijing University with a degree in mechanical engineering, Hu became involved with Communist youth activities and traveled abroad during the 1950s and 1960s as part of various youth delegations. He served as president of the All-China Students' Federation and an alternate member on the Secretariat of the Communist Youth League.

Hu was dismissed from all his posts during the Cultural Revolution and sent to the Ningxia Autonomous Region. When he returned to Beijing, Hu served as vice president of Qinghua University (1977-1978) and a member of the Secretariat of the Communist Youth League. In 1978 he regained his position as president of the All-China Students' Federation and from 1980 to 1982 served as mayor of Tianjin.

In 1982, Hu gained a seat on the Central Committee and served as director of the general office. In this position he controlled the distribution of information and resources within the Central Committee, deciding which issues were brought to the attention of the leadership and their priority. In 1985, Hu was named to the Politburo.

Like his close associate Zhao Ziyang, Hu Qili was considered a strong reformer who used his position within the party to push for greater economic opening. To the consternation of the conservative leadership, Hu also advocated a decreased role for the party in the economy. He was purged from the party along with Zhao Ziyang after the Tiananmen Square demonstrations of 1989.

Hu Yaobang (1915-1989)

Hu Yaobang, who served as general secretary of the Communist Party from 1982 to 1986, is credited with moving China away from orthodox Marxism and speeding its movement toward modernization and reform. He was forced to resign from China's top party position in 1987, however, for having made "mistakes on major issues of political principles."

Hu was born in Hunan Province in 1915. He joined the CCP in 1933 and worked as an organizer. One of the youngest participants in the Long March, Hu followed Deng Xiaoping to Beijing after the CCP victory in 1949 and became head of the Communist Youth League. In 1956 he was elected to the Central Committee.

During the Cultural Revolution, Hu was purged and sent to the countryside. He was restored to power with Deng in 1973, but denounced again in 1976—again with Deng. After Mao's death in 1976, Hu slowly regained

power. At the landmark third plenum of the Eleventh National People's Congress in December 1978, Hu was named to the Politburo and made head of the party's Organization and Propaganda Departments. In 1981, he was named to succeed Hua Guofeng as general secretary of the Communist Party.

Throughout his tenure as general secretary, Hu carried forth the reform agenda, often more enthusiastically than the older, more moderate members within the party leadership would have liked. Many conservatives considered Hu too liberal. Fearing the "spiritual pollution" that they believed inevitably followed greater opening to the outside world, the moderate leaders worried that Hu's plans would cause political instability within the country. They felt that these fears were borne out in the latter part of 1986, as inflation gained speed, the economy overheated, and students began demonstrating against the government and calling for greater political liberalization.

Because of the student unrest and continuing criticism of his policies by top-level officials, Hu was forced to resign in 1987. When he died in April 1989, students adopted Hu as a martyr. They viewed him as a man who had refused to bend with the political winds and who, as a result, paid a high political price. His death sparked the student protests that grew into the spring 1989 Tiananmen demonstrations.

Jiang Qing (1914-1991)

The third wife of Mao Zedong, Jiang Qing became well known as a member of the Gang of Four and is frequently held responsible for many of the atrocities that occurred during the Cultural Revolution. Arrested shortly after Mao's death in 1976, she and the other members of the Gang of Four were put on trial in 1980, and in 1981 she was sentenced to death, a punishment later commuted to life in prison.

Jiang was reportedly born in 1914 and raised largely by grandparents in Zhucheng, Shandong Province. She claims to have suffered a miserable childhood, a victim of poverty and her father's abuse. She studied in the provincial capital of Jinan until 1929, when she joined a theatrical troupe. She later received formal dramatic training and made several films in Shanghai between 1934 and 1937. When the Japanese invaded, she moved westward to Chongqing. In 1938 she made her way to Yan'an, the Communist capital, and became a drama instructor. She met Mao Zedong and became his mistress, joining the CCP in 1939. In the early 1940s Mao sent his second wife to Moscow for "medical treatment" and then divorced her in order to marry Jiang. (Mao's first wife, to whom he had been betrothed in childhood, was reportedly killed by the Kuomintang in 1930.)

Party officials, reportedly indignant at Mao's divorce of his second wife and the more than twenty-year age difference between Mao and Jiang, insisted that Mao could marry Jiang Qing only if she never exercised any political power. Hence, at the founding of the republic in 1949, Jiang had very little influence, although she became active in Chinese cultural circles.

Mao kept to this agreement until the outbreak of the Cultural Revolution in 1966, when Jiang Qing became one of its powerful leaders, acting as vice chairman of the Cultural Revolution Group. Jiang also became a leading member of what came to be known as the Gang of Four, a group of previously unknown radical party members who directed much of the Cultural Revolution activities. (The other members were Zhang Chunqiao, Yao Wenyuan, and Wang Hongwen.) Jiang was elected to the Central Committee in 1967 and later named to the Politburo. Her power, which stemmed from her ties to Mao, increased as his health deteriorated.

Politically, Jiang set herself against the moderates within the party and government, especially Deng Xiaoping, Liu Shaoqi, and Zhou Enlai. With the help of the others in the Gang of Four, she succeeded in stripping the former two of their power. She also ensured the appointment of several politically radical personalities to the Central Committee and Politburo and promoted "revolutionary operas" and other works to nurture the correct ideology among the masses. She continued to wield much power even after the fervor of the Cultural Revolution began to wane in the 1970s.

After Mao's death in 1976, however, Jiang's power crumbled. Only hours after Mao's passing she and the other members of the Gang of Four were arrested by his more moderate followers, who feared Jiang and her cohorts would attempt to fill the political vacuum left by Mao's absence. In 1981, Jiang was sentenced to death, with her sentence later commuted to life imprisonment. The Chinese government announced that Jiang had committed suicide in her jail cell on May 14, 1991, reportedly still unrepentant and suffering from throat cancer.

Martin Lee (1938-   )

Martin Lee, founder of Hong Kong's liberal United Democrats Party, has sought to improve the chances for a more democratic system in Hong Kong after the city reverts to Chinese control in 1997. His actions have frequently put him at odds with Beijing.

Martin Lee was born in Hong Kong in 1938, while his mother was on vacation in the colony. Lee's father was a general in the Kuomintang army who urged the KMT forces to maintain open lines of communication with the Communists. The family moved to Hong Kong permanently after the Communists gained control of the mainland.

Trained as a lawyer, Lee first entered the world of politics as head of the Hong Kong Bar Association from 1981 to 1983. During this time, Sino-British negotiations on Hong Kong's future were held, concluding with an agreement returning Hong Kong to China in 1997. At the time the agreement was signed, Lee favored this decision, believing that the colony could be insulated from shocks by Chinese guarantees to preserve Hong Kong's way of life after 1997. Lee served on the committee to draft Hong Kong's "Basic Law," which set forth the principles governing Hong Kong's transition.

Lee's attitude began to change in early 1989, as he and his colleague Szeto Wah came to doubt that the British attitude toward the transition was firm enough to ensure Hong Kong's interests and began to wonder whether the Basic Law would adequately protect the territory after 1997. At the same time, Lee and Wah formed the "Hong Kong Alliance," a mass organization to show Hong Kong's support for the burgeoning democracy movement on the mainland. Their actions brought Beijing's censure, as they were labeled "subversives" and expelled from the Basic Law drafting committee.

As Sino-British negotiations over Hong Kong continued, Lee has remained in the Hong Kong spotlight. Although his proposals have gained the support of many in Hong Kong, Beijing has repeatedly threatened to undo such proposals if they do not fall under the mainland's interpretation of the Basic Law.

Li Fuchun (ca. 1899-1975)

A protégé of Chen Yun, Li served as minister of heavy industry and later chairman of the State Planning Commission in the early 1950s, and was considered one of the most important economic planners of the early Communist regime. Born in 1899 near Changsha, Hunan, Li, like many other early revolutionary leaders, studied in France and Moscow and took part in the Long March. Appointed a vice premier in 1954 and a member of the Politburo Standing Committee in 1966, Li was purged during the later stages of the Cultural Revolution. He reappeared as vice premier in 1972 and died in 1975.

Li Ruihuan (1934-   )

Li Ruihuan, a pragmatic supporter of economic reforms, has expertise in trade unions and labor issues and has been a member of the Politburo since 1987.

Li was born in 1934 to a peasant family in Baodi County, north of Tianjin. A construction worker in Beijing during the 1950s, he also took engineering courses in his spare time. In 1959, he joined the CCP and in 1960 he was named a national model worker. Between 1965 and 1970, Li served as deputy party secretary of the Beijing Building Materials Bureau and was identified as vice chairman of the Beijing Trade Union in 1973.

Li was elected to the Standing Committee of the Fifth National People's Congress in 1978. That same year he became a member of the Standing Committee of the All-China Federation of Trade Unions and, in 1980, secretary of the Communist Youth League. For the next decade, Li served in various positions within Tianjin municipality, including mayor and deputy secretary.

In 1987, Li became a member of the Politburo of the Thirteenth Party Central Committee. After the Tiananmen Square demonstrations of 1989, Li became a member of the Politburo Standing Committee and a member of the Secretariat, where he was given the ideology portfolio. Li was named chairman of the Chinese People's Political Consultative Conference in 1993.

Li Xiannian (1907-1992)

A veteran of the Long March, Li Xiannian served China in several senior positions. In his later years, he was a member of the hard-line group who advocated a more restrained approach toward economic reform.

Li was born to a poor family on June 23, 1907, in Hongan County, Hubei. Li did not receive a formal education, but was trained as a carpenter. He joined the Nationalist forces for one year in 1927 and thereafter fought with the Communists. He took part in the Long March in 1935 and later led guerrilla forces against the Japanese in his native province. In 1945 he became an early member of the Communist Party's Central Committee and retained that position until his retirement in 1987. After his troops occupied the city of Wuhan in 1949 at the end of the civil war, he was made chairman of the provincial government of Hubei Province.

In 1952, Li was appointed mayor of Wuhan. In 1954 he was named vice premier and in 1956 he gained a seat on the Politburo. A year later, Li was named minister of finance. In this role he worked with Deng Xiaoping to reinvigorate the economy after the devastation of the Great Leap Forward. He also worked closely with Soviet advisers and was later said to have become suspicious of the government in Moscow.

Li survived the Cultural Revolution without being purged and in the mid-1970s again worked with Deng to repair the damaged economy. The two, however, increasingly became rivals; Li did not trust the capitalistic nature of the reforms introduced by Deng and his followers beginning in the late 1970s. Li held relatively conservative views and was believed to have played a role in the ousting of Hu Yaobang and Zhao Ziyang, two of Deng's protégés, in the latter 1980s.

Li was elected to the ceremonial post of president of the People's Republic in 1983 and visited the United States in 1985. He retired from the presidency in 1988 and was named head of the Chinese People's Political Consultative Conference. Li died in June 1992.

Lin Biao (1907-1971)

Born in Huangan County, Hubei Province, Lin was the son of a small handicraft factory owner. Lin joined the Communist Party in 1927 and played a key role as a CCP army commander in the war against the Japanese and later during the civil war against the Nationalists. After 1949, Lin was named commander of the Central-South China military district. In September 1954, he was made a vice premier. He was later added to the Politburo and elected vice chairman of the CCP.

Lin rose to the top of the leadership during the Cultural Revolution. He was responsible for the publication of the "Little Red Book" of Mao's quotations as well as for making it an important part of political education within the military. By 1966, he was named the second-ranking member of the Politburo, replacing Liu Shaoqi as Mao's heir apparent. Lin's most important post was head of the Military Affairs Committee. He was formally named Mao's successor in April 1969, but had begun to fall from Mao's favor by 1971. In that year, he is alleged to have plotted a coup against Mao and reportedly died in a plane crash while fleeing to Mongolia after the plot was uncovered.

Liu Huaqing (1916-   )

A career military officer, Liu was born in 1916 in Dawu County, Hubei. During the Sino-Japanese War, Liu served in the Red Army. After 1949, he was transferred to the Navy and served as political commissar and deputy commandant. In 1955, he was made rear admiral and in 1957 became vice chairman of the Scientific and Technological Commission for National Defense. Though he had served on the Cultural Revolution Group of the PLA, Liu was attacked and purged along with Nie Rongzhen in 1968. He reappeared in 1978 as vice minister of the State Scientific and Technological Commission and later deputy chief of the People's Liberation Army (PLA) General Staff. He was elected to the Central Committee and became commander of the navy in 1982. In 1987, Liu was appointed deputy secretary general of the Central Military Commission and became vice chairman in 1989. He was named to the Politburo Standing Committee in 1992.

Liu Shaoqi (1898-1969)

Once the second most powerful figure in China, Liu Shaoqi was a victim of the Cultural Revolution. Although he had served as president of the PRC and was at one time next in line to succeed Mao, he spent his final years imprisoned as a counterrevolutionary. He was posthumously rehabilitated in 1979.

The youngest of nine children, Liu was born in Ningxiang County, Hunan Province, in 1898. Educated in the Chinese classics, he went on to study in the provincial capital of Changsha. In 1920, he joined the Socialist Youth League and attended Sun Yat-sen University in Moscow, where he joined the CCP. Liu returned to China in 1922 to act as a labor organizer, organizing a series of strikes in Shanghai, Hunan, and Hubei. Next Liu went to Mao's Jiangxi Soviet and began organizing rural workers. Around this time, he asserted that an individual's social background, not his class background, determined class outlook. This formulation was integrated into Maoist thought and made it possible for the peasants to be considered part of the proletariat.

Liu began the Long March but left in order to travel to northern China, where, with Peng Zhen, he sought to organize students and intellectuals opposed to Chiang Kai-shek. In 1941, he was named political commissar of the New Fourth Army under Chen Yi. Because of his success in expanding the base of Communist control, Liu was called back to Yan'an and named head of the party Secretariat.

By the time the PRC was founded in 1949, Liu was the third-ranking member of the party after Mao and Zhu De. In 1954, he assumed the role of chairman of the National People's Congress and moved into the number two position. When Mao announced that he was stepping back from power in 1961, Liu was named his successor and officially hailed as Mao's "closest comrade in arms." For the next few years, Liu and Deng Xiaoping gained effective control of the country. Their major focus was on reversing the damage caused by the Great Leap Forward. In this effort, they downplayed the role of ideology and sought primarily to repair the economy.

In 1965 Mao emerged from his "retirement" and accused Liu and Deng of failing to consult him on various matters. Mao began the Cultural Revolution in the mid-1960s ostensibly to put the country back on the correct ideological track. In 1966, Mao branded Liu the "number one capitalist roader" and "China's Khrushchev." Liu was denounced and dismissed from all posts.

After being expelled from the CCP, Liu was imprisoned. In 1979 it was reported that he had died of pneumonia in prison in 1969. Liu was rehabilitated posthumously after Deng Xiaoping returned to power.

Peng Dehuai (1898-1974)

Once commander of the Red Army, Peng Dehuai was purged from the party in 1959 for criticizing Mao and the Great Leap Forward. Arrested during the Cultural Revolution, he died in 1974.

Peng was born in Xiangtan County, Hunan Province. He received little formal education and joined the army in 1918. When his commanding officer began a purge of Communists, Peng led his troops southward and formed his own army. In 1928 he joined the CCP and worked

with Mao Zedong and General Zhu De. He participated in the Long March and rose to deputy commander-in-chief of the Communist forces under Zhu during the Anti-Japanese War.

After the Communist victory in 1949, Peng commanded the Chinese forces during the Korean War. He replaced Zhu De as minister of defense in 1954. As minister, Peng stressed professionalism and sought to modernize China's military. In the spring of 1959, he led a military delegation to the Soviet Union and Warsaw Pact countries during which he is reported to have complained about Mao's Great Leap Forward policies and their effect on plans for military modernization. Peng believed that China's social and economic policies had a direct impact on China's military policies and that the military depended on rational economic policies in order to thrive.

Peng voiced these concerns in a "Letter of Opinion" addressed directly to Mao during the Lushan Plenum of 1959. Coming immediately after the Soviet Union decided to abrogate a 1957 agreement providing China with advanced military technology, Mao saw Peng's criticism as proof of his collusion with the Soviet Union and had him purged from the party. He was dismissed from his position as minister of defense and succeeded by Lin Biao.

Peng again entered the spotlight in 1965 after Yao Wenyuan (later a member of the Gang of Four) wrote a critique of a play entitled *Hai Rui Is Dismissed from Office,* saying that it symbolized Mao's tyrannical treatment of Peng. With the Cultural Revolution in full swing, Peng was arrested. He died in 1974, but was posthumously rehabilitated in 1978.

Peng Zhen (1902-   )

Peng Zhen, a close associate of Deng Xiaoping, has occupied a variety of positions, including mayor of Beijing and chairman of the National People's Congress. He was purged during the Cultural Revolution but regained most of his posts after 1979.

The son of a poor peasant family, Peng was born in Chuwu, Shanxi Province. After receiving a traditional education during his childhood, he joined the CCP in 1926 and became involved in organizing labor. He was imprisoned for his efforts in 1929. After his release in 1936, Peng joined Liu Shaoqi in organizing students in northern China. He continued after the beginning of the Sino-Japanese War. In 1942, he was named head of the Central Party School in Yan'an and played a key role in the "rectification" campaign through which Mao re-educated newer party members.

Peng was named political commissar in Manchuria under Lin Biao in 1946 and deputy director of the CCP's

Organization Department under Liu Shaoqi in 1948. After the founding of the People's Republic in 1949, he became mayor of Beijing, concurrently serving as chairman of the Beijing municipal party commission. He was elected to the Politburo in 1951. Three years later, Peng was elected vice chairman of the CPPCC. In 1956, he was named second-ranking member of the party Secretariat after Deng Xiaoping.

At the beginning of the Cultural Revolution, Peng was named chief of the "Group of Five," which attempted to limit the scope of the purge and to protect key moderate leaders. Because of his actions, Peng was accused of plotting a coup in February 1966 and purged of all his posts in June 1966.

Peng resurfaced in early 1979 and regained many of his former positions, including chairman of the Beijing municipal party committee. He was also elected to the Politburo. In 1981, Peng became chairman of the National People's Congress.

Peng retired from his posts in 1987. He reappeared briefly in 1989 to praise the military suppression of the Tiananmen Square demonstrations, but has rarely been seen in public since then.

Qian Qichen (1928-   )

A career diplomat, Qian has served in many ambassadorial posts and has represented China at various international organizations. He was appointed foreign minister in 1988 and was instrumental in handling tensions in China's foreign affairs in the wake of the Tiananmen incident of 1989.

Born in Tianjin in 1928, Qian was the second son of an electrical engineer. After the death of his father, the family moved to Shanghai, where Qian became involved in the underground student activities of the Communist Party. He joined the CCP in 1942 and worked briefly in the Soviet Union, administering the affairs of overseas students. Qian returned to Shanghai and began working for the newspaper *Da Gong Bao*. He served as deputy secretary of the student's district party committee and became a full member of the Communist Youth League, where he worked as a researcher in 1953.

Qian returned to the Soviet Union in 1954 to study at the Young Communist League School. While in Moscow he was made second secretary of the Chinese embassy. He later became deputy of the overseas students section and director of the research office. In 1963 he went back to Beijing, where he worked in the overseas students department of the Ministry of Education, and then as director of the ministry's foreign affairs office.

During the Cultural Revolution, Qian was sent to a labor reform camp. He reappeared in 1972 and once again became active in diplomacy. Before being named vice minister of foreign affairs and an alternate member of the

Central Committee in 1984, Qian served in China's embassy in the Soviet Union and as ambassador to Guinea-Bissau. He also headed the ministry's information department in Beijing and was director of Soviet and South Asian affairs. In 1985, Qian was elected to full membership in the Central Committee.

Qian succeeded Wu Xueqian as foreign minister in 1988. In 1991 he was named to the State Council, and in 1992 he was elected to the Politburo. Since 1993, Qian has also served on the Preparatory Committee of the Hong Kong Special Administrative Region.

Qiao Shi (1924-   )

Qiao was born in Dinghai, Zhejiang. The son of a landlord family, he attended university in Shanghai and joined the CCP in 1940. A participant in the Communist student movement, he served as the secretary of a district student committee for local underground organizations, including Shanghai. Around 1947, Qiao received his first major party appointment as deputy secretary of a district party committee in Shanghai.

From 1950 to 1962, Qiao served in several Communist Youth League posts. Beginning in 1955, he also held management positions at the Anshan and Jiuquan Iron and Steel Companies. Qiao went to work at the International Liaison Department of the CCP Central Committee in 1963. He was named deputy director of the Africa and Middle East division in 1965 and elected secretary of the Afro-Asian Solidarity Committee. He also headed several delegations to Communist bloc countries.

Purged during the Cultural Revolution, Qiao re-emerged in 1978 as deputy director of the International Liaison Department. He became its director in 1982.

In 1985 Qiao was named to the Politburo and in 1986 he became a vice premier of the State Council. Qiao has also served as director of the Organization Department of the Central Committee. Since being named chairman of the National People's Congress in 1993, Qiao has focused on strengthening the legal framework for economic reform. He has also orchestrated anti-corruption campaigns aimed at government and party officials.

Song Ping (1917-   )

A former Politburo and Standing Committee Member, Song oversaw such issues as family planning and the promotion of science and technology throughout China. Since his retirement in 1992, Song has remained active, conducting inspection tours and expressing his opinions on contemporary topics. He is considered a member of the more conservative group among China's top leadership.

Song was born in 1917 in Ju County, Shandong Province. He studied at the agricultural colleges of both

Beijing University and Qinghua University. Song joined the CCP in 1937 and studied at the Central Party School and the Institute of Marxism-Leninism in Yan'an. He later became a director of the Institute of Marxism-Leninism. During the mid-1940s, Song served as Zhou Enlai's political secretary and worked as editor of the *Chongqing Xinhua Daily*. In 1947, he was director of a department under the Harbin Trade Union Council.

After the founding of the People's Republic, Song was identified as secretary general of the cultural and educational department of the Northeast China Trade Union Council. In 1953, he was named director of the State Planning Commission's labor and wages planning bureau. Before the start of the Cultural Revolution, Song served as vice minister of labor and vice minister of the State Planning Commission. Until 1967, he was also believed to have held several positions in the Lanzhou military region.

In 1973, Song was identified as the secretary of the Gansu Provincial Communist Party structure, and in 1977 he was named the region's political commissar. Later that year, he was named to the Central Committee of the CCP. Song was named to the NPC Presidium in 1979 and became minister of the State Planning Commission in the early 1980s. Between 1984 and 1986, Song led numerous economic delegations abroad. In 1987 he was named director of the CCP's Organization Department and vice chairman of the Credentials Committee.

After the Tiananmen Square demonstrations of 1989, Song was elected a member of the Standing Committee and the Politburo. He was later appointed chairman of the China Family Planning Association. Song retired from his Standing Committee and Politburo posts in 1992, but still retained positions within the government. Throughout the latter stages of reform, Song has been known for his support for a greater government role in the economy.

Tian Jiyun (1929-   )

A native of Feicheng, Shandong Province, Tian Jiyun joined the Communist Party in 1945 and served after 1949 in a variety of financial and economic posts in Guizhou Province. He became director of Sichuan Province's Finance Department in 1977 and was made deputy secretary general of the State Council in 1981. In 1983 he became a vice premier and secretary general of the State Council. Tian joined the Politburo in 1985. After 1987, his focus shifted from economic policy to foreign economic relations and rural issues. Although a close aide of Zhao Ziyang, Tian survived Zhao's fall in 1989. In December 1990 he took over Yao Yilin's economic portfolio on the State Council. In April 1992 he became a member of the Politburo Central Committee and replaced Li Lanqing as vice premier in charge of foreign economic relations and trade. In March 1993 he was made vice

chairman of the National People's Congress Standing Committee. Tian is considered a strong proponent of economic reform.

Wang Dongxing (1916-   )

Mao's personal bodyguard, Wang was born to a poor peasant family in Jiangxi Province. By the 1950s, Wang had risen to the position of vice minister of security. He also commanded the 8341 unit, a security detail of 10,000 men used by Mao to spy on the Communist leaders it was supposed to protect. In 1966, Wang was named director of the general office of the Central Committee, giving him control over the day-to-day workings of the party. He became an alternate member of the Politburo in 1969 and a full member in 1973. Wang is said to have become disenchanted with the radicals whom he had served during the Cultural Revolution. He disassociated himself from them and took part in the arrest of the Gang of Four in 1976. Named a vice chairman of the Communist Party after Mao's death, Wang soon became the subject of much criticism for allegedly embezzling state funds. He was named to the Central Advisory Commission in 1987, but has not been seen frequently in public since then.

Wang Hongwen (ca. 1937-1992)

A member of the Gang of Four, Wang Hongwen helped form the Shanghai Workers' Revolutionary Rebel Headquarters during the Cultural Revolution and served as its deputy chairman under Zhang Chunqiao. Born to poor peasants in Jilin Province, he joined the army and fought in the Korean War. He later worked in a Shanghai textile mill until the Cultural Revolution catapulted him to fame. Wang was named to the Central Committee of the CCP in 1969 and became third-ranking member of the Shanghai Municipal Workers Party in 1971. He was said to be very close to Jiang Qing, Mao's wife. In 1972, he was made second vice chairman of the CCP, a position that placed him behind only Mao and Zhou Enlai in party rank. After Mao's death in 1976, Wang was arrested with the other members of the Gang of Four and sentenced to life in prison in 1981. He died in 1992 of a liver ailment.

Wu De (1909-   )

Wu De was born in 1909 in Hebei Province. After the CCP victory in 1949, Wu served in the party bureaucracy, as mayor of Tianjin and first secretary of the Jilin Provincial Party Committee. He was party first secretary of Beijing from 1973 until 1978. He was also named to the CCP Politburo in 1973. In 1976, Wu was acting chairman of the National People's Congress after the death of Zhu De. After the fall of the Gang of Four, Wu lost much of his political clout. He was stripped of all his posts except his Politburo membership in 1980, although he was elected to the CCP Central Committee's Central Advisory Commission in 1982 and again in 1987. He has made only rare public appearances since the mid-1980s.

Wu Xueqian (1921-   )

Wu, a career diplomat, was born in Shanghai in 1921. After graduating from the foreign languages department of Jinan University, Wu joined the CCP. By 1943, he was involved in the urban work department of the Central China Bureau and active in several underground party organizations in Shanghai. With the Communist victory in 1949, he was elected deputy director of the international liaison department of the New Democratic Youth League.

From 1950 to 1967, Wu led several youth delegations to Communist and third world countries. In 1957, he was elected to the Central Committee of the Communist Youth League and became vice chairman in 1958. Wu disappeared during the Cultural Revolution, but resurfaced in 1978. Later that year he was identified as deputy director of the CCP Central Committee's International Liaison Department.

In 1982, Wu was appointed minister of foreign affairs and elected to the Standing Committee. He was later named state councilor and in 1985 gained a seat on the Politburo. As foreign minister, Wu headed delegations to several sessions of the United Nations General Assembly. He became a vice premier of the State Council in 1988, the same year in which he was succeeded as foreign minister by Qian Qichen. Wu became vice chairman of the Chinese People's Political Consultative Conference in March 1993.

Yang Shangkun (1907-   )

Yang is a veteran of the Long March who has spent most of his career in the armed forces. Yang still wields substantial power despite his lack of formal positions within the government or party.

The son of a wealthy landowning family, Yang was born in 1907 in Sichuan Province. He studied at the Chongqing Sino-French Institute and Shanghai University, joining the CCP in 1927. Yang then studied in Moscow at the Sun Yat-sen University and returned to China in 1930. After working at CCP headquarters for two years, he joined the Jiangxi Soviet. In 1933, he served as director of the Political Department of the First Front Army under Zhou Enlai. During the Long March he was assigned to Peng Dehuai's Third Army Corps and later became its political commissar. Yang spent most of the civil war years in Yan'an, acting as secretary general of the Eighth Route Army headquarters.

After the Communist victory in 1949, Yang was appointed director of the staff office of the party's Central Committee. He also served as deputy secretary general under Deng Xiaoping. In 1956, he became a member of the Central Committee and an alternate member of the Secretariat. In 1964, he was named to the NPC Standing Committee.

At the beginning of the Cultural Revolution, Yang was accused of being one of four principal figures involved in an anti-party clique. He was branded a renegade traitor and counterrevolutionary. He reappeared in 1979 and was elected vice governor of Guangdong. Yang also served as first secretary of the Guangzhou military district. In 1980 he was made political commissar and in 1981 secretary general of the Military Commission of the Central Committee. Along with his half-brother, Yang Baibing (later a Politburo member himself), he continued to rise through the ranks of both the party and government. In 1988, Yang Shangkun was named president of the PRC, serving concurrently as vice chairman of the Central Military Commission.

Yang and Deng Xiaoping were reportedly involved in a power struggle after the 1989 Tiananmen incident. Deng accused Yang of trying to amass power—especially within the military—at his expense, given Deng's political troubles following the 1989 student protests. As a result, Yang was stripped of his official titles in 1993, but has remained visible in his home province of Sichuan. Yang Baibing was allowed to retain his posts.

Yao Wenyuan (1930-   )

Yao, a member of the Gang of Four, was born in 1930. An obscure literary critic in Shanghai, Yao rose to prominence after writing a critique of the popular play *Hai Rui Is Dismissed from Office,* which he claimed was a veiled critique of Mao for his treatment of Peng Dehuai in 1959. As a result of this essay and his ties to Jiang Qing, he emerged as chief spokesman and propagandist for the Cultural Revolution. In 1969 he was elected to the Politburo. After Mao's death, Yao was imprisoned along with the other members of the Gang of Four and in 1981 was sentenced to a twenty-year prison term.

Yao Yilin (1917-1994)

An associate of Chen Yun known for his role as an economic planner in the 1980s, Yao Yilin is credited with formulating plans for the controversial Three Gorges hydropower project on the Yangzi River. He has often been at odds with Deng Xiaoping regarding the pace and scope of economic reform.

Born in Anhui Province in 1917, Yao moved in 1935 to Beijing, where he joined the party and became a leader of the anti-Japanese movement. He attended Qinghua University but was expelled in 1936 after leading demonstrations against the Nationalist government of Chiang Kaishek. During the Sino-Japanese War, Yao served as secretary general of the North China Bureau of the CCP Central Committee and as party secretary of Tianjin municipality. Later, he took part in the armed uprising in eastern Hebei Province and served as director of the Propaganda Department in the region.

Yao was appointed vice minister of commerce after 1949 and became responsible for negotiating various trade agreements with China's Communist allies. He was elected an alternate member of the Central Committee in 1958 and became minister of commerce in 1960.

Yao was attacked at the start of the Cultural Revolution. He was stripped of all posts in 1967, but reappeared in 1973 as an alternate member of the Central Committee. In 1975 he served as acting minister of foreign trade and was elected a full member of the Central Committee. He was later reinstated to his position as minister of commerce.

In 1979, Yao was appointed vice premier, secretary general of the State Finance and Economic Commission under Chen Yun, and secretary general of the Central Committee. During the next year he was named to the Secretariat and served as director of the general office of the CCP Central Committee and minister of the State Planning Commission.

Yao was elected to the Politburo in 1985 and led delegations to the United States, the Middle East, and the Soviet Union. In December 1988 he was appointed chairman of the Three Gorges Project Examination Committee, which examined the controversial plan to build the largest hydroelectric dam in the world in Central China's Hubei Province. The project, which would supply China with one-eighth of its electric power needs, has subsequently been approved.

Despite his success in winning approval for this project, Yao was relieved of his formal posts in 1992, in part because of his ongoing tensions with Deng Xiaoping as well as his increasing age. Yao continued to adhere to his conservative economic views, advocating a slower pace of reforms and economic development. As one of the party elders, he continued to wield influence within the high levels of China's leadership until his death in December 1994.

Ye Jianying (1897-1986)

Once chairman of the National People's Congress and minister of defense, Marshal Ye Jianying was a veteran of the Long March and supporter of General Secretary Hua Guofeng. After Hua's fall from power, Ye lost much of his influence. He retired from the government in 1985.

Ye was born in Meizhou, Guangdong Province, to a middle-class family. He graduated from the Yunnan Military Academy in 1919 and joined the Communist forces sometime in the 1920s. He became friends with Zhou Enlai on the faculty of the Whampoa Military Academy, and in 1929 the two went to Moscow to receive advanced military training. They returned to China and took part in the Long March.

After the founding of the People's Republic in 1949, Ye was named mayor of Beijing and later mayor of Guangzhou. He also served as commander of the Guangdong military district, commander of the South China military region, and political commissar of Guangdong. In 1954 he was elected deputy for the People's Liberation Army to the National People's Congress and appointed vice chairman of the National Defense Council. Ye was promoted to marshal in 1955, one of only ten men holding China's highest military rank. During this period, Ye led several military delegations to other socialist states.

During the years of the Cultural Revolution, Ye maintained a low profile. In 1966 he was elected to the Politburo. He continued to hold his position in the Central Committee and to serve as vice chairman of the Military Commission on the Central Committee. In 1971, Ye succeeded Lin Biao as minister of national defense, although he was not officially named to the position until 1975. After the death of Mao Zedong, Ye became an ally of Mao's successor, Hua Guofeng. As Deng Xiaoping and his colleagues gained control of the government, Ye's influence began to wane. In his final years of public service, Ye maintained his Politburo and Central Committee standing and held ceremonial posts including chairman of the Presidium and vice chairman of the Central Military Commission. Ye resigned from his various posts in 1985, citing frailness and advancing age. He died in October 1986.

Zhang Chunqiao (1917-   )

Born in 1917 in Shandong, Zhang was a member of the Gang of Four. In his early career, Zhang did propaganda work for the Communists, rising to head the *Liberation Daily* and serving in various positions within the Shanghai Communist Party. During the Cultural Revolution, Zhang helped to form the Shanghai Revolutionary Committee and served as its chairman. He was later named chief of the Cultural Revolution Group. Before being arrested and purged from the party in 1976, Zhang served on the Politburo Standing Committee and acted as director of the general political department of the PLA. He received a death sentence in 1981, later commuted to life in prison.

Zhao Ziyang (1919-   )

Zhao Ziyang, a close associate of Deng Xiaoping, was a firm supporter of economic modernization before being removed from his top leadership posts after the 1989 Tiananmen Square demonstrations.

Zhao was born in 1919 to a family of grain merchants and landlords in Hua County, Henan Province. He attended secondary school in Kaifeng and Wuhan and joined the Communist Youth League in 1932. Unlike many in the older generation of China's leadership, Zhao was too young to take part in the Long March and had no military experience. During the first twenty years of the People's Republic, Zhao worked in various positions within the Guangdong provincial party apparatus, including political commissar of the Guangdong military district. In 1965, he was identified as the first secretary of the Guangdong Communist Party, the youngest first secretary at that time.

During the Cultural Revolution, Zhao was denounced and disappeared from public view, but he resurfaced in 1971 as secretary of the Inner Mongolia Communist Party. Zhao returned to Guangdong and was identified as chairman of the revolutionary committee in 1972.

In 1973, Zhao was elected to the CCP Central Committee. Within the next two years, he regained his positions as party first secretary of Guangdong and political commissar of the Guangdong military district.

Zhao became party chief of Sichuan, the most populous province in China, in 1976. In order to repair the devastation caused in the province by the Cultural Revolution, Zhao enacted sweeping reforms to enhance economic efficiency. These included expanding the size and number of privately owned plots, establishing a market for crop surpluses, and giving more freedom to factories to set prices for their products. Zhao's success in Sichuan earned him the attention of Deng Xiaoping. In 1979, he was elected a full member of the Politburo and made a vice premier of the State Council. He went on to become State Council premier, and in these posts Zhao worked with Hu Yaobang to further China's reform policies.

After Hu Yaobang's fall from power in 1987, Zhao took over as general secretary of the Communist Party. He called for China to adopt a more open economy despite inflationary pressures and was soon criticized by more conservative leaders who favored a contraction of what they saw as an overheated economy. In 1989, after student protests broke out in Tiananmen Square, Zhao adopted a conciliatory approach toward the demonstrators. At a meeting of the Asian Development Bank, he broke with the prevailing party view regarding the students and suggested that there was some justification for their protests. When he refused to take action against the students, he was charged with trying to split the party. Later that summer, Zhao and his senior aides were re-

moved from their posts and Zhao was placed under house arrest. He was not purged from the party, but has not resumed any public role. By early 1995 the party had yet to make a final decision on his case.

Zhou Enlai (1898-1976)

The PRC's first foreign minister, Zhou Enlai was born to a relatively wealthy family in Shaoxing County, Zhejiang Province, in 1898, and received his elementary training in the Chinese classics. In 1912 he matriculated at the Nankai Middle School and later attended Nankai University in Tianjin. During his college years, Zhou became an ardent nationalist and looked for ways to explain China's apparent fall from greatness.

While studying for a brief period in Japan, Zhou became involved in Chinese politics from afar, particularly the student-led May Fourth movement, which looked to China's past for an explanation of its weakness and looked to the outside world to help strengthen the country. At this time, he wrote for several Chinese publications and was jailed in 1919 because of these works. After his release in 1920, Zhou went to France with a group of Chinese students and again became involved in politics. He joined the CCP in 1922 and traveled through France and Germany, recruiting new party members among Chinese students in Europe.

Zhou returned to China in 1924 and began working at the Whampoa Military Academy. He was named deputy director of the political department under Chiang Kai-shek and later political commissar for the first division of the Nationalist Army. In 1926, Zhou traveled to Shanghai and worked as a trade union organizer. In 1927, he took part in an unsuccessful Communist rebellion against the Nationalists. His actions were fictionally portrayed in *Man's Fate,* a novel by André Malraux.

Next, Zhou went to study at Moscow's Sun Yat-sen University. He returned to Shanghai in 1929 and worked for the central party apparatus. When most members of the central party were purged, Zhou went to join the Jiangxi Soviet. There, Zhou was involved in power struggles that removed Mao Zedong from the top position of power. Zhou actually succeeded Mao in various army political positions. When Mao returned to power in 1935, however, Zhou moved to Mao's side. Later that year, he joined Mao on the Long March.

During the CCP's Yan'an days, Zhou acted as the Communists' chief negotiator with the Nationalist forces. In 1936, when Chiang Kai-shek was kidnapped by his own former followers, Zhou interceded to have him released. Zhou was also instrumental in helping establish the Communist-Nationalist united front against the Japanese. In 1945, Zhou was elected to the ruling Secretariat of the CCP, placing him among the top six men in the Communist hierarchy.

In 1949, Zhou was named premier of the People's Republic. As such, he served as principal administrator of the new bureaucracy as well as liaison between the Communist Party and other non-Communist groups. Most importantly, Zhou was also appointed foreign minister. He worked diligently but unsuccessfully in 1950 to get China admitted to the United Nations and tried to intercede with the United States during the Korean War. In 1954, he led China's delegation to the Geneva talks on Indochina.

Aside from border concerns, Zhou's main focus during the 1950s and early 1960s was China's position within the budding non-aligned movement. He is usually credited with China's expansion of relations with the third world at this time. In 1958, Chen Yi replaced him as foreign minister, although Zhou continued to dominate the country's foreign affairs apparatus.

Zhou weathered the Cultural Revolution relatively unscarred. He worked to limit the effects of the movement on other sectors, especially the country's nuclear development, oil production programs, and weapons research. He was also able to shield economic planners like Li Xiannian, who would later become president of the PRC.

After the Cultural Revolution ended, Zhou worked with others to rebuild the economy. He remained loyal to Mao, however, and apparently agreed on the appointment of Hua Guofeng as Mao's heir. In addition, Zhou sought to reopen ties to the West. He was instrumental in establishing contact with the United States and played a key role in the China visits made by Henry Kissinger and President Nixon. Zhou died of cancer in January 1976.

Zhu De (1886-1976)

The first commander-in-chief of the Red Army, Zhu De is often credited with plotting the military campaigns that resulted in victory for the Communist forces. Born in Yilong County, Sichuan, in 1886, Zhu's military career began with the warlord armies of southern China. After meeting Sun Yat-sen, Zhu went to Europe to study and met Zhou Enlai. He joined the CCP while in Germany but was expelled from the country in 1926 for taking part in numerous strikes and demonstrations. Although a member of the CCP, Zhu joined the Nationalist army when he returned to China.

In 1927, Zhu took part in the Communist attempt to seize Nanchang, known as the Nanchang Uprising. When the Red Army was defeated, Zhu fled southward and joined Mao's forces in 1928. He was named commander-in-chief of the Communist armies in 1930.

After the founding of the PRC in 1949, Zhu was named senior vice chairman of the new government. When the army was placed under the newly created Ministry of Defense in 1954, Zhu lost his position as commander-in-chief to Peng Dehuai. Zhu remained a senior member of the government until his death in 1976.

Zhu Rongji (1929-)

China's "economic czar" in the first half of the 1990s, Zhu Rongji generally favors active and pragmatic steps to further economic reform.

Zhu was born in 1929 in Changsha, Hunan. In 1947, he began his studies at Qinghua University and became an active member in many of the CCP-led student movements. Zhu joined the CCP in 1949.

After graduation, Zhu held several positions within the State Planning Commission. Because he took part in the Hundred Flowers movement, he was branded a rightist during the Cultural Revolution and sent to the countryside for five years.

Zhu re-emerged in the 1970s as an engineer with the Ministry of Petroleum Industry. In 1979 he was transferred to the State Economic Commission and put in charge of technical transformation. From 1983 to 1988 he served as vice minister of the State Economic Commission. In 1984 he was also elected vice president of the China Industrial Economic Association and head of Qinghua University's Economic Management Institute. In the fall of 1987, Zhu was elected an alternate to the CCP Central Committee and appointed deputy secretary of the Shanghai Municipal Party Committee. In 1988, he was named mayor of Shanghai, where he was known for his tough stance regarding political dissidents. Although Zhu has been a strong supporter of economic reforms, he appears relatively conservative in his attitude toward political liberalization.

Because of his "clear political stance" in subduing Shanghai students during the mid-1989 protests and his success in promoting foreign investment in China during the 1980s, Zhu gained the attention of the leadership in Beijing. In 1991 he was named to the Politburo and became a vice premier. When the State Council established a new and powerful Economic and Trade Office in 1992, Zhu was named to head it. He was also put in charge of the Securities Commission and in 1993 given the powerful role of governor of the People's Bank of China.

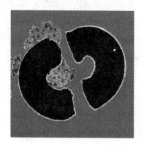

CHRONOLOGY

1911-1949

October 10, 1911. The 1911 Revolution against the Qing dynasty, led by Sun Yat-sen, began after a troop mutiny in Wuchang, Hubei Province.

February 1912. The infant Xuantong Emperor abdicated the throne, leaving Yuan Shikai, leader of the Beiyang Army (the most powerful army of the Qing dynasty), to establish a republican government in Beijing. Sun Yat-sen, who had already established his own provisional government in Nanjing, yielded control of the country to Yuan Shikai at this time.

December 1912. Sun Yat-sen formally established the Kuomintang (KMT or Nationalist) Party. Before the 1911 Revolution, the party was known as the Alliance Society, a group of provincial leaders who had pledged to work with Yuan Shikai to unify the country. It was the first political party established in China.

1913-1916. The new government proved short-lived. In 1914, Yuan suspended the parliament after power struggles with military governors in the south. The country then fell under the control of the Japanese military as a result of Japan's "Twenty-One Demands." At the end of 1915, Yuan Shikai declared himself emperor but was forced to end the monarchy in 1916. Yuan died later that year.

The period between Yuan Shikai's death and the formation of the Kuomintang government under Chiang Kai-shek in 1927 became known as the warlord era. Control of China rested in the hands of a group of warlords, each with independent control over his territory. This era represented a return to feudal patterns of rule.

May 4, 1919. In protest of the agreements reached at the Versailles Conference that failed to return Japanese territorial concessions to China at the end of World War I, students from Beijing launched mass demonstrations that later spread throughout China. The surge of nationalism exhibited during the demonstrations came to be known as the "May Fourth movement."

The May Fourth movement later expanded to include a "literary and cultural renaissance" among intellectuals in China. Ideas such as liberalism, social Darwinism, and later Marxism-Leninism caught on in China during this time.

July 1, 1921. The Chinese Communist Party was officially founded in Shanghai by twelve delegates including Mao Zedong. Individual party branches, or "cells," had been established earlier in several locales, including Shanghai, Changsha, and Beijing. At the first national meeting in Shanghai of the Chinese Communist Party (CCP), party members were called on to organize workers and to act as the "vanguard" of the proletariat with the ultimate aim of overthrowing the government.

1923-1926. In an attempt to build unity against the warlords and the Japanese, the KMT and CCP joined in a "united front" in 1923. After Sun Yat-sen's death in 1925, Chiang became leader of the KMT and its united front and in 1926 led the "Northern Expedition" to gain control of warlord areas in the north. Despite the success of the expedition, conflicts between the KMT and CCP continued.

April 1927. KMT troops under Chiang's command launched a surprise attack against Shanghai labor unions and radical activists, killing several important Communist leaders. This action destroyed the CCP-KMT united front and widened the split between the conservative and liberal factions of the KMT. Chiang Kai-shek, allied with the conservatives, went on to form his own Nationalist government in Nanjing, while Communist forces retreated to the south and created their own bases, called "soviets."

September 1931. Japanese troops bombarded the northeastern Chinese city of Shenyang and subjected its citizens to Japanese control.

February 1932-March 1934. Japan completed its occupation of Manchuria and established the puppet state of Manchukuo. The last of the Manchu emperors, Pu Yi, was inaugurated as the provincial dictator; on 1 March 1934 the Japanese installed Pu Yi as the Kangde Emperor.

October 1934. The KMT launched a military offensive in the south to rid the country of Communist influence. After the fall of their base at Jiangxi, the CCP retreated over six thousand miles to Yan'an in Shaanxi Province, in what came to be known as the "Long March." Of the more than 100,000 people who began the trek, only 20,000 survived.

December 12, 1936. Chiang Kai-shek was kidnapped in Xi'an, Shaanxi Province, by the former warlord of Manchuria, Zhang Xueliang, because of Chiang's appeasement of the Japanese invaders. Zhang insisted that fighting the Japanese take precedence over fighting the Communists. With the help of CCP negotiator Zhou Enlai, Chiang was released, ending what became known as the Xi'an incident.

July 1937. Japanese forces attacked Chinese troops at the Marco Polo Bridge outside Beijing. Three weeks later, Japan began a full-scale military offensive against China.

September 1937. To fight the Japanese more effectively, the CCP and KMT entered into a second united front, ten years after the first such effort had collapsed. The CCP proclaimed that it would abandon efforts at sovietization and focus on countering Japanese aggression, while the KMT promised to give up its attempts at military suppression of the Communists and seek a political settlement with the CCP.

March 1938. The recently formed CCP-KMT united front held a national congress and established a People's Political Council to advise the government. The congress adopted a "Program of Armed Resistance and National Reconstruction" to govern the wartime collaboration between the two parties and called for governmental, economic, and military reforms. The CCP-KMT cooperation remained largely symbolic, however, and gradually unraveled in practice.

April 1941. Japan and the Soviet Union signed a Treaty of Neutrality and Friendship, thereby ending any possibility of Soviet aid to the Nationalist government in China. During the earlier war years, the Soviet Union had supported both Chiang's Nationalist government and the Chinese Communist Party.

February 1942. The United States sent Lt. Gen. Joseph Stilwell to act as chief of staff for Generalissimo Chiang Kai-shek. In addition, the United States authorized a $500 million loan to Nationalist China. One year later, the two countries signed a treaty to relinquish U.S. extraterritorial and related rights in China. Washington also promised to ease immigration restrictions on Chinese citizens traveling to the United States. The first U.S. ambassador to China, Patrick Hurley, arrived in China in November 1944.

October 30, 1943. China was acknowledged as a "great power" in the "Declaration of Four Nations on General Security." According to the treaty, China had the right to participate with the United States, Soviet Union, and Great Britain in prosecuting war, organizing peace, and establishing the framework for international coopera-

tion. At the Cairo Conference in December of the same year, the other three powers agreed to help restore "territories Japan had stolen" to Chinese control.

March 1945. Chiang Kai-shek announced that a national assembly would be convened to draft a new constitution for the republic. Although the CCP was invited to join the assembly, its leaders refused, charging that the assembly would be a "congress of slaves" and demanding that Chiang be removed from office. To appease the CCP, Chiang invited Mao to join him and U.S. ambassador Hurley in Chongqing to confer on various issues. Chiang and Mao signed the "Double Ten" agreement to decrease hostilities, but tensions increased again in late October over Nationalist charges of CCP activity in Manchuria. There was also CCP-KMT fighting in Shanghai and Shandong Province.

January 1946. Chiang Kai-shek convened a Political Consultative Conference in Chongqing, at which he promised to recognize fundamental democratic rights and agreed to allow a coalition government under his leadership. Reductions in both KMT and CCP military forces were also agreed upon, and the CCP and KMT signed an accord to gradually unify their armies, although tensions between them were actually on the rise following Japan's surrender to the Allies in August 1945.

May 1946. After having been forced out of Nanjing in November 1937 by the approach of Japanese forces, the KMT government returned to the city. (In the interim, the Nationalists had moved their headquarters to Hankou and later to Chongqing.)

November 1946. The national assembly promised by Chiang in 1945 was held in Nanjing. Although most Communists and third-party delegates boycotted the assembly, Chiang described it as the beginning of constitutional government in China. Four days later, ongoing KMT-CCP negotiations regarding Manchuria were suspended and fighting between KMT and CCP forces resumed by the end of the month.

June 1947. The United States ended its arms embargo to China and began supplying the Nationalist forces with over $6.5 million worth of ammunition to aid in their fight against the Communists.

November 23, 1947. The first elections in China's history ended with the Nationalists winning the majority of seats. The government claimed that over 20 million citizens voted. On 25 December, the National Assembly adopted a new constitution.

April 1948. The U.S. Congress authorized a total of $463 million in aid to the Chinese Nationalists.

September 1948. CCP troops began winning ground with the fall of the industrial city of Jinan. During the next two months, the cities of Changchun and Shenyang fell to CCP control. Prompted by the CCP gains, Chiang asked for additional U.S. aid and sent his wife to the United States to request more support.

1949

January-May. After the fall of Beijing to the Communists on 31 January, the Nationalist government announced that it would enter peace talks with the CCP, but hostilities continued. By late May, Communist forces had gained control of numerous areas along the Yangzi River, including Nanjing, Wuhan, and Shanghai.

October 1. The People's Republic of China (PRC) was formally inaugurated. Two weeks earlier, the Chinese People's Political Consultative Conference (CPPCC) had adopted the Organic Law of the Central People's Government and ratified Mao Zedong's new "democratic program." Mao Zedong was named chairman and Zhou Enlai was named premier and foreign minister. The capital was established in Beijing. Within the next few months, the Soviet Union, Great Britain, and India recognized the new republic; the United States, however, refused to recognize the Communist government without consulting Congress and subsequently withdrew all diplomatic personnel from the country.

December. After the fall of both Chengdu and Chongqing to Communist forces, the Nationalist forces retreated to the island of Taiwan. Chiang Kai-shek reclaimed the presidency of Nationalist China in March 1950 and continued building his government from his new base in Taipei.

1950

February. China and the Soviet Union signed a Treaty of Friendship, Alliance, and Mutual Assistance. The treaty stipulated that both countries would recognize the independent status of the Mongolian People's Republic and that the 1945 treaty between the Soviet Union and Nationalist China was null and void.

April. Communist forces gained control of Hainan Island after forcing the evacuation of 125,000 Nationalist forces. One week later, the Nationalist government appealed to the United States for assistance to prevent a Communist invasion of Taiwan.

June 25. North Korean troops crossed the 38th parallel and invaded South Korea. They claimed that the invasion was a defensive action to preempt a South Korean invasion of the north. The same day, the UN Security Council adopted a resolution calling for a cease-fire.

June 27. In response to North Korea's decision to send troops across the 38th parallel into South Korea, U.S. president Harry Truman ordered the U.S. Seventh Fleet to protect Taiwan from possible Communist attack. Although the fleet did not take its position in the Taiwan Strait for almost a year, Truman's pronouncement marked an upgrading of the U.S. commitment to the Nationalist forces on Taiwan. In response, China began a campaign to "Resist America and Aid Korea."

June. China passed the Agrarian Reform Law, thus beginning the process of land reform by abolishing "feudal exploitation" by the land-owning class and by distributing land to the peasants. Further drives to collectivize agriculture took place throughout the 1950s.

August. Communist forces invaded Tibet and three months later took control of the capital at Lhasa. Before the fighting ended in March 1951, the People's Republic had claimed control over the region.

October-November. After amassing forces along the Korean-Manchurian border, the Chinese military crossed into North Korea and attacked South Korean troops. During previous weeks, Premier Zhou Enlai had warned the international community that China would intervene in the ensuing war if U.S. troops went into North Korea. By 26 November, 200,000 Chinese troops had begun a counteroffensive against UN troops.

December. The United States enacted an "informal" embargo on all U.S. exports to China, which remained in place for the next twenty-one years. Later in the month, President Truman froze all assets belonging to the People's Republic of China in the United States; China retaliated by freezing all U.S. assets in China.

1951

April. After canceling aid to Nationalist forces on Taiwan in January 1950, the United States resumed aiding the island government with the appointment of a 100-man Military Assistance Advisory Group. The first allocation of U.S. aid totaled $300 million.

May. Dean Rusk, assistant U.S. secretary of state, formally articulated the U.S. position on China claiming that the United States recognized the "national government of the Republic of China" in Taipei. Rusk claimed that the Beijing-based Communist government was under the control of the Soviet Union and, therefore, "not Chinese."

Late 1951. China initiated the "Three Anti's" campaign in Manchuria to fight corruption, waste, and bureaucratism. It targeted urban cadres, especially those working in economics and finance, and chastised them for their capitalist bias. The "Five Anti's" campaign began shortly thereafter in 1952, attacking those labeled as capitalists and members of the national bourgeoisie as well as Western-influenced intellectuals.

1952

August. Premier Zhou Enlai traveled to Moscow for the first Sino-Soviet negotiations since the signing of the bilateral treaty in February 1950. The two sides were said to have discussed the Korean crisis and its effect on the Chinese economy.

1953

February. U.S. president Dwight Eisenhower declared that the U.S. Seventh Fleet would no longer "protect" Communist China from the Nationalist forces on Taiwan. Chiang admitted that his forces were not adequately equipped to launch such an attack but noted that the KMT could "not afford to wait until we are fully prepared."

February 4. The Chinese government declared that the country's post-civil war recovery was complete and took steps to begin a five-year plan to develop the Chinese economy along the Soviet model. Soviet advisers and aid were provided to help the Chinese, and China established the State Planning Commission and economic ministries to oversee central economic planning.

March 5. Soviet premier Joseph Stalin died of a brain hemorrhage at the age of 73.

July. North and South Korea agreed to an armistice to end the Korean War. The agreement made stipulations for prisoner exchanges and established a demarcation line and a demilitarized zone. China reportedly had suffered one million casualties during the war. Because of foreign involvement, the war reinforced China's negative perceptions of the West and made China view the United States as the prime enemy.

1954

April-June. China and India signed an agreement in April to regulate trade and travel between the two countries. The two also reached agreement concerning the status of Tibet, although the border dispute between the two countries remained unresolved. China and India then issued a communiqué in June in which India promised to remain neutral in the cold war and China promised not to commit any act of aggression against India. This communiqué also marked the first use by China of the "Five Principles of Peaceful Coexistence," which thereafter guided Chinese foreign policy toward the third world. The principles included mutual respect for territorial integrity and sovereignty; nonaggression; noninterference in internal affairs; equality and mutual benefit; and peaceful coexistence.

September 3. Communist forces began shelling the Nationalist-held island of Quemoy (Jinmen). The next day, U.S. secretary of state John Foster Dulles ordered the Seventh Fleet to recommence patrolling the Taiwan Strait and on 7 September Nationalist forces began air strikes against the mainland.

September. The Chinese People's Political Consultative Conference adopted a formal constitution, thereby replacing the temporary government structures put in place by the Organic Law of the Central People's Government in 1949. The constitution established the National People's Congress (NPC) as a permanent representative organization of state authority, with a Standing Committee and delegates elected from more than 200,000 local assemblies. The CPPCC became an advisory body.

October. The Soviet Union promised to grant China a second credit of $130 million and to continue implementation of the provisions of the 1950 Sino-Soviet treaty, which had been delayed because of the Korean War.

December 2. The United States and the Republic of China on Taiwan signed a mutual defense treaty. The treaty stipulated that the two would develop and maintain their collective capacity to resist armed attack by "Communist subversion from without"; cooperate in economic development; consult on implementation of the treaty; and jointly meet an armed attack of either in the West Pacific. The Republic of China also promised to consult the United States before launching an attack on the mainland. The treaty did not make provisions for the Nationalist-held islands along the mainland coast.

The People's Republic of China maintained that the island of Taiwan was "entirely within the purview of China's sovereignty and purely an internal affair of China" and strongly protested the United States-Taiwan Mutual Defense Treaty. The Soviet Union supported this stand. The U.S. Senate ratified the treaty in February 1955.

1955

January 10. In addition to strikes on the Nationalist-held island of Quemoy, Communist forces began attacking the Dachen Islands, 200 miles north of Taiwan. The attacks were said to have been the largest of the ongoing civil war. One week later, Communist forces invaded Yijiang Island, which lies 210 miles north of Taiwan.

January 13. UN secretary general Dag Hammarskjöld ended a trip to Beijing during which he tried to secure the release of thirteen American prisoners. After the trip, Hammarskjöld expressed his belief that it would be useful if the People's Republic were allowed to enter the United Nations.

January. The U.S. House of Representatives passed what came to be known as the Formosa Resolution, which was a response to a request by President Dwight Eisenhower for authorization to use American armed forces to protect Taiwan and the Pescadore (Penghu) Islands. On 5 February, U.S. forces helped Nationalist forces withdraw from the Dachen Islands.

April. Chinese premier Zhou Enlai addressed delegates from twenty-nine Asian and African countries at the Bandung Conference in Indonesia. Zhou articulated the Chinese belief that the less developed countries of the world should "seek common ground" and, where necessary, act in union against the richer countries. The Bandung speech marked the beginning of what came to be known as the

"Bandung phase" of Chinese foreign policy, in which China sought to ease tensions along its border and to increase its contacts with African and Asian countries. During his remarks, Zhou also noted China's willingness to negotiate with the United States regarding the question of Taiwan.

May 30. China agreed to release 4 American airmen imprisoned on the mainland for two years. Beijing did not release another 11 prisoners charged with espionage until 1 August 1955, when Sino-U.S. negotiations were raised to the ambassadorial level. One month later, the Chinese released an additional 12 American civilians, while 29 Americans remained in Chinese prisons. For its part, Washington began to release some of the 129 Chinese nationals detained in the United States.

July 8. Beijing radio announced that China would provide $338 million in economic aid to North Vietnam. During a visit to Beijing, North Vietnamese leader Ho Chi Minh joined with the Chinese Communists in alleging that the United States wanted to prevent peaceful unification of Vietnam through elections.

1956

February. The Communist Party of the Soviet Union (CPSU) signaled a major policy change during its twentieth party congress with Premier Nikita Khrushchev's statement that a war with "capitalist imperialism" was no longer inevitable because of Soviet possession of nuclear weapons. He argued that there was an international trend toward peaceful coexistence and that other Communist parties should join the Soviet Union in finding a peaceful road to power. More importantly for China and Chairman Mao, Khrushchev delivered a detailed denunciation of Stalin and his "cult of personality." Mao Zedong feared that Khrushchev's speech would open the way for criticism of his own rule.

May. Mao launched what came to be known as the "Hundred Flowers movement," suggesting that the people of China should voice their criticisms of the Communist Party in order to strengthen it and signaling a liberalization of the Communist regime.

May 16. Great Britain decided to ease its informal embargo on exports to China by allowing "nonstrategic" items to be sent to the mainland.

July-August. Authorities of the Burmese government accused China of allowing thousands of troops to occupy territory in northeast Burma. Negotiations were already under way to resolve the growing tensions between the neighbors but broke off in August. Zhou Enlai later traveled to Burma to reach some agreement.

September. The eighth party congress adopted measures to shift emphasis away from sole leadership by Mao Zedong to a more collective leadership, giving Liu Shaoqi and Deng Xiaoping larger roles. The measures were an attempt to prevent a repeat of actions similar to Mao's 1955 collectivization drive. In response, Mao temporarily retreated to what was called the "second line" of leadership, leaving day-to-day administration of the country to others and instead focusing more on policy considerations.

1957

January 18. Despite tensions created by Khrushchev's February 1956 speech, Chinese and Soviet delegations led by Zhou Enlai and Nikolai Bulganin, respectively, signed an agreement to continue rendering support to the Near East and Middle East in order to prevent "aggression and interference" in these areas. The joint policy statement was a response to the Eisenhower Doctrine, which announced the U.S. intention to defend the Middle East from any country supported by international communism. During his trip to Moscow, Zhou declared China's belief that the Soviet Union was the world Communist leader.

February. Mao delivered a speech entitled "On the Correct Handling of Contradictions among the People," reiterating the idea that the Chinese people should be able to criticize the party.

April 20. The U.S. Department of State eased its "informal" embargo of exports to China, giving China an export status similar to that of the European Soviet bloc. The department also decided to allow a pool of American journalists to travel to China but maintained travel restrictions on other American citizens. (China would later refuse to accept visa applications from the journalists.)

May 7. The Republic of China and the United States signed an agreement that allowed for the positioning of *Matador* missiles on Taiwan. The missiles had a reported range of 600 miles and were capable of carrying nuclear warheads.

May 24. After a U.S. military court acquitted an American serviceman of the murder of a Taiwan citizen, anti-American riots broke out in Taipei. The almost 3,000 rioters raided the U.S. embassy and offices of the United States Information Agency and injured 13 Americans. In order to contain the hostilities, the Nationalist government declared martial law.

August. The Anti-Rightist campaign began as Peng Zhen accused critics who had emerged during the Hundred Flowers movement of holding antisocialist views. People with ties to the West also became targets of attack. By the end of the campaign in 1958, an estimated 400,000 to 700,000 intellectuals had been removed from their posts and sent to work in farms and factories.

October 15. China and the Soviet Union signed a secret agreement promising that the Soviet Union would help China develop its nuclear capacity. The agreement followed an official visit by Khrushchev to Beijing in July. The treaty was abrogated in June 1959.

1958

January. Mao began to advocate the simultaneous development of both industry and agriculture. He also sought to decentralize control of the country in order to weaken the central bureaucracy and used mass mobilization of the people to nurture ideological fervor and to achieve greater productivity. In a January 28 speech to the Supreme State Conference, he set the goal of catching up with Great Britain within fifteen years and thus began to sow the seeds of the Great Leap Forward.

February 19. The Chinese and Korean governments announced that Chinese forces would be withdrawn from Korea by the end of the year and called on other powers to remove their troops from the peninsula. (The United States announced that its forces would remain in the South.) The Chinese withdrawal was completed on 25 October.

May. The second session of the eighth party congress announced that China would implement Mao's plan for a Great Leap Forward. According to Mao, China needed to abandon the Soviet model of development with its emphasis on heavy industry and turn instead toward labor-intensive projects. With the Great Leap Forward, Mao hoped to match England in steel production within fifteen years by using "backyard furnaces." The resulting stress on quantity over quality and the lack of attention paid to agriculture led to massive industrial waste and famine in 1960 and 1961, when more than 19 million people died of starvation.

July. The government of China announced that it would begin a campaign to "liberate" Taiwan. In response, the Nationalists ordered a state of emergency on the Matsu (Mazu) and Pescadore Islands. One month later, the Communists began shelling Quemoy and the Tan (Dan) Islands. In September, the Nationalists claimed 3,000 civilian and 1,000 military casualties as a result.

August. An enlarged meeting of the Politburo adopted the Beidaihe Resolution, thereby formalizing the Great Leap Forward in agriculture. The resolution also established communes throughout the country. Because of the poor harvests in ensuing years, however, the commune system was reorganized in 1962.

September 4. The government of China laid claim to a twelve-mile zone off its coast. The government also included Quemoy, Matsu, and other islands in this claim and forbade foreign vessels and aircraft from entering the zone without prior permission.

September-October. The U.S. and Chinese ambassadors to Poland met in Warsaw to discuss the Taiwan Straits crisis. On 6 October, China declared a one-week ceasefire and on 25 October the Chinese government announced there would be a ceasefire every other day.

October 23. Chiang Kai-shek announced that although his goal was ultimately to reunify the country, he would not use force to do so. Instead, Chiang would implement Sun Yat-sen's "Three Principles of the People"—nationalism, democracy, and the people's livelihood—to regain the mainland.

December 17. During a Central Committee meeting, Mao Zedong announced that he would resign as chief of state in January 1959 to devote his energies full-time to being chairman of the Communist Party. Liu Shaoqi succeeded him as chief of state in April 1959.

1959

February 14. On the ninth anniversary of the signing of the Sino-Soviet Treaty of Friendship, Alliance, and Mutual Assistance, the countries signed another agreement asserting their "unbreakable unity." Moscow promised to provide China with $1.25 billion worth of equipment and industrial assistance, and the two sides signed a $1.75 billion trade agreement.

March 10. Riots broke out in the Tibetan capital of Lhasa. One week later, after Chinese troops fired on a crowd, Tibet's spiritual leader, the Dalai Lama, fled to India. Although the Tibetans declared their independence two weeks later, Zhou Enlai ordered the newly established government in Tibet to dissolve.

May 28. The International Olympic Committee announced that Nationalist China would no longer be recognized as the representative of China in the Olympics. The committee president said that if the People's Republic of China applied for membership, it would be accepted as the sole representative of China.

June. The Soviet Union secretly announced that it would withdraw nuclear assistance to China. In addition to canceling the 1957 technology and defense pact, the Soviet Union recalled all Soviet technicians working on projects in China.

August. During what came to be known as the Lushan Plenum, Mao Zedong purged Defense Minister Peng Dehuai after Peng reportedly criticized Mao's Great Leap Forward. Lin Biao replaced Peng as defense minister.

October 21. Tensions between China and India increased after fighting broke out in Kashmir. The clash prompted India to make "adequate military preparations" against future threats. The two sides held talks, which eventually broke down in May 1962.

1960

January. Burma and China signed a border agreement, a ten-year nonaggression treaty, and a treaty of friendship. During the next twelve months, China also signed treaties with Nepal (April), the Mongolian People's Republic (May), Cuba (September), and Cambodia (December).

April. The first published signs of the Sino-Soviet split appeared in the Chinese Communist Party's theoretical journal *Hongqi* (Red Flag) in an article entitled "Long Live Leninism." The article sought to prove the legitimacy of Mao Zedong Thought and stated that Mao, not Khrushchev, was the true heir to the Communist tradition. China hinted that Khrushchev was taking the Soviet Union toward revisionism with his plans for détente. The Soviet Union accused China of being too dogmatic.

December 6. Despite underlying tensions with the Soviet Union, China joined the other Communist countries of the world in issuing a manifesto of unity in the fight against capitalism. China's position was said to have been more aggressive than that of the Soviet Union. The manifesto claimed that the United States was the main force of aggression and rejected the American concept of brinkmanship.

December. China signed a Treaty of Friendship and Mutual Nonaggression with Cambodia and later began to supply the country with arms in support of its battle with the Vietnamese. China and Cambodia had established diplomatic relations in 1958 as part of China's attempt to counteract what it saw as growing ties between the Soviet Union and Vietnam.

1961

January 20. The Central Committee announced that, because of crop failures, the industrial policies adopted under the Great Leap Forward would be curtailed. China would later have to buy more than 6 million tons of wheat, barley, and flour from Canada to alleviate the food shortage.

July. After having met with U.S. president John F. Kennedy in June, Soviet premier Khrushchev sent a letter to all Communist leaders denouncing what he saw as China's overly aggressive policies and claiming that the mainland's China policy was risking war with the United States. Zhou Enlai countered Khrushchev's claims during the twenty-second congress of the CPSU in October. China continued to move away from the Soviet Union and in November pledged its alliance to Albania as a second axis in the Communist world.

1962

February 24. China warned that American involvement in South Vietnam was a direct threat to North Vietnam and that it also affected the security of China and Asia. The Soviet Union supported the Chinese claim. In April, Beijing estimated that within a fifteen-month period, fifty-two U.S. warships and sixty-four airplanes had invaded Chinese territorial space.

June 20. After reports of a buildup of Nationalist troops on the offshore islands, China began amassing troops on the mainland, sparking U.S. threats of retaliation if Taiwan was placed in danger.

September. The last Soviet consulates in China, in Shanghai and Harbin, were closed. China's trade with the Soviet Union was also reported to have decreased by more than 50 percent of its 1960 level over the past year.

October-November. Fighting along the Sino-Indian border erupted into a full-scale war when China opened an offensive and drove Indian troops across the border. India's prime minister, Jawaharlal Nehru, called on the United States for assistance. Hostilities continued until November 20, when China cleared the disputed territory of all Indian troops. Beijing declared a ceasefire the next day and announced that it would withdraw Chinese troops to a position twelve miles behind the original line. India refused to conduct further negotiations with Beijing.

December. In an effort to stabilize relations with its neighbors, China signed a boundary treaty with Mongolia governing the 2,500-mile border. Ten days later, Beijing signed an agreement with Pakistan regarding their common border and Chinese recognition of Pakistan's control over Kashmir. India also claimed control over Kashmir.

1963

February 27. Despite complaints about Chinese actions in India, Khrushchev announced that the Soviet Union would come to the aid of "any socialist country," including China. However, Khrushchev would later decline an invitation by the CCP to discuss bilateral relations, and China would continue to charge that the Soviet Union had become revisionist.

April. In an attempt to strengthen relations with China's neighbors, Liu Shaoqi embarked on a trip to several Southeast Asian countries, including Indonesia, Burma, Cambodia, and North Vietnam. Liu encouraged China's neighbors to oppose imperialist aggression. While in Burma he signed an aid package with the Burmese, a sign of appreciation for Burma's decision not to side with India during the Sino-Indian border war of 1962.

July 31. China denounced the signing of an Atomic Test Ban Treaty between the Soviet Union, the United States, and Great Britain. Beijing argued that it would not sign the treaty because it was not involved in the negotiations. France also refused to sign the treaty.

September 6. Hostilities broke out in the western Chinese province of Xinjiang, with reports of thousands of Kazakh nomads fleeing to the Soviet Union because of lack of food and religious persecution. The Kazakh tribesmen were said to have tried to elicit Soviet help in fighting the Chinese.

October 28. Chinese Foreign Minister Chen Yi made China's first official statement regarding its nuclear program, stating that it would be several years before China could test its nuclear weapons. Chen attributed China's lag in nuclear development to the country's lack of industrial capacity and the withdrawal of Soviet support.

December 14. Zhou Enlai began a two-month tour of Africa during which he visited Egypt, Algeria, Morocco, Albania, Tunisia, Ethiopia, Somalia, Mali, Ghana, and Guinea. Zhou was joined during part of the trip by Chen Yi. The two stressed the importance of relations between China and the African countries and called for a multilateral meeting similar to that held in Bandung in 1955. Zhou embarked on another trip to win the support of Asian states in February 1964. These anticolonial states in Asia, Africa, and Latin America became known as China's "intermediate zone."

1964

January 27. The government of France formally recognized China. In response, Taiwan broke relations with France on 10 February. The United States described the recognition as an "unfortunate step."

April 13. Polish officials sided with the Soviet position in the Sino-Soviet debate, claiming that China's actions were a "brazen and slanderous campaign" against the Soviet Leninist leadership. Earlier, Cuba had announced its support of the Soviet Union, although several African nations, Czechoslovakia, and Romania continued to support China.

July-August. With the escalation of U.S. forces in South Vietnam during the previous months, the *People's Daily* reiterated its support of North Vietnam, claiming that it would work to protect the peace and security of the socialist camp. China's concerns about the region were heightened by increased hostilities following a coup in Laos in April. Tensions again came to a head in August after the U.S. destroyer *Maddox* was attacked by North Vietnam.

October 16. China reportedly detonated its first nuclear bomb, followed by the successful detonation of a second bomb from the air in May 1965.

October-November. Soviet premier Khrushchev was forced to resign. He was replaced as party secretary by Leonid Brezhnev and as premier by Aleksei Kosygin. Two days later, Beijing extended "warm greetings" to the new Soviet leaders and expressed hope that the "fraternal, unbreakable friendship" between the two countries would continue to develop. Zhou Enlai joined other Communist leaders in celebrating the 47th anniversary of the Bolshevik Revolution in November.

1965

January. U.S. president Lyndon Johnson announced that aid to Taiwan had been a success and was no longer needed. On 30 June, the U.S. Agency for International Development announced the termination of nonmilitary aid to Taiwan. During a ten-year period, the United States reportedly gave $1.5 billion in economic aid to Taiwan.

January 30. Because of reports that China was training Congolese rebels within its borders, the government of Burundi announced that it would break diplomatic relations with China. Four days later, the government of Niger denounced the Chinese for having supported an unsuccessful revolt in that country in 1964.

February-March. The *People's Daily* published an editorial announcing that if U.S. troops crossed the 17th parallel into North Vietnam, China would join the fighting. The threat was repeated by Foreign Minister Chen Yi and Premier Zhou Enlai. The Soviet Union joined China and other Communist states in their support of the government of Hanoi.

July. China and North Vietnam concluded an agreement in which China promised to supply "equipment, whole sets of installations, and defensive and economic supplies" to North Vietnam. The Soviet Union and North Korea had concluded similar agreements with Hanoi.

September 2. Newspapers in China published an article by Defense Minister Lin Biao that called for a "People's War," emphasizing the use of rural revolutionary base areas to protect the Chinese mainland. Lin argued that current American hostilities in Vietnam provided a testing ground for the People's War theory and insisted that China had an unshakable commitment to the people of Vietnam. The theory of People's War implied, however, that China was not willing to fight the Korean War again and would not go to war in Vietnam in order to fight the Americans.

September 30. Indonesian president Sukarno was replaced during a coup by General Suharto. Because of the alleged backing of certain members of the Sukarno regime by the Indonesian Communist Party (PKI), the new government moved to eliminate the PKI and allowed anti-Chinese attacks within the country. On 10 December, the Chinese consulate in Medan was attacked by more than 2,000 demonstrators. The Chinese embassy in Jakarta was attacked in February 1966.

November 10. Yao Wenyuan, who was to become a member of the "Gang of Four," published an article attacking one of the deputy mayors of Beijing. The article came to be seen as the opening salvo in a campaign against all forms of culture and is considered a signal of the upcoming Cultural Revolution.

1966

April 10. Premier Zhou Enlai stated that China would not take the initiative in provoking war with the United States. Zhou did, however, stress the importance of the Vietnam War in Sino-American relations and reiterated China's support of Hanoi's struggle against "imperialist aggression."

May. In an effort to increase the army's role, Mao Zedong ordered the army to carry out some civilian tasks.

In what can be seen as the beginning stages of the Cultural Revolution, Mao called for the elimination of occupational differences. His orders were not made public for almost three months.

The Cultural Revolution heated up after a series of high-level Communist Party meetings and issuance of the "May 16 Circular," rejecting Peng Zhen's effort to limit the campaign to academic and intellectual circles. In June, the *People's Daily* began publishing articles suggesting that it was better to be "red" (revolutionary) than "expert" and that the people of China should rise up to destroy traditional feudal Chinese culture. The latter articles came to be considered the origin of the Red Guard movement.

July. The Chinese government closed the country to foreign visitors and suspended issuance of most visas except to those whose business was considered essential to the Chinese state. On 28 July, all universities and secondary schools were closed to give students the opportunity to participate in the Cultural Revolution. Although schools were supposed to reopen within six months, most stayed closed for several years. Primary schools reopened in December.

July 25. In an attempt to prove his continued good health, Mao Zedong (at the time seventy-two years old) was said to have taken a nine-mile swim in the strong currents of China's Yangzi River, watched by thousands of spectators.

August 8. The CCP Central Committee released a sixteen-point statement asserting that certain members of the party—including Liu Shaoqi and Deng Xiaoping—had taken the "capitalist road" and had to be removed. It called upon the masses to establish "cultural revolutionary groups" to attack what it labeled "antiparty, antisocialist rightists." The statement prohibited participation by peasants in the Cultural Revolution, while the activities of Red Guards were limited to the urban areas, to protect agricultural production.

August 18. Over a million Red Guards gathered in Tiananmen Square to hear speeches by Mao and Defense Minister Lin Biao. Mao officially recognized the Red Guards as leading the purge against the "antiparty, antisocialist rightists," and named Lin Biao their leader. By late fall of 1966, eight such rallies had been held in the square.

According to Mao's plans, the Red Guards were to lead the fight against traditional Chinese culture. In order to do so, they were allowed to spread throughout China destroying what they perceived as the "four olds" (old customs, old habits, old culture, and old thinking). Fighting broke out between the radical Red Guards and those committed to traditional Chinese culture.

September 15. The Red Guards' actions had become so worrisome that Zhou Enlai addressed a million of them, urging them to stop their campaigns. Because some feared that Red Guard actions would disrupt the autumn harvest, plans were instigated to suspend the movement temporarily during the fall.

October 1. On the 17th anniversary of the founding of the People's Republic, more than fifty diplomats from Soviet-bloc countries left the reviewing stand of Beijing's National Day parade in protest of Lin Biao's remark that the Soviet Union and the United States were colluding to plot a war in Vietnam.

October 27. China's official Xinhua (New China) News Agency announced that the country had successfully conducted a launch of its first atomic missile.

December. The Central Committee ordered all Red Guards to return home. Foreign news reported that the guards had caused disorder in several urban areas, including riots in Shanghai that led to the torture of a local party official. Meanwhile, Mao's wife, Jiang Qing, began her ascent within the party leadership and was later named to the "Cultural Revolution Group."

1967

January. A New Year's Day editorial in the *People's Daily* called for extending the Cultural Revolution into factories. Although leaders like Zhou Enlai opposed the idea, Red Guards were sent to rally the support of workers and peasants. Workers, however, resisted the directive, leading to a series of strikes—notably in Nanjing, Shanghai, and Fuzhou. The Cultural Revolution was said to have reached a turning point on 15 January when Mao ordered an "all-out general offensive" against his opponents. A 22 January editorial appearing in the *People's Daily* called on the Red Guards to "seize power." Three days later Xinhua News Agency heralded the anarchy brought about by the Red Guards within the country, proclaiming that "without anarchy, there can be no revolution." The army was later brought in to ensure that the Red Guards were able to carry out their activities.

February 5. The Red Guards established the Shanghai Commune, modeled after the Paris Commune of 1871.

February 11. After repeated complaints by the Soviet Union of mistreatment of its diplomats, China acted to abrogate the consular agreement with the country. Beijing also took steps to limit travel between the two countries.

February 23. The first public criticism of the Red Guards appeared in the CCP theoretical journal, *Hongqi,* which published an editorial criticizing the "shortcomings and mistakes" of the guards and claiming that they lacked experience and political maturity. In order to better educate youth, Mao placed the army in charge of political and military education within the country.

Summer. The Central Committee, State Council, Military Affairs Committee, and Cultural Revolution Group issued a joint order on 6 June seeking to curb the anarchy caused by the Red Guards. Called the "seven-point circular,'' it said that only the state had the power to carry out arrests and searches and that physical violence was forbidden. The circular had little effect and was followed by fighting in Wuhan, Guangzhou, and Fuzhou. In September, Mao called for restoration of the party apparatus in an attempt to stave off further unrest.

September 3. China announced plans to withdraw from the International Red Cross. Beijing cited the organization's domination by the United States as the reason for China's leaving.

September 25. Mao Zedong completed a tour of China, his first such tour since 1958, when he had surveyed the damage of the Great Leap Forward. Mao's trip was an attempt to appease many of the feuding Cultural Revolution factions within the country.

October 1. In a sign of China's diplomatic isolation, delegations from only five nations were present during the National Day activities in Tiananmen Square. During the course of the Cultural Revolution, China had been involved in arguments with more than thirty-two countries over the status of diplomats on the mainland.

1968

January 1. The Chinese government announced that it would expand plans to establish revolutionary committees, which would replace local party and government organizations in maintaining law and order. The original plan had been announced in January 1967 but was said to have encountered armed resistance from local leaders.

April 24. A Soviet journal, *Kommunist,* attacked Mao's Cultural Revolution policies, claiming that they were a sign of great power adventurist ambition, a deliberate break with Marxism-Leninism, and an impediment to industrial policy. Other articles criticized China for trying to prolong the Vietnam War and pushing the United States and the Soviet Union toward nuclear war.

July 1. Sixty-two countries, including the United States, the Soviet Union, and Great Britain, signed the Nuclear Nonproliferation Treaty (NPT). The People's Republic refused to sign the treaty because of the UN's refusal to recognize it as the legitimate government of China.

August 7. ''Mao Zedong Thought Propaganda Teams'' were established among workers in order to ''strengthen the sense of organization and revolutionary discipline'' in the country. A week earlier, the *People's Daily* had published an editorial ordering the masses to rely on and support the People's Liberation Army (PLA).

August 14. Foreign reports suggested that Beijing had begun to dissolve some of the Red Guard organizations. On 30 August, a *Beijing Review* article written by Cultural Revolution Group member Yao Wenyuan criticized the Red Guards for inciting the Chinese people to struggle against one another.

August 21. Soviet and East European military forces invaded Czechoslovakia in order to end what came to be known as the Prague Spring. Beijing reacted strongly to reports of the invasion, calling it ''fascist power politics played by the Soviet revisionist clique of renegades and scabs.''

September. All of China was reportedly under the control of the revolutionary committees formed in January, most of them dominated by the military. The implementation of revolutionary committees began the second stage of the Cultural Revolution.

October 4. Mao Zedong ordered urban youth (most of them Red Guards) to go to the countryside to ''learn from the masses.'' Known as the *xiafang* movement, the order called for the students to join the ''front line of agricultural production.'' Mao reasoned that going into the country would provide the youth ''an excellent opportunity to study.'' An estimated 15 million youth were affected by the *xiafang* campaign.

October 11. The twelfth plenum of the Eighth Central Committee moved to purge Chief of State Liu Shaoqi from the party. Liu had been attacked throughout the Cultural Revolution as a ''revisionist'' and ''capitalist-roader.'' Liu was removed from all posts and sent to reform through labor.

1969

March. Fighting broke out among Chinese and Soviet troops along the border near the disputed Zhenbao Island in the Ussuri River. Thirty-eight soldiers were said to have been killed in the hostilities, which were among the more than 600 skirmishes that took place in 1969.

March 23. Moscow heightened its criticism of Mao Zedong by obliquely comparing him to Adolf Hitler. The article, appearing in the Soviet Defense Ministry paper *Red Star,* described Mao as ''a traitor to the sacred cause of communism.''

April 1. The ninth CCP congress opened after an eight-year delay due to internal unrest in the country. A new constitution was approved and changes in the party leadership were formalized, placing many of the more radical figures of the party in high positions. The army's participation in the congress also increased, and Defense Minister Lin Biao was named Mao's heir.

May. The Chinese government announced that it could accept the status quo of the Ussuri river boundary as long as conflict could be averted. For its part, the Soviet Union hinted that continued hostilities could lead to preemptive Soviet strikes on China's nuclear installations.

May-July. China began to end its isolation from the rest of the world in May by appointing its first ambassador since the start of the Cultural Revolution. The appointment of an ambassador to Albania was followed by sixteen other appointments during June and July. China's full complement of ambassadors, however, was not in place until the end of 1970.

September. In an attempt to ease border tensions, Soviet premier Kosygin traveled to Beijing to participate in talks. Although the meetings were thought to have been unsuccessful, Beijing announced on 7 October that formal negotiations would be held later that month.

September 23. China conducted its first underground nuclear test.

November 7. The United States ended the Seventh Fleet's nineteen-year presence in the Taiwan Strait. The decision was said to have been precipitated by China's willingness to reopen the Warsaw Talks, which had been a forum for discussions of the U.S. and Chinese positions regarding Taiwan but had reached a stalemate in November 1968.

December 19. The United States announced that subsidiaries and affiliates of U.S. firms abroad would be allowed to engage in trading of nonstrategic goods with China. The action partly ended the informal ban of U.S. exports to China enacted in 1950.

1970

February 1. In the first official statement on foreign policy since 1967, the Chinese government expressed its support of Arab countries in their disagreements with Israel. Zhou Enlai sent a message to Egypt's president, Gamal Abdel Nasser, stating, "the Chinese people will forever remain the most reliable friend of [Egypt], Palestine, and other Arab countries."

April 22. The *People's Daily, Hongqi,* and the *Liberation Daily* published a joint article denouncing the Soviet invasion of Czechoslovakia and what came to be known as the Brezhnev Doctrine. The Chinese feared that the Soviet Union would try to apply the doctrine to China. They disagreed with Brezhnev's statements on limited sovereignty for Communist countries and the "supreme sovereignty" of the Soviet Union. The editorial concluded by stating that the doctrine introduced another element of disagreement in the Sino-Soviet dispute.

April 24. China launched its first satellite. The capsule was said to have weighed only 381 pounds and broadcast the song "The East Is Red" in addition to its normal broadcasts. That same day, Chiang Ching-kuo, son of Chiang Kai-shek and vice president of the Republic of China, escaped an assassination attempt while visiting New York City. The assailant was a member of the World United Formosans for Independence, a U.S.-based group advocating independence for Taiwan.

May. More than a week after U.S. forces moved in, the *Beijing Review* denounced the U.S. invasion of Cambodia as a "frantic provocation against the Chinese people." Analysts of China argued that the delay in publishing the criticism and the relative mildness of the statement suggested China's unwillingness to jeopardize improving Sino-American relations.

July 7. The French minister in charge of planning and territorial development led the first official French delegation to China since relations had been formalized in 1964. Zhou Enlai praised the delegates for France's adherence to neutrality.

July 10. The Reverend James Walsh, a Roman Catholic bishop in Shanghai, was released from prison after twenty years. Walsh had been arrested for "espionage and sabotage under the cloak of religion."

July 21. Classes resumed at Qinghua University in Beijing in the first reported instance of a university's return to normal activity since the start of the Cultural Revolution. A statement regarding the opening said that future admissions policy would emphasize students with worker and peasant backgrounds.

August 20. The *People's Daily* reported that rural medical technicians known as "barefoot doctors" were being trained in using herbs and medical care to treat the rural community in China. The doctors were hailed as a new element in China's medical revolution.

October–November. After eighteen months of negotiations, Canada formally recognized the People's Republic of China on October 12. The two countries signed a joint communiqué reaffirming their belief that Taiwan was an "inalienable part of the territory of China." Italy recognized China on 6 November, using the Canadian model to deal with the question of Taiwan.

December 31. In a move to limit arms transfers to Taiwan, the U.S. Congress deleted authorization for a loan of three submarines to the Republic of China. Earlier in the year, Congress rejected a plan to sell a squadron of F-4D fighter jets to Taiwan.

1971

February. China responded to the U.S.-assisted South Vietnam invasion of Laos by calling it a rabid act and grave provocation. As was the case after the invasion of Cambodia, however, the official Chinese criticism of the United States was considered relatively mild. The United States assured China that operations in Laos posed no threat to China.

February 25. During his state of the union address, U.S. president Richard Nixon expressed his desire to improve relations with China and stated that the United States was "prepared to see the People's Republic of China play a constructive role in the family of nations." The speech was the first time President Nixon had used the formal name adopted by the Communist regime in 1949.

March–April. The U.S. Department of State announced that restrictions on the use of U.S. passports for travel in China were to be removed. Less than a month later, China invited the U.S. ping-pong team to visit, and the team arrived in China on 10 April. Premier Zhou Enlai addressed the team and described recent events as a "new chapter" in relations between the two countries.

May 1. The *People's Daily* published an editorial defending the more moderate foreign policy pursued by China since the conclusion of the Cultural Revolution. The article followed an invitation by Mao Zedong to President Nixon to visit China.

June 10. The White House announced a full relaxation of the twenty-one-year embargo on U.S. trade with China. The embargo had been partly relaxed in 1969, when subsidiaries of American firms abroad were allowed to trade with China. Chinese exports to the United States were henceforth to be under the same restrictions as those from the Soviet Union and Eastern Europe.

July. President Richard Nixon announced that national security adviser Henry Kissinger had returned from a secret visit to China during which he had arranged for the president to make an official visit to Beijing in 1972. Kissinger's agreement with the Chinese based future Sino-American relations on three basic principles: Taiwan was a part of China; the political future of South Vietnam would be decided by Vietnamese; and all Asian disputes would be settled by peaceful means.

August 2. The United States announced that it would end its twenty-year opposition to China's participation in the UN. The United States did not approve, however, of taking away the Republic of China's seat in the organization. Both the mainland and Taiwan condemned America's "two-China" policy.

August 9. As a counterbalance to the warming of Sino-American relations, India and the Soviet Union signed a twenty-year Treaty of Peace, Friendship, and Cooperation. According to India, the treaty ensured that the Soviet Union would come to its assistance in the event of a Chinese or Pakistani attack.

August 26. Beijing announced that the revolutionary committees established during the Cultural Revolution had been replaced by provincial-level Communist Party committees.

September 13. Defense Minister Lin Biao and his family reportedly died in a plane crash while trying to escape to Mongolia. According to a report presented by Zhou Enlai during the tenth party congress, the "pro-Soviet" Lin had attempted to overthrow Mao in a coup and had made three assassination attempts on Mao before he was discovered. After Lin's death, Zhou Enlai became the second most powerful man in China.

October-November. The People's Republic of China was given Taiwan's seat in the UN. The resolution sponsored by Albania passed 76-35, with 17 abstentions. The United States voted against the resolution.

December. The Republic of China announced that it would hold its first elections since 1947. Chiang Kai-shek

had originally refused to hold elections again until the Nationalists reclaimed the mainland. The elections were held on 23 December 1972, with the KMT winning the majority of contested positions.

1972

February. President Nixon became the first U.S. head of state to visit the People's Republic of China. During ceremonies held in Beijing, Premier Zhou Enlai said that the "great differences" between the two countries should not hinder the normalization of relations between them. At the end of Nixon's visit, the two countries issued the Shanghai Communiqué and pledged to work toward normalization.

March. China and Great Britain reopened relations after a twenty-two-year hiatus. In their joint communiqué, Britain acknowledged China's claim to sovereignty over Taiwan. Within the year, the Netherlands, Greece, West Germany, and Australia also recognized the People's Republic.

July. Reports began to emerge that China's military was being rearmed and that emphasis was to be placed on training the regular army. The new program was a shift from the focus of political indoctrination advocated by Lin Biao. The announcement was followed by veiled criticism of the "Little Red Book" of Mao Zedong's quotations, including suggestions that Maoism should best be studied by reading complete texts rather than excerpts.

July 30. America's Associated Press and China's Xinhua News Agency agreed to exchange news and photographs. This signified the first regular news contact between the two countries since December 1949.

September 9. China agreed to buy Boeing 707s from the United States worth $150 million. The agreement also called for a supply of spare parts and the training of crews. Less than a week later, China agreed to buy half a million tons of wheat from the United States.

September 29. During a visit to China by Prime Minister Kakuei Tanaka, Japan and China released a communiqué affirming Japan's recognition of the PRC as the sole legitimate government of China. In December, Japan opened the Japan Interchange Association in Taipei in an attempt to maintain unofficial relations with Taiwan. This de facto arrangement came to be known as the "Japanese solution."

1973

January. Representatives from the United States, North Vietnam, South Vietnam, and the Vietcong signed a peace agreement in Paris that called for a ceasefire in Vietnam but that did not end the fighting in Cambodia. China's reaction to the agreement was favorable, noting that the U.S. presence in Vietnam had been a major source of tension in Sino-American relations.

May 1. Liaison offices were opened in Beijing and Washington to expand trade and deepen scientific and cultural relations. The two countries verbally agreed to grant the staffs of the offices diplomatic immunity and privileges. Although the offices were not formal embassies, the opening of the facilities in Washington signified a major concession by the Chinese, who had insisted that they would not establish a mission in any country that recognized Taiwan.

July. Chase Manhattan Bank announced on 4 July that it had agreed to establish a relationship with the Bank of China. The agreement marked the first time that a U.S. bank would represent a Chinese bank in the West since 1949. On 8 July, the U.S. Postal Service announced that it would begin parcel post delivery between China and the United States.

August 7. A campaign attacking Confucius began in a *People's Daily* editorial. The campaign was thought to be a veiled attack on Zhou Enlai by the more radical members of the Chinese leadership. The campaign continued into 1974.

August. The tenth party congress took on the task of institutionalizing the leadership changes resulting from the death of Lin Biao and the purge of his associates. Deng Xiaoping, who had been purged during the Cultural Revolution, was given back his posts. Zhou Enlai, however, had to defend the recent Chinese rapprochement with the United States against criticism from China's more radical leaders.

October 27. The *New York Times* reported that China would increase the number of militia units in the country. The Chinese justified the increase as an effort to prepare the country for possible attack by "Soviet revisionist social imperialism."

1974

January 19. South Vietnam and China began a two-day war over the uninhabited but oil-rich Paracel (Xisha) Islands. The Vietnamese were ousted from the islands on 20 January, but moved to occupy many of the Spratly (Nansha) Islands ten days later. China lodged verbal complaints but did not send troops. Taiwan also protested the occupation.

April 10. Vice Premier Deng Xiaoping enunciated China's new foreign policy during a speech to the UN General Assembly. According to the speech, the Soviet decision to act more like a superpower meant that the socialist camp no longer existed. Because of the simultaneous disintegration of the imperialist bloc, a new three-bloc structure was emerging in the world. The two superpowers (the United States and Soviet Union) formed one bloc, the other developed nations were in the second, and the

underdeveloped world was in the third. A more formal pronouncement of the "three worlds" theory was made in November 1978 and attributed to Mao.

October 11. The U.S. Congress repealed the 1955 Formosa Resolution, which had given the U.S. president the power to intervene in Taiwan. The administration had been pushing to repeal the resolution since 1971 in an attempt to ease the way for normalization of relations with China.

1975

January 13. The Fourth National People's Congress, the first congress since 1964, opened in Beijing. In addition to passing a new constitution, it confirmed the leadership group already in place. Zhou Enlai called for the "comprehensive modernization of agriculture, industry, national defense, and science and technology," an early formulation of the "Four Modernizations."

February 12. After a long hiatus, border talks between China and the Soviet Union reopened.

April 5. Chiang Kai-shek died at the age of 88 in Taipei. His son, Chiang Ching-kuo, was later named to succeed him.

April 18. China heralded the victory of the Khmer Rouge in Cambodia, labeling it a victory for Mao's concept of People's War. On 25 April, Prince Norodom Sihanouk, who had been living in exile in Beijing, returned to Cambodia as chief of state.

May 12. Vice Premier Deng Xiaoping arrived in France for an official visit. Deng was treated with the protocol normally reserved for a head of state. The increased status afforded to Deng reflected France's pleasure at being the first Western nation visited by a PRC official.

September. China and the European Economic Community opened formal relations. Earlier in the year, China had established relations with the Philippines and Thailand; relations were later formalized with Bangladesh.

A national conference on learning from Dazhai convened to discuss modernization of China's agriculture. The model for agricultural development was based on the Dazhai commune, which had become known for its self-reliance and ability to produce grain under severe conditions.

October 14. China accused the United States of interfering in its internal affairs following U.S. support of Tibetans fighting for the restoration of the exiled Dalai Lama.

December 5. U.S. president Gerald Ford completed a five-day visit to China. The visit was said to be cordial. Deng Xiaoping would later claim that Ford had agreed to accept China's three demands for normalization during the trip. A week later, after having implied that both superpowers were a threat to peace, the Chinese declared that the Soviet Union was the most dangerous source of war.

1976

January 8. Premier Zhou Enlai died of cancer at the age of seventy-eight. His death was considered a gain for the radical faction of China's leadership.

April. Zhou's January death sparked mass rallies in Tiananmen Square during the Qing Ming memorial festival. Mourners also showed their support for Vice Premier Deng Xiaoping, who had been subjected to increased criticism after Zhou's death.

April 7. The Central Committee chose Hua Guofeng to replace Zhou Enlai as premier and stripped Deng Xiaoping of all his positions, although he was allowed to remain in the party. Hua had previously served as vice premier and minister of public security. The radical members of the leadership had been critical of Deng in recent months because of his stress on pragmatism and economic development rather than on following the correct ideological stance.

April 15. After several years of tension due to border disputes, China and India announced that they would exchange ambassadors. Relations had been suspended since 1962, when border clashes led to war between the two states. On the same day, India also signed a five-year trade agreement with the Soviet Union.

April 26. Amid increasing recognition given to the People's Republic since its admittance to the UN, the government of South Africa went against the trend and recognized the Nationalist government on Taiwan as the legitimate government China.

July 28. A massive earthquake registering 8.2 on the Richter scale shook the city of Tangshan in Hebei Province. Beijing was hit by a tremor registering 7.9 on the Richter scale. China reported that the quakes were the strongest in more than 400 years and resulted in an estimated 655,000 deaths. Superstition suggested that the earthquakes were a sign of upcoming change.

September-October. Chairman Mao Zedong died on 9 September at the age of eighty-two. His death was followed by the arrest of the radical group in charge of many of the policies implemented during the Cultural Revolution (later known as the "Gang of Four"), along with thirty other high-ranking members of the party. Moderates within the leadership feared that the gang would move to fill the power vacuum left by Mao's death. Hua Guofeng was named to succeed Mao as chairman of the party and of the Military Commission; Hua also maintained his post as premier and therefore held the three most powerful positions in China.

December 25. Hua made his first major policy address since becoming CCP chairman. He vowed to remain loyal to the policies enacted by Mao and voiced opposition to

supporters of the Gang of Four. During his speech Hua hinted that ability would be emphasized over ideological loyalty yet proposed no major change from the Maoist line. On 26 December, Hua announced plans to purge the Gang of Four from the party.

1977

February 2. An article published in *Hongqi* signaled limited approval for some private agricultural and handicraft production. Such private production had been banned during the Cultural Revolution. The article also called for greater production of consumer goods such as bicycles, sugar, and salt.

February 26. Hua Guofeng ordered a drive to improve the Chinese army by emphasizing "know-how" over ideological correctness. The shift was accompanied by a loosening of control over cultural activities in May, when Beijing lifted a ban on the works of Shakespeare. Bans on works by Victor Hugo, Beethoven, Chopin, and Bach were also lifted on the principles of "making the past serve the present" and "making foreign things serve China."

July-August. The third plenary session of the Tenth Central Committee ended in Beijing. Hua Guofeng was formalized as chairman, and Deng Xiaoping was restored once again to his posts. Many party members who rose to the Central Committee during the Cultural Revolution were not re-elected. A Discipline Inspection Commission was established to weed leftists out of the party and improve party oversight. The meeting also led the way for the opening of the Eleventh Central Committee in August, during which the party adopted a new constitution and affirmed the policy of striving for the "Four Modernizations." Hua re-emphasized Chinese support for revolutionary struggles around the world and reaffirmed China's belief that all Communist parties should be independent and make their own decisions.

August 30. Yugoslav president Tito began a visit to Beijing. China had previously criticized Yugoslavia for abandoning communism and leaning toward revisionism, but—in a sign of its changing foreign policy—now welcomed Tito enthusiastically. The meeting was said to have been "warm and cordial," and Hua Guofeng made a reciprocal visit to Yugoslavia in August 1978.

September. Cambodian premier Pol Pot visited China as a sign of continued close relations between the two countries. In exchange for Cambodia's role as a buffer to Soviet-supported Vietnam, China had to endure the wrath of the international community for supporting the Khmer Rouge. A Chinese delegation visited Cambodia in December.

October 1. On the twenty-eighth anniversary of the founding of the PRC, the *People's Daily* published an editorial calling for a faster pace of construction and modernization within the country. The editorial urged the Chinese people to be both "red and expert." According to the editorial, only through study of science could China achieve the Four Modernizations.

October 6. After years of border tensions, China and the Soviet Union signed an agreement on navigation rights.

October. University entrance exams were reinstated. Youth were also allowed to move directly into college after high school, without first spending several years in the countryside. Graduate schools reopened in February 1978.

1978

February 26. The Fifth National People's Congress convened and was attended by many leaders who had been purged during the Cultural Revolution. During the congress, a new constitution was adopted. Hua Guofeng blamed the radical Gang of Four for the instability of recent years and outlined the main features of the Four Modernizations. He called for major increases in agricultural and industrial production while essentially remaining loyal to Mao's ideas.

July. China notified the Vietnamese government that it would recall its experts and stop technical and economic aid. Vietnam later signed a treaty of friendship with Moscow. China also suspended aid to Albania, charging the country with following an anti-Chinese course.

An American science and technology delegation visited Beijing, marking the official opening of scientific and technological exchanges between the two countries. The Communist press heralded the visit as the most significant since the visit of Nixon.

Vice Premier Li Xiannian announced that China would reverse its policy of not accepting foreign capital. Li told a representative from Japan's Mitsui Corporation that China would require a large amount of funds to modernize its economy and would be willing to accept investment from abroad. The following January, China promulgated its first law governing Sino-foreign joint ventures.

August 12. China and Japan signed a treaty of peace and friendship. According to Moscow, the agreement endangered détente and security in Asia.

December 15. The U.S. and Chinese governments announced that diplomatic relations would be restored as of 1 January 1979. The United States promised to recognize the People's Republic as the sole legitimate government of China and acknowledged Beijing's position that Taiwan was part of China. The United States also promised to end all official relations with Taiwan, although continuing relations on a "people-to-people" basis. China allowed the United States to continue to supply Taiwan with defensive weapons.

1979

January. Xinhua News Agency announced that property seized from those labeled "capitalist roaders" during the Cultural Revolution would be returned. There were also reports of further rehabilitations of party members purged during the Cultural Revolution.

January 1. The Chinese government announced that it had stopped bombarding the Nationalist islands of Quemoy and Matsu. Beijing also proposed talks with Taiwan to end the military confrontation and removed troops from the area on the mainland opposite the islands. The same day, the U.S. Mutual Defense Treaty with Taiwan was abrogated.

January 28. Vice Premier Deng Xiaoping arrived in the United States for a nine-day visit, during which President Jimmy Carter and Deng signed an agreement to establish a framework for a "new and irreversible course" in Sino-American relations and made plans for the opening of consulates in each country. A joint communiqué was issued at the end of Deng's visit that acknowledged that differences still existed between the two countries.

February 15. The government of Taiwan created the Coordinating Council for North American Affairs to act as the unofficial diplomatic counterpart to the newly established American Institute in Taiwan.

February-March. China invaded Vietnam on February 17. Xinhua labeled the Chinese action a "counterattack" brought about by repeated Vietnamese border incursions. Deng later said that the attack was a "punitive action" that would end within a month. China and Vietnam entered negotiations on 2 March and hostilities ended on 5 March. China formally withdrew from Vietnam on 16 March.

April 3. China announced that it would not renew the Treaty of Friendship with the Soviet Union scheduled to expire on 14 February 1980. The Chinese also called for talks with Moscow to decrease tensions between the two countries.

April 10. President Carter approved the Taiwan Relations Act, which legalized America's new relationship with Taiwan. According to the bill, America would continue to conduct relations with Taiwan and Taiwan would have a status separate from Beijing regarding matters of immigration and nuclear energy. The American Institute in Taiwan was given the power to conduct normal consular functions. In effect, the bill approved treatment of Taiwan as an independent state to which the United States would sell arms, lend money, and grant diplomatic immunity.

May. China and the United States signed a trade agreement on 14 May, paving the way for the United States to grant China most favored nation (MFN) trade status. With such status, tariffs on Chinese exports to the United States would be reduced by up to 75 percent. On 31 May, in a separate action, the U.S. Department of Commerce imposed import quotas on Chinese textile goods as a result of failure to reach agreement on China's level of textile sales.

August. Coudert Brothers announced that it would become the first American law firm to open an office in China since 1949. The office planned to handle legal affairs for U.S. firms doing business in China.

U.S. vice president Walter Mondale visited China and met with Deng Xiaoping. Mondale called for strengthening of bilateral ties, promised $2 billion worth of trade credits, and signed an agreement providing U.S. assistance in building a hydroelectric plant in China. Mondale became the first American leader to speak on Chinese national television.

September 26. Three days after reopening the first bilateral talks since 1964, China and the Soviet Union each accused the other of waging a propaganda campaign against it.

October 3. Criticism within China of Mao Zedong intensified with the publication of an article in the *People's Daily* stating that the late chairman was not a god. The article was one of many hinting at the fallibility of Mao and the disastrous decisions he made during the Cultural Revolution.

October 4. The first Sino-American joint venture contract was signed by the E-S Pacific Development Company of San Francisco and the China International Travel Service to build the Great Wall Hotel in Beijing.

October 15. Hua Guofeng, Chinese party chairman and premier, began a three-week tour of France, West Germany, Great Britain, and Italy. During his trip, Hua signed a series of agreements to increase trade and cultural exchanges.

October 16. Wei Jingsheng, an electrician at the Beijing Zoo who protested against the lack of political liberalism in China, was convicted of agitating for the overthrow of the government and sentenced to fifteen years in prison. Another political dissident, Fu Yueha, was tried on October 18 for organizing mass disturbances. She was sentenced to two years in prison.

November 19. Vice Premier Chen Muhua announced that China would work to control its rapid population growth and set a goal of bringing the rate of growth to zero by the year 2000.

November 27. The International Olympic Committee voted to admit the PRC. Taiwan would be allowed to participate under the name of the "Chinese Taipei Olympic Team" and would not be allowed to use its national flag or emblem. China did not participate in the 1980 Moscow Olympics, however, in protest of Soviet actions in Afghanistan.

November-December. Despite earlier calls for the people to voice their opinions in wall posters, the *People's Daily* began to attack the posters as advocating "anarchism" and "turning to foreigners for sympathy and support." Deng Xiaoping had previously praised the posters as a second Hundred Flowers movement. The "Democracy Wall" in downtown Beijing was closed on 6 December, and wall posters were banned the following month.

December 21. Monsignor Michael Fu Tieshan was consecrated as China's first Catholic bishop in fifteen years. Only two months earlier, the government allowed the first mass to be celebrated since 1964. The Vatican refused to recognize Bishop Fu, however, because he was ordained without Rome's approval.

December 25. Soviet forces invaded Afghanistan. This action drew criticism from members of the international community, many of whom boycotted the 1980 Moscow Olympics in protest. The Chinese government declared that the intervention would "spread the flames of armed rebellion into a conflagration" and pose a "threat to China's security."

1980

January 8. U.S. secretary of defense Harold Brown visited China in a sign of improving relations between the two countries. During his trip, Brown announced that the United States was willing to sell certain nonoffensive military equipment and high technology to China, including a ground station that would allow China to pick up Intelsat communications.

January 19. The Ministry of Foreign Affairs canceled border talks with the Soviet Union in protest of the December 1979 Soviet invasion of Afghanistan. The talks, which had begun in October 1979, were among the first signs of reduced tensions between the two countries since ideological differences chilled relations in the mid-1960s.

January 27. The Xinhua News Agency announced that the use of foreign currency would be prohibited in China. All economic transactions by foreigners would have to be conducted with foreign exchange currency (FEC), which would be issued by the Bank of China. (The use of FEC would be phased out in 1994.)

February 1. A trade agreement signed in 1979 between the United States and China went into effect after being approved by the U.S. Congress on January 24, 1980. The agreement called on both sides to strengthen economic and trade relations.

February. Sino-Vietnamese peace talks to negotiate border disputes broke off on 2 February; diplomats claimed that the time for discussion was not ripe. The two countries had held nine sessions within the previous ten months with limited results. China opposed Soviet assistance for Vietnam and Vietnam's ongoing involvement in Cambodia. Later in February, during a banquet in honor of Cambodian prime minister Khieu Samphan, Hua Guofeng promised that China would continue to oppose Vietnamese actions in his country and would support opposition forces in Cambodia against the Heng Samrin regime. Throughout the year, China launched several other protests against Vietnam, citing border incursions and other acts of violence.

February 12. The National People's Congress Standing Committee approved regulations to reinstate the awarding of academic degrees (bachelor's, master's, and doctorate) beginning 1 January 1981. (The granting of degrees was suspended during the Cultural Revolution years.) The Central Committee later passed the "Decision on Problems of Making Elementary Education Universal," which required implementation of universal elementary education by 1990. (The first postgraduate degrees were awarded in 1982.)

February 29. The fifth plenum of the twelfth CCP congress posthumously exonerated Liu Shaoqi, former chief of state of the PRC, of all crimes he was accused of during the Cultural Revolution. Liu had been attacked and jailed by the Gang of Four as the country's "number one capitalist roader" and later died of pneumonia while in prison. Liu was the most prominent of many former victims of the Cultural Revolution honored at this time.

March 14. In a major policy speech, Deng Xiaoping set forth two of the country's key foreign policy goals in the coming years: to contain Soviet expansionism and to work for the reunification of China. Although Deng at this time was in the process of slowly handing over control of day-to-day activities to Zhao Ziyang, he continued to exercise great influence over party decisions and to shape the economic reforms according to his own agenda.

March 19. The government of Taiwan allowed seventeen Chinese merchant fishermen, working on a Panamanian vessel docked in Taiwan, to visit Taipei. The visit by Chinese nationals was the first allowed by the government since KMT forces retreated to the island in 1949, when all travel to Taiwan from the mainland had been restricted.

April 30. The State Statistical Bureau (SSB) announced the results of the first comprehensive census conducted in China since 1949. The three-month census estimated the population of China (excluding Taiwan) at 970,920,000 in 1979. The SSB would conduct several other censuses throughout the decade.

April-May. The People's Republic of China was formally readmitted to the International Monetary Fund (IMF) in April and to its sister institution, the World Bank, in May, thereby becoming eligible for loans at considerably lower interest rates than the country could obtain from private foreign sources. Because of China's admittance into the IMF and the World Bank, the Republic of China (Taiwan) lost its standing within these lending institutions.

May 12. Fu Xukun became the first Chinese government worker known to have defected to the United States. Fu, serving as interpreter for a Chinese delegation visiting the United States, disappeared from his group and later resurfaced to ask for asylum from American authorities.

May 18. The government announced the successful launch of China's first multistage intercontinental ballistic missile (ICBM) from a point on the mainland. Said to have a range of approximately 6,000 miles, the missile landed somewhere in the Pacific Ocean.

May 22. General Secretary Hu Yaobang and Vice Premier Wan Li completed a visit to the Tibet Autonomous Region. They promised greater reforms aimed at relieving tensions between Tibet and Beijing and a relaxation of religious controls to allow for major religious observances such as the Lhasa Grand Prayer Ceremony, which had been outlawed twenty years earlier.

June 2. The National Administrative Commission of the Chinese Catholic Church and the Catholic Bishops College were established. A Chinese version of the Catholic Church had earlier been recognized in China. It held many of the same tenets as Roman Catholicism but did not pledge allegiance to the papacy of Rome. The new commission was to lead the clergy in observing the Chinese version of Catholicism within the country. It was also an attempt to increase nominal religious freedom. Several cathedrals and churches that had been closed during the Cultural Revolution were reopened.

June 23. The Ministry of Foreign Affairs sent a note to Vietnamese officials saying that continuation of Sino-Vietnamese talks were no longer appropriate because of Vietnamese hostilities along the border. The Chinese were specifically reacting to alleged Vietnamese incursions along the Sino-Vietnamese border at Yunnan as well as along the Thai-Vietnamese border. During the succeeding months, the Ministry of Foreign Affairs sent several diplomatic notes to the government of Vietnam voicing similar complaints.

Summer. A political crisis began to brew in Poland because of the Solidarity platform put forth by elements of Poland's labor force. China was reluctant to support the movement because of the possible precedent it could set for Chinese labor unrest. (Historically, the Chinese government always feared the rise of a labor-based urban opposition force.) Despite its hesitation in supporting the movement, China did criticize the Soviet position on the riots, insisting that the uprisings were an internal Polish problem that should be handled by the Polish government.

July 21. The Chinese government warned the Soviet Union and Vietnam against conducting oil or gas exploration near the Paracel and Spratly Islands. China re-emphasized that the islands had "always belonged to China" and that any action taken on the islands required China's permission. Sino-Soviet relations were already tense because of the conviction of Soviet spies in the northern province of Heilongjiang earlier in the month.

August 11. The first meeting of the Joint Economic Commission of China and West Germany was held in Beijing. It was the first such meeting between China and a major Western European state. The commission promised to continue to increase the level of contact between the two countries since the establishment of diplomatic relations in 1972 and to enhance bilateral trade and investment.

August 20. U.S. vice presidential candidate and former envoy to China George Bush visited Beijing. While in meetings with the Chinese, Bush tried to ease Chinese worries regarding presidential candidate Ronald Reagan's announced policy toward Taiwan. The U.S. Republican Party had always enjoyed relatively close relations with Taipei compared to the U.S. Democratic Party. During subsequent months, China protested Reagan's decision to sell arms to Taiwan and his hints at restoring relations with Taiwan.

August 18-23. At an enlarged meeting of the CCP Politburo, Deng delivered a speech "On the Reform of the System of Party and State Leadership." The speech suggested that the party needed to rectify itself in order to aid economic modernization and improve its image, which had been damaged during the Cultural Revolution.

August 31. In another step toward economic reform, the central government granted greater responsibility to regional governments for the planning and implementation of economic policy. The central government hoped that, with greater freedom to execute economic actions, the regional governments would be better able to promote efficiency in their operations and to capitalize on their unique comparative advantages.

September. The third session of the Fifth National People's Congress was held in Beijing. Deng Xiaoping, Chen Yun, Li Xiannian, Wang Zhen, and Xu Xiangqian resigned their State Council positions, citing old age. Ye Jianying was named NPC chairman and Zhao Ziyang replaced Hua Guofeng as premier. The congress also promulgated an income tax law concerning joint ventures with foreign investment. The one-child policy went into effect for all of China except minority areas. Finally, an amendment to article 45 of the constitution was passed suggesting that Chinese citizens no longer had the inherent right to "speak freely, air views fully, hold great debates, and write big-character posters."

September 17. Three agreements were signed between China and the United States during an official visit to Washington by Vice Premier Bo Yibo. The agreements expanded the vague, earlier agreements and set the groundwork for Sino-American relations regarding civil aviation, maritime transportation, and textiles. On October 17, Pan American Airlines was named to serve as the first commercial airline for direct travel between China and the United States.

October. The United States and Taiwan agreed to allow the American Institute in Taiwan and the Coordinating Council for North American Affairs to act as informal, nongovernmental organizations tasked with maintaining relations between the United States and Taiwan. The staffs of the two organizations, created in 1979, were granted diplomatic privileges and immunities, thereby establishing de facto government-to-government relations, although formal diplomatic relations did not exist. The Chinese government protested the agreement as interference in China's internal affairs and labeled it an open violation of the 1979 Sino-American communiqué that normalized bilateral relations.

October 9. After China's Ministry of Foreign Affairs lodged a formal protest with the Soviet government for incursions via Mongolia along the Inner Mongolian border, the *People's Daily* warned Moscow against continuing behavior that was "detrimental to continued development of relations." Later, the Ministry of Foreign Affairs again concluded that the time was not appropriate for Sino-Soviet talks. Previous talks had been canceled following the Soviet invasion of Afghanistan.

October 13. Democratic Kampuchea (Cambodia) was recognized by the United Nations. For China, the recognition lent support to its campaign for the withdrawal of Vietnamese forces from Cambodia. China also used the recognition as a sign of support for its policy of noninterference.

October 25. Kosygin resigned his position as CPSU chairman, citing health reasons. His action caused many in China to speculate that General Secretary Leonid Brezhnev was trying to solidify his control. Kosygin and Brezhnev reportedly disagreed on how to handle Soviet foreign policy, and Kosygin had recently gained favor with China's leaders. Chinese papers remarked that Kosygin's departure suggested that Brezhnev was successfully establishing one-man rule in the Soviet Union.

November. The Gang of Four and several associates were indicted for the "frame-up and persecution of party and state leaders, plotting to overthrow the political power of the dictatorship of the proletariat, and the persecution and suppression of large numbers of cadres and masses" during the Cultural Revolution. Their trial lasted from November 20 to December 29, and they were sentenced in 1981. The trial rekindled popular opposition to the Cultural Revolution and coincided with preliminary steps to produce an official history of the CCP, which would necessarily have to come to terms with the events of the Cultural Revolution.

December 3. The Chinese government called on the Dutch government to reconsider its decision to sell submarines to Taiwan. China called the proposed sale an act of interference in China's internal affairs. In protest of the

Dutch decision, Beijing recalled the Chinese ambassador to the Netherlands and downgraded diplomatic relations in January 1981.

December 16-25. At the Central Work Conference, the CCP distributed a circular calling for all cadres to unify their thinking on readjustment and economic reform. The circular argued that without proper thinking, reform would not be carried out smoothly. It called on party members to study documents regarding reform and to carry out reform wisely.

1981

January 1. The marriage law passed by the State Council came into effect, setting the minimum age for marriage at 22 and 20 for men and women, respectively. The new law also allowed for divorce as long as both sides consented and allowed women to retain their mother or father's surname. Together the laws were meant to adjust the marriage procedure to meet the needs of the modernizing, industrial society.

January 25. The Gang of Four and their associates were sentenced in Beijing. Mao's widow, Jiang Qing, and Gang of Four leader Zhang Chunqiao were sentenced to death, although their sentences were later commuted to life imprisonment. The other defendants were given jail terms ranging from sixteen years to life for their participation in the Cultural Revolution. None were given the chance for parole.

February 1. China's first large, high-flux test and research reactor came on line in the city of Chengdu in southwest China. The Chinese press hailed the indigenously designed and constructed reactor and claimed that the reactor would be instrumental in aiding research and development for a nuclear power reactor.

February 13. The conference of nonaligned movement foreign ministers ended in New Delhi and demanded the withdrawal of outside troops from Afghanistan and Cambodia. Zhao Ziyang represented the Chinese government and reiterated his country's stand against foreign interference in both countries. (In an attempt to improve its relations with the governments of the other countries, China had announced earlier that it would end its practice of supporting Communist insurgents in non-Communist developing countries.)

February 19. The People's Liberation Army issued guidelines on upholding the spirit of Lei Feng, an army officer who was killed in 1962 while trying to save others. Lei was held up as a model officer who symbolized the importance of loyalty to the party and the Chinese people. The Lei Feng campaign was another example of the army's attempt to maintain the "correct" spirit among its ranks. Lei Feng campaigns have often been used at times of social turmoil when the party needed to instill discipline and social order.

February 28. The government announced plans to slow down economic growth and contract output. It had called for a similar adjustment in 1979, but found itself unable to control all the various government agencies involved. Because of the vested interests in economic reform, some agencies again found ways to continue their projects despite the calls for economic tightening.

March. The IMF approved a $550 million loan to China to help finance its balance of payments deficit and stabilize the economy. Shortly thereafter, the government tried to raise more revenue and decrease inflation by issuing $3.3 billion worth of bonds.

April 8. Deng Xiaoping signaled China's willingness to improve relations with neighboring India in comments made while attending a meeting with a member of India's parliament. Relations between the two countries had been strained since 1962 because of border disputes and India's actions in Kashmir. In the months that followed, the two exchanged visits but continued to be hindered by persistent border questions.

April 15. The first Coca-Cola Company bottling plant opened in China in a factory owned by the China National Cereal, Oils, and Foodstuffs Import and Export Corporation. Many expected Coca-Cola to be a foreign currency earner, since only tourists and other foreigners could afford to purchase the drink.

May 9. To strengthen its opposition to the presence of Vietnamese forces in Cambodia and to Soviet support for those forces, the Chinese offered Prince Norodom Sihanouk arms and other weapons to help Cambodian opposition forces overthrow the Hanoi-sponsored Heng Samrin government in Phnom Penh. Earlier, China's fears of Soviet involvement were heightened when Soviet submarines sailed into Vietnam's Cam Ranh Bay. Later in the year, China's Ministry of Foreign Affairs filed a formal protest against Vietnam for its alleged incursions into the southern province of Yunnan.

May 29. Song Qingling, widow of Sun Yat-sen, died in Beijing. Song had served as honorary president of the country and was credited by some with helping to found the PRC. She was honored by the party as "a great patriotic, democratic, internationalist and Communist fighter known throughout the world." She was memorialized both by the mainland Chinese and those on Taiwan.

June. U.S. secretary of state Alexander Haig became the first high-ranking official in the administration of Ronald Reagan to visit Beijing. Haig, who believed China should be given a preeminent position in U.S. foreign policy as leverage against the Soviet Union, renewed U.S. promises to supply military equipment to China, signed cultural agreements, and made arrangements to open more consulates.

The sixth plenum of the Eleventh CCP Central Committee was held in Beijing. Hua Guofeng's fall from power was made official as Deng Xiaoping replaced him as chairman of the Military Commission and Hu Yaobang replaced him as party chairman. The Central Committee adopted a resolution on party history that tried to rationalize the events of the Cultural Revolution and to explain the role of socialism in shaping modern China. It declared that Mao Zedong had made mistakes in his later years but judged that 70 percent of his acts were good and only 30 percent were bad—the same formulation made in judging Stalin's deeds.

June 26. The foreign ministers of China and India began talks on border issues and a new air route to link the two countries. During the talks, the Beijing delegation proposed that China retain the territory captured in the 1962 border war while abandoning its claim to an area on the northwest side of India. No final agreement on the border was reached.

July. After formation of a coalition government in Cambodia on July 9, China presented its own three-point proposal to settle the problem of Cambodia during a UN-sponsored conference. The three points were: Vietnamese withdrawal of troops; respect for the people's right to self-determination; and guaranteeing a neutral and non-aligned status for Cambodia.

August 4. During a conference on disarmament in Geneva, the Chinese delegation asserted China's intention never to be the first country to use nuclear weapons or to use nuclear weapons against any nonnuclear state. In June, during a UN Arms Race Committee meeting, China's delegation expressed concern over the predominance of influence exercised by states with large nuclear arsenals. This was the basis of China's main objection to the nuclear nonproliferation treaty.

September 25. China launched three experimental satellites with one rocket—the country's first multilaunch. The satellites were launched from the Gobi Desert. It was only the eighth satellite launch since China began its space program in 1970 and was considered a major advance in the Chinese rocket/satellite program.

October 2. Deng Xiaoping voiced support for a nine-point proposal presented by Ye Jianying on the question of relations between Taiwan and the mainland. Specifically, the proposal called for the eventual reunification of the mainland and Taiwan. Focusing on the economic benefits of reunification, the proposal offered assistance to Taiwan and preferential treatment in its economic ties with the mainland. The government on Taiwan firmly dismissed the proposal.

November 2. An earlier article by Deng Xiaoping on "Rectifying the Party Style of Work" was printed in *Hongqi.* The article called on the party to "seek truth from facts" and to grasp certain principles of Mao Zedong Thought to aid in modernization. The article also called on party cadres to strengthen party traditions, to carry out self-criticisms, and to observe discipline. Many saw the article as the beginning of a party rectification campaign to weed out bad elements of the party, regain much of the credibility lost during the Cultural Revolution, and rejuvenate the party with younger members.

November 30. The fourth session of the Fifth National People's Congress opened in Beijing. The main focus of the conference was further reform of the economy. The congress concluded that adjustments made in experimental reforms in the rural sector were working and that agricultural reform should continue, along with greater emphasis on opening China's economy to the outside world. The congress also voted to extend the economic readjustment period until 1985.

December. Sino-Indian border talks began to falter despite earlier indications from high-ranking leaders that the two countries were ready and willing to improve relations. The reversal was precipitated by the Indian parliament's move to congratulate the government of Taiwan instead of mainland China on the seventieth anniversary of the 1911 Revolution. The talks ended on 20 May with an agreement that relations between India and China should be governed by the Five Principles of Peaceful Coexistence, China's overarching guide to foreign relations.

December 23. The Central Committee ended a meeting in which Chen Yun voiced opposition to expansion of the special economic zones (SEZs) and asserted that the state should retain its primary role in the economy. Hu Yaobang later countered by calling for more steps to encourage foreign investment to help modernize the economy. The two positions represented the growing divisions between conservatives and reformers in China. Meanwhile, the Central Committee established the China Investment Bank (CIB), which was to be responsible for raising funds abroad in order to support domestic investment and credit. The CIB would also act as the intermediary monetary body between China and the World Bank.

1982

January. In an attempt to increase investment in light industry, China reduced customs duties on imports of such items as energy, raw materials, and machinery for light industry and textile production. At the same time, China increased tariffs on imports of machinery and equipment already produced in China, thereby encouraging Chinese factories to continue to produce such equipment.

January 28. A Hong Kong newspaper reported an assassination attempt against Deng Xiaoping while he was touring Heilongjiang Province. A pro-Mao group was alleged to have fired shots at Deng's limousine. Deng was said to have been injured in the chest and flown to Beijing for medical attention.

February. The China National Offshore Oil Corporation (CNOOC) was established. As one of its first acts,

CNOOC extended invitations to forty-six foreign companies to bid on oil exploration along China's continental shelf, including the disputed Spratly Islands.

March. Thirteen of the State Council's vice premiers were replaced to make room for younger, more reform-minded leaders. The decision was made by the National People's Congress Standing Committee. Under new directives, there would be two vice premiers instead of the original thirteen. Furthermore, the number of ministries and commissions under the State Council would be reduced from ninety-eight to fifty-two, along with a 30 percent staff reduction.

March 5. The government of China freed 4,327 Nationalist soldiers and spies imprisoned since 1949. Although all the prisoners were given the chance to resettle in Taiwan, none decided to do so.

March 16. The Chinese Softball Association filed a formal protest against the secretary general of the International Softball Federation when the latter allowed the team from Taiwan to be referred to as the team from the "Republic of China." The complaint was rooted in continuing tensions over the status of Taiwan in relation to the mainland. The Chinese Softball Association later decided to withdraw from competition because of what was seen as undue recognition of Taiwan.

April 3. Sino-Mongolian meetings were held in the Mongolian capital of Ulan Bator to discuss border issues. The meeting was the first since the two countries had established a border protocol in 1964. China had always been wary of Mongolia because of its close ties to the Soviet Union. China and Mongolia share a 3,000-mile border. No formal agreement was reached regarding the status of the border.

May 1. China issued two documents governing the role of advertising within a socialist country. The documents asserted that advertising should play a positive role and should be supervised. Regulations were issued to deal with problems that might arise. Foreign ventures were held to the same guidelines. In late 1985 regulations would be passed to ban "slanderous propaganda, obscenity, and superstition" from advertisements.

May 8. Vice President Bush visited China and asked both Deng Xiaoping and Zhao Ziyang not to allow the question of Taiwan to be the sole determinant of Sino-American relations. Sino-American relations had been strained over the previous several months because of actions by the Reagan administration to give equal attention to Taiwan-American relations. Less than a month earlier, the Chinese foreign ministry had filed a complaint with the U.S. embassy regarding U.S. plans to sell military-related spare parts to Taiwan.

May 31. General Secretary Zhao Ziyang began an official visit to Japan, a sign of the growing closeness in relations between Japan and China. Although the Chinese still harbored deep resentment against Japan because of its actions before and during World War II, closer relations were seen as advantageous for economic reasons. Since normalizing relations, Japan had lent China more than $200 million per year.

July 30. The Politburo, in an enlarged meeting, discussed possible alternatives to life tenure, also known as the "iron rice bowl," for party leaders. The discussions laid the groundwork for the retirement of several party leaders in order to make room for younger cadres. Similar retirements took place within the National People's Congress. Several elder party leaders were named to a Central Advisory Commission that would provide guidance to current leaders, with Deng Xiaoping named its first chairman.

August 5. An argument regarding the wording of Japanese textbooks arose between China and Japan. The Chinese government protested a passage within a Japanese textbook describing the Japanese invasion of China simply as an "advance." China called on Japan to come to terms with its past acts of aggression. The dispute arose shortly after Zhao Ziyang had visited Japan to try to increase economic interactions.

September 1. The twelfth CCP congress opened in Beijing. The congress abolished the post of party chairman and instead re-established the post of general secretary. Deng stepped down as party leader and named Hu Yaobang to replace him. The party outlined the three major tasks for the 1980s as modernization, reunification with Hong Kong and Taiwan, and carrying out an independent foreign policy. A new party constitution was adopted and the congress ratified plans to quadruple the 1980 gross national product by the year 2000, despite growing disagreement between reformers and the "go slow" faction led by Chen Yun.

September. British prime minister Margaret Thatcher visited Beijing and promised to continue talks regarding the status of Hong Kong. (The British lease on Hong Kong was to expire officially on 1 July 1997.) Negotiations were held to discuss the peaceful return of Hong Kong to China's control. A joint statement announcing the start of the formal talks was issued on 1 July 1983.

October 5. China and the Soviet Union opened negotiations to improve bilateral relations, the first such talks in three years. China set down three obstacles to be overcome before normalization of relations could take place: an end to Soviet support of Vietnam and its occupation of Cambodia; an end to Soviet hostilities in Afghanistan; and the withdrawal of Soviet troops on the Sino-Soviet border. The Soviet Union would later comply with all three.

November 10. Soviet general secretary Leonid Brezhnev died in Moscow; Yuri Andropov was named to replace him. Foreign Minister Huang Hua led the funeral delegation from China. Although Huang made positive remarks regarding relations between the two countries,

China's decision to send a non-Politburo member as head of the delegation was taken as a sign that relations were still cool.

December 4. The National People's Congress ratified a new state constitution, which defined the NPC as the highest organ of state power. The new constitution called for re-establishment of the head of state, abolished the right to strike, expanded certain civil liberties, and made family planning a social "duty." The offices of president, premier, and other leading government posts were limited to two five-year terms.

December 20. Zhao Ziyang began a ten-nation tour of Africa to affirm China's support of third world countries. At the end of the tour, Zhao had secured agreements to increase the number of construction projects carried out by Chinese firms in African countries and to increase the level of trade.

December 29. The first "supermarket" in China opened in Beijing. Previously, all food items were sold in state-owned markets. Although stall owners still functioned under state control, the consolidation of sellers increased convenience to shoppers. Prices at the market were reported to be higher than those at the individual state-owned markets, but officials claimed that the added price was necessary to offset the increased cost of maintaining the supermarket.

1983

January 25. The Chinese Supreme Court commuted the death sentences of Gang of Four members Jiang Qing and Zhang Chunqiao. Both were said to have made "sufficient" progress during their first two years in prison. Their sentences were revised to life imprisonment.

February. U.S. secretary of state George Shultz paid a visit to Beijing. He discussed the question of Taiwan, China's technology transfers to other states, and trade and cultural issues. Shultz asserted that the United States would live up to the promises made under an August 1982 Sino-American communiqué that outlined a limit to U.S. arms sales to Taiwan and reiterated America's acceptance of the People's Republic as the sole government authority over China.

February 23. China declared that a Vietnamese offer of a partial withdrawal from Cambodia was a hoax. China called for nothing less than an unconditional withdrawal of Vietnamese troops from Cambodia and asserted that the Soviet Union should stop supporting Vietnamese forces.

March 18. China's minister of family planning received an award from the UN for work done to decrease China's population. Since it was begun in the latter part of the 1970s, China's one-child policy had reduced the population growth rate and helped increase the average life expectancy of Chinese citizens. The lower population

worked to increase the country's standard of living and aided plans for economic development.

April. China and India agreed to renew diplomatic ties, which had been suspended since border clashes took place in the early 1960s. Deng Xiaoping had expressed China's willingness to enter into border talks in April 1981. The attempt to improve relations was part of China's strategy of securing its borders in order to better deal with what it saw as the Soviet threat.

April 10. The Soviet Union and China signed a barter trade agreement through which the USSR would supply such goods as steel, timber, and cement to China in return for Chinese meat, cooking oil, and textiles. Sino-Soviet normalization talks broke off, however, because of Soviet insistence that third-country issues (namely, Vietnam) not be a subject of discussion.

April 13. The State Council passed regulations prohibiting the hunting of rare species within China. More than 160 such species were believed to inhabit the country.

April 23. Major Li Dawen of Taiwan, allegedly dissatisfied with the Nationalist government, defected to China via his U-6A spotter aircraft. Mainland authorities awarded him 150,000 yuan ($75,000). The practice of rewarding defectors would later be discontinued.

April 26. The People's Republic of China applied for membership in the Asian Development Bank (ADB). In doing so, Beijing protested Taiwan's membership within the bank. Membership in the bank would provide another source of low-interest funds for the country's economic development plans.

June 1. The State Council announced that state-owned enterprises would be made to pay taxes and that the state would no longer bear sole responsibility for enterprise losses. In exchange, state-owned enterprises would be allowed to retain after-tax profits instead of remitting all profits to the state. Certain state-owned enterprises—involved in defense, agriculture, telecommunications, and foreign trade—were exempt from the regulations because of their strategic importance to central authorities.

June 6. China participated in a meeting of the International Labor Organization (ILO) for the first time since the founding of the People's Republic of China. Although Nationalist China was a cofounder of the organization in 1917, it was ejected from its seat when the CCP took control of the country. The ILO restored China's seat in 1971, but China chose not to rejoin until 1983 after the ILO changed certain policies China had found inconsistent with its interests. The mainland was not charged for past-due membership bills.

June 21. The sixth session of the National People's Congress closed in Beijing. In addition to reporting on the government, strengthening anticorruption measures, and approving plans for social and economic development, the session elected new leaders. Li Xiannian was appointed president; Peng Zhen was named the National

People's Congress chairman; Zhao Ziyang was made premier of the State Council with Ulanfu as vice president; and Zhou Enlai's widow, Deng Yingchao, was elected to chair the Chinese People's Political Consultative Conference.

July. The first volume of Deng Xiaoping's *Selected Works* was published. The publication signaled Deng's successful consolidation of power within the party and codified his reform agenda. Publication of Deng's other works would follow.

July 1. The State Council declared that the People's Bank of China would act singularly and solely as China's central bank in an attempt to strengthen the government's ability to institute monetary changes within the economy. As the central bank, the People's Bank of China would be in charge of monitoring China's monetary policy and making decisions regarding the overall level of domestic credit. Commercial banks were established in order to handle industrial and commercial credits.

July 23. The government of Vietnam accused China of sending raiding parties across their border into northern Vietnam. The raiding parties allegedly burned down houses and planted land mines. In addition, Chinese fishing boats were charged with violating Vietnam's territorial waters. The denunciation was one of the more vocal from the Vietnamese in their ongoing conflict with China.

August 1. The Chinese government announced new exchange control regulations to attract foreign investors and investment.

August 19. President Reagan asked American federal courts to dismiss an Alabama state ruling that China had to pay a $41 million defaulted loan. The loan was issued in 1911 for funds to build a project in southern China. The Chinese government had rejected the September 1982 ruling on the grounds that it was not the government in power at the time of the loan.

September 16. Soviet deputy foreign minister Mikhail S. Kapitsa visited China for talks with Deputy Foreign Minister Qian Qichen. Kapitsa, in charge of East Asia and Southeast Asian affairs, was the highest-ranking Soviet official to visit China in more than twenty years.

October 1. A unified construction tax was put into effect for all projects except those involving energy, transportation, education, or medical facilities not detailed under the central plan. The tax would be charged against any project undertaken by a local unit. The tax would be 10 percent of the project cost and had to be paid for with private, nonborrowed funds. It was an attempt to improve central control over private investment.

October. China was admitted as the 113th member of the International Atomic Energy Agency (IAEA). As a member, China had to agree to allow inspection of its nuclear sites to verify that they were being used for peaceful purposes. China claimed its membership in the agency was further proof of its adherence to the principles of nonproliferation and the peaceful use of atomic energy, although the country was not yet a signatory of the NPT, which China contended was biased toward states that already had large nuclear arsenals.

October 31. The first exclusively Japanese-owned business opened in the Shenzhen Special Economic Zone. Previously, all investments were in the form of joint ventures with a Chinese firm or were enterprises owned by overseas Chinese. The new business was owned by Sanyo Corporation.

November 1. Qian Qichen voiced China's support for a ban on the world arms race in outer space. The proposal put forth by the UN would declare outer space a neutral zone to be used exclusively for peaceful purposes. In addition, he announced China's support for an agreement on chemical weapons.

November. The campaign against spiritual pollution, begun by Deng earlier in the year to reverse negative Western influences, was narrowed to affect only the literature and arts community. Zhou Yang, chairman of the China Federation of Literary and Art Circles, underwent a self-criticism in which he asserted that alienation was possible within a socialist society, but that socialism was still superior to capitalism. Hu Yaobang later defined spiritual pollution as "remarks and works of a very few people in theoretical circles and in fields of literature and art that are harmful to the Four Modernizations and to the stability and unity of the country."

December 15. A Chinese delegation was allowed to participate in a meeting of the General Agreement on Tariffs and Trade (GATT) regarding international trade in textiles (the multifiber agreement). Although China attended the meeting with only observer status, the delegation's presence marked the beginning of China's attempt to re-enter the trade regime. China's membership in GATT had been revoked in 1950.

December. After almost two years of diplomatic pressure from China and the downgrading of relations between the two countries, the Dutch government decided not to sell submarines to Taiwan. The December 1980 decision to sell submarines to Taiwan had sparked Chinese protests and the withdrawal of the Chinese ambassador to the Netherlands.

1984

January 1. The Central Committee distributed a circular demanding punishment for party members who abused their party privileges. The ruling applied to members who took advantage of their position in order to gain jobs, better housing, and other benefits for themselves or their relatives. The circular followed many calls by high-level party leaders to curb growing nepotism in their ranks.

January 10. At the invitation of U.S. president Ronald Reagan, Chinese premier Zhao Ziyang made an official visit to the United States. While in America, Zhao discussed Chinese reservations about stated U.S. policy toward Taiwan. Zhao then made an official visit to Canada.

January 24. Deng began a tour of China's SEZs to build support for the SEZs and their foreign investment programs amid growing criticism of them from certain elements within the party. Since the SEZs were established in the late 1970s, issues such as foreign control of resources and labor disputes had led many to question their appropriateness to China's goals. Deng's tour was meant to highlight the advantages of SEZs in helping the country strive for economic modernization.

February 1. The Central Committee implemented a second stage of land reform, allowing farmers to keep their land for fifteen years. Transfer of land among family members was acceptable as long as the transfer received approval from the rural leadership. Peasants were also given a greater role in making rural distribution decisions.

February 11. Soviet general secretary Yuri Andropov died in Moscow, fifteen months after the death of Leonid Brezhnev. A Chinese delegation led by Vice Premier Wan Li attended the funeral. During the trip, Vice Premier Wan affirmed China's commitment to better Sino-Soviet relations, commenting on the enduring friendship between the Chinese and Soviet peoples. Wan's status relative to Huang Hua, the delegation leader for Brezhnev's funeral, suggested the increasing importance being given by China to relations with the Soviet Union since 1982.

February 20. Several more Chinese cities—raising the number to 145—were opened to travel by foreigners. The cities, including Xianyang and Dali (Yunnan), were cited as scenic and historic areas of interest. Foreigners still needed permits before visiting the cities, and travel by journalists was still controlled.

February 28. The China National Conference on Economic Work stressed the need for higher productivity among China's workers in order to enhance China's modernization efforts. The conference was held in the wake of government measures in 1980 and 1981 to slow growth and decrease inflation.

March 5. President Li Xiannian began a visit to Pakistan, Jordan, Turkey, and Nepal. The visit, following Premier Zhao Ziyang's visit to African countries in December 1982, was a further sign of Beijing's desire to strengthen ties with the third world. The *People's Daily* heralded the trip as a success in improving "mutual understanding" and promoting friendship. It was Li's first foreign trip since being elected president.

March 26. China opened 14 coastal cities to foreign investment. Like the SEZs, the cities would attract foreign capital by offering tax breaks and other incentives. These cities were Dalian, Qinhuangdao, Tianjin, Qingdao, Yantai, Lianyungang, Nantong, Shanghai, Ningbo, Wenzhou, Fuzhou, Guangzhou, Zhanjiang, and Beihai.

April 2. The Chinese government endorsed the existence of nuclear weapons in Western Europe for the first time, justifying its position in terms of the need for defense against hostile Soviet forces and possible attack.

April. U.S. president Ronald Reagan made an official visit to China, during which the two countries agreed to avoid double taxation of U.S. companies operating in China and signed agreements on the peaceful uses of nuclear energy and on cultural exchange.

May. A new ruling required all Chinese citizens over the age of sixteen to carry identification cards, in an attempt to cut down on the number of migrants within the country. Without proper identification, urban residents would not receive a stipend or be considered for jobs. Assignment of housing was also based on proper identification.

May 9. China and West Germany signed an agreement to cooperate in developing methods for the peaceful use of nuclear technology. The two countries agreed to strengthen joint scientific research, as well as joint design, construction, and operations. West German chancellor Helmut Kohl made an official visit to China five months later.

May 10. The State Council announced provisional regulations giving state-owned enterprises greater decision-making power in economic affairs. Modeled after the household responsibility system begun in the rural areas, the goal of industrial reform was to bring about greater economic efficiency by granting more freedom. With the regulations in effect, the government would specify supply quotas, performance targets, and the enterprise's tax obligation. The enterprise manager could then decide how to invest any remaining profit.

June 11. Calling for a stronger rural household responsibility system, the Central Committee released a document suggesting that rural residents be given greater autonomy in choosing production and development strategies. It also called on the government to promote better training for rural workers.

June 13. China and Great Britain signed a statement establishing a working group to settle questions on the future of Hong Kong. The group would not hold any decision-making power. In April, the government had announced that Hong Kong residents would make up the governing body of the Hong Kong Special Autonomous Region after the colony was returned to China in 1997.

June 25. The State Economic Commission instituted a bonus system for state-owned enterprise workers. The system gave factory managers more autonomy over the use of surplus funds and the distribution of pay incentives.

July 10. Defense Minister Zhang Aiping visited the United States as part of a tour of Canada, France, the United States, and Japan. Zhang's visit signified the continuation of Sino-U.S. military cooperation despite tensions over the Reagan administration's stand on Taiwan. While in the United States, Zhang visited several military bases and defense contract corporations in Texas.

July 19. The China Council for the Promotion of International Trade opened China's first patent agency. The agency would help foreigners obtain patents for production in China and aid Chinese entrepreneurs seeking patents abroad.

September. British and Chinese negotiators signed a joint communiqué regarding the status of Hong Kong after 1997. The result of more than two years of talks, the communiqué outlined the return of Hong Kong to the People's Republic of China. Hong Kong was to retain its economic and social system for at least 50 years after its reversion to Chinese rule. Prime Minister Thatcher traveled to China in December to sign the agreement.

September 19. The government announced that the structure of foreign trade would be decentralized. Previously, only a handful of Chinese foreign trade companies had been allowed to trade on international markets. Under the new regulations, more foreign trade corporations would be established to facilitate trade between Chinese producers and foreign buyers.

October 20. The Central Committee passed its "Decision on the Reform of the Economic Structure." The plan envisioned a mixed economy, maintaining a state planning function that would concentrate on regulation rather than directing the agents of production. It sought to make greater use of Special Economic Zones and open cities in order to increase foreign investment.

October 30. The State Bureau of Nuclear Safety was formally established. In addition to helping the country live up to its IAEA commitments, the bureau would draft basic laws governing the use of atomic energy in China and formulate safety procedures to be used in the country.

November 11. On the thirty-fifth anniversary of its founding, the General Administration of Civil Aviation of China (CAAC) announced it would set up two international airline companies and three domestic flight companies. Individual provinces were encouraged to buy their own planes and set up regional airline service. Shortly thereafter, Xiamen Airlines was established in Fujian Province.

November 22. The second stage of party rectification began. All 40 million members of China's Communist Party were required to reapply for party membership over the next two years, and any member found guilty of wrongdoing was to be removed from the party. The first stage had focused on rebuilding the legitimacy of the party after the Cultural Revolution, while this stage emphasized consolidating party membership and weeding out unfit members. A similar rectification movement began in the PLA.

December. Editorials appeared in the *People's Daily* challenging the suitability of Marxism as the solution for China's problems. Among the many themes was the idea that "Marxism is not a dogma but a guide to action." Such arguments suggested that various interpretations of Marxism were now permissible and that to be Marxist a country need not fit the original mold perfectly.

December 21. Soviet deputy prime minister Ivan Arkhipov became the highest-ranking Soviet official to visit Beijing since the Sino-Soviet split. His visit had been scheduled originally for May but was allegedly canceled in response to U.S. president Reagan's successful trip. At the end of the visit, the two countries signed four treaties relating to economic, technical, and scientific exchanges.

1985

January 1. Deng Xiaoping's book, *Building Socialism with Chinese Characteristics,* was published. The book contained speeches given by Deng outlining his theories for reform and the implications for the party and the country as reform developed.

January 7. The first of many student protests during the year took place on the campus of Beijing University, this one protesting the elimination of stipends. These protests ended in a compromise with the university, but were followed late in the year by other student protests against the increasing closeness of Sino-Japanese relations.

January 19. U.S. chairman of the joint chiefs of staff General John Vessey ended an official visit to Beijing, during which he emphasized America's commitment to cooperation with China. The visit was part of ongoing attempts to enhance military relations between the United States and China and clarify the U.S. stand on Taiwan.

January 31. The *People's Daily* reported government plans to adjust prices for agricultural and industrial products into a two-tiered system. Once initial sales quotas were reached, the price of additional products sold would be determined by the market at the factory manager's discretion. Most agricultural procurement prices were also abolished; except for certain commodities, prices would be determined by the market.

February 9. The U.S. government decided to withdraw its commitment of $23 million to the United Nations Fund for Population Activities in China to show its opposition to China's birth control practices. China maintained that it did not carry out forced abortions.

March 3. An NPC delegation traveled to the Soviet Union at the invitation of the Supreme Soviet. The ten-day visit was the highest-ranking government-to-government exchange between the Soviet Union and China in two decades.

March 27. The third session of the Sixth National People's Congress adopted plans to move the country toward price reform. Many opposed the plan, however, because price reform entailed higher prices and increased inflation, and plans later had to be modified.

May 6. Deng Xiaoping confirmed plans to reduce the size of the PLA in order to modernize and improve it. The plan entailed decreasing the number of soldiers in uniform and refocusing some PLA industries on consumer goods production. The plan would also provide the means for higher education within the ranks and better technological training.

May 18. A scheduled visit of U.S. warships to the port of Shanghai was canceled because of a dispute over the ships' nuclear capacity. The visit would have been the first since 1949.

May 23. Universities, colleges, and private schools were granted more autonomy in decisions on admission, research, curricula, and administrative appointments. The State Education Commission also suggested that, to decrease expenditures, the system of free tuition for all students would be eliminated, with stipends and scholarships made available to needy students.

June 5. A document issued by the Ministry of Civil Affairs declared the end of commune restructuring and the replacement of communes with towns and township government. The dismantling of the communes was part of ongoing efforts to institute the household responsibility system.

July 16. Vice Premier Yao Yilin ended a trip to Moscow. During his visit, China and the Soviet Union signed two economic and trade agreements that included cooperation in the building of machinery, power engineering, and coal and chemical production.

July 22. President Li Xiannian visited the United States, the first Communist head of state to make an official visit there. During the visit the two countries agreed to an accord on the peaceful use of nuclear technology. The United States promised to proceed with plans to sell China a nuclear reactor—plans that had previously been stalled because of allegations that China was helping Pakistan develop nuclear devices.

September 22. During a celebration to mark the fortieth anniversary of the end of the War of Resistance against Japan, the CCP called for a third round of talks with Taiwan's Kuomintang government to discuss the idea of "one country, two systems."

September. The CCP underwent another major leadership change as ten of the twenty-four Politburo members were replaced by younger cadres. The move was designed to help eliminate "lifelong tenure" within the party and to promote a younger generation to assume everyday leadership of the party. The average age of the new appointees was fifty years old.

October 2. A Soviet delegation in China, headed by Supreme Soviet chairman Lev Tolkunov, agreed to begin the process of renormalization with China, beginning with the exchange of foreign ministers.

October 15. U.S. vice president Bush visited Beijing and met with Premier Zhao Ziyang, Vice Premier Wan Li, and General Secretary Hu Yaobang. Reports indicated that the most important topic of discussion was the question of Taiwan. Later in the month, Zhao traveled to New York to attend the fortieth anniversary of the founding of the United Nations.

November 23. Larry Wu Tai Chin, a retired analyst with the U.S. Central Intelligence Agency, was charged by the United States with spying for China. He was alleged to have received over $140,000 for information supplied to the Chinese while he was posted in Hong Kong with the Foreign Broadcast Information Service and to have provided classified materials after his retirement from the CIA in 1981.

December. The U.S. House of Representatives passed a textile bill that would have markedly decreased U.S. imports of Chinese textiles by limiting the number of goods that could be exported to the United States. President Reagan vetoed the bill. Later that month, the U.S. Department of Commerce announced that it would ease restrictions on exports of some U.S. products to China, including computers, semiconductors, and electronic instruments.

A group of students denouncing China's closer relations with Japan marched on Tiananmen Square. A few days later, other students rallied in Beijing to support Deng Xiaoping's program for greater opening to the world. They called on citizens to support the country's moves toward modernization and argued that increased ties with Japan were necessary for development.

December 22. Residents of western Xinjiang held protests against the government's atmospheric testing of nuclear weapons there. The majority of participants were members of China's minority Uighur nationality. Similar tests had also been conducted near the city of Urumqi.

1986

January 10. Zhao Ziyang announced China's intention to rejoin GATT. In 1982, China had begun attending GATT meetings with observer status and in 1984 took part in a textile agreement. Zhao admitted that the country would need time to bring China's trade structure into line with GATT provisions, but voiced China's belief that membership would be restored in due time.

January 13. As a follow-up to the February 1980 decision on compulsory education, the State Council signed a draft bill stipulating that compulsory education would be required for nine years. Citing education as of "strategic importance" to China's modernization, the bill made it illegal for any organization or individual to employ children before the completion of nine years of schooling.

January 17. In an effort to encourage grain production, the state lowered the grain quota to allow farmers to sell more grain on the open market. The government also offered farmers special loans to cover extra production costs.

February 10. The first technicians from the Soviet Union were sent to China since Soviet technical advisers were recalled in the early 1960s. The technicians were experts in the field of culture and education. The visits were the first exchange of personnel since the 1960s.

March 10. The People's Republic of China was formally admitted into the Asian Development Bank as the result of a compromise in which Taiwan would remain in the ADB under the name of Taipei, China.

March 13. The Chinese Film Bureau and the Ministry of Radio and Television were merged in order to increase central control over the ideological content of programming. The new ministry was named the Ministry of Radio, Film, and Television.

March 16. The first meeting of the Sino-Soviet Commission on Economic, Trade, Scientific, and Technological Cooperation was held to exchange ideas on how to further increase Sino-Soviet trade. The meeting also agreed to an exchange of engineers and technicians. In June, a Sino-Soviet scientific cooperation pact was established between the Chinese Academy of Sciences and the Soviet Academy of Sciences.

March 18. Hu Yaobang reiterated China's support for a political solution to the question of Cambodia. The proposed solution called for a tripartite government coalition to enter into negotiations with Vietnam regarding troop withdrawal. After the withdrawal and UN-observed cease-fire, a four-party coalition would be established, including the Heng Samrin faction, to oversee elections.

April. China signed an agreement with Sweden to launch a Swedish satellite in 1991 using China's *Long March 2* carrier rocket. The agreement was the first involving the launch of a foreign satellite by the Chinese.

April 23. Hong Kong officially joined GATT. (The colony had previously been represented by Great Britain.) China stated that Hong Kong's status in GATT would not change after the colony reverted to China in 1997. According to the provisions of the Sino-British Joint Declaration, Hong Kong, as a Special Administrative Region, would be a free port and would retain its ability to participate in international organizations and agreements, including GATT.

June 9. Communist Party General Secretary Hu Yaobang toured Western Europe in a trip heralded by China as "a new stage in China's friendly cooperation with Western Europe."

July 8. A domestic satellite communications network was officially put into operation. The network, designed to improve telephone and television communications, consisted of 300 relay stations and 5 ground stations in Beijing, Hohhot, Guangzhou, Lhasa, and Urumqi.

July 27. Zhao Ziyang completed a four-week goodwill visit to Romania, Yugoslavia, Greece, Spain, Turkey, and Tunisia. During his trip, Zhao reiterated China's adherence to the Five Principles of Peaceful Coexistence. On the trip, he worked to broaden areas of collaboration and to further develop economic and trade exchanges.

July 28. Soviet president Mikhail Gorbachev made a speech in the eastern port of Vladivostok that was viewed as a sign of the Soviet Union's willingness to decrease tensions in Asia. Along with a speech given in 1988 in Krasnoyarsk, this Vladivostok speech signaled a shift in Soviet policy from one of opposition to one of accommodation, compromise, and renewed friendship with China.

August 3. The Shenyang Explosion Prevention Equipment Factory in Liaoning Province became the first PRC factory allowed to go bankrupt.

August 5. The first stock market in China opened in Shenyang, Liaoning Province. The opening was part of a pilot study; other such markets might be opened depending on the performance of the Shenyang exchange. Foreigners were not allowed to buy shares. Another pilot stock program in Shanghai opened on September 26.

August 26. China's first non-government-owned bank opened in Shanghai. In addition to guaranteeing foreign loans and providing consulting services, the bank was to issue bonds, provide trust deposits in foreign currency, and offer loans in foreign exchange and Chinese yuan.

September. The National Defense University was established in Beijing. Consisting of three departments—basic military science, defense research, and advanced studies—the university was intended to train Chinese officers. More than 400 senior officers enrolled in studies there.

September 28. The sixth plenum of the twelfth party congress adopted "Guiding Principles for the Construction of Socialist Civilization," which affirmed China's commitment to Mao Zedong Thought and stressed the importance of socialist humanism. Deng also suggested that the country should undergo a level of political reform similar to Mao's 1956 Hundred Flowers movement.

October 1. Labor contracts were introduced in China. Henceforth, workers in state-owned enterprises were to be employed under contracts that terminate after a fixed number of years. Workers had the option to quit at the end of the period, or they could be fired by their enterprise.

October 27. China promulgated a law consisting of twenty-two provisions to encourage greater levels of foreign investment. Among the enticements, foreign ventures would receive greater tax breaks, access to bank loans, lower labor costs, and autonomy in hiring and firing workers. The regulations were aimed mainly at manufacturing industries.

November 3. The president of East Germany, Erich Honecker, completed a formal visit to China. His trip signified the growing ties between China and Eastern Europe. Two months earlier, Poland's president, Wojciech Jaruzelski, visited Beijing, becoming the first Polish president to visit China since 1959.

December. The NPC announced the establishment of the Ministry of Supervision, created to oversee the proper functioning of the government and to handle corruption within the bureaucracy.

December 19. Student demonstrations began in Shanghai and spread to Beijing, Nanjing, Hefei, Wuhan, Tianjin, and other cities over the next few weeks. The students demanded greater job mobility, better living conditions, open elections, and freedom of the press. Although authorities declared the protests illegal, General Secretary Hu Yaobang was hesitant to denounce the students or their mentors. More than 300 students were eventually arrested in Shanghai alone, and Hu's inaction during the student protests was later pointed to as a primary reason for his ouster as general secretary the following month.

1987

January 4. Hu Yaobang was dismissed as general secretary of the CCP because of his inaction during the student protest in December 1986 and because of mistakes made in implementing economic reform. At the same time, three prominent intellectuals—Fang Lizhi, Liu Binyan, and Wang Ruowang—were expelled from the party for advocating "bourgeois liberalization." Hu's formal resignation was announced almost two weeks later.

February 2. China's first credit card—the Great Wall card—was issued by the Bank of China in Beijing. The credit card was designed to handle transactions in yuan and was targeted primarily at businesses rather then individual consumers.

February 24. China and the Soviet Union announced an agreement to review the status of their common border. Border talks, suspended for over nine years, had been renewed on 8 February during meetings between Vice Foreign Minister Qian Qichen and his Soviet counterparts in Moscow.

April 8. Qingdao Brewery in Shandong Province was granted autonomy to import and export its beer products. It was among the first enterprises allowed to decide the level of its exports and to make independent contact with foreign buyers. Most other companies still had to establish trade contracts through centrally regulated foreign trade companies.

April 13. China and Portugal initialed a joint declaration on the future of Macao. Macao had been a colony of Portugal since the end of the Opium Wars and was to be administered by Portugal "permanently." Through the joint declaration, Portugal agreed to cede control of Macao to China in 1999, with Macao to retain its economic and political system for at least fifty years thereafter.

July 3. The Communist Party Central Discipline Inspection Commission took further steps to curb what it saw as rampant corruption in many government departments, following a June decision by the Supreme People's Court to pass out heavy penalties for economic crimes.

July 7. China commemorated the fiftieth anniversary of the Marco Polo Bridge incident, which marked the Japanese invasion of China. Press accounts faulted the Japanese for not coming to terms with and apologizing for its past deeds in China.

July 25. Inland river trade between China and the Soviet Union was re-established with the delivery of timber from China to the Soviet port of Lower Leninskoye. Inland river trade had been suspended for more than twenty years because of political tensions between the two countries and disagreement over boundaries within the rivers.

July 31. The PLA celebrated its sixtieth anniversary. Earlier in the year, the government announced completion of a one-million-troop cutback. The cutback, part of a plan to modernize the armed forces, sought to decrease the number of enlisted troops and to redirect military enterprises toward consumer production.

September 11. The ADB issued its first loan to China. The $100 million loan to the China Investment Bank was to promote technical innovations in light industry, electronics, and food enterprises. As of 1987, the CIB had also received loans worth more than $600 million from the World Bank.

September 14. The State Council established regulations for the country's nuclear energy production in order to ensure safe handling of nuclear materials. All nuclear materials were to be licensed, only trained personnel were to handle materials, and accounting and reporting systems were to be established.

October. The foreign ministry announced that the Tibet Autonomous Region would be closed to foreign tourists for an unspecified length of time. The announcement came after months of riots in Lhasa. Foreign correspondents based in Beijing were also asked to leave the region.

October 14. Journalists from Taiwan were allowed to visit the mainland, and Taiwan authorities began to allow citizens to visit relatives on mainland China. The move was a joint decision signaling the increasing ties between China and Taiwan.

November. Zhao Ziyang was elected general secretary of the CCP by the first plenum of the thirteenth party congress. He replaced Hu Yaobang, who had been dismissed in January. At the same meeting, Deng Xiaoping resigned from the Central Committee and Li Peng was approved as acting premier. During the congress, the party advanced the theory of the "primary stage of socialism" to explain the apparent contradictions between the ideal of a Communist economy and the trend toward marketization experienced by the Chinese economy since 1978. Because the Chinese economy was at the primary stage of socialism, the party reasoned that such capitalist tools were both appropriate and necessary.

November 24. The NPC announced that trial village committees would be given more latitude in governing themselves beginning 1 June 1988. The village committees law was an attempt to give the rural population greater voice in management and education within their communities. As of November 1987, there were reportedly 948,000 village committees in China.

November 30. The governments of China and Laos agreed to renew diplomatic relations, which had been broken off in 1978 because of tensions created by Laotian support of Vietnam and Chinese support of Laotian rebels. According to the agreement, relations between the two countries would be governed by the Five Principles of Peaceful Coexistence. During the talks, the two signed a trade agreement and China promised to stop supporting the rebels.

1988

January 14. Chiang Ching-kuo, president of Taiwan and son of Chiang Kai-shek, died in Taipei. Leaders on the mainland, including Zhao Ziyang, sent condolences and praise. They lauded Chiang for his adherence to a "one China policy" and his opposition to independence for the island of Taiwan. Lee Teng-hui was later named Chiang's successor.

January 15. The governments of China and Portugal exchanged documents on ratification of the Joint Declaration on the Question of Macao. The final agreement mirrors that of the 1984 Sino-British agreement on Hong Kong. Macao was set to revert to Chinese control in 1999 with the stipulation that the former colony would maintain its economic and social systems at least until 2049.

February 1. Border talks between China and the Soviet Union ended with the two sides agreeing to allow aerial photography of the region in question. Beijing maintained, however, that the presence of Soviet troops in Afghanistan precluded chances of a formal agreement settling border questions.

February 22. After remarks by Vietnam's Ministry of Foreign Affairs, the government of China reasserted its claim over the Spratly Islands in the South China Sea. In March, the Chinese Foreign Ministry strongly protested alleged Vietnamese intrusion on the islands, which ultimately led to armed naval conflict between the two countries.

March. Riots occurred in Lhasa, sparked this time by the end of the Tibetan Buddhist Grand Summons Ceremony and growing tensions between native Tibetans and Han Chinese settlers.

Yang Shangkun, vice chairman of the Central Military Commission (CMC), announced plans to reform the armed forces. During a session in June, the NPC Standing Committee approved plans to reintroduce ranks into the military. Ranks had been abolished in 1965 during the Cultural Revolution.

March 11. The China Federation of Handicapped People was established. Headed by Deng Pufang, Deng Xiaoping's son, who was paralyzed during the Cultural Revolution, the group's mission was to help China's handicapped population become better assimilated economically and socially.

April. At the first session of the Seventh NPC, Yang Shangkun was named president, Wang Zhen was named vice president, and Li Peng was formally approved as premier. Deng Xiaoping was elected chairman of the CMC, while party General Secretary Zhao Ziyang and Yang Shangkun were named vice chairmen.

April 13. Hainan was officially proclaimed a separate province of China by the NPC. The island, previously part of Guangdong Province, had been groomed as an export-processing zone throughout the 1980s.

American evangelist Billy Graham began a sixteen-day crusade throughout China. Graham met Premier Li Peng and they discussed issues of culture and education. Graham met with other leaders involved in China's social affairs, including the president of the China Christian Council.

June 3. An estimated 1,000 Beijing students conducted a protest march in front of the Ministry of Public Security to criticize the government's handling of crime within the city after a fellow student was beaten to death by a group of robbers.

June 26. The first Catholic bishops to be consecrated in China since 1955 were consecrated in a Shanghai ceremony. Bishop Sun Yanli and Bishop Sen Yifen were first ordained to the priesthood before the founding of the People's Republic. Their consecrations brought the total number of Christian bishops in China to eight.

July 1. The State Council published the first set of regulations for private enterprises in China. According to the regulations, a private enterprise is one employing more than eight people. The regulations stipulated that private enterprises must reinvest at least half their profits in the enterprise and that the salary of managers could be no more than ten times the amount of the average worker's salary.

July 18. The Ministry of Personnel announced plans for a new civil service system. Set to begin in 1989, the new system would at first affect only six agencies and ministries within the central government. The goal of the new system was to establish competitive examinations and a uniform wage scale for all employees.

July 28. The price of luxury items such as alcoholic beverages and cigarettes was allowed to vary according to market forces. Within weeks the prices of the goods increased dramatically. Because of this inflation and other inflationary pressures within the economy, the CCP Politburo announced plans for price and wage reform in an attempt to control prices. The People's Bank of China followed suit by increasing interest rates to further slow the economy.

September 7. China's first meteorological satellite was placed in solar-synchronous orbit. Named the *Fengyuan 1,* the satellite was to orbit the earth fourteen times a day. In order to boost its forecasting ability, scientists hoped to use the satellite in conjunction with projects undertaken in Taiwan.

September 8. In response to growing international questions about China's arms export policy, the foreign ministry outlined the three principles guiding arms export decisions. According to the Foreign Ministry, arms exports should enhance the receiver's "just defense capability," promote peace and stability, and not interfere in the internal affairs of the receiving country or other countries.

November. The governments of China and Mongolia signed a border treaty in Beijing after announcements of Soviet troop cutbacks. According to the treaty, the 1,860-mile border would be settled following the principle of the 1960 China-Mongolia Friendship Treaty.

November 10. The city of Xi'an held China's first disco dancing competition. Western disco and dancing had become increasingly popular throughout China since dance halls were allowed again in 1978.

December. Demonstrations in Tibet left one dead and thirteen injured. Hu Jintao was named Tibet's party secretary on 29 December to calm the unrest.

December 22. The China Art Gallery in Beijing presented the first exhibit of nude paintings in China. Two of the paintings in the exhibit were later removed because the models had been recognized and allegedly harassed.

December 24. Racial tension between Chinese and African students erupted in Nanjing during a party. Several students were injured. The tension spread to other cities in the following weeks, resulting in some African students asking to return home. The governments of Africa resisted the request, fearing possible negative effects on Sino-African relations.

1989

January 1. In an attempt to lessen the development gap between inland and coastal regions, the State Council and Central Committee approved policies that would use tax revenue from the coastal regions to fund projects in the relatively poor inner regions.

January 6. Fang Lizhi, who was stripped of his party membership in January 1987 for allegedly promoting "bourgeois liberalization," petitioned Deng Xiaoping for a general amnesty for political prisoners and for the release of Wei Jingsheng, a dissident jailed during the 1978 Democracy Wall movement.

February 6. China announced that its military and civilian personnel would take a more active role in UN peacekeeping operations. By doing so China hoped to raise its UN participation to the level of the four other members of the Security Council.

February 10. New riots broke out in Lhasa. After weeks of demonstrations and looting, troops of the Tibetan Military Region were sent to quell the disorder.

April 1. The Asian Development Bank, the Long-Term Credit Bank of Japan, and the First Interstate Bank of Hawaii became the first foreign banks to buy a stake in a Chinese-owned bank. They joined to buy a 25 percent share ($25 million) of Xiamen International Bank.

April. Hu Yaobang, former party general secretary, died on 15 April after suffering a heart attack. During the official day of mourning for Hu on April 22, university students gathered in Tiananmen Square to pay their respects and to protest against poor student living standards. Hu had been a symbol of support for the student movement since his actions during the student protests of 1986. Two days later, students staged a boycott of classes and began daily protests around Beijing. Zhao Ziyang, Hu's successor, adopted a moderate line toward the protesters and tried to work toward an agreement with them.

April 26. The *People's Daily* published an editorial condemning the student demonstrations as a form of antiparty and antisocialist turmoil. The wording of the editorial was meant as a warning to the students that their actions would not be tolerated by the leadership. The students, however, continued to press their demands for better living standards and an end to corruption within party ranks. Demonstrations continued, followed by a hunger strike by several students in Tiananmen Square.

April 28. In continuing its claim over the Spratly Islands, the government ordered Chinese forces to take over an atoll within the disputed island chain. The atoll was previously held by Vietnam.

May 18. Soviet president Mikhail Gorbachev ended his official visit to China, the first such visit by a Soviet leader since 1959. During his stay in Beijing, China and the Soviet Union had formally re-established diplomatic relations. However, his visit was overshadowed by the growing student protests and demonstrations in Tiananmen Square.

May 20. As a result of continued student protests, martial law was proclaimed in Beijing by Li Peng. The government was especially embarrassed by the student actions during Gorbachev's visit and the resultant foreign press coverage the demonstrators received. Despite the proclamation of martial law, many of the students remained in Tiananmen Square and were joined by workers and other citizens. The students erected a statue of the Goddess of Democracy in the square on May 30.

June 4. Having exhausted all attempts to persuade the students to leave Tiananmen Square, Deng Xiaoping ordered military troops into Beijing. Although the Chinese government reported only 300 deaths as a result of the ensuing violence, non-Chinese sources placed the death toll at at least 1,000 in Beijing and 300 in Chengdu.

June 9. Deng congratulated the military for its self-restraint during the military operations of 4 June and stressed the need for unity in the face of opposition. In later party meetings, Zhao Ziyang was blamed for allowing the students to get out of control and for trying to split the CCP. The meetings also blamed foreign influences for inciting a small minority of protesters blamed for carrying out the demonstrations.

June 23. The fourth plenum of the Thirteenth Central Committee ended in Beijing on 23 June. Its main focus was the disturbances at Tiananmen Square. The plenum removed Zhao Ziyang as general secretary and stripped him of his other positions within the party and government; three of Zhao's advisers were also formally relieved of their posts. Jiang Zemin was named the new general secretary.

June 26. The World Bank suspended consideration of seven loan applications for China because of foreign pressure resulting from Beijing's handling of the Tiananmen incident. The seven loans amounted to more than $780 million. All other loan activity was temporarily suspended.

August 20. The State Council announced that economic austerity measures would be extended past the previous two-year target. Premier Li Peng cited the economy's overheated performance to date, including an increase in industrial output of more than 10 percent and price increases of nearly 25 percent.

September 21. The Sino-Indian Commission held its first ministerial-level meeting. Sino-Indian relations had been re-established in April 1983 after a lapse of nearly twenty years. The commission agreed on the Chinese export of silk and silk yarn in exchange for Indian minerals and tea.

October 13. The Xinglong Observatory in Beijing unveiled China's largest telescope. The telescope was the result of fifteen years of development and a cost of roughly $6.7 billion. Scientists claimed the telescope to be the largest in Asia, with a capacity thirty times greater than any other Chinese telescope.

November 9. Moody's International Rating Service lowered China's rating from the most favorable rating of "A" to a "Baal" or medium-grade rating. As a result China had to pay higher interest rates for foreign loans. Banking analysts noted that the decrease was moderate given the increased political instability within the country.

November 11. Fourteen cases of AIDS were reported by the Beijing Health Department. According to the announcement, the cases were the result of exposure to foreigners. To stop the further spread of the disease, the city planned to monitor all those already infected with venereal disease and those having daily contact with non-Chinese residents.

November 12. The CCP Central Military Commission accepted Deng Xiaoping's resignation as its chairman and named Jiang Zemin to replace him. With his resignation, Deng no longer held any formal positions within the party or government except chairman of the National Bridge Society and of the Song Qingling Foundation.

1990

January 1. The British government gave full British citizenship to 50,000 select Hong Kong residents, which gave them the right to emigrate to Britain. China contended that the action was interference in its internal affairs, since the ruling would remain in effect after 1997.

January 6. After the fall of the Romanian government on December 22, 1989, China placed its police force on alert to stave off possible Chinese demonstrations. Romania and its former president, Nicolae Ceaucescu, had long been allies of China.

January 11. The state of martial law in Beijing, passed during the political turmoil of the past spring, was lifted. The government announced that the country was stable and congratulated itself for countering the rebellious factions. A week later the government released 573 people who had been detained as a result of their participation in the protests.

February 1. To the consternation of the Chinese government, Tibet's Dalai Lama, who had been living in exile, was awarded the Nobel prize for peace. The government labeled the award "outside meddling" in China's internal affairs and an "attempt by international imperialism to break up China's sovereign territory."

February 16. The NPC finished its draft of the Hong Kong Basic Law. The draft and a meeting held later in April made provisions for the establishment of the Hong Kong Special Autonomous Region on 1 July 1997, the establishment of a governing body for Hong Kong, and the formation of a committee to implement the Basic Law.

April 4. A meeting of the Seventh NPC ended with the suggestion that the country should guard against the type of "peaceful evolution" that plagued Eastern Europe. The congress stressed the importance of economic and political stability. Leadership changes were made in light of Deng Xiaoping's retirement in November 1989. Jiang Zemin was formally named chairman of the CMC. The meeting also resulted in promulgation of further rules governing Sino-foreign joint ventures.

April 23. Li Peng, in his first major trip abroad since the 1989 demonstrations in Tiananmen Square, became the first Chinese premier to visit the Soviet Union since

1964. During the visit, leaders of the two countries signed six agreements concerning trade, scientific exchange, border issues, and periodic consultations.

May 1. Beijing decided to lift martial law in Tibet, citing increased stability since the 1989 riots. Jiang Zemin further promoted Beijing's interests in the region with a ten-day tour in July. During his visit, Jiang met with religious and political leaders and praised the region for its work in developing the economy.

May 25. After hiding at the U.S. embassy since the 1989 Tiananmen incident, dissident scientist Fang Lizhi was allowed to leave China. His deteriorating health was cited as the major reason for Fang's release. Fang had been accused by the government of inciting the spring 1989 protests.

June 11. General Secretary Jiang Zemin outlined China's position on reunification, asserting that China's policy toward Taiwan was to establish "one China, with two systems." Jiang's speech came amid growing support for democracy on Taiwan. The following May, Taiwan's president, Lee Teng-hui, presented his own ideas regarding reunification and promised an end to the state of civil war between Taiwan and the mainland.

June 19. Acting in his capacity as chairman of the CMC, Jiang Zemin signed three regulations regarding the internal management and training of the PLA. The regulations stipulated that the party would maintain absolute control over the army and that it supported the political strengthening of the army. The regulations followed similar action to ensure that the army remain loyal to the government, especially in the event of further political instability. The training regulations were designed to promote military-wide standardization.

September 22. The eleventh Asian Games opened in Beijing. Thirty-seven delegations, including one from Taiwan, participated in the events. The Chinese government hoped that its successful hosting of the Asian Games would help in the country's bid to host the 2000 Olympics.

November 7. China broke diplomatic ties with Nicaragua after the latter decided to establish concurrent ties with Taiwan. Earlier in the year, China broke off relations with Guinea-Bissau as a protest against that country's ties with Taiwan. Despite increased relations with Taiwan, China continued to assert itself as the only legitimate government of China and dismissed any third country's attempt to act otherwise.

November 29. Having stopped processing loan applications from the Chinese government after the Tiananmen Square demonstrations, officials at the ADB reactivated review of Chinese loan applications. The ADB move followed an earlier decision by the World Bank and the Group of Seven to lift "sanctions" imposed on China since 1989. The United States remained the only country to continue enforcing such sanctions, although Washing-ton maintained contact with Beijing throughout the period.

1991

January 17. After the Security Council voted its approval, UN forces conducted air attacks on Iraq in an attempt to make the country withdraw its forces from Kuwait. (Iraq invaded Kuwait in August 1990.) China abstained from the vote, thereby giving tacit approval to the exercises.

January-February. Trials were held for students arrested during the Tiananmen incident of 1989. Most were given lenient sentences except for those whom Beijing decided represented the core of the group working with foreign influences. Others implicated in the incident were eventually allowed to leave the country.

May 1. The price of grain and cooking oil was adjusted by order of the State Council for the first time in twenty-five years. The price of the two staples had been set by the government in order to keep food costs down for urban residents. The adjustment was said to have been the result of consecutive above-average grain harvests and state surpluses.

May-July. Floods ravaged southern China, causing an estimated 80 billion yuan in damages. The floods affected eighteen provinces and claimed an estimated 3,000 lives. International aid poured in to help China cope with the disaster.

October. The dissolution of the Soviet Union led to heightened security concerns among the Chinese leadership and a growing resolve to strengthen the economy and keep tight control over political reform in order to avoid what were seen as mistakes made by the Soviet leadership.

November. The State Council issued a white paper on China's human rights practices. The document defined the primary human right as subsistence and economic development. It emphasized that different interpretations of human rights exist in different countries, claimed that the fundamental condition of China's population had improved since 1949, and highlighted the fair treatment of minorities within China.

November 10. An official visit by the general secretary of the Vietnamese Communist Party, Do Muoi, ended in Beijing. The visit marked the normalization of Sino-Vietnamese relations. Vo Van Kiet accompanied Muoi on his trip, which was held at the invitation of General Secretary Jiang Zemin and Premier Li Peng. Border discussions with Vietnam had been held throughout the 1980s. The main hindrance to improved relations had been Soviet support for Vietnam and Vietnam's support of the Heng Samrin government in Cambodia. Vietnam had since declared its intention to withdraw troops from Cambodia.

December 15. China's first nuclear power plant, Qinshan station, began operation. Located in Zhejiang Province, the station was designed and produced entirely within China. It was expected to supply an estimated 1.5 billion kilowatts of energy per year and was hailed as a major step forward in China's nuclear capabilities.

December. China moved to recognize eleven states within the Commonwealth of Independent States (CIS) that formerly belonged to the Soviet Union, following disintegration of the Soviet Union the previous fall and establishment of the CIS on 8 December. The recognition came less than two years after China and the Soviet Union had re-established relations. In the following months, China would also normalize relations with Belarus and the Baltic states. To show China's desire for smooth relations with the newly formed states, the minister for foreign economic relations and trade, Li Lanqing, visited the Central Asian republics.

1992

January 13. Bao Tong, Zhao Ziyang's adviser and alleged conspirator during the Tiananmen demonstrations of 1989, was sentenced to ten years in prison for subversion. The case against Zhao, who had been removed from his posts and placed under house arrest but remained a party member, was still undecided. Beginning in late 1992, references to Zhao's activities began to appear in various Chinese newspapers.

January 14. The State Council and the Central Committee sponsored the Central Ethnic Affairs conference to strengthen "the solidarity among people of all nationalities."

January 19-21. Deng made a tour of southern China, paying special attention to the SEZs. The trip was seen as an attempt to garner support for his reform policies, which after Tiananmen had increasingly been criticized as causing more harm than good. During the tour, Deng extolled South China for its progress.

February 25. The NPC Standing Committee passed a law on territorial waters and contiguous areas to solidify China's claim to the Spratly Island chain in the South China Sea. Five other Southeast Asian countries—Malaysia, the Philippines, Vietnam, Brunei, and Indonesia—and Taiwan also had claims to some of the islands.

March 12. China formally acceded to the Nuclear Nonproliferation Treaty. First effective on March 5, 1970, the treaty stipulates that member states will not transfer nuclear devices to countries without nuclear arsenals or help such countries achieve nuclear capability. Although China always claimed to support the overall prohibition and complete destruction of nuclear weapons, the leadership had complained that the NPT was biased in favor of those states with large nuclear arsenals. China would later send assurances to U.S. secretary of state James Baker

that it also intended to follow the guidelines in the Missile Technology Control Regime (MTCR).

April 3. The NPC approved plans for the controversial Three Gorges dam on the Yangzi River, which would create the largest hydroelectric plant in the world. Because building the dam would necessitate flooding much of the land surrounding the river site and relocating almost a million people, environmental and other groups opposed its construction. The government successfully argued, however, that the benefits of centrally planned flood control and greater power-generating capacity outweighed the scheme's problems.

April 16. China sent 47 military observers and 400 military engineers to Cambodia to help fulfill the 1991 Paris Peace Agreement that laid the groundwork for that country's political development after the withdrawal of Vietnamese troops. The Chinese government claimed that the personnel would aid in building necessary infrastructure but were not sent specifically to be part of UN peacekeeping operations.

April. KPMG Peat Marwick and Arthur Andersen joined with Chinese accounting firms to open the first joint-venture accounting firms in China. The openings signaled China's willingness to begin accepting Western standards of accounting.

July 31. China officially joined the Universal Copyright Convention (UCC), which protects copyrights related to literary, artistic, and academic works. The Chinese delegation noted that in joining the convention, China was signaling its desire to promote international exchanges in literature, arts, and science. The decision to join the UCC was ratified at the 26th session of the Standing Committee of the Seventh NPC. China had passed a copyright law in 1990.

August 24. China and South Korea restored diplomatic relations more than forty years after they fought each other during the Korean War. The two countries reported that their new relations would facilitate economic exchanges and pave the way for joint ventures between them. The re-establishment of Sino-South Korean ties was a blow to both North Korea and Taiwan.

September. The State Price Administration lifted price controls on 593 items and materials, ranging from soda ash to electrical machinery. Without set prices, producers would be allowed to determine their own prices according to market conditions. With the latest actions, the number of commodities directly priced by the central government dropped from 737 at the end of 1991 to only 89. The action was described by the central government as indicative of its willingness to undergo further reforms and economic liberalization.

October 7. Hong Kong governor Christopher Patten, appointed in April 1992, announced plans to increase the voting rights of Hong Kong citizens before Hong Kong's return to China in 1997. Beijing soundly rejected Patten's plans and claimed that the "liberalization scheme" violated the Hong Kong Basic Law. If the scheme were allowed to take effect, two-thirds of the colonial legislature's members would be selected through direct or indirect elections, up from a level of about one-third at the time of Patten's proposal.

October. The fourteenth party congress adopted the principle of a "socialist market economic system" for China, thereby supporting Deng Xiaoping's economic reform program. In addition to electing new Politburo members who supported the reform agenda, the congress re-elected Jiang Zemin as general secretary and replaced almost half the Central Committee. During the proceedings, the Central Advisory Commission, established in 1982 to accommodate older party members and make room for younger leaders, was abolished. The 1982 party constitution was also amended to institutionalize the move toward reform.

December 19. Russian president Boris Yeltsin completed a trip to China during which he signed a joint declaration on border questions. Because of domestic concerns, Yeltsin had to curtail his trip and was not able to visit the SEZs.

1993

February 20. The Beijing-Kowloon Railway Construction Headquarters was established by the State Council to oversee the construction of a 1,550-mile railway between the Chinese capital and Hong Kong. Work on the project began soon after the formation of the headquarters, at an estimated cost of 20 billion yuan.

March 12. North Korea announced its intention to withdraw from the NPT because of demands made on it to open two sites for inspection by the IAEA. The IAEA suspected North Korea of maintaining hidden nuclear-processing capability, which it believed was for nonpeaceful purposes. As North Korea's closest ally, China was encouraged to persuade North Korea to abide by the inspections and rejoin the treaty. The event became China's first post-cold war test as a regional leader.

March. The first plenum of the Eighth NPC elected Jiang Zemin China's president. (Jiang was already chairman of the CCP Central Committee and of the Central Military Commission.) The following appointments were also made: Rong Yiren as vice president, Li Peng as premier of the State Council, and Qiao Shi as chairman of the NPC Standing Committee. In addition to the appointments, the congress supported "building socialism with Chinese characteristics," including adding elements of a market economy.

April 29. The first high-level talks between China and Taiwan ended in Singapore. The talks were conducted by representatives of two groups founded in 1991: Taiwan's Straits Exchange Foundation and China's Association for Relations Across the Taiwan Straits. The two groups signed agreements on trade and communications as well as on such logistical issues as meeting plans and notarization of documents and mail. Although Beijing tried to put forward a plan for the PRC's ultimate sovereignty over Taiwan, no major agreements were made regarding the formal status of the two vis-à-vis each other.

August 25. The second plenary session of the CCP Central Discipline Inspection Commission ended in Beijing, passing resolutions to step up anticorruption efforts within the country. Corruption among high-level cadres had been a focus of discussion for several years and was seen as one of the underlying causes of the student demonstrations in 1989. Several party members accused of abusing their privileges had been executed in an attempt to demonstrate the party's seriousness in combating the problem.

September 23. Wei Jingsheng was released from prison just prior to completing his fifteen-year prison term. Wei had articulated his ideas for a "fifth modernization"—democracy—in a series of articles that attacked the leadership as autocratic. His release was timed to coincide with the International Olympic Committee's deliberations over the site of the 2000 Olympic Games. Despite its efforts to promote an image of political stability and freedom, Beijing was not chosen to host the Olympic games. Wei was later detained again after having met with the U.S. assistant secretary of state for human rights in April 1994.

November. The third volume of Deng Xiaoping's *Selected Works* was published, signaling an effort to codify Deng's reform agenda. The volume also sought to clarify Deng's role in the Tiananmen Square crackdown of 1989.

The third plenum of the Fourteenth Central Committee adopted plans to establish a "socialist market system." The plenum appeared to be a victory for the reformers within the party. The proposals adopted at the plenum suggested a gradual transformation of the economy into one based primarily on market mechanisms.

Jiang Zemin went to the United States to attend an Asia Pacific Economic Cooperation (APEC) meeting in Seattle. Jiang's meeting with U.S. president Bill Clinton was the highest-ranking meeting between Chinese and U.S. officials since the Tiananmen incident in 1989. The Seattle talks were held in conjunction with the APEC ministerial meeting and focused mainly on economic issues.

The Bank of China announced that as of January 1, 1994, China would eliminate the separate foreign exchange currency. Instead, all transactions would take place using the yuan. A new exchange rate would be formulated and the yuan would eventually become totally convertible in foreign exchange markets.

December 26. The hundredth anniversary of Mao Zedong's birth was celebrated throughout China, amid a renewal of public interest in Mao.

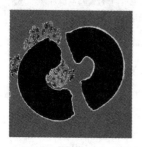

DOCUMENTS

Selections from the "Little Red Book" of Quotations from Chairman Mao

The "Little Red Book" of quotations from Chairman Mao Zedong, published at the outset of the Cultural Revolution, was carried and read by millions of Chinese students, peasants, workers, and Red Guards. The pages, about 3 1/2" by 5" in size, were bound by a bright red plastic cover with the title embossed in it. With a red ribbon attached as a marker, the 311-page booklet closely resembles a common prayer book or missal. (Unless otherwise stated, the source of each quotation is the first English edition of the book or pamphlet cited as published by the Foreign Languages Press, Beijing.)

I. The Communist Party

The force at the core leading our cause forward is the Chinese Communist Party. The theoretical basis guiding our thinking is Marxism-Leninism.

> Opening address at the first session of the First National People's Congress of the People's Republic of China (September 15, 1954).

If there is to be revolution, there must be a revolutionary party. Without a revolutionary party, without a party built on the Marxist-Leninist revolutionary theory and in the Marxist-Leninist revolutionary style, it is impossible to lead the working class and the broad masses of the people in defeating imperialism and its running dogs.

> "Revolutionary Forces of the World Unite, Fight Against Imperialist Aggression!" (November 1948), *Selected Works*, Vol. 4, p. 284.

Without the efforts of the Chinese Communist Party, without the Chinese Communists as the mainstay of the Chinese people, China can never achieve independence and liberation, or industrialization and the modernization of her agriculture.

> "On Coalition Government" (April 24, 1945), *Selected Works*, Vol. 3, p. 318.

The Chinese Communist Party is the core of leadership of the whole Chinese people. Without this core, the cause of socialism cannot be victorious.

> Talk at the general reception for the delegates to the Third National Congress of the New-Democratic Youth League of China (May 25, 1957).

A well-disciplined party armed with the theory of Marxism-Leninism, using the method of self-criticism and linked with the masses of the people; an army under the leadership of such a party; a united front of all revolutionary classes and all revolutionary groups under the leadership of such a party—these are the three main weapons with which we have defeated the enemy.

> "On the People's Democratic Dictatorship" (June 30, 1949), *Selected Works*, Vol. 4, p. 422.

We must have faith in the masses and we must have faith in the party. These are two cardinal principles. If we doubt these principles, we shall accomplish nothing.

> *On the Question of Agricultural Cooperation* (July 31, 1955), 3d ed., p. 7.

Armed with Marxist-Leninist theory and ideology, the Communist Party of China has brought a new style of work to the Chinese people, a style of work that essentially entails integrating theory with practice, forging close links with the masses and practicing self-criticism.

> "On Coalition Government" (April 24, 1945), *Selected Works*, Vol. 3, p. 314.

No political party can possibly lead a great revolutionary movement to victory unless it possesses revolutionary theory and a knowledge of history and has a profound grasp of the practical movement.

"The Role of the Chinese Communist Party in the National War" (October 1938), *Selected Works,* Vol. 2, p. 208.

As we used to say, the rectification movement is "a widespread movement of Marxist education." Rectification means the whole party studying Marxism through criticism and self-criticism. We can certainly learn more about Marxism in the course of the rectification movement.

Speech at the Chinese Communist Party's National Conference on Propaganda Work (March 12, 1957), 1st pocket ed., p. 14.

It is an arduous task to ensure a better life for the several hundred million people of China and to build our economically and culturally backward country into a prosperous and powerful one with a high level of culture. And it is precisely in order to be able to shoulder this task more competently and work better together with all non-party people who are actuated by high ideals and determined to institute reforms that we must conduct rectification movements both now and in the future, and constantly rid ourselves of whatever is wrong.

Ibid., pp. 15-16.

Policy is the starting point of all the practical actions of a revolutionary party, and manifests itself in the process and the end result of that party's actions. A revolutionary party is carrying out a policy whenever it takes any action. If it is not carrying out a correct policy, it is carrying out a wrong policy; if it is not carrying out a given policy consciously, it is doing so blindly. What we call experience is the process and the end result of carrying out a policy. Only through the practice of the people, that is, through experience, can we verify whether a policy is correct or wrong and determine to what extent it is correct or wrong. But people's practice, especially the practice of a revolutionary party and the revolutionary masses, cannot but be bound up with one policy or another. Therefore, before any action is taken, we must explain the policy, which we have formulated in the light of the given circumstances, to party members and to the masses. Otherwise, party members and the masses will depart from the guidance of our policy, act blindly and carry out a wrong policy.

"On the Policy Concerning Industry and Commerce" (February 27, 1948), *Selected Works,* Vol. 4, pp. 204-205.

Our party has laid down the general line and general policy of the Chinese revolution as well as various specific lines for work and specific policies. However, while many comrades remember our party's specific lines for work and specific policies, they often forget its general line and general policy. If we actually forget the party's general line and general policy, then we shall be blind, half-baked, muddle-headed revolutionaries, and when we carry out a specific line for work and a specific policy, we shall lose our bearings and vacillate now to the left and now to the right, and the work will suffer.

"Speech at a Conference of Cadres in the Shansi-Suiyuan Liberated Area" (April 1, 1948), *Selected Works,* Vol. 4, p. 238.

Policy and tactics are the life of the party; leading comrades at all levels must give them full attention and must never on any account be negligent.

"A Circular on the Situation" (March 20, 1948), *Selected Works,* Vol. 4, p. 220.

II. Classes and Class Struggle

Classes struggle, some classes triumph, others are eliminated. Such is history, such is the history of civilization for thousands of years. To interpret history from this viewpoint is historical materialism; standing in opposition to this viewpoint is historical idealism.

"Cast Away Illusions. Prepare for Struggle" (August 14, 1949), *Selected Works,* Vol. 4, p. 428.

In class society everyone lives as a member of a particular class, and every kind of thinking, without exception, is stamped with the brand of a class.

"On Practice" (July 1937), *Selected Works,* Vol. 1, p. 296.

Changes in society are due chiefly to the development of the internal contradictions in society, that is, the contradiction between the productive forces and the relations of production, the contradiction between classes and the contradiction between the old and the new; it is the development of these contradictions that pushes society forward and gives the impetus for the supersession of the old society by the new.

"On Contradiction" (August 1937), *Selected Works,* Vol. 1, p. 314.

The ruthless economic exploitation and political oppression of the peasants by the landlord class forced them into numerous uprisings against its rule. ... It was the class struggles of the peasants, the peasant uprisings and peasant wars that constituted the real motive force of historical development in Chinese feudal society.

"The Chinese Revolution and the Chinese Communist Party" (December 1939), *Selected Works,* Vol. 2, p. 308.

In the final analysis, national struggle is a matter of class struggle. Among the whites in the United States it is only the reactionary ruling circles who oppress the black people. They can in no way represent the workers, farmers, revolutionary intellectuals and other enlightened persons who comprise the overwhelming majority of the white people.

"Statement Supporting the American Negroes in Their Just Struggle Against Racial Discrimination by U.S. Imperialism" (August 8, 1963), *People of the World, Unite and Defeat the U.S. Aggressors and All Their Lackeys,* 2d ed., pp. 3-4.

It is up to us to organize the people. As for the reactionaries in China, it is up to us to organize the people to overthrow them. Everything reactionary is the same; if you don't hit it, it won't fall. This is also like sweeping the floor; as a rule, where the broom does not reach, the dust will not vanish of itself.

"The Situation and Our Policy After the Victory in the War of Resistance Against Japan" (August 13, 1945), *Selected Works,* Vol. 4, p. 19.

The enemy will not perish of himself. Neither the Chinese reactionaries nor the aggressive forces of U.S. imperialism in China will step down from the stage of history of their own accord.

"Carry the Revolution Through to the End" (December 30, 1948), *Selected Works,* Vol. 4, p. 301.

A revolution is not a dinner party, or writing an essay, or painting a picture, or doing embroidery; it cannot be so refined, so leisurely and gentle, so temperate, kind, courteous, restrained and magnanimous. A revolution is an insurrection, an act of violence by which one class overthrows another.

"Report on an Investigation of the Peasant Movement in Hunan" (March 1927), *Selected Works,* Vol. 1, p. 28.

Chiang Kai-shek always tries to wrest every ounce of power and every ounce of gain from the people. And we? Our policy is to give him tit for tat and to fight for every inch of land. We act after his fashion. He always tries to impose war on the people, one sword in his left hand and another in his right. We take up swords, too, following his example. ... As Chiang Kai-shek is now sharpening his swords, we must sharpen ours too.

"The Situation and Our Policy After the Victory in

the War of Resistance Against Japan" (August 13, 1945), *Selected Works,* Vol. 4, pp. 14-15.

Who are our enemies? Who are our friends? This is a question of the first importance for the revolution. The basic reason why all previous revolutionary struggles in China achieved so little was their failure to unite with real friends in order to attack real enemies. A revolutionary party is the guide of the masses, and no revolution ever succeeds when the revolutionary party leads them astray. To ensure that we will definitely achieve success in our revolution and will not lead the masses astray, we must pay attention to uniting with our real friends in order to attack our real enemies. To distinguish real friends from real enemies, we must make a general analysis of the economic status of the various classes in Chinese society and of their respective attitudes toward the revolution.

"Analysis of the Classes in Chinese Society" (March 1926), *Selected Works,* Vol. 1, p. 13.

Our enemies are all those in league with imperialism—the warlords, the bureaucrats, the comprador class, the big landlord class and the reactionary section of the intelligentsia attached to them. The leading force in our revolution is the industrial proletariat. Our closest friends are the entire semi-proletariat and petty bourgeoisie. As for the vacillating middle bourgeoisie, their right wing may become our enemy and their left wing may become our friend—but we must be constantly on our guard and not let them create confusion within our ranks.

Ibid., p. 19.

Whoever sides with the revolutionary people is a revolutionary. Whoever sides with imperialism, feudalism and bureaucrat-capitalism is a counter-revolutionary. Whoever sides with the revolutionary people in words only but acts otherwise is a revolutionary in speech. Whoever sides with the revolutionary people in deed as well as in word is a revolutionary in the full sense.

Closing speech at the Second Session of the First National Committee of the Chinese People's Political Consultative Conference (June 23, 1950).

I hold that it is bad as far as we are concerned if a person, a political party, an army or a school is not attacked by the enemy, for in that case it would definitely mean that we have sunk to the level of the enemy. It is good if we are attacked by the enemy, since it proves that we have drawn a clear line of demarcation between the enemy and ourselves. It is still better if the enemy attacks us wildly and paints us as utterly black and without a single virtue; it demonstrates that we have not only drawn a clear line of demarcation between the enemy and ourselves but achieved a great deal in our work.

> *To Be Attacked by the Enemy Is Not a Bad Thing But a Good Thing* (May 26, 1939), 1st pocket ed., p. 2.

We should support whatever the enemy opposes and oppose whatever the enemy supports.

> "Interview with Three Correspondents from the Central News Agency, the *Sao Tang Pao* and the *Hsin Min Pao*" (September 16, 1939), *Selected Works,* Vol. 2, p. 272.

Our stand is that of the proletariat and of the masses. For members of the Communist Party, this means keeping to the stand of the party, keeping to party spirit and party policy.

> "Talks at the Yan'an Forum on Literature and Art" (May 1942), *Selected Works,* Vol. 3, p. 70.

After the enemies with guns have been wiped out, there will still be enemies without guns; they are bound to struggle desperately against us, and we must never regard these enemies lightly. If we do not now raise and understand the problem in this way, we shall commit the gravest mistakes.

> "Report to the Second Plenum of the Seventh Central Committee of the Communist Party of China" (March 5, 1949), *Selected Works,* Vol. 4, p. 364.

1972 Shanghai Communiqué

At the conclusion of President Richard Nixon's historic trip to China in February 1972, the United States and China issued a joint communiqué in Shanghai. The communiqué addressed the common goals and essential differences remaining between the two countries, especially with regard to the question of Taiwan. The full text of the communiqué follows.

President Richard Nixon of the United States of America visited the People's Republic of China at the invitation of Premier Chou [Zhou] Enlai of the People's Republic of China from February 21 to February 28, 1972. Accompanying the President were Mrs. Nixon, U.S. Secretary of State William Rogers, Assistant to the President Dr. Henry Kissinger, and other American officials.

President Nixon met with Chairman Mao [Zedong] of the Communist Party of China on February 21. The two leaders had a serious and frank exchange of views on Sino-U.S. relations and world affairs.

During the visit, extensive, earnest and frank discussions were held between President Nixon and Premier Chou [Zhou] Enlai on the normalization of relations between the United States of America and the People's Republic of China, as well as on other matters of interest to both sides. In addition, Secretary of State William Rogers and Foreign Minister Chi Peng-fei [Ji Pengfei] held talks in the same spirit.

President Nixon and his party visited Peking [Beijing] and viewed cultural, industrial and agricultural sites, and they also toured Hangchow [Hangzhou] and Shanghai where, continuing discussions with Chinese leaders, they viewed similar places of interest.

The leaders of the People's Republic of China and the United States of America found it beneficial to have this opportunity, after so many years without contact, to present candidly to one another their views on a variety of issues. They reviewed the international situation in which important changes and great upheavals are taking place and expounded their respective positions and attitudes.

The U.S. side stated: Peace in Asia and peace in the world requires efforts both to reduce immediate tensions and to eliminate the basic causes of conflict. The United States will work for a just and secure peace; just, because it fulfills the aspirations of peoples and nations for freedom and progress; secure, because it removes the danger of foreign aggression. The United States supports individual freedom and social progress for all the peoples of the world, free of outside pressure or intervention. The United States believes that the effort to reduce tensions is served by improving communication between countries that have different ideologies so as to lessen the risks of confrontation through accident, miscalculation or misunderstanding. Countries should treat each other with mutual respect and be willing to compete peacefully, letting performance be the ultimate judge. No country should claim infallibility and each country should be prepared to reexamine its own attitudes for the common good. The United States stressed that the peoples of Indochina should be allowed to determine their destiny without outside intervention; its constant primary objective has been a negotiated solution; the eight-point proposal put forward by the Republic of Vietnam and the United States on January 27, 1972, represents a basis for the attainment of that objective; in the absence of a negotiated settlement the United States envisages the ultimate withdrawal of all U.S. forces from the region consistent with the aim of self-determination for each country of Indochina. The United States will maintain its close ties with and support for the Republic of Korea; the United States will support efforts of the Republic of Korea to seek a relaxation of tension and increased communication in the Korean peninsula. The United States places the highest value on its friendly relations with Japan; it will continue to develop the existing close bonds. Consistent with the United Nations Security Council Resolution of December 21, 1971, the United States favors the continuation of the ceasefire between India and Pakistan and the withdrawal of all military forces to within their own territories and to their own sides of the ceasefire line in Jammu and Kashmir; the United States supports the right of the peoples of South Asia to shape their own future in peace, free of military threat, and without having the area become the subject of great power rivalry.

The Chinese side stated: Wherever there is oppression, there is resistance. Countries want independence, nations want liberation and the people want revolution—this has become the irresistible trend of history. All nations, big or small, should be equal; big nations should not bully the small and strong nations should not bully the weak. China will never be a superpower and it opposes hegemony and power politics of any kind. The Chinese side stated that it firmly supports the struggles of all the oppressed people and nations for freedom and liberation and that the people of all countries have the right to choose their social systems according to their own wishes and the right to safeguard the independence, sovereignty and territorial integrity of their own countries and oppose foreign aggression, interference, control and subversion. All foreign troops should be withdrawn to their own countries.

The Chinese side expressed its firm support to the peoples of Vietnam, Laos and Cambodia in their efforts for the attainment of their goal and its firm support to the seven-point proposal of the Provisional Revolutionary Government of the Republic of South Vietnam and the elaboration of February this year on the two key problems in the proposal, and to the Joint Declaration of the Summit Conference of the Indochinese Peoples. It firmly supports the eight-point program for the peaceful unification of Korea put forward by the Government of the Democratic People's Republic of Korea on April 12, 1971, and the stand for the abolition of the "U.N. Commission for the Unification and Rehabilitation of Korea." It firmly opposes the revival and outward expansion of Japanese militarism and firmly supports the Japanese people's desire to build an independent, democratic, peaceful and neutral Japan. It firmly maintains that India and Pakistan should, in accordance with the United Nations resolutions on the India-Pakistan question, immediately withdraw all their forces to their respective territories and to their own sides of the ceasefire line in Jammu and Kashmir and firmly supports the Pakistan Government and people in their struggle to preserve their independence and sovereignty and the people of Jammu and Kashmir in their struggle for the right of self-determination.

There are essential differences between China and the United States in their social systems and foreign policies. However, the two sides agreed that countries, regardless of their social systems, should conduct their relations on the principles of respect for the sovereignty and territorial integrity of all states, nonaggression against other states,

noninterference in the internal affairs of other states, equality and mutual benefit, and peaceful coexistence. International disputes should be settled on this basis, without resorting to the use or threat of force. The United States and the People's Republic of China are prepared to apply these principles to their mutual relations.

With these principles of international relations in mind the two sides stated that:

• progress toward the normalization of relations between China and the United States is in the interests of all countries;
• both wish to reduce the danger of international military conflict;
• neither should seek hegemony in the Asia-Pacific region and each is opposed to efforts by any other country or group of countries to establish such hegemony; and
• neither is prepared to negotiate on behalf of any third party or to enter into agreements or understandings with the other directed at other states.

Both sides are of the view that it would be against the interests of the peoples of the world for any major country to collude with another against other countries, or for major countries to divide up the world into spheres of interest.

The two sides reviewed the longstanding serious disputes between China and the United States. The Chinese reaffirmed their position: The Taiwan question is the crucial question obstructing the normalization of relations between China and the United States; the Government of the People's Republic of China is the sole legal government of China; Taiwan is a province of China which has long been returned to the motherland; the liberation of Taiwan is China's internal affair in which no other country has the right to interfere; and all U.S. forces and military installations must be withdrawn from Taiwan. The Chinese Government firmly opposes any activities which aim at the creation of "one China, one Taiwan," "one China, two governments," "two Chinas," an "independent Taiwan" or advocate that "the status of Taiwan remains to be determined."

The U.S. side declared: The United States acknowledges that all Chinese on either side of the Taiwan Strait maintain there is but one China and that Taiwan is a part of China. The United States Government does not challenge that position. It reaffirms its interest in a peaceful settlement of the Taiwan question by the Chinese themselves. With this prospect in mind, it affirms the ultimate objective of the withdrawal of all U.S. forces and military installations from Taiwan. In the meantime, it will progressively reduce its forces and military installations on Taiwan as the tension in the area diminishes.

The two sides agreed that it is desirable to broaden the understanding between the two peoples. To this end, they discussed specific areas in such fields as science, technology, culture, sports and journalism, in which people-to-people contacts and exchanges would be mutually beneficial. Each side undertakes to facilitate the further development of such contacts and exchanges.

Both sides view bilateral trade as another area from which mutual benefit can be derived, and agreed that economic relations based on equality and mutual benefit are in the interest of the peoples of the two countries. They agree to facilitate the progressive development of trade between their two countries.

The two sides agreed that they will stay in contact through various channels, including the sending of a senior U.S. representative to Peking [Beijing] from time to time for concrete consultations to further the normalization of relations between the two countries and continue to exchange views on issues of common interest.

The two sides expressed the hope that the gains achieved during this visit would open up new prospects for the relations between the two countries. They believe that the normalization of relations between the two countries is not only in the interest of the Chinese and American peoples but also contributes to the relaxation of tension in Asia and the world.

President Nixon, Mrs. Nixon and the American party expressed their appreciation for the gracious hospitality shown them by the Government and people of the People's Republic of China.

The Four Modernizations

As China emerged from the late Mao years of political upheaval, its leaders set ambitious economic goals in an attempt to make up for lost time. These were embodied in Hua Guofeng's Ten-Year Plan (1976 to 1985), as well as in the goal of achieving the Four Modernizations—in agriculture, industry, science and technology, and national defense—by the year 2000. (The Four Modernizations were first proposed by Premier Zhou Enlai in the 1960s but became the banner of the early Deng Xiaoping era beginning in 1978.) Hua Guofeng summarized these lofty goals in the following speech delivered to the Fifth National People's Congress on February 26, 1978, entitled "Speed up Socialist Economic Construction."

In order to make China a modern, powerful socialist country by the end of the century, we must work and fight hard in the political, economic, cultural, military and diplomatic spheres, but in the final analysis what is of decisive importance is the rapid development of our socialist economy.

At the Third National People's Congress and again at the Fourth,[1] Premier Chou [Zhou Enlai], acting on Chairman Mao's instructions, put forward a grand concept for the development of our national economy which calls for the all-round modernization of agriculture, industry, national defense and science and technology by the end of the century so that our economy can take its place in the front ranks of the world. By the end of this century, the output per unit of major agricultural products is expected to reach or surpass advanced world levels and the output of major industrial products to approach, equal or outstrip that of the most developed capitalist countries. In agricultural production, the highest possible degree of mechanization, electrification and irrigation will be achieved. There will be automation in the main industrial processes, a major increase in rapid transport and communications services and a considerable rise in labor productivity. We must apply the results of modern science and technology on a broad scale, make extensive use of new materials and sources of energy, and modernize our major products and the processes of production. Our economic and technical norms must approach, equal or surpass advanced world levels. As our social productive forces become highly developed, our socialist relations of production will be further improved and perfected, the dictatorship of the proletariat in our country consolidated, our national defense strengthened, and our people's material well-being and cultural life substantially enriched. By then, China will have a new look and stand unshakably in the East as a modern, powerful socialist country.

The ten years from 1976 to 1985 are crucial for accomplishing these gigantic tasks. In the summer of 1975, the State Council held a meeting to exchange views on a prospective long-term plan. On the basis of a mass of material furnished by investigation and study, it worked out a draft outline of a ten-year plan for the development of our economy. The outline was discussed and approved by the Political Bureau. The "Gang of Four"[2] attacked the State Council meeting as "the source of the Right deviationist wind" and labeled the outline a "revisionist document." This was just plain slander and vilification. After the gang's downfall, the State Council revised and supplemented the outline in the light of China's fine political and economic situation and in accordance with the ardent desire of the whole nation to accelerate the Four Modernizations. The draft outline of the plan is now submitted to you for consideration.

According to the plan, in the space of ten years we are to lay a solid foundation for agriculture, achieve at least 85 percent mechanization in all major processes of farmwork, see to it that for each member of the rural population there is one mu[3] of farmland with guaranteed stable high yields irrespective of drought or waterlogging and attain a relatively high level in agriculture, forestry, animal husbandry, sideline production and fisheries. The plan calls for the growth of light industry, which should turn out an abundance of first-rate, attractive and reasonably priced goods with a considerable increase in per capita consumption. Construction of an advanced heavy industry is envisaged, with the metallurgical, fuel, power and machine-building industries to be further developed through the adoption of new techniques, with iron and steel, coal, crude oil and electricity in the world's front ranks in terms of output, and with much more developed petrochemical, electronics and other new industries. We will build transport and communications and postal and telecommunications networks big enough to meet growing industrial and agricultural needs, with most of our locomotives electrified or dieselized and with road, inland water and air transport and ocean shipping very much expanded. With the completion of an independent and fairly comprehensive industrial complex and economic system for the whole country, we shall in the main have built up a regional economic system in each of the six major regions, that is, the southwest, the northwest, the central south, the east, the north and northeast China, and turned our interior into a powerful, strategic rear base.

According to the ten-year plan, by 1985, we are to produce 400 billion kilograms of grain (440 million tons) and 60 million tons of steel. In each of the eight years from 1978 to 1985, the value of agricultural output is to increase by 4 to 5 percent and of industrial output by over 10 percent. The increase in our country's output of major industrial products in the eight years will far exceed that in the past 28 years. In these eight years, state revenues and investments budgeted for capital construction will both be equivalent to the total for the past 28 years. As fellow Deputies have reviewed the various economic targets in the ten-year plan, there is no need to list them now. The accomplishment of the ten-year plan will bring about tremendous economic and technological changes and provide the country with a much more solid material base, and, given another period of hard work over three more five-year plans, the stage will be set for China to take its place in the front ranks of the world economy.

The tasks set in the ten-year plan and the envisaged development over 23 years are gigantic, but the job can be done. We have a socialist system with its advantages which can ensure a rapid growth of the productive forces. Since the Cultural Revolution, and especially since the great struggle to expose and criticize the "Gang of Four," Chairman Mao's revolutionary line is better understood by the broadest masses, who are filled with a growing enthusiasm for socialism. We have a large population and abundant natural resources, and after 20-odd years of construction we have established a fairly solid material base and accumulated a rich store of experience, negative as well as positive. We have all the preconditions for speeding up economic growth. Of course, there will be difficulties ahead and arduous efforts are needed to surmount them. But there is no reason at all to be apathetic—to underestimate the favorable conditions, be pessimistic and think that this or that is impossible. In the

11 years from 1966 to 1976, despite serious interference and sabotage by Liu Shao-chi [Liu Shaoqi], Lin Piao [Lin Biao] and particularly the "Gang of Four," grain output still registered an annual increase of over 4.3 percent in a third of the provinces, municipalities and autonomous regions, with a maximum of 5.5 percent, and the value of industrial output went up annually by more than 12 percent likewise in a third of the provinces, municipalities and autonomous regions, with a maximum of 18.5 percent. With the smashing of the "Gang of Four," we believe that it is entirely possible for all the provinces, municipalities and autonomous regions to attain or exceed these rates of increase through their efforts. We are sure this splendid plan of ours can be fulfilled. . . .

To turn the plan into reality, we must also adopt effective measures and strive to solve a number of problems bearing on our whole economy.

First. Mobilize the Whole Nation and Go in for Agriculture in a Big Way.

Agriculture is the foundation of the national economy. If agriculture does not develop faster, there will be no upswing in our industry and economy as a whole, and even if there is a temporary upswing, a decline will follow, and there will be really serious trouble in the event of major natural calamities. We must have a clear understanding of this. Predominantly agricultural provinces must make an effort to develop agriculture, and predominantly industrial provinces must make still greater efforts. All trades and professions must do their best to support and serve agriculture. . . .

Second. Speed Up the Development of the Basic Industries and Give Full Scope to the Leading Role of Industry.

As the economy becomes modernized, the leading role of industry, and especially that of the basic industries, becomes more and more prominent. We must take steel as the key link, strengthen the basic industries and exert a special effort to step up the development of the power, fuel and raw and semi-finished materials industries and transport and communications. Only thus can we give strong support to agriculture, rapidly expand light industry and substantially strengthen the national defense industries.

In developing the basic industries, we must endeavor to strengthen our work in geology and in the opening up of new mines so that geological surveying and the mining industry will meet the needs of high-speed economic construction.

In developing the basic industries, we must be good at tapping the potential of the existing enterprises and at renovating and transforming them as well as at integrating this task with the building of new enterprises. In the next eight years, and especially in the next three years, our existing enterprises must be the foundation for the growth of production. We must make full use of existing equipment, make sure that complete sets of equipment are available, introduce technical transformation in a planned way and carry out extensive coordination between specialized departments. This will gain us time and speed and will save on investment. Meanwhile, the state plans to build or complete 120 large-scale projects, including ten iron and steel complexes, nine nonferrous metal complexes, eight coal mines, ten oil and gas fields, 30 power stations, six new trunk railways and five key harbors. The completion of these projects added to the existing industrial foundation will provide China with 14 fairly strong and fairly rationally located industrial bases. This will be decisive in changing the backward state of our basic industries. . . .

Third. Do a Good Job in Commerce and Develop Foreign Trade.

Socialist commerce is a bridge that links industry with agriculture, urban areas with rural areas and production with consumption. It is essential to make a success of commerce, for it promotes the rapid growth of the economy, consolidates the worker-peasant alliance and serves to meet the people's daily needs. . . . We should organize the exchange of industrial goods with agricultural products well, stimulate the interchange of urban and rural products, provide the markets with adequate supplies, appropriately expand commercial networks or centers, increase the variety of goods on the market, and improve the quality of service to customers. We should tighten price and market controls and deal resolute blows to speculation and profiteering.

There should be a big increase in foreign trade. In our export trade, attention should be given both to bulk exports and exports in small quantities. While expanding the export of agricultural and sideline products, we should raise the ratio of industrial and mineral products in our exports. We should build a number of bases for supplying industrial and mineral products and agricultural and sideline products for export. We should earnestly sum up our experience in foreign trade and, in accordance with the principle of equality and mutual benefit, handle our business transactions flexibly and successfully.

Fourth. Encourage Socialist Labor Emulation and Be Active in Technical Innovation and Technical Revolution.

The masses have a vast reservoir of enthusiasm for socialism. Socialist labor emulation is a good and important method of bringing the initiative and creativeness of the people into full play and of achieving greater, faster, better and more economical results in developing the economy. Each and every locality, trade, enterprise, establishment and rural commune and production brigade should fully mobilize the masses and bring about an upsurge in emulating, learning from, catching up with and

overtaking the advanced units, and helping the less advanced units. . . .

For our economy to develop at high speed, we must break free from conventions and use advanced techniques as much as possible. The broad masses have inexhaustible creative power and are fully capable of making a great leap forward in science and technology by relying on their own strength. Our workers, peasants and intellectuals should be creative and dauntless; they should dare to think, dare to speak out and dare to act and should unfold a widespread movement for technical innovation and technical revolution in urban and rural areas, coming up with new and better ways to do things and turning their talents to full account. All localities and departments must keep abreast of current developments in technology at home and abroad, work out plans and measures for employing and popularizing new techniques, strive to learn advanced science and technology, domestic and foreign, and must not get struck in a groove and rest content with old practices. We must increase technical exchanges and fight against the rotten bourgeois style of refusing to share information. Commendations and proper awards should be given to those units that have achieved marked successes in adopting new techniques, developing new technologies and turning out new products as well as to those collectives and individuals who have made inventions.

Fifth. Strengthen Unified Planning and Give Full Play to the Initiative of Both the Central and the Local Authorities.

Planned economy is a basic feature of the socialist economy. We must resolutely put an end to the anarchy resulting from the interference and sabotage of the "Gang of Four" and bring all economic undertakings into the orbit of planned, proportionate development. In formulating plans, we must follow the mass line, and both the central departments and the localities should do more investigation and study, endeavor to strike an overall balance, make the plans bold as well as sound and allocate manpower, material and money where they are most needed so that the various branches of the economy develop in coordination. A strict system of personal responsibility must be set up at all levels, from the departments under the State Council to the provinces, municipalities and autonomous regions right down to the grassroots units, so that each leading cadre has his clear-cut responsibilities and nothing is neglected. Fulfillment of the state plan will thus be effectively ensured. We must check up regularly on how the localities, departments and grass-roots units are carrying out their plans. We shall commend those who fulfill their plans satisfactorily and shall hold the leading cadres responsible where the plan is not fulfilled because of their poor work and bureaucracy. In the case of serious failures necessary disciplinary action will be taken. . . .

Sixth. Uphold the Principle of "From Each According to His Ability, to Each According to His Work" and Steadily Improve the Livelihood of the People.

Throughout the historical period of socialism, we must uphold the principles of "He who does not work, neither shall he eat" and "from each according to his ability, to each according to his work." In applying them we must firmly put proletarian politics in command, strengthen ideological and political work and teach and encourage everybody to cultivate the communist attitude towards labor and to serve the people wholeheartedly. With regard to distribution, while we should avoid a wide wage spread, we must also oppose equalitarianism and apply the principle of more pay for more work and less pay for less work. The enthusiasm of the masses cannot be aroused if no distinction is made between those who do more work and those who do less, between those who do a good job and those who do a poor one, and between those who work and those who don't. All people's communes and production brigades must seriously apply the system of fixed production quotas and calculation of work-points on the basis of work done and must enforce the principle of equal pay for equal work irrespective of sex. The staff and workers of state enterprises should be paid primarily on a time-rate basis with piecework playing a secondary role, and with additional bonuses. There should be pecuniary allowances for jobs requiring higher labor intensity or performed under worse working conditions. In socialist labor emulation, moral encouragement and material reward must go hand in hand, with emphasis on the former. As regards the reform of the wage system, the relevant departments under the State Council should, together with the local authorities, make conscientious investigation and study, sum up experience, canvass the opinions of the masses and then submit a draft plan based on overall consideration to the central authorities for approval before it is gradually implemented. . . .

We are not yet acquainted with many of the problems that crop up in economic construction. In particular, in many respects modern production remains an unknown kingdom of necessity to us. In accordance with Chairman Mao's instructions, the leading cadres at all levels must use their brains and assiduously study Marxism-Leninism, economics, production management and science and technology so as to "become expert in political and economic work on the basis of a higher level of Marxism-Leninism." We must study hard and work well, sum up experience, attain a better grasp of the laws governing socialist economic construction, master the art of guiding and organizing modern production, raise the level of economic management and do our economic work in an ever more meticulous, thoroughgoing, practical and scientific way, thus propelling the national economy forward at high speed. . . .

1. December 21, 1964, to January 5, 1965, and January 13-17, 1974.
2. Zhang Chunqiao, Yao Wenyuan, Jiang Qing, and Wang Hongwen.
3. One-third of an acre.

Normalization of U.S.-China Relations

The normalization of United States-China relations, announced in December 1978 after six months of intensive negotiations, heralded new foreign policy flexibility on both sides. Following are the texts of President Jimmy Carter's December 15, 1978, address, as delivered, announcing establishment of full diplomatic relations between the United States and the People's Republic of China; a U.S. statement released December 15; a People's Republic of China statement read by Chairman Hua Guofeng December 15; and an unofficial translation of a statement made by Nationalist Chinese president Chiang Ching-kuo December 16, 1978.

Carter's Speech

Good evening.

I would like to read a joint communiqué which is being simultaneously issued in [Beijing] at this very moment by the leaders of the People's Republic of China:

"Joint Communiqué on the Establishment of Diplomatic Relations Between the United States of America and the People's Republic of China, January 1, 1979:

"The United States of America and the People's Republic of China have agreed to recognize each other and to establish diplomatic relations as of January 1st, 1979.

"The United States recognizes the Government of the People's Republic of China as the sole legal government of China. Within this context, the people of the United States will maintain cultural, commercial and other unofficial relations with the people of Taiwan.

"The United States of America and the People's Republic of China reaffirm the principles agreed on by the two sides in the Shanghai communiqué of 1972 and emphasize once again that:

"—Both sides wish to reduce the danger of international military conflict.

"—Neither should seek hegemony [that is, a dominance of one nation over the other] in the Asia-Pacific region or in any other region of the world and each is opposed to efforts by any other country or group of countries to establish such hegemony.

"—Neither is prepared to negotiate on behalf of any other third party or to enter into agreements or understandings with the other directed at other states.

"—The Government of the United States of America acknowledges the Chinese position that there is but one China and Taiwan is part of China.

"—Both believe that normalization of Sino-American relations is not only in the interest of the Chinese and American peoples but also contributes to the cause of peace in Asia and in the world.

"—The United States of America and the People's Republic of China will exchange Ambassadors and establish embassies on March 1, 1979."

Yesterday, our country and the People's Republic of China reached this final historic agreement.

On January 1, 1979, a little more than two weeks from now, our two governments will implement full normalization of diplomatic relations.

As a nation of gifted people who comprise about one-fourth of the total population of the earth, China plays, already, an important role in world affairs—a role that can only grow more important in the years ahead.

We do not undertake this important step for transient tactical or expedient reasons. In recognizing the People's Republic of China, that it is the single government of China, we are recognizing simple reality. But far more is involved in this decision than just recognition of a fact.

Before the estrangement of recent decades, the American and the Chinese people had a long history of friendship. We have already begun to rebuild some of those previous ties. Now, our rapidly expanding relationship requires the kind of structure that only full diplomatic relations will make possible.

The change that I am announcing tonight will be of great long-term benefit to the peoples of both our country and China—and, I believe, to all the peoples of the world.

Normalization—and the expanded commercial and cultural relations that it will bring—will contribute to the well-being of our own nation, to our own national interest, and it will also enhance the stability of Asia.

These more positive relations with China can beneficially affect the world in which we live and the world in which our children will live.

We have already begun to inform our allies and other nations and the members of Congress of the details of our intended action. But I wish also tonight to convey a special message to the people of Taiwan—I have already communicated with the leaders in Taiwan—with whom the American people have had and will have extensive, close, and friendly relations.

This is important between our two peoples.

As the United States asserted in the Shanghai communiqué of 1972, issued on President [Richard] Nixon's historic visit, we will continue to have an interest in the peaceful resolution of the Taiwan issue.

I have paid special attention to ensuring that normalization of relations between our country and the People's Republic will not jeopardize the well-being of the people of Taiwan.

The people of our country will maintain our current commercial, cultural, trade, and other relations with Tai-

wan through nongovernmental means. Many other countries in the world are already successfully doing this.

These decisions and these actions open a new and important chapter in our country's history, and also in world affairs.

To strengthen and to expedite the benefits of this new relationship between China and the United States, I am pleased to announce that Vice Premier Teng [Deng Xiaoping] has accepted my invitation and will visit Washington at the end of January. His visit will give our governments the opportunity to consult with each other on global issues and to begin working together to enhance the cause of world peace.

These events are the final result of long and serious negotiations begun by President Nixon in 1972, and continued under the leadership of President [Gerald] Ford. The results bear witness to the steady, determined, and bipartisan effort of our country to build a world in which peace will be the goal and the responsibility of all nations.

The normalization of relations between the United States and China has no other purpose than this—the advancement of peace.

It is in this spirit, at this season of peace, that I take special pride in sharing this good news with you tonight.

United States Statement

As of January 1, 1979, the United States of America recognizes the People's Republic of China as the sole legal Government of China. On the same date, the People's Republic of China accords similar recognition to the United States of America. The United States thereby establishes diplomatic relations with the People's Republic of China.

On that same date, January 1, 1979, the United States of America will notify Taiwan that it is terminating diplomatic relations and that the Mutual Defense Treaty between the United States and the Republic of China is being terminated in accordance with the provisions of the Treaty. The United States also states that it will be withdrawing its remaining military personnel from Taiwan within four months.

In the future, the American people and the people of Taiwan will maintain commercial, cultural, and other relations without official Government representation and without diplomatic relations.

The Administration will seek adjustments to our laws and regulations to permit the maintenance of commercial, cultural, and other nongovernmental relationships in the new circumstances that will exist after normalization.

The United States is confident that the people of Taiwan face a peaceful and prosperous future. The United States continues to have an interest in the peaceful resolution of the Taiwan issue and expects that the Taiwan issue will be settled peacefully by the Chinese themselves.

The United States believes that the establishment of diplomatic relations with the People's Republic will contribute to the welfare of the American people, to the stability of Asia where the United States has major security and economic interests and to the peace of the entire world.

People's Republic of China Statement

As of January 1, 1979, the People's Republic of China and the United States of America recognize each other and establish diplomatic relations, thereby ending the prolonged abnormal relationship between them. This is an historic event in Sino-United States relations.

As is known to all, the Government of the People's Republic of China is the sole legal Government of China and Taiwan is a part of China. The question of Taiwan was the crucial issue obstructing the normalization of relations between China and the United States. It has now been resolved between the two countries in the spirit of the Shanghai Communiqué and through their joint efforts, thus enabling the normalization of relations so ardently desired by the people of the two countries.

As for the way of bringing Taiwan back to the embrace of the motherland and reunifying the country, it is entirely China's internal affair.

At the invitation of the U.S. Government, Teng Hsiao-ping [Deng Xiaoping], Deputy [Premier] of the State Council of the People's Republic of China, will pay an official visit to the United States in January 1979, with a view to further promoting the friendship between the two peoples and good relations between the two countries.

Taiwan Statement

The decision by the United States to establish diplomatic relations with the Chinese Communist regime has not only seriously damaged the rights and interests of the Government and the people of the Republic of China, but has also had a tremendously adverse impact upon the entire free world. For all the consequences that might arise as a result of this move, the United States Government alone should bear full responsibility.

In the past few years, the United States Government has repeatedly reaffirmed its intention to maintain diplomatic relations with the Republic of China and to honor its treaty commitments. Now that it has broken the assurances and abrogated the treaty, the United States Government cannot be expected to have the confidence of any free nation in the future.

The United States, by extending diplomatic recognition to the Chinese Communist regime, which owes its very existence to terror and suppression, is not in conformity with its professed position of safeguarding human rights and strengthening the capability of democratic nations to resist the totalitarian dictatorship.

The move is tantamount to denying the hundreds of millions of enslaved peoples on the Chinese mainland of their hope for an early restoration of freedom. Viewed from whatever aspect, the move by the United States constitutes a great setback to human freedom and democratic institutions. It will be condemned by all freedom-loving and peace-loving peoples all over the world.

Recent international events have proven that the United States' pursuance of the "normalization" process with the Chinese Communist regime did not protect the security of free Asian nations, has further encouraged Communist subversion and aggressive activities and hastened the fall of Indochina into Communist hands. The Government and the people of the Republic of China firmly believe lasting international peace and security can never be established on an unstable foundation of expediency.

Regardless of how the international situation may develop, the Republic of China, as a sovereign nation will, with her glorious tradition, unite all her people, civilian and military, at home and abroad, to continue her endeavors toward progress in the social, economic and political fields. The Chinese Government and the people, faithful to the national objectives and their international responsibilities, have full confidence in the future of the Republic of China.

The late President Chiang Kai-shek repeatedly instructed the Chinese people to be firm with dignity and to complete the task of national recovery and reconstruction. The Government and the people of the Republic of China have the determination and the faith, which they will exert their utmost, to work together with other free peoples in democratic countries to conquer Communist tyrannical rule and its aggressive policy. Henceforth, we shall be calm and firm, positive and hardworking. It is urged that all citizens cooperate fully with the Government, with one heart and one soul, united and determined to fight at this difficult moment.

Under whatever circumstances, the Republic of China shall neither negotiate with the Communist Chinese regime, nor compromise with communism, and it shall never give up its sacred task of recovering the mainland and delivering the compatriots there. This firm position shall remain unchanged.

Taiwan Relations Act of 1979

Following the normalization of U.S.-China relations on January 1, 1979, the U.S. Congress sought to reaffirm America's commitment to Taiwan's security through a bill (HR 2479) that became known as the Taiwan Relations Act, signed into law (PL 96-8) by President Jimmy

Carter on April 10, 1979. The major provisions are listed below.

Findings and Declaration of Policy
Sec. 2

(a) The President having terminated governmental relations between the United States and the governing authorities on Taiwan recognized by the United States as the Republic of China prior to January 1, 1979, the Congress finds that the enactment of this Act is necessary—
   (1) to help maintain peace, security, and stability in the Western Pacific; and
   (2) to promote the foreign policy of the United States by authorizing the continuation of commercial, cultural, and other relations between the people of the United States and the people on Taiwan.
(b) It is the policy of the United States—
   (1) to preserve and promote extensive, close, and friendly commercial, cultural, and other relations between the people of the United States and the people on Taiwan, as well as the people on the China mainland and all other peoples of the Western Pacific area;
   (2) to declare that peace and stability in the area are in the political, security, and economic interests of the United States, and are matters of international concern;
   (3) to make clear that the United States decision to establish diplomatic relations with the People's Republic of China rests upon the expectation that the future of Taiwan will be determined by peaceful means;
   (4) to consider any effort to determine the future of Taiwan by other than peaceful means, including by boycotts or embargoes, a threat to the peace and security of the Western Pacific area and of grave concern to the United States;
   (5) to provide Taiwan with arms of a defensive character; and
   (6) to maintain the capacity of the United States to resist any resort to force or other forms of coercion that would jeopardize the security, or the social or economic system, of the people on Taiwan.
(c) Nothing contained in this Act shall contravene the interest of the United States in human rights, especially with respect to the human rights of all the approximately eighteen million inhabitants of Taiwan. The preservation and enhancement of the human rights of all the people on Taiwan are hereby reaffirmed as objectives of the United States.

Implementation of United States Policy with Regard to Taiwan
Sec. 3

(a) In furtherance of the policy set forth in section 2 of this Act, the United States will make available to Taiwan such defense articles and defense services in such quantity as may be necessary to enable Taiwan to maintain a sufficient self-defense capability.
(b) The President and the Congress shall determine the nature and quantity of such defense articles and services based solely upon their judgment of the needs of Taiwan, in accordance with procedures established by law. Such determination of Taiwan's defense needs shall include review by United States military authorities in connection with recommendations to the President and the Congress.
(c) The President is directed to inform the Congress promptly of any threat to the security or the social or economic system of the people on Taiwan and any danger to the interests of the United States arising therefrom. The President and the Congress shall determine, in accordance with constitutional processes, appropriate action by the United States in response to any such danger.

Application of Laws; International Agreements
Sec. 4

(a) The absence of diplomatic relations or recognition shall not affect the application of the laws of the United States with respect to Taiwan, and the laws of the United States shall apply with respect to Taiwan in the manner that the laws of the United States applied with respect to Taiwan prior to January 1, 1979.
(b) The application of subsection (a) of this section shall include, but shall not be limited to, the following:
   (1) Whenever the laws of the United States refer or relate to foreign countries, nations, states, governments, or similar entities, such terms shall include and such laws shall apply with respect to Taiwan.
   (2) Whenever authorized by or pursuant to the laws of the United States to conduct or carry out programs, transactions, or other relations with respect to foreign countries, nations, states, governments, or similar entities, the President or any agency of the United States Government is authorized to conduct and carry out, in accordance with section 6 of this Act, such programs, transactions, and other relations with respect to Taiwan (including, but not limited to, the performance of services for the United States through contracts with commercial entities on Taiwan), in accor-

dance with the applicable laws of the United States.

(3) (a) The absence of diplomatic relations and recognition with respect to Taiwan shall not abrogate, infringe, modify, deny, or otherwise affect in any way any rights or obligations (including but not limited to those involving contracts, debts, or property interests of any kind) under the laws of the United States heretofore or hereafter acquired by or with respect to Taiwan.

(b) For all purposes under the laws of the United States, including actions in any court in the United States, recognition of the People's Republic of China shall not affect in any way the ownership of or other rights or interests in properties, tangible and intangible, and other things of value, owned or held on or prior to December 31, 1978, or thereafter acquired or earned by the governing authorities on Taiwan.

(4) Whenever the application of the laws of the United States depends upon the law that is or was applicable on Taiwan or compliance therewith, the law applied by the people on Taiwan shall be considered the applicable law for that purpose.

(5) Nothing in this Act, nor the facts of the President's action in extending diplomatic recognition to the People's Republic of China, the absence of diplomatic relations between the people on Taiwan and the United States, or the lack of recognition by the United States, and attendant circumstances thereto, shall be construed in any administrative or judicial proceeding as a basis for any United States Government agency, commission, or department to make a finding of fact or determination of law, under the Atomic Energy Act of 1954 and the Nuclear Nonproliferation Act of 1978, to deny an export license application or to revoke an existing export license for nuclear exports to Taiwan.

(6) For purposes of the Immigration and Nationality Act, Taiwan may be treated in the manner specified in the first sentence of section 202(b) of that Act.

(7) The capacity of Taiwan to sue and be sued in courts in the United States, in accordance with the laws of the United States, shall not be abrogated, infringed, modified, denied, or otherwise affected in any way by the absence of diplomatic relations or recognition.

(8) No requirement, whether expressed or implied, under the laws of the United States with respect to maintenance of diplomatic relations or recognition shall be applicable with respect to Taiwan.

(c) For all purposes, including actions in any court in the United States, the Congress approves the continuation

in force of all treaties and other international agreements, including multilateral conventions, entered into by the United States and the governing authorities on Taiwan recognized by the United States as the Republic of China prior to January 1, 1979, and in force between them on December 31, 1978, unless and until terminated in accordance with law.

(d) Nothing in this Act may be construed as a basis for supporting the exclusion or expulsion of Taiwan from continued membership in any international financial institution or any other international organization.

Overseas Private Investment Corporation

Sec. 5

(a) During the three-year period beginning on the date of enactment of this Act, the $1,000 per capita income restriction in clause (2) of the second undesignated paragraph of section 231 of the Foreign Assistance Act of 1961 shall not restrict the activities of the Overseas Private Investment Corporation in determining whether to provide any insurance, reinsurance, loans, or guaranties with respect to investment projects on Taiwan.

(b) Except as provided in subsection (a) of this section, in issuing insurance, reinsurance, loans, or guaranties with respect to investment projects on Taiwan, the Overseas Private Investment Corporation shall apply the same criteria as those applicable in other parts of the world.

The American Institute in Taiwan

Sec. 6

(a) Programs, transactions, and other relations conducted or carried out by the President or any agency of the United States Government with respect to Taiwan shall, in the manner and to the extent directed by the President, be conducted and carried out by or through

(1) The American Institute in Taiwan, a nonprofit corporation incorporated under the laws of the District of Columbia, or

(2) such comparable successor nongovernmental entity as the President may designate (hereafter in this Act referred to as the "Institute").

(b) Whenever the President or any agency of the United States Government is authorized or required by or pursuant to the laws of the United States to enter into, perform, enforce, or have in force an agreement or transaction relative to Taiwan, such agreement or transaction shall be entered into, performed, and enforced, in the manner and to the extent directed by the President, by or through the institute.

(c) To the extent that any law, rule, regulation, or ordinance of the District of Columbia, or of any State or political subdivision thereof in which the Institute is incorporated or doing business, impedes or otherwise interferes with the performance of the functions of the Institute pursuant to this Act, such law, rule, regulation, or ordinance shall be deemed to be preempted by this Act.

Services by the Institute to United States Citizens on Taiwan

Sec. 7

(a) The Institute may authorize any of its employees on Taiwan—

(1) to administer to or take from any person an oath, affirmation, affidavit, or deposition, and to perform any notarial act which any notary public is required or authorized by law to perform within the United States;

(2) to act as provisional conservator of the personal estates of deceased United States citizens; and

(3) to assist and protect the interests of United States persons by performing other acts such as are authorized to be performed outside the United States for consular purposes by such laws of the United States as the President may specify.

(b) Acts performed by authorized employees of the Institute under this section shall be valid, and of like force and effect within the United States, as if performed by any other person authorized under the laws of the United States to perform such acts.

Tax-Exempt Status of the Institute

Sec. 8

(a) The Institute, its property, and its income are exempt from all taxation now or hereafter imposed by the United States (except to the extent that section 11(a)(3) of this Act requires the imposition of taxes imposed under chapter 21 of the Internal Revenue Code of 1954, relating to the Federal Insurance Contributions Act) or by any State or local taxing authority of the United States.

(b) For purposes of the Internal Revenue Code of 1954, the Institute shall be treated as an organization described in sections 170(b)(l)(A), 170(c), 2055(a), 2106(a)(2)(A), 2522(a), and 2522(b).

. . .

Taiwan Instrumentality

Sec. 10

(a) Whenever the President or any agency of the United States Government is authorized or required by or pursuant to the laws of the United States to render or provide to or to receive or accept from Taiwan, any performance, communication, assurance, undertaking, or other action, such action shall, in the manner and to the extent directed by the President, be rendered or provided to, or received or accepted from, an instrumentality established by Taiwan which the President determines has the necessary authority under the laws applied by the people on Taiwan to provide assurances and take other actions on behalf of Taiwan in accordance with this Act.

(b) The President is requested to extend to the instrumentality established by Taiwan the same number of offices and complement of personnel as were previously operated in the United States by the governing authorities on Taiwan recognized as the Republic of China prior to January 1, 1979.

(c) Upon the granting by Taiwan of comparable privileges and immunities with respect to the Institute and its appropriate personnel, the President is authorized to extend with respect to the Taiwan instrumentality and its appropriate personnel, such privileges and immunities (subject to appropriate conditions and obligations) as may be necessary for the effective performance of their functions.

Separation of Government Personnel for Employment with the Institute

Sec. 11

(a) (1) Under such terms and conditions as the President may direct, any agency of the United States Government may separate from Government service for a specified period any officer or employee of that agency who accepts employment with the Institute.

(2) An officer or employee separated by an agency under paragraph (1) of this subsection for employment with the Institute shall be entitled upon termination of such employment to reemployment or reinstatement with such agency (or a successor agency) in an appropriate position with the attendant rights, privileges, and benefits which the officer or employee would have had or acquired had he or she not been so separated, subject to such time period and other conditions as the President may prescribe.

Reporting Requirement

Sec. 12

(a) The Secretary of State shall transmit to the Congress the text of any agreement to which the Institute is a party. However, any such agreement the immediate public disclosure of which would, in the opinion of the President, be prejudicial to the national security of the United States shall not be so transmitted to the Congress but shall be transmitted to the Committee on Foreign Relations of the Senate and the Committee on Foreign Affairs of the House of Representatives under an appropriate injunction of secrecy to be removed only upon due notice from the President.

(b) For purposes of subsection (a), the term "agreement" includes (1) any agreement entered into between the Institute and the governing authorities on Taiwan or the instrumentality established by Taiwan; and (2) any agreement entered into between the Institute and an agency of the United States Government.

(c) Agreements and transactions made or to be made by or through the Institute shall be subject to the same congressional notification, review, and approval requirements and procedures as if such agreements and transactions were made by or through the agency of the United States Government on behalf of which the Institute is acting.

(d) During the two-year period beginning on the effective date of this Act, the Secretary of State shall transmit to the Speaker of the House of Representatives and the Committee on Foreign Relations of the Senate, every six months, a report describing and reviewing economic relations between the United States and Taiwan, noting any interference with normal commercial relations.

Rules and Regulations
Sec. 13

The President is authorized to prescribe such rules and regulations as he may deem appropriate to carry out the purposes of this Act. During the three-year period beginning on the effective date of this Act, such rules and regulations shall be transmitted promptly to the Speaker of the House of Representatives and to the Committee on Foreign Relations of the Senate. Such action shall not, however, relieve the Institute of the responsibilities placed upon it by this Act.

Congressional Oversight
Sec. 14

(a) The Committee on Foreign Affairs of the House of Representatives, the Committee on Foreign Relations of the Senate, and other appropriate committees of the Congress shall monitor—

(1) the implementation of the provisions of this Act;

(2) the operation and procedures of the Institute;

(3) the legal and technical aspects of the continuing relationship between the United States and Taiwan; and

(4) the implementation of the policies of the United States concerning security and cooperation in East Asia.

(b) Such committees shall report, as appropriate, to their respective Houses on the results of their monitoring.

Definitions
Sec. 15

For purposes of this Act—

(1) the term "laws of the United States" includes any statute, rule, regulation, ordinance, order, or judicial rule of decision of the United States or any political subdivision thereof; and

(2) the term "Taiwan" includes, as the context may require, the islands of Taiwan and the Pescadores [Penghu], the people on those islands, corporations and other entities and associations created or organized under the laws applied on those islands, and the governing authorities on Taiwan recognized by the United States as the Republic of China prior to January 1, 1979, and any successor governing authorities (including political subdivisions, agencies, and instrumentalities thereof).

Authorization of Appropriations
Sec. 16

In addition to funds otherwise available to carry out the provisions of this Act, there are authorized to be appropriated to the Secretary of State for the fiscal year 1980 such funds as may be necessary to carry out such provisions. Such funds are authorized to remain available until expended.

Severability of Provisions
Sec. 17

If any provision of this Act or the application thereof to any person or circumstance is held invalid, the remainder of the Act and the application of such provision to any other person or circumstance shall not be affected thereby.

Effective Date
Sec. 18

This Act shall be effective as of January 1, 1979.

Chinese-Foreign Equity Joint Venture Law

The third plenum of the Eleventh Central Committee in December 1978 committed China to an open-door economic policy. This policy became more concrete in 1979 with passage of the Law of the People's Republic of China on Joint Ventures Using Chinese and Foreign

Investment, which led to a trickle of Sino-foreign joint venture signings in the early 1980s. China gradually promulgated more regulations dealing with foreign business in the 1980s, and the number of investment projects began to climb rapidly. The full text of the July 1979 joint venture law follows.

Article 1. With a view to expanding international economic cooperation and technological exchange, the PRC permits foreign companies, enterprises, other economic entities or individuals (hereinafter referred to as foreign participants) to incorporate themselves, within the territory of the PRC, into joint ventures with Chinese companies, enterprises or other economic entities (hereinafter referred to as Chinese participants) on the principle of equality and mutual benefit and subject to authorization by the Chinese Government.

Article 2. The Chinese Government protects, by the legislation in force, the resources invested by a foreign participant in a joint venture and the profits due him pursuant to the agreements, contracts, and articles of association authorized by the Chinese Government as well as his other lawful rights and interests.

All the activities of a joint venture shall be governed by the laws, decrees, and pertinent rules and regulations of the PRC.

Article 3. A joint venture shall apply to the Foreign Investment Commission of the PRC for authorization of the agreements and contracts concluded between the parties to the venture and the articles of association of the venture formulated by them, and the commission shall authorize or reject these documents within three months. When authorized, the joint venture shall register with the General Administration for Industry and Commerce of the PRC and start operations under license.

Article 4. A joint venture shall take the form of a limited liability company. In the registered capital of a joint venture, the proportion of the investment contributed by the foreign (participants) shall in general not be less than 25 percent. The profits, risks, and losses of a joint venture shall be shared by the parties to the venture in proportion to their contributions to the registered capital. The transfer of one party's share in the registered capital shall be effected only with the consent of the other parties to the venture.

Article 5. Each party to a joint venture may contribute cash, capital goods, industrial property rights, etc., as its investment in the venture.

The technology or equipment contributed by any foreign participant as investment shall be truly advanced and appropriate to China's needs. In cases of losses caused by

deception through the investment of outdated equipment or technology, compensation shall be paid for the losses.

The investment contributed by a Chinese participant may include the right to the use of a site provided for the joint venture during the period of its operation. In case such a contribution does not constitute a part of the investment from the Chinese participant, the joint venture shall pay the Chinese government for its use.

The various contributions referred to in the present article shall be specified in the contracts concerning the joint venture or in its articles of association, and the value of each contribution (excluding that of the site) shall be ascertained by the parties to the venture through joint assessment.

Article 6. A joint venture shall have a board of directors with a composition stipulated in the contracts and the articles of association after consultation between the parties to the venture, and each director shall be appointed or removed by his own side. The board of directors shall have a chairman appointed by the Chinese participant and one or two vice chairmen appointed by the foreign (participants). In handling an important problem, the board of directors shall reach decision through consultation on the principle of equality and mutual benefit.

The board of directors is empowered to discuss and take action on, pursuant to the provisions of the articles of association of the joint venture, all fundamental issues concerning the venture, namely expansion projects, production and business programs, the budget, distribution of profits, plans concerning manpower and pay scales, the termination of business, the appointment or hiring of the president, the vice (presidents), the chief engineer, the treasurer and the auditors as well as their functions and powers and their remuneration, etc.

The president and vice (presidents) (or the general manager and assistant general (managers) in a factory) shall be chosen from the various parties to the joint venture.

Procedures covering the employment and discharge of the workers and staff members of a joint venture shall be stipulated according to law in the agreement or contract concluded between the parties to the venture.

Article 7. The net profit of a joint venture shall be distributed between the parties to the venture in proportion to their respective shares in the registered capital after the payment of a joint venture income tax on its gross profit pursuant to the tax laws of the PRC and after the deductions therefrom as stipulated in the articles of association of the venture for the reserve funds, the bonus and welfare funds for the workers and staff members, and the expansion funds of the venture.

A joint venture equipped with up-to-date technology by world standards may apply for a reduction of or exemption from income tax for the first two to three profit making years.

A foreign participant who reinvests any part of his share of the net profit within Chinese territory may apply for the restitution of a part of the income taxes paid.

Article 8. A joint venture shall open an account with the Bank of China or a bank approved by the Bank of China.

A joint venture shall conduct its foreign exchange transactions in accordance with the foreign exchange regulations of the PRC.

A joint venture may, in its business operations, obtain funds from foreign banks directly.

The insurance appropriate to a joint venture shall be furnished by Chinese insurance companies.

Article 9. The production and business programs of a joint venture shall be filed with the authorities concerned and shall be implemented through business contracts.

In its purchase of required raw and semiprocessed materials, fuels, auxiliary equipment, etc., a joint venture should give first priority to Chinese sources, but may also acquire them directly from the world market with its own foreign exchange funds.

A joint venture is encouraged to market its products outside China. It may distribute its export products on foreign markets through direct channels or its associated agencies or China's foreign trade establishments. Its products may also be distributed on the Chinese market. Wherever necessary, a joint venture may set up affiliated agencies outside China.

Article 10. The net profit that a foreign participant receives as his share after executing his obligations under the pertinent laws and agreements and contracts, the funds he receives at the time when the joint venture terminates or winds up its operations, and his other funds may be remitted abroad through the Bank of China in accordance with the foreign exchange regulations and in the currency or currencies specified in the contracts concerning the joint venture.

A foreign participant shall receive encouragements for depositing in the Bank of China any part of the foreign exchange which he is entitled to remit abroad.

Article 11. The wages, salaries or other legitimate income earned by a foreign worker or staff member of a joint venture, after payment of the personal income tax under the tax laws of the PRC, may be remitted abroad through the Bank of China in accordance with the foreign exchange regulations.

Article 12. The contract period of a joint venture may be agreed upon between the parties to the venture accord-

ing to its particular line of business and circumstances. The period may be extended upon expiration through agreement between the parties, subject to authorization by the Foreign Investment Commission of the PRC. Any application for such extension shall be made six months before the expiration of the contract.

Article 13. In cases of heavy losses, the failure of any party to a joint venture to execute its obligations under the contracts or the articles of association of the venture, force majeure, etc., prior to the expiration of the contract period of a joint venture, the contract may be terminated before the date of expiration by consultation and agreement between the parties and through authorization by the Foreign Investment Commission of the PRC and registration with the General Administration for Industry and Commerce. In cases of losses caused by breach of the (contracts) by a party to the venture, the financial responsibility shall be borne by the said party.

Article 14. Disputes arising between the parties to a joint venture which the board of directors fails to settle through consultation may be settled through conciliation or arbitration by an arbitral body of China or through arbitration by an arbitral body agreed upon by the parties.

Article 15. The present law comes into force on the date of its promulgation. The power of amendment is vested in the NPC.

Xinhua Statement on U.S. Policy Toward Taiwan

After the United States normalized relations with China and terminated diplomatic relations with Taiwan, the American Institute in Taiwan (AIT) was established to replace the U.S. embassy in Taipei, and the Coordinating Council for North American Affairs (whose name changed to the Taipei Economic and Cultural Representative Office, or TECRO, in 1994) was established to represent Taiwan's interests in Washington, D.C. China's reaction to these developments, which it viewed as a violation of the agreement establishing diplomatic relations between the United States and China, follows. The statement was issued by Xinhua in October 1980.

An agreement that actually gives all diplomatic privileges to Taiwan representatives in the United States was signed here yesterday. This was an undisguised violation of the principles for the establishment of diplomatic relations between the United States and China.

The agreement was signed by the American Institute in Taiwan (AIT) and the Taiwan Coordinating Council for North American Affairs (CCNAA).

Asked by a Xinhua correspondent about the agreement, responsible officials of the State Department admitted today that the U.S. government is "quite aware of what the agreement is" and that it has made "no objection to it."

Under the agreement, the unofficial representatives of the United States in Taiwan and vice versa are made official diplomats in everything but name.

It says: "Each counterpart organization shall undertake to ensure that the other counterpart organization and its personnel will receive all privileges, exemptions, and immunities as set forth herein and to take all possible measures, as appropriate, to secure adequate protection of the other counterpart organization's premises and personnel, so as to facilitate proper execution of that organization's functions."

The privileges enjoyed by the two organizations include:

—the sending counterpart organization shall be free to communicate for all purposes related to the performance of its functions and shall enjoy inviolability for all correspondence related to its functions. The bag carrying the correspondence shall neither be opened nor detained.

—the wages, fees, or salaries of any designated employee of both sides shall be exempt from taxation imposed by the central and local authorities of the jurisdiction in which the receiving counterpart organization is located.

—the property and assets of the two organizations shall be immune from forced entry, search, attachment, execution, requisition, expropriation, or any other form of seizure or confiscation.

—designated employees of each side shall be immune from suit and legal process, and each sending counterpart organization shall enjoy in the territory in which the receiving counterpart organization is located the same immunity.

Commenting on the agreement, an American observer here said today, "In theory, the United States and Taiwan have only nongovernmental links, but in practice, virtually all the trappings of a full-blown diplomatic relationship are now in existence."

This is an open violation of the agreement between the United States and China and the joint communiqué on the establishment of diplomatic relations between the two countries. It is explicitly written in the communiqué: "The United States of America recognizes the government of the People's Republic of China as the sole legal government of China. Within this context, the people of the United States will maintain cultural, commercial, and other unofficial relations with the people of Taiwan."

It is common knowledge that as private organizations, both AIT and CCNAA have no rights to offer each other the privileges similar to those accorded diplomats. Why could they enjoy these privileges?

Answering this question by Xinhua, the State Department officials clung to the so-called U.S. "Taiwan Relations Act," and used it as a pretext for government support of the agreement.

It is known to all that the Taiwan Relations Act itself runs counter to the joint communiqué on the establishment of diplomatic relations between the United States and China. The act is nothing but a domestic act of the United States and can in no way serve as a legal basis for handling U.S.-Chinese relations.

It is recalled that after the normalization of Sino-U.S. diplomatic relations, the American government has repeatedly stated that the relations between the United States and Taiwan are "unofficial, nongovernmental."

Now the U.S. government publicly swallowed its own words. This is indeed surprising.

There is no doubt that the AIT and CCNAA agreement sponsored by the U.S. government and the Taiwan authorities will hurt the feelings of the Chinese people and give rise to widespread concern and indignation in China.

Reassessing Chinese Communist Party History

To legitimize the reversal of many of Mao's policies in the post-1978 era, as well as to explain the prosecution of Mao's wife and other members of the Gang of Four, the Chinese Communist Party began a policy of separating Mao's thought from his leadership qualities. As part of this effort, the sixth plenary session of the Eleventh Central Committee issued the following "Resolution on Certain Questions in the History of Our Party Since the Founding of the People's Republic" in June 1981. This document praises Mao's pre-1949 achievements and upholds the value of his political thought. However, it notes that many of his post-1949 political campaigns and methods had a detrimental effect on China's development, and it concludes that only 70 percent of Mao's achievements can be considered positive.

(1) The CCP has traversed sixty years of glorious struggle since its founding in 1921. In order to sum up its experience in the thirty-two years since the founding of the People's Republic, we must briefly review the previous twenty-eight years in which the party led the people in waging the revolutionary struggle for new democracy.

(2) The CCP was the product of the integration of Marxism-Leninism with the Chinese workers' movement and was founded under the influence of the October Revolution in Russia and the May Fourth movement in China and with the help of the Communist International [Comintern] led by Lenin. The revolution of 1911 led by Dr. Sun Yat-sen, the great revolutionary forerunner, overthrew the Qing dynasty, thus bringing to an end over two

thousand years of feudal monarchical rule. However, the semicolonial and semifeudal nature of Chinese society remained unchanged. Neither the Kuomintang nor any of the bourgeois or petty-bourgeois political groupings and factions found any way out for the country and the nation, nor was it possible for them to do so. The CCP and the CCP alone was able to show the people that China's salvation lay in overthrowing once and for all the reactionary rule of imperialism and feudalism and then switching over to socialism. When the CCP was founded, it had fewer than sixty members. But it initiated the vigorous workers' movement and the people's anti-imperialist and antifeudal struggle and grew rapidly and soon became a leading force such as the Chinese people had never before known.

(3) In the course of leading the struggle of the Chinese people with its various nationalities for new democracy, the CCP went through four stages: The northern expedition (1924-1927) conducted with the cooperation of the Kuomintang; the agrarian revolutionary war (1927-1937); the war of resistance against Japan (1937-1945) and the nationwide war of liberation (1946-1949). Twice, first in 1927 and then in 1934, it endured major setbacks. It was not until 1949 that it finally triumphed in the revolution, thanks to the long years of armed struggle in conjunction with other forms of struggle in other fields closely coordinated with it.

In 1927, regardless of the resolute opposition of the left wing of the Kuomintang with Song Qingling as its outstanding representative, the Kuomintang controlled by Chiang Kai-shek and Wang Jingwei betrayed the policies of Kuomintang-Communist cooperation and of anti-imperialism and antifeudalism decided on by Dr. Sun Yatsen and, in collusion with the imperialists, massacred Communists, and other revolutionaries. The party was still quite inexperienced and, moreover, was dominated by Chen Duxiu's right capitulationism, so that the revolution suffered a disastrous defeat under the surprise attack of a powerful enemy. The total membership of the party, which had grown to more than 60,000, fell to a little over 10,000.

However, our party continued to fight tenaciously. Launched under the leadership of Zhou Enlai and several other comrades, the Nanchang uprising of 1927 fired the opening shot for armed resistance against the Kuomintang reactionaries. The meeting of the Central Committee of the party held on 7 August 1927 decided on the policy of carrying out agrarian revolution and organizing armed uprisings. Shortly afterward, the autumn harvest and Canton uprising and uprisings in many other areas were organized. Led by Comrade Mao Zedong, the Autumn Harvest Uprising in the Hunan-Jiangxi border area gave birth to the First Division of the Chinese Workers and Peasants' Revolutionary Army and to the first rural revolutionary base area in the Jinggang mountains. Before

long, the insurgents led by Comrade Zhu De arrived at the Jinggang mountains and joined forces with it. With the progress of the struggle, the party set up the Jiangxi Central Revolutionary Base Area and the Western Hunan-Hubei, the Haifeng-Lufeng, the Hubei-Henan-Anhui, the Qiongya, the Fujian-Zhejiang-Jiangxi, the Hunan-Hubei-Jiangxi, the Hunan-Jiangxi, the Zuojiang-Youjiang, the Sichuan-Shaanxi, the Shaanxi-Gansu, and the Hunan-Hubei-Sichuan-Guizhou, and other base areas. The First, Second, and Fourth Front Armies of the Workers and Peasants' Red Army were also born, as were many other Red Army units. In addition, party organizations and other revolutionary organizations were established and revolutionary mass struggles unfolded under difficult conditions in the Kuomintang areas.

In the agrarian revolutionary war, the First Front Army of the Red Army and the Central Revolutionary Base Area under the direct leadership of Comrades Mao Zedong and Zhu De played the most important role. The front armies of the Red Army defeated in turn a number of "encirclement and suppression" campaigns launched by the Kuomintang troops. But because of Wang Ming's "left" adventurist leadership, the struggle against the Kuomintang's fifth "encirclement and suppression" campaign ended in failure. The First Front Army was forced to embark on the 25,000-*li* Long March and made its way to northern Shaanxi to join forces with units of the Red Army, which had been persevering in struggles there, and with its Twenty-Fifth Army, which had arrived earlier. The Second and Fourth Front Armies also went on their Long March, first one and then the other arriving in northern Shaanxi. Guerrilla warfare was carried on under difficult conditions in the base areas in South China from which the main forces of the Red Army had withdrawn. As a result of the defeat caused by Wang Ming's "left" errors, the revolutionary base areas and the revolutionary forces in the Kuomintang areas sustained enormous losses. The Red Army of 300,000 men was reduced to about 30,000 and the Communist Party of 300,000 members to about 40,000.

In January 1935, the Political Bureau of the Central Committee of the party convened a meeting in Zunyi during the Long March, which established the leading position of Comrade Mao Zedong in the Red Army and the Central Committee of the party. This saved the Red Army and the Central Committee of the party, which were then in critical danger, and subsequently made it possible to defeat Zhang Guotao's splittism, bring the Long March to a triumphant conclusion and open up new vistas for the Chinese revolution. It was a vital turning point in the history of the party.

At a time of national crisis of unparalleled gravity, when the Japanese imperialists were intensifying their aggression against China, the Central Committee of the party headed by Comrade Mao Zedong decided on and carried out the correct policy of forming an anti-Japanese national united front. Our party led the students' movement of 9 December 1935 and organized the powerful mass struggle to demand an end to the civil war and resistance against Japan, so as to save the nation. The Xi'an incident organized by Generals Zhang Xueliang and Yang Hucheng on 12 December 1936 and its peaceful settlement, which our party promoted, played a crucial historical role in bringing about renewed cooperation between the Kuomintang and the Communist Party and in achieving national unity for resistance against Japanese aggression. During the war of resistance, the ruling clique of the Kuomintang continued to oppose the Communist Party and the people and was passive in resisting Japan. As a result, the Kuomintang suffered defeat after defeat in front operations against the Japanese invaders.

Our party persevered in the policy of maintaining its independence and initiative within the United Front, closely relied on the masses of the people, conducted guerrilla warfare behind enemy lines, and set up many anti-Japanese base areas. The Eighth Route Army and the New Fourth Army—the reorganized Red Army—grew rapidly and became the mainstay in the war of resistance. The northeast Anti-Japanese United Army sustained its operations amid formidable difficulties. Diverse forms of anti-Japanese struggle were unfolded on a broad scale in areas occupied by Japan or controlled by the Kuomintang. Consequently, the Chinese people were able to hold out in the war for eight long years and win final victory, in cooperation with the people of the Soviet Union and other countries in the antifascist war.

During the anti-Japanese war, the party conducted a rectification movement, a movement of Marxist education. Launched in 1942, it was a tremendous success. It was on this basis that the seventh plenum of the Sixth Central Committee of the party in 1945 adopted the resolution on certain questions in the history of our party and soon afterward the party's seventh national congress was convened. These meetings summed up our historical experience and laid down our correct line, principles and policies for building a new-democratic new China, enabling the party to attain an unprecedented ideological, political, and organizational unity and solidarity.

After the conclusion of the war of resistance against Japan, the Chiang Kai-shek government, with the aid of U.S. imperialism, flagrantly launched an all-out civil war, disregarding the just demand of our party and the people of the whole country for peace and democracy. With the wholehearted support of the people in all the liberated areas, with the powerful backing of the students' and workers' movements and the struggles of the people of various strata in the Kuomintang areas and with the active cooperation of the democratic parties and nonparty democrats, our party led the People's Liberation Army in fighting the three-year war of liberation and in wiping out

8 million Chiang Kai-shek troops in the Liaoxi-Shenyang, Beiping-Tianjin, and Huai-Hai campaigns and in the successful crossing of the Changjiang (Yangzi) River. The end result was the overthrow of the reactionary Kuomintang government and the establishment of the great People's Republic of China. The Chinese people had stood up.

(4) The victories gained in the twenty-eight years of struggle fully show that:

(i) Victory in the Chinese revolution was won under the guidance of Marxism-Leninism. Our party had creatively applied the basic tenets of Marxism-Leninism and integrated them with the concrete practice of the Chinese revolution. In this way, the great system of Mao Zedong Thought came into being and the correct path to victory for the Chinese revolution was charted. This is a major contribution to the development of Marxism-Leninism.

(ii) As the vanguard of the Chinese proletariat, the CCP is a party serving the people wholeheartedly, with no selfish aim of its own. It is a party with both the courage and the ability to lead the people in their indomitable struggle against any enemy. Convinced of all this through their own experience, the Chinese people of whatever nationality came to rally around the party and form a broad united front, thus forging a strong political unity unparalleled in Chinese history.

(iii) The Chinese revolution was victorious mainly because we relied on a People's Army led by the party, an army of a completely new type and enjoying flesh-and-blood ties with the people, to defeat a formidable enemy through protracted people's war. Without such an army, it would have been impossible to achieve the liberation of our people and the independence of our country.

(iv) The Chinese revolution had the support of the revolutionary forces in other countries at every stage, a fact that the Chinese people will never forget. Yet it must be said that, fundamentally, victory in the Chinese revolution was won because the CCP adhered to the principle of independence and self-reliance and depended on the efforts of the whole Chinese people, whatever their nationality, after they underwent untold hardships and surmounted innumerable difficulties and obstacles together.

(v) The victorious Chinese revolution put an end to the rule of a handful of exploiters over the masses of the working people and to the enslavement of the Chinese people of all nationalities by the imperialists and colonialists. The working people have become the masters of the new state and the new society. While changing the balance of forces in world politics, the people's victory in so large a country, having nearly one-quarter of the world's population, has inspired the people in countries similarly subjected to imperialists and colonialist exploitation and oppression with heightened confidence in their forward march. The triumph of the Chinese revolution is the most important political event since World War II and has exerted a profound and far-reaching impact on the international situation and the development of the people's struggle throughout the world.

(5) Victory in the new-democratic revolution was won through long years of struggle and sacrifice by countless martyrs, party members, and people of all nationalities. We should by no means give all the credit to the leaders of the revolution, but at the same time we should not underrate the significant role these leaders have played. Among the many outstanding leaders of the party, Comrade Mao Zedong was the most prominent. Prior to the failure of the revolution in 1927, he had clearly pointed out the paramount importance of the leadership of the proletariat over the peasants' struggle and the danger of a right deviation in this regard. After its failure, he was the chief representative of those who succeeded in shifting the emphasis in the party's work from the city to the countryside and in preserving, restoring, and promoting the revolutionary forces in the countryside. In the twenty-two years from 1927 to 1949, Comrade Mao Zedong and other party leaders managed to overcome innumerable difficulties and gradually worked out an overall strategy and specific policies and directed their implementation, so that the revolution was able to switch from staggering defeats to great victory.

Our party and people would have had to grope in the dark much longer had it not been for Comrade Mao Zedong, who more than once rescued the Chinese revolution from grave danger, and for the Central Committee of the party, which was headed by him and which charted the firm, correct political course for the whole party, the whole people and the People's Army. Just as the CCP is recognized as the central force leading the entire people forward, so Comrade Mao Zedong is recognized as the great leader of the CCP and the whole Chinese people, and Mao Zedong Thought, which came into being through the collective struggle of the party and the people, is recognized as the guiding ideology of the party. This is the inevitable outcome of the twenty-eight years of development preceding the founding of the PRC.

(6) Generally speaking, the years since the founding of the PRC are years in which the CCP, guided by Marxism-Leninism and Mao Zedong Thought, has very successfully led the whole people in carrying out socialist revolution and socialist construction. The establishment of the socialist system represents the greatest and most profound social change in Chinese history and is the foundation for the country's future progress and development.

(7) Our major achievements in the thirty-two years since the founding of the People's Republic are the following:

(i) We have established and consolidated the people's democratic dictatorship led by the working class and based on the worker-peasant alliance, namely, the dictatorship of the proletariat. It is a new type of state power, unknown in Chinese history, in which the people are the masters of their own house. It constitutes the fundamental guarantee for the building of a modern socialist country, prosperous and powerful, democratic and culturally advanced.

(ii) We have achieved and consolidated nationwide unification of the country, with the exception of Taiwan and some other islands, and have thus put an end to the state of disunity characteristic of old China. We have achieved and consolidated the great unity of the people of all nationalities and have forged and expanded a socialist relationship of equality and mutual help among the more than fifty nationalities, and we have achieved and consolidated the great unity of the workers, peasants, intellectuals, and people of other strata and have strengthened and expanded the broad united front led by the CCP in full cooperation with the patriotic democratic parties and people's organizations and comprising all socialist working people and all patriots who support socialism and patriots who stand for the unification of the motherland, including our compatriots in Taiwan, Hong Kong, Macao, and Chinese citizens overseas.

(iii) We have defeated aggression, sabotage, and armed provocations by the imperialists and hegemonists, safeguarded our country's security and independence, and fought successfully in defense of our border regions.

(iv) We have built and developed a socialist economy and have in the main completed the socialist transformation of the private ownership of the means of production into public ownership and put into practice the principle of "to each according to his work." The system of exploitation of man by man has been eliminated, and exploiters no longer exist as classes, since the overwhelming majority have been remolded and now live by their own labor.

(v) We have scored signal successes in industrial construction and have gradually set up an independent and fairly comprehensive industrial base and economic system. Compared with 1952, when economic rehabilitation was completed, fixed industrial assets, calculated on the basis of their original price, were more than 27 times greater in 1980, exceeding 410 billion yuan; the output of cotton yarn was 4.5 times as great, reaching 2,930,000 tons; that of coal 9.4 times, reaching 620 million tons; that of electricity 41 times, exceeding 300 billion kWh; and the output of crude oil exceeded 105 million tons and that of steel 37 million tons; the output value of the engineering industry was 54 times as great, exceeding 127 billion yuan. A number of new industrial bases have been built in our vast hinterland and the regions inhabited by our minority nationalities. National defense industry started from scratch and is being gradually built up. Much has been done in the prospecting of natural resources. There has been a tremendous growth in railway, highway, water and air transport, and post and telecommunications.

(vi) The conditions prevailing in agricultural production have experienced a remarkable change, giving rise to big increases in production. The amount of land under irrigation has grown from 300 million *mu* in 1952 to over 670 million mu. Flooding by big rivers such as the Changjiang [Yangzi], Huanghe (Yellow River), Huaihe, Haihe, Zhujiang (Pearl River), Liaohe, and Songhuajiang has been brought under initial control. In our rural areas, where farm machinery, chemical fertilizers, and electricity were practically nonexistent before liberation, there is now a big increase in the number of agriculture-related tractors and irrigation and drainage equipment and in the quantity of chemical fertilizers applied, and the amount of electricity consumed is 7.5 times that generated in the whole country in the early years of liberation. In 1980, the total output of grain was nearly double that in 1952 and that of cotton more than double. Despite the excessive rate of growth in our population, which is now nearly 1 billion, we have succeeded in basically meeting the needs of our people in food and clothing by our own efforts.

(vii) There has been a substantial growth in urban and rural commerce and in foreign trade. The total value of commodities purchased by enterprises owned by the whole people rose from 17 billion yuan in 1952 to 226 billion yuan in 1980, registering an increase nearly thirteenfold; retail sales rose from 27 billion yuan to 214 billion yuan, an increase of 7.7 times. The total value of the state's foreign trade in 1980 was 8.7 times that of 1952. With the growth in industry, agriculture, and commerce, the people's livelihood has improved very markedly, as compared with preliberation days. In 1980, average consumption per capita in both town and country was nearly twice as much as in 1952, allowing for price changes.

(viii) Considerable progress has been made in education, science, culture, public health, and physical culture. In 1980, enrolment in the various kinds of full-time schools totaled 204 million, 3.7 times the number of 1952. In the past thirty-two years, the institutions of higher education and vocational schools have turned out nearly 9 million graduates with specialized knowledge or skills. Our achievements in nuclear technology, man-made satellites, rocketry, and so on, represent substantial advances in the field of science and technology. In literature and art, large numbers of fine works have appeared to cater to the needs of the people and socialism. With the participation of the masses, sports have developed vigorously, and records have been chalked up in quite a few events. Epidemic diseases with their high mortality rates have been eliminated or largely eliminated, the health of the rural and urban populations has greatly improved, and average life expectancy is now much higher.

(ix) Under the new historical conditions, the PLA [People's Liberation Army] has grown in strength and in quality. No longer composed only of ground forces, it has become a composite army, including the Naval and Air Forces and various technical branches. Our armed forces, which are a combination of the field armies, the regional forces, and the militia, have been strengthened. Their quality is now much higher and their technical equipment much better. The PLA is serving as the solid pillar of the people's democratic dictatorship in defending and participating in the socialist revolution and socialist construction.

(x) Internationally, we have steadfastly pursued an independent socialist foreign policy, advocated and upheld the Five Principles of Peaceful Coexistence, entered into diplomatic relations with 124 countries and promoted trade and economic and cultural exchanges with still more countries and regions. Our country's place in the United Nations and the Security Council has been restored to us. Adhering to proletarian internationalism, we are playing an increasingly influential and active role in international affairs by enhancing our friendship with the people of other countries, by supporting and assisting the oppressed nations in their cause of liberation, the newly independent countries in their national construction, and the people of various countries in their just struggles and by staunchly opposing imperialism, hegemonism, colonialism, and racism in defense of world peace. All of which has served to create favorable international conditions for our socialist construction and contributes to the development of a world situation favorable to the people everywhere.

(8) New China has not been in existence for very long, and our successes are still preliminary. Our party has made mistakes owing to its meager experience in leading the cause of socialism and subjective errors in the party leadership's analysis of the situation and its understanding of Chinese conditions. Before the Cultural Revolution there were mistakes of enlarging the scope of class struggle and of impetuosity and rashness in economic construction. Later, there was the comprehensive, long-drawn-out and grave blunder of the "Cultural Revolution." All these errors prevented us from scoring the greater achievements of which we should have been capable. It is impermissible to overlook or whitewash mistakes, which in itself would be a mistake and would give rise to more and worse mistakes. But, after all, our achievements in the past thirty-two years are the main thing.

It would be a no less serious error to overlook or deny our achievements or our successful experiences in scoring these achievements. These achievements and successful experiences of ours are the product of the creative application of Marxism-Leninism by our party and people, the manifestation of the superiority of the socialist system and the base from which the entire party and people will continue to advance, uphold truth and rectify errors—this is the basic stand of dialectical materialism our party must take. It was by taking this stand that we saved our cause from danger and defeat and won victory in the past. By taking the same stand, we will certainly win still greater victories in the future.

(9) From the inception of the PRC in October 1949 to 1956, our party led the whole people in gradually realizing the transition from new democracy to socialism, rapidly rehabilitating the country's economy, undertaking planned economic construction and, in the main, accomplishing the socialist transformation of the private ownership of the means of production in most of the country. The guidelines and basic policies defined by the party in this historical period were correct and led to brilliant successes.

(10) In the first three years of the People's Republic, we cleared the mainland of bandits and the remnant armed forces of the Kuomintang reactionaries; peacefully liberated Tibet; established people's governments at all levels throughout the country; confiscated bureaucrat-capitalist enterprises and transformed them into state-owned socialist enterprises; unified the country's financial and economic work; stabilized commodity prices; carried out agrarian reform in the new liberated areas; suppressed counterrevolutionaries; and unfolded the movements against the "three evils" of corruption, waste, and bureaucracy and against the "five evils" of bribery, tax evasion, theft of state property, cheating on government contracts, and stealing of economic information, the latter being a movement to beat back the attack mounted by the bourgeoisie.

We effectively transformed the educational, scientific, and cultural institutions of old China, while successfully carrying out the complex and difficult task of social reform and simultaneously undertaking the great war to resist U.S. aggression and aid Korea, protect our homes, and defend the country. We rapidly rehabilitated the country's shattered economy, which had been devastated in old China. By the end of 1952, the country's industrial and agricultural production had attained record levels.

(11) On the proposal of Comrade Mao Zedong in 1952, the Central Committee of the party advanced the general line for the transition period, which was to realize the country's socialist industrialization and socialist transformation of agriculture, handicrafts, and capitalist industry and commerce step by step over a fairly long period of time. This general line was a reflection of historical necessity.

(i) Socialist industrialization is an indispensable prerequisite to the country's independence and prosperity.

(ii) With nationwide victory in the new democratic revolution and completion of the agrarian reform, the contradiction between the working class and the bourgeoisie and between the socialist road and the capitalist road became the principal internal contradiction. The country needed a certain expansion of capitalist industry and commerce that were beneficial to its economy and to the people's livelihood. But in the course of their expansion, things detrimental to the national economy and the people's livelihood were bound to emerge. Consequently, a struggle between restriction and opposition to restriction was inevitable. The conflict of interests became increasingly apparent between capitalist enterprises on the one hand and the economic policies of the state, the socialist state-owned economy, the workers and staff in these capitalist enterprises and the people as a whole on the other. An integrated series of necessary measures and steps, such as the fight against speculation and profiteering, the readjustment and restructuring of industry and commerce, the movement against the "five evils," workers' supervision of production and state monopoly of the purchase and marketing of grain and cotton, were bound to gradually bring backward, anarchic, lopsided and profit-oriented capitalist industry and commerce into the orbit of socialist transformation.

(iii) Among the individual peasants, and particularly the poor and lower-middle peasants who had just acquired land in the agrarian reform but lacked other means of production, there was a genuine desire for mutual aid and cooperation in order to avoid borrowing at usurious rates and even mortgaging or selling their land again with consequent polarization, and in order to expand production, undertake water conservancy projects, ward off natural calamities and make use of farm machinery and new techniques.

The progress of industrialization, while demanding agricultural products in ever-increasing quantities, would provide stronger and stronger support for the technical transformation of agriculture, and this also constituted a motive force behind the transformation of individual into cooperative farming.

As is borne out by history, the general line for the transition period set forth by our party was entirely correct.

(12) During the period of transition, our party creatively charted a course for socialist transformation that suited China's specific conditions. In dealing with capitalist industry and commerce, we devised a whole series of transitional forms of state capitalism from lower to higher levels, such as the placing of state orders with private

enterprises for the processing of materials or the manufacture of goods, state monopoly of the purchase and marketing of the products of private enterprise, the marketing of products of state-owned enterprises by private shops, and joint state-private ownership of individual enterprises or enterprises of a whole trade, and we eventually realized the peaceful redemption of the bourgeoisie, a possibility envisaged by Marx and Lenin.

In dealing with individual farming, we devised transitional forms of cooperation, proceeding from temporary or all year-round mutual aid teams, to elementary agricultural producers' cooperatives of a semisocialist nature and then to advanced agricultural producers' cooperatives of a fully socialist nature, always adhering to the principles of voluntariness and mutual benefit, demonstration through advanced examples, and extension of state help. Similar methods were used in transforming individual handicraft industries. In the course of such transformation, the state-capitalist and cooperative economies displayed their unmistakable superiority.

By 1956, the socialist transformation of the private ownership of the means of production had been largely completed in most regions. But there had been shortcomings and errors. From the summer of 1955 onward, we were overhasty in pressing on with agricultural cooperation and the transformation of private handicraft and commercial establishments; we were far from meticulous, the changes were too fast, and we did our work in a somewhat summary, stereotyped manner, leaving open a number of questions for a long time. Following the basic completion of the transformation of capitalist industry and commerce in 1956, we failed to do a proper job in employing and handling some of the former industrialists and businessmen. But on the whole, it was definitely a historic victory for us to have effected, and to have effected fairly smoothly, so difficult, complex, and profound a social change in so vast a country, with its several hundred million people, a change, moreover, that promoted the growth of industry, agriculture, and the economy as a whole.

(13) In economic construction under the first Five-Year Plan (1953-1957), we likewise scored major successes through our own efforts and with the assistance of the Soviet Union and other friendly countries. A number of basic industries, essential for the country's industrialization and yet very weak in the past, were built up. Between 1953 and 1956, the average annual increases in the total value of industrial and agricultural output were 19.6 and 4.8 percent respectively. Economic growth was quite fast, with satisfactory economic results, and the key economic sectors were well-balanced. The market prospered, prices were stable. The people's livelihood improved perceptibly. In April 1956, Comrade Mao Zedong made his speech "On the Ten Major Relationships," in which he initially summed up our experiences in socialist construction and set forth the task of exploring a way of building socialism suited to the specific conditions of our country.

(14) The first National People's Congress was convened in September 1954, and it enacted the constitution of the PRC. In March 1955, a national conference of the party reviewed the major struggle against the plots of the careerists Gao Gang and Rao Shushi to split the party and usurp supreme power in the party and the state; in this way it strengthened party unity. In January 1956, the Central Committee of the party called a conference on the question of the intellectuals. Subsequently, the policy of "letting a hundred flowers blossom and a hundred schools of thought contend" was advanced. These measures spelled out the correct policy regarding intellectuals and the work in education, science, and culture and thus brought about a significant advance in these fields. Owing to the fact that the party enjoyed high prestige among the people for its correct policies and fine style of work, the vast numbers of cadres, masses, youth, and intellectuals earnestly studied Marxism-Leninism and Mao Zedong Thought and participated enthusiastically in revolutionary and construction activities under the leadership of the party, so that a healthy and virile revolutionary morality prevailed throughout the country.

(15) The eighth national congress of the party held in September 1956 was very successful. The congress declared that the socialist system had been basically established in China; that while we must strive to liberate Taiwan, thoroughly complete socialist transformation, ultimately eliminate the system of exploitation and continue to wipe out the remnant forces of counterrevolution, the principal contradiction within the country was no longer the contradiction between the working class and the bourgeoisie but between the demand of the people for rapid economic and cultural development and the existing state of our economy and culture, which fell short of the needs of the people; that the chief task confronting the whole nation was to concentrate all efforts on developing the productive forces, industrializing the country, and gradually meeting the people's incessantly growing material and cultural needs; and that although class struggle still existed and the people's democratic dictatorship had to be further strengthened, the basic task of the dictatorship was now to protect and develop the productive forces in the context of the new relations of production.

The congress adhered to the principle put forward by the Central Committee of the party in May 1956, the principle of opposing both conservatism and rash advance in economic construction, that is, of making steady progress by striking an overall balance. It emphasized the problem of the building of the party in office and the need to uphold democratic centralism and collective leadership, oppose the personality cult, promote democracy within the party and among the people, and strengthen the party's ties with the masses. The line laid down by the eighth national congress of the party was correct and it charted the path for the development of the cause of socialism and for party-building in the new period.

(16) After the basic completion of socialist transformation, our party led the entire people in shifting our work to all-around, large-scale socialist construction. In the ten years preceding the Cultural Revolution, we achieved very big successes despite serious setbacks. By 1966, the value of fixed industrial assets, calculated on the basis of their original price, was four times that in 1956. The output of such major industrial products as cotton yarn, coal, electricity, crude oil, steel, and mechanical equipment all recorded impressive increases. Beginning in 1965, China became self-sufficient in petroleum. New industries such as the electronic and petrochemical industries were established one after another. The distribution of industry over the country became better balanced. Capital construction in agriculture and its technical transformation began on a massive scale and yielded better and better results. Both the number of tractors for farming and the quantity of chemical fertilizers applied increased over seven times and rural consumption of electricity 71 times. The number of graduates from institutions of higher education was 4.9 times that of the previous seven years. Educational work was improved markedly through consolidation. Scientific research and technological work, too, produced notable results.

In the ten years from 1956 to 1966, the party accumulated precious experience in leading socialist construction. In the spring of 1957, Comrade Mao Zedong stressed the necessity of correctly handling and distinguishing between the two types of social contradictions differing in nature in a socialist society, and made the correct handling of contradictions among the people the main content of the country's political life. Later, he called for the creation of "a political situation in which we have both centralism and democracy, both discipline and freedom, both unity of will and personal ease of mind and liveliness." In 1958, he proposed that the focus of party and government work be shifted to technical revolution and socialist construction. This was the continuation and development of the line adopted by the eighth national party congress.

While leading the work of correcting the errors in the "Great Leap Forward" and the movement to organize people's communes, Comrade Mao Zedong pointed out that there must be no expropriation of the peasants; that a given stage of social development should not be skipped; that egalitarianism must be opposed; that we must stress commodity production, observe the law of value and strike an overall balance in economic planning; and that economic plans must be arranged with the priority proceeding from agriculture to light industry and then to heavy industry.

Comrade Liu Shaoqi said that a variety of means of production could be put into circulation as commodities and that there should be a double-track system for labor as well as for education in socialist society. The double-track system for labor refers to a combination of the system of the eight-hour day in factories, rural areas, and government offices with a system of part-time work and part-time study in factories and rural areas. The double-track system for education means a system of full-time schooling combined with a system of part-time work and part-time study. Comrade Zhou Enlai said, among other things, that the overwhelming majority of Chinese intellectuals had become intellectuals belonging to the working people and that science and technology would play a key role in China's modernization. Comrade Chen Yun held that plan targets should be realistic, that the scale of construction should correspond to national capability, that considerations should be given to both the people's livelihood and the needs of state construction, and that the material, financial and credit balances should be maintained in drawing up plans. Comrade Deng Xiaoping held that industrial enterprises should be consolidated and their management improved and strengthened, and that the system of workers' conferences should be introduced. Comrade Zhu De stressed the need to pay attention to the development of handicrafts and of diverse undertakings in agriculture. Deng Zihui and other comrades pointed out that a system of production responsibility should be introduced in agriculture.

All these views were not only of vital significance then, but have remained so ever since. In the course of economic readjustment, the Central Committee drew up draft rules governing the work of the rural people's communes and work in industry, commerce, education, science, and literature and art.

These rules, which were a more or less systematic summation of our experience in socialist construction and embodied specific policies suited to the prevailing conditions, remain important as a source of reference for us to this very day.

In short, the material and technical basis for modernizing our country was largely established during that period. It was also largely in the same period that the core personnel for our work in the economic, cultural and other spheres were trained and that they gained their experience. This was the principal aspect of the party's work in that period.

(17) In the course of this decade, there were serious faults and errors in the guidelines of the party's work, which developed through twists and turns.

[The year] 1957 was one of the years that saw best results in economic work after the founding of the People's Republic owing to the conscientious implementation of the correct line formulated at the eighth national congress of the party. To start a rectification campaign throughout the party in that year and urge the masses to offer criticisms and suggestions were normal steps in developing socialist democracy. In the rectification campaign a handful of bourgeois rightists seized the opportunity to advocate what they called ''speaking out and airing views in a big way'' and to mount a wild attack against the party and the nascent socialist system in an attempt to replace the leadership of the Communist Party. It was therefore entirely correct and necessary to launch a resolute counterattack. But the scope of this struggle was made far too broad and a number of intellectuals, patriotic people and party cadres were unjustifiably labeled ''rightist,'' with unfortunate consequences.

In 1958, the second plenum of the eighth national congress of the party adopted the general line for socialist construction. The line and its fundamental aspects were correct in that it reflected the masses' pressing demand for a change in the economic and cultural backwardness of our country. Its shortcoming was that it overlooked the objective economic laws. Both before and after the plenum, all comrades in the party and people of all nationalities displayed high enthusiasm and initiative for socialism and achieved certain results in production and construction. However, ''left'' errors, characterized by excessively high targets, the issuing of arbitrary directions, boastfulness and the stirring up of a ''Communist wind,'' spread unchecked throughout the country. This was due to our lack of experience in socialist construction and in adequate understanding of the laws of economic development and of the basic economic conditions in China. More important, it was due to the fact that Comrade Mao Zedong and many leading comrades, both at the center and in the localities, had become smug about their successes, were impatient for quick results and overestimated the role of man's subjective will and efforts.

After the general line was formulated, the ''Great Leap Forward'' and the movement for rural people's communes were initiated without careful investigation and study and without prior experimentation. From the end of 1958 to the early stage of the Lushan meeting of the Political Bureau of the party's Central Committee in July 1959, Comrade Mao Zedong and the Central Committee led the whole party in energetically rectifying the errors that had already been recognized. However, in the latter part of the meeting, he erred in initiating criticism of Comrade Peng Dehuai and then in launching a party-wide struggle against ''right opportunism.'' The resolution passed by the eighth plenary session of the eighth Central Committee of the party concerning the so-called antiparty group of Peng Dehuai, Huang Kecheng, Zhang Wentian, and Zhou Xiaozhou was entirely wrong. Politically, this struggle gravely undermined inner-party democracy from the central level down to the grass roots; economically, it cut short the process of rectification of the ''left'' errors, thus prolonging their influence. It was mainly due to the

errors of the Great Leap Forward and of the struggle against ''right opportunism,'' together with a succession of natural calamities and the perfidious scrapping of contracts by the Soviet government, that our economy encountered serious difficulties between 1959 and 1961, which caused serious losses to our country and people.

In the winter of 1960, the Central Committee of the party and Comrade Mao Zedong set about rectifying the ''left'' errors in rural work and decided on the principle of ''readjustment, consolidation, filling out, and raising standards'' for the economy as a whole. A number of correct policies and resolute measures were worked out and put into effect with Comrades Liu Shaoqi, Zhou Enlai, Chen Yun, and Deng Xiaoping in charge. All this constituted a crucial turning point in that historical phase. In January 1962, the enlarged central work conference attended by 7,000 people made a preliminary summing-up of the positive and negative experience of the ''Great Leap Forward'' and unfolded criticism and self-criticism. A majority of the comrades who had been unjustifiably criticized during the campaign against ''right opportunism'' were rehabilitated before or after the conference. In addition, most of the ''rightists'' had their label removed. Thanks to these economic and political measures, the national economy recovered and developed fairly smoothly between 1962 and 1966.

Nevertheless, ''left'' errors in the principles guiding economic work were not only not eradicated, but actually grew in the spheres of politics, ideology and culture. At the tenth plenary session of the party's Eighth Central Committee in September 1962, Comrade Mao Zedong widened and absolutized the class struggle existing only within certain limits in a socialist society and carried forward the viewpoint he had advanced after the antirightist struggle in 1957 that the contradiction between the proletariat and the bourgeoisie remained the principal contradiction in our society. He went a step further and asserted that, throughout the historical period of socialism, the bourgeoisie would continue to exist and would attempt a comeback and become the source of revisionism inside the party. The socialist education movement, unfolded between 1963 and 1965 in some rural areas and at the grass-roots level in a small number of cities, did help to some extent to improve the cadres' style of work and economic management. But, in the course of the movement, problems differing in nature were all treated as forms of class struggle or its reflections inside the party. As a result, quite a number of the cadres at the grass-roots level were unjustly dealt with in the latter half of 1964, and early in 1965 the erroneous thesis was advanced that the main target of the movement should be ''those party persons in power taking the capitalist road.'' In the ideological sphere, a number of literary and art works and schools of thought and a number of representative personages in artistic, literary and academic circles were subjected to unwarranted, inordinate political criticism. And there was an increasingly serious "left" deviation on the question of intellectuals and on the question of education, science, and culture. These errors eventually culminated in the "Cultural Revolution," but they had not yet become dominant.

Thanks to the fact that the whole party and people had concentrated on carrying out the correct principle of economic readjustment since the winter of 1960, socialist construction gradually flourished again. The party and the people were united in sharing weal and woe. They overcame difficulties at home, stood up to the pressure of the Soviet leading clique and repaid all the debts owed to the Soviet Union, which were chiefly incurred through purchasing Soviet arms during the movement to resist U.S. aggression and aid Korea. In addition, they did what they could to support the revolutionary struggles of the people of many countries and assist them in their economic construction. The third National People's Congress, which met between the end of 1964 and the first days of 1965, announced that the task of national economic readjustment had, in the main, been accomplished and that the economy as a whole would soon enter a new stage of development. It called for energetic efforts to build China step by step into a socialist power with modern agriculture, industry, national defense, and science and technology. This call was not fulfilled owing to the "Cultural Revolution."

(18) All the successes in these ten years were achieved under the collective leadership of the Central Committee of the party headed by Comrade Mao Zedong. Likewise, responsibility for the errors committed in the work of this period rested with the same collective leadership. Although Comrade Mao Zedong must be held chiefly responsible, we cannot lay the blame on him alone for all those errors. During this period, his theoretical and practical mistakes concerning class struggle in a socialist society became increasingly serious, his personal arbitrariness gradually undermined democratic centralism in party life, and the personality cult grew graver and graver. The Central Committee of the party failed to rectify these mistakes in good time. Careerists like Lin Biao, Jiang Qing, and Kang Sheng, harboring ulterior motives, made use of these errors and inflated them. This led to the inauguration of the "Cultural Revolution."

(19) The "Cultural Revolution," which lasted from May 1966 to October 1976, was responsible for the most severe setback and the heaviest losses suffered by the party, the state, and the people since the founding of the People's Republic. It was initiated and led by Comrade Mao Zedong. His principal theses were that many representatives of the bourgeoisie and counterrevolutionary revisionists had sneaked into the party, the government, the army, and cultural circles, and leadership in a fairly large majority of organizations and departments was no longer in the hands of Marxists and the people; that party persons in power taking the capitalist road had formed a bourgeois headquarters inside the Central Committee that pursued a revisionist political and organizational line and had agents in all provinces, municipalities, and autonomous regions, as well as in all central departments; that since the forms of struggle adopted in the past had not been able to solve this problem, the power usurped by the capitalist-roaders could be recaptured only by carrying out a great cultural revolution, by openly and fully mobilizing the broad masses from the bottom up to expose these sinister phenomena; and that the Cultural Revolution was in fact a great political revolution in which one class would overthrow another, a revolution that would have to be waged time and again.

These theses appeared mainly in the "16 May circular," which served as the programmatic document of the "Cultural Revolution," and in the political report to the ninth national congress of the party in April 1969. They were incorporated into a general theory—the "theory of continued revolution under the dictatorship of the proletariat"—which then took on a specific meaning. These erroneous "left" theses, upon which Comrade Mao Zedong based himself in initiating the "Cultural Revolution," were obviously inconsistent with the system of Mao Zedong Thought, which is the integration of the universal principles of Marxism-Leninism with the concrete practice of the Chinese revolution. These theses must be thoroughly distinguished from Mao Zedong Thought.

As for Lin Biao, Jiang Qing, and others, who were placed in important positions by Comrade Mao Zedong, the matter is of an entirely different nature. They rigged-up two counterrevolutionary cliques in an attempt to seize supreme power and, taking advantage of Comrade Mao Zedong's errors, committed many crimes behind his back, bringing disaster to the country and the people. As their counterrevolutionary crimes have been fully exposed, this resolution will not go into them at any length.

(20) The history of the "Cultural Revolution" has proved that Comrade Mao Zedong's principal theses for initiating it conformed neither to Marxism-Leninism nor to Chinese reality. They represent an entirely erroneous appraisal of the prevailing class relations and political situation in the party and state.

(i) The "Cultural Revolution" was defined as a struggle against the revisionist line or the capitalist road. There were no grounds at all for this definition. It led to the confusing of right and wrong on a series of important theories and policies. Many things denounced as revisionist or capitalist during the "Cultural Revolution" were actually Marxist and socialist principles, many of which had been set forth or supported by Comrade Mao Zedong himself. The "Cultural Revolution" negated many of the correct principles, policies and achievements of the seventeen years after the founding of the People's Republic. In fact, it negated much of the work of the Central Committee of the party and the people's government, including Comrade Mao Zedong's own contribution. It negated the arduous struggles the entire people had conducted in socialist construction.

(ii) The confusing of right and wrong inevitably led to confusing the people with the enemy. The "capitalist-roaders" overthrown in the "Cultural Revolution" were leading cadres of party and government organizations at all levels, who formed the core force of the socialist cause. The so-called bourgeois headquarters inside the party headed by Liu Shaoqi and Deng Xiaoping simply did not exist. Irrefutable facts have proved that labeling Comrade Liu Shaoqi a "renegade, hidden traitor, and scab" was nothing but a frame-up by Lin Biao, Jiang Qing, and their followers. The political conclusion concerning Comrade Liu Shaoqi drawn by the twelfth plenary session of the Eighth Central Committee of the party and the disciplinary measure it meted out to him were both utterly wrong. The criticism of the so-called reactionary academic authorities in the "Cultural Revolution," during which many capable and accomplished intellectuals were attacked and persecuted, also badly muddled the distinction between the people and the enemy.

(iii) Nominally, the "Cultural Revolution" was conducted by directly relying on the masses. In fact, it was divorced both from the party organizations and from the masses. After the movement started, party organizations at different levels were attacked and became partially or wholly paralyzed, the party's leading cadres at various levels were subjected to criticism and struggle, inner-party life came to a standstill, and many activists and large numbers of the basic masses whom the party has long relied on were rejected. At the beginning of the "Cultural Revolution," the vast majority of participants in the movement acted out of their faith in Comrade Mao Zedong and the party. Except for a handful of extremists, however, they did not approve of launching ruthless struggles against leading party cadres at all levels. With the lapse of time, following their own circuitous paths, they eventually attained a heightened political consciousness and began to adopt a skeptical or wait-and-see attitude toward the "Cultural Revolution," or even resisted and opposed it. Many people were assailed either more or less severely for this very reason. Such a state of affairs could not but provide openings to be exploited by opportunists, careerists, and conspirators, not a few of whom were escalated to high or even key positions.

(iv) Practice has shown that the "Cultural Revolution" did not in fact constitute a revolution or social progress in any sense, nor could it possibly have done

so. It was we and not the enemy at all who were thrown into disorder by the "Cultural Revolution." Therefore, from beginning to end, it did not turn "great disorder under heaven" into "great order under heaven," nor could it conceivably have done so. After the state power in the form of the people's democratic dictatorship was established in China, and especially after socialist transformation was basically completed and the exploiters were eliminated as classes, the socialist revolution represented a fundamental break with the past in both content and method, even though its tasks remained to be completed.

Of course, it was essential to take proper account of certain undesirable phenomena that undoubtedly existed in party and state organisms and to remove them by correct measures in conformity with the constitution, the laws, and the party constitution. But on no account should the theories and methods of the "Cultural Revolution" have been applied. Under socialist conditions, there is no economic or political basis for carrying out a great political revolution in which "one class overthrows another." It decidedly could not come up with any constructive program, but could only bring grave disorder, damage, and retrogression in its train. History has shown that the "Cultural Revolution," initiated by a leader laboring under a misapprehension and capitalized on by counterrevolutionary cliques, led to domestic turmoil and brought catastrophe to the party, the state, and the whole people.

(21) The "Cultural Revolution" can be divided into three stages:

(i) From the initiation of the "Cultural Revolution" to the ninth national congress of the party in April 1969. The convening of the enlarged Political Bureau meeting of the Central Committee of the party in May 1966 and the eleventh plenary session of the Eighth Central Committee in August of that year marked the launching of the "Cultural Revolution" on a full scale. These two meetings adopted the "16 May circular" and the "decision of the Central Committee of the CCP concerning the Great Proletarian Cultural Revolution" respectively. They launched an erroneous struggle against the so-called antiparty clique of Peng Zhen, Luo Ruiqing, Lu Dingyi, and Yang Shangkun and the so-called headquarters of Liu Shaoqi and Deng Xiaoping. They wrongly reorganized the central leading organs, set up the "Cultural Revolution Group under the Central Committee of the CCP" and gave it a major part of the power of the Central Committee.

In fact, Comrade Mao Zedong's personal leadership characterized by "left" errors took the place of the collective leadership of the Central Committee, and the cult of Comrade Mao Zedong was frenziedly pushed to an extreme. Lin Biao, Jiang Qing, Kang Sheng, Zhang Chunqiao, and others, acting chiefly in the name of the

"Cultural Revolution Group," exploited the situation to incite people to "overthrow everything and wage full-scale civil war." Around February 1967, at various meetings, Tan Zhenlin, Chen Yi, Ye Jianying, Li Fuchun, Li Xiannian, Xu Xiangqian, Nie Rongzhen, and other Political Bureau members and leading comrades of the military commission of the Central Committee sharply criticized the mistakes of the "Cultural Revolution." This was labeled the "February adverse current," and they were attacked and repressed.

Comrades Zhu De and Chen Yun were also wrongly criticized. Almost all leading party and government departments in the different spheres and localities were stripped of their power or reorganized.

The chaos was such that it was necessary to send in the PLA to support the left, the workers, and the peasants and to institute military control and military training. It played a positive role in stabilizing the situation, but it also produced some negative consequences. The ninth congress of the party legitimized the erroneous theories and practices of the "Cultural Revolution," and so reinforced the positions of Lin Biao, Jiang Qing, Kang Sheng, and others in the Central Committee of the party. The guidelines of the ninth congress were wrong, ideologically, politically, and organizationally.

(ii) From the ninth national congress of the party to its tenth national congress in August 1973. In 1970-1971 the counterrevolutionary Lin Biao clique plotted to capture supreme power and attempted an armed counterrevolutionary coup d'état. This was the outcome of the "Cultural Revolution," which overturned a series of fundamental party principles. Objectively, it announced the failure of the theories and practices of the "Cultural Revolution." Comrades Mao Zedong and Zhou Enlai ingeniously thwarted the plotted coup. Supported by Comrade Mao Zedong, Comrade Zhou Enlai took charge of the day-to-day work of the Central Committee, and things began to improve in all fields. During the criticism and repudiation of Lin Biao in 1972, he correctly proposed criticism of the ultraleft trend of thought. In fact, this was an extension of the correct proposals put forward around February 1967 by many leading comrades of the Central Committee who had called for the correction of the errors of the "Cultural Revolution." Comrade Mao Zedong, however, erroneously held that the task was still to oppose the "ultraright." The tenth congress of the party perpetuated the "left" errors of the ninth congress and made Wang Hongwen a vice chairman of the party. Jiang Qing, Zhang Chunqiao, Yao Wenyuan, and Wang Hongwen formed a gang of four inside the Political Bureau, thus strengthening the influence of the counterrevolutionary Jiang Qing clique.

(iii) From the tenth congress of the party to October

1976. Early in 1974 Jiang Qing, Wang Hongwen, and others launched a campaign to "criticize Lin Biao and Confucius." Jiang Qing and the others directed the spearhead at Comrade Zhou Enlai, which was different in nature from the campaign conducted in some localities and organizations where individuals involved in and incidents connected with the conspiracies of the counterrevolutionary Lin Biao clique were investigated. Comrade Mao Zedong approved the launching of the movement to "criticize Lin Biao and Confucius." When he found that Jiang Qing and the others were turning it to their advantage in order to seize power, he severely criticized them. He declared that they had formed a "Gang of Four" and pointed out that Jiang Qing harbored the wild ambition of making herself chairman of the Central Committee and "forming a cabinet" by political manipulation.

In 1975, when Comrade Zhou Enlai was seriously ill, Comrade Deng Xiaoping, with the support of Comrade Mao Zedong, took charge of the day-to-day work of the Central Committee. He convened an enlarged meeting of the military commission of the Central Committee and several other important meetings with a view to solving problems in industry, agriculture, transport, and science and technology, and began to straighten out work in many fields so that the situation took an obvious turn for the better. However, Comrade Mao Zedong could not bear to accept systematic correction of the errors of the "Cultural Revolution" by Comrade Deng Xiaoping and triggered the movement to "criticize Deng and counter the right deviationist trend to reverse correct verdicts," once again plunging the nation into turmoil.

In January of that year, Comrade Zhou Enlai passed away. Comrade Zhou Enlai was utterly devoted to the party and the people and stuck to his post until his dying day. He found himself in an extremely difficult situation throughout the "Cultural Revolution." He always kept the general interest in mind, bore the heavy burden of office without complaint, racking his brains and untiringly endeavoring to keep the normal work of the party and the state going, to minimize the damage caused by the "Cultural Revolution" and to protect many party and nonparty cadres. He waged all forms of struggle to counter sabotage by the counterrevolutionary Lin Biao and Jiang Qing cliques. His death left the whole party and people in the most profound grief.

In April of the same year, a powerful movement of protest signaled by the Tiananmen incident swept the whole country, a movement to mourn for the late Premier Zhou Enlai and oppose the Gang of Four. In essence, the movement was a demonstration of support for the party's correct leadership as represented by Comrade Deng Xiaoping. It laid the ground for massive popular support for the subsequent overthrow of the counterrevolutionary Jiang Qing clique. The Political Bureau of the Central Committee and Comrade Mao Zedong wrongly assessed the nature of the Tiananmen incident and dismissed Comrade Deng Xiaoping from all his posts inside and outside the party. As soon as Comrade Mao Zedong passed away in September 1976, the counterrevolutionary Jiang Qing clique stepped up its plot to seize supreme party and state leadership. Early in October of the same year, the Political Bureau of the Central Committee, executing the will of the party and the people, resolutely smashed the clique and brought the catastrophic "Cultural Revolution" to an end. This was a great victory won by the entire party, army and people after prolonged struggle. Hua Guofeng, Ye Jianying, Li Xiannian, and other comrades played a vital part in the struggle to crush the clique.

(22) Chief responsibility for the grave "left" error of the "Cultural Revolution," an error comprehensive in magnitude and protracted in duration, does indeed lie with Comrade Mao Zedong. But after all, it was the error of a great proletarian revolutionary. Comrade Mao Zedong paid constant attention to overcoming shortcomings in the life of the party and state. In his later years, however, far from making a correct analysis of many problems, he confused right and wrong and the people with the enemy during the "Cultural Revolution." While making serious mistakes, he repeatedly urged the whole party to study the works of Marx, Engels, and Lenin conscientiously and imagined that his theory and practice were Marxist and that they were essential for the consolidation of the dictatorship of the proletariat. Herein lies his tragedy. While persisting in the comprehensive error of the "Cultural Revolution," he checked and rectified some of its specific mistakes, protected some leading party cadres and nonparty public figures, and enabled some leading cadres to return to important leading posts. He led the struggle to smash the counterrevolutionary Lin Biao clique. He made major criticisms and exposures of Jiang Qing, Zhang Chunqiao, and others, frustrating their sinister ambition to seize supreme leadership. All this was crucial to the subsequent and relatively painless overthrow of the Gang of Four by our party.

In his later years, he still remained alert to safeguarding the security of our country, stood up to the pressure of the social imperialists, pursued a correct foreign policy, firmly supported the just struggles of all peoples, outlined the correct strategy of the three worlds, and advanced the important principle that China would never seek hegemony.

During the "Cultural Revolution" our party was not destroyed, but maintained its unity. The State Council and the PLA were still able to do much of their essential work. The Fourth National People's Congress, which was attended by deputies from all nationalities and all walks of life, was convened, and it determined the composition of the State Council, with Comrades Zhou Enlai and Deng Xiaoping as the core of its leadership. The foundation of China's socialist system remained intact, and it was possible to continue socialist economic construction. Our country remained united and exerted a significant influence on international affairs. All these important facts are inseparable from the great role played by Comrade Mao Zedong. For these reasons, and particularly for his vital contributions to the cause of the revolution over the years, the Chinese people have always regarded Comrade Mao Zedong as their respected and beloved great leader and teacher.

(23) The struggle waged by the party and the people against "left" errors and against the counterrevolutionary Lin Biao and Jiang Qing cliques during the "Cultural Revolution" was arduous and full of twists and turns, and it never ceased. Rigorous tests throughout the "Cultural Revolution" have proved that standing on the correct side in the struggle were the overwhelming majority of members of the Eighth Central Committee of the party and the members it elected to its Political Bureau, Standing Committee, and Secretariat. Most of our party cadres, whether they were wrongly dismissed or remained at their posts, whether they were rehabilitated early or late, are loyal to the party and people and steadfast in their belief in the cause of socialism and communism. Most of the intellectuals, model workers, patriotic democrats, patriotic overseas Chinese, and cadres and masses of all strata and all nationalities who had been wronged and persecuted did not waver in their love for the motherland and in their support for the party and socialism. Party and state leaders such as Comrades Liu Shaoqi, Peng Dehuai, He Long, and Tao Zhu and all other party and nonparty comrades who were persecuted to death in the "Cultural Revolution" will live forever in the memories of the Chinese people.

It was through the joint struggles waged by the entire party and the masses of workers, peasants, PLA officers and men, intellectuals, educated youth, and cadres that the havoc wrought by the "Cultural Revolution" was somewhat mitigated. Some progress was made in our economy despite tremendous losses. Grain output increased relatively steadily. Significant achievements were scored in industry, communications and capital construction, and in science and technology. New railways were built and the Changjiang [Yangzi] River bridge at Nanjing was completed; a number of large enterprises using advanced technology went into operation; hydrogen bomb tests were successfully undertaken and man-made satellites successfully launched and retrieved; and new hybrid strains of long-grained rice were developed and popularized. Despite the domestic turmoil, the PLA bravely defended the security of the motherland. And new prospects were opened up in the sphere of foreign affairs. Needless to say, none of these successes can be attributed in any way to the "Cultural Revolution," without which we would have scored far greater achievements for our cause. Although we suffered from sabotage by the counterrevolutionary Lin Biao and Jiang Qing cliques during the "Cultural Revolution," we won out over them in the end. The party, the people's political power, the people's army, and Chinese society on the whole remained unchanged in nature. Once again history has proved that our people are a great people and that our party and socialist system have enormous vitality.

(24) In addition to the above-mentioned immediate cause of Comrade Mao Zedong's mistake in leadership, there are complex social and historical causes underlying the "Cultural Revolution," which dragged on for as long as a decade. The main causes are as follows:

(i) The history of the socialist movement is not long and that of the socialist countries even shorter. Some of the laws governing the development of socialist society are relatively clear, but many more remain to be explored. Our party had long existed in circumstances of war and fierce class struggle. It was not fully prepared, either ideologically or in terms of scientific study, for the swift advent of the newborn socialist society and for socialist construction on a national scale. The scientific works of Marx, Engels, Lenin, and Stalin are our guide to action, but can in no way provide ready-made answers to the problems we may encounter in our socialist cause. Even after the basic completion of socialist transformation, given the guiding ideology, we were liable, owing to the historical circumstances in which our party grew, to continue to regard issues unrelated to class struggle as its manifestations when observing and handling new contradictions and problems that cropped up in the political, economic, cultural and other spheres in the course of the development of socialist society. And when confronted with actual class struggle under the new conditions, we habitually fell back on the familiar methods and experiences of the large-scale, turbulent mass struggle of the past, which should no longer have been mechanically followed.

As a result, we substantially broadened the scope of class struggle. Moreover, this subjective thinking and practice divorced from reality seemed to have a "theoretical basis" in the writings of Marx, Engels, Lenin, and Stalin because certain ideas and arguments set forth in them were misunderstood or dogmatically interpreted. For instance, it was thought that equal right, which reflects the exchange of equal amounts of labor and is applicable in the distribution of the means of consumption in socialist society, or "bourgeois right" as it was designated by Marx, should be restricted and criticized, and so the principle of "to each according to his work" and that of material interest should be re-

stricted and criticized; that small production would continue to engender capitalism and the bourgeoisie daily and hourly on a large scale even after the basic completion of socialist transformation, and so a series of "left" economic policies and policies on class struggle in urban and rural areas were formulated; and that all ideological differences inside the party were reflections of class struggle in society, and so frequent and acute inner-party struggles were conducted. All this led us to regard the error in magnifying class struggle as an act in defense of the purity of Marxism.

Furthermore, Soviet leaders started a polemic between China and the Soviet Union, and turned the arguments between the two parties on matters of principle into a conflict between the two nations, bringing enormous pressure to bear upon China politically, economically, and militarily. So we were forced to wage a just struggle against the big-nation chauvinism of the Soviet Union. In these circumstances, a campaign to prevent and combat revisionism inside the country was launched, which spread the error of broadening the scope of class struggle in the party, so that normal differences among comrades inside the party came to be regarded as manifestations of the revisionist line or of the struggle between the two lines. This resulted in growing tension in inner-party relations. Thus it became difficult for the party to resist certain "left" views put forward by Comrade Mao Zedong and others, and the development of these views led to the outbreak of the protracted "Cultural Revolution."

(ii) Comrade Mao Zedong's prestige reached a peak, and he began to get arrogant at the very time when the party was confronted with the new task of shifting the focus of its work to socialist construction; a task for which the utmost caution was required. He gradually divorced himself from practice and from the masses, acted more and more arbitrarily and subjectively, and increasingly put himself above the Central Committee of the party. The result was a steady weakening and even undermining of the principle of collective leadership and democratic centralism in the political life of the party and the country. This state of affairs took shape only gradually and the Central Committee of the party should be held partly responsible. From the Marxist viewpoint, this complex phenomenon was the product of given historical conditions. Blaming this on only one person or on only a handful of people will not provide a deep lesson for the whole party or enable it to find practical ways to change the situation. In the Communist movement, leaders play quite an important role. This has been borne out by history time and again and leaves no room for doubt. However, certain grievous deviations, which occurred in the history of the international Communist movement owing to the failure to handle the relationship between the party and its leader correctly, had an adverse effect on our party, too. Feudalism in China has had a very long history. Our party fought in the firmest and most thoroughgoing way against it and particularly against the feudal system of land ownership and the landlords and local tyrants, and fostered a fine tradition of democracy in the antifeudal struggle. But it remains difficult to eliminate the evil ideological and political influence of centuries of feudal autocracy. And for various historical reasons, we failed to institutionalize and legalize innerparty democracy and democracy in the political and social life of the country, or we drew up the relevant laws but they lacked due authority. This meant that conditions were present for the overconcentration of party power in individuals and for the development of arbitrary individual rule and the personality cult in the party. Thus, it was hard for the party and state to prevent the initiation of the "Cultural Revolution" or check its development.

(25) The victory won in overthrowing the counterrevolutionary Jiang Qing clique in October 1976 saved the party and the revolution from disaster and enabled our country to enter a new historical period of development. In the two years from October 1976 to December 1978, when the third plenary session of the Eleventh Central Committee of the party was convened, large numbers of cadres and other people most enthusiastically devoted themselves to all kinds of revolutionary work and the task of construction. Notable results were achieved in exposing and repudiating the crimes of the counterrevolutionary Jiang Qing clique and uncovering their factional setup. The consolidation of party and state organizations and the redress of wrongs suffered by those who were unjustly, falsely, and wrongly charged began in some places. Industrial and agricultural production was fairly swiftly restored. Work in education, science, and culture began to return to normal.

Comrades inside and outside the party demanded more and more strongly that the errors of the "Cultural Revolution" be corrected, but such demands met with serious resistance. This, of course, was partly due to the fact that the political and ideological confusion created in the decade-long "Cultural Revolution" could not be eliminated overnight, but it was also due to the "left" error in the guiding ideology that Comrade Hua Guofeng continued to commit in his capacity as chairman of the Central Committee of the CCP. On the proposal of Comrade Mao Zedong, Comrade Hua Guofeng had become first vice chairman of the Central Committee of the party and concurrently premier of the State Council during the "movement to criticize Deng Xiaoping" in 1976. He contributed to the struggle to overthrow the counterrevolutionary Jiang Qing clique and did useful work after that. But he promoted the erroneous "two-whatevers" policy, that is, "We firmly uphold whatever policy decisions

Chairman Mao made, and we adhere to whatever instructions Chairman Mao gave," and he took a long time to rectify the error. He tried to suppress the discussions on the criterion of truth unfolded in the country in 1978, which were very significant in setting things right.

He procrastinated and obstructed the work of reinstating veteran cadres in their posts and redressing the injustices left over from the past (including the case of the "Tiananmen incident" of 1976). He accepted and fostered the personality cult around himself while continuing the personality cult of the past. The eleventh national congress of the CCP, convened in August 1977, played a positive role in exposing and repudiating the Gang of Four and mobilizing the whole party for building China into a powerful modern socialist state. However, owing to the limitations imposed by the historical conditions then and the influence of Comrade Hua Guofeng's mistakes, it reaffirmed the erroneous theories, policies and slogans of the "Cultural Revolution" instead of correcting them. He also had his share of responsibility for impetuously seeking quick results in economic work and for continuing certain other "left" policies. Obviously, under his leadership it is impossible to correct "left" errors within the party, and all the more impossible to restore the party's fine traditions.

(26) The third plenary session of the Eleventh Central Committee in December 1978 marked a crucial turning point of far-reaching significance in the history of our party since the birth of the People's Republic. It put an end to the situation in which the party had been advancing haltingly in its work since October 1976 and began to correct conscientiously and comprehensively the "left" errors of the "Cultural Revolution" and earlier. The plenary session resolutely criticized the erroneous "two-whatevers" policy and fully affirmed the need to grasp Mao Zedong Thought comprehensively and accurately as a scientific system. It highly evaluated the forum on the criterion of truth and decided on the guiding principle of emancipating the mind, using our brains, seeking truth from facts, and uniting as one in looking forward to the future. It firmly discarded the slogan "take class struggle as the key link," which had become unsuitable in a socialist society, and made the strategic decision to shift the focus of work to socialist modernization. It declared that attention should be paid to solving the problem of serious imbalances between the major branches of the economy and drafted decisions on the acceleration of agricultural development. It stressed the task of strengthening socialist democracy and the socialist legal system. It examined and redressed a number of major unjust, false and wrong cases in the history of the party and settled the controversy on the merits and demerits, the rights and wrongs, of some prominent leaders. The plenary session also elected additional members to the party's central leading organs.

These momentous changes in the work of leadership signify that the party has re-established the correct line of Marxism ideologically, politically, and organizationally. Since then, it has gained the initiative in setting things right and is able to solve step by step many problems left over since the founding of the People's Republic and the new problems cropping up in the course of practice and carry out the heavy tasks of construction and reform, so that things are going very well in both the economic and political sphere.

(i) In response to the call of the third plenary session of the Eleventh Central Committee of the party for emancipating the mind and seeking truth from facts, large numbers of cadres and other people have freed themselves from the spiritual shackles of the personality cult and the dogmatism that prevailed in the past. This has stimulated thinking inside and outside the party, giving rise to a lively situation where people try their best to study new things and seek solutions to new problems. To carry out the principle of emancipating the mind properly, the party reiterated in good time the four fundamental principles of upholding the socialist road, the people's democratic dictatorship (i.e., the dictatorship of the proletariat), the leadership of the Communist Party, and Marxism-Leninism and Mao Zedong Thought. It reaffirmed the principle that neither democracy nor centralism can be practiced at each other's expense and pointed out the basic fact that, although the exploiters had been eliminated as classes, class struggle continues to exist within certain limits. In his speech at the meeting in celebration of the thirtieth anniversary of the founding of the PRC, which was approved by the fourth plenary session of the Eleventh Central Committee of the party, Comrade Ye Jianying fully affirmed the gigantic achievements of the party and people since the inauguration of the People's Republic while making self-criticism on behalf of the party for errors in its work and outlined our country's bright prospects. This helped to unify the thinking of the whole party and people. At its meeting in August 1980, the Political Bureau of the Central Committee set the historic task of combating corrosion by bourgeois ideology and eradicating the evil influence of feudalism in the political and ideological fields which is still present.

A work conference convened by the Central Committee in December of the same year resolved to strengthen the party's ideological and political work, make greater efforts to build a socialist civilization, criticize the erroneous ideological trends running counter to the four fundamental principles, and strike at the counterrevolutionary activities disrupting the cause of socialism. This exerted a most salutary countrywide influence in fostering a political situation characterized by stability, unity, and liveliness.

(ii) At a work conference called by the Central Committee in April 1979, the party formulated the principle of "readjusting, restructuring, consolidating, and improving" the economy as a whole in a decisive effort to correct the shortcomings and mistakes of the previous two years in our economic work and eliminate the influence of "left" errors that had persisted in this field. The party indicated that economic construction must be carried out in the light of China's conditions and in conformity with economic and natural laws; that it must be carried out within the limits of our own resources, step by step, after due deliberation, and with emphasis on practical results, so that the development of production will be closely connected with the improvement of the people's livelihood; and that active efforts must be made to promote economic and technical cooperation with other countries on the basis of independence and self-reliance.

Guided by these principles, light industry has quickened its rate of growth and the structure of industry is becoming more rational and better coordinated. Reforms in the system of economic management, including extension of the decision-making powers of enterprises, restoration of the workers' congresses, strengthening of democratic management of enterprises, and transference of financial management responsibilities to the various levels, have gradually been carried out in conjunction with economic readjustment. The party has worked conscientiously to remedy the errors in rural work since the latter stage of the movement for agricultural cooperation, with the result that the purchase prices of farm and sideline products have been raised, various forms of production responsibility introduced whereby remuneration is determined by farm output, family plots have been restored and appropriately extended, village fairs have been revived, and sideline occupations and diverse undertakings have been developed. All these have greatly enhanced the peasants' enthusiasm. Grain output in the last two years reached an all-time high, and at the same time industrial crops and other farm and sideline products registered a big increase. Thanks to the development of agriculture and the economy as a whole, the living standards of the people have improved.

(iii) After detailed and careful investigation and study, measures were taken to clear the name of Comrade Liu Shaoqi, former vice chairman of the Central Committee of the CCP and chairman of the PRC, those of other party and state leaders, national minority leaders and leading figures in different circles who had been wronged, and to affirm their historical contributions to the party and the people in protracted revolutionary struggle.

(iv) Large numbers of unjust, false, and wrong cases were re-examined and their verdicts reversed. Cases in which people had been wrongly labeled bourgeois rightists were also corrected. Announcements were made to the effect that former businessmen and industrialists, having undergone remolding, are now working people; that small tradespeople, peddlers and handicraftsmen, who were originally laborers, have been differentiated from businessmen and industrialists who were members of the bourgeoisie, and that the status of the vast majority of former landlords and rich peasants, who have become working people through remolding, has been redefined. These measures have appropriately resolved many contradictions inside the party and among the people.

(v) People's congresses at all levels are doing their work better, and those at the provincial and county levels have set up permanent organs of their own. The system according to which deputies to the people's congresses at and below the county level are directly elected by the voters is now universally practiced. Collective leadership and democratic centralism are being perfected in the party and state organizations. The powers of local and primary organizations are steadily being extended. The so-called right to "speak out, air views, and hold debates in a big way and write big-character posters," which actually obstructs the promotion of socialist democracy, was deleted from the constitution. A number of important laws, decrees, and regulations have been reinstated, enacted, or enforced, including the criminal law and the law of criminal procedure, which had never been drawn up since the founding of the People's Republic. The work of the judicial, procuratorial, and public security departments has improved and telling blows have been dealt at all types of criminals guilty of serious offenses. The ten principal members of the counterrevolutionary Lin Biao and Jiang Qing cliques were publicly tried according to law.

(vi) The party has striven to readjust and strengthen the leading bodies at all levels. The fifth plenary session of the Eleventh Central Committee of the party, held in February 1980, elected additional members to the Standing Committee of its Political Bureau and reestablished the Secretariat of the Central Committee, greatly strengthening the central leadership. Party militancy has been enhanced as a result of the establishment of the Central Discipline Inspection Commission and of discipline inspection commissions at the lower levels, the formulation of the "guiding principles for inner-party political life" and other related inner-party regulations, and the effort made by leading party organizations and discipline inspection bodies at the different levels to rectify unhealthy practices. The party's mass media have also contributed immensely in this respect. The party had decided to put an end to the virtually lifelong tenure of leading cadres, change the

overconcentration of power and, on the basis of revolutionization gradually reduce the average age of the leading cadres at all levels and raise their level of education and professional competence, and has initiated this process. With the reshuffling of the leading personnel of the State Council and the division of labor between party and government organizations, the work of the central and local governments has improved.

In addition, there have been significant successes in the party's effort to implement our policies in education, science, culture, public health, physical culture, nationality affairs, united front work, overseas Chinese affairs, and military and foreign affairs.

In short, the scientific principles of Mao Zedong Thought and the correct policies of the party have been revived and developed under new conditions and all aspects of party and government work have been flourishing again since the third plenary session of the Eleventh Central Committee. Our work still suffers from shortcomings and mistakes, and we are still confronted with numerous difficulties. Nevertheless, the road of victorious advance is open, and the party's prestige among the people is rising day by day.

(27) Comrade Mao Zedong was a great Marxist and a great proletarian revolutionary, strategist, and theorist. It is true that he made gross mistakes during the "Cultural Revolution," but, if we judge his activities as a whole, his contributions to the Chinese revolution far outweigh his mistakes. His merits are primary and his errors secondary. He rendered indelible meritorious service in founding and building up our party and the Chinese PLA, in winning victory for the cause of liberation of the Chinese people, in founding the PRC, and in advancing our socialist cause. He made major contributions to the liberation of the oppressed nations of the world and to the progress of mankind.

(28) The Chinese Communists, with Comrade Mao Zedong as their chief representative, made a theoretical synthesis of China's unique experience in its protracted revolution in accordance with the basic principles of Marxism-Leninism. This synthesis constituted a scientific system of guidelines befitting China's conditions, and it is this synthesis which is Mao Zedong Thought, the product of the integration of the universal principles of Marxism-Leninism with the concrete practice of the Chinese revolution. Making revolution in a large Eastern semicolonial, semifeudal country is bound to meet with many special complicated problems, which cannot be solved by reciting the general principles of Marxism-Leninism, or by copying foreign experience in every detail. An erroneous tendency of making Marxism a dogma and defying Comintern resolutions and the experience of the Soviet Union prevailed in the international Communist movement and in our party mainly in the late 1920s and early 1930s, and

this tendency pushed the Chinese revolution to the brink of total failure. It was in the course of combating this wrong tendency and making a profound summary of our historical experience in this respect that Mao Zedong Thought took shape and developed. It was systematized and extended in a variety of fields and reached maturity in the latter part of the agrarian revolutionary war and the war of resistance against Japan, and it was further developed during the war of liberation and after the founding of the PRC. Mao Zedong Thought is Marxism-Leninism applied and developed in China; it constitutes a correct theory, a body of correct principles, and a summary of the experiences that have been confirmed in the practice of the Chinese revolution, a crystallization of the collective wisdom of the CCP. Many outstanding leaders of our party made important contributions to the formation and development of Mao Zedong Thought, which are synthesized in the scientific works of Comrade Mao Zedong.

(29) Mao Zedong Thought is wide-ranging in content. It is an original theory that has enriched and developed Marxism-Leninism in the following respects:

(i) On the new-democratic revolution. Proceeding from China's historical and social conditions, Comrade Mao Zedong made a profound study of the characteristics and laws of the Chinese revolution, applied and developed the Marxist-Leninist thesis of the leadership of the proletariat in the democratic revolution, and established the theory of new-democratic revolution—a revolution against imperialism, feudalism, and bureaucrat-capitalism waged by the masses of the people on the basis of the worker-peasant alliance under the leadership of the proletariat. His main works on this subject include: "Analysis of the Classes in Chinese Society," "Report on an Investigation of the Peasant Movement in Hunan," "A Single Spark Can Start a Prairie Fire," "Introducing 'The Communist,'" "On New Democracy," "On Coalition Government," and "The Present Situation and Our Tasks." The basic points of this theory are:

(a) China's bourgeoisie consisted of two sections, the big bourgeoisie (that is, the compradore bourgeoisie, or the bureaucrat-bourgeoisie), which was dependent on imperialism, and the national bourgeoisie, which had revolutionary leanings but wavered. The proletariat should endeavor to get the national bourgeoisie to join in the United Front under its leadership and, in special circumstances, to include even part of the big bourgeoisie in the United Front, so as to isolate the main enemy to the greatest possible extent. When forming a united front with the bourgeoisie, the proletariat must preserve its own independence and pursue the policy of "unity, struggle, unity through struggle"; when forced to split with the bourgeoisie, chiefly the big bourgeoisie, it should have the courage and ability to wage a resolute armed struggle against the big bourgeoisie, while continuing to win the sympathy of the national bourgeoisie or keep it neutral.

(b) Since there was no bourgeois democracy in China and the reactionary ruling classes enforced their terroristic dictatorship over the people by armed force, the revolution could not but essentially take the form of protracted armed struggle. China's armed struggle was a revolutionary war led by the proletariat with the peasants as the principal force. The peasantry was the most reliable ally of the proletariat. Through its vanguard, it was possible and necessary for the proletariat, with its progressive ideology and its sense of organization and discipline, to raise the political consciousness of the peasant masses, establish rural base areas, wage a protracted revolutionary war, and build up and expand the revolutionary forces.

Comrade Mao Zedong pointed out that "the united front and armed struggle are the two basic weapons for defeating the enemy." Together with party-building, they constituted the "three magic weapons" of the revolution. They were the essential basis that enabled the CCP to become the core of leadership of the whole nation and to chart the course of encircling the cities from the countryside and finally winning countrywide victory.

(ii) On the socialist revolution and socialist construction. On the basis of the economic and political conditions for the transition to socialism ensuing on victory in the new-democratic revolution, Comrade Mao Zedong and the CCP followed the path of effecting socialist industrialization simultaneously with socialist transformation and adopted concrete policies for the gradual transformation of the private ownership of the means of production, thereby providing a theoretical as well as practical solution to the difficult task of building socialism in a large country such as China, a country that was economically and culturally backward, with a population accounting for nearly one-fourth of the world's total. By putting forward the thesis that the combination of democracy for the people and dictatorship over the reactionaries constitutes the people's democratic dictatorship, Comrade Mao Zedong enriched the Marxist-Leninist theory of the dictatorship of the proletariat.

After the establishment of the socialist system, Comrade Mao Zedong pointed out that, under socialism, the people had the same fundamental interests, but that all kinds of contradictions still existed among them, and that contradictions between the enemy and the people and contradictions among the people should be strictly distinguished from each other and correctly handled. He proposed that among the people we should follow a set of correct policies. We should follow the policy of "unity-criticism-unity" in political matters, the policy of "long-term coexistence and mutual supervision" in the party's relations with the democratic parties, the policy of "let a hundred flowers blossom, let a hundred schools of thought contend" in science and culture, and, in the economic sphere, the policy of overall arrangement with regard to the different strata in town and country and of consideration for the interests of the state, the collective, and the individual, all three.

He repeatedly stressed that we should not mechanically transplant the experience of foreign countries, but should find our own way to industrialization, a way suited to China's conditions, by proceeding from the fact that China is a large agricultural country, taking agriculture as the foundation of the economy, correctly handling the relationship between heavy industry on the one hand and agriculture and light industry on the other, and attaching due importance to the development of the latter. He stressed that in socialist construction we should properly handle the relationships between economic construction and building national defense, between large-scale enterprises and small and medium-scale enterprises, between the Han nationality and the minority nationalities, between the coastal regions and the interior, between the central and the local authorities, and between self-reliance and learning from foreign countries, and that we should properly handle the relationship between accumulation and consumption and pay attention to overall balance.

Moreover, he stressed that the workers were the masters of their enterprises and that cadres must take part in physical labor and workers in management, that irrational rules and regulations must be reformed, and that the three-in-one combination of technical personnel, workers, and cadres must be effected. And he formulated the strategic idea of bringing all positive factors into play and turning negative factors into positive ones so as to unite the whole Chinese people and build a powerful socialist country.

The important ideas of Comrade Mao Zedong concerning the socialist revolution and socialist construction are mainly contained in such major works as "Report to the Second Plenary Session of the Seventh Central Committee of the CCP," "On the People's Democratic Dictatorship," "On the Ten Major Relationships," "On the Correct Handling of Contradictions among the People," and "Talk at an Enlarged Work Conference Convened by the Central Committee of the CCP."

(iii) On the building of the revolutionary army and military strategy. Comrade Mao Zedong methodically solved the problem of how to turn a revolutionary army chiefly made up of peasants into a new type of people's army, which is proletarian in character, observes strict discipline, and forms close ties with the masses. He laid it down that the sole purpose of the people's army is to serve the people wholeheartedly. He put forward the principle that the party commands the gun and not the other way around. He advanced the three main rules of discipline and the eight points for attention and stressed the practice of political, economic, and military democracy and the principles of the unity of officers and soldiers, the unity of army and people, and the disintegration of the enemy forces. Thus he formulated by way of summation a set of policies and methods concerning political work in the army.

In his military writings such as "On Correcting Mistaken Ideas in the Party," "Problems of Strategy in China's Revolutionary War," "Problems of Strategy in Guerrilla War Against Japan," "On Protracted War," and "Problems of War and Strategy," Comrade Mao Zedong summed up the experience of China's protracted revolutionary war and advanced the comprehensive concept of building a people's army and of building rural base areas and waging people's war by employing the people's army as the main force and relying on the masses. Raising guerrilla war to the strategic plane, he maintained that guerrilla warfare and mobile warfare of a guerrilla character would for a long time be the main forms of operation in China's revolutionary war. He explained that it would be necessary to effect an appropriate change in military strategy simultaneously with the changing balance of forces between the enemy and ourselves and with the progress of the war. He worked out a set of strategies and tactics for the revolutionary army to wage people's war in conditions when the enemy was strong and we were weak. These strategies and tactics include fighting a protracted war strategically and campaigns and battles of quick decision, turning strategic inferiority into superiority in campaigns and battles, and concentrating a superior force to destroy the enemy forces one by one. During the war of liberation, he formulated the celebrated ten major principles of operation. All these ideas constitute Comrade Mao Zedong's outstanding contribution to the military theory of Marxism-Leninism. After the founding of the People's Republic, he put forward the important guideline that we must strengthen our national defense and build modern revolutionary armed forces (including the Navy, the Air Force and technical branches) and develop modern defense technology (including the making of nuclear weapons for self-defense).

(iv) On policy and tactics. Comrade Mao Zedong penetratingly elucidated the vital importance of policy and tactics in revolutionary struggles. He pointed out that policy and tactics were the life of the party, that they were both the starting point and the end result of all the practical activities of a revolutionary party and that the party must formulate its policies in the light of the existing political situation, class relations, actual circumstances, and the changes in them, combining principle and flexibility. He made many valuable suggestions concerning policy and tactics in the struggle against the enemy, in the united front, and other questions. He pointed out among other things:

- That, under changing subjective and objective conditions, a weak revolutionary force could ultimately defeat a strong reactionary force;
- that we should despise the enemy strategically and take the enemy seriously tactically;
- that we should keep our eyes on the main target of the struggle and not hit out in all directions;
- that we should differentiate among and disintegrate our enemies, and adopt the tactic of making use of contradictions, winning over the many, opposing the few and crushing our enemies one by one;
- that, in areas under reactionary rule, we should combine legal and illegal struggle and, organizationally, adopt the policy of assigning picked cadres to work underground;
- that, as for members of the defeated reactionary classes and reactionary elements, we should give them a chance to earn a living and to become working people living by their own labor, so long as they did not rebel or create trouble; and
- that the proletariat and its party must fulfill two conditions in order to exercise leadership over their allies: (a) lead their followers in waging resolute struggles against the common enemy and achieving victories; (b) bring material benefits to their followers or at least avoid damaging their interests and at the same time give them political education.

These ideas of Comrade Mao Zedong's concerning policy and tactics are embodied in many of his writings, particularly in such works as "Current Problems of Tactics in the Anti-Japanese United Front," "On Policy," "Conclusions on the Repulse of the Second Anti-Communist Onslaught," "On Some Important Problems of the Party's Present Policy," "Don't Hit Out in All Directions," and "On the Question of Whether Imperialism and All Reactionaries Are Real Tigers."

(v) On ideological and political work and cultural work. In his "On New Democracy," Comrade Mao Zedong stated: Any given culture (as an ideological form) is a reflection of the politics and economics of a given society, and the former in turn has a tremendous influence and effect upon the latter; economics is the base and politics the concentrated expression of economics.

In accordance with this basic view, he put forward many significant ideas of far-reaching and long-term significance. For instance, the theses that ideological and political work is the life-blood of economic and all other work and that it is necessary to unite politics and economics and to unite politics and professional skills, and to be both Red and expert; the policy of developing a national,

scientific, and mass culture and of letting a hundred flowers blossom, weeding through the old to bring forth the new, and making the past serve the present and foreign things serve China; and the thesis that intellectuals have an important role to play in revolution and construction, that intellectuals should identify themselves with the workers and peasants, and that they should acquire the proletarian world outlook by studying Marxism-Leninism, by studying society, and through practical work. He pointed out that "this question of 'for whom?' is fundamental; it is a question of principle" and stressed that we should serve the people whole-heartedly, be highly responsible in revolutionary work, wage arduous struggle, and fear no sacrifice. Many notable works written by Comrade Mao Zedong on ideology, politics and culture, such as "The Orientation of the Youth Movement," "Recruit Large Numbers of Intellectuals," "Talks at the Yan'an Forum on Literature and Art," "In Memory of Norman Bethune," "Serve the People," and "The Foolish Old Man Who Removed the Mountain," are of tremendous significance even today.

(vi) On party building. It was a most difficult task to build a Marxist, proletarian party of a mass character in a country where the peasantry and other sections of the petty bourgeoisie constituted the majority of the population, while the proletariat was small in number yet strong in combat effectiveness. Comrade Mao Zedong's theory on party building provided a successful solution to this question. His main works in this area include "Combat Liberalism," "The Role of the CCP in the National War," "Reform Our Study," "Rectify the Party's Style of Work," "Oppose Stereotyped Party Writing," "Our Study and the Current Situation," "On Strengthening the Party Committee System," and "Methods of Work of Party Committees." He laid particular stress on building the party ideologically, saying that a party member should join the party not only organizationally but also ideologically and should constantly try to reform his nonproletarian ideas and replace them with proletarian ideas.

He indicated that the style of work that entailed integrating theory with practice, forging close links with the masses, and practicing self-criticism was the hallmark distinguishing the CCP from all other political parties in China. To counter the erroneous "left" policy of "ruthless struggle and merciless blows" once followed in inner-party struggle, he proposed the correct policy of "learning from past mistakes to avoid future ones and curing the sickness to save the patient," emphasizing the need to achieve the objective of clarity in ideology and unity among comrades in inner-party struggle. He initiated the rectification campaign as a form of ideological education in Marxism-Leninism throughout the party, which applied the method of criticism and self-criticism. In view of the fact that our party was about to become and then became a party in power leading the whole country, Comrade Mao Zedong urged time and again, first on the eve of the founding of the People's Republic and then later, that we should remain modest and prudent, guard against arrogance and rashness, and keep to plain living and hard struggle in our style of work and that we should be on the lookout against the corrosive influence of bourgeois ideology and should oppose bureaucratism, which would alienate us from the masses.

(30) The living soul of Mao Zedong Thought is the stand, method, and viewpoint embodied in its component parts mentioned above. This stand, viewpoint, and method boil down to three basic points: To seek truth from facts, the mass line, and independence. Comrade Mao Zedong applied dialectical and historical materialism to the entire work of the proletarian party, giving shape to this stand, viewpoint, and method so characteristic of Chinese Communists in the course of the Chinese revolution and its arduous, protracted struggles and thus enriching Marxism-Leninism. They find expression not only in such important works as "Oppose Book Worship," "On Practice," "On Contradiction," "Preface and Postscript to 'Rural Surveys,'" "Some Questions Concerning Methods of Leadership," and "Where Do Correct Ideas Come From?" but also in all his scientific writings and in the revolutionary activities of the Chinese Communists.

(i) Seeking truth from facts. This means proceeding from reality and combining theory with practice, that is, integrating the universal principles of Marxism-Leninism with the concrete practice of the Chinese revolution. Comrade Mao Zedong was always against studying Marxism in isolation from the realities of Chinese society and the Chinese revolution. As early as 1930, he opposed blind book worship by emphasizing that investigation and study is the first step in all work and that one has no right to speak without investigation. On the eve of the rectification movement in Yan'an, he affirmed that subjectivism is a formidable enemy of the Communist Party, a manifestation of impurity in party spirit. These brilliant theses helped people break through the shackles of dogmatism and greatly emancipate their own minds.

While summarizing the experience and lessons of the Chinese revolution in his philosophical works and many other works rich in philosophical content, Comrade Mao Zedong showed great profundity in expounding and enriching the Marxist theory of knowledge and dialectics. He stressed that the dialectical materialist theory of knowledge is the dynamic, revolutionary theory of reflection and that full scope should be given to man's conscious dynamic role, which is based on and is in conformity with objective reality. Basing himself on social practice, he comprehensively and systematically elaborated the dialectical materialist theory on the sources, the process, and the purpose of knowledge and

the criterion of truth. He said that as a rule, correct knowledge can be arrived at and developed only after many repetitions of the process leading from matter to consciousness and then back to matter; that is, leading from practice to knowledge and then back to practice. He pointed out that truth exists by contrast with falsehood and grows in struggle with it, that truth is inexhaustible, and that the truth of any piece of knowledge, namely, whether it corresponds to objective reality, can ultimately be decided only through social practice.

He further elaborated the law of the unity of opposites, the nucleus of Marxist dialectics. He indicated that we should not only study the universality of contradiction in objective existence, but, what is more important, we should study the particularity of contradiction, and that we should resolve contradictions that are different in nature by different methods. Therefore, dialectics should not be viewed as a formula to be learned by rote and applied mechanically, but should be closely linked with practice and with investigation and study and should be applied flexibly. He forged philosophy into a sharp weapon in the hands of the proletariat and the people for knowing and changing the world. His distinguished works on China's revolutionary war, in particular, provide outstandingly shining examples of applying and developing the Marxist theory of knowledge and dialectics in practice. Our party must always adhere to the above ideological line formulated by Comrade Mao Zedong.

(ii) The mass line means everything for the masses, reliance on the masses in everything, and "from the masses, to the masses." The party's mass line in all its work has come into being through the systematic application in all its activities of the Marxist-Leninist principle that the people are the makers of history. It is a summation of our party's invaluable historical experience in conducting revolutionary activities over the years under difficult circumstances in which the enemy's strength far outstripped ours. Comrade Mao Zedong stressed time and again that as long as we rely on the people, believe firmly in the inexhaustible creative power of the masses, and hence trust and identify ourselves with them, no enemy can crush us, while we can eventually crush every enemy and overcome every difficulty. He also pointed out that in leading the masses in all practical work, the leadership can form its correct ideas only by adopting the method of "from the masses, to the masses" and by combining the leadership with the masses and combining the general call with particular guidance. This means concentrating the ideas of the masses and turning them into systematic ideas, then going to the masses so that the ideas are persevered in and carried through, and testing the correctness of these ideas in the practice of the masses. And this process goes on, over and over again, so that the understanding of the leadership becomes more correct, more vital, and richer each time. This is how Comrade Mao Zedong united the Marxist theory of knowledge with the party's mass line.

As the vanguard of the proletariat, the party exists and fights for the interests of the people. But it always constitutes only a small part of the people, so that isolation from the people will render all the party's struggles and ideals devoid of content as well as impossible of success. To persevere in the revolution and advance the socialist cause, our party must uphold the mass line.

(iii) Independence and self-reliance are the inevitable corollary of carrying out the Chinese revolution and construction by proceeding from Chinese reality and relying on the masses. The proletarian revolution is an internationalist cause that calls for the mutual support of the proletariats of different countries. But for the cause to triumph, each proletariat should primarily base itself on its own country's realities, rely on the efforts of its own masses and revolutionary forces, integrate the universal principles of Marxism-Leninism with the concrete practice of its own revolution, and achieve victory. Comrade Mao Zedong always stressed that our policy should rest on our own strength and that we should find our own road of advance in accordance with our own conditions. In a vast country like China, we must all the more rely mainly on our own efforts to promote the revolution and construction. We must be determined to carry the struggle through to the end and must have faith in the hundreds of millions of Chinese people and rely on their wisdom and strength. Otherwise, it will be impossible for our revolution and construction to succeed or to be consolidated even if success is won.

Of course, China's revolution and national construction are not and cannot be carried on in isolation from the rest of the world. It is always necessary for us to try to win foreign aid and, in particular, to learn all that is advanced and beneficial from other countries. The closed-door policy, blind opposition to everything foreign, and any theory or practice of great-nation chauvinism are all entirely wrong. At the same time, although China is still comparatively backward economically and culturally, we must maintain our own national dignity and confidence and there must be no slavishness or submissiveness in any form in dealing with big, powerful, or rich countries.

Under the leadership of the party and Comrade Mao Zedong, we never wavered, whether before or after the founding of new China, in our determination to remain independent and self-reliant and, no matter what difficulty we encountered, we never submitted to any pressure from outside; we showed the dauntless and heroic spirit of the CCP and the Chinese people. We stand for the peaceful coexistence of the people of all countries and their mutual assistance on an equal footing. While upholding our own independence, we respect other people's right to independence. The road of revolution and construction suited to the characteristics of a country has to be explored, decided on, and blazed by its own people. No one has the right to impose his views on others. Only under these conditions can there be genuine internationalism. Otherwise, there can only be hegemonism. We will always adhere to this principled stand in our international relations.

(31) Mao Zedong Thought is the valuable spiritual asset of our party. It will be our guide to action for a long time to come. The party leaders and the large group of cadres nurtured by Marxism-Leninism and Mao Zedong Thought were the backbone forces in winning great victories for our cause; they are and will remain our treasured mainstay in the cause of socialist modernization. While many of Comrade Mao Zedong's important works were written during the periods of new-democratic revolution and of socialist transformation, we must still constantly study them. This is not only because one cannot cut the past off from the present and failure to understand the past will hamper our understanding of present-day problems, but also because many of the basic theories, principles, and methodology set forth in these works are of universal significance and provide us with valuable guidance now and will continue to do so in the future.

Therefore, we must continue to uphold Mao Zedong Thought, study it in earnest and apply its stand, viewpoint, and method in studying the new situation and solving the new problems arising in the course of practice. Mao Zedong Thought has added much that is new to the treasure-house of Marxist-Leninist theory. We must combine our study of the scientific works of Comrade Mao Zedong with that of the scientific writings of Marx, Engels, Lenin, and Stalin.

It is entirely wrong to try to negate the scientific value of Mao Zedong Thought and to deny its guiding role in our revolution and construction, just because Comrade Mao Zedong made mistakes in his later years. And it is likewise entirely wrong to adopt a dogmatic attitude toward the sayings of Comrade Mao Zedong, to regard whatever he said as the unalterable truth, which must be mechanically applied everywhere, and to be unwilling to admit honestly that he made mistakes in his later years, and even try to stick to them in our new activities. Both these attitudes fail to make a distinction between Mao Zedong Thought—a scientific theory formed and tested over a long period of time—and the mistakes Comrade Mao Zedong made in his later years. And it is absolutely necessary that this distinction should be made.

We must treasure all the positive experience obtained in the course of integrating the universal principles of Marxism-Leninism with the concrete practice of China's revolution and construction over fifty years or so, apply and carry forward this experience in our new work, enrich and develop party theory with new principles and new conclusions corresponding to reality, so as to ensure the continued progress of our cause along the scientific course of Marxism-Leninism and Mao Zedong Thought. . . .

(32) The objective of our party's struggle in the new historical period is to turn China step by step into a powerful socialist country with modern agriculture, industry, national defense, and science and technology and with a high level of democracy and culture. We must also accomplish the great cause of reunification of the country by getting Taiwan to return to the embrace of the motherland. The fundamental aim of summing up the historical experience of the thirty-two years since the founding of the People's Republic is to accomplish the great objective of building a powerful and modern socialist country by further rallying the will and strength of the whole party, the whole army, and the whole people on the basis of upholding the four fundamental principles, namely, upholding the socialist road, the people's democratic dictatorship (i.e., the dictatorship of the proletariat), the leadership of the Communist Party, and Marxism-Leninism and Mao Zedong Thought. These four principles constitute the common political basis of the unity of the whole party and the unity of the whole people as well as the basic guarantee for the realization of socialist modernization. Any word or deed that deviates from these four principles is wrong. Any word or deed that denies or undermines these four principles cannot be tolerated.

(33) Socialism and socialism alone can save China. This is the unalterable conclusion drawn by all our people from their own experience over the past century or so and it likewise constitutes our fundamental historical experience in the thirty-two years since the founding of our People's Republic. Although our socialist system is still in its early phase of development, China has undoubtedly established a socialist system and entered the stage of socialist society. Any view denying this basic fact is wrong. Under socialism, we have achieved successes that were absolutely impossible in old China. This is a preliminary and at the same time convincing manifestation of the superiority of the socialist system. The fact that we have been and are able to overcome all kinds of difficulties through our own efforts testifies to its great vitality. Of course, our system will have to undergo a long process of development before it can be perfected. Given the premise that we uphold the basic system of socialism, therefore, we must strive to reform those specific features that are not in keeping with the expansion of the productive forces and the interests of the people, and to staunchly combat all activities detrimental to socialism. With the development of our cause, the immense superi-

ority of socialism will become more and more apparent.

(34) Without the CCP, there would have been no new China. Likewise, without the CCP, there would be no modern socialist China. The CCP is a proletarian party armed with Marxism-Leninism and Mao Zedong Thought and imbued with a strict sense of discipline and the spirit of self-criticism, and its ultimate historical mission is to realize communism. Without the leadership of such a party, without the flesh-and-blood ties it has formed with the masses through protracted struggles, and without its painstaking and effective work among the people and the high prestige it consequently enjoys, our country—for a variety of reasons, both internal and external—would inexorably fall apart and the future of our nation and people would inexorably be forfeited. The party leadership cannot be free from mistakes, but there is no doubt that, by relying on the close unity between the party and the people, it can correct its mistakes, and in no case should one use the party's mistakes as a pretext for weakening, breaking away from or even sabotaging its leadership. That would only lead to even greater mistakes and court grievous disasters. We must improve party leadership in order to uphold it. We must resolutely overcome the many shortcomings that still exist in our party's style of thinking and work, in its system of organization and leadership and in its contacts with the masses. So long as we earnestly uphold and constantly improve party leadership, our party will definitely be better able to undertake the tremendous tasks entrusted to it by history.

(35) Since the third plenary session of the Eleventh Central Committee, our party has gradually mapped out the correct path for socialist modernization suited to China's conditions. In the course of practice, the path will be broadened and become more clearly defined, but, in essence, the key pointers can already be determined on the basis of the summing up of the negative as well as positive experience since the founding of the People's Republic, and particularly of the lessons of the ''Cultural Revolution.''

(i) After socialist transformation was fundamentally completed, the principal contradiction our country has had to resolve is that between the growing material and cultural needs of the people and the backwardness of social production. It was imperative that the focus of party and government work be shifted to socialist modernization centering on economic construction and that the people's material and cultural life be gradually improved by means of an immense expansion of productive forces. In the final analysis, the mistake we made in the past was that we failed to persevere in making this strategic shift. What is more, the preposterous view opposing the ''theory of the unique importance of productive forces,'' a view diametrically opposed to historical materialism, was put forward during the "Cultural Revolution." We must never deviate from this focus, except in the event of large-scale invasion by a foreign enemy (and even then it will still be necessary to carry on such economic construction as wartime conditions require and permit). All our party work must be subordinated to and serve this central task—economic construction. All our party cadres, and particularly those in economic departments, must diligently study economic theory and economic practice as well as science and technology.

(ii) In our socialist economic construction, we must strive to reach the goal of modernization systematically and in stages, according to the conditions and resources of our country. The prolonged "left" mistakes we made in our economic work in the past consisted chiefly in departing from Chinese realities, trying to exceed our actual capabilities, and ignoring the economic returns of construction and management as well as the scientific confirmation of our economic plans, policies, and measures, with their concomitants of colossal waste and losses. We must adopt a scientific attitude, gain a thorough knowledge of the realities, and make a deep analysis of the situation, earnestly listen to the opinions of the cadres, masses, and specialists in the various fields and try our best to act in accordance with objective economic and natural laws and bring about a proportionate and harmonious development of the various branches of economy. We must keep in mind the fundamental fact that China's economy and culture are still relatively backward. At the same time, we must keep in mind such favorable domestic and international conditions as the achievements we have already scored and the experience we have gained in our economic construction and the expansion of economic and technological exchanges with foreign countries, and we must make full use of these favorable conditions. We must oppose both impetuosity and passivity.

(iii) The reform and improvement of the socialist relations of production must be in conformity with the level of the productive forces and conducive to the expansion of production. The state economy and the collective economy are the basic forms of the Chinese economy. The working people's individual economy within certain prescribed limits is a necessary complement to public economy. It is necessary to establish specific systems of management and distribution suited to the various sectors of the economy.

It is necessary to have planned economy and at the same time give play to the supplementary, regulatory role of the market on the basis of public ownership. We must strive to promote commodity production and exchange on a socialist basis. There is no rigid pattern for the development of the socialist relations of production. At every stage our task is to create those specific forms

of the relations of production that correspond to the needs of the growing productive forces and facilitate their continued advance.

(iv) Class struggle no longer constitutes the principal contradiction after the exploiters have been eliminated as classes. However, owing to certain domestic factors and influences from abroad, class struggle will continue to exist within certain limits for a long time to come and may even grow acute under certain conditions. It is necessary to oppose both the view that the scope of class struggle must be enlarged and the view that it has died out. It is imperative to maintain a high level of vigilance and conduct effective struggle against all those who are hostile to socialism and try to sabotage it in the political, economic, ideological, and cultural fields and in community life. We must correctly understand that there are diverse social contradictions in Chinese society that do not fall within the scope of class struggle and that methods other than class struggle must be used for their appropriate revolution. Otherwise, social stability and unity will be jeopardized. We must unswervingly unite all forces that can be united with and consolidate and expand the patriotic united front.

(v) A fundamental task of the socialist revolution is gradually to establish a highly democratic socialist political system. Inadequate attention was paid to this matter after the founding of the People's Republic, and this was one of the major factors contributing to the initiation of the "Cultural Revolution." Here is a grievous lesson for us to learn. It is necessary to strengthen the building of state organs at all levels in accordance with the principle of democratic centralism, make the people's congresses at all levels and their permanent organs authoritative organs of the people's political power, gradually realize direct popular participation in the democratic process at the grass roots of political power and community life, and, in particular, stress democratic management by the working masses in urban and rural enterprises over the affairs of their establishments. It is essential to consolidate the people's democratic dictatorship, improve our constitution and laws, and ensure their strict observance and inviolability. We must turn the socialist legal system into a powerful instrument for protecting the rights of the people, ensuring order in production, work and other spheres, punishing criminals, and cracking down on the disruptive activities of class enemies. The kind of chaotic situation that obtained in the "Cultural Revolution" must never be allowed to happen again in any sphere.

(vi) Life under socialism must attain a high ethical and cultural level. We must firmly eradicate utterly fallacious views that denigrate education, science, and culture, and discriminate against intellectuals, views that had long existed and found extreme expression during the "Cultural Revolution"; we must strive to raise the status and expand the role of education, science, and culture in our drive for modernization. We unequivocally affirm that, together with the workers and peasants, the intellectuals are a force to rely on in the cause of socialism and that it is impossible to carry out socialist construction without culture and the intellectuals. It is imperative for the whole party to engage in a more diligent study of Marxist theories, of the past and present in China and abroad, and of the different branches of the natural and social sciences.

We must strengthen and improve ideological and political work and educate the people and youth in the Marxist world outlook and communist morality; we must persistently carry out the educational policy that calls for an all-around development morally, intellectually, and physically, for being both Red and expert, for integration of the intellectuals with the workers and peasants and the combination of mental and physical labor; and we must counter the influence of decadent bourgeois ideology and the decadent remnants of feudal ideology, overcome the influence of petty-bourgeois ideology, and foster the patriotism that puts the interests of the motherland above everything else and the pioneer spirit of selfless devotion to modernization.

(vii) It is of profound significance to our multinational country to improve and promote socialist relations among our various nationalities and strengthen national unity. In the past, particularly during the "Cultural Revolution," we committed, on the question of nationalities, the grave mistake of widening the scope of class struggle and wronged a large number of cadres and masses of the minority nationalities. In our work among them we did not show due respect for their right to autonomy. We must never forget this lesson. We must have a clear understanding that relations among our nationalities today are, in the main, relations among the working people of the various nationalities. It is necessary to persist in their regional autonomy and enact laws and regulations to ensure this autonomy and their decision-making power in applying party and government policies according to the actual conditions in their regions. We must take effective measures to assist economic and cultural development in regions inhabited by minority nationalities, actively train and promote cadres from among them, and resolutely oppose all words and deeds undermining national unity and equality.

It is imperative to continue to implement the policy of freedom of religious belief. To uphold the four fundamental principles does not mean that religious believers should renounce their faith but that they must not engage in propaganda against Marxism-Leninism and Mao Zedong Thought and that they must not interfere with politics and education in their religious activities.

(viii) In the present international situation in which the danger of war still exists, it is necessary to strengthen the modernization of our national defense. The building up of national defense must be in keeping with the building up of the economy. The PLA should strengthen its military training, political work, logistical service, and study of military science and further raise its combat effectiveness so as gradually to become a still more powerful modern revolutionary army. It is necessary to restore and carry forward the fine tradition of unity inside the army, between the army and the government, and between the army and the people. The building of the people's militia must also be further strengthened.

(ix) In our external relations, we must continue to oppose imperialism, hegemonism, colonialism, and racism, and safeguard world peace. We must actively promote relations and economic and cultural exchanges with other countries on the basis of the Five Principles of Peaceful Coexistence. We must uphold proletarian internationalism and support the cause of the liberation of oppressed nations, the national construction of newly independent countries, and the just struggles of the peoples everywhere.

(x) In the light of the lessons of the "Cultural Revolution" and the present situation in the party, it is imperative to build up a sound system of democratic centralism inside the party. We must carry out the Marxist principle of the exercise of collective party leadership by leaders who have emerged from mass struggles and who combine political integrity with professional competence, and we must prohibit the personality cult in any form. It is imperative to uphold the prestige of party leaders and at the same time ensure that their activities come under the supervision of the party and the people. We must have a high degree of centralism based on a high degree of democracy and insist that the minority is subordinate to the majority, the individual to the organization, the lower to the higher level and the entire membership to the Central Committee. The style of work of a political party in power is a matter that determines its very existence. Party organizations at all levels and all party cadres must go deep among the masses, plunge themselves into practical struggle, remain modest and prudent, share weal and woe with the masses, and firmly overcome bureaucratism. We must properly wield the weapon of criticism and self-criticism, overcome erroneous ideas that deviate from the party's correct principles, uproot factionalism, oppose anarchism and ultraindividualism, and eradicate such unhealthy tendencies as the practice of seeking perquisites and privileges. We must consolidate the party organization, purify the party ranks, and weed out degenerate elements who oppress and bully the people. In exercising leadership over state affairs and work in the economic and cultural fields as well as in community life, the party must correctly handle its relations with other organizations, ensure by every means the effective functioning of the organs of state power and administrative, judicial and economic and cultural organizations, and see to it that trade unions, the Youth League, the Women's Federation, the Science and Technology Association, the Federation of Literary and Art Circles, and other mass organizations carry out their work responsibly and on their own initiative. The party must strengthen its cooperation with public figures outside the party, give full play to the role of the Chinese People's Political Consultative Conference, hold conscientious consultations with democratic parties and personages without party affiliation on major issues of state affairs, and respect their opinions and the opinions of specialists in various fields. As required of other social organizations, the party's organizations at all levels must conduct their activities within the limits permitted by the constitution and the law.

(36) In firmly correcting the mistake of the "continued revolution under the dictatorship of the proletariat," a slogan advanced during the "Cultural Revolution" that called for the overthrow of one class by another, we absolutely do not mean that the tasks of the revolution have been accomplished and that there is no need to carry on revolutionary struggles with determination. Socialism aims not just at eliminating all systems of exploitation and all exploiting classes but also at greatly expanding the productive forces, improving and developing the socialist relations of production and the superstructure and, on this basis, gradually eliminating all class differences and all major social distinctions and inequalities that are chiefly due to the inadequate development of the productive forces until communism is finally realized. This is a great revolution, unprecedented in human history. Our present endeavor to build a modern socialist China constitutes but one stage of this great revolution. Differing from the revolutions before the overthrow of the system of exploitation, this revolution is carried out not through fierce class confrontation and conflict, but through the strength of the socialist system itself, under leadership, step by step and in an orderly way. This revolution, which has entered the period of peaceful development, is more profound and arduous than any previous revolution and will not only take a very long historical period to accomplish but also demand the unswerving and disciplined hard work and heroic sacrifices of many generations.

In this historical period of peaceful development, revolution can never be plain sailing. There are still overt and covert enemies and other saboteurs who watch for opportunities to create trouble. We must maintain high revolutionary vigilance and be ready at all times to come out boldly to safeguard the interests of the revolution. In this new historical period, the whole membership of the CCP and the whole people must never cease to cherish lofty revolutionary ideals, maintain a dynamic revolutionary fighting spirit, and carry China's great socialist revolution and socialist construction through to the end.

(37) Repeated assessment of our successes and failures of our correct and incorrect practices of the thirty-two years after the founding of our People's Republic, and particularly deliberation over and review of the events of the past few years, have helped to raise immensely the political consciousness of all party comrades and of all patriots. Obviously, our party now has a higher level of understanding of socialist revolution and construction than at any other period after liberation. Our party has both the courage to acknowledge and correct its mistakes and the determination and ability to prevent repetition of the serious mistakes of the past. After all, from a long-term historical point of view the mistakes and setbacks of our party were only temporary whereas the consequent steeling of our party and people, the greater maturity of the core force formed among our party cadres through protracted struggle, the growing superiority of our socialist system and the increasingly keen and common aspiration of our party, army, and people for the prosperity of the motherland will be decisive factors in the long run. A great future is in store for our socialist cause and for the Chinese people in their hundreds of millions.

(38) Inner-party unity and unity between the party and the people are the basic guarantee for new victories in our socialist modernization. Whatever the difficulties, as long as the party is closely united and remains closely united with the people, our party and the cause of socialism it leads will certainly prosper day by day.

The resolution on certain questions in the history of our party, unanimously adopted in 1945 by the enlarged seventh plenary session of the Sixth Central Committee of the party, unified the thinking of the whole party, consolidated its unity, promoted the rapid advance of the people's revolutionary cause, and accelerated its eventual triumph. The sixth plenary session of the Eleventh Central Committee of the party believes that the present resolution it has unanimously adopted will play a similar historical role. This session calls upon the whole party, the whole army, and the people of all our nationalities to act under the great banner of Marxism-Leninism and Mao Zedong Thought, closely rally around the Central Committee of the party, preserve the spirit of the legendary foolish old man who removed mountains, and work together as one in defiance of all difficulties so as to turn China step by step into a powerful modern socialist country that is highly democratic and highly cultured. Our goal must be attained. Our goal can unquestionably be attained.

Nine-Point Proposal for Taiwan

On September 30, 1981, Marshal Ye Jianying, chairman of the Standing Committee of the National People's Congress, unveiled a nine-point program for the peaceful reunification of Taiwan and mainland China. The proposal signaled a new flexibility in China's attitude toward Taiwan and called for economic and cultural exchanges with Taiwan as well as the beginning of negotiations between the Kuomintang and the Communist Party. The text of the proposal follows.

Today, on the eve of the thirty-second anniversary of the founding of the People's Republic of China and at the approach of the seventieth anniversary of the 1911 Revolution, I wish, first of all, to extend my festive greetings and cordial regards to the people of all nationalities throughout the country, including the compatriots in Taiwan, Hong Kong, and Macao, and Chinese nationals residing in foreign countries.

On New Year's Day 1979, the Standing Committee of the National People's Congress issued a message to the compatriots in Taiwan, in which it proclaimed the policy of striving to reunify the motherland peacefully. The message received warm support and active response from the people of all nationalities throughout China, including the compatriots in Taiwan, Hong Kong, and Macao, and those residing abroad. A relaxed atmosphere has set in across the Taiwan Strait. Now, I would take this opportunity to elaborate on the policy concerning the return of Taiwan to the motherland for the realization of peaceful reunification:

(1) In order to bring an end to the unfortunate separation of the Chinese nations as early as possible, we propose that talks be held between the Chinese Communist Party and the Kuomintang of China [Taiwan— Ed.] on a reciprocal basis so that the two parties will cooperate for the third time to accomplish the great cause of national reunification. The two sides may first send people to meet for an exhaustive exchange of views.

(2) It is the urgent desire of the people of all nationalities on both sides of the straits to communicate with each other, reunite with their relatives, develop trade, and increase mutual understanding. We propose that the two sides make arrangements to facilitate the exchange of mail, trade, air and shipping services, and visits by relatives and tourists as well as academic, cultural, and sports exchanges, and reach an agreement thereupon.

(3) After the country is reunified, Taiwan can enjoy a high degree of autonomy as a special administrative region and it can retain its armed forces. The central government will not interfere with local affairs on Taiwan.

(4) Taiwan's current socioeconomic system will remain unchanged; so will its way of life and its economic and cultural relations with foreign countries. There will be no encroachment on the proprietary rights and lawful right of inheritance over private property, houses, land, and enterprises, or on foreign investments.

(5) People in authority and representative personages of various circles in Taiwan may take up posts of leadership in national political bodies and participate in running the state.

(6) When Taiwan's local finances are in difficulty, the central government may subsidize them [appropriately].

(7) For people of all nationalities and public figures of various circles in Taiwan who wish to come and settle on the mainland, it is guaranteed that proper arrangements will be made for them, that there will be no discrimination against them, and that they will have the freedom of entry and exit.

(8) Industrialists and businessmen in Taiwan are welcome to invest and engage in various economic undertakings on the mainland, and their legal rights, interests, and profits are guaranteed.

(9) The reunification of the motherland is the responsibility of all Chinese. We sincerely welcome people of all nationalities, public figures of all circles, and all mass organizations in Taiwan to make proposals and suggestions regarding affairs of state through various channels and in various ways.

Taiwan's return to the embrace of the motherland and the accomplishment of the great cause of national reunification is a great and glorious mission history has bequeathed on our generation. China's reunification and prosperity is in the vital interest of the Chinese people of all nationalities—not only those on the mainland, but those in Taiwan as well. It is also in the interest of peace in the Far East and the world.

We hope that our compatriots in Taiwan will give full play to their patriotism and work energetically for the early realization of the great unity of our nation and share the honor of it. We hope that our compatriots in Hong Kong and Macao and Chinese nationals residing abroad will continue to act in the role of a bridge and contribute their share to the reunification of the motherland.

We hope that the Kuomintang authorities will stick to their "one China" position and their opposition to "two Chinas" and that they will put national interests above everything else, forget previous ill will, and join hands with us in accomplishing the great cause of national reunification and the great goal of making China prosperous and strong, so as to win glory for our ancestors, bring benefit to our posterity, and write a new and glorious page in the history of the Chinese nation!

Constitution of the Chinese Communist Party

A new party constitution was adopted by the twelfth national party congress on September 6, 1982, replacing the 1977 party constitution. Amended in 1987 and 1992, the full text of the party constitution follows.

General Program

The Chinese Communist Party [CCP] is the vanguard of the Chinese working class, the faithful representative of the interests of the people of all nationalities in China and the force at the core, leading China's socialist cause. The party's ultimate goal is the creation of a communist social system.

The CCP takes Marxism-Leninism and Mao Zedong Thought as its guide to action.

Marxism-Leninism has revealed the universal law of the history of the social development of mankind and analyzed the insurmountable contradictions inherent in the capitalist system, pointing out that the socialist society is bound to replace capitalist society and ultimately develop into a communist society. The history of more than a century since the publication of the *Communist Manifesto* proves the correctness of the theory on scientific socialism and the strong vitality of socialism. Socialism essentially means to emancipate and develop productive forces, to eliminate exploitation and polarization and ultimately to realize common prosperity. The development and perfection of the socialist system is a protracted historical process. Despite twists and turns and relapses in the course of development, the inevitable replacement of capitalism by socialism is an irreversible general trend in the history of social development. Socialism is bound gradually to triumph along paths that are suited to the specific conditions of each country and are chosen by its people of their own free will. The Chinese Communists, with Comrade Mao Zedong as their chief representative, created Mao Zedong Thought by integrating the universal principles of Marxism-Leninism with the concrete practice of the Chinese revolution. Mao Zedong Thought is Marxism-Leninism applied and developed in China; it consists of a body of theoretical principles concerning the revolution and construction in China and a summary of experience therein, both of which have been proved correct by practice; it represents the crystallized, collective wisdom of the CCP.

The CCP led the people of all nationalities in waging their prolonged revolutionary struggle against imperialism, feudalism and bureaucrat-capitalism, winning victory in the new democratic revolution and establishing the PRC, a people's democratic dictatorship. After the founding of the People's Republic, it led them in smoothly carrying out socialist transformation, completing the transition from New Democracy to socialism, establishing the socialist system and developing socialism in its economic, political and cultural aspects.

Since the third plenum of the 11th CCP Central Committee was convened, the party, after summarizing both positive and negative experiences and by emancipating the mind and seeking truth from facts, has shifted the focus of the whole party's work to economic construction and implemented reform and opening up. It has gradually formed the theory, line, principles and policies on building socialism with Chinese characteristics by integrating the basic tenets of Marxism with the practice of socialist construction in contemporary China, thereby opening up a new era in the development of the socialist cause. The theory on building socialism with Chinese characteristics, which expounds on the fundamental issues related to building, consolidating and developing socialism in China and which inherits and develops Marxism, is a guide for the socialist cause to advance continuously in China.

Our country is now in the initial stage of socialism. This is an impassable stage for economically and culturally backward China in the drive for socialist modernization, which may take up to a hundred years. Socialist construction in our country must proceed from its own conditions and follows the road of socialism with Chinese characteristics. At the present stage, the principal contradiction in our country is that between the people's growing material and cultural needs and the backward level of our social production. However, because of domestic circumstances and foreign influences, class struggle will continue to exist within certain limits for a long time and may even sharpen under certain conditions; but class struggle is no longer the principal contradiction. The basic tasks of socialist construction in our country are to further liberate and develop the productive forces, to realize socialist modernization step by step and, to this end, to reform the aspects of and links in the relations of production and in the superstructure that are not suited to the development of the productive forces. It is imperative to uphold an ownership structure embracing diverse economic sectors with the public ownership of means of production as the main one; to apply the system of distribution with "to each according to his work" as the mainstay, supplemented by other modes of distribution; to encourage some people and areas to prosper before others; to reach common prosperity by eliminating poverty step by step; and continuously to satisfy the people's growing material and cultural needs on the basis of developed production and increased social wealth. The general starting point of and the criteria for appraising all our work should be conducive to developing the productive forces of our socialist society, increasing our socialist country's overall strength and raising the people's living standards. The strategic objective of our country's economic development is to quadruple the gross national product [GNP] of 1980 by the end of this century, and to have our per capita GNP reach the level of a moderately developed country by the middle of the next century.

The CCP's basic line for the initial stage of socialism is to lead and unite the people of all nationalities throughout the country to carry out economic construction as the central task, to uphold the four cardinal principles, to persevere in reform and opening to the outside world and to strive to build our country into a prosperous, powerful, democratic and civilized modern socialist country through our own arduous efforts.

In leading the socialist cause, the CCP must persist in regarding economic construction as its central task and all other work must be subordinated to and serve the central task. It is necessary to seize the opportunity to speed up development, to give full play to the role of science and technology as the primary productive force, to raise efficiency, quality and speed by relying on scientific and technological progress and improving workers' quality and to strive to push economic construction forward.

The foundation for our country is to uphold the four cardinal principles upholding the socialist road, the people's democratic dictatorship, leadership of the CCP and Marxism-Leninism-Mao Zedong Thought. In the whole process of socialist modernization, it is imperative to uphold the four cardinal principles and oppose bourgeois liberalization.

Reform and opening to the outside world are the only way to liberate and develop the productive forces. It is necessary fundamentally to reform the economic structure impeding the development of the productive forces and to institute a system of socialist market economy. Corresponding to this, reform should be carried out in the political structure and other fields. Opening includes opening to the outside and inside in an all-around way. Efforts should be made to develop economic and technological exchanges and cooperation with foreign countries; use more foreign funds, resources and technology; and draw on and assimilate all the achievements of civilization created by mankind, including developed Western countries' advanced methods of operation and management reflecting the law of modern production. In carrying out reform and opening to the outside, we should boldly explore, do pioneering work and blaze new trails in practice. The CCP leads the people, as they build a material civilization, in striving to build a socialist spiritual civilization. The building of socialist spiritual civilization provides the powerful mental impetus and intellectual support for economic construction, reform and opening to the outside world and helps create a favorable social environment. Major efforts should be made to promote education, science and culture, and it is necessary to respect knowledge and trained personnel; to raise the ideological, moral, scientific and cultural quality of the whole nation; to develop fine traditional national culture; and to bring about a thriving and developed socialist culture. It is essential to educate party members and the masses of people in the party's basic line, patriotism, collectivism and socialist ideology and to enhance their spirit of national dignity, confidence and self-improvement. Efforts should also be made to educate party members in lofty Communist ideals, to resist the corrosive influence of decadent capitalist and feudalist ideas, to eliminate all ugly social phenomena and to encourage the Chinese people to have lofty ideals, moral integrity, education and a sense of discipline.

The CCP leads the people in promoting socialist democracy, perfecting the socialist legal system and consolidating the people's democratic dictatorship. It upholds the system of people's congresses, the system of multiparty cooperation under the leadership of the Communist Party and the system of political consultation. It greatly supports the people in becoming masters of their own country and takes concrete steps to protect the people's right to run the affairs of state and society and to manage economic and cultural undertakings. It encourages the free airing of views. It establishes a sound system and process for democratic decision-making and democratic supervision. It strengthens state legislation and improves the implementation of the state law, gradually to incorporate all state undertakings into a legal framework. It enhances comprehensive control of public security and strives to maintain long-term social stability. It firmly cracks down on criminal acts and criminal elements who jeopardize state security and interests and who endanger social stability and economic development. It makes a strict distinction between and correctly handles the nature of two different contradictions, namely, the contradiction between ourselves and the enemy and the contradictions among the people.

The CCP upholds its leadership over the People's Liberation Army [PLA] and the other people's armed forces, strives to strengthen the building of the PLA and fully gives play to the PLA's role in consolidating national defense, in defending the motherland and in taking part in socialist modernization construction. The CCP upholds and promotes relations of equality, unity and mutual assistance among all nationalities in the country. It persists in implementing and improving the system of regional autonomy for minority nationalities. It makes great efforts to train and promote minority cadres and assists in the development of the economy and culture in areas inhabited by minority nationalities with a view to bringing about common prosperity and progress for all nationalities.

The CCP unites with all workers, peasants and intellectuals and with all the democratic parties, nonparty democrats and patriotic forces of all nationalities in China in further expanding and fortifying the broadest possible patriotic united front embracing all socialist working people and all patriots who support socialism, or who support the reunification of the motherland. It is necessary constantly to strengthen the unity of all people in the nation, including the unity of our compatriots in Taiwan, Xianggang (Hong Kong) and Aomen (Macao) and overseas Chinese, and accomplish the great task of reunifying the motherland according to the policy of "one country, two systems." The CCP stands for the vigorous development of relations with foreign countries and exerts efforts to create a favorable international environment for our country's reform, opening to the outside world and modernization construction. In international affairs, it adheres to the peaceful foreign policy of independence, maintains our country's independence and sovereignty, opposes hegemonism and power politics, safeguards world peace and promotes human progress. It stands for the development of state relations between China and other countries on the basis of the Five Principles of [Peaceful Coexistence] for sovereignty and territorial integrity, mutual nonaggression, noninterference in each other's internal affairs, equality and mutual benefit and peaceful coexistence. It constantly develops our country's good-neighborly and friendly relations with peripheral countries and enhances unity and cooperation with developing countries. It also develops relations with Communist parties and other political parties in other countries on the principles of independence, complete equality, mutual respect and noninterference in each other's internal affairs.

In order to lead Chinese people of all nationalities in attaining the great goal of socialist modernization, the CCP must closely follow the party's basic line, strengthen party building, persist in strict management of the party, carry forward its fine traditions and work style, enhance its fighting capacity and build the party into a strong core that leads all people in the nation constantly to advance along the road of socialism with Chinese characteristics. Four basic requirements must be met in party building.

First, it is necessary to adhere to the party's basic line. The entire party should unswervingly and always persist in unifying thinking and actions in line with the theory of building socialism with Chinese characteristics and the party's basic line. We should unify reform and opening with the four cardinal principles, comprehensively implement the party's basic line and oppose all erroneous tendencies of "leftist" and rightist deviation; while keeping vigilance against rightist deviation, main attention should be paid to guarding against "leftist" deviation. Building of various levels of leading bodies should be stepped up. Cadres who have done outstanding jobs and are trusted by the masses in the course of reform, opening and socialist modernization construction should be promoted. Hundreds and millions of successors to the cause of socialism should be trained and nurtured. All party organizations must ensure the implementation of the party's basic line.

Second, it is necessary to persist in mind emancipation and seeking truth from facts. The party's ideological line is to proceed from reality in all things, to integrate theory with practice, to seek truth from facts and to verify and develop truth through practice. In accordance with this ideological line, the entire party must make vigorous explorations, conduct bold experiments, work creatively, constantly study the new situation, sum up new experiences, solve new problems and enrich and develop Marxism through practice.

Third, it is necessary to serve the people wholeheartedly. The party has no special interests of its own apart from the interests of the working class and the broadest masses of the people. It always gives first priority to the masses' interests, shares weal and woe with them, maintains the closest ties with them and never allows party members to deviate and ride roughshod over them. The party practices the mass line in its work. While it does all things for the masses, it too relies on all things from the masses. As the party is sprung from the masses, it must return to the fold. It also converts its correct policy into the masses' voluntary actions. The issues of party style and the ties between the party and the masses are two issues that concern the life and death of the party. The party steadfastly opposes corruption and always works to improve party style and build a clean government.

Fourth, adherence to democratic centralism. Democratic centralism is the integration of centralism based on democracy and democracy under the guidance of centralism. It is the party's basic organizational principle as well as the application of the mass line in the conduct of party activities. Full play should be given to democracy within the party and the initiative and creativity of party organizations at all levels, and the broad ranks of party members should be brought into full play. It is necessary to exercise correct centralism to ensure unity of action throughout the ranks, and the prompt and effective implementation of decisions. It is necessary to strengthen a sense of organization and discipline and to see to it that everyone is equal before party discipline. In its internal political life, the party conducts criticism and self-criticism in the correct way, waging ideological struggles over matters of principle, upholding truth and rectifying mistakes. It is necessary to work to develop a political situation in which we have both centralism and democracy, both discipline and freedom, both unity of will and personal ease of mind and liveliness.

Party leadership consists mainly of political, ideological and organizational leadership. The party must adapt to the needs of reform, opening up and socialist modernization and step up and improve its leadership. It must concentrate on leadership over economic construction and organize and coordinate the forces of all quarters to carry out its work around economic construction with concerted efforts. The party must practice democratic and scientific decision-making, formulate and implement correct lines, principles and policies, do its organizational, propaganda and educational work well and make sure that all party members play their exemplary vanguard role. It must conduct its activities within the limits permitted by the constitution and the law. It must see to it that the legislative, judicial and administrative organs of the state and the economic, cultural and people's organizations work actively and with initiative, independently, responsibly and in harmony. It must strengthen leadership over the trade unions, the Communist Youth League, the Women's Federation and other mass organizations and give full scope to their roles. The party must adapt to the developments and changes of the situation, constantly improve its leadership style and method and raise its leadership level. Its members must work in close cooperation with the masses of nonparty people in the common effort to build socialism with Chinese characteristics.

Chapter I
Membership

Article 1. Any Chinese worker, peasant, member of the armed forces, intellectual or any other revolutionary who has reached the age of 18, who accepts the party's program and constitution and is willing to join and work actively in one of the party organizations, carry out the party's decisions and pay membership dues regularly may apply for membership of the CCP.

Article 2. Members of the CCP are vanguard fighters of the Chinese working class imbued with Communist consciousness.

Members of the CCP must serve the people wholeheartedly, dedicate their whole lives to the realization of Communism and be ready to make any personal sacrifices.

Members of the CCP are at all times ordinary members of the working people. Communist Party members must not seek personal gain or privileges beyond the personal benefits, job functions and powers as provided for by the relevant laws and policies.

Article 3. Party members must fulfill the following duties:
(1) Conscientiously study Marxism-Leninism-Mao Zedong Thought; study the theory on building socialism with Chinese characteristics and the party's line, principles and policies; study essential knowledge concerning the party; and acquire general, scientific and professional knowledge.
(2) Unswervingly implement the party's basic line, principles and policies; take the lead in participating in reform, opening up and socialist modernization; en-

courage the masses to work hard for economic development and social progress; and play an exemplary vanguard role in production and other work, study and social activities.
(3) Adhere to the principle that the interests of the party and people stand above everything, subordinate their personal interests to the interests of the party and people; be the first to bear hardships and the last to enjoy comforts; work selflessly for the public interests and make more contributions.
(4) Conscientiously observe party discipline and the laws of the state, rigorously guard party and state secrets, execute the party's decisions, accept any job and actively fulfill any task assigned them by the party.
(5) Uphold the party's solidarity and unity; be loyal to and honest with the party and match words with deeds; firmly oppose all factional organizations and small-group activities and oppose double-dealing and scheming of any kind.
(6) Earnestly practice criticism and self-criticism, be bold in exposing and correcting shortcomings and mistakes in work and resolutely fight negative and decadent phenomena.
(7) Maintain close ties with the masses, propagate the party's views among them, consult them when problems arise, keep the party informed of their views and demands in good time and defend their legitimate interests.
(8) Develop new socialist habits, advocate Communist ethics, and, as required by the defense of the country and the interests of the people, step forward in times of difficulty and danger, fighting bravely and defying death.

Article 4. Party members enjoy the following rights:
(1) To attend pertinent party meetings and read pertinent party documents and to benefit from the party's education and training.
(2) To participate in discussion at party meetings and in party newspapers and journals on questions concerning the party's policies.
(3) To make suggestions and proposals regarding the work of the party.
(4) To make well-grounded criticism of any party organization or member at party meetings; to present information or charges against any party organization or member concerning violation of discipline and of the law to the party in a responsible way and to demand disciplinary measures against such a member, or to demand the dismissal or replacement of any cadre who is incompetent.
(5) To vote, elect and stand for election.
(6) To attend, with the right of self-defense, discussions held by party organizations to decide on disciplinary measures to be taken against themselves or to ap-

praise their work and behavior, while other party members may also bear witness or argue on their behalf.

(7) In case of disagreement with a party decision or policy, to make reservations and present their views to party organizations at higher levels up to and including the Central Committee, provided that they resolutely carry out the decision or policy while it is in force.

(8) To put forward any request, appeal or complaint to a higher party organization up to and including the Central Committee and ask the organization concerned for a responsible reply.

No party organization, up to and including the Central Committee, has the right to deprive any party member of the above-mentioned rights.

Article 5. New party members must be admitted through a party branch and the principle of individual admission must be adhered to.

An applicant for party membership must fill in an application form and must be recommended by two full party members. The application must be accepted by a general membership meeting of the party branch concerned and approved by the next higher party organization; and the applicant should undergo observation for a probationary period before being transferred to full membership.

Party members who recommended an applicant must make genuine efforts to acquaint themselves with the latter's ideology, character, personal history and work performance; must explain to each applicant the party's program and constitution, qualifications for membership and the duties and rights of members; and must make a responsible report to the party organization on the matter. The party branch committee must canvass the opinions of persons concerned, inside and outside the party, about an applicant for party membership and, after establishing the latter's qualifications following a rigorous examination, submit the application to a general membership meeting for discussion.

Before approving the admission of applicants for party membership, the next higher party organization concerned must appoint people to talk with them, so as to get to know them better and help deepen their understanding of the party.

In special circumstances, the Central Committee of the party or the party committee of a province, an autonomous region or a municipality directly under the central government has the power to admit new party members directly.

Article 6. A probational party member must take an admission oath in front of the party flag. The oath reads: It is my will to join the Chinese Communist Party, uphold the party's program, observe the provisions of the party constitution, fulfill a party member's duties, carry out the party's decisions, strictly observe party discipline, guard party secrets, be loyal to the party, work hard, fight for Communism throughout my life, be ready at all times to sacrifice myself all for the party and the people and never betray the party.

Article 7. Probationary members have the same duties as full members. They enjoy the rights of full members except those of voting, electing or standing for election.

When the probationary period of a probationary member has expired, the party branch concerned should promptly discuss whether he is qualified to be transferred to full membership. A probationary member who conscientiously performs his duties and is qualified for membership should be transferred to full membership as scheduled; if continued observation and education are needed, the probationary period may be prolonged, but by no more than one year; if a probationary member fails to perform his duties and is found unqualified for membership, his probationary membership shall be annulled. Any decision to transfer a probationary member to full membership, prolong a probationary period or annul a probationary membership must be made through discussion by the general membership meeting of the party branch concerned and approved by the next higher party organization.

The probationary period of a probationary member begins from the day of the general membership meeting of the party branch which admits him as a probationary member. The party standing of a member begins from the day he is transferred to full membership on the expiration of the probationary period.

Article 8. Every party member, irrespective of position, must be organized into a branch, cell or other specific unit of the party to participate in the regular activities of the party organization and accept supervision by the masses inside and outside the party. Leading cadres of the party must also participate in democratic discussions at meetings of party committees or units. There shall be no privileged party members who do not participate in the regular activities of the party organization and do not accept supervision by the masses inside and outside the party.

Article 9. Party members are free to withdraw from the party. When a party member asks to withdraw, the party branch concerned shall, after discussion by its general membership meeting, remove his name from the party rolls, make the removal publicly known and report it to the next higher party organization for the record.

The party branch concerned should educate a party member who lacks revolutionary will, fails to fulfill the duties of a party member and is not qualified for membership, and should set a time limit by which the member must correct his mistakes; if he remains incorrigible after repeated education, he should be persuaded to withdraw from the party. The case shall be discussed and decided by the general membership meeting of the party branch concerned and submitted to the next higher party organization for approval. If the party member being persuaded to withdraw refuses to do so, the case shall be submitted to the general membership meeting of the party branch concerned for discussion and decision on the removal of his name from party rolls and the decision shall be submitted to the next higher party organization for approval.

A party member who fails to take part in regular party activities, pay membership dues or do work assigned by the party for six successive months without proper reason is regarded as having given up membership. The general membership meeting of the party branch concerned shall decide on the removal of such person's name from the party roll and report the removal to the next higher party organization for approval.

Chapter II
Organizational System of the Party

Article 10. The party is an integral body organized under its program and constitution and on the principle of democratic centralism. The basic principles of democratic centralism as practiced by the party are as follows:

(1) Individual party members are subordinate to the party organization, the minority is subordinate to the majority, lower party organizations are subordinate to higher party organizations and members of the party are subordinate to the national congress and the Central Committee of the party.

(2) The party's leading bodies of all levels are elected, except for the representative organs dispatched by them and the leading party members' groups in non-party organizations.

(3) The highest leading body of the party is the national congress and the central committee elected by it. The leading bodies of local party organizations are the party congresses at their respective levels and the party committees elected by them. Party committees are responsible and report their work to the party congresses at their respective levels.

(4) Higher party organizations shall pay constant attention to the views of the lower organizations and the rank-and-file party members, and solve in good time the problems they raise. Lower party organizations shall report on their work to, and request instructions from, higher party organizations; at the same time, they shall handle, independently and in a responsible manner, matters within their jurisdiction. Higher and lower party organizations should exchange information and support and supervise each other. Party organizations at all levels shall make it possible for party members to have a better understanding of and more participation in the party's affairs.

(5) Party committees at all levels function on the principle of combining collective leadership with individual responsibility based on division of labor. All major issues shall be decided upon by the party committees after democratic discussion. Members of the party committee shall effectively perform their duties according to collective decisions and division of labor.

(6) The party forbids all forms of personality cult. It is necessary to ensure that the activities of the party leaders be subject to supervision by the party and the people, while at the same time to uphold the prestige of all leaders who represent the interests of the party and the people.

Article 11. The election of delegates to party congresses and of members of party committees at all levels should reflect the will of the voters. Elections shall be held by secret ballot. The lists of candidates shall be submitted to the party organizations and voters for full deliberation and discussion. The election procedure of nominating a larger number of candidates than the number of persons to be elected may be used in a formal election. Or this procedure may be used first in a preliminary election in order to draw up a list of candidates for the formal election. The voters have the right to inquire into the candidates, demand a change, or reject one in favor of another. No organization or individual shall in any way compel voters to elect or not to elect any candidate.

If any violation of the party constitution occurs in the election of delegates to a local party congress, the party committee at the next higher level shall, after investigation and verification, decide to invalidate the election and take appropriate measures. The decision shall be reported to the party committee at the next higher level for checking and approval before it is formally announced and implemented.

Article 12. When necessary, party committees of and above the county level may convene conferences of delegates to discuss and decide on major problems that require timely solution. The number of delegates to such conferences and the procedure governing their election shall be determined by the party committees convening them.

Article 13. The formation of a new party organization or the dissolution of an existing one shall be decided upon by the higher party organizations.

Party committees at the central and local levels may send out their representative organs. When the congress of a local party organization at any level, including the grass-roots level, is not in session, the next higher party organization may, when it deems it necessary, transfer or appoint responsible members of that organization.

Article 14. When making decisions on important questions affecting the lower organizations, the leading bodies of the party at all levels should, in ordinary circumstances, solicit the opinions of the lower organizations. Measures should be taken to ensure that the lower organizations can exercise their functions and powers normally. Except in special circumstances, higher leading bodies should not interfere with matters that ought to be handled by lower organizations.

Article 15. Only the Central Committee of the party has the power to make decisions on major policies of a nationwide character. Party organizations of various departments and localities may make suggestions with regard to such policies to the Central Committee, but shall not make any decisions or publicize their views outside the party without authorization.

Lower party organizations must firmly implement the decisions of higher party organizations. If lower organizations consider that any decisions of higher organizations do not suit actual conditions in their localities or departments, they may request modification. If the higher organizations insist on their original decisions, the lower organizations must carry out such decisions and refrain from publicly voicing their differences, but have the right to report them to the next higher party organization.

Newspapers, journals and other means of publicity run by party organizations at all levels must propagate the line, principles, policies and resolutions of the party.

Article 16. When discussing and making decisions on any matter, party organizations must keep to the principle of subordination of the minority to the majority. A vote must be taken when major issues are decided on. Serious consideration should be given to the differing views of a minority. In case of controversy over major issues in which supporters of two opposing views are nearly equal in number—except in emergencies where action must be taken in accordance with the majority view—the decision should be put off to allow for further investigation, study and exchange of opinions, followed by another vote. Under special circumstances, the controversy may be reported to the next higher party organization for ruling.

When, on behalf of the party organization, an individual party member is to express views on major issues beyond the scope of existing decisions of the party organization, the content must be referred to the party organization to which the party member is affiliated for prior

discussion and decision; or must be referred to the next higher party organization for instructions. No party member, whatever his position, is allowed to make decisions on major issues on his own. In an emergency, when a decision by an individual is unavoidable, the matter must be reported to the party organization immediately afterwards. No leader is allowed to decide matters arbitrarily on his own nor to place himself above the party organization.

Article 17. The central, local and primary organizations of the party must all pay great attention to party building. They shall regularly discuss and check up on the party's work in propaganda, education, organization, discipline inspection, mass work and united front work. They must carefully study ideological and political developments inside and outside the party.

Chapter III
Central Organizations of the Party

Article 18. The national congress of the party is held once every five years and convened by the Central Committee. It may be convened before the due date if the Central Committee deems it necessary or if more than one-third of the organizations at the provincial level so request. Except under extraordinary circumstances, the congress may not be postponed. The number of delegates to a national congress and the procedure governing their election shall be determined by the Central Committee.

Article 19. The functions and powers of the national congress of the party are as follows:
(1) To hear and examine the report of the Central Committee;
(2) To hear and examine the report of the Central Discipline Inspection Commission;
(3) To discuss and decide on major questions concerning the party;
(4) To revise the constitution of the party;
(5) To elect the Central Committee; and
(6) To elect the Central Discipline Inspection Commission.

Article 20. The authority and functions of the national congress of party delegates are to discuss and decide on major issues; and to readjust and elect through by-election some members of the Central Committee and Central Discipline Inspection Commission. However, the number of members and alternate members of the Central Committee through readjustment and by-election must not exceed one-fifth of the total number of Central Committee members and alternate members who were elected at the national party congress.

Article 21. Each term of the party's Central Committee is five years. In case of the advancement or postponement of the convening of the national party congress, the Central Committee's term shall be correspondingly shortened or extended. Members and alternate members of the Central Committee must have a party standing of five years or more. The number of members and alternate members of the Central Committee shall be determined by the national congress. Vacancies on the Central Committee shall be filled by its alternate members in the order of the number of votes by which they were elected. The Central Committee meets in plenary session at least once a year and such sessions are convened by its Political Bureau. When the national congress is not in session, the Central Committee carries out its decisions, directs the entire work of the party and represents the CCP in its external relations.

Article 22. The Political Bureau, the Standing Committee of the Political Bureau and the general secretary of the Central Committee are elected by the Central Committee in plenary session. The general secretary of the Central Committee must be a member of the Standing Committee of the Political Bureau.

When the plenary session of the Central Committee is not in session, the Political Bureau of the Central Committee and its Standing Committee exercise the functions and powers of the Central Committee. The Secretariat of the Central Committee is an organization that runs day-to-day work for the Political Bureau of the Central Committee and its Standing Committee. Members of the Secretariat are nominated by the Standing Committee of the Political Bureau of the Central Committee and approved by the Central Committee in plenary session. The general secretary of the Central Committee is responsible for convening the meetings of the Political Bureau and its Standing Committee and presides over the work of the Secretariat.

Members of the Military Commission of the Central Committee are decided by the Central Committee.

The central leading bodies and leaders elected by each Central Committee shall, when the next national congress is in session, continue to preside over the party's day-to-day work until the new central leading bodies and leaders are elected by the next Central Committee.

Article 23. Party organizations in the Chinese PLA carry out their work in accordance with the instructions of the Central Committee. The General Political Department of the Chinese PLA is the political work organ of the military commission; it directs party and political work in the army. The organizational system and organs of the party in the armed forces will be prescribed by the military commission.

Chapter IV
Local Organizations of the Party

Article 24. A party congress of a province, autonomous region, municipality directly under the central government, city divided into districts or autonomous prefecture is held once every five years. A party congress of a county (banner), autonomous county, city not divided into districts or municipal district is held once every five years. Local party congresses are convened by the party committees at the corresponding levels. Under extraordinary circumstances, they may be held before or after their due dates upon approval by the next higher party committees. The number of delegates to the local party congresses at any level and the procedure governing their election are determined by the party committees at the corresponding levels and should be reported to the next higher party committees for approval.

Article 25. The functions and powers of the local party congresses at all levels are as follows:
(1) To hear and examine the reports of the party committees at the corresponding levels;
(2) to hear and examine the reports of the discipline inspection commissions at the corresponding levels;
(3) to discuss and decide on major issues in the given areas; and
(4) to elect the party committees and discipline inspection commissions at the corresponding levels.

Article 26. The party committee of the province, autonomous region, municipality directly under the central government, city divided into districts or autonomous prefecture is elected for a term of five years. The members and alternate members of such a committee must have a party standing of five years or more. The party committee of a county (banner), autonomous county, city not divided into districts or municipal district is elected for a term of five years. The members and alternate members of such a committee must have a party standing of three years or more. When local party congresses at various levels are convened before or after their due dates, the terms of the committees elected by the previous congresses shall be correspondingly shortened or extended. The number of members and alternate members of the local party committees at various levels shall be determined by the next higher committees. Vacancies on the local party committees at various levels shall be filled by their alternate members in the order of the number of votes by which they were elected.

The local party committees at various levels meet in plenary session at least twice a year.

Local party committees at various levels shall, when the party congresses of the given areas are not in session, carry out the directives of the next higher party organizations and the decisions of the party congresses at the corresponding levels, direct work in their own areas and report on it to the next higher party committees at regular intervals.

Article 27. Local party committees at various levels elect, at their plenary sessions, their standing committees, secretaries and deputy secretaries and report the results to the higher party committees for approval. The standing committees at various levels exercise the powers and functions of local party committees when the latter are not in session. They continue to handle the day-to-day work when the next party congresses at their levels are in session, until the new standing committees are elected.

Article 28. A prefectural party committee, or an organization analogous to it, is the representative organ dispatched by a provincial or an autonomous regional party committee to a prefecture embracing several counties, autonomous counties or cities. It exercises leadership over the work in the given region as authorized by the provincial or autonomous regional party committee.

Chapter V
Primary Organizations of the Party

Article 29. Primary party organizations are formed in enterprises, rural villages, offices, schools, scientific research institutions, city neighborhoods, PLA companies and other basic units, where there are three or more full party members.

In primary party organizations, the primary party committees, or committees of general party branches and party branches, are set up as the work requires and according to the number of party members, subject to approval by the higher party organizations. A primary party committee is elected by a general membership meeting or a meeting of delegates. The committee of a general party branch or a party branch is elected by a general membership meeting.

Article 30. A primary party committee is elected for a term of three or four years, while a general party branch committee or a party branch committee is elected for a term of two or three years. Results of the election of a secretary and deputy secretaries by a primary party committee, general party branch committee or party branch committee shall be reported to the higher party organization for approval.

Article 31. The primary party organizations are militant bastions of the party in the basic units of society. Their main tasks are:

(1) To propagate and carry out the party's line, principles and policies and decisions of the party Central Com-

mittee and other higher party organizations and their own party organizations; to give full play to the exemplary vanguard role of party members; and to unite and organize the cadres and the rank and file inside and outside the party in fulfilling the tasks of their own units.

(2) To organize party members to conscientiously study Marxism-Leninism-Mao Zedong Thought; study the theory of building socialism with Chinese characteristics and the party's line, principles, policies and decisions; study essential knowledge concerning the party; and study scientific, cultural and professional knowledge.

(3) To educate and supervise party members, improve their quality, enhance their party spirit, ensure their regular participation in the activities of the party organization, promote criticism and self-criticism, safeguard and enforce party discipline, see that party members truly fulfill their duties and protect their rights from encroachment.

(4) To maintain close ties with the masses, constantly seek their criticisms and opinions regarding party members and the party's work, protect their legitimate rights and interests and ensure good ideological and political work among them.

(5) To give full scope to the initiative and creativity of party members and the masses; discover, train and make recommendations for talented people; encourage them to contribute their wisdom and talent to the reform, opening up and modernization drive; and support them in these efforts.

(6) To educate and train activists asking to be admitted into the party, recruit party members on a regular basis and attach importance to recruiting outstanding workers, peasants and intellectuals working on the forefront of production and other fields of endeavor.

(7) To see that party and other nonparty functionaries strictly observe the state laws and administration discipline and the financial and economic regulations and personnel system; and that none of them infringe the interests of the state, the collective and the masses.

(8) To educate party members and the masses conscientiously to resist unhealthy tendencies and wage resolute struggles against various lawbreaking activities.

Article 32. Neighborhood, township and town primary party organizations and village party branches lead the work of their areas; support administrative, economic and mass self-management organizations; and ensure that such organizations fully exercise their functions and powers.

In a state-owned enterprise, the primary party organization shall give full play to its role as the political nucleus and perform its work around enterprise production and management. It shall ensure and supervise the implementation of party and state principles and policies in the enterprise; support the factory director (or manager) in performing his duties according to the law and uphold and improve the system of full responsibility for factory directors; rely wholeheartedly on the masses of workers and staff members and support the workers congress in performing its work; participate in making major decisions for the enterprise; strengthen itself; and lead ideological and political work as well as trade union and Communist Youth League organizations.

In an institution implementing the system of full responsibility for administrative leaders, the primary party organization shall give full play to its role as the political nucleus. In an institution where the system of full responsibility for administrative leaders is implemented under the leadership of the party committee, the primary party organization shall discuss major issues and decide on them and ensure that the administrative leader fully exercises his functions and powers.

In party and state offices at all levels, the primary party organizations shall assist the heads of these offices in fulfilling their tasks, improving their work, and exercising supervision over all party members, including the heads of these offices who are party members. However, they shall not lead the work of these offices.

Chapter VI
Party Cadres

Article 33. Party cadres are the backbone of the party's cause and public servants of the people. The party selects its cadres according to the principle that they should possess both political integrity and professional competence, persists in the practice of appointing people on their merit and opposes favoritism; it calls for genuine efforts to make the ranks of cadres more revolutionary, younger in average age, better educated and more professionally competent. The party should attach importance to the education, training, promotion and appraisal of cadres, especially the training and promotion of outstanding young cadres. Vigorous efforts should be made to reform the cadre system. The party should attach importance to the training and promotion of women cadres and cadres from among the minority nationalities.

Article 34. Leading party cadres at all levels must perform their duties as party members in an exemplary way as prescribed in Article 3 of this constitution and must meet the following basic requirements:

(1) Have a knowledge of the theories of Marxism-Leninism-Mao Zedong Thought and of the policies based on them that are needed to perform their duties; grasp the theory of building socialism with Chinese charac-

teristics; and strive to use the Marxist stand, viewpoint and method to solve practical problems.

(2) Resolutely implement the party's basic line, principles and policies, be determined to carry out reform and opening to the outside world, devote themselves to the cause of modernization and work hard to blaze new trails and make actual achievements in socialist construction.

(3) Persevere in seeking truth from facts, conscientiously make investigations and study, combine the party's principles and policies with the realities of their areas or departments, tell the truth, do practical work, work for actual results and oppose formalism.

(4) Be fervently dedicated to the revolutionary cause and imbued with a strong sense of political responsibility and be qualified for their leading posts in organizational ability, general education and professional knowledge.

(5) Correctly exercise the powers entrusted to them by the people, be honest and upright, work hard for the people, set an example, carry forward the style of hard work and plain living, forge close ties with the masses, uphold the party's mass line, conscientiously accept criticism and supervision by the masses, oppose bureaucratism and oppose the unhealthy trend of abusing one's power for personal gain.

(6) Uphold the party's democratic centralism, have a democratic work style, take the overall situation into account and be good at uniting and working with comrades, including those holding differing opinions.

Article 35. Party cadres should cooperate with nonparty cadres, respect them and learn open-mindedly from their strong points. Party organizations at all levels must be bold in discovering and recommending talented and knowledgeable nonparty cadres for leading posts and ensure that the latter enjoy authority commensurate with their posts and can play their roles to the full.

Article 36. Leading party cadres at all levels, whether elected through democratic procedure or appointed by a leading body, are not entitled to lifelong tenure and they can be transferred from or relieved of their posts.

Cadres no longer fit to continue work due to old age or poor health should retire according to state regulations.

Chapter VII
Party Discipline

Article 37. Party discipline is the code of conduct that party organizations at all levels and all party members must observe; it is a guarantee for safeguarding the party's solidarity and unity and the accomplishment of the party's tasks. Party organizations shall strictly enforce and safeguard party discipline. A Communist Party member must consciously act within the bounds of party discipline.

Article 38.   Party organizations shall criticize, educate or take disciplinary measures against members who violate party discipline, depending on the nature and seriousness of their mistakes and in the spirit of learning from past mistakes to avoid future ones, and curing the sickness to save the patient.

Party members who have seriously violated criminal law shall be expelled from the party.

It is strictly forbidden, within the party, to take any measures against a member that contravene the party constitution or the laws of the state, or to retaliate against or frame comrades. Any offending organization or individual must be dealt with according to party discipline or the laws of the state.

Article 39.   There are five measures of party discipline: warning, serious warning, removal from party posts, placing on probation within the party and expulsion from the party.

The period for which a party member is placed on probation shall not exceed two years. During this period, the party member concerned has no right to vote, elect or stand for election. A party member who during this time proves to have corrected his mistake shall have his rights as a party member restored. Party members who refuse to mend their ways shall be expelled from the party.

Expulsion is the ultimate party disciplinary measure. In deciding on or approving an expulsion, party organizations at all levels should study all the relevant facts and opinions and exercise extreme caution.

Article 40.   Any disciplinary measure against a party member must be discussed and decided on at a general membership meeting of the party branch concerned and reported to the primary party committee concerned for approval. If the case is relatively important or complicated, or involves the expulsion of a member, it shall be reported, on the merit of that case, to a party discipline inspection commission at or above the county level for examination and approval. Under special circumstances, a party committee or a discipline inspection commission at or above the county level has the authority to decide directly on disciplinary measures against a party member.

Any decision to remove a member or alternate member of the Central Committee or a local committee at any level from posts within the party, to place such a person on probation within the party or to expel him from the party, must be taken by a two-thirds' majority vote at a plenary meeting of the party committee to which he belongs. Under special circumstances, the Political Bu-

reau of the CCP Central Committee or the standing committees of local party committees at all levels may adopt a decision on disciplinary measures, which has to be confirmed when the committees meet in plenary session. Such a disciplinary measure against a member or alternate member of local committees at all levels is subject to approval by the higher party committees.

Members or alternate members of the Central Committee who have seriously violated criminal law shall be expelled from the party on the decision of the Political Bureau of the Central Committee; members and alternate members of local party committees who have seriously violated criminal law shall be expelled from the party on the decision of the standing committees of the party committees at the corresponding levels.

Article 41.   When a party organization decides on a disciplinary measure against a party member, it should investigate and verify the facts in an objective way. The party member in question must be informed of the decision to be made and of the facts on which it is based. He must be given a chance to account for himself and speak in his own defense. If the member does not accept the decision that has been adopted, he can appeal; the party organization concerned must promptly deal with or forward his appeal and must not withhold or suppress it. Those who cling to erroneous views and unjustifiable demands shall be educated by criticism.

Article 42.   Failure of a party organization to uphold party discipline must be investigated.

In the case of a party organization which seriously violates party discipline and is unable to rectify the mistake on its own, the next higher party committee should, after verifying the facts and considering the seriousness of the case, decide on the reorganization or dissolution of the organization; report the decision to the party committee higher up for examination and approval; and then formally announce and carry out the decision.

Chapter VIII
Party Organs for Discipline Inspection

Article 43.   The party's Central Discipline Inspection Commission functions under the leadership of the Central Committee of the party. Local discipline inspection commissions at all levels function under the dual leadership of the party committees at the corresponding levels and the next higher discipline inspection commissions. The local discipline inspection commissions serve a term of the same duration as the party committees at the corresponding levels. The Central Discipline Inspection Commission elects, in plenary session, its standing committee and secretary and deputy secretaries and reports the results to the Central Committee for approval. Local discipline inspection commissions at all levels elect, at their plenary sessions, their respective standing committees and secretaries and deputy secretaries. The results of the elections are subject to endorsement by the party committees at the corresponding levels and should be reported to the higher party committees for approval. The question of whether a grass-roots party committee should set up a discipline inspection commission or simply appoint a discipline inspection commissioner shall be determined by the next higher party organization in light of the specific circumstances. The committees of general party branches and party branches shall have discipline inspection commissioners.

The party's Central Discipline Inspection Commission shall, when its work so requires, accredit discipline inspection groups or commissioners to party or state organs at the central level. Leaders of the discipline inspection groups or discipline inspection commissioners may attend relevant meetings of the leading party organizations in the said organs as nonvoting participants. The leading party organizations in the organs concerned must support their work.

Article 44. The main tasks of the central and local discipline inspection commissions are as follows: To uphold the constitution and the other important rules and regulations of the party, to assist the respective party committees in rectifying party style and to check up on the implementation of the line, principles, policies and decisions of the party.

The central and local discipline inspection commissions shall carry out constant education among party members on their duty to observe party discipline. They shall adopt decisions for the upholding of party discipline; examine and deal with relatively important or complicated cases of violation of the constitution and discipline of the party or the laws and decrees of the state by party organizations or party members; decide on or cancel disciplinary measures against party members involved in such cases; and deal with complaints and appeals made by party members.

The central and local discipline inspection commissions should report to the party committees at the corresponding levels on the results of their handling of cases of special importance or complexity, as well as on the problems encountered. Local discipline inspection commissions should also present such reports to the higher commissions.

If a discipline inspection commission discovers violation of party discipline by any member of a party committee at the corresponding levels, it may conduct an initial verification of facts; if the case requires setting up of a file for investigation, it should report to the party committee at the corresponding level for approval; if the case involves a standing committee member of the

party committee, the commission should report such an offense to the party committee at the corresponding level and to the higher discipline inspection commission for approval.

Article 45. Higher discipline inspection commissions have the power to check up on the work of lower commissions and to approve or modify their decisions on any case. If decisions so modified have already been ratified by the party committee at the corresponding level, the modification must be approved by the next higher party committee.

If a local discipline inspection commission or such a commission at the basic level does not agree with a decision made by the party committee at the corresponding level in dealing with a case, it may request the commission at the next higher level to reexamine the case; if a local commission discovers cases of violation of party discipline by the party committee at the corresponding level or by its members, and if that party committee fails to deal with them properly or at all, it has the right to appeal to the higher commissions for assistance in dealing with such cases.

Chapter IX
Leading Party Members' Groups

Article 46. A leading party members' group shall be formed in the leading body of a central or local state organ, people's organization, economic or cultural institution or other nonparty unit. The main tasks of such a group are: To see to it that the party's line, principles and policies are implemented; to discuss and make decisions on major issues in their respective units; to unite with nonparty cadres and the masses in fulfilling the tasks assigned by the party and the state; and to guide the work of the party organizations of the department and those in the units directly under it.

Article 47. The members of a leading party members' group are appointed by the party committee that approves its establishment. The group shall have a secretary and deputy secretaries.

The leading party members' group shall subject itself to the leadership of the party committee that approves its establishment.

Article 48. Party committees may be set up in those government departments which need to exercise centralized and unified leadership over subordinate units. Procedures for electing such a committee and its functions, powers and tasks shall be provided separately by the Central Committee of the party.

Chapter X
Relationship between the Party
and the Communist Youth League

Article 49. The Communist Youth League of China [CYL] is a mass organization of advanced young people under the leadership of the CCP; it is a school where large numbers of young people will learn about Communism through practice; it is the party's assistant and reserve force. The CYL Central Committee functions under the leadership of the Central Committee of the party. Local CYL organizations are under the leadership of the party committees at the corresponding levels and of the higher organizations of the League itself.

Article 50. Party committees at all levels must strengthen their leadership over the CYL organizations and pay attention to the selection and training of league cadres. The party must firmly support the CYL in the lively and creative performance of its work to suit the characteristics and needs of young people and give full play to the league's role as a shock force and as a bridge linking the party with the broad masses of young people.

Those secretaries of league committees, at or below the county level or in enterprise and institutions, who are party members may attend meetings of party committees at the corresponding levels and of their standing committees as nonvoting participants.

State Constitution of the People's Republic of China (1982)

A new state constitution, the fourth since the founding of the People's Republic of China, was adopted in 1982. (Earlier constitutions date from 1954, 1975, and 1978.) Amendments to the fourth constitution were passed in 1988 and 1993 to reflect the new economic and political realities of a rapidly reforming China. The full text of the state constitution follows.

Preamble

China has one of the longest histories in the world. The people of all nationalities in China have jointly created a splendid culture and have a glorious revolutionary tradition.

Feudal China was gradually reduced after 1840 to a semicolonial and semifeudal country. The Chinese people waged wave upon wave of heroic struggles for independence and liberation and for democracy and freedom.

Great and earth-shaking historical changes have taken place in China in the twentieth century.

The 1911 Revolution, led by Dr. Sun Yat-sen, abolished the feudal monarchy and gave birth to the Republic of China. But the Chinese people had yet to fulfill their historical task of overthrowing imperialism and feudalism.

After waging hard, protracted and tortuous struggles, armed and otherwise, the Chinese people of all nationalities, led by the Chinese Communist Party (CCP) led by Chairman Mao Zedong, ultimately, in 1949, overthrew the rule of imperialism, feudalism and bureaucratic-capitalism, won the great victory of the new democratic revolution and founded the People's Republic of China (PRC). Thereupon the Chinese people took state power into their own hands and became masters of the country.

After the founding of the People's Republic, the transition of Chinese society from a new democratic to a socialist society was effected step by step. The socialist transformation of the private ownership of the means of production was completed, the system of exploitation of man by man eliminated and the socialist system established. The people's democratic dictatorship led by the working class and based on the alliance of workers and peasants, which is in essence the dictatorship of the proletariat, has been consolidated and developed. The Chinese people and the Chinese People's Liberation Army have thwarted aggression, sabotage, and armed provocations by imperialists and hegemonists, safeguarded China's national independence and security and strengthened its national defense. Major successes have been achieved in economic development. An independent and fairly comprehensive socialist system of industry has, in the main, been established. There has been a marked increase in agricultural production. Significant progress has been made in educational, scientific, cultural, and other undertakings, and socialist ideological education has yielded noteworthy results. The living standards of the people have improved considerably.

Both the victory of China's new democratic revolution and the successes of its socialist cause have been achieved by the Chinese people of all nationalities under the leadership of the CCP and the guidance of Marxism-Leninism and Mao Zedong Thought, and by upholding truth, correcting errors, and overcoming numerous difficulties and hardships. Our country is in the initial stage of socialism. The basic task of the nation is to concentrate its efforts on socialist modernization in accordance with the theory of building socialism with Chinese characteristics. Under the leadership of the CCP and the guidance of Marxism-Leninism-Mao Zedong Thought, Chinese people of all nationalities will continue to adhere to the people's democratic dictatorship and follow the socialist road, persist in reform and opening up, steadily improve socialist institutions, develop socialist democracy, improve the socialist legal system, and work hard and self-reliantly to modernize industry, agriculture, national defense, and science and technology step by step to turn China into a prosperous, strong, democratic, and culturally advanced socialist country.

The exploiting classes as such have been eliminated in our country. However, class struggle will continue to exist within certain limits for a long time to come. The Chinese people must fight against those forces and elements, both at home and abroad, that are hostile to China's socialist system and try to undermine it.

Taiwan is part of the sacred territory of the PRC. It is the lofty duty of the entire Chinese people, including our compatriots in Taiwan, to accomplish the great task of reunifying the motherland.

In building socialism it is imperative to rely on the workers, peasants and intellectuals and unite with all the forces that can be united. In the long years of revolution and construction, there has been formed under the leadership of the CCP a broad patriotic united front that is composed of democratic parties and people's organizations and embraces all socialist working people, all patriots who support socialism, and all patriots who stand for reunification of the motherland. This united front will continue to be consolidated and developed. The Chinese People's Political Consultative Conference is a broadly representative organization of the united front, which has played a significant historical role and will continue to do so in the political and social life of the country, in promoting friendship with the people of other countries, and in the struggle for socialist modernization and for the reunification and unity of the country. The system of multiparty cooperation and political consultation led by the CCP will exist and develop in China for a long time to come.

The PRC is a unitary multinational state built up jointly by the people of all its nationalities. Socialist relations of equality, unity, and mutual assistance have been established among them and will continue to be strengthened. In the struggle to safeguard the unity of the nationalities, it is necessary to combat big-nation chauvinism, mainly Han chauvinism, and also necessary to combat local-national chauvinism. The state does its utmost to promote the common prosperity of all nationalities in the country.

China's achievements in revolution and construction are inseparable from support by the people of the world. The future of China is closely linked with that of the whole world. China adheres to an independent foreign policy as well as to the Five Principles of [Peaceful Coexistence] for sovereignty and territorial integrity, mutual nonaggression, noninterference in one another's internal affairs, equality and mutual benefit, and peaceful coexistence in developing diplomatic relations and economic and cultural exchanges with other countries; China consistently opposes imperialism, hegemonism, and colonialism, works to strengthen unity with the people of other countries, supports the oppressed nations and the developing countries in their just struggle to win and

preserve national independence and develop their national economies, and strives to safeguard world peace and promote the cause of human progress.

This Constitution affirms the achievements of the struggles of the Chinese people of all nationalities and defines the basic system and basic tasks of the state in legal form; it is the fundamental law of the state and has supreme legal authority. The people of all nationalities, all state organs, the armed forces, all political parties and public organizations, and all enterprises and undertakings in the country must take the Constitution as the basic norm of conduct, and they have the duty to uphold the dignity of the Constitution and ensure its implementation.

Chapter 1. General Principles

Article 1. The PRC is a socialist state under the people's democratic dictatorship led by the working class and based on the alliance of workers and peasants.

The socialist system is the basic system of the PRC. Sabotage of the socialist system by any organization or individual is prohibited.

Article 2. All power in the PRC belongs to the people.

The organs through which the people exercise state power are the National People's Congress and the local people's congresses at different levels.

The people administer state affairs and manage economic, cultural, and social affairs through various channels and in various ways in accordance with the law.

Article 3. The state organs of the PRC apply the principle of democratic centralism.

The National People's Congress (NPC) and the local people's congresses at different levels are instituted through democratic election. They are responsible to the people and subject to their supervision.

All administrative, judicial, and procuratorial organs of the state are created by the people's congresses to which they are responsible and under whose supervision they operate.

The division of functions and powers between the central and local state organs is guided by the principle of giving full play to the initiative and enthusiasm of the local authorities under the unified leadership of the central authorities.

Article 4. All nationalities in the PRC are equal. The state protects the lawful rights and interests of the minority nationalities and upholds and develops the relationship of equality, unity, and mutual assistance among all China's nationalities. Discrimination against and oppression of any nationality are prohibited; any acts that undermine the unity of the nationalities or instigate their secession are prohibited.

The state helps the areas inhabited by minority nationalities speed up their economic and cultural development in accordance with the peculiarities and needs of the different minority nationalities.

Regional autonomy is practiced in areas where people of minority nationalities live in compact communities; in these areas organs of self-government are established for the exercise of the right of autonomy. All the national autonomous areas are inalienable parts of the PRC.

The people of all nationalities have the freedom to use and develop their own spoken and written languages and to preserve or reform their own ways and customs.

Article 5. The state upholds the uniformity and dignity of the socialist legal system.

No law or administrative or local rules and regulations shall contravene the Constitution.

All state organs, the armed forces, all political parties and public organizations, and all enterprises and undertakings must abide by the Constitution and the law. All acts in violation of the Constitution and the law must be looked into.

No organization or individual may enjoy the privilege of being above the Constitution and the law.

Article 6. The basis of the socialist economic system of the PRC is socialist public ownership of the means of production, namely, ownership by the whole people and collective ownership by the working people.

The system of socialist public ownership supersedes the system of exploitation of man by man; it applies the principles of "from each according to his ability, to each according to his work."

Article 7. The state-owned economy, namely the socialist economy under the ownership of the whole people, is the leading force in the national economy. The state ensures the consolidation and growth of the state-owned economy.

Article 8. In the rural areas, the responsibility system with the household contract linking output to payment as the main form, and other forms of cooperative economy such as producers', supply and marketing, credit and consumers' cooperatives, belong to the sector of socialist economy under collective ownership of the working people. Working people who are members of rural economic collectives have the right, within limits prescribed by law, to farm private plots of land, engage in household sideline production, and raise privately owned livestock.

The various forms of cooperative economy in the cities and towns, such as those in the handicraft, industrial, building, transport, commercial, and service trades, all belong to the sector of socialist economy under collective ownership by the working people.

The state protects the lawful rights and interests of the urban and rural economic collectives and encourages, guides, and helps the growth of the collective economy.

Article 9. Mineral resources, waters, forests, mountains, grassland, unreclaimed land, beaches, and other natural resources are owned by the state, that is, by the whole people, with the exception of the forests, mountains, grasslands, unreclaimed land, and beaches that are owned by collectives in accordance with the law.

The state ensures the rational use of natural resources and protects rare animals and plants. The appropriation or damage of natural resources by any organization or individual by whatever means is prohibited.

Article 10. Land in the cities is owned by the state.

Land in the rural and suburban areas is owned by collectives except for portions that belong to the state in accordance with the law; house sites and private plots of cropland and hilly land are also owned by collectives.

The state may in the public interest take over land for its use in accordance with the law.

No organization or individual may appropriate, buy, sell, or unlawfully transfer land in other ways. The right to the use of land may be transferred in accordance with the law.

All organizations and individuals who use land must make rational use of the land.

Article 11. The individual economy of urban and rural working people, operated within the limits prescribed by law, is a complement to the socialist public economy. The state protects the lawful rights and interests of the individual economy.

The state guides, helps, and supervises the individual economy by exercising administrative control.

The state permits the private sector of the economy to exist and develop within the limits prescribed by law. The private sector of the economy is a complement to the socialist public economy. The state protects the lawful rights and interests of the private sector of the economy and exercises guidance, supervision, and control over the private sector of the economy.

Article 12. Socialist public property is sacred and inviolable.

The state protects socialist public property; appropriation or damage of state or collective property by any organization or individual by whatever means is prohibited.

Article 13. The state protects the right of citizens to own lawfully earned income, savings, houses, and other lawful property.

The state protects by law the right of citizens to inherit private property.

Article 14. The state continuously raises labor productivity, improves economic results, and develops the productive forces by enhancing the enthusiasm of the working people, raising the level of their technical skill, disseminating advanced science and technology, improving the systems of economic administration and enterprise operation and management, instituting the socialist system of responsibility in various forms, and improving organization of work.

The state practices strict economy and combats waste.

The state properly apportions accumulation and consumption, pays attention to the interests of the collective and the individual as well as of the state and, on the basis of expanded production, gradually improves the material and cultural life of the people.

Article 15. The state practices a socialist market economy. The state strengthens economic legislation and perfects macrocontrol.

The state prohibits, according to the law, disturbance of society's economic order by any organization or individual.

Article 16. State-owned enterprises have decision-making power in operations within the limits prescribed by the law.

State-owned enterprises practice democratic management through congresses of workers and staff and in other ways in accordance with the law.

Article 17. Collective economic organizations have decision-making power in conducting economic activities on the condition that they abide by the relevant laws.

Collective economic organizations practice democratic management, elect and remove managerial personnel, and decide on major issues in accordance with the law.

Article 18. The PRC permits foreign enterprises, other foreign economic organizations, and individual foreigners to invest in China and to enter into various forms of economic cooperation with Chinese enterprises and other economic organizations in accordance with the law of the PRC.

All foreign enterprises and other foreign economic organizations in China, as well as joint ventures with Chinese and foreign investment located in China, shall abide by the law of the PRC. Their lawful rights and interests are protected by the law of the PRC.

Article 19. The state develops socialist educational undertakings and works to raise the scientific and cultural level of the whole nation.

The state runs schools of various types, makes primary education compulsory and universal, develops secondary, vocational, and higher education and promotes preschool education.

The state develops educational facilities of various types in order to wipe out illiteracy and provide political, cultural, scientific, technical, and professional education for workers, peasants, state functionaries, and other working people. It encourages people to become educated through self-study.

The state encourages the collective economic organizations, state enterprises and undertakings and other social forces to set up educational institutions of various types in accordance with the law. The state promotes the nationwide use of *putonghua* (common speech based on Beijing pronunciation).

Article 20. The state promotes the development of the natural and social sciences, disseminates scientific and technical knowledge, and commends and rewards achievements in scientific research as well as technological discoveries and inventions.

Article 21. The state develops medical and health services, promotes modern medicine and traditional Chinese medicine, encourages and supports the setting up of various medical and health facilities by the rural economic collectives, state enterprises and undertakings and neighborhood organizations, and promotes sanitation activities of a mass character, all to protect the people's health.

The state develops physical culture and promotes mass sports activities to build up the people's physique.

Article 22. The state promotes the development of literature and art, the press, broadcasting and television undertakings, publishing and distribution services, libraries, museums, cultural centers, and other cultural undertakings, that serve the people and socialism, and sponsors mass cultural activities.

The state protects places of scenic and historical interest, valuable cultural monuments and relics, and other important items of China's historical and cultural heritage.

Article 23. The state trains specialized personnel in all fields who serve socialism, increases the number of intellectuals, and creates conditions to give full scope to their role in socialist modernization.

Article 24. The state strengthens the building of socialist spiritual civilization through spreading education in high ideals and morality, general education and education in discipline and the legal system, and through promoting the formulation and observance of rules of conduct and common pledges by different sections of the people in urban and rural areas.

The state advocates the civic virtues of love for the motherland, for the people, for labor, for science and for socialism; it educates the people in patriotism, collectivism, internationalism, and communism and in dialectical and historical materialism; it combats capitalist, feudalist, and other decadent ideas.

Article 25. The state promotes family planning so that population growth may fit the plans for economic and social development.

Article 26. The state protects and improves the living environment and the ecological environment and prevents and remedies pollution and other public hazards.

The state organizes and encourages afforestation and the protection of forests.

Article 27. All state organs carry out the principle of simple and efficient administration, the system of responsibility for work, and the system of training functionaries and appraising their work in order constantly to improve quality of work and efficiency and combat bureaucratism.

All state organs and functionaries must rely on the support of the people, keep in close touch with them, heed their opinions and suggestions, accept their supervision, and work hard to serve them.

Article 28. The state maintains public order and suppresses treasonable and other counterrevolutionary activities; it penalizes actions that endanger public security and disrupt the socialist economy and other criminal activities, and punishes and reforms criminals.

Article 29. The armed forces of the PRC belong to the people. Their tasks are to strengthen national defense, resist aggression, defend the motherland, safeguard the people's peaceful labor, participate in national reconstruction, and work hard to serve the people. The state strengthens the revolutionization, modernization, and regularization of the armed forces in order to increase the national defense capability.

Article 30. The administrative division of the PRC is as follows:

(1) The country is divided into provinces, autonomous regions, and municipalities directly under the central government.
(2) Provinces and autonomous regions are divided into autonomous prefectures, counties, autonomous counties, and cities.
(3) Counties and autonomous counties are divided into townships, nationality townships, and towns.

Municipalities directly under the central government and other large cities are divided into districts and counties. Autonomous prefectures are divided into counties, autonomous counties, and cities.

All autonomous regions, autonomous prefectures, and autonomous counties are national autonomous areas.

Article 31. The state may establish special administrative regions when necessary. The systems to be instituted in special administrative regions shall be prescribed by law enacted by the NPC in the light of the specific conditions.

Article 32. The PRC protects the lawful rights and interests of foreigners within Chinese territory, and while on Chinese territory foreigners must abide by the law of the PRC.

The PRC may grant asylum to foreigners who request it for political reasons.

Chapter 2. The Fundamental Rights and Duties of Citizens

Article 33. All persons holding the nationality of the PRC are citizens of the PRC.

All citizens of the PRC are equal before the law.

Every citizen enjoys the rights and at the same time must perform the duties prescribed by the Constitution and the law.

Article 34. All citizens of the PRC who have reached the age of 18 have the right to vote and stand for election, regardless of nationality, race, sex, occupation, family background, religious belief, education, property status, or length of residence, except persons deprived of political rights according to law.

Article 35. Citizens of the PRC enjoy freedom of speech, of the press, of assembly, of association, of procession, and of demonstration.

Article 36. Citizens of the PRC enjoy freedom of religious belief.

No state organ, public organization, or individual may compel citizens to believe in, or not to believe in, any religion; nor may they discriminate against citizens who believe in, or do not believe in, any religion.

The state protects normal religious activities. No one may make use of religion to engage in activities that disrupt public order, impair the health of citizens, or interfere with the educational system of the state.

Religious bodies and religious affairs are not subject to any foreign domination.

Article 37. The freedom of person of citizens of the PRC is inviolable.

No citizen may be arrested except with the approval or by decision of a people's procuratorate or by decision of a people's court, and arrests must be made by a public security organ.

Unlawful deprivation or restriction of citizens' freedom of person by detention or other means is prohibited; and unlawful search of the person of citizens is prohibited.

Article 38. The personal dignity of citizens of the PRC is inviolable. Insult, libel, false charge, or frame-up directed against citizens by any means is prohibited.

Article 39. The home of citizens of the PRC is inviolable. Unlawful search of, or intrusion into, a citizen's home is prohibited.

Article 40. The freedom and privacy of correspondence of citizens of the PRC are protected by law. No organization or individual may, on any ground, infringe upon the freedom and privacy of citizens' correspondence except in cases where, to meet the needs of state security or of investigation into criminal offenses, public security or procuratorial organs are permitted to censor correspondence in accordance with procedures prescribed by law.

Article 41. Citizens of the PRC have the right to criticize and make suggestions to any state organ or functionary. Citizens have the right to make to relevant state organs complaints and charges against, or exposures of, violation of the law, or dereliction of duty by any state organ or functionary; but fabrication or distortion of facts with the intention of libel or frame-up is prohibited.

In case of complaints, charges, or exposures made by citizens, the state organ concerned must deal with them in a responsible manner after ascertaining the facts. No one may suppress such complaints, charges, and exposures, or retaliate against the citizens making them.

Citizens who have suffered losses through infringement of their civic rights by any state organ or functionary have the right to compensation in accordance with the law.

Article 42. Citizens of the PRC have the right as well as the duty to work.

Using various channels, the state creates conditions for employment, strengthens labor protection, improves working conditions, and, on the basis of expanded production, increases remuneration for work and social benefits.

Work is the glorious duty of every able-bodied citizen. All working people in state-owned enterprises and in urban and rural economic collectives should perform their tasks with an attitude consonant with their status as masters of the country. The state promotes socialist labor emulation, and commends and rewards model and ad-

vanced workers. The state encourages citizens to take part in voluntary labor.

The state provides necessary vocational training to citizens before they are employed.

Article 43. Working people in the PRC have the right to rest.

The state expands facilities for rest and recuperation of working people and prescribes working hours and vacations for workers and staff.

Article 44. The state prescribes by law the system of retirement for workers and staff in enterprises and undertakings and for functionaries of organs of state. The livelihood of retired personnel is ensured by the state and society.

Article 45. Citizens of the PRC have the right to material assistance from the state and society when they are old, ill, or disabled. The state develops the social insurance, social relief, and medical and health services that are required to enable citizens to enjoy this right.

The state and society ensure the livelihood of disabled members of the armed forces, provide pensions to the families of martyrs, and give preferential treatment to the families of military personnel.

The state and society help make arrangements for the work, livelihood, and education of the blind, deaf-mute, and other handicapped citizens.

Article 46. Citizens of the PRC have the duty as well as the right to receive education.

The state promotes the all-around moral, intellectual, and physical development of children and young people.

Article 47. Citizens of the PRC have the freedom to engage in scientific research, literary and artistic creation, and other cultural pursuits. The state encourages and assists creative endeavors conducive to the interests of the people that are made by citizens engaged in education, science, technology, literature, art, and other cultural work.

Article 48. Women in the PRC enjoy equal rights with men in all spheres of life, political, economic, cultural, and social, including family life.

The state protects the rights and interests of women, applies the principle of equal pay for equal work for men and women alike, and trains and selects cadres from among women.

Article 49. Marriage, the family, and mother and child are protected by the state.

Both husband and wife have the duty to practice family planning.

Parents have the duty to rear and educate their minor children, and children who have come of age have the duty to support and assist their parents.

Violation of the freedom of marriage is prohibited. Maltreatment of old people, women, and children is prohibited.

Article 50. The PRC protects the legitimate rights and interests of Chinese nationals residing abroad and protects the lawful rights and interests of returned overseas Chinese and of the family members of Chinese nationals residing abroad.

Article 51. The exercise by citizens of the PRC of their freedoms and rights may not infringe upon the interests of the state, of society, and of the collective, or upon the lawful freedoms and rights of other citizens.

Article 52. It is the duty of citizens of the PRC to safeguard the unity of the country and the unity of all its nationalities.

Article 53. Citizens of the PRC must abide by the Constitution and the law, keep state secrets, protect public property, and observe labor discipline and public order and respect social ethics.

Article 54. It is the duty of citizens of the PRC to safeguard the security, honor, and interests of the motherland; they must not commit acts detrimental to the security, honor, and interests of the motherland.

Article 55. It is the sacred obligation of every citizen of the PRC to defend the motherland and resist aggression.

It is the honorable duty of citizens of the PRC to perform military service and join the militia in accordance with the law.

Article 56. It is the duty of citizens of the PRC to pay taxes in accordance with the law.

Chapter 3. The Structure of the State

Section I. The National People's Congress

Article 57. The NPC of the PRC is the highest organ of state power. Its permanent body is the Standing Committee of the NPC.

Article 58. The NPC and its Standing Committee exercise the legislative power of the state.

Article 59. The NPC is composed of deputies elected by the provinces, autonomous regions, and municipalities directly under the central government, and by the armed forces. All the minority nationalities are entitled to appropriate representation.

Election of deputies to the NPC is conducted by the Standing Committee of the NPC.

The number of deputies to the NPC and the manner of their election are prescribed by law.

Article 60. The NPC is elected for a term of five years.

Two months before the expiration of the term of office of an NPC, its Standing Committee must ensure that the election of deputies to the succeeding NPC is completed. Should exceptional circumstances prevent such an election, it may be postponed by decision of a majority vote of more than two-thirds of all those on the Standing Committee of the incumbent NPC and the term of office of the incumbent NPC may be extended. The election of deputies to the succeeding NPC must be completed within one year after the termination of such exceptional circumstances.

Article 61. The NPC meets in session once a year and is convened by its Standing Committee. A session of the NPC may be convened at any time the Standing Committee deems this necessary, or when more than one-fifth of the deputies to the NPC so propose.

When the NPC meets, it elects a presidium to conduct its session.

Article 62. The NPC exercises the following functions and powers:

(1) to amend the Constitution;
(2) to supervise the enforcement of the Constitution;
(3) to enact and amend basic statutes concerning criminal offenses, civil affairs, the state organs, and other matters;
(4) to elect the president and the vice president of the PRC;
(5) to decide on the choice of the premier of the State Council upon nomination by the president of the PRC, and to decide on the choice of the vice premiers, state councilors, ministers in charge of ministries or commissions and the auditor general and the secretary general of the State Council upon nomination by the premier;
(6) to elect the chairman of the Central Military Commission and, upon his nomination, to decide on the choice of all the others on the Central Military Commission;
(7) to elect the president of the Supreme People's Court;
(8) to elect the procurator general of the Supreme People's Procuratorate;
(9) to examine and approve the plan for national economic and social development and the reports on its implementation;

(10) to examine and approve the state budget and the report on its implementation;

(11) to alter or annul inappropriate decisions of the Standing Committee of the NPC;

(12) to approve the establishment of provinces, autonomous regions, and municipalities directly under the central government;

(13) to decide on the establishment of special administrative regions and the systems to be instituted there;

(14) to decide on questions of war and peace; and

(15) to exercise such other functions and powers as the highest organ of state power should exercise.

Article 63. The NPC has the power to recall or remove from office the following persons:

(1) the president and the vice president of the PRC;

(2) the premier, vice premiers, state councilors, ministers, and the auditor general and the secretary general of the State Council;

(3) the chairman of the Central Military Commission and others on the commission;

(4) the president of the Supreme People's Court; and

(5) the procurator general of the Supreme People's Procuratorate.

Article 64. Amendments to the Constitution are to be proposed by the Standing Committee of the NPC or by more than one-fifth of the deputies to the NPC and adopted by a majority vote of more than two-thirds of all the deputies to the congress.

Statutes and resolutions are adopted by a majority vote of more than one-half of all the deputies to the NPC.

Article 65. The Standing Committee of the NPC is composed of the following: the chairman; the vice chairmen; the secretary general; and members.

Minority nationalities are entitled to appropriate representation on the Standing Committee of the NPC.

The NPC elects, and has the power to recall, all those on its Standing Committee.

No one on the Standing Committee of the NPC shall hold any post in any of the administrative, judicial, or procuratorial organs of the state.

Article 66. The Standing Committee of the NPC is elected for the same term as the NPC; it exercises its functions and powers until a new Standing Committee is elected by the succeeding NPC.

The chairman and vice chairmen of the Standing Committee shall serve no more than two consecutive terms.

Article 67. The Standing Committee of the NPC exercises the following functions and powers:

(1) to interpret the Constitution and supervise its enforcement;

(2) to enact and amend statutes with the exception of those which should be enacted by the NPC;

(3) to enact, when the NPC is not in session, partial supplements, and amendments to statutes enacted by the NPC provided that they do not contravene the basic principles of these statutes;

(4) to interpret statutes;

(5) to examine and approve, when the NPC is not in session, partial adjustments to the plan for national economic and social development and to the state budget that prove necessary in the course of their implementation;

(6) to supervise the work of the State Council, the Central Military Commission, the Supreme People's Court, and the Supreme People's Procuratorate;

(7) to annul those administrative rules and regulations, decisions, or orders to the State Council that contravene the Constitution or the statutes;

(8) to annul those local regulations or decisions of the organs of state power of provinces, autonomous regions, and municipalities directly under the central government that contravene the constitution, the statutes, or the administrative rules and regulations;

(9) to decide, when the NPC is not in session, on the choice of ministers in charge of ministries or commissions or the auditor general and the secretary general of the State Council upon nomination by the premier of the State Council;

(10) to decide, upon nomination by the chairman of the Central Military Commission, on the choice of others on the commission, when the NPC is not in session;

(11) to appoint and remove the vice presidents and judges of the Supreme People's Court, members of its judicial committee, and the president of the Military Court at the suggestion of the president of the Supreme People's Court;

(12) to appoint and remove the deputy procurators general and procurators of the Supreme People's Procuratorate, members of its procuratorial committee, and the chief procurator of the military procuratorate at the request of the procurator general of the Supreme People's Procuratorate, and to approve the appointment and removal of the chief procurators of the people's procuratorates of provinces, autonomous regions, and municipalities directly under the central government;

(13) to decide on the appointment and recall of plenipotentiary representatives abroad;

(14) to decide on the ratification and abrogation of treaties and important agreements concluded with foreign states;

(15) to institute systems of titles and ranks for military and diplomatic personnel and of other specific titles and ranks;

(16) to institute state medals and titles of honor and decide on their conferment;

(17) to decide on the granting of special pardons;

(18) to decide, when the NPC is not in session, on the proclamation of a state of war in the event of an armed attack on the country or in fulfillment of international treaty obligations concerning common defense against aggression;

(19) to decide on general mobilization or partial mobilization;

(20) to decide on the enforcement of martial law throughout the country or in particular provinces, autonomous regions, or municipalities directly under the central government; and

(21) to exercise such other functions and powers as the NPC may assign to it.

Article 68. The chairman of the Standing Committee of the NPC presides over the work of the Standing Committee and convenes its meetings. The vice chairmen and the secretary general assist the chairman in his work.

Chairmanship meetings with the participation of the chairman, vice chairmen and secretary general handle the important day-to-day work of the Standing Committee of the NPC.

Article 69. The Standing Committee of the NPC is responsible to the NPC and reports on its work to the congress.

Article 70. The NPC establishes a nationalities committee, a law committee, a finance and economic committee, an education, science, culture and public health committee, a foreign affairs committee, an overseas Chinese committee, and such other special committees as are necessary. These special committees work under the direction of the Standing Committee of the NPC when the congress is not in session.

The special committees examine, discuss, and draw up relevant bills and draft resolutions under the direction of the NPC and its Standing Committee.

Article 71. The NPC and its Standing Committee may, when they deem it necessary, appoint committees of inquiry into specific questions and adopt relevant resolutions in the light of their reports.

All organs of state, public organizations, and citizens concerned are obliged to supply the necessary information to those committees of inquiry when they conduct investigations.

Article 72. Deputies to the NPC and all those on its Standing Committee have the right, in accordance with procedures prescribed by law, to submit bills and proposals within the scope of the respective functions and powers of the NPC and its Standing Committee.

Article 73. Deputies to the NPC during its sessions, and all those on its Standing Committee during its meetings, have the right to address questions, in accordance with procedures prescribed by law, to the State Council, which must answer the questions in a responsible manner.

Article 74. No deputy to the NPC may be arrested or placed on criminal trial without the consent of the Presidium of the current session of the NPC or, when the NPC is not in session, without the consent of its Standing Committee.

Article 75. Deputies to the NPC may not be called to legal account for their speeches or votes at its meetings.

Article 76. Deputies to the NPC must play an exemplary role in abiding by the Constitution and the law and keeping state secrets and, in production and other work and their public activities, assist in the enforcement of the Constitution and the law.

Deputies to the NPC should maintain close contact with the units that elected them and with the people, listen to and convey the opinions and demands of the people and work hard to serve them.

Article 77. Deputies to the NPC are subject to the supervision of the units that elected them. The electoral units have the power, through procedures prescribed by law, to recall the deputies whom they elected.

Article 78. The organization and working procedures of the NPC and its Standing Committee are prescribed by law.

Section II. The President of the PRC

Article 79. The president and vice president of the PRC are elected by the NPC. Citizens of the PRC who have the right to vote and to stand for election and who have reached the age of 45 are eligible for election as president or vice president of the PRC.

The term of office of the president and vice president of the PRC is the same as that of the NPC, and they shall serve no more than two consecutive terms.

Article 80. The president of the PRC, in pursuance of decisions of the NPC and its Standing Committee, promulgates statutes; appoints and removes the premier, vice premiers, state councilors, ministers in charge of ministries or commissions, and the auditor general and the secretary general of the State Council; confers state medals and titles of honor; issues orders of special pardons;

proclaims martial law; proclaims a state of war; and issues mobilization orders.

Article 81. The president of the PRC receives foreign diplomatic representatives on behalf of the PRC and, in pursuance of decisions of the Standing Committee of the NPC, appoints and recalls plenipotentiary representatives abroad, and ratifies and abrogates treaties and important agreements concluded with foreign states.

Article 82. The vice president of the PRC assists the president in his work.

The vice president of the PRC may exercise such parts of the functions and powers of the president as the president may entrust to him.

Article 83. The president and vice president of the PRC exercise their functions and powers until the new president and vice president elected by the succeeding NPC assume office.

Article 84. In case the office of the president of the PRC falls vacant, the vice president succeeds to the office of president.

In case the office of the vice president of the PRC falls vacant, the NPC shall elect a new vice president.

In the event that the offices of both the president and the vice president of the PRC fall vacant, the NPC shall elect a new president and a new vice president. Prior to such election, the chairman of the Standing Committee of the NPC shall temporarily act as the president of the PRC.

Section III. The State Council

Article 85. The State Council, that is, the central people's government, of the PRC is the executive body of the highest organ of state power; it is the highest organ of state administration.

Article 86. The State Council is composed of the following:

The premier;
The vice premiers;
The state councilors;
The ministers in charge of ministries;
The ministers in charge of commissions;
The auditor general; and
The secretary general.

The premier has overall responsibility for the State Council. The ministers have overall responsibility for the respective ministries or commissions under their charge.

The organization of the State Council is prescribed by law.

Article 87. The term of office of the State Council is the same as that of the NPC.

The premier, vice premier, and state councilors shall serve no more than two consecutive terms.

Article 88. The premier directs the work of the State Council. The vice premiers and state councilors assist the premier in his work.

Executive meetings of the State Council are composed of the premier, the vice premiers, the state councilors and the secretary general of the State Council.

The premier convenes and presides over the executive meetings and plenary meetings of the State Council.

Article 89. The State Council exercises the following functions and powers:

(1) to adopt administrative measures, enact administrative rules and regulations and issue decisions and orders in accordance with the Constitution and the statutes;

(2) to submit proposals to the NPC or its Standing Committee;

(3) to lay down the tasks and responsibilities of the ministries and commissions of the State Council, to exercise unified leadership over the work of the ministries and commissions and to direct all other administrative work of a national character that does not fall within the jurisdiction of the ministries and commissions;

(4) to exercise unified leadership over the work of local organs of state administration at different levels throughout the country, and to lay down the detailed division of functions and powers between the central government and the organs of state administration of provinces, autonomous regions and municipalities directly under the central government;

(5) to draw up and implement the plan for national economic and social development and the state budget;

(6) to direct and administer economic work and urban and rural development;

(7) to direct and administer the work concerning education, science, culture, public health, physical culture, and family planning;

(8) to direct and administer the work concerning civil affairs, public security, judicial administration, supervision, and other related matters;

(9) to conduct foreign affairs and conclude treaties and agreements with foreign states;

(10) to direct and administer the building of national defense;

(11) to direct and administer affairs concerning the nationalities, and to safeguard the equal rights of minority nationalities and the right of autonomy of the national autonomous areas;

(12) to protect the legitimate rights and interests of Chinese nationals residing abroad and protect the lawful

rights and interests of returned overseas Chinese and of the family members of Chinese nationals residing abroad;

(13) to alter or annul inappropriate orders, directives, and regulations issued by the ministries or commissions;

(14) to alter or annul inappropriate decisions and orders issued by local organs of state administration at different levels;

(15) to approve the geographic division of provinces, autonomous regions, and municipalities directly under the central government, and to approve the establishment and geographic division of autonomous prefectures, counties, autonomous counties, and cities;

(16) to decide on the enforcement of martial law in parts of provinces, autonomous regions and municipalities directly under the central government;

(17) to examine and decide on the size of administrative organs and, in accordance with the law, to appoint, remove, and train administrative officers, appraise their work, and reward or punish them; and

(18) to exercise such other functions and powers as the NPC or its Standing Committee may assign it.

Article 90. The ministers in charge of ministries or commissions of the State Council are responsible for the work of their respective departments and convene and preside over their ministerial meetings or commission meetings that discuss and decide on major issues in the work of their respective departments.

The ministries and commissions issue orders, directives, and regulations within the jurisdiction of their respective departments and in accordance with the statutes and the administrative rules and regulations, decisions, and orders issued by the State Council.

Article 91. The State Council establishes an auditing body to supervise through auditing the revenue and expenditure of all departments under the State Council and of the local governments at different levels, and those of the state financial and monetary organizations and of enterprises and undertakings. Under the direction of the premier of the State Council, the auditing body independently exercises its power to supervise through auditing in accordance with the law, subject to no interference by any other administrative organ or any public organization or individual.

Article 92. The State Council is responsible, and reports on its work, to the NPC or when the NPC is not in session, to its Standing Committee.

Section IV. The Central Military Commission

Article 93. The Central Military Commission of the PRC directs the armed forces of the country.

The Central Military Commission is composed of the following: the chairman; the vice chairmen; and members.

The chairman of the Central Military Commission has overall responsibility for the commission.

The term of office of the Central Military Commission is the same as that of the NPC.

Article 94. The chairman of the Central Military Commission is responsible to the NPC and its Standing Committee.

Section V. The Local People's Congresses and the Local People's Governments at Different Levels

Article 95. People's congresses and people's governments are established in provinces, municipalities directly under the central government, counties, cities, municipal districts, townships, nationality townships, and towns.

The organization of local people's congresses and local people's governments at different levels is prescribed by law.

Organs of self-government are established in autonomous regions, autonomous prefectures, and autonomous counties. The organization and working procedures of organs of self-government are prescribed by law in accordance with the basic principles laid down in Sections V and VI of Chapter 3 of the Constitution.

Article 96. Local people's congresses at different levels are local organs of state power.

Local people's congresses at and above the county level establish standing committees.

Article 97. Deputies to the people's congresses of provinces, municipalities directly under the central government, and cities divided into districts are elected by the people's congresses at the next lower level; deputies to the people's congresses of counties, cities not divided into districts, municipal districts, townships, nationality townships, and towns are elected directly by their constituencies.

The number of deputies to local people's congresses at different levels and the manner of their election are prescribed by law.

Article 98. The term of office of the people's congresses of provinces, municipalities directly under the central government, counties, cities, and municipal districts is five years. The term of office of the people's congresses of townships, nationality townships, and towns is three years.

Article 99. Local people's congresses at different levels ensure the observance and implementation of the constitution, the statutes, and the administrative rules and regulations in their respective administrative areas. Within the limits of their authority as prescribed by law, they adopt and issue resolutions and examine and decide on plans for local economic and cultural development and for the development of public services.

Local people's congresses at and above the county level examine and approve the plans for economic and social development and the budgets of their respective administrative areas and examine and approve reports on their implementation. They have the power to alter or annul inappropriate decisions of their own standing committees.

The people's congress of nationality townships may, within the limits of their authority as prescribed by law, take specific measures suited to the peculiarities of the nationalities concerned.

Article 100. The people's congresses of provinces and municipalities directly under the central government, and their standing committees, may adopt local regulations, which must not contravene the constitution, the statutes, and the administrative rules and regulations, and they shall report such local regulations to the Standing Committee of the NPC for the record.

Article 101. At their respective levels, local people's congresses elect, and have the power to recall, governors and deputy governors, or mayors and deputy mayors, or heads and deputy heads of counties, districts, townships and towns.

Local people's congresses at and above the county level elect, and have the power to recall, presidents of people's courts and chief procurators of people's procuratorates at the corresponding level. The election or recall of chief procurators of people's procuratorates shall be reported to the chief procurators of the people's procuratorates at the next higher level for submission to the standing committee of the people's congresses at the corresponding level for approval.

Article 102. Deputies to the people's congresses of provinces, municipalities directly under the central government, and cities divided into districts are subject to supervision by the units that elected them; deputies to the people's congresses of counties, cities not divided into districts, municipal districts, townships, nationality townships, and towns are subject to supervision by their constituencies. The electoral units and constituencies that elect deputies to local people's congresses at different levels have the power, according to procedures prescribed by law, to recall deputies whom they elected.

Article 103. The standing committee of a local people's congress at and above the county level is composed of a chairman, vice chairmen, and members, and is re-

sponsible, and reports on its work, to the people's congress at the corresponding level.

The local people's congress at and above the county level elects, and has the power to recall, anyone on the standing committee of the people's congress at the corresponding level.

No one on the standing committee of a local people's congress at and above the county level shall hold any post in state administrative, judicial, and procuratorial organs.

Article 104. The standing committee of a local people's congress at and above the county level discusses and decides on major issues in all fields of work in its administrative area; supervises the work of the people's government, people's court, and people's procuratorate at the corresponding level; annuls inappropriate decisions and orders of the people's government at the corresponding level; annuls inappropriate resolutions of the people's congress at the next lower level; decides on the appointment and removal of functionaries of state organs within its jurisdiction as prescribed by law; and, when the people's congress at the corresponding level is not in session, recalls individual deputies to the people's congress at the next higher level and elects individual deputies to fill vacancies in that people's congress.

Article 105. Local people's governments at different levels are the executive bodies of local organs of state power as well as the local organs of state administration at the corresponding level. Local people's governments at different levels practice the system of overall responsibility by governors, mayors, county heads, district heads, township heads, and town heads.

Article 106. The term of office of local people's governments at different levels is the same as that of the people's congresses at the corresponding level.

Article 107. Local people's governments at and above the county level, within the limits of their authority as prescribed by law, conduct the administrative work concerning the economy, education, science, culture, public health, physical culture, urban and rural development, finance, civil affairs, public security, nationalities affairs, judicial administration, supervision, and family planning in their respective administrative areas; issue decisions and orders; appoint, remove, and train administrative functionaries, appraise their work, and reward or punish them.

People's governments of townships, nationality townships, and towns carry out the resolutions of the people's congress at the corresponding level as well as the decisions and orders of the state administrative organs at the next higher level and conduct administrative work in their respective administrative areas.

People's governments of provinces and municipalities directly under the central government decide on the establishment and geographic division of townships, nationality townships, and towns.

Article 108. Local people's governments at and above the county level direct the work of their subordinate departments and of people's governments at lower levels, and have the power to alter or annul inappropriate decisions of their subordinate departments and people's governments at lower levels.

Article 109. Auditing bodies are established by local people's governments at and above the county level. Local auditing bodies at different levels independently exercise their power to supervise through auditing in accordance with the law and are responsible to the people's government at the corresponding level and to the auditing body at the next higher level.

Article 110. Local people's governments at different levels are responsible, and report on their work, to people's congresses at the corresponding level. Local people's governments at and above the county level are responsible, and report on their work, to the standing committee of the people's congress at the corresponding level when the congress is not in session.

Local people's governments at different levels are responsible, and report on their work, to the state administrative organs at the next higher level. Local people's governments at different levels throughout the country are state administrative organs under the unified leadership of the State Council and are subordinate to it.

Article 111. The residents' committees and villagers' committees established among urban and rural residents on the basis of their place of residence are mass organizations of self-management at the grass-roots level. The chairman, vice chairmen, and members of each residents' or villagers' committee are elected by the residents. The relationship between the residents' and villagers' committees and the grass-roots organs of state power is prescribed by law.

The residents' and villagers' committees establish committees for people's mediation, public security, public health, and other matters in order to manage public affairs and social services in their areas, mediate civil disputes, help maintain public order, and convey residents' opinions and demands and make suggestions to the people's government.

Section VI. The Organs of Self-Government
of National Autonomous Areas

Article 112. The organs of self-government of national autonomous areas are the people's congresses and people's governments of autonomous regions, autonomous prefectures, and autonomous counties.

Article 113. In the people's congress of an autonomous region, prefecture, or county, in addition to the deputies of the nationality or nationalities exercising regional autonomy in the administrative area, the other nationalities inhabiting the area are also entitled to appropriate representation.

The chairmanship and vice chairmanships of the standing committee of the people's congress of an autonomous region, prefecture, or county shall include a citizen or citizens of the nationality or nationalities exercising regional autonomy in the area concerned.

Article 114. The administrative head of an autonomous region, prefecture, or county shall be a citizen of the nationality, or of one of the nationalities, exercising regional autonomy in the area concerned.

Article 115. The organs of self-government of autonomous regions, prefectures, and counties exercise the functions and powers of local organs of state as specified in Section V of Chapter 3 of the Constitution. At the same time, they exercise the right of autonomy within the limits of their authority as prescribed by the constitution, the law of regional national autonomy and other laws, and implement the laws and policies of the state in the light of the existing local situation.

Article 116. People's congresses of national autonomous areas have the power to enact autonomy regulations and specific regulations in the light of the political, economic, and cultural characteristics of the nationality or nationalities in the areas concerned. The autonomy regulations and specific regulations of autonomous regions shall be submitted to the Standing Committee of the NPC for approval before they go into effect. Those of autonomous prefectures and counties shall be submitted to the standing committees of the people's congresses of provinces or autonomous regions for approval before they go into effect, and they shall be reported to the Standing Committee of the NPC for the record.

Article 117. The organs of self-government of the national autonomous areas have the power of autonomy in administering the finances of their areas. All revenues accruing to the national autonomous areas under the financial system of the state shall be managed and used by the organs of self-government of those areas on their own.

Article 118. The organs of self-government of the national autonomous areas independently arrange for and administer local economic development under the guidance of state plans.

In exploiting natural resources and building enterprises in the national autonomous areas, the state shall give due consideration to the interests of those areas.

Article 119. The organs of self-government of the national autonomous areas independently administer educational, scientific, cultural, public health, and physical culture affairs in their respective areas, protect and cull through the cultural heritage of the nationalities, and work for the development and prosperity of their cultures.

Article 120. The organs of self-government of the national autonomous areas may, in accordance with the military system of the state and concrete local needs and with the approval of the State Council, organize local public security forces for the maintenance of public order.

Article 121. In performing their functions, the organs of self-government of the national autonomous areas, in accordance with the autonomy regulations of the respective areas, employ the spoken and written language or languages in common use in the locality.

Article 122. The state gives financial, material, and technical assistance to the minority nationalities to accelerate their economic and cultural development.

The state helps the national autonomous areas train large numbers of cadres at different levels and specialized personnel and skilled workers of different professions and trades from among the nationality or nationalities in those areas.

Section VII. The People's Courts
and the People's Procuratorates

Article 123. The people's courts in the PRC are the judicial organs of the state.

Article 124. The PRC establishes the Supreme People's Court and the local people's courts at different levels, military courts, and other special people's courts.

The term of office of the president of the Supreme People's Court is the same as that of the NPC; he shall serve no more than two consecutive terms.

The organization of people's courts is prescribed by law.

Article 125. All cases handled by the people's courts, except those involving special circumstances as specified by law, shall be heard in public. The accused has the right to defense.

Article 126. The people's courts shall, in accordance with the law, exercise judicial power independently and are not subject to interference by administrative organs, public organizations, or individuals.

Article 127. The Supreme People's Court is the highest judicial organ.

The Supreme People's Court supervises the administration of justice by the local people's courts at different levels and by the special people's courts; people's courts at higher levels supervise the administration of justice by those at lower levels.

Article 128. The Supreme People's Court is responsible to the NPC and its Standing Committee. Local people's courts at different levels are responsible to the organs of state power that created them.

Article 129. The people's procuratorates of the PRC are state organs for legal supervision.

Article 130. The PRC establishes the Supreme People's Procuratorate and the local people's procuratorates at different levels, military procuratorates, and other special people's procuratorates.

The term of office of the procurator general of the Supreme People's Procuratorate is the same as that of the National People's Congress; he shall serve no more than two consecutive terms.

The organization of people's procuratorates is prescribed by law.

Article 131. People's procuratorates shall, in accordance with the law, exercise procuratorial power independently and are not subject to interference by administrative organs, public organizations, or individuals.

Article 132. The Supreme People's Procuratorate is the highest procuratorial organ.

The Supreme People's Procuratorate directs the work of the local people's procuratorates at different levels and of the special people's procuratorates; people's procuratorates at higher levels direct the work of those at lower levels.

Article 133. The Supreme People's Procuratorate is responsible to the NPC and its Standing Committee. Local people's procuratorates at different levels are responsible to the organs of state power at the corresponding levels that created them and to the people's procuratorates at the higher level.

Article 134. Citizens of all nationalities have the right to use the spoken and written languages of their own nationalities in court proceedings. The people's courts and people's procuratorates should provide translation for any party to the court proceedings who is not familiar with the spoken or written languages in common use in the locality.

In an area where people of a minority nationality live in

a compact community or where a number of nationalities live together, hearings should be conducted in the language or languages in common use in the locality; indictments, judgments, notices and other documents should be written, according to actual needs, in the language or languages in common use in the locality.

Article 135. The people's courts, people's procuratorates, and public security organs shall, in handling criminal cases, divide their functions, each taking responsibility for its own work, and they shall coordinate their efforts and check each other to ensure correct and effective enforcement of law.

Chapter 4. The National Flag, the National Emblem, and the Capital

Article 136. The national flag of the PRC is a red flag with five stars.

Article 137. The national emblem of the PRC is Tiananmen in the center illuminated by five stars and encircled by ears of grain and a cogwheel.

Article 138. The capital of the PRC is Beijing.

Wan Li on the Household Responsibility System

Among the earliest of the post-1978 Dengist reforms was the transformation of agricultural production through institution of the "household responsibility system," which gave individual farmers the right to make production decisions and sell surplus agricultural production on open markets. Tried on an experimental basis throughout the country beginning in 1979, the system was officially sanctioned for nationwide implementation in early 1983. In the following speech, made on November 29, 1983, Vice Premier Wan Li candidly summarizes the new system and sets forth goals for the coming year.

The national conference on rural work has opened today [29 November]. The tasks of this conference are conscientiously to study the new situation of the past year, sum up fresh experiences, and solve new problems in order to adapt ourselves further to the new situation that has been created in the rural areas and to maintain and develop it. I would like to express some views on the following questions that are on your agenda for discussion and reference.

(I) On the Rural Situation and the Starting Point from Which to Solve Problems

This time last year, the party Central Committee con-

vened a national conference on ideological and political work in the rural areas and a national conference on rural work. Those attending these conferences further unified their understanding of some major problems in rural work and drafted document no. 1, which was issued for trial implementation after the Political Bureau discussed, revised, and adopted it. After the document was transmitted to lower levels, it received warm support from the whole party, the entire army, and the people of all nationalities throughout the country and further aroused the enthusiasm of large numbers of peasants, cadres, and intellectuals. Owing to the efforts of various relevant central departments as well as party committees and governments at all levels to implement the document, the excellent situation in the rural areas has further developed. This has been a year in which the output-related system of contracted responsibilities has been implemented in an all-around way and has developed in depth toward the restructuring of the rural economic system; a year in which the agricultural front has continued to advance with giant strides while overcoming natural disasters; a year in which rural commodity production has vigorously developed on an unprecedentedly large scale; and a year in which natural resources have been exploited in many areas to develop production comprehensively.

Over 90 percent of the peasant households have now adopted the output-related system of contracted responsibilities, which is based mainly on operation by households. People in some prosperous areas and areas with a higher level of mechanization once had doubts and misgivings about the output-related system of contracted responsibilities. After several years of observation and comparison, especially after this year's experimentation with it, they have chosen to adopt the output-related system of contracted responsibilities. After several years of observation and comparison, especially after this year's experimentation with it, they have chosen to adopt the output-related system of contracted responsibilities one after another. Some areas, after drawing on the experiences of other areas where this system was earlier adopted, have begun to surpass the latter in this regard. State farms have also started adopting measures to sign contracts with peasant households and have achieved very good results in this regard, and these measures are gradually being popularized. Considered as a great creation by the 800,000 peasants under the party's leadership, the output-related system of contracted responsibilities has already taken root in China. This system is not an expedient measure to solve the problem of providing the people with enough food and clothing; it is a reform of fundamental importance involving the entire rural economic system, and it is of immeasurable significance in building socialism with distinctive Chinese features.

What is more gratifying is the emergence in the country of a large number of specialized households and key households doing specialized jobs besides crop cultivation; they have achieved prosperity through their own labor. With these households providing the impetus, villages engaged mainly in certain types of specialized production have also appeared. On the basis of these specialized villages, towns and townships engaged in various types of specialized production on different scales as well as specialized products markets have been formed in some areas.

Undertakings of a developmental character have made noticeable progress in the past year, and some areas are working out their principles and plans for development step by step. However, we should also note that the rural areas' economic foundation and their ability to resist relatively serious natural disasters are still very weak. As far as some areas are concerned, the developments of the past few years are related to recovery. Peasants have generally and noticeably improved their livelihood, but developments in this regard are rather unbalanced. Peasants in a few localities still have considerable difficulties in making a living. Meanwhile, the problem of the superstructure not being suited to the relations of production has become increasingly outstanding as rural reforms in various fields have been expanding, the productive forces have been continuously increasing, and the diversification of the rural economic structure has been developing. A large number of bold reforms have been carried out in various fields, but generally speaking, more and more new and increasingly complicated problems have occurred, such as problems in circulation; problems in further improving the output-related system of contracted responsibilities, including problems in land readjustment and subcontracting; problems of further defining the policy of combining rural labor forces, funds, and natural resources in various forms; problems of reforming the economic system and the administrative management system in the rural areas; problems of spreading science and technology and universalizing cultural education; problems of improving operation and management, reducing production costs and achieving better economic results; problems of building water conservancy works, energy and transport facilities as well as small cities and towns; problems of strengthening ideological and political work and the building of a socialist material and spiritual civilization; and so forth.

We are faced with a series of major problems. While it is true that we are encountering an unprecedented excellent situation, we have certainly confronted many difficult problems that have been extremely complicated. Now is the crucial moment. If the problems are solved well, the situation in the rural areas will continue to develop and advance smoothly. Otherwise, the excellent situation already at hand will be hard to consolidate, and there is even the danger of losing it. In general, our problems are those that we have encountered in the course of advance.

We should not only be steadfast and full of confidence but should also face the difficulties squarely and take a cool and earnest attitude toward solving the difficult problems so that we might continue to push forward the vigorous rural economy and further tap the socialist enthusiasm and potentials of productive labor among the hundreds of millions of peasants and translate them into a realistic productive force.

Everyone now affirms the excellent rural situation, acknowledges that a number of difficult problems have appeared, and is ready to start solving these problems. However, all of us, from the top down, lack experience in leading large-scale commodity production. Many of our old experiences and conventional methods are not good enough to meet the present requirements, and moreover, some of those experiences and methods are out of date. For this reason, we must acquire new knowledge and improve our leadership work from the basic Marxist viewpoint of developing social productive forces and from the stand of developing rural commodity production on a large scale and building socialism with Chinese characteristics. Comrades of all departments must seriously think about what they are required to do in order to create a new situation in all fields of socialist construction. By proceeding from the overall interests of our country, they must deeply investigate and study the essence of some problems and the prospects of future development and foster a spirit of reform marked by boldness in exploring and advancing despite difficulties in building socialism with Chinese characteristics. In this way we will have a common language and the same ideological basis in solving the difficult problems before us.

(II) Further Emancipate the Mind, Seek Truth from Facts, and Solve the Question of Attitude toward Peasants

It would be very dangerous if our party were divorced from the masses of peasants who account for over 80 percent of the population of our country. If the 800 million peasants do not become well off, it will be impossible to quadruple the gross annual value of our agricultural and industrial production by the end of this century or to achieve the Four Modernizations. Because of this, we must at all times highly value and resolutely protect the enthusiasm of the hundreds of millions of peasants, bring such enthusiasm into full play, and further consolidate and reinforce the worker-peasant alliance. From what has happened in economic work this year, we can see that further efforts must be made to solve this question and that it is necessary to emphasize this continually.

With regard to the correct attitude toward peasants, our party has had very profound experiences and lessons in the past. Past experience has proved that whenever the party is carrying out a correct policy and is handling the relations among the state, collectives, and individuals properly, the peasants' enthusiasm will be great, agricultural production will rise, and the people of the whole country will have a better life. Whenever the party is implementing an improper policy which does excessive harm to the interests of individual peasants, the enthusiasm of peasants will diminish, agricultural production will decline, and the people of the whole country will not be able to have a good life.

More often than not, however, we forgot the pain after the scar was healed, and we repeated the previous mistakes over and over again. That went on until the convening of the third plenary session of the Eleventh CCP Central Committee, after which we have thoroughly resolved the issue of guiding ideology, set things right, and successively set forth a whole series of correct rural policies, which have given rise to an unprecedented situation. This situation is not easy to come by because it is the accomplishment of the joint efforts of all departments under the party's leadership as well as the results of the hundreds of millions of peasants' courageous work, searches and creation along the course charted by the third plenary session of the Eleventh CCP Central Committee. To maintain and develop this situation, we must adhere to the correct course and continue to bring the enthusiasm and creativeness of hundreds of millions of peasants into full play. Is it possible that this policy should still be viewed with skepticism?

Whether our policies can be carried out is related directly to how thoroughly we understand the extreme importance of protecting the peasants' enthusiasm. While making an overall review of the responsibility system that links output with individual economic benefits and giving it high evaluation, document no. 1 of this year also points out the trend of future development and sets forth new regulations about further relaxation of certain policies. For example, the peasants are allowed to handle the purchasing and marketing of their products after they have fulfilled the state's quotas; market their products at distant localities; purchase farm machinery or means of transportation individually or collectively; divert, within certain limits, their capital, technical know-how and labor, or pool them together in various ways; and so forth. Realizing that these policies are necessary for developing commodity production and for further arousing the peasants' enthusiasm, many localities have emancipated their minds even further and implemented these policies consciously and courageously while at the same time working in earnest to improve the management. Consequently, the peasants' enthusiasm has been further heightened, commodity production has flourished, and society's productive forces have been further set free. At the same time, however, the thinking of the leading cadres in some areas and departments is incompatible with the current situation and their actions have been irresolute. Consequently, the situation remains unchanged, their operation has become even more passive, many apparently feasible projects have not been started, and the peasants' enthusiasm has been dampened.

We can be sure that as long as our policies are proper and they have taken the peasants' legitimate interests into consideration, the peasants will follow the party and take the socialist course. We are absolutely sure that the 800 million peasants wholeheartedly support the policies adopted since the third plenary session of the Eleventh CCP Central Committee. On the whole, they already have contributed remarkably to the building of a socialist society with distinctive Chinese characteristics. This is the most essential and most important fact, which must not be viewed with skepticism even if there are still a few problems among the peasants and some shortcomings in our work, otherwise we will commit mistakes of principle.

At present, inadequate mental emancipation is conspicuously shown by certain people's attitude in their treatment of those peasants who have become well off. Certain people's worries that "polarization" might appear in the rural areas are unnecessary. The differences in affluence appearing in rural areas is simply a question of some people's becoming well off ahead of others, and not the result of some people's having exploited other people. Those peasants who have become well off since the third plenary session of the Eleventh CCP Central Committee are primarily those who have worked hard. This can be clearly seen from those key and specialized households that have come to the fore in recent years. Who are these peasants who make up these specialized and key households? Shanxi's Ying County has investigated and analyzed each of the county's 20,989 households engaged in specialized production and found that they are primarily made up of the following five groups of people. The first group is made up of brigade and production team cadres, or peasants who used to be cadres. These people, who make up 43 percent of those engaged in specialized production, have some business and administrative experience, and are particularly sensitive to the party's policies, so they accept them quickly and take actions earlier than others, and have thus become well-off families in the rural areas ahead of others. The second group is made up of educated youths and demobilized servicemen who have returned to the countryside, and army men transferred to civilian work. Generally speaking, these people—who make up 42 percent of the households—have at least junior high school education, and because they are educated and have all sorts of experience, they accepted government policies and acquired scientific and technical know-how quickly. The third group is skilled craftsmen. Under the contract system they are given a free hand in their work, making more money and performing their abilities to the fullest in various production and processing fields. They make up about 9 percent. The fourth group consists of able persons good at planning and management, who were criticized and suppressed during the period of leftist mistakes but refused to yield. They have faced the world and braved storms, have a large circle of friends and a wide field of vision, can make the right decisions in diversified undertakings and get rich quick. This group makes up about 5 percent. As for those who have had problems of one kind of another in the past or who have violated the law in their operations, their number is below 1 percent.

The findings of Ying County and other counties fully prove that the overwhelming majority of the peasants who became well-to-do early are the most enthusiastic and active elements, good at organizing the various productive factors, a group of leading figures who are cultured and skilled and have economic minds for the development of productive forces, and are the backbone force in developing commodity production from now on. Their economic and political conditions, social experiences and operational fields differ, and the levels and paces of their prosperity are also different, but their common experiences can be summed up in four words, namely, "get rich through diligence." Diligence consists of actively studying and learning science and technology, being good at absorbing various kinds of information, and improving management and operations. These traits, plus the courage to open up new lines of operation and take risks, and the willingness to work hard are the main source of the peasants' prosperity. There are a few people who take advantage of irrational prices and loopholes in the system to engage in evil practices and make money by fraudulent means, particularly some grass-roots cadres who use their power to seek personal gain, deliberately force down contract payments, and even obtain large loans and large amounts of materials by all kinds of illegal means. Cases like these are found all over. It is necessary opportunely to strengthen ideological and political work, rectify party style, strengthen management, and pay attention to preventing and correcting them. At any rate, however, these are only minor aspects and must not be confused with getting rich through diligence, still less to be regarded as the main aspect.

We should be good at guiding the peasants who have become well-to-do earlier than others, because our goal is to promote the development of the rural economy as a whole with common prosperity as the result, with peasants who have become rich first serving as examples. This year some provinces and autonomous regions have summed up the general experiences of the specialized and key households, refined and concentrated their essential characteristics and commended them. They affirmed mainly (1) models in getting rich through diligence, (2) pursuers, demonstrators, and disseminators of science and technology, and (3) advanced elements in building socialism in the rural areas. This means that the specialized and key households are greatly superior to the ordinary peasant households in labor intensity and diligence. They not only inherit and carry forward traditional skills but enthusiastically learn and absorb modern science and technology, breaking through the conservatism of the older generation of peasantry. They ardently support the party's present policies, have faith in the future development of socialism, and therefore have the vision and courage to expand reproduction. They abide by law and discipline, firmly follow state plans, overfulfill their state purchase quotas, get rich themselves without forgetting others and the entire village and lead the peasants in embarking on the road to common prosperity.

I think that the viewpoint of this kind of commendation is correct, and the method is appropriate. When we say that the peasants of the 1980s are a new type of socialist peasants, what we mean can be seen most clearly in the specialized and key households. I do not like setting proportions and figures about how many specialized and key households there should be. We should make a great effort to do a good job of helping the poor peasants. However, at the same time, we must support and protect the specialized and key households that have emerged in the process of making the rural areas prosper since the third plenary session of the Eleventh CCP Central Committee and also the peasants who have led the way in getting rich through diligence. It is they who have inherited and carried forward the fine traditions of the Chinese peasantry and who have also begun to acquire the qualities of commodity producers under the socialist system. Their experience merits careful study and summing up so that we can help them improve further and make contributions to building socialist modern agriculture of a Chinese type. First of all, we should affirm that they are the representatives of the advanced productive forces in today's rural areas, forerunners in the pursuit of common prosperity for the broad masses of the peasantry, and activists who have followed our party in carrying out in-depth rural economic reforms. When we say that we should further emancipate the mind, correctly treat the peasants and take care to treasure, firmly protect, and fully develop the peasants' enthusiasm, we mean primarily that we should treat the peasants who become well-to-do before others correctly. When the enthusiasm of this part of the peasants is protected, all peasants, including those who are now rather hard up, will have something to look forward to, and the goal of common prosperity will no longer be something unattainable.

Our country has a population of 1 billion, of whom 800 million are peasants. The situation of peasants has an important bearing on the development of the economy and the consolidation of political power in our country. . . .

(III) Get a New Understanding of the Rural Economy

As pointed out by document no. 1 of this year issued by

the party Central Committee, China's countryside is in a period of historical transition from a self-contained and semi-self-contained economy to large-scale commodity production, and from traditional agriculture to modern agriculture. This is the general trend and the general background for the economic activities of the Chinese peasants in the 1980s. We still cannot say that all comrades know very clearly the far-reaching significance of this historical transition. I often feel that our work in various fields is not well suited to the development of the situation.

A fundamental task in developing commodity production is to be adept at using the law of value to change products into commodities through various circulation links. The issue of the work of commodity circulation involves the price system, financial subsidies, and readjusting and restructuring the whole national economy. In the meantime, the present capacities of our warehouse installations and transport facilities are inadequate to cope with the trend of fast development of rural commodity production. All these are problems that cannot be resolved by individuals or a department alone. They require the coordinated efforts of all departments concerned, a certain amount of investment and take a certain period of time to resolve radically. However, I must point out a fact: Some policies, such as the policy of allowing the peasants to work in the field of rural commodity circulation in certain conditions, including long-distance transport of goods for sale, have been established and promulgated, but some comrades do not agree with them. Such comrades are either overly worried and refuse to implement the policies or do not exercise leadership in this regard, or engage in endless haggling and shifting of responsibilities. As a result, many problems that can be resolved have not been resolved. In many places astonishing quantities of fruits have become rotten, fresh milk soured, fish and shrimp spoiled, and grain mildewed, and the problem of difficulties in buying and selling is still quite common. The peasants of Qingxian County, Hebei Province, put up a couplet at the door of our purchasing station. The couplet reads: "Keep the good ones and sell the rotten." "While the rotten ones are put up for sale, the good ones will become rotten." The horizontal line on top reads: "Sell the old and keep the new." Isn't this bitter criticism sufficient to provoke deep thought? While putting great emphasis on developing socialist production, can we remain indifferent to such unreasonable and serious loss of our social wealth?

Of course, many comrades do not intentionally affect commodity production. They are unknowingly restricted by some old ideas either in an apparent or imperceptible way. In the past, because of the long-time shortage of materials, we had to solve our economic problems by using the supply system practiced during the years of war. This has left a deep impression in the minds of some

people, who misinterpret economic work as "control." As a result, the more control they exercise, the more scanty the supply. If we use the law of value properly to bring into full play the significant role of social needs in promoting social production, we will be able to enliven the market, and with the increase in sales there will be more, rather than less, commodities supplied to the market. Ours is a socialist country, and our economy is a planned economy in the main. We must have necessary quotas for unified and assigned procurement of commodities, but regulation through the market is also indispensable. We should proceed from the characteristics of commodity production and comprehensively consider how to suit our rural commodity circulation system and price policy to the needs of commodity production.

Some of the above-mentioned problems concerning commodity circulation cannot be avoided under current circumstances, while others may be partially or totally averted. When we mention the problems concerning commodity production, we must affirm the hard and diligent work done by the broad masses of staff members and workers on various fronts and the great achievements that they have scored. It should also be pointed out here that considerable contributions have been made by various departments to developing rural commodity production.

I have stated many times the concept that the principal contradiction at present is that the growth of production cannot meet the people's material and cultural needs. In view of this, a chief contribution that peasants should make to the modernization of our country is to supply commodities of better quality in greater quantities. In the final analysis, the party is required to lead the peasant masses to do this important work well. Many of our county party committee secretaries and county heads have elementary knowledge of agricultural production, but are quite unfamiliar with commercial, financial and trade work. County party committee secretaries should not act merely as "agricultural secretaries," still less as "grain secretaries." They must learn how to use the law of value to promote commodity production and circulation and must take care of the economic work as a whole.

We must clearly realize that, in addition to being an agricultural area, the Chinese countryside today is also a place with thriving environmental, economic, and social development. For that reason, beginning with the Central Committee, party committees at all levels must strengthen their leadership over rural work. Some localities have put it well: "Without agriculture, the situation will not be stabilized; without commercial work, the economy cannot be enlivened; without jobs, the people will not become affluent." Such an observation embodies profound truths compatible with our country's situation. It is hoped that secretaries of county party committees and other high-ranking cadres, as well as the state's various economic departments, will pay attention to guiding economic work with new ideas and new insights.

(IV) Effectively Carry Out Several Rural Projects for 1984

Without a doubt, the general trend of development of the rural areas in the future will be that they will become a modernized socialist countryside with distinctive Chinese characteristics. That fundamental course was charted by Comrade Deng Xiaoping. It is a gigantic task. As far as rural work is concerned, some projects have just been started, but some have not yet begun. We must continue to work hard and march forward courageously.

In addition to those mentioned before, the party's projects that must be properly carried out in 1984 also include the following:

First, the contract responsibility system based on the household operation with remuneration linked to output must continue to be improved. While this system has established its footing in all parts of the country, much work has to be done to consolidate and develop it. Because development is uneven, the emphasis of work should also differ accordingly. A relatively common issue is that we must encourage the peasants to invest in their land to increase soil fertility, and we must also allow appropriate concentrated use of land so that the needs of households engaged in specialized operations can be met gradually. I urge you to study how to make this project a success. When there is a sound agrarian system, there will be a reliable foundation for the system of contracted responsibilities with remuneration linked to output.

Second, the peasants' family operation must be improved, and various types of households engaged in specialized production must be energetically promoted. Family operation under the system of contracted responsibilities with remuneration linked to output has now become the foundation of the cooperative economy in China's countryside. Those specialized households appearing in various parts of the country are no longer a family operation in the traditional sense. In Shanxi's Yanbei prefecture, only 4 percent of the total number of rural families are specialized households engaged in grain production. This year [1983], they sold 340 million *jin* of grain to the state, or 75 percent of the total amount of grain the entire prefecture sold to the state. Experiences show that family operation can be vastly different in scale and accomplishment. Much work can be done in this respect. By no means should we reject the family operation whenever someone mentions that its economic performance should be enhanced and its operational scale should be expanded, thinking that this is tantamount to returning to the old path of making the business "large in size and collective in nature."

In disseminating the experiences of those families engaged in specialized production and in making the peasants' family operation even more vigorous, we must avoid flashy measures. The basic issue is that we must have good policies with which we can encourage the peasants to expand their family operation and achieve still better economic performance.

Along with the appearance and development of households engaged in specialized production other problems will emerge. The various policies and provisions stipulated in this year's document no. 1 must continue to be carried out. More specific regulations may be formulated to deal with those problems which have become quite conspicuous, and those which are still not clear should be put under further observation by carrying out penetrating, meticulous, and comprehensive investigation and study.

Third, we must do our best to improve all types of services. Commodity production can hardly be developed in rural areas if there is a lack of essential distribution channels, scientific and technical guidance, communications and transport facilities, means of production, and sources of information. Departments in charge of commerce, science and technology, communications and transport, manufacture of industrial goods for agricultural production and education must fully understand the peasants' earnest wishes, and continue to heighten their consciousness of serving the rural areas.

Fourth, we should develop various diversified undertakings in rural areas other than farming, and further readjust the agricultural production structure including running some processing industries suitable for rural areas within our capabilities.

With the development of diversified undertakings and the division of labor and trades, more and more peasants are bound to leave the land they have been tilling. It is inevitable historical progress. To develop the range of production, we should look to the vast mountainous and hilly areas, grasslands, water surfaces, sea areas and beaches and make use of more untapped economic resources. We should also look to cities, rural areas, and inside and outside the country and open up more markets. To develop the depth of production, we should promote multipurpose uses of resources at various levels and recycling materials to increase constantly the economical and economic benefits of agriculture. Work should be done in both areas.

Finally, I would like to talk about the party's ideological and political work in rural areas. I said last year that to build modern socialist agriculture with Chinese characteristics, we must simultaneously pay attention to building socialist material and spiritual civilizations. Without building the spiritual civilization, it is impossible to maintain the socialist orientation of economic development. The present rural situation is very good as a whole. However, in quite a few places, leadership is soft, weak and flabby; things are allowed to take their own courses; ideological and political work is weak; and these are serious unhealthy tendencies. Most obvious is that a few grass-roots cadres take advantage of their power and position to seek personal gains, for example, seizing farmland to build houses, obtaining through special connections chemical fertilizers, diesel oil, and other means of production that are in short supply, taking the lead in obstructing the use of land for key construction projects in order to get something from the state, and openly plundering state property. Some cadres secure "contracts" and take "shares." In some places, feudal superstitions run rampant and patriarchal forces are on the rise, disrupting normal production and social order. With opening to the outside world, smuggling, selling of smuggled goods, and other illegal activities are often found in rural areas. Some party members and cadres support and even directly participate in such activities. This has caused strong resentment among the masses and must be seriously dealt with. We must, through party rectification, do thoroughgoing and painstaking ideological and political work to support healthy trends, overcome unhealthy ones, energetically develop the "five stresses, four beauties, and three loves" activities and the campaign to build civilized villages and towns, and bring about a fundamental turn for the better in party style and social conduct. Party member comrades in rural areas not only should take the lead in getting rich through diligence, but should do good ideological and political work among the masses and lead them in building a new socialist countryside. The party Central Committee believes that by adhering to the policy of developing the socialist material and spiritual civilizations at the same time, new progress and development surely will be made in modernizing rural areas in the new year.

Joint Declaration of the Governments of the United Kingdom and Northern Ireland and China on the Question of Hong Kong

After two years of secret negotiations, representatives of the United Kingdom and the People's Republic of China initialed the following joint declaration on September 26, 1984, paving the way for China's resumption of sovereignty over Hong Kong on July 1, 1997.

The Government of the United Kingdom of Great Britain and Northern Ireland and the Government of the People's Republic of China have reviewed with satisfaction the friendly relations existing between the two Governments and peoples in recent years and agreed that a proper negotiated settlement of the question of Hong Kong, which is left over from the past, is conducive to the maintenance of the prosperity and stability of Hong Kong and to the further strengthening and development of the relations between the two countries on a new basis. To this end, they have, after talks between the delegations of the two Governments, agreed to declare as follows:

(1) The Government of the People's Republic of China declares that to recover the Hong Kong area (including Hong Kong Island, Kowloon, and the New Territories, hereinafter referred to as Hong Kong) is the common aspiration of the entire Chinese people, and that it has decided to resume the exercise of sovereignty over Hong Kong with effect from 1 July 1997.

(2) The Government of the United Kingdom declares that it will restore Hong Kong to the People's Republic of China with effect from 1 July 1997.

(3) The Government of the People's Republic of China declares that the basic policies of the People's Republic of China regarding Hong Kong are as follows:

(a) Upholding national unity and territorial integrity and taking account of the history of Hong Kong and its realities, the People's Republic of China has decided to establish, in accordance with the provisions of Article 31 of the Constitution of the People's Republic of China, a Hong Kong Special Administrative Region upon resuming the exercise of sovereignty over Hong Kong.

(b) The Hong Kong Special Administrative Region will be directly under the authority of the Central People's Government of the People's Republic of China. The Hong Kong Special Administrative Region will enjoy a high degree of autonomy, except in foreign and defense affairs, which are the responsibilities of the Central People's Government.

(c) The Hong Kong Special Administrative Region will be vested with executive, legislative, and independent judicial power, including that of final adjudication. The laws currently in force in Hong Kong will remain basically unchanged.

(d) The Government of the Hong Kong Special Administrative Region will be composed of local inhabitants. The chief executive will be appointed by the Central People's Government on the basis of the results of elections or consultations to be held locally. Principal officials will be nominated by the chief executive of the Hong Kong Special Administrative Region for appointment by the Central People's Government. Chinese and foreign nationals previously working in the public and police services in the government departments of Hong Kong may remain in employment. British and other foreign nationals may also be employed to serve as advisers or hold certain public posts in government departments of the Hong Kong Special Administrative Region.

(e) The current social and economic system in Hong Kong will remain unchanged, and so will the lifestyle. Rights and freedoms, including those of the person, of speech, of the press, of assembly, of association, of travel, of movement, of correspondence, of strike, of choice of occupation, of academic research, and of religious belief will be ensured by law in the Hong Kong Special Administrative Region. Private property, ownership of enterprises, legitimate right of inheritance, and foreign investment will be protected by law.

(f) The Hong Kong Special Administrative Region will retain the status of a free port and a separate customs territory.

(g) The Hong Kong Special Administrative Region will retain the status of an international financial center, and its markets for foreign exchange, gold, securities, and futures will continue. There will be free flow of capital. The Hong Kong dollar will continue to circulate and remain freely convertible.

(h) The Hong Kong Special Administrative Region will have independent finances. The Central People's Government will not levy taxes on the Hong Kong Special Administrative Region.

(i) The Hong Kong Special Administrative Region may establish mutually beneficial economic relations with the United Kingdom and other countries, whose economic interests in Hong Kong will be given due regard.

(j) Using the name of "Hong Kong, China," the Hong Kong Special Administrative Region may on its own maintain and develop economic and cultural relations and conclude relevant agreements with states, regions, and relevant international organizations.

The Government of the Hong Kong Special Administrative Region may on its own issue travel documents for entry into and exit from Hong Kong.

(k) The maintenance of public order in the Hong Kong Special Administrative Region will be the responsibility of the Government of the Hong Kong Special Administrative Region.

(l) The above-stated basic policies of the People's Republic of China regarding Hong Kong and the elaboration of them in Annex 1 to this Joint Declaration will be stipulated, in a Basic Law of the Hong Kong Special Administrative Region of the People's Republic of China, by the National People's Congress of the People's Republic of China, and they will remain unchanged for 50 years.

(4) The Government of the United Kingdom and the Government of the People's Republic of China declare that, during the transitional period between the date of the entry into force of this Joint Declaration and 30 June 1997, the Government of the United Kingdom will be responsible for the administration of Hong Kong with the object of maintaining and preserving its economic prosperity and social stability, and that the Government of the People's Republic of China will give its cooperation in this connection.

(5) The Government of the United Kingdom and the Government of the People's Republic of China declare that, in order to ensure a smooth transfer of government in 1997, and with a view to the effective implementation of this Joint Declaration, a Sino-British Joint Liaison Group will be set up when this Joint Declaration enters into force; and that it will be established and will function in accordance with the provisions of Annex II to this Joint Declaration.

(6) The Government of the United Kingdom and the Government of the People's Republic of China declare that land leases in Hong Kong and other related matters will be dealt with in accordance with the provisions of Annex III to this Joint Declaration.

(7) The Government of the United Kingdom and the Government of the People's Republic of China agree to implement the preceding declarations and the Annexes to this Joint Declaration.

(8) This Joint Declaration is subject to ratification and shall enter into force on the date of the exchange of instruments of ratification, which shall take place in Beijing before 30 June 1985. This Joint Declaration and its Annexes shall be equally binding. . . .

Deng Xiaoping on China's Economic Reform Program

China's economic reform program accelerated in the mid-1980s, a period sometimes referred to as the "second wave" of reforms, following the groundbreaking initiatives of the late 1970s that focused on the countryside. The second wave began in October 1984 with the Central Committee's decision to expand reforms into the urban economy. In these August 1985 remarks to the prime minister of Zimbabwe, Robert Mugabe, Deng Xiaoping briefly reviews the Maoist era and provides an overview of the 1978-1985 reform period.

We did a great deal of work between 1949, when the People's Republic of China was founded, and 1976, when Chairman Mao Zedong passed away. We were particularly successful during the period of transition from new democratic revolution to socialist revolution, in which we carried out agrarian reform and completed the socialist transformation of agriculture, handicrafts, and capitalist industry and commerce. We began to experience some trouble in 1957, when "left" ideology appeared. It was necessary for us to combat bourgeois rightists, but we went too far. The spread of "left" thinking led to the Great Leap Forward in 1958. That was a serious mistake. Disregarding objective conditions, we urged our people to go all out to make steel. This, together with a series of other "left" policies, resulted in great suffering. During the three years of economic difficulty from 1959 through 1961, industrial and agricultural output dropped, so commodities were in short supply. The people didn't have enough to eat, and their enthusiasm was greatly dampened. At that time our party and Chairman Mao Zedong enjoyed high prestige, and we explained to the people frankly why the situation was so difficult. We abandoned the slogan of the Great Leap Forward and adopted more realistic policies instead. It took us three years to recover. But our guiding ideology still contained remnants of "left" thinking. The year 1962 saw the beginnings of recovery, and in 1963 and 1964 things were looking up. But once again "left" thinking came to the fore. In 1965 it was said that certain persons who were in power in the party were taking the capitalist road. Then came the "Cultural Revolution," in which the "left" ideology was carried to its extreme. The "Cultural Revolution" actually began in 1965, but it was officially declared only a year later. It lasted a whole decade, from 1966 through 1976, during which time almost all the veteran cadres who formed the backbone of the party were brought down. It was they who were made the targets of the "Cultural Revolution." That is what we call the ultraleft trend of thought.

After the downfall of the Gang of Four, we began to set things to right, that is, to correct the ultraleft trend of thought. But we still maintained that it was necessary to uphold Marxism-Leninism and Mao Zedong Thought. When we met in 1981, I talked about keeping to the socialist road, upholding the people's democratic dictatorship, upholding leadership by the CCP, and upholding Marxism-Leninism and Mao Zedong Thought. Now we call these the Four Cardinal Principles. If we do not uphold them in our effort to correct ultraleft thinking, we shall end up "correcting" Marxism-Leninism and socialism.

We summed up our experience in building socialism in the past few decades. We had not been quite clear about what socialism is. What is the essence of Marxism? Another term for Marxism is communism. It is for the realization of communism that we have struggled for so many years. We believe in communism, and our ideal is to bring it into being. In our darkest days we were sustained by the ideal of communism. It was for the realization of this ideal that countless people laid down their lives. What is a communist society? It is one in which there is no exploitation of man by man, there is great material abundance, and the principle of "from each according to his ability, to each according to his needs" is applied. It is impossible to apply that principle without overwhelming material wealth. In order to realize communism, we have to accomplish the tasks set in the socialist stage. They are legion, but the fundamental one is to develop the productive forces so as to provide the material basis for communism. Socialism, whose ultimate aim is the realization of communism, should develop the productive forces and then demonstrate its superiority over capitalism. For a long time we neglected the devel-

opment of the socialist productive forces. From 1957 on they grew at a snail's pace. In that year the peasants' average annual net income was about 70 yuan, which meant that they were very poor. That figure was about the same as what a factory worker earned in a month. In 1966, when the "Cultural Revolution" was launched, the peasants' annual net income rose only slightly. Although peasants in some areas were better off, those in many other areas could barely manage to live from hand to mouth. Of course, even that was progress, compared with the old days. Still, it was far from a socialist standard of living. During the "Cultural Revolution" things went from bad to worse.

By setting things to right, we mean developing the productive forces while upholding the Four Cardinal Principles. To develop the productive forces, we have to reform the economic structure and open to the outside world. It is in order to assist the growth of the socialist productive forces that we absorb capital from capitalist countries and introduce their technology. After the third plenary session of the Eleventh Central Committee we began our reform step by step, starting with the countryside. The rural reform has achieved good results, and there has been a noticeable change in the countryside. Drawing on our successful experience in rural reform, we embarked on urban reform. Urban reform, a comprehensive undertaking involving all sectors, has been going on for a year now, ever since the second half of last year. Since it is much more complicated than rural economic reform, mistakes and risks are unavoidable, and that's something we are quite aware of. But economic reform is the only way to develop the productive forces. We have full confidence in urban reform, although it will take three to five years to demonstrate the correctness of our policies.

In the course of reform it is very important for us to maintain our socialist orientation. We are trying to achieve modernization in industry, agriculture, national defense, and science and technology. But in front of the word "modernization" is a modifier, "socialist," making it the "four socialist modernizations." The policies of invigorating our domestic economy and opening to the outside world are being carried out in accordance with the principles of socialism. Socialism has two major requirements. First, its economy must be dominated by public ownership, which may consist of both ownership by the entire people and ownership by the collective. Our publicly owned economy accounts for more than 90 percent of the total. At the same time, we allow a small proportion of individual economy to develop, we absorb foreign capital and introduce advanced technology, and we even encourage foreign enterprises to establish factories in China. All that will serve as a supplement to the socialist economy based on public ownership; it cannot and will not undermine it. While half the investment in a joint venture comes from abroad, the other half comes from the socialist sector, which will therefore also benefit from the growth of the enterprise. Half its profits go to the socialist sector, and the state collects taxes on all of them. An even more important aspect of joint ventures is that from them we can learn managerial skills and advanced technology that will help us to develop our socialist economy. We are also happy to have foreign businessmen launch wholly foreign-owned enterprises, on which we can also levy taxes and from which we can also learn technical and managerial skills. They will bring no harm to socialist ownership. As of now, there has been only limited foreign investment, far less than we feel we need. The second requirement of socialism is that there must be no polarization of rich and poor. If there is, the reform will have been a failure. We have given much thought to this question in the course of formulating and implementing our policies. Is it possible that a new bourgeoisie will emerge? A handful of bourgeois elements may appear, but they will not form a class. There will be no harm so long as we keep our socialist public ownership predominant, and so long as we guard against polarization. In the last four years we have been proceeding along these lines. In short, we must keep to socialism.

Let me add that when we talk about the open policy, we should be sure not to overlook the role played by the state apparatus. Our socialist state apparatus is so powerful that it can intervene to correct any deviations. To be sure, the open policy entails risks. Some decadent bourgeois things may be brought into China. But with our socialist policies and state apparatus, we shall be able to cope with them. So there is nothing to fear. Our comrades have published a collection of some of my speeches, entitled *Build Socialism with Chinese Characteristics*, which includes my opening speech at the twelfth national party congress. I don't know if you have read it.

We were victorious in the Chinese revolution precisely because we applied the universal principles of Marxism-Leninism to our own realities. In building socialism we have had both positive and negative experiences, and they are equally useful to us. I hope you will particularly study our "left" errors. History bears witness to the losses we have suffered on account of those errors. Being totally dedicated to the revolution, we are liable to be too impetuous. It is true that we have good intentions, that we are eager to see the realization of communism at an early date. But often our very eagerness has prevented us from making a sober analysis of subjective and objective conditions, and we have therefore acted in contradiction to the laws governing the development of the objective world. In the past China made the mistake of trying to plunge ahead too fast. We hope you will give special consideration to our negative experiences. Of course one can learn from the experience of other countries, but one must never copy everything they have done.

State Council Plan for Reforming China's State-Owned Enterprises

A key focus of urban reforms initiated in October 1984 was to make China's large state enterprises more efficient and to reduce their drain on the national budget. This State Council document from September 1985 lays out the early goals of state-enterprise reform. Making state enterprises more profitable has proved a difficult task, however, and ten years later remains a major goal of China's economic reforms.

In accordance with the CCP Central Committee's "decision on reform of the economic structure" and the guidelines laid down in a series of directives of the CCP Central Committee and the State Council, the key to restructuring the urban economic structure is instilling greater vitality in enterprises, particularly the large and medium-size state industrial enterprises. Invigorating enterprises means mainly implementing further established state policies, exercising powers delegated to the enterprises by the state, carrying out reforms effectively within the enterprises, and bringing their favorable conditions and potential into full play. At the same time, it is necessary to improve corresponding external conditions, to establish macroeconomic controls and management, and to create a favorable environment for enterprises' production and operation. To this end, the following stipulations on instilling greater vitality into large and medium-size state industrial enterprises are hereby laid down, in addition to acting on the "provisional regulations on giving greater decision-making power to state industrial enterprises," the "provisional regulations on improvement of the planning system," and the "provisional regulations on some policies on promotion of technological progress in state enterprises," which were promulgated or approved and transmitted by the State Council.

(1) Raise the level of management and operations and improve the quality of workers and staff members.

An enterprise should first set up a leading body that has a pioneering spirit and is efficient in management. The key to doing so is to have a competent factory director (manager). A factory director (manager) should know how to manage and operate and have knowledge of specialized technology; in particular, he should be bold in selecting and employing talented people. In selecting a factory director (manager), it is necessary to consider his educational background and ability and, in particular, his devotion to his work. A department in charge of enterprises may sign a contract with a factory director (manager) covering his tenure, objectives, and responsibilities. In the contract, responsibilities, powers, rewards, and punishments should be clearly defined in order to strengthen the enterprise operator's sense of responsibility and to arouse his enthusiasm.

It is necessary effectively to strengthen ideological and political work as well as cultural, technical, and professional training in order to raise the quality of workers and staff members. A good job should be done in dividing the work between the party and the government and in improving the system of democratic management by workers and staff members.

(2) Formulate strategies for operational development.

Under the guidance of the state plan and policies, an enterprise should formulate its short-term, intermediate, and long-term strategies for operational development, and decide on the orientation of its products in accordance with its conditions in personnel, technology, funds, and equipment; it should develop marketable, competitive products. It should change from a simple production mode to open production and management and increase continuously its ability to reform and improve itself. Where conditions permit, an enterprise should develop technology-intensive products. A department in charge of enterprises has the responsibility to direct and inspect the development of operational strategies by enterprises.

(3) Manage each level according to delegated authority within the enterprise.

On the premise of unified management, an enterprise is allowed to have reasonably small accounting units within itself in accordance with its trade and products. Where conditions permit, a workshop or factory branch may operate in a relatively independent way and exercise its decision-making power accordingly. The enterprise is still responsible for calculating the output value of its small accounting units, paying their taxes, and undertaking their debt obligations, and is responsible for their profits or losses.

(4) Do a good job in overall quality control.

All enterprises should follow correct guidelines, uphold the principle of "quality first," do a good job in overall quality control, and regard turning out quality products as their constant goal. Enterprises should do their basic work well. In accordance with state technological policies and consumer demands, enterprises should set or revise their quality standards, strictly enforce technological and labor discipline, and improve or strengthen their quality control and standards, as well as their metrological organizations and their means of inspecting and surveying. They should improve their economic responsibility and other management systems, stressing quality and strictly enforcing the system of proficiency assessment, and the system of rewards and punishment, in order to establish gradually a quality-guaranteed system.

(5) Lower consumption of materials and production costs.

All enterprises should take effective measures to lower their consumption of materials and to raise their rates of turning out finished products. The 1979 trial measures to reward those who economized in the use of fuel and raw and processed materials are to be implemented on a wider basis; the categories covered by the measures are increased from ten to twenty: coal, coke, electric power, gasoline, diesel oil, heavy oil, crude oil, gas, natural gas, imported steam, wood, rare and precious nonferrous metals in short supply, quality steel products and stainless steel, cast pig iron, soda ash, caustic soda, raw materials for chemical fiber, paper pulp, rubber and cement labeled above no. 325. At the same time, taking into account their own conditions and fuels and raw and processed materials other than those mentioned above that affect their production costs to a considerable extent, enterprises are allowed to make suggestions on readjusting the reward categories. Such suggestions will be put into practice after being approved by the people's government of a province, autonomous region, or municipality directly under the central government, or by a responsible department under the State Council, depending on the enterprise's order of subordination.

(6) Make multipurpose use of energy and natural resources.

Restrictions should be relaxed to allow enterprises to make use of waste gas, waste water, and industrial residues for production, and to retrieve various products; and they should be given preferential treatment in doing so provided that they maintain their original form of coordination and fulfill their contracts to the letter. Products made by them in such a way may be sold by themselves. In making multipurpose use of energy and natural resources, association and cooperation should be encouraged. If an enterprise itself does not benefit much by doing so, but society benefits noticeably from it, the tax department should reduce or remit its taxes.

An enterprise may reward a collective or individual who has actively made reasonable suggestions on the practice of the comprehensive utilization of energy and material resources for the purpose of reducing consumption and whose suggestions have resulted in a considerable reduction in the costs of products. Such bonuses may be drawn from the sum total of the money saved, at a certain percentage rate.

(7) Encourage enterprises to adopt one line of trade as the key one and to develop diversified operations at the same time.

An enterprise, after ensuring that the state plan will be fulfilled, may carry out its operations in a diversified way to develop many different kinds of products in accordance with market demand and on the basis of the area of its advantages. It may extend the line of its products or services.

In the case of a construction or labor service project that an enterprise has to build by relying on the forces of outside contractors, provided it can guarantee its completion of normal production, repair and maintenance work, it may undertake to build the project itself by organizing its surplus labor force to do it. As an encouragement, the enterprise may draw some bonuses and welfare funds at a certain percentage rate from the amount of expenditure saved after deducting the cost.

The tools and machine repair workshops of an enterprise, as well as its fleet of vehicles, warehouses, clubs, hospitals, canteens, kindergartens, and other service departments, may all be open to society on the basis of independent accounting and accepting responsibility for their own profits or losses. An enterprise, on the premise that it will persist in fulfilling the state plan and the task of producing its key products, may run a tertiary business either solely with its own capital, or as a joint venture with other investors. An enterprise carrying on diversified businesses should pay its taxes in accordance with the different taxable categories and tax rates for its respective products and respective trades.

(8) Develop lateral contracts between different enterprises.

Joint ventures or cooperation projects that cut across different trades, regions, cities and townships, and go beyond the ownership limits, will be permitted. In carrying out such ventures, however, persistent efforts must be made to adhere to the principles of equality, mutual benefits and voluntary participation and that large enterprises act as the principal participants or famous brand products take the lead. Defense industry enterprises and civil enterprises are encouraged to form associations for the production of products that are in demand on the market.

Active efforts should be made to develop joint scientific research and production ventures. An enterprise may join with a scientific research academy or institute or an institution of higher learning in the development of a new technology or product. It may also provide consultancy services either by itself or with the cooperation of such research units. Any benefits that accrue shall be divided among the parties concerned through consultations and in accordance with the relevant state regulations.

The profits made by a joint enterprise, after paying product taxes and business taxes in the place where it is located, shall be divided on the basis of the principle of "dividing first, paying taxes next." Where the total sum of wages is linked to the amount of taxes and profits delivered to the state, the percentage shares in the base figures of products taxes and business taxes shall be decided by the various parties to the joint venture through consultations. An enterprise has the right to make its own decision to enter into a joint venture. It also has the freedom to withdraw from it on the basis of the agreed terms.

(9) Improve the methods for the supply of materials and the marketing of products.

Energy and the principal raw materials needed for the purpose of fulfilling the mandatory targets assigned by the state should be provided at the prices set in the state plan. No unit is permitted to withhold any portion of any of the supplies for centralized distribution that are allotted an enterprise by the state. In the case of materials that are needed all year round and in large shipments or quantities, the supply departments and the departments in charge should get together the suppliers and customers to sign a contract by which such materials will be supplied directly by the contracted suppliers. The accounts will be settled by the enterprises that are independent accounting units. After the prerequisite that an enterprise can ensure its fulfillment of the state's mandatory plan for the transfer of materials, and also has a reasonable turnover reserve on hand, it may sell its products that are in excess of the production target and those means of production in store that are above the required reserve on the means of production market at negotiated prices. However, these negotiated prices must not exceed the price ceilings set by the state.

(10) Reduce appropriately the scope of the mandatory plan.

In assigning the production targets of the state's mandatory plan, some margin should be left for the enterprises. Even in the case of those products that are in short supply on the market, there should still be a margin established at a certain percentage rate for the enterprises concerned to have the incentive to exceed the production targets. The mandatory plan targets assigned to the enterprises by the state should be the same as those assigned and no departments or localities are permitted to raise the quota at each level. An enterprise must make sure the state's mandatory plan is fulfilled both in quality and in quantity.

In carrying out the state's mandatory plan assigned to the enterprises, a balanced relationship should be maintained carefully between the amount of the finished products to be transferred from the enterprise, and the supplies of major raw materials, energy, and other principal production conditions provided to it. When an enterprise has to procure some of the raw materials and energy needed for the production of products assigned by the state in the mandatory plan at negotiated prices, it should first try to absorb the extra expenditures incurred by itself. If this presents real difficulties, the price of that proportion of products that are produced with the raw materials and energy procured at negotiated prices can be raised to an appropriate extent, after obtaining the approval of the departments in charge, which act within their authority over commodity price control.

(11) Reduce regulatory taxes to increase the capability of the enterprises to transform themselves.

Regulatory taxes may be reduced or waived in a planned and systematic manner for the advanced enterprises with good economic results and a high regulatory tax rate. The State Economic Commission will make joint decisions together with the Ministry of Finance on which enterprises qualify for such reductions.

(12) Give some of the large enterprises the power to conduct business directly with foreign countries.

A small number of enterprises should be selected first on an experimental basis. The list of these enterprises selected for this purpose will be prepared by the State Economic Commission together with the Ministry for Foreign Economic Relations and Trade, and submitted for approval by the State Council. The approved experimental enterprises, under the guidance of the state's unified principles, policies, and plans for dealing with foreign countries, will have the power to hold talks and sign agreements with foreign businesses and can arrange technological imports, technological cooperation, joint operations, joint production, joint development, countertrade, processing of imported raw materials, assembly of imported parts, signing construction contracts and other business activities, directly with foreign partners, as long as these business operations are related to the export products of these enterprises themselves.

They can also import the equipment, instruments, and meters and spare parts that they need for themselves. Enterprises that produce export products may themselves in accordance with the principle that enterprises undertaking the task of fulfilling export plan are responsible for their own profits or losses import the various raw materials that are used exclusively for the purpose of their own production task (approval of the departments concerned must be obtained for the import of those raw materials that come under the unified control of the state) and organize independently the export of their products, as well as offering labor services and technical services. These enterprises can conduct such foreign operations by themselves or ask a foreign trade corporation to act as their agent. Meanwhile, it is necessary to actively develop joint industry and trade enterprises. Some enterprises may, with the approval of the state, also establish their offices in foreign countries and run factories abroad, either independently or jointly with other investors.

Enterprises authorized to deal directly with foreign firms may open foreign exchange accounts and the necessary renminbi accounts at the Bank of China, apply for foreign exchange loans from the Bank of China, and acquire and use foreign exchange according to the relevant state regulations.

(13) The liquidation and reorganization of companies.

This task should be carried out according to the State Council Circular on continuing to liquidate and reorganize companies. In accordance with the principle that government and enterprise responsibilities should be separate, a company is a legal economic entity engaging in production or providing a service; and it is an enterprise carrying out independent accounting, being responsible for its profits or losses, paying taxes in accordance with regulations, and being able to undertake economic responsibilities.

Units that are administrative organs but with the signboards of companies, which are unable to undertake economic responsibilities while still exercising the administrative functions of government organs, must first of all transfer the authority that should be delegated to their affiliated enterprises; and then they should cease operation, or be merged with other organs, or be changed into service companies in accordance with the actual situation; and if they have the approval of responsible departments, they can also be reinstated to become administrative organs again. All departments and regions must be firm in handling this question, and should not let such companies continue to withhold the authority the state has granted to large and medium-size enterprises, much less permit them to become first-grade administrative organs.

(14) All departments and cities should separate government responsibilities from those of enterprises, and should streamline their administration and delegate authority to the lower departments.

They should create a fine environment for production and operation for enterprises; do a good job in planning, coordinating, serving and supervising; provide professional guidance and management; evaluate the enterprises' economic and technical performance periodically; and guide the enterprises to improve their operation and management through providing them with the necessary information. Cities, in particular, should expedite the construction of various public facilities and improve their social services. They should direct and organize all forms of cooperation among enterprises, and promote and coordinate relations between enterprises and various other quarters. They should examine and correct the numerous irrational burdens that society has imposed on the enterprises, in order to protect the enterprises' legitimate interests and the property of the state. They must establish and improve the economic laws and urge those enterprises—when they have the resources—to employ full-time or part-time legal advisers so that they can administer their economic activities by legal means.

These regulations shall become effective on the day they are approved.

Should any previously promulgated regulations contravene these regulations, these regulations shall be followed. According to their actual situation, all regions and departments may formulate specific rules for implementation within the scope of the principles stipulated in these regulations.

Mikhail Gorbachev on Sino-Soviet Relations

The following review of Soviet domestic and foreign policy is excerpted from a speech by Soviet general secretary Mikhail Gorbachev, delivered in the Far Eastern Soviet port city of Vladivostok on July 28, 1986. Gorbachev's stated willingness to move from a position of confrontation to one of renewed friendship, compromise, and accommodation with China indicated a significant shift in Soviet policy toward China.

. . . The Far East is always associated in our minds with the immense expanses of the Land of the Soviets, stretching from the Baltic and the Black Sea to the Pacific Ocean. It is associated with the valor, industry, and steadfastness of the people who settled and defended this land, and with the novelty and scale of today's affairs. Vladimir Ilyich Lenin, with especial warmth, called the city of Vladivostok our very own city. The exploit of our fellow-countrymen, of those first pioneers who blazed the trail to the Pacific Ocean, will always remain in folk memory. We shall never forget the stormy nights of Spassk and the Volochayev days, the energetic assimilation of the region during the years of the first five-year plans, and the martial labor of the border troops on these hallowed borders of ours. The bravery and courage of the Far Eastern divisions and the sailors from the Pacific who fought near Moscow and Stalingrad and in the final battles of the Second World War in the East will live forever in the memory of the people. . . .

The Far Eastern region glorified by Arsenyev and Fadeyev has always been and will remain a region dear to the heart of the Soviet man. I am glad to have an opportunity to visit the Maritime Kray and to acquaint myself with your life and work, with what is being done in this region today and will be done tomorrow; the more so as in the plans defined by the twenty-seventh CPSU congress a special place is assigned to the Far East as to Siberia. . . .

Comrades, a little more than a year has passed since the April plenum of the Central Committee, and nearly five months since the ending of the work of the twenty-seventh party congress. All this time has been filled with active searches for new approaches to the solution of the urgent problems of Soviet society. It has been marked with a principled evaluation of what has been done, both what has been done and what has been left undone. We now have at our disposal an extensive program of action for the acceleration of the social and economic development of the country for a long time to come: one that takes account of both our own aspirations and the most important trends of world development. We also have the necessary setting out of this program in detail: the State Plan for the twelfth Five-Year Plan period, worked out from a profound analysis of the state of affairs and a search for reserves and for ways and means of ensuring the dynamic development of Soviet society.

The time has come to make ourselves responsible for implementing what we intend. Responsible on the widest scale, without making any allowances. The results of the work of the national economy for the first half of this year have already been summed up. They show that positive changes in the economy are gaining force, even if not to the same extent everywhere. We have succeeded in giving greater dynamism to economic processes and in raising the rates of growth of production and labor productivity. Measures for improving the situation in engineering, the fuel and power and agroindustrial complexes, ferrous metallurgy, chemicals, and petrochemicals and in several other sectors have begun to have an effect.

Social tasks too have been tackled better. More housing has been handed over for use. The number of facilities for social and cultural purposes being brought into use has increased. In places where the local bodies work dynamically and energetically, the supply of food products, industrial goods, and consumer services to the population has improved. Such changes can only be welcomed.

But we shall speak straight, comrades. The pleasing and encouraging improvements have been obtained first and foremost as a result of measures for strengthening labor, state, and plan discipline. People have had a more exacting approach to drawing up and fulfilling plans and bringing order into their affairs. They have started to work better. They have edged out drunkenness. And the positive results are already there.

But along with the general favorable indicators of the half-year, in some sectors the rates of growth fell in May and June. A number of ministries failed to cope with their plans. An irregular pace of production and an insufficiently effective use of what we have at our disposal continue to cause considerable difficulties, and quality of output has not shown any marked changes for the better. And you know that this is our common problem.

All this enables one to draw a quite definite conclusion: qualitative changes that would really have consolidated tendencies for accelerated growth have not taken place yet in the country. I think you understand and will agree that they could not have taken place, since the highly important measures of an economic, social, organizational, ideological, and other nature have only just started to be implemented and, of course, they cannot produce an immediate effect. Consequently, the increase in the rate of growth of national economy is not and, perhaps, even cannot yet, as I have already said, be stable.

This means that it is impermissible now to go to one of two extremes. It is naive and even harmful to assume that if economic indicators have risen, then the restructuring of our work has been fully embarked on and is progressing at full speed everywhere. This is yet far from being the case. In a whole number of the country's regions and industries they are only talking about restructuring and not setting it in motion. It is equally impermissible to give in to the difficulties of restructuring and the resistance or indifference of those accustomed to living by inertia and working in the old fashion.

It was rightly stressed at the twenty-seventh congress that we are starting on a task that is not simple and that we are posing for ourselves goals that are realistic yet difficult, that can only be achieved if we continually learn from life and constantly assimilate its experience, lessons, and new trends. In fact, we are just starting on this work, succeeding in some things and not so well in others. It is becoming more and more clear with time how complicated this task is and how large the volume of matters we are to tackle. But retreat we cannot and will not. There is simply no alternative to acceleration. We have had to speak about this on a number of occasions, and I should like to reiterate it here in Vladivostok once again.

What is meant is not that we should urge or persuade people to actions contrary to the laws of social development or try to bypass somehow or outwit these laws and existing conditions. In maintaining the course toward restructuring, the party and its Central Committee are proceeding from another premise—from the need to recognize these laws more profoundly and operatively and skillfully take account of them in our activities, and the pressing need to remove all impediments and obstructions, artificially created along these paths.

The tangible, objective results of the first half-year of the Five-Year Plan period prove that the Soviet people support the course of acceleration and support it in the most valuable way by deeds. Here in Vladivostok, just as wherever else I have to be in the course of fulfilling, let us say, my new obligations, I have been asking one and the same question: Is everything clear regarding the policy worked out by the party and proposed to the people, or are there any doubts? With great satisfaction I have also heard here, on Far East soil, warm support and approval for the party's policy directed toward the interests of the people, the interests of all Soviet people, every family, the interests of the country's future. It is important to direct this support, this mood of our people for struggle and the surmounting of difficulties with maximum returns and to the utmost effect towards solving the tasks set by the twenty-seventh CPSU congress.

It is from this position, comrades, that I should like to touch upon certain issues to do with the development of the Far East. I should like to consult, even perhaps continue the consultation that I have been having for three days now with you people of the Far East, as to how we can transform this region more swiftly, put its riches at the service of the Soviet people and meet more adequately and fully the demands of the people living here.

The Far East is traditionally called the country's outpost in the Pacific. This is undoubtedly true. But today this view can no longer be regarded as sufficient. The Maritime Kray and the Far East must be turned into a highly developed national economic complex. . . .

All that has been done in previous years provides a real precondition for this. Major enterprises have been built representing all industries. Mines and electric power stations have been commissioned, as have new railways, ferry crossings and ports. Hundreds of thousands of hectares of land have been improved. The Far East Scientific Center of the USSR Academy of Sciences has been set up, with a network of institutes. Qualified modern key workers and specialists have grown up. As a result, gross industrial production has almost trebled, and agricultural production has increased by over 50 percent. Today the Far East yields 40 percent of all fish caught in the country. Over the past four Five-Year Plan periods, 62 million square meters of housing have been built, which is equivalent to the erection of approximately seven cities like Vladivostok. While the growth in labor resources is still not sufficient, nevertheless the population has risen by 40 percent over the past twenty years. Overall, the country's economy now has a broad base on the coast of the Pacific Ocean.

However, in the light of the acceleration policy and from the positions of the twenty-seventh CPSU congress, we must pose a direct and acute question: Do the economic and social development, the standard of work of scientific institutions and the scale of their research in the Far East correspond to its growing role and the new tasks set by the party? Is the potential created there being used efficiently enough?

The strategic course towards accelerating socioeconomic development requires the implementation of a new regional policy, too. The party gives a prominent position in this to priority development of the eastern regions. In this connection, we are obliged to look attentively at the prospects for the economy of the Far East, and this must be done rapidly, taking into account the particular significance of the region. . . .

These are our common plans and concerns, comrades. They, better than any verbal contrivances, speak of the real intentions of the Soviet Union. And however much the ruling forces of imperialism may try to distort them, we openly and honestly have spoken, and will go on speaking to all peoples and governments: Yes, we need peace. Again and again we appeal to them to put a stop to the arms race, to end the nuclear madness, and eliminate nuclear arms, and to search persistently for political solutions to regional conflicts.

A phenomenon of enormous significance is taking place before our eyes. The notion that peace is needed by all is powerfully penetrating the consciousness of peoples even in places where the governments continue to regard weapons and war as a means of policy. It is needed by all precisely since a nuclear war would not be a clash merely between two blocs, between two confronting forces. It will lead to a global catastrophe threatening the destruction of human civilization.

Our initiatives for nuclear disarmament and a significant cut in conventional armaments and armed forces, for monitoring and improvement of the international situation, have been met in different ways. The friendly countries have come out in support of them. The countries of the socialist community quite rightly regard them as an integral part of the common line of socialism in the international arena. And not only because they . . . agreed with them, not only out of principled internationalist considerations, but also because both of us, we and they, are preoccupied with one and the very same exclusively peaceful effort—perfection of our societies.

On this basis impetus is being given to the beneficial process of drawing together, economic integration is being filled with new content, specific steps are being taken to create joint enterprises and associations, and living contacts among people are being broadened. In a word, a progressive, mutually advantageous process is taking place which deepens the cooperation and brotherhood between the peoples of the community. . . .

It would be right to say that our plans are regarded seriously and with interest by broad public circles, politicians, and representatives of the business world in the West who view things realistically, who are free of the paranoia of anticommunism, and who are not bound up with profits from the arms race. They also favor peace and cooperation, the development of healthy economic, scientific, and cultural relations with the Soviet Union. We welcome this approach. . . .

All this dictates the necessity of an urgent radical break with many conventional approaches to foreign policy, a break with the traditions of political thinking, with views on the problems of war and peace, on defense, on the security of specific states and on international security. One may understand, in this connection, our radical, in the full sense of the word, global proposals, such as the program for elimination of nuclear and other weapons of mass destruction in this century, for a complete ban on testing nuclear arms, for banning chemical weapons, for cooperation in the peaceful use of space and a whole number of other proposals which concern the whole world and all countries.

The main problem that has been confronting mankind today is the problem of survival; it is equally acute and urgent for Europe, Africa, America, and Asia. It takes a different shape, however, for each part of the world. And so since I am here in Vladivostok, it is natural to look at world political issues from the Asia-Pacific Ocean angle. Such an approach is justified on many counts. Above all because a large part of our country's territory lies east of the Urals, in Asia, Siberia, and the Far East. It is here that many all-union tasks put forward by the congress will be solved. Consequently the situation in the Far East as a whole, in Asia, and the adjacent oceanic expanses, where we have for a long time been permanent residents and sailors, is for us a national, state interest. . . .

Socialism is an integral factor in the grandiose and complex changes in this region. As a result of [the] Great October [Revolution of 1917] and the victory over fascism and Japanese militarism, as a result of the great Chinese revolution, after a new social order was established in Mongolia and in the land of Korea, whose people displayed unusual steadfastness in the struggle for a socialist future for their motherland, and then in Vietnam and Laos, socialism won a firm position in Asia.

But it was here that it had to face the most brutal and cynical opposition. The most vivid example of this is the example of Vietnam. Its heroic experience, and the lessons of its victory over imperialism, have yet again highlighted the unconquerable strength of the ideas of freedom and socialism.

It was here, here in Asia, that the concept of nonalignment was born, a movement that now includes in its orbit over a hundred states. It strives to give its answer to the challenge of the time, actively supports ending the division of the world into military blocs, and searches for its own ways of reducing the nuclear threat. Rejecting exploitation, the politics of conquest and neocolonialism, and condemning them, the nonaligned movement turns to humanity with an appeal for unity and cooperation in the struggle against the hunger and scandalous poverty of hundreds of millions of people.

The acknowledged leader of that movement is great India, with its moral authority and traditional wisdom, with its own particular political experience and huge economic potential. We assess highly the contribution it has already made to the cause of asserting the standards of equitable coexistence and justice in the international community. The friendly relations between the USSR and India have become a stabilizing factor on an international scale.

Japan has turned into a power of front-rank significance. The country that was the first victim of American nuclear weapons has covered a huge distance in a short time, and displayed striking accomplishments in industry and trade, education, science and technology. These successes are due not only to the meticulousness, self-discipline, and energy of the Japanese people, but to the three nonnuclear principles on which its international policy is officially based, although recently—and one cannot fail to draw attention to this—they, like the peaceful tenets of the Japanese constitution, are being circumvented more and more obviously.

But we see in Asia-Pacific much else too: people's dignity outraged by colonialism; the consequences of poverty, illiteracy, and backwardness. At the same time profound prejudices preserve conditions for mistrust and enmity between peoples, including those living within one state. Imperialism gambles on these difficulties and survivals of the past. As a result, local conflicts and ethnic and religious strife flare up and there is political instability. Everywhere where independence becomes a tangible international quantity, and where a threat arises to the exploitative interests of imperialism, it resorts to its favorite methods: economic blackmail, intrigues and plots against the leadership of the country concerned. It interferes in internal problems, supports separatists, and finances or actually arms counterrevolution and terrorists. The Punjab and the Tamil problem, which they also want to turn against India; the undeclared wars against Kampuchea and Afghanistan; the annexation of Micronesia; interference in the Philippines; and pressure on New Zealand—these examples alone are sufficient to show how the contemporary mechanism of imperialist intervention and dictate works.

The experience of history and the laws of growing interdependence, the demands for integration of the economy incline us to seek ways toward accord and toward setting up open links between states within the region and outside it. These states have tens, hundreds of problems crying out to be resolved, both those inherited from the colonial past and those arising from the contradictions of current development. But they are being dragged into blocs, which limit their freedom to dispose of their own resources, compel them to inflate their military budgets, drag them into the arms race and the militarization of the economy and all public life. All this deforms the processes of internal development, creates tension, and of course hinders the normalization of relations between nations and states.

The Soviet Union is also an Asia-Pacific country. This vast region's complex problems are familiar to it; it is directly touched by them. It is this which determines the balanced and large-scale view it takes of a gigantic part of the world that contains a mass of such varied states and peoples. Our approach to that part of the world is based on recognition and understanding of the realities existing here. At the same time our interest is not a claim to any kind of privilege and special position; no egoistic attempt to strengthen our security at someone else's expense; no seeking advantage to the detriment of others. We see our interest in pooling efforts, in cooperation that accords full respect to the rights of each people to live as it chooses and to resolve its own problems independently in conditions of peace. We are for building jointly new and just relations in Asia-Pacific.

I have recently had quite a few meetings with leaders of European states and various political figures from European countries. One cannot help comparing the situation in Asia with that in Europe. The Pacific region as a whole is not yet militarized to the same extent as the European region. Yet the potential for its militarization is truly enormous and the consequences extremely dangerous. To be convinced of this one only has to glance at the map. Some of the major nuclear powers are located here and powerful land armies and mighty navies and air forces have been created. The scientific, technological, and industrial potential of many countries on the western and eastern sides of the ocean makes it possible to boost any arms race. The situation is aggravated by the continuation of conflicts. Let us not forget that it was in Asia that American imperialism waged the two biggest wars since 1945, in Korea and Indochina. For four decades there has been no period lasting several consecutive years when the flame of military confrontation has not blazed; now in one spot in the Pacific Ocean area, now in another.

For better or for worse the Helsinki process of dialogue, talks, and agreements is in operation in Europe. This introduces some sort of stability and reduces the probability of armed conflict. This does not exist or virtually does not exist in the region that we are discussing. If there has been some change of late, then it is not for the better. Since the second half of the 1970s the United States has undertaken large-scale measures to increase military forces in the Pacific Ocean. It is under its pressure that the militarized Washington-Tokyo-Seoul triangle is taking shape. And although two of the three states in the region that possess nuclear weapons—the PRC and USSR—have pledged no first use, the United States has sited delivery vehicles for nuclear weapons and nuclear warheads in one of the crisis zones in the Korean peninsula and also delivery vehicles for nuclear weapons on Japanese territory. It has to be noted that militarization and the growth of the military threat in this part of the world are beginning to gather dangerous speed. The Pacific Ocean is turning into an arena of military and political confrontation. That is what gives rise to growing concern for the peoples who live here. It also alarms us, from all points of view, including that of the security of the Asiatic part of our country.

The Asia-Pacific strand of the Soviet Union's foreign policy is a component part of the overall platform of the CPSU's international activity, worked out by the April plenum and the twenty-seventh party congress. However, the platform is not a plan that can be applied to any situation, but rather principles and a method based on experience. Using this as a starting point, how could one conceive of a process of forming international security and peaceful influence in this vast region? First and foremost, the Soviet Union, in accordance with the principled line of the congress, will aspire to give more dynamism to its bilateral relations with all countries situated here without exception. We will comprehensively strengthen friendship and we are stepping up our diverse ties with [Mongolia, North Korea, Laos, and Cambodia]. We see our relations with our friends, relations built on the principles of equal rights and solidarity, as a component part of overall security in Asia and the Pacific Ocean.

At present, for example, the question of withdrawing a considerable number of Soviet troops from Mongolia is being examined with [that country's] leadership. We are ready to expand our ties with Indonesia, Australia, New Zealand, the Philippines, Thailand, Malaysia, Singapore, Burma, Sri Lanka, Nepal, Brunei, the Maldives Republic, all young and independent participants in the political life of the region. With some of them we already have diplomatic relations.

Speaking in a city from which, as they say, one could reach out a hand and touch the PRC, I should like to dwell on the most important issues in our relations with it. These relations are of particular importance for several reasons, starting with the fact that we are neighbors, that we have the world's longest land frontier and that for this very reason we are predestined, as are our children and grandchildren, to live side by side from this day forward and for all time. But of course that is not the only point. History has entrusted the Soviet and Chinese peoples with an exceptionally important mission. A great deal in international development depends on the two largest socialist states. In recent years there has been a noticeable improvement in our relations, and I want to confirm that the Soviet Union is ready at any time and at any level to discuss with China in the most serious way matters concerning supplementary measures to create an atmosphere of good-neighborliness. We hope that in the near future the frontier that divides us, I should like to say that unites us, will become a zone of peace and friendship.

Soviet people regard with understanding and respect the aim put forward by the CCP of modernizing the country and building in the long term a socialist society worthy of a great people. As far as one can judge, our priorities and those of China are similar: the acceleration of socioeconomic development. Why not support each other and cooperate in realizing our plans, where this is evidently to the benefit of both? The better our relations are, the more we can exchange experiences with each other.

We take pleasure in noting that a positive change has taken place in economic links. We are convinced that the mutually complementary nature of the Soviet and Chinese economies, which has been historically established, offers great opportunities for expanding these ties, including in the border regions. A number of major problems in cooperation are literally knocking at the door. We do not, for example, want the Amur frontier to be regarded as a water barrier. May the basin of this mighty river be a means of uniting the efforts of the Chinese and Soviet people in using the very rich resources and for water management projects there, for the common benefit. An intergovernmental agreement on this matter is already being jointly drawn up. The official border could pass along the main channel. The Soviet government is preparing a positive response on the matter of cooperation in building a railway to link the Xinjiang Uighur Autonomous Region and Kazakhstan. We have proposed cooperation with the PRC in space, which could include the training of Chinese cosmonauts. There are big opportunities for mutually beneficial exchange in the sphere of culture and education. We are ready for and sincerely desire all this. . . .

Our thoughts on security in the Asia-Pacific Ocean region are not made up out of thin air. They take into account experience past and present. The principles of Pancasila and Bandung have not sunk into oblivion and the positive examples of the truce in Korea, the 1954 Geneva conference on Indochina and the Indo-Pakistan agreement in Tashkent, live on in diplomatic experience. At the present time too we can see the efforts of a number of states to tackle in a practical way common economic problems and attempts to settle conflicts somehow.

There is much of positive value in the activity of ASEAN [Association for Southeast Asian Nations] and in bilateral contacts. After the idea of a Pacific Ocean community was rejected, the idea of Pacific Ocean economic cooperation is under discussion. We have approached it with an unprejudiced attitude and we are willing to join in deliberations about the possible foundations for such cooperation if, of course, it is conceived not according to a bloc, antisocialist plan imposed by someone, but as a result of free discussion without any kind of discrimination whatsoever. The already fairly extensive arsenal of scientific and political projects on the issue of creating a new world economic order and on the experience of integration in West and East could be a good basis for such discussion. We would propose a Pacific Ocean conference along the lines of the Helsinki conference, with the participation of all countries along the ocean, as an objective, if rather remote one. When and, of course, if, there is success in agreeing to its convocation, it will be possible to agree on where it should be held as well. One possibility is Hiroshima. Why should not that town, the first victim of nuclear evil, become a distinctive Helsinki for Asia and the Pacific Ocean?

Summing up, I want to stress again that we are in favor of including the Asia-Pacific area in the general process of creating an all-embracing system of international security, which was spoken of at the twenty-seventh CPSU congress. How do we envisage this in concrete terms? First of all, questions inevitably arise of a regional settlement. . . . Now I am going to deal with Southeast Asia and [Cambodia].

The Khmer people have made terrible sacrifices. This country, its town and villages were more than once subjected to American bombing. Through its suffering it won its right to choose its friends and allies, and it is unacceptable to try to draw it back into the tragic past and decide the future of this state in distant capitals, or even in the United Nations. Much here, as in other problems of Southeast Asia, depends on the normalization of Sino-Vietnamese relations. This is the sovereign affair of the governments and leaderships of the two countries. We can only express our interest in seeing the border between these socialist states becoming again a border of peace and good neighborliness, and a comradely dialogue renewed, with unnecessary suspicions and distrust being removed. The moment for this now seems propitious, and the whole of Asia needs it.

In our opinion there are no insurmountable obstacles to the establishment of mutually acceptable relations between the countries of Indochina and ASEAN. Given good will and conditions of noninterference from outside, they could settle their problems for the good of general Asian security at the same time.

There is the possibility of not only getting rid of the dangerous tension on the Korean peninsula but of beginning a movement along the path of solving the national problem of the whole Korean people. If one starts from truly Korean interests, there are no rational grounds for rejecting the serious dialogue being proposed by [North Korea].

Second, we are in favor of putting a barrier on the path of the proliferation and buildup of nuclear weapons in Asia and the Pacific. It is well known that the USSR has bound itself not to increase its medium-range nuclear missiles in the Asian part of the country. The USSR supports the declaration of the southern part of the Pacific Ocean as a nuclear-free zone, and calls on all the nuclear powers, either unilaterally or multilaterally, to guarantee its status. Implementation of the [North Korean] proposal for the creation of a nuclear-free zone on the Korean peninsula would be a serious contribution. The idea of creating such a zone in Southeast Asia has attracted the attention it deserves.

Third, we propose starting talks on reducing the activity of naval fleets, first and foremost of ships equipped with nuclear weapons, in the Pacific Ocean. A limitation on competition in the sphere of antisubmarine weapons would help to strengthen stability, in particular an accord to refrain from antisubmarine activity in certain zones of the Pacific Ocean. That would be a significant confidence-building measure. And in general I should like to say that if the United States were to renounce a military presence, say in the Philippines, we should not be found wanting in a response. We are, as previously, also decisively in favor of renewing the talks on turning the Indian Ocean into a zone of peace.

Fourth, the Soviet Union ascribes great importance to the radical reduction of armed forces and conventional weapons in Asia down to the limit of reasonable sufficiency. We are aware that it is necessary to resolve this issue in parts, gradually, starting with one particular region, say the Far East. In this context, the USSR is prepared to discuss with the PRC specific steps aimed at a balanced reduction in the level of land forces.

Fifth, the Soviet Union considers that the time has long since been ripe to put onto a practical footing the discussion of confidence-building measures and the non-use of force in the region. It is possible to start with simpler measures, for example, with measures for the security of maritime communications in the Pacific and also for preventing international terrorism. It would be possible to hold a conference to discuss and work out such steps in one of the Soviet coastal cities. By the way, in time it would also be possible to resolve the question of opening up Vladivostok to visits by foreigners. If it really proves possible to change the situation in the Pacific for the better, Vladivostok could become a major international center, a seat of trade and culture, a city of festivals, sporting meetings, congresses and scientific symposiums. We should like to see it as our wide-open window to the East. And then may it be, to use the phrase of our great Pushkin, that all flags will come to us as guests. . . .

Comrades, the present generation has inherited many difficult and agonizing problems and in order to move forward toward solving them we must get rid of the burden of the past and seek new approaches, guided by responsibility to the present and the future. The Soviet state calls upon all Asia-Pacific countries to cooperate for the sake of peace and security. Anyone who aspires to these goals, who hopes for a better future for his people, will find in us benevolent interlocutors and honest partners.

Mankind is living through a difficult, dramatic time but it has a reserve of toughness that enables it not simply to survive but to learn to live in a new civilized world, in other words, to live knowing no threat of war, to live in conditions of freedom when the highest criterion of all will be the good of man and development of the potential of the human personality. But that requires persistent struggle against the common enemy: the threat of universal destruction. Today, as never before, it is important to mobilize the potential of common sense, partnership, and reason existing in the world, in order to halt the slide toward disaster. Our resolution to do everything incumbent on us to this end is immutable: all can be sure of this, the peoples of all countries and states.

People's Daily Editorial on the 1989 Student Protests

Following former general secretary Hu Yaobang's death on April 15, 1989, student protests against the government gained strength in Beijing and other cities. On April 26, the People's Daily *raised the stakes by publishing a hard-line editorial that labeled the student-led movement a "planned conspiracy" that represented a "serious political struggle" confronting the entire country. The text of the editorial follows.*

In their activities to mourn the death of Comrade Hu Yaobang, Communists, workers, peasants, intellectuals, cadres, members of the People's Liberation Army, and young students have expressed their grief in various ways. They have also expressed their determination to turn grief into strength to make contributions in realizing the Four Modernizations and invigorating the Chinese nation.

Some abnormal situations have also occurred during the mourning activities. Taking advantage of the situation, an extremely small number of people spread rumors, attacked party and state leaders by name, and instigated the masses to break into the Xinhuamen in Zhongnanhai, where the party Central Committee and the State Council are located. Some people even shouted such reactionary slogans as "Down with the Communist Party." In Xi'an and Changsha, there have been serious incidents in which some lawbreakers carried out beating, smashing, looting, and burning.

Taking into consideration the feelings of grief suffered by the masses, the party and government have adopted an attitude of tolerance and restraint toward some improper words uttered and actions carried out by the young students when they were agitated with emotions. On 22 April, before the memorial meeting was held, some students had already turned up at Tiananmen Square, but they were not asked to leave as they normally would have been. Instead, they were asked to observe discipline and join in the mourning for Comrade Hu Yaobang. The students on the square were themselves able to consciously maintain order. Owing to the joint efforts by all concerned, it was possible for the memorial meeting to proceed in a solemn and respectful manner.

However, after the memorial meeting, an extremely small number of people with ulterior motives continued to take advantage of the young students' feelings of grief for Comrade Hu Yaobang to spread all kinds of rumors to poison and confuse people's minds. Using posters of both big and small characters, they vilified, hurled invective at,

and attacked party and state leaders. Blatantly violating the Constitution, they called for opposition to the leadership by the Communist Party and the socialist system. In some of the institutions of higher learning, illegal organizations were formed to seize power from the student unions. In some cases, they even forcibly took over the broadcasting rooms on the campuses. In some institutions of higher learning, they instigated the students and teachers to strike and even went to the extent of forcibly preventing students from going to classes, usurped the name of the workers' organizations to distribute reactionary handbills and established ties everywhere in an attempt to create even more serious incidents.

These facts prove that what this extremely small number of people did was not to join in the activities to mourn Comrade Hu Yaobang or to advance socialist democracy in China. Neither were they out to give vent to their grievances. Flaunting the banner of democracy, they undermined democracy and the legal system. Their purpose was to sow dissension among the people, plunge the country into chaos, and sabotage the political situation of stability and unity. This is a planned conspiracy and a disturbance. Its essence is once and for all to negate the leadership of the CCP and the socialist system. This is a serious political struggle confronting the whole party and the people of all nationalities throughout the country.

If we tolerate and connive at this disturbance and let it go unchecked, a seriously chaotic state will appear. Then, the reform and opening up, the improvement of the economic environment and the rectification of the economic order, construction and development, the control over prices, the improvement of our living standards, the drive to oppose corruption, and the development of democracy and the legal system expected by the people throughout the country, including the young students, will all become visionary hopes. Even the tremendous achievements scored in the reform during the past decade may be completely lost, and the great aspiration of the revitalization of China cherished by the whole nation will be hard to realize. A China with very good prospects and a very bright future will become a chaotic and unstable China without any future.

The whole party and the people nationwide should fully understand the seriousness of this struggle, unite to take a clear-cut stand to oppose the disturbance, and firmly preserve the hard-earned situation of political stability and unity, the Constitution, socialist democracy and the legal system. Under no circumstances should the establishment of any illegal organizations be allowed. It is imperative to firmly stop any acts that use any excuse to infringe upon the rights and interests of legitimate organizations of students. Those who have deliberately fabricated rumors and framed others should be investigated to determine their criminal liabilities according to law. Bans should be placed on unlawful parades and demonstrations and on such acts as going to factories, rural areas, and schools to establish ties. Beating, smashing, looting, and burning should be punished according to law. It is necessary to protect the legitimate rights of students to study in the class. The broad masses of students sincerely hope that corruption will be eliminated and democracy will be promoted. These, too, are the demands of the party and the government. These demands can only be realized by strengthening the efforts for improvement and rectification, vigorously pushing forward the reform, and making perfect our socialist democracy and our legal system under the party leadership.

All comrades in the party and the people throughout the country must soberly recognize the fact that our country will have no peace if this disturbance is not checked resolutely. This struggle concerns the success or failure of the reform and opening up, the program of the Four Modernizations, and the future of our state and nation. Party organizations of the CCP at all levels, the broad masses of members of the Communist Party and the Communist Youth League, all democratic parties and patriotic democratic personages, and the people around the country should make a clear distinction between right and wrong, take positive action, and struggle to firmly and quickly stop the disturbance.

Declaration of Martial Law in Beijing

The Tiananmen Square incident of May-June 1989 is often viewed as a turning point in modern Chinese history. The declaration of marital law on May 20, reproduced here, confirmed Li Peng's hard-line role in events and may have set the stage for the bloodbath that followed.

The State Council of the People's Republic of China this morning issued an order, signed by Premier Li Peng, to execute martial law in part of Beijing. Following is the full text of the order: In view of the fact that serious turmoil has taken place in Beijing and that social stability, people's normal life, and social order have been disrupted, and in order to firmly stop the unrest, to safeguard social tranquility in Beijing, to safeguard the life and property of the citizens, to protect public property, and to ensure the normal function of the central departments and the Beijing municipal government, the State Council decided, in accordance with the stipulations of clause 16 under Article 89 of the constitution of the People's Republic of China, to execute martial law in part of Beijing as from 10:00 on May 20, 1989, and that the order be implemented by the people's government of Beijing, which is to take concrete measures according to practical needs.

Chen Xitong's Report on the Tiananmen Incident

This June 30, 1989, report on the Tiananmen incident by Beijing mayor Chen Xitong presents the Chinese government's official version of events after the fact, including the key government allegation that the demonstrations constituted a "counterrevolutionary rebellion" with the goal of overthrowing the leadership of the Chinese Communist Party. It also alleges that political forces outside of the People's Republic had a hand in organizing the student demonstrations.

During late spring and early summer, namely, from mid-April to early June of 1989, a tiny handful of people exploited student unrest to launch a planned, organized, and premeditated political turmoil, which later developed into a counterrevolutionary rebellion in Beijing, the capital. Their purpose in plotting turmoil and rebellion was to overthrow the leadership of the CCP and subvert the socialist PRC.

The outbreak and development of the turmoil and the counterrevolutionary rebellion had a profound international background and social basis at home. As Comrade Deng Xiaoping put it, "this storm was bound to happen sooner or later. As determined by the international and domestic climate, it was bound to happen and was independent of man's will." In this struggle involving the life and death of the party and the state, Comrade Zhao Ziyang committed the serious mistake of supporting the turmoil and splitting the party, and had the unshirkable responsibility for the shaping and development of the turmoil. In the face of this very severe situation, the party Central Committee made correct decisions and took a series of resolute measures, winning the firm support of the whole party and people of all nationalities in the country.

Represented by Comrade Deng Xiaoping, proletarian revolutionaries of the older generation played a very important role in winning the struggle. The Chinese PLA, the armed police, and the police made great contributions in checking the turmoil and quelling the counterrevolutionary rebellion. The vast numbers of workers, peasants, and intellectuals firmly opposed the turmoil and the rebellion, rallied closely around the party Central Committee and displayed a very high political consciousness and the sense of responsibility as masters of the country.

Now, entrusted to so do by the State Council, I am making a report to the NPC Standing Committee on the turmoil and the counterrevolutionary rebellion, mainly the happenings in Beijing and the work of checking the turmoil and quelling the counterrevolutionary rebellion.

I. The Turmoil Was Brewed and Premeditated for a Long Time

Some political forces in the West always attempt to make socialist countries, including China, give up the socialist road, eventually to bring these countries under the rule of international monopoly capital and put them on the course of capitalism. This is their long-term, fundamental strategy. In recent years, they have stepped up the implementation of this strategy by making use of some policy mistakes and temporary economic difficulties in socialist countries. In our country, there was a tiny handful of people both inside and outside the party who stubbornly clung to their position of bourgeois liberalization and went in for political conspiracy. Echoing the strategy of Western countries they colluded with foreign forces, ganged up among themselves at home and made ideological, public opinion, and organizational preparations for years to stir up turmoil in China, overthrow leadership by the Communist Party, and subvert the socialist people's republic. That is why the entire course of brewing, premeditating and launching the turmoil, including the use of varied means such as stirring up public opinion, distorting facts, and spreading rumors, bore the salient feature of support by coordinated action at home and abroad.

This report will mainly deal with the situation since the third plenary session of the Thirteenth CCP Central Committee. Last September, the party Central Committee formulated the policy of improving the economic environment, straightening out the economic order and deepening the reform in an all-around way. This policy and the related measures won the support of the broad masses and students. The social order and political situation were basically stable. Firm evidence of this was the approval of Comrade Li Peng's government work report by an overwhelming majority (with a mere two votes against and four abstentions) at the National People's Congress in the spring of this year. Of course, the people and students raised many criticisms of some mistakes committed by the party and the government in their work, corruption among some government employees, unfair distribution, and other social problems. At the same time, they made quite a few demands and proposals for promoting democracy, strengthening the legal system, deepening the reform, and overcoming bureaucracy. These were normal phenomena. And the party and government were also taking measures to resolve them. At that time, however, there was indeed a tiny bunch of people in the party and society who ganged up together and engaged in many very improper activities overtly and covertly.

What deserves special attention is that, after Comrade Zhao Ziyang's meeting with an American "ultraliberal economist" on 19 September last year, some Hong Kong newspapers and journals, which were said to have close ties with Zhao Ziyang's "think tank," gave enormous publicity to this and spread the political message that "Beijing was using Hong Kong mass media to topple Deng and protect Zhao." In his article entitled "Big Patriarch Should Retire," published in Hong Kong's *Economic Journal*, Li Yi (alias Qi Xin), editor in chief of the reactionary *The Nineties* magazine, clamored for "removing the obstacle of extremely old men's politics" and "giving Zhao Ziyang sufficient power." Another article in *The Nineties* appealed to Zhao to be an "autocrat." Hong Kong *Emancipation* monthly also carried a lengthy article, saying that some people in Beijing had "overt or covert" relations with certain persons in Hong Kong media circles, which "are sometimes dim and sometimes bright, just like a will-o'-the-wisp" and that such subtle relations now "have been newly proven by a drive to topple Deng and protect Zhao launched in the last month." The article also said that "in terms of hopes of China turning capitalist, they settle on Zhao Ziyang."

To coordinate with the drive of "toppling Deng and protecting Zhao," Beijing's *Economics Weekly* published a dialogue on the current situation between Yan Jiaqi (research fellow at the Institute of Political Science under the Chinese Academy of Social Sciences) who had close ties with Zhao Ziyang's former secretary, Bao Tong, and another person. It attacked "the improvement of the economic environment and the straightening out of economic order," saying that it would lead to "stagnation." It also said that a big problem China was facing was "not to follow the old disastrous road of nonprocedural change of power as in the case of Khrushchev and Liu Shaoqi." It said that "nonprocedural change of power as in the cultural revolution will no longer be allowed in China." The essence of the dialogue was to whip up public opinion to cover up Zhao Ziyang's mistakes, keep his position and power, and push on with bourgeois liberalization with even less restraint. This dialogue was reprinted in full or parts in Shanghai's *World Economic Herald,* Hong Kong *Mirror* monthly, and other newspapers and magazines at home and abroad.

Collaboration between forces at home and abroad intensified toward the end of last year and early this year. Political assemblies, joint petitions, big- and small-character posters, and other activities emerged, expressing fully erroneous or even reactionary points. For instance, a large seminar "Future China and the World" was sponsored by the Beijing University Future Studies Society on 7 December last year. Jin Guantao, deputy chief editor of the "Toward the Future" book series and adviser to the society, said in his speech "attempts at socialism and their failure constitute one of the two major legacies of mankind in the twentieth century." Ge Yang, chief editor of the monthly *New Observer,* immediately stood up to "provide evidence" in the name of "the eldest" among the participants and a party member of dozens of years' standing, saying "Jin's negation of socialism is not harsh enough, rather it is a bit too polite."

On 28 January this year, Su Shaozhi (research fellow at the Institute of Marxism-Leninism-Mao Zedong Thought under the Chinese Academy of Social Sciences), Fang Lizhi, and the like organized a so-called neo-enlightenment salon at the Dule bookstore in Beijing, which was attended by more than 100 people, among them Beijing-based American, French, and Italian correspondents as well as Chinese. Fang described this gathering as "smelling of strong gunpowder" and "taking a completely critical attitude to the authorities." He also said "what we need now is action" and professed to "take to the streets after holding three sessions in a row." In early February, Fang Lizhi, Chen Jun (member of the reactionary organization "Chinese Alliance for Democracy") and others sponsored a so-called winter get-together of famed personalities at the Friendship Hotel, where Fang made a speech primarily on the two major issues of so-called democracy and human rights, and Chen drew a parallel between the 4 May movement and the Democracy wall at Xidan. Fang expressed the "hope that entrepreneurs, as China's new rising force, will join forces with the advanced intellectuals in the fight for democracy." At a press conference he gave for foreign correspondents on 16 February, Chen Jun handed out Fang Lizhi's letter addressed to Deng Xiaoping and another letter from Chen himself and thirty-two others to the NPC Standing Committee and the CCP Central Committee, calling for the amnesty and the release of Wei Jingsheng and other so-called political prisoners who had gravely violated the criminal law.

On 23 February, the Taiwan *United Daily News* carried an article headlined "Beginning of a Major Movement a Mega-Shock." It said "a declaration was issued in New York, and open letters surfaced in Beijing; as the thunder of spring rumbles across the divine land (China), waves for democracy are rising." On 26 February, Zhang Xianyang (research fellow at the Institute of Marxism-Leninism-Mao Zedong Thought under the Chinese Academy of Social Sciences), Li Honglin (research fellow at the Fujian Academy of Social Sciences), Bao Zhunxin (associate research fellow at the Institute of Chinese History under the Chinese Academy of Social Sciences), Ge Yang and thirty-eight others, jointly wrote a letter to the CCP Central Committee, calling for the release of so-called political prisoners.

Afterward, a vast number of big- and small-character posters and assemblies came out on the campuses of some universities in Beijing, attacking the Communist Party and the socialist system. On 1 March, for example, a big-character poster entitled "Denunciation of Deng Xiaoping: A Letter to the Nation" was put up at Qinghua University and Beijing University simultaneously.

The poster uttered such nonsense as "the politics of the Communist Party consists of empty talk, power politics, autocratic rule, and arbitrary decisions" and openly demanded dismantling parties and abandoning the Four Cardinal Principles (adherence to the socialist road, to the people's democratic dictatorship, to leadership by the Communist Party, and to Marxism-Leninism and Mao Zedong Thought). A small-character poster entitled "Deplore the Chinese" turned up at Beijing University on 2 March, crying for "totalitarianism" and "autocracy to be overthrown." On 3 March, there appeared at Qinghua University and other universities and colleges a "letter to the student masses" signed by the "Preparatory Committee of the China Democratic Youth Patriotic Association," urging students to join in the "turbulent current for 'democracy, freedom, and human rights' under the leadership of the patriotic democratic fighter Fang Lizhi."

On the campuses of Beijing University and other schools of higher learning on 29 March, there was extensive posting of Fang's article "China's Disappointment and Hope" written for the Hong Kong *Ming Pao Daily News.* In the article, Fang claimed that socialism had "completely lost its attraction" and there was a need to form political "pressure groups" to carry out "reforms for political democracy and economic freedom." But what he termed as "reform" actually is a synonym for total Westernization.

The big-character poster "Call of the Times," which came out in Beijing University on 6 April, questioned in a way of complete negation "whether there is any rationale now for socialism to exist" and "whether Marxism-Leninism fits the realities of China after all." On 13 April the Beijing Institute of Posts and Telecommunications and some other schools received a "Message to the nation's college students" signed by the "Guangxi University student union," which called on students to "hold high the portrait of Hu Yaobang and the great banner of 'democracy, freedom, dignity, and rule by law' " in celebration of the 4 May Youth Day.

Meanwhile, so-called democratic salons, freedom forums, and various kinds of "seminars," "conferences," and "lectures" mushroomed in Beijing's institutions of higher learning. The "democratic salon" presided over by Wang Dan, a Beijing University student, sponsored seventeen lectures in one year, indicative of its frequent activities. They invited Ren Wanding, head of the defunct illegal "Human Rights League," over to spread a lot of fallacies about the so-called new-authoritarianism and democratic politics. At one point they held a seminar in front of the statue of Cervantes, openly crying for the "abolition of the one-party system, forcing the Communist Party to step down and toppling the present regime." They also invited Li Shuxian, the wife of Fang Lizhi, to be their "adviser." Li fanned the flames by urging them to "legalize the democratic salon," "hold meetings here frequently," and "abolish Beijing municipality's ten-article regulations on demonstrations."

All this prepared, in terms of ideology and organization, for the turmoil that ensued. A *Ming Pao Daily News* article commented, "The contact-building and petition-signing activities initiated by the elite of Chinese intellectuals for human rights exerted enormous influence on students. They had long ago planned a large-scale move on the seventieth anniversary of the 4 May movement to express their dissatisfaction with the authorities. The sudden death of Hu Yaobang literally threw a match into a barrel of gunpowder." In short, as a result of the premeditation, organization, and engineering by a small handful of people, a political situation had already emerged in which "the rising wind forebodes a coming storm."

Comrade Hu Yaobang's death on 15 April prompted an early outbreak of the long-brewing student unrest and turmoil. The broad masses and students mourned Comrade Hu Yaobang and expressed their profound grief. Universities and colleges provided facilities for mourning by the students. However, a few people took advantage of this to oppose the leadership of the Communist party and the socialist system under the pretext of "mourning."

II. Student Unrest Was Exploited by the Organizers of Turmoil from the Very Beginning

This turmoil found expression first in the wanton attack and slanders against the party and the government and the open call to overthrow the leadership of the Communist party and subvert the present government as contained in the large quantity of big- and small-character posters, slogans, leaflets, and elegiac couplets. Some of the posters on the campuses of Beijing University, Qinghua University, and other schools abused the Communist party as "a party of conspirators" and an organization on the verge of collapse; some attacked the older generation of revolutionaries as "decaying men administering affairs of the state" and "autocrats with a concentration of power"; some called [out] the names of leading comrades of the CCP Central Committee one by one, uttering such nonsense as "the man who should not die has passed away while those who should die remain alive"; some called for "dissolving the incompetent government and overthrowing autocratic monarchy"; some cried for "the abolition of the CCP and the adoption of the multiparty system" and "the dissolution of party branches and removal of political workers from the mass organizations, armed forces, schools, and other units"; some issued a "declaration on private ownership," calling for "sounding the death knell of public ownership at an early date and greeting a new future for the republic"; some went so far as to "invite the Kuomintang back to the mainland and establish two-party politics," etc. Many big- and small-character posters used disgusting language to slander Comrade Deng Xiaoping, clamoring "down with Deng Xiaoping."

This turmoil, from the very beginning, was manifested by a sharp conflict between bourgeois liberalization and the Four Cardinal Principles. Of the program slogans raised by the organizers of the turmoil—either the "nine demands" first raised through Wang Dan, leader of an illegal student organization, in Tiananmen Square or the "seven demands" and "ten demands" raised later—there were two principal demands: one was to reappraise Comrade Hu Yaobang's merits and demerits the other was to negate completely the fight against bourgeois liberalization and rehabilitate the so-called wronged citizens in the fight against bourgeois liberalization. The essence of the two demands was to gain absolute freedom in China to oppose the Four Cardinal Principles and realize capitalism.

Echoing those demands, some so-called elitists in academic circles, that is, the very small number of people stubbornly clinging to their position of bourgeois liberalization, organized a variety of forums during the period and indulged in unbridled propaganda through the press. Most outstanding among the activities was a forum sponsored by the *World Economic Herald* and the *New Observer* in Beijing on 19 April. The forum was chaired by Ge Yang and its participants included Yan Jiaqi, Su Shaozhi, Chen Ziming (director of the Beijing Institute of Socioeconomic Science), and Liu Ruishao (of the Hong Kong *Wen Wei Po* Beijing office). One of their main topics was to "rehabilitate" Hu Yaobang; the other was to "reverse" the verdict on the fight against liberalization. They expressed unequivocal support for the student demonstrations, saying that they saw therein "China's future and hope." Later, when the Shanghai municipal party committee made the correct decision on straightening things out in the *World Economic Herald*, Comrade Zhao Ziyang, who consistently winked at bourgeois liberalization, refrained from backing the decision. Instead, he criticized the committee for "making a mess of it" and "landing itself in a passive position."

This turmoil also found expression in the fact that, instigated and engineered by the small handful of people, many acts were very rude, violating the constitution, laws and regulations of the PRC and gravely running counter to democracy and the legal system. They put up big-character posters en masse on the campuses in disregard of the fact that the provision in the constitution on "four big freedoms" (speaking out freely, airing views fully, holding great debates, and writing big-character posters) had been abrogated, and turning a deaf ear to all persuasion, they staged large-scale demonstrations day after day in disregard of the ten-article regulations on demonstrations issued by the standing committee of the Beijing municipal people's congress; late on the night of 18 and 19 April, they assaulted Xinhuamen, headquarters of the party Central Committee and the State Council, and shouted "Down with the Communist Party," something that never occurred even during the Cultural Revolution; they violated the regulations for the management of Tiananmen Square and occupied the square by force several times, one consequence of which was that the memorial meeting for Comrade Hu Yaobang was almost interrupted on 22 April; ignoring the relevant regulations of the Beijing municipality and, without registration, they formed an illegal organization, "solidarity student union" (later changed to "federation of autonomous student unions in universities and colleges") and "seized power" from the lawful student unions and postgraduate unions formed through democratic election; disregarding law and school discipline, they took by force school offices and broadcasting stations and did things as they wished, creating anarchy on the campuses.

Another important means that the small number of turmoil organizers and plotters used was to fabricate a spate of rumors to confuse people and agitate the masses. At the beginning of the student unrest, they spread the rumor that "Li Peng scolded Hu Yaobang at a Politburo meeting and Hu died of anger." The rumor was meant to spearhead the attack on Comrade Li Peng. In fact, the meeting focused on the question of education. When Comrade Li Tieying, member of the Politburo, state councilor, and minister in charge of the State Education Commission, was making an explanation of a relevant document, Comrade Hu Yaobang suffered a sudden heart attack. Hu was given emergency treatment right in the meeting room and was rushed to a hospital when his condition allowed. There was definitely no such thing as Hu flying into a rage.

On the night of 19 April, a female foreign language student at Beijing Teachers' University was run down by a trolley on her way back to school after attending a party. She died despite treatment. Some people spread the rumor that "a car of the Communist police knocked a student to her death," which stirred up the emotions of some students who did not know the truth.

In the small hours of 20 April, policemen whisked away those students who had blocked and assaulted Xinhuamen, and sent them back to Beijing University by bus. Some people concocted the rumor of "20 April bloody incident" alleging that "the police beat people at Xinhuamen, not only students, but also workers, women and children" and that "more than 1,000 scientists and technicians fell in blood." This further agitated some people.

On 22 April, when Li Peng and other leading comrades left the Great Hall of the People at the end of the memorial meeting for Comrade Hu Yaobang, some people perpetrated a fraud with the objective of working out an excuse for attacking Comrade Li Peng. First they started the rumor that "Premier Li Peng promised to come out at 12:45 [local time] and receive students in the square." Then they let three students kneel on the steps outside the East Gate of the Great Hall of the People for the purpose of handing in a "petition." After a while they said, "Li Peng went back on his word and refused to receive us. He has deceived the students." This assertion fanned strong indignation among the tens of thousands of students in Tiananmen Square and came very close to leading to a serious incident of assault on the Great Hall of the People.

Confused and incited by the rumors, the antagonism of young students against the government was greatly intensified. Using this antagonism, a very small number of people put up the slogan "The government pays no heed to our peaceful petition. Let's make the matters known across the country and call for a nationwide class boycott." This led to the serious situation in which 60,000 university students boycotted classes in Beijing and many students in other parts of China followed suit. The student unrest escalated, and the turmoil expanded.

This turmoil was marked by another characteristic, that is, it was no longer confined to institutions of higher learning in Beijing; it spread to the whole of society and to all parts of China. After the memorial meeting for Comrade Hu Yaobang, a number of people went to contact middle schools, factories, shops, and villages, made speeches in the streets, handed out leaflets, put up slogans and raised money, doing everything possible to make the situation worse. The slogan "Oppose the CCP" and the big-character poster "Long live class boycott and exam boycott" appeared in some middle schools. Leaflets "Unite with the workers and peasants, down with the despotic rule" were put up in some factories. Organizers and plotters of the turmoil advanced the slogan "Go to the south, the north, the east, and the west" in a bid to establish ties throughout the country. Students from Beijing were seen in universities and colleges in Nanjing, Wuhan, Xi'an, Changsha, Shanghai, and Harbin, while students from Tianjin, Hebei, Anhui, and Zhejiang took part in demonstrations in Beijing. Criminal activities of beating, smashing, looting, and burning took place in Changsha and Xi'an.

Political forces outside the Chinese mainland and in foreign countries had a hand in the turmoil from the very beginning. Hu Ping, Chen Jun, and Liu Xiaobo, members of the "Chinese Alliance for Democracy," which is a reactionary organization groomed by the Kuomintang, wrote "an open letter" from New York to Chinese university students, urging them to "consolidate the organizational links established in the student unrest and strive to carry out activities effectively in the form of a strong mass body." The letter told the students to "effect a breakthrough by thoroughly negating the 1987 movement against liberalization," "strengthen contacts with the mass media," "increase contacts with various circles in society," and "enlist their support and participation in the movement." Wang Bingzhang and Tang Guangzhong, two leaders of the "Chinese Alliance for Democracy," made a hasty flight from New York to Tokyo in an attempt to get to Beijing had have a direct hand in the turmoil. A number of Chinese intellectuals residing abroad who stand for instituting the Western capitalist system in China invited Fang Lizhi to take the lead, and cabled from Columbia University a "declaration on promoting democratic politics on the Chinese mainland" asserting that "the people must have the right to choose the ruling party" in a bid to incite people to overthrow the Communist party.

Someone in the United States, using the name "Hong Yan," sent in by fax "ten opinions on revising the constitution," suggesting that deputies to the national and local people's congresses as well as judges in all courts should be elected from among candidates without party affiliation, in an attempt to keep the Communist party completely out of the organs of power and judicial organs.

Some members of the former *China Spring Journal* residing in the United States hastily founded a "China democratic party." They sent "a letter addressed to the entire nation" to some universities in Beijing, inciting students to "demand that the conservative bureaucrats step down" and "urge the CCP to end its autocratic rule."

Reactionary political forces in Hong Kong, Taiwan, the United States, and other Western countries were also involved in the turmoil through various channels and by different means. Western news agencies showed unusual zeal. The Voice of America, in particular, aired news in three programs every day for a total of more than ten hours beamed to the Chinese mainland, spreading rumors, stirring up trouble, and adding fuel to the turmoil.

The facts listed above show that we were confronted not with student unrest in its normal sense, but with a planned, organized, and premeditated political turmoil designed to negate the Communist party leadership and the socialist system. It had clear-cut political ends and deviated from the orbit of democracy and legality, employing base political means to incite large numbers of students and other people who did not know the truth. If we failed to analyze and see the problem in essence, we would have committed grave mistakes and landed ourselves in an extremely passive position in the struggle.

III. 26 April People's Daily *Editorial*
Correctly Determined the Nature of the Turmoil

From the death of Comrade Hu Yaobang on 15 April to the conclusion of the memorial service on 22 April, Comrade Zhao Ziyang all along tolerated and connived at the increasingly evident signs of turmoil during the period of mourning, thus facilitating the formation and develop-

ment of the turmoil. In the face of the increasingly grave situation, many comrades in the central leadership and Beijing municipality felt that the nature of the matter had changed, and repeatedly suggested to Comrade Zhao Ziyang that the central leadership should adopt a clear-cut policy and measures to check quickly the development of the matter. But Zhao kept avoiding making an earnest analysis and discussion of the nature of the matter. At the end of the memorial meeting for Comrade Hu Yaobang, comrades in the central leadership again suggested to Zhao that a meeting be held on 23 April before his visit to the Democratic People's Republic of Korea. Instead of accepting this suggestion, Zhao went to play golf as if nothing had happened. Because he took such an attitude, the party and the government lost a chance to stop the turmoil.

On the afternoon of 24 April, the Beijing municipal party committee and people's government reported to Comrade Wan Li. At his proposal, members of the Standing Committee of the Politburo met that evening, with Comrade Li Peng presiding, to analyze and study earnestly the development of the situation. A consensus was reached that all signs at that time showed we were confronted with an anti-party and anti-socialist political struggle, which was conducted in a planned and organized way and manipulated and instigated by a small handful of persons. The meeting decided that a group for stopping the turmoil be established in the central leadership, and at the same time requested the Beijing municipal party committee and people's government to arouse the masses fully, try to win over the majority and isolate the minority in a bid to put down the turmoil and stabilize the situation as soon as possible.

The following morning, Comrade Deng Xiaoping made an important speech, expressing his full agreement with and support for the decision of the Politburo Standing Committee and making an incisive analysis of the nature of the turmoil. He pointed out sharply that this was not a case of ordinary student unrest, but political turmoil aimed at negating the leadership of the Communist Party and the socialist system. Deng's speech greatly enhanced the understanding of the cadres and increased their confidence and courage in quelling the turmoil and stabilizing the overall situation.

The *People's Daily* editorial on 26 April embodied the decision of the Politburo Standing Committee and the spirit of Comrade Deng Xiaoping's speech, and pointed to the nature of the turmoil. At the same time, it made a clear distinction between the tiny handful of persons who organized and plotted the turmoil and the vast number of students. The editorial made the overwhelming majority of the cadres feel sure about the matter and pointed out the direction of their action, enabling them to work with a clear-cut stand.

After the editorial was published in the *People's Daily,*

the Beijing municipal party committee and people's government, under the direct leadership of the CCP Central Committee and the State Council, convened in quick succession a variety of meetings inside and outside the party, upholding the principle and seeking unity of understanding; cleared up rumors and set people's minds at ease through various forms; supported school leaderships, party and youth league members and backbone students by encouraging them to work boldly, and advised and dissuaded those students who took part in demonstrations; and worked hard to win over the masses by conducting a variety of dialogues. The dialogues, between the State Council spokesman Yuan Mu and other comrades and students, between leaders of relevant central departments and students and between principal leaders of the Beijing municipal party committee and people's government and students, achieved good results.

Meanwhile, earnest work was done in the factories, villages, shops, primary and secondary schools, and neighborhoods to stabilize the overall situation and prevent the turmoil from spreading to other sectors of society. Various provinces, municipalities, and autonomous regions did a good job in their respective localities in accordance with the spirit of the editorial to prevent the situation in Beijing from influencing other parts of the country.

The clear-cut stand of the 26 April editorial forced the organizers and plotters of the turmoil to make an about-face in strategy. Before the publication of the editorial, large numbers of posters and slogans were against the Communist Party, socialism, and the Four Cardinal Principles. After the publication of the editorial, the illegal Beijing "federation of autonomous student unions in universities and colleges," issued on 26 April "no. 1 order of the new student federation" to change their strategy, urging students to "march to Tiananmen under the banner of supporting the Communist Party" on 27 April and putting forth such slogans as "Support the Communist Party," "Support socialism," and "Safeguard the constitution." It also, at the suggestion of Fang Lizhi, changed such subversive slogans as "Down with the bureaucratic government," "Down with the corrupt government," and "Down with the dictatorial rule," into ones like "Oppose bureaucracy, oppose corruption, and oppose privilege"—slogans that could win support from people of various circles.

The Japanese Jiji News Agency then dispatched from Beijing a news story entitled "Young Officials Form a Pro-democracy Group," describing some figures in Zhao Ziyang's so-called think tank as "young officials of the CCP Central Committee and the government" and saying that they "made frequent contacts with representatives of the new autonomous student unions at Beijing's universities and colleges, including Beijing University, Qinghua University, People's University, and Beijing Teachers'

University, which took part in the demonstrations, and offered advice to the students." It also said that, during the mass demonstrations on 27 April, the students held up "placards 'supporting socialism' and 'supporting the leadership of the Communist Party.' They did so at the instruction of the group."

Leaders of the student unrest originally planned to stage "a 100-day demonstration and a student strike of indefinite duration." But they lost such enthusiasm after the publication of the editorial.

Compared with the demonstration on 27 April, the number of students taking part in the one held on 4 May dropped from over 30,000 to less than 20,000, and the onlookers also decreased by a big margin. After the 4 May demonstration, 80 percent of the students returned to class as a result of the work done by party and administrative leaders of various universities and colleges. After the publication of the *People's Daily* 26 April editorial, the situation in other parts of the country also tended to stabilize quickly. It was evident that, with some more work the turmoil, instigated by a small handful of persons by making use of the student unrest, was likely to calm down. A host of facts show that the *People's Daily* 26 April editorial is correct and indeed played its role in stabilizing the situation in the capital and the whole country as well.

IV. Comrade Zhao Ziyang's Speech on 4 May Was the Turning Point in Escalating the Turmoil

When the turmoil was close to subsiding, Comrade Zhao Ziyang, who was the CCP general secretary, adopted a changeable attitude of contradicting himself. At first, when the Politburo Standing Committee solicited his opinions during his visit to Korea, he cabled back explicitly expressing "full agreement with the policy decision made by Comrade Deng Xiaoping on handling the current turmoil." On 30 April, after he returned home, he once again expressed, at a meeting of the Politburo Standing Committee, his agreement with Comrade Deng Xiaoping's speech and the determination of the nature of the turmoil as made in the 26 April editorial, maintaining that the handling of the student unrest in the previous period was appropriate.

A few days later, however, when he met with representatives attending the annual meeting of the Asian Development Bank on the afternoon of 4 May, he expressed views diametrically opposed to the decision of the Politburo Standing Committee, to Comrade Deng Xiaoping's speech, and to the spirit of the editorial. Firstly, when the turmoil had already come to the surface, he said "there will be no big turmoil in China"; secondly, when a host of facts had proven that the essence of the turmoil was the negation of the leadership by the Communist Party and the socialist system, he still insisted that "they are by no means opposed to our fundamental system. Rather they are asking us to correct mistakes in our work''; thirdly, although facts had shown that a tiny handful of people was making use of the student unrest to instigate turmoil, he merely said that it was "hardly avoidable" for "some people to take advantage of this," thus totally negating the correct judgment of the party Central Committee that some people were creating turmoil.

This speech of Comrade Zhao Ziyang's was prepared by Bao Tong beforehand. Bao asked the central broadcasting station and CCTV to broadcast the speech that very afternoon and repeat it for three days running. He also asked the *People's Daily* to print the speech on the front page the following day and carry a large quantity of positive responses from various sectors. Differing views were held up and not allowed to appear even in confidential reading matter. Comrade Zhao Ziyang's speech, publicized through the *People's Daily* and certain newspapers, created serious ideological confusion among the masses and the cadres, while inflating the arrogance of the organizers and plotters of the turmoil.

The vast difference between Comrade Zhao Ziyang's speech and the policy of the party Central Committee evoked many comments at home and was also discerned by the media abroad. A Reuters dispatch said Zhao's remarks "constituted a sharp contrast to the severe reproof to students a week before" and "a major revision in the judgment of the previous week." An article in *Le Monde* of France on 6 May stated that "the party leader (referring to Zhao Ziyang) seemed to make the development of the situation favorable to himself."

The distribution of the speech resulted in ideological confusion among leading officials at various levels, party and youth league members, and the backbone of the masses, particularly those working at universities and colleges. They were at a loss in their work, and many voiced their objection. Some people asked, "There are two voices in the central leadership. Which is right and which is wrong? Which are we supposed to follow?" Some queried, "We are required to be at one with the central leadership, but with which one?" Others complained, "Zhao Ziyang plays the good man at the top while we play the bad ones at the grass roots." Cadres in universities and colleges and backbone students generally felt "betrayed" and had heavy hearts, and some even shed sad tears. Work at the universities and colleges was bogged down in a completely passive situation.

At that time, the Beijing municipal party committee and people's government were also in a difficult plight. Although they knew opinions differed in the central leadership, they had to tell the low levels against their will that the central leadership was of one opinion with "some stressing this and others stressing that." They had to ask the central leadership for instructions on many things, but Comrade Zhao Ziyang, as general secretary, was reluctant to call a meeting. In the face of strong demands by the Beijing municipal party committee and people's government, he reluctantly convened a meeting on 8 May. However, he refused to hear the briefing by Beijing authorities. At the meeting some comrades said Comrade Zhao Ziyang's speech on 4 May did not accord with the spirit of the 26 April editorial. Zhao retorted, "I'll bear the responsibility if I made incorrect remarks." At another meeting, some comrades said that comrades working at the grass roots complained that they "had been betrayed." Comrade Zhao Ziyang rebuked, "Who has betrayed you? It was only during the Cultural Revolution that people were betrayed." In those days, quite a few people from top to bottom echoed the Hong Kong and Taiwan newspapers, repeatedly attacking the Beijing municipal party committee and people's government and comrades working at the grass roots. Demonstrating hooligans yelled, "The Beijing municipal party committee cannot escape the criminal responsibility of making false reports to deceive the central leadership." In the face of the worsening situation, certain measures under consideration could not be implemented.

In contrast, organizers and plotters of the turmoil were encouraged by Comrade Zhao Ziyang's speech. Yan Jiaqi, Cao Siyuan (director of the Research and Development Institute of the Stone Company), and others said that "things have turned for the better. It is necessary to mobilize the intellectuals to support Zhao Ziyang." Zhang Xianyang said "Aren't we advocating making use of the students? Zhao Ziyang is now doing just this."

Egged on by Comrade Zhao Ziyang and plotted by a few others, leaders of the "autonomous student unions" of Beijing University and Beijing Teachers' University declared to resume their class boycott that night. Many other universities followed suit and organized "pickets" to prevent students willing to resume class from going to the classroom.

After that, a new wave of demonstrations surged ahead. On 9 May, several hundred journalists from more than thirty press organizations took to the streets and submitted a petition. About 10,000 students from a dozen universities including Beijing, Qinghua, and People's Universities, Beijing Teachers' University, and the University of Political Science and Law, staged a demonstration, supporting the journalists, distributing leaflets, and calling for a continued class boycott and a hunger strike.

Henceforth, the situation took an abrupt turn for the worse and the turmoil was pushed to new heights. Influenced by the situation in Beijing, the already calmed situation in other parts of China became tense again. Shortly after Comrade Zhao Ziyang's speech, a large number of student demonstrators assaulted the office buildings of the Shanxi provincial party committee and provincial government in Taiyuan on 9 and 10 May. They also assaulted the ongoing international economic and technological cooperation fair, the import and export commodities fair, and the folk arts festival. This created a very bad impression both at home and abroad.

V. Use Hunger Strike as Coercion to Escalate the Turmoil

Good and honest people asked if the lack of understanding, consideration, and concession on the part of the government had caused the students to make so much trouble.

The facts are just the opposite. From the very beginning of the turmoil, the party and government fully acknowledged the students' patriotism and their concern about the country and people. Their demands to promote democracy and reform, punish official profiteers, and fight corruption were acknowledged as identical with the aspirations of the party and government, which also expressed the hope of solving the problems through normal democratic and legal procedures.

However, such good aspirations failed to win an active response. The government proposed to exchange views and increase understanding through dialogues via various channels, levels, and forms.

Yet the illegal student organization put forward very strict conditions as terms of the dialogue. They demanded that their partners to the dialogues "must be people holding positions at or above member of the Standing Committee of the Politburo of the party Central Committee, vice chairman of the NPC Standing Committee and vice premier"; "a joint communique on every dialogue must be published and signed by both parties"; and dialogues should be "held in locations designated in turn by representatives of the government and students."

These bore nothing like [the characteristics of] a dialogue, but rather of setting the stage for political negotiations with the party and government.

Even under such circumstances, the party and government still took the attitude of utmost tolerance and restraint, with the hope of continuing to maintain the channels for dialogue in order to educate the masses and win over the majority.

At two o'clock in the early morning of 13 May, leaders of the "federation of autonomous student unions in universities and colleges" raised the demand for a dialogue, which was accepted two hours later by the General Office of the party Central Committee and that of the State Council. However, the students ate their own words and canceled the dialogue at daybreak.

On the morning of 13 May, the bureau for letters and visits of the General Offices of the party Central Committee, the State Council, and the NPC Standing Committee again notified them of the decision to hold the dialogue with students on 15 May.

Despite their agreement, the students began their maneuver over the number of participants in the dialogue. After the government agreed to their first proposed list of twenty people, they then demanded the number be raised to two hundred. Without waiting for further discussion, they went on to criticize "the government's insincerity in holding dialogue." Only four hours after they were informed of the dialogue, they hastily made public the long-prepared "hunger strike declaration" launching a seven-day fast that involved 3,000 people and subsequently a long occupation of Tiananmen Square.

May 13 was chosen as the starting date of the hunger strike "to put pressure on them because of Gorbachev's China visit," said Wang Dan, leader of the "federation." The very small number of people who organized and plotted the turmoil used the fasting students as "hostages" and their lives to blackmail the government in a vile fashion, making the turmoil even more serious.

During the student hunger strike, the party and government maintained an attitude of utmost restraint and did everything they could in various aspects. First of all, staff members of various universities and leading officials at all levels and even party and state leaders went to Tiananmen Square to see the fasting students on many occasions and gave them ideological advice.

Second, efforts were made to help the Red Cross Society mobilize 100 ambulances and several hundred medical workers to keep watch at the fasting site day and night; 52 hospitals were asked to have nearly 2,000 beds ready so that students who suffered shock or illness because of the hunger strike could get first aid and timely treatment.

Third, all sorts of materials were provided to alleviate the sufferings of the fasting students and ensure their safety. The Beijing municipal party committee and people's government mobilized workers, officials, and vehicles to provide the fasting students with drinking water, edible salt, and sugar via the Red Cross Society day and night. The municipal environmental sanitation bureau sent sprinklers and offered basins and towels for the fasting students. Adequate supplies of medicine preventing sunstroke, cold, and diarrhea were provided by pharmaceutical companies and distributed by the Red Cross Society. The food organizations sent a large amount of soft drinks and bread to be used during emergency rescue of the students. A total of 6,000 straw hats were provided by commercial units and 1,000 quilts were sent by the Beijing Military Region Command, in response to the city authorities' request, to protect the fasting students from heat during the day and cold at night. To keep the hunger strike site clean, makeshift flush toilets were set up and sanitation workers cleaned the site at midnight. Before the torrential rain on 18 May, 78 buses from the public transport company, and 400 thick boards from the materials bureau were sent to protect the fasting students from rain and damp. No fasting student died in the seven-day hunger strike.

However, all this failed to evoke any positive response. Facts told people time and again that the very small number of organizers and plotters of the turmoil were determined to oppose us to the very end and that the problem could not be solved even with tolerance on 1,000 occasions and 10,000 concessions.

It needs to be pointed out in particular that Comrade Zhao Ziyang did not do what he should have done when the situation quickly deteriorated, but instead stirred up the press by incorrectly guiding public opinion, making the already deteriorated situation more difficult to handle.

In his 6 May meeting with comrades Hu Qili and Rui Xingwen, both then in charge of propaganda and ideological work in the Central Committee, Comrade Zhao Ziyang said that the press "has opened up a bit and there have been reports about the demonstrations. There is no big risk in opening up a bit by reporting the demonstrations and increasing the openness of news." He even said, "Confronted with the will of the people at home and the progressive trend worldwide, we can only guide our actions according to circumstances." Here, he even described the adverse current against communism and socialism as the "will of the people at home" and a "progressive trend worldwide."

His instructions were passed on to major press units in the capital the same day and many arrangements were made afterward. As a result, the *People's Daily* and many other national newspapers and periodicals adopted an attitude of full acknowledgment and active support for the demonstrations, sit-ins, and hunger strike, devoting lengthy coverages with no less exaggeration. Even some Hong Kong newspapers expressed their surprise over this unique phenomenon.

Under the incorrect guidance of the public opinion, the number of people who took to the streets to support the students increased day by day as the momentum grew after 15 May. The number of people involved grew from tens of thousands to 100,000 and several hundred thousand, in addition to the 200,000 students who came from other parts of the country to show their support for the fasting students.

For a time, it looked as if refusal to join in the demonstrations meant being "unpatriotic" and refusal to show support was equal to "indifference to the survival of the students." Under such circumstances, the fasting students were made to ride the tiger and found it difficult to get off. Many parents of the students and teachers wrote to or called leading organs, press organizations, radio, and television stations, asking them not to force the fasting students onto the path of death and to show mercy in saving the children and stopping this kind of "deadly public opinion."

This did not work, however. The students' hunger strike and the residents' demonstrations threw social order in Beijing into a mess and seriously disrupted the Sino-Soviet summit, which was closely followed worldwide, forcing some changes on the agenda, with some activities even canceled.

Meanwhile, demonstrations in major cities and even provincial capitals registered a drastic increase in the number of people involved, while people also took to the streets in some small and medium-sized cities, producing a large scale involvement and a serious disturbance never seen since the founding of the People's Republic.

In order to support the students and add fuel to the flames of turmoil, some so-called elitists who took a stubborn stand in favor of bourgeois liberalization, cast off all disguises and came to the fore. On the evening of 13 May, the big-character poster "We can no longer remain silent" appeared at Beijing University. It was written by Yan Jiaqi, Su Shaozhi, Bao Zunxin, and others, urging intellectuals to take part in the big demonstrations they had sponsored to support the students' hunger strike.

On 14 May "Our urgent appeal for the current situation" was jointly made by twelve people including Yan Jiaqi, Bao Zunxin, Li Honglin, Dai Qing (reporter with the *Guangming Daily),* Yu Haocheng (former director of the Masses Publishing House), Li Zehou (research fellow at the Philosophy Institute of the Chinese Academy of Social Sciences), Su Xiaokang (lecturer at the Beijing Broadcasting Institute), Wen Yuankai (professor at the China University of Science and Technology), and Liu Zaifu (director of the Literature Institute under the Chinese Academy of Social Sciences). They demanded that the turmoil be declared a "patriotic democracy movement" and the illegal student organization be declared legal, saying that they would also take part in the hunger strike if these demands were not met. This appeal was published in the *Guangming Daily* and broadcast on the China Central Television. These people also went to Tiananmen Square many times to make speeches and agitate. They slandered our government as "an incompetent government," saying that, through the fasting students, "China's bright future can be envisioned."

Then the people formed the illegal "Beijing union of intellectuals" and published the 16 May declaration, threatening, with countercharges, that "a promising China might be led into the abyss of real turmoil" if the government did not accept the political demands made by the very small number of people.

As the situation became increasingly serious, Comrade Zhao Ziyang used the opportunity of meeting Gorbachev on 16 May to deliberately direct the fire of criticism at Comrade Deng Xiaoping and to make the situation even worse. Right at the beginning of the meeting, he said "Comrade Deng Xiaoping's helmsmanship is still needed for the most important issues. Since the thirteenth national party congress, we have always reported to Comrade Deng Xiaoping and asked for his advice while dealing with the most important issues." He also said that this was "the first time" that this "decision" by the Chinese party had been disclosed to the public.

On the following day, Yan Jiaqi, Bao Zuxin, and others published their most furious and vicious 17 May declaration. They came out with slurs such as "Because the autocrat controls unlimited power, the government has lost its own sense of obligation and normal human feelings"; "despite the Qing dynasty's death seventy-six years ago, there is still an emperor in China though he is without such a title and a senile and fatuous autocrat." "General Secretary Zhao Ziyang declared publicly yesterday afternoon that all decisions in China must be approved by this decrepit autocrat," they said quite openly. In their hoarse voices they shouted "gerontocratic politics must end and the autocrat must resign."

Some newspapers and periodicals in Hong Kong and Taiwan echoed their reactionary clamor. The Hong Kong newspaper *Express* published an article on 18 May entitled "Down with Deng and Li, But Not Zhao." It said, "Zhao Ziyang's speech was full of indications that the foul atmosphere at home now was caused by Deng Xiaoping's helmsmanship"; "at present the masses are eager to get rid of Deng and Li, while Zhao's role is almost open upon calling." It also added, "It would be a good piece of news for Hong Kong if Deng could be successfully ousted and China's reforms embark on the path of legal rule with the realization of democracy." Against the backdrop of such screams, slogans smearing Comrade Deng Xiaoping and attacking Comrade Li Peng were all around. Some demanded that "Deng Xiaoping step down," while others said, "Li Peng, step down to satisfy the people." Meanwhile, slogans like "Support Zhao Ziyang," "Long Live Zhao Ziyang," and "Zhao Ziyang should be promoted to chairman of the Central Military Commission" could be seen and heard in the demonstrations and at Tiananmen Square.

Plotters of the turmoil attempted to use the chaos as an opportunity to seize power. They distributed leaflets, proclaiming the founding of the "preparatory committee to the people's conference of all circles in Beijing" to replace the municipal people's congress. A call was made to establish a Beijing regional government to replace the legal Beijing municipal people's government. They attacked the State Council, which was established in accordance with the law, as "pseudo-government." They also spread rumors saying that the Foreign Ministry and a dozen other ministries had already "declared independence" from the State Council and that about thirty countries in the world had broken diplomatic relations with our country. After the rumor that "Deng Xiaoping has stepped down" was made, some went to demonstrations carrying a coffin, burned Comrade Xiaoping's ef-

figy and set off firecrackers on Tiananmen Square to celebrate their "victory." The situation in Beijing became increasingly serious, with anarchy viciously spreading and many areas sinking into complete chaos and white terror. If our party and government did not take resolute measures under such circumstances, another vital chance would be missed and further great irredeemable damage could be done. This end would by no means be permitted by the broad masses of the people.

VI. The Government Had No Alternative But to Declare Martial Law in Parts of Beijing, a Correct Measure

To safeguard the social stability in the city of Beijing, to protect the safety of the life and property of the citizens and ensure the normal functioning of the party and government departments at the central level and of the Beijing municipal government, the State Council had no alternative but to declare martial law in parts of Beijing as empowered by clause 16 of Article 89 of the PRC constitution and at a time when police forces in Beijing were far too inadequate to maintain normal production, work, and living order. This was a resolute and correct decision.

The decision on taking resolute measures was announced at a meeting called by the central authorities and attended by cadres from the party, government and military in Beijing on 19 May. Comrade Zhao Ziyang, persisting in his erroneous stand against the correct decision of the central authorities, neither agreed to speak at the meeting together with Comrade Li Peng, nor agreed to preside over the meeting. He did not agree even to attend the meeting. By so doing, he openly revealed his attitude of separating himself from the party before the whole party, the whole country, and the whole world.

Before this, members of the Standing Committee of the Politburo of the party Central Committee met to discuss the issue of declaring martial law in parts of Beijing on 17 May. On the same day, a few people who had access to top party and state secrets gave away the information out of their counterrevolutionary political considerations. A person who worked with Comrade Zhao Ziyang said to the leaders of the illegal student organization, "The troops are about to suppress you. All the others have agreed. Zhao Ziyang was the only one who was against it. You must get prepared."

On the evening of 17 May, Bao Tong summoned some people from the Political Structural Reform Research Center of the party Central Committee for a meeting. After divulging the secret on declaring martial law, he made a "farewell speech" in which he warned those attending not to reveal the schemes worked out at the meeting, saying that anyone who revealed them would be a "traitor," a "Judas." On 19 May, Gao Shan, deputy bureau director of this Political Structural Reform Research Center, hurried to the Economic Structural Reform Institute to pass on to those who were holding a meeting the so-called instructions from "above." After that, the meeting, presided over by Chen Yizi (the institute director), drafted a "six-point statement on the current situation" in the name of the Economic Structural Reform Research Institute, the Development Institute of the China Rural Development Research Center under the State Council, the Institute of International Studies of the China International Trust and Investment Corporation, and the Beijing Association of Young Economists. The statement, which was broadcast at Tiananmen Square and distributed widely, demanded "the publicizing of the inside story of the decision making of the top leadership and the divergence of opinions at the top level of leadership" and "the convening of a special session of the NPC and a special congress of the CCP." It also urged the students on Tiananmen Square to "end their hunger strike as soon as possible," hinting that the government "would adopt extreme measures (military control)."

Soon after that, some people, who identified themselves as employees of the State Commission for Restructuring the Economy, went to Tiananmen Square to deliver a speech in which they said, "With deep grief and extreme anger, we now disclose a piece of absolutely true news. General Secretary Zhao Ziyang has been dismissed from his post." The speakers called on workers, students, and shopkeepers to carry out nationwide strikes and cited the masses to "take immediate action to fight a life-and-death struggle." The speech was soon printed in the form of a *People's Daily Extra,* which was widely distributed. On the same evening, leaflets entitled "Several Suggestions on the Tactics of the Student Movement" were found at Beijing railway station and other public places. It said that "at present, hunger strike and dialogue should no longer be our means and demands. We should hold peaceful sit-ins and raise clear-cut new political demands and slogans: (1) Comrade Ziyang must not be removed; (2) a special CCP national congress must be convened immediately; and (3) a special session of the NPC must be held immediately." It also said that people "shouldn't be terrified by the troops who were coming" and that "this attitude should be explained and publicized time and again to the students before the troops' arrival." Some leaders of the autonomous students federation of Beijing colleges and the Beijing autonomous workers union who have been arrested also confessed that, at about 4 P.M. on 19 May, someone holding a piece of paper and identifying himself as a staff worker of a certain organization under the party Central Committee went to the "Tiananmen Square headquarters" and revealed the news that martial law was about to be declared.

As a result of the close collaboration between a small number of people who had access to top party and state secrets and the organizers and schemers of the turmoil,

the organizers made timely adjustment to their tactics. That night, forty-five minutes before the meeting called by the central authorities and attended by cadres from the party, government and military institutions in Beijing, they changed the hunger strike to a sit-in in a bid to mislead the people and give them the false impression that since the students had already ended their hunger strike it was not necessary for the government to declare martial law. By so doing they also gained time to organize people and coerce those who were in the dark to set up roadblocks at major crossroads to stop the advance of the troops and to continue to mislead public opinion and confuse people's minds. While viciously cursing Comrade Deng Xiaoping and other proletarian revolutionaries of the old generation, saying that "we don't need Deng Xiaoping's wisdom and experience," they lavished praise on Comrade Zhao Ziyang by saying that "the country is hopeless without Ziyang as the party leader" and "Give us back Ziyang." They also plotted to rally forces for greater turmoil, claiming that they were going to mobilize 200,000 people to occupy Tiananmen Square and to organize a citywide general strike on 20 May. Harmonizing with Comrade Zhao Ziyang's three-day sick leave, which started on 19 May, they spread the word that a "new government" would be established in three days' time.

Under the extremely urgent circumstances, the party Central Committee and the State Council decided resolutely to declare martial law in parts of Beijing, starting at 10 A.M., 20 May, to prevent the situation from worsening and to grasp the initiative to stop the turmoil so as to give support to the broad masses, who were opposed to the turmoil and longed for stability. However, as the organizers and schemers of the turmoil had learned of our decision before it was implemented, there were tremendous difficulties and obstacles for the troops in entering the city.

On the eve of the declaration of martial law and on the first two days after it was declared, all major crossroads were blocked. More than 220 buses were taken away and used as roadblocks. Traffic came to a standstill. Troops who were to enforce the martial law were not able to arrive at their designated places. The headquarters of the party Central Committee and the State Council continued to be surrounded. Speeches inciting people could be heard everywhere on the streets. Leaflets spreading rumors could be seen everywhere in the city. Demonstrations, each involving several tens of thousands of people, took place one after another and Beijing, our capital city, fell into total disorder and terror. During the following few days, the martial law troops managed to enter the city by different ways. Meanwhile, the armed police and police continued to perform their duties by overcoming tremendous difficulties. Urban and suburban districts organized workers, residents, and government office workers, as many as 120,000 people altogether, to maintain social order. The outer suburban counties also sent out militiamen. The concerted efforts of the troops, police, and civilians helped improve transport, production, and order in the capital and people felt more at ease. But the very small number of people never stopped for a single day their activities to create turmoil and never changed their goal of overthrowing the leadership of the Communist Party. Things were developing day by day towards a counterrevolutionary rebellion.

One of the major tactics of the organizers and schemers of the turmoil after martial law was declared was to continue to stay on Tiananmen Square. They wanted to turn the square into a "center of the student movement and the whole nation." Once the government made a decision, they planned to stage a strong reaction at the square and form an "anti-government united front." These people had been planning to incite incidents of bloodshed on the square, believing that "the government would resort to suppression if the occupation of the square continues" and "blood can awaken people and split the government."

To ensure that the situation on the square could be maintained, they used funds provided by reactionary forces both at home and abroad to improve their facilities and install advanced telecommunications devices, spending 100,000 yuan a day on average. They even started illegal purchase of weapons. By using the tents provided by their Hong Kong supporters, they set up "villages of freedom" and launched a "democracy university" on the square, claiming that they would turn the university into "the Huangpu [Whampoa] Military Academy of the new era." They erected a so-called goddess statue in front of the Monument to the People's Heroes. The statue was named initially the "Goddess of Liberty," but its name was later changed to "Goddess of Democracy," showing that they took American-style democracy and freedom as their spiritual pillar.

Fearing that the students who took part in the sit-in could not hold on, Liu Xiaobo and other behind-the-scene schemers went up onto the front stage and performed a four-man farce of a 48-to-72 hour hunger strike so as to pep up the students. They said, "As long as the flags on the square are still up, we can continue our fight and spread it to the whole country until the government collapses."

Taking advantage of the restraint that the government and the troops still exercised after martial law was declared, the organizers and plotters of the turmoil continued to organize all kinds of illegal activities. Following the establishment of the "autonomous students federation of Beijing colleges," the "Beijing autonomous workers union," the "fasting contingent," the "Tiananmen Square headquarters" and the "union of the capital's intelligentsia," they set up more illegal organizations such as the "patriotic joint conference of people from all walks of life in the capital for upholding the constitution," and the "autonomous union of Beijing residents." In the name of the Research Institute for Restructuring the Economic System, the Development Institute of the China Rural Development Research Center under the State Council, and the Beijing Association of Young Economists, they openly sent telegrams to some of the troops in an attempt to incite defection. They were engaged in such underground activities aimed at toppling the government as organizing a special team in charge of molding public opinion and making preparations to launch an underground newspaper.

They organized their sworn followers in taking a secret oath, claiming "under no circumstances should we betray our conscience, yield to autocracy, and bow to the emperor of China of the 1980s." Wan Runnan, general manager of Stone Company, listed the following six conditions for retreating from Tiananmen Square when he called together some leaders of the autonomous students federation of Beijing colleges in an international hotel: "To withdraw the troops, cancel martial law, remove Li Peng, ask Deng Xiaoping and Yang Shangkun to quit, and let Zhao Ziyang resume his post." During the meeting, they also planned to organize "a great march to claim victory at midnight." Moreover, as they believed that there was almost no hope of solving problems within the party after Comrade Zhao Ziyang asked for sick leave, they pinned their hopes on an emergency meeting of the Standing Committee of the NPC.

Yan Jiaqi, Bao Zunxing and others sent a telegram to the leaders of the NPC Standing Committee, saying that "as the constitution is being wantonly trampled on by a few people, we hereby make an emergency appeal for the holding of an emergency meeting of the NPC Standing Committee immediately to solve the current critical problems."

Inspired by a certain member of the NPC Standing Committee, the Stone Research Institute of Social Development circulated a petition to convene such an emergency meeting. After getting the signatures of several members of the NPC Standing Committee, it sent urgent telegrams to the NPC Standing Committee members outside Beijing. Conspiratorially, they said nothing about their true purpose in those letters and telegrams in an attempt to deceive those comrades who did not know the truth. They even went so far as to usurp the names of those comrades to serve their ulterior motives.

After doing all this, Yan Jiaqi and Bao Zunxing published an article in Hong Kong's *Ming Pao Daily News,* entitled "Solve China's Present Problems in a Democratic and Legal Way: A Letter to Li Peng," which called on "every member of the NPC Standing Committee and every deputy to the NPC to cast a sacred vote to abolish martial law and dismiss Li Peng as premier."

Organizers and instigators of the turmoil also

unbridledly agitated for and organized violent action. They enlisted local hooligans, ruffians, and criminals from other parts of the country, ex-convicts who had not turned over a new leaf, and people with a deep hatred of the Communist Party and the socialist system to knock together "dare-to-die corps," "flying tiger teams," "the volunteer army," and other terrorist organizations, threatening to detain and kidnap party and state leaders and seize state power by means of "attacking the Bastille." They distributed leaflets to incite counterrevolutionary armed rebellion, advocating that "a single spark can start a prairie fire" and calling for establishing "armed forces that might be called the people's army," for "uniting with various forces, including the Kuomintang in Taiwan," and for "a clear-cut stand to oppose the Communist party and its government by sacrificing lives."

They declared that they would settle accounts with the party and the government after the event and even prepared a blacklist of those to be suppressed. The Hong Kong-based *Ming Pao Daily News* published a "dialogue" on 2 June between Liu Xiaobo, one of the organizers and planners, and "a mainland democratic movement leader," in which Liu said, "We must organize an armed force among the people to bring about Zhao Ziyang's comeback."

The activities of the instigators of the riots have strong financial backing. In addition to the materials worth some hundreds of thousands of yuan from the Stone Company, they also got support from hostile forces overseas and other organizations and individuals. Some people from the United States, Britain, and Hong Kong offered them nearly US $1 million and tens of millions of Hong Kong dollars. Part of the money was used for activities to sabotage the enforcement of martial law. Anyone who took part in establishing obstacles to stop traffic and block army vehicles could get 30 yuan a day. Also they set high rewards for rioters burning military vehicles and beating soldiers, promising to offer 3,000 yuan for the burning of a vehicle and several thousand yuan for capturing or killing soldiers.

A high-ranking official from Taiwan launched a campaign to "send love to Tiananmen" and took the lead in donating 100,000 Taiwan dollars. A member of the Central Committee of the Kuomintang in Taiwan suggested that 100 million Taiwan dollars be donated to establish a so-called fund to maintain flesh and blood ties with and to support the mainland democratic movement. Some people of the Taiwan arts and cultural circles also launched "a campaign to support the democratic movement on the mainland." A letter by the autonomous students federation of Beijing colleges to "Taiwan friends in art circles" said that "we heartily thank you and salute you for your material and spiritual support at this crucial moment."

All this shows that the turmoil planned, organized, and premeditated by a few people could not be put down merely by the government's making some concessions or just issuing an order to impose martial law, contrary to the imagination of some kind-hearted people.

They had made up their minds to unite with all hostile forces overseas and in foreign countries to launch a battle against us to the last. All one-sided goodwill would lead only to their unscrupulous attack against us, and the longer the time the greater the cost.

VII. How Did a Small Minority of People Manage to Incite the Counterrevolutionary Rebellion?

The Chinese PLA undertakes not only the sacred duty of "strengthening national defense, resisting aggression, and defending the motherland" but also the noble responsibility of "safeguarding the people's peaceful labor, participating in national reconstruction, and working hard to serve the people," which are provided for in Article 29 of the constitution of China. It was precisely to carry out the tasks entrusted to them by the constitution that the troops entered the city proper and safeguarded social order.

After the announcement of martial law in some areas of the capital on 20 May, the troops, despite repeated obstructions, were mobilized to march toward the city proper in accordance with a deployment plan and by different ways to take up appointed positions.

The handful of organizers and plotters of the rebellion were well aware that they would have no way to continue their illegal and counterrevolutionary activities and their conspiracy would come to nothing if the martial law troops took up all positions in the center of Beijing. Therefore, they started to create trouble deliberately and did their best to aggravate the unrest, which eventually developed into a counterrevolutionary rebellion.

On 1 June the Public Security Bureau detained a few of the ringleaders of the illegal organization known as the "federation of autonomous workers' unions." The agitators of the rebellion then took advantage of this opportunity to incite some people to surround and attack the offices of the Beijing municipal public security bureau, the municipal party committee and government and the Ministry of Public Security.

On the evening of 2 June a police jeep on loan to the Chinese central television station was involved in a traffic accident in which three people died. None of the victims were students. This was deliberately distorted as a provocation by martial law troops. The conspirators attempted to seize the bodies and parade them in coffins, stirring up the people and making the atmosphere extremely tense. After this incitement and uproar they lit the fire of the counterrevolutionary rebellion.

Just after midnight on 3 June, while the martial law troops were heading for their positions according to schedule, agitators urged crowds to halt military and other motor vehicles, set up roadblocks, beat soldiers, and loot trucks of materials at Jianguomen, Nanheyan, Xidan, Muxidi, and other crossroads. Some twelve military vehicles were halted by crowds near Caohezhuang. Soldiers marching past the Yanjing Hotel were stopped and searched by rioters, and military vehicles parked in front of the Beijing Telegraph Office had their tires slashed and were surrounded with road dividers.

Around dawn, military vehicles on the Yongdingmen bridge were overturned, others at Muxidi had their tires slashed and a group of 400 soldiers in Caoyangmen was stoned. In the Liubukou and Hengertiao areas, military vehicles and soldiers were surrounded by unruly crowds.

Around 7 A.M., some rioters swarmed over military vehicles that had been halted at Liubukou and snatched machine-guns and ammunition. From Jianguomen to Dongdan and in the Tianpiao area, martial law troops were cut off, surrounded, and beaten. On the Jianguomen flyover some soldiers were stripped and others severely beaten.

Later in the morning, troops in the Hufangqiao area were beaten by rioters and some were blinded. The mob prevented injured soldiers from reaching hospitals by deflating ambulance tires and the victims were dragged from the vehicles. From Hufang Road to Taoranting Park, twenty-one military vehicles were surrounded and halted. Policemen escorting the soldiers were beaten and wounded by the rioters.

From noon onward, many of the soldiers trapped by mobs and barricades at the Fuyoujie, Zhengyilu, Xuanwumen, Hufangqiao, Muxidi, and Dongsi crossroads were injured and their equipment, including helmets, military caps, raincoats, water containers, and bags, was stolen. At Liubukou policemen tried several times to recover a military truck loaded with arms and ammunition from an enraged mob but failed. The consequences, had they been stolen or exploded, would have been dreadful. They were then forced to use teargas to disperse the rioters and recapture the dangerous cargo.

About the same time, mobs began to surround and assault buildings, state housing organizations and establishments of vital importance, including the Great Hall of the People, the Propaganda Department of the CCP Central Committee, and the Ministry of Radio, Film, and Television, as well as the west and south gates of Zhongmanhai. Dozens of policemen and guards there were injured.

As the situation rapidly deteriorated, the instigators of the upheaval became more vicious. At about 5 P.M., the ringleaders of the illegal organizations known as the "Beijing federation of autonomous students unions of universities and colleges" and the "federation of autonomous workers' unions" distributed knives, iron bars, chains, and sharpened bamboo sticks, inciting the mobs to kill soldiers and members of the security forces. In a broadcast over loudspeakers in Tiananmen Square, the "federation of autonomous workers' unions" urged the people "to take up arms and overthrow the government." It also broadcast how to make and use Molotov cocktails and how to wreck and burn military vehicles.

A group of mobs organized about 1,000 people to push down the wall of a construction site near Xidan and stole tools, reinforcing bars, and bricks, ready for street fighting. They planned to incite more people to take to the streets the next day, a Sunday, to stage a violent rebellion in an attempt to overthrow the government and seize power at one stroke.

At this critical juncture, the party Central Committee, the State Council, and the Central Military Commission decided to order troops poised on the outskirts of the capital to enforce martial law to forcibly march in and quell the counterrevolutionary rebellion.

VIII. How Did the Counterrevolutionary Rebels Injure and Kill People's Liberation Army Soldiers?

Since the enforcement of martial law in Beijing, the martial law troops heading for Beijing proper tried their best to avoid conflicts, exercising great restraint. After the 3 June riot happened, and before the troops entered the city, the Beijing municipal government and the headquarters of the martial law enforcement troops issued an emergency announcement at 6:30 P.M., which said, "All citizens must keep off the streets and not go to Tiananmen Square as of the issuing of this notice. Workers should remain at their posts, and other citizens must stay at home to ensure their safety." The announcement was broadcast over and over again on television and radio.

At about 10 P.M. on 3 June, most of the martial law troops heading for Beijing proper from various directions entered urban districts successfully, but they had been halted at barricades set up at the main crossroads. Even so, the troops were still quite restrained, while the counterrevolutionary rioters took the opportunity to beat and kill soldiers, to steal military materials, and burn military vehicles.

From 10 P.M. to 11 P.M. the same day, at Cuiweilu, Gongzhufen, Muxidi, and Xidan, twelve military vehicles were burned. Some people threw bricks at soldiers. And some rioters pushed trolley buses to the crossroads, set them on fire and blocked the roads. When fire engines got there, they were also smashed and burned.

Around 11 P.M. three military vehicles were wrecked and one jeep was overturned at Hufangqiao, and military vehicles on the Andingmen flyover were surrounded. In Chongwenmen Street, a regiment of soldiers was surrounded, and on the Jianguomen flyover, thirty military vehicles were halted by barricades, and another three-hundred military vehicles were halted near the Beijing Mining School. Trying to persuade the rioters to let them through, members of the PLA from warrant officers to generals were beaten up or kidnapped.

To avoid conflicts, the barricaded military vehicles in Nanyuan Sanyingmen made a detour. When they reached the south gate of the Temple of Heaven [Tiantan], they were halted again and many of these vehicles were wrecked and burned. One military vehicle was halted in Zhushikou, and a group of people swarmed over it. When a man who looked like a cadre came up and tried to persuade them to leave it alone, he was severely beaten and no one knows whether or not he died.

Just after dawn on 4 June, more military vehicles were burned. Several hundred military vehicles on dozens of road crossings in Tiantan Dongche Road, the north gate of the Temple of Heaven, the west exit of the Qianmen subway, Qianmen Donglu, Fuyou Street, Liubukou, Xidan, Fuxingmen, Nanlishilou, Muxidi, Lianhuachi, Chegongzhuang, Donghuamen, Dongzhimen, Dabeiyao, Hujialou, Beidougezhuang and Jiugongxiang in Chaoyang district and Daxing county were attacked with Molotov cocktails and handmade flamethrowers. Some soldiers were burned to death, and some others were beaten to death. In some areas, several dozen military vehicles were burning at the same time.

At the Shuangjing intersection, more than seventy armored personnel carriers were surrounded and machine-guns ripped from twenty of them. From Jingyuan intersection to Laoshan crematorium, more than thirty military vehicles were burning at the same time. Some rioters with iron bars and oildrums waited at the intersection to stop and burn passing motor vehicles. And many military vehicles carrying food, bedding, and clothing were hijacked to unknown places.

Several mobs drove stolen armored personnel carriers along the Fuxingmen flyover area firing their guns. The "federation of autonomous workers' unions" claimed in their own broadcast that they had stolen a military transceiver and a cipher code book. The mobs also assaulted civilian installations and public buildings. Shop windows including those of the Yanshan department store in Xicheng district were broken. Pine trees in front of Tiananmen gate and the western part of Chairman Mao's Memorial Hall were burned. Some public buses, fire engines, ambulances, and taxis were also wrecked and burned. Some people even drove a public bus loaded with oildrums toward the Tiananmen rostrum and attempted to set fire to it. They were stopped by martial law troops on the southern side of Golden Water Bridge.

The especially unbearable thing was that the mobs not only attacked military vehicles and took part in beating, smashing, looting, and burning in an unbridled way, but they also murdered soldiers in various bestial ways. At about dawn on 4 June, some mobs beat up soldiers with bottles and bricks at the Dongdan crossroads. At Fuxingmen, a military vehicle was surrounded and twelve soldiers were dragged off the vehicle. They were searched and severely beaten. Many of them were badly injured. In Liubukou, four soldiers were surrounded and beaten up, and some were beaten to death. In the Guangqumen area, three soldiers were severely beaten. One was rescued by some bystanders, and the other two have not yet been found. In Xixingsheng Lane in Xicheng district, more than twenty armed policemen were beaten up by mobs; some were badly injured, and the others' whereabouts are unknown. In Huguosi, a military vehicle was halted, and soldiers on it were beaten up and detained as hostages. Submachine guns were snatched. A truck full of bricks was driven from Dongjiao Minxiang to Tiananmen Square, and people on the truck shouted, "if you are really Chinese, come up to smash the soldiers."

After dawn, the rioters' atrocities toward the PLA soldiers became extremely detestable. A police ambulance was carrying eight injured soldiers to a hospital when it was halted by mobs. They beat a soldier to death and shouted that they would do the same to the other seven. In front of a bicycle shop in Qianmen Street, three soldiers were severely beaten by hooligans, who threatened anyone who tried to rescue them. On Chang'an Avenue a military vehicle broke down suddenly and was attacked right away by about 200 rioters. The driver was killed inside the cab. About 30 meters to the east of the Xidan intersection, another soldier was beaten to death. Then the mob poured gasoline over his body and set fire to it. In Fuchengmen, another soldier's body was hung over the flyover after he had been savagely killed. In Chongwenmen, a soldier was thrown from the flyover and burned alive. The rioters wildly clamored that it was "lighting a heavenly lantern." Near the Capital cinema on West Chang'an Avenue, an officer was beaten to death, disemboweled and his eyes plucked out. His body was then strung up on a burning bus.

In the several days of the rebellion, more than 1,280 military vehicles, police cars and public buses were wrecked, burned, or otherwise damaged. Of the vehicles, over 1,000 were military vehicles, more than 60 were armored personnel carriers, and about 30 were police cars. More than 120 public buses were destroyed as well as more than 70 other kinds of motor vehicles. During the same period, arms and ammunition were stolen. More than 6,000 martial law soldiers, armed police, and public security officers were injured, and the death toll reached several dozens. They sacrificed their blood and even their precious lives to defend the motherland, the constitution, and the people. The people will remember their contributions forever.

Such heavy losses are eloquent testimony to the restraint and tolerance shown by the martial law troops. The PLA is an army led by the CCP and serves the people wholeheartedly. They always are ruthless to the enemy, but kind to the people. They were able to defeat the 8 million Kuomintang troops armed by U.S. imperialism during the war years and able to defeat U.S. imperialism, which was armed to the teeth to effectively safeguard the sacred territory and territorial waters and airspace of our country. So why did they suffer such great casualties in quelling the counterrevolutionary rebellion? Why were they beaten and even killed, even when they had weapons in their hands? It is just as Comrade Deng Xiaoping pointed out, "It was because bad people mingled with the good, which made it difficult for us to take the firm measures that were necessary." It also showed that the PLA love the people and are unwilling to injure civilians by accident. The fact that they met death and sacrificed themselves with generosity and without fear fully embodies the nature of the PLA. Otherwise how could there be such a great number of casualties and losses? Doesn't this reflect that the army defends the people at the cost of its own life?

In order to quell the counterrevolutionary rebellion and to avoid more losses, the martial law troops, having suffered heavy casualties and been driven beyond forbearance, were forced to fire in the air to open the way forward after repeated warnings.

During the counterattack, some rioters who wreaked havoc were killed. Because there were numerous bystanders, some were knocked down by vehicles, some were trampled on or hit by stray bullets. Some were wounded or killed by ruffians who had seized rifles.

According to the information we have so far gathered, more than 3,000 civilians were wounded and over 200, including 36 college students, died during the riot. Among the nonmilitary casualties were rioters who deserved the punishment, people accidentally injured, doctors, and other people who were carrying out various duties on the spot. The government will seriously deal with the problem arising from the deaths of the latter two kinds of people.

Due to a rumor spread by the Voice of America and some people who deliberately wished to spread rumors, people talked about a "Tiananmen bloodbath" and that "thousands or even tens of thousands of people fell in a pool of blood." The facts are that, after the martial law troops reached Tiananmen Square at 1:30 A.M., the Beijing municipal government and the martial law headquarters issued an emergency notice, which stated "A serious counterrevolutionary rebellion occurred in the capital this evening" and "all citizens and students in Tiananmen Square should leave immediately to ensure that martial law troops will be able to accomplish their tasks." The notice was broadcast repeatedly for three hours through loudspeakers. The sit-in students gathered around the Monument to the People's Heroes in the southern part of the square. At around 3 A.M., they sent representatives to the troops to express their desire to withdraw from the square voluntarily and this was welcomed by the troops.

At 4:30 A.M., the martial law headquarters broadcast the following notice: "It is time to clear the square and the martial law headquarters accepts the request of the students to be allowed to withdraw." At the same time, another notice on quickly restoring normal order to the square was issued by the municipal government and the headquarters and broadcast. After hearing this, several thousand students organized hand-in-hand pickets and started to leave the square in an orderly manner, carrying their own banners and streamers at about 5 A.M.

The troops vacated a wide corridor in the southeastern corner of the square to ensure the smooth and safe departure of the students. At the same time, a few students who refused to leave were forced to leave by martial law troops in accordance with the demand of the "notice." By 5:30 A.M., the square-clearing operation had been completed.

During the whole operation no one, including the students who refused but were forced to leave, died. Tales of "rivers of blood" in Tiananmen Square and the rumormongers themselves "escaping from underneath piles of corpses" are sheer nonsense.

The counterrevolutionary rebellion was put down with Tiananmen Square returning to the hands of the people and all martial law enforcement troops taking up their assigned positions.

During the quelling of the counterrevolutionary rebellion, the PLA and the police, regardless of sacrifice, fought valiantly and performed immortal feats. Many people gave first aid to the wounded and rescued besieged soldiers, rendering their cooperation and support to the martial-law enforcement troops. Many good people said touching deeds emerged during the event.

Due to the counterrevolutionary rebellion, Beijing has suffered heavy losses in its economy, and losses in other fields cannot be counted in terms of money. Workers, peasants, and intellectuals are now working hard to make up for the losses. Now, order in the capital has fundamentally returned to normal and the situation throughout China is also tending to become smooth, which shows that the correct decision made by the party Central Committee has received support from the Chinese people of all nationalities. Yet, the unrest and the rebellion are not completely over, as a handful of counterrevolutionary rioters refuse to recognize defeat and still indulge in sabotage, and even dream of staging a comeback.

In order to achieve thorough victory, we should mobilize the people completely, strengthen the people's democratic dictatorship and spare no effort to ferret out the counterrevolutionary rioters. We should uncover instigators and rebellious conspirators, and punish the organizers and schemers of the unrest and the counterrevolutionary rebellion, that is, those who obstinately stuck to the path of bourgeois liberalization and carried out political conspiracies, those who colluded with overseas and other foreign hostile forces, those who provided illegal organizations with top secrets of the party and state, and those criminals who committed the atrocities of beating, smashing, grabbing, and burning during the disturbances. We should make a clear distinction between two different types of contradictions and deal with them accordingly, through resolute, hard, and painstaking work. We must educate and unite people as much as possible and focus the crackdown on a handful of principal culprits and diehards who refuse to repent. On this basis, we will retrieve all the losses suffered in the unrest and the counterrevolutionary rebellion as soon as possible. For this, we must rely on the people, try to increase production, practice strict economy, and struggle arduously.

Chairman, vice chairmen, and Standing Committee members, our country's just struggle to quell the unrest and the counterrevolutionary rebellion has won the understanding and support of the governments and people of many countries. We extend our wholehearted gratitude for this. However, there are also some countries, mainly the United States and some West European countries, which have distorted the facts, spread slanderous rumors, and even uttered so-called condemnations and applied sanctions to our country to set off an anti-China wave and wantonly interfere in our country's internal affairs. We deeply regret this. As for all the outside pressure, our government and people have never submitted to such things, not this time nor any time. The rumors will be cleared away, and the truth and facts will come out.

Our country will unswervingly take economic construction as the central task and persist in the Four Cardinal Principles and in reform and opening up to the outside world. Our country will, as always, adhere to our independent foreign policy of peace, continue to develop friendly relations with all countries in the world on the basis of the Five Principles of Peaceful Coexistence, and make our contributions to the safeguarding of world peace and the promotion of world development.

Hong Kong Basic Law

The policies set forth in the 1984 Sino-British Joint Declaration on Hong Kong form the basis of the Basic Law of the Hong Kong Special Administrative Region of the PRC. The Basic Law Drafting Committee, comprising more than fifty mainland and Hong Kong representatives, began work in 1985. After several rounds of revisions, the law was finally endorsed by both sides of the drafting committee in February 1990 and promulgated by China's National People's Congress on April 4, 1990. The text of the law, which goes into effect on July 1, 1997, follows.

Preamble

Hong Kong has been a part of China's territory since ancient times, but it was occupied by Britain after the Opium War in 1840. On 19 December 1984, the Chinese and British governments signed the Joint Declaration on the Question of Hong Kong, affirming that the government of the People's Republic of China (PRC) will resume the exercise of sovereignty over Hong Kong with effect from 1 July 1997, thus fulfilling the long-cherished common aspiration of the entire Chinese people for the recovery of Hong Kong.

In order to uphold national unity and territorial integrity and to maintain Hong Kong's prosperity and stability, and taking account of the history of Hong Kong and its realities, the PRC has decided that upon China's resumption of the exercise of sovereignty over Hong Kong, a Hong Kong Special Administrative Region [SAR] will be established in accordance with the provisions of Article 31 of the Constitution of the PRC and that under the principle of "one country, two systems," the socialist system and policies will not be practiced in Hong Kong.

The basic policies of the PRC regarding Hong Kong have been elaborated by the Chinese government in the Sino-British Joint Declaration. In accordance with the Constitution of the PRC, the National People's Congress [NPC] hereby enacts the Basic Law of the Hong Kong SAR of the PRC, prescribing the systems to be practiced in the Hong Kong SAR in order to ensure the implementation of the basic policies of the PRC regarding Hong Kong.

Chapter I
General Principles

Article 1. The Hong Kong SAR is an inalienable part of the PRC.

Article 2. The NPC authorizes the Hong Kong SAR to exercise a high degree of autonomy and enjoy executive, legislative, and independent judicial power, including that of final adjudication, in accordance with the provisions of this law.

Article 3. The executive authorities and legislature of the Hong Kong SAR shall be composed of permanent residents of Hong Kong in accordance with the relevant provisions of this law.

Article 4. The Hong Kong SAR shall safeguard the rights and freedoms of the residents and other persons in the region in accordance with law.

Article 5. The socialist system and policies shall not be practiced in the Hong Kong SAR and the previous capitalist system and way of life shall remain unchanged for fifty years.

Article 6.   The Hong Kong SAR shall protect the right of private ownership of property in accordance with law.

Article 7.   The land and natural resources within the Hong Kong SAR shall be the state property of the PRC. The government of the Hong Kong SAR shall be responsible for their management, use and development and for their lease or grant to individuals, legal persons, or organizations for use or development. The revenues derived shall be exclusively at the disposal of the government of the Hong Kong SAR.

Article 8.   The law previously in force in Hong Kong, that is, the common law, rules of equity, ordinances, subordinate legislation, and customary law shall be maintained, except for those that are inconsistent with the law or have been amended by the legislature of the Hong Kong SAR.

Article 9.   In addition to the Chinese language, English may also be used as an official language by the executive authorities, legislature, and judicial organs of the Hong Kong SAR.

Article 10.   Apart from displaying the national flag and national emblem of the PRC, the Hong Kong SAR may also use a regional flag and regional emblem. The regional flag of the Hong Kong SAR is a red flag with a bauhinia having a five-star pistil. The regional emblem of the Hong Kong SAR has a bauhinia having a five-star pistil at the center, surrounded by the characters "Hong Kong Special Administrative Region of the PRC" and the words "Hong Kong" in English.

Article 11.   In accordance with Article 31 of the Constitution of the PRC, the systems and policies practiced in the Hong Kong SAR, including the social and economic systems, and the system for safeguarding the fundamental rights and freedoms of its residents, the executive, legislative, and judicial systems, and the relevant policies, shall be based on the provisions of this law.

No law enacted by the legislature of the Hong Kong SAR shall be inconsistent with this law.

Chapter II
Relationship Between the Central Authorities and the Hong Kong SAR

Article 12.   The Hong Kong SAR shall be a local administrative region of the PRC, which shall enjoy a high degree of autonomy and come directly under the central people's government.

Article 13.   The central people's government shall be responsible for foreign affairs relating to the Hong Kong SAR.

The Ministry of Foreign Affairs of the PRC shall establish an office in Hong Kong to deal with foreign affairs.

The central people's government shall authorize the Hong Kong SAR to deal with relevant external affairs on its own in accordance with this law.

Article 14.   The central people's government shall be responsible for the defense affairs relating to the Hong Kong SAR.

The government of the Hong Kong SAR shall be responsible for the maintenance of the public order of the Hong Kong SAR.

Military forces sent by the central people's government to be stationed in the Hong Kong SAR for defense shall not interfere in the local affairs of the Hong Kong SAR.

The government of the Hong Kong SAR may, in times of need, ask the central people's government for assistance from the garrison in the maintenance of public order and in disaster relief.

In addition to abiding by the national laws, members of the garrison shall abide by the laws of the Hong Kong SAR.

Expenditure for the garrison shall be borne by the central people's government.

Article 15.   The central people's government shall appoint the chief executive and the principal officials of the executive authorities of the Hong Kong SAR in accordance with the provisions of Chapter IV of this law.

Article 16.   The Hong Kong SAR shall be vested with executive power. In accordance with the relevant provisions of this law it shall, on its own, manage the administrative affairs of the Hong Kong SAR.

Article 17.   The Hong Kong SAR shall be vested with legislative power.

Laws enacted by the legislature of the Hong Kong SAR shall be reported to the NPC Standing Committee for the record. The reporting for record shall not affect the entry into force of such laws.

If the NPC Standing Committee, after consulting its Committee for the Basic Law of the Hong Kong SAR, considers that any law enacted by the legislature of the Hong Kong SAR is not in conformity with the provisions of this law regarding affairs within the responsibility of the central authorities or the relationship between the central authorities and the Hong Kong SAR, it may return the law in question but it shall not amend it. Any law returned by the NPC Standing Committee shall immediately cease to have force. This cessation shall not have retroactive effect, unless otherwise provided for in the laws of the Hong Kong SAR.

Article 18. The laws of the Hong Kong SAR shall be this law, the laws previously in force in Hong Kong as stipulated in Article 8 of this law, and the laws enacted by the legislature of the Hong Kong SAR.

National laws shall not be applied in the Hong Kong SAR except for those listed in Annex III to this law. The laws listed in Annex III to this law shall be applied locally in the Hong Kong SAR by way of promulgation or legislation.

The NPC Standing Committee may make additions to or deletions from the list of laws in Annex III after consulting its Committee for the Basic Law of the Hong Kong SAR and the government of the Hong Kong SAR. Laws listed in Annex III to this law shall be confined to those relating to defense and foreign affairs as well as other laws outside the limits of the autonomy of the Hong Kong SAR as specified by this law.

In case the NPC Standing Committee decides to declare a state of war or, by reason of turmoil within the Hong Kong SAR that is beyond the control of the government of the Hong Kong SAR and endangers national unification or security, decides that the Hong Kong SAR is in a state of emergency, the central people's government may decree the application of the relevant national laws in the Hong Kong SAR.

Article 19. The Hong Kong SAR shall be vested with independent judicial power, including that of final adjudication.

Courts of the Hong Kong SAR shall have jurisdiction over all cases in the Hong Kong SAR, except that the restrictions on their jurisdiction imposed by Hong Kong's previous legal system and principles shall be maintained.

Courts of the Hong Kong SAR shall have no jurisdiction over cases related to national defense, diplomacy, and other acts of the state. Courts of the Hong Kong SAR shall obtain a statement from the chief executive on questions concerning national defense, diplomacy, and other facts of the state whenever such questions arise in any legal proceedings. This statement shall be binding on the courts. Before issuing such a statement, the chief executive shall obtain a certificate from the central people's government.

Article 20. The Hong Kong SAR may enjoy other powers granted to it by the NPC, the NPC Standing Committee and the central people's government.

Article 21. Chinese citizens who are residents of the Hong Kong SAR shall be entitled to participate in state affairs in accordance with law.

In accordance with the assigned number of seats and the election method specified by the NPC, Chinese citizens among the residents of the Hong Kong SAR shall elect deputies of the Hong Kong SAR to the NPC to participate in the highest organ of state power.

Article 22. Departments of the central people's government as well as provinces, autonomous regions, and municipalities shall not interfere in the affairs that the Hong Kong SAR administers on its own in accordance with this law.

If there is a need for departments of the central people's government as well as provinces, autonomous regions, and municipalities to set up offices in the Hong Kong SAR, they must have the consent of the government of the Hong Kong SAR and the approval of the central people's government.

All offices set up in the Hong Kong SAR by the departments of the central people's government, or by provinces, autonomous regions, and municipalities and the personnel of these offices shall abide by the laws of the Hong Kong SAR.

People from other parts of China must apply for approval for entry into the Hong Kong SAR. The number of people allowed to take up residence in the Hong Kong SAR shall be determined by the competent departments of the central people's government after soliciting the opinions of the government of the Hong Kong SAR.

The Hong Kong SAR may establish an office in Beijing.

Article 23. The Hong Kong SAR shall enact laws on its own to prohibit any act of treason, secession, sedition, subversion of the central people's government, and theft of state secrets; prohibit foreign political organizations or groups from carrying out political activities in the Hong Kong SAR; and prohibit political organizations and groups in the Hong Kong SAR from establishing contacts with foreign political organizations or groups.

Chapter III
Fundamental Rights and Duties of the Residents

Article 24. Residents of the Hong Kong SAR (hereinafter referred to as "Hong Kong residents") shall include permanent residents and nonpermanent residents. The permanent residents of the Hong Kong SAR shall be
(1) Chinese citizens born in Hong Kong before or after the establishment of the Hong Kong SAR;
(2) Chinese citizens who have ordinarily resided in Hong Kong for a continuous period of no less than seven years before or after the establishment of the Hong Kong SAR;

(3) Persons of Chinese nationality born outside Hong Kong to those residents listed in categories (1) and (2);

(4) Persons who are not of Chinese nationality but who have entered Hong Kong on a valid travel document, who have ordinarily resided in Hong Kong for a continuous period of no less than seven years, and who have taken Hong Kong as their place of permanent residence before or after the establishment of the Hong Kong SAR;

(5) Persons under twenty-one years of age born in Hong Kong to residents listed in category (4) before or after the establishment of the Hong Kong SAR; and

(6) Persons other than those residents listed in categories (1) to (5) who had the right of abode only in Hong Kong before the establishment of the Hong Kong SAR.

The above-mentioned residents shall have the right of abode in the Hong Kong SAR and shall be qualified to obtain, in accordance with its law, permanent identity cards that state their right of abode.

The nonpermanent residents of the Hong Kong SAR shall be persons who, in accordance with its law, shall be qualified to obtain Hong Kong identity cards but shall have no right of abode.

Article 25.   All Hong Kong residents shall be equal before the law.

Article 26.   Permanent residents of the Hong Kong SAR shall have the right to vote and the right to stand for election in accordance with law.

Article 27.   Hong Kong residents shall have freedom of speech, of the press and of publication; freedom of association, of assembly, of procession, and of demonstration; and the right and freedom to form and join trade unions and to strike.

Article 28.   The freedom of person of Hong Kong residents shall be inviolable.

No Hong Kong resident shall be arbitrarily or unlawfully arrested, detained or imprisoned. Arbitrary or unlawful search of the body of any resident or deprivation or restriction of his/her freedom of person shall be prohibited. The torture of any resident or arbitrary or unlawful deprivation of his/her life shall be prohibited.

Article 29.   The homes and other premises of Hong Kong residents shall be inviolable. Arbitrary or unlawful search of, or intrusion into, a resident's home or other premises shall be prohibited.

Article 30.   The freedom and privacy of communication of Hong Kong residents shall be protected by law. No

department or individual may, on any grounds, infringe upon the residents' freedom and privacy of communication, with the exception that the relevant authorities may censor communication in accordance with legal procedures to meet the needs of public security or of investigation into criminal offenses.

Article 31.   Hong Kong residents shall have freedom of movement within the Hong Kong SAR and freedom of emigration to other countries and regions. They shall have freedom to travel and freedom of entry and exit. Unless restrained by law, the bearers of valid travel documents shall be free to leave the Hong Kong SAR without special authorization.

Article 32.   Hong Kong residents shall have freedom of faith.

Hong Kong residents shall have the freedom of religious belief and the freedom to preach and to carry out and participate in religious activities in public.

Article 33.   Hong Kong residents shall have freedom of choice of occupation.

Article 34.   Hong Kong residents shall have freedom of academic research, of literary and artistic creation, and of other cultural pursuits.

Article 35.   Hong Kong residents shall have the right to confidential legal advice, access to the courts, and choice of lawyers for timely protection of their legitimate rights and interests, and for representation in the courts, and the right to judicial remedies.

Hong Kong residents shall have the right to institute legal proceedings in the courts against the actions of the executive organs or their personnel.

Article 36.   Hong Kong residents shall have the right to social welfare as prescribed by law. The welfare benefits and retirement insurance of the labor force shall be protected by law.

Article 37.   The freedom of marriage of Hong Kong residents and their right to raise a family freely shall be protected by law.

Article 38.   Hong Kong residents shall enjoy the other rights and freedoms safeguarded by the laws of the Hong Kong SAR.

Article 39.   The "Provisions of the International Covenant on Civil and Political Rights," the "International Covenant on Economic, Social, and Cultural Rights," and international labor conventions as applied to Hong Kong shall remain in force and shall be implemented through the laws of the Hong Kong SAR.

The rights and freedoms enjoyed by Hong Kong residents shall not be restricted unless prescribed by law. Such restrictions shall not contravene the provisions of the preceding paragraph of this article.

Article 40. The legitimate traditional rights and interests of the indigenous inhabitants of the New Territories shall be protected by the Hong Kong SAR.

Article 41. Persons in the Hong Kong SAR other than Hong Kong residents shall, in accordance with law, enjoy the rights and freedoms of Hong Kong residents prescribed in this chapter.

Article 42. Hong Kong residents and other persons in Hong Kong shall have the obligation to abide by the laws in force in the Hong Kong SAR.

Chapter IV
Political Structure
Section I. The Chief Executive

Article 43. The chief executive of the Hong Kong SAR shall be the head of the Hong Kong SAR and shall represent the region.

The chief executive of the Hong Kong SAR shall be accountable to the central people's government and the Hong Kong SAR in accordance with the provisions of this law.

Article 44. The chief executive of the Hong Kong SAR shall be a Chinese citizen of no less than forty years of age who is a permanent resident of the region, does not have the right of residence in any foreign country, and has ordinarily resided in Hong Kong for a continuous period of twenty years.

Article 45. The chief executive of the Hong Kong SAR shall be selected by election or through consultations held locally and be appointed by the central people's government.

The method for selecting the chief executive shall be specified in the light of the actual situation in the Hong Kong SAR and in accordance with the principle of gradual and orderly progress. The ultimate aim shall be the general election of the chief executive nominated by a nominating committee with a broad representation according to democratic procedures.

The specific method for selecting the chief executive is prescribed in Annex I, "Method for the Selection of the chief executive of the Hong Kong SAR."

Article 46. The term of office of the chief executive of the Hong Kong SAR shall be five years. He or she may serve for no more than two consecutive terms.

Article 47. The chief executive of the Hong Kong SAR must be a person of integrity, dedicated to his or her duties.

The chief executive, on assuming office, shall declare his or her assets to the chief justice of the Court of Final Appeal of the Hong Kong SAR. This declaration shall be put on record.

Article 48. The chief executive of the Hong Kong SAR shall exercise the following powers and functions:

(1) To lead the government of the region;

(2) To be responsible for the implementation of this law and other laws that, in accordance with this law, apply in the Hong Kong SAR;

(3) To sign bills passed by the Legislative Council and to promulgate laws;

To sign appropriations bills passed by the Legislative Council and report the budget and final accounts to the central people's government for the record;

(4) To decide on government policies and to issue executive orders;

(5) To nominate and to report to the central people's government for appointment the following principal officials: secretaries and vice secretaries of departments, directors of bureaus, commissioner against corruption, director of the Commission of Audit, head of the Police Division, head of the Entry Affairs Division and director of Customs; and to propose to the central people's government the removal of the above-mentioned officials;

(6) To appoint or remove judges of the courts at all levels in accordance with legal procedures;

(7) To appoint or remove public office bearers in accordance with legal procedures;

(8) To implement the directives issued by the central people's government in respect of the relevant matters provided for in this law;

(9) On behalf of the government of the Hong Kong SAR, to deal with external affairs and other affairs as authorized by the central authorities;

(10) To approve the introduction of motions regarding revenues or expenditure to the Legislative Council;

(11) To decide, in light of security and vital public interests, whether government officials or other personnel in charge of government affairs should testify or give evidence before the Legislative Council or its committees;

(12) To pardon persons convicted of criminal offenses or to commute their sentences; and

(13) To handle petitions and complaints.

Article 49. If the chief executive considers that a bill passed by the Legislative Council is not compatible with the overall interests of the Hong Kong SAR, he or she may return it to the Legislative Council within three months for reconsideration. If the Legislative Council passes the original bill again by no less than a two-thirds majority, the chief executive must sign and promulgate it within one month, or act in accordance with the provisions of Article 50 of this law.

Article 50. If the chief executive refuses to sign the bill passed by the Legislative Council for a second time, or the Legislative Council refuses to pass an appropriation bill or any other important bill introduced by the government, and if a consensus still cannot be reached after consultations, the chief executive may dissolve the Legislative Council.

The chief executive shall consult the Executive Council before dissolving the Legislative Council. The chief executive may dissolve the Legislative Council only once in each term of his or her office.

Article 51. If the Legislative Council refuses to pass an appropriations bill introduced by the government, the chief executive may apply to the Legislative Council for temporary appropriations. If appropriation of public funds cannot be approved because the Legislative Council has already been dissolved, the chief executive may approve temporary short-term appropriations according to the level of the previous fiscal year's expenditure prior to the election of the new Legislative Council.

Article 52. The chief executive must resign under any of the following circumstances:
(1) If he or she loses the ability to discharge the functions of his or her office due to serious illness or other reasons;
(2) If, after the Legislative Council has been dissolved because the chief executive twice refused to sign a bill it passed, and the new Legislative Council has passed by a two-thirds majority the original bill in dispute, but the chief executive still refuses to sign it; or
(3) If, after the Legislative Council has been dissolved because it refused to approve an appropriations bill or any other important bill, the new Legislative Council still refuses to pass the original bill in dispute.

Article 53. If the chief executive of the Hong Kong SAR is not able to discharge his or her duties for a brief period, such duties shall temporarily be assumed by the administrative secretary, financial secretary, or secretary of justice, in this order.

In the event that the office of chief executive becomes vacant, a new chief executive shall be selected within six months in accordance with provisions of Article 45 of this law. During the period of vacancy, his or her duties shall be assumed according to the provisions of the preceding paragraph.

Article 54. The Executive Council of the Hong Kong SAR shall be an organ for assisting the chief executive in policy making.

Article 55. Members of the Executive Council of the Hong Kong SAR shall be appointed by the chief executive from among the principal officials of the executive authorities, members of the Legislative Council and public figures. Their appointment or removal shall be decided by the chief executive. The term of office of members shall not exceed that of the chief executive who appoints them.

Members of the Executive Council of the Hong Kong SAR shall be Chinese citizens who are permanent residents of the region and who do not have the right of residence in any foreign country.

The chief executive may invite other persons concerned to sit in on meetings of the Council as he or she deems necessary.

Article 56. The Executive Council of the Hong Kong SAR shall be presided over by the chief executive.

Except for the appointment, removal, or disciplining of officials and the adoption of measures in emergencies, the chief executive shall consult the Executive Council before making important policy decisions, introducing a bill to the Legislative Council, enacting subsidiary legislation or dissolving the Legislative Council.

If the chief executive does not adopt a majority opinion of the Executive Council, he or she shall put his or her specific reasons on record.

Article 57. A Commission Against Corruption shall be established in the Hong Kong SAR. It shall function independently and be accountable to the chief executive.

Article 58. An Audit Commission shall be established in the Hong Kong SAR. It shall function independently and be accountable to the chief executive.

Section II. The Executive Authorities

Article 59. The government of the Hong Kong SAR shall be the executive authorities of the region.

Article 60. The head of the government of the Hong Kong SAR shall be the chief executive of the region.

The Department of Administration, Department of Finance, Department of Justice, bureaus, divisions, and commissions shall be established in the government of the Hong Kong SAR.

Article 61. The principal officials of the Hong Kong SAR shall be Chinese citizens who do not have the right of residence of any foreign country, who are permanent residents, and who have ordinarily resided in Hong Kong for a continuous period of fifteen years.

Article 62. The government of the Hong Kong SAR shall exercise the following powers and functions:
(1) Formulating and implementing policies;
(2) Managing administrative affairs;
(3) Managing the external affairs authorized by the central people's government under this law;
(4) Drawing up and introducing budgets and final accounts;
(5) Drafting and introducing bills, motions, and subsidiary legislation; and
(6) Designating officials to sit in at the meetings of the Legislative Council and speak on behalf of the government.

Article 63. The Department of Justice of the Hong Kong SAR shall be the authority handling criminal prosecutions, free from any interference.

Article 64. The government of the Hong Kong SAR must abide by the law and shall be accountable to the Legislative Council of the region in the following areas implementing laws passed by the council and already in force; presenting regular reports on its work to the council; answering questions raised by members of the council; and obtaining approval from the council for taxation and public expenditure.

Article 65. The previous system of establishing advisory bodies by the executive authorities shall be maintained.

Section III. The Legislature
Article 66. The Legislative Council of the Hong Kong SAR shall be the legislature of the region.

Article 67. The Legislative Council of the Hong Kong SAR shall be composed of Chinese citizens who are permanent residents of the region and who do not have the right of residence in any foreign country. Permanent residents of the region who are not Chinese citizens, or who have the right of residence in a foreign country, may also be elected members of the Legislative Council; however, such members should not exceed 20 percent of the total members of the Legislative Council.

Article 68. The Legislative Council of the Hong Kong SAR shall be decided by election.
The method for forming the Legislative Council shall be specified in light of the actual situation in the Hong Kong SAR and in accordance with the principle of gradual and orderly progress. The ultimate aim shall be the selection of all the members of the Legislative Council through general election.
The specific method for forming the Legislative Council and the voting procedures for bills and motions are prescribed in Annex II, ''Method for the Formation of the Legislative Council of the Hong Kong SAR and Voting Procedures.''

Article 69. The term of office of the Legislative Council of the Hong Kong SAR shall be four years, except the first term, which shall be two years.

Article 70. If the Legislative Council of the Hong Kong SAR is dissolved by the chief executive in accordance with the provisions of this law, it shall, within three months, be reconstituted by election as prescribed by Article 68 of this law.

Article 71. The chairman of the Legislative Council of the Hong Kong SAR shall be elected from among the members of the Legislative Council.
The chairman of the Legislative Council of the Hong Kong SAR shall be a Chinese citizen no less than forty years of age, who does not have the right of residence in any foreign country, who is a permanent resident of the region, and who has ordinarily resided in Hong Kong for a continuous period of twenty years.

Article 72. The chairman of the Legislative Council of the Hong Kong SAR exercises the following powers and functions:
(1) Presiding over meetings;
(2) Deciding on the agenda, giving priority to bills introduced by the government for inclusion on the agenda;
(3) Deciding on the time of meetings;
(4) Calling special meetings during the recess;
(5) Calling emergency meetings at the request of the chief executive; and
(6) Other powers and functions as prescribed in the rules of procedure of the Legislative Council.

Article 73. The Legislative Council of the Hong Kong SAR shall exercise the following powers and functions:
(1) Enacting, amending, or repealing laws in accordance with the provisions of this law and legal procedures;
(2) Examining and approving budgets submitted by the government;
(3) Approving taxation and public expenditure;
(4) Hearing and debating the policy addresses of the chief executive;
(5) Raising questions on the work of the government;

(6) Holding debates on any issue concerning public interests;

(7) Endorsing the appointments and removals of the judges of the Court of Final Appeal and the chief judge of the High Court;

(8) Receiving and dealing with complaints from Hong Kong residents;

(9) If a motion initiated jointly by one-quarter of the members of the Legislative Council accuses the chief executive of a serious breach of the law or a dereliction of duty, and if he or she still refuses to resign, the council may, after passing a motion for investigation, give a mandate to the Chief Justice of the Court of Final Appeal to form and chair an independent investigating committee. The committee shall be responsible for carrying out the investigation and reporting its findings to the council. If the committee considers the evidence sufficient, the council may pass a motion of impeachment by a two-thirds majority and report it to the central people's government for a decision; and

(10) Summoning, as required when exercising the above powers and functions, the persons concerned to testify or give evidence.

Article 74.   Members of the Legislative Council of the Hong Kong SAR may introduce bills in accordance with the provisions of this law and legal procedures. Bills that do not relate to public expenditure or the structure and operation of the government may be introduced individually or jointly by members of the council. Written consent of the chief executive shall be required before bills relating to government policies are introduced.

Article 75.   The quorum for the meeting of the Legislative Council of the Hong Kong SAR shall be no less than one-half of its members.

The rules of procedure for the Legislative Council shall be established by the council on its own, but they shall not be inconsistent with this law.

Article 76.   A bill passed by the Legislative Council of the Hong Kong SAR shall take effect only after it is signed and promulgated by the chief executive.

Article 77.   Members of the Legislative Council of the Hong Kong SAR shall not be legally liable for speeches made at meetings of the council.

Article 78.   Members of the Legislative Council of the Hong Kong SAR shall not be subject to arrest when attending or on their way to a meeting of the Legislative Council.

Article 79.   The chairman of the Legislative Council shall declare that a member of the council is no longer qualified for the office under any of the following circumstances:

(1) When he or she loses the ability to discharge the functions of his or her office due to serious illness or other reasons;

(2) When he or she, with no valid reason, is absent from meetings for three consecutive months without the consent of the chairman of the Legislative Council;

(3) When he or she loses or renounces his or her status as a permanent resident of the Hong Kong SAR;

(4) When he or she accepts a government appointment and joins public service;

(5) When he or she is bankrupt or fails to comply with a court order to repay debts;

(6) When he or she is convicted and sentenced to imprisonment for one month or more for a criminal offense committed within or outside the Hong Kong SAR and is relieved of his or her duties by a motion by two-thirds of the members of the Legislative Council present; or

(7) When he or she is censured for misbehavior or breach of oath by a vote of two-thirds of the members of the Legislative Council present.

Section IV. Judicial Organs

Article 80.   The courts of the Hong Kong SAR at all levels shall be the judicial organs of the region, exercising the judicial power of the region.

Article 81.   The Court of Final Appeal, the High Court, district courts, magistrates' courts, and other special courts shall be established in the Hong Kong SAR. The High Court shall comprise the Court of Appeal and the Court of the First Instance.

The judicial system previously in practice in Hong Kong shall be maintained except for those changes consequent upon the establishment of the court of Final Appeal of the Hong Kong SAR.

Article 82.   The power of final adjudication of the Hong Kong SAR shall be vested in the Court of Final Appeal of the region, which may invite judges from other common law jurisdictions to sit on the Court of Final Appeal as required.

Article 83.   The structure, powers, and functions of the courts of the Hong Kong SAR at all levels shall be prescribed by law.

Article 84.   The courts of the Hong Kong SAR shall decide cases in accordance with the laws applicable in the region as prescribed in Article 18 of this law and may refer to precedents of other common law jurisdictions.

Article 85. The courts of the Hong Kong SAR shall exercise judicial power independently and free from any interference. Members of the judiciary shall be immune from legal action in respect of their judicial functions.

Article 86. The principle of trial by jury previously practiced in Hong Kong shall be maintained.

Article 87. In criminal or civil proceedings in the Hong Kong SAR the principles previously applied in Hong Kong and the rights previously enjoyed by the parties to the proceedings shall be maintained.

Anyone who is lawfully arrested shall have the right to a fair trial by the judicial organs without delay and shall be presumed innocent until convicted by the judicial organs.

Article 88. Judges of the courts of the Hong Kong SAR shall be appointed by the chief executive on the recommendation of an independent commission composed of local judges, persons from the legal profession and other eminent persons.

Article 89. A judge of a court of the Hong Kong SAR may be removed only for inability to discharge the functions of his/her office, or for misbehavior by the chief executive on the recommendation of a tribunal appointed by the chief justice of the Court of Final Appeal and consisting of no fewer than three local judges.

The chief justice of the Court of Final Appeal of the Hong Kong SAR may be investigated only for inability to discharge the functions of his/her office, or for misbehavior, by a tribunal appointed by the chief executive and consisting of no fewer than five local judges and may be removed by the chief executive on the recommendation of the tribunal and in accordance with the procedures prescribed in this law.

Article 90. The chief justice of the Court of Final Appeal and the chief judge of the High Court of the Hong Kong SAR shall be Chinese citizens who are permanent residents of the region and have no right of abode in foreign countries.

In addition to the procedures prescribed in Articles 88 and 89 of this law, the appointment and removal of judges of the Court of Final Appeal and the chief judge of the High Court of the Hong Kong SAR shall be made by the chief executive with the endorsement of the Legislative Council of the region and reported to the NPC Standing Committee for the record.

Article 91. The Hong Kong SAR shall maintain the previous system of appointment and removal of members of the judiciary other than judges.

Article 92. Judges and other members of the judiciary of the Hong Kong SAR shall be chosen by reference to their judicial and professional qualities and may be recruited from other common law jurisdictions.

Article 93. Judges and other members of the judiciary serving in Hong Kong before the establishment of the Hong Kong SAR may all remain in employment and retain their seniority with pay, allowances, benefits, and conditions of service no less favorable than before.

The government of the Hong Kong SAR shall pay to judges and other members of the judiciary who retire or leave the service in compliance with regulations as well as to those who have retired or left the service before the establishment of the Hong Kong SAR, or to their dependents, all pensions, gratuities, allowances, and benefits due to them on terms no less favorable than before, and irrespective of their nationality or place of residence.

Article 94. On the basis of the system previously operating in Hong Kong, the government of the Hong Kong SAR may make provisions for local lawyers and lawyers from outside Hong Kong to work and practice in the region.

Article 95. The Hong Kong SAR may, through consultation and in accordance with law, maintain judicial relations with the judicial organs of other parts of the country, and they may render assistance to each other.

Article 96. With the assistance or authorization of the central people's government, the government of the Hong Kong SAR may make appropriate arrangements with foreign states for reciprocal judicial assistance.

Section V. District Organizations

Article 97. District organizations that are not organs of political power may be established in the Hong Kong SAR, to be consulted by the government of the region on district administration and other affairs, or to be responsible for providing services in such fields as culture, recreation, and environmental sanitation.

Article 98. The powers and functions of the district organizations and their composition shall be prescribed by law.

Section VI. Public Servants

Article 99. Public servants serving in all government departments of the Hong Kong SAR must be permanent residents of the region, except where otherwise provided for in Article 101 regarding public servants of foreign nationalities in this law and except for those below a certain rank as prescribed by law.

Public servants must be dedicated to their duties and be responsible to the government of the Hong Kong SAR.

Article 100. Public servants serving in all Hong Kong government departments, including the police department, before the establishment of the Hong Kong SAR, may all remain in employment and retain their seniority with pay, allowances, benefits, and conditions of service no less favorable than before.

Article 101. The government of the Hong Kong SAR may employ British and other foreign nationals previously serving in the public service in Hong Kong, or those holding permanent identity cards of the region, to serve as public servants at all levels, but only Chinese citizens among permanent residents of the region who have no right of abode in foreign countries may fill the following posts: the secretaries and vice secretaries of departments, directors of bureaus, Commissioner Against Corruption, Director of Audit, Commissioner of Police, Director of Immigration and Commissioner of Customs.

The government of the Hong Kong SAR may also employ British and other foreign nationals as advisers to government departments and, when required, may recruit qualified candidates from outside the region to professional and technical posts in government departments. These foreign nationals shall be employed only in their individual capacities and shall be responsible to the government of the region.

Article 102. The government of the Hong Kong SAR shall pay to public servants who retire or leave the service in compliance with regulations as well as to those who have retired or left the service in compliance with regulations before the establishment of the Hong Kong SAR, or to their dependents, all pensions, gratuities, allowances, and benefits due to them on terms no less favorable than before and irrespective of their nationality or place of residence.

Article 103. The appointment and promotion of public servants shall be on the basis of their qualifications, experience and ability. Hong Kong's previous system of recruitment, employment, assessment, discipline, training, and management for the public service, including special bodies for their appointment, pay and conditions of service, shall be maintained, except for any provisions for privileged treatment of foreign nationals.

Article 104. The chief executive, principal officials, members of the Executive Council and of the Legislative Council, judges of courts at all levels and other members

of the judiciary in the Hong Kong SAR must be sworn in according to law when assuming office to pledge support for the Basic Law of the Hong Kong SAR of the PRC and loyalty to the Hong Kong SAR of the PRC.

Chapter V
Economy
Section I. Public Finance, Monetary Affairs, Trade, Industry, and Commerce

Article 105. The Hong Kong SAR shall, in accordance with law, protect the right of individuals and legal persons to the acquisition, use, disposal, and inheritance of private property and their right to compensation for lawful deprivation of their property.

Such compensation shall correspond to the real value of the property concerned and shall be freely convertible and paid without undue delay.

The ownership of enterprises and the investments from outside the region shall be protected by law.

Article 106. The Hong Kong SAR shall have independent finances.

The Hong Kong SAR shall use its financial revenues exclusively for its own purposes and they shall not be handed over to the central people's government.

The central people's government shall not levy taxes in the Hong Kong SAR.

Article 107. The Hong Kong SAR shall follow the principle of keeping expenditure within the limits of revenues in drawing up its budget, strive for a fiscal balance, avoid deficits, and ensure that the budget is commensurate with the growth rate of its gross domestic product.

Article 108. The Hong Kong SAR shall practice an independent taxation system.

The Hong Kong SAR shall, taking the low tax policy previously pursued in Hong Kong as reference, enact laws on its own concerning types of taxes, tax rates, tax reductions, exemptions, and other matters of taxation.

Article 109. The government of the Hong Kong SAR shall create an appropriate economic and legal environment for the maintenance of the status of Hong Kong as an international financial center.

Article 110. The monetary and financial systems of the Hong Kong SAR shall be prescribed by law.

The government of the Hong Kong SAR shall, on its own, formulate monetary and financial policies, safeguard the free operation of financial business and financial market, and regulate and supervise them in accordance with law.

Article 111. The Hong Kong dollar, as the legal tender in the Hong Kong SAR, shall continue to circulate.

The authority to issue Hong Kong currency shall be vested in the government of the Hong Kong SAR. The issue of Hong Kong currency must be backed by 100 percent reserve fund. The system regarding the issue of Hong Kong currency and the reserve fund system shall be prescribed by law.

The government of the Hong Kong SAR may authorize designated banks to issue or continue to issue Hong Kong currency under statutory authority, after satisfying itself that any issue of currency will be soundly based and that the arrangements for such issue are consistent with the object of maintaining the stability of the currency.

Article 112. No foreign exchange control policies shall be applied in the Hong Kong SAR. The Hong Kong dollar shall be applied in the Hong Kong SAR. The Hong Kong dollar shall be freely convertible.

Markets for foreign exchange, gold, securities, and futures shall continue.

The government of the Hong Kong SAR shall safeguard the free flow of all capital within, into, and out of the region.

Article 113. The Exchange Fund of the Hong Kong SAR shall be managed and controlled by the government of the region, primarily for regulating the exchange value of the Hong Kong dollar.

Article 114. The Hong Kong SAR shall maintain the status of a free port and shall not impose any tariff unless otherwise prescribed by law.

Article 115. The Hong Kong SAR shall pursue the policy of free trade and safeguard the free movement of goods, intangible assets, and capital.

Article 116. The Hong Kong SAR shall be a separate customs territory.

The Hong Kong SAR may, using the name "Hong Kong, China," participate in relevant international organizations and international trade agreements, including preferential trade arrangements, such as the General Agreement on Tariffs and Trade and arrangements regarding international trade in textiles.

Export quotas, tariff preferences, and other similar arrangements, which are obtained by the Hong Kong SAR or which were obtained and remained valid, shall be enjoyed exclusively by the region.

Article 117. The Hong Kong SAR may issue its own certificates of origin for products in accordance with prevailing rules of origin.

Article 118. The government of the Hong Kong SAR shall create an economic and legal environment for encouraging investments, technological progress, and the development of new industries.

Article 119. The government of the Hong Kong SAR shall formulate appropriate policies to promote and coordinate the development of various trades such as manufacturing, commerce, tourism, real estate, transport, public utilities, services, agriculture and fishery, and pay attention to environmental protection.

Section II. Land Leases

Article 120. All leases of land granted, decided upon or renewed before the establishment of the Hong Kong SAR, which extend beyond 30 June 1997, and all rights in relation to such leases, shall continue to be recognized and protected under the law of the region.

Article 121. As regards leases of land granted or renewed where the original leases contain no right of renewal, during the period from 27 May 1985 to 30 June 1997, which extend beyond 30 June 1997 and expire not later than 30 June 2047, the lessee is not required to pay any additional premium as from 1 July 1997, but an annual rent equivalent to 3 percent of the rateable value of the property at that date, adjusted in step with any changes in the rated value thereafter, shall be charged.

Article 122. In the case of old schedule lots, village lots, small houses, and similar rural holdings, where the property was on 30 June 1984 held by, or in the case of small houses granted after that date, where property is granted to, a lessee descended through the male line from a person who was in 1898 a resident of an established village in Hong Kong, the previous rent shall remain unchanged so long as the property is held by that lessee or by one of his lawful successors in the male line.

Article 123. Where leases of land without a right of renewal expire after the establishment of the Hong Kong SAR, they shall be dealt with in accordance with laws and policies formulated by the region on its own.

Section III. Shipping

Article 124. The Hong Kong SAR shall maintain Hong Kong's previous systems of shipping management and shipping regulation, including the system of management concerning seamen.

The government of the Hong Kong SAR shall, on its own, define its specific functions and responsibilities in respect of shipping.

Article 125. The Hong Kong SAR shall be authorized by the central people's government to continue to maintain a shipping register and issue related certificates under its legislation, using the name "Hong Kong, China."

Article 126. With the exception of foreign warships, access for which requires the special permission of the central people's government, ships shall enjoy access to the ports of the Hong Kong SAR in accordance with the laws of the region.

Article 127. Private shipping businesses and shipping-related businesses and private container terminals in the Hong Kong SAR may continue to operate freely.

Section IV. Civil Aviation

Article 128. The government of the Hong Kong SAR shall create conditions and take measures for the maintenance of the status of Hong Kong as a center of international and regional aviation.

Article 129. The Hong Kong SAR shall continue the previous system of civil aviation management and keep its own aircraft register in accordance with provisions laid down by the central people's government concerning nationality and registration marks of aircraft.

Access of foreign aircraft to the Hong Kong SAR requires the permission of the central people's government.

Article 130. The Hong Kong SAR shall be responsible on its own for matters of routine business and technical management of civil aviation, including the management of airports, the provision of air traffic services within the flight information region of the Hong Kong SAR, and the discharge of other responsibilities allocated to it under the regional air navigation procedures of the International Civil Aviation Organization.

Article 131. The central people's government shall, in consultation with the government of the Hong Kong SAR, make arrangements providing for air services between the region and other parts of the PRC for airlines incorporated in the Hong Kong SAR and having their principal place of business in Hong Kong and other airlines of the PRC.

Article 132. All air service agreements providing for air services between other parts of the PRC and other states and regions with stops at the Hong Kong SAR and for air services between the Hong Kong SAR and other states and regions with stops at other parts of the PRC shall be concluded by the central people's government.

In concluding the air service agreements referred to in the first paragraph of this article, the central people's government shall take account of the special conditions and economic interests of the Hong Kong SAR and consult the government of the Hong Kong SAR.

Representatives of the Hong Kong SAR may partici-pate, as members of the delegations of the government of the PRC, in air service consultations with foreign governments concerning arrangements for such services referred to in the first paragraph of this article.

Article 133. Acting under specific authorizations from the central people's government, the government of the Hong Kong SAR may
(1) renew or amend air service agreements and arrangements previously in force;
(2) negotiate and conclude new air service agreements providing routes for airlines incorporated in the Hong Kong SAR and having their principal place of business in Hong Kong and rights for over-flights and technical stops; and
(3) negotiate and conclude provisional arrangements with foreign states or regions with which no air service agreements have been concluded.

All scheduled air services to, from, or through Hong Kong that do not operate to, from, or through the mainland of China shall be regulated by the air service agreements or provisional arrangements referred to in this article.

Article 134. The central people's government shall give the government of the Hong Kong SAR the authority to:
(1) negotiate and conclude with other authorities all arrangements concerning the implementation of the air service agreements and provisional arrangements referred to in Article 133 of this law;
(2) issue licenses to airlines incorporated in the Hong Kong SAR and having their principal place of business in Hong Kong;
(3) designate such airlines under the air service agreements and provisional arrangements referred to in Article 133 of this law; and
(4) issue permits to foreign airlines for services other than those to, from, or through the mainland of China.

Article 135. Airlines incorporated and having their principal place of business in Hong Kong and civil aviation-related businesses there prior to the establishment of the Hong Kong SAR may continue to operate.

Chapter VI
Education, Science, Culture, Sports,
Religion, Labor, and Social Services

Article 136. On the basis of the previous educational system, the government of the Hong Kong SAR shall, on its own, formulate policies on the development and improvement of education, including policies regarding the educational system and its administration, the language of instruction, the allocation of funds, the examination system, the system of academic awards, and the recognition of education qualifications.

Community organizations and individuals may, in accordance with the law, run educational undertakings of various kinds in the Hong Kong SAR.

Article 137. Educational institutions of all kinds may retain their autonomy and enjoy academic freedom. They may continue to recruit staff and use teaching materials from outside the Hong Kong SAR. Schools run by religious organizations may continue to provide religious education, including courses on religion.

Students shall enjoy freedom of choice of educational institutions and freedom to pursue their education outside the Hong Kong SAR.

Article 138. The government of the Hong Kong SAR shall, on its own, formulate policies to develop Western and traditional Chinese medicine and to improve medical and health services. Community organizations and individuals may provide medical and health services in accordance with law.

Article 139. The government of the Hong Kong SAR shall, on its own, formulate policies on science and technology and protect by law achievements in scientific and technological research, patents, discoveries, and inventions.

The government of the Hong Kong SAR shall, on its own, decide on the scientific and technological standards and specifications applicable in Hong Kong.

Article 140. The government of the Hong Kong SAR shall, on its own, formulate policies on culture and protect by law the achievements and the legitimate rights and interests of authors in their literary and artistic pursuits.

Article 141. The government of the Hong Kong SAR shall not restrict the freedom of religious beliefs, interfere in the internal affairs of religious organizations, or restrict religious activities that do not contravene the law of the Hong Kong SAR.

Religious organizations shall, in accordance with law, enjoy the rights to acquire, use, dispose of, and inherit property and the right to receive financial assistance. Their previous property rights and interests shall be maintained and protected.

Religious organizations may, according to their previous practice, continue to run seminaries and other schools, hospitals, and welfare institutions and to provide other social services.

Religious organizations and believers in the Hong Kong SAR may maintain and develop their relations with religious organizations and believers elsewhere.

Article 142. The government of the Hong Kong SAR shall, on the basis of maintaining the previous systems concerning the professions, work out on its own the methods of assessing the qualifications for professional practice for the various professions.

Persons with professional qualifications or qualifications for professional practice obtained prior to the establishment of the Hong Kong SAR may retain their previous qualifications, in accordance with the relevant regulations and codes of practice.

The government of the Hong Kong SAR shall continue to recognize the professions and the professional organizations recognized prior to the establishment of the Hong Kong SAR, and these organizations may, on their own, assess and accredit professional qualifications.

The government of the Hong Kong SAR may, as required by developments in society and in consultation with the parties concerned, recognize new professions and professional organizations.

Article 143. The government of the Hong Kong SAR shall, on its own, formulate policies on sports. Nongovernmental sports organizations may continue to exist and develop in accordance with law.

Article 144. The government of the Hong Kong SAR shall maintain the policy previously practiced in Hong Kong in respect of subventions for nongovernmental organizations in fields such as education, medicine and health, culture, art, recreation, sports, social welfare, and social work. Staff previously serving in subventioned organizations in Hong Kong may remain in their employment in accordance with the previous system.

Article 145. On the basis of the previous social welfare system, the government of the Hong Kong SAR shall, on its own, formulate policies on the development and improvement of this system in the light of economic conditions and social needs.

Article 146. Voluntary organizations providing social services in the Hong Kong SAR may, on their own, decide their forms of service, provided that the laws of the Hong Kong SAR are not contravened.

Article 147. The government of the Hong Kong SAR shall formulate labor laws and policies on its own.

Article 148. The relationship between nongovernmental organizations in fields such as education, science, technology, culture, art, sports, the professions, medicine and health, labor, social welfare, and social work as well as religious organizations in the Hong Kong SAR and their counterparts on the mainland shall be based on the principles of nonsubordination, noninterference and mutual respect.

Article 149. Nongovernmental organizations in fields such as education, science, technology, culture, art, sports, the professions, medicine and health, labor, social welfare, and social work as well as religious organizations in the Hong Kong SAR may maintain and develop relations with foreign countries and other regions and with relevant international organizations. They may, as required, use the name "Hong Kong, China" in the relevant activities.

Chapter VII
External Affairs

Article 150. Representatives of the government of the Hong Kong SAR may participate, as members of delegations of the government of the PRC, in negotiations conducted by the central people's government at the diplomatic level and directly affecting the Hong Kong SAR.

Article 151. The Hong Kong SAR may, on its own, using the name "Hong Kong, China," maintain and develop relations and conclude and implement agreements with states, regions, and relevant international organizations in appropriate fields, including the economic, trade, financial and monetary, shipping, communications, tourism, cultural, and sports fields.

Article 152. Representatives of the government of the Hong Kong SAR may participate, as members of delegations of the government of the PRC, in international organizations or conferences in appropriate fields limited to states and affecting the Hong Kong SAR, or may attend in such other capacity as may be permitted by the central people's government and the international organization or conference concerned, and may express their views, using the name "Hong Kong, China."

The Hong Kong SAR may, using the name "Hong Kong, China," participate in international organizations and conferences not limited to states.

The central people's government shall take the necessary steps to ensure that the Hong Kong SAR shall continue to retain its status in an appropriate capacity in those international organizations of which the PRC is a member and in which Hong Kong participates in one capacity or another.

The central people's government shall, where necessary, facilitate the continued participation of the Hong Kong SAR in an appropriate capacity in those international organizations in which Hong Kong is a participant in one capacity or another, but of which the PRC is not a member.

Article 153. The application to the Hong Kong SAR of international agreements to which the PRC is or becomes a party shall be decided by the central people's government, in accordance with the circumstances and needs of the Hong Kong SAR and after seeking the views of the government of the Hong Kong SAR.

International agreements to which the PRC is not a party but which are implemented in Hong Kong may continue to be implemented in the Hong Kong SAR. The central people's government shall, as necessary, authorize or assist the government of the Hong Kong SAR to make appropriate arrangements for the application to the Hong Kong SAR of other relevant international agreements.

Article 154. The central people's government shall authorize the government of the Hong Kong SAR to issue, in accordance with law, passports of the Hong Kong SAR of the PRC to all Chinese citizens who hold permanent identity cards of the Hong Kong SAR, and travel documents of the Hong Kong SAR of the PRC to all other persons lawfully residing in the Hong Kong SAR. The above passports and documents shall be valid for all states and regions and shall record the holder's right to return to the Hong Kong SAR.

The government of the Hong Kong SAR may apply immigration controls on entry into, stays in and departures from the Hong Kong SAR by persons from foreign states and regions.

Article 155. The central people's government shall assist or authorize the government of the Hong Kong SAR to conclude visa exemption agreements with states or regions.

Article 156. The Hong Kong SAR may, as necessary, establish official or semiofficial economic and trade missions in foreign countries and shall report the establishment of such missions to the central people's government for the record.

Article 157. The establishment of foreign consular and other official or semiofficial missions in the Hong Kong SAR shall require the approval of the central people's government.

Consular and other official missions established in Hong Kong by states that have formal diplomatic relations with the PRC may be maintained.

According to the circumstances of each case, consular and other official missions established in Hong Kong by states that have no formal diplomatic relations with the PRC may be permitted either to remain or be changed to semiofficial missions.

States not recognized by the PRC may only establish nongovernmental institutions in the Hong Kong SAR.

Chapter VIII
Interpretation and Amendment of the Basic Law

Article 158.   The power of interpretation of this law shall be vested in the NPC Standing Committee.

The NPC Standing Committee shall authorize the courts of the Hong Kong SAR to interpret on their own, in adjudicating cases before them, the provisions of this law that are within the limits of the autonomy of the region.

The courts of the Hong Kong SAR may also interpret other provisions of this law in adjudicating cases before them. However, if the courts of the region, in adjudicating cases before them, need to interpret the provisions of this law concerning affairs that are the responsibility of the central people's government, or the relationship between the central authorities and the region, and if such interpretation will affect the judgments on the cases, the courts of the region shall, before making their final judgments that are not open to appeal, seek an interpretation of the relevant provisions from the NPC Standing Committee through the Court of Final Appeal of the region. When the NPC Standing Committee makes an interpretation of the provisions concerned, the courts of the region, in applying those provisions, shall follow the interpretation of the NPC Standing Committee. However, judgments previously rendered shall not be affected.

The NPC Standing Committee shall consult its committee for the Basic Law of the Hong Kong SAR before giving an interpretation of this law.

Article 159.   The power of amendment of this law shall be vested in the NPC.

The power to propose amendments to this law shall be vested in the NPC Standing Committee, the State Council, and the Hong Kong SAR. Amendment proposals from the Hong Kong SAR shall be submitted to the NPC by the delegation of the region to the NPC after obtaining the consent of two-thirds of the deputies of the region to the NPC, two-thirds of all the members of the Legislative Council of the region, and the chief executive of the region.

Before a proposal for an amendment to this law is put on the agenda of the NPC, the Committee for the Basic Law of the Hong Kong SAR shall study it and submit its views.

No amendment to this law shall contravene the established basic principles and policies of the PRC regarding Hong Kong.

Chapter IX
Supplementary Provisions

Article 160.   Upon the establishment of the Hong Kong SAR, the laws previously in force in Hong Kong shall be adopted as laws of the region except for those which the NPC Standing Committee declares to be inconsistent with this law. If any laws are later discovered to be inconsistent with this law, they shall be revised or cease to have force in accordance with the procedure as prescribed by this law.

Documents, certificates, contracts and rights, and obligations valid under the laws previously in force in Hong Kong shall continue to be valid and be recognized and protected by the Hong Kong SAR provided that they are not inconsistent with this law.

Report of China's State Council on Human Rights in China

The Tiananmen incident led to worldwide condemnation of the Chinese government's handling of the affair and to increasing international scrutiny of the human rights situation in China. In response to persistent criticism of the country's human rights record and reports of ongoing violations, China's State Council issued a "white paper" on human rights in November 1991, excerpted below.

Preface

It has been a long-cherished ideal of mankind to enjoy human rights in the full sense of the term. Since this great term—human rights—was coined centuries ago, people of all nations have achieved great results in their unremitting struggle for human rights. However, on a global scale, modern society has fallen far short of the lofty goal of securing the full range of human rights for people the world over. And this is why numerous people with lofty ideals are still working determinedly for this cause.

Under long years of oppression by the "three big mountains"—imperialism, feudalism and bureaucrat-capitalism—people in old China did not have any human rights to speak of. Suffering bitterly from this, the Chinese people fought for more than a century, defying death and personal sacrifices and advancing wave upon wave, in an arduous struggle to overthrow the "three big mountains" and gain their human rights. The situation in respect to human rights in China took a basic turn for the better after the founding of the People's Republic of China. Greatly treasuring this hard-won achievement, the Chinese government and people have spared no effort to safeguard human rights and steadily improve their human rights situation, and have achieved remarkable results. This has won full confirmation and fair appraisal from all people who have a real understanding of Chinese conditions and who are not prejudiced.

The issue of human rights has become one of great significance and common concern in the world community. The series of declarations and conventions adopted by the UN have won the support and respect of many countries. The Chinese government has also highly appraised the Universal Declaration of Human Rights, considering it the first international human rights document that has laid the foundation for the practice of human rights in the world arena.

However, the evolution of the situation in regard to human rights is circumscribed by the historical, social, economic, and cultural conditions of various nations, and involves a process of historical development. Because of tremendous differences in historical background, social system, cultural tradition, and economic development, countries differ in their understanding and practice of human rights. From their different situations, they have taken different attitudes toward the relevant United Nations conventions. Despite its international aspect, the issue of human rights falls by and large within the sovereignty of each country. Therefore, a country's human rights situation should not be judged in total disregard of its history and national conditions, nor can it be evaluated according to a preconceived model or the conditions of another country or region. Such is the practical attitude, the attitude of seeking truth from facts.

From their own historical conditions, the realities of their own country and their long practical experience, the Chinese people have derived their own viewpoints on the human rights issue and formulated relevant laws and policies. It is stipulated in the Constitution of the People's Republic of China that all power in the People's Republic of China belongs to the people. Chinese human rights have three salient characteristics.

First, extensiveness. It is not a minority of the people or part of a class or social stratum but the entire Chinese citizenry who constitutes the subject enjoying human rights. The human rights enjoyed by the Chinese citizenry encompass an extensive scope, including not only survival, personal, and political rights but also economic, cultural, and social rights. The state pays full attention to safeguarding both individual and collective rights.

Second, equality. China has adopted the socialist system after abolishing the system of exploitation and eliminating the exploiting classes. The Chinese citizenry enjoys all civic rights equally irrespective of money and property status as well as of nationality, race, sex, occupation, family background, religion, level of education, and duration of residence.

Third, authenticity. The state provides guarantees in terms of system, laws and material means for the realization of human rights. The various civic rights prescribed in the constitution and other state laws are in accord with what people enjoy in real life. China's human rights legislation and policies are endorsed and supported by the people of all nationalities and social strata and by all the political parties, social organizations, and all walks of life.

As a developing country, China has suffered from setbacks while safeguarding and developing human rights. Although much has been achieved in this regard, there is still much room for improvement. It remains a long-term historical task for the Chinese people and government to continue to promote human rights and strive for the noble goal of full implementation of human rights as required by China's socialism.

In order to help the international community to understand the human rights situation as it is in China, we present the following brief account of China's basic position on and practice of human rights.

I. The Right to Subsistence—The Foremost Human Right the Chinese People Long Fight for

It is a simple truth that, for any country or nation, the right to subsistence is the most important of all human rights, without which the other rights are out of the question. The Universal Declaration of Human Rights affirms that everyone has the right to life, liberty, and personal security. In old China, aggression by imperialism and oppression by feudalism and bureaucrat-capitalism deprived the people of all guarantee for their lives, and an innumerable number of them perished in war and famine. To solve their human rights problems, the first thing for the Chinese people to do is, for historical reasons, to secure the right to subsistence.

Without national independence, there would be no guarantee for the people's lives. When imperialist aggression became the major threat to their lives, the Chinese people had to win national independence before they could gain the right to subsistence. After the Opium War of 1840, China, hitherto a big feudal kingdom, was gradually turned into a semicolonial, semifeudal country. During the 110 years from 1840 to 1949, the British, French, Japanese, U.S., and Russian imperialist powers waged hundreds of wars on varying scales against China, causing immeasurable losses to the lives and property of the Chinese people.

- The imperialists massacred Chinese people in untold numbers during their aggressive wars. In 1900, the troops of the eight allied powers—Germany, Japan, Britain, Russia, France, the United States, Italy, and Austria—killed, burned and looted, razing Tanggu, a town of 50,000 residents, to utter ruins, reducing Tianjin's population from 1 million to 100,000, killing countless people when they entered Beijing, where more than 1,700 were slaughtered at Zhuangwangfu alone. During Japan's full-scale invasion of China, which began in 1937, more than 21 million people were killed or wounded and 10 million people mutilated to death. In the six weeks beginning from 13

December 1937, the Japanese invaders killed 300,000 people in Nanjing.

- The imperialists sold, maltreated, and caused the death of numerous Chinese laborers, plunging countless people in old China into an abyss of misery. According to incomplete statistics, more than 12 million indentured Chinese laborers were sold to various parts of the world from the mid-nineteenth century through the 1920s. Coaxed and abducted, these laborers were thrown into lockups, known as ''pigsties,'' where they were branded with the names of their would-be destinations. Between 1852 and 1858 40,000 people were put in such ''pigsties'' in Shantou alone, and more than 8,000 of them were done to death there. Equally horrifying was the death toll of ill-treated laborers in factories and mines run by imperialists across China. During the Japanese occupation, no less than 2 million laborers perished from maltreatment and exhaustion in Northeast China. Once the laborers died, their remains were thrown into mountain gullies or pits dug into bare hillsides. So far more than 80 such massive pits have been found, with over 700,000 skeletons in them.
- Under the imperialists' colonial rule, the Chinese people had their fill of humiliation and there was no personal dignity to speak of. The foreign aggressors enjoyed ''extraterritoriality'' in those days. . . .
- Forcing more than 1,100 unequal treaties on China, the imperialists plundered Chinese wealth on a large scale. Statistics show that, by way of these unequal treaties, the foreign aggressors made away with more than 100 billion taels of silver as war indemnities and other payments in the past century. Through the Sino-British Treaty of Nanjing, the Sino-Japanese Treaty of Shimonoseki, the International Protocol of 1901 and five other such treaties alone, 1.953 billion taels of silver in indemnity were extorted, sixteen times the 1901 revenue of the Qing government. The Treaty of Shimonoseki alone earned Japan 230 million taels of silver in extortion money, about four and a half times its annual national revenue. The losses resulting from the destruction and looting by the invaders in wars against China were even more incalculable. During Japan's full-scale war of aggression against China (1937-45), 930 Chinese cities were occupied, causing $62 billion in direct losses and $500 billion in indirect losses. With their state sovereignty impaired and their social wealth plundered or destroyed, the Chinese people were deprived of the basic conditions for survival.

In face of the crumbling state sovereignty and the calamities wrought upon their lives, for over a century the Chinese people fought the foreign aggressors in an indomitable struggle for national salvation and independence. The Taiping Heavenly Kingdom Movement, the Boxers Movement, and the Revolution of 1911, which overthrew the Qing dynasty, broke out during this period. These revolutionary movements dealt heavy blows to imperialist influences in China, but they failed to deliver the nation from semicolonialism.

A fundamental change took place only after the Chinese people, under the leadership of the Chinese Communist Party, overthrew the Kuomintang reactionary rule and founded the People's Republic of China. After its birth in 1921, the Chinese Communist Party set the clear-cut goal in its political program to ''overthrow the oppression by international imperialism and achieve the complete independence of the Chinese nation'' and to ''overthrow the warlords and unite China into a real democratic republic''; it led the people in an arduous struggle culminating in victory in the national democratic revolution. . . .

The Chinese people have won the basic guarantee for their life and security.

National independence has protected the Chinese people from being trodden under the heels of foreign invaders. However, the problem of the people's right to subsistence can be truly solved only when their basic means of livelihood are guaranteed.

To eat their fill and dress warmly were the fundamental demand of the Chinese people who had long suffered cold and hunger. Far from meeting this demand, successive regimes in old China brought even more disasters to the people. In those days, landlords and rich peasants who accounted for 10 percent of the rural population held 70 percent of the land, while the poor peasants and farm laborers who accounted for 70 percent of the rural population owned only 10 percent of the land. The bureaucrat-comprador bourgeoisie who accounted for only a small fraction of the population monopolized 80 percent of the industrial capital and controlled the economic lifelines of the country. The Chinese people were repeatedly exploited by land rent, taxes, usury, and industrial and commercial capital. . . .

Ever since the founding of the People's Republic of China in 1949, the Chinese Communist Party and the Chinese government have always placed the task of helping the people get enough to wear and eat on the top of the agenda. For the first three years of the People's Republic, the Chinese people, led by their government, concentrated their efforts on healing the wounds of war and quickly restored the national economy to the record level in history. On this basis, China lost no time to complete the socialist transformation of agriculture, handicraft industry, and capitalist industry and commerce, thus uprooting the system of exploitation, instituting the system of socialism and, for the first time in history, turning the people into masters of the means of production and beneficiaries of social wealth.

This fired the people with soaring enthusiasm for building a new China and a new life, emancipated the social productive forces and set the economy on the track of unprecedented growth. Since 1979, China has switched the focus of its work to economic construction, begun reform and opening to the outside world, and set the goal of building socialism with Chinese characteristics. This has further expanded the social productive forces and enabled the nation to basically solve the problem of feeding and clothing its 1.1 billion people. ...

The problem of food and clothing having been basically solved, the people have been guaranteed the basic right to subsistence. This is a historical achievement made by the Chinese people and government in seeking and protecting human rights.

However, to protect the people's right to subsistence and improve their living conditions remains an issue of paramount importance in China today. China has gained independence, but it is still a developing country with limited national strength. The preservation of national independence and state sovereignty and the freedom from imperialist subjugation are, therefore, the very fundamental conditions for the survival and development of the Chinese people. Although China has basically solved the problem of food and clothing, its economy is still at a fairly low level, its standard of living falls considerably short of that in developed countries, and the pressure of a huge population and relative per-capita paucity of resources will continue to restrict the socioeconomic development and the improvement of the people's lives. The people's right to subsistence will still be threatened in the event of a social turmoil or other disasters.

Therefore it is the fundamental wish and demand of the Chinese people and a long-term, urgent task of the Chinese government to maintain national stability, concentrate their effort on developing the productive forces along the line that has proved to be successful, persist in reform and opening to the outside world, strive to rejuvenate the national economy and boost the national strength, and, on the basis of having solved the problem of food and clothing, secure a well-off livelihood for the people throughout the country so that their right to subsistence will no longer be threatened.

II. The Chinese People Have Gained Extensive Political Rights

While struggling for the right to subsistence, the Chinese people have waged a heroic struggle for democratic rights.

The people did not have any democratic rights to speak of in semifeudal, semicolonial China. The Revolution of 1911 led by Dr. Sun Yat-sen, the great forerunner of bourgeois-democratic revolution, overthrew the feudal Qing dynasty and gave rise to the Republic of China. He hoped to establish a Western-style democratic system in China, but the fruits of the revolution were snatched by Yuan Shikai, a feudal warlord. The parliament became a mere instrument for warlords in power struggle, and there occurred the scandal of the "parliament of pigs" and the bribery in electing a president. His dream unfulfilled, Dr. Sun died in sorrow and indignation, which found expression in his famous admonition "The revolution has not yet succeeded." Many Chinese had cherished illusions about the U.S.-supported Chiang Kai-shek government. However, Chiang turned out to be just another warlord under whose fascist rule millions of democracy-seeking people perished in bloody massacres. He adopted a nonresistance policy toward the Japanese invasion while stepping up the civil war, ignoring opposition from the Chinese Communists, patriots, and democrats from all walks of life and the broad masses of the people. He launched the all-out civil war after the victory of the War of Anti-Japanese Resistance, again violating the ardent wish for peace, democracy, and reconstruction of the Communist Party, the democratic parties and the people throughout China. Driven beyond the limits of forbearance, the people rose up in arms and in the end toppled Chiang's reactionary rule.

Since the very day of its founding, the Chinese Communist Party has been holding high the banner of democracy and human rights. It encouraged and assisted Dr. Sun in reorganizing the Kuomintang, effected the cooperation between the Kuomintang and the Communist Party and launched the Northern Expedition against the reactionary rule of the warlords. After Chiang Kai-shek betrayed the democratic revolution, the party united all patriots and democrats and led the people in a struggle against civil war, hunger, autocracy, and persecution. In the liberated areas it established democratic governments, drew up laws that guaranteed the people's democratic rights, and resolutely implemented its own democratic program. The democratic system in the liberated areas attracted numerous patriotic and democratic fighters and became the hope of the entire people. Under the party's leadership, the Chinese people overthrew the Kuomintang reactionaries' dictatorial rule and founded the democratic and free People's Republic of China.

The Chinese people gained real democratic rights after the founding of new China. In explicit terms the constitution stipulates that all power in the People's Republic of China belongs to the people. That the people are masters of their own country is the essence of China's democratic politics. By stating that the People's Republic of China is a socialist state of the people's democratic dictatorship led by the working class and based on the alliance of workers and peasants, the constitution has established the status of the workers, peasants, and other working people as masters of the country and thus invested the people who were at the bottom rung of the social ladder in old China with lawful democratic rights. Equality of men and women, as provided by the constitution, has enabled women, who account for half the Chinese population, to gain the same rights as men in politics, economy, culture, society, and family life. The stipulation that all nationalities in China are equal has ensured that all the nation's minority nationalities enjoy equal democratic rights with the Han people.

To guarantee that the people are the real masters of the country with the right to run the country's economic and social affairs, China has adopted, in light of its actual conditions, the people's congresses as the state's basic political system. Deputies to the people's congresses at all levels are chosen through democratic elections. The Constitution stipulates that all citizens of the People's Republic of China who have reached the age of eighteen have the right to vote and stand for election, regardless of nationality, race, sex, occupation, family background, religious belief, education, property status, or length of residence, with the exception of persons deprived of their political rights by law.

Taking into consideration its vast territory, large population, inconvenient transportation, and relatively low economic and cultural development, China has adopted an election system appropriate to its actual conditions. That is, deputies to people's congresses at the county level or below are elected directly, while those to people's congresses above the county level are elected indirectly. This election system makes it possible for the people to choose deputies whom they know and trust. The election system has been improved in recent years on the basis of past experience. For instance, more candidates are posted than the number of deputies to be elected, instead of an equal number as before.

The right to vote has been widely exercised by the Chinese people. According to statistics from the 1990 county- and township-level direct elections, 99.97 percent of the citizens at eighteen years of age or above enjoyed the right to vote. Generally speaking, upward of 90 percent of the voters participate in the elections held in the various provinces, autonomous regions, and municipalities.

The most striking characteristic of China's electoral system is that elections are not manipulated by money and that deputies are not elected on the basis of boasting and empty promises but according to their actual contributions to the country and society, their attitude in serving the people and their close relations with the people. It is clear from the election results that the elected are broadly representative, that is, representative of people of all social strata and all trades and professions. Of the 2,970 deputies to the Seventh National People's Congress, 684, or 23 percent, are workers and farmers; 697, or 23.4 percent, are intellectuals; 733, or 24.7 percent, are government functionaries; 540, or 18.2 percent, are democratic party members and patriots with no party affiliation; 267, or 9 percent, are from the People's Liberation Army; and 49, or 1.6 percent, are returned overseas Chinese.

The National People's Congress is the supreme organ of state power. It has legislative power, and elects or removes the president and vice presidents of the People's Republic of China, the chairman of the Central Military Commission, the president of the Supreme People's Court and procurator-general of the Supreme People's Procuratorate; and appoints or removes the premier, vice premiers, state councilors, ministers, ministers in charge of commissions, the auditor-general, and the secretary general. All administrative, judicial, and procuratorial organs of the state are created by the National People's Congress, responsible to it and supervised by it.

Following the principle of democratic centralism, the National People's Congress adopts major policy decisions after full airing of opinions; once adopted, these policies are carried out in a concerted effort. In this way, the People's Congress can not only represent the people's common will but also become instrumental for the people in running state, economic, and social affairs. Coming from among the people, the people's deputies are responsible to the people and supervised by the people; their close contact with the masses and wide knowledge of the actual situation enable them to fully reflect the people's wishes, formulate laws suited to reality, and supervise the work of government organs.

The Chinese Communist Party is the ruling party of socialist China and the representative of the interests of the people throughout the country. Its leadership position has been the result of the historical choice made by the Chinese people during their protracted and arduous struggle for independence and emancipation. The leadership of the party is mainly an ideological and political leadership. The party derives its ideas and policies from the people's concentrated will and then turns them into state laws and decisions that are passed by the National People's Congress through the state's legal procedures. The party does not take the place of the government in the state's leadership system. The party conducts its activities within the framework of the constitution and the law and has no right to transcend the constitution and the law. All party members, like all citizens in the country, are equal before the law.

The system of multiparty cooperation and political consultation under the leadership of the Communist Party is the basic political system that gives expression to people's democracy. It guarantees that all social strata, people's organizations, and patriots from various quarters can express their opinions and play a role in the country's political and social life. There are in China eight democratic parties apart from the Communist Party; they are the Revolutionary Committee of the Chinese Kuomintang, the China Democratic League, the China Democratic National Construction Association, the China Association for Promoting Democracy, the Chinese Peasants and Workers Democratic Party, the China Zhigongdang

(Party for Public Interest), the Jiu-San Society (3 September Society), and the Taiwan Democratic Self-Government League.

Cooperation between the Communist Party and these democratic parties took shape during the democratic revolution before 1949, the year new China was founded. The leading role of the Communist Party in the cooperation is recognized by the democratic parties as it has been evolved in long years of common struggle. These democratic parties shared with the Communist Party the same basic political ideas whether in the struggle for overthrowing the "three big mountains" or during the period of building new China. Enjoying political freedom and organizational independence, all these democratic parties have developed greatly. They are neither parties out of office nor opposition parties, but parties participating in state affairs.

As China's ruling party, the Communist Party repeatedly asks these democratic parties for their opinions on every major state affair and consult with them for solutions. Relations between the Communist Party and the democratic parties follow the guideline of "long-term coexistence and mutual supervision, treating each other with full sincerity and sharing weal or woe." Full play has been given to the role of the democratic parties in participating in and discussing state affairs, democratic supervision and uniting all the people. Many members of the democratic parties have assumed leading posts in organs of state power, government departments, and judicial organs. Of the nineteen vice chairmen elected by the Seventh National People's Congress at its first session, seven are members of democratic parties. Nearly 1,200 members of the democratic parties and personages with no party affiliations are holding leading posts in governments above the county level.

The Chinese People's Political Consultative Conference (CPPCC) consists of representatives of all the political parties and people's organizations and from among patriots and democrats who support socialism and the reunification of the motherland. New China's first central people's government was elected by the first Chinese People's Political Consultative Conference. After the establishment of the National People's Congress as the supreme organ of state power, the CPPCC became an organization of the patriotic united front. It provides a forum for discussions on major state policies and principles and big issues in social life and plays a supervisory role through suggestions and criticisms. The CPPCC usually convenes simultaneously with the people's congress at the corresponding level. The system of political consultation has played an important role in promoting democracy.

China attaches great importance to the promotion of democracy at the grass-roots level so as to guarantee that citizens can directly exercise their political rights. Neighborhood committees are the grass-roots democratic organizations in urban areas, and their counterparts in rural areas are village committees. As self-governing organizations established by the people, these committees deal with matters concerning public welfare and residents' well-being while assisting local governments in mediating family and neighborhood disputes, conducting ideological education, and maintaining public order. Most Chinese enterprises have adopted the system of workers' congress, which is the basic form of democratic management through which workers participate in the decision-making and management of the enterprises and supervise the enterprise leaders. Over the last few years, virtually all directors and managers of large and medium-size state enterprises have been examined and their work appraised with the participation and supervision of the workers' congresses.

The constitution provides for a wide range of political rights to citizens. In addition to the right to vote and to be elected mentioned above, citizens also enjoy freedoms of speech, the press, assembly, association, procession, and demonstration. There is no news censorship in China. Statistics show that of all the newspapers and magazines in China, only one-fifth are run by party and state organizations, and the others belong to various democratic parties, social organizations, academic associations, and people's organizations. By law citizens have the right to intellectual property, such as copyright, and the right to publication, patent, trademark, discovery, invention, and scientific and technological achievement. It is a matter of personal freedom for a citizen to decide what book he will write, what point of view he will use in writing it, and which publishing house he will choose to have his book published. Statistics show that an overwhelming majority of the 80,224 titles of books printed in 1990 with a total impression of 5.64 billion copies were signed by individual authors. As to the freedom of association, the 1990 statistics showed that there were 2,000 associations, including societies, research institutes, foundations, federations, and clubs. All these associations operate freely within the framework of the constitution and the law.

The constitution also rules that citizens have the right to criticize and make suggestions regarding any state organ or functionary and the right to make to relevant state organs complaints or charges against, or exposures of, any state organ or functionary for violation of the law or dereliction of duty.

The constitution provides that freedom of the person of citizens of the People's Republic of China is inviolable. Unlawful detention or deprivation of citizens' freedom of the person by other means and unlawful search of the person of citizens are prohibited; the personal dignity of citizens is inviolable, and insult, libel, false accusation or false incrimination directed against citizens by any means is prohibited; the residences of citizens are inviolable and unlawful search of, or intrusion into, a citizen's residence is prohibited; freedom and privacy of correspondence are protected by law, and those who hide, discard, damage, or illegally open other people's letters, once discovered, shall be seriously dealt with, and grave cases shall be prosecuted.

The constitution provides that China implements the system of people's democratic dictatorship, which combines democracy among the people and dictatorship against the people's enemies. To guarantee the people's democratic rights and other lawful rights and interests, China pays great attention to improving its legal system. It has promulgated and put into effect a series of major laws, including the constitution, the Criminal Law, the Law of Criminal Procedure, the General Provisions of the Civil Law, the Law of Civil Procedure, and the Law of Administrative Procedure. During the 1979-1990 period, the National People's Congress and its Standing Committees made 99 laws and 21 decisions on legislative amendments and passed 52 resolutions and decisions on legal matters; the State Council formulated more than 700 administrative laws and regulations; and the people's congresses and their standing committees of various provinces, autonomous regions and municipalities, and provincial capital cities formulated numerous local laws and administrative rules and regulations, of which more than 1,000 were about human rights.

The unity between rights and duties is a basic principle of China's legal system. The constitution stipulates that every citizen is entitled to the rights prescribed by the constitution and the law and at the same time must perform the duties prescribed by the constitution and the law, and that in exercising their freedoms and rights, citizens may not infringe upon the interests of the state, of society, or of the collective, or upon the lawful freedoms and rights of other citizens. Legally, citizens are the subjects of both rights and duties. Everyone is equal before the rights and duties prescribed by the constitution and the law. No organization or individual may enjoy the privilege of being above the constitution and the law.

Practice of the past forty-odd years since liberation proves that the socialist democracy and legal system adopted by China are suited to the country's actual conditions and that the people are satisfied with it. It goes without saying that the building of this democratic politics and this legal system is no smooth sailing. There were times when democracy and law were seriously violated, such as happened during the "Cultural Revolution" (1966-76). Nevertheless, the Communist Party, backed by the people, corrected these mistakes and set the nation's socialist democracy and legal system back to the course of steady development. Upholding the general policy of reform and opening to the outside world and giving great attention to building socialist democratic politics, China is striving to improve and strictly enforce the socialist legal system and continuing the work to reform and improve the political system—all for the purpose of ensuring that the people can fully enjoy their civic rights and better exercise their political right of running the country.

III. Citizens Enjoy Economic, Cultural, and Social Rights

The human rights advocated by China encompass not only the right to subsistence and the civic and political rights, but also economic, cultural, and social rights. The Chinese government pays due attention to the protection and realization of the rights of the country, the various nationalities, and private citizens to economic, cultural, social, and political development.

Socialist China eliminated the system of exploitation of man by man, thus making it possible for the first time in history for all working people to secure the right to equal economic development. China upholds the socialist system of public ownership of the means of production as the mainstay while at the same time permitting and encouraging the appropriate development of other economic sectors as supplements to the socialist economy. It will neither adopt a unitary public ownership system, which is divorced from the nation's current level of development of productive forces, nor practice privatization, which tends to shake the dominant position of public ownership in the national economy.

Public ownership of the means of production constitutes the basis of China's socialist economic system. It guarantees that the major means of production in society are possessed by all the working people through the ownership by the whole people and the collective ownership by the laboring masses. The working people enjoy the right to manage, control, and use the means of production. According to statistics, the total social investment in fixed assets in China came to 444.9 billion yuan in 1990, of which 291.9 billion yuan, or 65.6 percent, was invested in units owned by the whole people, and 52.9 billion, or 11.9 percent, in collectively owned units. That is to say, the bigger share (77.5 percent) of the social investment in fixed assets is owned by the state and the collectives of the laboring masses.

The distribution system adopted in China is mainly based on the principle of "from each according to his ability, to each according to his work." At the same time, the government allows and encourages some people to become rich first by the sweat of their brow and through legitimate business activities. Those who get rich first can then help others, so that common prosperity can be achieved. This brings into play the enthusiasm of the laboring masses and at the same time prevents polarization. China is one of the nations that registers the lowest income gap in the world. According to 1990 statistics, the 20 percent of urban dwellers with the highest spendable incomes earn only 2.5 times as much as the 20 percent with the lowest incomes. This very fact has made it possible for China, an economically underdeveloped country, to guarantee the livelihood of its 1.1 billion people and avoid social confrontation resulting from polarization.

Economic equality has motivated the laboring people to a great extent and brought about speedy growth of the Chinese economy. Over the past forty-odd postliberation years and particularly in the past decade and more since the adoption of the policy of reform and opening to the outside world, China has all along [been] in the front rank of the world in terms of the rate of economic growth. The annual increase of GNP [gross national product] was 6.9 percent during the 1953-90 period and 8.8 percent during the 1979-90 period. China now leads the world in the output of many important products, including grain, cotton, pork, beef, mutton, cloth, coal, cement, and television sets; and it has also emerged as one of the world's biggest producers of steel, crude oil, electricity, and synthetic fibers.

With the growth of the national economy, the overall living standards of the Chinese people have greatly improved. . . .

Now that the Chinese people have solved the basic problems of food and clothing, they are working their way toward a well-to-do life. According to statistics, in 1990 every hundred rural families owned 118.3 bicycles and 44.4 television sets; and every hundred urban households owned 188.6 bicycles, 111.4 television sets, 42.3 refrigerators and 78.4 washing machines. In addition, the housing conditions of Chinese residents have improved, with the 1990 average per-capita living space increased to 7.1 square meters from 3.6 square meters in 1978 for urban dwellers and to 17.8 square meters from 8.1 square meters in 1978 for rural inhabitants. The speeds at which the economy grows and the people's living standards improve in new China are not only something inconceivable in old China, but also among the highest in the world community.

The right to work is a basic right of the citizens. In old China, people were deprived of the right to work according to their own will. This right was controlled by the landlords and capitalists, the owners of the means of production. The working people were constantly threatened by the prospect of unemployment. When China was liberated in 1949, a total of 4,742,000, or 60 percent of the total labor force in the cities, were jobless.

It is stipulated in the constitution that Chinese citizens have both the right and the duty to work. The government took all sorts of measures and solved the problem of unemployment, thereby enabling the masses of the working people to take part in socialist construction as masters of the society. In the 12 years between 1979 and 1990, a total of 94 million new jobs were created in urban areas.

With the expansion of the productive forces, the problem of rural surplus labor emerged as a major issue. The Chinese government has adopted the policy for some of the farmers to "leave the field but remain in the village," and, by vigorously developing rural enterprises and encouraging individual households to run industrial and sideline occupations along specialized lines, found the fundamental way out for the surplus labor force in rural areas. Since 1985, the unemployment rate in urban areas has remained at around 2.5 percent, which is fairly low compared with other countries in the world.

The constitution provides that public property and the legitimate property of citizens are protected. Public property owned by the state, collective property owned by the working people, and the legitimate property owned by individuals are all protected by law. Any organization or individual is thus forbidden to occupy, seize, share out, or destroy such properties. It is also forbidden to seal up, withhold, freeze, or confiscate such properties by illegal means. The state protects the citizens' ownership and inheritance rights to their legitimate income, savings, housing, and other legitimate properties. The rights of use and contract management of state-owned land, forests, mountains, grassland, uncultivated land, beaches, and waters obtained by units under public ownership and collective ownership and private citizens through legal means are protected by law. Whoever infringes upon such rights shall be dealt with by legal means.

At present, there are more than 90,000 private enterprises in China. Like the properties of units under public ownership or collectively owned by the laboring people, the legitimate properties of private enterprises are under the protection of law and shall not be illegally seized, sealed up, or confiscated. The Chinese government also provides legal protection to foreign investment, joint ventures with Chinese and foreign investment, and solely foreign-owned enterprises in China.

The right of education is an important prerequisite for the overall, free development of human beings. In old China, the majority of the working people did not have such a right. With only less than 20 percent of school-age children going to school, more than 80 percent of the total population were illiterate. After the founding of new China, the government took various measures to guarantee the citizens' right of education by devoting great efforts to the development of education. . . .

Since China adopted the policy of reform and opening to the outside world, the number of students studying abroad has been rapidly increasing. Since 1978, China has sent 150,000 students in various disciplines of learning to study in 86 countries and regions. So far almost 50,000 of them have returned after finishing their studies, and over 100,000 of them are staying abroad. After the political incident of 1989, the number of Chinese going abroad to study has not decreased but has increased to some extent.

In 1990, China completed its plan of sending 3,000 government-sponsored students abroad for academic pursuits. Meanwhile, about 6,000 students were sent to foreign countries by various units, and 20,000 (not including those enrolled in Australian- and Japanese-language schools) paid their own way to study abroad.

According to statistics of departments concerned in Beijing, Shanghai, and Guangzhou, more than 3,000 students have returned from overseas and have started work at their new posts during the past two years. In the meantime, more than 5,700 students have returned to countries where they study after coming home to visit relatives, take vacation, or do short-term jobs. According to international norms, Chinese students who are sponsored by the government to study abroad have the duty to return to serve their home country. The Chinese government, always valuing returned students and creating favorable working conditions for them upon return to China, has set up special organizations to take direct responsibility in receiving and arranging suitable jobs for returned students. More than seventy postdoctoral mobile research centers and short-term working stations have been set up by the Chinese Academy of Sciences and various universities, offering fine research and living conditions for those who have returned. Moreover, the Chinese government and related departments have set up a number of foundations to raise funds for scientific research and to aid returned students in research and teaching activities.

The Chinese citizens enjoy freedom of scientific research and literary and artistic creation. In order to promote the development of scientific research and to bring about cultural and artistic prosperity, the Chinese government upholds the guideline of "serving the people and socialism" and the principle of "letting a hundred flowers blossom and a hundred schools of thought contend.". . .

China has formed a legal system to protect intellectual property rights. A trademark law and a patent law have been promulgated and put in force. On 1 June 1991, a copyright law went into effect. According to 1990 statistics, more than 270,000 valid trademarks have been registered; and 66 countries and regions have applied for patent rights in China. By the end of 1990, American enterprises alone have applied for registration of 12,528 patent rights in China.

Public health facilities are a necessary guarantee for the human rights of life and health. In old China, health organizations and technicians were in short supply and at a low level and the majority of them were concentrated in urban areas. After the founding of new China, a public health network was gradually established. Covering all the cities and countryside, this network includes many kinds of health organizations at various levels and employs different types of public health workers. . . .

With the development of medical and public health undertakings, the incidence of infectious and endemic diseases has been drastically reduced. Such highly infectious diseases as leprosy, cholera, the plague, and smallpox have been basically eradicated. Snail fever, Kaschin-Beck disease, the Keshan disease, and other endemic diseases have come under control. The development of medical care and epidemic prevention has greatly improved the health of the Chinese people. . . .

The Chinese nation has a fine tradition of respecting elderly people. This tradition has been carried forward in new China. Senior citizens have the right to material assistance from the state and society. By the end of 1990, there had been 23.01 million people in the whole country living on retirement pensions. The proportion of the number of retired workers to the number of workers still in service is 16. In 1990, the pension for an average retired worker was 60 percent of the average pay for a worker in service, which ensured the livelihood of senior citizens in retirement, who also had the help and care of people from all walks of life.

In urban areas, one of the major tasks of neighborhood committees is to help widowed senior citizens and safeguard their rights and interests. Welfare institutions and senior citizen homes have been set up respectively by the state and the collective enterprises to provide board and lodging and other free services for senior citizens without relatives to depend on. In rural areas, childless and infirm old people are guaranteed food, clothing, housing, medical care, and burial expenses by society and collectives. The legal rights of senior citizens are protected by law; it is forbidden to abuse, insult, slander, ill-treat, or abandon them. Adult offspring have the obligation to provide for their parents.

China attaches great importance to guaranteeing the rights of women, children, and teenagers.

According to the constitution, women share equal rights with men in political, economic, cultural, social, and family life. Like men, they have the right to elect and to be elected. A considerable percentage of people's deputies and officials at various levels are women. Of the people's deputies elected in 1988 to the seventh National People's Congress, 634, or 21.3 percent, were women. At present, 5,600 women serve as judges in the people's courts. The state lays special stress on training and promoting women cadres. The number of women serving in government offices has increased from 366,000 in 1951 to 8.7 million; this accounts for 28.8 percent of the total number of civil servants.

In China, men and women get equal pay for equal work. Working women enjoy the right of special labor protection and labor insurance. The total number of women workers in China has increased from 600,000 in 1949 to 53 million. Women's right to education is also duly respected. In 1990, the total number of female students at school reached 78.81 million. These included 700,000 college students, 21.56 million middle-school students, and 56.56 million primary school students, accounting for 33.7, 42.2, and 46.2 percent respectively of the total number of students at school and college.

The state also pays special attention to protecting women's right to freedom of choice in marriage and forbids mercenary and arranged marriages and other acts of interference in other people's freedom of marriage. The judicial departments have taken stern measures according to law against criminals engaged in the sale of women.

The state has formulated laws and regulations to protect children. It is strictly forbidden to ill-treat and sell children and to use child labor. In order to safeguard the life and health of children, the state has issued a decision on strengthening and improving the health care in nurseries and kindergartens, and formulated special regulations to prevent and treat diseases such as infantile paralysis [polio], smallpox, diphtheria, and tuberculosis. China enjoys a relatively high rate of health care for children and of schooling for school-age children compared with other developing countries. The rate of inoculated children in China has almost reached the average level of developed countries. . . .

IV. Guarantee of Human Rights in China's Judicial Work

The aim and task of China's judicial work is to protect the basic rights, freedoms, and other legal rights and interests of the whole people in accordance with law; protect public property and citizens' lawfully owned private property; maintain social order; guarantee the smooth progress of the modernization drive; and punish the small number of criminals according to law. All this shows that China attaches great importance to human rights protection in the administration of justice.

China's public security and judicial organs follow the following principles in carrying out their duties: (1) All citizens are equal in regard to the applicability of law. In accordance with the law, each citizen's legal rights and interests shall be protected, and any citizen's offenses against the law and his criminal activities shall be looked into; (2) China's public security and judicial organs shall base themselves on facts and regard the law as the criterion in the conduct of all cases; (3) the procuratorate and the court shall independently exercise their respective procuratorial and judicial authority. They shall only obey the law and not be interfered with by any administrative organ, social organization, or person. While dealing with criminal cases, the people's court, the people's procuratorate, and the public security organ shall divide their work according to law, cooperate with, and moderate one another. They should exercise their authority only within the scope of their own responsibilities and not [be]

allowed to supersede one another. Procuratorial organs shall oversee whether the activities in public security organs, courts, prisons and reform-through-labor institutions are legal. These principles of justice are clearly stipulated in China's law, and they provide the legal guarantee for safeguarding human rights in the state's judicial activities. . . .

(4) No "Political Prisoners" in China

In China, ideas alone, in the absence of action that violates the criminal law, do not constitute a crime; nobody will be sentenced to punishment merely because he holds dissenting political views. So-called political prisoners do not exist in China. In Chinese criminal law "counterrevolutionary crime" refers to crime that endangers state security, that is, criminal acts that are not only committed with the purpose of overthrowing state power and the socialist system, but that are also listed in Articles 91-102 of the Criminal Law as criminal acts, such as those carried out in conspiring to overthrow the government or splitting the country, those carried out in gathering a crowd in armed rebellion, and espionage activities. These kinds of criminal acts that endanger state security are punishable in any country. In 1980, in handling the case of the Lin Biao and Jiang Qing counterrevolutionary cliques, the special court of the Supreme People's Court strictly implemented this principle by prosecuting members of the cliques according to law for their criminal acts while leaving alone matters concerning the political line.

(5) Prison Work and Criminals' Rights

At present there are, in all, 680 prisons and reform-through-labor institutions in China, holding 1.1 million criminals in detention. The rate of imprisonment is 0.99 per thousand of the total population. Compared with the rate of imprisonment of 4.13 per thousand in one of the Western developed countries according to 1990 statistics of its Ministry of Justice, China's rate is quite low.

China's prisons and reform-through-labor institutions receive, strictly according to law, criminals sent to them to enforce sentences passed by the courts. If they find the relevant legal documents not complete or the judgment not yet in effect legally, they have the legal right to refuse to take the persons in custody. Prisons and reform-through-labor institutions should notify a criminal's family members of his whereabouts within three days after taking him into custody. According to China's law, most prisoners are allowed to serve their sentences in the area where they reside to make it convenient for their family members to visit them and for the units where they used to work to help educate them. The allegation that in China some citizens are sent to labor camps without trial or sent away in some form of exile within the country is a distortion of the system whereby prisons and reform-through-labor institutions in China take criminals into custody; it is a groundless fabrication. . . .

The prisons and reform-through-labor institutions in China are designed not merely to punish the criminals but to educate them and turn them into law-abiding citizens by organizing them to take part in physical labor, learn legal and ordinary knowledge, and master productive skills. Prisoners who have taken educational or technical training courses and passed examinations given by local education or labor departments are given certificates corresponding to their levels of education or technical grades. The validity of such certificates is recognized in society. . . .

China's law stipulates that prisoners who really show repentance and have rendered meritorious service can, upon rulings of the people's courts, have their sentences commuted or be put on parole. In 1990, 18 percent of the criminals in custody were accorded such treatment.

Thanks to the humanitarian, scientific, and civilized management of the prisons and reform-through-labor institutions, the recidivism rate has for many years stood at 6 to 8 percent. Many prisoners have returned to society and become key members or engineers in their enterprises, and some of them have become model workers or labor heroes. Compared with the situation in one developed country in the West, where, according to 1989 judicial statistics, 41.4 percent of ex-prisoners returned to jail, China has come a long way in reforming and educating criminals. . . .

(6) Prison Labor

China's law stipulates that all prisoners able to work should take part in physical labor. This is also the practice adopted in many countries worldwide. China's policy of reforming criminals through labor is designed to help those serving prison terms mend their old ways by acquiring the labor habit and fostering a sense of social responsibility, discipline, and obedience to the law. This policy enables criminals in custody to stay healthy through a regular working life and avoid feelings of depression and apathy resulting from a prolonged monotonous and idle prison life. It also helps them learn productive skills and knowledge of one kind or another so that they can find a job after being released from prison and avoid committing new crimes because of difficulties in making a living. China's policy of reforming criminals through labor is not simply for the purpose of punishment; it is a humanitarian policy conducive to the reform, and the physical and mental health, of the criminals. . . .

Prison labor products are mostly used to meet the needs within the prison system, and only a small quantity enters the domestic market through normal channels. The export of prison products is prohibited. China's foreign trade departments, which handle the export of Chinese commodities in a unified way, have never granted foreign trade rights to reform-through-labor institutions.

(7) Education Through Labor and the Rights of Those Being Educated Through Labor

The work of education through labor in China is based on the 1957 Decision on Education Through Labor and other regulations adopted by the Standing Committee of the National People's Congress. Education through labor is not a criminal but an administrative punishment. Education-through-labor administrative committees have been set up by the people's governments of various provinces, autonomous regions, municipalities as well as large and medium-size cities, and the work is under the supervision of the people's procuratorates. It is stipulated that those eligible for education through labor should meet the requirements of relevant laws and regulations. For example, they should be at or above the age of sixteen and have upset the public order in a large or medium-size city but refused to mend their ways despite repeated admonition, or they have committed an offense not serious enough for criminal punishment. The decision to put a person under education-through-labor is made through a strict legal procedure and under a system of legal supervision in order to avoid subjecting the wrong person to the program. . . .

Those undergoing education through labor are entitled to civic rights prescribed by the constitution and the law, except that they must comply with the measures taken according to the regulations on education through labor to restrict some of their rights. For instance, they are not deprived of their political rights and have the right to vote according to law; they have the freedom of correspondence and the right to take time off during festivals and holidays; during the period of education through labor they are allowed to meet with their family members, those who are married can live together with their spouses during visits, and they can be granted leave of absence or go home to visit family members during holidays. Those who have acquitted themselves well while being educated may have their term reduced or be released ahead of time. Every year about 50 percent of the people undergoing the education-through-labor program have their term reduced or are released ahead of time.

The education-through-labor institutions follow the policy of educating, persuading and redeeming the offenders, with the emphasis on redeeming. Classes are opened, and instructors assigned, in these institutions to conduct systematic ideological, cultural, and technical education. . . .

V. Guarantee of the Right to Work

A citizen's right to work is the essential condition for his right to subsistence. Without the right to work, there will be no guarantee for the right to subsistence. The constitution and the law provide that citizens have the right to work, rest, receive vocational training, and be paid for their labor and that they have the right to labor protection and social security.

Having a job is the direct embodiment of the right to work. In China, with its large population and weak economy, employment is an outstanding social issue. . . .

After the founding of new China, the people's government attached great importance to this problem and took various practical measures to ensure employment. In less than four years, virtually all the unemployed left over from old China started work again. Since then, with the annual population growth of 14 million, employment has always been a cardinal issue in China's economic life. For a considerably long period of time, job-waiting people in urban areas basically counted on the government for job placements and most of them were employed in public works. . . .

The Chinese government pays special attention to the protection of female workers. In July 1988, the State Council promulgated Regulations on Labor Protection of Female Workers, laying down specific guidelines. For example, it is forbidden to make female workers engage in particularly strenuous work or work harmful to their physiological well-being. Also stipulated are concrete protections for female workers during the menstrual period, and also during pregnancy, maternity leave, and breast-feeding, at which periods their basic wages must remain the same and their work contracts cannot be terminated. In recent years, a child-bearing fund has been established in many places to offer living subsidies to women during breast-feeding and leave. . . .

VI. Citizens Enjoy Freedom of Religious Belief

There are many religions [practiced] in China, such as Buddhism, Daoism, Islam, Catholicism, and Protestantism. Among them Buddhism, Daoism, and Islam are more widely accepted. It is difficult to count the number of Buddhist and Daoist believers, since there are no strict admittance rites. Minority nationalities such as the Hui, Uighur, Kazakh, Tatar, Tajik, Uzbek, Kyrgyz, Dongxiang, Salar, and Bonan believe in Islam, a total of 17 million people. There are 3.5 million and 4.5 million people in China following Catholicism and Protestantism respectively.

China's constitution stipulates that citizens enjoy freedom of religious belief. The state protects normal religious activities and the lawful rights and interests of the religious circles. The Criminal Law, Civil Law, Electoral Law, Military Service Law, and Compulsory Education Law and some other laws make clear and specific provisions protecting religious freedom and equal rights of religious citizens. No state organ, social organization, or individual may compel citizens to believe in, or not to believe in, any religion; nor may they discriminate against citizens who believe in, or do not believe in, any religion.

State functionaries who illegally deprive a citizen of the freedom of religious belief shall be investigated, and legal responsibility affixed where due according to Article 147 of the Criminal Law.

The government has established departments of religious affairs responsible for the implementation of the policy of religious freedom. During the "Cultural Revolution," the government's religious policy was violated. After the "Cultural Revolution," especially since China initiated the reform and opening to the outside world, the Chinese government has done a great deal of work and made notable achievements in restoring, amplifying and implementing the policy of religious freedom and guaranteeing citizens' rights in this regard.

With the support and help of the Chinese government, religious facilities destroyed during the "Cultural Revolution" have gradually been restored and repaired. By the end of 1989, more than 40,000 monasteries, temples, and churches had been restored and opened to the public upon approval of the governments at various levels. Houses and land used for religious purposes are exempted from taxes. Temples, monasteries, and churches that need repair but lack money get assistance from the government. . . .

There are now eight national religious organizations in China. They are the China Buddhist Association, the China Daoist Association, the China Islamic Association, the Chinese Patriotic Catholic Association, the National Administration Commission of the Chinese Catholic Church, the Chinese Catholic Bishops College, the Three-Self Patriotic Movement Committee of the Protestant Churches of China, and the China Christian Council. There are also 164 provincial-level and more than 2,000 county-level religious organizations.

All religious organizations and all religious citizens can independently organize religious activities and perform their religious duties under the protection of the constitution and the law. There are forty-seven religious colleges in China, such as the Chinese Institute of Buddhist Studies, the Institute of Islamic Theology, the Jinling Union Theological Seminary of the Chinese Protestant Churches in Nanjing, the Chinese Catholic Seminary, and the Chinese Institute of Daoist Studies.

Since 1980, more than 2,000 young professional religious personnel have graduated from religious colleges and more than 100 religious students have been sent to twelve countries for further studies. China has more than ten religious publications and about 200,000 professional religious personnel—nearly 9,000 of them are deputies to the people's congresses and members of the Chinese People's Political Consultative Conference at various levels. Along with deputies and members from other circles, they participate in discussions of state affairs and enjoy equal democratic rights politically. . . .

Guided by the principles of independence, self-rule, and self-management, Chinese religions oppose any outside control or interference in their internal affairs so as to safeguard Chinese citizens' real enjoyment of freedom and right to religious belief. Before the founding of the People's Republic of China, China's Catholic and Protestant churches were all under the control of foreign religious forces. Dozens of "foreign missions" and "religious orders and congregations" carved out spheres of influence on the Chinese land, forming many "states within a state."

At that time there were 143 Catholic dioceses in China, but only about twenty bishops were Chinese nationals—and they were powerless—a good indication of the semifeudal and semicolonial nature of the old Chinese society. Chinese Catholic and Protestant circles resented this state of affairs and, as early as the 1920s, some insightful people proposed that the Chinese church do its own missionary work, support itself and manage its own affairs. But these proposals were not realized in old China. After the founding of new China, Chinese religious circles rid themselves of foreign control and realized self-management, self-support, and self-propagation. The Chinese people finally control their own religious organizations.

The Chinese government actively supports Chinese religious organizations and religious personnel in their friendly exchanges with foreign religious organizations and personnel on the basis of independence, equality, and mutual respect. International relationships between religious circles are regarded as part of the nongovernmental exchange of the Chinese people with other peoples of the world. In recent years, Chinese religious organizations have established and developed friendly relations with more than seventy countries and regions and sent delegations to many international religious conferences and symposiums. Chinese religious groups have joined world religious groups such as the World Fellowship of Buddhists, the Supreme Council for Islamic Affairs, the World Conference on Religion and Peace, the Asian Conference on Religion and Peace, and the World Council of Churches. ...

VII. Guarantee of the Rights of the Minority Nationalities

China is a unified, multinational country, with fifty-six nationalities in all. The Han people take up 92 percent of the total population of the country, leaving 8 percent for the other fifty-five nationalities. To realize equality, unity, and common prosperity among the nationalities is China's basic principle guiding relationships between nationalities. The constitution provides that all nationalities in the People's Republic of China are equal. The state protects the lawful rights and interests of the minority nationalities and upholds and develops the relationship of equality, unity, and mutual assistance among all of China's nation-

alities. Discrimination against and oppression of any nationality are prohibited, and any acts that undermine the unity and create splits among the nationalities are also prohibited. The constitution clearly stipulates that in striving for unity among all its nationalities, China opposes great-nation chauvinism, especially great-Han chauvinism, as well as local nationalism. ...

At present, there are throughout the country 159 national autonomous areas, including five autonomous regions, 30 autonomous prefectures and 124 autonomous counties (or banners). National autonomous areas exercise all rights of self-government in accordance with the Law of the People's Republic of China on Regional National Autonomy and may work out autonomous rules and specific regulations according to local political, economic and cultural characteristics. Without violating the constitution and the law, autonomous regions have the right to adopt special policies and flexible measures; autonomous organs can apply for permission to make alterations or desist from implementing resolutions, decisions, orders, and instructions made by higher-level state organs if they are not in accordance with the situation in autonomous regions. Organs of self-government have the right to handle local financial, economic, cultural, and educational affairs. In regions where people of a number of nationalities live together or in scattered communities, more than 1,500 national townships were established so as to enable minority nationalities to enjoy equal rights to the fullest.

In new China the political rights of minority nationalities are ensured.

Before liberation, the minority nationalities, like the majority of the Han people, suffered under severe oppression by the reactionary ruling class. The oppression in some areas took more savage and cruel forms than in others. For instance, in old Tibet, over 95 percent of Tibetans, from generation to generation, were serfs attached to officials, nobles, and lamaseries. According to the 13-Article Code and 16-Article Code, which had been enforced for several hundred years in old Tibet, Tibetans were divided into three classes and nine grades. The lives of ironsmiths, butchers, and women, who were declared an inferior grade of inferior class in explicit terms, were as cheap and worthless as a straw rope. This feudal serf system with its hierarchy of three classes and nine grades was bolstered by cruel punishments such as gouging out eyes, cutting off feet, removing the tongue, chopping off hands and arms, pushing an offender off a cliff, or drowning. Under such circumstances, the human rights of the majority of laboring people were out of the question.

After new China was founded, the old system was abolished and democratic reforms were carried out in one minority area after another. In Tibet, the serfs shook off their chains, and are no longer serf-owners' private property that can be bought, sold, transferred, bartered, or used to clear a debt, no longer to suffer the above-mentioned savage punishments, and no longer divided into the three classes and nine grades. Thanks to the democratic reform, the minority nationalities, oppressed for generations, obtained the freedom of person and human dignity, won basic human rights and for the first time became masters of their own destiny. . . .

VIII. Family Planning and Protection of Human Rights

The Chinese government implements a family planning policy in the light of the constitution, with the aim of promoting economic and social development, raising people's living standards, enhancing the quality of its population and safeguarding the people's rights to enjoy a better life.

China is a developing country with the biggest population in the world. Many people, little arable land, comparatively inadequate per-capita share of natural resources, plus a relatively backward economy and culture—these features spell out China's basic national conditions.

The population, which is expanding too quickly, poses a sharp contradiction to economic and social development, the utilization of resources, and environmental protection, places a serious constraint on China's economic and social development, and drags improvement of livelihood and the quality of the people. By the end of 1990, the mainland population had reached 1.14 billion. With such an immense population base, China, despite the implementation of birth control, still sees a yearly net increase of 17 million people, a number equal to the population of a medium-size country. . . .

More than a quarter of the annual addition to the national income is consumed by the new population born during the same year. As a result, funds for accumulation have to be cut, and the speed of economic growth slowed down. The rapid swelling of the population has brought about many pressures on the country's employment, education, housing, medical care, communications, and transportation.

Faced with the gravity of this situation, the government, in order to guarantee people's minimum living conditions and to enable citizens not only to have enough to eat and wear but also to grow better off, cannot do as some people imagine—wait for a high level of economic development to initiate a natural decline in birthrate. If we did so, the population would grow without restriction, and the economy would deteriorate steadily.

Hence, China has to strive for economic growth by trying in every possible way to increase the productive forces, while at the same time practice the policy of family planning to strictly control population growth so that it may suit economic and social development. This is the only correct choice that any government responsible

to the people and their descendants can make under China's given set of special circumstances. . . .

China's population policy has two objectives: control of population growth and improvement in quality of the population. Work in this field not only encourages couples of child-bearing age to have fewer children but also provides them with maternal care, baby care, and advice on optimum methods of child-bearing and child-rearing. These services include premarital checkups, genetic consultation, prenatal diagnosis, and care during pregnancy to help couples have sound, healthy babies.

Drowning or abandoning female infants, a pernicious practice left over from feudal society, occurs much less often now, but has not been stamped out entirely in some remote areas. China's law clearly forbids the drowning of infants and other acts of killing them. The government has adopted practical measures for handling these kinds of criminal offenses according to law.

China's family planning policy fully conforms to Item 9 of the United Nations' Declaration of Mexico City on Population and Growth in 1984, which demands that "countries which consider that their population growth rate hinders their national development plans should adopt appropriate population plans and programs." It also accords with the UN World Population Plan of Action which stresses that every country has the sovereign right to formulate and implement its own population policy.

Some people who censure China's family planning policy as "violating human rights" and "inhuman" do not understand or consider China's real situation. But some others have deliberately distorted the facts in an attempt to put pressure on China and interfere in China's internal affairs. China has only two alternatives in handling its population problem: to implement the family planning policy or to allow the birthrate to grow blindly. The former choice enables children to be born and grow up healthy and live a better life, while the latter one leads to unrestrained expansion of population so that the majority of the people will be short of food and clothing, while some will even tend to die young. Which of the two pays more attention to human rights and is more humane? The answer is obvious. . . .

X. Active Participation in International Human Rights Activities

China recognizes and respects the purposes and principles of the Charter of the United Nations related to the protection and promotion of human rights. It appreciates and supports the efforts of the UN in promoting universal respect for human rights and fundamental freedoms, and takes an active part in UN activities in the human rights field. China advocates mutual respect for state sovereignty and maintains that priority should be given to safeguarding of the right of the people of the developing countries to subsistence and development, thus creating the necessary conditions for people all over the world to enjoy various human rights. China is opposed to interfering in other countries' internal affairs on the pretext of human rights and has made unremitting efforts to eliminate various abnormal phenomena and strengthen international cooperation in the field of human rights.

In April 1955, Chinese Premier Zhou Enlai signed the "Draft Final Communiqué of the Asian-African Conference" (also known as the "Bandung Declaration") at the Asian and African Conference held in Bandung, Indonesia. The communiqué declared that the conference fully supports the fundamental principles concerning human rights laid down in the UN Charter, and made the "respect for fundamental human rights and for the purposes and principles of the Charter of the United Nations" the first of the ten Principles of Peaceful Coexistence.

In May of the same year, Zhou Enlai, speaking at an enlarged session of the Standing Committee of the National People's Congress, said that "the ten principles contained in the Bandung Declaration also include respect for fundamental human rights and for the purposes and principles of the Charter of the United Nations. . . . All these are the principles that have been consistently advocated by the Chinese people and adhered to by China."

In his speech during the general debate at the forty-first session of the United Nations General Assembly held in 1986, the Chinese foreign minister, when mentioning the twentieth anniversary of the International Covenant on Civil and Political Rights and International Covenant on Economic, Social, and Cultural Rights, pointed out that "the two covenants have played a positive role in realizing the purposes and principles of the UN Charter concerning respect for human rights. The Chinese government has consistently supported these purposes and principles."

In September 1988, the Chinese foreign minister pointed out in his speech at the forty-third session of the United Nations General Assembly that the "Universal Declaration of Human Rights" is "the first international instrument that systematically sets forth the specific contents regarding respect for and protection of fundamental human rights. Despite its historical limitations, the Declaration has exerted a far-reaching influence on the development of the postwar international human rights activities and played a positive role in this regard."

China has taken an active part in the UN activities in the sphere of human rights. Since resuming its lawful seat in the United Nations in 1971, China has sent its delegation to attend every session of the UN Economic and Social Council and of the UN General Assembly, and has taken an active part in deliberation of human rights issues and stated its views on the issue of human rights, making its contributions to enriching the connotation of the concept of human rights.

Chinese delegations attended as observers the UN Human Rights Commission's sessions in 1979, 1980, and 1981. China was elected a member of the Human Rights Commission at the first regular session of the UN Economic and Social Council and has been a member ever since. Since 1984 the human rights affairs experts recommended by China to the Human Rights Commission have been continually elected members and alternate members of the Subcommission on Prevention of Discrimination and Protection of Minorities. The Chinese members have played an important role in the subcommission. They have become members of the Working Group on Indigenous Populations and the Working Group on Communications affiliated with the subcommission. China has taken an active part in drafting and formulating international legal instruments on human rights within the UN, and has sent delegates to participate in working groups charged with drafting these instruments, including the UN convention on the rights of children, the international convention on the protection of the rights of all migrant workers and their families, the convention against torture and other cruel, inhuman, or degrading treatment or punishment, the declaration on the right and responsibility of individuals, groups, and organs of society to promote and protect universally recognized human rights and fundamental freedoms, and the declaration on the protection of rights of persons belonging to national, ethnic, religious, and linguistic minorities. The meetings of these working groups paid much attention to the suggestions and amendments put forward by China.

Since 1981 China has participated in every session of the governmental experts group organized by the UN Commission on Human Rights to draft the declaration on the right to development and made positive suggestions until the declaration on the right to development was passed by the forty-first session of the UN General Assembly in 1986. China energetically supported the commission on human rights in conducting worldwide consultation on the implementation of the right to development and supported the proposal that the right to development be discussed as an independent agenda item in the human rights commission. China has always been a cosponsor country of the human rights commission's resolution on the right to development.

Since 1980 the Chinese government has successively signed, ratified, and acceded to seven UN human rights conventions, namely, the convention on the prevention and punishment of the crime of genocide, the international convention on the suppression and punishment of the crimes of apartheid, the convention on the elimination of all forms of discrimination against women, the international convention on the elimination of all forms of racial discrimination, the convention relating to the status of refugees, the protocol relating to the status of refugees, and the convention against torture and other cruel, inhuman, or degrading treatment or punishment. The Chinese government has always submitted reports on the implementation of the related conventions, and seriously and earnestly performed the obligations it has undertaken.

China has always upheld justice and made unremitting efforts to safeguard the right of third world countries to national self-determination and to stop massive infringements on human rights. As is well known, China has for many years made unremitting efforts to seek a just and reasonable resolution of a series of major human rights issues, including the questions of Cambodia, Afghanistan, the occupied Palestinian and Arab territories, South Africa and Namibia, and Panama.

China pays close attention to the issue of the right to development. China believes that as history develops, the concept and connotation of human rights also develop constantly. The declaration on the right to development provides that human rights refer to both individual rights and collective rights. This means a breakthrough in the traditional concept of human rights and represents a result won through many years of struggle by the newly emerging independent countries and the international community, a result of great significance.

In the world today the gap between the rich and the poor becomes wider and wider. Social and economic growth in many developing countries is slow, and one-third of the population in developing countries still live below the poverty line. To the people in the developing countries, the most urgent human rights are still the right to subsistence and the right to economic, social, and cultural development. Therefore, attention should first be given to the right to development.

China appeals to the international community to attach importance and give attention to the developing countries' right to development and adopt positive and effective measures to eliminate injustice and unreasonable practice in the world economic order. An earnest effort must be made to improve the international economic environment, alleviate and gradually eliminate factors disadvantageous to developing countries, and establish a new international economic order. Factors that have a negative influence on the right to development, such as racism, colonialism, hegemonism, and foreign aggression, occupation, and interference, must be eliminated. A favorable international environment must be created for the realization of the right to development.

Over a long period in the UN activities in the human rights field, China has been firmly opposed to any country's making use of the issue of human rights to sell its own values, ideology, political standards, and mode of development, and to any country's interfering in the internal affairs of other countries on the pretext of human rights, the internal affairs of developing countries in particular, and so hurting the sovereignty and dignity of many developing countries.

Together with other developing countries, China has waged a resolute struggle against all such acts of interference and upheld justice by speaking out from a sense of fairness. China has always maintained that human rights are essentially matters within the domestic jurisdiction of a country. Respect for each country's sovereignty and noninterference in internal affairs are universally recognized principles of international law, which are applicable to all fields of international relations, and of course applicable to the field of human rights as well.

Section 7 of Article 2 of the United Nations Charter stipulates that ''nothing contained in the present charter shall authorize the United Nations to intervene in matters which are essentially within the domestic jurisdiction of any state.''

The declaration on the inadmissibility of intervention in the domestic affairs of states and the protection of their independence and sovereignty, the declaration on principles of international law concerning friendly relations and cooperation among states in accordance with the United Nations Charter, and the declaration on the inadmissibility of intervention and interference in the internal affairs of states, which were all adopted by the United Nations, contain the following explicit provisions: ''no state or group of states has the right to intervene directly or indirectly, for any reason whatsoever, in the internal or external affairs of any other state,'' and ''every state has the duty to refrain from the exploitation and the distortion of human rights issues as a means of interference in the internal affairs of states, of exerting pressure on other states or creating distrust and disorder within and among states or groups of states.''

These provisions of international instruments reflect the will of the overwhelming majority of countries to safeguard the fundamental principles of international law and maintain a normal relationship between states. They are basic principles that must be followed in international human rights activities. The argument that the principle of noninterference in internal affairs does not apply to the issue of human rights is, in essence, a demand that sovereign states give up their state sovereignty in the field of human rights, a demand that is contrary to international law. Using the human rights issue for the purpose of imposing the ideology of one country on another is no longer a question of human rights, but a manifestation of power politics in the form of interference in the internal affairs of other countries. Such abnormal practice in international human rights activities must be eliminated.

China is in favor of strengthening international cooperation in the realm of human rights on the basis of mutual understanding and seeking a common ground while reserving differences. However, no country in its effort to realize and protect human rights can take a route that is divorced from its history and its economic, political, and cultural realities. A human rights system must be ratified and protected by each sovereign state through its domestic legislation. As pointed out in a resolution of the UN General Assembly at its forty-fifth session, "Each state has the right freely to choose and develop its political, social, economic, and cultural systems."

It is also noted in the resolution of the forty-sixth Conference on Human Rights that no single mode of development is applicable to all cultures and peoples. It is neither proper nor feasible for any country to judge other countries by the yardstick of its own mode or to impose its own mode on others. Therefore, the purpose of international protection of human rights and related activities should be to promote normal cooperation in the international field of human rights and international harmony, mutual understanding, and mutual respect. Consideration should be given to the differing view of human rights held by countries with different political, economic, and social systems, as well as different historical, religious, and cultural backgrounds. International human rights activities should be carried on in the spirit of seeking common ground while reserving differences, mutual respect, and the promotion of understanding and cooperation.

China has always held that to effect international protection of human rights, the international community should interfere with and stop acts that endanger world peace and security, such as gross human rights violations caused by colonialism, racism, foreign aggression and occupation, as well as apartheid, racial discrimination, genocide, slave trade, and serious violation of human rights by international terrorist organizations. These are important aspects of international cooperation in the realm of human rights and an arduous task facing current international human rights protection activities.

There is now a change over the world pattern from the old to the new, and the world is more turbulent than before. Hegemonism and power politics continue to exist and endanger world peace and development. Interference in other countries' internal affairs and the pushing of power politics on the pretext of human rights are obstructing the realization of human rights and fundamental freedoms. In the face of such a world situation, China is ready to work with the international community in a continued and unremitting effort to build a just and reasonable new order of international relations and to realize the purpose of the United Nations to uphold and promote human rights and fundamental freedoms.

The Law on Territorial Waters and Their Contiguous Areas of the People's Republic of China

Adopted by the National People's Congress on 25 February 1992, this law attempts to solidify China's claim to the Spratlys and other disputed islands in the South China Sea. (Malaysia, the Philippines, Vietnam, Brunei, and Indonesia also have claims to some of these islands.) Passage of the law was seen by many observers as a sign of China's more aggressive foreign policy stance in the early 1990's, following a period in which it maintained a relatively low profile after the 1989 Tiananmen incident.

Article 1. This law is formulated in order to enable the People's Republic of China (PRC) to exercise its sovereignty over its territorial waters and its rights to exercise control over their adjacent areas, and to safeguard state security as well as its maritime rights and interests.

Article 2. The PRC's territorial waters refer to the inland waters contiguous to its territorial land.

The PRC's territorial land includes the mainland and its offshore islands, Taiwan and the various affiliated islands including Diaoyu Island, the Penghu Islands, the Dongsha Islands, the Xisha Islands, the Nansha Islands, and other islands that belong to the PRC.

The PRC's inland waters refer to the waters along the datum line of territorial waters facing the land.

Article 3. The extent of the PRC's territorial waters measures twelve nautical miles from the datum line of the territorial waters.

The PRC's datum line of territorial waters is designated with the method of a straight datum line, formed by joining the various base points with straight lines.

The external boundary of the PRC's territorial waters refers to the line, every component point of which has a nearest distance of twelve nautical miles from the datum line of the territorial waters.

Article 4. The PRC's contiguous areas refer to the waters that are outside of but adjacent to its territorial waters. The extent of the adjacent areas has a width of twelve nautical miles.

The external boundary of the PRC's contiguous areas is a line, every component point of which has a nearest distance of twenty-four nautical miles from the datum line of the territorial waters.

Article 5. The PRC exercises sovereignty over its territorial waters and the aerial space over the territorial waters, as well as the seabeds and underground earth of its territorial waters.

Article 6. Nonmilitary foreign vessels enjoy the right of harmlessly passing through the territorial waters of the People's Republic of China according to law.

To enter the territorial waters of the People's Republic of China, foreign military vessels must obtain permission from the government of the People's Republic of China.

Article 7. While passing through the territorial waters of the People's Republic of China, foreign submarines and other submersible craft must sail on the surface of the sea and display their flags.

Article 8. While passing through the territorial waters of the People's Republic of China, foreign vessels must abide by the laws and statutes of the People's Republic of China and must not harm the peace, security, and good order of the People's Republic of China.

Foreign nuclear-powered vessels and other vessels carrying nuclear, toxic, or other dangerous materials must produce certain certificates and take special preventative measures to pass through the territorial waters of the People's Republic of China.

The government of the People's Republic of China has the right to adopt all necessary measures to prevent and stop the harmful passage of vessels through its territorial waters.

Foreign vessels that violate the laws and statutes of the People's Republic of China shall be dealt with according to law by relevant departments of the People's Republic of China.

Article 9. To ensure navigation safety and satisfy other requirements, the government of the People's Republic of China may require foreign vessels passing through its territorial waters to use designated navigational channels or prescribed sea lanes. Concrete methods should be issued by the government of the People's Republic of China or its relevant responsible departments.

Article 10. The relevant responsible organs of the People's Republic of China shall have the right to evict foreign military vessels or vessels owned by foreign governments and used for noncommercial purposes that violate the laws or regulations of the People's Republic of China while passing through the territorial waters of the People's Republic of China. Losses or damages caused shall be borne by the nation whose flag is being flown by the vessel in question.

Article 11. Any international or foreign organization or individual who intends to conduct activities connected with scientific research or marine work shall first seek the approval of the People's Republic of China or its relevant responsible departments and abide by the laws and regulations of the People's Republic of China.

Whoever is found illegally entering the territorial waters of the People's Republic of China to conduct activities connected with scientific research or marine work in violation of the preceding provisions shall be handled by the relevant organs of the People's Republic of China according to law.

Article 12. Foreign air carriers may not enter the air above the territorial waters of the People's Republic unless they do so in accordance with agreements or accords that the governments of their countries have signed with the People's Republic of China, or they have been approved or accepted by the government of the People's Republic of China or organs it has authorized.

Article 13. The People's Republic of China has the authority to exercise powers within its adjacent areas for the purpose of guarding against or punishing conduct that violates laws and regulations regarding security, customs, finance, health, or entry-exit control within its land territories, inland waters, or territorial seas.

Article 14. When authorities of the People's Republic of China have reason to believe that a foreign ship has violated the laws and regulations of the People's Republic, they may exercise the right to chase it.

The chase begins when the foreign ship or one of its small boats, or other ships of ships being chased are operating for the mother ship in inland waters, territorial seas, or adjacent areas of the People's Republic of China.

If the foreign ships are in adjacent areas of the People's Republic of China, the chase may proceed only when the rights of the relevant laws and regulations in Article 13 of this law have been violated.

As long as the chase is not interrupted, it may continue outside the territorial seas of the People's Republic of China or its adjacent areas. The chase stops when the ship being chased enters the territorial seas of its own country or a third country.

The right to chase in this article is exercised by military ships or military air carriers of the People's Republic of China, or by ships or air carriers authorized by the government of the People's Republic of China to perform official duties.

Article 15. The datum line of territorial seas of the People's Republic of China shall be announced by the government of the People's Republic of China.

Article 16. The government of the People's Republic of China shall draw up relevant regulations in accordance with this law.

Article 17. This law becomes effective upon promulgation.

Jiang Zemin on the Socialist Market Economy

China's fourteenth party congress, convened in the fall of 1992, set the goal of establishing a socialist market economy in China and emphasized a faster pace of reform to achieve that goal. In this speech to the third plenum of the party congress, delivered November 14, 1993, General Secretary Jiang Zemin summarizes China's current situation as the country sets out to implement these and other important changes.

Comrades: The third plenary session of the Fourteenth CCP Central Committee will come to an end today [14 November]. This is a successful session of historical significance. The "Decision of the CCP Central Committee on Some Issues Concerning the Establishment of a Socialist Market Economic Structure" adopted at the session specifies—in line with Comrade Deng Xiaoping's theory on building socialism with Chinese characteristics and the guidelines of the fourteenth CCP National Congress—the goals and basic principles for restructuring the economy set by the fourteenth CCP National Congress, further expands those goals and principles in some areas, and formulates a program of action to restructure the economy. It will surely exert a major and far-reaching impact on China's reform, opening, and socialist modernization drive.

I would like to take advantage of this opportunity to bring up some points with regard to the current situation, the implementation of the "decision," and ways to build up the party and exercise effective party leadership.

I. On the Current Situation

Under the guidance of Comrade Deng Xiaoping's important speeches in early 1992 and the guidelines of the fourteenth CCP National Congress, we have opened up a new situation in work in all sectors over the past year. The economy is growing vigorously, fresh progress has been made in implementing measures of reform and opening up aimed at establishing a socialist market economic system, and new achievements have been scored in all other undertakings. Today, the country enjoys economic development, political stability, national unity, and social progress. The overall situation is decidedly good.

This year, the economy has maintained its momentum of fast growth on top of the breakneck growth recorded in 1992. The gross national product grew by 13.3 percent in the first three quarters. It is expected that this high growth rate will be maintained for the whole year. Industrial production by enterprises at the village level or higher is expected to grow by about 21 percent. A comparatively good harvest has been reported in the agricultural sector. As for some prominent contradictions and problems that have emerged in the course of the breakneck economic growth, the CCP Central Committee and State Council have taken a series of measures to solve them. Particularly the measures we have taken since June to strengthen and improve macroeconomic regulation and control and to rectify order in the banking and other economic sectors have—thanks to the common efforts of all quarters over the past few months—yielded positive results. The situation in the banking sector is stabilizing. The overheated development in real estate and development zones as well as the excessive growth in investment have been brought under control. The construction of key state projects has picked up speed and inflation has, more or less, been brought under control. Prices in the foreign exchange swap market have decreased and have basically returned to normal. By and large, no IOUs were issued in procuring agricultural and sideline products harvested in the summer; funds for autumn-harvested crops have been allocated. Prices of major capital goods including steel products have come down again. The situation in terms of state revenues and expenditures has improved somewhat. Income has continued to increase in both urban and rural areas. The economy as a whole is developing in a sound manner.

Facts have borne out that the measures taken by the CCP Central Committee and State Council to strengthen and improve macroeconomic regulation and control are absolutely correct and necessary. Judging from the current trends, we will still be able to maintain a rather fast economic growth rate and bring about the sustained, rapid, and healthy development of the national economy.

Reform and opening up have picked up pace noticeably this year. Many major reform measures are either being carried out or will soon be promulgated. This year, we have seized the opportunity and taken big steps in implementing price reforms by freeing the prices of many industrial capital goods. Over 90 percent of the counties (cities) have lifted price controls on grain procurement and procurement and selling prices. The degree of the application of market prices has, on the whole, risen continuously. Opening up to the outside world has continued to develop both in scope and in depth, and there has been a new upsurge in foreign investment in China. One of the main characteristics for strengthening and improving macroeconomic regulation and control is the idea of solving the contradictions and problems in the march forward by deepening reforms and by employing mostly economic and legal means supplemented, certainly, with the necessary administrative means. Practice has shown that this approach is successful. This has provided us with valuable experience, showing us that the fundamental way to solve the deep-seated problems in economic and social development lies in deepening reform.

The present social and political situation in the country is also good. This year has seen the transition from the old leading bodies to the new, following the smooth change of terms in people's congresses, governments and committees for the Chinese People's Political Consultative Conference at the central as well as local levels, and the convening of national congresses, one after another, for mass organizations such as the Communist Youth League, the All-China Women's Federation, and the All-China Federation of Trade Unions. New progress has been made in building a socialist democracy and legal system with the formulation of some major laws and regulations. Propaganda and ideological work have been strengthened. The central authorities have paid attention to promoting clean administration and the anticorruption struggle, with the Central Discipline Inspection Commission and the State Council having made specific arrangements that are currently being implemented in earnest by various localities and departments. Even closer ties have been forged between the party and the masses following the investigation and handling of some serious and major cases and the checking of some malpractice. The social and economic order has been maintained, thanks to the further strengthening of the comprehensive management of public security, the prompt defeat of domestic and foreign hostile forces' plots to create disturbances, and the proper handling of some emergencies.

Generally speaking, developments and changes in the international situation also are favorable to us. The world will likely enjoy a relatively long period of peace following the end of the confrontation between East and West. The further improvement of our nation's relations with neighboring countries, in particular, is conducive to creating an international environment favorable to economic construction. A worldwide economic structural readjustment would help us attract foreign investment and technology. The Asia-Pacific region's growing influence on the world also is favorable for us.

In short, the present domestic and international situation is comparatively favorable, and we really are facing a great opportunity for reform and development. There are not many historical opportunities like this. We must seize the favorable opportunity; quicken the pace of reform; open up to the outside world and modernize; and further enhance our composite national strength. It was based exactly on this consideration that the Central Committee Political Bureau had suggested that the third plenary session of the fourteenth CCP Central Committee make a decision on the issue of establishing a socialist market economic system, seek a common understanding and uniform steps throughout the party, vigorously deepen reform, and promote economic development. We believe that our nation's reform, opening up to the outside world, and modernization will take on a new aspect after this plenary session.

II. Several Issues Concerning the Implementation of the "Decision"

Since the fourteenth CCP National Congress determined the goal of establishing a socialist market eco-

nomic system, comrades from different quarters have hoped for a further step forward in formulating a more complete and systematic argument on the socialist market economic system to facilitate better organization and advancement of the reform of the economic structure. We all noticed that while market mechanisms are playing an increasingly important role in our economic life, the sluggishness of reform in certain fields has adversely affected the establishment of a new system and the healthy development of the national economy. We have made breakthroughs and accumulated experience in reforms in various fields over the past decade or so, and we also have conditions ready for bringing about the overall advancement of the reform. We now need to formulate an overall plan and to stress standardization in our system and policies. Although the basic framework outlined by the decision of this plenary session for the socialist market economic system still needs to be examined and continuously improved in practice, its existence can enhance our ability to anticipate the kind of guidance needed for the reform work and make the reform even more fruitful.

The "Decision" is rich and all-embracing in its contents, with all fifty of its articles being of great significance. Here I would like to present a few opinions on implementing the guidelines of the "Decision":

(1) Correctly Handle the Relations Between Reform and Development

With fairly favorable conditions at home and abroad and with China's great potential for economic development, it is possible to maintain a reasonably high growth rate for a long period. It is necessary for us to focus on economic development, seize the current favorable opportunities, and concentrate our efforts on improving the economic situation. Comrade Deng Xiaoping is absolutely correct when he says that "development is the last word" and "the final resolution of the problems lies in developing the economy." We should follow the guiding spirit of the plenary meeting and waste no time in introducing various already-prepared reform measures so as to create a favorable structure and conditions for the economy. In arranging economic work, it is necessary to pay attention to creating a flexible environment. New thinking is also needed for development, which should truly be directed at focusing on economic performance rather than on the same old road of extensive management, which indiscriminately seeks greater output value and expands the extent of investment. The state can become rich and strong and the people's livelihood can be improved only when production is improved and more wealth is created. The experience of many years tells us that we should pay attention to two major things at all times: strengthening the role of agriculture as the foundation of the national economy and improving state-owned large- and medium-sized enterprises.

As for agricultural problems, the CCP Central Committee has already convened a meeting and formulated general and specific policies. It is imperative conscientiously to carry out these policies to ensure the stable development of agriculture and the overall rural economy. From now forward, more efforts should be made to improve state-owned large- and medium-sized enterprises. The reinvigoration of China's economy depends mainly on state-owned large- and medium-sized enterprises. Many problems now facing us can be solved by deepening reforms. The reform of state-owned large- and medium-sized enterprises is a key point and a difficult point in China's efforts to improve its economic structure.

The "Decision" has been a big step forward in the thinking about improving enterprises because it has distinctively pointed out the problems of building a modern enterprise system. The "Decision" summarizes the basic characteristics of the modern enterprise system and points out the orientation for the reform of enterprises. It is imperative to deepen thoroughly the reform of enterprises in accordance with the requirements of the "Decision" so as to truly improve state-owned enterprises and to enable it to play a guiding and backbone role in economic development. This is not only an important economic issue that affects the development of the national economy as a whole but also an important political issue that affects the destiny of socialism. We should work hard to resolve this issue.

(2) Correctly Handle the Relations Between Strengthening Macrocontrol and Developing the Role of the Market

A socialist market economy is integrated with the basic system of socialism. The establishment of a socialist market economy seeks to enable the market to play a fundamental role in the allocation of resources, under the state's macrocontrol. The macrocontrol of the state and the role of the market mechanism, both of which are essential requirements of the socialist market economic structure, are integrated, mutually supplementary, and mutually promoting. To change the traditional planned economic system, it is necessary to emphasize the importance of fully permitting the market's fundamental role in allocating resources. If we fail to do so, there will be no socialist market economy. But we should also see the negative aspects of spontaneity, rashness, and sluggishness existing in the market. Such weaknesses and inadequacies need to be amended and overcome by the state's macroguidance and control of market activities. In today's world, there is not a single country whose economy is not under the government's control. Being a socialist country, China should improve and is more qualified to improve the macrocontrol.

The current problems are: The market is not completely permitted to play its role in many respects, and there exist the phenomena of unbridled development and a chaotic economic order in the market. We should actively cultivate and develop the market system, continue to carry out the reform of the price and commodity circulation system, develop the factors of production market, and improve and strengthen the control, management, and supervision of the market. Practices in 1993 also show that to establish a socialist market economic structure, it is necessary to work hard both in giving full play to the role of market regulation and in strengthening macrocontrol. The key points of the work for each period may be different. According to various actual conditions, sometimes more emphasis will be placed on the role of the market and sometimes on the macrocontrol by the state. But, while emphasizing one aspect, we must not neglect or pay no attention to the other side.

(3) We Must Give Equal Emphasis to Two Fronts and Do Well in Both

In the course of implementing reform, opening up, and the modernization drive, we must consistently persist in the principle of giving equal emphasis to two fronts and doing well in both. Having learned a profound lesson in this regard, we must never repeat the mistake of emphasizing one to the neglect of the other.

At a time when everyone is focusing on promoting reform and opening up and developing the economy, we must not overlook the promotion of spiritual civilization. Emphasizing the principles and tasks of promoting socialist spiritual civilization, the "Decision" sets out some requirements, particularly in pointing out that under a socialist market economy, we should actively propagate the need to persist in a correct outlook on life and a civilized, healthy lifestyle and work to promote public and professional ethics. All these remarks have specific aims. It is a fact of life that money worship, extreme individualism, decadent lifestyles, and other social evils are spreading, some of which have developed to quite a serious extent. We must take resolute steps to combat them. We must unequivocally encourage what is right, overcome what is evil, and promote in the whole society a good social climate that is eminently healthy, progressive, and positive. We must carry forward our fine national culture and traditions, learn from the fruits of all advanced foreign civilizations and, moreover, never mistake their dregs for their best parts. . . .

Continued efforts should be made to carry out the fight against corruption. Building a clean government and combating corruption constitute essential conditions for the establishment of the socialist market economic structure. These also have a great bearing on the destiny of the ongoing reform and on the destiny of the party and the country. The Central Committee's line, principles, and policies for the anticorruption struggle are clear and specific, and they enjoy the heartfelt support of the vast ranks of cadres and people. The focal points of this struggle are leading party and government bodies, law-enforcement departments, and economic administrative departments, as well as the investigation and prosecution of major cases. Party members, high- and middle-ranking cadres in particular, must heighten their awareness and set a good example by being honest and observing discipline. As for those corrupt elements, we must punish them in accordance with state laws and party discipline, no matter who they are. We must not tolerate or abet their wrongdoing. The fight against corruption is a long-term and arduous task and should be carried out with unremitting effort. We must see to it that the targets set by the Central Committee for the different periods of this struggle are attained.

(4) Fully Mobilize All Positive Factors and Bring the Initiatives of All Sides into Play

Whether in the past revolutionary war or during the current reform, opening, and modernization construction, only by closely relying on the broad mass of cadres and the masses, by fully bringing into play the initiatives of all sides, and by pooling the wisdom and efforts of everyone can we expect to achieve success. We have always stressed the need to bring into play the initiatives of both the central government and local governments. The "Decision," by giving full consideration to our country's actual conditions and to work in localities, formulated the direction and principles of the reforms of the fiscal, taxation, and financial systems. The purpose of employing a tax-sharing system, of a rational division of jurisdiction between the central and local governments, and of determining the revenue-expense ratio between the central and local governments in a rational manner is to straighten out the economic relationship and to standardize economic activities. Strengthening the central bank's regulatory and supervisory functions over the currency, practicing a separation between the funds of a political nature and those of a commercial nature, and attaining a unified exchange rate constitute a major reform of the financial system, which involves readjusting the relationship between the interests of the central government and those of localities.

A reform of fiscal, taxation, and financial structures is required to develop a socialist market economy, which not only is compatible with accepted international practices but also takes into account China's characteristics and reality. By so doing, it will be conducive to giving play to the initiatives of the central government and that of localities, doing an even better job of economic construction, and attaining coordinated socioeconomic development. When dealing with the relationship between the central government and localities, the central government should give consideration to localities' difficulties. As for localities, they should establish the concept of the national interest. Whereas the national interest should take care of

local interests, local interests should subordinate themselves to the national interest. The fact that a consensus over the reform plan for fiscal, taxation, and financial structures has been reached through discussion and coordination shows that everyone has taken the national interest into consideration and that everyone upholds the concept of the national interest. We should fully understand the far-reaching significance of the reform, and with one heart and one mind and with joint efforts, we should accomplish the reform tasks.

Our country is a vast country. Economic development in various regions is rather imbalanced. Because there are historical reasons for the regional imbalances, it will take time to narrow these gaps. The policy and principles of the party and the state are to exploit the advantages of both the economically developed and the less-developed regions. Our basic principle in this respect is clear. It is advisable for economically developed regions to make full use of their own advantageous conditions and existing foundation to achieve even faster development, to raise the economy rapidly to new heights, to help promote development in less-developed regions, and to make an even greater contribution to the country's modernization undertaking. To realize gradually the goal of common prosperity, the state has adopted policies to support vigorously economic development in less-developed regions of central and western China.

With the deepening of reform and the expansion of reform, regions in central and western China have gradually improved their conditions for developing the economy. Through their own efforts and with the state's support, it is completely possible that they can gradually accelerate the pace of development by fully bringing into play their advantages, including natural resources and other advantages.

When dealing with the relationship between the state, enterprises, and staff members and workers, it is necessary to bring initiatives into play. Within the enterprises, it is necessary to give full play to the enthusiasm of the party organization, of management personnel and of all staff members and workers. Among the people, it is necessary to bring into play the initiatives of workers, farmers, intellectuals, and people from various circles. It is necessary to enhance national unity and to bring into play the initiatives of all nationalities in the nation. We should develop the enthusiasm of trade unions, Communist Youth League organizations, women's federations, and other mass organizations as well as democratic parties. Mobilizing the initiatives of the broad mass of cadres and the masses depends on deepening reform and perfecting various systems; and it is also necessary to rely on ideological and political work to exploit our political advantages.

All in all, our principle is to give full play to the initiatives of all sides, to mobilize all positive factors, to turn negative factors into positive ones, and to devote all our energy to the great undertaking of socialist modernization construction. By so doing, our reform, opening and economic construction will be provided with the broadest and deepest mass foundation and will keep on developing with great vigor.

III. On Strengthening Party Building and the Leadership of the Party

Establishing a socialist market economic structure and accelerating the pace of modernization are great historical tasks in the new period. To lead this unprecedented pioneering work and to achieve success, our party must effectively strengthen its own ideology, organization, and work style.

(1) It Is Necessary to Strengthen the Party's Ideological Construction and to Arm the Whole Party with Comrade Deng Xiaoping's Theory of Building Socialism with Chinese Characteristics

A party, a nation, and a country, especially a big party like ours and a country composed of people of fifty-six different nationalities with a population of more than 1 billion, must have correct theoretical guidance and powerful spiritual support. Now we are in the midst of a profound social change in the course of reform, opening up, and modernization, and great changes are taking place in social relations and the social and economic outlooks. To assume the historical responsibility for leading this great change, our party must have correct theoretical guidance and powerful spiritual support. Otherwise, the whole party and the whole country cannot have strong rallying power, will lack unity as did the old China, and cannot have great strength. Ideological construction is the foundation for improving our organization and work style. Comrade Deng Xiaoping's theory of building socialism with Chinese characteristics has brought forward and developed Mao Zedong Thought, and it is contemporary Marxism in China. We must use this theory to arm the whole party, the whole army, and people of all nationalities of our country. The party Central Committee has made a decision about studying the third volume of the *Selected Works of Deng Xiaoping,* and so comrades of the whole party, especially leading cadres at and above the county level, must conscientiously study it in the light of actual conditions. We should carry forward the Marxist study style of combining theory with practice, seriously study the original works, have a good grasp of their essence, and implement the guidelines in line with the actual situation of various departments and localities. You comrades here are members and alternate members of the CCP Central Committee and responsible comrades of the party, government, army, and mass organizations, and so you must take the lead in studying well the book to increase your political, ideological, and leadership quality and enhance your consciousness of firmly implementing the party's basic line. This is a matter of fundamental importance in successfully promoting reform, opening up, and the modernization drive.

(2) It is Necessary to Strengthen the Building of the Party

The strength of the party lies in the unity of the party and in good organization and strict discipline. To strengthen the party's organizational construction, we have to do many things. Here I only want to stress three points. First, it is imperative to implement firmly the party's principle of democratic centralism. Only by adhering to the principle of democratic centralism can we unify our understanding and steps. Party organizations at various levels must consciously place the interests of the party and state at the top spot; their local interests must be subordinated to the interests of the whole; their immediate interests must be subordinated to long-term interests; and they must take the overall situation into consideration, guarantee the implementation of various principles and policies of the party Central Committee, and maintain a high degree of unity politically, organizationally, and in their actions. The practices of not carrying out orders and not banning things that should be banned are extremely unfavorable to our cause and will not be tolerated by party discipline. Second, it is necessary to enhance the building of the party's grass-roots organizations. The party's grass-roots organizations are the party's foundation. Only with a solid foundation can the entire party be assured of having powerful fighting strength and withstand the test of any upheavals. Implementing the "Decision" requires the joint efforts of all levels of party organizations. Grass-roots party organizations are also required to carry out hard and meticulous work and help translate the party's decision into the action of the masses. It is necessary to make great determination to build the party's grass-roots organizations into a fighting force that will unite and lead the masses to realize the party's goals. Third, it is necessary to enhance the building of all levels of leading bodies. The key lies in following the principle of making the contingent of cadres more revolutionary, younger in average age, better educated, and professionally more competent, and in selecting and promoting cadres who meet the requirements of being able and having political integrity. To help our party organizations retain vigor and vitality, it is necessary to promote those cadres, particularly young and middle-aged cadres, who are loyal to the cause of the party, who vigorously promote reform, opening and modernization construction, to all levels of leading posts.

(3) Enhance Investigation and Study; Improve Work Style and Ways of Thinking

Time is advancing. The situation is evolving. New situations and new problems keep coming up. All levels of leading bodies and leading cadres should strive to improve leadership styles and methods so as to keep up with the pace of the times. It is necessary to treat this matter at the same level as raising the level of leadership and administration. With so much work to do, all levels of the party's leading cadres, senior-level cadres in particular, should comprehensively implement the guidelines set forth at the fourteenth CCP National Congress and the decision adopted at the present plenary session, improve their ability to master the overall situation, and arrange work in all respects. Since next year will be a very important year to promote reform and the tasks will be very arduous and demanding, we must properly handle the relationship between reform, development, and stability, and strive to maintain a stable political environment and a sound economic environment. All levels of leaders should not only know well their advantageous conditions and seize favorable opportunities, but also foresee well contradictions and difficulties in the course of progress and do a good job in a down-to-earth manner.

It is necessary to grasp correctly and handle well major theoretical and practical problems, to persist in materialist dialectics, avoid one-sidedness and metaphysics, remove interference, and always and unwaveringly adhere to the party's basic line. We should go deep down to the front line of reform and construction; conduct serious investigation and study; discover problems in a timely manner; proceed from reality; work creatively; constantly sum up experiences; and be good at utilizing experiences created by the masses to guide their progress. The CCP Central Committee has on many occasions called on all levels of leading cadres to step up investigation and study. It will be impossible for a leader to perform his duty well if he makes light of investigation and study, if he does not understand well his work, if he is blind to reality. If we can squeeze a little bit more time for studying, cut back time spent on socializing, do a little more investigation and study, refrain from acting subjectively, do more concrete things, and stop making empty speeches, then we will be able to greatly raise our leadership level.

Comrades!

Our country is now in a very important historical period. The burden on our shoulders is onerous. We carry enormous responsibilities. We should, in a spirit of bearing a high sense of responsibility toward the party, the state, and the Chinese nation, always and steadfastly follow Comrade Deng Xiaoping's theory on building socialism with Chinese characteristics and the party's basic line; hold fast to the central task of the economic construction; unwaveringly develop a socialist market economy, socialist democratic politics, and socialist spiri-

tual civilization; emancipate the mind; seek truth from facts; work with one heart and one mind; display a pioneering and enterprising spirit; rely on our own efforts; build an enterprise through arduous effort; and strive to build our country into a rich, strong, democratic, civilized, and modern socialist country!

President Clinton on U.S. Policy Toward China

Following China's Tiananmen incident of June 1989, an annual debate took place in the United States over extension of most favored nation (MFN) trading status to China. In May 1994, however, in renewing China's MFN status, U.S. president Bill Clinton made the decision to "delink" human rights from the MFN decision and inaugurated a new U.S. policy of constructive engagement with China. The text of his May 26 statement follows.

Our relationship with China is important to all Americans. We have significant interests in what happens there and what happens between us.

China has an atomic arsenal and a vote and a veto in the UN Security Council. It is a major factor in Asian and global security. We share important interests, such as in a nuclear-free Korean peninsula and in sustaining the global environment.

China is also the world's fastest-growing economy. Over $8 billion of United States exports to China last year supported over 150,000 American jobs.

I have received Secretary [of State Warren] Christopher's letter recommending, as required by last year's executive order—reporting to me on the conditions in that executive order. He has reached a conclusion with which I agree, that the Chinese did not achieve overall significant progress in all the areas outlined in the executive order relating to human rights, even though clearly there was progress made in important areas, including the resolution of all emigration cases, the establishment of a memorandum of understanding with regard to how prison labor issues would be resolved, the adherence to the Universal Declaration of Human Rights, and other issues.

Nevertheless, serious human rights abuses continue in China, including the arrest and detention of those who peacefully voice their opinions and the repression of Tibet's religious and cultural traditions.

The question for us now is, given the fact that there has been some progress but that not all the requirements of the executive order were met, how can we best advance the cause of human rights and the other profound interests the United States has in our relationship with China?

I have decided that the United States should renew Most Favored Nation trading status toward China. This decision, I believe, offers us the best opportunity to lay the basis for long-term sustainable progress in human rights and for the advancement of our other interests with China.

Extending MFN will avoid isolating China and instead will permit us to engage the Chinese with not only economic contacts but with cultural, educational, and other contacts, and with a continuing aggressive effort in human rights—an approach that I believe will make it more likely that China will play a responsible role, both at home and abroad.

I am moving, therefore, to delink human rights from the annual extension of Most Favored Nation trading status for China. That linkage has been constructive during the past year, but I believe, based on our aggressive contacts with the Chinese in the past several months, that we have reached the end of the usefulness of that policy, and it is time to take a new path toward the achievement of our constant objectives. We need to place our relationship into a larger and more productive framework.

In view of the continuing human rights abuses, I am extending the sanctions imposed by the United States as a result of the events in Tiananmen Square. And I am also banning the import of munitions, principally guns and ammunition, from China.

I am also pursuing a new and vigorous American program to support those in China working to advance the cause of human rights and democracy. This program will include increased broadcasts for Radio-Free Asia and the Voice of America, increased support for non-governmental organizations working on human rights in China, and the development, with American business leaders, of a voluntary set of principles for business activity in China.

I don't want to be misunderstood about this. China continues to commit very serious human rights abuses. Even as we engage the Chinese on military, political, and economic issues, we intend to stay engaged with those in China who suffer from human rights abuses.

The United States must remain a champion of their liberties.

I believe the question, therefore, is not whether we continue to support human rights in China but how we can best support human rights in China and advance our other very significant issues and interests. I believe we can do it by engaging the Chinese. . . .

The actions I have taken today to advance our security, to advance our prosperity, to advance our ideals, I believe are the important and appropriate ones. I believe, in other words, this is in the strategic economic and political interests of both the United States and China, and I am confident that over the long run this decision will prove to be the correct one.

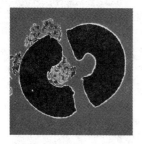

BIBLIOGRAPHY

CHAPTER 1
Imperial China—Origins to 1911

Bodde, Derk. *Chinese Thought, Society, and Science: The Intellectual and Social Background of Science and Technology in Pre-Modern China.* Honolulu: University of Hawaii Press, 1991.

Chang, Hsin-pao. *Commissioner Lin and the Opium War.* Cambridge: Harvard University Press, 1964.

Chang, Kwang-chih. *The Archaeology of Ancient China.* New Haven, Conn.: Yale University Press, 1963.

—. *Shang Civilization.* New Haven, Conn.: Yale University Press, 1980.

Chen, Kenneth. *Buddhism in China: A Historical Survey.* Princeton, N.J.: Princeton University Press, 1964.

deBary, William Theodore, Wing-tsit Chan, and Burton Watson, comps. *Sources of Chinese Tradition.* New York: Columbia University Press, 1964.

—. *The Chinese Language: Fact and Fantasy.* Honolulu: University of Hawaii Press, 1984.

Ebrey, Patricia. *Chinese Civilization and Society: A Sourcebook.* New York: Free Press, 1981.

Fairbank, John King. *China: A New History.* Cambridge: Harvard University Press, 1992.

Fung, Yu-lan. *A History of Chinese Philosophy,* trans. Derk Bodde. Princeton, N.J.: Princeton University Press, 1952-1953.

Gasster, Michael. *Chinese Intellectuals and the Revolution of 1911: The Birth of Modern Chinese Radicalism.* Seattle: University of Washington Press, 1969.

Gernet, Jacques. *A History of Chinese Civilization.* New York: Cambridge University Press, 1982.

Hucker, Charles O. *China's Imperial Past: An Introduction to Chinese History and Culture.* Stanford: Stanford University Press, 1975.

Jochim, Christian. *Chinese Religions: A Cultural Perspective.* New York: Prentice-Hall, 1986.

Keightley, David N. *The Origins of Chinese Civilization.* Berkeley: University of California Press, 1983.

Kratochvil, Paul. *The Chinese Language Today.* London: Hutchinson, 1968.

Levenson, Joseph R. *Confucian China and Its Modern Fate,* vol. 1: *The Problem of Intellectual Continuity;* vol. 2: *The Problem of Monarchical Decay;* vol. 3: *The Problem of Historical Significance.* Berkeley: University of California Press, 1958, 1964, 1965.

Loewe, Michael. *Imperial China: The Historical Background to the Modern Age.* New York: Praeger, 1966.

Meskill, John T. *An Introduction to Chinese Civilization.* Lexington, Mass.: D. C. Heath, 1973.

Michael, Franz. *China Through the Ages: History of a Civilization.* Boulder, Colo.: Westview Press, 1986.

Mote, Frederick W. *Intellectual Foundations of China.* 2d ed. New York: McGraw-Hill, 1989.

Ramsey, Robert S. *The Languages of China.* Princeton, N.J.: Princeton University Press, 1987.

Reischauer, Edwin O., and John K. Fairbank. *East Asia: The Great Tradition.* Boston: Houghton Mifflin, 1960.

Ropp, Paul S., ed. *Heritage of China: Contemporary Perspectives on Chinese Civilization.* Berkeley: University of California Press, 1990.

Schwartz, Benjamin I. *The World of Thought in Ancient China.* Cambridge: Harvard University Press, 1985.

Skinner, G. William. *The City in Late Imperial China.* Stanford: Stanford University Press, 1977.

Teng, S. Y., and J. K. Fairbank. *China's Response to the West: A Documentary Survey, 1839-1923.* 2d ed. Cambridge: Harvard University Press, 1979.

Thomas, Stephen. *Foreign Intervention and China's Industrial Development, 1870-1911.* Boulder, Colo.: Westview Press, 1984.

Thompson, Laurence G. *Chinese Religion: An Introduction,* 4th ed. Belmont, Calif.: Wadsworth Press, 1988.

Wakeman, Frederic, Jr. *The Fall of Imperial China.* New York: Free Press, 1975.

Wright, Arthur F., and John K. Fairbank, eds. *Chinese Thought and Institutions.* Chicago: University of Chicago Press, 1957.

Wright, Mary Clabaugh, ed. *China in Revolution: The First Phase, 1900-1913.* New Haven, Conn.: Yale University Press, 1968.

CHAPTER 2
Republican China (1911-1949)

Ch'i, Hsi-sheng. *Warlord Politics in China, 1916-1928.* Stanford: Stanford University Press, 1976.

Chow, Tse-tsung. *The May Fourth Movement: Intellectual Revolution in Modern China.* Cambridge: Harvard University Press, 1960.

Clubb, O. Edmund. *Twentieth Century China.* 3d ed. New York: Columbia University Press, 1978.

Eastman, Lloyd, ed. *The Abortive Revolution: China under Nationalist Rule, 1927-1937.* Cambridge: Harvard University Press, 1974.

Fairbank, John King. *China: A New History.* Cambridge: Harvard University Press, 1992.

Feuerwerker, Albert. *Economic Trends in the Republic of China, 1912-1949.* Ann Arbor: University of Michigan Center for Chinese Studies, Michigan Papers in Chinese Studies Number 31, 1977.

Grieder, Jerome. *Intellectuals and the State in Modern China: A Narrative History.* New York: Free Press, 1981.

—. *Hu Shih and the Chinese Renaissance: Liberalism in the Chinese Revolution, 1917-1937.* Cambridge: Harvard University Press, 1970.

Hsu, Immanuel C. Y. *The Rise of Modern China.* 4th ed. New York: Oxford University Press, 1990.

Jordan, Donald A. *The Northern Expedition: China's National Revolution of 1926-1928.* Honolulu: University of Hawaii Press, 1976.

Link, Perry. *Mandarin Ducks and Butterflies: Popular Fiction in Early Twentieth-Century Chinese Cities.* Berkeley: University of California Press, 1981.

Nathan, Andrew. *Peking Politics, 1918-1923: Factionalism and the Failure of Constitutionalism.* Berkeley: University of California Press, 1976.

Rawski, Thomas. *Economic Growth in Prewar China.* Berkeley: University of California Press, 1989.

Rigby, Richard. *The May Thirtieth Movement: Events and Themes.* Canberra: Australian National University Press, 1980.

Schiffrin, Harold Z. *Sun Yat-sen and the Origins of the Chinese Revolution.* Berkeley: University of California Press, 1968.

Schran, Peter. *Guerrilla Economy: The Development of the Shensi-Kansu-Ninghsia Border Region, 1937-1945.* Albany: State University of New York Press, 1976.

Schwarcz, Vera. *The Chinese Enlightenment: Intellectuals and the Legacy of the May Fourth Movement of 1919.* Berkeley: University of California Press, 1986.

Spence, Jonathan D. *The Gate of Heavenly Peace: The Chinese and Their Revolution, 1895-1980.* New York: Viking Press, 1981.

—. *The Search for Modern China.* New York: W. W. Norton, 1990.

Tien, Hung-mao. *Government and Politics in Kuomintang China, 1927-1937.* Stanford: Stanford University Press, 1972.

Tuchman, Barbara. *Stilwell and the American Experience in China.* New York: Bantam, 1984.

Wilbur, C. Martin. *The Nationalist Revolution in China, 1923-1928.* New York: Cambridge University Press, 1984.

—, and Julie Lien-ying How. *Missionaries of Revolution: Soviet Advisers and Nationalist China, 1920-1927.* Cambridge: Harvard University Press, 1989.

CHAPTER 3
Maoist China (1949-1978)

Barnett, A. Doak. *China and the Major Powers in East Asia.* Washington, D.C.: Brookings Institution, 1977.

Barnouin, Barbara. *Ten Years of Turbulence: The Chinese Cultural Revolution.* New York: K. Paul International, 1993.

Chesneaux, Jean. *China, the People's Republic, 1949-1976.* 1st American ed. New York: Pantheon Books, 1979.

Dietrich, Craig. *People's China: A Brief History.* New York: Oxford University Press, 1986.

Fairbank, John King. *China: A New History.* Cambridge: Harvard University Press, 1992.

Federal Research Division, Library of Congress. *China: A Country Study.* 4th ed. Area Handbook Series. Ed. Robert L. Worden et al. Washington, D.C.: U.S. Government Printing Office, 1988.

Gittings, John. *China Changes Face: The Road from Revolution 1949-1989.* Oxford: Oxford University Press, 1989.

Harrison, James P. *The Long March to Power: A History of the Chinese Communist Party, 1921-1972.* New York: Praeger, 1972.

Hinton, Harold C., ed. *Government and Politics in Revolutionary China: Selected Documents, 1949-1979.* Wilmington, Del.: Scholarly Resources, 1982.

Hsu, Immanuel C. Y. *The Rise of Modern China.* 4th ed. New York: Oxford University Press, 1990.

Hsueh, Chün-tu. *Revolutionary Leaders of Modern China.* New York: Oxford University Press, 1971.

Karnow, Stanley. *Mao and China: A Legacy of Turmoil.* 3d ed. New York: Penguin Books, 1990.

—. *Mao and China: Inside China's Cultural Revolution.* New York: Viking Press, 1984.

Li, Zhisui. *The Private Life of Chairman Mao.* New York: Random House, 1994.

MacFarquhar, Roderick, and John K. Fairbank, eds. *The Cambridge History of China,* vol. 14, *The People's Republic,* part 1: The Emergence of Revolutionary China 1949-1965. Cambridge: Cambridge University Press, 1987.

—. *The Cambridge History of China,* vol. 15, *The People's Republic,* part 2: Revolutions within the Chinese Revolution 1966-1982. Cambridge: Cambridge University Press, 1991.

MacFarquhar, Roderick. *The Origins of the Cultural Revolution,* vol. 1. *Contradictions Among the People 1956-1957.* Oxford: Oxford University Press, 1974.

—. *The Origins of the Cultural Revolution,* vol. 2. The Great Leap Forward 1958-1960. New York: Columbia University Press, 1983.

Meisner, Maurice. *Mao's China and After: A History of the People's Republic.* Rev. ed. Transformation of Modern China series. New York: Free Press, 1986.

Salisbury, Harrison E. *The New Emperors: China in the Era of Mao and Deng.* Boston: Little, Brown, 1992.

Schurmann, Franz. *Ideology and Organization in Communist China.* Berkeley: University of California Press, 1968.

Spence, Jonathan D. *The Search for Modern China.* New York: W. W. Norton, 1990.

White, Lynn T., III. *Policies of Chaos: The Organizational Causes of Violence in China's Cultural Revolution.* Princeton, N.J.: Princeton University Press, 1989.

Whiting, Allen S. *Chinese Domestic Politics and Foreign Policy in the 1970s.* Ann Arbor: Center for Chinese Studies, University of Michigan, 1979.

Wilson, Dick. *Mao Tse-tung in the Scales of History.* New York: Cambridge University Press, 1977.

CHAPTER 4
Deng's China (1979-1989)

Barnett, A. Doak, and Ralph N. Clough, eds. *Modernizing China: Post-Mao Reform and Development.* Boulder, Colo.: Westview Press for School of Advanced International Studies, Johns Hopkins University, 1986.

Fewsmith, Joseph. *Dilemmas of Reform in China: Political Conflict and Economic Debate.* Armonk, N.Y.: M. E. Sharpe, 1994.

Goldman, Merle. *Sowing the Seeds of Democracy in China: Political Reform in the Deng Xiaoping Era.* Cambridge: Harvard University Press, 1994.

Harding, Harry. *China's Second Revolution: Reform After Mao.* Washington, D.C.: Brookings Institution, 1987.

Hinton, Harold C., ed. *The People's Republic of China, 1979-1984: A Documentary Survey.* 2 volumes. Wilmington, Del.: Scholarly Resources, 1986.

Hsu, Immanuel C. Y. *China without Mao: The Search for a New Order.* 2d ed. New York: Oxford University Press, 1990.

Kau, Michael Ying-Mao, and Susan H. Marsh, eds. *China in the Era of Deng Xiaoping: A Decade of Reform.* Armonk, N.Y.: M. E. Sharpe, 1993.

Kim, Samuel S., ed. *China and the World: Chinese Foreign Policy in the Post-Mao Era.* Boulder, Colo.:

Westview Press, 1984.

Nathan, Andrew. *China's Crisis: Dilemmas of Reform and Prospects for Democracy.* Studies of the East Asian Institute. New York: Columbia University Press, 1990.

Salisbury, Harrison E. *The New Emperors: China in the Era of Mao and Deng.* Boston: Little, Brown, 1992.

Smil, Vaclav. *China's Environmental Crisis: An Inquiry into the Limits of National Development.* Armonk, N.Y.: M. E. Sharpe, 1993.

Terrill, Ross. *China in Our Time.* New York: Simon and Schuster, 1992.

The Tiananmen Incident and Post-Deng China

Chang, King-Yuh, ed. *Mainland China After the Thirteenth Party Congress.* Boulder, Colo.: Westview Press, 1990.

Goldstein, Steven M. *China at the Crossroads: Reform After Tiananmen.* Ithaca, N.Y.: Foreign Policy Association, 1992.

Goodman, David S., and Gerald Segal, eds. *China in the Nineties: Crisis Management and Beyond.* New York: Oxford University Press, 1991.

Gu, Zhibin. *China Beyond Deng: Reform in the PRC.* Jefferson, N.C.: McFarland, 1991.

Hicks, George, ed. *The Broken Mirror: China After Tiananmen.* Chicago: St. James Press, 1990.

Joseph, William A., ed. *China Briefing, 1994.* Boulder, Colo.: Westview Press, 1994.

Ogden, S., et al., eds. *China's Search for Democracy: The Student and Mass Movement of 1989.* Armonk, N.Y.: M. E. Sharpe, 1992.

Overholt, William H. *The Rise of China: How Economic Reform Is Creating a New Superpower.* New York: W. W. Norton, 1993.

Saich, Tony, ed. *The Chinese People's Movement: Perspectives on Spring 1989.* Armonk, N.Y.: M. E. Sharpe, 1990.

Unger, Jonathan. *The Pro-Democracy Protest in China.* Armonk, N.Y.: M. E. Sharpe, 1991.

CHAPTER 5
Politics and China's Second Revolution:
The Quest for Modernization

Bartke, Wolfgang. *Who's Who in the People's Republic of China.* 2d ed. New York: Saur, 1987.

Chang, Maria Hsia. "China's Future: Regionalism, Federation, or Disintegration." *Studies in Comparative Communism,* vol. 25, no. 3, September 1992.

Chang, Parris. *Power and Policy in China.* 3d ed. Dubuque, Iowa: Kendall/Hunt, 1990.

Clarke, Christopher. "China's Transition to the Post-Deng Era." In *China's Economic Dilemmas in the 1990s: The Problems of Reforms, Modernization, and*

Interdependence. Washington, D.C.: Joint Economic Committee, April 1991.

Dreyer, June Teufel. *China's Political System.* New York: Paragon House, 1993.

Hamrin, Carol Lee. *China and the Challenge of the Future: Changing Political Patterns.* Boulder, Colo.: Westview Press, 1990.

Lieberthal, Kenneth G., and Bruce J. Dickson. *A Research Guide to Central Party and Government Meetings in China, 1949-1986.* Armonk, N.Y.: M. E. Sharpe, 1989.

—, and David M. Lampton, eds. *Bureaucracy, Politics, and Decision Making in Post-Mao China.* Berkeley: University of California Press, 1992.

—, and Michel Oksenberg, eds. *Policy Making in China: Leaders, Structures, and Processes.* Princeton, N.J.: Princeton University Press, 1988.

MacFarquhar, Roderick. *The Politics of China 1949-1989.* New York: Columbia University Press, 1993.

McCormick, Barrett L., Su Shaozhi, and Xiao Xiaoming. "The 1989 Democracy Movement: A Review of the Prospects for Civil Society in China." *Pacific Affairs,* vol. 65, summer 1992.

Miller, H. Lyman. "Holding the Deng Line." *China Business Review,* January-February 1993.

—. "Some Perspectives on China's Fourteenth Party Congress." *Washington Journal of Modern China,* vol. 1, no. 2, spring 1993.

Perry, Elizabeth J., and Ellen V. Fuller. "China's Long March to Democracy." *World Policy Journal,* vol. 8, fall 1991.

Ristaino, Marcia. "The Impact of the Soviet Coup on China and Reform." *Washington Journal of Modern China,* vol. 1, no. 2, spring 1993.

Saich, Tony. "The Fourteenth Party Congress: A Programme for Authoritarian Rule." *China Quarterly,* December 1992.

Shue, Vivienne. "China: Transition Postponed?" *Problems of Communism,* January-April 1992.

Yu, Peter Kien-hong. "Regional Military Separatism in Communist China." *Global Affairs,* vol. 8, spring 1993.

Zhang Zhou. "An Analysis of Some of the Objectives of China's Modernization." *Social Sciences in China,* vol. 14, autumn 1993.

CHAPTER 6
The Dragon Stirs:
China's Economy Under Reform

Banister, Judith. *China's Changing Population.* Stanford: Stanford University Press, 1983.

Byrd, William A. *The Market Mechanism and Economic Reforms in China.* Armonk, N.Y.: M. E. Sharpe, 1991.

—, and Lin Qingsong, eds. *China's Rural Industry:*

Structure, Development, and Reform. Oxford/New York: Oxford University Press for the World Bank, 1990.

Chao, Kang. *The Development of Cotton Textile Production in China.* Cambridge: Harvard University Press, Harvard East Asian Monographs Number 74, 1977.

Chung, Jae Ho. "The Politics of Agricultural Mechanization in the Post-Mao Era." *China Quarterly,* June 1993.

Eastman, Lloyd F. *Family, Fields and Ancestors: Constancy and Change in China's Social and Economic History 1550-1949.* New York: Oxford University Press, 1988.

Eckstein, Alexander. *China's Economic Revolution.* Cambridge: Cambridge University Press, 1977.

Grub, Phillip D., and Jian Hai Lin. *Foreign Direct Investment in China.* New York: Quorum Books, 1991.

Harding, Harry. "The Problematic Future of China's Economic Reforms." In *China's Economic Dilemmas in the 1990s: The Problems of Reforms, Modernization, and Interdependence.* Washington, D.C.: Joint Economic Committee, April 1991.

Hsu, Robert C. *Economic Theories in China 1979-1988.* Cambridge: Cambridge University Press, 1991.

Keidel, Albert. "China's Economy After the Fourteenth Party Congress: Sequenced Stages of Reform." *Washington Journal of Modern China,* vol. 1, no. 2, spring 1993.

Lardy, Nicholas R. *China in the World Economy.* Washington, D.C.: Institute for International Economics, 1994.

—. *Economic Growth and Distribution in China.* Cambridge: Cambridge University Press, 1978.

—. *Foreign Trade and Economic Reform in China.* Cambridge: Cambridge University Press, 1992.

Needham, Joseph. *Science and Civilization in China,* vol. 1. Cambridge: Cambridge University Press, 1965.

Perkins, Dwight H. *China: Asia's Next Giant?* Seattle: University of Washington Press, 1986

—, and Shahid Yusuf. *Rural Development in China.* Baltimore: Johns Hopkins University Press, 1984.

Perry, Elizabeth J., and Christine Wong, eds. *The Political Economy of Reform in Post-Mao China.* Cambridge: Harvard University, Center for East Asian Studies, 1985.

Prime, Penelope B. "The Economy in Overdrive: Will It Crash?" *Current History,* vol. 92, no. 575, September 1993.

Prybyla, Jan. *Reforming China and Other Socialist Economies.* Washington, D.C.: American Enterprise Institute Press, 1990.

Putterman, Louis. "Institutional Boundaries, Structural Change, and Economic Reform in China: An Introduction." *Modern China,* vol. 18, no. 1, 1992.

Riskin, Carl. *China's Political Economy: The Quest for Development Since 1949.* New York: Oxford University Press, 1987, 1988, 1991.

Sicular, Terry. "Plan and Market in China's Agricultural Commerce." *Journal of Political Economy,* vol. 96, no. 2, 1988.

White, Gordon. *Riding the Tiger: The Politics of Economic Reform in Post-Mao China.* Stanford: Stanford University Press, 1993.

World Bank. *China, Socialist Economic Development* (A World Bank Country Study), vol. 1: *The Economy, Statistical System, and Basic Data;* vol. 2: *The Economic Sectors: Agriculture, Industry, Energy, Transport, and External Trade and Finance.* Washington, D.C.: World Bank, 1983.

—. *China, Socialist Economic Development* (A World Bank Country Study): External Trade and Capital. Washington, D.C.: World Bank, 1988.

—. *World Development Report 1992: Development and the Environment.* New York: Oxford University Press for the World Bank, 1992.

Xue Muqiao. *China's Socialist Economy.* Beijing: New China/Foreign Languages Press, 1981.

CHAPTER 7
Chinese Foreign Policy Post-Tiananmen

Garver, John W. *Foreign Relations of the People's Republic of China.* Englewood Cliffs, N.J.: Prentice-Hall, 1993.

Hao, Yufan, and Guocang Huan, eds. *The Chinese View of the World.* New York: Pantheon, 1989.

Harding, Harry, ed. *China's Foreign Relations in the 1980s.* New Haven, Conn.: Yale University Press, 1984.

Kim, Samuel S. *China In and Out of the Changing World Order.* Princeton, N.J.: Center for International Studies, Princeton University, 1991.

—, ed. *China and the World: Chinese Foreign Relations in the Post-Cold War World.* 3d ed. Boulder, Colo.: Westview Press, 1994.

Robinson, Thomas W., and David Shambaugh, eds. *Chinese Foreign Policy: Theory and Practice.* New York: Oxford University Press, 1994.

Whiting, Allen S., ed. *Chinese Foreign Relations.* New York: Annals of the American Academy of Political and Social Studies, 1992.

Bilateral and Regional Issues

Atlantic Council of the United States and National Committee on U.S.-China Relations. *United States and China Relations at a Crossroads.* Washington, D.C.: Atlantic Council, 1993.

Bartke, Wolfgang. *The Agreements of the People's Republic of China with Foreign Countries, 1949-1990.* 2d ed. Munich: Institute of Asian Affairs, Hamburg, 1992.

Calabrese, John. *China's Changing Relations with the Middle East.* London: Kegan Paul International, 1991.

Chang, Parris H., and Martin H. Lasater. *If the PRC Crosses the Taiwan Strait: The International Response.* Lanham, Md.: University Press of America, 1992.

Chen, Min. *The Strategic Triangle and Regional Conflicts: Lessons from the Indochina Wars.* Boulder, Colo.: Lynne Rienner, 1992.

Clough, Ralph N. *Reaching Across the Taiwan Strait.* Boulder, Colo.: Westview Press, 1992.

Dittmer, Lowell. *Sino-Soviet Normalization and Its International Implications, 1948-1972.* Seattle: University of Washington Press, 1992.

Harding, Harry. *A Fragile Relationship: The United States and China Since 1972.* Washington, D.C.: Brookings Institution, 1992.

Hood, Steven J. *Dragons Entangled: Indochina and the China-Vietnam War.* Armonk: M. E. Sharpe, 1992.

Lin Zhiling and Thomas W. Robinson, eds. *The Chinese and Their Future: Beijing, Taipei, and Hong Kong.* Washington, D.C.: American Enterprise Institute, 1993.

Robinson, Thomas W., ed. *New Ideas and Concepts in Sino-American Relations.* Washington, D.C.: American Enterprise Institute, 1992.

Shambaugh, David. *Beautiful Imperialist: China Perceives America, 1972-1990.* Princeton, N.J.: Princeton University Press, 1991.

Shuichi Ono. *Sino-Japanese Economic Relationships: Trade, Direct Investment, and Future Strategy.* Washington, D.C.: World Bank, 1992.

Wang Gungwu. *China and the Overseas Chinese.* Singapore: Times Academic Press, 1991.

Other Special Topics in Foreign Relations

Amnesty International. *China: Continued Patterns of Human Rights Violations.* New York: Amnesty International, 1992.

Asia Watch. *Continuing Religious Repression in China.* New York: Asia Watch, 1993.

Jacobson, Harold K., and Michel Oksenberg. *China's Participation in the IMF, the World Bank, and GATT.* Ann Arbor: University of Michigan Press, 1990.

Kent, Ann. *Freedom and Subsistence: China and Human Rights.* New York: Oxford University Press, 1993.

Smil, Vaclav. *China's Environmental Crisis: An Inquiry into the Limits of National Development.* Armonk, N.Y.: M. E. Sharpe, 1993.

Wilhelm, Alfred D., Jr. *The Chinese at the Negotiating Table: Style and Substance.* Washington, D.C.: National Defense University Press, 1994.

CHAPTER 8
Society and Culture in Contemporary China

Aird, John S. "China: Surprising Census Results." *China Business Review,* March 1983.

Andors, Phyllis. *The Unfinished Liberation of Chinese Women: 1949-1980.* Bloomington: Indiana University Press, 1983.

Banister, Judith. *China's Changing Population.* Stanford: Stanford University Press, 1987.

Davin, Delia. *Woman-Work: Women and the Party in Revolutionary China.* New York: Oxford University Press, 1979.

Davis, Deborah, and Ezra Vogel, eds. *Chinese Society on the Eve of Tiananmen: The Impact of Reform.* Cambridge: Harvard Council on East Asian Studies, 1990.

Dreyer, June Teufel. "Traditional Minorities Elites and the CPR Elite Engaged in Minority Nationalities Work." In *Elites in the People's Republic of China,* ed. Robert A. Scalapino. Seattle: University of Washington Press, 1972.

Fang Lizhi. *Bringing Down the Great Wall: Writings on Science, Culture, and Democracy in China.* New York: Alfred A. Knopf, 1991.

Friedman, Edward. "Reconstructing China's National Identity: A Southern Alternative to Mao-Era Anti-Imperialist Nationalism." *Journal of Asian Studies,* February 1994.

Gilmartin, Christina K., Gail Hershatter, Lisa Rofel, and Tyrene White, eds. *Engendering China: Women, Culture, and the State.* Cambridge: Harvard University Press, 1994.

Gladney, Dru C. *Muslim Chinese: Ethnic Nationalism in the People's Republic.* Cambridge: Harvard University Press, 1991.

—. "Representing Nationality in China: Refiguring Majority/Minority Identities." *Journal of Asian Studies,* February 1994.

Greenblatt, Sidney L. *The People of Taihang: An Anthology of Family Histories.* White Plains, N.Y.: International Arts and Sciences Press, 1972.

—. "Campaigns and the Manufacture of Deviance in Chinese Society." In *Deviant Behavior in Chinese Society,* ed. Richard Wittingham Wilson, Amy Auerbacher Wilson, and Sidney Leonard Greenblatt. New York: Praeger, 1977.

Harding, Harry. *Organizing China: The Problem of Bureaucracy 1949-1976.* Stanford: Stanford University Press, 1981.

Haub, Carl. "China's Fertility Drop Lowers World Growth Rate." *Population Today,* June 1993.

Hayhoe, Ruth. "China's Universities Since Tiananmen: A Critical Assessment." *China Quarterly,* June 1993.

Honig, Emily, and Gail Hershatter. *Personal Voices: Chinese Women in the 1980s.* Stanford: Stanford University Press, 1988.

Kalish, Susan. "In China, The Peak Childbearing Years Have Peaked." *Population Today,* January 1993.

Kallgren, Joyce K., ed. *Building a Nation-State: China After Forty Years.* Berkeley: Institute of East Asian Studies, Center for Chinese Studies, 1990.

Link, Perry, Richard Madsen, and P. Pickowicz. *Unofficial China: Popular Culture and Thought in the People's Republic of China.* Boulder, Colo.: Westview Press, 1989.

Lipman, Jonathan N., and Stevan Harrell. *Violence in China: Essays in Culture and Counterculture.* Albany: State University of New York Press, 1990.

MacInnis, Donald E. *Religion in China Today: Policy and Practice.* Maryknoll, N.Y.: Orbis Books, 1989.

Manion, Melanie. *Retirement of Revolutionaries in China: Public Policies, Special Norms, Private Interests.* Princeton, N.J.: Princeton University Press, 1993.

Orleans, Leo A. *Every Fifth Child: The Population of China.* Stanford: Stanford University Press, 1972.

Pye, Lucian W. "The State and the Individual: An Overview Interpretation." *China Quarterly,* September 1991.

—. *The Mandarin and the Cadre: China's Political Cultures.* Ann Arbor: University of Michigan, Center for Chinese Studies, 1988.

—. *The Spirit of Chinese Politics.* Cambridge: Harvard University Press, 1992.

Rosen, Stanley. "The Effects of Post-4 June Re-education Campaigns on Chinese Students." *China Quarterly,* June 1993.

Rosenblum, Arthur L., ed. *State and Society in China: The Consequences of Reform.* Boulder, Colo.: Westview Press, 1992.

Rozman, Gilbert, ed. *The East Asian Region: Confucian Heritage and Its Modern Adaptation.* Princeton, N.J.: Princeton University Press, 1993.

Schell, Orville. *Discos and Democracy: China in the Throes of Reform.* New York: Doubleday, 1987.

Schoenhals, Martin. *The Paradox of Power in a People's Republic of China Middle School.* Armonk, N.Y.: M. E. Sharpe, 1993.

Shen Tong. *Almost a Revolution.* Boston: Houghton Mifflin, 1990.

Stacey, Judith. *Patriarchy and Socialist Revolution in Socialist China.* Berkeley: University of California Press, 1983.

Tian, H. Y. "The New Census of China." *Population Today,* January 1991.

—. "China: Demographic Billionaire." *Population Bulletin,* April 1983.

Tu Wei-ming, ed. *China in Transformation.* Cambridge: Harvard University Press, 1994.

Vogel, Ezra. *Canton Under Communism: Programs and Politics in a Provincial Capital, 1949-1968.* New York: Harper and Row, 1969.

—. *One Step Ahead in China: Guangdong Under Reform.* Cambridge: Harvard University Press, 1989.

Walder, Andrew. "Workers, Managers and the State: The Reform Era and the Political Crisis of 1989." *China Quarterly,* September 1991.

Weller, Robert. *Resistance, Chaos and Control in China: Taiping Rebels, Taiwanese Ghosts and Tiananmen.* Seattle: University of Washington Press, 1994.

Zeng Yi, Tu Ping, Gu Baochang, Wu Yi, Li Bohua, and Li Yongping. "Causes and Implications of the Recent Increases in the Reported Sex Ratio at Birth in China." *Population and Development Review,* June 1993.

Zhang Xinxin and Sang Ye. *Chinese Lives: An Oral History of Contemporary China.* New York: Pantheon Books, 1987.

CHAPTER 9
Modernizing the Chinese Military

Allen, Kenneth W. "People's Republic of China People's Liberation Army Airforce." Washington, D.C.: Defense Intelligence Agency, DIC-1300-445-91, May 1991.

Bullard, Monte R., and Edward O'Dowd. "Defining the Role of the PLA in the Post-Mao Era." *Asian Survey,* vol. 26, June 1986.

Byrnes, Michael T. "The Death of a People's Army." In *The Broken Mirror: China After Tiananmen,* ed. George Hicks. Chicago: St. James Press, 1990.

Cheng Hsiao-shih. *Party-Military Relations in the PRC and Taiwan. Paradoxes of Control.* Boulder, Colo.: Westview Press, 1990.

Cheung, Tai Ming. "PLA Buying Weapons, Equipment from Russia." *Far Eastern Economic Review.* April 9, 1993.

China's Defense Industrial Trading Companies. Defense Intelligence Agency, 1990.

Dreyer, June Teufel, ed. *Chinese Defense and Foreign Policy.* China in a New Era series. A Professors World Peace Academy Book. New York: Paragon House, 1988.

Folta, Paul H. *From Swords to Plowshares? Defense Industry Reform in the PRC.* Boulder, Colo.: Westview Press, 1992.

Gallagher, Joseph P. "China's Military Industrial Complex: Its Approach to the Acquisition of Modern Military Technology." *Asian Survey,* vol. 27, no. 9, September 1987.

Godwin, Paul H. B. *The Chinese Communist Armed Forces.* Maxwell Air Force Base, Ala.: Air University Press, June 1988.

Gregor, A. James. "The People's Liberation Army and China's Crisis." *Armed Forces and Society,* vol. 18, fall 1991.

Hahn, Bradley. "China's Submarine Fleet." *Navy International,* February 1989.

Handbook of the Chinese People's Liberation Army. Washington, D.C.: Defense Intelligence Agency, DDB-2680-32-84, November 1984.

Jencks, Harlan W. "Civil-Military Relations in China: Tiananmen and After." *Problems of Communism,* May-June 1991.

Joffe, Ellis. "The Tiananmen Crisis and the Politics of the PLA." In *China's Military: The PLA in 1990/1991,* ed. Richard Yang. Boulder, Colo.: Westview Press, 1991.

Kan, Shirley A. "China's Military: Roles and Implications for U.S. Policy Toward China." *CRS Report to Congress.* Washington, D.C.: Library of Congress, October 1993.

Latham, Richard J., and Kenneth W. Allen. "Defense Reform in China: The PLA Air Force." *Problems of Communism,* May-June 1991.

Lee, N. "Chinese Maritime Power Towards Modernization." *Naval Forces.* 1990.

Lewis, John W., Hua Di, and Xue Litai. "Beijing's Defense Establishment: Solving the Arms-Export Enigma." *International Security,* vol. 15, spring 1991.

Lin, Chong-pin. "From Panda to Dragon: China's Nuclear Strategy." *National Interest,* spring 1989.

U.S. Congress. Foreign Affairs Committee. *Technology Transfer to China.* Washington, D.C.: U.S. Government Printing Office, 1987.

Wortzel, Larry M. *China's Military Modernization: International Implications.* Westport, Conn.: Greenwood Press, 1988.

CHAPTER 10
China's Relations with Hong Kong, Taiwan, and Tibet

Hong Kong

Baldinger, Pamela. "The Birth of Greater China." *China Business Review,* May-June 1992.

Chan, Ming K., and David J. Clark, eds. *The Hong Kong Basic Law: Blueprint for Stability and Prosperity Under Chinese Sovereignty?* Armonk, N.Y.: M. E. Sharpe, 1991.

Ching, Frank. *Hong Kong and China: For Better or for Worse.* New York: Asia Society/Foreign Policy Association, 1985.

Harding, Harry. "The Emergence of Greater China." *American Enterprise,* vol. 3, May-June 1992.

Miners, Norman. *The Government and Politics of Hong Kong.* New York: Oxford University Press. 1991.

Rafferty, Kevin. *City on the Rocks: Hong Kong's Uncertain Future.* New York: Penguin Books, 1991.

Sung Yun-wing. *The China-Hong Kong Connection: Key to China's Open Door Policy.* New York: Cambridge University Press, 1991.

U.S. Congress. Senate Committee on Foreign Relations. Subcommittee on East Asian and Pacific Affairs. *Hong Kong's Reversion to China and Implications for U.S. Policy.* Hearings April 2, 1992. 102d Congress, 2d sess. Washington, D.C.: U.S. Government Printing Office, 1992.

Taiwan

Clough, Ralph N. *Island China.* Cambridge: Harvard University Press, 1978.

—. *Reaching Across the Taiwan Strait: People-to-People Diplomacy.* Boulder, Colo.: Westview Press. 1993.

Cohen, Marc J. *Taiwan at the Crossroads: Human Rights, Political Development, and Social Change on the Beautiful Island.* Washington, D.C.: Asia Resource Center, 1988.

Gold, Thomas B. *State and Society in the Taiwan Miracle.* Armonk, N.Y.: M. E. Sharpe, 1986.

Hickey, Dennis Van Vranken. *United States-Taiwan Security Ties: From Cold War to Beyond Containment.* Westport, Conn.: Praeger, 1994.

Lasater, Martin L. *U.S. Interests in the New Taiwan.* Boulder, Colo.: Westview Press, 1991.

Long, Simon. *Taiwan: China's Last Frontier.* New York: St. Martin's Press, 1991.

Myers, Ramon H., ed. *A Unique Relationship: The United States and the Republic of China Under the Taiwan Relations Act.* Stanford: Hoover Institution Press, 1989.

Simon, Denis Fred, and Michael Y. M. Kao, eds. *Taiwan: Beyond the Economic Miracle.* Armonk, N.Y.: M. E. Sharpe, 1992.

Tien, Hung-mao. *The Great Transition: Political and Social Change in the Republic of China.* Stanford: Hoover Institution Press, 1989.

Tibet

Goldstein, Melvyn C. *A History of Modern Tibet, 1913-1951: The Demise of the Lamaist State.* Berkeley: University of California Press, 1989.

Institute for Asian Democracy. *Tibet: Options for U.S.-China Policy.* Washington, D.C.: Institute for Asian Democracy, 1993.

National Committee on U.S.-China Relations. *Tibet: Issues for Americans.* New York: NCUSCR, 1992.

Nyandak, Tinley. "Tibet: The Undying Nation." *Freedom at Issue,* no. 108, May-June 1989.

U.S. Congress. Senate Committee on Foreign Relations. *U.S. and Chinese Policies Toward Occupied Tibet.* Hearing, July 28, 1992. 102d Congress, 2d sess. Washington, D.C.: U.S. Government Printing Office, 1993.

Periodicals

Asian Wall Street Journal Weekly
Asiaweek
Asian Survey
Australian Journal of Chinese Affairs
Beijing Review
China Business Review
China Quarterly
Far Eastern Economic Review
Issues and Studies
Journal of Asian Studies
Journal of Contemporary China
Journal of East Asian Affairs
Journal of Northeast Asian Studies
Pacific Affairs
Pacific Review
Washington Journal of Modern China

Annuals

Asian Security
Asian Strategic Review
Asian Survey (January issue)
Central Intelligence Agency, Report on the Chinese Economomy
China Briefing
Current History (September issue)
Commentary (September issue)
Far Eastern Economic Review Yearbook
Hong Kong, Annual Report
Pacific Economic Outlook

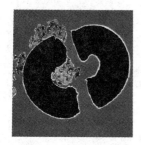

INDEX

Page numbers in **boldface** refer to biographical sketches.